those you trust

by
SARA ALLEN STEWART

Those You Trust © 2015 Sara Allen Stewart
All rights reserved.
ISBN: 069252696X
ISBN-13: 978-0692526965
Library of Congress Control Number: 2015915289
Sara Allen Stewart, Spokane, Washington

Edited by Dani Gonzalez

Cover Artist: Angel Dettlaff
artwork.angel.dettlaff@gmail.com
www.artworkangeldettlaff.jimdo.com

Cover Editor: Jaime Roy
www.jaimeroy.com

This book is dedicated to my Father,
Allen Burnett Knox.
Thank you for all the hours filled with Dr. Seuss,
Peanuts, and navigational technical manuals.
I love and miss you.

These two lovely ladies encouraged me, challenged me, helped me with formatting, and were very good at giving that extra push I needed.

22Random Ninja22
Insideimasadrainbow

I also want to personally thank the following individuals. These amazing people inspired me to write with their stories, their kind words, and their beautiful hearts. Most are writers themselves and have chosen to have their pennames listed here. Keep an eye out for them... they will be doing AMAZING things!

Dani (who also did the editing)
Erika Vela, LittleWing, Sarah – swagUPwindowsDOWN
Chocolate-Colombo, CrumpetCapers, Evix, LazyLazyWriter
Raven, Sophie, Rikke Anderson, Jasmine-TotallyLosingIt
Talida Mueller, Dona, EpicallyObsessed, Carly Jones
Syasya, Annabellex2, Chany-btrslovesong
Jamie Nelson, ksjf2012, Ajay B.

Some others I want to thank include my Aunt Nina and Uncle John, who provided a safe haven when needed.

My friends Adrianne (Andii), Janet, Leon, Ed, E'lise, and Kari. People who have been there for me when no one else was.

Robin Marr Loeper, my friend who helped me find the cover artist.

Dr. G and Susan G. who taught me that it's never too late to reinvent yourself as long as you do it with honesty, honour, a bit of humour, and a whole lot of Marty Robbins.

Last, and certainly least, I wish to thank my former employer for deciding to throw away his dedicated and loyal, long-term staff. You always said we were like a family....too bad it was so much like my own. So thank you for two years of unemployment, after ten years of service, in this terrifying economy. Without it, I never would have found my way back to the written word. With any luck, you'll be seeing a lot more of me.

Chapter 1~ Those You Trust

To anyone who doesn't know him, Kendall Knight seems like any typical fourteen-year-old boy. He has blond hair, cut a little shorter on the sides and back than in the front, his bangs often falling in front of his eyes. His eyes are green and he has dimples in both his cheeks, which become significantly more pronounced when he smiles, which he does often. He is the youngest of his friends, if only by a few months, but is considered the unofficial leader of the tight-knit little group. He has a younger sister whom he adores, even if she does get on his nerves at times. He does well in school, loves hockey, video games, scary movies, and skating on the pond in the park that is close to his house.

To anyone who does know him, Kendall is all these things and more. To his mom, Jennifer Knight, he is a loving and devoted son.

Jen is a petite woman with auburn hair and blue eyes. She has worked at the Shakopee Steak House for about ten years, starting out as part-time and then shifting to full-time after her husband, Will, had been killed in a car accident nearly seven years earlier. She sometimes struggled to make ends meet, and relies heavily upon Kendall to take care of his little sister and the house. She often worries that she places too much responsibility on him, but he always assures her that he can handle it.

To anyone who knew William Knight, they can see how much Kendall is like his father, both in looks and manner. Will had been blond with eyes that shifted between blue and green, depending on what colour he was wearing or on his mood. While Will's hair had a bit of curl to it, Kendall's is straight and his eyes are all green. Jen hopes Kendall will be tall like his father. Other similarities include a laid-back nature, a love for pulling pranks, and a good sense of humour. They also shared a strong will, a fiercely protective nature, and a stubborn streak that runs a mile wide. Will and Kendall had been extremely close and the boy was devastated when his father died.

Will's best friend was Antonio Garcia. Antonio and his family had moved to Minnesota from Missouri when he was four. The Garcias had moved next door to the Knights and the boys had been inseparable from the start. They grew up together, attended college together, joined the police academy together, and were partners on the force for several years. Jennifer Thornton and Sylvia Montoya also grew up as best friends and when the two couples started dating, married, and had families of their own... they became godparents to each other's children. The families were closer than any blood relations they knew and it extended to two other families, the Mitchells and the Diamonds.

Carlos is Antonio and Sylvia's only child, and is several months older than Kendall is. People often mistake his gentle and childlike nature for naiveté', but he is actually very observant of the world around him. His quiet wisdom surprises many people who assume the happy-go-lucky boy is lacking intellectually. He is sweet and kind to everyone, but once a certain line is crossed, he lets you know in no uncertain terms that he isn't afraid to fight for what he believes in. Like Kendall, he is definitely his father's son and the two boys have grown to have the same close friendship that their fathers had.

James Diamond met Kendall and Carlos in preschool when they were all three. His mother is Brooke Diamond, the owner/CEO of one of the top modeling agencies in the

Midwest. He has grown up learning about fashion and how to present one's self when in public. He is considered by many to be shallow because of his attention to such things, but he is actually one of the kindest and most protective people that Kendall had ever known.

Logan Mitchell joined the group of friends when they were seven. He and his mom, Joanna, moved back to Shakopee from Texas after his parent's divorce. He is the top student at Shakopee Middle School and his dream is to become a doctor. He has always read at an advanced level and can often be found with his nose in one of the many textbooks that he has found online. People call him names like "nerd" or "geek" but it never phases him. He is quick to assist anyone having trouble with their studies and tutors many of the younger students. He is well liked by everyone except for a few select bullies whom he tries to avoid. He isn't really afraid of them, he is actually very quick on his feet and can outrun most of them. His friends, however, won't tolerate such treatment of the studious boy and have spent many hours in detention for going after someone who has mistreated their friend.

After Will died, Kendall began taking on responsibilities that no child should have to bear, but he took being the man of the house very seriously. There are times when he feels lost, alone, or unsure of what to do, and that is when he turns to Antonio. That is why he was now sitting on the porch swing on the Garcia's front porch, waiting for Antonio to return home from his patrol shift.

∞

It was already dark on this early November day and Kendall was shaking from more than the cold. He sat there, watching the snowfall and felt a shiver go through him. "At least it's from the cold," he thought, as his mind began replaying what was one of the most confusing and frightening days in his young life.

It all started when Jen called home from work around seven the evening before. Kendall had just come inside after shoveling the walk and answered the phone, "Hey mom."

"It's about time someone answered, I've called three times," Jen gently admonished.

"Sorry, I was out shoveling, I don't know where Katie went," Kendall said looking around for his sister.

"It's alright sweetheart, I know this is short notice but Elaine called in sick, we're already down two people and there's no one else to cover. I need you to warm up dinner for you and your sister and make sure Katie gets her bath and put to bed on time." "No problem mom. Don't worry about it, we'll be fine."

"Thanks Sweetie, I'll see you both in the morning then." "Bye mom," Kendall said and hung up the phone.

"Katie, why didn't you answer the phone?" Kendall called out as he went to the fridge and pulled out the leftover casserole that was in there. He popped it in the microwave and went to find his seven year old sister, who was being surprisingly quiet that evening.

"Katie, what are you up to? Mom has to work late so we need to get homework going and pick things up a little."

When he didn't get an answer, he walked upstairs to her room and knocked on her door. "Katie, are you in there?" He heard a little moan and opened the door. Katie was lying on her bed, holding her stomach.

"Are you okay?" he asked as he made his way over to her bedside.

She shook her head and mumbled, "I don't feel well."

Kendall put his hand on her forehead and found her very warm to the touch. He jumped up and ran to grab the thermometer. "Here, hold this under your tongue," he quietly instructed. Twenty seconds later it read 101.2, "Katie-Bug, you have a fever. What hurts?"

"My stomach and my head both hurt. I feel like I'm going to throw up, but I haven't yet," she told him.

"Okay, I'm going to get you something for your fever, just yell if you need me. I'll be right back though." He went to the kitchen and poured some ginger ale into an old sippy cup.

Then he went back into the bathroom, got two children's Tylenol, and grabbed the trash bin, just in case.

"Here you go Baby Sis, take these but drink slowly." he said as he helped her sit up. He sat next to her as she took the pills and drank a little more of the ginger ale.

She lay back down shivering a little so Kendall pulled her soft fleece blanket up around her. "Thanks Big Brother," she said in a quiet voice.

"Anything for you Baby Sis, but if you have to puke aim for the bin, okay?"

She grinned at him knowing he didn't handle that kind of thing well. "What'll you give me if I make it?"

"Respect and lots of hugs," he said.

Katie sniffled, "I prefer cash."

"Would you prefer to clean it up yourself?" Kendall teased back.

"Okay, okay I'll aim," she said pushing her lower lip out.

"That is not gonna work where puke is concerned. I'm going to go down and eat dinner, but I'll be back up soon. I have a ton of homework, so I'll do it up here where I can keep an eye on you." "Okay, thanks Kendall," Katie nodded. She closed her eyes, hoping to rest a little.

"Call me if you need anything," Kendall whispered to her as he headed downstairs.

After eating his dinner and cleaning up the dishes, Kendall grabbed his backpack and headed back upstairs. He looked in and saw Katie sleeping peacefully so he went into his own room, which was right across the hallway. He left the door open in case she needed him.

He groaned as he looked at the stack of books and papers he still had to do. He started on his math and had worked on it for about fifteen minutes when he heard retching coming from Katie's room. He jumped up and ran across the hallway where he found her throwing up into the trash bin.

He sat next to her rubbing her back, "It's okay Katie-Bug, I'm here." He grabbed a ponytail band from her night table and quickly tied her hair back so that she didn't get anything gross on it.

After a couple of minutes, she stopped throwing up and looked at him crying, "My tummy hurts really bad Kendall!"

"I know, let's take your temperature again and then I'm going to call Logan and see what he recommends, okay?"

She nodded and lay back down as Kendall grabbed the thermometer again. Her temperature was still at 101, so Kendall called Logan on his cell.

"Hello," Logan answered.

"Hey Loges, I have a question about something medical. Katie has a temperature of 101 and just threw up whatever it was she ate today. She says her head and stomach both hurt so I gave her a couple of Tylenol and ginger ale about an hour ago but her temperature still hasn't gone down." "It hasn't gone up though, right?" Logan asked.

"Nope still the same," Kendall replied.

"The stomach flu is going around so there isn't much else you can do except give her Tylenol every six hours and try and keep her hydrated. I would also take her temperature every hour just to make sure it isn't going up. Rest is really the best thing, if she can get any. Do you want me to come over and help out?" Logan asked his friend.

"No, that's okay. Thanks though, I'll call back if I have any more questions," Kendall smiled.

"Okay, I hope she feels better soon. See you tomorrow."

"Okay, bye Logan. Thanks again," Kendall said. He hung up and went back to sit next to Katie.

"Logan says it's probably the stomach flu and it pretty much has to run it's course," Kendall told her.

She sighed and rolled over on her side hugging her stomach, "Okay, I'm a little tired now so I'll try and sleep."

"Good girl," Kendall said to her as he kissed her cheek. "I'm going to go clean out the trash bin and then try and finish my homework."

He went into the bathroom dumping the contents into the toilet, quickly flushing before he had to add to it. He rinsed the bin out and returned it to Katie's bedside.

Twenty minutes later Katie cried out for him and he ran to her room, finding her with her head in the trash bin. After four hours of on again, off again vomiting, Kendall gave up on trying to get any homework done and turned on the small television in Katie's room.

About three hours later, he woke up when he heard the front door open. He carefully made his way to the hall so he didn't wake up Katie, who was finally resting peacefully. He saw his mother walking up the stairs and put his finger to his lips to shush her in case he startled her.

"What are you still doing up, don't you have school tomorrow?" Jen asked.

"Katie's been sick all night, Logan thinks it's the flu that's going around," he told her.

Jen groaned, "Okay sweetie, thank you so much. You get to bed now and I'll take over."

"She's actually sleeping pretty well right now, so maybe she'll be good for the rest of the night," Kendall said, stifling a yawn.

She kissed him on the forehead and pushed him towards his room, where he gratefully collapsed onto his own bed.

∞

Kendall woke up to an annoying beeeeep beeeeep, and threw his alarm clock across the room. Remembering Katie and the night before, he ran across the hall to her room and found that she was not in her bed.

He walked down to his mom's room and knocked quietly. "Come in Kendall" Jen said. He peeked in and saw Katie curled up in bed next to their mother.

"How is she?" he asked quietly.

"Her temperature is almost back to normal and she's been sleeping most of the night. You did a great job sweetheart!"

Kendall smiled and gave his mom a quick kiss on the cheek. "I have to get ready for school," he told her and ran to get ready.

After a quick shower and then breakfast, Kendall headed out to school. He hadn't thought to ask his mom for notes to explain why his homework wasn't done, but his teachers were pretty understanding and he knew they would call and confirm with his mom if they had any questions. He might get into trouble every now and then, but they all knew he was a good kid.

He ran into Logan at his locker. "Hey, how's Katie? You look like crap," Logan commented.

"Good morning to you too. She's doing a lot better this morning, Thanks for your help last night," Kendall said as he opened his locker.

James walked up behind him, "Dude what is with your hair, do you NEVER comb it?"

Kendall just looked at him and rolled his eyes, "We can't all be morning beauties like you James."

"True, true," James replied. "Couldn't you at least try? After all, we do hang out and I wouldn't want it getting around that my best friend doesn't know how to comb his own hair."

Kendall just rolled his eyes again and stuck his tongue out at him.

"Katie was sick all night, so give him a break," Logan told James.

"My Katie-Kat is sick! Is she okay?" James asked Kendall while pulling him closer to him. As Kendall started to answer, James pulled out his comb and tried to run it through Kendall's unruly hair.

"Ow! Yes, she's doing much better this morning," Kendall yelled.

"Hold still," James instructed as he finally got Kendall's bangs to stop sticking up. "There, not perfect but much better."

"Thank you and where exactly did you learn to comb other people's hair?" Kendall asked as he pushed James away.

"Well it wouldn't be so much work if you tried using a proper conditioner once in a while," James retorted.

Before Kendall could make a scathing reply the first bell rang, and they headed to first period math.

∞

The day went by rather slowly and Kendall struggled to pay attention in class, but three hours of sleep was not much to go on. All of his teachers had been understanding and had given him until Monday to hand in his assignments. He was hoping to get most of it done that night so he could hand it in tomorrow and have the weekend free.

He figured the only thing he wouldn't be able to finish was his English paper and the five-page questionnaire that the Mr. Deesie, the new teacher, had given them all. He and Logan had last period English together so they were going to meet James and Carlos after class and walk to hockey practice together. Dismissal bell rang and the students all gathered their books and headed out.

"I'll meet you out front after you talk to Mr. Deesie," Logan told Kendall.

"Great, it should only take a couple of minutes," Kendall smiled.

After everyone else had left, Kendall approached his teacher's desk. He was a little apprehensive, as he didn't really know the teacher very well. Mr. Deesie had taken over for Mrs. Cramer who had retired last June.

He was about forty-five, with blue eyes and thinning dark hair, cut short. He was about 5'10" and a little on the stocky side. He was always immaculately dressed, wearing a button down shirt, slacks, and sometimes a sweater vest. He seemed pleasant enough, although he addressed his students by their surnames instead of their first, which most of the kids found strange.

"Mr. Dessie, could I ask you about the assignments due tomorrow?" Kendall asked.

"What about them?" Mr. Deesie asked, looking up from his desk. He folded his hands in front of him, looking at the boy.

Kendall found himself wishing he'd asked Logan to stay with him. Mr. Deesie had a way of staring at you that was a bit unsettling.

"Um, well you see my sister was sick all last night and my mom had to work a double shift so I didn't have time to get much done. I was hoping I could get an extension until Monday. I can have it here first thing Monday morning before classes start," Kendall promised.

"I see, have a seat please Mr. Knight," Mr. Deesie said, indicating one of the desks in the front row.

"Okay," Kendall said, a bit confused.

Mr. Deesie stood up with his hands clasped behind his back and began to pace back and forth in front of the teen." Mr. Knight, do you know why we have assignment deadlines?" Kendall started to reply but Deesie put his finger up and said, "Wait until I am finished." "Sorry," Kendall muttered and watched his teacher pace in front of him.

"We have assignment deadlines because we have class deadlines. We have class deadlines because we have school deadlines. If we do not finish on time, it pushes everything out of order and we fall behind. I do not like to fall behind. The assignment that is due tomorrow will account for HALF of your quarterly grade. Do you understand that?"

"Yes, but that doesn't change the fact that I was up all night with my sick baby sister. There was no one else to take care of her," Kendall explained.

Mr. Deesie stopped in front of Kendall and looked down at him. "Was I finished speaking Mr. Knight?

Kendall just shrugged, looking at him unsure of what he should say.

"I was not," the teacher said, answering his own question. "Also, we do not shrug in my class."

Okay, my teacher is a whack job, Kendall thought to himself. As Kendall tried to think of a way to get out of the rest of the lecture, he realized that the teacher was no longer standing in front of him.

Kendall jumped as the man placed his hands on his shoulders still ranting about deadlines and what he expected from his students. Deesie started rubbing small circles on Kendall's neck with his thumb and the boy felt very uncomfortable. He gently tried to shrug the man's hands off him, but to no avail.

Mr. Deesie suddenly went silent. "What did I say about shrugging?"

"You know Mr. Deesie, you're absolutely right. I need to run home and get to work on this assignment right away," Kendall said, suddenly feeling unnerved. He moved to stand, but Deesie's firm grip wouldn't allow it.

"I am not finished speaking and I did not say that you were excused. I also did not say that I would NOT grant you an extension," Mr. Deesie said.

Kendall was now thoroughly confused by the teacher, but before he could say anything Deesie bent down and whispered into his ear, "How badly do you need this extension?"

"W-What do you mean?" Kendall managed to stammer out.

"You heard me," Deesie said. He reached down and kissed Kendall on the neck running his fingers through the blond hair. He released his hold on the teen, walked to the door and locked it repeating, "How badly do you need this extension?"

Kendall sat there in shock for a moment, his mind failing to comprehend what his teacher was proposing. "Why did you lock the door?" Kendall asked, standing up quickly.

"I am waiting for an answer, Mr. Knight. How badly do you need this extension?" Deesie asked for the third time, walking around the desk towards Kendall.

"I have to get to hockey practice and my friends are waiting out front for me," Kendall told the man backing away and trying to go around the teacher's desk to get to the door.

Deesie just smiled and continued to advance slowly. "I believe that being on the hockey team requires a passing grade Mr. Knight. Am I correct in assuming this?"

Kendall stopped and looked at him, angry now, "I'll tell the principal and coach what you've said and done!"

Deesie just laughed. "Who is going to believe you? Do you really think they will take the word of a teenager, who has had authority issues in the past, over that of a well-respected teacher?"

Although inside the teacher's words caused doubt, Kendall stood his ground. "Yes, because it's the truth!"

Deesie gave him a twisted smile, "Keep telling yourself that sweetheart."

Kendall made a dash for the door, unlocked it, and raced out.

Chapter 2~ Papi

Kendall quickly stopped at his locker and grabbed his backpack, throwing his books into it as he ran to the front doors. He needed to talk to someone who would believe him and knew the answer when he saw his friends waiting on the front steps.

"What took you so long?" Logan asked.

"Yeah, and why do you look like you're gonna hurl?" James asked as he noted that Kendall's face was pale and that he was shaking slightly.

"I-I'm not really feeling very well, you should probably go to practice without me. I don't think I can make it," Kendall told them.

Logan reached up and tried to feel his forehead, but Kendall pushed his hand away. Logan gave him a surprised and hurt look.

"Sorry, I just don't want you to get sick if I have the flu," he explained to his friend.

"Okay, but I will be calling to check on you after practice. If you need anything before then, just give me a call," Logan told him.

"Okay, thanks Loges," Kendall smiled. He watched as his friends started for the rink, and then, turned and walked the other way.

Carlos hadn't said anything, but he knew something was up with his blond friend. Kendall never missed practice, PERIOD. He looked back and watched as his friend walked away, knowing that something was wrong.

∞

Kendall's mind raced from one thought to another as he walked. He could not believe that Deesie was a creeper. He knew he had to get the assignment done tonight and turned in first thing tomorrow, and had no idea how he was going to accomplish that. He would just have to do his other assignments this weekend and turn them in on Monday, since he had already gotten extensions for those.

First, though, he needed to speak to the one person he knew could help him, Antonio Garcia.

So Kendall waited, sitting on his godparent's porch swing. He worked on his English assignment for as long as the sun was up. He managed to finish the questionnaire by the time it was completely dark, and then he sat, watching the snow. He was still so tired from getting no sleep the night before that he decided to nap a bit. He pulled his legs up onto the swing and the gentle swaying lulled him to sleep.

It was about 5:15 pm when Antonio Garcia pulled into his driveway. He walked up the path to his porch and went into the house.

He went upstairs and changed out of his uniform and into regular clothes, and then headed out to shovel the walkway before his wife and son got home. He turned on the porch light, walked out the door, and was surprised to find Kendall sleeping on his porch swing. He reached down and gently shook the boy's shoulder, softly calling his name.

"Hey buddy, what are you doing sleeping out here in the cold?"

Kendall awoke with a start, confused as to why he was so cold and stiff. He saw Antonio smiling down at him with concern in his eyes.

Kendall swung his legs off the swing and started shivering from the cold. "H-Hi, Papa G, sorry about that."

"Kendall, why are you sleeping out here in the cold? Shouldn't you be at practice with the other boys?" Antonio asked.

"I really need to talk to you about something, Papi. Something happened at school today and I-I'm not sure what to do," Kendall whispered, still trembling from the cold.

Antonio knew it had to be something serious—Kendall only called him "Papi" when he was frightened or sad. He leaned the shovel against the house, gently took Kendall's arm and guided him into the warm house.

Antonio led Kendall to his study, sat him down on the couch, and wrapped a blanket around him. Then he went into the kitchen and quickly made some hot chocolate for the both of them. They sipped their hot chocolate and Antonio waited for Kendall to warm up a bit before questioning him. He watched Kendall and knew the boy was trying to figure out how to say whatever it was that he needed to say.

"Doing a little better?"

Kendall nodded. "Yeah, a little. Thanks for the hot chocolate. I didn't realize how cold it was."

"So, what's going on?" Antonio asked gently.

Kendall tried to think of how to begin, so he started with the night before, telling Antonio about Katie being sick all night and how he didn't get much done in the way of homework or sleep. Antonio listened patiently, knowing these details were somehow important to what was bothering the boy and that it might take some time to get to the root of the problem.

Finally, Kendall got to the part where he asked his teachers for extensions.

"Most of the teachers were really understanding about it and told me I can turn my work in on Monday."

"Most? Who had a problem with it?" Antonio asked.

"M-Mr. Deesie, the new English teacher," Kendall told him.

"Okay, what was his problem?"

Antonio noticed that Kendall was no longer looking up and he was subconsciously clenching and unclenching his hands. At this point Antonio got extremely worried about what he was going to hear.

Kendall finally continued. "I stayed after class to ask Mr. Deesie if I could turn my assignment in on Monday. I still have a paper to finish, and he gave us a long questionnaire to fill out, so he can figure out exactly how much we know about English, literature and things like that. He told me to take a seat up front, and started lecturing me about how important it is to turn our work in on time. I guess because it makes him look bad otherwise."

"Did you explain to him about your sister being sick?" Antonio asked.

"I tried, but he didn't really seem to care about that. He told me that he wasn't finished speaking and that we don't shrug, whatever that's supposed to mean."

Antonio smiled and shook his head knowing Kendall's low tolerance for what he deemed to be pointless rules. "Go on."

"I guess I started to tune him out, trying to figure out how I could just leave, when I realized he was standing behind me. He started holding onto my shoulders, still talking about what's expected of his students and he s-started rubbing my neck. I started to get a little nervous and wasn't sure what to do."

Antonio nodded his expression neutral but his heart in his throat. "Go on."

"I finally told him that I agreed with him and that I should get home and get started right away. I tried to stand up, but he wouldn't let go. He said he wasn't finished speaking and that he hadn't excused me yet."

Kendall paused and took another sip of his cocoa. He started shivering again, but Antonio knew it wasn't from the cold. He smiled softly, reached over, and patted the boy's hand, encouraging him to go on.

"Then he whispered in my ear and asked me how badly I needed the extension. I asked him what he meant and he k-kissed me on the neck," Kendall said quietly.

Antonio inhaled sharply. "Kendall, look at me."

Kendall looked up at Antonio and he saw the concern in the older man's eyes. "Did he do anything else to you?" Antonio asked.

Kendall shook his head, "N-No."

"You're sure?" Antonio gently prodded.

"H-He didn't touch me again, but he l-locked the door and asked me how badly I needed the extension. Then he pointed out that I needed a passing grade to play hockey."

"He locked the door? You're absolutely certain about that?"

"Yes, I heard the click when he turned it, and I had to unlock it when I left."

"Okay, what then?" Antonio asked, trying to keep his voice even.

"T-Then he started walking towards me, and I told him I'd tell the principal and coach," Kendall told him.

"What did he say to that?" Antonio asked.

"He asked me if I really thought that they'd believe me over him. I told him, yes, because it was true. He told me to keep believing that and called me s-sweetheart."

"What happened next?" Antonio asked.

"He kept coming towards me, but I ran around his desk and got the door open. I got my stuff from my locker and met the guys outside," Kendall told him.

They both sat quietly for a few minutes, Antonio trying to decide what steps to take next, and Kendall just wishing he had stayed home today. "Did you tell the other boys about this?" Antonio asked Kendall.

"No, I haven't told anyone but you. I feel bad. I told them I was feeling sick so I could skip practice and come talk to you. I really didn't want anyone else to know. What if they don't believe me?" Kendall asked quietly as he found himself shivering again.

Antonio smiled softly at his godson and pulled him into a famous Garcia bear hug. "There is no way they would take that man's word over yours," he told him.

Kendall hugged him back, thankful for the safety he felt in Antonio's arms. "Thanks, Papi. I didn't know where else to go," he whispered.

"I'm going to make a phone call. I want you to stay in here and keep warm, and then I'll drive you home," Antonio instructed.

"Okay," Kendall nodded.

Antonio walked back into the kitchen and called his partner's cell phone.

"Aren't we done for the day?" Officer John Bennet joked as he answered the call.

"Not by a long shot," Antonio said. "I need you to meet me at the station in half an hour. We have a problem regarding a new middle school teacher, and I want to get right on this before something really bad happens."

"I'll see you there," Bennet replied, all trace of humour gone from his voice.

Chapter 3~ Meeting the Deadline

A few minutes later, Antonio and Kendall arrived at the Knight house. Antonio parked in the street and turned the lights off. "Okay Mijo, I'm going to head down to the station. Bennet is going to meet me there, and we're going to run a background check on this Deesie and see what turns up. I don't think we should tell your mom about this quite yet. She'd head right down there and confront him, which might complicate the investigation. Are you alright with that?"

Kendall nodded. "It's not like I want to talk to my mom about something like this anyway."

Antonio smiled. "I know you don't. Do you think you'll be able to get that paper finished tonight?"

"Oh, I'm definitely finishing it, even if I have to stay up all night," Kendall said.

"Good. Tomorrow hand in your work as usual and leave immediately after class. I don't want you staying behind, and make sure you're always with someone," Antonio instructed.

"Okay, but what if he tells me to stay after class?" Kendall asked, trying to think of anything that could go wrong.

"Tell him you can't and leave. I'm very serious about this, Kendall. I do not want you in there alone with him. I also want you to let me know if you see him approaching any other students after class. Alright?"

Kendall smiled at Antonio. "Will do!"

Antonio smiled back. "Alright, you should get inside. Try and not stay up too late, and call Logan if you need help finishing your paper. I'll call your cell once we find something out."

Kendall nodded, opened the door, and got out. Before he could close the door, Antonio called out to him. "Kendall, you did good today, son. I'm proud of you."

Kendall smiled. "Thanks Papi."

∞

Kendall started up the sidewalk and walked the short distance to his house.

"Hey mom, I'm home!" Kendall announced as he walked in the door.

Jennifer walked out of the kitchen where she was making dinner. "Hey sweetie, you're home a little early. How was practice today?"

"Umm, I didn't actually go to practice. I didn't get much of my homework done last night and Papa G offered to help me with a couple of the problems," Kendall told her.

"That was nice of him," she said, kissing his cheek.

"I still have a paper to finish, so I'm gonna head up and get started. How's Katie feeling?"

"She's doing much better, no temperature, and she's actually keeping food down," Jen told him.

"Thank God! I really don't think I could handle much more puke. She throws up a lot for someone so small!" Kendall said, heading up the stairs.

"Yes she does." Jen laughed as she went back to the kitchen.

He poked his head into Katie's room. "Hey Katie-Bug! How are you feeling? The guys all asked about you and said they hope you feel better."

She was sitting up on her bed playing video games. "I do, I haven't hurled once this afternoon," she said, waving him off as she tried to concentrate on the game.

"Okay, I'll let them know. Do you need anything before I get started on my homework?"

"Nope, I think I'm good. Thanks for staying with me last night, it really did make me feel better," she said, smiling.

"Anything for you, Baby Sis," he smiled back.

∞

Kendall had barely gotten started on his paper when his cell rang—it was Logan. "Hey Loges, how was practice?"

"Not too bad, there were a couple of other guys out sick, so coach just had us practice passing and such. How are you feeling?"

"I'm, okay. I think I'm mostly tired. I took a nap and feel a little better. I'm working on my English assignment now, so I can hand it in tomorrow," he said.

"Mr. Deesie wouldn't give you an extension?" Logan asked.

"No, apparently he doesn't believe in them. He told me we have deadlines for a reason, blah, blah, blah. I'm trying to get it done now. I finished the questionnaire, and I'm about two-thirds finished with the actual paper," Kendall told him as he typed away on his laptop.

"You do know that this paper is half of this quarter's grade, right?" Logan asked.

"Yeah, Mr. Deesie made that painfully clear," Kendall said.

"Do you need any help? I'm finished and can come over and give you a hand," Logan offered.

"No, I think I've got this handled. I know what I need to write, I just have to get it typed up, thanks!"

"No problem. Why don't you email me your paper before you print it up and I'll proofread it and organize the footnotes for you?" Logan said.

"Really? That would be great! I hate proofreading. It takes me longer to do that than it does to actually type it up."

"That's because your typing skills suck, you never know when to start and stop a paragraph, and I'm not even going to get into your lack of punctuation skills," Logan teased.

Kendall rolled his eyes. "I'm not even going to reply to that. Mostly because I don't want to do the proofreading, but just so you know, that was just mean."

Logan chuckled. "The truth hurts, buddy. By the way, how is Katie feeling?"

Kendall laughed back. "She's feeling much better tonight. No hurling today and she's able to concentrate on her video games."

"Well, at least her priorities haven't changed. Give her a hug for me and let me know when you send your paper," Logan said.

"Will do for both! Thanks again, Loges! Talk to you later." Kendall hung up and concentrated on his typing, deliberately ignoring paragraph placement.

Three hours later, Kendall called Logan to let him know he was getting ready to email the paper.

"Send it on over and I'll give you a call before I send it back. It'll probably take me a couple of hours. Maybe you should try and get some rest until then, you don't want to come down with what Katie had," Logan suggested.

"I think I'll do just that. Thanks Logan, I really do appreciate this. I don't know what I'd do without you!" Kendall told his friend.

Logan smiled, thinking back on all the times Kendall had literally saved his butt from bullies. "I'm happy to do it. After all, someone has to keep my correcting skills up-to-date."

Kendall smirked. "You're a funny guy tonight, aren't you?"

"I do what I can," Logan said, laughing.

∞

Antonio reached the police station about fifteen minutes after dropping Kendall off at home. He saw John's car already there and smiled. He knew his partner of five years was as dedicated as they came, and he was lucky to have him.

He walked into the station and went straight to his office.

Bennet looked up as Antonio walked in. "So, what's going on? Who's the teacher and what's the problem?" Bennet asked as he followed Antonio into his office. He listened carefully as his partner relayed his conversation with Kendall.

"Okay, why don't we just go pick this perv up then?" he asked when Antonio had finished.

Antonio shook his head. "Several reasons."

"Such as?"

"One, Deesie made sure to point out to Kendall that it would be his word against his and as there were no witnesses, that's pretty much the case. Two, Deesie claims that he's well respected in the teaching community. I want to check that out first. We need to see if there have been complaints of any kind filed against this man. My hunch is there aren't. If he had ever been investigated for something like this, there would have to be a record of it, and there's no way he would have been hired as a teacher here. At least, I hope he wouldn't have. Three, Kendall just turned fourteen and I really don't want to traumatize him with any publicity until we have all the facts. While it's a nice theory that they don't release the name of a minor in these cases, you and I both know somehow people always find out," Antonio explained.

"Okay then, we'll have Sally start a background check on Mr. Robert Deesie and see what we come up with. What's the plan if there's nothing on him?" Bennet asked.

Antonio sighed. "Then we have to get proof of what happened, which means asking my godson to wear a wire while confronting this guy. Something I really don't want to do."

"Understood. So, I guess we make sure we find all of this perv's dirty little secrets, no matter how well hidden," Bennet said with a smile.

"Exactly," Antonio said.

Chapter 4~ Deesie

Robert Deesie leads a structured life. His clothing is always clean and pressed, even his 400 thread count Egyptian cotton pajamas. His shoes are always proper dress shoes, polished so that he can see his face in them. If you looked in his closet, you would find the wooden hangers spaced precisely two inches apart, so that nothing creases. His shoes are set out precisely one and a half inches apart, so as not to scuff.

He has no ornamentation in his house, with the exception of a few well-placed antique mirrors.

His kitchen is immaculate. There is nothing on the counters, with the exception of a stainless steel toaster oven (regular toasters are barbaric and leave too many crumbs). His dishes are white, some might say plain looking, others elegant.

In the living room, there is a burgundy and gold tapestry sofa, rather dated, but in perfect condition. Two dark burgundy leather-sitting chairs were placed, one on either side of the fireplace. Over the mantel is a full-size mirror. The coffee table is dark wood and has several books of art and poetry, placed just so. There is one silk potted palm in an oriental pot sitting next to the front window—real plants leave a mess.

In his study, there are the usual books one might find in the home of an educator, with others that were hidden under false covers. On the walls a few accolades that he has acquired, nicely framed.

He has no family photos on the walls, no trinkets or knick-knacks that would collect dust.

His basement is much the same as the rest of the house. An immaculate laundry room with racks for drying personal items. Clean but otherwise empty, with the exception of one room, where there sits a locked antique trunk. In the trunk are various little souvenirs he has collected over the years.

Things you might find in anyone's keepsake box, except these items did not really belong to Robert Deesie. They belonged to a variety of young people that he has come across over the years. Personal items he took as reminders of his time with them, even a few photos. Every now and then, he will take out the key, open the trunk, and look at these things, sometimes smiling, sometimes crying. Always by the time he is finished though, there is hunger in his eyes.

Chapter 5~ Rumours

About an hour later, Antonio pulled back into his driveway. He smiled as he got out and was greeted by his son, who had been shoveling the walkway.

"Hey Papi!" Carlos yelled from where he was standing in the snow, where it was nearly a foot deep.

"Hey Carlitos, how was school today?"

"Okay. Kendall got sick and didn't make it to hockey practice. I guess Katie has the flu and he was up all night with her. Where were you?" Carlos asked, noticing his father was already wearing his street clothes, which was strange. He usually came home wearing his police uniform.

"I had to run back to the station, John needed help with something. So, do you know what's for dinner?" Antonio asked.

"I think Mami made chicken tonight."

"Good, I'm starving." He smiled as he put his arm around his son's shoulders and they walked into the house together.

After dinner, Sylvia and Antonio were in the kitchen cleaning up after dinner. "So, what's bothering you?" Sylvia asked her husband.

"What do you mean?" he asked.

"You've been distracted all evening, and I did notice that you were not in uniform when you got home. Which means you went back out, which means something happened," Sylvia surmised.

Antonio smiled at her. "John just needed help with something, so I ran down to the station to give him a hand."

"Something important I take it?"

"Why do you say that?"

Sylvia just looked at him, arms crossed, with a knowing look on her face.

"What?" Antonio asked as she arched an eyebrow at him. The one person he could never bluff was his wife. "Really sweetheart, everything's fine. I'm going to go help Carlitos with his homework," he said as he headed up the stairs.

A short while later, Antonio was helping Carlos finish his math homework. "Papi, can I talk to you about something?" Carlos asked.

"You know you can talk to me about anything Mijo," Antonio smiled.

"I'm worried about Kendall. He looked really strange after school. He said he wasn't feeling well, but I don't think that was all," Carlos said quietly.

"Didn't you say he was tired from being up all night with Katie? That could be part of it," Antonio said.

"I know, but he *never* misses hockey practice. Remember last year when he had bronchitis and the doctor told him to stay home? He still went to practice. The year before that, he played the day after dislocating his knee."

Antonio held his hand up before Carlos could continue with a complete rendition of Kendall's medical history. "Mijo, I know you're worried, but maybe he just didn't feel well. He was probably exhausted after being up with Katie all night. Sometimes even the strongest get tired and need to take a break."

"Maybe," Carlos said, although he looked unconvinced.

"Carlos, if you're worried, give him a call. If he doesn't answer, it means he's probably getting some well-deserved rest. If he does answer, then maybe hearing his voice will make you feel better."

Carlos smiled at Antonio. "Okay, I'll give him a call and see how he's feeling. Thanks Papi."

Antonio ruffled his son's hair and kissed him on the forehead. "Anytime Mijo."

∞

Kendall groaned as his ringing phone woke him up. "Hello?"

"Hey, I'm sending your paper back. It looks good, at least B material. Are you sleeping?" Logan asked, as he listened to his friend yawn.

"I was," Kendall said, yawning again.

"Sorry about that, I should have just printed it up and brought it to you in the morning," Logan said.

"No, that's okay, really. Thanks for all your help. You're sure it's B worthy?" Kendall asked.

"Definitely. I thought Fahrenheit 451 was an interesting choice for your subject. I like Ray Bradbury, although I haven't read much of his writing," Logan said.

"I wanted to pick something that was going to be unique, and I really like the book," Kendall told him.

"Well you did a good job with it. I'm sending it back to you now. Make sure you get some more sleep, and stay home if you start feeling sick. I'll print up a copy and take it in just in case."

"Okay, thanks Loges. Goodnight." Kendall smiled.

"Night Kendall."

Kendall got up, turned his laptop and printer on, and a couple of minutes later he had his assignment printed out and safe in his folder. He fell back onto his bed and was just starting to nod off, when his phone rang again.

He groaned as he answered. "Hello?"

"Hey Kendall, I just wanted to call and check on you," Carlos said.

"Hey Carlos, I'm okay, just tired is all," Kendall replied.

"Are you sure? You looked pretty wiped after school," Carlos asked, still feeling that something was off with his friend.

"Yeah, I'm fine. I got some homework done and was just going back to bed."

"Back to bed?"

"Yeah, I finished my English assignment and sent it to Logan for proofreading. He called a few minutes ago to let me know he was sending it back," Kendall told him.

"I glad he does that for us. I hate proofreading," Carlos said.

"Me too." Kendall laughed.

"Are you sure there's nothing bothering you? You know I'm here for you, right?" Carlos asked him.

Kendall smiled and silently cursed that Carlos could be so insightful. "I know you are. I'm okay, I'm just really tired."

"Okay, call me if you need anything, my phone is right here," Carlos said.

"I will, thanks buddy. I'll see you in the morning."

"Okay, goodnight Kendall."

"Night Los," Kendall said. He finally fell into a fitful sleep, dreaming of running down elongated school corridors, unable to find his way out.

∞

Outside a man was walking down the street and paused, as if to fix the laces on his boots. He looked at the house across the street and smiled a twisted smile as he watched the upstairs lights go off.

∞

Kendall awoke the next morning completely exhausted. He jumped in the shower, hoping it would wake him up a bit. After the steam from his shower had cleared, he looked in the mirror. He looked paler than usual and had dark circles under his eyes. He quickly splashed some cold water on his face and brushed his teeth. He ran his fingers through his hair as he went downstairs to grab some breakfast. His mom and Katie were already up and in the kitchen.

"Morning," he said as he walked in and grabbed a bowl for some cereal.

"Sweetie, you look terrible. Do you feel alright?" Jen asked as she put her hand on his forehead.

"I'm fine, I was just up late finishing my English assignment, it's due today."

"Well, you don't have a fever, but if you start feeling sick call me. Okay?"

"I will," he promised as he poured some cereal into his bowl.

"I have the late shift tonight, and Katie is going for a sleepover at Molly's. There's some leftover soup in the fridge, or I can leave you some money for pizza," Jen told him.

"Soup's fine, mom. We don't have practice tonight, so is it okay if the guys come over and watch a movie?" Kendall asked.

"Of course, but only if you're feeling okay. Wait, if the boys are coming over, they are not going to want soup. I'll leave money for pizza," she said, grabbing her purse.

"You're the best," Kendall told his mom, kissing her cheek.

"I know...By the way, NO pillow, water, snowball, chocolate chip, marshmallow, or popcorn fights! Especially in the house!" Jen said.

Kendall rolled his eyes. "Mom, we're not seven anymore."

"Didn't that just happen last month at James' house?" Katie smirked.

"Stop helping," Kendall ordered.

Kendall finished his breakfast, rinsed his bowl, and headed out for school. He made sure his phone was on vibrate, so he could keep it in his pocket in case Antonio called him. Carlos caught up with him about two blocks from school.

"Hey, how are you feeling?" Carlos asked his friend.

"I feel okay, just a little tired. My mom said you guys could come over for pizza and a movie tonight. She's working late and Katie won't be there to bug us."

"Sounds good, I'll call and ask my mom at lunch." Carlos smiled.

As they continued walking, Carlos started feeling queasy. "Kendall I think I'm going to puke."

Kendall looked at his friend, who had turned pale. "Can you make it to school?"

"I really don't think so," Carlos mumbled right before throwing up on the sidewalk.

"I'm going to call your mom so she can and come get you."

"Okay," Carlos whimpered, right before throwing up again.

Kendall quickly dialed the Garcia home and Sylvia answered. "Hi Mama G, it's Kendall. Carlos just got sick about a block from school. He doesn't think he can walk anymore."

"Tell him to hold on, I'm on my way."

"Okay, uh, you might want to bring a bucket for the car ride home," Kendall told her as he watched Carlos throw up again.

"Okay, thanks sweetie. I'll be there in a couple of minutes."

"Hey buddy, your mom's on her way," Kendall told Carlos as he rubbed his friend's back.

"Okay, thanks Kendall," Carlos said as the nausea eased a bit.

"No problem, buddy, it'll be okay. It's probably just the flu, like Katie had and it only lasted one day. Maybe we can do pizza and a movie next weekend."

Carlos nodded miserably. He looked embarrassed by the puke on the ground. Kendall smiled at his friend and quickly kicked snow over it.

A couple of minutes later, Sylvia pulled up next to them and got out. "Sweetie, are you doing okay?"

Carlos looked at his mom, bottom lip quivering, and shook his head no.

"Let's get you home and into bed. Thank you so much for staying with him, Kendall," Sylvia said as she opened the passenger door for her son.

"Anything for Carlos, Mama G," he said, helping his friend into the car and handing him the bucket he saw sitting on the floor. "Take care buddy! I'll call and check on you later."

Carlos waved goodbye as the car pulled away, and then quickly put his head in the bucket.

Kendall took off at a slow jog, realizing he was going to be late if he didn't hurry. He got to his locker just before first bell. He put his backpack in the locker and was pulling out his math book when someone slammed into him, pushing him against the lockers. He looked up and saw Jason Banks smirking as he quickly walked off.

What's his issue today? Kendall wondered.

Jason was one of the resident bullies at the school, but usually avoided Kendall and his friends since the day they let him know that beating on Logan and trying to lock him in his own locker was not going to be tolerated. They had issues every now and then, but the older boy (he had been left back twice) had finally figured out it wasn't worth going up against the four friends.

Kendall was on his way to first period and realized he was getting some strange looks from people. The next thing he knew, someone grabbed his arm and pulled him into the boys' restroom.

Logan had ahold of him and was visibly shaken. "Kendall, what happened yesterday?" Logan asked quietly.

"What are you talking about?" Kendall asked, thoroughly confused.

"What happened after English? Jason is telling everyone that he heard you proposition Mr. Deesie in exchange for an extension."

"What do you mean proposition?" Kendall asked.

"He's telling everyone that you offered to go down on Mr. Deesie for an extension."

"That is NOT what happened, Jason wasn't even there!" Kendall yelled, visibly angry, now that he realized what Logan was saying.

"Then what happened? You were obviously upset after talking to him."

"I told you what happened. He said he doesn't give extensions. Do you really think I would do something like that?" Kendall asked his voice suddenly quiet.

Logan looked at his friend and saw the hurt in his eyes. "O-Of course not, I-I just wanted to warn you about what's being said. We were all worried about you last night, and now Jason is spreading this like it's wildfire," Logan stammered.

The bell rang and Kendal walked past Logan and out the door. He entered the classroom with his head up and walked straight to his desk. He sat down, pulled out his book and papers, and ignored everyone around him, including Logan.

All the while Kendall's mind was racing, and he felt as if his heart might explode out of his chest at any moment. He could feel eyes on him and heard whispering around him.

Logan kept trying to catch his eye, but Kendall wouldn't look his way. He felt horrible and knew he should have handled things differently. He could hear the whispers too and turned several times to glare at the speakers. He knew his friend would never do what they were saying and that was probably what he should have opened their conversation with, but he'd been in shock.

The bell rang and Kendall gathered his things and headed out the door without looking back. Logan raced to keep up with him, but decided he should probably get ahold of James, who had been excused from first and second periods, because he had a dental appointment.

"CALL ME! ASAP," Logan sent in a text to James.

He finally caught up with Kendall at their lockers and took ahold of his arm again. "Kendall, please talk to me. I don't believe it and I handled that badly. I'm really sorry," Logan begged.

Kendall looked at him and it broke Logan's heart to see him so hurt. His eyes were wide and watery, his face ashen—he looked completely miserable. "So you do believe me?" Kendall asked quietly.

"Of course I do. I was just freaking out by what people were saying. I mean, it's Jason Banks and he has bullied most of the people in this school. You think they would be smart enough to take that into account. He probably just figured if he started a nasty rumour, it would be payback for all the times you put him in his place."

"Probably," Kendall said, but he had a sick feeling that this was not something that Jason had planned.

"Have you seen Carlos? We should probably let him know what's going on," Logan said.

"He got sick when we were walking to school and Mama G had to pick him up. I think he has the same thing Katie had. He was throwing up all over the sidewalk."

"Okay, we can call him later then. I already messaged James," Logan said.

Kendall nodded, thinking he should call Papi and tell him what was going on.

"It's going to be okay, really. Do you want to skip?" Logan asked his friend.

They had separate classes now, and he didn't want to leave Kendall alone. James usually had first and second period with Kendall, and Carlos had second and third, but with them not there, Logan thought maybe they should just go hang out somewhere.

"No, I'm not letting them have the satisfaction," Kendall said.

"Somehow I was afraid you were going to say that." Logan sighed. When the bell rang, they both set out to their respective classes.

"Thanks Loges," Kendall said as they parted. Logan watched his friend walk through what seemed to be a sea of people and prayed he would be alright.

Logan got to second period and took his seat. He heard a voice behind him. "Still friends with the manwhore I see," Jason remarked. People around them snickered.

"Why don't you shut up before someone puts YOU in a locker?" Logan retorted.

"Logan, is there a problem?" Mr. Westin asked.

"No sir," Logan replied still glaring at Jason.

"Then perhaps we can begin class, if you are quite sure you're finished?"

"Yes sir, sorry."

∞

Kendall handled second period the same way he did as first—ignoring everyone around him, doing his work, and then leaving as soon as class was over. When he was sitting in third period, he felt a hand on his arm.

"Hey Kendall, don't take what that jerk face is saying seriously. People are stupid to believe anything that bully has to say. Especially since he's beaten most of them up," Jenny Tinkler told him, smiling warmly.

Kendall smiled at Jenny. "Thanks Jenny, I'm sure it'll blow over soon."

"You and the guys have always been there for me, and I'm not gonna let some idiot convince me that you're something you're not," Jenny promised.

Kendall smiled at her again, and then winced as she totally missed her seat and landed on the floor, twice. She smiled broadly at him and managed to get into her seat without further complication on the third try.

Kendall quickly called Antonio after third period. There was no answer so Kendall left a message. "Hey Papi, can you give me a call?"

He ran into Logan at their lockers. It was lunch period, and Logan told him that James would meet them outside.

He opened his locker and some papers, that had been folded and pushed through the slots, fell out. Logan grabbed one and unfolded it. He quickly crumpled it, shocked by the graphic drawing on it.

"What did it say?" Kendall demanded, grabbing one of the other papers and reading it. "Manwhore for rent. Will do anything for a good grade. Call Kendall at ***-****."

Kendall just stared at it.

Logan snatched the paper from Kendall and read it. He gathered them all up and shoved them into his backpack, not wanting anyone to pull them out of the trash. "Come on," he said, grabbing Kendall by the arm and dragging him out the front door.

While James was waiting for the guys out front, someone handed him a flyer and laughed. He unfolded it and couldn't believe what was on it. He looked to see who had given it to him. He saw a couple of kids laughing. They were standing next to Jason Banks. James stormed over to him and grabbed him by his jacket.

"What is this?" James demanded.

"What's the matter, you didn't know your little friend offers to do "favours" in exchange for grades?" Jason smirked.

"You should be careful about what you say," James warned.

"What's the term? Squid pro clo?" Jason laughed.

"That's "quid pro quo," you idiot, and you should probably run right now," James advised.

"Oh yeah?" Jason said with a cocky grin on his face.

"Oh yeah," James growled. Jason laughed and stayed where he was, until he saw the look on James' face, and then he ran.

Logan and Kendall came out of the building at this time or James would have chased him down. He figured he would get another chance later on.

"What is going on?" James yelled.

"Shut up and come on," Logan hissed, still pulling a shocked Kendall along with him.

∞

They didn't look back, or they may have seen a certain teacher in the window, smiling. Once they were out of sight, he took a seat at his desk, pulled out a folder, and opened it. He perused the copy of Kendall Knight's student file, something he had managed to copy while the principal's assistant was out of the office. He found what he was looking for and picked up the phone.

A woman's friendly voice came on the phone. "Steak House, this is Denise speaking. How may I help you?"

"Hello, I'm not sure if you can tell me, but my wife and I were there last week and the hostess was incredibly kind, and we'd like to pay another visit while she's there."

"As long as you aren't asking for any personal information, it's allowed. Do you know her name?" Denise asked.

"I think her name tag said, Jennifer. She was the nicest lady, my wife and I were already impressed with your establishment, but she made us feel right at home. It's a long drive from St. Paul though, so I wanted to make sure she'd be there."

"Jen is very sweet!" Denise agreed as she checked the schedule. "You're in luck, she works tonight and tomorrow night. If you wanted to make a reservation, I'd be happy to do that for you," Denise offered.

"That's wonderful! I'll have to call you back after I speak with my wife. I'm not sure what time she wanted to go."

"I understand. Just give me a call back when you know, and we'll get you on the list," Denise told him.

"Thank you, I'll do just that," Deesie said and hung up. He sat back, smiling as he read the file once more. "I've waited so long, but soon we'll be together," he said, looking at Kendall's school picture.

Chapter 6~ Broken Trust

The boys kept going until they reached the park about four blocks away. Logan had a firm hold on Kendall, and James actually had to rush to keep up. All the way there, Logan kept wondering about why this was happening and what they were going to do about it. It had to be Jason's sick way of getting even with them for all the times they went up against him. He knew Jason hated them all, but especially Kendall.

∞

Jason did not like being put in his place and two years ago, when Kendall saw him pounding on Logan after school, he'd ended up on his back, with Kendall wailing on him like there was no tomorrow.

In spite of the fact that Kendall was two years younger and was half the size of the bully, it was Jason who limped away that day. A week later, Jason had tried to exact revenge by beating on Logan again, and was in the process of trying to shove the door shut on the locker he'd just put Logan into, when he heard another battle cry and Jason went flying down the hallway, with Kendall on top of him.

This time, Jason recovered and had thrown Kendall off and was proceeding to kick the crap out of him, when another body hit him. Logan had jumped onto his back, yanking at his ears and hair, anything to get him to stop.

Jason smashed backwards into the wall and Logan lost his hold on the huge boy. Just as Jason was getting ready to unleash another round of abuse, he was hit by a third body as Carlos landed on his back, and then a fourth as James threw himself at Jason's legs, knocking him to the floor.

Before he knew it, Jason was effectively pinned to the floor with Kendall sitting on top of him, arms crossed, asking, "Have you had enough? Because we can do this all day."

Jason glared daggers at him but nodded his face red with anger as he stopped struggling.

"Good, now this is what's going to happen," Kendall said in a very low voice. "You are going to leave Logan and everyone else alone, or we are going to fold YOU in half and lock you in your own locker. Understand?" Jason just looked up at him, fuming.

"I asked if you understand." Kendall said, still sitting on top of the bully, calmly looking down at him, eyebrow raised.

Jason finally nodded and Kendall stood up, grabbing Logan's arm and pulling him up with him. Carlos and James both let go, and they all stood together, no one saying a word.

Jason had gotten up and looked at the four of them, debating on whether he should try going after them. He wisely chose to turn around and walk away.

∞

They finally stopped at the oak tree that overlooked the pond. "What is going on?" James asked again.

He looked at his two friends. Logan's face was flushed with anger, and he still hadn't released his grip on Kendall. Kendall's face, on the other hand, was expressionless and he was pale.

James took ahold of the hand that was holding onto Kendall's arm and gently began prying the fingers loose.

'You need to tell me what's going on!" James pleaded.

Logan opened his backpack and took out the papers he had shoved into it. "This is the crap that Jason has been spreading around all morning," he said, handing them to James.

As Logan explained what Jason was telling everyone at school, James looked at the papers, each one worse than the last. His jaw clenching tighter and tighter. After he'd finished looking at them all, he handed them back to Logan. He saw that Kendall was now sitting under the tree, looking at the pond. His expression was far away and detached, the dark blue pond reflecting in his eyes, making them a cold and strange mix of blue and green.

"Where's Carlos?" James asked Logan.

"Home sick, he has the stomach flu," Logan said.

"We do NOT let him see these," James said. Logan nodded in agreement.

James walked over and sat down next to Kendall. "You doing okay, buddy? You're awfully quiet."

Kendall nodded. His mind was racing, wondering what he should say and desperately hoping that Papi would call him back soon.

"Are you sure?" His friend's calm demeanor worried James. He expected him to be yelling, maybe throwing things. Sitting here quietly under the tree was NOT something he would call a normal Kendall reaction.

Kendall sighed. "What do you want me to say, James? Jason finally figured out a way to get even."

Logan came over and sat on the other side of Kendall. "Well, what are we going to do about it?"

"Nothing," Kendall replied quietly.

"Nothing?" Logan and James yelled.

"Nothing," Kendall repeated. "Think about it, if we go in there and cause a scene, it's just going to get worse. It's Friday. If we just get through the rest of today, it'll probably blow over by the end of the weekend. People will have a chance to think about it and realize it's just Jason being a jerk."

Logan was surprised by his friend's logic, and had to admit it made sense.

James, on the other hand, was turning several different shades of red, and for a moment, Logan thought he might actually pass out.

"James, breathe," Kendall told him.

James nodded, took a deep breath and then shrieked, "HOW CAN WE NOT DO SOMETHING?!"

"James..." Kendall started.

"We can't let him get away with something this bad! I mean, it's one thing to call people names like nerd, geek, shrimp—sorry Logan. Or to pick them up like a toddler and try and lock them in their own locker—sorry again, Logan, but this goes WAY too far!"

"He won't get away with it and... ouch!" Logan said, smacking him on the arm for his previous comments. "But Kendall is right. If we make a big deal about this now, then he looks guilty. If we just play it cool, give people a chance to THINK about it, and then we can deal with Jason after things calm down. I mean, it's not like Mr. Deesie is accusing Kendall of this, it's Jason, and everyone knows he's a liar."

The mention of Deesie made Kendall want to vomit, but he was careful to stay calm. He knew Deesie had to be behind this somehow. The door had been closed, and Jason was one of the first ones to leave after class.

Papi, please call, he thought, hoping that Antonio had found something, anything on Deesie. He took a deep breath and said, "We should get back."

"Are you sure? Maybe we should just skip the rest of the day," Logan suggested.

Kendall stood up and put his hands out to help his friends up. "I am not running away."

James and Logan looked at each other and then at Kendall. They each took an offered hand and stood up. "Let's do this then," they said together. Kendall just shook his head and smiled at them.

A few minutes later, they were back at school and at their lockers. They pulled out their assorted textbooks and folders and got ready to head to class. "Okay, we meet back here after EVERY class," James instructed. He wanted to make sure that both of his friends were okay.

"Agreed," Kendall and Logan said.

The next two classes were a blur to Kendall. He did the same as he had that morning, ignoring everyone. He just wanted to get through to the end of the class. He kept checking his phone, but nothing from Antonio yet.

That means they haven't found anything either, he thought miserably.

He decided he would just go over to the Garcia's after school to check on Carlos, and maybe Antonio would be home soon after. He could show him the one paper he had managed to keep from Logan and tell him about the others.

The bell finally rang and Kendall headed to his locker. He opened it and was grabbing his English book and folder, when someone slammed him into the lockers.

"Hey Kenny, watcha doing? Getting ready to take care of business?" Jason snarled at him.

Kendall rolled his eyes and attempted to detach himself from the bully's hands. "Get off me, Jason."

Jason slammed him back again. "Make me." He smiled.

Kendall smiled back and Jason felt a tap on his shoulder. He looked over his shoulder to see one furious brunet. "Remember when I told you to run earlier?" James whispered. "DO IT AGAIN!"

Jason took off at a dead run down the hallway and out of sight.

"Thanks James," Kendall said.

"No problem. I like it when he runs. Although he has terrible form," James smiled.

"What's going on?" Logan asked as he walked up behind them.

"Not much, just making sure Jason gets his exercise," James told him, pulling out his comb to straighten any wayward strands.

"Okay, do I even want to know what that means?" Logan asked.

"Kendall Knight to the office please, Kendall Knight to the office," the voice of Tara Shipley, the Principal's assistant, came over the loudspeaker

Kendall sighed, "Now what?"

"Cheer up, at least you get to see the future Mrs. Diamond," James said with a dreamy smile as he thought of the pretty brunette with the big blue eyes.

Kendall and Logan both rolled their eyes.

"Give me your homework and I'll take it to class," Logan instructed.

"Thanks Logan," Kendall said and handed it to him. He headed off towards the office, wondering what was going on now.

"Meet us back here after class," James yelled after him.

Kendall waved an acknowledgement before he turned down the next corridor. He walked into the office and greeted the assistant, who sat behind a large brown desk. "Hi Ms. Shipley, you called me down?"

"Hi Kendall, have a seat and Principal Lane will be right with you."

Kendall sat down and tried to figure out what he'd done to be called to the office, when Principal Lane opened the door and called him in. Kendall got up and followed her into her office.

Principal Janice Lane was a well-dressed blonde with her hair cut into an efficient bob. She was in her late forties and loved her job. She'd always loved working with children and believed that there is good in all of them. She was patient and kind, well-liked by the students,

faculty, and parents. She always made people feel at ease, and at this moment was wondering exactly how to approach the situation at hand.

"Hello Kendall, have a seat," she told him as she sat down at her desk.

He sat in one of the chairs in front of her desk.

"So, do you want to tell me what's been going on the last couple of days?" she asked.

"Um, well Jason seems to be having a problem with me, but other than that, not much," Kendall said.

"Oh yes, Jason. I will be speaking with him on Monday. Kendall, I'm talking about the problem between you and Mr. Deesie," she said carefully.

Kendall's heart nearly stopped. "Mr. Deesie?"

"Yes, do you want to tell me about it?" Principal Lane asked.

"There's not really much to tell. I had to ask him for an extension on an assignment yesterday, because Katie was sick and I was up with her all night. He really didn't seem like he wanted to. He said that deadlines are important, so I made sure to get it done so I could hand it in on time. Logan's turning it in for me now," Kendall told her.

"Poor Katie, how is she doing today? I hear this twenty-four hour bug is awful," Principal Lane asked.

"She's much better, thanks. Now Carlos has it. He got sick on the way to school this morning."

The Principal sighed. "I guess it is that time of year."

"Was that all?" Kendall asked, hoping to get out of there as soon as possible.

She folded her hands and rested her chin on them. "Kendall, do you understand what it means to make an inappropriate suggestion?"

"I'm not sure what you mean," he said quietly.

"Mr. Deesie came to me and told me about the conversation he had with you after class yesterday."

"What about it?" Kendall asked. His stomach was starting to do flip-flops, and he was really hoping that he wasn't going to throw up right then and there.

She sighed again. "Kendall, I know things are difficult for you sometimes, with your mom having to work so much, you having to help take care of Katie, and trying to squeeze in all the things that go along with being a kid. I understand when you and the boys play your little pranks. I even find some of them funny. But, there are limits as to what can be tolerated and offering sexual favours in exchange for an extension or better grade is one of those things that cannot be tolerated."

"What!" Kendall jumped up from the chair. He couldn't believe this was happening. "I did NOT offer that perv anything! All I did was ask for an extension and HE is the one who suggested something!" Kendall shouted. He was furious now.

"Kendall, sit down now! I will not be screamed at!"

Kendall debated on just leaving, but decided he needed to get this fixed. He returned to his seat and tried to stop shaking.

∞

Logan walked into Mr. Deesie's English class and was greeted with the usual smile. "Good afternoon, Mr. Mitchell."

Logan smiled back and went to his desk. "Please hand your assignments forward," Mr. Deesie said after the bell rang.

He then proceeded to go to the first desk in every row and pick them up. After gathering all of the papers, he cleared his throat. "I'm afraid there is a very serious matter that I need to discuss with you all. There was an unfortunate breech of conduct here by a student yesterday. After speaking with Principal Lane, it was decided that she will deal with the offending student and I will discuss with you exactly what behaviour can be tolerated in this class. Indeed, in this school."

Logan stared ahead in disbelief. That was why Kendall had been called to the office.

Mr. Deesie continued, "I understand there might be some confusion as to what behaviour may be deemed offensive, so Principal Lane and I drew up this basic guideline of what is inappropriate. If you have any questions regarding any of this, please know that you can come to Principal Lane, the guidance counselor, or me. While there is a possibility the comments were said in jest, they were inappropriate nonetheless. The student in question is being counseled by Principal Lane and it will be recommended that they see Mrs. McGrath on a regular basis until they understand their misdeed completely."

Jason snickered, causing others to do so as well.

"Mr. Banks, is there something you would like to say?" Mr. Deesie asked.

"No sir," Jason replied, looking over at Logan with a smirk.

"It is also to be understood that bullying, ridiculing, muttering demeaning comments, OR the passing of papers with offensive comments or drawings will also NOT be tolerated. Is this perfectly clear?" Mr. Deesie said, glancing around the room with a final look at Jason.

"Yes, sir," they all replied.

"Good. As this has been a difficult day, I want you to all read quietly, and you may leave as soon as the bell rings," Mr. Deesie said.

Logan felt like he had been sucker punched. What Jason had said was true.

∞

Things were not going much better in Principal Lane's office.

"Kendall, you have to understand that I can't just let this go. These are VERY serious charges."

"Which are LIES!" Kendall yelled frantically.

"Kendall, please calm down and lower your voice. Why don't you tell me your version of what happened, quietly please," she said, rubbing her temples.

Kendall took a deep breath, trying to calm down. Principal Lane got up and poured a cup of water from the cooler. She handed it to Kendall and told him to take a drink, and that was when she noticed his shaking hands. She looked at him more closely and saw his pale face, the dark circles under his eyes, and the look of panic that he was trying to keep down. She made note of the rapid breathing and eyes that would water with tears he was not allowing to fall. In an instant, she began to question the accusation.

"Kendall, tell me what happened."

He looked at her. "Why bother? You won't believe me anyway, he said you wouldn't."

With that, he got up and walked out. For a moment, she contemplated following him. Instead, she picked up her phone and called out to the front desk. "Tara, please bring me Mr. Deesie's personnel file."

∞

Kendall walked out of the office, and then ran to the bathroom. He rushed into a stall and emptied the contents of his stomach. He couldn't believe this. Deesie was setting him up and everyone was falling for it. He flushed and sat next to the toilet in case he had to vomit again. He tried to calm his breathing and closed his eyes for a few moments. He heard the final bell ring and got up. He washed his hands and splashed some cold water on his face. He needed to find Logan and James.

∞

After the final bell, Logan raced out of the classroom. He made his way over to James' classroom and grabbed him by the arm as soon as he came through the door.

"What's wrong? Is Kendall okay?" James asked him. Logan's face was red and James could tell he was angry about something.

"Read this," Logan said, giving him the paper that Deesie had handed out.

James' eyes widened as he read it. "What is this?"

Logan told James what Mr. Deesie had said in class. How he'd chewed Jason out for what he'd done.

"This has to be some kind of mistake," James whispered.

"This is from Principal Lane, there's no mistake," Logan said, indicating the paper he had just given to James.

∞

Kendall made his way through the hallway to his locker. He opened it up and put on his jacket and grey beanie. He grabbed his backpack and waited for the guys. A few minutes later, Logan and James walked up. Kendall immediately knew something was off with his two friends.

Logan looked at him, anger flashing in his eyes. "Well, Kendall, is there something you want to tell us?"

"Like the TRUTH, maybe?" James added in anger, completely ignoring Kendall's slightly confused face.

"What?" Kendall asked quietly, looking from Logan to James.

"What REALLY happened yesterday?" Logan asked angrily, shoving the paper from Deesie at him.

Kendall looked at the paper and his face went pale again. "I told you what happened," Kendall insisted, desperately wishing Antonio would call so he could tell them what had really happened.

"Really, then why is the PRINCIPAL going to recommend that you go to counseling? I can't believe you would do something like this, much less LIE to your best friends about it!" Logan said, practically shouting now.

"We were worried sick about you all day, and it turns out we can't even trust you!" James muttered.

Kendall stood there, just looking at them. He was in too much shock to say anything. They thought he had lied to him, that he was guilty of the horrible thing that Jason said he had done. For a minute, he thought he might pass out. Instead, he pushed past them and went out the front door.

They went out right after him and James grabbed his arm. "What's the matter, you don't have anything to say for yourself?"

Kendall looked at them, unshed tears glistening in his eyes. "Go to hell," he whispered as he pulled away and ran his heart shattering with every step.

They watched as Kendall ran away from them, wondering what could have possessed him to do something like this. James suddenly had doubts...this was Kendall. They had known each other for most of their lives, and he had never done anything to break their trust. He looked at Logan.

"Are you sure about this?"

"James, it's not like when another student accuses someone of something like this. This is a teacher for God's sake, and the Principal drew this paper up, and Kendall was in her office all last period, being talked to about this."

"I guess... I just would have hoped he could talk to us about it," James said quietly.

"Well, he didn't. In fact, he lied to our faces," Logan fumed.

∞

Robert Deesie watched the boys from his classroom window and smiled. He turned and went back to his desk, laughing quietly to himself.

Chapter 7~ Uncovered Truths

Officer Sally O'Hara was a 12-year veteran of the Shakopee Police Department and the second in command, under Chief Garcia. She had graduated top of her class in criminal law with a minor in computer forensics. She worked both field and on the desk, and tonight, she was in the office, tracking down any information that she could find on Robert Deesie.

She smiled and shook her head as the phone rang and she saw it was Antonio.

"Sally, anything yet?"

"Not yet Boss. I promise I'll let you know as soon as I find something, although things might go a little faster if I didn't have to keep answering the phone."

"It hasn't been that many," he said.

"Eight and counting," Sally told him.

Bennet chuckled at the sound of exasperation in her voice. "Give her a break, Garcia. She's doing everything she can."

"I know, I know. I just hate waiting," Antonio grumbled.

"I will give you a call the minute I find something," she promised.

"Thanks Sally." He sighed and hung up.

∞

Everything Sally had pulled up on Robert Philip Deesie was clean. He never even had a speeding ticket. Ten years ago, he was named "Teacher of the Year" two years running at the private school he taught at in Chicago. Everyone she spoke with said he was an incredible teacher, who excelled in working with special needs children. The principal said they had been sorry to see him go, but five years ago, his fiancé had been offered an amazing job in Toledo, so he had taken a position in a public school there.

The school in Toledo had nearly the same to say as the one in Chicago. Students, faculty and parents all adored him. A year ago, he took a sabbatical, no record of marriage, so people assumed it was because he and his fiancé had broken up. He'd applied for and been offered the position at the middle school here.

∞

"Look, you know as well as I do that if there's something out there, Sally will find it. It's easy to find the good stuff, but it takes time to find the dirt. I know it's out there, but you have to give her a chance to find it," John told his partner.

"I know. I just hate the thought that a pedophile is a teacher in our schools," Antonio said.

"Look, on the bright side, it's Friday. You know Sally will work all through the weekend if that's what it takes. By Monday, we'll be locking the little perv up for good."

Antonio smiled at his partner's optimism. "I hate it when you do that."

"What?" John asked innocently.

"Make things sound so logical."

John just laughed at him.

"Laugh it up, it's just because I'm not use to it," Antonio added with a smirk.

∞

Kendall ran until he found himself back at the park. He collapsed under the oak tree, hugging his knees to his chest. He hadn't felt such pain since his dad had died. No, not even then. His dad couldn't help dying, and he wasn't completely alone then.

What was he going to do? His best friends, his brothers, thought he was a pervert and a whore. He would never forget the look of anger and betrayal on their faces, or their angry words.

God, when did everything go so wrong? Why does everything always have to be so hard? He sat there for a few minutes, his head on his knees, trying to calm down.

"Daddy, what do I do?" he whispered.

He sat quietly, listening to the sounds around him and watching the ducks on the pond. *In a few weeks, the pond will be frozen solid and we'll be able to go skating*, he thought. *We... If I don't figure out a way to fix this, there won't be a "we."*

Suddenly he knew what he had to do. He grabbed his backpack and pulled out his MP3 player. He scrolled through the features, until he found what he was looking for. Then he got up and headed back to school.

Once he got there, he headed to the library and logged onto one of the computers. He found a site that explained Minnesota State laws and found what he needed. He turned on his MP3 player and put it in his shirt pocket. He pulled out his phone, turned on the video application, and put it in his jacket. He took a deep breath and headed toward the classroom, hoping Deesie was still there.

Kendall looked in and saw the man sitting at his desk, grading papers. Taking another deep breath, he went in and closed the door behind him.

"Mr. Deesie, I need to talk to you."

"Well, well, Mr. Knight, I cannot say that I'm surprised to see you here. Take a seat," he said, indicating the desks in front of him.

"I'll stand, thank you," Kendall said, refusing to sit down.

Deesie gave him an annoyed look. "Have it your way then. What can I do for you today?"

"You can try telling people the truth. I know you had Jason spread those lies about what happened."

Deesie just smiled at him. "Having trouble getting people to believe in our innocence, are we?"

"You won't get away with this," Kendall said, watching the man carefully.

Deesie got up from the desk and walked to the door, locking it again. "We wouldn't want anyone walking in on our private conversation, would we?"

"Yeah, w-well what if I told you I was recording this conversation so it d-doesn't matter if the door is locked or not?" Kendall stammered at him.

Deesie looked at the boy. "Exactly how would you be doing that? I see no video or tape recorder?"

"There are a lot of things that can record... digital cameras, phones, lots of things," Kendall said.

"Really? Very curious, perhaps I could see your phone then?"

"W-Why?" Kendall asked nervously.

"Just show me," Deesie instructed.

Kendall reluctantly pulled his phone out of his pocket. Deesie picked it up and looked at it. The video function was on and was set to record. He shook his head, clicked delete, and then turned the phone off. "Mr. Knight, how stupid do you think I am?" he asked, handing the phone back to the boy. Kendall snatched it away from Deesie with a frustrated look on his face.

"Now, where were we? Oh, yes what can I do for you today? Or rather, what are you willing to do for me? I should tell you, I have been grading the assignments that were handed in and your paper is, inadequate, to say the least. I'm afraid you will be getting a D, which will result in your unfortunate removal from the hockey team."

"My paper was good and I deserve more than a D!" Kendall yelled.

"Then you probably won't be pleased to learn that your friend, Mr. Mitchell's paper is also far below my expectations, and he will be receiving a C, bringing his average down to a B. Perhaps he was too busy helping you with your paper to do a better job on his own?" Deesie suggested.

Kendall was now visibly upset, thinking this was one more thing to add to the list of his offenses.

"Logan did not help me with my paper, and he finished his assignment long before it was due!"

"Regardless of what you claim, the grades will stand, unless you can convince me otherwise, and I am certain that Mr. Mitchell will not be too pleased. I believe that he wants to go to medical school. He has worked so hard to keep his record flawless. A shame really," Deesie said, as he walked towards the boy again.

Kendall shook his head. "You stay away from me."

Deesie stopped walking and just stared at him.

After a moment, Kendall asked quietly, "What do I have to do?"

"Just be nice to me," Deesie purred.

"Why don't you just spell it out?" Kendall demanded.

"Hmmm, interesting thought. Let's make it easy for you and go back to the basics. You DO remember your ABC's?"

"What?" Kendall asked, thoroughly confused by the question.

Deesie began to walk a wide circle around the boy. "Let's start with A, as in you ask me what I want you to do and you always do what I ask. B is for blowjob, but don't worry, I like giving as much as receiving. I find youth is just so... tasty. Finally, C is for copulate, although not the literal translation, of course. If you need definitions for these words I can provide them."

Kendall seriously thought he might throw up.

"Well, are we in agreement?" Deesie asked.

"No!" Kendall shook his head and made for the door.

"I wouldn't turn me down if I were you. I will give you until Monday to change your mind. After that, the grades stand," Deesie warned.

Kendall unlocked the door and ran out. Once outside, Kendall pulled his earbuds out of his backpack and plugged them into the MP3 player.

"Please, please, please!" he prayed. He listened for a moment and smiled, feeling hope for the first time in what had to be the longest day of his young life. He grabbed his backpack and headed home.

∞

Kendall ran into his house and up the stairs to his room. He grabbed a flash drive from his desk and plugged his MP3 player into the computer.

"Kendall, is that you?" Jen called up to him.

"Yeah, hi mom."

"Is everything okay? You usually let me know when you get home," she said.

Kendall went downstairs and kissed his mom on the cheek. "Sorry about that, just something I needed on the computer."

"Where are the boys? Aren't they coming over for the night?"

"Um, no... Carlos is sick, so we're going to do it another time," Kendall explained.

"Oh no, is it what Katie had?"

"Yeah, he started throwing up on the way to school. Mama G had to pick him up. I thought I'd go over and see how he's doing, try and cheer him up," Kendall told her, hoping that Carlos didn't hate him yet.

"That's a good idea, sweetheart. Why don't you take them the soup I made? If Carlos is as sick as Katie was, Sylvia probably doesn't feel like cooking."

"You want me to carry a pot of soup to their house?" Kendall laughed.

"I'll drop you off, smarty pants. You can walk home when you're through visiting. I should be ready to go in about twenty minutes."

"Okay, sounds good. Gives me time to finish up what I was doing," Kendall said, walking back upstairs.

After the files had been transferred to the flash drive, Kendall took an envelope and wrote 'Papi' on it. He dropped the flash drive inside and wrote a quick note on the paper that Jason had put in his locker. He sealed it and shoved it into his pocket.

∞

Tara had pulled out the personnel file on Robert Deesie and taken it into the principal. "You know, it's a lot easier if I just pull it up on the computer," she said with a smile.

"I know, but I like to read the written responses. You can learn so much by the way people answer things on paper," Janice said.

"You're just afraid that you'll delete the year's fiscal reports again." Tara laughed.

Janice smiled at the memory of the unfortunate incident. "I hate computers."

"They aren't too fond of you either," Tara teased.

"Tara, what do you think of Mr. Deesie?" Janice asked her assistant and friend. She knew all of the students liked her assistant. She also knew that Tara paid very close attention to what went on in the school. She was a second set of eyes and ears and could always be relied upon for an honest answer.

"Honestly, not very much," Tara said.

"Why?"

"He just doesn't seem to fit with what I would expect of a middle school teacher. I know he taught in a fancy school in Chicago, but the guy dresses and speaks as if he should be teaching in a University. I don't think the kids can relate to him very well. He's always calling them by their surnames and he doesn't really seem that interested in their thoughts or ideas. It's like he wants things his way or else."

Janice nodded in agreement.

The main door to the office opened and Tara went out to see who it was.

"Hi, Ms. Shipley," Jenny Tinkler waved, sending the cup of pens that were on the desk flying across the room.

"Hi, Jenny, don't worry about the pens, I'll get them," she told the girl, afraid that other things would soon become airborne. "What can I do for you, sweetie?"

"I just have a question about the paper Mr. Deesie handed out in class. He said we could ask Principal Lane about it if we were confused, and well, I am," she said with another bright smile.

"What paper?"

Jenny handed her the paper. "He said Principal Lane drew up this guideline for us about behaviour, and I just want to make sure I know what it means."

Tara looked at the paper, "He said Principal Lane drew this up?"

"Yeah," Jenny said.

"Okay, let me take it to her. Have a seat and Jenny. DON'T touch anything else. You know the procedure."

Jenny smiled at her again and sat down in one of the chairs, tucking her hands underneath her and crossing her ankles, tucking them under the chair. Tara smiled at her and went back into the office.

"Janice, do you know anything about this?" Tara asked, as she handed the paper to her.

Janice looked at it and muttered, "What the hell is this?"

"Jenny brought it in. She said Mr. Deesie handed them out in class and told them that you drew it up."

"No, I didn't. Is Jenny still here?" she asked, frowning.

"Yes, she's sitting out there in neutral," Tara said.

Janice smiled and walked out and heard first-hand from Jenny exactly what had happened today. After sending Jenny on her way with no other incidents, Janice asked Tara her opinion on the whole matter.

"You know, I adore Kendall, he's a great kid. I can't see him doing what Mr. Deesie is claiming he did. I honestly don't think he has that much experience. He just turned fourteen and while that doesn't really mean much in today's world, Jennifer and the other boys' parents have all done a very good job of making sure that their kids don't grow up too fast. They still have sleepovers playing video games and watching Disney movies... Please don't tell Carlos I spilled the beans about that!" Tara asked.

Janice smiled. "Secret is safe with me."

"What are your thoughts about him?" Tara asked.

"I don't know, the officials I spoke with at the other schools all spoke so highly of him, but it just doesn't seem to be the case here," Janice said.

"I know Kendall has had to grow up faster than he should have, but that doesn't mean he's lost his innocence. As I said, I don't really care for Mr. Deesie. I don't think he treats the kids like they matter, like you do."

"Meaning?" Janice asked.

"You treat the kids like their opinions count, that they have a voice. They know they can come to you and be treated with respect and consideration. They know you won't let them down."

Janice sighed, closed her eyes and then whispered, "Until today."

Tara thought for a moment that Janice was going to cry and her eyes watered as well. "So... what are we going to do about it?"

∞

Janice Lane was upset to say the least. She headed to Mr. Deesie's classroom, going over what she needed to discuss with him. She looked in and saw him sitting there, looking out the window, with an odd expression on his face. "Robert, I think we need to chat, if you have time."

"Certainly, Principal Lane, what can I do for you?" He smiled.

"Please, it's Janice. We need to talk about Kendall Knight. I spoke with him this afternoon, and there seems to be some confusion as to what happened."

"Confusion?"

She handed him the paper that Jenny had given her. "Yes, I also want to ask you about this. I understand the students were led to believe that I drew this up and approved of it. This document was something we'd discussed as a possibility, and you had no authorization to hand it out until I, and our legal representatives, went over it."

"I do apologize, Janice. I thought we had agreed it was necessary to let the children know what is unacceptable, especially with what was being spread around by the other students today. I am admittedly uncomfortable with the topic of... well, you know."

"Sex?" she asked.

He nodded with a slight blush. "I sincerely believed this was the best way to reach them and now realize that I crossed the line. I am truly sorry. It will not happen again, I assure you. As for Mr. Knight, as I indicated, it could very well been something that I took out of context and it is just unfortunate that another student overheard the exchange."

Janice sighed deeply before responding, "Kendall told me it was you who made an inappropriate suggestion, not he. Also that you told him that I wouldn't believe him if he did come and talk to me about it."

"T-That's absurd," Deesie stammered. "Why would I lie about such a thing? The boy is obviously troubled and would benefit from a good psychologist."

Janice sat there, looking at him. "You do understand that I have to hear BOTH sides of the story? I am not making any accusations, Robert. I am just explaining to you that I have to consider all sides of this matter. Monday I will be chatting with the other students in his classes

to see if they have noticed any odd behaviour. It's possible that something happened at home, so I'll be speaking with his mother as well."

A flash of something indescribable crossed his face, but was quickly gone. "I understand," he said in a calm voice.

"Robert, please don't worry, I'm responsible for everything that goes on here, and I'm certain we can get this matter cleared up quickly."

"Of course," he said, giving her a small smile.

"Have a nice weekend and I'll see you on Monday," Janice said as she headed back to her office.

"Yes... Monday," he said.

∞

"How did it go?" Tara asked when Janice came in.

Janice shook her head. "Can you get me Antonio Garcia's number please?"

"It went that well?" Tara asked as she quickly pulled the Garcia's file up on the computer.

"Yes," Janice said.

∞

Sally was patiently awaiting a file from Chicago. She had been working for over twelve hours trying to find out everything there was to know about Robert Deesie. She knew Antonio was impatient only because he was worried sick at the moment. The older cop may not show much, but she could tell. Hell, she was scared to think there was a possible pedophile actually teaching at the school. It was days like these that made her glad she didn't have kids of her own yet.

She decided she would call Antonio before he called in again. She called his cell instead of tying up radio.

"Garcia," he answered.

"Hey Boss, before you ask, NO, I don't have anything else, yet. I'm waiting on info from the school in Chicago. It's taking longer because they just became automated three years ago and only put the information of active staff into their system. I have a great girl working on scanning all of his info into the system now, and she'll send it over as soon as she's finished."

"Alright," he sighed.

"There was also a glitch somewhere along the line between Toledo and here. They think their info was scrambled because what came through didn't quite match what they have there. As soon as I have it all, I'll call you. Maybe you should, I don't know, run home, grab a bite to eat, see your kid?"

Antonio laughed. "Have I been that annoying?"

"I adore you, but yes," Sally said with a smile.

"Sorry," he said sheepishly.

"Don't be. If you weren't annoying the hell out of me, I'd think something was wrong." Sally laughed.

John laughed at the expression on Antonio's face. "You have to admit, you had that coming."

Antonio rolled his eyes as he checked his phone. "Damn it, I always forget to check for missed calls. Kendall called three times." Antonio listened to the messages and quickly hit return call. He cursed again when it went straight to voicemail.

∞

Jennifer dropped Kendall off at the Garcia's and drove off to work.

A frazzled Sylvia answered the door. "Hi sweetie, Carlos will be glad to see you, he's getting bored."

Kendall laughed and walked in carrying the pot. "My mom made soup and thought you might like to have it for dinner after dealing with a sick kid all day."

Sylvia smiled broadly. "I love your mom, this is perfect. Do you want to stay?"

"No thanks, I just thought I'd check in on Carlos and head home. I'm still trying to catch up on sleep from the other night with Katie."

"I know how that goes. On top of being sick, Carlos had nightmares all day, so hopefully you can cheer him up." She sighed.

"I'll try, Mama G."

"Thank you," she said as she kissed his forehead.

Kendall carried the soup into the kitchen for her. "I have something to drop off for Papa G. Is it okay if I leave it in his study?"

"Sure sweetie, he should be home soon," Sylvia smiled.

"Thanks." Kendall went into the study and left the envelope for Antonio on his desk, and then headed upstairs to Carlos' room and knocked quietly, in case his friend was sleeping.

"Come in," he said in a sad little voice.

"Hey Carlitos, how are you doing, buddy?" Kendall asked.

Carlos was wearing flannel pajamas with ducks on them and curled up under about three brightly coloured fleece blankets. "Better, I haven't puked for almost two hours."

Kendall sat down next to Carlos. "That's good. You should be feeling better soon. Katie only puked for about seven or eight hours and then felt better. My mom sent some homemade soup and it helped Katie. Are you sure you're okay? You look sad."

Carlos looked at him, his lower lip trembling. "I had bad dreams all day and they scared me."

"They were just dreams, Carlos, they can't hurt you. Do you want to talk about them?"

Carlos shook his head. "I'll get scared again."

"No you won't. Didn't you know that once you tell a bad dream to someone who loves you, it goes away? My grandpa told me that," Kendall told him.

"Really?"

"Yup, just ask Katie. So why don't you tell me about them?" Kendall suggested as he ruffled his friend's already unruly hair.

"Well, the one that scared me the most was where we were in school and there was nobody else there. Just you, me, James, and Logan."

Kendall looked away for a moment at the mention of their two friends.

"What's wrong?" Carlos asked noticing the look on his friend's face.

"Nothing Carlos, just a little tired. Go on," Kendall urged.

Carlos looked at him suspiciously but continued. "The halls were empty and it echoed when we walked or talked. It was really creepy, it felt like someone was after us and we started running. Then somehow, Logan and James got outside. I kept calling for them to help us get out, but they kept running away. I don't think they heard me. You and I kept running, even though we couldn't see anything. The halls kept getting longer and longer. It was almost like I couldn't breathe sometimes. Then you were a little ahead of me and a door closed with you on the other side. I couldn't get it open, and I kept yelling for you. I heard you pounding and calling my name on the other side and then you stopped. I kept yelling and yelling, but you never came back!" Carlos was nearly crying now.

"Carlitos, you know I would NEVER leave you behind. No matter what, I would never leave your side," Kendall promised, hugging Carlos as he tried to calm his distressed friend.

"Kendall, you don't understand. You didn't leave me behind—there was something on the other side of the door that took you away, and I couldn't save you!" Carlos sobbed.

"Carlos, look at me. I'm right here and everything's okay. Everyone has bad dreams like that, but that's all they are. There are way too many real things to be scared of to worry about dreams."

"Like what?" Carlos sniffed.

"Well, like spiders, clowns, Big Bird..." Kendall tried naming off all of the things he knew scared Carlos.

Carlos sniffed and nodded. "Those are scary things."

"What happens when you see a spider?" Kendall asked.

"Someone squishes it."

"Big Bird?"

"Someone turns the channel."

"Clowns?"

"We all run away screaming like little girls." Carlos smiled, remembering when they'd run into a clown at the mall last year.

"Well, we ran... James screamed like a girl." Kendall laughed. "Remember what Logan told you the last time you had nightmares? Nightmares are just a... something... something... manifestation of something or other of our subconscious." Kendall was trying to remember the exact words Logan had used, but had been laughing too hard at the image of Big Bird running after Carlos trying to peck his hockey helmet.

"I remember," Carlos said.

"Anyway, it's probably because you and I were walking to school when you got sick and had to leave, that's all," Kendall said.

Carlos nodded. "That makes sense, I guess."

"Of course it does." Kendall smiled.

Carlos sat up and looked at his friend. "Why did you look sad earlier?"

Kendall sighed. "I kinda had a fight with James and Logan, but everything's going to be alright. I figured out a way to fix it."

"What was it about?"

"I really don't want to talk about it right now, okay? We'll talk about it later, when you're feeling better. I'm here to cheer you up, remember?"

"How can I be happy if you're sad?" Carlos asked.

"Because I'm not sad right now. I'm here with you and everything's good. You'll feel better tomorrow, and I can come play video games if you want."

"Will you tell me then?" Carlos asked, pushing his lower lip out.

"Yes, I'll tell you then," Kendall promised.

"I'll hold you to that you know."

"I know, Los. After we both get a good night's sleep, everything will be better. I should get going before it gets too late. If you need me, just call. Even if it's because you're having a bad dream," Kendall said as he stood up to leave.

"I will, thanks Kendall. See you tomorrow?" Carlos said snuggling into his blankets.

"You bet. Bye Carlos."

"Bye Kendall," Carlos yawned.

Kendall went downstairs. "Bye Mama G!"

"Are you sure you don't want to stay for dinner?" Sylvia asked, as she came out from the kitchen.

"No thanks, I'm pretty tired. My mom left soup at home for me. I told Carlos I'd come back and play video games with him tomorrow, if that's okay?"

"Of course, and tell your mom thanks for the soup. She's a lifesaver," Sylvia said as she gave him a kiss on the cheek.

"Will do!" Kendall smiled as he headed out the door.

∞

Janice Lane called the Garcia home.

"Hello Sylvia, it's Principal Lane."

"Hi Janice, how are you?"

"I'm doing alright. How is Carlos this evening? We missed him at school today."

Sylvia laughed. "He's doing much better, thank you. He just had a friend visit and he's resting now."

"Good. Could you have Antonio give me a call when he has a chance? It's pretty important," Janice asked.

"Sure, did you want to call him at the station?"

"No, I don't want to bother him at work. It's not an emergency, just a couple of concerns I have about something."

"Alright, I'll give him the message as soon as he gets in," Sylvia said.

"Thank you. Have a good evening."

"You too Janice." Sylvia hung up the phone and went back into the kitchen to make a tray for Carlos.

Antonio got home about ten minutes later. "How is my lovely wife tonight?" he called out.

Sylvia came out of the kitchen, hair pulled hastily into a ponytail and her shirt sporting some kind of stain. "She's tired, needs a long hot bath, and the only reason we're not eating frozen pizza is because Jen sent soup." She smiled as she kissed him.

"Hard day?" He smiled.

"Your son... puking all morning and then nightmares when he finally fell asleep."

"My poor boy," he said.

"You can take his tray up to him in a minute," she told him.

"Of course." He smiled again. They walked into the kitchen together. "Smells good," he said.

"It does, it was so nice of Jen to send it over. Oh, that reminds me, Kendall left something for you in your study," Sylvia told him as she spooned some soup into a mug for Carlos.

"Kendall was here, when?"

"About an hour ago, why?"

"I'll tell you all about it later," he said as he walked to his study.

Antonio found the envelope and opened it. He pulled out the flash drive, wondering what his godson had done. He booted up his computer, plugged the flash drive in, and waited.

∞

Sally was at the station, still waiting, when she saw a message received flash across her screen. "Thank God, maybe this will have the answers Antonio needs," she said. She continued waiting as the information downloaded onto her computer.

∞

Kendall walked home, cutting through the park, all the while hoping Antonio wouldn't be mad at him for what he'd done. He really didn't think he could handle another person being angry with him.

He smiled as he remembered poor Carlos all wrapped up in his blankets. He had looked like he was five years old, not fourteen. Kendall shuddered as he remembered Carlos' dream. *He has some pretty wild ones*, he thought. He hoped Carlos could get some sleep tonight and would feel well enough to hang out tomorrow. He hated feeling so alone, and right now, Carlos was the only friend he had left.

He was lost in thought, but looked up once he got to the sidewalk, waiting for a car to pass before he crossed the street. He was halfway down the block when he had a strange feeling that he was being watched and stopped to look around. A sedan about a block back suddenly turned down the side street and out of sight. Kendall shivered and quickly walked the rest of the way home.

∞

A few minutes later, Robert Deesie arrived at home. He went in and quietly took off his galoshes and hung up his coat and scarf. He went into the kitchen to make some tea. He turned on the stove and placed the teapot on the burner, pulled down a single cup and saucer and his special blend of tea. He was humming as he waited for the water to boil.

When the teapot finally whistled, he poured the water into the cup and waited for his tea to steep.

He thought back on the conversation he had had with Principal Lane. *Stupid woman, she thinks she is so much better than I am,* he thought.

"How dare she interfere with my plans," he fumed. He suddenly screamed in fury, throwing the cup and saucer across the counter, where they smashed into pieces. He continued to pull dishes down, smashing them one by one on the counter and floor. Once all of the dishes were broken, Deesie headed upstairs to his bedroom.

∞

Antonio sat at his desk and waited. As soon as the flash drive finished loading, he clicked on it, opening the file. The first thing he heard was Kendall's voice, "Papi, please don't be mad..."

∞

Sally sighed in relief as the information finished downloading. She clicked on "open" and started reading through the material. She read all of the school's files on Robert Deesie, the list of merits he had accumulated while working there, the photo clippings from both award ceremonies when he was named, "Teacher of the Year."

"They loved this guy and it seems with good reason," she said to herself. There was a photo of him and a group of people at the going away party they had thrown for him when he had transferred to Toledo.

Sally had a funny little feeling something was off as she looked at the smiling photo of Deesie and the others. She quickly pulled up the Toledo file, then the pulled up the basic info file she'd originally run. She quickly logged into the Chicago police central database.

While she was waiting for login confirmation, she pulled up another screen and logged into Toledo's database. When she was finally confirmed on both sites, she began typing furiously... pulling up the info she was looking for. She inhaled sharply as the data came across the screens.

"Holy shit, holy shit, holy shit! John get in here now!" Sally yelled as she picked up the phone and dialed Antonio's cell.

Bennet had come running the minute he heard Sally's language. She might have a wild Irish temper at times, but she rarely cursed. "What! What is wrong?"

Sally gestured at the computer screen, and for a moment, he couldn't figure out what she was going on about.

"Holy shit! Tell him I'm on my way to get him!" John yelled, heading for the door.

∞

Once Kendall got home, he locked up, warmed up some soup, and ate in silence, sitting at the kitchen table. When he finished, he washed his dishes and headed upstairs, where he took a nice long, hot shower. Then he put on his green plaid flannel pajama bottoms and grey top.

He checked the computer, hoping that maybe James or Logan had messaged him. His email account showed he had received over 100 messages and his inbox was full. He opened the first couple and swallowed hard.

"Hey whore, can I pay you to take care of a few things?"

"Loser, you can't get your grades the regular way..."

Kendall slammed the laptop closed and tried very hard to control the emotions threatening to overwhelm him. "It'll all be over soon, everyone will know what really happened and things can go back to normal," he told himself. He lay down on his bed and closed his eyes, hoping to get some sleep.

∞

Antonio was halfway through listening to the file, when his cell rang. "Antonio, John is on his way to pick you up. We have everything we need to arrest Deesie!" Sally said, her tone angry, yet controlled.

"So do I," Antonio said quietly and hung up.

Sally stared at the receiver in shock. "What the hell did he find...? Did he just HANG UP on me?"

∞

Antonio finished listening to the recording of the conversation of Kendall and Deesie. He was beyond furious. It was a good thing that Deesie was nowhere near him at the moment, because he would have killed him on the spot.

∞

At that moment, Deesie was putting his suitcase in the back seat, next to his precious trunk. He placed his shaving kit next to it. He was humming quietly to himself as he pulled out of the garage and began driving down the road.

∞

John Bennet pulled into the Garcia driveway and sprinted for the door. He started pounding on it, and Sylvia was very surprised to see him standing there with his fist raised to pound again.

"John, what's wrong?" Sylvia asked, opening the door wider to let him in.

"Antonio?"

"Study," she said, following him as he raced for the study.

"You are not going to believe what Sally found!" John said.

"You're not going to believe what I have here either," he told his partner. He pushed John to his chair and had him sit down and then he restarted the message.

While John listened to the recording, Antonio tried calling Kendall's cell again. It still went directly to voicemail. "Damn it, Kendall, where are you?" he said.

He called the Knight's home phone and it rang.

∞

Kendall was in another fitful sleep, this time dreaming of clowns chasing him down long, dark corridors, and Big Bird standing in the kitchen eating cereal with giant spiders. He woke up thinking he had heard a phone ringing and listened for a moment. When he didn't hear anything, he nodded off back to sleep.

∞

John Bennet was a 20-year veteran of the police force, and he had seen and heard a lot of things. What he had heard on that recording, coupled with what he had seen at the station, made his blood run cold.

"Car's out front, let's go," he told his partner. Antonio nodded and they headed towards the door.

Sylvia followed right behind them. She had heard a good portion of the recording and was angry, scared, and more than a little nauseated. "Wait, where are you going? Are you going to get Kendall?"

"After we arrest Deesie. Honey, if Kendall calls, tell him to stay home and I'll pick him up on the way back," he said as he kissed her on the forehead.

"Okay, let me know when you're on your way," she begged.

"I will. We really need to go now," he kissed her again and walked out the door.

Bennet started the car, and once they pulled away from the Garcia home, turned on the siren and lights.

Antonio was on the radio, requesting backup at 1127 E. Rale Drive, instructing that sirens and lights be turned off two blocks from the address.

They arrived at the house in just a few minutes. John and Antonio got out of the car and cautiously walked up to the house. They drew their weapons and Antonio knocked on the door, standing to the side and yelled, "POLICE, OPEN UP!"

Bennet stood on the other side of the door, and when there was no answer, he kicked the front door open.

Antonio covered Bennet as he walked into the house. "Robert Deesie, this is the police! Please come into the living room with your hands raised above your head!"

No answer. They looked around the living room and saw all of the mirrors had been broken. The furniture was overturned, a plant torn out of its pot. There were books thrown everywhere, some torn in half. The other team of officers joined them and they proceeded through the house, looking for the man. Antonio and Bennet got to Deesie's bedroom and called an all clear.

"Antonio, look!" John said. He was standing at the closet. The only things hanging there were empty hangers. "Looks like he took off," Bennet said.

Antonio looked at his partner for a moment, and then realization struck the both of them.

A look of horror crossed Antonio's face. "Kendall!" he said as he ran for the front door, John right behind him.

Chapter 8~ Gone

Antonio got to the car first, jumping in the driver's side. He started the car and began to pull away, barely giving John time to get in before speeding off. Antonio handed his cell to his partner.

"Call Kendall's house, tell him to make sure the doors and windows are locked and not to answer the door for anyone except us. Let him know that we'll be there in just a few minutes."

Bennet nodded and scrolled through the contact list and found the Knight's number. It rang six times and the machine picked up, it's robotic tone telling them to leave a message.

"No answer," he told Antonio. He leaned back and sighed in frustration, trying to get his head straight. They needed to get to Kendall before anything happened.

"Damn it, try his cell," Antonio said. There was a feeling of cold panic beginning to build in his chest, and he eased up on the gas when he realized he was already going 50 mph.

"Went straight to voicemail," Bennet said quietly, looking out the window to avoid his partner's panic-stricken face.

Antonio didn't say anything, trying to calm himself and concentrating on getting to the Knight's house in one piece. He didn't need to get into an accident now—Kendall needed him.

Two minutes later, they arrived. Antonio had been driving without the siren and turned off the lights as they reached the Knight's block.

It was dark and quiet, and a slight breeze was blowing. Antonio and John quickly made their way up the walkway to the porch. Antonio carefully tried the front door. It was locked and there was no sign that it had been tampered with.

Please let everything be alright, he prayed as he pulled out his keys and found the spare to his friend's house.

He and Bennet drew their weapons as Antonio quietly opened the door. They stepped inside and looked quickly around, the living room was clear. There was no sound in the dark house. Bennet looked at his partner and signaled that he was going to move forward. Antonio nodded, and they headed for the kitchen.

John quickly looked in, and not seeing any movement, switched on the light. Antonio stepped in behind him, and his heart dropped when he saw the window on the back door—it was broken.

Then he looked around the kitchen. The dish rack that normally sat on the counter was now in the sink, and there were dishes scattered on the floor and counter. The towel rack that used to hang next to the sink was on the floor, the towels flung across the room. The bowl that normally held fresh fruit was smashed to pieces, and the apples it had been holding were scattered around on the floor.

Bennet was already on the radio requesting back up. He looked over and saw his partner standing there, staring at the island in the middle of the kitchen.

Antonio was pale, his fists were clenched, and his eyes were filled with anger as he stared at what he saw there.

Bennet quickly moved to his partner's side and followed Antonio's gaze.

He moved closer to the island and saw blood on the corner, as well as a few strands of blond hair stuck to it. The blood had run down the side and formed a small pool on the floor below it. Then he saw small drops of blood leading to the back door.

"Stay here," he said quietly.

He made his way to the back door, careful to avoid everything on the floor. With one hand, he slowly opened the door, reached over, and flipped on the back light. Bennet saw one set of footprints leading up to the back porch. He stepped out, carefully avoiding the footprints. Looking closer, he saw another set of footprints leading away, drops of blood behind them.

Dessie must have carried Kendall out over his shoulder, he thought, turning around to go back inside. He saw something lying in the snow next to the porch and carefully reached down and picked it up. It was a grey beanie and there was blood on it.

He got back inside and saw that Antonio was no longer in the kitchen. "Damn it," he cursed. He quickly moved to the living room, nothing. Bennet heard someone moving around upstairs and followed the sound, where he found Antonio in a bedroom that he assumed was Kendall's.

The walls were green and a twin bed was in the corner next to a large window. Clothes were scattered around, mixed in with hockey gear and sticks. Posters and pictures adorned his walls, some were of the four boys together.

"Rest of the house is clear," Antonio said, looking up at John. He saw the grey beanie John was holding. "That's Kendall's."

"I thought as much," Bennet replied softly. "There's only one set of footprints out back, so he must have been carrying him."

Antonio nodded before looking around the room. Nothing looked different to him. It looked like a typical fourteen-year-old boy's room.

"Do you see anything that might be missing?" John asked, not knowing what to say as he looked around.

"Nothing obvious, we'll have to ask Jen to be sure," Antonio said. He cringed inwardly at the thought of telling her that a suspected pedophile has taken her son. Not something he wants to tell any parent, much less his friend. "His jacket is gone from the coat rack."

Antonio walked around the room before stopping in front of the dark brown desk and opening the laptop lying on top of it. When the screen came on, it showed the last thing Kendall had been looking at. On it were the cruel messages from people at his school. Antonio glared angrily at the sight.

A call came over the radio, saying the other team was there. "I'll handle this," John told his partner.

Antonio nodded distractedly, continuing to read a few of the messages.

Bennet called out as he headed down the stairs. "House is all clear. We are looking for Robert Deesie. He is a suspect in the possible kidnapping of Kendall Knight."

Bennet continued issuing orders, "We need forensics to start gathering evidence. He broke in, coming and going through the back door. There are signs of a struggle in the kitchen, so be careful, there are broken dishes everywhere. There are viable footprints out back, so follow them and find out where that son of a bitch was parked." With that, the officers immediately got to work.

Bennet got on the radio to the station. "Sally, get an APB out on Robert Deesie. We need to contact the state police... we have a possible kidnapping. Send them the make, model, and license of Deesie's car. Make sure they have an accurate description of Deesie and one of Kendall Knight. Also, send them all of the information that you received earlier."

"Consider it done," Sally said, already on the computer and forwarding all of the information on to the Minnesota State Patrol.

When she was finished with that, she prepared a write up and photos for a nationwide Amber Alert. Then she prepared a full report for the FBI, just in case. They were going to need all the help they could get, and they were going to need it fast.

Chapter 9~ Kendall

Kendall was a fairly light sleeper, but the last two days had left him drained and near exhaustion.

After waking from a few strange dreams, he finally fell into a deep sleep. He didn't hear the sound of glass breaking downstairs, or the sound of footsteps treading up the stairs. He didn't hear the door to his bedroom open or the footsteps that halted at his bed. He didn't see the dark figure, standing there silhouetted against the hallway light. He didn't feel the blankets being pulled back, so that the figure standing there could look down at him. Admiring the child who was finally sleeping so peacefully.

He wasn't aware of anything until he felt a sudden heaviness upon him. He awoke with a start and tried to call out, but found his mouth covered by a gloved hand. The other hand had taken ahold of his hands and was holding them above his head.

The figure bent down. "Shhh..." he whispered into the boy's ear. "You stay quiet, behave yourself, and do exactly as I say, or we will wait for your pretty mother to get home, so I can officially meet her. Do I make myself perfectly clear?"

Kendall looked up at Robert Deesie's smiling face and nodded.

"Good boy. Now I am going to remove my hand, and you will remain quiet."

Kendall nodded again, his face colourless from shock.

Deesie removed his hand and continued looking down at the blond as he pulled a necktie from his pocket. He proceeded to tie Kendall's hands together, and then got off of him. He pulled Kendall up into a sitting position.

"Now, we are going for a little trip, and you will continue to behave yourself, understood?" Deesie asked.

Kendall was visibly shaking now but nodded.

"Very good, sweetheart, now stay there while I get a few things," Deesie ordered as he began to search the room.

Deesie grabbed an empty blue backpack from the closet. He pulled a couple of hoodies from their hangers and then went to the dresser. He pulled out a few shirts, jeans, socks, and boxers and carefully packed them into the backpack. Then he grabbed a pair of grey Vans sneakers and put them in the front pouch. He zipped the backpack up and tossed it to Kendall.

"Let's go," he ordered, pulling Kendall up from his bed and toward the door.

After they got down the stairs, he took the backpack, grabbed Kendall's hands, and removed the tie. He grabbed Kendall's jacket and held it up. "Arms in."

Kendall complied. Deesie zipped it up and then retied Kendall's hands. He took the grey beanie that was with the jacket and put in on Kendall's head. "Boots?" he asked, and Kendall pointed to the mat by the door. Deesie grabbed them and forced Kendall's feet into them. He tightened and tied them. "We wouldn't want you to trip and hurt yourself now would we?"

He handed the backpack to Kendall and pushed him towards the kitchen. "Start walking, sweetheart."

Kendall's mind was racing, trying to come up with an option. He decided on the easiest and most obvious and turned, swinging the backpack with all his might. It hit Deesie in the chest and sent him flying back towards the doorway.

Deesie quickly recovered and jumped up, making a grab for the boy, but Kendall had gotten around to the other side of the center island.

Kendall grabbed the large glass fruit bowl and threw it at the dark haired man. It bounced off Deesie's shoulder and he yelped in pain. Deesie's face was now red with anger, his eyes burning with fury as he glared at the boy.

Kendall made a run for the backdoor, but failed, Deesie was much quicker than he looked. He grabbed the boy by his dark blue jacket and flung him across the room with surprising strength. Kendall hit the counter by the sink knocking the dish rack into the sink.

He grabbed a bowl that was lying there and turned to throw it, but Deesie was already on him.

The man shoved him back up against the sink and Kendall instinctively latched on to one of the towels hanging there, trying to maintain his balance. A moment later, the entire thing came crashing down. Deesie made a move to grab him, Kendall tried to dodge but failed.

Deesie had grabbed ahold of the boy by the collar. "What did I tell you?"

He grabbed Kendall by the back of his neck and slammed his head down onto the corner of the island. He held him there with one arm lying across his neck, his other arm pushed up against Kendall's back effectively pinning him to the counter.

Kendall's vision was blurry and black spots started to fill in. He could feel blood running down his face. He tried to wriggle free from the larger man, but found he couldn't move.

He could hear the anger in Deesie's voice as he pushed himself against the boy. "What did I tell you? It looks like we will be waiting for your mother to get home. Don't worry though, sweetheart, I will let you watch. It'll be your first lesson."

"No, no please, I'll do what you say! I promise I won't fight you anymore! Please leave my mom alone!" Kendall pleaded.

Deesie stayed silent for a moment, listening as the boy choked back sobs. He leaned over, pressing the length of his body against Kendall. "You will do exactly what I say from now on or I WILL come back here and your family will pay the price. Do you understand?"

"Y-Yes, just please don't hurt her!" he begged on the verge of collapsing. The pain in his head was almost unbearable and he felt dizzy.

Deesie smiled and loosened his hold on the blond. Before Kendall could straighten up all the way, he grabbed the back of Kendall's head and slammed him back down onto the counter.

Kendall could no longer fight the darkness.

Deesie kept his hold on the boy and turned him around so he was facing him. Taking ahold of Kendall's tied hands, he bent down a little, so he could pick him up and throw him over his left shoulder.

Reaching down with his right hand, he grabbed the backpack. He carefully stepped over the assorted items that now littered the floor. He opened the back door and stepped outside, turning awkwardly due to the unconscious boy on his back, and managed to pull the door closed.

He then headed out through the backyard, and then through the yard of the neighbour on the right. He'd made certain to take the route with the least light and quickly made his way to his car, which was parked on the next street over.

He opened the trunk and laid Kendall inside, throwing the backpack in next to him. Deesie closed the trunk and walked around, getting into the driver's side.

He smiled, humming as he drove away.

Chapter 10~ Hearing the Truth

Antonio closed Kendall's laptop, unplugged it and stood up. He slid it into the black case that was sitting next to the desk and walked downstairs into the living room.

Bennet was standing near the large white bookcases, discussing something with another officer. They both looked edgy and nervous.

"John, when you're finished there we need to go pick up Jen," Antonio said.

Bennet nodded at Antonio and finished speaking with the other officer. He walked over to his shaken partner. "Do you want me to do this?" John asked quietly.

Antonio shook his head. "We need to stop and pick Sylvia up, Jen's going to need her." He didn't want to think of how Jen would react. No parent wants to hear that their child has been taken, especially by a pedophile.

Bennet squeezed Antonio's shoulder. He knew the adult Garcias and Knights had been friends since they were kids. "What are you going to say?"

"I have no idea. I never thought I'd have to tell the wife of my late best friend that her only son has been injured and taken by a pedophile, and we have absolutely no idea where he is!" Antonio snapped angrily.

Bennet was taken aback by Antonio's tone, but knew it wasn't directed at him. As badly as he felt about the missing boy, he knew Antonio was dying inside. He knew in some way, his partner was blaming himself for this.

"Let's go," John said, heading for the door.

The drive to the Garcia home was quiet, and both men were trying to figure out why Deesie had chosen to do this now. In his conversation with Kendall, he'd told him that he had until Monday to make up his mind, so why now?

Antonio cleared his throat. It was dry and felt like he'd been swallowing sand. "I'm sorry I snapped at you, John. I really..."

Bennet held his hand up, interrupting him. "Nothing to be sorry about, that's what friends are for."

Antonio gave him a grateful smile and then turned and stared out the window. They pulled into the Garcia driveway and got out, heading to the door in silence.

They were greeted by Sylvia, and after one look at their faces, she could tell something was wrong. "Where's Kendall, I thought you were bringing him here?" she said, trying to keep her voice steady, but faltered as her husband took her into his arms.

"Deesie took him," Antonio whispered holding her tight as he desperately tried to maintain control of his emotions.

"Oh God, no!" Sylvia face turned pale as she clutched her husband and choked back a sob.

Antonio stood there holding her for a moment, holding her. He kissed her forehead. "We have to go get Jen, she doesn't know yet."

"Let me get my coat. Wait, we can't leave Carlos here alone, he still has a fever," Sylvia said, fighting back tears.

"Call Joanna and see if she can come stay with him," Antonio suggested.

Sylvia nodded and dialed the Mitchell's number. "Jo, would it be possible for you to come and stay with Carlos for a little while? He's sick and Antonio and I need to run an important errand."

"Of course, is everything alright?" she asked, noting that Sylvia's voice sounded strained.

"I'll fill you in when you get here, okay?" she said, looking at her husband, who was standing there, eerily calm.

"Okay, I'm on my way," Joanna said as she hung up.

"She'll be right over, I didn't want to tell her over the phone," Sylvia said as she hugged Antonio tightly.

They stood in silence, each lost in their own thoughts. A few moments later, Joanna Mitchell pulled up outside the Garcia home. She walked up to the house and Sylvia answered the door before she could knock.

"Thanks for coming so quickly," Sylvia said as she ushered her in.

"Alright, what's wrong?" Joanna asked, looking at the three distraught people standing there.

Antonio quickly filled her in on what had occurred over the past few hours.

"Oh my God," Joanna said, turning slightly pale.

"Carlos doesn't know yet, he was sleeping the last time I looked in on him. I think we should tell the boys together, they're going to need each other," Sylvia told her.

"I'll give Brooke a call and tell her what's going on. I'll have her pick up Logan and she can bring both of the boys over after we've taken care of Jen," Joanna said as she fought to hold back tears.

Sylvia nodded and gave her a quick hug and then the Garcias and Bennet headed out the door.

∞

Jennifer Knight loves her job at the steakhouse. She works as the hostess, helps to wait tables, and sometimes fills in as a cook. All of the patrons love her for her patience (especially with their rowdy children) and her positive attitude. She loves people and doesn't mind the hard work, even the late night shifts. The only thing that does bother her is that it takes away precious time with her kids. She wonders if she should go back to school, maybe get her teaching certificate. However, working and school equals even less time with Katie and Kendall. Maybe in a couple of years, she keeps telling herself.

∞

Jen was busy on the phone, making reservations, when she saw Antonio and Sylvia walk in. She gave them a quick smile and a wave. A waitress came over to seat them, but Antonio explained that they weren't there to eat and waited for Jen. When Jen was finished with her call, she walked over and immediately knew something was off with her two friends. Her heart dropped when she saw the cautious look on Antonio's face and the tears that shone in Sylvia's eyes.

"What is it? What's happened?"

Antonio cursed himself for not knowing how else to say it, so he just came out and told her. "Jen, I need you to come with us, something's happened with Kendall," he said gently.

She didn't say anything, just nodded. She knew they wouldn't be there if it weren't serious, and she didn't want to completely lose it in front of everyone. One of the other waitresses quickly ran and grabbed her things for her.

Antonio and Sylvia each stood on one side of her, putting their arms around her shoulders and led her out to the car. "Jen, let me have your car keys," Antonio said.

She handed him her purse and he found them on top. "John, please follow us in her car," he said, tossing the keys to his partner and pointing at Jen's light coloured sedan. Bennet nodded and headed for the car.

Antonio opened the back door of his patrol car and Sylvia climbed in, pulling Jen after her. Then he got into the driver's seat and took a deep breath. He explained how Deesie had broken into their house and taken Kendall.

"Jen, I hate to ask this of you now, but I really need you to go through Kendall's room and tell me if you see anything missing. It'll help us determine what Deesie's plans are," Antonio said quietly.

Jen remained silent, but nodded. Sylvia kept her arms around her friend as they drove to the Knight house. They arrived a short time later. Police were still there trying to gather as much evidence and information as they could. Antonio opened the car door and helped the two women out. They walked up to the house, a Garcia on either side of Jen. She avoided looking at the neighbours who were watching the scene.

They walked in and Antonio led Jen up the stairs to Kendall's room. He didn't want her going into the kitchen. "Okay, take your time and tell me if you see anything missing," he said gently.

Jen nodded and her eyes swept across her son's room, it looked like it always did. Not seeing anything obvious, she went to the closet and opened it.

She stood back looking inside. "His blue backpack, two hoodies—one grey, one green. One pair of grey Vans sneakers." She moved to the dresser and opened the top drawer. "Two long sleeve t-shirts, one blue with an Incubus logo, one green, plain. Two short sleeved t-shirts, one black and one red, both plain." She opened the next drawer. "Two pairs of blue jeans, one pair of black jeans." She went through the rest of the dresser listing missing clothing.

Antonio was writing the list of items down as she moved through the room. "His laptop," she said.

"I have it," Antonio told her. She gave him a slight nod.

"The small framed photo of the boys at the cabin last year, it was on top of his dresser," she said as she continued looking around.

Antonio wrote it down. "Anything else?"

"I don't see anything," she said quietly. Her heart felt like it was going to burst out of her chest and she felt slightly dizzy. "My baby," she whispered to herself.

"Okay, we should go," Antonio told her.

"NO! I want to stay here. What if Kendall tries calling? What if we miss him?!" She was suddenly very shaky and near tears, the feeling of hysteria building.

Putting his hands on her shoulders, he looked into her eyes. "Jen, we'll have all calls forwarded to our house."

Jen shook her head.

"Honey, you can't stay here, it's a crime scene and we need to let the officers do their job. When they're done, they will lock up and call. I know it's hard, but it's the best chance we have to find Kendall," Sylvia said as she wrapped her arms around her friend, who was now sobbing. She gently guided Jen through the door and down the stairs.

A few minutes later, they pulled into the Garcia driveway, Bennet right behind them. Sylvia still had her arms around Jen, who was having trouble walking. Antonio got out and they both half carried the distraught mother up the steps. Jo opened the door and enveloped Jen and Sylvia both in a hug. They helped Jen to the sofa and she sat with her head on Sylvia's shoulder, Jo rubbing her back.

"Should we call Brooke, or wait a bit?" Joanna asked Sylvia.

"Let's wait a few minutes. I want to get her into bed before we have to worry about the boys," Sylvia said quietly.

Joanna nodded in agreement.

About ten minutes later Jen's sobs had quieted to soft weeping. "Come on, honey, you need to lie down for a while," Sylvia whispered to her friend.

Jen shook her head. "I need to be awake in case something happens."

"You know we'll wake you. You need to rest, Katie's going to need you to be strong for her," Sylvia said, pulling Jen up from the couch.

"Oh my God, Katie! How am I going to tell her?" Jen sobbed, thinking of the small brunette. Katie idolized her older brother. How is she suppose tell her seven-year-old what has happened?

"We'll worry about that tomorrow. She's safe where she is, and hopefully by morning we'll have good news," Sylvia said, leading Jen to the guest room that was next to Antonio's study.

Jo picked up the phone and called Brooke Diamond. "You should head over," she said when Brooke answered the phone.

"We're on our way," Brooke said, grabbing her purse and calling for her son.

Sylvia sat Jen on the bed, knelt down, pulled off her shoes and sat next to her. Jen's sobs had ceased, but tears still fell from her eyes. She looked at Sylvia in desperation. "This isn't real, I can't lose him." Her breathing picked up and she started shaking.

Sylvia put her arms around her friend and gently rocked her back and forth. "It's going to be okay, we're not going to lose him. Antonio will find him and bring him home," she softly whispered.

Jen held on to her and they sat there in silence until Jen's eyes started to droop. Sylvia helped her lie down and covered her with the blanket. She sat for another moment, and then quietly got up and left the room.

Antonio, John, and Joanna were standing in the kitchen quietly talking. Sylvia joined them and started a pot of coffee. It was going to be along night. "What are we going to say to the boys?"

Antonio sighed. "All we can do is tell them what's happened and that we're working hard to find him, and then John and I need to get back to the station. Sally has been coordinating things there, but we need to go through the information we have and try to figure out Deesie's next move. I'm going to take Kendall's laptop in and have her go through the messages on there to see if there's anything we can use."

A flash of anger went through him at the memory of the messages he had read. He was also going to have Sally match the email addresses to the people who had sent them and have a "little chat" with them as soon as he had Kendall back home.

He sighed again. "We need to speak with Jason Banks as well. From the sounds of it, Deesie may have coerced him into harassing Kendall today."

"Damn, I completely forgot. Janice Lane called before you got home. She said she needed to talk to you about something, it sounded important," Sylvia told Antonio.

"We need to let her know what's going on anyway, it might as well be now," he said, reaching for the phone.

∞

Janice Lane had gone home feeling depressed and more than a little tired.

They had been so excited when the school board hired Robert Deesie, she had felt lucky to get him. Not many teachers with accolades like his wanted to move to a small town. They certainly couldn't afford to pay him what Chicago had, even what Toledo had for that matter. He'd assured them that money was not a priority, that as he got older, he wanted to lead a more serene life away from the big city.

Now her mind was filled with doubts, and as she thought back on the events of the day, she grew more troubled. He had passed the background checks with flying colours. She, herself, had spoken to the principal at the Toledo school, the man repeating how sorry they were to see him go. How the students and teachers all adored him.

"So why isn't that the case here? He seems aloof to the staff, Tara certainly can't stand him, and the students don't seem able to connect with him," she said to herself. Now this situation with Kendall Knight.

As much as she hated to think that something was missed during all of the background checks and the extra precautions she had taken, there must have been something.

Kendall might get into trouble, and he might have a temper, but he had never lied to her. He and the other boys always owned up to any pranks or stunts they pulled, usually with a smile and always with an apology.

She had never seen Kendall like he was today. He was definitely shaken up and seemed almost uncertain. Of what, she didn't know, although with his final statement before walking out of her office, she had a fairly good idea of what it might be.

The phone rang, interrupting her thoughts. "Hello."

"Hi Janice, you needed to talk to me?" Antonio asked.

"Thank you so much for getting back to me. I'm a little worried about something that happened at school today," she said and proceeded to tell him about the events of the day.

In turn, Antonio told her everything that had occurred that evening.

Janice sat down quickly, afraid she might faint. "What can I do?" She should have paid closer attention to how Kendall was acting. She could have helped him. She mentally chastised herself.

"I'm not sure at the moment. If I think of anything, I'll give you a call," he promised.

"Please let me know if you hear anything or if Jennifer needs anything," Janice said, crying now.

"I will, Janice, thank you." Antonio hung up.

"Well?" Sylvia asked.

Antonio turned and began explaining what Janice had called about when he heard a small voice speak.

"Papi, what happened to Kendall?" Carlos was standing in the doorway, near tears, having heard his father's part of the phone conversation.

Antonio walked over to his son. "Mijo, what are you doing up?"

"I heard people down here and came to see who it was. What happened, Papi?" Carlos' voice was raspy, fear evident in his tone. He was starting to panic as he looked at the faces of his parents.

Antonio was about to answer, when there was a knock at the front door.

Sylvia looked from her son to her husband, nodded and went to answer the door. "Come sit down Mijo. Logan and James are here and we'll discuss of this all together," Antonio said putting his arms around his son. They walked into the living room, followed by Joanna and Bennet.

Sylvia opened the door and Brooke walked in with James and Logan in tow. The boys were confused as they looked at their parents and Bennet.

"W-What's going on?" James asked.

"Boys, have a seat," Antonio said as he sat down next to Carlos.

Once everyone had taken a seat Logan asked, "Where's Mama K? I saw her car out front."

"She's resting dear," Joanna answered.

"Where are Kendall and Katie?" James asked.

Antonio looked at the boys and took a deep breath, tightening his hold on his own son. "Boys... I'm afraid there's something we need to tell you. Kendall came to me yesterday, because a teacher made a pass at him. He was very upset and asked me what to do about it. I told him that we were going to investigate the teacher, but apparently, someone at school started spreading lies about what really happened. Kendall took it upon himself to go back and get this teacher to make advances again, this time he recorded it."

Antonio paused for a moment glancing from boy to boy and decided against telling them why Kendall had really gone back. The boys were going to be heartbroken as it was, he didn't want to intensify the feelings of guilt that he knew they would soon have.

"He dropped a copy of the recording here, and in the meantime, Officer O'Hara discovered some other things about this teacher. We went to arrest him and found that he'd already packed his things and left." He paused for another moment, and the boys could tell he was having difficulty going on.

Carlos was already crying, knowing what it was his father was going to say. He knew Kendall had been troubled when he visited. *I should have bugged him for more information, but I just let him go*, Carlos thought with a sob.

Logan could feel the fear building in his chest and was desperately trying not to have a panic attack. The guilt was beginning to wash over him as he remembered the last conversation he had had with Kendall.

James sat there quietly, his fists clenched. "Mr. Deesie did something to Kendall, didn't he?"

Antonio nodded, suddenly having difficulty finding his voice, John jumped in. "We tried several times to call Kendall, but there was no answer. We went to his house to pick him up and bring him here, but when we got there, we found the glass on the back door broken and Kendall was gone."

By now, all three boys were crying and their parents held them close.

Antonio kissed Carlos on the head, and as he wiped his son's tears from his cheek, looked at the boys. "We ARE going to find Kendall and bring him home. We all need to be strong for him, for each other, and especially for Jen and Katie. I need to get back to the station, but I think it might be a good idea if you boys stayed the night," he said, looking at Brooke and Joanna.

"I think it might be a good idea if we all stay here tonight," Brooke suggested, and Joanna nodded in agreement.

"The boys can share Carlos' room and we'll figure the rest out later," Sylvia said.

Antonio and Bennet grabbed their jackets and headed for the door. Carlos got up and ran after his father who pulled him into a hug. "It'll be alright, Mijo. We're going to bring him home." He kissed Carlos on top of the head and gently pushed him into his mother's waiting arms, and then he and Bennet left.

Chapter 11~ The Call

Antonio and John arrived at the station about fifteen minutes later, to find Sally hard at work, sifting through a mountain of information. She had a whiteboard up, listing the possible timeline and posting evidence as it came in.

"Hey Boss," she said without looking up from her computer screen. "I have the APB running statewide and a report ready if we need to call in the FBI. I prepared an Amber Alert with the most recent photos I could find of Kendall and Deesie. I also have traces running on all of Deesie's credit cards in case he uses them. I got one report that he stopped and took $1,000 and send the report to the FBI, since they have more resources than we do, and we're going to need the help. Let's wait on the Amber Alert for now."

"Uh, why?" John asked.

"Several reasons... One: He doesn't know that we're investigating him. Two: That Kendall recorded their conversation. Three: That I spoke with Janice Lane about her conversation with him. Four: He doesn't know that we know that he's gone or that he has Kendall. He's probably figuring that no one will notice Kendall is missing until morning. That gives us a slight advantage in that he doesn't know that we're already looking for him. So we'll start the Amber Alert tomorrow morning."

"That makes sense. So what's the next step?" Bennet asked his partner.

Sally interrupted, "The next step is the Boss goes over what I found out about Mr. Robert Deesie."

Antonio nodded, taking the papers that Sally had printed up for him and started looking them over. After a few minutes, he rubbed his tired eyes. "Sally, could you just give me the run down?"

She nodded and immediately launched into her findings. "So, when I finally got the information from Chicago and Toledo, something wasn't adding up. Then I took a closer look at the photos that Chicago sent of Deesie's going away party and the records that I pulled from the DMV. The pictures didn't match. They also didn't match the yearbook photos from Toledo. I took his background check back further and guess what I found?"

Antonio looked at her, "What?"

"Robert Deesie has a younger brother, Stephen Marcus Deesie, who spent fifteen years in the Illinois State Penitentiary for four counts of child molestation, one count for the kidnapping and rape of a non-consensual minor, and numerous counts for possession of child pornography."

"That's all he got?!" John yelled.

"Yes, the DA offered him a deal, reducing his sentence on two conditions. First, that he confess to the molestation/rape charges, so the children wouldn't have to testify in court. The parents were all amiable to this, because they didn't want their kids traumatized any further. Then he had to play mole and help them uncover the names of the others on the internet porn sites he used. This led to the arrest and conviction of TWO county officials and several prominent businessmen. He was sentenced to twenty years, but got out in fifteen because of good behaviour. Not a mark against him in prison."

"Well isn't that special? So now he's free to run around and do it all over again," John muttered angrily.

"I agree, but getting angry about it isn't going to help us now," Antonio told him. "Go on Sally."

"Fourteen months ago, Stephen Deesie was released from prison. About a year ago, Robert Deesie took a sabbatical from the school in Toledo. I spoke with the principal in Toledo and apparently, Deesie had emailed them, saying he was going through a very stressful personal time and that he needed a break from teaching. No one there ever spoke with him again. He also broke up with his fiancé of nearly five years, Karen Johnson. I tracked her down, and she said that when she got home one evening, all of his personal items were gone and he had left her an email, breaking up with her. He said he couldn't handle the pressures of teaching anymore and that he resented her success. She never actually spoke with him then and hasn't spoken with him since."

Sally handed Antonio two of the papers. "Robert Deesie as we know him and Robert Deesie as the rest of the world knows him."

Antonio was looking at copies of two drivers licenses. The first was Minnesota license of a man about 5'10" with thinning dark hair, blue eyes, and a stocky build. The second was an Ohio license of a man about 6'1" with thick dark hair, hazel eyes, and a slim build.

Sally handed him another paper. "This is Stephen Deesie's mug shot." It matched the photo of the man in the Minnesota license.

"So... where's the real Robert Deesie?" John asked, looking from Antonio to Sally.

"I'm afraid that we probably know the answer to that." Antonio sighed putting his head in his hands.

Kendall woke up in darkness. He was disoriented and his head felt like it was going to explode.

He felt dizzy. He was lying down and couldn't see anything. It felt like everything was moving in a strange, twisted way. He tried to stretch out and found he was only able to move so far, his legs hitting against something before he could straighten out all the way.

Then he remembered what had happened and tried to stop the feeling of panic building in his chest. He realized he was in the trunk of a car and that the car was moving. It moved slightly to the side as if it was taking a turn. *No, no, no,* he thought.

Trying to keep calm, he started feeling around to see if there was anything he could use as a weapon. He felt his backpack, but nothing else. The panic was building again, and now he was feeling sick to his stomach. He really did not want to throw up in the small, enclosed space, so he tried lying still and taking deep breaths.

While lying there, he felt something in his pocket, reached in, and found his cell phone. He had forgotten all about it after the confrontation with Deesie at school. Deesie hadn't thought to search his jacket.

Kendall turned the phone back on and punched in a phone number.

∞

Antonio, John, and Sally were still going over the evidence. He had given Sally the list of items missing from Kendall's room, and she had added it to the board.

"Okay, so he packed clothing for Kendall, which means he intends on keeping him alive," Sally said.

"For now," John responded in a bitter tone before she shot him a warning look. "Sorry," he whispered in apology.

"It's okay, but let's try and stay positive, please?" Sally asked.

John nodded, God, he was tired. He couldn't even begin to think of how exhausted Antonio must be. He glanced at his partner, who was looking at the board.

"With the exception of Kendall's jacket, he packed only lightweight clothing, so either he's planning on keeping him inside or he's heading someplace warm.

Thoughts... opinions?" Antonio asked.

They were contemplating this when Antonio's cell rang. "Garcia," he answered, still looking at the board. He almost dropped the phone when he heard Kendall's voice, which was small and urgent.

"Papi?"

"Kendall? Son, where are you? Are you alright? "Antonio asked, looking at John in shock.

Sally jumped on the computer and punched in Antonio's cell number to put a trace on the call.

"I think I'm in a car trunk, it feels like we're moving," Kendall whispered, near tears at the sound of his godfather's voice.

"Why didn't he take your phone?" Antonio asked.

"He took it away from me and turned it off at school, when he thought I was recording with it. I took it back and put it in my jacket pocket. I forgot it was there. He didn't search my jacket before we left my house. I just woke up and found it. My head hurts really bad Papi. I'm scared." Kendall was trying to keep his voice quiet. He didn't want to be found with the phone.

Antonio's heart was breaking at the sound of fear in the boy's voice. He remembered what he'd seen in the Knight's kitchen.

"Kendall, I know your head was hurt. Are you alright otherwise?"

"I think so."

"Good. You're going to be okay, we're going to find you. Did he say anything about where he might be taking you?" Antonio asked.

"No, he didn't say anything about that," Kendall said.

"We can track the GPS on his cell," Sally whispered to Antonio.

He nodded. "Listen Mijo, we can track your phone, but you have to keep it on. Is there any place you can hide it so he won't find it?"

"Maybe under the mat in the trunk," John said.

"What if he ditches the car, though?" Sally pointed out.

"Kendall, is there any place on you that you can hide it? Is there an inside pocket he might not find? Antonio asked.

"No... Wait a second, I have an idea," Kendall said.

Antonio could hear rustling around and anxiously waited for Kendall to come back on the line.

Kendall twisted his hands, which were still tied, and partially unzipped his jacket. Reaching inside, he started pulling at a loose thread on the quilted lining. Once he had a large enough opening, he pushed his fingers into it, deepening the hole, and hoping it didn't tear too much.

After a moment, Kendall picked up the phone. "I tore a small hole in the inside of my jacket. It'll fit in there, and he shouldn't be able to find it."

Antonio smiled. "Good job! As soon as we hang up, I want you to put it in there. We'll be able to track it as long as the phone is on."

"I don't want to hang up," Kendall whispered, his voice breaking.

"Kendall, I don't want you to hang up either, but if he finds the phone, he'll take it from you. The charge on your phone should last long enough for us to track you. It shouldn't take too long, Mijo. There are a lot of people looking for you. You'll be home soon, I promise," Antonio explained, trying to keep his own voice from breaking.

"Okay. Can you do something for me though? Can you tell my mom and Katie that I love them? The guys too?" Kendall asked quietly.

"Of course I will," Antonio said, sitting down, his legs suddenly weak.

"Thank you." Kendall paused a moment. "Okay, I'm going to hang up now. I love you, Papi," Kendall said.

"I love you too, Mijo," Antonio whispered back.

Kendall hung up and made sure to turn the ringer volume off. Then he worked the phone into the small hole inside his jacket. He laid back and closed his eyes, praying that Antonio would find him soon.

Antonio sat staring at his phone, Bennet sitting next to him.

Sally finished up on the computer and told Antonio, "They're running the GPS trace on his phone. It may to take a little while, because they're moving, but they should have something for us soon." She started making notations about the call on the whiteboard as she avoided looking at Antonio. She was pretty sure that if she looked into his eyes right now, she'd lose it. The unexpected call had them all shaken.

"He is one brave kid," John said softly, his hand on Antonio's shoulder.

Antonio nodded. "I know. I just hope it's enough to get him through this."

Chapter 12 ~ Regrets

Back at the Garcia house Sylvia, Joanna, and Brooke were sitting in the kitchen, quietly talking. Jen was still asleep and they were hoping she would sleep through the night.

They were all remembering the night she lost Will. She had cried and held her children, but then "Mommy Mode" kicked in and she had pulled herself together for Kendall and Katie. She kept going, taking care of everyone else, including her distraught friends. Then about a month after the funeral, the Garcia's had received a frantic call from Kendall. "Mommy won't wake up!" their panic-stricken godson had cried. They had rushed over to meet the ambulance and found Jen passed out, completely non-responsive.

At the hospital, the doctors told them she was suffering from malnutrition and severe exhaustion. She was in the hospital for three days and she was not too happy about it. She also wasn't happy to find that her three friends had arranged for one of them to be there with her for the following two weeks, making sure she ate and rested.

When she would get surly with them, they just ignored it and pointed out that she needed to remain strong for her children, and she couldn't do that if she ran her health into the ground. She finally realized she couldn't do it all and that it was okay to accept help, especially from those who love her.

In the living room, Carlos, James, and Logan sat next to one another on the couch. Carlos was curled up asleep, still clutching a fuzzy blanket. His fever was gone, but he was exhausted from being sick all day, and now the emotional toll of finding out that his best friend had been taken by a possible pedophile.

James and Logan sat in silence, staring at the Tom and Jerry cartoon on TV. They were still in shock and terrified at the thought of what could be happening to their friend.

"We called him a liar," James said in a small voice.

"I know," Logan sighed.

"We accused him of offering to... do *that* to Mr. Deesie," James said.

"I know," Logan said, his voice starting to break.

"We should have been there for him and we turned our backs on him. He RAN away from us because we hurt him so bad!" James said, choking back a sob. His eyes watered as tears started to build up.

"I know, I know, I know!" Logan's voice was increasing in volume with every word. "It's MY fault! How could I actually believe ANYTHING that Jason Banks said?"

"What did you do?" Carlos asked quietly. He was now wide awake and looking at them with a horrified expression on his face.

"We betrayed him, Carlos," James said, trying to hold back the tears. He went on to explain what had happened at school that day.

Carlos sat quietly, watching his brokenhearted friends, trying to think of a way to comfort them. Then a flash of anger went through him and he decided at that moment they didn't deserve comforting. Pulling back his hand, he slapped each of them across the face.

James and Logan were suddenly quiet at the shock of being struck by their friend. Carlos rarely got angry, and when he did, it was a frightening sight, and right now, he was VERY angry. "HOW could you do that? He needed you and you turned your backs on him?" Carlos screamed at them.

"We know, Carlos," Logan cried.

The mothers heard the commotion and came-running in. "What is going on?" Sylvia asked, looking at Logan and James, who were sitting there, each holding a red cheek, and one enraged Carlos.

Carlos ignored their mothers standing there and continued. "What about standing by each other no matter what? What about ALWAYS being there for each other? What about our FRIENDSHIP?!"

"Carlos, stop!" Sylvia ordered, grabbing ahold of her nearly hysterical son. "You're going to wake up Jen," Sylvia said as she wrapped her arms around her son and he started to cry. "Mijo, you need to calm down."

Brooke and Joanna stood there in shock and looked at their respective sons. "What is Carlos talking about?" Jo quietly asked the boys, who at this point were crying again. They sat next to each other, Logan holding his head and James staring straight ahead, as tears fell freely from his eyes.

"James, what happened?" Brooke asked, as she sat next to him. He wrapped his arms around his mother, burying his face in her shoulder.

"Logan, please tell us what's going on," Joanna begged as she sat next to him and pulled him into her arms.

Twenty minutes later, the boys had managed to get everything out and were now sitting quietly with their mothers still holding them. Sylvia had pulled Carlos into Antonio's recliner and sat next to him, gently stroking his hair. "Carlitos, you need to apologize for hitting James and Logan," Sylvia instructed.

"Sorry," he muttered, not looking at them.

"Carlos, I don't care how upset you are, we do not hit each other in anger," Sylvia said firmly.

"It's okay, Mama G, we deserved it," Logan whispered. James nodded in agreement.

"No, it's not okay. You need to forgive each other and yourselves. You need to be there for each other, especially now," Sylvia told him. Brooke and Jo nodded in agreement.

Carlos looked at his brothers, tears making his vision hazy. "I'm sorry. I shouldn't have hit you, I was just so mad. It's just that after everything..."

"We know. We screwed up and don't blame you if you hate us. We don't blame K-Kendall if he hates us t-too," James said.

"What? I don't hate you! Why would you think Kendall hates you? He loves you," Carlos said.

"What we did was the worst thing ever. He RAN away from us, Carlos," Logan whispered.

"Well, I know for a fact that he DOESN'T hate you," Carlos said. His voice was rising again.

"Carlos, stay calm and explain quietly," Sylvia warned again.

Carlos nodded. "I know, because he came here after school to check on me. He was trying to cheer me up, but when I mentioned you guys, he got a sad look on his face. I asked him what was wrong and he wouldn't tell me everything, just that you guys had had a fight but that everything was going to be okay, because he figured out a way to fix it."

Both James and Logan looked at him. "How?" Logan asked.

"He wouldn't tell me anything else, and then he tried to cheer me up about the bad dream I had. Before he left, he promised he'd tell me tomorrow, only now he's NOT coming back and we don't know where he is," Carlos sobbed. "I should have made him tell me, maybe he'd be here now instead of... gone."

Half an hour later, the mothers had led the boys upstairs to try to get some sleep. They piled the blankets on the floor and all three collapsed into them.

When Sylvia checked on them a little later, they had finally fallen asleep—James in the middle, one arm around each of the other boys. Logan had a fuzzy blanket curled up under his

cheek, and Carlos had taken his stuffed puppy, laid it on James' shoulder, and had his head resting on it.

She made sure they were all covered and kissed each boy on the head. She watched them for a moment and then smiled sadly, backing out of the room.

∞

Deesie drove until about 3 am, having gone a little over 250 miles.

He pulled into the next town and found an all-night drug store. He went in and purchased bandage materials, duct tape, ibuprofen, a sleep aid, and other assorted items. He asked the cashier for directions to the nearest decent motel and smiled appreciatively when she gave him directions. He wished her a good morning, and humming, got back into the car and drove to a dark, vacant lot. He got out again and opened the trunk.

Putting his hand over Kendall's mouth, he shook him. "Wake up."

Kendall woke with a start, trying to figure out where he was and what was happening. His green eyes went wide when he saw Deesie, and he tried to fight down the panic he felt building in his chest again.

"Stay quiet or else," Deesie hissed as he pulled the boy up and out of the trunk.

"You are going to sit up front and be quiet, or spend the night freezing in the trunk. Do you understand?"

Kendall nodded, trying not to fall over. His head was spinning and he felt nauseated again.

"We will take care of your head once we get to the motel," Deesie told him.

He pushed the boy to the passenger door, opened it, and pushed him inside. Reaching down, he fastened the seat belt, stopping for a moment when he was at eye level with Kendall.

"We wouldn't want to risk you getting hurt if there was an accident, would we, sweetheart?" Deesie smiled, his hand lingering on Kendall's waist. The boy shuddered, pushing himself as far back into the seat as possible. Deesie smiled again and shut the door.

They arrived at the motel a few minutes later.

"Stay in here and don't make any sounds. If you try anything, I will make you regret it. Understand?" Deesie threatened.

Kendall nodded. His head throbbed and his body hurt—he could barely stand much less run.

Deesie locked the doors and went inside the office. He rang the bell at the counter and the night manager came out. "I need a room for the night please," he told the man who was half-asleep.

"Just you?" the man asked.

"My son and I," Deesie told him.

"Sixty dollars for the night. Ice and vending machines are on the first floor."

"That's fine." Deesie smiled as he handed the man cash.

"Check out time will be 5 pm," the clerk said, looking at the clock and handing Deesie the key.

"Perfect." Deesie smiled.

Chapter 13~ The First Night

Deesie got into the car and pulled into the parking spot in front of the room. Reaching into the back seat, he pulled out the bag from the drugstore. He got out, grabbed Kendall's backpack from the trunk, went to the passenger door, and opened it. He unfastened Kendall's seatbelt and pulled him out of the car, pushing the backpack into his hands.

"Walk," he ordered, keeping his hand on the boy's collar.

They got into the room, and he pushed Kendall into the bathroom. "I want you to take a shower. Make sure you wash your hair thoroughly, it's matted with blood," Deesie said, pulling a small bottle of shampoo out of the bag. "I'll take care of your head once you're finished."

Kendall took the bottle and just stood there for a minute. He was NOT going to take a shower with Deesie in here.

Deesie seemed to have read his thoughts. "Don't worry, sweetheart. While you are showering, I am going to grab my bag from the car. Remember, the car is right outside the door and I will only be a moment, so if you try anything..." Deesie warned, giving him a twisted smile.

Kendall nodded and held up his hands. "I can't shower with this on."

Deesie untied his hands and walked out of the bathroom, closing the door behind him.

Kendall leaned against the bathroom sink and looked in the mirror. He was shocked, although not surprised, to see his face covered in dried blood. He had a laceration about 1 ½" long on the left side of his forehead, just below the hairline. His hair was matted tightly to his head, and he knew it was going to hurt scrubbing it clean. His left eye was slightly swollen, and his cheek already had a noticeable bruise on it. He was still incredibly dizzy. Everything seemed to shift around him, and his head was throbbing.

He started the shower, running the water until the room was steamy. He steadied himself against the bathroom counter, undressed, and then quickly got into the shower, pulling the curtain closed. He stood there for a moment, letting the hot water flow over his tired and sore muscles before attempting to put his head under the running water.

He nearly screamed when the water hit the wound and he braced himself against the wall. After a moment, he reached for the shampoo and poured a small amount into his hand. He gingerly scrubbed at the area, wincing as the water hit it, rinsing the blood and shampoo away. When he finished, he grabbed a towel, wrapped it around his waist, and carefully stepped out.

"Are you almost finished in there?" Deesie yelled through the door.

"Yes, just dressing," Kendall said, and quickly pulled on his clothes.

"Need help?" Deesie asked in a suggestive tone.

"NO!" Kendall snapped, pulling his shirt over his head as fast as he could.

The door opened and Deesie stood there. "Watch your tone," he warned. Kendall just nodded, having frozen in front of him.

"Sit there." Deesie pointed at the toilet.

Kendall sat and Deesie pulled alcohol and the bandage material from the bag. "Hold still," he ordered as he poured alcohol onto a cotton ball. Kendall hissed in pain as Deesie rubbed it onto the wound. "Aw, does that hurt, sweetheart? I guess maybe you should have done what you were told and this wouldn't have happened." He smiled as he cleaned up the area.

Kendall bit his lower lip to keep from crying out in pain as Deesie worked. When Deesie finally finished cleaning the area, he put a couple of butterfly bandages on it, pulling the edges of the wound together. Then he put a large gauze bandage over the whole thing. He grabbed Kendall's chin, forcing him to look up so he could check his eyes. "Your eyes are contracting and dilating fine, so I don't think you have a concussion."

Next, he grabbed a cup and filled it with water. He handed it to Kendall along with three pills, two were white and oval, and the other was small, round, and blue. "Take these."

"What are they?" Kendall asked suspiciously.

"Ibuprofen and something to help you sleep. Now take them or I will shove them down your throat!" Deesie snapped.

Kendall took the cup and pills and swallowed them.

Deesie grabbed Kendall and pulled him up. "Time for bed." Kendall froze, suddenly terrified of what the older man was going to do to him.

"Move!" Deesie ordered, pushing Kendall into the bedroom.

Looking around, Kendall saw two beds, a small table with two chairs, and a small television. Deesie pushed him to the bed that was furthest from the door. Deesie pulled back the covers. "Sit."

Kendall did as he was told and Deesie tied his hands again. "Lie down," Deesie said, pushing Kendall down and then covering him with the blankets.

"I am going to take a shower now, and I am leaving the door open. If you try to leave or call for help, you will be punished. Understand, sweetheart?"

Kendall looked up at him and nodded.

"Good." Deesie reached over and pulled the cord off of the phone that was on the table between the beds. He grabbed some clothes from his suitcase and went into the bathroom.

Kendall lay there, hoping that the ibuprofen would kick in soon. At least, he prayed it was ibuprofen. He could hear Deesie in the bathroom as he hummed to himself in the shower. After a few minutes, Kendall's eyes started to get heavy and he found himself fighting sleep.

I should just give into it, he thought, but he was terrified of what might happen while he slept.

Deesie finished up and went back into the bedroom. He looked over at the boy. "Still awake, I see. Good, let's go over a few rules then, shall we?" he said as he walked over to Kendall's bed. He sat down and ran his fingers through the blond's still damp bangs.

Kendall cringed and tried to turn away from the man's touch. Suddenly Deesie gripped his hair and whispered, "Rule number one, you will do what I say, PERIOD. NO questions or arguments will be tolerated. Number two, if you try and run away, you will severely regret it once I get my hands on you. Number three, you are not to speak to anyone, unless I say it's alright."

He leaned over the boy. "Number four, you are MINE. I will do what I want with you, when I want to do it. If you fight me on anything, you will not enjoy it. I will, but I can guarantee that you will not. Do you understand me?"

Kendall looked at him for a moment and then nodded.

"Good," Deesie whispered into his ear and then placed a lingering kiss on the boy's cheek, and then one on his forehead.

"Sleep tight, sweetheart," he said as he got up and went to his own bed. He reached over and turned out the light.

Kendall lay there, shivering and praying that Antonio would find him soon. A few moments later, the combination of exhaustion and the pills he had taken, sent Kendall into a deep, dreamless sleep.

∞

Stephen Deesie laid there, trying to fall asleep. He thought of everything that had happened, all of his plans ruined. That stupid woman, Principal Lane, questioning him and taking the word of the boy over his. She had not come out and said so, but he could tell from

her body language. He started to get angry again. "Now is not the time to lose it," he told himself.

He needed to relax and tried controlling his breathing. He glanced over at Kendall, who was finally sleeping soundly. He smiled to himself and got up. He grabbed the handi wipes he had purchased and walked over to the other bed. He looked down at Kendall, walked around, and got in on the other side. When the boy didn't move, he got closer and rolled Kendall onto his right side.

He slipped his right arm under Kendall and wrapped it around his chest. He put his left arm around Kendall's waist and pulled the blond into a tight hug, snuggling into the back of his neck. He lay there for a few moments, taking in the scent of the boy, his breath picking up. He started nuzzling Kendall's neck and ear and pulled him even tighter. Letting out a quiet moan, he started rubbing up against the boy and started to kiss the tender flesh below his ear. Kendall stirred a little but remained asleep, the sleeping pill doing its job.

Deesie smiled again, and then began rubbing against him harder, increasing the friction to his now hardening member.

'You are mine," he growled. He slipped his left hand under the boy's shirt, running his hand up and down the firm abdomen and chest. He rolled onto his back and grabbed a handi wipe from the package.

Then, reaching down, he freed himself from his pajama bottoms. With his right arm, he held Kendall tightly and with his left slowly started rubbing himself until he was nearly erect. Then he started pumping himself harder, moaning and clutching the sleeping teen tightly. He increased the rate, his hand moving up and down at a fast pace. His moans got louder, and he turned his head, biting the blond's left shoulder, wishing desperately that he could have his way with the teen now.

"It's not time yet," he told himself as he brought himself closer to climaxing. He quickly placed the handi wipe over himself and then he came, moaning loudly, back slightly arched, next to the boy who slept on, blissfully unaware of what had just taken place next to him.

Deesie stayed there for another few minutes, holding Kendall and smiling to himself. It had been too long, he thought. Finally, he released his hold on the teen and went to his own bed, where he quickly fell asleep.

∞

It was almost 2 am and Sally was still processing information as it came in. The FBI was sending agents to assist with the case, but they wouldn't arrive until later. In the meantime, she was still waiting for a location from the GPS trace they had running on Kendall's phone, but the fact that they were still on the move was causing delays. The only thing they knew for certain was that Deesie was driving east on Interstate 94 and hadn't stopped yet. Antonio had decided that he and Bennet would take the department SUV and start following the same route. This way, when Deesie stopped and they were able to get a lock on his location, they wouldn't be far behind.

Antonio gave Sylvia a quick call to let her know what was going on.

The moms were still sitting in the kitchen, finishing their second pot of coffee, when the phone rang. Sylvia glanced at the caller ID and quickly answered. "Antonio, anything new?"

"We might have caught a break. Kendall has his cell and called me. His cell has a GPS chip, and Sally has a trace running on it. They're still on the move, but we know in what direction, so John and I are heading out to follow them. Once they stop, we should be able to get an exact location," Antonio quickly explained.

"Should I wake Jen and tell her?" Sylvia asked. Brooke and Jo were looking at her, trying to find out what was going on. She gestured for them to wait a minute.

"Not yet, wait until we have something definitive. She needs the rest, and I would rather she sleep right now. Let her know when she wakes up, though. With any luck, we'll have a location on them by then and Kendall will be on his way home," Antonio told her.

"What if Deesie finds the cell?"

"Kendall tore a hole inside his jacket and hid it there. It should be safe, although the charge won't last more than a day, but by then, we should have a pretty good idea of where they are," Antonio told her.

"Alright, good."

"Also... Kendall sent a message to Jen, Katie, and the boys. He wants them to know that he loves them. Could you tell them for me in the morning?" Antonio asked quietly.

"I will, first thing," Sylvia promised, eyes tearing up again. "Please be careful and keep us informed. I love you."

"I will, sweetheart. Talk to you soon," Antonio said.

"What's going on?" Brooke demanded.

"Shhhh... We don't want to wake Jen up," Sylvia whispered. She explained what Antonio had told her.

"So, this is good news?" Joanna asked.

"Let's hope so," Sylvia said.

Chapter 14~ Advantage Lost

Deesie woke up at about 7 am. He felt quite refreshed and smirked as he looked over at Kendall, who was still sound asleep. He quickly dressed, and walked to the manager's office to buy a newspaper. He took it back to the room and looked through the classifieds.

Finding what he wanted, he reattached the phone cord and made a call. After hanging up, he walked over to where Kendall was still sleeping soundly. "Wake up," he said, shaking Kendall. After a moment, the boy half opened his green eyes, looking around in confusion.

"W-What's going on?" he asked, his speech slurred.

"I am going out for a while and you are going to stay here and sleep. I won't be gone long and this is to ensure that you don't try anything," Deesie told him, grabbing the duct tape.

He pulled a strip off and wrapped it around Kendall's ankles. He removed the necktie from Kendall's wrists and pulled his arms behind his back, wrapping a strip of duct tape around his wrists. Then, he took the necktie and tied it around Kendall's head for a makeshift gag.

"I will be right back, and if I find you've tried anything, I will beat you within an inch of your life. Understand sweetheart?"

Kendall nodded, closing his eyes, the effects of the sleeping pill not having worn off yet.

Deesie went to his car, pulled the rest of his belongings out, and put them in the room. He checked the trunk, and finding a small spot of blood, laid the mat over it. He then placed the "Do Not Disturb" sign on the room's door handle, got in the car, and drove away.

He stopped at the first coffee place he found and ordered an espresso. "Where would I find a used car lot?" Deesie asked the barista.

She gave him directions, and he smiled and gave her a large tip. He drove to the car lot and parked. It was still early, but one salesperson came out and greeted him.

"Good morning sir, how may I help you on this lovely Saturday?'

Deesie looked at the man's nametag and returned the smile. "Well Doug, my son and I are driving back home and he's not feeling too well, so we need to fly the rest of the way."

"I'm so sorry to hear that. Nothing serious, I hope," the man said in concern.

"He's been ill for some time now. We're going to visit his grandparents. Unfortunately, he can't tolerate the car ride anymore, so I was hoping you could take it off my hands."

Doug smiled as he walked over and inspected the car. "It's an older model, but the mileage isn't too bad. The interior is in great condition." He turned the engine on and listened for a moment. "Sounds good! No pinging, engine runs nice and smooth."

He got out, checked the tires, and opened the trunk. "Everything looks good. I can't give you top dollar, but I can give you a fair deal."

"Sounds good." Deesie smiled, offering Doug his hand.

They went into the sales office and came to an agreement. Doug offered Deesie $3,500 and went to write a check, but Deesie stopped him. "I really need cash. I'm from out of state and don't have access to a bank here, especially since it's the weekend. I really need to get my boy to Boston to see his grandparents."

"We don't keep a lot of cash on hand, but let me see what I can do," Doug said.

"I appreciate it," Deesie said with a sad smile.

A few minutes later Doug returned. "All I can offer you for cash is $2,800, and that will clean us out. I can write you a check for the difference," he said apologetically.

Deesie thought about it for a moment. "You know Doug that will be just fine. I appreciate your help, I truly do."

Doug smiled. "I'll go get the papers drawn up then."

He shook Doug's hand again. "Would it be alright if I borrowed your phone? I have a friend who said he'd pick me up once I'm finished."

"Of course," Doug smiled as he went to write up the paperwork for the purchase. Deesie pulled out the ad he had torn from the paper and dialed the number.

While they finished business, a red Ford Explorer pulled up. "My friends are here. I can't tell you how much I appreciate your help, Doug." Deesie smiled and offered his hand again.

"It was so nice to meet you too, Robert. I really hope your son gets better. You two have a safe trip," Doug said.

"Thank you," Deesie said as he walked out the door. He went over to the Explorer, and after speaking with the driver for a moment, got in on the passenger's side.

∞

About 6 am, Sally got a location confirmation for Kendall's phone. She immediately got on the radio to Antonio. "Boss, we have a location for the GPS, they're in Fergus Falls. We're hoping to lock onto an exact location soon."

Bennet looked at Antonio. "We're over an hour away."

"Sally, call the local sheriff and send them the information we have on Deesie. Maybe they can check out the local motels and locate his car," Antonio instructed.

"Already done," she said.

∞

Deesie pulled into the motel parking lot and unlocked the door of the room. He looked in and saw Kendall was still out. He carried his trunk out, put it into the back of the SUV, and locked it up.

He went back into the room and walked over to Kendall. He pulled the duct tape off and removed the tie from his mouth. "Time to wake up, sweetheart," he said, shaking the boy.

Kendall opened his eyes and looked up at Deesie, panic rising again.

"Get up and get dressed, we're leaving," Deesie said, pulling him up.

Kendall stumbled to his backpack, grabbed it, and went into the bathroom. His head wasn't as painful, but felt thick and he was slightly disoriented. He still felt dizzy, but not as nauseated.

He stood at the sink, filled the cup with water and rinsed his mouth, and then drank the rest. He looked in the mirror and saw he was very pale and the bruises more prominent on his face. His bangs hung down low enough that they nearly covered the bandage on his forehead.

He pulled clean clothes from his bag and started to change. His muscles were stiff and sore. Looking down, he saw bruises on his chest and abdomen. He probably had them on his back as well, he thought, trying to see in the mirror. He noticed an oddly shaped bruise on his shoulder. "What is that?" he said. He touched it and found it was sore to the touch.

The bathroom door flew open, and an enraged Deesie stood there. "What did I tell you?" he growled at the boy.

Before Kendall could say anything, Deesie had him by the throat, closing off his air supply. The boy tried pulling Deesie's hands away, gasping for air. His vision was starting to fade when he suddenly hit the floor, released from the man's grip.

He coughed and started gulping in air as Deesie grabbed him by the hair and forced a t-shirt over his head. He dragged him into the bedroom and threw him onto the floor.

"Get your boots and coat on NOW!" he hissed, grabbing the backpack and shoving everything else into it. As soon as Kendall had put them on, Deesie grabbed him by the arm and

pulled him up. "One word, one look, one gesture to ANYONE and you are dead. Do you understand me?" Deesie spat.

Kendall's eyes were wide with panic, wondering what was going on. One minute he was asleep, then he was dressing, then Deesie was choking him.

Deesie grabbed him by the throat again. "I said, DO YOU UNDERSTAND?" Kendall nodded, fear evident in his eyes.

Deesie pushed Kendall's backpack into his hands and held onto him tightly as they walked out the door. He pulled him to the red SUV and Kendall looked at him in confusion. "Get in," Deesie ordered, pushing Kendall through the back passenger door. "Buckle up, and don't think you can get out through the door or window, the child safety locks are on," he told him, slamming the door.

Kendall's mind raced as he tried to control the fear washing over him, wondering what had set the man off.

Deesie got into the driver's seat and drove away. They drove for about ten minutes, until Deesie found a secluded area. He stopped the SUV and got out. Walking around to Kendall's door, he opened it and stared at the teen. "What is this?" he asked quietly, holding an object up. His face was expressionless, but his tone was angry.

Kendall looked at Deesie's hand and his heart nearly stopped. Dread filled him as he looked from his cell phone back to Deesie's face.

At the motel, Deesie had been packing up the rest of his things and knocked Kendall's jacket onto the floor. He grabbed it and felt something strange under the left arm. Looking inside the jacket, he saw a small hole. Reaching inside, his fingers touched something hard. He grabbed ahold of it and pulled it out. It was the boy's phone. He remembered it from the other day, when he had taken it away from him. Looking at it, he cursed. He quickly turned it off, knowing they can be traced.

Deesie continued staring at the boy. "What is this?"

"M-My phone," Kendall replied.

"Hidden in your jacket, power on, volume off," Deesie stated.

Kendall nodded, his eyes now showing defiance.

"What exactly did you think you would accomplish with this?" Deesie asked.

"I just want to go home," Kendall said.

"Well, that's not going to happen, sweetheart. I can guarantee that." Deesie pulled him out and slammed him back against the SUV.

Kendall started to struggle, and Deesie punched him in the stomach. Kendall doubled over and Deesie pushed him to the ground and began kicking him. Kendall curled up on the ground, covering his head with his hands, hoping it would end soon.

After a couple of minutes, Deesie stopped and grabbed the front of Kendall's jacket. "I should kill you right here and now, but then I wouldn't be able to have any more fun with you." He straddled Kendall and looked down at the terrified teen. He just stared down at him for a few moments, and then he started grinding himself into Kendall's hips. The boy's eyes went wide, a look of horror in them, and he tried to hit the man, but Deesie grabbed his hands and held them above his head.

"This is going to happen. Maybe not at this moment, but it is going to happen. It will be up to you as to how it goes. I can be nice about it...," he said, gently stroking the blond's hair and then caressing his cheek. "Or I can be rough," he whispered into Kendall's ear. Then Deesie slammed his lips onto Kendall's and forced his tongue into the boy's mouth. Kendall gagged, trying not to vomit. Deesie kissed him hard for a moment and then latched onto Kendall's bottom lip, biting down hard.

Kendall never stopped struggling and tried to wriggle away from the older man. Deesie sat up, looked down at him, and then backhanded him, first with one hand and then the other, repeatedly. Blood began to flow freely from Kendall's nose and freshly split lip.

Suddenly, he was free as Deesie released his hold on him and stood up. Deesie kicked him in the ribs one last time, before hauling him up and pushing him back into the SUV. He grabbed the tie, retied Kendall's hands, and then reached into his backpack and pulled out the pajama top the boy had worn the night before. He wiped the blood off of Kendall's face and then slammed the door shut. He drove back to town and stopped at the motel. He looked at the boy, who was nearly unconscious in the backseat and told him to stay where he was. He got out and went back into the room. A couple of minutes later he came back out, leaving the "Do Not Disturb" sign on the door, and got back into the SUV and drove away.

∞

Sally got a message that Kendall's cell signal was gone. *Damn, it probably died,* she thought. A few moments later, she received another message that the signal was back. "Weird, maybe there was a glitch," she said.

The trace on the phone had finally given them an exact location, but before she could call Antonio, the phone rang and she answered to a very distraught Janice Lane.

"I received an email from Robert Deesie a few moments ago, saying that he's resigning because of recent events and he realizes our school just isn't a good fit for him."

"Okay, please stay calm. Can you send me the email?" Sally asked and gave Janice the link.

"Alright, I'm sending it now," Janice said.

"Thanks for calling us so quickly. We can trace the email to the computer from where he sent it. I'll let you know when we find something," Sally said.

"Thank you, Sally," Janice said.

"You're welcome. I'll talk to you later." Sally hung up, still working on the computer. When the information she requested finally came across the screen, she was not happy.

She got on the radio to Antonio. "Boss, we finally have an exact location on the cell trace. They're at the Fergus Falls Motel on Main Street. Also, Janice Lane just called in, she received an email from Deesie saying that he's resigning..." Sally went silent as the IP address she was tracing came across the screen.

"Okay, and...?" Antonio said.

"Oh no... Boss, the email was sent from Kendall's cell phone."

Bennet looked at Antonio. Deesie had found the phone. "We're almost there," he told Antonio.

"Sally, get the Sheriff from Fergus Falls there, NOW!" Antonio yelled.

"They're already on their way," Sally said.

"We're two minutes out," John told him as they entered the town, siren and lights going. He turned them off before reaching the motel. Bennet pulled into the parking lot and Antonio was out of the car before it stopped. The local sheriff was there with the manager and Antonio ran up to him.

"They're in room twelve, no sign of movement and no car, but the key hasn't been returned," Sheriff Johansen told him.

"Give me the key to the room," Antonio instructed the manager, who handed him the pass key.

They headed down to the room and saw the "Do Not Disturb" sign. Antonio listened at the door and heard nothing. Bennet stood on the other side of the door, the sheriff and his men stood by as back up.

Antonio knocked and there was no answer. He nodded to John who took the key and quickly opened the door. They went in, weapons drawn. No one was in the room. Bennet checked the bathroom and called an all clear.

"Damn it," Antonio swore.

John had noticed something and walked over to the table. "Antonio, over here."

Antonio walked over to Bennet and looked at the table. On it sat Kendall's cell phone, and next to it was a long-sleeved grey shirt, still damp with blood.

Chapter 15~ Setbacks

Antonio stood there, holding Kendall's shirt, looking it over carefully. "There are no holes or tears and the blood is primarily on the outside of the shirt," he said as he headed out the door, Bennet right behind him.

"Hold up, where are you going?" John called after him.

"I'm going to find them," Antonio said, still walking towards their SUV.

"Antonio... Antonio stop!" John yelled. "You have no idea where they're headed. Sheriff Johansen has sent his men to patrol the primary roads in and out of town. They have the description of his car, he won't get past them."

"What if they already got through BEFORE the patrols were set up?" Antonio yelled back.

"Because he set them up when Sally first called him over an hour ago, and we know that they were here after that," John said calmly, indicating the shirt that Antonio still clutched in his hands. "Or the blood would be dry."

Antonio took a deep breath, trying to stop the feelings of panic and absolute helplessness he felt at that moment. He knew John was right, but he couldn't just stand there and do nothing. He drew in another deep breath and tried to clear his head. He felt tears starting to burn at his eyes, but refused to let them fall.

Bennet put his hands on his partner's shoulders. "Antonio, we need to take a step back for a minute and figure out our next step, which does NOT include just driving off in some random direction. That won't do anyone any good."

Antonio nodded in agreement and gave his friend a small smile. "Sorry, I know you're right. I just..."

"I told you before, that's what friends are for. Now let's go talk to the manager and see if he can tell us anything that might be useful. Then we need to get a hot meal and some rest," John said.

Antonio started to shake his head, but John stopped him before he could say anything. "We're not going to do Kendall any good if we collapse from exhaustion. It's been how long since we've eaten? Even longer since you've slept. So we're going to get a couple of hours of rest and then take turns sleeping on the road." His tone left no room for argument and Antonio knew he was right.

Antonio rubbed his hand over his exhausted face. "You're right, let's go talk to the manager and then find a place to grab a bite."

Half an hour later, they were seated at a local diner, eating breakfast. The day manager at the motel had called in the night manager, and he knew nothing. All they found out was that Deesie paid in cash and he hadn't seen a boy with him, although Deesie paid for the double, claiming his son was with him.

When they were finished with their meal, they headed back to the motel for a couple of hours of sleep. Sheriff Johansen had promised to let them know if anything turned up.

Before turning in, Antonio called home to let them know what was going on.

Sylvia and the other mothers were sitting in the kitchen. Jen had awoken at about seven and joined them. They had switched to tea, and when the boys woke up, they made breakfast, which no one really ate. Even Carlos had just picked at his food.

Finally, the boys went into the living room and turned on the television, flipping through the channels until they found an old episode of Spongebob Squarepants. They sat there, staring at the TV, not saying much, but sitting in close proximity of one another.

Jen cleared the table and started on the dishes, needing something to do. She hadn't said much and wasn't crying anymore, but her eyes were still red and puffy.

Katie was still at Molly's house, unaware of what had happened the night before. It was Molly's eighth birthday today and her party started at noon. Jen decided to wait until after the party to tell Katie, hoping that Kendall would be on his way home by then.

The phone rang and the women froze. Sylvia looked at the caller ID and answered in a calm voice. "Hi honey, how are things going?" Jen turned and looked at her.

"Hi sweetheart. We traced Kendall's phone to Fergus Falls before the signal died. It showed they were here within the last couple of hours. The sheriff had already set up patrols to check all the main routes in and out of town before we got here. They have a full description, so we're hoping to narrow it down soon. The FBI should be arriving at the station there any time now, and then we're going to activate the Amber Alert. Tell Jen and the boys that we're hoping to have something soon. John and I are going to get a little rest and I'll call you with anything else," Antonio told her, praying they would have good news soon.

"Okay Antonio, get some rest and we'll talk to you later." Sylvia hung up and smiled at Jen, trying to remain positive. Something told her that Antonio wasn't telling her everything, but she wasn't about to question him on it. The boys had heard the phone ring and ran into the kitchen, and were standing with their mothers. Sylvia smiled again, hugging both Jen and Carlos, and repeated what Antonio had told her.

"So they know what town he's in? This is good news, right?" James asked hopefully.

"Of course it is. Papa G will find Kendall and they'll be home in no time," Jen said as she gathered all the boys into her arms and hugged them.

Sylvia, Brooke, and Joanna looked at one another, their expressions filled with hope but uncertainty. They just hoped it was true. They were going to have to keep a very close eye on Jen until her son was home.

∞

"Not telling them about Deesie finding the phone?" Bennet asked Antonio.

"Not right now. There's no reason to panic them at this point. I don't want Jen breaking down until we know more." Antonio sighed, rubbing his head and hoping that it was the right decision.

"I don't blame you, and there's still a good chance that the road patrols will find them."

"I hope so, John. I don't think I've ever felt this helpless," Antonio said as he lay back and closed his eyes.

"I know, get some rest," Bennet said as he went into the bathroom to take a hot shower.

∞

Sally had filled FBI Agent Christian Bower in on everything, and it was decided that since she was managing everything on her end so well, that his expertise would best be utilized at the site, so he was on his way to Fergus Falls.

She had managed to get some sleep in Antonio's office,. She was grateful that she had never needed too much sleep to function well. She was still processing evidence and had arranged for someone to take care of the Knight's kitchen as soon as it had been cleared. From the photos she had seen, she didn't want Jennifer going in and seeing what had happened.

The FBI had given her limited access to their data site so she could coordinate with them as more information came in. They had also activated the Amber Alert. Kendall and Deesie's photos and information were now being broadcast nationwide.

She called Janice Lane to let her know what had happened and to discuss arranging an assembly meeting at the school on Monday morning. The students would need to be informed one way or another, and some of them needed to be questioned. She would discuss Jason Banks with Antonio the next time he checked in, to see if he wanted Jason interrogated now about his connection with Deesie, or if he wanted to wait on it.

Personally, she would like to bring him in and scare the hell out of him after what he had done. She knew Jason's home life wasn't ideal and he had gotten into trouble before, but he had crossed some major lines this time.

Her computer let her know she had a message, and she pulled up the report. It was the Minnesota DMV, reporting that a late model Toyota Sedan, owned by Robert Deesie, had been sold to the "The Falls" used car lot in Fergus Falls, MN. No purchase by Deesie had been reported.

Sally immediately got on the phone to the car lot and identified herself. She was put through to the salesman who had handled the purchase, Doug Janson.

"Good morning, this is Doug Janson. How may I help you?" he asked in a friendly voice.

"Mr. Janson, I just need to ask you a few questions about the car you purchased this morning from Robert Deesie."

"Oh yes, Robert. What did you need to know?" he asked curiously.

"The DMV reported the sale of a gray 1990 Toyota Camry. Did he purchase another vehicle you?"

"No, his son is ill and they're going to fly home to Boston. He said the boy can't handle the road trip any longer. Why, what's the problem? He had all of the proper paperwork: title, registration, driver's license, even the insurance papers," Doug told her.

"Was the boy with him? Did you see him at all?" Sally asked, ignoring his questions.

"No, he had friends pick him up. I assumed they were staying with them and that his son was there," he said.

"He had friends with him?"

"No, he called them when we were finished and they came to pick him up. Can you please tell me what's going on?" Doug sounded panicked now.

"Mr. Deesie is a suspect in an ongoing investigation, and don't worry, you didn't do anything wrong. In fact, you did everything right. Most places would have waited until Monday to file their reports with the DMV. Can you give me the phone number from which he made the call to his friends?"

Doug gave her the number. "I can't tell you how much you've helped, Doug. I'm going to have to send someone from the sheriff's office to pick up the car, though. It's important evidence in this investigation. They'll give you the proper paperwork. Thank you again."

Sally hung up and punched in the phone number that Doug had given her. Getting a name and address, she picked up the phone and called Sheriff Johansen. She explained what she'd found and gave him the information regarding Marvin and Anne Scott. He told her that he actually knew them. They were a very nice older couple, and he would go and speak with them about their dealings with Deesie.

Sally got back on the computer and put in a request to the airport in Fergus Falls. No one named Robert Deesie had booked a flight either online or in person. She got on the phone, spoke with the security there, and made sure they received the information from the Amber Alert

.∞

Sheriff Johansen called Sally after speaking with the Scotts. "Hi Sally, it turns out the Scott's are NOT friends of Deesie. He called them first thing this morning about a 1996 Ford Explorer they had for sale. He told them that he and his son are on a vacation of sorts and rented a place in the mountains. He said his wife had left him a few months ago and that the boy has been getting into trouble ever since. Said he decided to take some time off from work and spend some quality time with him. He told them he realized that he was going to need a

four-wheel drive vehicle and the local car lot didn't have what he was looking for. They picked him up from there, he test-drove it, and they came to an agreement. He paid $2,500 in cash for it. I've already got the patrols looking for it."

He gave her the info on the Explorer and she pulled and changed the Amber Alert information. "Thanks Sheriff, I'll let Chief Garcia know," she said.

Sally called Antonio's cell. "Hello?" a sleepy voice answered.

"Hey Boss, I know you need the rest, but we have some new information you need."

"What is it?" he asked, instantly alert.

Sally went on to tell him about Deesie selling his car and purchasing the Explorer. She gave him the information on the SUV and let him know that the alerts had been activated.

"Thanks Sally," Antonio said and hung up.

"What's going on?" Bennet asked.

"Deesie got rid of his car this morning and bought another. We have been looking for the wrong car all morning. We're heading out in ten minutes," he told his partner as he headed for the bathroom to take a quick shower.

"To where?" Bennet asked.

"Same direction we were heading before. He told the people that he bought the car from that they were heading for the mountains. He is going to want to be somewhere fairly isolated, and he bought a four-wheel drive, so that makes sense. Besides, I am NOT just going to sit around doing nothing. If we need to alter our course later, we will," he said as he closed the door.

∞

Deesie drove out of town, smiling when the patrols didn't bother to try to stop him. They weren't looking for an SUV, so they just waved him through. He stayed on I-94 for another two hours before turning off and heading for the next decent sized town. He found another secluded place just a few miles outside of town and stopped. He got out and opened the back door.

Kendall sat hunched over, semi-conscious, and didn't respond when Deesie first shook him. "Wake up!" Deesie commanded slapping his face.

Kendall looked up with a start, his expression filled with fear as he tried to back away from the man.

Deesie got in the back seat and grabbed Kendall by the arm roughly. "I am going to stop for supplies in a few minutes, and I'm going to make sure you don't cause any problems," he told the teen as he pulled a strip of duct tape off the roll. He wrapped it around Kendall's ankles and then put a small piece across his mouth. He pushed him down onto the floor. "You stay down there until I say. Do you understand me, sweetheart?"

Kendall just nodded at him. His head was throbbing again, and he had a shooting pain in his side. He thought he might have a cracked rib or two. He just wanted to sleep, to let the darkness help him forget everything for a while.

Deesie got back in the front and drove to the town. He pulled into the local sporting goods store and looked back at Kendall again. "Behave!" he hissed as he got out, locking the doors.

Half an hour later, Deesie walked out with several items, including a small tent, sleeping bags, a camp stove, some medium weight climbing rope, and a 22-gauge rifle with ammunition.

He loaded up the SUV and got in, giving a quick glance to the teen still lying on the floor. He seemed to be sleeping, so Deesie pulled out and headed to the next stop, a drugstore. He bought a first aid kit and extra bandage materials.

Next, he headed to a grocery store and bought some basic supplies. He drove back towards the interstate, pulling over at the same spot that he had on his way in. He pulled further off the road and got out of the SUV. Opening the door to the back seat, he took the tape off the boy's ankles and pulled Kendall out. "Wake up!" he ordered.

Kendall woke up slowly and looked at Deesie. He started shaking, remembering the last time the man had pulled him out of the car.

"Sit down, sweetheart. We need to clean you up," Deesie said, pulling out the first aid kit.

He pulled the tape from Kendall's mouth and his lip started bleeding again. Taking the cotton pads, Deesie poured alcohol on them and started cleaning Kendall's face. The boy winced at the burning sensation but said nothing. Deesie changed the bandage on his forehead, and then handed him some ibuprofen and a bottle of water. "Swallow those."

Kendall took the pills and drank a little more of the water.

Deesie took the bottle away and shook his head, smirking. "Need to save it for later."

Kendall's left eye was definitely black now and still swollen slightly. The right side of his lower lip had been split open and his jaw was decorated with blue and purple bruises as well.

"You're just going to be all kinds of pretty colours soon," Deesie said, laughing.

Kendall just looked up at him, defiance still in his eyes. He might be hurt, but he wasn't going to give the perv the satisfaction of knowing how much.

"That attitude is going to get you into more trouble," Deesie warned, taking note of the look the boy had given him.

He reached over and ran his hand up Kendall's cheek. When he reached hair, he yanked hard. "Remember what I told you, I can be nice or I can be rough," he smirked. He took a finger and traced the teen's lips. "So beautiful," he whispered.

Kendall just looked at him in horror, suppressing the shudder that ran along his spine. Deesie leaned over and ran his tongue over the boy's mouth, pushing it in between his lips. Kendall kept his teeth firmly clenched, refusing to allow him access. Deesie smiled his breath hot on Kendall's pale and defiant face.

"What is rule number four, sweetheart? You are mine."

When the teen still refused to unclench his jaw, Deesie smiled again. This time, his mouth moved to the boy's neck and he started licking along his pulse point and then latched on with his teeth. Kendall gasped in surprise, but quickly closed his mouth in case Deesie tried to kiss him again. The man continued sucking at his neck for a moment and then released him, leaving dark blue and purple marks on the tender skin. Kendall pulled away in disgust, his stomach churning at the thought of the man's touch.

Deesie looked at him in amusement. "Soon we'll be somewhere that when I want something from you, I will just take it." He looked the boy up and down and then pulled him up and pushed him back into the SUV. "In case you're wondering, sweetheart, I want it all," he whispered into Kendall's ear.

Once Kendall was buckled back into the SUV, Deesie slammed the door and walked to the driver's side, humming to himself in pure sadistic joy.

Kendall sat in the back, feeling sick again. *Papi, please find me soon!*

Chapter 16~ Escape

Antonio and Bennet had just finished checking out of the motel when Sheriff Johansen called. "Garcia, my deputy, stationed on the east side of town, just called in. He remembered seeing a red Ford Explorer pass through, heading for I-94 about three hours ago. He didn't think anything of it because they were looking for the sedan Deesie was driving before. I've already alerted the Highway Patrol."

Antonio smiled. "Thanks Sheriff, that helps a lot. Bennet and I are heading out now, thanks for all of your help."

"Sorry we couldn't do more, but I hope you find your boy soon. Make sure to keep me informed," Johansen said.

"Will do, Sheriff. Thanks again," Antonio said.

"Well?" John asked.

"We're going east. A deputy remembered seeing the Explorer three hours ago," Antonio, said as he got into driver's seat of their SUV.

"At least that's something," John said reassuringly.

"Could you get on the line to Sally and let her know what's going on?" Antonio asked as he pulled away from the motel.

John nodded and turned on the radio. "Hey Sally, this is Bennet. We're heading east on I-94, about three hours behind Deesie."

"Okay, Agent Bower is on his way there. He should be there shortly. I'll let him know so he can follow, and you guys can meet up somewhere en route."

"Sounds good. Anything else come through?" Bennet asked.

"No, but I wanted to ask the Boss if he wants me to have Jason Banks brought in and questioned now or later?" Sally asked.

"Do it now, he might know something we can use," Antonio told her.

"Will do, Boss. I'll let you know," Sally said.

"Thanks Sally. Have you gotten any rest?" Antonio asked.

"Yup, enough for now. I'll talk to you as soon as I find out anything."

"Sounds good, thanks," Antonio said.

"I don't know how she does it. I swear, she can sleep for one or two hours and run circles around everyone for the next twenty," Bennet remarked.

"We're lucky to have her." Antonio smiled.

"You mean we're lucky she's on OUR side. She can be one scary lady when she's pissed off," Bennet said.

Antonio smiled and nodded.

"I wonder which is worse, a Latin temper or an Irish one?" John asked.

"Do you REALLY want to find out?" Antonio asked. He had seen both his wife and Sally angry, and quite frankly, he was afraid of BOTH.

"Not really," John said.

"Wise choice, my friend." Antonio laughed.

∞

At the Garcia house, Jo and Brooke had both run home for a quick shower and change of clothing.

Jen had showered and borrowed some of Sylvia's clothing, since she hadn't been able to get any of her own from home. Sylvia and Jen were going to pick up Katie as soon as their friends returned.

The boys had also showered and dressed, and were now hanging out in Carlos' room, playing video games. Their mothers wanted them to stay close by, mostly for peace of mind, and the boys didn't seem inclined to argue.

Jo and Brooke returned. Each with a bag packed with things for themselves and their sons. They were all planning to stay at the Garcia's until this ordeal was over. As soon as they arrived, Jen and Sylvia got ready to leave.

"Are you sure you don't want to stay here? I can go with Sylvia to get Katie," Joanna offered.

"No, I really need to be the one to tell her, and she'll know something's wrong if I'm not there. Thank you though," she said, giving her friend a hug.

∞

Sylvia and Jen drove to Molly's house in silence. Sylvia was trying to figure out what it was her husband hadn't told her. Meanwhile, Jen was trying to think of a way to tell her baby girl that a very bad man had taken the big brother she adores.

They pulled up in front of Molly's house and got out and walked up to the door. They could hear the giggling of little girls from the street and both smiled.

Molly's mom, Judy, answered. "Hi Jen, Sylvia! Come and join the chaos."

About seven little girls were running around, chasing or being chased by one another.

"Would you like something to eat or drink?" Judy asked.

"No thanks, we really need to get going. It looks like they had fun," Jen said, smiling.

"They did. It's going to take a week to recover but I love it!" Judy said, laughing.

Katie ran up. "Hey Mom! Hi Mama G! Do I have to go?"

"I'm afraid so, sweetheart. Go get your things and tell Molly goodbye," Jen said, kissing her on the head.

"Okay." Katie pouted, looking at her mom.

"Not going to work." Jen smiled.

"Man, I'm slipping," Katie said, running to get her things.

They got into Sylvia's car, Jen getting into the backseat with Katie. She put her arm around her daughter, but before she could say anything, Katie asked, "What's going on? Why did Mama G drive you here? Why have you been crying?"

"Katie, please give me a chance to speak," Jen said softly.

"Mom..."

"Katie, something happened last night. Someone broke into our house and... and..." Jen looked at her youngest child and thousands of memories flooded her mind, overwhelming her.

"Mom, please tell me!" Katie was frightened now. Her mother had never sounded so strange.

Sylvia jumped out of the car and got into the backseat, on the other side of Katie. She put her arm around her and grabbed Jen's hand, holding it tightly. "Katie, someone broke into your house last night and took Kendall. Papa G is looking for him and he's close behind. Your brother will be home soon, safe and sound. You and your mom are going to stay with Carlos and me until they get home. Logan, James, and their moms are there too," Sylvia told her.

Katie let a few tears fall as both moms hugged her. "Papa G is the best, and if anyone can find Kendall, he will."

"That's right, sweetheart. Papa G will find him." Sylvia hugged her again.

She got back into the driver's seat and drove them home. They arrived back at the Garcia's a few minutes later and headed inside.

The boys heard them come in and went downstairs to check on Katie. They were surprised to see her leading her mom to the couch, telling her to lie down and rest. Katie

grabbed the blanket from the back of the couch and covered her mom. She took her bag into the guest room and came back out. "Hey guys, is everyone okay?"

They all nodded. "You want to come up and play video games or watch a movie?" Carlos asked.

"Sure, that's a good way to pass the time," she said and walked up with them.

The moms all looked at each other in concern—Katie was acting as if nothing were wrong.

Once upstairs, they decided to watch a movie and Carlos chose *Toy Story*. They were all settling in, when Katie said she would go make some popcorn and headed downstairs as the opening credits ran.

"Guys, I'm really worried about her," Logan said.

"Well, she's a lot like Mama K, always taking care of everybody else first," Carlos pointed out.

James and Logan nodded.

"Hey, someone open the door, my hands are full!" Katie yelled a few minutes later. Logan and Carlos jumped up. Carlos opened the door and Logan took the tray from her. She just stood there for a minute, not moving.

"Katie..." Carlos whispered.

She looked up, tears streaming down her small round face and threw herself into James' awaiting arms, sobbing. He picked her up and sat down on the bed, cradling her small, shaking form. Logan set the tray down and sat on one side of them, Carlos on the other. They put their arms around James and Katie and all held on tightly to one another.

∞

Kendall tried to sleep as much as he could in the car. He was hoping to stay awake as long as he could that night. Deesie had him completely freaked out. He leaned his head against the tinted back window, watching the road go by. He had no idea where they were going. He just hoped Papi would find him soon.

The ride had consisted of Deesie humming something or silence. Apparently, he didn't believe in radios, so Kendall was startled when the man started speaking.

"So you're probably wondering how I became a teacher."

"Not really," Kendall mumbled.

"It was quite simple really. I just took my brother's place," Deesie told him.

"Your brother?"

"Yes, he was a wonderful teacher, everyone loved him. I loved him... But sometimes, bad things happen to good people," he said in a neutral tone.

Kendall had a very bad feeling about this conversation, but he hoped he could find out something useful. "So, if you're not Robert?"

"I'm Stephen, Robert's little brother."

"What happened to your brother?" Kendall asked quietly.

"I told you, I took his place. You see, no one was going to give me a job. Hell, I had a hard time finding a decent place to live. Seems people don't want convicted sex offenders around. When the opportunity arose, I took it. It is amazing how much easier things got after that. I don't have to register and people leave me alone."

Kendall's heart sank and he felt very sick to his stomach at this point.

Deesie started rambling on about his "deeds" and Kendall tried to block the images that were now going through his head. The car stopped a short time later and he looked out the window. They were at a roadside motel, well off the beaten path, and there were individual units instead of rooms. He didn't see any other cars around, and he felt an overwhelming urge to run. Maybe he would be able to get away and hide in the woods. At this point, he would rather take his chances out there.

"Did you hear me?" Deesie said. Kendall looked at him and shook his head.

"I said, stay here and behave or I will make sure you regret it. As you can see, there is no one else around, so if things get a little loud, no one will bothered by it." Deesie winked as he got out and headed to the office.

Kendall tried the door, but the stupid child safety lock was on. He was thinking about climbing up to the front and going out that way, when he saw Deesie coming out. He sat back, trying to come up with a plan.

"That was easy. It's the off-season, so he said I could take my pick of units. Guess which one I chose, sweetheart?" he asked as he got back in and drove to the unit furthest from the office.

Deesie opened Kendall's door and pulled him out. He grabbed Kendall's backpack and handed it to him. Still holding on to the boy's arm, he grabbed his own suitcase and shaving kit from the SUV. He closed the door and locked it.

"Walk," he said, pushing the boy in front of him.

It's now or never, Kendall thought as he took a deep breath and turned, hitting Deesie with the backpack for the second time, this time in the head. He took off at a dead run for the woods, dodging the shrubs that lined the driveway.

Chapter 17 ~ Caught

Deesie hit the gravel driveway with a thud. He laid there for a moment, in shock. Then rage kicked in and he tore after the boy, jumping the shrubs like hurdles, howling like the mad man he was.

Kendall ran, dodging trees and branches. He stopped for a moment to try to get his bearings. It was only a half moon, but he could see fairly well, which was both good and bad. He could see to run, but it also meant that Deesie could see to follow him.

He heard Deesie yell and he took off running again. He could hear the man behind him, so he veered to the right, hoping to lose him. Kendall ran for a few minutes and then stopped to catch his breath. His sides hurt, ribs aching from the beating he had taken that morning.

God, it's only been a day. He thought, listening carefully for sounds of the older man.

Hearing none, he started walking at a fast pace to try to give his burning lungs a rest. He had no idea where he was, but anywhere was better than the motel with that perv. He knew the road was to his left and not a clue what was to the right.

It was cold here, but luckily, no snow yet. The air was crisp and clear, sounds carrying for quite a distance. If he could just find a place to hide until morning, then maybe Deesie would leave, and he could go back to the motel and call for help.

Kendall thought about climbing a tree, but with the moon's half-light, there was a chance he could be seen.

He started looking around and found a small area inside an old dead tree. He tucked himself into it, curling up to conserve body heat.

He could hear Deesie still looking for him, but it was impossible to tell where he was. Sounds seemed to come from everywhere in the quiet night.

∞

Deesie was furious! That little bastard had hit him again and taken off. After the initial shock of hitting the ground, he had been up and after the teen in a heartbeat. He wasn't far behind when his foot caught on a root and he hit the ground for a second time. He got up and listened for a minute. He heard the sounds of crunching leaves and took off in that direction.

After a few minutes, he slowed his pace, realizing that he could no longer hear any sounds of the boy.

Damn it, he's hiding somewhere, Deesie thought. He began walking very carefully, knowing the boy would be able to hear him coming if he wasn't quiet.

A calm had come over him as the thrill of the hunt took hold. A twisted smile adorned his lips, and he was almost giddy with excitement. He didn't know if he should kill the boy or thank him when he found him.

No, not kill him. There would be no fun in that. His smile widened thinking of what he was going to do to the teen once he got his hands on him again.

He stopped walking and stood completely still, head cocked, listening for any sounds. He heard nothing, but smiled when he saw a small wisp of fog coming from the area of an old tree. He exhaled and watched his breath form the same kind of fog. Smiling again, he slowly walked over to the tree.

"Hello sweetheart," Deesie said looking down at the teen curled up inside the tree.

Kendall's heart nearly stopped when he saw Deesie standing there.

The man reached down, grabbed the boy by the arm, and hauled him up. Kendall took advantage of the fact that they were on uneven ground and shoved his whole body against the larger man, knocking him over. Kendall took off running again, this time in the direction of the road.

Deesie cursed and jumped up, setting off after the boy again.

Kendall was trying to keep up a fast pace, but exhaustion was quickly taking over. He realized he had not eaten since the night before and had had very little water. He could hear Deesie behind him and desperately looked for a place to hide. He saw an area thick with trees and shrubs and headed for it.

∞

Deesie followed the fleeing teen at a slow and steady pace. He would stop every few moments to listen for the sound of footsteps, and then continue. He knew the boy would be tiring soon, since he had not fed him and he was still recovering from the beating he had given him earlier.

He started calling out in singsong, "Come out, come out, wherever you are." He stood quietly again, listening. His face broke out into a twisted smile again and he took off running.

Kendall was almost to the trees when something hit him from the side. He cried out in pain as he hit the ground, and then was flipped over onto his back and pinned down. He looked up into the face of one very angry Stephen Deesie.

"You are going to be VERY sorry!" Deesie hissed.

Kendall started struggling, trying to get out from underneath the man, but Deesie put his hands around the teen's throat and started squeezing slowly.

"Stop fighting me or I will choke you until you pass out," he ordered.

Kendall stopped moving and Deesie relaxed his hold on his throat. "Good boy, now get up," he growled.

He pulled the boy up, keeping one hand on the teen's arm, and the other holding tightly to his hair. He half dragged him back to the motel, stopping at the SUV. He opened the back door and pulled out one of the bags from the sporting good's store. Still holding the boy's hair tightly, he reached down and grabbed his shaving kit and suitcase.

He shoved Kendall towards the room, kicking the blond's backpack over to the door. Deesie opened the door and pushed the boy through, and then bent down and grabbed the backpack. He locked the door behind him.

"You want to continue disobeying me?" Deesie yelled as he backhanded him.

Kendall's head whipped to the side from the force of the blow, and he hit the floor. Kendall quickly got to his knees, but Deesie grabbed him before he could stand. He unzipped Kendall's jacket, pulled it off, and threw it on the floor. He hit him again. "Do you? Answer me!"

Kendall just looked up at him, defiance in his eyes.

Grabbing the bag he had taken from the SUV, Deesie pulled a pair of handcuffs out and latched them onto the boy's wrists. "You are going to be VERY sorry by the end of this night," Deesie hissed into Kendall's ear.

He pushed him back to the floor, and reaching down, yanked off Kendall's boots and socks. He pulled Kendall up and dragged him into the bathroom. He put the plug in the tub and turned the cold water on.

Kendall tried to back out of the bathroom, but Deesie grabbed him and forced him against the wall, pinning him there.

Once the tub was full, he took ahold of Kendall's shirt and pushed him towards the tub, forcing him in fully dressed. Kendall yelled and tried to climb out, but Deesie pushed him back, this time grabbing his hair and holding him under the water for a few seconds. When he pulled him back up, Kendall was coughing and spitting the freezing water. Deesie did it again and Kendall was kicking and desperately clawing at the sides of the tub.

Kendall came back up, choking on more water.

Deesie repeated this for almost ten minutes. By the time he was finished, Kendall was barely moving. He hauled the half drowned teen out of the tub, leaving him coughing and gasping for air on the bathroom floor.

Kendall lay there, shivering uncontrollably and unable to move, both from lack of oxygen and terror.

Deesie had gone into the bedroom and returned with his shaving kit.

"You like to run away? I WILL stop that from happening again." He smiled as he pulled an item from the bag. "Do you know what pressure points are? You have them everywhere, but when you injure the ones on your feet, it makes it very painful to walk."

Kendall started shaking his head and tried to sit up. Deesie smiled and knelt beside him, grabbing Kendall's right foot. He ran his hand along the heel and stopped at the outer edge. With his finger, he measured about a quarter of an inch in and then slowly inserted a long, thick tapestry needle.

Kendall screamed in agony as Deesie twisted it back and forth before pulling it back out.

Deesie repeated the action again in the middle of his heel, and then again on the inside of his foot. He smiled down at the boy as he moved his hand up to the ball of his foot and inserted the needle there and then again at the area under his little toe, repeating the twisting action.

Kendall lay on the floor, nearly hyperventilating from the pain. The needle had penetrated the muscle in five different places.

Deesie got up and poured alcohol over the needle, carefully disinfecting it, before putting it back into the case.

Pulling Kendall's foot up, he poured the alcohol over it, making sure to hit every wound. Kendall yanked his foot away and curled up on the floor.

He grabbed Kendall's backpack and threw it next to him. "Get ready for bed," he ordered and left the boy to change.

Kendall was shivering so badly he had difficulty opening his backpack. He pulled out the flannel pajama bottoms and a long-sleeved t-shirt. He realized his hands were still cuffed, so he couldn't change his shirt, but changed out of his wet jeans. He pulled a towel down from the towel rack and tried to dry his shirt as much as possible, and then lay there shivering. His foot felt like it was on fire.

Deesie came back a few minutes later and looked down at him. "That's right, we need to take those off," he said, pointing to the cuffs. His voice was quiet, and he seemed almost gentle, as he reached for the boy's hands. Kendall backed into the wall, distancing himself from the older man.

"We need to get that wet shirt off, sweetheart," Deesie told him as he knelt down and unlocked the cuffs.

Kendall sat there, not moving as he watched the man. Deesie grabbed the towel from him and then pulled the boy to his feet. Kendall cried out when his foot hit the floor and he grabbed ahold of the sink, so he could take his weight off it.

Deesie smiled smugly and then reached over and pulled the teen's wet shirt over his head. Kendall gasped in surprise and froze when the man took the towel and started drying him off. Deesie stood behind him and started drying Kendall's hair, and then moved to his shoulders and back.

Then he wrapped his arms around him and started rubbing the towel up and down his chest and abdomen. Deesie laid his head on Kendall's shoulder, staring at him in the mirror.

The boy had gone white from shock and was shaking. "Shhh..." Deesie whispered in a comforting tone. Then he kissed Kendall's neck and pulled him against him. He dropped the towel and he ran his fingers slowly back and forth across the boy's abdomen, continuing to kiss his neck and along his shoulder.

Kendall began struggling and tried to push away, but the man held him too tightly. Deesie grabbed a handful of blond hair and pulled his head to the side, giving him access to Kendall's pulse point. He bit down before sucking at it, hard.

"No, no, no," Kendall chanted, trying once more to pull away.

Deesie moved his hand from around Kendall's waist and started caressing the boy's chest, fingers tracing little swirls across the soft skin. He finally removed his mouth from Kendall's throat and admired the deepening purple mark.

"Walk," he ordered, pushing the boy to the bedroom.

Kendall stumbled, unable to walk on his right foot, and fell to his knees.

Deesie grabbed him around the waist and half carried him to the bed furthest from the door. He practically threw Kendall onto the bed. He started humming as he went back into the bathroom and grabbed the dry t-shirt. He went back into the bedroom and handed it to the shaken teen, smiling down at him.

Kendall quickly pulled the shirt over his head, not taking his eyes off the man.

Deesie sat down on the bed and leaned over the boy, caressing his cheek. "From now on, every night you will kiss me goodnight," he said bending down and putting his lips on Kendall's. "When I do this, you will open your mouth. If you don't, I WILL make you," he said, running his tongue along the boy's bottom lip.

Kendall looked up at him, shivering uncontrollably, not answering.

Deesie ran his tongue along the soft lip once more and was again denied access.

"I see you are unwilling to take even the simplest of commands. Sweetheart, your life is going to become VERY difficult if you do not start obeying me." Deesie said as he ran his tongue along the boy's lip for the third time.

Kendall's jaw remained clenched. He was not going to willingly make out with this perv.

"I warned you," Deesie said. One hand was yanking the blond hair as the other closed around Kendall's throat. After a moment, the boy gasped for breath and Deesie slammed his mouth onto Kendall's.

Deesie released his hold on Kendall's throat and his hand roamed up under his shirt. Kendall tried to wriggle free, but Deesie was too strong. After a couple of minutes, he pulled away, breathless, and taking a finger, traced the boy's lips.

Kendall felt like he was going to pass out from the combination of pain and disgust.

"You are going to learn to obey me, ONE way or the other," he said as he took the handcuffs and reattached them to Kendall's wrists. He pulled the covers up over the boy and laughed as he walked into the bathroom. Deesie ran the hot water and took a shower, smiling to himself.

"It's been a rather good night," he said, as he dressed for bed. He grabbed the bottle of sleeping pills and poured two into his hand. He filled a cup with water and took them out to Kendall. "No ibuprofen for you tonight, but take these," he said, handing them to the boy.

Kendall's hands were shaking as he took the pills and water and then swallowed them.

"Poor boy, still cold?" Deesie asked smugly. He bent down and kissed the boy on the forehead. "Goodnight, sweetheart." He chuckled as he climbed into his own bed and turned off the lights.

Chapter 18~ Evaluations and Possible Locations

Agent Christian Bower caught up with Garcia and Bennet at a rest stop about two hours east of Fergus Falls. After introductions, they all sat down at one of the resident picnic tables that were bolted down.

Bower launched right into his findings and concerns for this case. "I have copies of all the reports from Deesie's previous crimes, as well as what your Officer O'Hara has put together. I also have copies of Deesie's mental evaluations, which were lacking, to say the least."

"Meaning?" Antonio asked.

"They classified Stephen Deesie as a pedophile and stopped there. I don't believe the evaluations were nearly extensive enough. Pedophiles target children from some misguided 'love' for them. True pedophiles want relationships only with children. Yet Deesie had a seemingly normal adolescence, even dating the same girl for nearly two years. Now, it is possible that the relationship was to hide his true nature, but after speaking with his former girlfriend, they had a normal physical relationship as well. They broke up because he became increasingly possessive of her and his moods started shifting. One minute loving, the next angry, because she didn't do something the way he wanted it done."

"So you don't think he's a pedophile?" John asked, confused.

"Not in the textbook sense. I think a more accurate diagnosis would be he is a sexual sadist with pedophilic tendencies. True pedophiles prefer a certain type—most of their victims share a similar physical characteristic. Deesie's victims that we know about, were both genders, ranged in ages 8-12, and were of varying ethnic backgrounds."

"Great," Bennet mumbled, shaking his head.

"There were also no signs of him being interested in children until he hit his thirties. Going back a little further, we found that he had had several physical altercations with people closer to his own age, while he was in his twenties. People of both genders, who fought back. In cases where charges were pressed, a settlement was made out of court, paid by his parents. After three such cases, his parents cut him off financially," Bower told them.

"So why switch to kids?" John asked.

"The possibility is he began focusing on children, because they couldn't fight him. That he could intimidate them into remaining silent. His last victim was a 12-year-old boy, who was taken on his way home from running an errand for his mother. Deesie had him for ten days, in the basement of his house, before he was found. During that time, he abused him physically, mentally and emotionally."

He handed Antonio the file on the boy and he started reading it. Antonio felt his stomach clench at the photos of the dark haired child.

The first one was of the boy with his family at an outing of some sort. He was smiling broadly. An arm draped around someone that Antonio assumed was an older brother. A school photo, same broad smile, eyes twinkling happily.

Then the photos at the hospital after he had been found, noticeably thinner. Bruises in all stages of healing covered his small body. What Antonio noticed most was the light was now gone from those once happy, brown eyes.

"Also, something that was not made clear was that he was perusing child porn sites, not for personal satisfaction, but to find out the identities of members on those sites, and then blackmailing them," Bower stated.

"So, he's a coward and a thief?" John said, shaking his head.

"And so much more," Antonio said, closing the file.

Bower cleared his throat. "There are also concerns about your relationship with the victim. It was not recommended that you continue on this investigation, with your emotional involvement. However..." he started, looking at Antonio.

Antonio stood up, his face suddenly flushed and his eyes flashing.

"Oh shit," Bennet muttered.

"That VICTIM has a name!" Antonio yelled, interrupting Bower. "His name is KENDALL, and he came to me because this freak made advances toward him. He came to ME because he trusts me, and if you think I am going ANYWHERE before I find him and bring him home, you are greatly mistaken. The fact that he is my godson..."

"Garcia, let me finish," Bower said, holding his hands up.

"Antonio, let him say what he needs to say. You and I both know WE are not leaving until we have Kendall back," John said, putting his hand on Antonio's arm and pulling him back down to the bench.

Antonio nodded and sat back down, his arms crossed and jaw clenched.

"As I was trying to explain, I believe removing you from this case would be a mistake. You know the vict... you know Kendall and how his mind works. You know what to look for if he's able to leave a sign. He's a smart kid. He showed that by immediately going to you with what happened. He also thinks outside the box, and that's going to work in his favour."

"How so?" John asked.

"Think about what he's done so far. He recorded Deesie trying to blackmail him, deliberately allowing the man to think he was recording with his phone, and FIND it, all the while recording with his MP3 player. Then he calls Garcia after he found his cell, and then again, tearing a hole in his jacket to hide it. He can think on his feet, even when he's afraid. That's going to work in his favour," Bower said.

Antonio nodded and visibly relaxed. "So what's our next step?"

∞

Sally sent a patrol car to pick up Jason Banks for questioning. She opted to bring him in as opposed to speaking to him at his house...she wanted the home turf advantage. After Jason was brought in, she had him wait in the interrogation room for a few minutes.

She watched through the two-way mirror, and when he finally started showing signs of getting antsy, she went in. "Hey Jason, I hear you've been up to no good again."

"I don't know what you're talking about." He smirked, folding his arms.

"Really? Because I heard that you were passing out some very interesting papers at school yesterday."

"Is that illegal?" he asked with a snort.

"Not necessarily, it depends on what was on them, and why," Sally said, sitting across from Jason and just looking at him.

"Just jokes, ya know?"

Sally didn't say anything but sat back and continued staring at him.

"Look, he deserved it. He and those friends of his have been giving me trouble for years," Jason said.

"By trouble, you mean defending themselves and others from you and your little bullying peons?"

"Whatever." Jason sat back, shaking his head.

"Jason, I know that Mr. Deesie put you up to it. What I want to know is... What did you get out of it?" Sally stated.

"Yeah, how do you know he put me up to it?"

"How else would you have known what to write, draw, and whatever else you did on those papers?" Sally asked, still staring.

"Maybe I heard what happened?" he replied smugly.

"Well in that case, you're in a lot more trouble than I thought," she said.

"What do you mean?"

"Well, if you heard what happened, then you know what he said and tried to do to Kendall Knight. Since you failed to report it, that makes you guilty of failing to report a crime," she told him.

"What?" Jason was definitely getting nervous now. He was starting to sweat and tapping his foot under the table.

The phone buzzed and Sally picked it up. "Thanks Johnson," she said, standing up, still looking at Jason. "I'll be right back. You might want to reconsider your previous statements."

Sally walked out into the main office, where Mrs. Banks was standing, furious. "What have you arrested my son for? You can't talk to him without a lawyer!"

"Mrs. Banks, Jason has not been arrested, YET. He is being questioned regarding the activities of a teacher at his school. Since he has not been charged, we are allowed to question him without an attorney or parent present," Sally told her.

"Well, what about this teacher, what is this all about?" Mrs. Banks asked.

"I'll have Officer Johnson explain it to you," Sally said, indicating the older officer at the desk, who came and took the woman's arm. He took her to one of the smaller offices while Sally went back to the interrogation room.

"Well, Jason, have you decided to tell me the truth?" she asked, sitting back down.

"Is Mr. Deesie in trouble?"

"You could say that," she said.

"Why?"

"You haven't figured that out yet?" Sally asked, amazed at the boy's slowness to grasp the situation.

Jason just sat there, looking like a deer caught in the headlights.

"Okay, let me make this easy for you. Listen carefully, as this is your only chance to avoid any serious trouble here, understand?" Sally said.

Jason nodded.

"Good. Mr. Deesie made sexual advances toward Kendall. After a conversation with Principal Lane, he resigned by email, AFTER kidnapping Kendall. We are currently searching for them. So I'm going to ask you once more, exactly what do you know about Deesie and what happened that night?" She sat back in her chair and watched him closely.

Jason's face had lost all colour, and he dropped his head into his hands. "No, this isn't happening."

"I'm trying to help you, Jason. If anything happens to Kendall, you can, and will, be held as an accessory. You're sixteen, which means you can, and will, be tried as an adult," Sally said as she reached over and put her hand on his arm.

Jason looked up at her miserably.

"Jason I know you get into trouble, but I also know your home life isn't the greatest. I know your dad tells you that you'll never be more than he was, and I think he's wrong about that. Kids in that situation tend to act out, and I don't think you're really a bad kid. I think you've made some bad choices and have a problem controlling your baser impulses, but that shouldn't condemn you to time in prison. You have your whole life ahead of you, and I really don't want to see that happen. Jason, please, is there anything you can tell me that might help?"

"I really don't know anything. Mr. Deesie called me in after class and said he knew I have a problem with Kendall and the guys. He asked me if I wanted to play a prank on Kendall and get even with him. I said sure, why wouldn't I? So he gave me these papers and told me what to say, that's all I swear." Jason was shaking now.

"Did he say anything about where he might go on a vacation or anything like that? Anything at all, no matter how unimportant it might seem?"

"I'm sorry, he never did. That was the first time I ever really talked to him. Do you think he's going to hurt Kendall? I mean, I know we never got along, but..." Jason asked quietly.

"I hope not, but right now we just don't know," she said, giving his hand a comforting squeeze. She stood up and opened the door. "You can go now, but if you remember anything at all, please call me."

"I will, thanks for believing me," Jason said as he walked out. He met his mother at the door, who had quieted down considerably.

"Jason thanks again," Sally called to him. She wanted his mom to know that Jason had been a big help.

He waved and gave her a small smile.

"You know, Mr. Deesie didn't say anything that day, but a couple of weeks ago, he was talking about famous writers from the Midwest. He said something about one of them being born in Osseo," Jason said.

"Okay?"

"He said a friend of his lived in a small town near there, and when he stayed with him, they drove over to Osseo and went to the guy's house or something. Ap... something, I think. I know it started with an A." Jason's brow was furrowed as he tried to remember. He was actually surprised he remembered that much.

"It started with an A, near Osseo?" Sally asked, trying to remember her local geography.

"Yeah, I'm sorry, I don't remember the whole thing," Jason apologized.

Sally went over and hugged him. "You have no idea how helpful you've been."

Jason blushed. His mom smiled at Sally and mouthed, "Thank you."

The Banks went on their way and Sally got on the computer and pulled up the state map. She found three towns that began with an A, within a 200-mile radius of Osseo.

Sally got on the radio with Antonio. "Boss, we have a possible location." She told him about her conversation with Jason and gave him the names of the three towns.

∞

Deesie woke up at about 3 am, feeling restless and looked over at Kendall, who was sleeping in the next bed.

He watched him for a few minutes and saw the boy shivering. He debated for a moment and decided he would rather have the boy healthy to start with. After immersing him in freezing water, he didn't want him catching pneumonia. He would need to feed him in the morning as well. He got up, grabbed an extra blanket from his bed, and walked over to the sleeping boy.

He sat down next to him for a few minutes, watching the blond sleep. He reached over and brushed some bangs out of the teen's eyes. *He really is quite unique,* the man thought as his heart rate picked up.

Smiling to himself, he pulled the covers off the boy, and reaching down, pulled the pajama bottoms down so that Kendall's hips were exposed. He pushed his shirt up a little and placed gentle kisses on the boy's abdomen, His right hand gently rubbed Kendall's thigh, and the boy stirred a bit but slept on. Moving his mouth from the teen's navel to his left hipbone, Deesie bit down hard and started sucking.

After a minute, he pulled off, smiled, and went back to the task at hand. A moment later, he pulled off again, this time satisfied with the purple mark.

Deesie pulled Kendall's pajama bottoms back up and his shirt back down. Then he pulled the covers back up and laid the extra blanket on top of him, tucking it in. He bent down and kissed Kendall on the forehead. He went back to his own bed, smiling to himself, having decided to leave a little "love" mark like that every night.

∞

At about 7 am, Deesie awoke again and got up. Kendall was still sound asleep. "Those over-the-counter sleeping pills work well," Deesie said to himself.

He went into the bathroom to shave and get dressed. He packed up his shaving kit, smiling at the little case that held his needles. He had learned long ago that the simplest things could cause the greatest pain. He went back into the bedroom and packed up his suitcase.

Then he walked over to Kendall's bed and sat down. "Rise and shine, sweetheart," Deesie said, shaking the boy.

It took a moment for Kendall to open his eyes, and when he did, he pushed away from the man sitting next to him.

"Uh, uh, uh," Deesie chastised him, grabbing ahold of the boy's arm. "You do NOT pull away from me."

Kendall just looked at him, jaw clenched in case Deesie tried to kiss him again, the memory of last night still vivid in his mind.

"Lose the attitude, sweetheart. I mean it," Deesie said as he took the boy's hands and pulled him closer. "You need the cuffs off to shower, so hold still."

Kendall didn't say anything as Deesie removed the cuffs and then stood up and moved away from him. When Kendall tried to stand, an incredible shooting pain went up his right leg and he yelped.

"Need help?" Deesie asked, smirking at him.

Kendall glared at him and gingerly tried to take a step, but then stopped. He looked over at Deesie, who was still smirking at him, and turning his foot to the side, limped over to his backpack and picked it up.

He walked into the bathroom and closed the door. Once the door was closed, he quickly braced himself against the sink. He reached over and turned on the water for the shower. While it was warming up, he pulled clean clothes out and laid them on the counter. He undressed as quickly as possible and stepped into the tub, leaning against the wall to keep the pressure off his foot.

He soaped up and rinsed off as fast as he could. Everything hurt, and he wished he could let the hot water run over him longer, but he didn't trust Deesie to stay out. He sat down on the side of the tub, quickly dried off, and pulled his clothes on. After a couple of minutes, he got to his feet, grabbed his backpack, and limped back out into the bedroom.

He made his way to one of the chairs in the room and sat down. He pulled on socks and then his boots, wincing at the pain in his foot as it made contact with the boot. His foot still hurt like hell, but the sock and boot cushioned his foot, relieving some of the pressure.

"Here," Deesie said, tossing him a granola bar and a bottle of juice.

"Thanks," Kendall mumbled as he opened the juice and took a sip.

"After you eat, you can have some ibuprofen. I don't need you getting sick in the car," Deesie said as he grabbed their bags and headed out the door.

Kendall watched Deesie leave, and as soon as the door closed, he got up and limped to the bed. Earlier, he had noticed a pad and pen on the table between the beds. He grabbed the items, quickly tucking them under his shirt. He got back to the chair just as Deesie walked back in.

"Hurry up, I want to get on the road as soon as possible," Deesie said.

Kendall quickly ate the granola bar, and Deesie handed him the promised ibuprofen. "Let's go," Deesie said, grabbing Kendall by the arm and pulling him up.

Kendall grabbed his jacket and put it on, limping out the door behind the man. He climbed into the SUV and Deesie slammed the door behind him. Deesie got into the driver's seat and drove up to the manager's office to return the key.

"Stay here," he said, looking back at the boy. Then he grinned. "That's right, I don't need to worry about you running off again anytime soon."

Kendall glared at him and Deesie pointed his finger at him in warning. Deesie got out and walked to the office.

Kendall pulled out the pen and pad and quickly scribbled out a note. He folded it and put it in his pocket, and then hid the items in the pouch on the back of the seat in front of him.

Deesie walked into the office and dinged the little bell. The elderly man came out and looked at him nervously.

"Just checking out," Deesie told him, setting the key on the counter.

The man nodded as he wrote out the receipt and handed it to Deesie. "H-Have a good day."

"Everything alright?" Deesie asked, watching him closely.

"Y-Yes," the man stammered, smiling at Deesie.

Deesie could hear the television on in the room the old man had come from and caught the words "Amber Alert." The old man looked up at Deesie and saw the other man staring at him. Deesie smiled as he walked into the other room, where he saw first Kendall's, and then his picture, come across the screen.

Deesie looked around the little room and saw the phone sitting next to the chair that the old man had vacated. He walked back out and looked down at the other man, who was avoiding eye contact. "Something you want to ask me?"

"N-No, I don't know nothing, ain't seen nothing," the old man claimed, desperation in his voice.

"Is that true? Did you call the police?" Deesie asked softly, putting his hands around the old man's throat.

The man shook his head, clawing at Deesie's hands.

"Are you sure?" Deesie asked as he tightened his hold on the fragile throat.

The old man nodded as he gasped for air.

"I don't believe you," he hissed into the man's ear and proceeded to choke the life out of him. When the old man had stopped struggling, Deesie released his hold on him, and he crumpled to the floor like a rag doll.

Deesie calmly went back out to the SUV and opened Kendall's door. He grabbed him by the arm and yanked him out. Kendall's eyes went wide.

"What's wrong?"

Deesie dragged him into the office and behind the counter, where the old man lay. "This is because of YOU! It is YOUR fault this man is dead!"

He pushed Kendall towards the man and he stumbled, falling next to him. Kendall looked at the older man, seeing the terror that had been frozen on his face at the moment of death.

He reached over and gently touched his cheek. "No, no, no! Why would you kill him? He wasn't strong enough to fight you! He never did anything to you!" Kendall was angry now and didn't care if Deesie hurt him.

Deesie grabbed him by the collar and pulled him close. "He called the police because YOUR picture is all over the news. He died because of YOU and don't you ever forget that!" Deesie hissed at him.

He pulled Kendall to his feet and started towards the door. Kendall resisted and Deesie lost his grip and Kendall fell to the floor. "You better get your ass in that car or there will be a repeat of what happened last night with a few little extras thrown in!" Deesie yelled, as he grabbed Kendall again and half carried him to the SUV.

He pushed Kendall into the back and slammed the door shut. He hurried around, got into the driver's seat, and pulled out, heading for the interstate.

Kendall sat back in shock, his eyes filled with tears as he thought of the old man lying there, all alone on the cold floor. He refused to let them fall. Deesie would not make him cry, no matter what.

Back at the motel, the television continued to blare and a little old man lay dead after trying to help a young boy who had been taken by a very bad man. Next to him was a piece of

notepaper and on it was written, "Please call Antonio Garcia at ***-***-****. We are driving a red Ford Explorer, license plate *** ***. It was signed, *Kendall Knight.*

Chapter 19~ Notes

Sally had spent most of the night coordinating with the law enforcement departments in the towns of Andover, Apply Valley, and Anoka. She made sure they had all the information from the Amber Alert, as well as any other information they might need. She also sent the information to the police in Osseo, since Deesie had mentioned he had been there.

At about 8am, she was starting to get tired and was thinking about taking a nice little catnap in Antonio's office, when a call came in from the state police. She took the information and got on the radio to Antonio and Bennet.

"Boss, where are you guys at?"

"Hey, Antonio's sleeping. What's going on?" John asked.

"The state police got a call from a roadside motel about an hour ago. The owner, Randolph Crowley, said he had seen the Amber Alert on TV and recognized Deesie. He checked in last night around eight using the name, Marc Philips. He told Mr. Crowley he was traveling with his son, but that he never saw the boy."

Bennet reached over and started shaking Antonio. "Wake up, we've got a lead."

"Go on, Sally," John said as Antonio rubbed his eyes and tried to stretch out in the small area.

"The State Police went to investigate the story, hoping to get there before they checked out...," she said.

Antonio was fully awake now. "What, where?"

"Let her finish," John said quietly, he had a bad feeling about where this was going.

"They found Mr. Crowley, age 72, dead in the office. There was no one else at the motel," she told them.

"What happened to Crowley?" Antonio sighed in frustration.

"Apparent asphyxiation, they think he was strangled. There was no sign that he put up a struggle. Boss, they found something else. Next to Mr. Crowley, on the floor, was a piece of notepaper from the motel."

"And?" Antonio asked.

"It was a handwritten note. It said, please call Antonio Garcia at ***-***-****. We are driving a red Ford Explorer, license plate *** ***. They said it was signed by Kendall Knight."

"Where is this motel?" Antonio asked.

She gave them the directions and John pulled over and turned the car around. Antonio called Bower to let him know what had happened and where they were heading. About forty-five minutes later, Bennet pulled the SUV into the motel parking lot, with Bower close behind. Patrol officer Andrews greeted them.

"What have you found out?" Bennet asked, as they walked to the office.

"Not much," Andrews told him. "Mr. Crowley lived here alone ever since his wife died five years ago. Doesn't get too many guests here, being ten miles off the interstate. He has his regulars, but the only guest registered here within the last week was Marc Philips, who checked in last night."

"Marc Philips, a combination of Stephen and Robert's middle names," John said.

Antonio nodded. "What about this note that was found?"

Andrews handed him a plastic evidence bag with a small note inside.

"This is Kendall's handwriting," Antonio confirmed. "Is this the motel's notepaper?"

Andrews nodded.

He was relieved. No one had actually seen the boy since he had disappeared, and the note confirmed that he was alive. At least, he was this morning.

Bennet seemed to be reading his thoughts and put his hand on his partner's shoulder. "We'll find him, this is proof he's alive. We just need to figure out which way they went."

"Did you find anything in the room?" Antonio asked.

"Nothing out of the ordinary—a granola bar wrapper and juice bottle were on the table. Other than that, nothing. We've sent those in to see if we can get prints," Andrews said.

"Let's go take a look, see if there's anything you might notice," John said to Antonio.

Bower stayed and spoke with Andrews, while Antonio and John walked down to the last unit. They walked in and looked around, not seeing anything obvious. Bennet went to check out the bathroom, while Antonio looked around in the bedroom.

He saw that both beds had apparently been slept in and sighed in relief. He pulled back the covers from the first bed and found nothing. He moved to the second bed, pulled the covers back, and found a few drops of blood near the foot of the bed. This concerned him a lot.

"John, can you come and take a look at this?"

Bennet came out of the bathroom and went over to Antonio. "What is it?"

Antonio pointed at the spots. "What do you think?"

Bennet looked around and found another spot of blood that was barely noticeable in the carpet. "I'm not sure, it's just a couple of drops, and they're at the foot of the bed. Could be he hurt his foot. I smelled rubbing alcohol in the bathroom, which would go along with a small injury."

Antonio nodded but didn't say anything.

Bennet looked at his partner. "NO, I know what you're thinking, and if that were the case, there would be a lot more blood and it wouldn't be down there."

Antonio nodded. John was right. Now was not the time to panic. Kendall was alive and they needed to concentrate on finding him, period.

∞

Deesie had gotten back on the interstate and was still heading east. He had ranted for the first twenty minutes or so, and was now driving in silence.

Kendall sat in the back with his head against the window. He kept thinking about the old man lying dead in the office. He wondered if he had a family somewhere and how long it would be before someone found him.

This was so messed up.

He looked at Deesie in the front seat and wondered what he would do next. He closed his eyes and nodded off for a little while but woke when he heard Deesie speaking.

"Are you listening to me?" Deesie asked.

Kendall looked at him and shook his head. "I was asleep."

"I said we will be camping out for the next few nights so there won't be any more trouble. I'm going to stop at the next town and pick up a few more supplies."

Kendall nodded and looked back out the window.

A few hours later, they pulled into a small town. Deesie drove to a local market and parked on the far side of the parking lot. There was a park on the north side of the market, where kids were playing soccer.

"Give me your hands," Deesie said, pulling the cuffs out.

Kendall leaned forward, with his hands extended, and Deesie latched the cuffs onto his wrists. "Do I really need to tell you to behave?"

Kendall just sat back and looked at him.

"Your attitude is going to get you hurt VERY soon at this rate, sweetheart. I will be back in a few minutes. Don't try anything or someone else will get hurt," Deesie hissed as he got out and locked the doors.

Kendall watched him walk through the market doors and grabbed the pen and pad from the seat pouch. He wrote the same message that he had back at the motel. He folded the paper, slipped it into his pocket, and put the pen and pad away.

He sat, looking out the window, watching people go in and out, families doing their weekly shopping. He thought about home and wished he were there with his family. He missed them so much and he had never felt so alone.

For a moment, he debated on trying to climb into the front seat and getting out, but there were too many people around, and he was afraid Deesie would make good on his promise to hurt someone else. He sighed, thinking back to the little old man. "It's all my fault."

He saw a little boy, probably a couple of years older than Katie, kick the ball across the grass, close to the SUV. Kendall immediately rolled the window down as far as it would go.

"Hey, kid can you give this to your mom?" he asked, holding the folded note out the window.

The little boy looked at Kendall suspiciously.

"Look, I know you shouldn't talk to strangers, I don't want anything, just take this to your mom, please?" Kendall pleaded as he dropped the paper out the window. "Don't pick it up until we leave. In fact, don't even come near here until we're gone, that way you're safe."

The little boy looked at him again and then nodded.

Kendall smiled at him. "Thank you! Thank you so much! Now go back to your friends until we leave, okay?"

The little boy turned and ran back to his friends. Kendall quickly rolled the window back up, hoping the little boy would remember to get the paper.

A few minutes later, Deesie came out with a couple of bags and loaded them into the back of the SUV. He got in, started the engine, and pulled out.

Kendall watched through the window until he couldn't see the park anymore.

Well, it was worth a try, he thought.

∞

The boys playing in the park had finished their game and started to head home, when 9-year-old Ian Wayne remembered his promise to the boy in the red truck. He ran back to where they had been parked and looked for the paper. He found it a minute later—it had blown a short way across the parking lot. He grabbed it, shoved it into his jeans pocket, and quickly headed home for dinner.

∞

Deesie drove for a couple of more hours on the interstate, and then pulled off at an exit. He drove until they came to a quiet wooded area, and pulled off, driving as far as he could off the road. "We'll stay here tonight," he said as he parked and got out. He went around to Kendall's door and opened it.

The boy got out and Deesie closed the door. "This is for your attitude earlier," he said, backhanding Kendall, who hit the side of the SUV and then fell to his knees.

Deesie grabbed his hair and forced him to look up. "I should take advantage of where you are at the moment," he smirked, pulling Kendall towards him.

The teen's eyes went wide with horror when he realized what Deesie was talking about and tried to push away from him.

Deesie bent down and smiled. "We'll leave that for later, we need to get camp set up before dark."

He released his hold on Kendall and walked to the back of the SUV. "Soon sweetheart, very soon." Kendall rose slowly, leaning against the SUV to support his weight until he was able to stop shaking.

Chapter 20~ Camping Out

Ian Wayne ran home and dashed in the house, knowing he was late for dinner.

"Ian Christopher Wayne, where have you been?" his mother called out.

"Sorry mom, we were playing soccer and I forgot about the time," he answered, quickly washing his hands.

"Sit," his mother said, indicating the empty dining room chair. He took his seat next to his dad and across from his older sister. "You were supposed to be home over half an hour ago, young man. You still have chores to do and you have school tomorrow," she scolded.

"I know, mom, I'm sorry. We were just wrapped up in the game," he said, taking a spoonful of mashed potatoes from a bowl.

His older sister smirked at him and he kicked her under the table.

"Ow, mom..." she whined.

"Stop it, both of you," their dad ordered.

Ian smirked back at his sister and began devouring his dinner. After dinner, Ian took out the trash while his sister did the evening dishes.

Afterwards, they would all settle in for the evening and have family movie time.

Mr. Wayne was watching the local news while waiting for his family to join him. Ian walked into the living room and looked over at the news alert.

"I saw him."

"Saw who?" his dad asked.

"The boy on TV," he said, pointing at the picture of Kendall as the Amber Alert came across the screen again.

"Really? You saw THAT boy?" his dad asked, shaking his head, thinking back to when his son insisted that The Rock was the substitute math teacher.

"Dad, I really saw him! We were playing soccer in the park and he was in a red truck at the market," Ian insisted.

"Ian, do you know what an Amber Alert is? It means that a child has been taken, so if this is a joke, it's NOT funny," his dad said seriously.

"I'm serious! Look, he gave me a note and asked me to give it to my mom!" He searched his pockets for the note. "See!" he said, holding it out to his dad.

His dad took the paper from him and read it. "Ian did you go near him or the man he was with?" he asked, his tone suddenly urgent.

"No, he was the only one in the truck, sitting in the backseat. He asked me to give the note to mom, but not to pick it up until they left. He said I should go back to my friends until they were gone, so I did. I almost forgot and went back to get it. Did I do something wrong?" Ian asked, worried by the look on his dad's face.

"No, you didn't do anything wrong. I'm sorry I didn't believe you, son. Why don't you go pick out a movie while I talk to your mom?" His dad smiled.

"Okay," Ian replied, walking to the video cabinet. "Adults are SO confusing," he mumbled.

∞

Sally received a call from a store in Watertown. The owner had seen the Amber Alert that afternoon and remembered Deesie coming in the day before and purchasing some things. She got a list of the items and thanked the man for calling.

Sally got on the radio. "Hey Boss, I just got a call from a sporting goods store in Watertown. The owner said Deesie came in early yesterday afternoon and purchased camping supplies, including a tent, sleeping bags, camp stove, lantern, hunting knife, handcuffs, and a 22 gauge rifle with two boxes of ammo."

"Okay Sally, thanks. Alert the state police and the FBI that he's armed."

"Already done," she said.

"Have I told you that I think you're absolutely amazing?" Antonio asked.

"Not today, but I know you do. Thanks Boss." She smiled.

"Great, psycho has a gun," John muttered.

"I know," Antonio sighed.

A few minutes later, Antonio's cell rang. "Garcia."

"Hello, is this Antonio Garcia?"

"Yes, this is Officer Garcia, who is this please?"

"My name is Christopher Wayne. I'm calling because my son brought home a note this afternoon with your number on it."

"A note with my number? Does it say anything else?" Antonio asked, motioning for Bennet to pull over.

"Yes," Mr. Wayne read the rest of the note to Antonio. "My son, Ian, said that a boy in a red truck asked him to give it to his mom."

"Where are you?" Antonio asked.

Mr. Wayne gave him directions.

"Okay, we'll be there within the hour. I'm going to need to speak to your son."

"Alright, we'll be waiting," Mr. Wayne said and hung up.

Antonio called Bower and told him about the call he had just received. It was decided that Bower would keep going and they would all meet up again later.

Thirty-five minutes later, John and Antonio pulled up in front of the Wayne home. They got out and walked up to the door, which was opened by a wide-eyed, dark haired little boy. "Dad, there are policemen here!"

Mr. Wayne came to the door and welcomed the two officers. They sat down on the couch and Mr. Wayne handed Antonio the note. "Same notepaper and Kendall's handwriting," he said, handing the note to John.

"This is Ian," his dad said, introducing the small boy.

"Am I in trouble?" he asked, looking a little worried.

"No son, we're here because of the note you were given. Can you tell me more about it?" Antonio asked with a smile.

"What do you want to know?" Ian asked.

"Well, can you tell me about the boy who gave it to you? Where you were, what you were doing at the time?" Antonio asked.

"I was playing soccer in the park with my friends. Ben kicked the ball too far, almost into the parking lot and I went to get it. A boy opened the back window and asked me if I'd take the note to my mom. He dropped it out the window, and said he knew I wasn't supposed to talk to strangers but asked me to take the note to my mom. Then he told me not to get it then, but to wait until they had left, so I'd be safe. Then he told me I should go back to my friends, so I did. I almost forgot the note when we finished playing, but I ran back and found it."

Antonio pulled out his cell phone and scrolled down. "Is the boy you saw in this picture?" he asked, showing the phone to Ian.

The boy looked and saw four boys with their arms around each other, all smiling and holding hockey sticks. "Him," he said, pointing to the blond.

"Did the boy seem like he was okay?"

"I guess, but he had a black eye and a cut on his lip. He was also wearing a funny bracelet."

"Funny bracelet, like this?" John asked, pulling out his handcuffs.

"Yeah." Ian nodded.

Antonio and Bennet looked at each other. "Did he happen to say where they were going?" Antonio asked hopefully.

"No, he didn't."

"Thank you so much, Ian. I can't tell you how helpful you have been. Your parents should be very proud of you," Antonio said, standing up and shaking the boy's hand.

"We are," Christopher said. "I hope you find the missing boy soon. I take it you know him personally?"

"My godson and I hope we find him soon too," Antonio said, shaking his hand.

John and Antonio headed back to their car. "Where to now?" John asked his partner.

"I guess we keep going the way we've been going. They don't seem to stray too far from the interstate," Antonio said.

∞

Deesie opened the back of the SUV and started pulling out camping gear. "Come and get this," he told Kendall.

Kendall limped over and Deesie removed the cuffs and handed the tent to him. "Put it over there," Deesie instructed, pointing to a small clearing a few feet off. Kendall walked over and dropped it where Deesie had pointed.

"Catch!" the man yelled as he threw a sleeping bag at the teen, who barely missed being hit in the face with it. Deesie laughed. "What's the matter, sweetheart? Daddy never taught you how to play catch?"

Kendall just glared at him and walked back to grab more of the gear. He pulled out the camp stove and lantern and carried it over to the tent.

They spent the next half an hour setting things up, and Deesie went to grab some of the canned goods he had picked up at the market. He opened two cans of soup and put them on the stove.

They sat there in silence for a while, and then Deesie looked over at the boy. "So, do you have a girlfriend?"

"No, why?"

"Just curious. I guess that means you don't have too much experience with things." The man smirked.

Kendall rolled his eyes and just looked at the trees.

"What's the matter, sweetheart? Do you get embarrassed by questions like that?" Deesie asked as he stirred the soup.

"What happened to your brother?" Kendall asked.

Deesie looked at him, irritated at the change of subject. "Let's just say you probably don't want to know the answer to that, sweetheart."

"Why did you kill that old man? If he'd already called the police, letting him live wouldn't have changed anything," Kendall said.

"I told you, he died because of you. If your picture hadn't been all over the news, he wouldn't have seen it and he wouldn't have called the police!" Deesie yelled.

"But he never saw me, he only saw you," Kendall pointed out.

Deesie continued stirring the soup. *If that's true and the old man didn't call the cops, he didn't have to worry about them finding them anytime soon,* he thought.

Deesie poured the soup into two mugs and handed one to Kendall. Kendall took it, watching Deesie closely. The man sat down to his right and started eating, lost in thought.

"Eat up, sweetheart. I want to get an early start tomorrow," Deesie ordered.

Kendall slowly drank the soup from the mug, blowing on it from time to time. A few minutes later, they had both finished and Kendall rinsed the mugs with a little of the bottled water Deesie had brought out.

Deesie threw his backpack at him. "Get ready for bed."

"We're not sleeping in our clothes?"

"No, and do what you're told without questioning me. Change in the tent while I change out here, since you are so shy," he mocked.

Kendall took his boots off and climbed into the tent, where he quickly changed into his flannel pajama bottoms. He left his t-shirt on since he was running out of clean ones and Deesie had taken his pajama top the other day.

"Get out here," Deesie ordered.

Kendall sighed and crawled out of the tent. Deesie grabbed his backpack and tossed it to the side. Then he grabbed Kendall and pulled him up. "We still have the little matter of your disobedience from this morning to deal with," he said, pushing the teen to the ground.

Kendall sat, still watching the man as he grabbed his shaving kit. He pulled out the little back case that held the needles. Still smiling, he pulled out a needle about six inches long and crouched in front of the boy.

"You are going to learn to obey me, sweetheart. Now, I could put this into your knees, but I think I want you to be able use them later," he said, giving Kendall a dirty little smile.

Kendall just stared ahead, trying to control the panic that was building in his chest.

"I could pierce your ears," he suggested, rubbing the needle along the side of the blond's head.

Suddenly he grabbed him and pushed him onto his stomach.

Kendall yelped and tried to get back up, but Deesie put his knee in the small of his back and held him down. He pushed Kendall's shirt up above his shoulders and then straddled him. He bent down and kissed the boy's ear, and then ran his tongue down his spine.

"No!" Kendall yelled, trying to wriggle away, nearing full panic.

"Relax sweetheart, it's not time for that... yet," Deesie whispered. He reached down, took Kendall's earlobe in his mouth, and sucked on it while running his hands up and down the blond's sides.

"I would stay still if I were you, you don't want this breaking off," Deesie warned as he sat back up.

With his left hand, he held the boy's neck steady as he took the needle and inserted it up under Kendall's left shoulder blade, running parallel to the bone, until only about an inch remained out. He slowly wiggled it back and forth and Kendall screamed. He pulled it out halfway, and then pushed it back in at a slightly different angle. Deesie did this six more times, smiling every time Kendall screamed out in pain. He finally pulled the needle out all the way and ran his hands over the teen's back.

He leaned back down, kissed the boy's neck, and then bit down. He started sucking at the tender flesh until it was just the right shade of bluish purple. The boy underneath him lay there, panting from the pain that continued to burn in his shoulder.

"Keep making that noise, sweetheart, it's turning me on," Deesie whispered and then stood up. He reached down and pulled Kendall's shirt back down, and then knelt beside him, gently stroking his hair.

"I wouldn't have to hurt you as much if you would just OBEY me," Deesie said, suddenly tightening his grasp on the blond hair.

The man got up, grabbed a bottle out of his shaving kit, and handed Kendall two sleeping pills and a little water. "Now, swallow these and get to bed."

The boy grabbed the pills and took a sip of water.

"Go to bed now," Deesie ordered, still smirking.

Kendall managed to limp to the tent and crawled into the sleeping bag. He was shaking from pain and fear, wondering how much longer he could take this. He tried to shake off the pain, but it felt like shards of glass were impaling the muscles in his shoulder.

He rolled over onto his right side and continued shaking. He knew it wasn't just the pain. He had been hurt worse in hockey practice. It was wondering what else Deesie would try. The man kept hinting at things he was going to do, and he really didn't think he could handle that.

He took the pills Deesie had given him, and reaching down, rolled the top if his sock down a bit with the pills tucked inside. He was almost asleep when Deesie crawled in and unzipped his own sleeping bag.

The next thing he knew, Deesie was hovering over him. "Time for my goodnight kiss, sweetheart," he whispered, pushing Kendall onto his back. He ran his tongue along the teen's bottom lip, but the boy's jaw remained firmly clenched. He gave him a second chance, and when he was still denied, sighed in frustration.

He grabbed Kendall's hair and yanked hard with one hand, his other closing around the boy's throat. He started squeezing, but Kendall still refused to cooperate.

"If you pass out, I will do MORE than just kiss you," Deesie said. After another moment, Kendall unclenched his jaw and Deesie kissed him deeply.

After a couple of minutes, he pulled off, and smiling, looked down at the boy. "Goodnight sweetheart." He smirked and then crawled into his own sleeping bag.

Kendall rolled back onto his right side, his stomach clenching as he tried not to vomit up the soup he had just eaten.

∞

Antonio, John, and Bower met at another rest stop and compared notes.

"At least we've been heading in the right direction. It seems like we're usually within an hour or two of where they've been," Bennet said.

"True, but the fact that he knows about the Amber Alert and has now murdered someone means that they probably won't be staying in any more motels," Bower said.

"With the camping equipment, they could stay anywhere and not be seen for days," Antonio agreed.

"I contacted the Parks Departments and all of the Ranger Stations will be notified and sent all of the information. It's not camping season and anyone who is out there should be easily found. I doubt Deesie would go to any actual camp grounds, and in this cold, clear weather, smoke will be easily seen and smelled," Bower said.

"Hopefully," John said.

"My main concern is finding exactly where he's heading. My people have been trying to locate any friends, in or out of prison, who lived in the Osseo area, and so far haven't turned up anything," Bower told them.

"Hopefully Kendall is able to continue leaving notes, at least we can track them that way," Antonio said.

Bennet and Bower both nodded.

"Kendall may be the only way we do find them. He's a smart boy, I don't know that I would have thought about leaving notes, or hiding a cell phone inside a tear in my coat, and that's after YEARS of training, mind you," Bower said.

Antonio and John both smiled. "He is a special boy," Antonio said.

"All of your boys are special," John told him, patting him on the back.

"True," Antonio agreed, smiling.

He remembered Halloween this year. The boys had dressed as scarecrows and flopped, seemingly lifeless, in chairs on the porch. When kids would come up to trick or treat, they would jump to life, scaring them. Sylvia had to be quick out the door with the candy that night after one little girl dressed as a witch turned around and started hitting the boys with her broom. Poor Logan got a welt across his cheek that lasted a few days.

Was that really just a few days ago? Antonio thought wearily.

He needed to call home soon and let them know what was going on. He missed his family, but he was not going home until they were all safely together again.

Chapter 21 ~ Updating the Folks Back Home

At the Garcia home, Sylvia and Jen were making dinner for the group and discussing the call they had received from Janice Lane earlier. She had asked if one of the mothers could join her and Sally O'Hara at the school assembly tomorrow.

"I can do it, really," Jen told Sylvia.

"I seriously don't think that would be a good idea, Jen."

The last thing Jen needed was to walk into an auditorium with hundreds of people, all staring at her in pity. Someone was bound to say something to set her off, and she would either burst into tears, or get angry and start yelling. They were also going to be discussing the papers that Jason Banks and his friends had passed around, and Jen did not need to hear what people had been saying to, and about her son.

Sylvia knew Jen had started focusing on everyone else's needs and fears in order to hide from her own, so she decided to use that to her advantage.

"Katie is staying home tomorrow, and with the boys going to the assembly, she's going to need you here." She was, in fact, very worried about her little goddaughter as well as their boys.

∞

Sylvia remembered going upstairs to check on the kids yesterday and found all four of them huddled together on the floor. Katie had broken down, and then she had fallen asleep in James' arms. The boys had moved to the floor, James sitting with his back against the bed, Katie curled up protectively in his arms. James was softly singing, Hush Little Baby to her, making up more passages as he went along. It was her favourite lullaby and Kendall always teased Katie that the only reason she liked it was because it involved the baby getting things.

Carlos and Logan had been sitting on either side of them, watching the muted TV, all of them had been crying.

She had quietly backed out and left them to comfort each other, and later, when she had gone back up to call them for dinner, she found all four sound asleep.

James was still sitting with his back to the bed, holding Katie. His head had fallen forward, and his chin was resting on Katie's head. Carlos was sleeping with his head across James' knees and Logan with his head on James' shoulder. It would have been picture perfect, except for the reason they were here. Their brother was missing... the picture was incomplete.

∞

"They're just going to be letting the students and parents know what's happened and offer counseling if the kids need it. Then they'll go into the importance of telling someone if anyone makes you feel uncomfortable. I've helped Janice with these type of assemblies before, and it's pretty standard stuff, really not something to worry about," Sylvia said, trying to convince Jen.

Jen looked at her friend, still uncertain.

"Please, just let me do this," Sylvia asked, her bottom lip going out, and doing her very best imitation of Carlos when he wanted something.

"Oh my God! I KNEW that's where he got it. You keep trying to blame it on Antonio!" Jen laughed.

Sylvia smirked at her.

"Alright, alright, I know when I'm beaten," Jen said, hands up.

"I hear laughter," Brooke said as she walked into the kitchen.

"We were just discussing the assembly tomorrow. Sylvia convinced me to let her do it by using the 'Carlos pout' on me," Jen told her.

"I thought that was Antonio's legacy." Brooke smiled.

"You are SWORN to secrecy," Sylvia said, pointing at her two friends.

Brooke and Jen held up their left hands, right hands over their hearts. "We swear."

"To quote our darling little Logie-Bear, I need new friends," Sylvia said, sticking her tongue out.

"Jo and the kids should be back any minute," Brooke said as she started setting the table. Joanna had insisted that the kids needed to get out of the house for a while, and had taken them to the mall. None of them had really wanted to go, but had agreed that she was right.

Jen sat down suddenly.

"What's wrong?" Brooke asked, sitting next to her.

"I am an awful mother! My baby is out there, God knows where, and I am here LAUGHING like there's nothing wrong!" Jen cried.

Brooke looked at Sylvia and put her arm around Jen. "First of all, you are not an awful mother. You are a wonderful mom—all of the kids adore you. Do you really think Kendall wants you sitting around here, crying your eyes out? How do you think that would make him feel? Part of being strong means being able to laugh when you can and crying when you have to, so don't feel guilty for either. We're all going to get through this together, and when Antonio brings our boy home, there will be a celebration the likes of which this town has never seen."

Jen sat quietly for a moment and then hugged Brooke. "You're right, Kendall wouldn't want that. Thank you."

Brooke hugged her back. "Let's finish getting dinner ready, those boys are going to EAT tonight if I have to spoon feed each one of them."

Jen smiled, knowing full well that Brooke would do it. The boys had just picked at their food for the last two days. Carlos wouldn't even finish the corndogs his mom had made for him.

The phone rang and Sylvia answered. "Hi sweetie, how are things going?"

"We caught a bit of a break. Is Jen there?" Antonio asked.

"Yes, she and Brooke are right here. Joanna and the kids should be home any minute," she said, gesturing for Jen and Brooke to join her.

"Honey, can you put me on speaker?"

"Of course," she said and set the phone on the counter.

"Okay, this morning the State Police received a call from a motel about ten miles off of the interstate. He told them that he thought the man who had checked in the night before was Deesie. He also told them he hadn't seen a boy, but that the man had said his son was with him, sleeping in the car," Antonio told them.

"Were they there?" Jen asked quietly.

"They had been. Kendall actually left a note with my name and number on it, as well as the make, model, and license of the SUV that they're driving," Antonio replied.

"That's good though, right?" Brooke asked.

Antonio sighed. He had been debating on whether to tell them about the murder or not, but as it would most likely be on the news, he decided they should hear it from him. "Yes, but that's not all. When the state police got there, they found the owner dead. He'd been strangled."

"Oh my God!" Jen said, putting her head in her hands. Sylvia and Brooke both put an arm around her.

"Go on, honey," Sylvia said.

"This afternoon, John and I met up with Agent Bower, and while we were talking, I received a call. A man said that while he was watching TV, his son, Ian, told him that he had

seen the boy that was on TV. At first, his dad didn't believe him, but Ian was insistent and said the boy had given him a note, which he gave to his dad. We drove over and met with them. The note had the same information on it as the one from the motel, and it was definitely Kendall's handwriting. I showed Ian a picture from my cell that had all of the boys in it, and he picked Kendall out as the one that he'd spoken with," Antonio told them.

"He spoke with him? Was he okay, is he hurt, what did he say?" Jen asked.

"Yes, he spoke with him, he said he looked okay. They were parked at a market and Deesie was inside, I presume shopping, and Kendall was sitting in the back of the SUV. Ian and his friends were playing at the park next door to the market, and Kendall managed to get his attention when their soccer ball was kicked too far. He asked Ian to take the note to his mom, but told him to stay away until they left. After the boys were done playing, Ian ran back, grabbed the note, and took it home. He gave it to his dad, who called me. That wasn't too long ago, so we know they're close by and that's very good news," Antonio told them.

"Why didn't Kendall just run away while Deesie was in the market?" Brooke asked.

"Ian said that Kendall was wearing a funny bracelet. John showed him his handcuffs and he said that's what it looked like," he said.

'Okay, so someone's seen him just a little while ago, and he was okay. So that's good news," Sylvia said hugging Jen again.

Joanna, Katie, and the boys walked in the front door. "Hi, we're back!" Jo called out.

Brooke looked out from the kitchen and put her finger to her lips. "Shhh, Antonio is on the phone."

"Papi!" Carlos said, running for the kitchen.

"Is that my boy?" Antonio smiled as he heard Carlos' voice.

"Yup, where are you now?" Carlos asked.

"Still on the interstate, Mijo. What are you boys up to today?" Antonio asked.

"Mama M took us to the mall. We didn't really want to go, but she said we should. We got ice cream and played in the arcade for a while."

The others had come in. Katie was getting a piggyback ride from Logan. She quickly jumped off and ran to her mom. "Did you find him?" Katie asked.

"Not yet, Mija, but we spoke to a little boy who saw him. Your Mami will tell you all about it. John and I are going to stop and grab a bite to eat, and I want ALL of you to stay strong, alright? With any luck, we'll all be home soon," Antonio told her.

"Okay, Papa G. Bye!" Katie said and turned to hug her mom.

"Goodbye for now, I'll speak to you soon," Antonio said.

"Bye," everyone said as Sylvia took the phone off speaker.

"Goodbye darling," she said before she hung up.

They all sat down to dinner, where Jen and Sylvia shared what Antonio had told them, leaving out the part about Deesie killing the owner of the motel. The children did not need to know that right now.

∞

Deesie woke up in a cold sweat, his heart pounding. "This is all YOUR fault," he said, looking over at Kendall. The boy just had to ask about Robert.

It wasn't really a dream he had awoken from, but a memory. One that he didn't want, because in spite of what people might think, he had actually loved his brother very much. He started replaying the events of that night in his mind.

∞

Robert trying to be supportive, always wanting to help him. What Robert didn't understand was the only way to help him was to give him his identity, and he could never do that while he was alive. He remembered the sadness in Robert's eyes when Stephen had told him he had been chased out of yet another apartment. Robert had offered him money for a hotel, knowing his brother couldn't get a job because of his record. Never pity from Robert,

only sadness. No wonder everyone loved him. Robert had tried, unsuccessfully, to calm his brother down and had gone to make him a cup of tea.

That's when Stephen had taken the knife and kitchen towel, and walking up behind his brother, had quickly slit his throat, covering it with the towel, so as not to leave a huge mess.

Stephen sat there, cradling his brother's body, weeping. After an hour or so, he had taken a comforter from the closet and wrapped Robert gently in it. Karen, Robert's fiancé, wouldn't be home until tomorrow, so he had time to do things right. He found Robert's keys and carried him to the car in the garage, gently lying him in the trunk. Then he went in and packed all of Robert's clothing, photos, and other personal items.

After making sure that everything was clean, he locked up and got in the car.

He drove out of town to a place that overlooked the river. Robert had always loved fishing, so this spot was perfect. He took the shovel he had grabbed from the garage and dug a very deep hole. When he was finished, he gently pulled his brother out of the car and carried him to the grave. He climbed in and pulled Robert in after, gently lying him down. He made sure that Robert was wrapped up tightly and then climbed out. He filled in the grave and found a couple of large rocks, placing them at the top. He sat there and cried again, telling his brother how sorry he was and how much he loved him. When he was all cried out, he got into the car and drove away, never looking back.

∞

Deesie looked over at the sleeping boy again and crawled out of his sleeping bag. He made his way over to Kendall and quietly unzipped his bag. He crawled in next to the sleeping teen and wrapped his arms around him. After a couple of minutes, he slipped his hand under the teen's shirt and started nuzzling his neck.

Kendall's eyes snapped open as he felt someone touching him.

Deesie felt the boy tense up and smiled his twisted smile. "Are we waking up sweetheart?" Deesie asked, pulling Kendall tighter.

Chapter 23~ Stranger Danger

Deesie finished and pulled Kendall's pajama bottoms back up. He lay down next to the boy, running his tongue over his own lips. "Mmmm you taste good, sweetheart," he whispered, kissing the boy's ear. "Did you pay close attention?"

Kendall continued staring up, not answering, his expression empty and body limp.

"I asked you a question," Deesie said.

"No."

"I told you that you needed to pay attention so you can learn what I want," Deesie said firmly, his tone angry and demanding.

Kendall turned his head and looked Deesie in the eyes. "If you try and put THAT in my mouth, you won't get it back," he stated and turned to look back up at the ceiling.

"I was going to wait until morning to punish you for hitting me, but with that smart attitude of yours, I think we'll do it now," Deesie said angrily.

He got up and crawled out of the tent and Kendall heard him open the SUV door. He heard Deesie moving around outside, cursing once, and then he was back, pulling Kendall out of his sleeping bag and grabbing the boy's jacket.

He unhooked one of the cuffs. "Put your jacket on."

Kendall pulled it on and zipped it without a word.

"No zipper," Deesie said, reattaching the handcuffs and unzipping the jacket.

He pulled Kendall towards a tree just past the tent. Kendall stumbled, without his boots on, his foot was extremely painful and he had a hard time walking. Kendall saw a rope thrown over a large limb and started to back up.

"Where do you think you're going, sweetheart? Don't you like your new accommodations?" Deesie asked, smirking.

He grabbed the teen's arms, took the end of the rope, and ran it between the boy's hands. Then he threw it over the limb. He grabbed the end again, walked over to the trunk of the tree, and wrapped it around the base, pulling it tight.

Kendall screamed in pain as his arms were pulled above his head when the rope tightened around the middle of the handcuffs. His shoulder felt like it was on fire again, and the pressure was almost unbearable.

Deesie smiled cruelly and pulled on the rope again. This time, Kendall's feet left the ground, putting all the weight on his arms, and the boy screamed again. Deesie let the rope slide from his hands for a moment, Kendall landed on his feet, and his injured foot gave out.

Deesie laughed. "What's the matter, sweetheart, not having any fun?"

Kendall was trying to catch his breath when Deesie repeated the previous action. After a few minutes, he tied the rope off. Kendall was standing with his arms pulled halfway above his head, in agony every time he moved.

Deesie walked up to the boy and looked at him smugly. He pulled back his hand and slapped Kendall hard across the face. "You WILL start obeying me!"

Kendall just looked at him, shivering from pain and the cold.

Deesie grabbed Kendall on both sides of the head and kissed him hard. "Goodnight sweetheart, sleep tight." He laughed, walking back to the tent.

Once inside, he found the handi wipes and took care of himself, picturing the boy the whole time.

∞

Kendall tried pulling on the rope, hoping it would give a little, but it was fastened tight and he had very little strength left. He found if he stayed completely still, the pain in his shoulder wasn't as bad, but it meant having to stand fully on both feet. He was only in his socks, and the pressure on his injured foot caused shooting pains up his leg. Standing on one foot didn't work for long, and he had no idea what to do. He was too far from the tree to rest against it. His head was pounding, he felt sick to his stomach, and to top it all off...it was already freezing out and Deesie had made sure to leave his jacket open.

He was so tired and everything hurt so much, he just wanted to go home.

He felt disgusting and wished he could take a hot shower and scrub Deesie's touch away. His mind began racing from thought to thought. He wondered if anyone had found the old man at the motel, if the little boy had given his mom the note, if Papi would be able to find him without the cell phone, how his mom and Katie were. God, he missed them all so much. Tears filled his eyes as he thought of home, but he snapped out of it before they fell. Crying wasn't going to help, and he certainly wasn't going to give the pervert the satisfaction.

∞

A couple of hours later, Deesie went out to check on the boy. He was surprised that he hadn't heard any more screaming, considering the position the boy was in.

He had been hoping the boy would beg for mercy, and would have granted it, IF the teen agreed to 'practice' his newly taught lesson. He smirked to himself, thinking of the boy's reaction when he woke up to find him holding him, and again as he had realized his body was going to react to the stimulation Deesie gave it. STILL the blond fought him, refusing to do as he was told, and then having the nerve to threaten him.

What he had told the teen was true, he did enjoy a good challenge, but enough was enough.

He found Kendall standing where he had been left, both feet on the ground. The boy had found after a few minutes of standing completely still, that the pain in his leg dulled to a throbbing ache, and preferred it to the excruciating pain in his shoulder.

"Hello sweetheart, how is everything going?" Deesie chuckled.

Kendall stayed silent and just watched the man.

Deesie circled the boy, hoping to make him nervous. "So are you going to play nice?"

Kendall didn't answer.

Deesie came up from behind him, grabbed his hair, and yanked his head back. "I ASKED you a question," Deesie growled, tired of the lack of cooperation from the teen. He walked around to the front of the boy and slapped him. Then he put his foot on Kendall's right foot and slowly pushed down.

Kendall cried out in pain. "Answer me!" Deesie demanded.

Kendall looked at him and through gritted teeth hissed, "No, I won't play nice."

Deesie yelled in fury and punched Kendall in the stomach. The rope prevented him from doubling over but the force of the blow caused Kendall to lose his footing and he screamed as his shoulder was jolted.

After a moment, Kendall looked at him and stood up straight again.

Deesie could not believe the nerve of this child, and his patience was gone for the night. He pulled back and punched Kendall in the face, effectively knocking the teen out cold.

Deesie went to the rope and dropped the boy to the ground. Then, throwing him over his shoulder went back to the tent and dumped him onto his sleeping bag. He climbed back into his own bag and rolled over, falling asleep within minutes.

∞

Sylvia, Brooke and the boys drove to the school in silence. The mothers had decided that the boys should attend the assembly, but they would go home afterwards. Principal Lane

had already agreed that they should have a couple of days off and arranged for their homework to be sent home with them.

They arrived and parked. Sylvia headed to the gym to meet up with Sally, while Brooke took the boys and headed for the office to pick up their homework.

The assembly was going to be held during first period and kids were putting coats and backpacks into their lockers. The boys got sympathetic looks from many of the kids, and a few others looked down when they walked by, not wanting to make eye contact.

Logan figured it was because of the papers that Jason had spread around, and he had heard that several of the kids had emailed Kendall. He didn't really want to know what the emails said, but he felt his guilt and shame rise to the surface again, remembering the last time he had seen his friend.

They were almost to the office when Jason Banks walked up to them.

"Look guys, I'm rea—" he started, but before he could finish, Carlos let out a scream and attacked the other boy.

James and Logan stood there, stunned, and then tried to pull their friend off the other boy.

Janice Lane and Tara came running from the office and watched the scene in shock.

James and Logan would no sooner pull Carlos off, when he would break free and land on Jason again, still swinging. Jason didn't fight back, he let the younger boy hit him, never trying to strike him back.

Brooke got to them and reached over and pulled Carlos off, wrapping her arms around him. "Carlos! Stop it right now. I know you're angry at him, but enough!"

James and Logan stood between them and Jason, afraid of what would happen if Carlos got loose again. But the boy had crumpled in Brooke's surprisingly strong arms and started to cry. "He hurt him!"

"I know, baby," Brooke said in a soothing tone, wiping the tears from the boy's face. "This is no way to handle it, though. Jason has been trying to help and is sorry for what he did."

"He's a LIAR! He LIKES hurting people!" Carlos screamed.

Jason slowly stood up. "He's right, I am mean to people. I did hurt Kendall to get back at him, but I never would have done it if I knew what Mr. Deesie really was, I swear! I am so sorry, Carlos. If I could take it all back, I would." Jason stood there looking down.

James and Logan looked at him in disbelief, not knowing what to say. Jason was crying.

Tara went to Jason and put her arms around him. "Come with me, sweetie, let's get you cleaned up," she said and led him down the hall to the nurse's office.

"Come with me, boys," Janice Lane said, walking back into her office.

They followed her, James and Logan still in shock by the fact they saw Jason crying. Brooke still had her arms around Carlos, who had quieted down, and was just sniffling now and then.

"Carlos, you know that behaviour is unacceptable. You cannot go around hitting people because you are angry with them. It is one thing to defend yourself, but it is quite another to be the instigator," Principal Lane said sternly.

Brooke went to say something in defense of the boy, but Janice held up her hand to silence her. James and Logan looked at each other, eyes wide in amazement. One does NOT silence Brooke Diamond.

"That being said, I completely understand WHY you did it, and there will be no consequences, provided you apologize to Jason for hitting him. Sorry Brooke, I just wanted to get that out before the protests began." Janice smiled.

Brooke gave Janice a half smile and took a deep breath. "No, you were right." She turned and looked at Carlos. "Carlos, you need to apologize before we leave today. I know Jason has done some very bad things, and while he may have deserved it, sinking to his level does not accomplish anything."

Janice smiled at the fact Brooke had still managed to get her opinion in.

Carlos nodded. "I'll say I'm sorry for hitting him, but not for calling him a liar and... he's still mean," Carlos said stubbornly, crossing his arms across his chest.

"That will be fine," Janice told him.

She pulled three folders from her desk and handed one to each of the boys. "Here are your lessons for the week. If you need any assistance just call in and the teacher for that class will help you."

The boys took the folders and nodded.

She walked over and put one arm around James and the other one around Logan's shoulders. "I know this seems like an impossible situation right now, and that words won't help how you feel, but we need to stay strong. I truly believe that Chief Garcia will be bringing Kendall home soon." She hugged the boys tightly. "The assembly will be starting soon, so we should get down to the gym now."

Brooke nodded and stood up. "Let's go."

She walked down the hallway with her arm still around Carlos, and Janice with her arms around James and Logan. Normally, the boys would be embarrassed to be seen walking through the school with their principal hugging them, but right now, they took comfort in the embrace of the older woman.

Parents and children were walking into the gymnasium and taking seats amongst the bleachers. Brooke took the boys and walked to the far end, sitting on the bottom row. The teachers and staff were seated in chairs, lining the wall and the podium, which had been brought down to the floor level with chairs for Principal Lane, Sally, and Sylvia.

When it seemed like people had settled in, Janice took the podium.

"Please everyone, quiet down. We have a lot to get through today, so if everyone is ready, I would like to get started."

As the noise diminished, Janice continued. "I think that everyone knows why we are here today, either from here or the news. A few months ago, we hired a teacher, Robert Deesie, from Toledo. He had an impeccable reputation and all of our background checks showed that he was definitely someone we would want on our staff. It turns out that the man who portrayed himself as Robert Deesie was, in fact, his brother."

She looked at Sally and nodded to her. "Officer Sally O'Hara will be taking the podium now, to further explain and to answer any questions you might have."

Sally stood up and walked to the podium. "Most of you know me from past assemblies and the annual winter coat drive. At this time, all we have been able to confirm regarding Stephen Deesie, is that he has somehow assumed his brother's identity. To be clear, Principal Lane followed ALL of the proper procedures in hiring a new staff member, even going above and beyond by calling and speaking to his previous employers herself."

A student waved her hand. "So what happened to the real Robert, then?"

"Right now, we have no knowledge of Robert Deesie's location, but it is believed that he was most likely killed by Stephen," Sally answered.

"Yes?" Sally said, nodding to a parent waving her hand.

"Do you have any idea where he is and if he still has Kendall Knight?"

"At this time, we do not know the location, but have confirmed with different sources, that Kendall is alive and with him. That being said, if ANYONE has any idea where Deesie may have gone, from either classroom conversations or any other sources, PLEASE let me know. Any detail no matter how small, may be important and will be checked out. Also, if any of you were approached by Deesie and he acted inappropriately, please tell Principal Lane or another staff member."

"I heard on the news that the police found a man murdered in a motel yesterday. Did Deesie have anything to do with that?" Another parent asked.

Sylvia and Brooke both tensed. The boys didn't know about the motel manager, and they silently cursed the parent who asked.

Sally smiled sadly. "Unfortunately there are murders every day. When a case, such as a kidnapping, becomes high profile, people try and tie all of the local crimes together, when in fact, they may have absolutely nothing to do with one another."

Sylvia glanced around. Everyone seemed satisfied with that answer. She was going to have to tell Antonio that Sally deserved a huge raise.

"Now I'd like to talk about the Stranger Danger training that became so popular years ago. I believe that this concept has caused more harm than good, because it teaches children that they should consider outsiders as the only threat. The fact is, most abuse, molestations, and kidnappings, are committed by someone they or their parents know."

"Parents, when a child is abused by someone they know, they are less likely to tell, thinking that they won't be believed. Every family should have a zero tolerance policy for people who make their children feel uncomfortable, and I don't care if it's the next-door neighbor or their grandpa. If your child is afraid, there is a reason, so listen to and BELIEVE them. It could be a simple misunderstanding, but it could also be something serious."

"Kids, if someone makes you feel uncomfortable, either with the way they're speaking to you or the way they touch you, it doesn't matter who that person is. Whether it's a parent, sibling, neighbor, family friend, ice cream man, teacher, TELL someone. If the first person doesn't listen, TELL someone else. If you have to, call the police yourself, someone there will listen. I guarantee it."

"Something else I need to address here today is..." Sally stopped and looked down as her phone vibrated. She looked at the text message and smiled. "I need to take this, so Principal Lane will take over to speak with you about spreading rumours and propaganda," she said as she headed for the nearest door.

Sylvia and Brooke looked at one another, and Sylvia got up and followed Sally.

∞

Sally returned the call the minute she hit the hallway. "Officer O'Hara here, what's going on?"

The person on the other end identified themselves as a deputy with the sheriff's department from Stearns County. "We found an unidentified body, of what appears to be a young male, in Baker's Lake this morning. We think it might be the boy you're looking for."

"Did you identify by photo?" Sally asked her heart in her throat.

"He's been in the water too long for that. He'll need to be identified by dental records," the deputy said.

"Are you kidding me? Did you even read the reports sent out? Kendall Knight was confirmed alive YESTERDAY! He didn't even go missing until Friday night! You people better get your heads out of your proverbial asses or I will be driving over and kicking you there!" Sally yelled.

She hung up, taking a deep breath, trying to calm down. Turning around, she saw Sylvia standing there. Sally was so angry that tears were pooling in her blue eyes. Sylvia grabbed her and pulled her into a hug.

"Stupid, ignorant, dumb ass people who don't actually READ the damn reports," Sally said, as she cried into Sylvia's shoulder.

Sylvia held the younger woman, letting her get it out. She realized that Sally had been on the go, without a break, since Friday. Sally and John had both known the boys for years, from the police station, to events around town, to family gatherings at the Garcia home.

After a couple of minutes, Sally took a deep breath. "I'm sorry for losing it, everything that's going on, and then some IDIOT, who can't do their job right, tells me they found a body that's been in the lake for a week or more, and thought it was Kendall."

"Honey, you have no reason to apologize. You've been at it for four days straight, and I really don't know how you do it. The fact that, not only are you incredible at your job, but that you actually care so much, just overwhelms me. We are so lucky to have you here," Sylvia said trying to comfort her.

"Thank you, but I feel like such a big baby right now. Crying when there's still so much to do."

"You cry because you care. I'll tell you something else. I would LOVE to see that deputy right now. You scared the hell out of me and I was just listening. I can just imagine him heading for the border right now," Sylvia said, smiling.

"Well, I guess we should probably get back in there. I hate crying. Do I look all teary?" Sally asked, wiping her eyes.

"You look fine," Sylvia told her as they headed back in.

Sally walked back up to the podium as Janice was finishing up the discussion about the papers that had been handed around about Kendall. She looked at Sally, who nodded and smiled.

Janice went to sit back down and Sally took over. "Sorry about that, with Chief Garcia and Officer Bennet on the road, we're a little short-handed."

Brooke caught Sylvia's eye and looked at her questioningly. Sylvia shook her head and mouthed, "Everything's okay." Brooke sighed in relief and nodded.

Sally took a deep breath and continued. "The last thing we need to address today is the matter of cyber bullying. Kendall received a lot of VERY nasty emails. I have his laptop, and as soon as time allows, I will be connecting the email addresses with their owners. So, we are willing to offer a one-time deal and it is over by the end of the school day. If you sent one of these emails to Kendall and you go to Principal Lane admitting it, you will not be charged. If you sent one and do not admit it, you will be charged, and most likely spend any free time you have, providing community services."

Many of the kids exchanged looks and shuffled nervously on the bleachers.

"Also, if you are on any extra-curricular teams, such as football, cheerleading, etc., you will be removed and banned from these activities for ONE year. So, I urge you to do the right thing and realize there are consequences to your actions," Sally said firmly.

Janice returned to the podium. "Any students who wish to take advantage of this offer can stop by the office and leave their email address with Tara. Parents, I recommend if your child did participate in this harassment, that you limit their internet access for a few weeks. If there are no more questions or concerns, we'll wrap this up. Counseling will be provided to any student, or parent, who feels they need it."

Sally walked over to Sylvia and Brooke, and the boys joined them.

"Did something happen?" Logan asked Sally.

"No kiddo, everything's okay. Someone phoned in with some faulty information, and I just needed to clear it up," Sally told him.

"Really, that's all it was?" Carlos asked.

"Yes, Mijo," Sylvia said, hugging her son. "Let's get home and you boys can get started on your homework."

Carlos and James groaned while Logan smiled.

"There's something WRONG with you," James told Logan.

"What? I like learning," Logan replied defensively.

"Boys, please..." Sylvia said, rolling her eyes as they all headed out the door.

Sally laughed. "I think my job is easier than yours."

"Some days I would agree with you," Sylvia said.

On the way out, they passed by Jason Banks and his mother. Carlos went up to him and took a deep breath. "I'm sorry for hitting you, I shouldn't have done that."

Jason nodded. "That's okay, I deserved it. I am really sorry about Kendall."

Carlos nodded and went to join the others.

Sylvia looked at Brooke. "What was that all about?"

"I'll tell you later," Brooke said.

Deesie woke up about six, still angry at the teen. He looked over at Kendall, who was still out, and made a decision. "I'll get two birds with one stone this time." He chuckled to himself.

He crawled over to the boy and checked to make sure he was actually breathing. His face was considerably more bruised, and his left eye swollen again from the blow he had received. Deesie started to shake him. "Wake up!" he commanded.

After a couple of minutes, Kendall's eyes fluttered open for a moment.

"I said, WAKE UP!"

Kendall groaned in pain, but tried to move away from the man once his vision focused.

"I have an errand to run, and you are staying here. I won't be gone long, and when I return, we are going to prepare a little something for Principal Lane," Deesie said with a twisted smile.

Kendall was still having a hard time focusing as Deesie grabbed his legs, and he kicked out in reflex. Deesie grabbed ahold firmly. "Would you prefer the tree, sweetheart?"

Kendall shook his head and the man wrapped duct tape around his ankles. Deesie unlocked the cuffs and flipped the boy over, securing his hands behind his back.

Kendall cried out in pain as his shoulder hit the ground. "Want me to kiss it and make it better?" Deesie leered.

Kendall shook his head as he tried to find a less painful position.

Deesie grabbed Kendall's boots. "I'm taking these just in case by some miracle you get loose."

The man walked out of the tent and zipped it closed. He walked to the SUV, laughing to himself again. He and Kendall would be having a little fun when he got back. "Well, at least I will," he smiled.

He got in the SUV and drove off, heading for the nearest town.

Chapter 24~ The Ranger

Ranger Dan Thompson was out making the rounds in his territory, checking out campgrounds and rest stops. He had been with the Minnesota State Forestry Department for over twenty years and was due to retire soon. He had bought a place with a little land near Red Wing. He loved his job and was actually considering going for another five years. He was only forty-six, working another five years would add to his retirement considerably, and he knew he was going to miss it. He loved the wilderness, the people, all of it. Some days it was hard, and others, he could just sit back and enjoy the beauty of the woods.

He pulled down a side road that led to the river. He had chased off many illegal fishermen and was surprised people still wanted to be on the river this time of year. The fish weren't really biting and it was damn cold out.

He saw something to his left and backed up to take a closer look. He saw a small tent. Shaking his head, he pulled up a few yards off. He didn't see a car anywhere near, although there were recent tracks in the dirt.

He called into dispatch and let them know what he'd found. He got out, walking towards the tent, where he saw the usual camping equipment set up. Looking around, he saw a climbing rope was hung over a large tree limb, just behind the tent.

That's strange, he thought.

"Hello, Forest Service. Anyone around?" He called out again as he walked to the tent. "Anyone here?"

Still nothing.

The tent was zipped closed, so he carefully opened it, identifying himself again. He looked inside and saw someone lying on their right side.

"Forest Service, everything alright here?"

He heard a small moan and took a closer look. "Oh my God! Son, what happened to you?" he said, kneeling down beside Kendall. The boy was barely conscious, his face badly bruised, his hands cuffed behind his back, and his feet taped together.

"No more," the boy said in a weak voice.

"I'll be back in just a minute," Thompson told him and ran for his Jeep. He got on the radio. "Dispatch, this is Ranger Thompson, Station 11. I have a teenage boy, about ten miles out from the station and about a mile due south of the river. He's been beaten and left, tied up in a tent, in a clearing here."

A dispatcher came on the radio. "Be advised that State Police has issued an Amber Alert for a 14-year-old boy, who was taken from his home on Friday. He and his abductor are believed to be in the area. The fugitive, Stephen Deesie, is to be considered armed and dangerous. He is driving a 1996, red Ford Explorer."

"Copy that, Dispatch. No vehicle in sight. Probably shouldn't move the boy, but I'm going to risk it, since we don't know where the fugitive is."

"Copy that. Will inform the State Police and have emergency vehicles standing by."

"Copy that. Have them meet me back at the station," Thompson replied.

"Copy that. Will send emergency vehicles and police to Forestry Station 11."

He went back to the tent and leaned down, speaking gently to Kendall. "You're going to be alright son. I'm going to get you out of here." He pulled the tape off the boy's legs but couldn't do anything about the handcuffs at that time.

Kendall came around and panicked to find someone trying to pull him up.

"It's alright. I'm not going to hurt you. My name's Dan and I'm here to help you."

Kendall could have wept in relief.

"Do you think you can walk if I help you?" Thompson asked.

Kendall nodded and the older man put his arm around the teen's waist.

"What's your name?" Thompson asked.

"K-Kendall," the boy managed to get out.

"Well Kendall, let's get you someplace safe and warm." Thompson smiled reassuringly as he half-carried the boy out of the tent.

∞

Deesie walked into the nearest large store and purchased a few things, including a disposable cell phone. He made sure it had the applications he wanted, as well as internet service.

He stopped and bought an espresso from a coffee stand and headed back to camp. He was almost there when he saw something white through the trees, so he stopped the SUV and rolled down the window. He could hear a voice saying, "It's going to be alright."

Deesie got out, opened the back of the SUV, grabbed the rifle, and loaded it. He quietly walked towards the clearing, his weapon raised.

∞

Thompson helped Kendall to his Jeep. The boy was freezing and having a hard time walking. The ranger knew he was in pain. "Just a little further, son. It's going to be alright," Thompson said, as he reached for the door handle.

Kendall was leaning against the ranger for support when he heard a loud noise. The man suddenly jolted forward and then fell back, taking Kendall with him. Not sure what had happened, Kendall looked over at the man, who was lying with his eyes closed, blood seeping from his chest.

"Dan, w-what...?" the boy stammered, unable to help the bleeding man.

"Where did you think you were going, sweetheart?" Deesie asked.

Kendall shook his head. "No, no, no. What did you do?"

Deesie grabbed him by the hair, pulling him away from the dying ranger.

"This IS your fault. If you had behaved yourself last night, we would have been long gone. Instead, you had to fight me again, and now that man is going to die, because of YOU!" Deesie hissed at the boy.

Kendall looked down at the fallen ranger and began rocking back and forth on his knees, with Deesie's words echoing in his mind.

"We have to go! I am going to bring the car over here, you STAY put," Deesie growled.

Kendall didn't move or say anything. He just stared in shock at Dan Thompson lying there, bleeding out.

Deesie pulled the SUV around and started throwing supplies in the back. He grabbed the sleeping bags, Kendall's backpack, and his suitcase from the tent, and then pulled the SUV over to the Ranger's Jeep.

He grabbed Kendall by the arm and pushed him into the back. "You can't just leave him here like this!" Kendall screamed at him, struggling to get back to the ranger.

"Watch me," Deesie said coldly as he gave the boy a final shove and slammed the door. "No more camping out! We will be driving straight through, now," he said as he got in the driver's seat and pulled away.

"With the exception of one quick stop," Deesie said to himself, smiling.

Chapter 25~ The Photo Session

Sally had just gotten back to the station when a call came in from the forest service. She immediately got on the radio to Antonio and Bennet.

"Hey Boss, I just got a call from the forest service. Seems a ranger came across an illegal campsite in his territory. He found a teenage boy beaten and tied up inside a tent. No one else was in the area. He called in for emergency vehicles and state police. They're waiting for him at Ranger Station 11. They think it could be Kendall."

"Directions?" Antonio asked.

Sally gave him the directions to the ranger's station. John pulled off at the next exit as Antonio plugged the information into the GPS. Normally, he hated the thing, but it had more information than their maps when it came to the off-road areas.

John looked at it. "Not far at all."

"Glad you can understand that stupid thing," Antonio said.

"It's fairly simple. You just need to give it a chance and NOT smack it when you think it's taking too long." John laughed.

"Maps are more reliable," Antonio grumbled.

"Sometimes," John admitted.

"Although you don't have to fold a GPS."

Antonio rolled his eyes at his partner. "Just get us there."

∞

Deesie drove until he found another off-road motel. He pulled in and parked outside the office. "You know the drill," he warned Kendall. He pulled a baseball cap over his head, got out, and walked into the office, returning a few moments later. He got back in, drove to the furthest unit, and parked in front. He got out and opened Kendall's door, pulling the boy out. He kept a tight hold on Kendall as he grabbed his backpack and the bag from the store. He pushed the teen to the door, opened it, and pushed him inside.

Throwing the bags on the bed, Deesie looked at Kendall. "Go shower and make sure you get all of the blood off of you." He removed the handcuffs and pulled the boy's jacket off him. "We need to clean this up, too."

Kendall realized it had the ranger's blood on it. He stood there, staring at his jacket, not moving or saying anything.

"I told you to go shower! We need to get on the road again, but there is something I need to do first," Deesie said angrily.

"What?" Kendall asked suspiciously.

"A little message for Principal Lane and it involves YOU, so go shower!" Deesie snapped. He threw Kendall's backpack at him and then pulled two items from the store bag. "Put these on with your black jeans," he instructed, handing Kendall a black tank top and a white, long-sleeved button down shirt.

"Why?" Kendall asked.

He grabbed the teen by the hair and Kendall yelped.

"I do not have to explain things to you. Just do what you are told. If you are having trouble comprehending what I have told you, I will be happy to scrub you down and dress you myself!" he said with his twisted smile.

Kendall grabbed the items and limped into the bathroom, closing the door behind him. He turned the water on, letting it run to warm up. He was freezing and could feel a tightness in his chest. He looked at his reflection in the mirror and realized why his head was hurting.

The entire left side of his face was bruised and his eye was swollen again. He had a small cut just below his eyebrow and there was blood on the right side of his face. He realized it was Ranger Dan's blood. He was still in shock that Deesie had shot the man and then just left him to die. He felt so bad. The man was trying to help him, and now he was dead because of him.

The room was beginning to steam up, so he set the clean clothes out on the counter and pulled off his dirty ones.

Something fell on the floor when he pulled off his socks, and he realized it was the sleeping pills that Deesie had given him the night before. He quickly picked them up and tucked them into a small pocket in his backpack.

He slowly climbed into the shower and let the hot water run over him. His entire body hurt, and he couldn't even lift his left arm anymore, his shoulder hurt so much. His foot was doing a little better, but it still hurt to put weight on it for any length of time without having a stabbing pain shoot up his leg.

He awkwardly lathered his hair with his right hand and then let the hot water rinse it clean. He scrubbed himself clean and grabbed a towel.

He stepped out of the shower and sat down on the closed toilet. He dried off and pulled on his boxers and jeans. It took a moment to get the tank top on, and there was no way he could do up all the buttons on the shirt. He pulled his socks on, but Deesie still had his boots. He stood up slowly, not feeling very steady at all, and sat down again.

"Are you done in there, or do you need help drying off again?" Deesie yelled through the door.

"I'm coming," Kendall snapped.

Deesie opened the door. "Too bad."

Kendall rolled his eyes and stood up.

"Watch the attitude, sweetheart. Let's get this done so we can get on the road," Deesie said as he grabbed the boy's arm.

He pulled Kendall into the bedroom and pushed him to the bed. "Sit and button the shirt all the way," Deesie ordered.

"I can't."

Deesie walked to him and started buttoning it up the rest of the way. He looked down at the teen and finger combed the damp blond hair, smiling every time Kendall flinched.

"Now, you will do what I say or else," Deesie threatened. "Sit back up against the headboard and cross your legs."

"Why?" Kendall asked.

Deesie walked back over to him and grabbed his right foot, squeezing it hard. Kendall yelped in pain.

"Because I SAID so, now do it."

Kendall scooted back, until his head rested against the headboard, and crossed his legs.

"Look at me," Deesie instructed, holding up a cell phone. Kendall heard the click as the man took a photo.

"Good, now put your arms behind your head and look at me."

"I can't lift my left arm."

"Fine, just your right then," Deesie snapped.

Kendall did as he was told and Deesie took another photo. The man walked over to him and unbuttoned the shirt, pushing it open, and took another photo. "Sit up and pull your left leg up," Deesie said.

Kendall was getting very nervous, but did as he was told. The man reached down and pushed the shirt off his right shoulder, so that the skin was exposed, and took another photo.

"Very nice." Deesie smiled as he looked at the photos. "Now shirt off and lie down."

"Why?" Kendall asked again.

Deesie walked over and slapped him.

"Stop questioning me and DO what I tell you. If you don't, I will walk up to the office and do something to the nice couple who run this place."

Kendall bit his lower lip and did as the man asked.

Deesie took a few more photos, pushed the shirt further up, and unzipped the jeans more. Kendall sat up and pushed the shirt back down, trying to cover himself. "Stop it!" he yelled.

Deesie grabbed him and pushed him back down. "Stay still," Deesie hissed as he pushed the shirt back up and pulled the jeans open. "Now smile."

Kendall was shaking and refused to look at the phone anymore. Deesie smiled at the teen's discomfort.

"Tank top off," he ordered. When the boy just sat there, he went over and pulled it off over his head, and pushed him so he was lying back on the pillows again. Kendall crossed his arms over his chest, but Deesie grabbed his hands and pulled them down. "Would you like me to cuff you?"

Kendall shook his head.

"Now stay there," Deesie said and took a couple of more photos. Deesie watched him for a moment and licked his lips. "Jeans off."

Kendall shook his head, sat up, and pulled his legs up to his chest, staring at the man defiantly.

Deesie took a photo of the boy in that position and walked back over to him. "Remember what I said earlier? Do you really want MORE people to die because you won't do what you are told?" Deesie asked, pointing to the hunting knife on his belt for emphasis.

Kendall just glared at him.

"Or, maybe we should go back and pick up your friend...the tall one with the dark hair. That might be a fun addition, and it's not really that far away," Deesie said with a wink.

"You leave them alone!" Kendall yelled.

Deesie looked at him and smiled. "Then take your jeans off."

Kendall took a deep breath and pushed his jeans down. Deesie grabbed them and pulled them off completely, and then pulled off his socks. "Lie down and look away from me." Kendall had no problem looking the other way as he heard the camera function click.

"Sit up and look at me." Kendall sat up, hugging his knees again, but refused to look at the man.

"LOOK at me," Deesie hissed.

Kendall didn't lift his head but raised his eyes, looking at Deesie through his bangs.

"That's VERY nice. Janice is going to love these. Now boxers off, and if you do as you're told, I won't take advantage of the situation," Deesie leered.

"What do you mean Janice is going to love these?" Kendall asked quietly.

Deesie sat next to him and started stroking the boy's leg. "It means that I am sending these to her as a little token of appreciation."

Kendall was suddenly feeling very sick to his stomach at the thought of his principal seeing him naked.

"What's the matter, sweetheart, are you shy? Don't like the idea of someone seeing your body in all its' splendor? If you're nervous, I can help you relax," Deesie said, squeezing Kendall's knee.

"No, don't!" Kendall begged.

"Then boxers off or I will send her a video of a re-enactment of what you learned last night," Deesie threatened.

Kendall was shaking even more, but did as the man instructed.

Deesie took several more photos of the boy, forcing him to turn over or spread his legs further. "Now, touch yourself," the man said, biting his lower lip.

Kendall looked at him in horror. "No! I won't do that, I don't care what you do to me. Why can't you just leave me alone!" he screamed, curling up into a ball. He began shaking uncontrollably.

Deesie smiled and ran his fingers down the boy's spine. "Fine, we're finished for now, sweetheart."

He threw Kendall's backpack at him again. "We need to leave. Put on your jeans and a different shirt. I'll grab your boots from the car."

Kendall reached down and grabbed his clothes. He quickly dressed, feeling dirty again. He was losing hope that anyone would find him, or that he would ever see home again.

Deesie came in and tossed the teen his boots. "Hurry up."

Kendall grabbed his backpack, and Deesie grabbed the other bag and the boy's jacket.

They got to the SUV and Kendall got in the back. "Clean your jacket with these," Deesie said, giving him a few handi wipes.

The boy took them and started wiping his jacket with them as Deesie ran in to give the manager the key.

Kendall reached for the pen and pad of paper. *Why bother?* He thought and went back to cleaning the ranger's blood from his jacket.

He was just finishing up with it, when Deesie got back to the SUV. "Where do you want me to put these?" Kendall asked, showing him the bloody wipes.

Deesie handed him a plastic bag. "Put them in here. Now, before we go, I need to send a message to someone," Deesie said smugly, as he pulled out his cell and typed in Janice Lane's email address.

He laughed as he drove off and then started humming.

∞

Antonio and Bennet were almost to the ranger's station when they got a call from Sally.

"Boss, I just got a call from Forest Service dispatch. Ranger Thompson never showed up, so they went looking for him."

"And?"

She paused for a moment before continuing. "They found him at the campsite. He has been shot, and there's no sign of Kendall or Deesie. They don't expect Thompson to make it."

"Where's the campsite?" Antonio asked. Sally gave him the directions and he punched it into the GPS and turned around, heading back the way they had just come.

They arrived at the campsite about ten minutes later. There were rangers and State Police going over the area.

They got out of the SUV and one of the rangers came up. "Ranger Dodd," he said, holding out his hand.

"Chief Garcia and this is Officer Bennet. How's your man?" Antonio asked.

"Not good. He was shot in the back and lost a lot of blood. They think the bullet may have hit a lung. It went all the way through and lodged in the Jeep door. It looks like it may have been a 22. It's amazing he was alive at all."

"I'm sorry about this. Have you found anything?" Antonio asked.

"We're still processing the site, but they left in a hurry. Didn't take the tent, camp stove, dishes, and there's a climbing rope thrown over the limb of the tree there. I don't know why," Dodd said, pointing to the tree.

"No personal items?" Bennet asked.

"Not that we've found."

"How did you find Ranger Thompson?" Antonio asked.

"He'd called in, saying he was bringing the boy to the station and to have the emergency vehicles meet him there. When he didn't show up, they called in to dispatch, and we

came to check it out. Found him lying next to his Jeep, barely alive, no sign of anyone else around, just the abandoned campsite," Dodd said.

"Damn it! He cannot be too far away!" Antonio yelled.

"State Police are already covering the exits and rest stops for the next fifty miles," Dodd said.

"Is it alright if we have a look around?" John asked.

"Sure thing, maybe you can see something we don't."

"Come on," Bennet said, putting his hand on Antonio's shoulder.

They headed for the camp, hoping Kendall had left another clue.

∞

Janice Lane had just returned from her lunch and sat down to check her emails. There were several from parents who hadn't been able to attend the assembly that morning.

She forwarded them on to Tara, who would answer them later. She clicked on one email that had an attachment.

"Principal Lane... I thought you might appreciate this as much as I am. ENJOY!"

She opened the attachment and stared at the first picture in horror. "Oh my God!"

Tara had heard Janice cry out and ran in. "What's wrong?"

Janice gestured towards the computer as she desperately tried to get a hold of her emotions. Tara's hands flew to her mouth in shock as she saw the message and photo of Kendall. His face was so bruised, and he looked so sad and alone.

Chapter 26~ The Email

Sally answered the phone to a nearly hysterical Tara Shipley. She couldn't make out what the woman was trying to say.

"Tara, TARA, please slow down, I can't understand you," Sally said calmly.

Tara took a deep breath. "Please, you have to get over here. Principal Lane just received an email that... I don't know!"

"Okay, I need you to SLOW down. Now, what does the email say?" Sally asked, trying to keep the other woman calm and focused.

"I can't explain it, please just get over here!" Tara was now sobbing.

"I'll be there in ten minutes," Sally said, heading out the door. Sally pulled up in front of the middle school a few minutes later. She was worried. Nothing ever rattled Tara Shipley, and the woman was clearly unnerved.

She walked to the main office, and hearing voices in the Principal's office, she knocked and walked in. She found Janice Lane and Tara sitting on the small couch. Both women had been crying but seemed to be calming down for the moment. Sally walked over, knelt down, and took ahold of a hand from each of the women. "What happened?" she asked quietly.

Janice pointed to her computer. "I'm going to go take a look, alright?" Sally asked.

Janice nodded and Sally stood up and walked to the desk. She sat down and moved the mouse to clear the screensaver. She clicked on the email and was not prepared for what she saw. There were nearly two dozen photos of Kendall attached to the email, along with a taunting message to Janice.

She took a deep breath and clicked on the first photo to enlarge it. Kendall was sitting back on a bed, wearing a white button-down shirt and black jeans. His face was badly bruised, and he looked exhausted and in pain. The next photo showed him in the same position, with his shirt open. They continued like that, until the boy was no longer wearing anything. She could tell that he was being posed, and he was not looking at the camera in most of the photos. She could also see that his body was nearly covered in bruises.

Deesie was trying to break him, and had now added humiliation to the physical abuse. In the few photos that showed Kendall actually looking at the camera, she saw sadness and pain, but there was also defiance in his eyes. The one that broke her heart was where Kendall was hugging his legs, head down, with only his eyes raised to look at the camera. She prayed Deesie had not broken Kendall yet.

"Hang on, baby, we're going to find you."

Sally grabbed the phone and called the FBI agent, who was working the case from Quantico. She explained about the email and forwarded it on to her—she was going to let them handle that part. She forwarded it to the station, so she could go over it as well. She needed to call Antonio and tell him about this. To say he was not going to take this well, was a massive understatement. Deesie had better hope that someone else finds him first, because once Antonio saw these, there was no telling what he would do.

She turned and looked at Janice and Tara.

"I know this whole thing is horrifying and a complete shock. It may be Deesie's way of getting even with you for questioning his motives before. He probably figured he could hurt

both you and Kendall this way. I need to get back to the station, but if you get any more emails, don't open them. Just call me and then forward them on to me at the station."

"Thank you, Sally. I didn't know what to do," Janice said, her voice still shaky.

"Why don't you go home and get some rest? You look like you're ready to collapse," Sally suggested.

"I'll drive you home and stay for a while," Tara offered.

Janice nodded. "Thank you, I think I'll take you up on that, but after last bell."

"You're welcome," Tara smiled. She stood up and walked Sally out.

Halfway down the hall, an excited voice called out, "Officer Sally!"

Sally turned just as Jenny Tinkler came running up, slamming into her. They both hit the floor with Jenny half lying on top of Sally.

"Hi Jenny, can you get up, please?" Sally asked.

"Sorry!" Jenny apologized and hopped up.

Tara reached a hand down to Sally, who groaned as she stood up.

"Jenny, you know you're supposed to WALK down the halls," Tara scolded.

"I'm so sorry, but I heard Officer Sally was here and needed to tell her something," Jenny said.

"It's okay, Jenny. What did you need?" Sally asked.

"Well, you said to tell you if Mr. Deesie had ever talked about anyplace special?"

"Yes. Why? Do you know someplace he might go?" Sally asked, not entirely hopeful.

"Well, in class one day, we were talking about local writers. He told us how he was visiting his cousin one day, and they drove to Osseo to hear Garrison Keillor speak. He was saying how the writer is from Anoka, and it was totally worth the five and a half hour drive to hear him," Jenny rambled on.

"Jenny, Anoka is less than half an hour from Osseo," Sally pointed out.

"Huh, they didn't go to Anoka," Jenny said.

"Okay, I'm totally confused, sweetie. Could you just tell me where Mr. Deesie and his cousin drove FROM?" Sally asked, rubbing her temples.

"A small town just outside of Appleton," Jenny said.

"Appleton, Wisconsin?" Sally asked.

"Yeah, that's it." Jenny smiled.

"Jenny, this is VERY important... Are you sure he said Appleton?" Sally asked.

"Yeah, I know he did, because my aunt lives there and we visit her every summer. He said his cousin has a cabin up near the Oneida Reservation. It's outside a little town called, um... Jamieson. I may be clumsy, but I have a great memory," Jenny said proudly.

"Jenny, I owe you big time!" Sally said as she ran out the door.

∞

Sally got to the station and immediately got on the line with Quantico, telling them about Deesie's cousin. The agent said she would track it down and get back to her.

She got on the phone with Bower and told him about the town in Wisconsin. Bower was checking out the Andover area and said he would head in that direction and await confirmation.

She took a deep breath and got onto the radio to Antonio. "Hey Boss, you there?"

Bennet answered, "Hey, it's John. What's going on?"

"We're waiting for a confirmed location of a cabin in Wisconsin that belongs to a relative of Deesie. It's near a small town called Jamieson, outside of Appleton, near the Oneida Reservation," Sally told him.

"Are we sure about this?" Bennet asked.

"Well, they've been heading in that direction, and it goes along with what Jason was trying to remember. One of the other students came to me and said that Deesie had told them that he had visited Osseo to hear a writer from Anoka speak. He told them it was over a five hour drive, which puts them near Appleton," Sally explained.

"They'll be getting off of I-94 then," Antonio said.

Bennet nodded in agreement.

Sally took a deep breath, not really wanting to tell him about the photos. "Antonio, t-there's something else. Janice Lane received an email from Deesie from a generic account. The message said, *Principal Lane... you might appreciate this as much as I am.* There was an attachment with it."

"Which was?" John asked.

"Approximately two dozen photos of Kendall," Sally said quietly.

"Sally, what about the photos?" Antonio could tell she was having a hard time telling him something.

"They were taken in a room somewhere and..." Sally said, realizing she was holding back a sob. She silently cursed her lack of emotional control.

"Honey, what was in the photos?" Antonio asked gently, not wanting to hear the answer.

Sally took another deep breath. "Deesie took photos of Kendall as he made him undress. It looked like he was posing him. He was covered in bruises, and he looked so... hurt."

Antonio's jaw was clenched and the colour had drained from his face. "Send them to me."

"I'm not sure that's a good idea, Boss," Sally warned.

"Sally, SEND them. That's an order," Antonio said firmly.

"Pull off the road first, please," Sally pleaded.

"Alright, pulling off," Antonio said as he headed for the next exit. He pulled over and parked on the side of the road. "Send them now, please."

Sally forwarded the email to Antonio, grateful that his phone had a small screen. Antonio opened the email and clicked on "open attachment." His face was expressionless as he looked at the photos of his young godson, twenty-two of them, each one worse than the last.

John's eyes went wide, and he stopped looking at them after the thirteenth. He watched Antonio process what he was looking at and he knew that Deesie should be very afraid of what would happen once they caught up to him.

After a few minutes, Antonio closed the internet application. "John, will you drive please?"

Bennet nodded, got out, and went around to the driver's side.

Antonio was still sitting there, so John opened the door and his partner looked up.

Antonio got out and walked over to the passenger's side. Before he got into the car, he walked a few feet away, bent over, and vomited.

A few minutes later, he and Bennet were on their way to Jamieson, Wisconsin.

Chapter 27 ~ Doc

Deesie was sticking to the back roads for the most part, avoiding the interstate. They should make Jamieson before dark. He would have to stop and load up on supplies—food, gas for the generator, probably a few clothes for the boy. Once they got to the cabin, he did not want to leave for a while. He wanted to spend time with his prize.

He looked in the rearview mirror and watched Kendall for a moment. The boy was sleeping with his head leaning against the window. He smiled, thinking of his little photo session. It had really sent the boy to the edge. He should be much easier to handle now.

He wished he could see Principal Lane's face when she opened that email. Who knows, maybe it would do the uptight little bitch some good.

Kendall started coughing again—he had been coughing on and off since they left the motel.

Deesie sighed. "Figures he would get sick right before we get someplace where we'll have plenty of time and privacy."

He decided to pull off at the next town and pick up some cough and cold medicine. He needed coffee anyway. He should also probably get them a hot meal, since they had not eaten since the night before.

He pulled into the next decent-sized town and found a drug store. "Wake up, sweetheart," he told Kendall.

When he got no answer, he reached back, grabbed the teen's leg, and squeezed. "I said wake up!"

Kendall's eyes opened and he looked at Deesie.

"Give me your hands," Deesie ordered, pulling out the handcuffs.

Kendall reached forward and the man locked them around his wrists. Kendall lay back against the seat coughing, he felt terrible. His chest was tight, he was freezing, and his head was killing him.

"I'm going in here to pick up some medicine for you. Stay put and behave, or there will be consequences," Deesie threatened.

Kendall was silent and sat looking out the window, his eyes drooping again.

Deesie was back out in about ten minutes and found the boy sleeping again. "Wake up and take this," he said, measuring out some cough medicine in the little cap.

Kendall reached up, took it from the man, and swallowed it.

"Take these and drink this," Deesie said, handing the teen two ibuprofen and a bottle of Gatorade. Kendall took the pills and swallowed them with a sip of the Gatorade. Then he sat back and leaned his head back against the window.

Deesie pulled into a fast food place and got in line for the drive-thru. He ordered two meals and handed one back to Kendall, who just sat it on the seat next to him.

"Eat," Deesie commanded.

"I'm not hungry."

"You eat that or I will pull over and feed it to you," Deesie threatened.

Kendall pulled out the burger, took a bite, and then put it back in the bag.

"You are pushing it, sweetheart," Deesie growled.

"I don't feel well," Kendall said and leaned back against the window.

"Fine, eat it once the medicine kicks in. It's your problem if it's cold," Deesie told him.

Kendall closed his eyes and fell back to sleep.

∞

Sally got the call from Quantico, confirming that Deesie did have a cousin who owned a cabin near the lake, just outside of Jamieson.

She got on the radio to Antonio. "Hey Boss, we got confirmation on a cabin seven miles north of Jamieson. Deesie's cousin, Theodore Farley, owns it."

"Thanks Sally. Are you doing okay there?" Antonio asked.

"Doing better since we know where they're heading. You and John okay?"

Antonio looked at Bennet, who nodded. "Same here."

Bennet looked at the GPS. "We should be there in approximately seven hours."

"Punch it and get us there in six," Antonio instructed.

"Let me know when you get close and I'll coordinate with Bower and the Appleton Sheriff's Department," Sally said.

"Will do," Antonio said. "Sally... thank you."

"Anything for you, Boss. Get there fast, but get there safe." Sally smiled.

"Will do."

∞

Kendall and Carlos were in the school hallway when a door shut between them. He could hear Carlos on the other side, screaming and trying to get to him. Kendall couldn't move, he couldn't call out, just listen to Carlos screaming for him.

The next thing he knew, Carlos was standing in front of him. "You said you'd never leave me behind," Carlos said accusingly.

"I didn't want to leave, Carlos. I want to be home," Kendall told him.

"Then why did you give up?" Carlos asked him as he started to cry.

"Please don't cry! I didn't give up. I just don't know what to do anymore!" Kendall started crying too.

"You just have to fight," Carlos told him. "Please fight, Kendall. Please come home!"

Then Carlos was gone and the door opened.

Kendall awoke with a start. He was shaking and started coughing.

"Take some more of this," Deesie said, tossing the bottle of cough syrup back to him.

Kendall took a cap full of the nasty-tasting stuff and sat the bottle in the cup holder. He took a drink of the Gatorade that he had opened earlier. His mind was racing as he tried to remember the dream, but all he could hear was Carlos telling him to fight and come home.

After a few minutes, he fell back to sleep, head against the window.

Deesie pulled off the road about two hours outside of Jamieson. Kendall was still sleeping, but he wasn't coughing anymore.

"Wake up!" Deesie ordered.

Kendall opened his eyes and looked at the man.

"We're going to be getting there soon and..." Deesie started to say.

"Where?" Kendall asked.

"Your new home, sweetheart, and DON'T interrupt me again! As I was saying, since we are going to be there awhile, people will know you're there. So, the story goes like this... You are my nephew. Your parents were killed in a car accident about a week ago, which explains why you look the way you do. I am bringing you to the cabin for rest and rehabilitation, as recommended by the doctors. Your name is Philip, and you are not to speak to anyone, except to answer yes or no. Any smart-ass attitude you give will be blamed on the trauma of losing your parents, but once I get you alone, you will be sorry. Do you understand me?"

Kendall looked at him. "Yes."

"If you don't behave, we can always have another photo session, only this time, maybe with a bit more action," Deesie leered.

Kendall just looked out the window again.

Deesie laughed as he pulled the SUV back out onto the road.

Kendall reached over and grabbed the bag of food sitting next to him, and slowly ate the burger. He was going to need his strength.

∞

They got to Jamieson and Deesie pulled in front of the General Store.

"We are going to see how you do in here, so give me your hands," Deesie said.

Kendall extended his hands and Deesie took off the cuffs. "You remember what I told you, sweetheart," Deesie warned as he got out of the SUV. He walked around, opened Kendall's door, and took his arm. To anyone looking, it seemed as if he was helping the boy out, but Kendall knew differently.

"Behave," Deesie hissed as they walked towards the door. Kendall just kept his head down, avoiding eye contact with anyone who might be looking. It wasn't like he wanted anyone to see him like this.

Deesie grabbed a cart. "You push so that you have something to lean on."

They walked down the aisles and Deesie grabbed supplies, putting them in the cart. They went through the checkout and Deesie smiled at the checker.

"Hi, just passing through?" she asked.

"No, staying up at the lake for a while," Deesie said with a smile.

"Gets cold this time of year," she warned.

"We're staying at a relative's place, they have a good generator. Just needed to get away for a while, family tragedy," he said sadly, as he placed a hand on Kendall's shoulder.

Kendall cringed at his touch and the man squeezed down.

She gave them a sad smile. "Oh, I'm so sorry. I hope that a nice quiet vacation will help. You might want to make sure you have chains for your car. The roads tend to get a bit difficult after it snows."

"Already have them, thank you." Deesie smiled as he paid the bill. "I'm sure we forgot something and will see you again soon."

"Have a good evening," she said as they walked out the door.

"You did very well, sweetheart," Deesie whispered into Kendall's ear.

Kendall got into the SUV as Deesie loaded his purchases into the back.

They stopped at the gas station next, where Deesie filled six 5-gallon cans for the generator. While he was paying for the gas, Kendall grabbed the pen and pad, scribbled out a note, and put it in his pocket. The next stop was the market, where Deesie bought groceries and more cold medicine.

"It's going to take a while to get things set up there, so we're stopping at the diner. You WILL NOT speak to anyone except to say yes or no. If you try anything, you will be sorry. We are going to be almost ten miles from town, in the middle of nowhere, so I won't care how much you scream. Understood, sweetheart?"

Kendall looked at him and nodded.

They got out, with Deesie holding onto Kendall's arm, and walked into the fifty's-styled diner.

∞

There were a few people in the diner, including a tall man with curly blond and gray hair. He looked to be in his late forties or early fifties.

Jacob Akins was the local veterinarian and a lifelong resident of Jamieson. He was well respected and loved by everyone in the community, always taking an interest in the people in his town. At the moment, he was interested in the two newcomers who had just walked through the door.

As he sat at the counter sipping his coffee, he thought the man looked familiar. He watched as they headed for a booth near the back of the diner. The man didn't let go of the boy until they sat down across from one another.

"Hey Maddie, what do you think the story is there?" he asked the waitress, slightly nodding his head in the newcomers' direction

"I don't know, Doc, but I'm sure you'll find out." She smiled as she grabbed two sets of utensils wrapped in napkins and headed to the booth.

"Good evening, gentlemen," she said cheerfully to Deesie and Kendall as she placed the utensils in front of them.

"Good evening," Deesie said, smiling at her.

"Can I get you started with something to drink?"

"I'll have coffee, black, and my nephew will have milk," Deesie replied.

"Okay, I'll have that right up for you. Specials are in the front of the menu, and I'll take your order when you're ready." She smiled again.

"Perfect," Deesie said.

Maddie went back to the counter, poured the drinks, and returned to the booth. "There you are," she said, setting the drinks in front of them.

"Thank you. I think we're ready to order. We will both have the chicken dinner," Deesie said.

"Two chicken dinners it is," she said and went back to the counter to place the order.

Doc Akins walked over to the booth. "Hi, I'm Doc Akins. I'm sorry to bother you, but you look familiar."

"Well, my cousin has a cabin near here, and I use to visit him quite a bit. Maybe we met when I was visiting?" Deesie suggested.

"Maybe. Who's your cousin?" Doc asked.

"Theodore Farley, he has a cabin by the lake," Deesie said. He was getting nervous at being questioned and wondered if this Doc had seen the Amber Alerts.

"I know Ted. He hasn't been up here in quite some time. So you're either a Farley or a Deesie?" Doc asked with a smile.

"Robert Deesie. This is my nephew, Philip," he said, indicating Kendall.

"What happened to you, son?" Doc asked, taking note of all the bruises on his face.

Kendall glanced up and then looked at Deesie, not saying anything.

Deesie stood up and took Doc by the arm, walking away from the booth. "Sensitive subject, he and his parents were in a car accident about a week ago. They were both killed, and he was lucky to walk away with just some minor injuries. The doctors recommended taking him away for a while, so we came up here for a few weeks. He doesn't say much, still in shock. I'm hoping some time up here will do him some good."

"I'm sorry about that, losing both parents has got to be hard for someone so young. I have a boy close to his age, maybe after you get settled, he and Philip should get together and hang out for a while. Sometimes it's easier to open up to someone your own age," Doc offered.

"That would be really nice, I'm sure he'd like that," Deesie replied, shaking Doc's hand and smiling.

"You got everything you need in case the snow hits?" Doc asked.

"I think so," Deesie replied, watching Maddie take their dinners to their table. "It looks like our food is ready. It was nice speaking to you, hopefully the boys can get together soon," he said as he headed back to his booth.

"Nice talking to you, too," Doc said, going back to the counter.

"Well?" Maddie asked. He quietly told her what Deesie had told him.

"That is so sad, poor little guy," she said.

"Yeah, I have a feeling that's not quite the whole story," Doc said, sipping on his coffee again.

"Why is that?" Maddie asked him.

"I may be just an old country vet, but I can tell a fresh bruise from an old one. I can also tell when someone is afraid to talk, as opposed to not wanting to."

"You think he's beating him?" Maddie asked.

"Someone is, and since he's the only other one with him..." Doc said quietly.

Another man came up and greeted Doc and Maddie. Doc whispered to him for a moment and the man nodded and quickly left, returning a few minutes later.

"Eat so we can get out of here. Stupid nosey country hicks," Deesie hissed at Kendall.

They both ate in silence. When they were nearly finished, Doc came up again. "You know, I was going to ask if you have a radio. Not much in the way of cell service up there, and if the snow hits, a radio is really the only way of getting ahold of anyone if there's an emergency."

"Uh, no I don't have a radio," Deesie said.

"Well, I just happen to know someone with a spare and he's happy to loan it to you." Doc smiled, taking Deesie by the arm and pulling him towards the counter.

"O-Okay," Dessie stammered as he threw a warning glare at Kendall.

"This is Matt, and he'll show you how to use it," Doc said, smiling again.

Matt handed Deesie the radio and proceeded to explain how to use it.

In the meantime, Maddie had headed back for the booth to clear the table. Without looking at Kendall, she spoke. "Honey, I don't know what's going on here, but if you need help, all you have to do is say so."

Kendall froze, unsure of what to do. He didn't want Deesie to hurt anyone here, and he knew that he would. "I'm not supposed to talk to anyone. You need to go, he'll hurt you," he whispered to her. Then he reached into his pocket and slipped a folded note next to the plate. He was getting nervous. Deesie kept looking over at them as Maddie busied herself with the dirty dishes.

"Okay honey, you boys have a nice evening," she said in a normal voice as she walked away from Kendall.

Matt had finally finished explaining how to use the radio, and Deesie walked over for the check. He paid the bill. "It was wonderful, thank you."

"You boys come back soon!" Maddie smiled.

"We will," Deesie said as he walked to the booth and grabbed his jacket. "Come on," he hissed to Kendall. The boy stood up and put on his jacket and they headed for the door.

Kendall glanced over at Doc, who gave him a reassuring smile. Deesie put an arm around the boy's shoulders and guided him out the door.

"Doc," Maddie said, handing him the note.

Doc quickly read it and asked Maddie for the phone.

Chapter 28~ The Cabin

Deesie pulled off the dirt road about a mile outside of town and got out of the SUV. He walked around to Kendall's door and opened it. He grabbed the tie he had used before and moved to wrap it around Kendall's head.

"What are you doing?" Kendall asked, pulling back.

Deesie grabbed him by the jacket and pulled him closer. "Don't question me and don't pull away when I touch you. You don't need to see where we are going, so I am blindfolding you," Deesie growled.

"Why don't you want me to see where we're going?" Kendall asked as Deesie wrapped the cloth around his head.

"What did I JUST tell you? Don't question me!" Deesie said and slapped the boy across the face. Kendall yelped and Deesie grinned, pulling the boy closer. "I like it when you make noises, sweetheart," he whispered into the boy's ear.

A shiver went down his spine, and the next thing Kendall knew, he was gagging as the man shoved his tongue into his mouth.

"I should just do you right here," Deesie said as he pushed the boy back onto the seat and climbed in. He unzipped Kendall's jacket and began running his hands up and down his torso. He gripped the blond's hair tightly as he ran his tongue along his jaw line, nipping here and there. Kendall struggled to get the man off him, but he was pinned against the seat.

Then Deesie started grinding his hips into the boy and Kendall hit panic mode. "No! Get off of me!" Kendall screamed, desperately trying to wriggle free. He started coughing uncontrollably, unable to catch his breath. Deesie stopped and looked down at the panicked teen, annoyed. He pulled the boy up, so he was sitting and could catch his breath.

As soon as the coughing slowed down, Deesie pushed the boy onto the floor of the SUV. "Stay there until we get to the cabin," he snapped as he slammed the door. He got back in the driver's seat and started driving, taking a turn here and there and humming happily to himself. "We are going to have such fun, sweetheart!"

∞

Antonio and Bennet were about two hours outside of Jamieson when his cell rang. "Garcia," he answered.

"Hi, you don't know me, but a boy left a note with your name and number on it. My name is Jacob Akins. The boy and an older man were at the local diner here."

"I'm Chief Antonio Garcia," Antonio said, indicating to John to pull over. "Where are you located? How did the boy look? Was he alright?"

"I'm in Jamieson, Wisconsin. The boy was pretty banged up. The man claimed he was the boy's uncle. He said there was a car accident about a week ago and that the boy lost both parents."

"We're already on our way there. Are they still in town?" Antonio asked.

"No, they took off a few minutes ago for a cousin's cabin, about seven miles outside of town. The boy slipped Maddie, the waitress here, a note, asking that someone call this number and said his name is Kendall," Doc told him.

"His name is Kendall and he was kidnapped last Friday, by a man posing as a school teacher. This man is armed and dangerous. He killed a motel manager and shot a forest ranger," Antonio said.

"I knew there was something off about that guy. How long before you get here?" Doc asked.

Bennet looked at Antonio. "I can push it, but the roads are getting icy."

"No, don't risk it, we can't help Kendall if we're killed on the road," Antonio sighed.

"Then about two hours," John said, looking at the GPS.

"Probably two hours," Antonio told Doc.

"We don't have a local Sheriff's office here, the nearest one's in Appleton. Why don't you come to my clinic here in town and you can use it for whatever you need?" Doc offered.

"Clinic?" Antonio asked.

"I'm the local veterinarian and have a small office here."

"That would be perfect, thank you," Antonio said gratefully.

"Happy to do what I can," Doc said, and then gave them directions to his clinic.

Antonio got on the radio. "Hey Sally, you there?"

"Yeah Boss, what's going on?"

"Just got a call from Jacob Akins in Jamieson. Kendall and Deesie just left the diner there, and Kendall managed to slip a note to the waitress. Apparently, Akins was suspicious of Deesie and got him talking. Deesie claimed Kendall is his nephew and had been in an accident, but Akins didn't buy the story. Akins is the local vet there, so we're going to meet up with him at his clinic and use it as base," Antonio told her.

"Was Kendall okay?"

"He said he was pretty banged up, which is why I'm sure Deesie made up the story about an accident," Antonio said.

"How much longer until you get there?" Sally asked.

"About two hours."

"Okay, I'll get on the line with Bower and the Appleton Sheriff."

"Good, thanks Sally." Antonio smiled. "Have you heard anything about Ranger Thompson?"

"He made it through surgery. The bullet hit the lower part of his left lung. He's still in critical condition and hadn't regained consciousness the last time I called. He had lost a lot of blood and the doctors are amazed he's made it this far. Hopefully that's a good sign though," Sally told him.

"Hopefully," Antonio said sadly. "We'll call you when we get to Jamieson."

"Okay Boss."

∞

Deesie pulled into the driveway next to the cabin. "We're here," he announced cheerfully.

He got out, walked around, and opened Kendall's door. "Time to get out, sweetheart," he said, pulling the boy up.

Kendall groaned. Being on the floor, he had felt every bump on the dirt road and everything hurt.

Deesie pulled him out of the SUV and held him around the waist as he pulled off the blindfold. "Home, sweet home," Deesie said and he kissed the teen on the neck. He held onto Kendall for a moment and then released him. Kendall shuddered from the disgust he felt at the man's touch.

Kendall looked at the cabin. It was nice looking from the outside, a little smaller than his grandfather's. It had a large front porch and the trees and brush had been cleared around it for about 300 yards in every direction. The windows were boarded up and it seemed well cared for.

Deesie had opened the back of the SUV and pulled out a couple of bags. "Take these," he told the boy as he grabbed a couple more. Kendall took the bags and followed Deesie up to the cabin. The man opened the door and ushered Kendall inside. "Put those over in the kitchen. I'm going to go get the generator running before it gets dark," he said as he headed back out the door.

Deesie grabbed two of the gas cans and headed around to the back of the cabin. Kendall put the bags on the counter and looked around. A simple living room was to the right as you walked in the front door, furnished with a couch and two chairs. There was a large fireplace on the outer wall. There was a wood stove in the middle of the room between the living room and kitchen, which was to the left. There was a small dining room on the left as you walked in with a table and benches.

There was a hallway leading to the back of the cabin, two doors on each side. Kendall heard a motor start as Deesie started up the generator. He walked out to the porch and Deesie came around the side of the cabin.

"Let's get the rest of the supplies in," the man said.

Kendall limped over to the SUV, picked up more of the bags, and carried them inside. Deesie was right behind him. After they unloaded the vehicle, Deesie handed Kendall his backpack and led him back to one of the rooms at the end of the hall.

He opened the door. "This is your room for now. I'll be right next door."

The bathroom was across from Deesie's room, and there was a third bedroom across from Kendall's.

Kendall tossed his backpack onto the bed and sat down. He was so tired and his chest was still tight. He could feel congestion building in it. He just wanted to climb into bed and go to sleep, but he was terrified of what would happen again.

Deesie walked into the room and tossed a bag at him. "It'll take about an hour for the water to heat up so you can take a shower," he said and walked out.

Kendall looked inside the bag and found some flannel pajamas, sweats, t-shirts, and a couple of flannel shirts. He could hear Deesie out in the front room taking boards off the windows. He went to the windows in his room and tried prying one of the boards loose, but they were tightly secured. He sighed and walked out into the living room.

"Do you know how to use a wood stove?" Deesie asked the boy as he continued pulling boards down.

"Yes." Kendall said as he went to the wood box and pulled out what he needed. "Matches?"

Deesie pointed to a box on the counter and Kendall grabbed it. After a few minutes, the fire was going and the room was starting to warm up.

"Good boy," Deesie said, walking by Kendall and running his hand through the boy's hair.

Deesie went to the hall closet, pulled out some sheets and blankets, and handed the linens to the teen. "Go make your bed."

Kendall took them and went back to his room. He had trouble making the bed but eventually finished.

"Water is warm enough. Go shower," Deesie yelled back to him.

Kendall grabbed the flannel pajama bottoms and a long-sleeved t-shirt. He walked into the bathroom and closed the door. He turned on the water and looked in the mirror. He could barely recognize himself with all the bruises, cuts, and swelling on his face. Looking at his chest and arms, he saw there were more bruises. He tried looking at his back in the mirror and saw bruises there, as well as the hickeys that ran along his neck. He noticed another mark on his left hip and couldn't remember when Deesie had done that.

"Hurry up in there! Don't use all the hot water," Deesie yelled.

Kendall quickly showered and pulled on the clean clothes. He gathered his things and opened the door, jumping when he saw Deesie standing there smiling at him. "Squeaky clean, sweetheart?"

Kendall walked past him and down to his room. Deesie was right behind him. "Unpack everything and get back out to the living room when you're finished."

Kendall started pulling the clothes out of the bag and put them in the small dresser.

"Bring your boots up with you," Deesie yelled. Kendall sighed, wondering what the perv was up to now. He grabbed his boots and limped out to the main room.

Deesie took his boots. "These stay with me. We don't want you running off, now do we? Sit down," Deesie ordered, pointing to the couch.

Kendall sat down with Deesie right next to him. "So this is what's going to happen, sweetheart. We are going to stay here and enjoy each other's company for a while."

He ran his fingers up and down Kendall's arm as he spoke. "If you behave, you won't get hurt. If you don't behave... well, let's just say that you will wish you had. We are far away from everyone, and as I said before, you can scream and no one will hear you. In fact, you probably will scream." Deesie smirked as he nuzzled Kendall's neck.

Kendall just stared straight-ahead, jaw clenched.

"See, that's the attitude I'm talking about," Deesie said as he grabbed Kendall's chin and forced him to look at him. "That is what will get you into trouble. But..." he said, kissing Kendall's neck below his ear, "I can be forgiving to a point."

Kendall raised his arm and covered his mouth as he had a coughing fit.

"You need to go to bed. I want that cold gone as soon as possible, and you better hope that I don't get it," Deesie snapped.

"YOU kissed me, not the other way around," Kendall said.

Deesie backhanded him. "You just NEVER learn, do you?"

Kendall held his stinging cheek. *What's one more bruise?* He thought. He took a little satisfaction in knowing that he could irritate the man.

Deesie stormed off to the bathroom and grabbed the cough syrup, ibuprofen, sleeping pills, and glass of water.

"Take these," he said as he handed Kendall first the cough syrup, then the ibuprofen, and then the sleeping pills.

"Go to bed, sweetheart. We can begin our quality time tomorrow."

Kendall walked to the bedroom and closed the door, wishing there was a lock on it. He quickly took the two little blue pills he had palmed and put them in his backpack with the other ones. He climbed into bed but couldn't sleep at first, his thoughts keeping him awake. He wondered if the waitress had called Papi. She was so nice and had seemed so worried. He also knew he couldn't wait forever for someone else to save him, and his eyes started to close as he came up with a plan.

After about an hour, Deesie headed to his bedroom. First, he looked in on the boy who was sleeping soundly. He walked into the room and pulled back the covers, looking down at the teen. He reached down and pushed the leg of Kendall's pajamas up, until his thigh was exposed. Deesie bent down to leave his nightly "love mark" on him. He was nipping and sucking at Kendall's right thigh when the boy stirred, but didn't waken. Deesie continued with his task, and when it was the bluish-purple colour that he liked, he pulled the pajama leg back down and covered the boy with the blankets. Smiling to himself, he left the room, closing the door behind him.

Kendall opened his eyes after he heard the man leave. *Well, that explains the other marks,* he thought, more determined than ever to get out of this place

Chapter 29 ~ A Plan of Action

Bennet and Antonio pulled into Jamieson about 7:15 pm. They found Doc Akins' place with no trouble and were greeted by the man when they knocked on the door. They went inside and found agent Bower had already arrived.

"So what's the plan?" John asked.

"We go get Kendall," Antonio stated.

"It's not going to be that simple," Bower said.

Antonio raised an eyebrow. "Why is that?"

"Doc, maybe you should explain," Bower suggested.

Antonio and John looked at the man expectantly.

"Sure thing," Doc said as he walked over to the map. "The cabin is a little over seven miles through the woods. There's only one dirt road going in or out of the area, and Deesie would be able to hear anyone coming from over a mile away," he explained, pointing to an area on the map.

"What about using the trees as cover?" Antonio asked.

"I've been up to that cabin many times. Farley made sure there was a clearance between three and five hundred yards around the cabin for safety's sake. In case of fire or hunters out not paying attention. Point is if Deesie happens to be looking, he will see you. Going up there in the dark gives you no advantage, because he will hear you coming," Doc told them.

Antonio walked over to the map and pointed to a small area. "If we park here and walk in, he wouldn't be able to see or hear much."

"The issue is, neither would we," Bower pointed out.

Bennet could tell that Antonio was getting frustrated. Hell, so was he. They were so close, but he knew that Doc and Bower were right. Traipsing around in the strange woods, in below freezing temperatures, was not a solid plan.

He put his hand on Antonio's shoulder. "They're right. Deesie doesn't know that we know where he is. Right now, we have the element of surprise on our side, and we don't want to lose that. So we get a hot meal, some sleep, and start out at first light. By this time tomorrow, we'll be on our way home, Kendall with us. Deesie will be on his way either to prison or to hell."

Antonio rubbed the bridge of his nose. He knew they were right, but damn it anyway. He just wanted Kendall safely away from that monster. Truth be told, he wanted Deesie dead and that actually concerned him a lot. He had never hated anyone the way he hated that man.

"It's really the best plan of action," Doc said gently.

"I know, I just..." Antonio sighed.

"I understand. Now let's get you boys something to eat. The diner is just down the road, and you can talk to Maddie—she's the one who spoke to your boy," Doc said with a smile.

Antonio nodded and the men headed down the street. Once they were there and had placed their orders, Antonio called Sally.

"Hey Boss, you're there?"

"Yeah, we got here about half an hour ago. We came up with a plan, and now we're grabbing something to eat," Antonio sighed.

"So, what's wrong?" Sally asked, hearing a strain in Antonio's voice.

"We're going to have to wait until morning. The cabin is too far out, and Deesie would know we're coming."

"I was afraid it was something like that. I know you're anxious, but Deesie doesn't know you're coming and tomorrow will be here soon enough," she said.

"I know, I just want this over," he said quietly.

"Tomorrow it will be and the three of you will be on your way home. Deesie will be locked up, hopefully forever this time," she said encouragingly. "Are you going to call home and let them know?"

"Yeah, after we finish eating," he told her as he saw the food being carried to their table.

"Very good! I had a cleaning service go in, take care of the Knight home, and found someone to repair the window on the back door. Do you want me to get someone over there to change the locks as well?"

"That would be great, Sally. I have told you that you're amazing, right?" He smiled.

"Yes, but one never gets tired of hearing it." She laughed. "Keep me updated."

"Will do," Antonio said as he headed to the table. The food did smell good.

While they were eating, Maddie told them what she had seen and heard. She smiled sadly, as she told them about the note Kendall slipped to her while Doc kept Deesie occupied with the radio. "He seemed so worried about what would happen to me."

"He was. Deesie already killed one man and critically injured another. Kendall doesn't want anyone to get hurt, especially because of him," Antonio said with a weary smile.

"He's a little young to take on that kind of responsibility," Maddie said.

"He's always been that way," Antonio told her. Maddie smiled at Antonio and squeezed his shoulder as she turned and walked back to the counter.

"You boys are going to need a place to stay tonight. You're welcome at my place, plenty of room there. It's only a couple of miles outside of town," Doc offered.

"We don't want to put you out," Antonio said.

"That's not an issue. My son is staying at a friend's house tonight and there are enough beds to go around," Doc told him.

"We'd love to, thank you," Bennet answered for the group.

Antonio looked at him.

"What? I, for one, would appreciate a warm, soft bed as opposed to that cold, hard seat in the car," John said.

"It's settled then, you boys follow me out and we'll get you settled in." Doc smiled.

Antonio sighed, shaking his head in defeat. "Fine, I know when I'm beat."

"Can I get that in writing for future reference?" John smirked. Antonio rolled his eyes and stood up.

They arrived at the Akins home a few minutes later. It was a lovely two-story farmhouse that had been in the family for three generations. There was a big barn and other outbuildings. It reminded Antonio of a picture from Norman Rockwell.

They pulled up and a huge yellow Labrador retriever came running up to greet them.

"This here's Samson," Doc said as the lab ran from man to man, tongue hanging out of a face with a perpetual doggy smile on it. "House!" Doc snapped his fingers and the dog ran back to the front porch and sat waiting.

"Impressive!" John commented.

"Thanks! He's still young and hasn't learned all of his manners yet, but he tries... sometimes. Tends to forget them when new people come around, or if there's food involved." Doc laughed.

"Sounds like Carlos!" John laughed as he patted Antonio's shoulder. Antonio just looked at him.

"What? Fun-loving, adorable smile on his face, loves everyone, and lives for food," John said defensively.

"Yeah, YOU explain that comment to his Mami." Antonio smirked, punching his partner in the arm.

"Ouch... I will!" Bennet said while holding his arm. "Wait, you're not really gonna tell her, right?" he asked, suddenly worried. "Antonio?"

Antonio just followed Doc into the house, leaving Bennet to wonder if he should be concerned for his life. Bower patted Bennet on the shoulder, laughing. "I think you should be worried," he said and walked up to the house.

∞

Once Doc had shown them to their rooms, Antonio called home.

Sylvia answered. "Hi honey, where are you? How are things?"

Antonio smiled when he heard his wife's voice. "Actually, I have some news. Where is everyone?"

"Let me call them," Sylvia said.

He heard her call out to everyone and then the phone was on speaker. "Go ahead, sweetheart," Sylvia said.

"Hey everyone, I have some news. We've tracked Deesie to Jamieson, Wisconsin. It's a small town outside of Appleton. Deesie has a relative, who has a cabin here," Antonio told them.

"Are they there?" Jen asked anxiously.

"I have several people who've confirmed they saw both Deesie and Kendall this afternoon. Deesie bought some supplies and they ate at the diner here in town. Kendall spoke to the waitress and slipped her a note with my number on it. We're staying with the local vet tonight, since he's seen both of them and spoke with Deesie. He told him that Kendall is his nephew and that they're staying at his cousin's place."

"Well, are you going after them?" Brooke asked.

"We're going out at first light. The cabin is deep in the woods, and Deesie would see us coming if we went out tonight. The Appleton Sheriff's Department will be sending some men, and Bower has agents coming in to meet us in the morning," Antonio explained.

"So not until morning?" Jen asked, near tears again.

"I know it's hard. I'm not happy about it either. The good news is that Deesie doesn't know we've found them, and we really don't want to lose the element of surprise," Antonio told her.

"Alright, so tomorrow you'll all be coming home," Jen stated, trying to smile as she hugged Katie.

"Tomorrow we will all be heading home," Antonio promised.

∞

Deesie woke up about 5 am and made a pot of coffee. He started a fire in the wood stove and then sat down and poured himself some cereal. When he was finished eating, he walked to Kendall's room and opened the door. He had heard the boy coughing on and off throughout the night and brought the cough medicine with him.

He sat down on the bed, next to the boy, and brushed his bangs back from his forehead. The cut from Friday night seemed to be healing alright and some of the bruises were starting to turn yellowish in colour. He ran his fingers down Kendall's cheek. It would be so easy just to have his way with him now, but he enjoyed drawing it out. The anticipation was as good as the act itself and the look in those green eyes when the boy thought something more was going to happen, was priceless.

He smirked to himself as he pulled the covers down and crawled up onto the bed. He pushed Kendall's legs apart slightly and sat on his knees between them. He put his hands on Kendall's hips and reached down and started running his mouth along the boy's neck whispering, "Time to wake up, sweetheart."

He felt the boy suddenly tense and smiled to himself.

Kendall felt someone on top of him and woke with a start. Deesie was kissing his neck and telling him to wake up. He instinctively pushed at the man. "Get off of me!"

"That's not a very nice way to say good morning." Deesie smirked, as he ran his hands up Kendall's sides. "We will be teaching you some manners," the man said as he got off the bed, smiling.

Kendall took a couple of deep breaths, trying to calm himself down.

"Get up and get dressed," Deesie ordered as he left the room, slamming the door behind him.

Kendall got up and dressed quickly, layering three shirts. Then he grabbed his backpack and put some extra clothing in it, along with the Vans that Deesie had originally packed. Then he pulled the five pills out that he had hidden in it and put them in his pocket. He took the backpack and shoved it under the bed. He saw the cough medicine, poured a capful, swallowed it, and sat the bottle back on the table.

Kendall limped out into the kitchen, where Deesie was pouring himself a cup of coffee.

The man smirked at him again and sat down at the table. "Cereal is on the counter. While you are eating, I am going to take a shower. I take it I can trust you NOT to run off?" Deesie chuckled as he walked into the bathroom.

Kendall heard the water as Deesie started the shower. After a couple of minutes, he took the pills from his pocket and crushed them in-between two spoons. He quickly stirred them into Deesie's coffee and rinsed the spoons off, putting one away while he used the other for his cereal.

Kendall was just finishing his cereal when Deesie came out of the bathroom. Kendall got up, took his bowl to the sink, and began washing the dishes.

After a few minutes, Deesie moved over to the couch, sipping his coffee. "You are going to learn a few valuable lessons. We are going to become VERY close and I am going to do things to you that you've never dreamed of. Like I told you last night, I don't want your cold, but luckily, there are plenty of other things we can do that don't involve using your mouth."

The man yawned and rested his head back on the couch. Kendall went to sit at the kitchen table and watched the man closely. Deesie had finished his coffee and was still mumbling something, so Kendall waited.

After about half an hour, the man was snoring and Kendall moved. He went to the bedroom and grabbed his backpack, pulling out his shoes. He put them on and hissed. They were tighter than his boots were and put pressure on his foot, but after a minute Kendall was able to ignore it. He grabbed the cough medicine and threw it into the backpack.

Walking quietly up the hallway, he could hear Deesie still snoring, so he went into the bathroom. He grabbed the ibuprofen from the counter, popped two in his mouth, and then he tossed the bottle into his backpack.

He made his way to the kitchen, where he grabbed some granola bars and a couple of bottles of Gatorade, putting them into his backpack as well.

He made his way slowly to the front door, watching Deesie the whole time. He carefully pulled his jacket off the hook next to the door and slipped it on. He didn't have any gloves or a hat with him, so he pulled Deesie's gloves from his jacket pocket and took them. He slowly opened the door and slipped through, closing it quietly behind him.

He made his way off the porch and over to the SUV, going to the side that wasn't visible to the cabin.

Reaching down, he pulled the cap off one the tire valves, and taking a small stick, depressed the valve, letting the air out. He moved to the other tire and did the same thing, until both tires on the passenger side were flat.

He stood up and carefully made his way around the back of the cabin, coming out on the other side. He followed the driveway for a little while, making sure he was going the right way, and then walked into the trees, keeping the road in sight.

Chapter 30~ Runaway Rabbit

Antonio woke up about 4:30 am, hearing someone moving around. He yawned and got up, quickly dressed, and then walked down the hallway to the kitchen.

"Hey, sorry. I didn't mean to wake you up. Did you get any sleep?" Doc asked, smiling.

"Yeah, some. I can't thank you enough for putting us up here, not to mention all your help with this case," Antonio said.

"We all do what we can. Coffee?" Doc asked, offering a cup of the steaming hot liquid to him.

"Perfect, thank you. Do you always get up this early?" Antonio asked, taking the offered cup.

"Gotta feed the stock and check on my mare. She's ready to foal any day now."

"Need some help?" Antonio offered.

"I'm not one to turn away someone willing to pitch hay or gather eggs. You might want to put on my extra pair of muck boots. They might be a little large, but better than nothing," Doc recommended.

"Sounds good." Antonio laughed as they headed out the back door. They stopped and pulled on the work boots and headed to the barn.

After about a half an hour of tossing hay to horses, breaking ice on the watering troughs, and fighting with possessive chickens for eggs, Antonio was wide awake and hungry. The sun wasn't up yet, but it was peaceful, and Antonio could definitely appreciate the quiet beauty of the place. It was a nice change of pace from sitting in the car and driving all day.

He took a deep breath and prayed. "Please let us find Kendall today and please let him be alright."

Doc startled him when he came up behind him and placed a hand on his shoulder. "Don't worry, you'll have your boy back today," he said and then walked back to the house.

What is the man, psychic? Antonio wondered as he followed him back to the house carrying a basketful of fresh eggs.

Back in the kitchen, Doc started mixing up biscuits for breakfast. "Hope you boys like a big breakfast."

"I know I do. I am so tired of the fast food we've been eating. What can I do to help?" Antonio asked.

"Well, biscuits will take about ten minutes to bake, so if you want to start cooking up some of the bacon that's in the fridge, and then we'll just make a big batch of scrambled eggs." Doc smiled.

The men busied themselves preparing the meal, and both Bower and Bennet were drawn to the kitchen by the homey smells.

"I think I've died and gone to Heaven," John said as he deeply inhaled the aromas surrounding him.

Antonio rolled his eyes at the sight of his partner standing there with his eyes half closed and the goofiest grin on his face. "Really? You're almost drooling."

"What? Do you know how long it's been since I had a real home-cooked meal? In fact, I think the last time was at your house," John said.

"Well, don't count on any more meals after Sylvia finds out that you compared her son to a dog." Antonio smirked.

"I was JOKING! You know... trying to lighten the mood by making an obscure comparison for humour's sake?" Bennet said defensively.

Antonio just looked at him. "I really don't think Sylvia will see it that way."

"No one said you have to tell her," John pointed out.

"You expect me to LIE to my wife?"

"It's not a LIE if you don't tell her... Fine, I'll plead insanity, telling her that after being trapped in a car with you for five days straight, I cracked," Bennet said smugly.

"Are you sure it's not the two of you who are married?" Bower asked, walking over to help Doc.

Both of their jaws dropped as they looked at the FBI Agent.

"Sounds like a fair question to me... Breakfast is served," Doc told them.

After breakfast, Bennet and Bower cleaned up, while Antonio spoke with the Appleton Sheriff. They had agreed to meet at Doc's office at 7 am and would head out for the cabin from there.

"I think I should go with you," Doc said.

"Not a good idea to have a civilian in the possible line of fire," Antonio explained.

"Well, this civilian knows the area like the back of his hand and is an experienced tracker. Also, if anyone needs medical attention, I was a fully trained medic in Desert Storm and I've kept my license up-to-date. I'm also a good shot if need be," Doc told him.

"I have to admit, I'm impressed." Antonio smiled. "Alright, we can definitely use you, but you need to stay in the background. I don't want to have to explain to your family if anything happens to you," Antonio said, pointing to a family portrait that hung above the mantle.

The picture showed Doc standing with one arm around a beautiful dark haired woman. Her eyes were hazel with amber highlights and she had a dazzling smile. His other arm was around a tall boy with the same dark hair as his mother but curly. He had his mother's eyes, but his smile was all Doc's, wide and friendly.

Doc smiled. "Just me and my boy now. We lost Laura two years ago to a drunk driver."

"I'm so sorry," Antonio said quietly.

"So am I. She was quite a woman, full of fire. I guess we balanced each other out." Doc smiled.

"Your son looks like her, except for the curly hair," Antonio said.

"Yup, boy got lucky there. Her good looks and my disposition." Doc laughed.

"Good combination." Antonio smiled.

Bennet and Bower walked out of the kitchen. "Are we about ready to go?" John asked.

"Yup, let's go get your boy," Doc said, putting a hand on Antonio's shoulder.

"Yeah, let's go get him," Antonio agreed with a determined smile.

∞

James and Logan woke to full-fledged screaming and jumped up, confused as to where it was coming from. James ran and switched on the light. They found Carlos on the floor thrashing about in his blankets, sound asleep but screaming at full volume. Logan attempted to free his friend from the blankets, and as soon as he was loose of them, James grabbed him and pulled him tightly to his chest.

"Carlos, wake up," Logan said gently as he stroked his friend's dark hair. Carlos was still struggling, but James was able to hold onto him and Logan finally coaxed him awake.

'Hey buddy, were you having a bad dream?" Logan asked gently.

Carlos didn't answer, just looked around, trying to figure out where he was. He couldn't understand why he couldn't move, and when he realized that James was holding him, stopped trying to get away. He leaned back into his friend's arms and sobbed.

"Carlos, please, what is it?" Logan asked again.

"K-Kendall... It was so cold and there was red all over the ice!" Carlos choked out.

James and Logan looked at each other. "Carlos, it was just a dream," James whispered.

"Yeah, you heard Papa G last night. They know where he is and they're going to bring him home today," Logan said, trying to soothe his friend. "Why don't you tell me what was in the dream?"

Carlos calmed down a little. "We were playing hockey at the pond and we were all having fun. T-Then I looked over and Kendall was lying on the ice, and it was red all around him. He was so cold and we couldn't wake him up."

"Okay, well... we've all been really scared about what's been going on. The weather's colder, and we were just talking yesterday about how the pond will be frozen enough to go skating on, remember? So, all of our fears, combined with the hope that Kendall comes home today, and the fact we were talking about playing hockey, manifested into a nightmare," Logan told him.

"Why was it red?" Carlos sniffed.

"Well, Papa G said that the people who saw Kendall said he was banged up. That, with the fact that one of us almost always gets hurt the first time we go out on the pond made you think of blood," Logan explained.

"I guess that makes sense," Carlos said.

"Sure it does," James said, hugging Carlos.

Sylvia was watching the scene from the doorway, having come running at the sound of her son's screams. She smiled at the boys comforting one another and nodded when she caught Logan's eye.

He smiled at her and nodded back that they were okay. Sylvia closed the door and prayed that this would be over today and that the boys would all be together again soon.

∞

Kendall slowly made his way through the woods, far enough away from the road so he could hide, but close enough to keep it in sight. The sun was finally up all the way, but the temperature was still below freezing, and the sky looked like it might snow at any time.

He really wished he had his boots. His sneakers were not much protection from the cold and they were not as cushioned, so he could feel pain in his right foot every time he took a step. He had put Deesie's gloves on and had his jacket zipped up as high as it would go.

"Ten miles isn't really THAT far," he kept telling himself. He knew he had to get as far away as he possibly could before Deesie woke up, and he hoped he could figure out which way town was. He knew Deesie had turned a couple of times on the way to the cabin. He just needed to find out where.

He had been walking for over an hour when he heard something that made his blood run cold.

"Where are you, you little shit?!" Deesie screamed.

Kendall could tell that the man's voice was carrying from a distance, but he took off at a faster pace, pulling back further from the road.

Chapter 31 ~ Pursuit

The last thing Deesie remembered was telling his little plaything what they would be doing in the near future. He remembered feeling pleasantly relaxed as he laid back on the couch, sipping his warm coffee. It was the most relaxed he had been in days. He smiled to himself as his mind wandered to all the incredible things he was planning on doing to the boy, so much fun planned.

The next thing he knew, he was dreaming of Robert and his brother's blood on his hands. Then he was at the river, putting Robert in the cold ground and crying at the loss.

Dessie jerked awake feeling very strange. "What the hell is wrong with me?" He was groggy and his limbs felt like they weighed a hundred pounds each.

He looked around, but the boy was not in the living room or kitchen. He tried to get up, but found he was a little dizzy, and then it hit him. The other night while camping, Kendall had woken up so quickly.

"He hasn't been taking the sleeping pills, he's been hiding them. Little shit DRUGGED me!"

He got up and steadied himself against the wall. After a minute, rage took over and he started going from room to room. "Where are you? You better hope I don't find you, because when I do, I am going to pound you into the ground!"

He went to his own room and checked in the closet. The boy's boots were still there. He went back into the living room and saw Kendall's jacket was gone.

"Well, he won't get far with only socks on his feet. This time I will make sure he can't walk at all!" Deesie growled, as he grabbed his own coat.

He ran to the SUV and got in. As he backed up, he noticed that it lagged and seemed to be sinking on the passenger's side. He got out and checked to see what was going on and saw the two flat tires. Enraged, he started screaming. "Where are you, you little shit?! You are going to PAY for this!"

Deesie grabbed the hunting knife, handcuffs, and rifle from the back of the SUV. He looked around to see if there were any footprints, but the ground was too cold. He headed off down the driveway, figuring that Kendall would follow it, trying to get back to town.

∞

Kendall was trying to keep up a fast pace, but his foot felt as if it was on fire again. Looking around, he found a thin but sturdy branch that he could use as a walking stick, and being able to lean on it helped a bit. He could hear Deesie screaming obscenities every now and then, but Kendall knew he was a couple of miles ahead of him for now and hoped he could keep it that way.

∞

At Doc Akins' clinic, the four men met up with the sheriff and three deputies from Appleton. Four additional FBI agents showed up a few minutes later. Deesie had taken Kendall across state lines, which made this a federal case. The agents were insisting that the officers be used as back up, not first-on-scene responders.

Before Antonio could say anything, Bower cut in. "Chief Garcia and Officer Bennet have been on this case since day one. They know the suspect and they know Kendall Knight. Given the nature of the crime and the potential harm to the child, there is a very good chance that he

will respond ONLY to someone he knows. He has known Officer Garcia his entire life and trusts him. He also knows Officer Bennet, so they WILL be on front line response. Doc Akins is a local tracker and a fully trained medic. He will be accompanying us as well."

One of the agents grumbled a bit and Antonio looked at him. "Look, I don't give a damn about jurisdictional mandates. I'm not here because I want to collar the bad guy. I don't care if he's tried in state courts or federal courts. I'm here for my godson, and anything beyond that is up to you."

Bower smiled and looked around. "So, we're in agreement then?" he asked in a tone that left no room for question.

After that was settled, they looked at the map and decided the best plan would be to park about two miles from the cabin and hike in, leaving two deputies with the vehicles so they could drive in when needed. The men headed out with Bower, Garcia, Bennet, and Doc sharing an SUV. Doc driving and the other men followed them out, since Doc was the one who knew the area.

"Thanks for that back there," Antonio said to Bower.

"Not a problem, everything I said was true. Besides, it's not as if anyone could have stopped you. This way you aren't arrested for interfering in a federal case, which would have resulted in a LOT of paperwork for me. I hate paperwork," Bower said, smiling.

Antonio smiled and looked out the window. As much as he was glad that this was almost over, he was afraid of what they would find once they got there. They had no idea what physical or emotional condition Kendall was in. He had been able to avoid thinking about it too much in the last couple of days, but now he had to. In his mind, all he could see were the photos of Deesie's last kidnap victim and then the photos Deesie had sent to Janice Lane.

He looked up when he felt the SUV stop and saw Bennet looking at him. "He's going to be okay, he's a strong boy with an amazing family. No matter what help he needs after we get him back, he'll get it."

Antonio smiled at his partner. "I hope so."

"No, you KNOW so. You can't give up on this before he's even home," John said firmly.

"I'm not, I'm just... scared," Antonio admitted.

"Well, snap out of it. He needs you to be strong. God knows he's been strong throughout this whole thing, we can't wimp out on him now."

Antonio looked at his partner and smiled. "Good pep talk."

"Good enough for you NOT to tell Sylvia what I said?"

Antonio snorted. "No, that's just too good not to share."

John sighed. "You suck."

Doc and Bower had been watching the interaction and just smiled and shook their heads.

"What?" John asked, noticing the expression on their faces.

"Not a thing." Doc laughed.

"I still think you should be worried," Bower said as he got out of the SUV.

Antonio smiled smugly at his partner as he joined Bower. "You ALL suck," John mumbled.

Once they were all there, they broke up into teams and headed out. The plan was to travel off-road and surround the cabin once they arrived. The FBI had brought a thermal scanner to determine where in the cabin Deesie and Kendall were located. This would give them an advantage in that they wouldn't be going in completely blind.

Antonio, Bennet, Doc, and Bower made up the first team. They were all wearing a protective vest and, with the exception of Doc, carried both a rifle and handgun. Doc was packing his rifle, binoculars, and a med kit that he always kept on hand.

Doc led them about fifty yards off the road and they headed for the cabin, walking at a brisk pace. After about ten minutes, Doc pulled up and put his finger on his lips.

They all listened carefully and heard someone off in the distance yelling, "Come back here you little shit or it will be all the worse for you when I get my hands on you!"

Antonio and John looked at one another. "Deesie," Antonio hissed and started in the direction of the voice.

Doc grabbed him. "Wait, we need to go slow. The sounds out here carry, and he's further off than you think. If we tip him off that we're here, we lose the advantage."

"He's right. Obviously, he doesn't have Kendall at the moment. We should split up and look for him," Bower suggested.

Antonio nodded in agreement.

Bower got on the radio and let the other teams know. One team would go to the cabin and check it out. If no one were there, they would wait, hiding in the woods. The other team was going to circle around the other way and hopefully catch up to Deesie before he found Kendall.

∞

Kendall had to stop for a couple of minutes to catch his breath. He pulled out the cough meds and swallowed a capful, and then he drank a little Gatorade. His chest hurt and he could hear himself wheeze every now and then. He started coughing and muffled the sound with his arm. He looked up to see it had started to snow. *Really? This is fair!* He thought sarcastically.

As soon as he caught his breath, he took off again. He heard Deesie screaming again and realized the man sounded closer, so he began to run, using the stick for balance.

∞

Deesie had taken off down the road at a run. He had been unconscious for almost two hours and he wasn't sure how far Kendall had gone. He realized the boy was too smart to stay on the road, so after about a mile, he moved to the woods. Every few hundred yards, he would stop and listen. He smiled when he heard someone coughing softly and headed in that direction.

Deesie stopped after a few minutes and listened again. He could hear leaves crunching. His face broke into a twisted smile. "Come out, come out wherever you are!" he called out in singsong.

He was done with the teen's defiant attitude and had decided that once he caught up with the boy, he was going to break him completely. He had always wondered what it would be like to have sex in the woods. Today he planned on finding out. He thought about the satisfaction he would feel holding the boy down and making him his. Then he was going to drag his little ass back to the cabin and beat him senseless. Tomorrow, he would begin his "lessons" again, until the blond did exactly as he was told and how.

∞

Antonio, John, Bower, and Doc separated and began walking in horseshoe formation, with Bennet and Bower on point. They moved slowly, listening carefully for any sounds. They all heard Deesie singing, "Come out, come out," and realized they were close.

They kept going in the same direction with the officers pulling their handguns. Bower signaled to widen the search perimeter, and they panned out a few more yards in both directions. They were still within earshot but were just out of sight of one another. Bower had gotten back on the radio to let the other team know that they needed to come around and hopefully catch Deesie in the middle.

∞

Kendall could hear Deesie close behind and continued running. He slipped a couple of times but managed to stay on his feet. He had just crossed a small clearing and was among the trees again, when he hit something hard and almost fell. Shocked that he was still upright, Kendall looked up into the smiling face of John Bennet.

"Hey kid, need a ride home?" John asked, feeling happier than he had in days.

Kendall was in shock and just nodded. He could feel tears begin to surface and wanted to collapse.

John pulled out his radio. "Anto—"

A shot rang out and Kendall fell forward as Bennet was thrown backwards, still clutching the teen's arms.

Chapter 32~ Found

Antonio heard Bennet on the radio and then a shot. He immediately took off, running in the direction of his partner's last position. He stopped to listen, heard a blood-curdling scream, and took off running again.

"John!" Kendall screamed as the man fell to the ground, blood gushing from the head wound.

"John, please don't die! No..." The older man didn't respond, but Kendall could see his chest rise and fall and knew he wasn't dead yet.

Suddenly, a pair of arms wrapped themselves around his waist and pulled him up and away from Bennet. "You are in so much trouble, sweetheart," Deesie hissed into his ear.

Kendall kicked out and hit at the man, trying to get back to Bennet. "STOP or I will shoot him again," Deesie threatened.

Kendall immediately stopped moving as he watched Deesie point the rifle at John. Deesie reached down, took the officer's handgun and half-carried Kendall back across the clearing.

∞

Antonio slowed down and went carefully through the trees, his handgun drawn and ready. He heard a low moan and made his way towards the sound. He found Bennet lying on the ground, blood all over his face.

He got on the radio. "Doc, Bower, we need assistance. I have an officer down. We are approximately 500 yards due east of my last position."

He checked his partner's pulse and found it strong. He checked the wound on his head but couldn't really tell how bad it was. John moaned again and Antonio held his hand. "It's going to be okay, buddy. You're going to be alright."

Doc arrived with Bower close behind. "Any idea what happened?"

"No, he was on the radio and then I heard the shot and a scream. I found him like this," Antonio told him.

Doc examined Bennet. "Good news is it seems to be superficial. Bad news is he's gonna have quite a headache for a while."

"Thank God," Antonio said in relief.

Bower was looking around and saw footprints in the fresh snow. First there were two sets,then one, and then two again. "Someone else was close."

"I think it was Kendall who screamed," Antonio said.

Bower got on the radio to have someone meet them at the road, so they could get Bennet out of there.

"You two take John up to the car. I'm going to follow these footprints," Antonio said.

"I don't think that's a good idea. The man is armed and will use you and Kendall against one another," Bower told him.

"You said yourself that I may be the only one Kendall responds to. If you get John out of here now, you can meet up with me in a few minutes. It won't be hard since it's not snowing that hard yet," Antonio stated.

"He's right, we're wasting time. Let's get John up to the car and get back," Doc said.

"Alright, but you hang back and do not engage unless absolutely necessary," Bower told Antonio.

Antonio nodded and headed off, following the footprints.

∞

Deesie went as fast as he could, holding Kendall around the waist. He headed away from the cabin, figuring that the police were already there. He stopped for a moment, and keeping ahold of Kendall, pulled him around so they were face to face. "You are going to be VERY sorry for all of this, sweetheart."

He looked around and pulled the boy towards a denser grove of trees. The snow wasn't reaching the ground there yet and it would be harder for someone to find them. He took Kendall's backpack, threw it on the ground, and slapped the walking stick that the boy was still holding from his hand. Pulling out the handcuffs, he put them on the teen's wrists and forced him to sit down on the ground. He looked to see if they had been followed yet, and not seeing anyone, grabbed Kendall's hair and forced him to look in his eyes.

"To be clear, I will kill anyone who comes after us. When we are safe, you and I are going to 'consummate' our little friendship right here in the woods. Then we are going to find a way out of here and I am going to make your life a living hell for as long as I let you live. Do you understand me?" Deesie growled.

Kendall just looked at him, his green eyes full of hate.

Deesie grabbed the boy by the throat and squeezed. "I said do you understand me?"

Kendall stayed silent, hoping the man would just kill him already.

Deesie released him suddenly as he heard a noise. He grabbed Kendall and pulled him up behind a tree, with one arm around his waist holding him tight, and his other hand covering his mouth.

They watched as Antonio made his way across the clearing and into the trees.

"One sound and he is dead," Deesie whispered as he took his hand away from Kendall's mouth. He reached into his pocket and pulled out Bennet's handgun.

Kendall's heart dropped as he saw Antonio get closer.

Antonio followed the footprints cautiously and saw them head into a grove of trees. There were no footprints he could follow, so he moved slowly. He saw something on the ground and recognized Kendall's backpack.

Deesie suddenly appeared from behind a tree with a tight grip on Kendall, holding Bennet's revolver to the boy's head. "Drop your weapons or I kill him here and now."

Antonio put his hands up slowly. "Let's just talk about this calmly."

Deesie cocked the revolver. "I said, drop your weapons NOW!"

There was no way Antonio could make it to him before he hurt Kendall. All he could do at the moment was buy time until Bower and the others followed.

Antonio put his revolver on the ground and then lowered his rifle. "Stephen, you need to stop before this goes any further. Do you really want to hurt him? He's a boy with his life just beginning, he's never hurt anyone."

"So you know who I am. Even after two interviews and a thorough background check, that stupid woman, Lane, never figured it out. It really is amazing how easy it was to fool her. So sure of herself and everything that she does, and yet look at where we are. I took one of her precious students and there wasn't a thing she could do about it. There's nothing you can do about it either," Deesie said as he pulled Kendall a little tighter to him. He gave Antonio a suggestive leer as he moved his hand down Kendall's torso. The boy instinctively started trying to pull away and Deesie laughed.

"No, leave him alone!" Antonio ordered angrily.

Deesie stopped laughing and glared at Antonio. "Stop talking. Drop the radio too."

Antonio did as he was told, watching Deesie closely. He could see the pain and fear in Kendall's eyes and looked at him reassuringly.

"Take out your handcuffs, put them on, and throw the key," Deesie instructed. Antonio took the cuffs from his belt and hooked them around his own wrists, dropping the key where he stood.

"What's your name?" Deesie asked Antonio.

"Garcia."

"I've seen you around the school, your son goes there," Deesie said.

Antonio remained silent.

He pulled Kendall tighter and whispered, "He's one of your little friends, isn't he, sweetheart?"

"How long have you known each other?" Deesie asked Antonio.

Antonio had a very bad feeling as to where this was going. "The boys have been friends for a few years. Why?"

"How long, hmm? Are your families close? I think they are. I can see it in his eyes," Deesie whispered to Kendall.

When the boy didn't reply, he grabbed his hair and yanked his head back. "I asked you a question."

Deesie released his hair when Kendall started coughing and wheezing again. Kendall had a hard time catching his breath and he felt like he might pass out.

"Don't die yet, we still need our quality time," Deesie whispered as he kissed Kendall on the neck.

Antonio took a step forward. "Don't do it," Deesie warned. "Sit there," he told Antonio, indicating a tree about twenty feet away. "Don't move or he pays the price," Deesie told him as he tightened his hold on Kendall.

Antonio walked to the tree, watching the man carefully, gauging the distance between them.

Deesie whispered to Kendall, "Remember what I told you was going to happen earlier? Well, now we have an audience."

He pulled Kendall a little further back into the trees, but to where Antonio could still see. "No!" Kendall yelled as Deesie turned him around and pushed him to the ground.

"What are you doing?" Antonio yelled at him.

"Putting on a little show for you," Deesie said, giving him his twisted smile.

Antonio moved to get up, but Deesie held the gun to Kendall's head. "Uh uh uh, I wouldn't if I were you."

Kendall started trying to push the man away, but Deesie unzipped his jacket and just smiled down at him. Then he grabbed a hold of the flannel shirt and tore it open. He pushed the t-shirt up and started kissing Kendall's chest.

"NO!" he screamed at the man.

Antonio was furious. He couldn't move or Deesie would hurt Kendall, but he couldn't just sit there and do nothing either. "Kendall, look at me. LOOK at me, Mijo, please," Antonio said, trying to remain calm.

Kendall could hear Antonio, but he was desperately trying to move away from the man on top of him. Finally, he looked over to Antonio.

"It's okay. It's going to be alright. Just look at me and don't think about it," Antonio said, his voice breaking.

"Papi, please..." Kendall whispered, his eyes pleading.

"Leave him alone!" Antonio screamed, never having felt so helpless.

Deesie looked at Garcia as he ran his tongue along Kendall's throat. He bit down and whispered. "Don't worry, sweetheart. When we're through, one bullet will take care of all his problems."

Deesie laughed and Kendall felt the man's weight shift as he moved off of him for a split second. Kendall looked up at him and hit at the man, who grabbed his hands. Kendall moved his legs so Deesie was in-between them and not on him. Deesie bent down towards him

and Kendall turned his head to look at Antonio, who was still trying to reassure the boy. Then he looked back up at Deesie, who smiled and said, "You are going to scream for me, sweetheart."

Kendall looked at Deesie, sudden fury in his green eyes. "No, I'm not," he hissed between clenched teeth.

Kendall wrapped his legs around the man's waist and pulled him down just as he slammed his head upward. He felt the cartilage in Deesie's nose crush against his forehead and the man screamed, falling backwards. Kendall pulled his left leg up, and as Deesie sat back up howling in fury, Kendall kicked up and caught the man under the jaw with his foot. Deesie went flying off of him. Kendall flipped over onto his stomach, got up, and ran for the walking stick. He turned just as Deesie got close, and swung the stick hard, hitting the man fully on the hip. The branch broke, but Deesie was slowed. Deesie reached up, grabbed the stick, and pulled it hard, throwing Kendall into a tree.

Antonio was on Deesie before he could move for the boy again.

The men fought for control of the situation. Deesie had lost the gun somewhere during the fight but still had the knife. He finally pinned Antonio, who was fighting at a disadvantage with his cuffed hands. Deesie pulled the knife from the sheath on his belt and raised up, grasping it with both hands, screaming the whole time.

"NO!" Kendall screamed and threw himself on top of Antonio, pushing the part of the stick he was still holding up against Deesie to keep him away.

Suddenly, everything stopped as he realized the man had impaled himself on the broken stick. Kendall looked up in shock at the man, who now had a piece of wood the circumference of a broom handle, sticking through his abdomen. Blood began seeping around the stick and from the man's mouth. Antonio reached around the boy and pushed the man off them. He grabbed Kendall and pulled him away from the man. The boy was staring at Deesie, his eyes wide with horror. He started shaking uncontrollably, not saying anything.

Antonio cupped Kendall's face in his hands. "Look at me, Mijo." Kendall looked into the soft, brown eyes, still unable to speak. Antonio pulled the boy close and put his arms around him.

Suddenly, they heard a wild scream and Deesie was up and running towards them, stick still protruding from his abdomen. Antonio shielded Kendall and a shot rang out, stopping Deesie in his tracks, half of his head gone. Antonio looked in the direction of the shot and saw Doc standing there holding his rifle.

"Don't look up, you don't need to see this," Antonio told Kendall. The boy curled in towards his godfather, still not saying anything.

"Keep your head down, but put your arms around my neck," Antonio said gently.

Kendall reached up and put his arms around Antonio. He stood up, determined to get the boy away from the horrific scene. It wasn't easy carrying him with his hands cuffed together, and he honestly felt like he was going to collapse at any moment.

Suddenly, a soft, deep voice said, "Give him to me." Doc reached over and took Kendall from him.

The boy jumped at the other man's touch. "It's alright, Mijo, you've met Doc. He helped us find you," Antonio said gently, brushing back the boy's bangs. His forehead was bleeding from the impact with Deesie's face, and it was already turning a dark purple.

"Let's get you both out of here," Doc said.

Antonio went over and grabbed Kendall's backpack, his radio, and weapons. He stopped and found the key he had dropped and unhooked the handcuffs as he hurried after Doc and Kendall.

Suddenly, the area was overrun with deputies and FBI. Doc and Antonio ignored them and headed for the car.

They got to the SUV and Bennet was lying in the back compartment. His head was bandaged and he was suffering from the worst headache of his life. He had regained

consciousness as Doc and Bower carried him to the vehicle but refused to leave until they had Kendall.

He looked over at Antonio. "Deesie?"

"Dead," Antonio answered quietly.

Antonio sat in the back seat and Doc handed Kendall to him. Kendall curled up into a ball, his face pressed against Antonio. He was clutching the man's shirt with both hands.

Antonio reached down and unlocked the cuffs on his wrists. Doc tried to look him over, but Kendall shied away from his touch. The boy was shaking and had another coughing fit.

"I'd say let's head out for the hospital, but he's in shock and probably hypothermic, so I think we should stop at my clinic first. I can get him started on some warm fluids and hopefully take care of that head," Doc said as he got into the driver's seat.

Antonio nodded as he held Kendall tight, a tear of relief rolling down his cheek.

Chapter 33~ Hypothermia and Headaches

Doc drove slowly down the dirt road, trying to avoid as many bumps as he could. He looked in the rearview mirror and watched Antonio holding Kendall.

"Antonio, does he feel warm or cold to the touch?"

Antonio felt Kendall's cheek. "He's really cold."

"See if you can keep him awake until we get him warmed up. We should be there in about ten minutes," Doc instructed.

Antonio stroked Kendall's hair. "Kendall, wake up son. I need you to try and talk to me." When he got no response, Antonio patted his cheek, "Kendall, wake up. I need you to stay awake for me."

The only response he got was a small whimper.

"I can't get him to wake up, Doc, and he's not shivering anymore," Antonio said, his concern growing.

"Alright, John hold on. I'm going to speed up, which means the ride gets bumpier," Doc warned.

John braced himself and winced at every bump but said nothing. They arrived at Doc's clinic about five minutes later. Doc jumped out and opened Antonio's door. He took Kendall from Antonio, and as soon as he got out, Doc handed him back to his godfather.

"We'll be right back for you, John," he told Bennet as he ran to the clinic door and unlocked it.

He led Antonio down a small hallway to his office. "Put him on the couch, it's warmer in here," Doc instructed. "Do you think you can manage with John or do you want me to get him?" Doc asked as he grabbed some blankets and sweats, that he kept there, out of his closet.

"I can get him, just take care of Kendall, please," Antonio said as he headed back to the SUV.

Doc grabbed his med kit, pulled out the thermometer, and placed it in Kendall's ear. He cursed when he saw the boy's temperature was 89.5. He pulled off the teen's wet sneakers and socks. Then he wrapped his arm around his thin waist and pulled him up so he could remove his jacket and flannel shirt. Both were soaked with melted snow and blood. He grabbed bandage scissors from his bag and cut off the t-shirts, and was shocked to see the condition the boy was in—there were bruises and welts everywhere.

He quickly pulled the sweatshirt over the boy's head, wanting to get him into it before Antonio got back in.

Next, he cut off the jeans and found massive bruising on his legs as well. He pulled the sweatpants onto the boy as Antonio half-carried John through the door and sat him in the overstuffed chair by the window.

Doc tucked the heavy blankets around Kendall. "Stay with him, his temperature is too low. I'm going to grab some warm fluids and supplies," Doc said as he quickly ran to one of the exam rooms to get what he needed.

He returned a couple of minutes later with everything he might possibly need. He pulled strips of tape off and stuck them to the side of the couch so they were within easy reach. Next, he placed a tourniquet around Kendall's right arm.

"Hold his arm steady for me," he instructed Antonio as he opened a catheter. Antonio held the boy's arm out straight for Doc, but turned his head when Doc inserted the catheter into Kendall's vein.

Doc capped the catheter and taped it in place. Next, he grabbed the bag of fluids, which already had a line attached, and hung it from the light fixture above the couch. He removed the cap, attached the line directly to the catheter, and taped it securely. He twisted the dial to open full flow.

He watched the line to make sure it was flowing properly and then grabbed his stethoscope. He placed in on Kendall's chest and listened to first his heart and then his lungs.

"Okay, his heart sounds good, but we're not moving him until his temperature is up to 95 degrees and he's responsive. His lungs are crackly though and he's wheezing a lot, so chances are he has pneumonia."

"What is his temperature?" Antonio asked.

"It was a little over 89 before I got him out of those wet clothes. He should start warming up soon. I have another bag of fluids in the incubator to replace this one when it runs out. He's pretty dehydrated," Doc told him.

Doc started cleaning the wound on his forehead. "How did this happen?"

"He head-bashed Deesie," Antonio said.

Doc checked Kendall's eyes. "His eyes are responding properly, so I don't think he has a concussion. Speaking of... How's your head, John?" Doc asked as he got up to check on the man.

"Well, I've felt better, but I'll be fine." John smiled.

"We're lucky it was just your head. I don't know what we'd have done if he'd hit anything important," Antonio teased his friend.

John just looked at him, "When my thoughts clear, I will come up with a crushing retort."

"So... never," Antonio said smugly.

"You suck," John sighed.

Doc just shook his head at the two, glad that they were able to joke after everything that they had been through the last few days.

John looked at Antonio. "Shouldn't you call home and let them know we have Kendall and that he's safe?"

"I was going to wait until we got to the hospital, but maybe you're right. I want to wait until he's awake, though," Antonio said. "I'm going to give Sally a call and let her know what's going on."

Antonio pulled out his cell and called the station.

"Hey Boss, what's going on?" Sally asked.

"Hey Sally, I wanted to call and give you an update. We found Kendall. We're at Doc's clinic in Jamieson, because he's suffering from hypothermia and shock. We'll be taking him to Appleton County Hospital as soon as he's stable enough to move... John too," Antonio told her.

"What happened to John?"

"Deesie shot him. The bullet grazed his head and he has a possible concussion," Antonio told her.

"Where's Deesie?"

"Dead... Doc shot him. I'll explain everything in detail once we get home. Could you do me a favour and call Janice Lane and let her know?" Antonio asked.

"Sure thing, Boss. Have you called home yet?"

"No. I will as soon as Kendall wakes up though, which should be any time now," Antonio said.

"How is he, besides the shock and hypothermia?" she asked, not sure if she wanted to know the answer.

"We won't really know for sure until we get him to the hospital. We knew he was pretty bruised from the photos. As for anything else, I just don't want to think about it right now," he told her.

"I understand. Give Kendall and John my love. We'll all be happier when you're all safely home. I'll give Janice a call and let her know and tell her to keep it quiet for now. Before I forget, we did get some good news today. Ranger Thompson regained consciousness and his condition has been upgraded to serious but stable."

"That's great! Thanks Sally, you're the best," Antonio said, smiling.

"I know, but thanks for telling me," she teased.

"Alright, I'll talk to you later, probably after we get to the hospital and get these two checked in," Antonio said.

"Okay, talk to you then," Sally said, hanging up.

Antonio went back in to the office and sat next to Kendall. He touched his cheek and was glad to feel he was getting warmer. He looked over at John, who was starting to nod off.

"John, wake up! No sleeping until we get to the hospital. If you need, I can call someone and have them take you now."

"Nope, I'm fine. Not leaving you guys, so just wake me up if you see me trying to sleep," John said.

"Okay." Antonio smiled at his partner, thinking again how lucky he was to have him.

Doc came back in and checked Kendall's temperature again. "93.6." He checked the fluids and hung the other bag, switching the lines. "Why don't you try talking to him and see if you can get him to come around?" Doc suggested.

Antonio nodded. "Kendall, hey buddy, it's Papi. Please wake up now."

Kendall stirred and tried to shift onto his right side. He moaned as he moved and tried kicking out his legs.

"Hey, it's okay, Mijo. You're safe now," Antonio said softly.

Kendall started coughing and panicked when he couldn't seem to catch his breath.

"DOC!" Antonio yelled.

"Sit him up, but hold him and don't let him pull out the catheter!" Doc said as he ran for his portable oxygen machine. He wheeled the machine over and plugged it in, pulling out a new mask and opening it.

Antonio pulled Kendall up and was holding him with his right arm pinned, so the catheter remained intact.

Kendall was in a full-blown panic attack, not being able to breath and not knowing who was holding onto him. He tried to scream, but nothing came out and he couldn't seem to draw a breath.

"Hold him to you, so that his head is over your shoulder," Doc instructed.

Antonio did as he was told and Doc was able to place the oxygen mask over Kendall's face. He turned it on full. Kendall struggled against it, but Antonio and Doc held on firmly.

"Damn it, breathe, I don't want to have to intubate you," Doc said.

"Doc..." Antonio begged.

Kendall's chest was heaving as he tried to breathe, and Doc could see his lips were turning blue.

"Hold him," Doc said as he removed the mask, and pinching Kendall's nose closed, he reached over, forced a breath into the boy's mouth, and then inhaled deeply. He did it once more and then replaced the mask.

A few seconds later, Kendall took a small breath on his own and then another. After a minute, his breathing was almost normal and he had collapsed against Antonio.

John had been watching, feeling completely helpless. Once Kendall was breathing, he looked at Doc. "What was that?"

Doc looked at him and smiled. "An old rancher's trick. When you have a newborn sheep, goat, or something smaller, and they can't breathe, it's a way to test to see if their lungs

are working properly. Sometimes their bodies just don't know how to breathe until you show them. Doesn't happen that often, but if they seem healthy and their lungs have been cleared, it works. Only works on the smaller animals though, because you've got to be able to fill their lungs and then suck it back out."

"The things you learn that you never knew you didn't really want to know," John quipped.

"What?" Antonio asked him.

"Never mind. I know what I meant," John said.

Kendall was lying against Antonio. He was shaking but breathing normally now.

"What would have happened if it didn't work?" John asked.

"Then I would have intubated him, and we would have had to call an ambulance to transport you boys now. Luckily, that wasn't the case."

Doc grabbed a couple of pillows from the closet and piled them on the couch. "Try lying him down now," Doc told Antonio.

Antonio gently lay Kendall back on the pillows. The boy stirred and his eyes fluttered open and then closed again.

"Kendall, can you hear me?" Antonio asked him.

Kendall opened his eyes again, trying to focus his vision. He shifted onto his right shoulder, trying to take the pressure off his left, whimpering as he moved.

"Let me check him," Doc said. When he moved to lift the sweatshirt, Kendall pulled away, eyes wide.

"It's okay, Mijo, it's Doc and he's only trying to help," Antonio said as he pulled Kendall up into his arms again.

He could feel the boy tense as Doc lifted the shirt and again as Doc touched his back. Antonio just held him, stroking his hair, telling him that it was alright. Kendall relaxed at Antonio's reassurances, until Doc reached his left shoulder blade and he screamed.

"What the hell? It looks like a small puncture wound here at the base of his shoulder blade. There's a large localized hematoma here and his shoulder's warm," Doc said.

"Deesie threw him against a tree," Antonio said.

"Maybe," Doc said unconvinced. "The hospital will be able to check it out further."

Antonio helped Kendall lay back down on his right side. "Is that better?"

Kendall looked up at him, his eyes filling with tears. "P-Papi, he killed John. He shot him in the head." His voice was raspy and weak.

Antonio was confused, and then he realized that Kendall didn't know that John was alive and sitting there, right behind him. "No, no Mijo. John is not dead. The bullet just grazed him."

Kendall shook his head. "I saw him. He was all bloody and wouldn't wake up! So many people hurt because of me."

John heard and struggled to get up.

Doc pointed at him. "Wait." He pushed his desk chair over and helped John into it. Then he pushed the chair over to the couch, next to Kendall.

"Hey buddy. I'm okay, see," John said, reaching down and taking the boy's hand. "I promised you a ride home and I'm going to see that you get it."

Kendall was confused and was trying to process everything that he had seen. He couldn't seem to put his thoughts into any rational order and finally just accepted that it was really John sitting there.

"I thought..." Kendall said, suddenly very tired.

"Hey, he hit me in the head. Couldn't possibly do any damage there," John said, smirking at Antonio.

Antonio smiled and looked from his partner to his godson, who was now sleeping.

Doc checked Kendall's temperature again and it was up to 95.4. "We can leave for the hospital as soon as the fluids are done," Doc told Antonio.

"Okay. John can you sit here with him while I call home?" Antonio asked.

"Sure thing," John replied.

Antonio went and sat in the chair that Bennet had vacated and called home.

∞

Everyone was on edge at the Garcia home. The boys hadn't slept after Carlos' nightmare, and everyone jumped whenever the phone rang.

Jen was baking in the kitchen, trying to keep her mind occupied, and Brooke paced the house nearly wearing a path in the floors. Joanna was trying to keep the children distracted with a board game and Sylvia had joined them.

The phone rang and Sylvia checked the caller ID. "Antonio!"

"Hi honey, can you put me on speaker?"

"Jen, Brooke, come in here!" Sylvia called, as she sat the phone on the table and hit the speaker button. Both women came running in and took a seat on the couch.

"Everyone's here sweetie," Sylvia told him.

"We have Kendall. We're going to be heading for the Appleton County Hospital in a few minutes. He's doing okay, but we need to get him checked out," he told them.

"Where are you now? Can I speak to him?" Jen asked.

"We're at Doc Akins' clinic in Jamieson, and he's actually sleeping right now. He's in shock and hypothermic, so we brought him here to get him warmed up. Doc is a licensed medic and has been taking good care of him. His temperature is much better now, so we'll be leaving soon. I'll give you a call from the hospital after they examine him, and he should be able to talk by then."

"What about Deesie?" Brooke asked.

"He's dead. He won't be hurting anyone else," Antonio said.

"Is everyone else alright?" Sylvia asked.

"Deesie shot John, but the bullet just grazed him. He's doing okay, but he'll be checking into the hospital as well," Antonio said.

"You're okay, right Papi?" Carlos asked.

"I'm fine, Mijo. Just anxious to get home now." Antonio smiled.

"When do you think that will be?" Jen asked.

"Honey, it all depends on what the doctors say. I'm thinking they'll keep them both overnight, so hopefully we'll be on our way home tomorrow," Antonio said softly.

Jen looked like she would cry again. "I was hoping..."

'I know, Jen, but we need to make sure he's okay. I know it's hard, but he's safe and not leaving my sight," Antonio said reassuringly. "We'll call you from the hospital as soon as he's able to talk, okay?"

"Okay." Jen smiled. "Please give him a hug and tell him I love him, that we ALL love him," she said as she looked around the room. "The same with John, and tell Doc Akins, thank you."

"I will. We better get going now. It won't be too much longer before we're home, I promise."

"Antonio, thank you," Jen whispered.

"You don't have to thank family for looking after their own. Talk to you soon." He smiled.

He hung up and walked over to Kendall and John. He bent down, kissed Kendall on the head, and gave John a hug. "That's from the family at home."

John smiled and chuckled. "I feel so special right now... so close to you."

"Shut up," Antonio retorted, rolling his eyes.

Chapter 34~ The Hospital

Antonio looked at the clock. He couldn't believe it was barely noon. It felt like he had been awake for days. They were just getting ready to head out for Appleton. Doc was capping off Kendall's catheter and wrapping it.

"Okay, I'm going to help John out first, he'll ride shotgun, and then we'll get you and Kendall situated in the backseat," Doc said.

Antonio looked at him. "Doc, you don't have to drive in with us, you've done more than enough."

"Don't be ridiculous, Kendall needs someone to hold onto him and John isn't strong enough. I'll just have my boy drive over and pick me up after school," Doc told him.

Antonio smiled gratefully. "I really don't know what we would have done without you. Kendall and I would both be dead now."

Doc just smiled. "We all do what we can," he said softly as he walked over to John and helped him up. "Let's get you out."

Antonio went over to the couch and sat next to Kendall, who had been sleeping peacefully for the better part of an hour now. He hated to wake him, but he didn't want to frighten him by just picking him up.

"Kendall, it's time for us to go now, you need to wake up for a minute. You can go back to sleep in the car."

Kendall stirred, pulling the blanket tighter.

"It's time to get up, sleepyhead." Antonio laughed as he pulled on the blanket gently.

Suddenly Kendall snapped awake and pulled back, not sure where he was.

"It's okay. It's Papi, you're safe and we're here in Doc's clinic, remember?" Antonio asked softly.

Kendall's eyes focused and he relaxed as he saw Antonio.

"Are you okay now?" Antonio asked.

The boy took a deep breath and nodded.

"Good. We're getting ready to go now. Doc is helping John out to the car," Antonio said.

"John... he's okay, right?" Kendall asked in a small voice.

"He's fine, Mijo, just a headache, remember?"

Kendall nodded as he struggled to put the events of the day into some kind of order, but his mind was still foggy. "Are we going home?"

"Soon, we have to get you and John checked out at the hospital first," Antonio told him.

"I don't want to go to the hospital, I want to go home." Kendall started rocking back and forth. He didn't want anyone to see or touch him, and he knew they would.

Antonio hugged him. "We will, I promise. But we need to make sure that you're both alright."

"I don't want to go!" Kendall repeated, trying not to panic.

"I know you don't, but it's going to be okay. I'll be with you the whole time, I'm not going to let anyone hurt you," Antonio promised.

Doc came back into the office. "Everything okay in here?" he asked, seeing the look on Kendall's face.

"It'll be fine, he's just worried about going to the hospital," Antonio explained.

"Well, I don't blame you there. I'm not much for hospitals myself. John really needs to get his head checked out though, he might have a concussion," Doc explained to the boy. "Plus, you don't want to be on the road and have another coughing spell where you can't breathe, do you?"

Kendall thought about it, he didn't really remember what happened, but it didn't sound like something he wanted to happen again. "N-No, not really."

"Well, the sooner we get there and get the two of you checked out, the sooner you'll be on your way home. The best thing when you have to do something you don't want to do is to just get it over with and move on with things." Doc smiled.

Kendall looked at Doc and Antonio and sighed. He knew he could trust them, but he still didn't want to go.

The two men gave him a moment and finally he nodded. "Okay."

"That's my boy." Antonio smiled.

"You promise you'll stay with me?"

"I'm not leaving your side," Antonio promised again.

Kendall looked at Doc. "Will you stay with John?"

"Of course I will. Now why don't we get going?" Doc smiled.

Kendall's shoes and jacket were still wet, so Doc put them into a bag while Antonio wrapped one of the blankets around Kendall. "Put your arm around my neck, Mijo."

Kendall wrapped an arm around Antonio's neck and Antonio put one arm around the boy's waist and the other under his legs and lifted him off the couch. Doc led the way to the SUV and opened the door. Antonio helped Kendall inside, got in next to him, and then buckled them both in. Doc got into the driver's seat.

"I called ahead and they're expecting us, so you boys can get right in."

"Thanks Doc. How long do you think it'll be before we get there?" John asked.

"Well, if the roads are good, less than an hour, a little longer if it's icy."

"Sounds good." John was getting tired and really wanted something for his headache.

Kendall was already half asleep and leaning against Antonio. A few minutes later, he was sound asleep and Antonio was holding him.

∞

They arrived at the hospital close to an hour later. Doc ran inside to let the emergency personnel know they were there and grabbed a wheelchair for John.

An intern brought a gurney out for Kendall, but Antonio waved them off as he picked up the sleeping boy. "Kendall, it's time to wake up, we're at the hospital," Antonio whispered as he carried the teen inside.

"Hmmm?" Kendall mumbled.

"Time to wake up, we're here," Antonio told him again.

Kendall opened his eyes and curled in towards Antonio, shaking, sensing too many people around him.

"It's alright, we're going into a room," Antonio told him as he followed a nurse through the waiting area.

She led them down the hallway and stopped at a room. "We're going to put you in here for now. Your doctor will be here momentarily," she told John.

Doc nodded and pushed John into the room.

A couple of minutes later, Dr. Natalie Talbot introduced herself and looked at Bennet's head. She was about fifty with auburn hair and soft brown eyes that smiled when she did.

"Well, looks like we need to send you up for a CT scan and make sure there's no permanent damage, and maybe a couple of stitches."

"Stitches? I HATE needles!" John whined.

"You got shot in the head and you're worried about a couple of stitches?" Doc laughed.

"It's NOT funny! I hate needles!" John repeated defensively. "A bullet is really fast and it's over before you know it happened, but stitches take FOREVER, and they poke you with that stingy stuff to numb it!"

"Well, we could forego the stingy stuff if you like," Dr. Talbot said, smiling.

"But then I'll feel the stitches!" John complained.

"How OLD are you?" Doc asked, still laughing at him.

"Needles hurt!" he declared, pouting as the nurse wheeled him out of the room.

"How are you, Doc, and how's that son of yours?" Dr. Talbot asked.

"We're doing alright, Natalie, thank you. Some days are better than others, but you know how it is." Doc smiled.

∞

Dr. Talbot had been the doctor on duty the night Laura had been killed. After he had received the call, he broke every speed limit getting there. He had come in to find Natalie holding Laura's hand and telling her that her family was on the way and not to be scared. There was nothing they could do for her—both kidneys damaged beyond repair and other internal injuries, but Natalie had stayed with her until Doc and Jake Jr. arrived.

Laura died just a little while later, and while he sat there holding the lost love of his life, Natalie held his son and told him it was alright to cry and to let it all out.

Doc had been impressed by her empathy, and they had been friends ever since.

During the summer, her husband, Doc, and their kids would go fishing, and then they would have a cookout afterwards.

∞

"That I do," she said softly. "Are you going to wait here for your friend?"

"If that's alright."

"Of course it is." She smiled.

Antonio lay Kendall on the hospital bed and sat next to him, stroking his hair and telling him it was going to be alright. The teen was shaking again, more from nervousness than cold, but Antonio made sure he was covered with the warm blanket from Doc's office. The hospital blankets were so thin, and he knew from experience they did little to warm you.

A man in his late 50's or early 60's walked in and introduced himself as Dr. Shaw.

Antonio stood and shook his hand. "I'm Antonio Garcia and this is Kendall Knight. I think Doc Akins called ahead to explain things?"

Dr. Shaw glanced at the clipboard in his hand. "Yes, it seems so. Well, how are we doing?" Shaw asked Kendall.

Kendall just looked at him and curled up as far back against the bed railing as he could.

"Well, we can't examine you like that, so why don't you sit up and scoot over to the edge of the bed?" Shaw instructed.

Kendall looked at Antonio and shook his head.

"Dr. Shaw, could I speak to you for a minute?" Antonio asked, becoming annoyed with the man's attitude.

"Just a moment," Shaw said as he rang for a nurse. "Are you Kendall's guardian?"

"I'm his godfather and have his mother's authorization for care. Why?"

"Then I'm afraid I'll have to ask you to step out. It's doctor's discretion as whether to allow non-family members in an exam room, and I think he'll do better without you here."

A male nurse walked past Antonio and over to Kendall.

"Now, wait just one damn minute! I am the boy's godfather and I am the police officer who is responsible for his care. I WILL be present. If you need me to, I'll get his mother on the phone and you can speak to her," Antonio said, his voice rising.

"Nurse Peters, please get the boy into a gown so I can examine him," Shaw instructed. "Mr. Garcia, we have rules tha—"

"Don't touch him, he's still in shock!" Antonio interrupted, warning the nurse.

"PAPI!" Kendall screamed as the nurse took ahold of his arm. He pulled away and fell back over the bed railing, onto the floor. He crawled under the bed, curling himself into a ball and screaming, holding his arms over his head.

Antonio lost it and shoved past the doctor. "GET AWAY FROM HIM!" he screamed at the nurse, who had pushed the bed against the wall and was now trying to pull Kendall out from under it by his foot. He grabbed the nurse and pulled him away from the boy. "I will arrest you for assault if you take ONE MORE STEP!" Antonio growled when the nurse made a move towards him.

Shaw had walked back to the call button and was calling for security when Dr. Talbot and Doc came running in, having heard the commotion from next door. Dr. Talbot ordered Nurse Peters out of the room and turned to confront Shaw, but Doc was there before she could say a word.

Doc took one look at Antonio trying to comfort the boy, who was now somehow on the floor, and grabbed Shaw by the collar, pulled him out of the room, and pushed him up against the wall in the hallway. He had dealt with this self-righteous prig before and had a pretty good idea of what had happened.

"Now you listen to me. That boy has been through hell the last few days, and the LAST thing he needs is some sanctimonious, over-bearing, dim-witted doctor with a God complex, manhandling him. That OFFICER in there is his godfather and he will stay with Kendall for as long as the boy wants him there! You are a disgrace to your profession and the main reason I cannot stand most human doctors. I don't know how so many of you lose your humanity, but you do. You better hope on the day you need a good doctor that someone better than you is available," Doc said in a low voice. "Now get the hell away from here before I lose my temper!" Doc yelled as he pushed the man down the hallway and away from Kendall's room.

∞

Antonio was trying to calm Kendall down. The boy had stopped screaming, but he was now curled into a tight ball and not responding to anyone.

"I am so sorry, Dr. Shaw is not known for his sympathetic nature and I'm not even going to try and excuse it. Peters is Dr. Shaw's usual assigned nurse, but was clearly the wrong choice for this patient's care," Natalie said.

"I don't think he even read the damn file," Antonio said angrily.

"Probably not in depth," Natalie admitted. "Do you think you can get him up and back on the bed?"

"Mijo, I need to get you off of this cold floor, okay?" Antonio whispered. Kendall didn't respond, so Antonio slowly put his arms under the boy and picked him up. Doc grabbed the bed and pulled it closer and Antonio lay Kendall down on it. Sitting next to him, Antonio ran his fingers through the boy's hair, trying to soothe him.

Natalie dimmed the lights. "Just sit in here with him for a while. I'll come and check on you in a bit, and we'll see how he's doing then."

Antonio nodded. "Thank you."

Natalie and Doc left the room and she closed the door gently behind them. "That was a pretty little scene I must say," she said, arching an eyebrow at Doc.

"Well, I can't stand that man and I am NOT sorry for what I said. He's had it coming for quite some time now."

She smiled at him. "You do know he will try and press charges?"

"Let him, I know a few things about the good Dr. Shaw that I think he'd rather remain unspoken," Doc said.

"You amaze me, do you know that? You are the sweetest, most even-tempered person I've ever known, and yet, when someone crosses the line, you go all papa bear on them." Natalie smiled.

'That's a good thing though, right?"

"A very good thing. Now I'm going to go over the file that Shaw should have read, and you can fill me in with whatever you know," she said.

"Good plan," Doc said as they walked to the admissions desk.

∞

Antonio sat with Kendall, just speaking to him quietly. He told him about Doc's home and how he had collected eggs from actual chickens and threw hay out to the cows and horses. He told him about Doc's mare that was ready to have her baby anytime now and how she had taken carrots from him.

"Maybe we can come back and visit here this summer. Doc says the fishing is great and you boys can go horseback riding with his son. What do you think?" Antonio asked.

Kendall didn't say anything, but moved and put his arms around Antonio's waist, holding him tightly.

"It's alright, it's been a hell of a week, and what just happened was wrong. I broke my promise to you and I'm sorry," Antonio said quietly, his voice breaking.

"No you didn't," Kendall whispered.

"Yes, I did. I promised you that no one here would hurt you and they did."

"Wasn't your fault. Can we really come back and visit Doc?" Kendall asked.

"We sure can. How are you feeling now?"

"Everything hurts," Kendall told him.

"Would it be okay if Dr. Talbot checked you out? She seems really nice," Antonio asked hopefully.

Kendall looked at him and nodded, curling up against Antonio's chest. "I'm not going anywhere and that's a promise I'm keeping," Antonio said, holding the boy tight.

A few minutes later, Dr. Talbot and Doc came back in. "How are you two doing?" she asked.

"Better." Antonio smiled. "Kendall said that you can check him out, but I AM staying."

"Of course you are. Oh, and just to let you know, your friend next door, John, has a mild concussion. He had to have four stitches, but he's going to be just fine. I do want to keep him for the night so we can monitor him though," she told them.

"Not a problem," Antonio said.

"Kendall, can you tell me how you're feeling?" Natalie asked.

"Everything hurts," he said quietly.

"Okay, what hurts the most?" she asked.

'My chest and back."

"Is it okay if I listen to your lungs?" she asked softly. "Doc thinks you might have pneumonia."

Kendall looked at her and nodded, sitting up but staying within contact of Antonio.

"Okay, could you lift your sweatshirt just a little?" Natalie asked, putting her stethoscope to her ears.

Kendall bit his lower lip, and she waited for a moment, until he slowly raised the shirt.

She smiled and slowly placed the stethoscope on his chest and listened for a moment. "I'm going to put this on your back now, okay?" He nodded and she slowly moved the instrument to his back and listened. "Looks like Doc was right, although I didn't really doubt it. Do you know what it means to have crackly lungs?"

Kendall shook his head no.

"Here, take this," she said, handing him the stethoscope. "Now if Antonio will allow it, you can listen to his lungs for a minute and I'll show you the difference."

Antonio nodded and she took the chest piece and placed it on Antonio's chest. "Put those in your ears, and if Antonio would take a deep breath?"

Antonio did as he was asked, smiling at her. He was grateful that she was good with trauma victims.

"Okay, did you hear a whoosh when he inhaled?"

Kendall nodded.

"That's a clear lung. Now, I'm going to take the chest piece and put it back on your chest, okay?"

When he nodded, she placed it over his lung. "Now take a breath and listen."

Kendall took a breath and looked at her.

"Did you hear a sound like someone crinkling paper?"

Kendall nodded again.

"That is the congestion in your lungs. It's caused by fluid build-up, which means you're going on antibiotics." She smiled.

"Okay," he said quietly.

"Now, we need to check out those bruises, and Doc said your shoulder is bothering you. Would you be willing to put on a gown? You can keep your sweatpants on, but it would be easier to examine your back without the sweatshirt. I can leave the room until you're ready."

Kendall sighed, taking the gown from her. "You don't have to leave."

"Okay, how about I just turn around then?" She smiled, turning her back so he could change.

He tried to pull the shirt up, but couldn't raise his arm too far, so Antonio helped him out of it. Antonio tried not to show any emotion as he saw the bruising up close, but felt sorrow and anger course through his veins again. Kendall sat with his legs over the side of the bed so Dr. Talbot could look at his back.

"Are you ready?" Natalie asked as she walked over to the bed.

Kendall nodded, and she carefully pushed the gown open so she could get a better look at his back. She winced when she saw all the bruises and the hematoma Doc had described. She carefully touched the boy's shoulder blade and he pulled away.

She pulled the gown closed and looked at him. "Honey, I think we need to start you back on some fluids. That way we can get you on some IV antibiotics and something for the pain. How does that sound?"

Kendall looked at Antonio, who nodded.

"You're not going to make me go to sleep are you?" Kendall asked.

"Not if you don't want me to, but the pain medicine will make you a little sleepy. I think you need it though. Your shoulder really hurts, doesn't it?" she asked softly.

He sighed again and nodded.

"Is it alright then? Antonio will stay here with you, I promise."

Kendall nodded again.

"Okay, let me get the nurse to get the IV line set up. NOT that nurse," she said, seeing the sudden panic on his face. "He's gone home for the day and is not allowed in here. Nurse Patrick will set up the line, and since Doc already placed a catheter, it will only take a minute." She smiled.

A few minutes later, the fluids were running and Kendall was leaning against Antonio. Natalie came in and explained that she was going to inject the antibiotic, ampicillin, into the fluid bag, and then some morphine into the catheter port on his hand. He watched her closely, and after a few minutes, found himself starting to get sleepy.

"Okay honey, I'm going to look at your shoulder a little more closely now," Natalie said as she pushed the gown down slightly. She located the small puncture wound that Doc had told her about and carefully pushed against his shoulder blade. He whimpered a little but didn't pull away. She examined the rest of his back and then asked Antonio to help her lay Kendall back. Once he was lying on his back, she pulled the gown up to examine his chest. The boy seemed to be sleeping now, so she wanted to get this done quickly.

She gestured for Antonio to come closer so she could talk to him quietly.

"Okay, I'm going to examine his legs now. Doc said they're pretty bruised as well. I'm going to cover him from the waist down with a drape in case he comes around, because I don't want him feeling vulnerable. I understand we probably need to take photos and run a rape kit?"

Antonio nodded. "Yes, I need to know what happened, if at all possible."

"Okay, we're going to get that done now, and then get him settled into a room. Do you think he'd want to be in with John?"

"That would be great. I can sleep in a chair and keep an eye on them," he said.

She nodded and gave instructions to Nurse Patrick.

Antonio sat at the head of the bed, so Kendall would see him if he woke up while Dr. Talbot performed the rest of the exam. She quickly took photos and sent the camera out before he woke up, not wanting him to see it. When she was done, she and the nurse got Kendall back into the sweats and covered him with the blanket.

"So there aren't any physical signs of sexual assault, although you and I both know that's not definitive, and it doesn't mean other things didn't happen."

Antonio nodded. "What else did you find?"

"Well, the bruising on his torso and legs were caused by severe blows from either a fist or foot. He has several bruised ribs, but no broken ones. There are a few bruised areas that appear to be bite marks, but with all the other bruising, it's hard to tell at this point. The puncture wound on his shoulder looks like it was made by a needle of some sort, and the muscle is severely traumatized and possibly separated from the scapula, which is causing all of the pain. He also has puncture wounds on the bottom of his right foot, which are spaced out and deep into the muscle."

"So they were deliberate?" Antonio asked.

"All of these wounds were deliberate, and that's not even taking into account the emotional and psychological trauma. He's going to need counseling and a lot of understanding."

"He'll get it," Antonio said.

"I know he will," she said, patting him on the shoulder. "I'm going to have him moved into the room before he wakes up, and have them bring in a cot for you. No reason for you to sleep on a chair."

"Thank you for everything."

"You're welcome. I'll be in to check on him in a while," she said as she pressed the call button for the nurse.

Antonio went back to Kendall's bedside and sighed. "It's going to be alright, whatever you need, you'll get."

∞

A little while later, Kendall had been taken to the room he was to share with John, who was sitting up in bed, talking to Doc. "How is he?"

"He should be okay," Antonio said, relaying what Dr. Talbot had found.

"Thank God for small favours," Bennet said.

"True, but we won't know everything that happened until Kendall tells us," Antonio said.

John looked at his partner. "He'll be okay."

Antonio smiled. "How's your head?"

"Better since I have drugs." John grinned.

"Good." Antonio laughed.

Kendall stirred and Antonio went to sit next to him. "Papi, where are we?"

"We're in your hospital room. You get to share with John, and they're going to bring in a cot so I can sleep next to you," Antonio told him. "How are you feeling?"

"Meh head's thick," he slurred.

"That would be the morphine, it's normal. How about I call home, so you can talk to your Mami?"

Kendall nodded.

Antonio quickly dialed home.

"Hi sweetie! How is everyone?" Sylvia asked.

"Hi honey, everyone is doing okay. They gave Kendall some pain medication and I wanted him to talk to Jen before he falls asleep."

"Let me get her," Sylvia said and called Jen.

"Hello?" Jen answered anxiously.

"Hey Jen, someone here wants to say hi." He held the phone up to Kendall's ear. "Mijo, it's your Mami."

Kendall heard his mom calling him. "Kendall... baby, how are you?"

"M-Mama, 's'that you?"

"Yes baby, it's mama," Jen said, her voice breaking.

"Hi mama, you okay?"

"I'm fine now," she said, tears filling her eyes.

"Katie and the guys okay?"

Jen quickly put the phone on speaker. "Everyone's fine, baby, we're just so glad to hear your voice."

Everyone had come running, and were now gathered around the phone.

"Kendall!" Katie yelled.

He smiled a little as his eyes closed. "Hey Katie-Bug."

"Why does your voice sound so funny?"

Antonio's voice came back on the line. "They gave him something for pain and it's making him sleepy. I'll have him call again when he's awake."

"Hi Papi!" Carlos yelled.

"Hey Carlos, are you boys doing okay?" Antonio asked. He was worried about James and Logan, knowing they felt guilty about what had happened at school that day.

"Better now," James said, smiling.

"Good. Well, I'm going to get off here for now. We'll call back later when Kendall is able to talk more," Antonio promised.

"Okay," they all said at once.

"Bye for now," Antonio said and hung up.

Jen was crying, but this time it was because she had heard Kendall's voice. Her friends were hugging her, and everyone felt a surge of relief knowing that he was safe and would soon be home.

Chapter 35~ Wrong!

Antonio, John, and Doc were talking quietly in the room while Kendall slept, when Antonio's cell rang. "Garcia."

"Hey, where are you guys at?" Bower asked.

"We are at the Appleton County Hospital. We checked both Bennet and Kendall in," Antonio said.

"Are they doing alright?"

"So far. Are you heading this way?" Antonio asked.

"Yeah, I should be there in half an hour or so. Do you guys need anything?"

"I think we're good, thanks." Antonio smiled.

"Okay, see you soon then," Bower said, hanging up.

"Bower is on his way here," he told the others.

A few minutes later, a tall, dark-haired boy, about 16, knocked on the door before entering. "Hi Dad," he whispered, noticing the sleeping boy.

"Hey Jake, come on over here. I want you to meet some people," Doc said, waving his son in. "This is Antonio Garcia," he said, nodding towards the man sitting next to him. "That's John Bennet in the bed. This is my son, Jacob Jr. We call him Jake or JJ."

"Nice to meet you," Jake smiled as he shook hands with them.

"That's Kendall sleeping over there. He's Antonio's boy," Doc told him. "How was school? Did you get that science project done?"

"Yeah, Jeff and I were up until about two, but we finally got it done." His son smiled.

"Good. Look, why don't we go grab you boys something decent to eat? The food in the cafeteria here is awful," Doc offered.

"You don't have to do that," Antonio said.

"Speak for yourself, real food sounds good," John interrupted. "I hate hospital food."

"And stitches, don't forget stitches." Doc laughed.

Bennet put his finger to his lips, making a slicing motion across his throat.

Antonio looked at them. "Am I missing something?"

"Inside joke," John quickly said.

"Mmhmmm," Antonio said skeptically. "Doc?"

"Don't do it. I will NEVER hear the end of it," Bennet begged.

"Maybe if you tell him about the stitches, he'll forget about the D.O.G. thing," Doc said.

John looked at Doc. "You suck, big time."

"That's right, I almost forgot about that." Antonio smirked.

"Damn it!" John said, covering his head with the blankets.

∞

Back home, the boys were sitting in Carlos' room, doing their schoolwork. Carlos was just finishing his math, and James was working on his literature assignment.

Logan had finished his assignments the day before, and was now attempting to read "A Tale of Two Cities," but he had been reading the same page for the last hour.

"Logan, can you check these for me?" Carlos asked.

"When you're done," Logan answered, not looking up.

"I am done," Carlos declared, tossing the paper to his friend.

Logan sighed and picked up the paper, quickly looking it over. "Double check problems four and nine," he said, tossing it back in Carlos' general direction.

"What's wrong with you?" James asked.

"Nothing, I'm just trying to read my book," Logan said.

"You haven't turned the page once, and you would normally have half the book read by now," James pointed out.

"Yeah Logie, I could have read more than you have by now," Carlos stated.

"Whatever," Logan grumbled.

Carlos and James looked at each other. James closed his book, walked over, and sat down next to Logan. "What's wrong?"

Logan sighed. "Why does something have to be wrong?"

"Because there is," Carlos said, sitting on the other side of his friend.

"Fine, you want to know what's wrong? EVERYTHING IS WRONG! This whole week is WRONG! Us being here doing homework instead of being in class is WRONG! Carlos having nightmares about bloody ice is WRONG! Not having hockey practice is WRONG! Our mothers crying when they think we can't hear them is WRONG! Katie being scared to leave the house in case something happens to one of us is WRONG!" Logan yelled.

"Logan..." James started.

KENDALL BEING BEATEN UP AND GOD KNOWS WHAT ELSE HAPPENED TO HIM... IS WRONG!" He stood up and threw his book across the room, his face red and eyes beginning to tear. "But you want to know what the most WRONG thing is? I turned my back on my best friend, I made him cry, I called him a liar, and I BELIEVED the worst about him."

"Loges..." Carlos said.

"I took the word over someone I can't stand and of someone I don't even know, over that of my best friend. Do you know that Jenny QUESTIONED the paper that Deesie handed out? Did I? NO! I just believed what I read, and then I convinced James it was true! THAT'S WHAT'S WRONG!"

He covered his face with his hands and fell to his knees, sobbing. James reached out and grabbed him, pulling him close. "Logan, we're both to blame for the way we treated him. The only thing we can do is apologize and hope he forgives us. And you know what? He will, because that's what friends do."

Carlos sat, looking at his two distraught brothers, and then ran to get his mom.

James pulled Logan in closer and put his chin on his head, rocking him back and forth slowly. "We screwed up, but you know Kendall. He doesn't hate us. You heard him on the phone, he wanted to know if we were okay. Would he have asked that if he hated us?"

"James, you questioned it, remember? You asked if I was sure, and I told you yes. I never questioned it. I never thought for a second a teacher would lie about something like that," Logan said, still crying.

"That's because they're not supposed to," Sylvia said from the doorway.

She walked in and knelt beside the two boys, wrapping her arms around them. "Mijos, you're supposed to be able to trust your teachers, to be able to go to them when you need help. That is why they run background checks and do multiple interviews. However, very bad people are sometimes also very smart and get through the cracks. That is why it's important to have someone you trust to go to, and that is what Kendall did. The ONLY person to blame in this is Deesie. Kendall could never hate you."

"But..." Logan began.

"No buts. Come with me. I want you to hear something," Sylvia said, pulling them up, having decided that drastic action was needed.

She led the three boys down to Antonio's study, closed the door, and sat down at his computer. She pulled up the file that had been downloaded from Kendall's flash drive.

"Okay, now I want you to listen to this. This is a very disturbing conversation, and I normally wouldn't allow you boys to hear it, but I think you need to. I want you to pay special attention to what Kendall says at the beginning."

"What is it Mami?" Carlos asked.

"Remember when Kendall told you he'd found a way to fix things?"

Carlos nodded.

"Well, what he did was go back to the school and record Deesie. Now remember, this is AFTER Deesie handed out the papers in class. Logan, I want you to remember what Deesie told you in the classroom and compare it to the way he speaks to Kendall on here," she said, looking at him.

Logan nodded.

She pressed play and they heard Kendall's voice come over the speaker. His voice sounded rushed, as if he was trying to get it all out in one breath.

"Papi, please don't be mad at me! I know you told me not to be alone with Mr. Deesie, but something else happened at school today, and I had to do something. He got Jason Banks to start rumours about me and there were papers all over the school. I should have listened to Logan and James and just skipped the rest of the day with them, but I had to be stubborn about it and stay. If I had listened to them, Mr. Deesie wouldn't have lied to Logan in class. Then he handed out these papers, talking about inappropriate behaviour in school. He told everyone that I offered to do... something in exchange for an extension, which I didn't. But he's a teacher and everyone believed him, even Principal Lane. He said they would believe him, and they did."

"Logan showed me the paper that Mr. Deesie handed out, and said he also told everyone that I had to go to counseling for making inappropriate suggestions. They think I lied to them, and they were so mad. They think I betrayed them, Papi. You know I can take a lot, but I can't take losing them. So I went back and checked the laws on recorded evidence, and it said that if you tell the person you're recording a conversation, then it's admissible in court. So that's what I did, and now you can arrest him so he can't hurt anybody else and everything will be fixed and can go back to normal. SO, PLEASE don't be mad at me for doing this. I really can't take someone else being mad at me today."

There was a pause as Kendall took a breath. "I'll be at home tonight. Mom has the late shift and Katie is spending the night at Molly's because her birthday is tomorrow. Thanks for everything, Papi... I love you."

Next the conversation between Kendall and Deesie came on and they listened to the whole thing in silence.

Sylvia watched them, and as soon as the recording was over, she turned off the computer. "Kendall did not and does not hate you. You are his friends, his brothers, and he was willing to do anything to keep you. He knew what kind of man Deesie was, and he fought back against him and he won. Is it fair that you do any less? Are you going to allow Deesie to beat you?"

"How do we win against him if he didn't hurt us?" Logan asked.

"Didn't he? Do you really think he didn't know what he was doing by playing you against Kendall? Now you're sitting here, hating yourself and believing that Kendall hates you, because of what Deesie did."

Sylvia knelt in front of Logan and James, taking their hands in hers. "You win by forgiving yourselves. You forgive yourselves because Kendall doesn't blame you, and if he did, he would forgive you. You win by being there for each other no matter what, and by TALKING about it when something bothers you, instead of keeping it all bottled up inside. You win by realizing how much you are all loved, and that by standing together, you can do anything."

Logan looked at her. "But what if Kendall is... different? He's been through so much, and trauma can change people. What if nothing is ever the same again?"

Sylvia hugged him, "Then we help him find his way back to us, no matter how long the wait, and we do that together."

Chapter 36~ Delayed

Kendall woke up to the sound of soft voices and slowly opened his eyes. He saw Antonio sitting next to John on his bed. They were eating sandwiches and talking to Doc, who was sitting in a chair next to a teenage boy.

He shifted in his bed a little and realized that he really didn't feel well. His chest was tight, his throat hurt, and he felt very dizzy.

As he tried to speak, he started coughing and couldn't stop. He could feel himself starting to panic again. Antonio and Doc both jumped up and ran to his bedside, one on either side. Doc pressed the call button and then raised the incline of the bed. He and Antonio helped Kendall sit up to aid with his breathing. While it helped a bit, but he still couldn't take a deep breath.

Nurse Patrick came in, pulled the oxygen mask down from the wall, and went to place it on Kendall, but he pulled away from her. Doc took it from her and put it to the boy's face and she turned it on. She pulled a stethoscope from the instrument rack and tried to listen to Kendall's lungs. He jumped when she went to put it under his sweatshirt.

"I'm going to call Dr. Talbot in," she said and reached for the phone to page Dr. Talbot.

Antonio was speaking to him, trying to reassure him, and Kendall tried to focus, but everything was so fuzzy. He felt so strange and didn't like it.

Dr. Talbot came in and went over to Kendall. She took her stethoscope and showed it to him. "Honey, I need to listen to your lungs, is that alright?"

He looked at her, trying to recall who she was, and then remembering, nodded.

Doc lifted Kendall's shirt a little, and when he didn't pull away, Natalie placed the stethoscope on his chest and listened. "Okay, we're going to get you started on a nebulizer to help open your airways."

Dr. Talbot nodded to the nurse, who ran to get the equipment needed.

Natalie took a thermometer and placed it in Kendall's ear. "Well, he's not hypothermic anymore. His temperature is 103.4. We need to get these sweats off him and get him into something that won't hold the heat in. Do you think he'll let you change him out of the sweatshirt?" she asked Antonio.

"I can try."

Natalie grabbed a gown from the closet and handed it to Antonio. He smiled reassuringly at Kendall. "Mijo, we need to change you into something cooler, so I'm going to help you get your shirt off and put this on, okay?"

Kendall shook his head. There were WAY too many people around him at the moment.

"Why don't we step out," Natalie said to Doc and Jake as she slid the curtain between John and Kendall's beds. "We'll be right outside," she told Antonio.

He nodded, waited until everyone had gone, and a couple of minutes later tried again. This time, Kendall allowed him to take the sweatshirt off and pull the gown around him.

Antonio helped him lie back and took his hand. "It's going to be okay. I know you don't feel well right now, but you'll be back on your feet in no time."

Natalie looked in and Antonio nodded to her. She walked in with the nebulizer the nurse had brought.

"Kendall, this is a nebulizer and it's going to help you breathe better. We use it just like the oxygen mask, but it's going to smell a little funny because of the medicine. Before we do that though, do you think you can swallow a couple of Tylenol? We need to get your fever down."

He nodded and she handed him the two tablets and held a glass of water, so he could sip from it. "Okay, now can we get this on you?" She smiled, holding the nebulizer mask.

Kendall looked at her and the little machine and nodded. She removed the oxygen mask and replaced it with the nebulizer mask, and turned it on. "We're going to need to do this every three to four hours, until the antibiotics start doing their job."

Kendall nodded again, scrunching his nose at the funny smell.

"I need to talk to Antonio for a minute, but we'll be right over here," she told him, pointing to the doorway.

Antonio followed her. "What's going on? Shouldn't he be feeling better by now, and why does he seem so out of it?"

Natalie sighed. "I think we have several things going on. His blood work was normal, except for a high white blood cell count, which is normal with an infection such as pneumonia. With the combination of his injuries, exhaustion, shock, the pneumonia causing the fever, and possible hypoxemia, it's put a strain on his immune system. If his fever doesn't come down in the next hour, we're going to add another antibiotic, as well as an injectable antipyretic. We're also going to change his pain meds to Torbugesic, because morphine can suppress the respiratory system."

"He's going to be alright though, right?" Antonio asked as an overwhelming sense of helplessness came over him.

"I think he's going to be just fine. We only started treatment a few hours ago, it's just going to take some time," Natalie reassured him.

"He's a strong boy and a fighter," Doc reminded Antonio.

"I know. It's just..." Antonio started.

Doc put his arm around Antonio's shoulders. "You've had a hell of a week worrying about what was happening to your boy, almost losing your friend, and not being home with the rest of your family. But they're both safe and they're both going to be okay. You'll all be on your way home soon and can start to put this all behind you."

Antonio took a deep breath. "Thanks, Doc. I know you're right, I just hate seeing him like this."

"I know, but Natalie is the best and he'll be feeling better in no time."

Antonio smiled at them. "I guess I better call home and let them know we'll probably be here longer than we thought. His mom is not going to be happy."

"Do you want me to call her?" Natalie asked.

"No, I called earlier so she could hear Kendall's voice before he fell back to sleep. I didn't really go into detail about what's happened, so I should let them know about everything anyway. Thanks, though."

"Okay, well I'll be close in case you need me to speak with her about anything," Natalie said.

He nodded and walked back into the room and pulled the curtain open between John and Kendall's beds.

"What's going on?" John asked.

"Looks like we'll be here a little longer than we thought," he said and explained what Natalie had told him.

"Okay, well a couple of days in bed isn't going to hurt me. Maybe by then I can help with the drive back home."

Antonio looked over at Kendall, who was finally resting peacefully. "I'm going to go into the hall and call home to let them know what's going on. I'll be right outside the door, so if he wakes up, just yell for me, okay?"

"Sure thing," John said.

Doc, Jake, and Natalie were still chatting in the hallway. "You going to call her now?" Doc asked.

"Yeah, might as well get it over with." Antonio sighed.

"We'll go back in and keep John company until you're done then," Doc said, wanting to be there if Antonio needed someone to talk to.

"Thanks Doc." Antonio smiled as he called home.

Sylvia answered, but before she could say anything he said, "Honey don't say anything yet. Everything is fine, but I need to talk to you for a minute."

"Okay," she said in a neutral tone.

"Where are the kids?"

'We sent them to the skating rink," she said.

"Katie too?"

"Yes," she said.

"Good. Okay, we're going to be here for a little longer than we thought, and I know Jen isn't going to be happy about it," he told her.

"Why?"

"Kendall has pneumonia and developed a fever. They need to keep him on an IV with antibiotics and pain meds. I know Jen, and she's going to want to drive here, but it's really not a good idea."

"Yes she will." Sylvia sighed.

"Okay, well why don't you call her and put me on speaker. I can also let you know what happened with Deesie."

He heard her call Jen, and then the phone was on speaker. "Antonio?" Jen asked.

"Hey, I thought I'd call you with an update and fill you in on more of the details."

"Okay. How is Kendall? Is he still sleeping?" she asked.

"Yeah, he's sleeping. Look Jen, the doctor thinks he may need to be here longer than she originally thought. He has pneumonia and is dehydrated, so she wants to keep him on an IV with antibiotics. He also needs to use a nebulizer for now. He has a fever, but the antibiotics should take care of that soon."

"How much longer?" she asked.

"I'm not sure, honey. Hopefully only a day or so."

"Maybe I should drive out there," she said.

"I really don't think that's a good idea. The roads are not the best, so it'll take you between eight to twelve hours to get here. If Kendall hears you're driving all this way, he'll start worrying and that won't help things either. I know you miss him, and we all really want to be home as well. Katie and the boys need you there, and I'll have him call as soon as he's able."

Jen sighed. She knew he was right, but she hated being away from her son when he needed her. Even though she was terrified of the answer, she took a deep breath and asked, "What else happened to him? What did Deesie do to him?"

"First, the doctor did a rape kit, and there was no sign that he was sexually assaulted. We don't know what else might have happened, because he hasn't really been able to talk much. He has a lot of bruises, some lacerations, and his left shoulder is injured."

"So Deesie didn't...?" Jen asked quietly.

"According to what the doctor saw, that most likely didn't happen," he said reassuringly.

Tears of relief flowed down her cheeks and Sylvia was hugging her. "Thank God!"

"Jen, it's a long story, and I'll tell you everything when we get home. Just know that you should be very proud of him. He was so strong and kept his wits about him the whole time. In fact, he saved my life...," he said.

"What?" Sylvia and Jen said in unison.

"After we found them, Deesie and I were fighting and he had me pinned. He was just about to knife me, when Kendall threw himself on top of me, holding up a stick to keep him away. Deesie impaled himself on it. I thought that was it for him, but then Deesie got up a minute later and Doc shot him," Antonio explained.

"Oh my God," Sylvia said in shock.

"There's a lot more to tell, but it can wait until we get home. Bottom line is, we're all alive and will be home as soon as Kendall can safely travel. I'll call you often, and you can call me anytime. John and Kendall are in the same room and they're bringing in a cot for me, so I'll be right next to him," Antonio told them.

"Okay, but if it's going to be longer than a day or two, I WILL be driving there," Jen said.

"I know you will, but with any luck we'll be on our way home by Friday. So give everyone my love and let them know that we'll be home soon. I'll have Kendall call again as soon as he's able to talk."

"Okay, thank you, Antonio. I-I don't know what we would have done without you," Jen said quietly.

"We take care of family, remember?"

"Always." She smiled as they hung up.

Chapter 37 ~ Statements

Bower got to the hospital and asked for Kendall's room number.

He walked in to find Antonio, John, Doc, and Jake Jr. still chatting. Antonio put his finger to his lips and pointed to Kendall, who was finally sleeping again. Natalie had put him on an oxygen line and monitors, and the nurse was to check his temperature every 30 minutes.

"How's he doing?" Bower asked quietly.

Antonio told him what Dr. Talbot had found and that she had the photo card and copy of his file ready for the agent.

"I need to get statements from all of you," Bower told Antonio, John, and Doc. "I'll need to get Kendall's when he's able."

The men all nodded. "Who first?" John asked.

"Why don't we start with you? What happened right before you got shot?" Bower asked.

"Uh, well... we had panned out, and I was just getting to a clearing, when something ran into me. I thought it was an animal, and when I looked down I saw it was Kendall, I think we both almost had a heart attack at that point. I remember I was holding onto him and I asked him if he wanted a ride home... And then nothing until I woke up on the way to the car," John told him.

"How's your head by the way?" Bower asked, smiling.

"It's fine, just a mild concussion. I should be up and around in no time," John said.

"Don't forget you had to have stitches." Doc said helpfully.

"Shut. Up," John ordered.

Doc just smiled.

"I will get that story before we leave," Antonio told his partner.

Bennet glared at both Doc and Antonio. "NOT if I have anything to say about it. Isn't it a violation of doctor/patient privilege?"

"Only if you're a basset hound," Doc told him.

"I MEAN because it was between me and MY doctor," he said, rolling his eyes.

"But your doctor isn't the one threatening to tell." Antonio smiled smugly.

"You ALL still suck," John grumbled.

The nurse came in then. She checked Kendall's monitor and took his temperature.

"What is it?" Antonio asked.

"103.6. I'm going to let the doctor know. I think she wants to add another antibiotic," she said as she paged Dr. Talbot.

Antonio sighed as he looked down at Kendall. "At least he's resting quietly now."

Natalie came in a couple of minutes later and had the nurse add doxycycline to the fluid bag. "His temperature hasn't gone up that much. I'm hoping that adding the second antibiotic will bring the fever down soon. All of his other readings are normal, so we should see improvement by morning at the latest. How did things go with his mom?"

"She was disappointed and wanted to drive here, but I talked her out of it. If he's not ready to go home by Friday, I expect she'll be on her way," Antonio said.

"Moms... What can you do?" Natalie smiled.

"True." He smiled back.

"How is my other patient?" she asked, walking over to check on John.

"I'm fine, thanks," he said sullenly.

"Why so glum?"

"He..." John said pointing at Doc, "keeps threatening to tell Antonio about my stitches."

"What's to tell? They're right there in your head," she said confused.

"Not THAT part," he said.

"Oh, okay. Now I understand. Doc, are you being mean?" she asked with a smile.

"Who... me?" he asked with a broad smile.

She shook her head and laughed. "Be nice, he's had a bad day."

"I am ALWAYS nice," he said in a hurt tone.

"Tell that to Dr. Shaw. I think he wet himself." She smirked.

"HE had it coming. HE is lucky I didn't put him through a wall!" Doc said, all joking gone from his voice.

"Something I should know?" Bower asked.

"Only that Shaw is one of the most hateful and disgusting people on this planet. If I saw him standing in the road, I wouldn't slam on the brakes," Doc hissed.

"Wow! I think I missed something," John said.

Doc filled him and Bower in on what had happened with Kendall. "That is just the tip of the iceberg my friends."

"Unfortunately, it's true," Natalie agreed.

"Why doesn't the hospital just fire him?" John asked, shocked by Doc's obvious hatred of the man.

"Because he's on the board of directors and is vested in the actual corporate part," she told him.

"It's the ONLY way he's held on to his license. He couldn't cut in Chicago, even as a second rate doctor, so he came here and invested his savings, buying his way onto the board," Doc said bitterly.

Bower smiled and patted Doc on the back. "Well, as I OWE you a huge favour for helping us out, I think I might be able to do something about this."

"Such as?" Doc asked.

"Why don't you let me work out the details? I'm sure you'll hear about something soon. Consider it an early Christmas gift," Bower said.

Doc and Natalie both smiled.

"Now that's a scary sight," John said, looking at the three of them.

"Okay, Doc, let's get your statement now." Bower laughed.

"Let's see... You had gone north and I took the south, into the trees. I heard yelling and made my way in. I saw Kendall running, and he grabbed a branch or something and hit Deesie, who was chasing him. The branch broke and Deesie caught ahold of the end and threw the boy into a tree. A second later, Antonio tackled him, and they were too close together for me to get a clear shot. Then Deesie was on top of Antonio and I saw him raise up, but before I could shoot, Kendall was on top of Antonio, still holding the stick. I think he was just trying to keep Deesie away, but the idiot came down and ran himself through with it. Antonio pushed him off them and pulled Kendall away. Next thing I knew, Deesie is up and screaming, running at them with a knife, damn stick still in his gut. I fired and hit him in the head. He stayed down that time. By the time I got to Antonio, he had Kendall up and was trying to carry him out. I took the boy from him, and Antonio grabbed their gear and we went to the car."

"Wow, I missed a lot," John said.

"It wasn't a pretty sight," Doc told him.

"I imagine not," John agreed.

"Are you in any condition to give me your statement?" Bower asked Antonio.

"Sure, but let's step out in the hallway, in case Kendall wakes up. John, let him know where I am if he does and call for me," Antonio said.

"Will do," Bennet promised.

Out in the hallway, Antonio told Bower everything that had happened in the woods, the clinic, and then at the hospital.

"I'll need to speak with Kendall about what happened too. Including everything that occurred from the time he was taken, until he was brought here," Bower told Antonio.

"I know, hopefully he'll be in better condition tomorrow," Antonio said.

"Some of the questions aren't going to be easy ones for him to answer. How do you think he'll do with it?" Bower asked, concerned. "I can arrange to have a psychologist here if you think it will help."

"I don't think adding another stranger into the mix is going to help matters. Maybe Dr. Talbot could help. He doesn't seem to be afraid of her," Antonio suggested.

"I'll ask her then. Why don't you guys get some rest, and I'll be in touch soon. If you need anything at all, just call me. I'll be staying in town here."

"Thanks, I will." Antonio said, shaking Bower's hand.

As Bower started to leave, Antonio said, "Christian thanks for everything. I really appreciate all that you did."

Bower smiled. "You're welcome, Antonio. I'm glad it all worked out and you got your boy back safe."

Antonio went back into the room, thinking about the days ahead of them and hoped everything would be alright. He smiled at his friends, who were talking quietly again, and went over to check on Kendall.

He brushed a few unruly bangs out of the teen's eyes. "You need a haircut."

Kendall stirred a little and a moment later opened his eyes. "Hi Papi," he said, his voice raspy and low.

"Hey, how are you feeling now?"

"Tired and my head hurts a little," Kendall answered as he pawed at the oxygen tube in his nose.

"Leave it alone, you need it," Antonio said, pulling his hand down.

"Feels funny," Kendall complained.

"I know, but leave it there," Antonio ordered.

Kendall sighed and tried to turn a little, wincing every time he moved.

Antonio helped him shift his left shoulder up a little. "Better?"

Kendall nodded.

"You feel up to calling home?" Antonio asked. Kendall smiled and nodded.

Antonio dialed his house and Brooke answered. "Hello."

"Hi Brooke, I have someone here who wants to say 'hi' again, before he falls back to sleep," Antonio said.

"Just a minute," Brooke said and called out for Jen.

"Hello," Jen answered. She had been outside helping Carlos shovel the walk and sounded out of breath.

"Hey, Jen. Someone's awake and wanted to give you all a quick call," he said and put the phone up to Kendall's ear.

"Hi mama."

"Hi baby. How are you feeling now, any better?"

"Little bit. My throat is a little sore though, so it's hard to talk. What's everybody doing?" Kendall asked.

"Well, everyone is running in, hoping they can talk to you, so I'm going to put you on speaker."

"Okay," he said.

"Kendall!" Carlos squealed.

"Hey, Carlitos. You feeling better?"

"I am now!"

Kendall swore he could actually hear him smiling.

"Hi Kendall," James said quietly.

"Hey Jamie. I miss you guys so much," Kendall said, his voice breaking.

"Not as much as we miss you," James said, tearing up but smiling.

"Katie, you there?" Kendall asked.

"Yeah, Big Brother," Katie said.

"Hug James, will you?"

"Sure thing," she said and threw her arms around James, who hugged her back, trying not to cry.

"Hi Kendall. Are they treating you alright there?" Brooke asked.

"Yeah Mama D. Dr. Talbot and her nurse are really nice. Where's Loges?"

"Oh honey, he ran some errands with his mom and Mama G. They're going to be so sad they missed your call," Jen told him.

Kendall's face fell a little.

"We can call Mama G's cell," Antonio whispered to him.

Kendall nodded. "Papi's going to call Mama G, so we can talk to him."

"Okay, that's a great idea, baby. I know he misses you." Jen smiled.

Kendall started coughing, so Antonio took the phone. "We'll give you a call later, okay?"

"Okay, thanks Antonio." Jen said.

"Bye everyone, we'll talk soon." He smiled as everyone yelled goodbye and hung up.

"Are you okay?" he asked Kendall.

He coughed for a couple of minutes, nodding as he caught his breath. "Can we call Logan?"

"You bet." Antonio smiled and called his wife's cell.

Sylvia answered a few seconds later. "Antonio?"

"Hey honey, is Logan with you?"

"Yes."

"Someone here wants to talk to him," he said.

Sylvia looked at Logan and gestured for him to come over. "Someone is on the phone for you," she said, handing it to him.

Logan took the phone and looked at her. "What do I say?"

"What about, hi?" Kendall suggested.

"Hi Kendall... How are you feeling?" Logan asked.

"Better now that I got to talk to everyone." Kendall smiled.

"Kendall, I'm so..." Logan started.

"Don't," Kendall ordered. "I miss you and I love you and that's all there is to say."

Logan was near tears, but Sylvia was hugging him and smiling.

"Okay, I miss you and I love you, too. So get better and come home soon," Logan said, sniffling.

"Will do."

Logan handed the phone back to Sylvia.

"Are you doing alright, Mijo?"

"Yeah, just really tired right now. Here's Papi. I love you," Kendall said as he handed the phone back to Antonio. He closed his eyes and was soon fast asleep.

Chapter 38~ The Interview

A few minutes later, the nurse came in and checked on Kendall. "His temperature is down to 101.1, so it's going in the right direction," she told Antonio.

"Thank God," he said, smiling.

"I'll be back for his breathing treatment in a half an hour," she said and went to finish her rounds.

Doc smiled at Antonio. "Well, I guess we should take off for now. We've got stock to feed. I'll check in on you boys in the morning, and if you need anything at all, you have my number."

"We can't thank you enough, Doc, really," Antonio said.

"No thanks necessary. I'm just glad you boys are alright and will be able to head home soon." Doc smiled.

"See you later, Doc. It was nice to meet you, Jake," John said.

"Nice to meet you too." Jake smiled, shaking first John's hand and then Antonio's.

"We'll talk later," Doc said, patting Antonio on the back.

"Bye Doc... Jake," Antonio said.

"I don't know about you, but I need a nap." John yawned a few minutes later.

"Get some sleep," Antonio told his friend.

Antonio pulled a chair up next to Kendall's bed and just watched him for a few minutes. He couldn't believe everything that had happened in the last five days, and everything they still had to face. He smiled at his godson and thought about how much he looked like Will.

Your dad would be so proud of you, he thought. He sighed, thinking about how much he missed his friend.

He found the TV remote and turned on the local news, with the volume on low. Soon he nodded off and slept until the nurse returned for Kendall's breathing treatment. She gently woke Kendall so she could place the mask on him. Moments later, he was sleeping again and slept through the rest of the treatment.

The nurse patted Antonio on the shoulder. "I'll have them bring in the cot, so you can get some real sleep."

"That would be great, thank you," he said, yawning.

A few minutes later, the cot was set up next to Kendall's bed and Antonio was soon fast asleep.

∞

The night nurse came in at around one in the morning for Kendall's next treatment. "Kendall, it's time for your breathing treatment," she said. He didn't respond, and they had strict orders to make sure that he knew they were there before touching him. "Kendall," she said louder and he stirred. "Come on, sweetheart, it's time to wake up for your treatment."

Kendall heard the word "sweetheart" and snapped awake.

"NO! STAY AWAY! DON'T TOUCH ME!" he screamed. He started thrashing around, trying to escape his blankets.

Antonio and John were both awake the instant they heard him scream.

"Kendall, it's okay. It's Papi, you're safe," Antonio said, trying to calm the boy, but all Kendall heard was Deesie's voice.

The monitors started going off as Kendall's heart rate and blood pressure soared. The nurse was in shock, not knowing what had happened, but quickly moved to page the doctor on call.

Antonio couldn't get Kendall to respond to him—he just kept screaming. Afraid that the boy was going to hurt himself, he pushed the side railing down and pulled Kendall to him. He held him tightly to his chest with one arm, and with the other held his head to his shoulder.

"It's okay, Mijo, you're alright. No one is going to hurt you. Kendall, please listen, it's me," Antonio whispered as he sat there, gently rocking Kendall back and forth.

"He's here! He's going to hurt you! He killed John! He's going to hurt you! You have to run!" Kendall repeated again and again.

The doctor came in and ordered a sedative, and a couple of minutes later, Kendall quieted down. He was still trembling and telling Antonio to run. Antonio just sat there, holding the boy tightly, stroking his hair.

"No, Mijo, everyone's safe. He's not going to hurt you anymore. He's not going to hurt anyone ever again, I promise."

John had gotten out of bed and was sitting on the other side of Kendall's bed. "What the hell happened?"

"I don't know. I was asleep and woke up when I heard him scream." Antonio looked at the nurse, "Did you come in before or after he started screaming?"

"Before. I was trying to wake him up for his breathing treatment. I didn't touch him. We have orders not to until he's awake. I called his name a couple of times, and when he started to wake up, I told him why I was here, and suddenly his eyes were open and he started screaming," she said.

"You're sure you didn't touch him, even by accident?" John asked.

"No, I swear. I was holding the nebulizer and calling to him," she replied, obviously distraught.

"What were your exact words?" John asked, trying to figure out what had set the boy off.

She thought back. "I called him the first time, telling him it was time for his breathing treatment. When he didn't respond, I said his name again. He moved a little, so I said, 'come on, sweetheart. It's time to wake up,' and that's when he screamed."

John thought for a moment, and then asked Antonio, "Didn't you say Deesie called Kendall 'sweetheart' in the classroom the first time he made an advance?"

Antonio nodded.

"He did it again on the recording that Kendall made. It looks like we might have a word trigger," John said.

Antonio sighed and nodded.

"I'm confused. Did I start this?" the nurse asked.

"No, you didn't do anything wrong, but if you could put on his chart for no one to use the word 'sweetheart,' that would be a big help," John told her.

"I will. I'll come back in a little while for his breathing treatment," she told Antonio.

He nodded and whispered, "Thank you."

"Another thing. Why does he keep thinking I'm dead?" John asked.

"Well, I'm pretty sure he's never seen anyone he cares about get shot before, and he hasn't really been that lucid since we found him. I think he was dreaming about what happened in the woods, and that's why he thought I was going to get hurt."

"Damn," John said.

"Exactly."

The rest of the night was uneventful. Antonio slept sitting up in Kendall's bed, holding him, and John slept on Antonio's cot.

∞

Doc found them that way the next morning as he came in, carrying breakfast for them. He set the bag of food down and shook John's shoulder.

"Hey, what's going on here?"

John woke up yawning. "Hey Doc, what are you doing here?"

"Had to pick up some supplies, so I thought I'd bring you boys a decent breakfast. What happened?"

"Long night. Kendall woke up with nightmares and the doctor had to sedate him," John told him.

"Poor kid. Has Natalie been in yet?" Doc asked as he handed a container of food to John.

"I don't think so. Thank you so much for bringing real food." John smiled as he took the offered meal.

Antonio woke up when he heard the two men talking. He yawned and looked down at Kendall, who he was still cradling in his arms. He kissed him on the head, and then slid him over, so he was lying on his right side, facing John. He covered him with the blanket and stood up. He stretched, wincing as he realized how stiff his back was.

"Breakfast?" Doc said, handing him a container.

"Bless you." Antonio smiled, taking the food. "I didn't expect to see you this early."

"Well, my mare foaled last night, so I was up and needed to pick up a few things. I thought I'd just stop by and see how things are going," Doc told them.

"Not so good," Antonio said.

"So I heard. The boy's bound to have some bad dreams though," Doc told him.

"I know. I just wish he could get some peace for now. Bower's coming in today to try and take a statement, and I'm not sure Kendall's going to handle it well at all." Antonio sighed.

"If he's not ready to talk about it, he's not ready. It's not like they're waiting to charge the man. He's dead," Doc pointed out.

"True enough," Antonio agreed.

∞

Dr. Talbot came in as the men were finishing their breakfast. "Good morning. I hear we had a difficult night?"

"Yeah, you could say that," John said.

"What happened?" she asked.

Antonio told her about Kendall's nightmare as she checked his chart.

"Okay, once he's doing better physically, we might want to put him on something for anxiety. Antonio, do you think you could wake him so I can check him out?" Natalie asked.

Antonio nodded. "Kendall, can you wake up for me?"

Kendall stirred and stretched his legs out. "Hmmmm?"

"Time to wake up, Mijo, Dr. Natalie needs to see how you're doing."

"Hmmm... 'kay." Kendall opened his eyes and rubbed them.

"How are you feeling this morning?" Natalie asked him.

"Tired," he mumbled.

"I bet you are. It's been a long week for you. Is it alright if I take your temperature and listen to your lungs?"

"Mmmhmm," he yawned.

She smiled and placed the thermometer in his ear. "Look at that, 99.4. Your temperature is almost normal."

She put the stethoscope on his chest. "Still crackly, but we're making progress," she said, smiling down at him. "Are you hungry?"

He made a face and shook his head.

"You're going to need to try and eat something soon. Is your stomach bothering you?"

"No, not hungry," he said.

"Well, you're going to have to try and eat something. I can't release you until you're eating and drinking on your own," she told him.

Kendall sighed. "Maybe later?"

"Alright, but I want you to have something in your stomach by noon," she said.

"He will. I'll get you whatever you want, Mijo," Antonio said.

Kendall nodded and realized John was lying on Antonio's cot. "Hi John, why are you there?" Kendall asked, confused.

"You don't remember last night?" Natalie asked.

"I talked to everyone at home and then got sleepy," he told her.

"That's the last thing you remember?" she asked.

"Yeah," he said, trying to remember anything else. "Why?"

"You had a bad dream, that's all," Antonio said.

"I don't remember."

"It's alright, don't worry about it, that's normal," Natalie told him.

"Okay," he said, his brow furrowed as he tried to remember.

"Don't give yourself a headache over it," John said.

"Hey, you want to see something?" Doc asked Kendall.

"What?"

Doc pulled a small video camera from his jacket pocket, went over, and stood next Antonio. He turned it on and turned the screen towards Kendall. "That is Midnight Shadow's new foal. He was born at 3:15 this morning."

Kendall watched the baby horse lying next to his mother, and then he suddenly stood up on shaky legs. The foal started to walk around the stall and soon was running around his mother, getting use to his new world.

Kendall smiled as he watched. "Look at him, that's so cool. He can already run?"

"Doesn't take them long. You'll have to come and visit him sometime." Doc smiled.

"Really?"

"You betcha," Doc said.

Antonio smiled at the boy watching the mare and her foal on the small screen. "Thanks Doc," he whispered.

Doc smiled and gave him a wink.

∞

Kendall had just finished his next breathing treatment, when Bower came in.

"Good morning," he said.

"Hey Christian," Antonio said, hoping that using the agent's first name would help put Kendall at ease.

"Kendall this is Agent Christian Bower with the FBI. He helped us find you," Antonio said.

"Hello," Kendall said shyly, pulling closer to Antonio.

"Hi Kendall, are you feeling any better today?" Bower smiled.

Kendall nodded, watching the man closely.

"John, why don't you and I head down to the cafeteria and see if there's anything Kendall might like there," Doc suggested.

John looked at Antonio, who nodded. "Sure, maybe there'll be pudding or something. Does that sound good?" he asked Kendall.

The boy just looked at him, eyebrow raised, suddenly very nervous. He pushed himself back against the pillows and pulled his legs up.

"It's alright, Mijo, Christian just needs to ask you a couple of things," Antonio said reassuringly.

"Why?"

Bower went and sat at the foot of the cot. "We just need to know a few things."

"Like what?"

"Well, could you tell me what happened the night that Deesie took you from home?" Bower asked.

Kendall looked at Antonio, who sat next to him. Antonio put his arm around him. "It's okay, really. I'm not going to leave you."

Kendall sighed. "Not much to tell. I woke up and he was there. He told me to behave or he would wait for my mom to get home. He tied my hands up with his necktie, I think. He took some stuff from my closet and dresser and put them in my backpack."

"Okay, and then?" Bower asked.

"We went downstairs, and he made me put on my jacket and boots. He gave me my backpack and pushed me towards the kitchen," Kendall told him.

When the boy didn't continue, Bower said, "There were some broken dishes, things pulled from the wall..."

Kendall was looking at his hands. "I hit him with my backpack and tried to get away. He caught me though and hit my head on the island. I don't remember after that."

Bower smiled gently. "Do you remember calling Antonio from the car?"

Kendall sighed again. "Yes."

"Can you tell me about it?"

"I woke up and found my cell phone in my pocket. I called Papi, and he said they were looking for me and asked if I could hide it somewhere, so they could track it. I tore a hole in my jacket and hid it in there."

"And then?"

"Later he woke me up and made me get in the front seat. We drove to a motel and he told me to behave, went in, and paid for a room. When we went inside the room, he told me to take a shower and wash my hair, because there was blood all over, so I did."

"Was he there when you showered?" Bower asked.

"NO! I closed the door, showered, and then got dressed. When I was done, he cleaned my forehead and bandaged it. Then he gave me some ibuprofen and a sleeping pill," Kendall said as he started clenching and unclenching his hands.

Antonio took one of his hands and held it.

Kendall looked at him. "Why do we have to talk about this? He's dead, right?"

"It'll be okay," Antonio said, hugging him.

"I know this is hard, Kendall, but it's important that we know as many details as possible," Bower said.

"Why? He's dead," the boy repeated stubbornly. He did *not* want to talk about this.

"Kendall, please... Can you tell us what happened next?" Antonio asked.

Kendall rolled his eyes. "I got into bed and he told me there were four rules."

"What were they?" Bower asked.

"Number one was that I had to do what he said. Two, was if I ran away, he'd punish me when he caught me. Three, was I was not supposed to talk to anybody."

Bower looked at Antonio. "What was number four?"

"That I was his... Can we stop now?"

"Just a little bit longer, please?" Antonio asked.

The boy sighed and his agitation was becoming more apparent.

"After that, did you go to sleep?" Bower asked.

Kendall nodded.

"What happened when you woke up?" Antonio asked.

"He woke me up once, saying he had to do something, so he taped my hands and feet. But I was still really tired, and I think I fell back to sleep."

"And then?" Bower asked.

Kendall's voice was rushed as he tried to get through the next part as fast as he could. "He woke me up later and told me to get dressed, so I went into the bathroom to change. I was dressing and he came in screaming at me. He was asking me what I did, but I didn't know what

he was talking about. Then he started to choke me, and I thought I was going to die, but he let me go. He pulled me out into the bedroom and made me get my jacket and boots on. We left, but got into a different car, and he said not to try anything because the child locks were on. We drove for a few minutes and he stopped."

Kendall started to feel dizzy and nauseated.

"What happened next, Mijo?" Antonio asked.

"He got out of the car and opened the door. He was holding my cell phone. I don't know how he found it. He was really mad and he hit me. Then he started kicking me, and I just covered my head and waited for him to stop."

Kendall's voice went monotone as he recalled the events, and he started to shake. "Then he was on top of me and telling me that it was going to happen, but I wouldn't know when."

"What was going to happen?" Bower asked.

Kendall's monitors started going off, but he continued as if he had not heard Bower's question. "He said he could be nice or he could be rough, and then he kissed me, and I couldn't breathe because his tongue was making me gag. Then he bit me and sat back up and started hitting me."

Kendall's breathing was becoming erratic and he felt oddly detached. He could hear voices, but they were muffled, as if he was under water, and he could only see shadows.

Dr. Talbot ran in just as Kendall lost consciousness.

Chapter 39~ Nightmares

"What happened?" Dr. Talbot asked.

"I was asking him a few questions about what had happened and he passed out," Bower told her.

"NO more questions, no more inquiries until he is physically and emotionally able to handle it," she ordered.

Kendall was pale and his breathing was fast and erratic. She removed the oxygen tube from his nose and replaced it with the mask. "Calm down, honey, it's alright," she whispered. After a few minutes, his heart rate slowed to normal and his breathing regulated.

Kendall was aware that there were people around him. He could sense Antonio's presence. He could feel him holding his hand and his fingers running through his hair. Voices were coming and going, but he couldn't make out any words, only sounds. He recognized Antonio and Dr. Talbot's voices and then they were gone.

He was in the woods, trying to run. He could hear Deesie behind him and desperately tried to run faster. Everything hurt and he couldn't breathe. He was trying to find home, but didn't know which way to go. He knew what the man would do to him if he caught him, and he would rather die.

Suddenly, someone had ahold of him and he tried to pull away.

"Uh uh uh, sweetheart. You're mine," Deesie whispered as he pushed him down.

He could feel hands all over him, and he tried to push them away, but found he couldn't move. He tried to scream, but no sound came from his mouth.

He looked around frantically and saw Antonio sitting under the tree.

"PAPI! Please help me!"

His godfather just sat there, and Kendall realized there was blood all over him.

"I told you one bullet would take care of his problems," Deesie said as he pushed down against the terrified boy. "No, no, no! Papi!" Kendall sobbed.

Suddenly, he was in the school and running down the hallways. He could hear his friends calling for him, but he couldn't find them. He looked in one of the classroom doors and saw Deesie's English room—students sitting at their desks, listening to the teacher drone on and on about lessons.

Deesie walked over to Logan and put his arms around him. He started to kiss the boy's neck. "You need to learn your abc's." Kendall pounded on the door, yelling at Deesie to leave his friend alone, but the man just looked at him, smiling his twisted smile.

The room went dark, and he could hear Carlos screaming for him down the hallway. He ran, calling for him, and came to another classroom. The door was locked, but he knew his friend was inside.

The light came on in the room and through the window, he saw Carlos sitting on the floor, holding his dead father, crying. "This is your fault!" Carlos screamed at him.

"I'm sorry!" Kendall cried. "Carlos, please!"

"Your fault!" his friend screamed again.

He turned away from the scene and saw someone lying on the floor a little further down the hallway. He made his way to them, his heart threatening to explode from his chest. He looked

down and saw the little old man from the motel. He was dead. His eyes were wide open and he had a look of absolute terror on his face.

"See what you did, sweetheart?" He heard Deesie's voice all around him.

Kendall ran down the hall, away from the dead man, trying to open doors as he tried to escape. One opened and he ran in and closed the door. He heard Deesie's voice behind him and he turned. The man was standing there with a stick through his stomach. There was blood spurting from the wound, and Kendall looked down to find he was still holding the stick—he couldn't let go.

He looked back up and Deesie was gone. Standing there was James, blood flowing from his mouth.

"Kendall, why?" James asked as he fell to the ground.

Kendall woke up screaming.

Antonio was there, holding him and telling him it was alright, that he was safe. Kendall knew it was a dream and that he should feel safe, but all he could see were his friends broken or bleeding, and it was his fault.

Dr. Talbot came running back in and had to give Kendall another mild sedative.

He finally quieted, and Antonio sat there holding him, trying to fight the tears, but found that he couldn't hold them in any longer.

"I'm sorry, Mijo. I should have been there. I should have answered my damn phone that day and pulled you out of school. I should have sent someone to your house before we went after Deesie. I promised your Papi I would take care of you and I failed. I couldn't protect you, and I broke my promise to your dad and to you. I'm so sorry, Mijo." Antonio was sobbing now. It was all just too much.

John went to his partner and stood there, with his hands on his shoulders. He wanted to speak words of comfort to his friend, but decided the best thing to do was just to let him cry.

A few hours later, Antonio was sitting on Kendall's bed, still holding the sleeping boy. John was sitting in a chair, watching TV with the volume turned down. Doc had left a couple of hours before, after making sure both Antonio and Kendall were doing alright. He told John he would call to check on them later.

Antonio hadn't said anything since he had broken down and John didn't push him. He knew his partner took his responsibilities very seriously, and it killed Antonio to know that someone he loved was in pain, especially when there was nothing he could do about it.

A while later, John looked over and Antonio was starting to nod off, and he decided his friend needed to get some real sleep.

He got up and walked over to him. "Antonio, go sleep in my bed. I'll stay here with Kendall."

"No, I need to be here when he wakes up," Antonio said stubbornly.

"You're not going to do him any good by exhausting yourself," John pointed out.

He walked over to his bed and pushed it next to Kendall's. "Move," he ordered, pointing to the bed.

Antonio was about to protest and John just pointed again. "Now!" he said firmly. "I'll be here on the other side."

Antonio sighed and gently helped Kendall lie back against his pillows. He went and laid down on the other bed, while John sat next to Kendall on the other side.

∞

A couple of hours later, Kendall opened his eyes and looked around, confused. He saw John sleeping in the chair next to him, and turning his head, saw that the other bed had been pushed next to his and Antonio was sound asleep on it.

Kendall pushed his blankets off and crawled over the railing, onto the other bed, and curled up next to Antonio. The monitors beeped as he moved, but he was already sound asleep by the time the nurse came in to check on him.

John woke up when the nurse came in and was surprised to see Kendall gone. He looked over and couldn't help but smile at the boy curled up next to Antonio, the teen holding on to the older man's hand. The nurse moved the IV bag to the other side of the bed, so the line didn't pull out, and then covered Kendall with a blanket.

"Why don't you sleep in this bed?" she told John, who thought that was a wonderful idea. He laid down and was soon fast asleep.

∞

Antonio woke up the next morning, surprised to find Kendall sleeping next to him. The boy had curled his hand inside Antonio's larger one and seemed to be sleeping peacefully. He looked over and saw John was snoring softly in the next bed.

He looked at his watch and realized it was 7 am. "Damn, I slept for almost ten hours."

He moved to get up, but Kendall wrapped his arms around Antonio's arm, holding on tightly. He smiled and kissed him on the head. "Mijo, I need to get up."

"Hmmm?" Kendall mumbled.

"It's morning, I need to get up," Antonio repeated.

"Hmm... 'kay," but he made no move to release him. Antonio laid back and just held him for a few more minutes.

The nurse came in for a breathing treatment, so Antonio had to wake Kendall this time. "Son, it's time to wake up, you need your meds," he whispered, gently shaking the boy's hand, which was still firmly clutching his arm.

Kendall opened his eyes slowly.

"Good morning, Kendall! It's time for your nebulizer treatment. Is it alright if I put the mask on you now?" the nurse asked, smiling at him.

He nodded and rolled onto his back, wincing at the pain in his shoulder.

She placed the mask over his face and turned on the machine. "I'll be back in half an hour to take it off," she told him, and left to finish her other duties.

"I HATE morning people!" John moaned.

Antonio laughed at him and Kendall mumbled, "Me too," under the mask.

After the nurse returned and removed the nebulizer, an orderly brought in breakfast for the three.

"I'm running down to the cafeteria and getting something else. Their food may not be good, but it has to be better than this," John declared, poking at what looked to be poached eggs.

"Yeah, that's a good idea," Antonio agreed.

Kendall looked at the bowl of lumpy oatmeal and thought he was going to throw up. He pushed it away and rolled over, holding his stomach.

"Are you okay?" John asked, noting the boy had gone pale. Kendall shook his head and pointed to the bowl.

"Can't say I blame you there," he said.

Antonio grabbed the tray and pushed it away. "Are you going to be sick?" Kendall shook his head, desperately hoping it was the truth.

A few minutes later, his stomach calmed down and he was able to sit back up.

"You need to eat something, Kendall. Dr. Talbot said you can't go home until you do," Antonio reminded him.

"I'm not hungry."

"That's because you haven't eaten in a long time. How about I go get us some breakfast from the cafeteria? Do you want cold cereal, eggs, or maybe toast?" Antonio asked.

Kendall shook his head.

"Don't get the pudding. I'm pretty sure you're not supposed to be able to cut it with a knife," John warned.

"How about a shake? A plain vanilla shake?" Antonio suggested.

Kendall sighed. He knew Antonio wasn't going to let him get away without trying something, so he nodded.

"Okay then." Antonio smiled. "I'll find something more edible for us," he told John.

"Thank you," John said gratefully as Antonio headed down to the cafeteria.

John looked over at Kendall. "Kendall, can I ask you something?"

Kendall looked at him and nodded.

"Are you afraid to go home? Is that why you don't want to eat?"

Kendall looked down and didn't answer.

John went over and sat down next to the boy. "What's wrong?"

Kendall didn't speak at first. "What are they going to think?" he asked quietly.

"Who?" John asked.

"Everybody. Are they going to think that...?" Kendall faltered.

"No one is going to think anything, except how glad they are to have you home," John told him.

"But..."

"You listen to me, the people who love you are the only ones that matter. You know and they know that nothing happened. Even if it had, it wouldn't be your fault. Nothing that happened was your fault, NOTHING. Deesie is the only one at fault here, period," John stated.

"He killed those people because of me. That's my fault," Kendall whispered.

"What people?" John asked.

"The old man at the motel, the ranger, he almost killed you and Papi." Kendall was near tears.

John put his arm around the boy. "First, Ranger Thompson is not dead. He was badly wounded, but he is alive and out of intensive care. I don't know why we didn't think to tell you, but with everything that's happened, we forgot, and I'm sorry about that."

"H-He's not dead? But he shot him in the back,. There was blood everywhere. He tried to help me and I couldn't do anything."

"When he didn't show up to meet the emergency vehicles, they went to find him. They got to him just in time. As for the old man at the motel, there was nothing you could have done. Deesie was insane and he was going to hurt anyone who got in his way. That man called and let us know you were there and brought us that much closer to finding you. He knew what he was doing and that Deesie was dangerous, but it was more important for him to do the right thing. I think he'd be happy to know it wasn't in vain," John told him.

"What was his name?" Kendall asked.

"Mr. Crowley. I'm not sure of his first name. I can find out though," John said.

Kendall nodded.

"Kendall, can I ask you something else? You don't have to answer or give me any details, but I think it might help us help you," John asked gently.

Kendall looked at him and nodded.

"We know that Deesie didn't... you know. Can you tell me if he did other things that were inappropriate? No details just nod or shake your head."

Kendall looked down at his hands and bit his lower lip. There were moments when the humiliation and shame of what happened threatened to overwhelm him.

John watched him as he gave a faint nod.

"Okay buddy. I don't need to know any more, but when you're ready to talk about things, we'll all be here for you," John said.

Chapter 40~ The Trigger

Antonio returned a few minutes later with a tray of food, at least that's what he chose to believe it was. He set the tray down, handed a plate to John, and handed a cup to Kendall.

"Thank you," Kendall said as he took the shake.

He took a sip and Antonio smiled. "That's my boy."

John took a bite of the eggs. "I may have been wrong about this being better than the actual hospital meal."

"I agree. I think I'll run out and get something for lunch, if that's alright?" Antonio said, looking at Kendall.

Kendall looked at the food, made a face and nodded. "I don't want you to starve."

John laughed. "You think it looks bad? Try eating it," he said, taking a forkful of the food and holding it towards the boy.

Kendall shook his head and sat back further on his bed. "I'll puke on you," he warned.

Antonio smiled as he watched Kendall threaten Bennet. "I'd take him seriously if I were you," he warned his partner.

Natalie came in. "How are my boys today?"

"My head's healing, but your cafeteria is trying to kill me," John told her.

She looked at his plate and frowned. "That is why I bring my lunch."

"Have you tried to eat?" she asked Kendall.

"He looked at his oatmeal and almost lost it, so I went and got him a shake," Antonio told her.

She smiled at Kendall. "Have you had any of it?"

"A little."

"Drink it," she ordered, smiling.

He took a sip for her.

"Good?" she asked.

He nodded as he sat the cup back down.

She picked it up and handed it back to him. "Then DRINK it."

He sighed in defeat and took another sip, and when he went to set it back down, she looked at him. "I can do this ALL day," she told him, arching an eyebrow.

He rolled his eyes and took another sip. Antonio watched the exchange and smiled.

"Can I take your temperature and listen?" Natalie asked Kendall. He nodded, so she pulled out her stethoscope and put it on his chest. "Sounds better. Are you coughing as much?"

Kendall shook his head no.

"Good," she said as she placed the thermometer in his ear. "99.2, I'd call that normal. We'll be sending you home on antibiotics and pain meds though," she told him. She checked his fluid line and watched the monitors for a moment.

"Is it alright if I check out your shoulder?"

He sighed but nodded.

She pushed the gown off his shoulder blade and involuntarily winced at the sight. "Is it bothering you much?"

"Sometimes. It hurts to lie on it or move a lot."

"Honey, can you tell me how it was injured? I want to make sure that I'm doing the right thing for you," she said.

Kendall sat there for a moment and sighed. "He got mad and poked me with needles."

"Just needles, not anything with a syringe?"

"Just needles. They were long and fat," he said.

"Same thing with your foot?"

He nodded. "He said something about pressure points, and he pushed the needle in and moved it around."

Antonio's face was flushed with anger, but John caught his eye and shook his head slightly. Antonio took a deep breath and released it. Kendall was opening up a little and he wasn't going to jeopardize that.

"Which did he do first, your shoulder or your foot?" Natalie asked.

"My foot."

"What day?' she asked in a conversational tone.

He thought for a moment. "I think it was Saturday night."

"Why was he angry?" she asked as she lifted his foot to look at it.

"I ran away."

Antonio and John looked at one another in surprise.

She pushed on the bottom of his foot a little and he hissed a little. "It looks like it's healing fine. Does it feel any better?"

He nodded. "A little."

She smiled. "Good. You ran away?"

Kendall nodded.

"I'm going to wrap your foot for some cushioning. Where were you when you ran away?" she asked as she pulled a bin with bandage materials from under the counter.

"The motel in the woods."

"How did you get away?" Natalie asked, keeping her tone neutral as she worked.

"We were walking to the room and I hit him in the head with my backpack and ran."

"It was really cold that night. How long were you out there?" she asked, wrapping his foot.

"I'm not sure. He was mad when he found me though."

"So he took you back to the motel and punctured your foot?" she asked, finishing with his foot.

Kendall nodded.

"Is that the only thing he did?" she asked as she started to change the bandage on his forehead.

Kendall shook his head and sighed. She was trying to help and he didn't have to tell her everything. "First he filled the bathtub with cold water and kept pushing me under."

Antonio inhaled sharply and then coughed a little to hide it when Kendall looked at him.

"Well, that, along with being out in the cold so long, probably contributed to the pneumonia," she said.

Kendall yawned a little.

Natalie smiled as she helped him to lie back. "When did he hurt your shoulder?"

"Hmmm, the next night. He was mad because I didn't want to leave the old man at the motel."

Kendall's eyes were starting to droop a little. "Then he got mad after I told him I wasn't paying attention so I could learn and do the letter B to him after he showed me how he wanted it done. So he tied me to a tree. Then he hit me, and I woke up and the ranger was bleeding and dying," Kendall said softly in one breath as he fell back to sleep.

Antonio and John stared at Natalie in shock. "How did you get him to talk to you?" John asked.

"Well, I was non-confrontational, kept it medically based. I was busy doing different things, so it kept diverting his attention, and... I pushed the little red button on his fluid pump," She smiled.

"Sneaky." John laughed.

"What is this letter B he was talking about?" she asked.

Antonio remembered the recording. "Deesie told him he had to learn his abc's and made it sexually based."

"But, Kendall wouldn't do it, so that's why Deesie got mad," John pointed out.

"No, but he said that Deesie showed him how he wanted it done. I think he just told us one of the things that was done to him," Antonio said quietly.

Natalie rubbed his shoulder. "He'll sleep for a couple of hours and probably won't remember everything, so I wouldn't dwell on it for now."

Antonio nodded. "Thanks Natalie that was extremely helpful, no matter how disturbing."

"I'll be back later," she said, patting John on the shoulder as she left.

∞

About an hour later, Antonio's cell rang. "Garcia."

"Hi Papa G," Katie said.

"Hey Mija, what are you up to?"

"I was wondering if I can talk to Kendall. I wanted to ask him something," she told him.

"He's taking a nap right now. How about I have him give you a call when he's awake?"

"Okay," she said, sounding disappointed.

"What's everyone up to?"

"Not much. James and Carlos are doing schoolwork, but Logan is already done with his. We're going to go to the park later, to see if the pond is frozen enough to skate on it. We're not going to skate though. We want to wait until Kendall is home first. Mom and Mama G are going to our house later to make sure everything is ready for when we go home. That's why I wanted to talk to Kendall. Papi, do you think he'd switch rooms with me?" she asked.

"I don't know, honey. Why do you want to switch rooms?"

"Well, I was worried he might have bad dreams because of what happened and thought if we switched rooms, maybe he wouldn't. My room is bigger anyway, and that way when the guys come and stay, they would have more room. We can paint it and move everything over. I know the guys would help," Katie said.

"Katie, that's such a nice thing you want to do. I'm not sure if he'll want to switch rooms or not, but I promise I'll have him call as soon as he's awake." Antonio smiled.

"How's he feeling today?" she asked quietly.

"He's feeling much better, and I'm hoping we can come home tomorrow. Just remember, he'll tire quickly for a while, and he won't be able to do too much," Antonio told her.

"I know. How does he look?"

"Well, he has a lot of bruises and a few cuts. His left shoulder is hurt and will take a while to heal all the way," he said.

"But, does he look the same?"

"I'm not sure what you mean, Mija. What do you mean, by the same?"

"I don't know. Just... the same," she said quietly.

"Katie, your brother still looks like your brother, just a little banged up," he told her, confused by what she meant.

"Mom said that when Kendall comes home, he might be different, because sometimes people who live through trauma change. She said not to expect things to be the same for a while," she said quietly.

"I think she meant that he might be a little quieter, maybe not as up for doing things as he usually is. But after some time, he'll be okay," he told her.

"Are you sure?"

"He's already doing much better, and once he's home with everyone, I'm willing to bet that he'll get better even faster." Antonio smiled.

"Okay, but make sure he calls so I can ask him. Mom said we can paint tonight if he wants to."

"I will, now you tell everyone that we said hi, and we'll call back later," Antonio said.

"Okay, Papa G, talk to you later!" Katie said, hanging up.

∞

Doc knocked quietly at the door. "How are we doing today?"

"Much better," Antonio said, smiling.

"Good. I thought I'd see if you need someone to make a food run. I hear the cafeteria is trying to kill people," he said, smirking at John.

"YES! And they are. That kind of cooking should be illegal," John stated.

"Afraid I have to agree with John on that one. I've tasted some lousy hospital and cafeteria food, but this place is the worst," Antonio said.

Doc smiled. "Well, there's a great sandwich place close by."

"That sounds perfect. Why don't you go with him, Antonio? You should get out for a few minutes," John told him.

"What if Kendall wakes up and I'm not here?"

"You already told him that you were going to go and grab lunch, and he's doing much better today. He will be fine. You won't be gone that long."

Antonio nodded. "Okay, we'll be back soon."

∞

Antonio had to admit that getting out of the hospital was nice. He hadn't realized how much he missed the fresh air, so he and Doc walked to the sandwich shop. They placed their orders, and while they waited, Doc asked, "Kendall's doing better today?"

Antonio nodded. "Yeah, he slept through the night and actually drank part of a shake this morning. Hopefully he'll eat his sandwich."

"I hear Natalie was able to get him to talk a little?"

"She's amazing and sneaky. We learned a few things that'll hopefully help us understand what he went through."

"She has her ways." Doc smiled.

Antonio told him about Katie's phone call. "She's only seven and worried about her brother having nightmares."

"It's going to a long road for everyone," Doc said.

"I'm afraid so," Antonio said sadly.

They picked up their order and headed back for the hospital. "You know, I was going suggest that once the boys are released, you make a short side trip on your way home," Doc said.

"Where to?" Antonio asked.

"I thought Kendall might like to stop by and see the foal. He seemed really taken with him. Might be good to see something beautiful after the hell he's been through. I happen to be very good friends with his doctor and am pretty sure I can arrange to have him released before the usual time. If you boys left here around seven, you would be at my place around eight. I could make you a decent breakfast, and we can take the boy out to the stables," Doc said.

Antonio thought about it for a moment. "You know, I think that might be perfect. It may be just what he needs."

∞

They got back to the hospital to find Kendall had woken up and was watching cartoons with John.

John saw them and smiled. "Food!"

"You and your stomach," Antonio said.

"Hey Kendall, I heard you like turkey," Doc said as he handed the boy a bag.

"Thank you." He smiled as he set the bag on the table.

"Kendall, please try and eat a little," Antonio said.

The boy sighed and took the sandwich out of the bag. He took a couple of bites and set it back down.

"Here's an ice tea to wash it down," Doc said, handing him a bottle.

"Thank you," Kendall said as he took the bottle and opened it. He had half of it gone before he knew it, not knowing how thirsty he actually was. A few minutes later, he had eaten half of the sandwich. "Papi, I'm full."

"Good job! Before I forget, you need to call Katie. She called to ask you something while you were sleeping," he said, handing Kendall his cell.

"What did she want?" Kendall asked.

"Well, if you call her, you'll find out," Antonio told him.

Kendall rolled his eyes and dialed the Garcia home.

Sylvia answered. "Antonio?"

"No Mama G, it's me. Papi said Katie called and wanted to talk to me."

"Hi sweetheart, let me get her!"

Kendall froze and then visibly shuddered, looking at the phone.

"Kendall, what's wrong?" Antonio said.

The boy looked at him and then shook his head. "N-Nothing, it's okay."

"Are you sure?"

He nodded.

"Kendall?" Katie's voice came on the line.

"Hi Katie-Bug, Papi said you called while I was sleeping."

"How are feeling today, Big Brother?"

"Better, how's everyone there?"

"Everybody's okay, but Carlos is mad because I spit marshmallows further than he did."

"You CHEATED!" Carlos yelled in the background.

"How can you CHEAT at spitting, genius?" she asked smugly.

"Because you squish two together and then suck on them until they're mushy and no one can tell," Kendall said.

"Shhh, those are trade secrets," she whispered into the phone.

"He can't hear me," Kendall pointed out.

"I wanted to ask you something and you don't have to if you don't want to, but I really want to do it for you, and we can paint and everything tonight," Katie rushed the words out in her excitement.

"What?" Kendall asked, thoroughly confused.

"Your room," Katie said.

"What about my room?"

"I wanted to know if it's okay if we switch rooms. My room is bigger and it was yours first anyway. That way when the guys come over, you have more room for everyone. Mom said we could paint it and move everything tonight. So can we?" Katie asked.

"Katie, you love your room," Kendall said.

"I can love my new room just as much. Mom said we can get new curtains and I can paint it any colour I want. Besides, I love you more, and this way maybe you won't have any bad dreams or anything," Katie whispered.

Kendall was quiet for a moment, not knowing what to say. "Tell you what. You can do whatever you want. If you really want to switch, we can. ONLY if you really want to. Okay?" he said softly.

"Thanks Kendall, I really do want to! Do you still want green walls or another colour?" Katie asked.

"Surprise me, but no PINK!"

"Would I do that to you?" she asked innocently.

"Maybe I should tell someone else that part," he said, suddenly worried that his room would be a montage of pink and purple with fluffy pillows and unicorn posters.

"Don't you trust me?" she asked.

"Can you put mom on?"

"She's at the store."

"Then put Mama G on, Papi wants to talk to her anyway," Kendall instructed.

"Fine. Love you, Big Brother," Katie said.

"I love you too, now put Mama G on." He smiled.

Sylvia was laughing as she got back on the line. "PLEASE don't let her paint my room pink or anything," he begged.

"I won't sweetheart, I promise," Sylvia said.

Kendall froze again, smile gone.

Antonio jumped up and took the phone. "Sylvia? Hi honey, what's going on there?" he asked, as he walked out of the room. "Honey, what did you just say to Kendall?"

"What? I promised him I wouldn't let Katie paint his room pink. Why, what's wrong?" she asked in concern.

"Did you happen to call him sweetheart?" Antonio asked.

"Yes, why? What's wrong?"

"Honey, we think it's a word trigger. Deesie would call him that before he would hurt him. Could you let everyone know that?"

"Oh my God is he alright?" she asked, near tears.

"He's fine, honey, it's just going to take some time, that's all. Some good news is that we might be able to come home tomorrow. Dr. Talbot will be in to check on Kendall later, and if his temperature is still normal and he's breathing alright, she might release him."

"That is good news. Are you sure he's alright? I feel terrible."

"Honey, he's fine, really. I should have told you the other day. Please don't stress out about it, just let everyone know, alright?" he said softly.

"Alright, give him a hug for me."

"Will do. Give my love to everyone, and I'll call as soon as we know if we get to come home," he said.

"Bye honey," Sylvia said.

Antonio went back in the room and John had distracted Kendall by asking him what his little sister was up to.

"I bet your room is gonna be all pink and pretty when you get home," John teased.

Kendall looked at him and groaned.

"No it won't be, Mami promised she'll make sure that there are no 'girly' colours allowed in the room. However, she did mention that John's house needs some renovation and maybe we should surprise him the next time he leaves on vacation," Antonio said, winking at Kendall.

"Hey, not cool!" John said.

Kendall smiled at Antonio. "I'm tired."

"Go to sleep then," Antonio told him, pulling the blankets up for him.

Kendall was soon fast asleep.

"Is Sylvia okay?" John asked.

Antonio nodded. "She felt terrible, but I told her there was no way she could have known, and just to let everyone else know."

"Good," John said.

Natalie came in a few minutes later. "I see you got some decent food." She smiled.

"Yes, thanks to Doc and Antonio," John said.

She went over to Kendall's bed and pulled the thermometer out. "98.9, still normal. Did he eat anything?"

"Yes, he ate half a sandwich and drank almost a full bottle of ice tea," Antonio told her.

"Well, since his temperature has been normal for over twelve hours, his breathing has improved, and he's actually eating a little, I think we can let you boys go tomorrow." She smiled.

'That'll make everyone happy," Antonio said, smiling back.

"Kendall will need to be on antibiotics for a couple of weeks, and I'm going to prescribe some pain meds and a portable nebulizer for him. We can fill those here though, so you don't have to worry about finding a pharmacy. I also might wrap his shoulder and send a sling with him. It's not so bad when he's quiet, but if he's up, moving around, it's probably going to start bothering him more. He's going to need to be seen by his pediatrician for a follow-up, and he might need physical therapy for his shoulder as well."

"Whatever he needs. Natalie, I can't thank you enough," Antonio said.

She smiled. "Well, don't forget to come back and visit on a non-patient basis. I hear Doc invited your boys out to his place this summer, so maybe we can all go fishing or something then."

"That would be great," Antonio said.

"I'll be back to check on things later." She smiled as she left.

The three men sat, talking for a while, and Kendall stirred. He started kicking out his feet and whimpering.

Antonio jumped up and grabbed his hand. "Kendall, wake up."

Kendall opened his eyes and looked at Antonio. "Hmmm?"

"I think you were having a bad dream," Antonio said.

"Don't remember," Kendall told him.

"That's alright. Guess what, Mijo? Dr. Natalie said we can go home tomorrow."

"Really?"

"Mhm, so we should be able to leave early and be home by tomorrow night," Antonio told him.

Kendall smiled as he closed his eyes. He opened them again and looked at Antonio. "Mama G won't let Katie paint my room pink, right?"

"No, she won't let her paint it pink. I promise."

Chapter 41 ~ Going Home

"When is mom going to be home?" Katie asked for the third time since getting off the phone with her brother.

"She'll be here in a little while, be patient," Sylvia said.

"But we have a lot to do!" Katie whined.

"Katie, we'll get it all done, I promise. They won't be home until tomorrow night, so that gives us the rest of today, tonight, and all of tomorrow to get it done." Sylvia laughed.

"Katie, why don't we go online? There's a website where you can pick a type of room similar to the one you want to paint, and see what the colours will look like on the walls. That way we'll know what to get ahead of time," Logan suggested.

"Okay!" She smiled as they headed upstairs to look at Logan's laptop.

"It's nice to see them excited for something," Joanna said.

"It's been a long week," Sylvia said.

"Yes it has, but things will be back to normal in no time." Jo smiled.

"I hope so." Sylvia sighed, recalling her conversation with Antonio.

Jen and Brooke came in with James and Carlos in tow. The boys were carrying grocery bags for their mothers. "Thank goodness, Katie was driving me crazy waiting for you." Sylvia smiled.

"I guess we need to run to the hardware store next," Jen said.

"Logan managed to distract her by showing her an online site where she can pick out colours ahead of time," Jo told her.

"Good, maybe we can get the groceries put away first then," Jen said, walking into the kitchen.

A few minutes later, Katie came running down the stairs. "Mom, I know what colours to get! Can we go now?"

"Katie, inside voice, please," Jen scolded.

Katie rolled her eyes. "But I've been waiting like, forever!"

"It's been like twenty minutes," Logan pointed out.

Katie turned, crossed her arms, and raised her eyebrow at him.

"Or... like... forever," he said.

"Katie, please don't frighten the boys," Sylvia said.

"What colours did you decide on?" Jen asked her daughter.

Katie handed her printout, showing two shades of green. One a deep rich colour, the other more muted and subtle. "Very nice! Did you find anything for your room?" Jen asked.

She handed her another printout with different shades of blues and purples. "I haven't decided yet. Can we go now?"

"Why don't you and Katie go to the hardware store and the boys and I can head over to the house and start moving the furniture out. I'll stop at the station and pick up the new house keys for you," Sylvia suggested.

"Brooke and I can meet you later and bring dinner," Jo said.

"Sounds good," Jen said and they all headed out.

A little while later, Sylvia and the boys pulled into the Knight's driveway. "Are you boys ready to get to work?" she asked, smiling.

They nodded and got out. They found themselves walking slowly to the door. "Okay, what's wrong?" she asked when she realized they weren't next to her any longer.

"It's just... we haven't been here since..." James said hesitantly.

"Oh honey, I'm sorry I didn't even think about that." She sighed, mentally cursing herself for the second time that day. "Are you worried about what you'll find?"

The boys all nodded and she smiled softly. "There's nothing bad in there, I promise. Sally even had the house cleaned for Jen, so when they come home, it's ready for them. The door has been fixed and the locks have been changed. Mama D and Mama M are going to run to the market later so they have groceries. Do you need to stay out here for a while?"

"I think I'm good," James said, looking at his two friends.

Carlos and Logan smiled and nodded as well. They went inside and headed up to Katie's room, and between the four of them, soon had it emptied of its contents.

Jen and Katie showed up a little while later, and the boys ran down and carried in the paint and supplies. The next hour was spent taping windows, fixtures, and covering the wood floor with tarp.

Jen looked at her daughter. "You're SURE you want to do this?"

Katie rolled her eyes. "Mom, I told you like a thousand times now, YES!"

"A thousand times, really Katie?" Logan teased.

She turned around and crossed her arms again, just looking at him.

"W-Well, I guess it c-could have been a thousand," he stammered.

"Katie, please don't scare the boys before we paint," Sylvia asked.

James and Carlos laughed at Logan. "You're scared of a 7-year-old!" Carlos laughed.

Katie turned and looked at Carlos, giving him the same stare. He quickly went over and stood behind his mom. Katie turned to James. "Do you have anything to say?"

He gave her his most dazzling smile. "I love you?"

"Katie, don't hurt the boys, we need them." Jen laughed.

Logan smirked at his two friends. "Who's afraid of a 7-year-old?"

Three hours later, the room had its first coat of paint on the walls. Brooke and Jo showed up with groceries for the house and pizza for the group, so they all settled down into the living room to eat. "So, Katie, would you like to come with me for a while?" Brooke asked.

"Why?" Katie asked curiously.

"Well, I thought since you're redoing your brother's room, that maybe we should find something special for him." Brooke smiled.

"Brooke, you don't have to do that," Jen said.

"Oh pshhh. I was just thinking maybe a new comforter or something like that. That is if Katie will help me pick it out," Brooke said.

"Really? That would be awesome!" Katie squealed.

"Katie, nothing pink or girly. I promised your brother," Sylvia said.

Katie rolled her eyes. "Would I do that to my big brother?"

"Katie," Jen warned.

"Fine, maybe we can find something hockey related," she said, a slight pout on her lips.

"That's my good girl." Jen smiled as she started clearing away the paper plates.

Brooke and Katie left for the department store, while the boys gave the bedroom a second coat of paint.

"It looks pretty good," Logan said.

"Yeah! I think he'll like it," Carlos agreed.

"Well, we better get this stuff cleaned up and the brushes soaking," James told them as he started putting the lids back on the paint cans.

"Don't you think it looks good?" Carlos asked.

"Yeah, it looks great," James said as he continued to clean up.

"James?" Logan asked.

"What? It looks great, okay. Kendall is going to like it... It's just different," James told him.

"That's kinda the point, buddy," Carlos said.

"I know. It's just going to take some getting used to, that's all. Just drop it, okay?" James said as he took the brushes into the bathroom and put them to soak in the bucket.

A few minutes later, the paint, tape, and supplies had been put away and everyone was getting ready to leave. Jen realized someone was missing and went back upstairs.

"James, we're ready to go."

She heard something coming from Kendall's old room and quietly opened the door.

James was sitting on the floor with his back against Kendall's bed, his head down, softly crying.

She went over and sat next to him. "Sweetie, what is it?"

He shook his head and continued crying into his arms.

Jen put her arms around him. "Baby, it's alright. Please tell me what's wrong."

He mumbled something into his arms that she couldn't understand.

She cupped his face in her hands and made him look at her. "James, please tell me."

"I d-didn't protect him. I'm the strongest and I'm supposed to protect them. I failed, and now he's hurt and everything's changing," James whispered.

"James, you didn't fail anyone. Sometimes things are beyond our control and just happen. It's not right and it's not fair, but that's life," she told him.

"You don't understand! Kendall figures things out, decides what needs to be done, and takes action first. Logan is always there when we need help learning or understanding something. Carlos can always make people smile and feel good about anything, no matter what. I'm the one who takes care of them when someone tries to hurt them, I protect them!" James explained.

"I know, honey, but you can't protect them from life, and sometimes life is..." Jen said.

"Wrong," James finished.

"I was going to say hard, but I guess wrong fits too," she said as she brushed his bangs back.

"I should have done something," James said.

She hugged him and sighed. "Baby, we all feel like there should have been something we could have done. The truth is there was no way to know what was going to happen. Deesie was a horrible man, who liked to hurt people, and it's unfortunate there are people like that in the world. All we can do is be there for each other and get through this together. Okay?"

He sniffed and nodded. "I know it's just..."

"It's just that sometimes you need to let it out and that's perfectly understandable," she said, kissing his forehead. "Are you ready to go?"

He nodded again.

She stood up and offered him her hand. "We'll move everything over tomorrow?"

He stood up and gave her a small smile. "Yeah, we'll have it ready when he gets home."

∞

Kendall was still sleeping when Agent Bower stopped by. He didn't want to stress Kendall out, so he and Antonio spoke in the hallway.

"How's he doing today?" Bower asked.

"It was a long night, but he's doing much better today. Dr. Talbot is releasing him in the morning," Antonio told him.

"That's great. I'm sorry about what happened yesterday. We will eventually need to find out what happened."

"I know. Dr. Talbot actually got a few more details today," Antonio said and told him about her conversation with Kendall.

"Well, that explains what the case of needles was for. We found it among Deesie's belongings, along with a few other things. He had a trunk filled with trophies from past victims,

some we didn't know about. I found this in there." Bower pulled out the small framed photo of the boys that had been sitting on Kendall's dresser. "I thought he might want this back."

Antonio smiled. "Thanks Christian, I appreciate it."

"So you're heading for home tomorrow?"

Antonio nodded. "We're going to surprise Kendall with a little side trip to Doc's first. He got Natalie to release the boys early enough, so we should be home by tomorrow night."

"Ah, yes... Doc. When you see him, can you tell him to check in with Dr. Talbot in about a week? I promised them an early Christmas present and found it sooner than I thought." Bower gave a mischievous grin.

"What did you do?" Antonio asked.

"Only making sure that people in positions of authority follow the law." He grinned.

"You guys are going to have to keep me informed." Antonio laughed.

"I'm sure one of us will. You have a safe trip home, and I'll be in touch in a few weeks to see where Kendall's at with being able to handle any more questions." Bower smiled.

"Sounds good," Antonio said, shaking Bower's hand.

∞

Kendall woke up a couple of times during the night, but all in all, it was quiet. Nurse Patrick came in around 6:30 am to wake them.

"Dr. Talbot will be in soon with your prescriptions and to say goodbye." She smiled as she removed Kendall's catheter.

"Thank you." He smiled.

"I'm going to jump in the shower," John said and headed for the bathroom.

"Papi, I don't have anything to wear," Kendall told him.

"Your backpack's in the car and we grabbed your shoes and jacket. I think your jacket is ruined. I have an extra one in the car. It'll be a little big, but at least it'll be warm. I'll grab them when John gets done."

Kendall nodded. "Okay, thanks."

John finished and came out a few minutes later, so Antonio went to the SUV and grabbed the backpack and his jacket. When he got back, he helped Kendall stand, and the boy grabbed his backpack and headed for the bathroom.

"You yell if you need any help," Antonio said.

"I will, thanks Papi," Kendall said as he closed the door.

Kendall was a little dizzy. He hadn't been on his feet much the last couple of days. He sat down, removed the wrap from his foot, and turned on the water. Once it was warm, he shed the gown and sweats and stepped under the stream of water. He stood there for a few minutes, just letting the warm water flow over him, and then attempted to wash his hair. It was harder than he thought, but he managed to get his hair lathered and rinsed. When he finished washing, he reluctantly stepped out of the shower. It had felt really good.

He wrapped a towel around himself and opened his backpack. He found some clean clothes that were his and left the ones Deesie had bought lying on the floor. He found he couldn't pull his t-shirt over his head and sighed. He found a new toothbrush and paste, so he brushed his teeth and then looked in the mirror. His face was still bruised, but the colours were changing from deep purple and black to a bluish purple and yellow.

His eye wasn't swollen anymore and the first laceration on his forehead was healing well. The newer one from Deesie's face was still a little swollen and painful if he touched it. He looked at his neck and chest and shuddered at all the marks Deesie had left. He wished they would scrub away.

Sighing again, he wrapped the towel around his shoulders and opened the door. "I can't get my shirt on," he whispered.

Antonio came over and helped him pull it on.

"Thank you," Kendall said. He grabbed his backpack and limped back to his bed.

Antonio quickly showered and dressed. "Aren't those your clothes in the bathroom?"

Kendall shook his head. "No, HE bought them, I don't want them."

"Okay, I'll let the nurse know. Maybe they have a place for donations," Antonio said.

Natalie came in a few minutes later. "How are my boys this morning?" she asked cheerfully.

"I think everyone's doing well this morning." Antonio smiled.

She had brought a bag with various items and pulled them out, explaining what they were. She held up a prescription bottle. "Antibiotics, one twice daily, you need to eat with them." She held up another bottle. "Pain meds, one every 6-8 hours, USE them." She pulled out a roll of elastic wrap. "This is for your foot if you need it."

She pulled out a small box, took out the portable nebulizer, and showed them how to work it. "Twice a day for the next three days and then as needed. I want you to go to your doctor for a recheck in one week, and they can re-evaluate things then."

Kendall nodded.

She pulled out another box. "This is a shoulder immobilizer. I want you to wear it when you're up doing things. Limiting the movement will help the muscle heal faster. Can I show you how to put it on?"

Kendall nodded, and she wrapped it around his waist first, and then wrapped the thin band around his upper arm, and another onto his forearm. "It's like a sling, but it offers more stability, and it's a bit more adjustable for comfort's sake. You can loosen it around the waist a little if it's putting too much pressure on your bruised ribs," she explained.

"Okay, thank you," Kendall said.

"No problem, honey. Is it alright if I check your temperature and lungs?"

Kendall nodded and she took his temperature. "98.8, perfect."

Then she pulled out her stethoscope. "Sounds much better, but still a little crackly. Not nearly as much as when you first got here, though."

He smiled at her. "Thanks for everything."

"You're welcome. Can I give you a hug?" she asked.

He blushed a little and nodded.

She wrapped her arms around him. "You take care and keep in touch. I'm going to miss the three of you."

"We will," Kendall said.

"Well, you boys better hit the road. You have a long drive ahead of you," Natalie said.

"Thanks for everything, Natalie," Antonio said, hugging her.

"And you!" she said, hugging John. "Don't forget those stitches need to come out in another ten days."

"I won't, thanks for taking care of us," John said, hugging her back.

"Well... someone has to," she said, smiling. "Come back and visit."

"Will do!" John smiled.

The nurse brought in a wheelchair. "That's for you, I can walk," John told Kendall.

Kendall rolled his eyes and made a face but sat in the chair. The nurse let Antonio push him to the entrance door and he left John and Kendall there as he went to get the SUV.

Kendall was nervous and knew people were looking at him. John put his hand on his shoulder and squeezed, and when he saw Antonio drive up, pushed Kendall out the door. He helped Kendall into the backseat and climbed in next to him.

Antonio pulled out of the hospital parking lot and headed towards Jamieson. "There are a couple of pillows in the back if you get tired," he told Kendall.

"Okay, thanks Papi," Kendall said.

"We'll do your first breathing treatment when we stop for lunch."

"Okay," Kendall said, yawning. "This shoulder thing feels funny."

"I know but you'll get used to it. I had to wear one when I dislocated my shoulder a couple of years ago, remember?" Antonio said.

"Mmmhmm," Kendall said as he closed his eyes.

John reached back and grabbed a pillow. He put it on his shoulder and pulled Kendall over, so he could rest against him. A little while later, Antonio looked in the rearview mirror and saw the pillow was now in John's lap, and Kendall's head was resting on it and he was sleeping peacefully. John had his head back and was snoring quietly, his arm resting on Kendall's shoulder.

Antonio shook his head and smiled.

∞

Antonio pulled into Doc's driveway about forty-five minutes later. He got out and opened Kendall's door. "Mijo, time to wake up, we made a quick stop."

Kendall rubbed his eyes and yawned. "Huh?"

"I thought we'd stop and say goodbye to Doc," Antonio told him as he shook John's shoulder. "John, wake up."

John opened his eyes. "Where are we?"

"Doc's place. He offered to make breakfast for us." Antonio smiled.

"Yes!" John said and got out of the SUV.

Doc came out to greet them with Samson running ahead. "Oh no you don't, you already got me into trouble once," John said to the dog.

Samson ran over to Antonio, who had his arm around Kendall's waist, and then sat in front of the pair, looking at them expectantly. Kendall reached down and scratched the dog's head, who then started running around happily, his whole body seemed to be wagging.

Kendall chuckled. "He's so happy and friendly. He reminds me of Carlos."

John looked over the boy's head and gave Antonio a triumphant smile.

"HE can say that," Antonio said as they continued up to the house.

"Hey... that's not fair!" John yelled after them.

Doc offered his hand to help Kendall up the stairs and the teen took a hold of it. "I hope you boys are hungry, I made biscuits with gravy, scrambled eggs, and sausage."

"Sounds good, Doc." Antonio smiled.

They went inside and Doc led them into the kitchen. "Wash up, have a seat, and we can eat."

Kendall used the sink first and then Doc pulled a chair out for him. "Plenty to eat. If you would rather have something else, I can do that."

"This looks good, thank you." Kendall smiled as he sat down.

A few minutes later, plates had been dished up and the men were eating. Kendall took a bite every now and then, but he really wasn't very hungry.

"Kendall, please eat a little more," Antonio asked.

Kendall sighed and took a few more bites. "I'm sorry, it really is good, I'm just not very hungry," he told Doc.

"It's going to take a while for you to build up your appetite," Doc said, smiling.

After they had finished and the table had been cleared, Doc sat down and looked at Kendall. "So, how would you like to meet Midnight Shadow's foal?"

"Really?" Kendall smiled.

"Really. We'll need to find you some boots to wear. Jake has several pairs he's outgrown. Let me see your foot."

Kendall lifted his foot and Doc carefully pulled off his shoe.

"Be right back." He winked and went out into the mud porch. He came in a moment later. "I think these will fit," he said, kneeling down and helping Kendall get the boots on.

"Can you walk in them alright?" Doc asked as he took Kendall's hand and helped him up.

"I think so, they feel fine," Kendall told him.

"Good," Doc said as he handed Kendall the jacket he had been wearing.

They walked out the back door and headed to the stables. Doc had taken Kendall's good arm, helping him manage the uneven ground. Once they got to the stables, Doc took Kendall to the fence. "Stand here and I'll send them out."

Kendall did as he was told, and a moment later, a beautiful black horse came trotting out with a smaller version of herself following. Doc came back out and handed Kendall a handful of carrots. "Midnight loves these, just make sure you let go when she grabs ahold or she'll pull you over," he said.

Kendall nodded and held a carrot out for the horse. She snorted a few times, but finally made her way over and took the offering. He gave her another one and she put her head over the fence and nuzzled his forehead.

"Looks like you made a friend." Doc laughed.

Kendall gave her another carrot and she pulled back and chomped happily away on it, while her foal made his way over to the fence. Kendall held out his hand and the foal walked over and bumped it with his nose. The next thing he knew, the foal had latched onto his fingers and was nursing on them.

Doc laughed. "Apparently you've made two friends."

Kendall tried to pull his hand back, but the foal was very happily sucking on his fingers and refused to release him. It tickled and Kendall started giggling.

Midnight Shadow came back over and put her head back over the fence, asking for more carrots. Kendall only had the one hand to work with, so Doc came over and handed her the last two and she stood there, eating them contentedly.

John pulled out his phone and quickly took a couple of pictures of the scene. He nudged Antonio and showed him. "I think we should send these home, what do you think?"

Antonio smiled and nodded.

John quickly typed a text and sent it to Sylvia and Sally's phones.

After about half an hour, the horses decided it was time to go back in and Doc opened their door for them.

They walked back to the house and Kendall went to take off the boots, but Doc stopped him. "Why don't you keep those? Jake outgrew them three years ago."

"Thanks Doc." Kendall smiled and went to wash the foal's saliva off his hand.

The three men walked into the living room. Antonio smiled at Doc. "I can't thank you enough. That's something incredible that he'll never forget."

"Well, I can't believe Midnight took to him so quickly. Usually she'll grab a carrot and run," Doc told him.

Kendall followed them a moment later. "Papi, could I use your phone for a minute?"

"Sure, you calling home?" he asked, handing Kendall his cell.

"Yeah, I wanted to ask James something."

"Why don't you sit in here and I'll get these two another cup of coffee before you go?" Doc told him.

Kendall smiled and sat on the couch, and when the others went back into the kitchen, he dialed James' cell. Kendall had been feeling strange since the dream where James had died, and he just wanted to reassure himself that his friend was alright.

"Hello," James answered.

Kendall smiled in relief. "Hi James, it's Kendall."

"Hey, what are you doing? Are you on your way home?" James asked.

"Yeah, we stopped to eat and will be leaving in a few minutes. I just wanted to call and..." Kendall's voice failed him.

"What's wrong?" James asked, suddenly worried.

"I-I just had a bad dream and wanted to make sure you were okay. I know it's stupid, but..."

"It's not stupid, and I'm glad you called. I can't wait for you to get home tonight, everybody's so happy," James told him.

"Can I ask you a favour?" Kendall whispered.

"You can ask me anything."

"I know you guys have been staying at Carlos' and you probably want to go home, but would you stay with me for a couple of nights? I just... I'm a little scared to stay alone," Kendall whispered almost in tears. He would never admit he was afraid to any of his friends but James.

It was an unspoken rule that James was the protector in their group, with Kendall as his backup. However, on the extremely rare occasions that Kendall felt threatened, James was there.

"You know I will, buddy. For as long you need me to be there," James told him.

"Thanks James, I really appreciate it."

"You don't have to thank me, I'll always be here for you," James said.

Kendall smiled. "See you tonight."

"See you tonight, little brother." James smiled.

Chapter 42~ Homecoming

Since James was up, he decided to shower and dress. Then he went to wake Carlos and Logan. "Come on you guys, get up, we have a lot to do today!"

The other two boys groaned and pulled the blanket over their heads. James reached down and pulled it off. "Rise and shine!"

They groaned again and Carlos threw his pillow at him. "Okay, I tried to be nice," James warned them as he reached down and grabbed a hold of the blanket the boys were lying on. He pulled it up hard and Carlos and Logan went flying off, landing against the wall, with Carlos on top of Logan.

"Hey!" they both yelled.

James just smiled. "Time to get up!"

"But I'm tired," Carlos whined as he buried his head in Logan's shoulder.

"Hey, get off of me!" Logan said, pushing Carlos over.

"Come on, you guys! They're on their way home, and we still have a lot to do in Kendall's room," James told them.

The other boys smiled and jumped up. "I get the shower first!" Logan yelled. With eight people in the house, whoever was last in usually had to shower in cold water.

"No, I do!" Carlos yelled back as they pushed each other back and forth, running down the hallway.

"You always use all the hot water!" Logan complained, as he got to the bathroom first. He looked at Carlos, smirking, and locked the door behind him.

Carlos stood there pouting.

"Don't worry, I already used the rest of the hot water." James smiled as he walked past his friend.

"Ha, that'll teach him!" Carlos grinned happily. "Hey wait, that means I won't have any either."

James laughed as he headed downstairs. "See? Problem solved."

The moms were already up and sitting in the kitchen and talking over coffee.

"Good morning," James said, smiling as he walked in.

"Good morning, sweetheart," Brooke said, kissing him on the cheek.

Sylvia realized she still needed to tell everyone about Kendall's word trigger. They had been so busy last night and everyone seemed to be happy for the first time in days, she hadn't wanted to ruin it.

"As soon as everyone is here, I need to let you know a couple of things that Antonio told me yesterday."

"Is everything alright?" Jen asked.

"Yes, it's just that they found a word trigger, and I want to let everyone know what it is and that there might be more that we don't know about yet," Sylvia explained.

"What's a word trigger?" James asked as Logan and Carlos came in.

"Well, sometimes people develop what they call 'triggers,' and it can be anything...a sound, a smell, something they see, and sometimes it's just a word. So we just need to avoid using that word until he's doing better," she explained.

"What's the word?" Jen asked.

"Sweetheart, maybe sweetie. Antonio said that's what Deesie would call Kendall," Sylvia told them.

"What happens when he hears the word?" Jen asked.

"It can trigger a panic attack, flashbacks, any number of things," Logan interjected.

"Exactly, so we just need to be careful about using that word for now. It will be more of a 'mom' thing, since I don't think you boys go around using the word, 'sweetheart' that often. But if you notice anything else that's become a trigger, please let us know immediately," Sylvia said.

The boys all nodded.

After breakfast, they got ready to head over to the Knight house to finish working on Kendall's new room.

Sylvia grabbed her cell, which had been charging on the counter, and noticed she had a new message. She opened it and called everyone over.

"I got a message from John. It says, 'We stopped at Doc Akin's place to say goodbye and Kendall made a new friend.' Look at this," she said and turned the screen so everyone could see.

There were two photos of Kendall standing next to a fence. On the other side of the fence was a big black horse eating something and a baby horse that had Kendall's fingers in its mouth. There was a tall man with curly blond hair that they assumed was Doc, and he was smiling. Kendall was wearing a black jacket that was too big for him and one arm wasn't in its sleeve. Even from the distance that the photo was taken, the bruises on his face were clearly visible and shocked them. However, the one thing they all noticed was the smile on his face as he was looking at the baby horse.

As they looked at the pictures, they felt hope, because at that moment in the photo, Kendall was happy and they knew he wasn't lost to them.

They all headed over to the Knight home in high spirits and soon had Kendall's room in order. The boys had moved the furniture in, while Jen and Sylvia moved the clothing from his old closet to the new one. Jo and Brooke transferred his posters and photos to the new room. Since there was more wall space, they spread them out a bit more. James found a couple of large padded c- hooks and hung Grandpa Knight's vintage hockey stick over his desk. By noon, the room was finished and looked great.

"His room hasn't been this clean in years! I can't thank you all enough. This is going to be such a nice surprise." Jen smiled, as she looked around.

"He'll love it," Carlos said happily.

"Yes he will swe... honey," Jen corrected quickly. "I need to get out of the habit of saying that word."

"We all do," Sylvia said. "Who wants lunch? I think we should go out and treat ourselves to a nice meal."

Everyone thought that was a great idea and decided to head over to Applebee's for lunch.

∞

Antonio, John, and Kendall said their goodbyes to Doc and were on the road by 9 am. John offered to drive the first half of the trip, since he was feeling better and wasn't supposed to drive after dark. Antonio agreed and sat in the backseat with Kendall. The boy slept a good part of the way, and Antonio woke him when they were ready to stop for lunch.

"What do we want?" John asked.

"Someplace with a drive-thru?" Kendall asked. He really didn't want to go in somewhere and be stared at again.

"Good idea," Antonio said, sensing the boy's discomfort. "Then we need to do your nebulizer treatment."

Kendall nodded.

John soon found a place, and they ordered their food and parked, so they could eat. "You need to eat with your meds and it's time for a pain pill," Antonio told Kendall.

Kendal picked at his food again, but Antonio got him to eat half of his burger. Then he gave Kendall his pill and pulled out the nebulizer. They got it going, and Kendall sat there, breathing the medicated mist in.

"Papi, do they know how I look?" he asked quietly under the mask.

"What do you mean?"

Kendall pointed to the bruises on his face. He was worried everyone would freak out if they weren't warned. He had been banged up and had many bruises and injuries over the years, but he had never looked like this, and he was a little scared at how they would react.

"They know you were beaten up, but do you want me to call them and make sure they're prepared?" Antonio asked.

Kendall nodded, "Please, I just don't want..."

Antonio smiled. "I'll give them a call now, while you are having your treatment."

Kendall nodded. "Thank you."

"I need to stretch my legs anyway," Antonio said as he got out of the SUV. He called home and there was no answer, so he called Sylvia's cell.

"Antonio?" she asked when she answered.

"Yes honey. How's everything going there?"

"Perfect, we finished Kendall's room a little while ago and decided to go out for lunch. Where are you?"

"We should be leaving Wisconsin in another hour or so, depending on the roads. It started to snow about an hour ago, so we're taking it slow. Kendall wanted me to call because he's a little worried about how everyone is going to react to the way he looks," Antonio said.

"Why is that?" Sylvia asked.

"Well, he's pretty bruised and has a few lacerations. Almost every part of his face is a different colour, and when we went through the hospital, a few people were shocked, and I think he's afraid the same thing will happen when we get home. I never thought about it until he said something, because John and I have been with him for the last few days. Although he's healing, he does look pretty bad. So if you could let everyone know?" Antonio asked.

"Of course, although we did see a little in the photos that John sent this morning. I'll make sure everyone knows how extensive it is. I also warned everyone about the word 'sweetheart.' I never realized how often I use that word, so it's going to be a challenge to keep up on it."

"I know it is, but hopefully once we get him into counseling, it'll help him work through that," Antonio said.

"Do you know what time you'll be home?"

"Not really. I'm hoping by eight tonight, but it really depends on the weather," he told her.

"Okay, well I'll let everyone know."

"Okay honey. Well, I think we're ready to get back on the road. I'll give you a call later, alright?"

"Talk to you later, swe... honey, ugh. This is not going to be easy."

Antonio smiled. "You can always say it in Spanish."

"Talk to you later, amorcito," she smiled.

"Same here," he laughed.

"You're impossible," she said.

"I know, but you love me anyway," he smirked.

"Some days more than others," she retorted.

∞

They drove for another three hours, when Antonio had John pull over so they could switch places. He didn't want his partner pushing himself too hard.

Around 6 pm, he pulled into a small town so they could grab some dinner. There were no drive-thru places, so he ran into a local restaurant and ordered three sandwiches to go.

They sat in the parking lot and ate.

After Kendall had eaten half his sandwich, John gave him his antibiotic and another pain pill.

While they were finishing, Antonio made a quick call home.

"Hello," Carlos answered.

"Hey Mijo, what are you up to?" Antonio asked his son.

"Papi! We're just getting ready to eat dinner. Where are you?"

"Still a few hours out, buddy. It's starting to snow again, so we're taking it slow," Antonio told him. "Is Mami there?"

Yeah, I'll get her," he said and called Sylvia to the phone.

"Hello," she answered.

"Hi honey, just letting you know we're going to be a little longer than we hoped. It's snowing, so we're going to take it slow, so probably not until nine or ten tonight. Why don't you see if Jen wants to stay over? Kendall will probably be ready to sleep for the night by the time we get home."

"Okay, I'll ask her. If that's the case, maybe the other boys should stay the night as well, or do you think that might be too much for him?" Sylvia asked.

"I think that's a good idea." He smiled.

"Hold on for a minute and I'll ask now," Sylvia said.

She called Jen in, who thought it would probably be for the best. No reason to move him around too much tonight, especially after such a long drive. It was agreed that while everyone would stay to meet them when they got home, Joanna and Brooke would go home after, while the boys stayed the night.

"She thinks it's a good idea and says thank you. I think she's a little nervous about going home, and this way, I can stay with them for part of the day tomorrow," Sylvia said quietly.

"Good plan. I was wondering about that. We're going to head back out, and we'll see you all soon."

"Okay, drive carefully and we'll be waiting!" Sylvia smiled.

∞

A few hours later, Antonio pulled into town and dropped John off at his house. "Get some sleep," he told his partner as he got out of the SUV.

"Will do. Talk to you later." John yawned. "Take care, kiddo. I'll see you later," he said, reaching in and hugging Kendall.

"Bye John. Thanks," Kendall whispered.

"You need anything, you call me," John told him.

"I will." Kendall smiled.

A few minutes later, Antonio pulled down his street and pulled over. "Are you ready for this?" he asked.

Kendall nodded. "Just nervous."

"I know, Mijo. If you get overwhelmed, just say so. Everyone knows what you've been through and will understand," Antonio told him.

Kendall took a deep breath and nodded.

"That's my boy," Antonio said as he pulled up the street and into his driveway.

Antonio got out and opened Kendall's door for him.

Inside, Carlos squealed. "They're home!"

"Carlos, calm down! Kendall might get freaked out if we all jump him when he walks in the door," Logan told him.

Carlos took a deep breath and nodded, but he was so excited, he found it hard to stay still. Sylvia went over and put her arm around him to help him stay quiet.

Antonio and Kendall walked to the porch, where Kendall stopped. He suddenly felt very shy and a little sick to his stomach. He felt like he did on his first day of school and looked at Antonio, trying not to panic.

"Take a deep breath and we'll go slowly. Just remember that everyone here loves you and they've missed you so much," Antonio said as he wrapped his arm around the boy.

"I know, I just... I don't know. I feel weird," Kendall said.

"Once you get inside, everything will be okay, you'll see," Antonio reassured him.

Kendall nodded and they walked up the steps.

Jen opened the door as they got to it and smiled at her son.

"Hi baby," she said as tears started to fall.

"Hi Mama," he said as she took him in her arms and kissed his forehead. She stood there, holding him for a moment, and Antonio ushered them inside.

Everyone was quiet for a moment, and then Katie ran to her brother, throwing her arms around his waist. The three of them stood there like that for a couple of minutes, until Jen released her hold and picked Katie up so she could kiss her brother.

Kendall looked around shyly, unable to meet anyone's eyes. He knew how he looked, and he was still worried about what they thought.

Carlos couldn't hold it back any longer and ran to him. "Kendall!" he said as he gently hugged his friend. "I've missed you so, so much!"

Logan came over and hugged him next. "Kendall..."

"Logan, no more of that," Kendall warned.

Logan nodded and smiled at his friend.

Brooke went over to him and kissed his cheek. "Welcome home, honey."

Kendall smiled shyly. It felt so weird to feel this way around the people he has known and loved his whole life, but he felt so uncertain of himself.

Joanna came over and hugged him. "I'm glad you're back, baby."

"Thank you."

Kendall looked over at James, who came over and gently took the younger boy into his arms and hugged him. Kendall hugged him back.

"Welcome home, little brother," James whispered.

Chapter 43~ One Word

A short while later, the bags had been brought in and Jen had settled Kendall onto the couch, Katie curled up next to him. The other boys were sitting close by and had put in a movie, and Sylvia was in the kitchen making popcorn and hot chocolate for them.

The parents were sitting around the table having tea. Brooke and Joanna were going to be leaving soon, and Antonio wanted to fill them in on a few things first.

"How have the boys been doing?" Antonio asked.

"They've had good days and bad. Carlos has been having nightmares, and Logan broke down the other day," Sylvia told him.

"James had a moment last night," Jen said.

"I think they were all doing much better today though," Joanna said.

"Yes, I think fixing up Kendall's room really helped them. They were so proud of the work they did and promised Katie that when she's ready, they'll be there to do her room." Sylvia smiled.

"Nothing pink or girly in Kendall's room, right?" Antonio asked.

"Don't be silly, there is nothing pink in his room. Beautiful greens and we got him a new blue comforter," Brooke promised.

Sylvia laughed as she saw the wary look on her husband's face. "Nothing pink and I didn't see anything girly, I double checked," she told him as she carried the tray of snacks out into the living room.

He smiled in relief.

She set the tray down on the table, smiled, and went back to the kitchen. "Come see this," she said quietly.

The other parents got up and followed her into the other room.

James had a pillow on his lap and Kendall's head was lying on it. He was lying on his right side, sound asleep. Katie was curled up hugging Kendall's waist, also asleep. Carlos was sitting on the floor in front of Kendall, his head resting against James' knee, Kendall's hand resting on his shoulder. Logan was sitting on the other side of Kendall, with his friend's feet resting in his lap.

"We should get him up to bed," Antonio said.

"No, let's wait a little while. They all need this right now." Jen smiled.

They stood and watched for a moment and went back into the kitchen. "I think they're going to need to spend some time together. Since it's the weekend, maybe the boys could come and stay?" Jen asked, looking at her friends.

"Of course," Jo said, and Brooke nodded as well.

"Good idea. I'll need to talk to them too, once we put Kendall to bed though," Antonio said.

"What about?" Jen asked.

"You already know about the word trigger, but he's also been having some really bad nightmares. He wakes up screaming, not knowing where he is or who's there with him."

"What were they?" Sylvia asked.

"He couldn't remember, and the doctors had to sedate him twice. He slept really well last night and on the ride home, so hopefully he won't have anymore, but we just won't know unless it happens," Antonio told them.

Jen was quiet for a moment and bit her lip. "What else happened to him?"

"We don't really know everything, he hasn't told us much. Agent Bower asked him a few questions the other day, but it triggered a panic attack, so the doctor made him leave. Dr. Talbot did get him to talk to her a little, but I think we should wait and talk about that when the kids aren't around," he told her.

"After they go to bed then?" Jen asked.

He looked at her and nodded.

"Well, I should get home. I'll pack up some things for Logan and drop them off tomorrow," Joanna said.

"Same here. We'll see you tomorrow," Brooke said, hugging Jen.

Jen nodded. "Thank you for everything, I couldn't have made it without all of you."

"We should get the kids to bed too," Sylvia said.

Jen nodded and they all walked out together.

Brooke went to James and kissed his cheek. "I'll see you tomorrow, darling."

He smiled. "Okay mom, goodnight."

"I'll see you tomorrow as well," Jo said, kissing Logan.

"Night mom," Logan said.

Antonio walked them to their cars, and when he went back inside, smiled at the boys. "I think it's time for everyone to get some sleep."

They all nodded in agreement. It had been a long day.

"Where's everyone going to sleep?" he asked.

"Katie is staying with me. So, the boys together?" Jen asked, looking at them.

"Yeah, Kendall can have my bed and we can sleep on the floor," Carlos said, smiling.

The other two boys nodded in agreement.

Antonio reached down and carefully removed Katie's arms from her brother's waist and handed her to Carlos. "Here Mijo, please take her to their room."

Carlos took the sleeping girl from his father and started carrying her to the bedroom.

Jen knelt down beside her sleeping son and kissed him on the cheek. "Time for bed sweetheart," she said, realizing her mistake too late.

Kendall inhaled sharply and his eyes flew open. He started screaming as he tried to push away from anyone who was touching him, trying to escape. Jen fell back onto the floor sobbing, and Sylvia grabbed her, pulling her away from the couch so Antonio could get to Kendall. Logan stood up quickly, unsure of what to do, and James tried to hold onto Kendall but lost his grip on the smaller boy as he pulled away.

"NO! STAY AWAY FROM ME!" he screamed as he kicked out.

His eyes were unfocused and he had no idea where he was or what was happening, he just wanted to get away.

Antonio grabbed him and pulled him against his chest, holding him tightly. "Shhh, it's alright. You're safe, Mijo."

Kendall was close to hyperventilating, and Antonio wrapped his arms and legs around the boy to prevent him from hurting himself or anyone else. Antonio slowly rocked the screaming boy back and forth, trying to quiet him.

His screams woke Katie, who moved so suddenly that Carlos nearly dropped her.

"Kendall!" she cried as she slipped from Carlos' grasp and ran for her brother.

Logan saw her coming and caught her, pulling her away from the scene. He picked her up and took her into the bedroom, pulling Carlos along with them. Logan closed the door and sat down on the bed, holding Katie. She was fighting him, desperate to get to her brother.

"Katie, stop, you can't help him! Let Papa G take care of him!" He held her close and she finally collapsed against his chest sobbing.

Carlos sat next to them, clearly in shock. "What happened?"

"Mama K went to wake him up and accidentally called him sweetheart. He woke up panicking, trying to get away," Logan explained, trying not to cry as he heard his friend still screaming in the other room.

"What are we going to do?" Carlos whispered, as he also tried not to cry.

∞

They still couldn't get Kendall to wake up or to calm down, and he was now having difficulty breathing. Antonio made a decision. "Sylvia, get the car. We need to get him to the hospital."

She nodded, and James moved to Jen and held her while Sylvia ran for the door.

"My fault, it's all my fault," she kept chanting, sitting there in James' arms, shock evident on her tear-stained face.

"Take care of her," Antonio said as he picked Kendall up and headed out the door.

They got to the hospital and Sylvia ran ahead of Antonio to get help.

They got Kendall into a room and Antonio quickly told the doctor what had happened. The doctor gave Kendall a sedative and then put him on oxygen, until his breathing regulated.

Sylvia called Joanna and Brooke, explaining what had just happened, and they both headed back to her house. They got there to find Jen sitting on the floor, cradled in James' arms. She was crying softly, her head on his shoulder.

Logan, Carlos, and Katie had come out when they no longer heard screaming, and James explained that Mama and Papa G had taken Kendall to the hospital. They were sitting on the couch, Logan still holding Katie.

"James, do you think you can get her to the bedroom?" Brooke asked.

He nodded and helped Jen up, supporting most of her weight. He got her to bed and Brooke took over.

James walked back into the living room and sat next to his friends, putting his arms around them. "It's going to be okay."

Joanna sat next to Logan and took Katie from him. "Why don't you boys go get ready for bed? Kendall is probably going to have to stay the night at the hospital, and you're going to need your rest."

"Not until we know how Kendall is," Logan said.

"Honey, I know you're worried, but it could be hours," Joanna explained.

"I don't care. I'm not sleeping until I know he's okay," Logan said, trying not to cry.

The other boys nodded in agreement.

"Alright, but go get your pajamas on and come back down. You can watch a movie or something until we hear from Antonio," Joanna said.

They agreed and went up to change.

"As for you, my little love, you stay right here with me," Jo whispered to Katie, who was still quietly crying.

∞

After the sedative finally started working, they moved Kendall into a private room. The doctor recommended putting Kendall on an anti-anxiety medication, although there was no guarantee it would be a hundred percent effective.

"Will he be able to go home tomorrow?" Antonio asked.

"He should be able to, provided that he's responsive and calm," the doctor said.

"I'm staying with him tonight, in case he has another episode," Antonio said.

"That's not really in accordance with hospital policy," the doctor told him.

"I'm a police officer and he is a kidnap victim. I'm not trying to be rude or anything, but hospital policy really doesn't matter to me at this point," Antonio told him.

"Understood. The nurse will be back to check on him in a while." The doctor smiled.

"I better get home and check on Jen and the kids. I was so hoping that tomorrow would be a happy day," Sylvia said, hugging Antonio.

Antonio kissed her. "It might still be a good day. This is just a little setback. It's going to take time for everything to get back to normal."

"If it ever does," Sylvia said.

"Now, you listen, I'm going to tell you what John told me. He needs us to be strong. God knows he's been strong throughout this whole thing. We can't wimp out on him now," Antonio quoted his partner.

"You're right, it's just everyone was so happy, and he was finally safe with us at home. Jen is going to keep blaming herself for this," Sylvia said.

"Then you tell HER what John said."

"Will do," she said as she smiled at her husband.

She went over and kissed Kendall on the forehead. "You rest and then come home tomorrow, Mijo."

"I'll call you in the morning when we're ready to leave," Antonio said.

Sylvia nodded and walked out the door. She got home about fifteen minutes later and walked in to find all the children waiting up.

"He had to stay?" James asked.

She nodded. "He had to be sedated, so Papi is staying with him tonight."

"He's okay though, right?" Logan asked.

Sylvia nodded. "How's Jen?"

"Brooke is still sitting with her," Joanna said.

Sylvia nodded. "Why don't you boys go to bed? Kendall should be home tomorrow, and you all need some sleep."

They nodded and got up.

"Katie, you want to stay with us tonight?" Logan asked.

She nodded. He went over and took the little girl from his mother, and they all headed upstairs.

Sylvia and Joanna went to check on Jen. Brooke was sitting on the bed and Jen had fallen asleep next to her.

"How is he?" Brooke whispered.

"Sedated, they're keeping him tonight. Antonio is staying with him."

Brooke nodded. "I'll stay with Jen tonight. You two go get some sleep."

"Are you sure?" Joanna asked.

Brooke nodded. "We're fine here. If I need you, I'll call."

Sylvia and Joanna both headed upstairs to try to get some sleep.

∞

At the hospital, Antonio sat in the chair next to Kendall's bed. He thought about everything they had been through and shook his head. One week of hell.

Kendall had survived beatings, torture, illness, and degradation, and now all it took was one word for everything to fall apart. A word his mother had used since before the boy was born. A word that use to represent love and affection, now all it caused was fear and pain. It was all so wrong, and he had no idea how to fix this.

He sighed and ran his fingers through his godson's hair. "We'll figure this out, I promise, Mijo."

Chapter 44~ Not Alone

Sylvia went to check on the children at about one. She found the boys sleeping on the floor, James in the middle again, with his arms around his brothers. They had probably fallen asleep with him comforting them. She knew that Katie had been in the bed before, but now she was on the floor with her arms wrapped around Logan's waist.

She went downstairs to check on Jen and Brooke and found both were sound asleep. She sighed, trying to believe what Antonio had said. Everything was going to be alright, it was just going to take time.

She went over, pulled the blanket up over her two sleeping friends, and then headed back to her own room.

∞

Kendall awoke around 3 am. He looked around in confusion and saw Antonio sleeping in the chair next to him. "Papi where are we?" he asked in a quiet voice.

Antonio woke up immediately. "Hey Mijo, are you alright?"

"I dreamed we were home, and then I heard my mom crying," Kendall said.

Antonio smiled. "It wasn't a dream. We were home for a little while."

"Why are we here?" Kendall asked, feeling panic starting to build.

"You kind of had a bad dream and couldn't breathe. We had to bring you to the hospital, and they gave you something to help."

"I don't remember. What's wrong with me, why can't I remember?"

"You were asleep, Mijo. Everything is alright now," Antonio said soothingly.

"Was my mom crying?"

"She was just worried, that's all. She's still at my house and resting," Antonio said, concerned that Kendall was going to work himself up into another attack. "You need to rest so you can go home in the morning, alright?"

The nurse came in to check on him because the monitors had showed an elevation in Kendall's heart rate. "Is everything alright in here?"

Kendall pulled back when she got too close for comfort.

"Everything is fine, thank you. He just woke up not knowing where he was," Antonio told her.

"Do we need something to help us sleep?"

"I think he's fine, thank you," Antonio said, starting to become annoyed. He hated when people spoke in the third person.

"Well, if we need something, just push the button," she told him.

He nodded and rolled his eyes once she had left the room. "She's no Nurse Patrick, is she?"

Kendall smiled and shook his head. "I want to go home."

"We will, the doctor just needs to check on you in the morning, and then we can leave," Antonio told him.

"I'm sorry, Papi. So much trouble..." Kendall whispered as he closed his eyes.

Antonio sighed. "Oh Mijo, none of this is your fault. How do I make you understand that?"

Antonio cursed Deesie and the fact that he got off so easily by dying, while the people he hurt had to go on, trying to pick up the pieces of their shattered lives.

∞

Sylvia woke up around 6 am and went downstairs to start a pot pf coffee. She found Jen sitting there at the table.

"How are you doing?" she asked, hugging her friend.

"I can't do this," Jen stated.

"What so you mean?" Sylvia asked.

"I can't do this," Jen repeated, her face void of expression.

"Do what?" Sylvia asked, her concern growing more by the second.

Jen's eyes looked empty, her voice completely calm. "I can't fix this. All I'll do is hurt him."

"Jen, everything's going to be alright. We're all going to help," Sylvia told her.

"It won't work, I can't do it."

"Well, exactly what do you plan on doing then?" Sylvia said, her voice rising. She was getting angry now.

"I can't do it," Jen said again.

"Well you DAMN WELL better figure out how to do it, because your son needs you now more than ever!" Sylvia was yelling now, trying to get through to her friend.

Jen just sat there. Sylvia grabbed her by the forearms and pulled her around to face her. "Are you listening to me?"

Brooke came running out. "What is going on?"

"I can't do it," Jen said again.

Sylvia slapped her hard across the cheek. The last few days had been hard, but this was too much. "HOW DARE YOU GIVE UP ON HIM!"

Jen shook her head and grabbed her cheek. "What? What are you talking about? Who am I giving up on?"

Sylvia stopped in shock. "What do you mean what am I talking about? Jen, what's the last thing you remember?" Sylvia asked softly.

"We were sending the kids to bed, and I slipped and called Kendall sweetheart. He woke up screaming and Antonio had to take him to the hospital. I was sitting in bed crying, Brooke was with me, and then you were here yelling at me. Did you HIT me?" she asked, still holding her cheek.

"You must have been sleepwalking. Can you remember what you were dreaming about?" Brooke asked.

"I was in the hospital and watching Kendall as he slept. I bent down and kissed him. He woke up screaming, but I couldn't comfort him, he just kept crying and trying to get away from me. Then Will was there, and I remember telling him I can't do it. He was saying something, but I couldn't hear him, he was fading away, and I kept telling him I just can't do it anymore," Jen was crying.

"Jen, I'm so sorry! I should have known something was wrong when you seemed to look right through me," Sylvia said, hugging her.

"What did you think I was talking about?" Jen asked, hugging her back.

"All you would say was, 'I can't do this,' that all you would do is hurt him. You just kept repeating it, and I thought you meant..."

"You thought I was giving up on Kendall?" Jen asked.

Sylvia nodded.

"That's what he said," Jen whispered.

"What who said?" Brooke asked her.

"Will, when I told him I can't do it alone. He was telling me that I'm not alone," Jen said, smiling sadly.

∞

Kendall woke up about 7 am and saw Antonio sleeping in the chair next to his bed. His head hurt and his chest felt tight again. "Papi," he whispered.

Antonio woke up and smiled. "Hey, how are you feeling?"

"I have a headache, but can we go home? I don't want to stay here."

"As soon as the doctor checks on you," Antonio said, brushing Kendall's bangs out of his eyes. "You still need a haircut."

Kendal rolled his eyes and smiled.

The nurse came in a few minutes later to check on him. "How are you feeling this morning?"

"Better. Can I go home?" Kendall asked.

"The doctor will be in around nine to check on you and will decide then," she told him.

Kendall sighed.

"I'll have them bring you some breakfast," the nurse said as she left.

"I'm going to make a quick call home, okay?" Antonio said.

Kendall nodded.

Antonio stepped into the hallway and called home.

"Hello," Sylvia answered.

"Hi honey, how is everyone?" he asked.

"The kids and Jo are still sleeping, and I sent Jen back to bed. She was sleepwalking earlier and scared the hell out of me," Sylvia said, relaying what had happened.

Antonio sighed. "We're going to have to find counseling for both of them, maybe the other kids too."

"I know. Brooke knows a couple, and Janice might have a recommendation as well," Sylvia told him.

"Good. We'll call on Monday and see about getting them in. I am worried about what will happen if Kendall has a panic attack like he did last night. There is no way Jen will be able to hold him. I almost lost my grip until he calmed down a little," Antonio said.

"Brooke said James is going to stay with them for a while. I think he's strong enough if need be. Hopefully he won't have another attack, though. Why didn't he react like that when I called him that on the phone?"

"I think maybe because he was awake. He reacted but managed to snap himself out of it when I spoke to him," Antonio told her.

"How is he this morning? Is he awake yet?" Sylvia asked.

"Yes, he woke up a little while ago. He really wants to go home. He woke up about three and was confused about where we were."

"I can imagine. Are you going to bring him here or to his house?" she asked.

"Why don't you see what Jen wants to do? She might want to stay with us for a few days, which wouldn't be a bad idea. Is Kendall's room large enough for a second bed?"

"Yes, why?"

"Well, if James is going to be staying there, we might want to set something up for him," Antonio recommended.

"That's a great idea. I'll run down and see about getting another twin bed. It'll give us something to do this morning." She smiled.

"Okay, I'll give you a call once the doctor releases Kendall," Antonio said.

"Alright honey." She smiled, hanging up.

"Did I hear someone needs to go shopping?" Brooke asked.

∞

A little while later, the boys and Katie came down and wandered into the kitchen.

Sylvia smiled. "Good morning. What does everyone want for breakfast? I'll fix anything you want."

"I'm not really hungry," Logan said, and the others nodded in agreement.

"Well, you need to eat something, and then we have a few things to do before Kendall comes home."

"IS he coming home?" Carlos asked.

"Carlitos, of course he is. I spoke with Papi, and they're just waiting for the doctor to release him. Look, I know last night was scary, but you all have to understand this is NOT going to be easy for anyone. We all have to work together and support one another. We're going to find a counselor to help Kendall work through this. As frightened as we were last night, Kendall is more frightened, worried that things will never be the same," she said, looking into the sad faces of the children.

"So you need to decide if you're going to be able to be there for him, because chances are this IS going to happen again. You need to be honest with yourselves, because if you say that you'll be there and then aren't, it could do more harm than good. I'm pretty sure he will understand if you need time," Sylvia explained.

They looked at one another. "I'm in," James said, putting his hand out and looking at Logan and Carlos. They both smiled and put their hands on top of his.

Sylvia smiled. "Good. Now, what did you all want for breakfast?"

After they had eaten, Brooke and Joanna took the kids shopping for a new bed. After they found one, they headed to the Knight home and quickly had it assembled, made up, and topped with a matching comforter.

Then they headed back to the Garcia's to wait for word on Kendall.

∞

Jen had woken up again and sat in the kitchen, sipping coffee with Sylvia.

"Jen, I can't apologize enough for earlier. I feel terrible, I should have known better," Sylvia said.

"You had no way of knowing what was going on. I don't blame you for anything, including being angry when you thought I was giving up. In fact, I should thank you for it. You have always been there, not only for me but also for the kids. I'm so thankful that they will be protected, no matter what. That means more to me than anything."

The phone rang and Sylvia answered. "Antonio?"

"Hi honey, we're heading home now. So what's the plan?"

"Well, we're all here, so why don't you come home? We can decide the rest later." She smiled.

"Okay, then we'll be home in a few."

"Antonio and Kendall are on their way here," she told Jen.

Jen smiled nervously. "Hopefully I don't slip up again."

"Antonio thinks it was because he was asleep. When I called him that on the phone, he was able to snap out of it. Of all the words in the world that bastard could have used..."

"I know. I've always called the kids that. I didn't even think about it when I went to wake him," Jen said.

"We also need to realize that he's probably going to hear it in other places, as well as sweetie, and we're going to have to stay on top of it," Sylvia told her.

"I know. This isn't going to be easy." Jen sighed.

"No, but we will get through it," Sylvia told her.

"Yes, we will," Jen agreed.

Chapter 45~ A Good Day

Antonio pulled into the driveway, parked, and got out. He opened Kendall's door, and reaching down, picked him up. They had forgotten to grab Kendall's things, so he was wearing Antonio's jacket and no shoes, so Antonio carried him up to the house.

Sylvia opened the door and Antonio put Kendall down, steadying him for a moment.

Jen was standing there, unsure of what to do, and finally hugged him and helped him to the couch. "I'm so sorry, baby."

"Mom, it's okay, it's not your fault. My mind is just all... weird right now," he told her. Kendall felt awful. His mom was blaming herself because his head was all screwed up.

"How about some breakfast?" Sylvia said.

Kendall shook his head, but Antonio nodded. "You didn't eat at the hospital and you have to take your medicine."

Kendall rolled his eyes. "I'm not hungry."

"Well, that's too bad, because you're eating. We also need to do your breathing treatment and show your mom how to work the nebulizer," Antonio told him.

Kendall sighed as his mom led him back to the kitchen. "Where is everybody?" Kendall asked quietly. He wouldn't blame everyone for leaving after last night.

"They're out running a few errands and should be back any minute," Sylvia said as she made scrambled eggs and toast for them.

"Mmmm... coffee," Antonio said, pouring himself a cup.

Jen poured Kendall a glass of juice and handed it to him, along with his antibiotic. "Did they give you anything for pain at the hospital?"

Kendall shook his head, so Jen handed him a pain pill.

"I don't want them. It doesn't really hurt right now and they make me sleepy," he said.

"Kendall..." Jen said.

"Please mom, I'll take one later. I'm tired of being tired all the time."

Jen sighed. "Alright, but you're taking one in an hour."

Kendall nodded.

Sylvia set a plate of food in front of him and Antonio sat next to him, eating his own breakfast. Kendall just picked at his food.

"Kendall, please eat something," Antonio said.

Kendall sighed and took a few bites. He really wasn't hungry, and he honestly didn't feel very well right now. Soon, he started nodding off.

"Okay buddy, let's give you your treatment, and then you need some more sleep," Antonio said.

He put his arm around Kendall's waist and helped him upstairs. Kendall went into the bathroom and changed into his flannel pajamas. He asked Antonio for help with his shirt, and after he was changed, Antonio led Kendall into the guest room next to Carlos' room. Kendall laid down, suddenly very tired.

Jen had grabbed Kendall's backpack and the bag from the hospital and brought them to Antonio.

First, he gave Kendall a pain pill, and then Antonio showed her how to work the nebulizer. She sat next to her son and ran her fingers through his hair. She smiled as he fell

asleep, and when the half an hour was over, she gently removed the mask and covered him with a blanket.

She kissed him on the forehead. "I love you, baby, and I'm so happy you're home."

∞

Jen headed downstairs, surprised to see that everyone was back since she hadn't heard them come in.

"How's Kendall?" Katie asked quietly.

"He's doing much better. He's just taking a nap. What were you all out doing?"

"Well, we figured it might be helpful to have at least one of the boys stay with you for a while, and we decided Kendall's room could handle an extra bed," Brooke told her.

"You didn't have to do that," Jen said.

"Yes she did. It's hard to get my beauty sleep lying on the cold, hard floor." James smiled as he kissed Jen on the cheek.

Jen put her hand on his cheek and smiled. "You could lie on a bed of rocks every night of your life and you would still be beautiful."

"Barf!" Katie said, making a gagging noise.

"Hey!" he warned. "I think I found the TICKLE BUG!" he said, holding up his hand. He wiggled his fingers and started chasing Katie around, poking her sides.

"No! Carlos, get the tickle bug!" Katie squealed.

Carlos started chasing James, trying to grab his hands, so James turned and took off after Carlos. "The tickle bug will not be stopped!"

"Guys, Kendall's trying to sleep," Logan pointed out.

All three stopped suddenly and looked at him and then at each other. Logan saw the looks on their faces and started shaking his head frantically. "No, no, no!"

"The tickle bug wants to go outside!" Carlos yelled as James tackled Logan and pulled him out the front door, Carlos and Katie close behind.

"Stop it!" Logan squealed. "Mom, help!"

Jo smiled at her son, who was now pinned down by James and Carlos, Katie straddling him and tickling him under the arms.

"Sorry swe... honey! The tickle bug is immune to mothers," she told him as she closed the door.

"Well, on that note, I'm going up to take a nap," Antonio said.

"Alright, I'll call you for lunch," Sylvia said, giving him a quick kiss.

Antonio headed upstairs, looked in on Kendall, who was still fast asleep, and then collapsed onto his own bed for the first time in over a week.

"We should probably make some hot chocolate for the little bugs," Joanna said.

"Good idea." Jen laughed as they went to make a tray of hot chocolate and snacks for the kids.

A few minutes later, James, Carlos, and Katie came back in, with Logan following.

His hair was seriously mussed and he had snow clinging to his backside. His face was red and he was pouting. "I'm going to go change, since I'm now all covered in snow," he said, glaring at the other three.

"Oh Logie, don't be mad. You know we love you," Katie said.

"I need new friends," he said as he stomped up the stairs, sending the other three into a fit of giggles.

Logan changed into some dry clothes and heard Kendall coughing in the next room. He went in to check on him. "Hey, you doing okay, buddy?"

Kendall opened his eyes and smiled. "Hey," he said and then started coughing again.

"Let me get you some water," Logan said and ran into the bathroom and filled a cup. He took it to Kendall and helped him sit up to drink it, soothingly rubbing Kendall's back until the coughing subsided. "Are you okay now?"

Kendall nodded and lay back down. "Thanks Loges."

"How are you feeling?" Logan asked.

"My chest is kinda tight again, but the breathing thing helped."

"Breathing thing? Oh, the nebulizer." Logan smiled.

"Yeah," Kendall said.

"Well, I should let you get some sleep," Logan said, standing up to leave.

Kendall grabbed his hand. "Please stay, just for a little while."

"Sure. You want me to read to you?"

"That would be great." Kendall smiled.

"Let me grab my book," Logan said and ran to Carlos' room to get it.

"What is it?" Kendall asked as Logan sat next to him.

"A Tale of Two Cities, by Charles Dickens."

"Who?" Kendall asked.

"Charles Dickens. He wrote *Oliver, David Copperfield, A Christmas Carol.*" Logan said, listing titles until Kendall recognized one.

"He wrote a *Muppet Christmas Carol*?" Kendall asked, confused as he closed his eyes.

"Close enough." Logan laughed as he started reading aloud.

∞

About a half an hour later, Jen went up to check on Kendall and found Logan sitting next to him on the bed, quietly reading. Kendall was sleeping curled up next to his friend. Logan had his arm resting on the pillow above Kendall's head, and Kendall was tucked into the crook of his arm. She smiled and quietly went back downstairs.

∞

Antonio woke up about an hour later, feeling more rested than he had in quite a while. He stretched, yawning, and got up. He went to check on Kendall, and was surprised to see Logan sleeping next to Kendall, a book sitting open next to him and his chin resting on top of Kendall's head.

Antonio went downstairs to find the other boys and Katie playing video games. The moms were in the kitchen sitting around the table. Jen seemed more relaxed, and they were all drinking tea and talking quietly. They smiled when Antonio came in.

"I should go check on Kendall," Jen said and went to get up.

"I just looked in on him. He's still sleeping and Logan's with him," Antonio told her.

She nodded and sat back down.

"I guess we should go over a little of what I know before he wakes up." Antonio sighed.

"Okay." Jen nodded.

"Do you want us to go?" Jo asked.

"No, I think we all need to know as much as possible, so we're better prepared to help. I'm just going to give you a quick summary, and then we can go into more details later, when the kids aren't around," Antonio said.

First, he checked to make sure that the kids were still in the living room, and then sat in a chair where he could see if one of them decided to come into the kitchen.

"As I told you, he wouldn't say much to Agent Bower, he just went over what happened the night Deesie took him. That was enough to send him over the edge and he had a massive panic attack. Dr. Talbot had to sedate him. The next day, she checked on him and kept him distracted while asking him questions that had to do with some of his injuries. We found out the second night, at the motel where Mr. Crowley was murdered, Kendall actually managed to run away for a while."

"Where did he go?" Jen asked.

"The motel is in the middle of nowhere, and he tried to hide in the woods, but Deesie eventually found him. He said Deesie was really angry, and when they got back to the room, he kept submerging him in cold water in the tub."

"Oh my God," Sylvia said, taking Jen's hand.

"That's not all—he also took a large needle and punctured the muscles on the bottom of his right foot so he couldn't run away again. Then he gave Kendall a set of four rules that he expected him to obey."

"What were the rules?" Jen asked quietly.

Antonio told them what Deesie's rules were, keeping a close eye on the living room as he spoke.

Jen was looking like she might faint, so Antonio stopped for a few moments. "Maybe we should continue this later?"

She smiled and shook her head. "No, I'm okay. Please, I need to know what happened."

Antonio nodded. "After he killed Mr. Crowley, Deesie decided they were going to camp out to avoid any further problems. He was angry that Kendall hadn't obeyed him that morning, so he punished him again. He took the needle, and this time, put it up under his shoulder blade and injured the muscles there. That's why he needs to wear the shoulder stabilizer. It's going to take a while for it to heal." He stopped and gave them a moment before continuing.

"Now, Natalie had given Kendall his pain medication, or I don't think he would have told her what else happened that night. I don't think he meant for it to come out, and I don't think he remembers telling her, so we don't say anything until he's ready to talk about it. Agreed?"

They all nodded and Jen took a deep breath, Sylvia holding one hand and Brooke the other.

"Okay, well when Deesie first made an advance towards him, he told Kendall that he needed to learn his abc's." Antonio paused. This was *not* an easy conversation. "He made them sexually based and told Kendall what he expected. Now, Kendall didn't go into any detail, he just told Natalie that Deesie had tied him to a tree because he refused to pay attention when Deesie showed him how he wanted the letter B done."

"Letter B?" Sylvia asked.

Antonio sighed. Damn, this was hard. "It stood for blowjob."

"Oh my God!" Jen cried.

"No, he didn't force Kendall to give him one. I think what he meant by Deesie showing him, is that Deesie did that to him," Antonio rushed the last sentence out.

"Excuse me," Jen said, standing up. She put her hand over her mouth and ran for the bathroom, Joanna following to comfort her.

"I think that's enough for today. We'll go over the rest later when things have settled down. I'll let her listen to the recording and tell her about the rest. There are some things I haven't had time to go over with any of you about, but she needs to take it slow, and I need to confirm some things first," Antonio said.

Jen came back a few minutes later, looking pale.

"I'm sorry, honey, we'll finish this later when everyone has had a chance to get settled and some real rest," Antonio told her.

She nodded. She didn't think she could handle any more anyway.

Antonio hugged her and kissed her on the head. "It'll be okay, I promise."

She hugged him back. "I know it will be. It's just so hard."

"I know. Look, why don't you all stay the night again and we can make it a fun night for the kids? Movies, pizza, and sugar of all types. You can get a fresh start tomorrow, and we'll make sure you have everything you need at home," Antonio said.

"That sounds good." She smiled.

∞

Kendall stirred, waking Logan. "Hey buddy, you okay?"

"Hmmm?" Kendall asked.

"You doing alright?" Logan asked again.

Kendall yawned. "I think so."

"You want to go downstairs? I think the guys are playing video games," Logan asked.

"Sure," Kendall said, his voice was raspy and his throat was hurting.

Logan helped Kendall up and they made their way slowly down the stairs. Kendall stumbled a little, so Logan put an arm around his waist to steady him.

"Thanks." Kendall smiled.

"No problem. If you fall, just aim for me," Logan said.

They got down the stairs without any more incidents and Logan helped Kendall over to the couch, and he sat next to Carlos. Carlos put his arm around Kendall and hugged him.

"Hey Carlitos. Who's winning?"

"I am, who else?" Katie smirked.

"She cheats," James accused.

"You're just jealous that I'm five levels above you," she stated smugly.

"Because you cheat," he repeated.

"How can I cheat, genius? I'm sitting right here playing the game at the same time you are."

"Because you get online and check the cheat sheets ahead of time," Kendall said.

"AH HA!" James shrieked.

"Trade secrets!" Katie said, pinging Kendall with her finger.

Kendall laughed at her and started coughing again, so Carlos rubbed his back.

"I'm going to make you some tea with honey," Logan said, getting up.

Logan went into the kitchen and noticed the parents all sitting around, not speaking. "Is everything okay?"

"Yes honey, we were just discussing how we should have a fun night tonight. How about movies and pizza?" Jen asked.

"Sounds good, I'm just going to make Kendall some tea. He's coughing and I think his throat is bothering him."

'You are so swe... kind," Jen said and got up to help.

"It's okay, I've got this." Logan smiled.

Jen smiled back and kissed him on the cheek. "Thanks swe... HONEY. Thanks honey. I'm going to have so much trouble with this."

"You'll do fine, Mama K." Logan smiled as he poured the tea into a mug and then added a spoonful of honey. He took the mug out to Kendall and then sat to watch the battle between Katie and the other two boys.

After a while, they decided to watch a movie and all settled down together. Sylvia and Joanna took them some sandwiches and hot chocolate for lunch and everyone ate, with the exception of Kendall.

"Kendall, you should eat something," Logan said.

Kendall sighed and took a couple of bites of his sandwich. A few minutes later, he was nodding off, so Carlos moved and put Kendall's feet up on the couch, while Logan put a pillow under his head. Carlos covered him with the fleece blanket that was on the back of the couch.

"He didn't eat much and he's lost a lot of weight," Logan said, remembering how light his friend felt when he helped him down the stairs.

"Maybe we can make him a shake or something when he wakes up. We're going to have to keep a close eye on him," James said.

They all agreed, knowing it was going to be a battle with their friend. He was stubborn and could be very difficult when he decided he didn't want to do something.

They were watching another movie when Kendall whimpered a little and kicked his legs out.

James was there immediately, being careful not to grab his friend. "Kendall, wake up buddy."

Kendall whimpered again, so James brushed his bangs back. "Kendall, wake up. You're okay," James said a little louder.

Kendall opened his eyes. "Hmmm?"

"I think you were having a bad dream," James said.

"Don't 'member," Kendall told him.

"It's okay, you don't have to remember." James smiled.

"Okay." Kendall smiled and yawned.

"You want to pick the next movie?" Carlos asked.

"That's okay, you pick," Kendall said.

"Spiderman?" Carlos asked, knowing it was one of Kendall's favourites.

"Sounds good." Kendall smiled.

∞

The rest of the afternoon was quiet. It was cold and snowing again, and everyone seemed content to remain inside. Brooke and Joanna left around 4 pm with strict instructions that they be called if Jen or anyone needed anything.

About six, Sylvia and Jen got ready to go pick up dinner for the group.

"Who wants to go get pizza and pick out a couple of movies?" Sylvia asked.

"ME!" Carlos said and jumped up and ran to put on his boots and jacket.

"I'll go, too," Logan said, hoping to find a movie that didn't involve just shooting zombies.

"We'll be back in a little while," Sylvia said as they left.

James ran out after them. "Logan, don't forget to get Kendall a shake or something."

Logan nodded.

"What's that about?" Jen asked.

"We just noticed Kendall wasn't eating a lot and could use the calories," Logan answered.

She smiled at him. "Have I told you just how special you boys are?"

Logan blushed. "Thanks, Mama K."

After about twenty minutes of arguing at the video store, they settled on a couple of movies, two having been vetoed by the moms. They stopped and picked up the pizzas and went through a drive-thru to get Kendall a chocolate shake.

They arrived back home and everyone settled in to eat their dinner, and Carlos put the first movie in. James was keeping a close eye on Kendall and handed him his plate when he hadn't taken a bite after ten minutes. Kendall smiled and took a couple of bites and then set the plate back down.

James handed him his shake. "I know you're not very hungry, but at least drink this, okay?"

Kendall looked at him and sighed. "Okay." He took the glass and sipped on it throughout the rest of the movie.

They were halfway through the second movie and Kendall had fallen asleep, his head resting on the arm of the couch.

"We should probably get him to bed," Antonio said and went to get up.

"I can get him, Papa G," James said as he stood up.

"Are you sure?"

"Yeah, he doesn't weigh that much," he said as he bent down and carefully picked up his friend.

Logan followed them and pulled the covers back on Carlos' bed. James gently laid Kendall down, and Logan covered him up.

"I'll stay with him," James said.

"Are you sure?" Logan asked.

"Yeah, you stayed with him this morning." James smiled, sitting on the bed next to Kendall.

He picked up the TV remote and turned it on, putting the volume on low. Soon he nodded off and woke up when Logan and Carlos came in.

"What time is it?"

"About eleven," Logan said.

James got up and went to brush his teeth and put on his pajamas. Soon, everyone was ready for bed—the boys settling into the blankets on the floor. Jen and Sylvia came in, tucked everyone in, and then went to turn in themselves.

"How are they?" Antonio asked Sylvia when she went into their bedroom.

"All is well." She smiled.

"Thank God." He smiled back as he kissed her.

∞

About an hour later, James heard Kendall whimpering and jumped up.

"Kendall, it's okay. You're safe."

Kendall opened his eyes. "Bad dream," he said in a shaky voice.

"It's okay, I've got you," James told him as he lay down next to him and wrapped his arms around him. Kendall sighed and closed his eyes.

James pulled him close, lying his chin on top of Kendall's head. "Nobody's going to hurt you while I'm here," James promised.

Chapter 46~ Will It Get Back To Normal?

Antonio got up, checked on the boys about 3 am, and found them all sleeping soundly.

James was on the bed with Kendall, making him wonder if the boy had had another nightmare. He was concerned about Jen being able to handle Kendall if he did have a panic attack and was glad that James would be staying with them for a few days.

Yesterday had been a good day for all of them, in spite of the discussion he had to have with Jen. He mentally groaned thinking of everything he still needed to tell her. He would let her decide what she was ready for, but that didn't mean it was going to be any easier.

He walked over and pulled the blankets up over Carlos and Logan. He grabbed an extra blanket from the closet and put it over James and Kendall. He smiled as he looked at them. He was so proud of all his boys. He closed the door partway and went back to bed.

∞

Kendall woke up about 4 am and found he was still being held firmly in James' protective embrace. He wiggled a little, but James didn't loosen his grip.

"James… James," he whispered.

"Huh, what's wrong, are you okay?"

"I just need to use the bathroom," Kendall said.

"Okay. Do you need help?" James asked, yawning.

"Uh, no, I just need you to let go of me a little," Kendall told him.

"Oh, sorry," James said, releasing his friend.

"It's okay, thanks." Kendall smiled and got up.

When he was finished, he looked back in the room and saw James sleeping soundly, sprawled across the bed.

He smiled as he looked at his three friends. He knew they were all going to be watching him closely, and as much as he loved them, they could definitely overdo it at times. However, since he was the same way, he could hardly get mad at them for it.

He decided that he wasn't tired at the moment and went downstairs. He curled up in Antonio's recliner and looked out the window. It was snowing again and the world looked fresh and bright. He was still sitting there watching the snow, when Antonio came down at 5 am to make some coffee.

"Kendall, what are you doing up?"

"Couldn't sleep anymore."

"You're feeling alright though?" Antonio asked.

Kendall smiled. "I'm fine, just wanted some time…"

"To yourself?" Antonio finished.

Kendall nodded. "I'm sorry, I know that sounds bad, but it just feels like someone's always watching me."

"It doesn't sound bad, it's understandable. Between the hospital, me, your mom, and the boys, you haven't had a moment alone for the last few days."

"I don't mind it, really. I just have a hard time thinking when someone is always trying to take care of me," Kendall said.

"What are you thinking about?"

Kendall shrugged. "I don't know… things."

"Things?"

"Like how I'm going to miss hockey this season. How to keep my mom from freaking out every time I walk out the door from now on. How I really don't want to go back to school with everybody knowing... things."

"That's a lot to think about." Antonio smiled, sitting on the arm of the chair. Kendall scooted over so Antonio could sit next to him. "You do know your mom's going to find a counselor for you and that they'll probably start you on some anti-anxiety meds, right?" Antonio told him.

"I don't need someone to talk to and I HATE being medicated," Kendall said.

"Mijo, I know you think that, but you need help dealing with everything that's happened and to stop the panic attacks."

"I don't want to talk to somebody I don't know," Kendall said stubbornly.

"What if it was someone you do know, that's worked with kids before?" Antonio asked him.

"Who?" Kendall asked suspiciously.

"Well, Sally's done a lot of counseling with kids, and you like her. She already knows what happened, so you wouldn't have to go into that too much," Antonio told him. "That's if your mom agrees. She may want you to go to an actual psychologist, but that doesn't mean you can't talk to Sally as well."

"Maybe," Kendall said quietly.

"Think about it, okay?" Antonio asked.

Kendall nodded. "I will."

"That's my boy. Could you tell me something?"

"What?" Kendall asked.

"How did you get away from Deesie that day?"

"Oh, umm... he would give me sleeping pills at night and I just pretended to take them. When we got to the cabin, he took my boots and figured I couldn't run away without them. I guess he forgot that he packed my shoes. So that morning, when he was in the shower, I crushed up the pills and put them in his coffee. It took about an hour, but he finally fell asleep and I left."

Antonio looked at him. "I am seriously impressed."

Kendall smiled at him. "Thanks."

"So, what else is bothering you?" Antonio asked.

Kendall shrugged and looked out the window.

"Kendall..."

"I just feel... I don't know... tired of everything being different."

"I know, but things will get back to normal. I promise," Antonio said, hugging him.

"How do you know?"

"Because I have faith that they will."

"But, how do you KNOW?" Kendall asked.

"Because I believe in you and everyone who loves you."

Kendall raised an eyebrow and smirked. "If you don't know, you can just say so."

"Smart aleck," Antonio said, ruffling Kendall's hair.

Kendall smiled at him and they both sat there for a few minutes, watching the snow.

∞

James was dreaming that he and the guys were on the pond skating and goofing off. Kendall slipped and he caught him. "Forget how to skate?" he teased, holding up his smaller friend.

"You wish," Kendall retorted, sticking his tongue out at James. Logan and Carlos were laughing in the background. Everyone was having fun.

Suddenly it was dark and he heard Logan and Carlos screaming at him to hold on, not let go of Kendall. He was holding Kendall by the arm and realized something was pulling them

towards the darkness. Kendall was being pulled away and James held onto his hand, trying to keep him from being pulled further into the darkness.

"James!" Kendall screamed as he was suddenly pulled from his friend's grasp.

James woke with a start, his heart pounding. Kendall was no longer there, but he remembered he had gone to use the bathroom. "Over an hour ago," he said to himself, looking at the clock. He jumped up and tripped, his feet catching in the blankets, and he almost landed on Carlos. He rolled up and ran for the bathroom to find it empty.

"Kendall... Kendall where are you?" James whispered as he ran from room to room.

Not finding his friend, he raced down the stairs. "Kendall! Where are you?" James was panicking.

Antonio came out of the kitchen. "James, what's wrong?" he said, grabbing him by the arm.

"I can't find him, he's gone!"

Antonio pulled James closer to him. "Mijo, who's gone?"

"Kendall, I woke up and he's gone."

James was close to tears and Antonio realized the teen was not completely awake. "James, wake up! He's right here, see?" Antonio said, pulling him into the kitchen.

Kendall looked at them in confusion. "What's wrong?"

James looked over when he heard Kendall's voice. "Where were you?"

"I couldn't sleep, so I came downstairs. You were asleep, so I didn't want to wake you up," Kendall told him.

"I dreamed... I don't know what I dreamed. But you were gone and we couldn't find you," James said, his voice breaking. "When I woke up, you weren't there."

Kendall got up and went to his friend. "I'm sorry, I'm right here, James. Everything's okay."

James pulled Kendall into a hug, still shaking.

"James... hurts," Kendall whispered as his friend held him a little too tightly. James loosened his grip but didn't let go. He was crying now.

Antonio rubbed James' back. "It's okay, see, everyone's safe."

Kendall looked over James' shoulder at Antonio and sighed, his heart breaking at his brother's sobs.

Nothing is ever going to be the same again, Kendall thought sadly.

Chapter 47 ~ Caring for Kendall

About an hour later, Sylvia went downstairs to find Antonio sitting on the couch watching an old movie on TV. He had a pillow on his lap and James lay on one side and Kendall on the other, their heads meeting in the middle. Antonio had an arm resting on a shoulder of each boy.

"What's this? Did Kendall have another nightmare?"

Antonio shook his head. "James."

She sighed and hugged her husband from behind. "What are we going to do?"

"I think I'm going to talk to Sally about working with them. She's counseled so many kids, and the boys all know her, so I think they might be more willing to open up to her than they would to a stranger. They know she cares," Antonio said.

"Good idea. Breakfast?"

"That would be great. I already made coffee." He smiled.

She kissed him on the cheek and headed into the kitchen. A little while later, she came out. "I have some pancakes ready. Why don't you see if these two are hungry while I scramble up some eggs?"

Antonio gently shook James. "Mijo, breakfast is ready."

James yawned and turned over, eyes still closed, so he tried waking Kendall. "Kendall, time to get up. Breakfast is ready."

Kendall opened his eyes. "Hmmm?"

"Breakfast," Antonio repeated.

"Not hungry."

"Well, I am, and you're lying on me, so..." Antonio laughed.

"You're eating," James said as he sat up.

"No," Kendall said, pulling the pillow over his head.

"Come on," James ordered, grabbing the pillow away.

"No," Kendall said, pulling the blanket down on him from the back of the couch.

Antonio got up and out of the way, interested to see who was going to win the battle of wills. Both boys were tired but extremely stubborn.

"Kendall, you need to eat and that's that," James warned.

Kendall didn't reply, just pulled the blanket tighter around himself.

James tried reasoning. "You have to take your antibiotics, and you have to eat with those, so come on."

When Kendall still didn't answer, James pulled on the blanket, but he wouldn't let go. "I warned you," James said and he bent down and picked the smaller boy up, blanket and all.

Kendall squealed. "James, put me down!"

"Nope, you're eating," he said as he carried his friend back to the kitchen.

Antonio followed them into the kitchen and Sylvia looked up, surprised to see James delivering Kendall to the table. He sat him in a chair and stood behind him. Kendall untangled himself from the blanket and went to stand up, only to find James' hands on his shoulders. Kendall looked up and glared at his friend.

James just smiled. "You're eating or I'm feeding you. Your choice."

Antonio sat down next to him. "Pancake?" He smiled as he put one on Kendall's plate.

Kendall rolled his eyes and sighed. "Fine, I'll eat."

James stood there, still holding him.

"I said I'll eat, so you can sit down," Kendall told him.

"Yeah, take a bite first," James ordered.

"I'll take a bite once you sit down," Kendall said stubbornly.

Antonio and Sylvia looked at each other and nodded. Sylvia went to James and took him by the shoulders. "You sit here," she said, pushing him into the chair next to Kendall.

Kendall looked at James and smiled. "Ha..." he said and Antonio pushed a bite of pancake into his mouth.

Kendall choked a bit but swallowed.

"Ha," James said smugly as he put a pancake onto his own plate.

Kendall looked at Antonio. "Hey, you need to eat, so I took advantage of the distraction. Besides, my breakfast is getting cold waiting for you two."

Kendall sighed, but he knew he wasn't going anywhere until he ate, since his chair was firmly situated between Antonio and James. Half an hour later, Kendall managed to eat a pancake and a couple bites of scrambled eggs. James and Antonio had long since finished but waited.

"Happy?" Kendall asked as he choked down the last bite.

"Yes," James said, smiling at his friend.

"Good job, sweethe... honey," Sylvia quickly corrected.

Kendall started shaking a little and looked down, but a few seconds later, he smiled at her. "Thanks."

"How about you take the first shower so there's hot water?" James said, getting up.

"Okay." Kendall got up and followed James upstairs.

"Damn it!" Sylvia cursed, near tears.

Antonio got up and hugged her. "It's alright, honey. He's fine."

"That's not the point. What if he weren't alright?"

"But he IS alright. It didn't even last as long as it did when he heard it on the phone."

"Is it wrong that I hate that man so much?"

"Not at all. I think we all hate him more than words can say," Antonio told her, kissing her cheek.

∞

Kendall went into the bathroom and started the shower. He stood under the warm flowing stream for a few minutes. It took him a while to wash and rinse his hair, but once he was done, he got out and dried off. He pulled on some jeans and realized he still couldn't get his shirt on over his head. He sighed and opened the door. "James, are you there?"

"Yeah," James said.

"I can't get my shirt on." Kendall sighed.

James went in and found Kendall with the towel wrapped around his shoulders. "Don't look," Kendall said, embarrassed by the marks that still covered him.

"Don't be ridiculous. I can't help if I can't see. It's okay, really," James told him, taking the t-shirt.

Kendall bit his lower lip and sighed, dropping the towel.

James helped him pull on his t-shirt and smiled. "They don't look so bad and they're healing. You'll see. They'll be gone in no time."

"I know how I look," Kendall whispered, pulling his flannel shirt on over the t-shirt.

"Let me fix your hair," James said, grabbing his comb. A minute later, he had the unruly mop of hair combed down. "There, now when it dries it'll look normal instead of like you stuck your finger in a light socket."

Kendall rolled his eyes. "Thanks," he said quietly, but still wouldn't meet his eyes.

"Kendall, look at me," James said.

Kendall looked at James. "There's nothing to be ashamed of or embarrassed about. So you have some bruises, we have ALL had bruises. They heal and go away and we forget they were even there."

"They're not all bruises," Kendall whispered, looking down.

"Wha... oh," James said as he realized what Kendall had just told him. "That doesn't matter either, and you really can't tell the difference."

"But..."

"But what?" James asked gently.

"I just feel... dirty knowing they're there," Kendall confided.

James hugged him. "You're not dirty. You didn't ask for any of this and you need to stop thinking like that."

Kendall sighed. "I know. It's just..."

"Hard and wrong," James finished.

"Yeah."

"I know little brother. But you don't have to worry about that again, I promise," James told him.

"Thanks James." Kendall smiled.

"Anytime. Now I want to get my shower before Logan and Carlos get up and start fighting about hot water. Don't forget to take your medicine, okay?"

"Okay, thanks," Kendall said, heading downstairs to find his medications.

∞

A couple of hours later, everyone was up, showered, and fed.

Kendall was upstairs taking his nebulizer treatment with Logan helping and being absolutely fascinated with the workings of the little machine. He was going over the history and how advanced the machines had become, and Kendall finally tuned him out.

His shoulder was bothering him a bit, so he shifted on the pillow. Before he came up, his mom had asked if he had taken his medicine. He told her he had taken his antibiotic and then gone into how James and Antonio had tricked him into eating. So far, she hadn't caught on that he never mentioned taking the pain pill. He hated them. He would rather be in a little pain than feel like a zombie.

He realized Logan was still talking about the nebulizer. "Logan, when I don't have to use it anymore, you can have it."

"Really?" Logan asked, excited.

"Yes, it's yours. If you promise to STOP talking about it."

"Just trying to help with your education," Logan said.

"When am I ever going to use information on the history of the nebulizer?" Kendall asked, his voice muffled by the mask.

"You can never tell, there might be a pop quiz someday," Logan retorted, making a mental note to ask his teacher if they could add it to the study list. When his treatment was over, Logan helped him get everything packed up. They would be heading over to the Knight house in a little while.

"Kendall?" Logan said.

"Yeah?"

"Are you nervous about going home?" Logan asked.

Kendall shrugged. "A little, I guess."

"That's normal, but everything looks great and we'll be staying with you."

"I know, Loges. Thanks." He smiled. On the inside, he was getting nervous and he hated the fact that his friends' lives were being disrupted.

∞

A little over an hour later, they pulled into the Knight driveway. Katie, Logan, and James rode in the Knight car, Carlos and Kendall in the Garcia's. Antonio and Sylvia were going to stay for a little while and help everyone get settled.

The boys were going to stay the night and walk to school from the Knight's. Logan and Carlos would go home the next night, and James would stay the rest of the week. The boys had already decided amongst themselves that they would alternate until Kendall felt safe and no longer had panic attacks or nightmares.

They got out and walked up to the house, but Kendall trailed behind a little, suddenly very nervous.

Antonio noticed his hesitation and wrapped an arm around the boy. "It's okay, Mijo," he whispered and helped him up the steps.

The other boys had grabbed the bags and started up the stairs. Kendall stood there, looking around for a minute and took a deep breath. Katie grabbed his hand. "Come on, I want you to see your room," she insisted, trying to pull her big brother up the stairs. When he didn't move, she turned and pouted at him.

"Katie, give him a minute, the room will still be there," Jen told her.

"I'm sorry," Katie said as she realized Kendall hadn't been home since the bad man took him. She never thought about her big brother being scared. *Home is supposed to be safe. It isn't fair,* she thought, her eyes filling with tears.

Kendall looked down at her and noticed her face. "Hey, are you going to show me or not?" he asked, trying to smile.

She looked up at him, smiling back and held onto his arm as they walked slowly up the stairs. Once they hit the landing, Katie started pulling him into his new room. "Close your eyes."

"Katie..."

"Please?" She pouted.

Kendall closed his eyes and allowed his little sister to guide him into the bedroom. "Okay, open them," Katie said, excitement in her voice.

Kendall opened his eyes and looked around. "Wow." He smiled, taking in the freshly painted walls, the photos and posters that had been transferred, and the hockey stick hung carefully above his desk.

"Do you really like it?" Katie asked.

"I love it," he told her and bent down to hug her.

"Mama D helped me pick out the comforters, and she got another bed so the guys would have a place to sleep."

"You did a great job, Katie-Bug, but what about your room?"

"I still need to pick out colours and things. The guys said they'd help when I decide."

He sat down on the bed and looked at her. "Katie, you're a pretty special little sister, you know that?"

"Of course I do!" She smirked and then hugged him tightly around the waist. "Don't ever leave me again," she said and then ran out the door.

"I'll do my best." He sighed.

The guys came in. "So, what do you think?" Carlos asked.

"It's great. Thanks, you guys."

"We can change whatever you don't like," Logan said, noticing a sadness in his friend's eyes.

"Nope, it's perfect." Kendall smiled.

∞

After a while, they headed downstairs to the living room where their parents were sitting and talking.

"Boys, can we talk to you for a minute?" Jen asked.

"Sure Mama K!" Carlos said and they all sat down.

"We think that it would be a good idea for all of you to have someone to talk to about what's happened and to help you deal with things," Antonio said.

"You mean like a psychiatrist?" Logan asked.

"No, we were thinking more along the lines of a counselor, someone who's worked with kids who've suffered different types of trauma," Antonio said.

"Like who?" James asked.

"Well, we were thinking Sally O'Hara, since you all know and like her. I already spoke with her and she said she would be happy to set aside some time each week for all of you, either together or separately. However you want to do it," Antonio told them.

"I think it's a good idea," Logan said.

James agreed. "I'm okay with it."

Carlos said, "Me too, I love Sally."

Antonio looked at his godson. "Kendall?"

He nodded. "Sure."

"Honey, I still want you to see an actual psychologist for a while too," Jen said.

"Mom..."

"Kendall, please. Just for a little while. I'm going to see someone too."

Kendall sighed. "Fine, but just for a little while."

She kissed him on the cheek. "Thank you, baby. Now, how about some lunch?"

"Sounds good," Antonio said.

"I'll give you a hand," Sylvia said, getting up and following her friend back to the kitchen.

Carlos patted Kendall's shoulder. "It'll be okay, buddy, really. It might even be fun. You like Sally and who knows, maybe the psychologist will be just as nice."

Kendall just looked at him. "Carlos, sometimes your enthusiasm is really annoying."

"I know, but you have to admit I'm adorable!" He grinned.

Kendall rolled his eyes and shook his head.

Antonio laughed. "I'm going to go give your moms a hand."

He got up, walked back to the kitchen, and then stopped for a moment. He realized he hadn't been there since the night Kendall had been taken and flashed back to the condition the kitchen had been in when he first got there. He took a deep breath and continued in.

"Honey, are you okay?" Sylvia asked, noticing her husband seemed a little pale.

He smiled. "Fine, just a little tired. Need help?"

"Sure!" Jen said handing him a tray loaded with sandwiches.

He took them out to the dining room. The moms were close behind with a tray of fruit and glasses with milk. Jen called the kids. "Come on, you guys. Lunch!"

They all went into the dining room and James quickly guided Kendall to a chair between him and Antonio. He smiled smugly as he held the tray of sandwiches in front of Kendall.

Kendall looked at him and rolled his eyes but took half a sandwich from the plate. Antonio took the tray from James and placed another half sandwich on Kendall's plate, smiling. Kendall glared at them both and sighed.

Logan and Carlos started laughing at the expression on Kendall's face. Kendall looked at them and they looked away, still giggling. Kendall raised an eyebrow. "Katie..." he smiled at his little sister, who was seated between his two friends.

Katie smiled and nodded at her big brother. Reaching up, she grabbed each boy by the ear and twisted.

They immediately stopped laughing. "Ow, ow, ow!" they both cried.

"Katie..." her mother warned.

"Just teaching them some table manners, mom." She smiled innocently and winked at her brother.

∞

After lunch, the kids went into the living room to watch a movie.

"Kendall, did you take a pain pill yet?" Jen asked.

"Ummm."

"Kendall!"

"No, I feel fine, really."

Jen came out with the pill bottle and a glass of water. "You're supposed to take these."

"Mom, I don't need it," Kendall insisted.

"Kendall..." she warned.

"How about I take one before bed?"

"That's fine, because that's when the next one is due to be taken."

"They make me sleepy and I'm tired of sleeping," he argued.

She sighed. "Take half of one now and a full one at bedtime."

"Fine," he said, taking the glass.

Jen broke the pill in half and handed it to him. He swallowed it and handed her the glass. "Thank you, swe... honey," Jen said.

Kendall sighed. "You're welcome."

∞

Half an hour later, Kendall started nodding off and Katie grabbed a blanket and covered him.

Antonio came in. "You guys have been all cooped up for a couple days now, why don't you go outside for a while?"

"What if Kendall wakes up though?" Carlos asked.

"He'll be fine. We're here, and you boys need to work off some of that pent up energy. Now go!"

"We could go and see how the pond is coming along," Logan said.

The others nodded in agreement, and moments later, were bundled up and heading to the park.

"So, what do you think about this counseling thing?" James asked his friends.

"It's probably a good idea," Logan said.

"Especially if it's Sally, she's awesome!" Carlos smiled.

"True. How do you think Kendall is going to handle it?" James asked.

"I think he'll do fine with Sally. I don't know about a psychologist though. He doesn't like talking about things with strangers," Logan said.

"But Mama K said he only has to go for a little while, so maybe it'll be okay," Carlos said.

"Maybe," James said doubtfully.

They got to the park and sat under the oak tree for a while. Logan went to check the ice marker. "Four inches. Another inch and it'll be ready."

"Good, maybe Kendall will be ready to come out by the time it's frozen enough," Carlos said hopefully.

"He's not going to go out until those bruises are almost gone," James told him, remembering how embarrassed his friend was this morning.

"But that could take weeks!" Carlos said sadly.

"Well, we could do some night skating, then maybe he won't care too much," Logan said, putting his arm around Carlos' shoulders. "Just remember, we have to be patient and not push him too hard."

"I know. I just want things to be the way they were." Carlos sighed.

James smiled sadly. "Us too, buddy."

They were getting ready to head back to the Knight house, when Jason Banks walked up. Carlos and Logan both tensed and James moved in front of them. "What do you want, Jason?"

Jason put his hands up. "I just wanted to ask how Kendall's doing. Officer Sally said he was home."

"Why do you care?" Carlos snapped.

"Carlos, it's okay," Logan whispered, remembering the last time they had seen Jason.

"He's doing better," James told him.

"Good, I'm glad," Jason nodded. "Well... bye," he said and turned to leave.

"Jason thanks for asking," Logan said.

"Sure." Jason smiled and walked off.

"That was weird," James said.

"I know, Jason being nice. I guess anything's possible," Logan remarked.

"I still think he's mean," Carlos said, crossing his arms.

"You know, people can change for the better," Logan told him.

"Maybe, but I still don't trust him," Carlos replied stubbornly.

"You don't have to, buddy," James said.

They walked back to the house and found Antonio and Sylvia getting ready to leave. Kendall was sitting up watching TV, but still looked tired.

Sylvia kissed him. "We'll see you later, Mijo."

Kendall smiled. "Okay."

Antonio reached down and hugged him. "If you get worried or need anything, you call me, alright?" Kendall nodded and Antonio kissed him on the forehead.

Logan and James hugged them and said goodbye and Carlos walked them to the car. "Bye Mami, bye Papi."

"Goodbye Carlitos," Sylvia said, giving her son a kiss on the cheek.

"We'll see you tomorrow," Antonio said as he hugged Carlos. "You call if anyone needs anything. Make sure you give Mama K a hand, okay?"

"Will do!" Carlos smiled.

Antonio and Sylvia pulled out of the driveway. "Are you okay?" Sylvia asked.

Antonio nodded. "Just worried."

She smiled. "Everything will be alright. The kids and Jen are all going to go to counseling and one of the boys will be there if she needs them."

"I know, just the cop in me, I guess."

"Or the Papi," she suggested.

He smiled. "Maybe."

∞

The rest of the day was quiet, and after dinner and a few video games, the boys got ready for bed. Kendall was nervous, and he knew it was because Antonio wasn't there. He felt safe with Antonio in close proximity, and although he didn't say anything, the other boys could tell. He didn't argue with his mom about taking a pain pill. Kendall figured that if he could sleep through the night without waking up, it would be easier.

Jen went and tucked them in, Kendall in his bed, Carlos on the other. James and Logan slept on the floor in between the beds, with James next to Kendall.

"Are you boys comfortable? I can get a couple of extra blankets," Jen offered.

"I think we're fine. Goodnight, Mama K." James smiled.

"Goodnight boys," she said and walked across the hallway to tuck Katie in.

Kendall was trying to get comfortable, but there was a lump under his bottom sheet that kept poking him. "What the?" He reached under and pulled out the object.

"What's wrong?" Logan asked, turning on the table lamp. All three of the boys burst out laughing.

"Katie! So NOT funny!" Kendall yelled as he looked at the large stuffed purple unicorn with a glittery horn.

They could hear Katie laughing hysterically across the hallway. Kendall looked at his friends, who immediately stopped laughing.

"What, it's not pink!" Katie yelled back, still laughing. The other boys started giggling again.

"Shut up!" Kendall ordered, glaring at them. Logan turned out the light again, and with the exception of a muffled giggle here and there, it was quiet.

∞

Soon, everyone was fast asleep. It was about 2 am when Kendall heard whispering.

"Come out, come out wherever you are. It's time for your lessons, sweetheart."

Kendall found himself in the forest and could hear Deesie's voice all around him. He tried to run, but felt a sharp pain in his knee. He reached down and pulled out a long needle.

Suddenly, someone was on top of him, tearing at his clothes, biting his neck. He tried to scream, but nothing came out and he couldn't breathe. He heard Antonio calling to him in the background, and when he turned his head, he saw him lying there in a pool of blood.

"PAPI, NO!" he screamed, sound finally coming out.

"It's all your fault, sweetheart," Deesie said as he reached down and started choking him.

James heard Kendall stir and woke. He sat next to his friend. "Kendall, are you okay?"

He got no response, but Kendall suddenly started kicking and gasping as if he couldn't breathe. James turned the light on. "Kendall, wake up. Kendall, BREATHE!" he yelled, trying to wake his panicking friend.

Logan and Carlos awoke quickly. "What do we do?" Carlos asked.

"Go get Mama K," Logan told him, and he moved to the other side of Kendall's bed.

"Kendall, please wake up! You're home and safe, we're here with you," James said.

"See if you can get him up so he can breathe easier," Logan said.

James wrapped his arms around Kendall and pulled him, so he was sitting up in bed. He held him tightly to his chest. "Kendall, it's okay, you need to wake up," Logan said, stroking the blond bangs back.

Jen came running in with Carlos. Logan jumped up and Jen sat down. "Calm down, baby, it's mama. Please wake up. Honey, please…"

After a minute, Kendall's breathing slowed and he collapsed against James. His hair was matted to his forehead with sweat, and he was shaking.

"Baby, wake up," Jen said gently.

He opened his eyes. "Mama?"

"That's right, you're home and you're safe. It was just a bad dream."

"Don't remember," he said his voice raspy.

"It's okay, you don't have to remember." She smiled, running her fingers through his damp hair.

Carlos heard a small sound and looked over to see Katie standing in the doorway, tears streaming down her face. He went over, picked her up, and carried her to her room. "It's okay, Katie. He's waking up now."

She just held onto him, sobbing. He rocked her back and forth and started singing "Hush Little Baby" to her.

"Do you want me to sleep in here with you tonight?" he asked as she quieted down. She nodded and he tucked her back into bed. He grabbed a blanket from the closet and curled up at the foot of her bed.

Once they finally had Kendall back to sleep, Jen went and checked on Katie. She smiled when she saw Carlos curled up at the foot of Katie's bed and her daughter had scooted down and was now hugging Carlos' arm to her.

Chapter 48~ Psychology

Jen woke up about 6 am. She had not slept well. She kept replaying the previous night over and over in her mind. She had to get Kendall help today. He couldn't keep going on like this. None of them could.

She looked in on the boys and smiled sadly.

James still had Kendall wrapped tightly in his arms, and Logan had somehow managed to curl up on the other side of Kendall. They were all sound asleep. She checked in on Katie and Carlos and found they were still in the same positions they had been in when they fell asleep.

She went downstairs and made some coffee and decided to make the boys a nice breakfast, and quickly mixed up some waffle batter. She made a few, put them in the oven to stay warm, and went back upstairs. She woke Carlos and Katie first and then went in to wake the others.

"Logan, it's time to get up. Breakfast is ready," she whispered as she gently shook him.

"Morning Mama K," he said quietly as he got up and headed downstairs.

Jen walked around the bed.

"James, it's time to get up."

"Hmm?" James mumbled.

"It's time for breakfast."

"Okay, be right there," he said, yawning. "Do you want me to wake Kendall up?"

"No, let him sleep for now," she said.

James nodded and gently unwrapped himself from his friend and got up. He pulled the blankets back up over Kendall and headed downstairs.

Logan helped Jen serve up breakfast and they all ate quietly. "So, are you boys ready to go back to school?" Jen asked, smiling.

James and Carlos groaned.

"I am," Logan said.

"You're always ready for school. You're the only person I know who's happy when summer break is OVER," Carlos teased.

"What? I like learning," Logan retorted.

"Boys..." Jen laughed.

"How are you doing, Mama K?" James asked.

She sighed. "I think we've all been better. I'm going to find someone for Kendall to see today, even if I have to go through the entire phone book. Sylvia said Principal Lane or Sally might know someone, so I'll start with them."

"Do you want me to stay home and help?" James asked. He was worried about what would happen if Kendall had a panic attack and Jen was the only one home.

She smiled at him. "No swee... honey, you need to get back to school. Your mom will be coming over later this morning."

"Okay, but call if you need anything, okay? I'll have my cell on vibrate."

"I will, thank you."

∞

After breakfast, the boys went to get ready for school. Carlos used the upstairs shower and James the one on the main floor. Logan packed his things packed and waited his turn.

Kendall whimpered in his sleep and Logan went over and sat next to him. "Kendall, wake up," he said gently. When he got no response, he tried again. "Kendall, come on, buddy, wake up."

Kendall woke suddenly and jumped back against the headboard.

"Whoa... it's okay, it's just me," Logan said soothingly.

Kendall focused on Logan's voice and relaxed a little. He was shaking and clenching his hands. "Logan?"

"Yeah, it's me," Logan said softly.

"Sorry," Kendall said in a raspy voice.

"Don't apologize. Are you alright?"

"Yeah."

"Another bad dream?" Logan asked.

"Don't remember."

"It's okay, I never remember mine either. It's still pretty early. Why don't you try getting some more sleep?" Logan smiled.

"I don't want to sleep."

"Well, why don't you just rest until we're ready for school then?" Logan suggested.

Kendall nodded and lay back down. He was soon sound asleep. Logan was sitting next to Kendall, his hand on his shoulder, when Carlos came in.

"Everything okay?" Carlos asked.

"He woke up confused. I think he was having another bad dream."

Carlos sighed. "Maybe one of us should stay with him."

"Mama K said she's going to get him in to see someone, and we need to get back to class before we fall behind," Logan told him.

"I know."

"I don't like leaving them either. Maybe we can come over after school and stay for a couple of hours," Logan said.

"I think I'll let Papi know what happened last night," Carlos said.

"That's probably a good idea. Can you stay with him while I shower?"

Carlos nodded and sat next to his friend.

James came in. "Hey Carlos, have you got your things packed?"

"No, I think I'll just stop and pick them up after school."

"Are you okay, buddy?" James asked.

Carlos shook his head. "Just worried."

James sighed. "Me too, but things will get better."

"Promise?"

"I promise."

Kendall heard voices and opened his eyes. "Hey."

"Morning!" Carlos said and hugged him.

"How are you feeling?" James asked.

"Headache," Kendall said.

"I'll ask your mom what you can take," James said and went to find her.

Jen came in a couple of minutes later with two Tylenol and a glass of juice. "Here you go, honey."

"Thank you," Kendall said, taking the pills and juice.

Logan came in. "We better get going or we're going to be late."

The other two boys nodded and grabbed their backpacks. "We'll walk Katie, Mama K," James said, kissing her cheek. Logan and Carlos both kissed her goodbye and headed downstairs.

"Thanks boys, there are lunches packed for you on the table!" she called after them.

"How are you doing?" she asked Kendall, brushing his hair off his forehead.

"I'm okay. Just a little headache is all."

"Well, I'm going to fix you some breakfast, which you need to eat. Then I'm going to find someone for us to see today."

"Mom, I really don't want to talk to anybody," Kendall told her.

"I know, but you can't keep going on like this. You need someone to talk to about this, someone who knows how to help you work through it."

"Why can't I just talk to Sally?"

"You can talk to Sally, but I also think you need professional help. Someone who can take an objective point of view," she explained. "Now, I'm going to get something for you to eat, and then you need to get ready."

Kendall nodded but didn't say anything.

"Kendall, please don't be difficult. I need someone to talk to someone about this too. I know it's hard, but I don't want what happened when your dad died to happen again," Jen said quietly. "The truth is, honey, I'm scared... Please?"

He sighed. "Okay, I'll try."

"Thank you, baby. Why don't you jump in the shower while I fix your breakfast?"

"Okay," he said. He grabbed some clothes and went to shower. When he finished, he realized there was no one to help him with his t-shirt. There was no way he was asking his mom, so he just put on the flannel shirt and buttoned it up all the way.

He headed downstairs and went to the kitchen, where he found Jen on the phone trying to make an appointment. She smiled at him and put a plate with a waffle and some fruit on it in front of him. He took a couple of bites while she tried another office.

Finally, she hung up. "Well, no one that Sally or Janice recommended is available for 1-2 weeks. So I guess I'll check out the yellow pages."

She was on the phone for over a half an hour before finding a psychologist that could take both of them that day.

"Okay, ten for me and eleven for you. I'm going to get dressed." She kissed his cheek and headed upstairs.

Yay, Kendall thought as he cleared his plate of the barely eaten food and rinsed it.

∞

Jen and Kendall sat in the waiting room of Dr. Richard Graham. Jen was filling out paperwork. The office had already called Appleton County Hospital for Kendall's records, so she was filling in the rest of their histories.

Kendall sat with his coat zipped up as far as it would go and a dark blue beanie pulled down over his head. People stared when they saw the bruises on his face and he didn't like it.

Jen took the paperwork up to the receptionist, who took it from her with a smile. "So, Brooke will be meeting us here, and then she's going to come over for a while today," Jen told Kendall.

"That's good," he said, slumping down.

"Honey, I know you're nervous, but try and relax a little. Brooke should be here before I go in, so you won't be out here alone."

A moment later, the receptionist called Jen's name. She looked at Kendall, "Honey, I..."

"It's fine, mom, just go." He smiled.

"Are you sure?"

"Yes, I'll be fine. I'm sure Mama D will be here any minute."

"Okay. If you need anything..."

"Mom, just go."

Jen got up and followed the assistant into the doctor's office.

∞

Dr. Graham was a pleasant looking man in his mid-fifties. He had neatly trimmed salt and pepper hair and blue eyes. He had been practicing for over twenty years, and so far had a large success rate with his patients, mostly due to his use of psychogenic drugs, not his knowledge or amiable nature.

He greeted Jen. "Welcome, Mrs. Knight. I understand we will be seeing both you and your son today?"

"Yes, I believe the hospital sent his records?" she asked, sitting down.

"Yes, I see that they did." Dr. Graham smiled, looking through the files. "Seems you've all had a rough month."

"You could say that."

"Where would you like to start today?" he asked.

"I'm not sure."

"Why don't you tell me a little about what's been happening between you and Kendall?"

"Well, I guess I'm just worried about finding the best way to help him through this." She went on to explain what had happened with Deesie, Kendall's injuries, his nightmares, and panic attacks.

"That is a lot for someone to deal with. How are you coping with it?"

"The first couple of nights were alright, since we were staying with friends, but last night was hard. He had a nightmare and we couldn't get him to wake up at first. Then he never remembers what it was he was dreaming. He woke up with a headache, he doesn't want to eat, and he doesn't want to talk about it. I know the only reason he agreed to come here today was because I guilted him into it, but I just didn't know what else to do."

"Tell me, does he usually have trouble confiding in people?"

"No, he can usually discuss things with someone. If not with me, he has his friends or his godparents. His godfather is the only reason we got him back. In fact, he's the one Kendall went to when Deesie first made an advance towards him. Antonio is a wonderful man, he and Kendall's dad were best friends since they were about four. His wife and I have been friends since the fourth grade."

"Where is Kendall's dad?"

"He died almost seven years ago," Jen told him.

"So, Antonio is a good father figure then?"

"Absolutely." She smiled.

"Do you think he might, perhaps, play too large a role in Kendall's life?"

"What do you mean by too large a role?" Jen asked.

"You said Kendall initially went to him with this problem. Why not you?"

"Well, Kendall does try and protect me from things and Antonio is a policeman, so I guess it made sense to him."

"I see. Tell me, do you rely on a lot of outside sources for support?" Dr. Graham asked.

"Meaning?"

"Sometimes it's easier to allow other people to handle things, rather than to face them ourselves. It is especially hard for single parents, such as yourself, to deal with a severe crisis on their own. When you have others who are willing to jump in and take over, it makes it difficult for you to take back control. The end result becomes that you can't reconnect and you lose a bit of yourself in the process. I can definitely see why you cannot get through to your son when a crisis develops. He turns to someone else, in this specific case, Antonio."

"I'm not sure that's quite the case," Jen said.

"Who has Kendall confided in?"

"Well..."

"Who took over when a crisis developed the other night? Who decided to take Kendall, YOUR son, to the hospital, and who stayed there with him?" Dr. Graham pointed out. "Who is deciding what you hear and when you should hear it? Has he even told you everything?"

"No, you don't understand. The Garcias are family. The same with the Mitchells and the Diamonds. We all look out for one another. Antonio asked me how much I'd be able to handle, and when I couldn't take any more, he stopped," Jen explained.

Dr. Graham looked at her and nodded. "I understand... but here we are, and you have no idea how to reach your son. Does that sound right to you?"

"No," Jen said quietly, suddenly doubting her choices over the last couple of weeks.

"Well, we're going to help you learn how to reach Kendall on your own. We will also help Kendall learn how to face his fears and deal with them." Dr. Graham smiled.

"How?" she asked.

"Well, I would first recommend that you limit Kendall's contact with Antonio for now. He needs to learn to confide in you, and we need to put him on a strong anti-anxiety medication to help him cope with the nightmares and panic attacks. After he starts the medication, I am going to recommend using a type of 'immersion' therapy. You said when he hears the word 'sweetheart,' he has a flashback of sorts, and so you have tried to avoid using it. Unfortunately, it is a commonly used word and we need to desensitize him to it. So, after he starts the medication, I want you to use the word, including waking him with it."

"Are you sure about this? He is only fourteen, and I don't know if separating him from Antonio is a good idea, and he and Carlos are so close. You didn't see him when I accidentally woke him by calling him 'sweetheart.' He couldn't breathe."

Dr. Graham smiled. "That's what the medication is for—to eliminate the anxiety, so we can get him back to normal. Jennifer, I'm not going to force you to do anything that you don't feel comfortable doing, but if you really want your son whole again, you really need to consider what you're willing to do to reach him."

She nodded.

He sat down and typed out a prescription. "Now, why don't I meet with Kendall and he and I can have a nice chat? You can fill this prescription while he and I talk. There is a pharmacy right downstairs. Why don't we also make another appointment for both of you tomorrow?" He smiled, handing her the prescription.

Jen took it and nodded. "Thank you."

"We'll see you tomorrow then." He smiled.

Jen went back to the waiting room to find Brooke sitting next to Kendall, showing him something on her phone. "Hi," Brooke said, smiling brightly.

"Hi Brooke, thanks for coming."

The receptionist called Kendall's name. He sighed and got up. Jen kissed him on the cheek. "Just relax, he's very nice."

Kendall nodded and followed the assistant down the hallway.

"How did it go?" Brooke asked.

"Alright, I guess," Jen said and told her about what Dr. Graham had recommended.

"Jen, are you sure about that? That doesn't sound like something a child psychologist would recommend," Brooke asked.

"Well, his credentials say he's fully trained in all ages and aspects of psychological traumas. Maybe we do rely on Antonio too much."

"Do you really think Kendall is going to be okay with that?" Brooke asked.

"Well, hopefully Dr. Graham can get him to talk and we won't have to worry about it. He said I don't have to do anything I'm not comfortable with. I need to go fill this for Kendall," she said, walking to the elevators.

"Please don't make any rash decisions," Brooke asked, already deciding she was going to check into this Dr. Graham's professional background.

"I won't." Jen smiled, but she already doubted her ability to see the situation clearly. *That is WHY I decided to get help from a professional, isn't it?* She asked herself.

∞

Dr. Graham greeted Kendall when he walked into his office. "Hello Kendall, please have a seat. How are we today?"

"I'm doing okay," Kendall answered as he took the chair Dr. Graham indicated with his hand.

"Is that the truth?" Dr. Graham asked smiling.

Kendall already didn't like him. "Why wouldn't it be?"

"Well, your mother said you're having bad dreams."

"People have bad dreams all the time," Kendall said.

"True, however most people haven't gone through what you have in the last few weeks."

Kendall shrugged. "Bad things happen to people all the time."

"We're not going to get very far if you don't start actually answering the questions," Graham said.

"I did answer the question," Kendall pointed out.

"Really?"

"You asked how I was, I said I was okay."

Dr. Graham smiled. "Do you have issues with authority, Kendall?"

"I guess it depends," Kendall said.

"On?"

"If I believe they're an authority figure or not," Kendall told him.

"Does it really matter what you believe? A person who is in charge of a situation is an authority figure, period."

Kendall raised an eyebrow and just looked at him.

Dr. Graham was already getting frustrated with this boy and tried a different tact. "Why don't you tell me what's important in your life."

"My family, my friends," Kendall said.

"Do you consider your friends to be like family?" he asked, recalling the conversation with his mother.

"Yes."

"Why?"

"Because they are."

"That's not really an answer. You do understand that they aren't REALLY your family, don't you?" Graham asked.

"That's your opinion."

"You're kind of a smart ass, aren't you?" Dr. Graham asked.

Kendall looked at him and stood up. "I think I'm done here. Nice to meet you," he said and walked out. Kendall went and waited for the elevator.

His mother and Brooke stepped out and he stepped in. "Kendall, where are you going?" Jen asked as the doors closed.

Brooke pushed the call button, and when the doors opened, they got in and went to the ground floor, where they found Kendall waiting patiently by the car.

"Kendall what happened?" Jen asked.

"I am NOT seeing him again," Kendall said.

"Kendall, why are you acting like this?"

"Why don't we talk about this at home?" Brooke suggested.

Jen opened the doors and Kendall got in without saying another word.

Chapter 49~ Uncertainty

"Good Morning," Antonio said as he walked into the station. "This is for you," he said, handing Sally a large cup of hot Chai tea, her favourite.

"Morning Boss and thank you. Aren't you taking a few days off?"

"Yeah, I just thought I'd stop by and pick up my mail and Kendall's laptop, if you're finished with it." He smiled.

"I am. I printed and then deleted all of the messages and cleared the history. All but two of the kids admitted to sending the emails, so I thought you might want to speak with them?"

"Yes I do," Antonio said.

Sally handed him the printouts. "There you go. How's everyone doing?"

"Alright, I think. First night was rough. Kendall ended up back at the hospital, but he seems to be doing better."

"Good. I already called the other boys. I'll meet with them in a group this afternoon after school. I also tweaked this and wanted to know what you think. I thought it might be easier for Kendall to answer on paper than have to actually talk about it for now."

Antonio took the paper from her. "Isn't this the information sheet you came up with for rape victims?"

A couple of years ago Sally had created a template of the questions commonly asked to victims of assault. She realized that many victims found it easier to write down what they had experienced, instead of talking about it. She had simplified it by creating a checklist and a place to write down how many times something happened, and an area where they could write down anything they wanted to add. She'd taken it to one of the DA's, and they'd managed to get it approved by the local courts, so that it was now as admissible as a sworn statement in cases of extreme trauma, provided it's witnessed by an officer or a court representative.

"Yeah, I tweaked it and changed a few of the questions. I thought if I had him fill this out, instead of trying to get it out of him verbally, we might get further."

"This is great! Are you going to be seeing him soon?"

"I haven't heard anything from him or Jen. I figure it'll be a few days until I do. I thought I would take this over later though and see if we can get it out of the way. When you take him his laptop, give him this," she said handing him a small box. "I had them replace his cell phone, new number and everything. They transferred his data to the new phone, so he should be ready to go."

Antonio smiled. "You amaze me, you know that?"

"I know. Your mail is on your desk." She smirked.

"Thank you," he said and went in to get some of the paperwork cleared from his desk. He sat down and sifted through the papers dealing with what he needed to and setting the rest aside. There was a large manila envelope and he picked it up, smiling when he saw the return address was Doc's. He opened it and read the letter.

Dear Antonio,

Jake worked all Friday night on these, and I wanted to get this off to you as soon as they were done. After hearing about Kendall's nightmares, he made a dreamcatcher for him. His mother taught him how to make them when he was little. He made one for you, too. The

legend goes that the night air is filled with dreams, both good and bad. The dreamcatcher, when hung where you sleep, swinging freely with the air, catches the dreams as they flow by. The good dreams know the way, slipping through the outer holes and slide down the soft feathers so gently, that many times, the sleeper doesn't know that they're dreaming. The bad dreams, not knowing the way, get tangled in the web and perish with the first light of the new day.

The outer ring is wrapped with the hair from Midnight Shadow's mane. The center webbing is from her foal's, which, by the way, we named Shadow's Knight. There are also five bracelets. Jake made one for each of the boys and Kendall's little sister. They're made with a combination of Midnight and the foal's hair. We hand carved the beads last year from an elk antler we found. You boys take care and keep in touch.

— Doc and Jake

Antonio pulled out the contents, two dream catchers about seven inches in diameter, each adorned with several beads and three strands with a feather woven into each. The bracelets were beautifully braided, with a bead about a half an inch long. Each bead was carved with a different pattern, and there was a silver clasp on each bracelet. The kids were going to love them.

He put them back in the envelope and grabbed the laptop, phone, and his coat. "I'll see you later, Sally. Thanks again, for everything."

"Not too soon though, and you're welcome."

"No, not too soon... By the way, you need some time off too," he said sternly.

"Already scheduled for next week." She smiled.

"Alright, I'll talk to you later." Antonio smiled as he left.

∞

"Kendall, please tell me what happened," Jen pleaded as they drove home.

Kendall sat in silence, looking out the window. *Not his family! What did that jerk know about it anyway?* He fumed. He stole a sideways glance at his mom, wondering what Graham had told her.

They pulled into the driveway and got out. Brooke pulled up behind them. She had already called her office to have a background check run on this Dr. Graham. She was worried about what he had recommended to Jen. It didn't sound right at all. Kendall's behaviour had compounded her concern. The man said or did something to make the boy act that way.

Damn it, they have already been through enough, she thought. She got out and followed them into the house.

After they went inside, Kendall started up the stairs.

"No, you need to tell me what happened," Jen ordered.

"I don't like him."

"That is not an answer," Jen said.

Kendall looked at her. "That's what HE kept saying. He would ask me something, I'd answer, and he either accused me of lying or told me it wasn't an answer. Then he said our friends are NOT family, and when I told him that's his opinion, he called me a smart ass! So I left." Kendall turned around and walked upstairs, slamming his door.

Jen sighed. "What am I supposed to do now?"

"Honey, we'll find him another psychologist, one that specializes in children," Brooke told her.

"There's no one available for a week, at the earliest!"

"Let me make a couple of calls. I'll find someone," Brooke said.

"No, Dr. Graham is right. I need to take control of the situation and I'll find someone. Until I do, Kendall is going to have to see Dr. Graham."

"Jen, I really don't think that's a good idea. He's already so upset, and with everything else," Brooke said gently.

"Well, that's not your call, is it?" Jen snapped.

Brooke looked at her in shock.

"I'm sorry... it's just that he is right. I DO need to start taking care of things on my own. I can't go running to everyone when I have a problem."

"Jen, that's what friends are for. We support one another and help each other through things," Brooke said.

"Really? When was the last time you needed me to handle a problem for you? When was the last time ANY of you needed me to fix something for you? Brooke, all I do is take. I can't even get through to my own son! He doesn't come to me, he goes to Antonio and it has to stop."

"Jen, you can do something for me now," Brooke said gently.

"What?"

"Get a second opinion. Please?" Brooke asked.

Jen sighed. "I'll call one of the others that Sally recommended and make an appointment. BUT, we are still seeing Dr. Graham until then."

"That's all I ask," Brooke said sadly.

"I'll make us some lunch" Jen said and went into the kitchen.

∞

Kendall sat at his desk and doodled. With no computer or cell, he was pretty much cut off from talking to anyone else. He was tired and not feeling very well. His chest was still tight and he should probably use the nebulizer. *Forget it,* he thought. He went to lie down and was soon fast asleep.

∞

Jen made some sandwiches and cut up some fruit. She put a plate on a tray, along with a bottle of ice tea and the new medication that Dr. Graham had prescribed.

"Why don't you let me take it up?" Brooke offered.

"I can do it."

"I know you can, I just haven't heard how Kendall likes his new room. Did he find the 'surprise' Katie got for him?" Brooke asked.

"Yes, the other boys thought it was hysterical. I heard them giggling on and off for quite a while. Katie was laughing so hard... It was nice to hear them laughing." Jen smiled.

"Well, let's get his lunch to him and I can offer to get him something 'special' for her room." Brooke smiled.

They went upstairs and Brooke knocked on Kendall's door. "Kendall, lunch is ready."

Not getting an answer, she opened the door. Kendall was sleeping, so Jen set the tray on his desk. She sat down next to him and gently shook him. "Honey, I brought you some lunch."

"Hmmm?"

"Lunch."

"I'm not hungry," he said, closing his eyes again.

"Kendall, you need to eat and you need to take your medication," Jen said.

"I already took it after breakfast."

"No honey, your new medication. Dr. Graham prescribed an anti-anxiety medication to help with your nightmares," she explained.

"No, I'm not taking it."

"Kendall..." Jen warned.

"I don't trust him and I'm not taking anything he prescribed," Kendall told her.

"Kendall, you will stop being difficult and do what you're told," Jen said firmly.

Kendall looked at her. "I'll eat, but I'm not taking anything he prescribed."

Brooke noticed that Kendall's breathing was becoming laboured. "Kendall, are you feeling alright?"

He shook his head. "My chest hurts and I'm tired."

"I'll get the nebulizer. Where did we put it?" Jen asked.

"It's in the bathroom," he said.

Jen went to find it and Brooke sat next to him. "It'll be okay, honey. I'm doing some checking on this Dr. Graham and we're going to get you in to see someone else. Until then... just try and go along with your mom for now, okay?"

"I don't like him."

"I know. I don't like him either. We'll get this figured out," she promised.

"Okay, thanks Mama D."

Jen came back in with the nebulizer and set it up. Kendall breathed in the medicated mist and fell asleep.

Jen sighed. "He's so tired all the time."

"Give it some time, it's only been a few days and he's still recovering. It can take weeks to recover from pneumonia, and with everything else he's been through," Brooke said.

"I know. I just wish things were back to normal. I hate seeing him like this. I hate seeing ALL of the kids stressed out and afraid, never knowing what's going to happen next."

"Well, luckily our kids are strong and care enough about each other to stay strong. They'll be fine, and soon this will all be just a memory," Brooke told her.

"A memory we don't want," Jen whispered.

Brooke hugged her. "I agree, but that's all it will be."

Jen gently shook Kendall. "Honey, I'm going to take the mask off now, and I want you to eat."

"Hmmm, okay," he said, yawning.

Brooke brought the tray over to him and set it on the table next to the bed. "Thanks Mama D."

She smiled. "Eat, and I'm starving, so we should go eat too."

Jen nodded and followed Brooke downstairs.

Kendall slowly ate his lunch and managed to get most of it down. When he was finished, he lay back down and was quickly asleep.

Brooke and Jen ate lunch in the kitchen. "So, what did Dr. Graham prescribe for Kendall?"

"Lorazepam, one every eight hours," Jen told her, reading the label.

Brooke made a mental note to check out the medication as well.

∞

There was a knock at the door, and Jen answered to find Antonio standing there.

"Come on in." She smiled.

"I thought I'd drop off Kendall's laptop. Sally traded his cell phone in and had all of his numbers transferred onto it. Also, Doc sent him and the boys something."

"Brooke and I are having lunch. Are you hungry?" Jen asked.

"No, I'm good. Thanks." He smiled.

"Antonio, could I ask you a few things?"

"Of course, anything," he said.

"Why don't you take Kendall's things up to him first, and then we can sit in the kitchen and talk," Jen said.

"Sure. Is he feeling any better?"

"He just had a breathing treatment. He said his chest was hurting."

"He'll be up and around in no time," Antonio said and then headed upstairs.

He found Kendall sleeping, an empty plate on the table next to him. "Kendall," he said, gently shaking the boy.

"Hmmm? I ate, mom," he mumbled.

"That's good, but I'm not your mom." Antonio laughed.

Kendall opened his eyes. "Papi?" He reached up and hugged the man tightly. He was shaking.

"Hey. What's this, Mijo? Did you have a bad dream?"

Kendall shook his head.

"What's wrong?"

"We went to see a doctor today, and I don't like him. Mom and I already fought about it and now he wants me to take pills, and I won't. He accused me of lying, said my friends don't count as family, called me a smart ass, and I think he told mom the same thing, and I don't want to go back!" Frustrated, Kendall had rushed it all out in one breath.

"Wait, he accused you of lying and called you names?" Antonio asked.

Kendall nodded.

"That doesn't sound right. What did your mom say?"

"She told me to quit being difficult and do what I was told. I don't know what to do. I don't want to go back, and I'm NOT taking the pills," Kendall said.

"Okay, we'll get it all sorted out," Antonio promised.

"Mama D said that, too."

"Does Brooke know what happened?"

Kendall nodded.

"Okay, well don't worry about it now. I brought your laptop back and Sally got your phone replaced."

"Really? That's great, thank you," Kendall said, happy that he was no longer cut off from the world.

"Doc sent something for you and the other kids." Antonio smiled as he handed him the manila envelope.

Kendall looked in and pulled out the contents. "Read the letter," Antonio said.

Kendall read the letter. "Wow, these are really nice. His son made these?" he asked, looking at the dreamcatcher and bracelets.

"He did."

"I'll have to write them a letter and thank them. Do you think it'd be okay if I sent Ranger Thompson a card, and maybe one to Mr. Crowley's family, if he had any?" Kendall asked.

"I think they'd really like that." Antonio smiled. "Let me hang this for you," he said and took the dreamcatcher. He attached it to one of the hooks on the curtain rod.

"Thanks Papi." Kendall smiled.

"Why don't you get some more sleep and NO more bad dreams from now on," he said as he kissed Kendall on the forehead.

"Okay. Talk to you later?"

"You bet." Antonio smiled as he grabbed the tray. Antonio took the tray into the kitchen where Jen and Brooke were sitting, finishing their lunch.

"Well, he ate everything," he told them.

"Thank God," Jen said.

She sighed when she saw the pill still sitting on the tray. She picked it up and put it back in the bottle.

"What did you want to talk about, honey?" Antonio asked her.

"Well, Kendall and I went to see a psychologist this morning, and he said I may be depending on you all too much. I think he may be right. I mean, you've had to deal with so much through this whole thing. You were away from your family while we stayed with your family. You took care of Kendall at the hospital in Appleton and then again here. He thinks we might be becoming too dependent on you and that I need to take control of the situation and do things for myself," Jen told him.

"Okay, first of all, us taking care of one another is just something we've always done. Do you remember when Sylvia's dad died? We ended up being gone for almost a month. You took care of Carlos that whole time, and he had never been away from us that long. You stayed up with him when he cried at night. You made him his favourite comfort foods. We didn't have to worry once that whole month, because we knew he was with you. Second, I would have been on the road looking for ANY child that Deesie took. It's my job, it's what I do."

He took her hand and one of Brooke's. "We are family, not bound by blood, but by something just as strong. I will always be there for all of you, and I know you'll be there for me."

Jen and Brook smiled.

Jen jumped up and hugged Antonio. "Thank you! You have no idea what that means."

"Is there anything else?"

"Can you tell me more of what happened?" Jen asked.

"Are you sure you're ready to hear more?"

Jen nodded.

"Okay, let me know if you need me to stop."

"I will," she promised.

"What do you want to know first?"

"Why Kendall?" she asked.

"Well, we think he fixated on him when he asked for an extension for his assignment. Deesie took advantage of the fact he asked for help and attempted to exchange favours. Kendall told him no and threatened to tell. Deesie just laughed it off. I guess thinking that no one would believe him. Kendall came to me and we started an investigation. The next day, Deesie had gotten Jason Banks to spread rumours, in the form of flyers, about Kendall, and people started to believe them. That's why I took his laptop. Some of the kids sent him some pretty unfriendly emails, and we tracked them down and they're being dealt with."

Jen nodded. "Okay, and then?"

"Apparently Deesie had gone to Janice Lane, accusing Kendall of making an inappropriate offer in exchange for the extension. She called Kendall into the office and was talking to him about it, when Deesie told the class the same thing. He handed out a paper, saying that Principal Lane had written it, explaining what behaviour wasn't allowed. He also made a point to chew Jason out in front of everyone. That with the fact Kendall had skipped practice the night before and the fact that he had been called to the office during class, convinced most of the students it was true. When Logan and James confronted him about it, he told them it was all a lie, but the fact that a teacher, supposedly backed up by the principal, was telling them this, made them doubt Kendall."

"The boys are heartbroken by the fact they listened to Deesie," Brooke told Jen.

"I know. It wasn't their fault." Jen smiled sadly. "What happened next?"

"Kendall was understandably upset and decided he needed to fix the problem as soon as possible. He took his phone and his MP3 player and set them to record, and then he went back and confronted Deesie. He tricked him into thinking he was recording with his phone, and Deesie took it and turned it off. All the while, he was recording with his MP3 player. He dropped it off at my house when he was visited Carlos that day."

"What was on the recording?"

"It might be easier if you listen to it. It's on my home computer, so when you're ready, you can come over and listen to it," Antonio suggested.

Jen nodded. "Okay, that might be easier."

"Anything else?"

"I know that Deesie didn't... and that he probably did do the other things to him. Do you know if anything else like that happened?"

Antonio sighed. "Not really. Sally's going to bring over something for Kendall to work on that should tell us more."

"What is it?"

"She came up with this document that helps victims explain what happened without actually having to talk about it until they're ready. It'll give us have a better idea of how to help him," Antonio said.

"Okay, I think that's enough for now, unless there's something you think I should know now?" Jen asked.

"I think you should know everything, but we need to go at a pace that doesn't overwhelm you. I think once Sally works with Kendall a little, it'll make it easier," Antonio told her.

"You're right. I'll give Sally a call and set something up."

"She's seeing the other boys later today, so whenever you're ready."

"Okay, I'll give her a call in a little while then."

"Good. Kendall said something about sending cards to Ranger Thompson and Mr. Crowley's family, so I'll have Sally get those addresses for him," Antonio said, standing up.

"Thank you, Antonio," Jen said, kissing him on the cheek.

"You're welcome. We'll see you later."

"Let me walk you out. I wanted to ask you about the game coming up," Brooke said.

"Wow, an escort. I could get use to this." He smiled as Brooke took his arm.

Jen laughed and shook her head. "Talk to you later."

"Okay, what happened?" Antonio asked Brooke quietly.

Brooke explained what Jen had told her and what had happened with Kendall. "I called my office and they're running a background check on Dr. Graham. I have never heard of a psychologist recommending that someone get rid of their support. Kendall was so upset. He wouldn't say anything all the way home, and then he and Jen got into it a little."

Antonio sighed. "He said something along those lines when I went up to see him."

"I'm really worried about her. I thought she was going to lose it when Kendall told her he wasn't taking anything Graham prescribes. I understand that she wants things to get back to normal and she's terrified of what might happen when Kendall has a nightmare or panic attack, but I'm not sure she understands that throwing pills at the problem isn't going to actually FIX it," Brooke said.

"No, it won't," Antonio agreed.

"Just so I'm not a total liar, what time is the game on Saturday?"

"Ten." Antonio laughed.

"Thank you, I'll let you know what I hear," Brooke said, kissing his cheek.

"Please do," Antonio said.

Brooke went back inside and found Jen sitting in the kitchen. "You alright, honey?"

Jen nodded. "I called Sally. She'll come over before she meets with the boys."

"Good," Brooke said, patting her arm.

"Do you think I'm doing the right thing?" Jen asked.

"About?"

"Making Kendall see Dr. Graham until I can get him in somewhere else."

"I think you're doing what you think you need to," Brooke answered carefully.

"But is it the RIGHT thing?"

Brooke sighed. "I think if the reason is for him to have someone to talk to about this, then no. He isn't going to talk to someone he doesn't trust."

"Sally got him an appointment with a Dr. Jenkins next Tuesday. She specializes in working with children," Jen said.

"Well, that's good, isn't it?"

"What do we do until then?" Jen asked.

"We take one day at a time and go slowly," Brooke said.

"I'm still going to see Dr. Graham tomorrow. A lot of what he said made sense."

"Well, if you feel comfortable with him, then that's what you need to do. I still hope you'll consider getting another opinion though," Brooke said, worried that Graham would still try to convince Jen that she should go it alone.

"I will," Jen promised.

Chapter 50~ The Boys' First Day Back

The boys had an uneventful morning at school. People would give them a sad or embarrassed smile every now and then, but otherwise, everything seemed normal. A few asked how Kendall was doing and seemed happy when they heard he was doing well and should be back soon. Their teachers told them there wouldn't be a problem if they needed more time for assignments.

Lunchtime was pretty much the same. The boys sat together and James called the Knight house to see how things were going.

"Hello," Jen answered.

"Hi Mama K, we were just checking in."

"Everything's fine. Sally's coming over in a little while to talk to Kendall."

"Good. We're going to meet with her after school, so I won't be there right away. Unless you need me?"

Jen smiled. "No, I think we're doing fine here, take as long as you need. Do you think you could stop by the office and pick up Kendall's lessons?"

"Sure, anything else?" James asked.

"No, I think that was it. Thanks sweetheart," Jen said and hung up.

"What's wrong?" Carlos asked, noticing a strange look on James' face.

"Mama K called me sweetheart."

"That was nice," Carlos said.

"No genius, we're supposed to AVOID that word," Logan reminded him. "She probably just slipped. Moms use that word a lot."

"Maybe," James said unconvinced.

Jenny Tinkler came running over. "Hey guys!"

"Hi Jenny!" the boys responded on high alert.

Carlos saw Jenny's right foot catch on the back of her left one, reached out, and caught her before she hit the floor. He pulled her onto the bench next to him.

"Thanks Carlos!" She grinned.

"Actually, we owe you a big thank you," Carlos said, hugging her.

"For what?"

"Because you helped Papi find Kendall," Carlos said, hugging her again.

"I didn't do that much," she said, blushing.

"Jenny, if you hadn't remembered the name of the town where Deesie's cousin had a cabin, they probably wouldn't have found Kendall before something really bad happened," Logan said as he hugged her.

"You guys..." she said, embarrassed by the sudden display of affection.

James got up, went over, and gave her a big hug too. "No Jenny, because of you we got him back, and we can never thank you enough for that."

Jenny sniffed a little, not use to such positive attention. "How is Kendall?"

"He's doing better. Hopefully he can come back to school next week," Logan told her.

"That's good. I miss him."

The bell rang and James and Carlos groaned.

"Next class," Logan announced happily.

"There is something wrong with you," James said as they headed to their next class.

∞

The rest of the day went well, until Logan went to his English class. He walked in and stopped before he reached his desk. He looked at Kendall's empty seat and then to the front of the classroom at the substitute teacher. His stomach started doing flip-flops and he fought down the urge to vomit right on the spot. He took a deep breath and started for his desk, stopped, and then ran out of the room. He ran into the restroom and threw up his lunch.

He sat there for a minute and heard someone come in. "Logan, are you okay?"

"Yeah, I'm fine." He opened the stall door to find Jason standing there looking worried. "Are you sure?"

Logan nodded. "I-I'm good, thanks."

"Good. Mr. Lawrence said you can skip English, so I brought you the assignment," he said, handing Logan the papers.

Logan reached out and took them from the larger boy. "I better get back," Jason said and turned to go.

"Jason."

"Yeah?"

"Thanks."

"No problem." Jason smiled as he headed back to class.

Logan spent the rest of last period in the library, working on his English assignment. He was nearly finished when the last bell rang. He finished the question he was working on and then gathered up his books and headed for his locker.

James and Carlos were already there waiting. "Are you okay?" Carlos asked, noticing that Logan looked a little more pale than usual.

"I'm fine," he said.

"You weren't in English. I stopped by the classroom," James said.

"Mr. Lawrence excused me, so I was doing my homework in the library," Logan explained.

"Did Jason say something?" Carlos asked, knowing Jason was in that class.

"Actually, yeah. I had a mini panic attack and left before class started. He followed me into the bathroom and asked if I was alright. He even spoke to Mr. Lawrence and brought me my assignment," he told him, smiling a little.

"Jason... Jason BANKS?" Carlos clarified.

"Yes Carlos... Jason Banks. I told you people can change," Logan said.

"I guess they can." James smiled.

Carlos looked less certain but trusted his friends. "Okay, I'll try and believe that."

Logan smiled as he opened his locker. A piece of paper fell out and Carlos picked it up for him. Logan unfolded it and turned white, his hands shaking.

"What is it?" James said, grabbing the paper from Logan.

He quickly read it and turned five shades of red. "Come on!" he growled, grabbing Carlos and Logan by the arms.

James hauled them into the principal's office. "We need to see Principal Lane NOW!"

"James, what's wrong?" Tara asked, jumping up.

"THIS IS WRONG!" he screamed, waving the paper at her.

Janice came running out. "What is going on out here?"

"This..." James said, his eyes filling with angry tears.

She took the paper from him and read it, her face flushing with anger. "Come in, boys," she said, ushering them into her office. "Tara, please get Antonio Garcia down here immediately."

Janice got the boys settled on her couch and grabbed a cup of water for James. "Drink."

He took it, his hands still shaking.

"Where did you find that?"

"It was in my locker," Logan said quietly.

"Was that the only one?" she asked.

"I think so."

"What is it?" Carlos asked.

"You don't need to see it," James said.

"I have a right to know what's going on," Carlos said.

Janice looked at James and he nodded.

She held the paper up for Carlos to read, and his eyes filled with tears. "Why would anyone say something like that?"

Janice handed him a tissue. "I don't know, but I'm going to find out. Do you have any idea who might have done this?"

The boys thought for a minute. "No," James and Logan both said.

"I would have said Jason, but he's been trying to be nice and helped Logan when he got sick in English," Carlos said.

"Are you sick, Logan?" she asked.

He shook his head. "Just a little panic attack, although I feel sick now."

"You're sure?"

He nodded.

Carlos heard Antonio's voice in the outer office, jumped up, and ran to his father. "Papi!"

Antonio hugged his son. "What happened, Mijo?"

"Antonio, in here," Janice called.

He walked into her office, his son still clinging to his waist. "Carlitos, I need to breathe."

Carlos relaxed his hold and Antonio hugged him. "Go sit with your brothers so I can talk to Janice."

Carlos did as he was told and sat down next to James, who wrapped an arm around his shoulders and the other around Logan's.

"This was in Logan's locker," Janice said, handing Antonio the paper.

He took it and read it, his jaw clenching in anger. The paper was printed, "Hey losers, too bad they found your little buddy so fast. The slut should have got what was coming to him. Who knows, maybe he did. He probably liked it. Do you think he dreams about Mr. Deesie touching him? Do you think it makes him wish he was back there…?" The paper continued in that manner for quite a while, each question or statement worse than the last.

Antonio took a deep breath and looked at his boys. "You all read this?"

They nodded.

"Okay, we don't tell Kendall or Jen about this. Janice and I will track down who did this and they will be charged. Do you have any idea who might have done this?" Antonio asked them.

The boys all shook their heads.

"Okay, there were two people who didn't admit to sending an email. We'll start there," Antonio told Janice.

She nodded. "I'll get a list of students who logged onto the library computers today."

"I'll give you a call later then," Antonio said. "Come on, boys, I'll drive you home."

"We're supposed to meet with Sally," Logan told him.

"Where are you meeting her?"

"We were just going to go to the station," Carlos said.

"Perfect, I can work on a few things there and then I'll take you all home. Now let's go get your things."

"I needed to pick up Kendall's assignments," James said.

"I have them here, honey," Janice said, handing him a folder with Kendall's name on it.

"Thank you… I'm sorry about, well…yelling," James said.

"You have nothing to be sorry for. If you boys need more time, let me know," Janice told them.

"Thank you," they all said.

"I'll be in touch," Antonio said as they left.

Sally knocked on the Knight's door.

Jennifer answered. "Hi Sally, thanks for being able to see him here."

"Not a problem. It's easier for people to open up in familiar surroundings." She smiled.

Jen led Sally upstairs and knocked on Kendall's door. Not getting a response, she opened it to find Kendall still sleeping. "Kendall, Sally's here," Jen said, gently shaking him.

"Hmmm?"

"Sally's here to talk to you," Jen told him.

"Okay," he said, sitting up.

"Hey kiddo." Sally smiled.

"Hi Sally," Kendall said shyly.

"I'll leave you two alone. Do you need anything, honey?"

"No, I'm good," Kendall said.

Jen smiled and left, closing the door behind her.

"How are you doing?" Sally asked as she sat on the other bed.

Kendall shrugged.

Sally watched him for a moment, taking in the averted eyes, the slight shaking of his hands, the down turned mouth that usually had a hint of a smile. "Antonio said Katie switched rooms with you and they all decorated it. It's really nice. How do you like it?" she asked.

"They did a great job and it's nice that there's room for the extra bed."

"But...?"

"I don't know, I just wish Katie hadn't been so worried that she gave up her room for me," he said quietly.

"It's hard to suddenly be the one who has to take from someone. Especially when you're the one use to looking out for that someone?" Sally asked.

Kendall nodded.

"You're a great big brother, Kendall, and you've helped to raise a great little sister. I don't know many little girls who would willingly give up their room, much less come up with the idea," Sally said.

"Katie's pretty special." He smiled.

"Yes she is. So stop feeling guilty about it and enjoy the fact that she loves you so much."

"I'll try."

"Is there anything in particular that you want to talk about?" Sally asked.

"Not really."

"Okay, let me suggest some things then, and if you don't want to talk about it, we won't," she said.

"That's a switch," he commented.

"What is?" Sally asked.

"Nothing."

"Okay, let's set some ground rules. You don't have to answer me if you don't want to, you can ask me anything you want, and I will answer you honestly. However, if you make a comment like the one you just did, you need to clarify it for me... Okay?"

Kendall sighed and nodded.

"So...?"

"My mom and I went to see a psychologist this morning and I don't like him."

"Fair enough. Why don't you like him?" Sally asked.

"He said my friends don't count as family, and when I told him that was his opinion, he called me a smart ass. My mom and I already argued about it because she was talking to me like he was."

"How was she talking to you?" Sally asked.

"She'd ask me a question and when I answered, she said it wasn't an answer. When I told her I wasn't going to take anything he prescribed, she got mad and told me I need to stop being so difficult. I tried explaining that I don't trust him, but she didn't want to hear it."

"Okay, can you tell me exactly why you don't trust him?" Sally asked.

"I don't know. He's just... phony. He asks a question, and when you answer it, he either accuses you of lying or says it's not an answer. I don't like being talked to like I'm four years old. I'm also worried about what he told my mom. I heard her arguing with Mama D a little while ago and I think it was about him. She said I have to go back, but I'm not going."

"Well, I don't blame you for not liking being talked down to, that's not okay. He also shouldn't have called you a smart ass, even if you were being one, which I'm not saying you were. I'm just saying they are supposed to maintain a professional demeanor. Your mom didn't say anything about that?" Sally asked.

"No."

"Okay, I do know that we made an appointment with Claudia Jenkins next week. She's very nice and specializes in child psychology. I think you'll really like her. Do you know who recommended this psychologist to your mom?"

"She couldn't get in with anyone until next week and she wanted us to go today, so she found him in the yellow pages," Kendall told her.

"Wait, she's seeing him too?"

"Yeah, why?"

"So he's not a child psychologist?" she asked.

"I don't know what he is."

"What's his name?"

"Dr. Graham."

"Do you know his first name?" she asked.

"I think it's Richard. I really wasn't paying much attention."

"Okay then, I'll run a little check on him," Sally told him.

"Mama D already is. She said she didn't like him either."

"Well, if Brooke Diamond is on the case, I won't worry about it for now." Sally smiled.

"Okay." He smiled back.

"Now, I have something I'd like you to work on. I know you don't want to talk about what happened, that's why I have this," she said, pulling out a clipboard with the statement sheet on it.

"What it is?" Kendall asked nervously.

Sally explained the paperwork to him. "Do you think you can answer some questions this way?"

Kendall sighed. "I think so. We don't have to talk about it though, right?"

"No, we don't have to talk about it until you're ready. I do have to stay here while you answer the questions though, so it's admissible in court."

"Why does it have to go to court?"

"It's not that there will be a court appearance or anything, it's just so that it's admissible as actual evidence without you having to make a verbal statement," she told him.

"Okay," Kendall said, taking the clipboard from her.

"Now, if there's something you don't understand, just ask."

He nodded as he took it from her. He read it first, and Sally could tell he was nervous, but he started filling it out. "Umm, what does this mean?" he asked, covering his other answers with his hand.

Sally looked at the question and sensed his discomfort. "Tell you what, let's make this easy."

She grabbed his laptop, turned it on, and pulled up a legal terminology website. "Just type in anything you don't understand and you'll find it. Not all of the questions will pertain to you, so don't worry about answering them all."

Kendall smiled gratefully. "Thanks."

"No problem." She smiled. She looked over when she heard him type something else in and watched his eyes go wide at whatever the explanation was. "You doing okay?"

He nodded and blushed. Kendall finished about a half an hour later and handed Sally the clipboard. He felt very tired and couldn't look her in the eyes.

Sally took the clipboard. "I just need you to sign and date it here, while I watch."

He nodded and took the clipboard back and signed it where she indicated.

Sally took the clipboard back and slipped it into her bag without looking at it. "Are you doing okay?"

He nodded. "I'm just tired."

"Well, I think that's more than enough for today. Is it okay if I come back and see you tomorrow?"

Kendall smiled and nodded.

"There's one more thing I want you to do though," she said, pulling a small box out of her bag.

"What?"

"This is just a small digital camera. I want you to start taking pictures of things," she said, handing him the box.

"Why?"

"Well, photography is one of the ways I relax, and I've found that the photos a person takes shows the world the way they're seeing it at the moment. I want to see the way you see the world," she explained.

"What do I take pictures of?"

"Whatever you want, no matter what it is. If you feel like taking a video, you can do that too," Sally told him.

"Okay."

"I'm going to give one to each of the other boys, too," she told him.

"What if they want to take pictures of me?" he asked, feeling panic building as he remembered the last time someone took his picture.

"They won't if you don't want them to."

"How does this help?" he asked.

"Do you know what you'd find if you looked on my home computer?"

Kendall shook his head.

"Probably over 20,000 photos, and that's not including the ones I have stored on my external drive. I take my camera everywhere and take pictures of everything. Your mood changes the way you see something. I can take a photo of something one day, and take another of the exact same thing the next day, and you can see the difference."

"How?"

"The way you hold the camera, the way you stand, if you create a shadow or not, many subtle things. It's easy when I look at mine, because I know how I do these things depending on the mood I'm in. It's a little hard to explain, but does any of this make sense?"

Kendall thought for a moment and nodded. "I think so."

"Good. Tomorrow I'll bring my laptop and show you what I mean, okay?"

"Okay." Kendall smiled, trying to stifle a yawn.

"Call me if you need anything, it doesn't matter what time. I put my cell number into your phone."

"Thanks Sally."

"You're welcome, kiddo. I will see you tomorrow. Get some more sleep."

Kendall nodded and lay back down.

Sally went downstairs and found Jen and Brooke sitting in the living room, talking.

"Well?" Jen asked.

"He did really well, he even managed to answer the questions we needed for his statement," Sally told her.

"What did you find out?" Jen asked.

"I haven't gone over it yet. I didn't want to stress him out by reading it while he was there. I'll go over it later and let you know as soon as possible."

"Okay." Jen nodded.

"I'm meeting with the other boys, and Kendall wants me to come back tomorrow, so I'll see you then." Sally smiled.

"Thank you so much, Sally," Jen said.

"I'm happy to do it. I'll talk to you later."

"Okay," Jen said as she opened the door for Sally.

"Well, the fact that he was able to answer the questions is good news," Brooke said.

Jen nodded. "I hope so."

∞

Antonio pulled up to the station and saw Sally getting out of her car. "Looks like we got here on time."

The boys just looked out the windows, not saying anything.

"Boys, I know this is hard, but I want you to try and stay positive. I'm going to find out who wrote that and they'll be severely punished," Antonio told them.

"I'm just worried about Kendall going back to school now," Logan said and the other boys agreed.

"I know you are, but we'll take care of this before he goes back, I promise. Now let's get in and I'll start working on it while you chat with Sally."

They nodded and everyone got out and went into the station.

"Hey Sally," Antonio said.

"Hi boys! Just head into the first room there," Sally said, pointing at a door.

The boys nodded and went in quietly.

"Okay, what's going on Boss?"

Antonio showed her the paper and explained what had happened. She nodded and headed into the room with her bag.

Sally spent an hour with the boys, and by the end, they were actually smiling. She gave them each a camera and told them what she had told Kendall.

"When the memory card is full, bring it in and we'll see what you've done. Take photos of whatever catches your eye. However, Kendall doesn't want you taking any pictures of him, and I want you all to honour that request."

"He doesn't look that bad, Sally," Carlos said.

"I know, honey, that's not the whole reason though."

"What is the reason?" Logan asked.

"Let's just say, for now, it's a really good reason. Trust me on this, okay?"

The boys all agreed, although they still wondered why.

"So, when do you guys want to meet again?" Sally asked.

"We have practice tomorrow, so Wednesday after school?" James said.

"Perfect. If any of you need to talk or anything else before then, just give me a call," Sally said, handing them each a card with her number on it.

They all walked out to the lobby together and Antonio came out. "Everybody ready to go?"

They nodded.

"Okay, I'll drop Logan off at home and James at Kendall's?" Antonio asked.

"Actually, I left my bag at Kendall's, so I can walk home from there," Logan said.

"No, I'll drop you off at home. Is your mom home yet?"

"Probably not. I think she had a few houses to show today," Logan said.

"Then you can call and tell her you'll be at my house. You can either stay over, or she can pick you up from there," Antonio said. There was no way any of his boys was staying alone right now.

"It's okay, Papa G, I'll be fine," Logan said.

Antonio just looked at him.

"Or... I can stay at your house," Logan said, smiling.

"Good choice." Antonio laughed as he opened the door.

They pulled up in front of the Knight house a few minutes later and got out.

James knocked on the door and Jen answered. "Honey, remind me to give you a key. Come on in, boys, Antonio."

"Hi mom," James said and went and kissed his mother on the cheek.

"Hello darling, how was school?"

"It was okay," he said, looking at the other boys. "I brought Kendall's assignments, Mama K."

"Thank you, sweetie," she said, taking the folder from him.

James looked at her. *That's twice,* he thought.

"Well, I'm going to go shovel the walk before it gets dark," he said.

Logan and Carlos had run upstairs to grab their bags and found Kendall sitting up on his bed, just staring at the ceiling.

"Hey, how are you feeling?" Logan asked.

"I'm feeling okay. How was school?"

"It was okay. James brought your assignments home for you, so if you need help, let me know. I'll be over at Carlos' until my mom get home. You sure you're okay?"

Kendall smiled and nodded. "Just a little tired."

Carlos noticed the dream catcher. "Hey where did that come from?"

"Doc Akins' son, Jake, made it. That reminds me..." Kendall grabbed the manila envelope. "He also made these, one for each of us," he said as he handed them each a bracelet.

"Wow, what are these made from?" Logan asked.

"Here's the letter, it explains it," Kendall said, handing him the paper.

Logan read it aloud. "That was so nice of them."

"These are so cool!" Carlos said.

"They are," Kendall agreed, smiling at Carlos' enthusiasm.

Kendall got up to walk his friends downstairs.

"Papi, look what Doc sent us!"

"I know, Mijo, he sent them to the station. We'll have to send Doc and Jake a thank you card." Antonio smiled.

Carlos nodded as he showed Brooke his bracelet.

"You two ready to go?" Antonio asked.

Logan and Carlos nodded and kissed Jen and Brooke goodbye.

"See you guys later." Kendall smiled as they left.

"Dinner will be in about half an hour," Jen said.

"I'm going to go out and keep James company," Kendall said, grabbing his jacket and going out the door. He walked over to James. "Thanks for doing this."

"No problem. At least you have a short walkway." James smiled.

"How was school?" Kendall asked.

James shrugged. "Pretty much the same, Jenny says, hi."

"Tell her, hi, for me tomorrow."

"Will do," James said as he put the shovel away. "Should you be out in the cold?"

"Trust me, it was colder inside this morning," Kendall told him.

"What do you mean?" James asked.

Kendall shook his head. "Just a disagreement. I'll tell you later."

James looked at him. "Promise?"

Kendall nodded. "Promise."

Chapter 51 ~ Deception

The boys went inside and headed upstairs to get started on their homework. Kendall groaned when he looked at two weeks' worth of assignments. "I'm never going to get all of this done."

James looked at the pile of papers. "Why don't you just concentrate on one subject at a time? If you need help, we can call Logan."

Kendall nodded, pulled out his math book, and sifted through the papers until he found his math assignments. "Well, these don't look too bad."

James smiled. "Yeah, wait until you get to social studies."

Kendall groaned again. "I hate social studies."

James laughed at him. "So... what happened today?"

Kendall sighed. "My mom and I went to see this psychologist. I don't like him, and now she's mad because I won't go back or take the pills he gave her for me."

"You do need to talk to someone though."

"I know. Sally found someone else, but I can't get in until next week. My mom wants me to go see Dr. Graham until then, but I told her I won't."

"Is he that bad?"

"I don't know. My mom seems to like him. All I know is he said you guys are not my family, and he got mad when I told him that was his opinion. I think he told my mom the same thing, and I'm worried she might have listened. She and your mom were arguing earlier. I'm pretty sure it was about him."

"Mama K would never say we aren't family," James said.

Kendall shrugged. "I don't know anything anymore. I really hope not."

"Boys, dinner!" Jen called up.

James looked at Kendall, who made no attempt to move. "Come on, you need to eat."

"I ate today," Kendall said.

"Good! Now it's time to eat again," James said, pulling Kendall up and pushing him out the door.

Everyone sat down for dinner, James sitting next to Kendall.

"So, how was school today?" Jen asked.

"Mrs. Oliver said we're having auditions for the Christmas play and wants me to try out," Katie said.

"Are you going to?"

"I don't know. It's an awful lot of work. I thought maybe I'd help with ticket sales," Katie told her.

"Well, then they'll be playing to a sold out house," Brook said, smiling.

"How was your day, James?" Jen asked.

"It was fine. School, and then we met with Sally."

"How did that go?" Brooke asked.

"It went fine. We're going to meet again on Wednesday after school, because we have practice tomorrow," James told her.

"Good. I really like Sally," Brooke said.

"She's pretty cool and she's easy to talk to," James agreed.

He looked at Kendall and kicked him under the table. Kendall looked at him and James nodded towards his plate. Kendall rolled his eyes and took another bite.

Jen smiled at the silent interaction. James could always get Kendall to do something he didn't want to do. *If only I could get through to him like that*, she thought sadly.

After dinner, the boys helped clear the table and Jen gave Kendall his antibiotic, and then handed him the other pill.

He shook his head and handed it back to her. "Kendall, please just take it."

"I'm sorry, mom, I don't want it," he said and went back to rinsing the dishes.

"Sweetheart, you have to understand it's for your own good."

Kendall froze and dropped the plate he had been rinsing. He started shaking.

James looked at Jen in shock. "Kendall, it's okay. Come on. Let's go finish up some of your homework." He grabbed Kendall by the arm and pulled him upstairs.

"Jen, what the hell was that? You deliberately called him that!" Brooke said angrily.

"Dr. Graham said we have to desensitize him to it. It's a commonly used word, and if he doesn't get over it, he could have an attack in public when none of us is around. What would happen then?" Jen said defensively.

"I'm pretty sure he's not going anywhere without one of us with him for a while, and isn't this something that takes time to work through? He's been home less than four days," Brooke pointed out.

"I am well aware of how long my son has been home! Do you think I like any of this? He doesn't want to eat, he won't talk about anything, and he won't let me in!" Jen yelled in frustration.

"Honey, you have to give him time. None of this is going to go away overnight. I know it's hard, but trying to rush him through it is not going to help. If he's not ready, then he's not ready," Brooke explained.

"I don't know what to do anymore," Jen said, slamming a dish down on the counter.

"Jen, I wish I could make it all go away, but I can't and neither can you. We just have to deal with this on a day to day basis," Brooke said softly.

"No, *WE* don't, *I* do. He's my son, he's my problem!"

"No, *we* are all here for you and Kendall. Jen, you can't do this alone, no one could."

"Brooke, I know you're trying to help, but you can't fix this for me. I have to work through this on my own," Jen said.

Brooke sighed. "Jen, please."

"Brooke, enough. I have to try to do this on my own. I promised you I'll get a second opinion, and I will. Now, please just drop it," Jen snapped.

"Alright, I'm sorry. I don't want to argue, just know I'm here for you, and please stop doubting yourself," Brooke pleaded.

Jen smiled. "I know you're here for me, and I truly appreciate it. You have all done so much and I don't mean to be ungrateful. Things are just so... different right now."

"I know they are, but it will get better. Just realize it's going to take time, and please, remember that you don't have to do this alone," Brooke said.

"I know, but I'm a big girl, and I need to start doing things for myself."

Brooke sighed, knowing she wasn't going to get any further with her stubborn friend tonight. *I'll give Sylvia and Joanna a call later*, she thought. She also didn't like the fact Jen had just called Kendall a problem.

Brooke smiled softly. "Well, I should get going. Jo will be here tomorrow, and before you say anything else, you do need someone here while the boys are in school. If Kendall does have a nightmare or panic attack, you can't hold him by yourself. So until he's better, one of us will be here."

"Alright, that makes sense. Thank you," Jen said.

"No thanks necessary, you would do the same for any of us."

"Yes I would," Jen said, hugging Brooke.

∞

A couple of hours later, Jen went upstairs and tucked Katie in. She knocked on Kendall's door.

"Come in," James said. He was sitting on the bed watching TV, and Kendall was at his desk, still working on his homework.

"How's it coming?" she said as she went over to the desk.

"Alright."

"Honey, I'm sorry about earlier," she said.

"It's okay," he replied, continuing to work on his math.

"Lights out in ten minutes, alright?" she said, kissing him on top of the head.

"Okay."

"Goodnight James," she said and went over and kissed him goodnight.

"Night Mama K." He got up and followed her out. "Are you okay?"

"No, but hopefully I will be. I hope that we all will be. I'm sorry about earlier."

He just hugged her. "It's okay. I love you, Mama K."

"I love you too. Bed in ten minutes."

He nodded and went back into the room. "You doing okay, buddy?"

"Yeah, just trying to get this paper done."

"That's not what I meant," James said.

"I know."

"Well?" James asked, pulling the paper away from Kendall.

"James, I need to finish that," he said, trying to grab the paper back.

"Then tell me what I want to know."

"Just give it back."

James held it above his head. "Then answer me."

"You are such a pain in the butt," Kendall said, trying to grab it once more.

"Let's face it, buddy, I'm taller than you, and unless you get a growth spurt in the next few minutes, you're not getting this back until you answer me."

Kendall glared at him.

"Well?"

"What do you want me to say? That everything sucks right now? My mom blames herself because my head is all screwed up and she tries to fix it by talking to someone that completely freaks me out. That I'm mad right now because she won't listen to me?" Kendall said, sitting on his bed.

James sat down and put an arm around his shoulder. "Yes, that's what I wanted to hear. Because I am listening and I will always listen. All you have to do is talk to me."

"I hate this."

"I know, but it's going to get better, it's just going to take time," James said.

"I just want to be normal again," Kendall whispered.

James pulled Kendall closer. "You're normal, little brother, it's just everything else that's messed up right now."

∞

The rest of the night was uneventful. Kendall stirred once or twice, but James would call to him and he would settle back into sleep. The alarm went off at 6 am and James groaned and turned it off. Kendall opened his eyes, but then turned over and fell back to sleep.

James jumped in the shower, and half an hour later, was ready for school. He knocked on Katie's door to find her still sleeping. "Hey Katie-Kat, time to get up."

Katie yawned. "Morning James."

"Morning. I think your mom's still sleeping, so how about we get ourselves ready for school?"

"Okay," she said, getting up.

James went downstairs and pulled out a couple of bowls and some cereal. He made lunch for Katie and himself while he waited for her to come downstairs.

Jen heard someone moving around and looked at the clock. "I forgot to set my alarm!" she said, jumping out of bed.

She bumped into Katie as she came out of the bathroom.

"Morning mom."

"Good morning, Katie. I'm sorry, honey, I overslept."

"It's okay. James woke me up and he's making breakfast."

Jen smiled and walked with her daughter downstairs. James was just finishing making their lunches when Katie and Jen walked into the kitchen.

"Good morning, James! Thank you so much for getting everything started."

"Not a problem, Mama K," he said, pouring some cereal for Katie and himself.

Jen put on a pot of coffee. "I'm going to run up and get dressed," she said, heading back upstairs.

"How are you doing, Katie?" James asked.

She shrugged.

"What's wrong?"

"I just wish everybody was happy again," she said.

"I know me too." He sighed.

"Maybe soon?" she asked hopefully.

"Soon," he agreed.

∞

Once she had showered and dressed, Jen went in to wake Kendall. "Honey, it's time to get up... Kendall." She gently shook him.

He opened his eyes, "Morning mom."

"Good morning, sleepyhead. You need to get up and get dressed. I have an appointment at nine," she said.

"Okay." He sighed.

She went back down and Kendall got up and went to take a shower. By the time he finished, James had come back up to get his backpack.

"James, can you help me with my shirt?"

"Sure." James went in and helped Kendall pull his t-shirt on. He grabbed his comb and started on the mop of blond hair.

"I can comb my own hair, you know," Kendall said.

"Yes, but not well." James smirked.

Kendall rolled his eyes. "Ow!" he yelped as James hit a tangled patch.

"One word... conditioner. There, much better."

"Thank you, I think," Kendall said, rubbing his head.

"Anytime... really, especially when we go out in public together," James teased.

Kendall raised an eyebrow at him. "You should remember that we're staying in the same room. Many things could happen."

"Such as?" James asked.

"I don't know... corn syrup in your shampoo, purple Kool-Aid in the shower head, so many things," Kendall said as he headed downstairs.

James laughed and then thought about it for a moment. He went back into the bathroom and took his shampoo and conditioner bottles and hid them in the back of the hall closet.

A few minutes later, Katie and James left for school while Jen and Kendall had breakfast. He ate half a bowl of cereal and Jen gave him his antibiotic. Jen had already called and made an appointment with the pediatrician for Thursday and the psychologist that Brooke had recommended for her the next Friday.

"Okay, so you have an appointment with Dr. Sharpe at ten for the day after tomorrow, and I have an appointment with Dr. Hill next Friday," she told him.

Kendall nodded.

"I'm still going to see Dr. Graham today, and I need you to come with me, because Mama M won't be free until after eleven."

"I can stay by myself," Kendall told her.

"No, you can't. Bring your homework so you have something to do while you're waiting."

"Okay." He sighed.

"Thank you, baby."

"You're welcome."

"Hey, how about we stop by the mall after and get you a new jacket?"

Kendall was wearing last year's jacket, which was a little too small because his other had been ruined.

"Mom, I really don't want to go out in public looking like this. Can we do it later?"

"Okay, whenever you're ready, but I want you to layer until we get you a new one." She smiled.

"Okay, thanks mom."

"Well, we better get going," she said.

Kendall went upstairs, grabbed a backpack, and put the rest of his math homework in it. He grabbed a hoodie, put it on, went back downstairs, and put his jacket on over it.

They arrived at Dr. Graham's office about twenty minutes later. Kendall sat near the door as Jen signed in. He pulled out his homework and started working on it.

"How much do you have left?" Jen asked.

"Three pages of math, and then everything else."

"You'll get through it fine." She smiled.

"I hope so. There's like a thousand pages."

"A thousand?" she asked.

"Well, it seems like a thousand."

The receptionist called Jen's name. "Back in a while," she said, kissing his cheek.

"Okay."

Jen followed the assistant to the back, while Kendall continued working on his math.

"Good morning, Jennifer, how are we doing this morning?" Dr. Graham smiled.

"Alright, I guess," she said, sitting down.

"That was not a positive sounding answer."

"Kendall's just not very happy," she said.

"Yes, I heard he doesn't want to come back," Dr. Graham frowned.

"No, I found someone else that he agreed to see. I'm sorry, especially after you got us both in so quickly."

"Well, you have to do what makes him comfortable. Just remember though, you are the parent," Dr. Graham said.

"I know. I just need to find someone he'll talk to, and he refused to come back."

"Of course, I understand. Please don't berate yourself, you need to do what you think is right."

"Thank you for understanding," she said.

He smiled. "Perhaps he'll be feeling better once the anti-anxiety medication begins taking effect."

She sighed. "He refuses to take it."

"I see, well that is disappointing. It would make such a big difference in his recovery. Perhaps his new doctor can get him to take it."

"I tried, but he said he doesn't trust you and won't take anything you prescribe," Jen said quietly.

"I'm sure you did your best. Children today have such strong wills and have difficulty seeing that we only want what is best for them."

"I'll ask his pediatrician if she can get him to agree to take it. He has an appointment on Thursday," she told him.

"Very good, then. Now, did you have time to think about what we discussed yesterday?"

"Some of it. I do need to start taking care of some things myself, but I'm not sure limiting Kendall's contact with Antonio is such a good idea," she said quietly.

"Why is that?"

"They're very close. He's also very close with Carlos, Antonio's son. They have been best friends since birth. I did try calling him sweetheart while he was awake."

"And...?"

"Well, it didn't go very well," she said, shaking her head.

"What happened?" he asked.

"Well, first he froze and then dropped the plate he was holding. When he started shaking, James took him upstairs to calm him down. He was upset the rest of the night," she said.

"James?"

"Another best friend. He's been staying with us in case Kendall wakes up with a nightmare. He's a strong boy and can hold him," Jen explained.

"I see. You do understand that if he takes the medication, there won't be a need for others to jump in?"

"Yes, but he won't take it," Jen said uncomfortably.

He got up and sat on his desk in front of her chair. "Why don't you let me talk to him about it? I can give him the literature on it. I'll make it clear that there are no hard feelings and that I only want to help until he can get into the other doctor."

"I really don't think he'll go for it."

"Do I have your permission to try?" he asked.

She sighed. "I guess it can't hurt to ask."

"Very good. Give me a few minutes then, and hopefully he'll agree." Graham smiled.

She nodded.

∞

Dr. Graham went into a room two doors down and called to his nurse. He went over to the locked drug cabinet and opened it, pulling out a vial of injectable Lorazepam. "Could you please bring Kendall Knight in here? Just tell him his mother needs him."

The nurse went out and knelt next to Kendall. "Dr. Graham sent me out. He said your mother needs you."

"Is she okay?"

"I'm sure she's fine, but it did sound urgent."

Kendall got up and followed her back into one of the rooms. Dr. Graham came in as soon as he saw Kendall enter the room.

"Where's my mom?"

"She's next door, Kendall. She wanted me to discuss the benefits of the medication I prescribed and I told her I would try," Dr. Graham told him.

Dr. Graham handed something to the assistant. "Now, why don't we try and reason this out?" he asked as he locked the door.

"Why did you lock the door?" Kendall asked. He could feel panic rising in his chest.

"So we could discuss this reasonably without you running away. I'm sure you're perfectly capable of having an adult conversation, you're a smart boy."

"I want to leave, please open the door," Kendall said.

"Well, I wouldn't be fulfilling my duties as your doctor then."

"You're NOT my doctor! Now let me out!"

"Calm down so we can discuss this reasonably," Dr. Graham ordered.

Kendall went to the door and tried to open it, but Dr. Graham pulled him back.

"Don't touch me! Get off!" Kendall screamed, trying to push the doctor away.

"Now be a good boy and take your medicine like your mother wants," he said, pulling up Kendall's sleeve.

"No! Leave me alone!" Kendall yelled, trying to get out of the older man's grasp.

With only one good arm, he couldn't get away, and Dr. Graham held him tightly as the nurse injected the liquid into the muscle of his right arm.

"No! Leave me alone!" Kendall screamed again.

A moment later, he started to feel strange and Dr. Graham pulled him over to the couch and sat with him on it. Kendall found it incredibly difficult to concentrate, and when his muscles relaxed, Dr. Graham released him.

"There's a good boy," he said as Kendall's eyes closed.

Chapter 52~ Dr. Graham

Brooke walked into Diamond Fashions Inc. for the first time in nearly two weeks. "Good morning, Emily," she said to her assistant.

"Good morning, Mrs. Diamond, it's so nice to see you back." Emily smiled as she followed Brooke into her office. "Papers that require your immediate approval are on your desk, those that can wait are in your box. The advertising department is waiting to hear your decision on which models you want to use for the spring line, the photos from the modeling agency are on top."

"Thank you, Emily. You have taken good care of things while I was gone. Do you have that information on Dr. Graham for me yet?"

"Yes, it's right here along with the information on Lorazepam," she said, pulling a file from the pile of papers.

"Thank you, dear."

"I took the liberty to check out a few more psychologists in town, and there are very few I would go to, much less take my child to. Also, an interesting fact, did you know that psychologists are not allowed to prescribe or dispense medications? They're supposed to go through a medical doctor or a licensed psychiatrist," Emily told her.

"Then how is it Dr. Graham was able to prescribe anything?" Brooke asked.

"Well, it turns out there are two states which will issue a special certificate to psychologists, provided they take a 2-year pharmacology course, which he did when he lived in Louisiana. Many psychologists work in conjunction with a primary medical provider, and that's how they get around the law. Graham kept his dispensing license up-to-date and orders his drugs through an office that he keeps in Baton Rouge. I'm assuming he then has them shipped here through a private courier. As a backup, he works in conjunction with a general practitioner by the name of Louis Davis. Dr. Davis hasn't actually been practicing much in the last two years," Emily told her.

"Why would he go through all that trouble?" Brooke asked.

"Because after he received his dispensing certificate, his salary nearly tripled," Emily said.

"He wrote a prescription for Kendall and Jen filled it at the pharmacy downstairs though," Brooke told her.

"Yes, but her bill from his office probably includes a prescription fee that many doctors work into their charges," Emily said.

"Slick bastard," Brooke growled.

"Exactly. If someone claims that he filled or had written the prescription, he has the GP to fall back on. There's no record of anyone filing a malpractice claim against him, so either he hasn't been caught..."

"Or he paid them off himself," Brooke finished.

Emily nodded.

"Emily, I have some things I need to take care of, which might take a while. What I would like you to do is go through the photos and choose five models that you like for the spring line. Also, fax this information over to Officer Sally O'Hara at the police station and get ahold of Jack Barr. I want him to do a complete investigation into Dr. Graham and tell him I

expect something that we can use against him in court," Brooke told her as she put the file into her briefcase.

"You want ME to choose the models?" Emily asked in shock. Brooke always chose the models, colours, and designs for her company. Brooke took her business very seriously, and so far had never allowed anyone to make one of these decisions.

Brooke looked at Emily and smiled. "You've done a fantastic job for me since you started four years ago. You have proven not only your knowledge, loyalty, and commitment, but also your willingness to go the extra mile. I trust you."

Emily smiled back. "I don't know what to say."

"You don't have to say anything, dear. Call me on my cell if you need me."

Emily nodded.

Brooke grabbed her cell and made a quick call. "Sylvia, is Antonio there?"

"Yes, why?"

"Good, I'll be there in twenty minutes. I need to talk to you both about something," she said as she walked out the door.

∞

Jen waited nervously for Dr. Graham to come back. *There is no way he is going to be able to talk Kendall into anything,* she thought. It was almost impossible to change Kendall's mind once he had made it up. She prayed she was doing the right thing. Dr. Graham was right about her having to take more control over their lives. She couldn't keep running to her friends whenever there was a problem. Her children needed to be able to rely on her, not be a burden everyone else.

"Will, what do I do?" she silently asked her husband. She found her thoughts wandering lately, she couldn't keep them on a coherent track.

She was so confused and tired. Her dreams were filled with images of someone in black coming in and hurting her children. She would hear them screaming for her and couldn't help them, she failed them. Just like she had failed Kendall, the night the Deesie broke in and took him. She should have been home taking care of him, but she wasn't. She always told her children there were no such things as monsters—she was so wrong.

Not knowing what Deesie had done to her son was slowly killing her inside, and she didn't know how to reach him. He didn't trust her, and why should he? She hadn't protected him. Instead of turning to her, he looked to Antonio and the boys for support. She wanted to cry every time she looked at his bruised face, every time he needed help because he couldn't use his arm much yet. She just wanted to hold him and never let him go, but she was afraid.

She was brought out of her reverie by a yell. She listened closely and heard another. *Oh please, don't be Kendall!* She thought as she opened the door.

She saw Dr. Graham come out of the room two doors down, looking disheveled.

"What happened, what is it?" she asked him.

"It's alright. I was explaining to Kendall the benefits of the medication and he worked himself into a panic attack. I had to give him an injection, because he started having difficulty breathing," he said, smiling sadly.

"Oh my God!" Jen said as she ran down the hall.

She opened the door to the room Dr. Graham had just come from and saw Kendall lying on the couch, his eyes closed. The nurse was standing next to him, and Dr. Graham dismissed her when he came in.

Jen sat next to Kendall on the couch and ran her fingers through his hair.

Dr. Graham knelt next to her. "I gave him an injection of the Lorazepam. It will take care of any anxiety for the next eight to ten hours. If you think you can get him to take a pill tonight around seven, he should be alright through the night," he said, patting her shoulder.

"What if he won't take it?" she asked, her eyes filling with tears.

"Well, with younger patients, parents sometimes put the pill in applesauce or something like that. They don't even know they're taking it. After a few days, he should notice a difference in the way he feels and appreciate your efforts."

"I don't know. I don't like the idea of tricking him into doing something I know he doesn't want to do," she said, uncertainty in her voice.

"It is, of course, up to you, Jennifer, but you need to remember that YOU are the parent here. Sometimes parents have to make difficult choices, and sometimes it makes their children angry or unhappy. Ultimately, you have to do what is best for your son. Do you think going on like this is good for him or you?" Graham asked her.

She looked down at Kendall and sighed. "No."

"Think of when he was very small. Would you have let him put his finger in a light socket or get into the cabinet where you keep the cleaning supplies? No. It's the same principal really—you had to protect him, sometimes from himself, and that's what you need to do now."

"That makes sense," she agreed.

"Why don't you stay in here with him for a while? He should come around in the next half an hour and we'll help you get him to your car. He will probably sleep on and off for the rest of the day." Graham smiled.

She nodded. "Thank you."

∞

It was cold and dark. Kendall looked around but couldn't see anything. Then he saw a light in the distance and started walking towards it. He realized he was in a hallway lined with doors. When he tried one, he found it was locked.

Suddenly, he heard a faint whispering. "Come out, come out wherever you are."

He could hear footsteps coming towards him and he turned and ran.

"It's time to play, sweetheart," the voice said, coming from in front of him now. Something started pushing against him, holding him tight against the wall. A mouth was on his, a tongue gagging him, making it hard to breathe, hands roaming up and down his body. He pulled away and frantically began trying the doors. One opened and ran in and slammed it closed behind him. Someone started knocking at the door.

"Where are you, you little shit? You are going to be VERY sorry once I get my hands on you!" the voice hissed.

Kendall backed away from the door as Deesie shook the handle, trying to get in.

Suddenly, he fell over something and hit the floor, his hands in something wet and warm. The door opened and the light came on. Deesie stood there, with the stick protruding from his abdomen. He walked towards Kendall, who scooted back and hit something soft. Looking down, he saw Antonio lying there, blood flowing from his chest.

Kendall started shaking.

"Kendall, honey, it's okay. Mama's here," Jen said softly, brushing his bangs back.

His breathing became rapid and erratic. "Papi!"

"Kendall, please wake up. It's alright," Jen pleaded.

His breathing finally slowed and his eyes fluttered open and then closed again.

"Baby, can you hear me?"

He opened his eyes again. "Mom?" he asked in confusion.

She smiled at him. "Yes, you're okay."

He looked around. "Where are we?"

"Dr. Graham's office, you had a panic attack and were having trouble breathing. He had to give you something to calm you down," she told him.

"No," he shook his head as he desperately tried to remember what had happened. He knew something was wrong, but couldn't concentrate. "Why can't I remember?" His voice sounded strange to him, raspy, and his words slurred together.

"Don't worry about it now. We need to get you home. Do you think you can stand?" Jen asked softly.

Everything felt heavy, but he forced himself to move. He couldn't remember why, but this was a bad place and he didn't want to be here anymore.

"Go slowly. Let me call Dr. Graham and he'll help you," Jen told him as she moved for the door.

"No! I don't want him," Kendall said and pushed himself up.

"Kendall, you're going to fall!" Jen said, rushing back to him.

He pushed himself off the couch and stumbled towards the door. Jen grabbed his good arm and wrapped it around her shoulder. "Honey, please let me call someone to help."

He shook his head and continued walking for the door.

"Okay, let's just take it slowly," Jen said, frustrated that he wasn't listening. She opened the door and they stepped into the hallway.

"Let me help you there," Graham said, reaching over to take Kendall's arm.

The boy pulled back and fell against the wall. "Stay away," he hissed.

"Kendall, you will stop being so rude! He's only trying to help you and this attitude is just going to get you into trouble," Jen told him firmly.

Kendall stared at her for a moment. "Leave me alone!" He got up and stumbled past them. He was feeling trapped and everything was starting to close in.

"I'm so sorry, Dr. Graham," Jen said as she went to catch up with Kendall.

"Applesauce!" he called after her.

She looked back at him and nodded.

Kendall grabbed his jacket and backpack, and made his way to the elevator. The door had opened almost as soon as he got there, and Jen barely slipped in through the doors before they closed.

"I am so disappointed in you," she said angrily.

He didn't say anything, and as soon as the doors opened, he stumbled through them and got to the outside door. He looked around, trying to get his bearings. He could hear his mother calling him but ignored her and took off running as fast as he could. He fell once and got back up, turning at the corner.

Jen stood there in shock as she watched her son run away from her. She got into the car and followed him, but by the time she turned the corner, he was gone.

∞

Kendall made his way through an alley and ended up on one of the side streets. He was getting very dizzy, his head was pounding, and it was getting hard to breathe. His chest felt like it was on fire and his legs felt as heavy as lead. He was sure people watching him, but when he looked up, no one was there.

He found a bench and sat down. "What's wrong with me?"

He remembered his phone and pulled it out of his pocket. He dialed the first number on it. "Please answer, please answer," he begged.

"Hello?"

"Carlos... Can you find me?" Kendall choked out.

"Kendall, is that you?"

"Yes, can you come get me? Please..."

"Where are you?" Carlos had been on his way to second period when his phone rang. He was now running down the hall, trying to find James or Logan.

"I-I don't know, someplace downtown," Kendall said.

Carlos saw James as he walked into his classroom and raced down the hall. He went into the room and grabbed James, pulling him out.

"Carlos, what are you doing?"

"Call my dad, tell him we have to find Kendall," Carlos said.

"WHAT?!"

Carlos just pointed at his phone and then at James. "Kendall, try and find a street sign or something. I need to know where you are before I can come get you," Carlos said.

James pulled his phone out and dialed the Garcia home.

Antonio answered. "Hello."

"Papa G, something's wrong. Kendall is on the phone with Carlos and asked him to find him. He's trying to find out where he is now."

Kendall looked around. "Market, someplace on Market, near the doctor's office."

"Okay, Market, not far from Dr. Graham's office," Carlos said.

James repeated it to Antonio. "Tell Carlos to keep him on the phone and that I'm on my way. Meet me out front," Antonio told James, running out the door.

"Papi's on his way here, come on," James said, pulling Carlos down the hall.

"Kendall, Papi's on his way to get us, and then we'll find you. Stay on the phone, okay?"

"Okay... Carlos, I don't feel well."

"I know, buddy. You'll be okay, we're on our way," Carlos told him. He was terrified. He had never heard Kendall sound so strange.

"I'm getting Logan," James said as he raced off down the hall towards Logan's classroom.

Carlos waited at the front door and saw his dad pull up just as James and Logan came running to the doors.

"Kendall, are you still there?" Carlos asked as he got into the car.

Antonio gestured for Carlos to hand him the phone. "Kendall, what happened, Mijo? Kendall... are you there?" he asked, but there was no answer.

"Papi?" Kendall's voice was raspy and he was slurring his words badly.

"Kendall, what happened?"

"Can't 'member, but I think something bad happened. I can't think and it's hard to breathe."

"Where's your mom?" Antonio asked.

"I-I ran away from the doctor's office," Kendall whispered.

"Okay, we're close to Market. Do you know where on Market you are?"

"I'm on a bench somewhere."

His voice was weak, and Antonio could barely hear him. "Kendall...Kendall, keep talking."

The boys were all watching out the windows. "There he is!" Logan yelled, pointing to a bench about a block away.

Antonio pulled up and parked. "Stay here."

He got out and walked cautiously to the bench. He didn't want to frighten him. "Kendall, it's Papi."

Kendall looked up. He was white as a sheet and was having trouble breathing. "Papi, I can't..."

Antonio caught him as he passed out.

Chapter 53~ Prescription for Malpractice

The doorbell rang at the Garcia home and Sylvia answered the door.

"Brooke, come in. Antonio had to go, there was an emergency," she said and told Brooke about the phone call.

"Well, I found out some very interesting things about Jen's psychologist, and as soon as my investigators have finished, Dr. Richard Graham will be going down so fast and so far that he's going to have to find an escalator UP to hell," Brooke smiled coldly.

"Honey, you know I love you... but you scare the crap out of me sometimes."

"Oh... you are just too sweet!" Brooke said, flashing her a dazzling smile.

∞

Jen drove around the block and then a few blocks towards home. She headed back towards the doctor's building when she found no sign of Kendall. "What did I do?" she said, cursing herself. She pulled over and called the Garcia home.

Sylvia looked at the number on caller ID. "It's Jen," she said, looking at Brooke. She took a deep breath. "Hello?"

"Sylvia, I-I can't find Kendall. I said something horrible to him and he ran away. I don't know what's wrong with me. I can't believe what I did." Jen was now sobbing.

"Calm down, honey, and tell me what happened," Sylvia said.

Jen took a ragged breath and told her about Dr. Graham speaking with Kendall. Then the panic attack and what happened after.

"Why did he run away from you?" Sylvia asked.

"On the elevator ride down, I-I..." Jen stammered.

"Jen, what happened?" Sylvia asked.

"I told him I was disappointed in him, and when we got outside h-he ran away from me. I can't find him. What am I going to do?"

"Jen, first you need to calm down. Where are you?" Sylvia asked.

"I'm back at Dr. Graham's office building. I was hoping Kendall would come back here."

"Alright, listen to me. I'm going to come and get you, so STAY there. We'll figure this out, okay?" Sylvia asked.

"Okay. I-I'm so scared." Jen was sobbing again.

"It's alright, I'll be right there. Don't go anywhere!" Sylvia instructed.

"I won't," Jen promised.

Sylvia hung up and went to get her coat and purse. "You didn't tell her that Antonio is getting Kendall?" Brooke asked.

"No, I don't want her driving right now. I'll tell her when I pick her up."

"Why don't I wait here? She wasn't very happy with me yesterday and she might be more willing to open up to you if I'm not there. Besides, I would be sorely tempted to go up to Dr. Graham's office and push him out a window," Brooke said.

Sylvia nodded. "I know the feeling. If Antonio calls, please let him know."

"I will. I'll give Jo a call as well," Brooke said.

Sylvia nodded as she ran out the door.

∞

The boys watched as Antonio walked over to Kendall and saw him collapse into Antonio's arms. James jumped out of the car, the other boys right behind him.

Antonio picked Kendall up. "Grab his things... James get the door!"

Carlos grabbed Kendall's backpack and James opened the back door and got in. Antonio handed Kendall to him, took off his own jacket, and handed it to James. "Put this over him, he's cold."

James did as he was told while Logan got into the front seat and Carlos climbed in on the other side of the backseat, pulling Kendall's feet onto his lap. James held Kendall tightly and could hear the wheezing as his friend struggled to breathe.

"He's really pale and he's not breathing very well," James said in a shaky voice.

"I know. We'll be at the hospital in a couple of minutes. It's going to be alright," Antonio said, trying to reassure the boys.

They pulled up to the hospital entrance and Antonio jumped out. He took Kendall from James and carried him inside, the boys close behind.

"Boys, please take a seat out here," the nurse instructed as she led Antonio into a room.

James started to follow, but Logan grabbed his arm and pulled him to some chairs. Carlos followed and sat down next to them. "Things are never going to get better, are they?" he asked quietly.

"I don't know, Carlitos. I think it's going to take a long time," Logan told him.

"It's not fair," Carlos said, putting his head in his hands.

"I know, it really isn't," Logan said sadly, as he hugged his friend.

∞

"What do we have going on here?" Dr. Davidson asked Antonio as he started to examine Kendall.

Antonio explained what had happened in the last two weeks. "I'm not sure about this morning. He was with his mom, she had an appointment with her psychologist, and something happened. He called my son, said he had run away from his mom, and asked Carlos to get him. He said he was having trouble breathing and that something had happened, but he didn't know what. He wasn't making much sense."

"Is he taking anything?" Dr. Davidson asked.

"Amoxicillin and Tramadol for pain," Antonio told him.

"He's not on ANYTHING else?" the doctor asked firmly.

"No. They wanted to put him on an anti-anxiety medication, but he refused to take it. Why?" Antonio asked, not liking the implication.

"See his eyes?" Dr. Davidson said as he raised an eyelid and shined a light into Kendall's eye. "They're both fully dilated. His breathing is laboured, and not from the pneumonia. His oxygen saturation and his blood pressure are both low. He either took or was given something."

"He wouldn't have taken anything. It's a battle to get him to take a pain pill when he needs it," Antonio insisted.

"Do you know what the medication is that he refused to take?"

"No, but I know someone who does," he said and quickly dialed Brooke's cell.

"Hello, Brooke Diamond."

"Brooke, I need to know what medication Dr. Graham prescribed for Kendall," Antonio said.

"Lorazepam. Why?"

"We're at the hospital. Kendall couldn't breathe and then he collapsed. The doctor thinks he either took or was given something," Antonio told her.

"That son of a bitch!" Brooke hissed. "Jen called a little while ago in hysterics. She said Graham tried to convince Kendall to take the pills. He told her Kendall had a panic attack, so he gave him an injection of Lorazepam to calm him down. She said after he woke up, he was having trouble walking and told her that he wanted to leave because it was a bad place. He ran away from her after she said something she shouldn't have. "

"An injection of Lorazepam," Antonio told the doctor as he listened to Brooke.

"Any idea how much?" Davidson asked.

"Brooke, did she say how much he gave him?" Antonio asked.

"No, she didn't. Antonio, she didn't even know he had done it. She wasn't with them," Brooke said.

Antonio looked at Davidson and shook his head. "Okay, I'll call you in a little while."

"We're going to treat this as an overdose and get him started on some Flumazenil to counter the effects of the Lorazepam," Dr. Davis said.

The nurse inserted a catheter and Davidson instructed her to give a slow push of 0.2ml of Flumazenil.

"So, exactly what's happening with him?" Antonio asked the doctor.

"Well, first of all, injectable Lorazepam is not really indicated for children under the age of 18, unless it's for seizures. Second, it is not something you give someone who is having respiratory issues. This would include pneumonia. Third, if you do give an injection, you do NOT leave your patient unattended for several hours," Dr. Davis explained.

"Would that have caused the confusion and trouble speaking?" Antonio asked.

Dr. Davidson nodded. "Those are just a few of the side effects. Now, who prescribed this?"

"Dr. Graham, I don't know his first name," Antonio said.

"Is Dr. Graham a general practitioner?" Davidson asked.

"No, a psychologist."

"Do you know which GP he works with... the one who gave the injection?"

"No... Brooke said HE gave Kendall the injection," Antonio said, putting things together as he remembered what Brooke had told him.

Antonio pulled out his phone and called Brooke back.

"Hello, Brooke Diamond."

"Brooke, I need you to come to the hospital, bring everything you have on Graham, please."

"On my way," she said grabbing her briefcase and coat.

Chapter 54~ Pranks with Purpose

Sylvia found Jen still sitting in her car, just staring out the windshield. Sylvia got out and knocked on the driver's window. It took a moment for Jen to look at her, but she finally did and opened the door.

Sylvia reached in and took her arm, pulling her into a hug. "It's going to be okay, Jen. Kendall called Carlos, he and Antonio went to get him. They should be at our house by the time we get there," Sylvia told her as she opened her car door and helped Jen in.

Jen just sat there, looking out the window as she and Sylvia drove to the Garcia home. They pulled into the driveway and saw Jo's car there. Brooke's was gone and Antonio wasn't back yet. Sylvia helped Jen out and Jo got out of her car and took Jen's other arm.

"Where's Brooke?" Sylvia asked Joanna.

"She was gone when I got here, so I waited outside. Maybe she got called back into the office," Joanna suggested.

"Maybe," Sylvia said as they went inside.

Joanna helped Jen take her coat off and then led her over to the couch. "Honey, what happened?" she asked her stricken friend.

"I hurt him," she whispered.

"I'll go make us some tea," Sylvia said. She was hoping Jen would talk to Jo, and truth be told, she was a little upset with her right now, and she was trying to get it under control.

Joanna smiled. "That would be nice. It's a little chilly out."

Sylvia left the other two women, went into the kitchen, and put the kettle on.

Where did Brooke go? She wondered.

∞

Brooke got to the hospital about ten minutes after getting off the phone with Antonio. She was furious, which meant she was calm and VERY focused at the moment.

She parked and walked into the emergency room. She went up to the desk. "I need Kendall Knight's doctor, please," she told the nurse.

"Are you a relative?" she asked.

"Yes, and he's expecting me."

She heard James call out. "Mom, what are you doing here?"

"Hello darling, Papa G called me. I have some information he needs," she said, hugging her son.

"What kind of information?"

"On Dr. Graham and the medication he gave Kendall," she told him as she walked him back to the other boys.

"What do you mean, 'medication he gave Kendall'? Kendall wouldn't take it," James said.

"I know. You wait here. I'll be back in a few minutes, and then we're going to run a few errands." She smiled.

All three boys got a chill from the tone in her voice. She went back over to the desk and followed the nurse back.

"James, I love your mom... but she scares me," Logan whispered.

James and Carlos both nodded in agreement.

∞

Antonio was standing next to Kendall's bed, holding his hand. As soon as he was stable, they were going to be moving him to a private room. The Flumazenil was working, and his breathing had improved, but Dr. Davidson wanted to keep him for the night to be certain the Lorazepam was clearing his system.

A voice interrupted his thoughts. "How is he?" Brooke asked.

"Doing a little better now."

"Poor baby," she said as she kissed Kendall on the forehead.

She pulled out the file and handed it to Antonio. "We should probably call Sylvia, she and Jen should be back at the house by now," Brooke said.

"Let me read this first," Antonio said, opening the file.

"There are some very interesting things in there, and my people are doing a more in depth investigation as we speak," Brooke told him.

Antonio nodded and continued reading. "You're sure Jen said that Graham gave Kendall the injection?"

"That's what she said."

"According to Dr. Davidson, Graham isn't allowed to administer injections, even if the GP was standing right there. So as soon as Kendall is settled in, I'll be getting a warrant issued," Antonio told her.

"I had Emily fax all of this information to Sally, so hopefully it helps," Brooke said.

"Your guy is a licensed investigator?"

"Yes, one of the best." Brooke smiled.

"Then this should be all we need." Antonio smiled back.

∞

Joanna was still trying to coax a more coherent answer from Jen. "Can you tell me what happened?"

Jen sighed and told her what she had already told Sylvia. Jo was a little shocked. "Honey, what were you feeling at the time?"

"Don't you mean thinking?" Jen asked.

"No, what were you feeling? Were you angry, frightened, sad...?"

"All of those, I guess. He just wouldn't listen to me. I was trying to help and he looked at me like I was...I don't know."

"Jen, don't you think the medication might have had something to do with that? He'd just woken up and was confused," Joanna said.

"Maybe, or maybe he just doesn't want me there."

"You know that's not true. Did you ever stop to think that he hasn't even had time to process what's been going on, especially since he's been sick? Honey, he has ALWAYS tried to protect you and Katie. He might subconsciously be doing that even now. While his protective nature is something we have all just accepted, regardless of his age... he is still just a child. He's not really talking to anyone about this yet. It's going to take time," Jo pointed out.

"He called out for Antonio, not me. He knows I failed him and that I can't protect him," Jen said.

"Is that why you're pushing him away?" Jo asked. "Because you're jealous that Antonio was able to help him. Antonio is a police officer—he would have tried to help ANYONE in that situation, and don't forget he is Kendall's godfather. Someone you and Will chose because you trusted him, because you knew he would be there if needed."

Jen looked at her in shock. "I am not pushing him away! I am trying to figure out how to help him."

"Honey, I'm not trying to hurt you, but ever since you woke him up that first night, you've kept your distance. I think you blame yourself for causing it, and now you're trying to find someone to help him deal with it because you're afraid you can't. Jen, you're in panic mode and you need to stop and think about it. If he doesn't trust someone and has told you so, then

you need to respect that. He does need someone to help him deal with it, but he needs you too. By that, I mean he needs you to listen to what he says, and to understand he needs time to heal. It's not going to happen right away. It could take months or even years, and the drive-thru approach this Dr. Graham seems to take isn't going to help Kendall or you."

Jen sat there. "I just want him back."

"You HAVE him back, but you have to accept that things are going to be different for a while and listen to what he's trying to say. Honey, he needs you, but when was the last time you just went to him and held him?"

Jen looked down at her hands. "I don't know."

Joanna hugged her. "Then, when he gets home, sit down and just hold him, because that's what he needs from you right now. He needs his mom."

∞

"Why don't I take the boys for a while? We'll go run a couple of errands and then get some lunch," Brooke suggested.

"That might be a good idea. I need to give Sylvia a call and let her and Jen know what happened," Antonio said.

"Alright then, I'll give you a call in a little while," Brooke said, giving him a quick hug.

"Thanks Brooke." Antonio smiled.

∞

Brooke went back to the waiting room. "Kendall is doing better and they're waiting to get him into a room, so why don't we go and have a little fun?" Brooke said, wrapping her arms around the three boys and ushering them out to her car.

"Mom, where are we going?" James asked as they drove towards downtown.

"How would you boys like to play a prank on someone who REALLY deserves it?"

The boys looked at each other, smiled, and nodded. "I think we're in," James said.

First, they stopped at the market, where the boys ran in and picked up a few things. Next, they stopped at a small bakery.

"Okay boys, run over to the florist shop across the street and get as many helium balloons as you can," she said, handing James some money.

The boys ran across the street while she went in and ordered a small round cake with a message on it. A few minutes later, they pulled up a block from a parking garage and got out.

"Alright, now you boys go through the public entrance, while I walk around to the private. I'll text you once the coast is clear and tell you where I am," Brooke said.

The boys nodded, each carrying a small bag while Brooke took the balloons and cake box. She walked down to the entrance and smiled at the attendant. "I was hoping you could help me."

"If I can," the attendant said.

"Well, my fiancé's birthday is tomorrow and I just got called out of town on business. We had a very special dinner planned tonight, and he's very sad I can't make it. I wanted to surprise him with a cake and balloons, just to let him know how sorry I am, but I can't find my keys. I know it's probably against the rules, but if you could possibly let me into the car so I could leave these for him, I would be forever grateful," she said, smiling with a little pout evident on her lips.

"I don't know... I could get into a lot of trouble giving you someone's keys."

"Oh, you don't have to give me the keys. If you could just open the doors and I could leave these. Then he won't know I misplaced my silly keys again," she said.

He was still trying to decide when she touched his arm. "Of course, I'm happy to contribute to your favourite charity as well," she said, flashing a fifty-dollar bill.

"Well, since I'm not actually giving you the keys, I don't see the harm in it. Who's your fiancé?" he asked, smiling back.

"Richard Graham."

He looked on the wall and found the keys. "His car is on the next level down. May I help you with those?" he said, offering to take the balloons.

"Aren't you sweet?" she gushed.

She followed him to an older model Mercedes and he opened the door for her. She sat the cake on the seat and took the balloons. "I can't tell you how much I appreciate this. It's going to mean so much to my little Dicky."

He snickered a little at the nickname.

"I can lock it up when I'm finished," she said.

"I don't know, I mean...," he stammered.

"Well, I need to write him a note, and it is on the personal side, if you know what I mean. I'll be happy to let you know when I'm done, if you want to double check the doors."

"I guess that'll be okay, just make sure you lock it up tight," he said.

"I promise." She smiled, tying the balloons to the ski rack.

The minute he was out of sight, she sent a text to James' phone, and a couple of minutes later, the boys arrived, sticking close to the walls. James reached up and taped a piece of black cloth over the security camera that monitored the area.

"Alright, I'll keep watch," she said and walked over to the entryway.

The boys got busy. James opened the cap to windshield wiper fluid and added distilled water mixed with red raspberry Kool-Aid. Logan opened the trunk and disconnected the taillights, while Carlos let the air out of all four tires.

"It feels like we should do more," James mused.

"I think that's enough. He'll get message," Brooke said as she opened the cake box, making sure that the top was clearly visible from the driver's seat.

On the small cake, written in elegant gold icing, were the words, Be Very Afraid!

∞

Antonio had noticed Kendall move slightly and sat next to him on the bed. "Kendall, can you wake up? You're safe, Mijo. You're here with me, and your Mami is on her way."

Kendall moved slightly and Antonio brushed his bangs back. "Kendall, please wake up."

The teen's eyes fluttered open and then closed. It took so much effort just to do that much. He could feel someone holding his hand and knew it was Antonio. "Papi," he managed to get out.

"That's right, Mijo, it's Papi. You're safe and soon you'll be feeling better."

Kendall shook his head. "They'll never go away."

"Who'll never go away?" Antonio asked.

"He killed you, you were in the room and the blood was everywhere. He's going to hurt everyone, and I don't know how to stop him," Kendall whispered.

The heart monitor started beeping.

"Kendall, calm down. No one hurt me, I'm right here. You're safe and your Mami is coming," Antonio tried reassuring the boy.

Kendall shook his head again. "No, no I don't want to see her. She's mad at me... She thinks I'm bad because I don't like him. He's bad and I don't want to go back. Don't make me go back! He locks you in, they always lock you in!" Kendall pleaded.

He was shaking and his eyes were moving back and forth at an incredible rate.

The nurse came in and immediately called for the doctor. Dr. Davidson arrived a moment later. "What happened?"

"He woke up a couple of minutes ago and was afraid and confused," Antonio told him.

Dr. Davidson looked into Kendall's eyes. "Give another slow push 0.2 ml of Flumazenil," he said to the nurse.

She nodded and went to get the vial. The doctor pulled it up and she began administering it.

"What's going on, what's with his eyes?" Antonio asked.

"It's called nystagmus and it's another side effect from the Lorazepam. Another dose of the Flumazenil should take care of it. It's probably going to take a good twenty-four hours for his system to clear," he told Antonio.

Antonio sighed. Graham had better find a good attorney, he thought as he watched his godson trembling.

Kendall had already calmed down a little by the time the nurse was finished.

Antonio sat next to him. He could see the boy's eyes still moving rapidly under his closed eyelids. A VERY good attorney, he thought again.

He heard a knock on the door and Sylvia and Jo stepped in, holding on tightly to Jen.

He smiled and stood up. "Let's talk outside for a minute," he said, putting an arm around Sylvia and Jen.

"I'll stay with Kendall," Joanna said.

"Thanks Jo." Antonio smiled.

"What's going on?" Jen asked.

Antonio told her what Dr. Davidson had said and what he had done for Kendall so far.

"So he's allergic to the medication?" Jen asked.

Antonio sighed. "Not exactly. Dr. Davidson said an injection of Lorazepam isn't something they usually give children under 18, unless it's for seizures. It can cause difficulty breathing, confusion, and now something is going on with his eyes. He gave him something to counter the injection, but said it'll probably be twenty-four hours before it's out of his system."

"Then why did Dr. Graham give it to him?" Jen asked.

"I don't know, Jen, but I do need to confirm something. Were you IN the room when he gave Kendall the shot?" Antonio asked.

"No, he was talking to him about taking the medication and said he had a panic attack. He said he started having trouble breathing, so he gave him the shot. I don't understand why

he'd give him something that causes breathing problems, when he was having breathing problems."

"The reason the injection made it hard to breathe is because he has pneumonia. It's not something you give someone with respiratory problems. He had Kendall's medical chart, right?" Antonio asked.

"Yes, they faxed it from Appleton."

"Then he should have known, but that's not our biggest problem with this. Jen, he's not licensed to prescribe anything, much less give an injection of a controlled substance," he told her.

"What? I don't understand," Jen said.

"Psychologists are not medical doctors and apparently he's working through a loophole. We're investigating him now and will probably be arresting him soon," Antonio told her.

Jen just stood there. "Can I see my son?"

"Of course, Jen. Come on," Sylvia said as she wrapped an arm around her.

They walked in. Joanna was sitting next to Kendall, softly singing a lullaby. "Go to sleep, my teddy bear," she sang, stroking his hair.

Jo got up and went to stand by Antonio so Jen could sit next to him. "Baby, please wake up," she whispered, holding his hand.

∞

Kendall heard someone singing softly and soft fingers in his hair. He knew the song from somewhere, but he couldn't remember where. It was so hard to concentrate on anything and his head hurt. Then the singing was gone and someone else was whispering to him, and he knew the voice. It echoed in his mind... *I am so disappointed in you.*

He pulled away. "I don't want to go back, it's a bad place."

"Honey, you're not ever going back, I promise. I am so sorry," Jen said. As she reached up to stroke his cheek, he turned his head.

The heart monitor started beeping. "NO, I don't want it! Leave me alone! I don't want it, it hurts!" he screamed.

Jen fell back as he pushed away from her. Antonio caught her before she hit the floor and pushed her towards Sylvia and Joanna. He grabbed Kendall before he fell over the railing on the other side of the bed and held onto him.

The nurse and Dr. Davidson came running in, and Dr. Davidson ordered an injection of Torbugesic.

Kendall quieted seconds after the nurse administered it.

Sylvia and Joanna had ushered Jen out of the room and found a place for her to sit. She was white as a sheet and tears were flowing freely down her cheeks. "What have I done?" she sobbed.

A moment later, Dr. Davidson came out and knelt in front of her. "Mrs. Knight, please don't take anything that happened in there to heart. He's confused because of the Lorazepam and one of the side effects is hallucinations. Kendall is not aware of what's going on around him. Probably the easiest way to explain it is to think of it as night terrors. A nightmare that happens when you are not quite awake and yet not totally asleep. I know it's difficult right now, but he should be much better by morning. I would recommend that you not be alone tonight, and if you think you need it, I can send something with you to help you sleep. I gave him a mild sedative and he should sleep for the next few hours without further incident."

"Thank you, doctor," Sylvia said. He nodded and walked over to the nurse's station.

"It's my fault! I took him there and I let this happen."

"Honey, please don't. It's not your fault, you were trying to find help. You didn't know Graham would do something like this, and he will be held accountable," Sylvia told her.

"I made him go with me," Jen said.

"Yes, but you weren't taking Kendall to see him, Graham tricked you into that," Jo pointed out.

"Does it matter?" Jen cried. She was close to hysterics. "Kendall pushed me away! He's afraid of me!"

Sylvia snapped. She grabbed Jen by the shoulders and shook her twice. "STOP IT! Stop it right now! I am DONE with this! You are not to blame for this. Kendall is not to blame for this! Graham is an opportunistic son of a bitch who preyed on your fears and the love you have for your child. He has probably done it before and we are going to put a stop to it. Kendall loves you and is not responsible for what is going on in his head right now. "

"But..." Jen said.

"NO BUTS! You heard the doctor and you WILL listen to what he said. If you can put such stock into what a charlatan like Graham tells you, then you can damn well listen to a REAL doctor and the people who love you! Now, we're going to take Dr. Davidson up on his offer and get something to help you sleep. You and Katie are going to stay with us tonight, and after the doctor releases Kendall tomorrow, we are going to pick him up and you are going to apologize for what you said earlier. Then you are going to spend some quality time with your son and stop hiding behind baking, dishes, and everything else that you busy yourself with. Understood?" Sylvia said.

Jen looked at her and nodded.

"Good," Sylvia said, hugging her. "Now let's get that prescription and then get you to bed."

∞

Brooke and the boys arrived not long after the other moms left. They stopped to grab some sandwiches and brought one for Antonio. They got to Kendall's room and found Antonio sitting in a chair next to the sleeping boy.

"How is he?" Brooke asked, handing Antonio the bag.

He shook his head. "He's still having reactions to the drug and had to be sedated when Jen came in. He was terrified she was going to take him back to Graham and almost pushed her to the floor and himself off the other side of the bed. He's quieted down, and Dr. Davidson said it should be clearing his system by tomorrow. Have you heard anything from your man?"

"Well, we were a little preoccupied. Let me call Emily and find out," she said.

"Preoccupied with what?" Antonio asked, noting the look on her face. He looked at the three boys, who were all avoiding eye contact.

"Brooke... is there something I should know?"

"Of course not, darling, I just took the boys on a short adventure."

"Brooke... is this adventure something the station is going to be called about?"

"The answer to your question that implied we committed a felony of some sort is... no." She smiled.

He raised an eyebrow. "Good."

"Perhaps a misdemeanor, but not a felony." She smirked as she pulled out her phone.

He looked at the boys, who smiled nervously and he shook his head. "I DON'T want to know," he told them.

A moment later, she told him that Emily had already faxed what her investigator had found, to Sally.

"Thank you. Can you stay with Kendall for a couple of hours? I'll be back after I check a few things out at the station," Antonio asked.

"Of course I will," she said.

"Okay boys, I'll drop you off at my house. Logan, your mom is there with Sylvia and Jen, and if one of you could go pick up Katie after school and take her there, please?" Antonio asked.

"Sure thing, Papa G," James said.

"I want to stay here, Papi, please," Carlos asked.

"Carlos, don't you have practice tonight?"

"Please Papi..." Carlos gave him his best pout.

Antonio sighed. "Alright, you can stay for a little while. Maybe Brooke can give you a ride home when I get back?"

"Of course I will," Brooke said, patting Carlos on the shoulder.

Antonio, James, and Logan left. Carlos sat next to Kendall on the bed and turned the TV on with the volume on low.

"Mama D?"

"Yes dear?" Brooke said as she worked on her tablet.

"You're not going to get into trouble, are you?"

"For what?"

"You know..."

"Oh that, pish-tosh. That was simply a way of letting Dr. Graham know that he should be careful about what he does."

"What do you think he'll do when he finds his car like that?"

Brooke just smiled. "Hopefully he'll run screaming like the coward he is."

"I hope he pees his pants," Carlos said.

"That would be funny too, dear."

An hour later, Brooke looked up from her tablet and smiled. Carlos had fallen asleep and pulled Kendall over, so his head was resting on his chest and he had wrapped his arm protectively around his brother's shoulders.

∞

When Dr. Graham left the office at 6 pm, he saw balloons tied to his ski rack. "What is this all about?" he said as he walked up to the car, watching the thirty brightly coloured balloons floating above his car. He untied them from his car and tied them to a nearby post. He opened his car and got in, and then saw the box sitting on the passenger seat. His blood ran cold when he read the message on the cake and he quickly slammed his door closed and locked it. He started the car, put it into reverse, and heard a horrible squealing and grinding noise as his car jerked and then refused to move. He got out and saw his tires completely flat and resting on the rims. Completely spooked, he ran to the attendant's office to get help.

Chapter 56~ Hissy Fit

The ride to the Garcia home was quiet, each of the mothers lost in their own thoughts. Jen looked out the window, thinking back on the events of the last couple of weeks. So much had happened in such a short period of time.

She was trying to believe what Dr. Davidson had told her. That Kendall didn't know what was happening, but all she could hear were his screams as he tried to get away from her. She kept replaying the morning in her mind. She had never been disappointed in either of her children. She didn't know why she had said something so cruel to him. The sight of him running away from her would be forever burned in her memory.

She took a deep breath. Sylvia and Joanna are right. I can't fix this by pretending everything is normal when it isn't. I can't help him get better if I don't realize how hurt he is.

Sylvia pulled into the driveway and they all walked quietly up to the house. Once inside, Sylvia went into the kitchen to make the tea she had started a couple of hours before. Joanna and Jen followed her and they sat in the kitchen.

"How you doing, honey?" Joanna asked Jen.

"Better," she said.

"Are you sure?" Sylvia asked.

She nodded. "Yes, everything you said is true. I need to listen to the real doctors and the people who love us. I need to quit hiding from Kendall and pretending I can make everything better by making cookies and trying to push pills at him. I realized I haven't even really hugged him since he got home on Friday night. I was trying to go on like nothing's happened."

Sylvia handed her a cup of tea. "Luckily hugging him is something you can do when he gets home tomorrow."

"If he'll let me," Jen said.

"Don't wait and don't ask... just DO it," Jo told her.

Jen smiled and nodded.

Sylvia handed Jen the sedative Dr. Davidson had prescribed. "Now take this and then you're getting some real sleep. Someone will pick up Katie and bring her here, and tomorrow we'll bring Kendall home. It's up to you, but we would be happy to have you stay here for a few days. If not, one of us will be at your house during the day, one of the boys at night."

When Jen went to speak, Sylvia pointed her finger at her. "NO arguments, this IS the way it's going to be, so deal with it."

Jen smiled. "I was just going to say thank you. I don't know what I would do without all of you."

"Oh... well, you're welcome," Sylvia hugged her. "You're not going to find out, because we're not going anywhere."

"What do you think Brooke was up to today?" Joanna asked.

Sylvia shook her head. "I don't know, but I'm sure we'll find out.

∞

A few minutes later, Antonio dropped James and Logan off at the house.

"Where's Carlos?" Sylvia asked, noticing her son was missing.

"He wanted to stay with Kendall for a while. Brooke is with them. The boys will go pick up Katie, and I'm going to run to the station. I'll be back later," he said, kissing her goodbye.

"Are you boys alright?" Jen asked.

"Yeah Mama K, we're fine. How are you doing?" Logan asked.

"I'm okay, swe... I'm okay, honey. I think I'm going to go lie down now," she said, hugging the boys and then heading to the bedroom.

"Is she really okay?" Logan asked his mom.

"She's trying, honey. It's going to be a long road though."

"So, what did you boys do today?" Sylvia asked.

"Ummm, I think I have homework," James said, heading upstairs.

"Me too," Logan squeaked, quickly following his friend upstairs.

Sylvia and Joanna looked at each other. "Brooke," they said in unison.

∞

Sally greeted Antonio as he walked into the station. "Hey Boss, the reports from Jack Barr are on your desk. He found a few things that might prove useful. How's Kendall doing?"

"Thanks Sally. He's resting now," Antonio told her as he went into his office. He picked up the first folder and started reading through the papers.

∞

A few minutes later, Bennet walked in. "Hey there!"

"Aren't you on medical leave?" Sally smiled.

"I'm bored, besides, the doctor gave me a clean bill of health," he said, handing her the release form.

"Good thing it was just your head." Sally smirked as she took the form.

"HA. HA," he retorted.

"Good one! A bullet to your head has made you cleverer! Boss is in his office, go get brought up to speed."

John just looked at her for a moment and then gave up trying to respond. He knocked on Antonio's door. "Hey partner, what's up?"

"Hey John, how are you feeling?"

"Fine, brought my release slip in. Why the intense paper rage?" he asked, watching Antonio angrily turn a page.

Antonio told him everything that had gone on regarding Richard Graham.

"Are you freaking kidding me? After everything else that happened, now the kid has to deal with some..." he took a deep breath and stopped himself before he launched into a string of expletives.

"Here, read this," Antonio said, handing him the file. "Sally..."

Sally popped her head in. "I already have calls into all four families that Graham settled with. I heard from the Tanners, they really don't want to get involved but will send a copy of their son's file. Still waiting on the other three. I also spoke with Ryan at the DA's office and he'll get a warrant issued when you're ready, but it would be better if Kendall confirmed that Graham gave him the injection."

Antonio nodded. "Thanks Sally."

"No problem."

John shook his head as he read the file. "So this guy messed these families up. Why settle?"

"Malpractice is VERY hard to prove against therapists, because there are so many different treatment methods. It's especially difficult in Louisiana," Sally told him.

"What's so special about Louisiana?"

"Psychologists can prescribe medications there."

"What... Who thought that was a good idea?" John asked.

"I don't know, they've refused the bill in every other state but New Mexico," she said.

"Sally, did the Tanners say they have any medical evidence backing up their son's reaction and withdrawal from the medication he was given?" Antonio asked.

"Yes, they're including it with the copy of his psychological reports. They're also sending a copy of the autopsy report, as well as the funeral notices. While they say they don't want to get involved, I think they're hoping someone takes this son of a bitch down. I think they need an acknowledgment that someone pushed their son towards suicide," Sally told him.

Antonio nodded. "We're going to see they get it. That's why we're going to take this slow and do it right."

Sally and John looked at him, nodded, and smiled.

"I'm going to get back to the hospital. Let me know if you hear from any of the other families, or if anything else comes up," Antonio said.

"Will do, Boss. Tell Kendall, hi, for me and I'll stop by and visit him soon. That reminds me, did you want to go over his statement sheet?" Sally asked.

"Yeah, if you have a copy I'll go over it tonight."

"Sure thing." Sally quickly ran off a copy and put it in an envelope for him.

"Thanks Sally, I'll see you later."

"Okay, let me know if you need anything."

"Will do." He smiled.

∞

He got back to the hospital and found Brooke working on her tablet. Carlos asleep on the bed holding onto Kendall. He smiled at the two boys, remembering all the times they had shared a crib when they were babies.

"Aren't they adorable?" Brook whispered.

"Yeah, they are. I do think they would object to the word 'adorable' though. How were things?"

"He slept the whole time. Carlos fell asleep about half an hour ago," Brooke told him.

Antonio nodded. "Okay, thanks Brooke. Jen and Jo are at my house. Jen and Katie are staying the night."

He went over and gently shook Carlos' shoulder. "Carlitos, it's time to go home, Mijo."

Carlos yawned. "Hi Papi. Do I have to go? I wanna stay here with you and Kendall."

"I don't think they'll let you stay here," Antonio told him.

Carlos sighed and pouted. "Tell them I have to."

"Carlos..."

"Please Papi? That way when Kendall wakes up, he knows I found him."

"He'll know," Antonio said, ruffling Carlos' hair.

Kendall stirred and whimpered and Carlos held him tighter. Carlos looked at Antonio, his brown eyes sad. "He NEEDS me, Papi."

Antonio sighed. "As long as the nurses say it's alright."

"Why don't I go ask?" Brooke smiled and walked out to find the nurse's desk.

Carlos smiled widely. "I get to stay."

"Carlos, she hasn't even asked yet...Never mind," he said, thinking about who was doing the "asking."

Brooke returned a few moments later. "It's fine if you stay, darling," she told Carlos. "I'll head over to your house and see how things are going there," she said to Antonio.

"Thanks Brooke. By the way, Sally is handling things at the station, and as soon as we have everything we need, Graham will be arrested."

"I want to be there."

"That's not normal procedure, but I think a phone call can be arranged." He smiled.

"That's all I ask. Call if you need anything," she said.

"I think we'll be fine. Thanks Brooke."

She went over and kissed Kendall on the head and then Carlos on the cheek. "Goodnight dear, I'll see you tomorrow."

"Night, Mama D."

∞

A couple of hours later, the police station received a phone call from a panic-stricken man.

Officer Johnson was trying to speak to the man, but he kept getting shrieked at. Sally was just getting ready to head out for the night, when Johnson held the phone away from his ear and rolled his eyes.

"Dr. Graham, please, if you would just let me get a word in..." Johnson said.

Sally stopped and motioned for Johnson to hand her the phone, which he gladly did.

"Hello, this is Officer O'Hara. How may I help you?"

"This is Dr. Richard Graham. I am trying to get someone here because my car was broken into and vandalized."

"I'm sorry to hear that. Where is your car located?"

"At the private section in the St. Joseph Doctor's Building parking garage."

"Don't they have attendants there?" she asked.

"Yes, but apparently no one saw anything!" he yelled, looking at the attendant angrily.

Sally smiled. "Why don't you tell me what happened to your car?"

"Someone left balloons tied to it and a cake on the front seat!"

"Is it your birthday? Maybe a friend was trying to surprise you," she suggested.

"It is NOT my birthday! No one has keys to my car but the attendant and me. There was a very disturbing message on the cake, and whoever did it also flattened all of my tires."

"Your tires were slashed?" she asked, mentally groaning.

"No, the attendant thinks the air was just let out. He used a small pump to test one."

Thank God, she thought to herself. "Well, there is a chance they just lost air."

"ALL FOUR TIRES!" he screamed.

"Dr. Graham, if you do not lower your voice, I will end this call. Yes, it is possible for all four tires to lose air. The weather has turned considerably colder, and if the valves weren't sealed properly, they would leak a little going from a cold environment to a warm one."

She was trying not to laugh at the expression on Johnson's face. He knew she was embellishing things as she went along and was laughing into his arm.

"Well... What about the cake and balloons?"

"We don't really send out a patrol car when someone LEAVES a gift for someone. If you like, you can drop it off here and we can look at it. You said there was a message on it?"

"Yes, someone wrote, 'Be Very Afraid' on it!" he yelled.

Sally shook her head. "Do you have any idea who might have left it?"

"If I KNEW who left it, I wouldn't be talking to you, now would I?!"

Sally arched an eyebrow. "Well, perhaps you can tell me one more thing then?"

"What?" Graham fumed.

"What flavour is the cake?"

She pulled the phone away from her ear as he shrieked and slammed the receiver down.

"Well... THAT was rude," she said calmly, before erupting into laughter.

Chapter 57 ~ Insight

Antonio sent Carlos to get something for them to eat.

Kendall had opened his eyes when Carlos got up to go down to the cafeteria, but went right back to sleep. His eyes were back to normal and he was breathing much easier now.

Carlos came in with a bag and handed it to Antonio. "Did he wake up?"

"No, he just opened his eyes for a second."

"Okay," he said, sitting next to Antonio to eat his sandwich. "Papi?"

"Yes?"

"Why is Mama K so mad at Kendall?"

"What? Jen isn't mad at Kendall," Antonio told him.

"Yes she is, she's mad at you too," Carlos stated as he took another bite.

"Why do say that?"

He shrugged.

"Carlos, I want an answer," Antonio said firmly. "Has she said something?"

"No."

"Then why do you think she's mad?"

"Just the way she looks sometimes."

"How does she look?" Antonio asked.

"Like... I don't know, mad."

Antonio sighed. "Okay, let's try it this way... WHEN did she look mad?"

"When you and James got Kendall to eat, when you got him to take his medicine, when you brought him home from the hospital on Saturday."

"Are you sure it was anger and not concern?" Antonio asked.

Carlos thought about it. "No. I don't really know how to describe it, Papi. She looked mad and then sad, and then it was gone."

"Why do you think she's mad, Mijo?" Antonio asked.

Carlos shrugged again.

"Carlos..."

Carlos sighed. "I think she's upset because you could help him and she couldn't. I think that's why she made him go to Dr. Graham too, because she wanted to help him so badly and he was the only one they could get in to see."

Antonio sat there, contemplating what Carlos had said as they finished their meal.

He couldn't understand why Jen would be upset. They had always taken care of one another's children. Then again, Jen hadn't been thinking too clearly either. He sighed. He needed to talk to her about this.

"Carlos, do you feel like I've been spending too much time with Kendall? That I've been ignoring you and your Mami?"

"Why would I think that?"

"Well... I was gone for a while and then stayed with him at the hospital and now again."

Carlos smiled. "Papi, he needs us right now. We're supposed to be there for family, right?"

'That's right, Mijo, we are. I just want to make sure that you don't feel like I'm neglecting you."

"Kendall is my brother and if he needs you, then that's where you should be."

"You're a pretty special kid, you know that?"

Carlos smiled. "Can you do me a favour and remember that just in case?"

"I don't want to know," Antonio said, wondering what Brooke and the boys had been up to.

∞

They finished eating and Carlos sat next to Kendall and watched cartoons, while Antonio started reading Kendall's statement sheet. The further he read, the angrier he became as he looked at the boxes checked yes. Generalized touching, inappropriate touching, kissing, open mouth kissing including with tongue, biting with intent of leaving marks upon skin, given fellatio, hitting, kicking, choking.

Antonio stopped reading. He felt sick to his stomach, even though he knew this definitely was not the worst case they had ever seen. Far from it. Kendall had been lucky, considering what could have happened, but still, it was just so wrong. He felt his eyes begin to water and rubbed them.

"Are you okay, Papi?"

"Yeah, just a little tired. I think I'm going to run down and grab some coffee."

"Okay," Carlos said.

"Do you want anything?"

"No, I'm good. Maybe a bottle of ice tea for Kendall, in case he wakes up?"

Antonio smiled and nodded. He folded the paper, put it in his pocket, and headed down to the cafeteria. Antonio gave Sylvia a quick call.

"Hi honey," she answered.

"Hi, how are things going there?"

"Okay, we just finished up dinner and the kids are watching TV."

"How's Jen?"

"She's doing better. She took one of the sedatives Dr. Davidson prescribed and is getting some much-needed sleep. You sound strange, is everything okay there?" Sylvia asked.

"Everything's fine. Kendall is sleeping and Carlos is watching cartoons. He wants to stay the night, so I told him it was okay."

"Brooke said something like that. Jen, Katie and the boys are staying here tonight. I'm going to try and talk Jen into staying here for a couple of days," Sylvia said.

"Honey, do you think there's a chance that Jen's upset that Kendall has needed me for the last few days?"

"I don't know. I haven't really thought about it. Why?" she asked.

"Carlos seems to think she might be."

"She hasn't said anything," Sylvia said.

"I know, maybe it's subconscious. He was pretty adamant about it. He said that she looked sad and mad a couple of times."

"Well, I guess it's possible. She keeps blaming herself for not being able to help him. She could have some latent jealousy. She's not thinking clearly and it would go along with her panicked attempts to find someone to help him," Sylvia told him.

"Okay, I'm going to need to talk to her and make sure that we're okay." Antonio sighed.

"She's doing a lot better now. We talked after the episode at the hospital and she realized she hasn't been handling this well at all. So, I'm hoping when Kendall comes home tomorrow, that she reaches out to him instead of hiding from him."

"I hope so too, honey. Well, I had better get back to the boys. I'll see you in the morning," he said.

"Goodnight honey. Give the boys a kiss for me."

"Goodnight, I will. I love you."

Sylvia smiled. "I love you too, amorcito."

∞

Antonio went back to the room and pulled a chair closer to the bed. He and Carlos sat there and watched cartoons together.

A couple of hours later, Antonio looked over and saw that Kendall had woken up and was watching the TV. He hadn't moved, so Carlos hadn't noticed yet.

Antonio smiled. "Hey buddy, how are you feeling?"

When Kendall didn't answer, he got up and sat next to him. "Are you doing okay?"

Kendall didn't say anything but nodded slightly.

"Kendall, do you know where you are?"

He nodded again.

"Guess what? I get to stay here with you!" Carlos told him.

Kendall looked at him and gave him a small smile.

"Kendall, look at me," Antonio said. The boy looked up at him. "It's going to be alright. I know things seem impossible right now, but they will get better. It's all been so much for you to try and take in, but we are going to get through this," Antonio told him as he brushed the bangs out of his eyes. "You still need a haircut."

Kendall just looked at him sadly and closed his eyes.

Carlos looked at Antonio. "Papi, why won't he say anything?"

"I don't know, Mijo, it's probably still the medication," Antonio said softly, but his heart told him that wasn't entirely the case.

Carlos leaned over and pulled Kendall over, so that his head was resting on his shoulder. He wrapped his arms around him and whispered softly. "I found you today and I'm not letting go."

Chapter 58 ~ Distant

Sylvia was worried about Antonio, he had sounded so strange on the phone. Why did Carlos think Jen was angry?

"Jo, when you and Jen were talking, did she say anything about being upset or angry with Antonio?"

Joanna thought back. "She didn't say she was angry, but I do think she's upset that Antonio was able to help Kendall when she couldn't. I pointed out he's a police officer and that's his job. I think she was also hurt because when Kendall woke up in Graham's office, he called for Antonio. I think it's more a matter of her blaming herself then anger."

"That's right, she said something about that on the phone when she called after Kendall ran away from her," Sylvia said.

"Why, what's going on?"

"Carlos told Antonio he thinks Jen is mad at him for being able to help Kendall," Sylvia told her.

"It's probably just all the frustration and helplessness she feels," Joanna said.

"I hope so, but it worries me that the kids might be picking up on it," Sylvia said.

"Well, I think she's thinking a bit more clearly now. We can talk to her about it later if you're worried."

"I think Antonio is going to talk to her, it might be better that way," Sylvia said.

Joanna smiled. "It hasn't been easy on him either. He's trying to make sure everyone is okay. When all of this has settled down, maybe the two of you should get away for a weekend."

Sylvia smiled. "That would be nice, but I have a feeling it's going to be a while."

∞

He heard voices come and go, some he recognized others he didn't. Then it was silent, and when he opened his eyes, no one was there. He looked around the small sterile room and got up. He walked out into the hallway and it was empty. He listened carefully and couldn't hear anything, so he started down the hall, looking for a way out. He heard a noise behind him, but when he looked, there was nothing there. He found the nurse's station and it was empty, so he picked up the phone and dialed Carlos' number. It rang, and a moment later, he heard a phone ring in one of the rooms. He sat the phone on the desk and walked towards the room. He put his hand on the doorknob, turning it slowly and then pushed the door open...

Kendall woke with a start, trying to take a deep breath. He closed his eyes, forced himself to slow his breathing, and then opened his eyes again. Antonio was sleeping in the chair and Carlos was lying in the bed next to him. He felt his arm around his shoulders. He wiggled free and climbed out of the bed, pulling the IV stand with him. He went into the bathroom and closed the door. He was dizzy and felt sick to his stomach, so he sat on the floor next to the toilet, leaning his head against the wall.

∞

Antonio woke when he heard the monitors go off and saw that Kendall was gone. "Carlos, where's Kendall?" he asked, shaking his son.

Carlos opened his eyes. "Hmm? I don't know," he said, jumping up.

Antonio checked the closet while Carlos checked the bathroom. "Papi," he said, pointing.

Antonio walked over and looked in. Kendall was asleep on the floor. "Thank God. Kendall, wake up. What are you doing on the floor?" he asked as he gently shook his shoulder.

Kendall jumped back and hit the wall, shaking.

"You're okay, it's Papi. We need to get you back to bed," Antonio said softly as reached over to help him up off the floor.

Kendall looked at him and took his hand and Antonio pulled him up. He put an arm around his waist and helped him back to his bed.

"Are you okay?" Antonio asked.

Kendall nodded and closed his eyes.

The nurse had come in to check on things. "Is everything alright?"

"I think so," Antonio said.

The nurse made sure that the monitor was hooked onto Kendall's finger and that the IV line was sound. "If you need anything, just push the call button."

"Thank you," he said.

Antonio sat down in the chair and Carlos stood next to him. "Papi, was he sleepwalking?"

"I don't know, maybe. Try and get some more sleep, Mijo."

Carlos nodded and got into the bed next to Kendall. He put his arm around his shoulders, and a few moments later, Kendall rolled over and hugged him tightly.

Antonio smiled at the boys and soon they were all fast asleep.

∞

The next morning, Sylvia checked on Jen and found her still sleeping. She woke the kids for school and made breakfast while they got ready.

Once they had showered and dressed, they went down and sat at the kitchen table, but only picked at their food.

"I can make you something else," Sylvia offered.

"No, this is fine, Mama G. I'm just not very hungry," Logan said. James and Katie nodded in agreement.

"I know, honey, but you need to eat something. Katie, I think you're all staying here for a couple of days, so we can go over and pick up some things after school. Boys, if you want to stay, you can run home after school and get what you need. If not, just let me know, okay?"

"I'm staying," James said.

Logan nodded. "Me too. We have an appointment with Sally after school though."

Sylvia smiled. "Okay. Should we see if Sally just wants to meet you here?"

"I'll give her a call after first period," Logan said.

Sylvia nodded. "Look, I know yesterday was a setback, but Kendall will be home today and we can get back on track. None of this was his or Jen's fault, so we need to help them move past it."

"That's a lie," Katie said.

Sylvia looked at her. "What's a lie, Mija?"

"If mom had listened to Kendall, NONE of yesterday would have happened. We would be home now and he wouldn't have had to go back to the hospital!" Katie yelled angrily. She got up and ran upstairs.

"I'll go," James said and followed Katie upstairs.

"Sorry Mama G, it's just getting to her," Logan said.

"I know... it's getting to all of us. Are you okay?"

"As good as any of us is, I guess," Logan said.

∞

James knocked on the bedroom door. "Katie-Kat, can I come in?" Not getting an answer, he slowly opened the door and saw Katie lying on the bed, her face in the pillow.

James sat next to her on the bed and rubbed her back. "Katie, I know it's hard right now, but you've got to give your mom a break."

"Why?"

"She's doing the best she can, she didn't mean for what happened yesterday to happen. You know she would do anything to protect any of us."

"Except LISTEN!" Katie said, her voice muffled by the pillow.

James sighed. "Katie, she didn't take Kendall to see Graham, she went to see him. Obviously, it was a bad choice, but she thought she needed someone to talk to."

"She has people to talk to."

"I know, but she thought someone who wasn't close to the situation might help her to help Kendall better. Look, Graham tricked her and it's HIS fault Kendall's in the hospital. I know she said something she shouldn't have, but she feels really bad about it."

"She should feel bad, moms aren't supposed to say those kinds of things," Katie stated.

"I know."

"I just want my brother back," she said, hugging him.

"I know. We all do, but it's going to take a while for him to feel better, and we all have to help. That means NOT being mad at your mom too, because if she's feeling bad, then Kendall will feel guilty about it. He already feels guilty about all of this, even though none of it's his fault. Papa G is going to make sure Graham pays for what he did... And if you're good, I'll tell you what we did yesterday," he promised.

"What did you do?"

"If you promise to try and be understanding to your mom and SWEAR not to tell anyone, I'll tell you on the way to school, okay?"

"Is it good?"

"It's great," he said, giving her a devious smile.

∞

About 9 am, Dr. Davidson stopped in to examine Kendall before releasing him.

"Are you feeling better?" he asked.

Kendall nodded.

"Follow my finger with just your eyes," he said, moving his finger back and forth and then up and down.

Kendall did as he was asked.

"Very good. Any more trouble breathing or any dizziness?"

Kendall shook his head.

Antonio gestured to Davidson and pulled him aside. "He hasn't said a word since yesterday afternoon."

"Not at all?"

Antonio shook his head.

"Alright," he said and went back over to Kendall.

"I'll have the nurse come in and remove your catheter, but I need to hear you speak. One of the side effects of the Lorazepam is difficulty speaking. So, how are you feeling this morning?"

"Fine."

"Can you tell me who this is?" he asked, pointing to Carlos.

Kendall sighed. "Carlos and that's Papi."

"Okay, I'll have the nurse come and remove the catheter, and you can get dressed while we get the paperwork done," Dr. Davidson said with a smile.

Kendall nodded.

After the nurse removed the catheter, Kendall went into the bathroom to dress.

Carlos waited for him in the room while Antonio spoke with Dr. Davidson. "So, any idea what's going on? He's not acting right."

"Well, yesterday took a lot out of him. The initial reaction to the medication was physically and emotionally difficult. He is still experiencing a type of withdrawal and could still suffer a few side effects. I'll send the literature home with you, so you know what they are. He's

probably going to be very tired and should just rest for the next couple of days. Make sure he eats and continues with his antibiotics, his lungs are still not completely clear. If you need more, I can get a refill for you," Dr. Davidson said.

Antonio nodded. "I'll see how many he has and get it refilled if needed. Thank you."

"No problem. If you have any questions, I'll be here until six," Dr. Davidson said.

"Thanks, I appreciate all of your understanding with this," Antonio said, shaking his hand.

"You're very welcome." Dr. Davidson smiled as he went to finish his rounds.

Antonio went back into the room and found the boys getting their jackets on. "Alright, let's get home. Carlos, we need to get you in for at least your afternoon classes."

Carlos groaned. "But Papi..."

"No 'buts' Carlos and you're supposed to see Sally this afternoon."

Carlos poked out his bottom lip.

"Not going to work, Mijo." Antonio laughed.

∞

They arrived at home about fifteen minutes later and Carlos helped Kendall up the porch.

Sylvia and Jen heard them at the door and walked into the living room to meet them. Sylvia had a firm grip on Jen's arm. "Remember, just tell him you're sorry and hold him."

"Hi honey," Antonio said as he and the boys walked in.

"Are you hungry?" Sylvia asked as she pushed Jen forward a little.

"I'm starving," Antonio said.

"Me too!" Carlos piped in as he helped Kendall take off his jacket.

"How about you, Kendall?" Jen asked.

Kendall shook his head.

"Just a little?" she asked, walking over to him.

Sylvia pulled Carlos and Antonio towards the kitchen, leaving Jen and Kendall in the living room.

Kendall shook his head again, not looking up.

Jen hesitated a moment and then hugged him. "I'm so sorry, baby. I'm so, so sorry."

She held onto him tightly and cried into his shoulder.

"It's okay, I'm just tired," he whispered, pulling away and then heading upstairs.

Jen sat on the stairs and cried.

Chapter 59~ The First Step

Kendall walked upstairs, went into the guest room, and sat down on the bed. He sat there for a few minutes, just looking at the wall.

He knew his mom was reaching out, but he didn't know how to let her in. He was so tired and confused, he didn't know what to do. He wouldn't do the one thing she had asked of him, and he knew she was just trying to help. She was a good mom and had every right to be disappointed in him.

He wished he could remember what had happened, but all he knew was that she was angry because of his attitude... Where else had he heard that?

"I'm losing my mind," he said as he curled up on the bed and tried to sleep.

∞

Sylvia heard Jen crying and looked out to see her sitting alone on the stairs. She went over, sat next to her, and put an arm around her shoulders. "What happened?"

Jen shook her head. "He just stood there. When I told him I was sorry, he just said it was okay."

"That's good then," Sylvia said.

"No, it's not. He wouldn't look at me, he wouldn't hug me back. He pulled away and said he was tired and went upstairs."

Antonio was listening and went over. Reaching down, he took Jen's hand. "Come with me, we need to talk."

"Honey, can you take Kendall something to eat and his antibiotic?" he asked Sylvia as he guided Jen to his study.

Sylvia nodded as Antonio closed the door.

Carlos watched his dad take Jen into his study and close the door. "What's going on?" he asked his mom.

"Papi is just going to explain some things to Mama K. Now eat up and go get ready for school. I'm going to fix something for Kendall to eat."

Carlos groaned at the thought of school. "He's not going to eat."

"He'll eat a little, he needs his antibiotic. Maybe just some yogurt and toast," she said as she pulled out a plate.

Carlos finished his breakfast and went upstairs to shower and change. He didn't find Kendall in his room, so he checked the guest room. He saw Kendall curled up on the bed. "Hey buddy, you doing okay?"

Kendall nodded.

"I'm going to grab you some of my pajamas, and if you want to jump in the shower when I'm done, I can help you with your shirt," Carlos offered.

"Okay," Kendall said quietly.

Carlos went back into his room, pulled some flannel pajamas out of his dresser drawer, and grabbed himself some clean clothes for school. "Here you go," he said, setting the pajamas on the dresser.

"Thanks."

"No problem, I'll be out in a few minutes," Carlos said and went in and started his shower.

Sylvia came up with a tray a moment later. "Honey, I brought you some breakfast. I know you're not very hungry, but you need to take your antibiotic. So just take a few bites, okay?"

Kendall sat up and Sylvia put the tray on the nightstand. She sat down next to him. "Just some toast and yogurt, okay?"

He nodded and took a couple bites of toast. Sylvia handed him a glass with some juice and his amoxicillin.

Take these or I will shove them down your throat.

He looked at Sylvia and took the glass and pill with shaky hands.

"Are you alright, Mijo?" she asked, noticing a strange look flash across his eyes.

He nodded and swallowed the pill.

"Try and finish as much as you can." She smiled, brushing his hair back.

He nodded.

"Do you need anything else?"

He shook his head no.

"I'll be back up in a little while to check on you, try and get some sleep," she said, kissing him on the forehead.

Kendall nodded and took a spoonful of yogurt. He wasn't hungry, but he knew the medicine would make him sick to his stomach if he didn't eat. He finished it by the time Carlos was ready for school.

"Shower's free," he said as he sat next to Kendall.

Kendall got up, grabbed the pajamas, and went into the bathroom. He sighed when he realized he couldn't get his t-shirt off. He opened the door. "Carlos?"

"Yeah buddy?"

"Can you help me get this off, please?"

"No problem." Carlos smiled and went into the bathroom. He helped ease the shirt over Kendall's head.

He stood there in shock. He hadn't seen Kendall without his shirt since he had gotten home and couldn't believe all the bruises.

Kendall quickly backed away and pulled the shirt around himself. "Sorry, I forgot."

"Kendall... no. I'm sorry. I knew..." Carlos stammered, his eyes tearing up.

"It's not your fault. Just go, okay?"

Carlos nodded and went out into the hallway.

Kendall closed the door and turned on the water. It was already warm, so he got in and stood under the warm, steady stream. He closed his eyes and tried to calm his breathing down. *Great, now Carlos feels bad. Why can't I go one day without hurting someone?*

He finished showering and put on the flannel pajamas that Carlos had loaned him. He opened the door and was surprised to see Carlos waiting there.

"Are you alright?" Carlos asked.

Kendall looked at him and nodded. "Are you?"

Carlos nodded and then hugged Kendall gently. "I'm sorry, I knew you were banged up, I just didn't realize how bad."

"It's not your fault, Carlos."

"I know. I'm just sorry. I wish I could make it all go away."

Kendall hugged him back. "Me too. I think I'm going to go lie down."

"I'll see you after school. James and Logan will be coming over too," Carlos told him.

Kendall nodded and went back into the bedroom.

"Bye Kendall, get some rest!" Carlos said as he headed downstairs.

"Carlitos, are you ready for school? What's wrong, Mijo?" Sylvia asked when she saw the look on his face.

"Kendall... he's all bruised... I made him feel bad," he said, and unable to hold it in any longer, started crying.

Sylvia hugged him. "I'm sure you didn't. I know it looks bad, but Papi said it looks much worse than it is and he's getting better every day."

He nodded and she wiped the tears from his cheeks. "I know it's hard, baby. Maybe you should talk to Sally about it?"

Carlos nodded.

"Okay, let's get you to school," she said as she handed him his jacket.

He grabbed her coat and held it for her. "My little caballero."

He blushed. "Mami..."

She laughed at him. "NOW you're shy. You mooned the entire opposing team at the hockey playoffs last year, and you blush when I call you my little gentleman."

"Mom," he whined as they headed out the door.

∞

Antonio sat Jen in front of his computer. "It's time you hear what happened that day at school," he said as he opened the file of Kendall's recording.

She sat there and listened to the entire thing without saying a word. Tears were streaming down her face as she heard the conversation between Kendall and Deesie.

Antonio watched her and hoped he was doing the right thing. She needed to know what had happened so they could move forward and start healing. When the recording was over, he gave her a moment. "Are you alright? Because there's more you need to know."

She took a deep breath and nodded. He handed her the copy of Kendall's statement sheet. "Read as much as you can. It took me a while to finish it."

She took it from him, her hands shaking, and started to read. He watched her closely to make sure she was doing alright. She was very pale and looked like she might get sick.

"Honey, if you need to stop, then do."

She shook her head and finished reading the sheet. "He did all of this to my son?"

Antonio nodded. "That's why this is going to take time, Jen. Probably a long time. Consider all of this happening, plus Deesie telling him that he was the reason he killed Mr. Crowley. Honey, he witnessed two people get shot, one of whom he knows and cares about, Deesie telling him it was all because of him. It would be hard for an adult to handle, much less a child."

She took a couple of deep breaths. "What do I do?"

"You get him the right kind of help and you listen when he tries to tell you something. I know you're upset right now, but the fact is he's still in shock. I'm sorry, but you add Graham into the equation, and that's probably put us back to square one."

Antonio went on to tell her what Brooke had found out about Graham, and the fact that as soon as they had everything they needed, he would be charged.

"Before you start saying this is all your fault again, it's not. Yes, you should have listened to Kendall, but you didn't go there with the intention of Graham seeing him. No, you shouldn't have said what you did, but you're in a fragile state too. You need to realize it's going to take time for Kendall to get over that too. You need to stop blaming yourself and start dealing with this, otherwise neither of you is going to recover. Sally said she gave you the name of someone who specializes in child psychology and traumas, and that's a good start."

Jen nodded. "Okay, I'll do what I need to. I just don't know how to reach him, and it hurts to think that..."

"He can talk to me?" Antonio finished.

She nodded.

"Jen, this isn't a popularity contest. He didn't turn to me because he loves me more than you. He turned to me because I was there. Because I know what happened and he doesn't have to tell me, and I'm trained in this and know when not to push him. Also, he's always tried to protect you, and in all honesty, no boy wants to discuss the fact he was molested with his mother."

Jen nodded. "I know you're right, it's hard to accept that he's closing himself off from me."

"I know, but you have to deal with it and show him that none of this is his fault, because right now, he's blaming himself for everything, including what happened yesterday. So, I'm going to tell you what I would want someone to tell me... Suck it up and get over it. Don't take it personally, because he isn't trying to hurt you or anyone else. He's trying to process this and has no idea how to do it. Our first priority is *Kendall*, everything else comes second," Antonio told her.

Jen smiled at him and nodded. "I am glad you're here for him, I just want him to know that I am too."

He hugged her. "He does, Jen, just give it some time."

Sylvia knocked on the door. "Anyone want coffee?"

"That would be great, honey," Antonio said, getting up.

"It does sound good," Jen said.

"Coffee is on. I'm going to go grab Kendall's tray," Sylvia said.

∞

Kendall had fallen asleep after a few minutes and kept fighting off the feeling that someone was standing there watching him. He would wake up and find no one there and fall back to sleep. "Stop being stupid," he told himself. He finally fell into a sound sleep.

He felt someone climb on the bed next to him. Suddenly someone was on top of him, pressing down and he couldn't move or breathe.

"It's time, sweetheart," he heard Deesie whisper in his ear. He tried to move as he felt hands move up and down his body. It felt like he was being pushed through the mattress. 'What was rule number four?" Deesie whispered as he bit down on Kendall's neck.

∞

Sylvia knocked quietly on the door, and when Kendall didn't answer, opened it slowly. The bed had been slept in but there was no one in the room. "Kendall?" She looked in the bathroom and he wasn't there or in Carlos' room. "Kendall, where are you?"

Not getting an answer, she yelled for Antonio.

Antonio and Jen came running up the stairs. "What is it?" he asked.

"I can't find Kendall. He's not in the bathroom or the bedrooms."

"Check the closets, he crawled out of bed and was in the bathroom last night," Antonio said as he pushed back the shower curtain to check the tub.

Jen checked the closet in the guest room. "Not here!" she said, beginning to panic.

"Calm down, Jen. He's here somewhere. The front door is still locked," Antonio told her.

Sylvia pulled open Carlos' closet door. "In here!"

Kendall had crawled into the back of the closet and curled up into a ball and was sound asleep. Antonio and Jen went into Carlos' room, and Antonio pulled the shoes and clothes that were on the floor out.

He looked at Jen and pointed. "Get in there and go to your son."

"What if he doesn't want me?" Jen asked, suddenly afraid.

"Seriously? After the conversation we just had?"

She looked at him, took a deep breath, and crawled into the closet next to Kendall. She took another breath and put her hand on his shoulder. "Kendall, wake up. We need to get you back into bed." When he didn't respond, she called to him a little louder. "Kendall, wake up, honey. Why are you in the closet?"

He moved a little. "Hmmm?"

"Baby, we need to get you off the floor and back into bed. Can you get up?"

He opened his eyes and jumped back. "He's here, he was here!"

"Who was here?" Jen asked softly.

He looked at her. "What?"

"You said he was here, who is here?"

He shook his head in confusion.

"It's okay, baby, nobody here is going to hurt you. You need to come out so we can get you back to bed."

Kendall nodded and she got up and put her hand down to help him up. He looked at her hand and then took it as he crawled out. She put her arm around him, walked him into the other bedroom, and tucked him in. She sat next to him until he was asleep again. Antonio and Sylvia watched from the hallway in case they were needed. Jen got up once Kendall was sleeping and kissed him on the head.

She closed the door quietly as she left. "Thank you," she said, hugging Antonio.

"You know that's just the first step," he said.

Jen nodded. "I know, but it's one step closer than I was this morning."

Chapter 60~ Silence

Carlos found Logan and James in the cafeteria. "Hey guys."

"Hey Carlitos. How did last night go?" James asked.

Carlos sat down and shrugged. "Okay, I guess."

"What's wrong, buddy?" Logan asked.

"I don't know... I guess it's just everything. I helped Kendall with his shirt this morning and... I just wasn't expecting him to look that bad."

"I'm sorry, Carlos. I should have warned you. I know it looks bad now, but he's getting better," James said, patting his friend on the back.

"I hope so. Mami said I should talk to Sally about it."

"That's a good idea. I already called her and she's going to meet us at your house at about four. She's going to go over a little earlier and talk to Kendall," Logan told him.

"Good luck with that, he isn't talking much to anyone," Carlos said sadly.

"What do you mean?" James asked.

"He didn't talk at all last night and not much this morning. I mean, he talked to me a little, but that was pretty much it."

"It could be the medication," Logan told him.

"Maybe," Carlos said doubtfully.

∞

The boys continued with their day, checking in with one another after each class. They hadn't found who it was that left the note in Logan's locker, so they were keeping a close eye on one another.

When it was time for last period, Logan took a deep breath and walked into his English class.

He made his way to his desk and sat down. A moment later, he felt a hand on his shoulder. "It's okay," Jason said.

Logan looked at him and nodded. "Thanks Jason."

The class seemed to drag, and Logan found his thoughts drifting. His eyes would wander to Kendall's empty seat and he wondered how his friend was doing. He tried to pay attention as Mr. Lawrence gave the reading assignment, and was grateful when the bell rang.

"Logan, can I see you after class please?" Mr. Lawrence asked.

Logan nodded and remained in his seat as the other students left. "I'm sorry, Mr. Lawrence. I know I was kind of zoning out," Logan said apologetically.

"It's alright, Logan, I know this whole thing has been unnerving for you. I was just going to ask if you would prefer that I just give you your assignments and you can spend final period in the library. At least until things are closer to normal for you."

Logan sighed in relief. "That would be incredibly helpful. I'm just having a hard time concentrating."

"I've already cleared it with Principal Lane, and all you need to do is sign in and out with the librarian," Mr. Lawrence told him.

"Thank you so much," Logan said.

"You're welcome. If you need any help, just check with me at the end of final period and we can go over the material."

"I will thank you again," Logan said as he got up and ran to find his friends.

He met up with James and Carlos at his locker and they headed over to Carlos' house.

∞

Sally arrived at the Garcia's about one. Antonio answered the door. "Hi Sally."

"Hey Boss. How did things go last night?"

"About as well as can be expected, I guess. Kendall's upstairs. He was sleeping last I checked. Jen and Sylvia ran over to Jen's house and then to run some errands. Jen and the kids are going to stay here for a couple of days and she needed to get some things for them."

"How's he doing?" Sally asked.

Antonio sighed. "I honestly don't know. It seems like we took a huge step backwards. I had a long talk with Jen, I had her listen to the recording Kendall made and read the statement sheet. She may not have been totally ready for all of that, but she needs to know what Kendall went through before she can begin to understand how to help him."

Sally nodded in agreement.

"I'm really worried about Kendall. Right now, he isn't speaking much at all. Last night, in the hospital, I woke up because the monitors were going off. He had gotten out of bed and we found him sleeping on the bathroom floor. This morning, Sylvia went up to get his breakfast tray and he wasn't in the bedroom. We checked all the rooms upstairs and found him curled up in the back of Carlos' closet, sound asleep."

"Damn, he was doing so well the other day when I spoke with him. Has he said anything about what happened in Graham's office?" Sally asked.

Antonio shook his head. "I don't know. He is so confused right now. I'm not sure he remembers much. Dr. Davidson said he could still be feeling the effects of the medication and the literature he sent home says that Lorazepam can cause short-term memory loss, that's why they use it as a sedative before surgeries."

"Well that's just great. Speaking of Graham, we heard from the other three families and they will help as long as the DA can get the waivers they signed revoked. Ryan doesn't think it should be too hard, considering the circumstances. He's working on the legalities of it now," Sally told him.

"Good."

"I tracked down the two students who emailed Kendall and sent the names onto Janice Lane. She's going to have a nice long chat with them, and since Dylan Mason is on the football team, he'll be pulled and banned for the next year. Chelsie Cameron was out sick the day of the assembly, so I told Janice to use her judgement based on Chelsie's attitude when she speaks to her," Sally said.

"Thanks Sally, I can't tell you what it means to me knowing you've got my back."

Sally smiled. "Why don't I go see if Kendall will still talk to me?"

"Second door on the right," Antonio said.

She nodded and headed up the stairs.

∞

Sally knocked on the door and slowly opened it. Kendall was curled up on the bed asleep, so she knocked a little louder. "Hey kiddo," she called out. Kendall opened his eyes. "Is it okay if I come in?"

He nodded and sat up.

"Hell of a couple of weeks, huh?"

Kendall nodded again, not really looking at her.

"So, do you want to talk for a while?"

He shook his head, still not looking up.

"Okay, you don't have to. I do need to ask you a couple of things, so maybe you could just nod or shake your head?"

He sighed and nodded.

"Do you remember what happened in Graham's office yesterday?"

Kendall shook his head no.

"Nothing at all? Not going there or him giving you an injection?"

He shook his head again but rubbed his arm where he had received the shot.

"Is your arm bothering you?"

He nodded.

"Is that the arm he gave you the shot in?"

Kendall shrugged.

"Can I see it?"

He sighed and held his arm up to her.

She smiled and held his hand for a moment before pushing up his sleeve.

"Oh honey." She winced as she saw the dark bruise at the injection site on his bicep. Then she saw another bruise that encircled his arm just above the elbow. She could clearly make out marks of individual fingers.

Sally held his hand for a moment. "Kendall, I need to take a picture of these bruises, okay? Nothing else, just your arm, so we can use it as evidence against Graham."

Kendall pulled his arm away and shook his head no.

"Honey, please? I promise I won't take any other photos. We really need this to help stop him from hurting someone else."

Kendall didn't respond.

"We can put the pillow on your lap and you can lay your arm on it. That way all we see will be your arm, nothing else."

Kendall closed his eyes and then nodded.

Sally pulled out her small digital camera and laid a pillow across Kendall's legs. He pushed his sleeve up and he laid his arm across it.

"I'm just going to turn your arm a little so I can get a good picture, okay?"

He nodded and she angled his arm so that she could get a picture of both bruises.

"I'm going to take one more, a close-up of the finger marks, and then we'll be done."

She quickly took the picture and pulled Kendall's sleeve down. "Thank you. I know that was hard, but you did great," she said as she put the camera away.

"So, you aren't talking too much. Is your throat hurting?"

He shook his head no.

"Just not in the mood?"

Kendall shrugged.

"Okay, you don't have to talk. I don't suppose you've had a chance to take any pictures of your own?"

He shook his head.

"Well, that's understandable. However, now I am going to give you an assignment. I want you to take at least ten photos by tomorrow afternoon. They can be of anything. I'll be giving the other boys a project too, and they know that they're not supposed to take your picture. I didn't tell them why."

Kendall nodded.

"Are you still having bad dreams? Antonio said they found you asleep in the closet this morning."

Kendall bit his lower lip and nodded.

"Do you remember them at all?"

He didn't respond.

"Maybe just a little...?" Sally prodded.

He gave a slight nod.

"Are they about Deesie?"

He nodded.

"Any about what happened yesterday?"

Kendall shrugged.

"Kendall, are you mad at your mom for what happened yesterday?"

He looked at her and shook his head.

"Are you angry with yourself?"

He looked down and didn't respond.

"I want you to listen to me, none of what happened with Deesie or Graham is your fault. They're both solely to blame for their actions, and I don't want you to start believing that you had it coming or that you in anyway encouraged their behaviour. Deesie was a sadistic psychotic, and because he's dead, there's no way of knowing why he chose you. It could be as simple as you asking for more time for your assignment and he felt a connection because you needed something from him. By the way, you needing that time was for a very legitimate reason that every other teacher understood."

Kendall just shrugged.

"As for Graham, he's victimized other families with his so-called treatments and will be held accountable for what he's done. We have four families who have come forward that settled out of court with him. He's not going to get away with this anymore."

Kendall just sat there, looking at the window.

"Okay kiddo, I'll let you get some more rest. If you need anything, call me anytime, even if it's just to know there's someone on the other line."

Kendall nodded. "Thanks," he whispered.

She smiled. "I'll stop by tomorrow and check on you."

He nodded.

∞

Sally went downstairs. "Well?" Antonio asked.

She shook her head. "I talked. He either nodded or shook his head no. The only thing he said was thanks, when I told him to call me if he needed anything."

"Damn it," Antonio said.

"He's been having nightmares about Deesie and I think he's remembering them, that's why he's hiding. I think he's sleepwalking, trying to get away. He doesn't remember what happened with Graham, but did you see his arm?" she asked.

"No, why?" Antonio asked.

She pulled out the camera and showed him the photos she took.

Antonio looked at them. "I didn't even notice those while we were at the hospital."

"You were a little preoccupied. There is a positive side to these bruises, we can now add assault to the charges and we have the proof," she pointed out.

"True, I'll be glad when we get the green light from Ryan and we can get this over with," Antonio said.

"Me too."

"Hey, let me make you some lunch. I need to get Kendall to eat too," he said, walking into the kitchen.

"Sounds good," Sally said, following him. "By the way... Did I mention that we got a call from one Dr. Richard Graham last night?"

"No... Is this something I NEED to hear?"

"Only for amusement's sake. It seems someone paid his car a visit yesterday and left some balloons and a cake for him," Sally told him. She decided to omit the part about the tires, as there wasn't any real damage.

"This was bad, why?"

"Apparently there was a message on the cake and it freaked him out a bit."

"What was the message?"

"Be very afraid." Sally smirked.

"Sounds like good advice to me," Antonio said, smiling at her.

"That's what I thought. Apparently, he thinks otherwise. What can you do? Clearly some people just don't like getting advice from outside sources."

"Clearly," he agreed, handing her a plate with a roast beef sandwich.

"I'm going to take this up to Kendall," he said, picking up the tray.

"Why don't we eat upstairs with him? I don't like that he's starting to isolate himself," Sally said, grabbing the other plates.

"Good idea." He smiled.

∞

Half an hour later, they had finished their lunch. Kendall had eaten half of his sandwich and then fallen asleep. He hadn't said a word throughout the meal.

"I'm going to have to let the boys know that Kendall's sleepwalking so they can keep an eye on him at night," Antonio said.

"Maybe have them lock the bedroom door at night as long as they're in there with him," Sally suggested.

Antonio nodded.

"Hopefully Dr. Jenkins will be able to help him with all of this. I just hope he's willing to talk to her," Sally said.

"I know. Graham really set things back," Antonio said angrily.

"Don't worry, he'll get what's coming to him," Sally promised.

∞

Chelsea Cameron and Dylan Mason were waiting to see Principal Lane.

The intercom buzzed. "Tara, please send in Chelsea Cameron."

Tara smiled at Chelsea and opened the door for her, closing it after she entered.

"This is so stupid," Dylan complained.

"Maybe you should have thought about that BEFORE sending an email to Kendall Knight, and then again when you ignored the immunity offered at the assembly," Tara said firmly.

"Stupid little jerk got what was coming to him," Dylan muttered under his breath.

"What was that?" Tara asked.

"Nothing, Ms. Shipley."

"Dylan, just a friendly word of advice... lose the attitude BEFORE you speak with Principal Lane. She might be more willing to give you a break, especially considering your position on the football team, if you're actually sorry for what you did."

"Whatever," he said. If I get kicked off the team for this, that little smartass will pay, he thought to himself.

∞

Principal Lane was seated at her desk when Tara showed Chelsea in. She smiled at the girl. "Please have a seat. Chelsea, I understand that you were home sick the day of the assembly. Your mother confirms this, so if you're willing to apologize for your behaviour, then no further action will be needed."

"I am really sorry, Principal Lane. I don't know why I thought it was funny at the time, but it wasn't, and I feel really badly about it. I'll even apologize to Kendall in person. Everyone just..."

Janice smiled. "Chelsea, I do understand about peer pressure, but all of you need to realize just how cruel you were, and how much words can hurt."

"I do. I will NEVER do anything like that again. My parents even took the internet off of my laptop for the next month, not that I really feel like using it right now."

"Alright, I believe that you regret your actions, and since your parents are handling things on their end, we can afford to let it go this time. However, if there's another incident like this and you're involved, you will not be granted leniency again."

Chelsea nodded. "I understand, thank you."

"Alright, you can go back to your class now," Janice said, seeing the girl to the door.

"Dylan, please come in," Janice said and held the door as he walked into her office.

"Have a seat," she told him as she sat down at her desk. "So, do you want to explain why you didn't come forward when given the opportunity?"

He snorted. "Because I think what I do at home is my own business."

"Not when it involves bullying another student, it isn't," Janice said firmly.

"Whatever."

"Dylan, do you understand how much trouble you're in? You sent FOUR threatening and contemptuous emails to Kendall Knight. Not only will there be consequences here at school, but the police are also involved, and if they decide to pursue this, you can be charged."

"Only because that little freak's friend is the chief of police," he mumbled.

"That's enough. I will not tolerate name calling!" Janice sighed. "I'm sorry, Dylan, but since you obviously are unrepentant, I'm suspending you for two weeks and you are OFF the football team for the remainder of the year."

"You can't do that!" he yelled.

"I'm sorry, Dylan, but you've been given every opportunity to avoid this situation and you've made your choice. I'll be calling your parents and discussing this at length with them. I'll have your teachers put together your assignments for the next two weeks, and you'll be responsible for seeing that the work is done. You are excused," she said, standing up and walking to the door.

"This isn't over!" he fumed.

"Goodbye Dylan." Janice opened the door. "Tara, please notify Dylan's teachers that he'll need his assignments for the next two weeks."

"Right away," Tara said.

∞

The boys got to Carlos' house to find Sally sitting there, talking to Antonio.

"Hey guys. How was school?"

"Good." Logan smiled. James and Carlos both rolled their eyes.

"I'll give you some privacy." Antonio smiled and went to his study.

"So, yesterday was tough," Sally said.

They all nodded.

"Anyone want to talk about it?"

"It's just a lot to try and understand," Logan said.

"I know it is. Carlos, your dad tells me you handled the call from Kendall very well. You stayed calm and relayed the information that you got from Kendall to James. Antonio was very impressed with the way all of you worked together to find Kendall, and then again at the hospital. You boys should be very proud of yourselves and each other. Not with just the way you handled yesterday, but throughout this whole ordeal."

They all smiled.

"Thanks Sally," James said.

"Is there anything else you boys want to talk about? Maybe about what you did yesterday afternoon?" she asked, smiling.

"Like what?" Logan said, his voice squeaking.

"W-We don't know what you're talking about," James stammered.

She just looked at them, arching an eyebrow. "Who let the air out of the tires?"

The boys looked at one another and Carlos raised his hand.

She nodded. "The balloons and cake?"

"Uh..." James started.

"Never mind let me guess... Your mom?"

The boys looked at each other, unwilling to inform on Mama D.

"Anything else I should know?"

"Like what?" Logan said, his voice still breaking.

She looked at him and James. "Well, while Carlos let the air out of the tires, what were you two doing?"

"I kind of replaced his windshield wiper fluid with Kool-Aid," James admitted.

She nodded, trying not to smile. "What kind?"

"Red raspberry."

"Good choice," she said as she looked at Logan. "And you?"

"I kind of... disconnected his tail lights," he told her.

"Is that all?" she asked them.

They nodded.

"But we didn't do anything that actually damaged his car," Carlos pointed out.

"We just wanted..." James said.

She nodded and patted him on the shoulder. "So, I have an assignment for you. I want you each to take at least ten pictures of your favourite things."

"Wait, we're not in trouble?" Carlos asked.

"For what?"

"But we just told you..." Logan said.

"Hey, I'm off duty and I'm actually amazed at your restraint. I probably would have done a lot more," she said.

"Like what?" Carlos asked curiously.

"Well, not that I would EVER admit to doing anything, like say, taking a piece of fish and wrapping it around a chunk of onion and securing it in someone's tailpipe with some netting and tape. I definitely would not tell you to make sure it's a small piece so that it doesn't block the exhaust. Or that after someone has been driving for say, half an hour, they start smelling cooking fish, and after a while, it smells like rotting fish."

All three boys looked at her in shock.

"Sally, I LOVE you!" Carlos said, throwing his arms around her.

Sally smirked and hugged him back.

Chapter 61 ~ Bloody Nose

Tara knocked on Janice's door after Dylan left. "Come in," Janice said wearily.

"That wasn't pleasant," Tara commented.

"No, it wasn't. I need to call Antonio. I think we know who it was that left the note in Logan's locker."

"Do you think Jason's involved? He and Dylan are buddies."

"I know, but Jason seems to have done a complete turnaround. I hate to think he'd still be involved in this," Janice said.

"I hope not. He seemed genuinely remorseful when he heard about Kendall. All of his teachers have reported he's doing better in his classes, and Coach Williams says he's been helping him with strategies and coaching the junior players on the football team," Tara told her.

Janice smiled. "At least one good thing has come of this, then."

"It could be Dylan's angry about Jason's change of heart. He and Todd Rickard were pretty tight with Jason, and now..." Tara said.

"Did Todd send an email to Kendall?"

"Yes, but he took advantage of the immunity."

"I'll give Antonio a call and talk to him about this. I warned Dylan there was a chance the police would get involved. Maybe he should talk to Dylan's parents—it might have more impact coming from Antonio," Janice said.

"The Masons seem like nice people. They always show up for school functions and games. They even volunteered to work a booth this Halloween for the band fundraiser," Tara said.

"Alright, can you get me both the Mason and Rickard home numbers, please?" Janice asked.

"Right away." Tara smiled and went to pull up the information on her computer.

∞

Sally was just finishing up with the boys, when Sylvia, Jen, and Katie came in.

"Hi Sally! Can I steal the boys to help bring in the groceries?" Sylvia asked.

"Absolutely. I was just getting ready to take off. When did you boys want to meet again?"

"We have practice tomorrow, which we can't miss, so Friday?" Logan asked.

"Friday it is then. Here or somewhere else?"

"I think here is fine. In fact, why don't you stay for dinner afterwards?" Sylvia suggested.

"That's sounds great, thanks! I'll see you all on Friday then." She smiled and walked out with the boys.

"I'm going to go see Kendall," Katie said, running up the stairs. Katie checked Carlos' room and didn't see him, so she opened the guest room door and found him sleeping soundly.

"Kendall, wake up! I missed you!" she said as she ran over and jumped on the bed next to her brother.

"Kendall!" she called. Not thinking about it, she decided to wake him the way she had always done and jumped on him. "Kendall, wake up!"

Kendall woke up screaming, "NO! GET OFF ME!" He threw his hands up to keep whoever was on him away, catching Katie in the face. She fell back off the bed while Kendall scrambled off the other side and crawled under it, hiding his head in his arms and shaking.

Jen and the boys were out getting the last of the grocery bags, while Sylvia and Antonio were talking and putting away groceries in the kitchen.

They heard Kendall scream, a thump, and then Katie scream.

"Oh no," Antonio said as he ran up the stairs with Sylvia right behind him. Katie was already in the hallway, holding her bleeding nose. "Baby, what happened?" Sylvia asked as she pulled the little girl into the bathroom.

"It's my fault, I scared him," Katie cried.

Antonio went in the bedroom and didn't see Kendall. He saw the blanket and pillow on the floor. "Kendall, where are you?"

He heard a small whimper, and looking under the bed, saw Kendall curled up in a tight ball.

"Kendall, it's okay, you're safe here." Not getting a response, he tried to reach for the boy, but decided against grabbing him. Antonio pushed the bed so he could reach Kendall, and knelt down next to him. "Mijo, it's alright it was just Katie. She didn't mean to scare you." He reached out and touched Kendall's shoulder. When he didn't pull away, pulled the boy up into his arms and held him.

∞

Jen and the boys came in and heard Katie crying.

"Katie?" Jen said as she rushed up the stairs. She saw Sylvia and Katie in the bathroom, Sylvia holding a damp washcloth to Katie's nose.

"Oh my God! What happened?" Jen asked.

"I'm okay, mom, really."

"Katie, what happened?" Jen asked again.

"I scared Kendall. He was sleeping and I jumped on him... I forgot," Katie said, her brown eyes welling with tears.

"Oh Katie," Jen said, hugging her daughter. "Let's go get some ice on that."

Katie nodded and she and Jen went downstairs.

The boys had followed Jen up and heard what happened. James looked in the guest room and saw Antonio holding Kendall, trying to wake him up slowly.

"Is he okay?"

"I think so," Antonio said.

"Why is the bed over there?" Carlos asked, noticing that it was now against the closet door.

"He was under the bed when I found him. It was the only way I could get him out," Antonio explained. "Logan, can you go check on Katie?" Logan nodded and went downstairs to check on the little girl.

Sylvia went into the guest room. "How is he?"

Antonio shook his head. "Did Katie say what happened?"

"She was excited to see him, and when he didn't wake up when she called him, she jumped on him."

"Is she alright?"

"Just a bump on the nose, it's already stopped bleeding. He's going to feel terrible when he realizes what happened," Sylvia said.

"I know. James, Carlos can you push the bed back this way so I can get him up on it?"

The boys nodded and together got the bed back into place. Antonio lifted Kendall up off the floor and laid him on the bed, covering him.

He sat next to the teen. "Mijo, can you wake up? Kendall, I need you to wake up now," Antonio said.

Kendall groaned and covered his eyes with his hand.

"Boys, stay with him. I'm going to see what I can give him for pain," Antonio instructed as he went to find the literature on Lorazepam.

"Carlos, can you turn down the light?" James asked.

Carlos nodded and dimmed the overhead and went to sit on the other side of Kendall. "It's okay, buddy. Papi will get you something for your head."

Kendall started shaking, and James sat closer and pulled him up, so his head was resting on his chest. "It's okay. Do you know what happened?"

"Dream... someone on me... couldn't breathe. My head hurts," Kendall whispered.

"I know, Papi's getting you something to make it better," James said, looking at Carlos.

Antonio came back in with some Tylenol. "Here Mijo, you can have this for the pain."

Kendall took the pills and James helped him steady the glass of water.

"Are you doing any better?" Antonio asked and Kendall nodded his head. "Okay, try and get some rest and I'll bring you up some dinner later," Antonio said.

Kendall nodded and closed his eyes.

"I'll stay with him," James said.

"I'll get started on my homework and then we can switch," Carlos said.

James smiled and nodded.

∞

In the kitchen, Katie kept fidgeting away from the ice pack that Logan was trying to hold against her nose.

"Katie what possessed you to jump on him?" Jen asked.

"I'm sorry, mom, I wasn't thinking about it. It's how I always wake him up," Katie said, still teary-eyed.

"I can't believe he hit you," Jen said, shaking her head.

"He didn't hit me. He was trying to push me away and accidentally hit my nose," Katie said, quick to defend her brother.

"Honey, I didn't mean it like that. I just mean that you need to be more careful around him. He's not himself."

"I know, mom! I said I was sorry."

"It's okay, Katie, we all have to be more careful right now," Logan said.

"I know," she said sadly.

Antonio came in. "How are you, little one?" Antonio asked, picking Katie up and looking at her nose. "Hmmm, a little puffy. Does this hurt?" he asked, gently tweaking her nose. She giggled and shook her head no. "Well, I think you need ice cream," he said.

She smiled broadly.

"How about AFTER dinner?" Jen said.

He looked at Katie. "No, I think I need to make an executive decision here and proclaim dessert before dinner tonight."

Jen and Sylvia looked at each other and shook their heads.

"What can we do? We have five normal-aged children and one OLD one," Sylvia said, poking Antonio in the ribs.

He just looked at Katie and winked.

Chapter 62~ Food Fight

While the kids and Antonio ate their ice cream, Sylvia and Jen made an actual meal for them, consisting of spaghetti with meatballs and a green salad.

The phone rang and Antonio answered. "Hello."

"Hi Antonio, it's Janice Lane. I think I might know who put the note in Logan's locker."

"Who?" he asked as he walked to his study.

"Dylan Mason. He logged onto one of the library computers on Monday morning during his study period. He sent four of the emails to Kendall and didn't take advantage of the immunity we offered. I spoke with him a little while ago and he was rather belligerent about the whole subject," she told him.

"How so?"

"Tara told me he was making comments while he was waiting to meet with me, and he told me he didn't believe he needed immunity because he can do whatever he wants from home. He was calling Kendall names, and when he refused to lose the attitude, I suspended him and pulled him from the football team. I thought I would see if you would rather be the one to speak to his parents. They seem to be very nice people. Tara says they're always at the games cheering Dylan on and helping out with school functions, so I'm not sure what Dylan's story is."

"Yeah, I do want to speak with them. Do you have their address?"

Janice gave it to him.

"I'll let you know what they say," he told her.

"Thank you, Antonio. How's Kendall doing?"

He told her about the setback they had with Dr. Graham.

She sighed. "Damn, well give him and Jen my best. Have her let me know before he comes back, so I can chat with his teachers about what we need to do to make his return easier."

Antonio smiled. "Will do. Thank you, Janice."

Antonio called John. "Hey, can you go with me to speak to one of the students' parents? I just got a call from Janice Lane, and she thinks she knows who put the note in Logan's locker."

"Sure thing. I'll swing by and pick you up in about twenty minutes."

"Thanks John." Antonio smiled as he hung up.

He went back into the kitchen. "Who was that?" Sylvia asked.

"Janice, she had some information about one of the students and she wants me to go speak to their parents. John will be here in about twenty minutes to pick me up."

"Good, then you can both have dinner before you go out," Sylvia said.

Antonio nodded. "I'm going to run up and change into my uniform, since this is official business."

"Must be serious," Sylvia said.

"It is," he said, giving her a quick kiss before heading upstairs.

He popped his head in to check on Kendall. "How are you two doing up here?"

"Okay. He's sleeping again."

"Dinner will be ready soon. I have to go out for a little while, so do you think you can get him to eat something?" Antonio asked.

"Sure thing, Papa G." James smiled.

"James, just so you know, I'm really proud of you, son. You've all been so incredible throughout this whole thing."

James smiled. "Thanks Papi, that really means a lot."

Antonio smiled back and then went to change.

∞

Bennet knocked on the Garcia door and Carlos answered. "John!" he yelled, hugging the man.

"Carlos... can't breathe," he said, hugging the boy back.

"Sorry, we're just getting ready to eat. Mami and Mama K made spaghetti."

"That sounds good." John smiled.

"John, how's your head?" Sylvia asked, giving him a kiss on the cheek.

"My head's fine, but I think Carlos cracked a rib. That kid can hug." He smiled.

"Yes he can. Come in and grab some dinner before you go out," she said.

"Hey John," Antonio said while coming down the stairs.

"Hey, so who are we going to talk to?"

"Dylan Mason's parents. I'll tell you more on the way."

Sylvia grabbed both men by the arms and lea them into the dining room. "Sit and eat first."

"Have I mentioned how much I LOVE your cooking?" John said as Sylvia set a plate in front of him.

"Hey John, did you tell her about Samson yet?" Antonio asked.

John choked on a bite of food. "NO!"

"Who's Samson?" Sylvia asked.

"No one, no one at all," John insisted, glaring at Antonio.

Everyone looked at Antonio, curious now.

"I'll tell you later, honey," Antonio said as he started eating his dinner.

"In that case, I'm going to need seconds," John declared, watching his partner closely.

Antonio just looked at him and smirked.

After they finished eating, the two men got ready to leave.

"Logan, can you take a tray up for James and Kendall? James is going to try and get him to eat something," Antonio asked.

"Sure thing, Papa G," Logan said and went into the kitchen to fix a couple of plates.

Antonio and John headed out. "I'll be home late, honey. I'm not sure how long this is going to take," Antonio said, kissing Sylvia goodbye.

"Bye John." She smiled.

"Bye... Hopefully I'll see you later," he said, kissing her on the cheek and glaring at Antonio again.

"You will be telling me what this is about," she stated to her husband. He just smiled and walked out with his partner.

"Just so you know... you suck," John told his partner as they got into the car.

Antonio just laughed.

∞

They pulled up to the Mason house about ten minutes later. Antonio had brought the emails Dylan had sent to Kendall as well as the note from Logan's locker.

He knocked on the door and Lydia Mason answered.

"Hello. Can I help you?" she asked, looking at the two officers.

"Mrs. Mason, we need to speak with you about Dylan," Antonio said.

She sighed and stepped aside. "Please, come in."

She called her husband. "Ted, the police are here to discuss Dylan."

Ted Mason came in from the kitchen looking tired. "What has he done this time?"

"Mr. Mason, did Dylan discuss with you what happened at school today?"

"He said he's been suspended and taken off the football team. He was angry, and that's all he would say. I was going to call and speak with Principal Lane tomorrow to find out the whole story," he said.

"Were you aware Dylan was one of the students that sent Kendall Knight emails regarding the Mr. Deesie matter?" Antonio asked.

Lydia nodded. "Principal Lane told us, but Dylan refused to apologize. We told him this would happen, but he wouldn't listen."

Antonio handed them the copies of the emails, as well as a copy of the note.

Ted Mason took them and read them, shaking his head. "I don't know what's wrong with the boy. We've tried everything. We've taken him to three different counselors, tried positive reinforcement, grounding, taken away privileges—nothing has helped. He's gotten so big in the last year that, quite frankly, he scares me. I just don't know what to do anymore," he said apologetically.

"Where is he now?" Bennet asked.

"He's over at his friend Todd's house," Lydia told him.

"Todd Rickard?" Antonio asked.

She nodded.

"Alright, does Dylan have a laptop, or does he use a home computer?" Antonio asked.

"He has his own laptop, and you can have it," Ted said.

"We have your permission to go through it?" Antonio asked.

"Yes. In fact, if you want to, you can go through his room," Ted told him.

Antonio looked at Bennet and nodded.

"I'll show you," Lydia said, leading them upstairs.

She opened the door, which had a sign saying, "STAY OUT... THIS MEANS YOU!" on it.

"I'll leave you to it," she said and went back downstairs.

"Charming," John muttered as he looked at the walls covered in posters of half-naked girls with crude comments written on them, and others of what looked like modern day monsters killing people.

Antonio opened the laptop and turned it on while John went through the bookshelves and then Dylan's dresser.

"Nothing here," he said as he went to look over Antonio's shoulder.

"This kid is seriously disturbed, look at these websites," he said, scrolling through the history.

"Three on serial killers, five on white power, one on adult porn. How the hell is he able to get into these sites?" Antonio asked.

"Because all you have to do is click the button that says you're an adult. If they're free they don't actually make you prove it," John said.

"Okay, let's take this to Sally and have her check it thoroughly. Did you check the closet or bed yet?"

"Not yet," John said as he opened the closet door.

Antonio went over to the bed and looked under, but there was nothing there. He checked in between the mattresses and found the usual magazines that so many teen boys think their parents don't know about. He pushed them around, but found one didn't move and he pulled it out. In between the pages was a hunting knife wrapped in a cloth.

"Why do you think he's hiding this?" Antonio asked.

John looked over. "Something to ask him about."

They heard yelling and Dylan came bursting into the room. "What do you think you're doing in my room?"

The kid was big, about 6'2 and definitely had a football player's build. Antonio could understand why his parents were afraid of him. However, he was no match for the two police officers and Dylan was smart enough to realize that.

"Perhaps you can tell me why you have this hidden in your mattress?" Antonio asked, holding up the knife.

"That's mine!" Dylan yelled.

"Yeah genius, we figured that. Now ANSWER the question," Bennet said.

Mr. Mason had come in. "Where did you find that? That's my grandfather's antique Buck Knife. It was locked in a safe box."

"Well, apparently Dylan found a way to get it. It was hidden under his mattress. We'll need to take this in for evidence, but I'll see that it gets back to you," Antonio told him.

"Dylan, what were you thinking?" Ted asked his son.

"They're framing me. They must have found it and planted it there," Dylan claimed.

"How exactly could we have done that?" John asked him.

"I don't know, but you did!" the teen yelled.

"You either calm down and answer my questions here, or I take you in and you can answer them at the station," Antonio told him firmly.

"What questions?"

"Let's start with the emails you sent to Kendall Knight. Why did you send them?" Antonio asked.

Dylan laughed. "Because the little freak deserved it, but you should already know that. Isn't your kid one of his friends?" the boy taunted.

Antonio took a deep breath. "Did you put a note in Logan Mitchell's locker on Monday?"

"What note?" Dylan asked smugly.

"Garcia, give him a break. There is no way Dylan here could have written that note. Too many big words," Bennet said.

Dylan flashed him a dirty look. "Goes to show what you know. I have a B average in English."

"So you admit you wrote it, then?" John asked.

"I..." Dylan realized his mistake too late.

"Your parents have given us permission to take your laptop. If we find ANYTHING on it that even sounds remotely threatening, I will be hauling your butt in and charging you. Do you understand me?" Antonio said through gritted teeth as he stood, almost nose to nose with the teen.

Dylan was smart enough to take a step back as he realized he might have pushed things too far.

"I ASKED you a question," Antonio said quietly.

Dylan nodded.

"Good. Mr. and Mrs. Mason, I am very sorry about all of this. You'll be hearing from my office in the next couple of days, and I'll get your grandfather's knife back to you," Antonio said as he walked out of the bedroom.

Bennet smirked at Dylan as he followed his partner down the stairs.

"Can you believe that kid?" Bennet asked Antonio as they drove to the station.

"No, I really can't," Antonio said.

∞

Logan took the tray up to the guest room. "Hey buddy, dinner," he told James as he set the tray on the nightstand.

James smiled. "Thanks, that smells really good." He gently shook Kendall. "Time for dinner, Kendall."

Kendall opened his eyes and looked around confused.

"How's your headache?" Logan asked.

"Okay."

"You need to eat something," James told him.

Kendall shook his head.

"Well, you can either eat it on your own, or I can chew it up and feed it to you," James said.

Logan looked at him. "Gross. Were you watching NatGeo again? Because that's the only time you come up with stuff like that."

James smiled. "It was the only thing on and I couldn't reach the remote."

Logan looked at Kendall. "Just take a few bites, okay? Because I really don't want to see him try that."

Kendall smiled at him and then got a strange look on his face. "Where's Katie? I thought I heard her crying earlier. Was it a dream?"

Logan looked at James. "Um, she's fine. She's downstairs finishing her homework with Carlos."

Kendall saw the look pass between his friends. "What's wrong?"

"Nothing, you just need to eat so you can take your antibiotic," James said as he set the tray on Kendall's lap.

"I want to see Katie," he said, suddenly worried.

"After you eat we'll go downstairs and you can see everyone," Logan said.

Kendall looked at him suspiciously and took a couple of bites. James ate his dinner quickly.

"I'm going down for seconds, be right back." James rushed downstairs. "Katie, let me see your face for a minute."

"Why?" she asked.

"Because Kendall remembers hearing you cry, and if he realizes he hurt you... Damn, there's a bruise."

"Language," Jen said from the kitchen where she was doing the dishes.

"Sorry."

"What's going on?" Sylvia asked.

"Kendall remembers hearing Katie cry, and if he sees this bruise, he's going to freak."

"Honey, if he already remembers that much, then he's going to remember the rest. If he asks, I think it'd be best just to tell him what happened," Sylvia told him.

"Are you sure we can't just cover it up or something?" James asked.

"Then when he does remember, he'll know we lied to him," Sylvia pointed out.

"I guess, but..."

"It'll be fine. It was an accident after all."

"Try this," he said, pulling Katie's hair over her face.

"James, really?" Sylvia asked.

"Okay... Although I think she can totally make that look work. Wasn't there an actress a really long time ago who use to wear her hair like that?"

"Yes, but Katie isn't an actress, and Veronica Lake did NOT wear her hair over her nose, only over one eye. You know, so she could still see," Sylvia told him.

James sighed. "Do you have his antibiotic?"

Sylvia nodded and went into the kitchen to get it.

James tried pulling Katie's hair down, just a little.

"James..." Sylvia said.

"Just helping her straighten it," he said as he finger combed the long brown locks.

"Here," Sylvia said, handing him the pill and a glass of milk.

"Thanks." He smiled and headed back upstairs.

"I don't want Kendall to feel bad," Katie said.

"Oh Mija, it'll be okay," Sylvia said, hugging her.

∞

James walked back into the guest room, where Logan was trying to convince Kendall to eat a little more.

"Here's your antibiotic," James said, handing the pill and milk to Kendall.

"Thanks," he said quietly.

"Try and eat a little more," James said, sitting down next to him.

Kendall shook his head.

"Look, it's your favourite, so eat four more bites, okay?"

Kendall took another bite and pushed the tray away.

"That was only one," James said, pushing the tray back towards Kendall.

Kendall looked at him and pushed it away again.

James raised an eyebrow, reached down, took a bite of the spaghetti, and made a show of chewing it.

"Take another bite, or I FEED you this one," he said, pointing to his mouth and leaning towards Kendall.

Kendall leaned back into the pillows and pushed the tray back towards James.

Logan watched. Interested to see how this was going to play out. He was pretty sure if James actually tried putting the pre-chewed food in Kendall's mouth, he would puke.

James grabbed a fork, spit the food out onto it, and held it towards Kendall.

"Your choice," he said as he pushed the tray back towards his friend.

Kendall quickly reached over, pulled the fork down, and released it, and the food hit James in the face.

James sat there for a minute. "Huh... I did not see that coming."

Logan was holding his sides since he was laughing so hard.

James reached over, picked up a handful of spaghetti, and moved to shove it in Kendall's face, when Logan stopped him.

"James, not a good idea," he said, still laughing.

James looked at Kendall and back at Logan and mashed the spaghetti into Logan's face.

Logan stopped laughing. "That was so NOT cool!" he sputtered.

James was laughing at him so hard he fell off the bed.

"Not nice," Logan declared as he left the room and walked over to the bathroom to clean himself off.

∞

Carlos and Katie could hear laughter and went running upstairs. They saw Logan covered in spaghetti and started laughing.

"Oh yeah, real funny," he said, trying to get the spaghetti out of his hair.

James was still giggling on the floor and Kendall was shaking his head at them.

Sylvia and Jen had followed the sound of laughter to see what was going on and both women covered their mouths so they didn't laugh at poor Logan.

"FOOD FIGHT!" Carlos yelled.

"NO!" Sylvia said and grabbed her son before he could completely destroy the bedroom.

"Aww, mom," Carlos whined.

"No!" Sylvia repeated. "Go downstairs and get the basket with the cleaners." Carlos pouted. "NOT going to work, now go!" Sylvia ordered.

A few minutes later, Logan was spaghetti free and the bedroom was cleaned up.

Antonio got home. "Hey, where is everyone?"

"Up here, honey," Sylvia called down.

"What happened here?" he asked.

"HE thought it would be funny if I wore Kendall's dinner," Logan said, pointing at James.

"Hey, HE started it," James said, pointing at Kendall. "If you'd let me hit him with the spaghetti, YOU wouldn't have gotten it."

"YOU are the one who tried to feed him chewed up food," Logan pointed out.

"Only because he wouldn't eat."

"Really?" Logan said.

"Boys! First, chewed up food, really? Second... I can't even think of a second after the first." Antonio chuckled.

No one had noticed Kendall get up and walk over to Katie. He put his hand on her shoulder and looked at her. "What happened to your face?"

Suddenly everyone was quiet.

"It was an accident," she said.

Antonio caught Jen's eye. She nodded and gave a small gesture to Sylvia. Sylvia and Jen grabbed the boys and pulled them out the door.

"Katie, I hit you, didn't I? It wasn't a dream!"

She threw her arms around his waist. "No, it was my fault, I jumped on you when you were sleeping and scared you. I fell off the bed, that's all!"

He started shaking and tried to pull away from her, but she wouldn't let go. "Katie, let me go."

"No, I won't! It wasn't your fault, Kendall, it was an accident!"

"Katie, please... I'm going to be sick!"

Antonio pulled Katie away as Kendall ran for the bathroom, slamming the door behind him.

Antonio picked Katie up. "James!"

James came running up the stairs.

"Take her to her mother," Antonio said, handing a sobbing Katie over to James.

Katie wrapped her arms around James' neck and continued crying as he took her downstairs.

Antonio knocked on the bathroom door. He could hear Kendall retching on the other side. "I'm coming in."

He opened the door and found Kendall throwing up what little he had eaten. He sat next to the boy and rubbed his back until he finished.

He got a cup of water for Kendall. "Drink this."

Kendall took a sip. He was shaking and started rocking back and forth.

Antonio put his arms around him and pulled him over. "Mijo, it was an accident. She wasn't thinking and jumped on you. You both landed on the floor. It was no one's fault."

Kendall wasn't really hearing him, all he could think of was that he hurt his baby sister. The sister he had always vowed to protect. Her face was bruised and her nose was swollen. He put his head in his hands and pulled at his hair.

Antonio took the boy's face in his hands. "Kendall, you didn't hurt her, it was an accident."

Kendall wouldn't look at him, but he wrapped his arms around Antonio's waist, holding on tightly. "What's wrong with me?"

Antonio hugged the boy back. "There's nothing wrong with you, Mijo, you just need time to heal."

He sat there and held his godson until he was asleep, and then he picked him up and carried him to Carlos' room. He laid him on the bed and covered him up with the blankets. He brushed Kendall's bangs back and sighed. "Things will get better, I promise."

Chapter 63~ Adjustments

Antonio closed the bedroom door and went downstairs. Everyone was sitting in the living room quietly watching TV.

"How is he?" Jen asked. Katie was sitting in her lap, her head on her mother's shoulder.

"He's sleeping," Antonio said, turning off the TV. "There are some things we need to talk about and now seems as good a time as any."

"What is it?" Jen asked.

Antonio thought about it for a moment, trying to decide the best way to explain it.

"First..." he said as he reached over and took Katie from her mom and looked at her, "you are NOT to blame for what happened. It's not your fault, and it's not Kendall's fault. We just have to be patient and understand that some bad things have happened and Kendall dreams about them. When he's sleeping, he doesn't know what's going on around him, and if we startle him, he gets frightened. He's starting to remember the dreams, and because of that, he's started sleepwalking, trying to get away. So, we need to be extra careful, making sure we lock the front and back doors, and remember NOT to grab him or startle him in any other way. We found him in the bathroom at the hospital last night and in the closet this morning."

He hugged Katie. "Are you doing better?"

She nodded and hugged him back.

"Why don't you go watch TV in my study? I need to talk to the boys for a minute," he said, putting her down.

Jen stood up and took Katie's hand. "Come on, honey, and then we need to get you ready for bed."

Katie sniffled and took her mom's hand and they left the room.

"I think it's time for you to know more about what happened when Kendall was with Deesie. Some of it will be difficult to hear, so if it gets to be too much, let me know. I think it's important that you know, so you can understand why he reacts the way he does."

The boys looked at one another and nodded.

Antonio went on to tell them about the motel manager Deesie had murdered, the shootings of Ranger Thompson and Bennet. How Kendall had escaped twice and how he had saved Antonio's life in the woods. He told them about the questions Kendall had answered on the statement sheet and stopped to give the boys a few moments to absorb it all.

Sylvia went over and sat between Carlos and Logan, both of whom had tears in their eyes. James just sat there quietly, his face pale and his jaw set. Antonio got up, sat between James and Logan, and put his arms around both boys.

"There's a little more, but if you want me to stop, I will."

"No, we need to hear everything," James said, the other two boys nodding in agreement.

Antonio took a deep breath. "Sylvia, I haven't told you or Jen about this yet. I don't think she can handle it right now."

Sylvia nodded. "Okay."

"After Deesie shot Ranger Thompson, he took Kendall to a motel room and took some photos of him. Some very BAD photos and he sent them to Principal Lane. That's why Sally told you not to take any pictures of him," Antonio explained.

Carlos started crying and buried his head in Sylvia's shoulder, who also had tears running down her cheeks. She pulled Carlos and Logan closer, both boys allowing themselves to be held.

James sat there for a moment before jumping up and running out the front door.

Antonio was right behind him. "James!"

James ran down the block and stopped at the corner. Antonio caught up with him and grabbed him. "James..."

"IT'S NOT FAIR! How can somebody DO something like that? Him and Graham and... How can people be so..."

Antonio wrapped his arms around the shivering teen. "I know, Mijo, it's not fair. There's no excuse for any of it, but Deesie is dead and Graham WILL be paying for what he's done."

James cried into Antonio's shoulder as they walked back to the house.

After Antonio and Sylvia got the boys calmed down, he told them about Dylan Mason.

"I want you boys to be very careful and stick together. He's been suspended, but I really don't trust him or his friend Todd Rickard," Antonio told them.

"They're Jason's football buddies," Carlos said.

'I know, but we don't have any reason to believe that Jason is involved in this anymore. If it turns out he is, we'll deal with him as well," Antonio promised.

The boys nodded.

"Do any of you have any questions?"

They all shook their heads no.

"Why don't you boys head on up to bed then? Kendall's in your bed Carlos, I don't want him alone," Antonio said.

"He won't be," James said as he walked upstairs.

Logan and Carlos followed him. "I'll be up in a little while to check on you," Sylvia said.

Sylvia went over to Antonio and hugged him. "We're going to have to tell Jen about everything sooner or later."

"I know," he said, kissing her forehead.

They went up about an hour later and found the boys had stationed themselves around the bed—James and Carlos on each side and Logan at the foot. If Kendall got up, one of them would know it.

∞

At about 4 am, Kendall heard a voice.

He felt someone pressing down on him, and a hand on his mouth. "Hello, sweetheart, what did I tell you about running away from me?" There were fingers around his throat and someone was squeezing. He gasped, trying to draw a breath and suddenly a mouth was on his. He gagged at the intrusion, trying to break free.

Kendall opened his eyes and no one was there. He climbed out of the bed and crawled to the closet door, trying to stay quiet.

Logan opened his eyes when he felt someone brush by him and saw Kendall crawl into the closet. He crawled after him and softly called him. Not getting a response, he looked in and saw Kendall curled up near the back, sound asleep. Not sure what to do, he decided to go in after his friend. He touched Kendall's shoulder and he pulled back a little but otherwise remained still. Logan pulled his blanket in and lay down next to Kendall, pulling the blanket over the both of them.

When James woke up a couple of hours later, he saw Kendall was gone. He sat up quickly, and looking around, saw that Logan was missing as well. He saw the closet door open and walked over. He smiled when he saw Logan curled up next to Kendall in the small space.

He shook Logan's foot. "Hey, everything okay?"

Logan yawned, and trying to stretch, realized where he was. "Yeah, he crawled in here a while ago. I didn't want to wake him up."

"Let's see if we can get him out."

Logan nodded and yawned again. "Kendall, it's time to get up," he said and gently shook his friend's shoulder.

"Hmmm?"

"Time to get up," Logan said, yawning again.

Kendall opened his eyes. "Where are we?"

"Carlos' closet," Logan said.

"Why?"

"You were sleep walking and kind of crawled in here," Logan explained.

"I don't remember."

"That's because you were asleep. Let's get out of here," Logan said.

Logan crawled out first and then helped Kendall out.

"Why don't you try and get some more sleep?" James suggested.

Kendall nodded and climbed back into the bed, his eyes closing as soon as his head hit the pillow.

Carlos woke up hearing the other boys. "Morning," he yawned.

"Morning Carlos," James and Logan said.

"I'm going to jump in the shower," Logan said, grabbing his backpack.

"I'll go start breakfast. Can you stay here with Kendall?" James asked Carlos.

Carlos nodded and sat on the bed next to his friend, and James headed downstairs.

Carlos sat there, thinking about what his dad had told him the night before and felt his eyes tear up again.

"I should have made you tell me that day. I should have made you stay with us. I'm so sorry," he whispered to Kendall.

He sat there, lost in his thoughts, when Logan came back in. "Carlos, are you okay?"

Carlos looked up and nodded.

"You don't look okay," Logan said.

"Just thinking."

Logan sighed and sat next to him. "I know, but we have to move forward. If you keep dwelling on everything, it's going to drive you crazy."

"I know, I just keep thinking about how scared he must have been."

Logan patted Carlos on the shoulder. "We can't do anything about that, but we can help him now. Why don't you go jump in the shower and I'll stay here?"

Carlos smiled, got up, and grabbed some clothes and went into the bathroom.

Logan sat next to Kendall and watched him sleep. "You will get better, we all will."

∞

Antonio woke up and got up quietly so Sylvia could sleep a little longer. He heard someone showering, looked in Carlos' bedroom, and saw Logan sitting next to Kendall.

"How did you boys sleep?"

Logan laughed a little. "Well, I slept in the closet for half the night."

"Kendall?"

Logan nodded. "There are times it's good to be short."

Antonio smiled. "I'll go get breakfast started. Let's see if we can get him to come down and eat today."

Logan nodded.

Antonio found James in the kitchen setting the table. "Good morning. How are you feeling?"

James shrugged. "Okay, I guess."

"It's a lot to deal with, I know," Antonio said, squeezing James' shoulder.

James nodded.

"So, what do we want for breakfast this morning? I can make almost anything," Antonio said.

"I'm fine with cereal," James said.

"Good, my specialty," Antonio said, pulling some boxes from the cupboard. "That... and toast."

James smiled and went to grab the milk from the refrigerator. He saw some fruit and pulled some strawberries out. "I think I'll make Kendall a smoothie. It might be easier to get him to drink one than to fight with him about eating again."

"Good idea. There are some bananas, and add some cream for calories," Antonio said, pulling out the small carton.

James smiled as he threw the concoction into the blender. When it was blended thoroughly, he poured it into a tall glass.

"Let's see if we can get him to come down. I think Jen said he has an appointment with Dr. Sharpe today anyway," Antonio told him.

James nodded and headed upstairs.

Carlos was now out of the shower and dressed. "Breakfast is ready." James smiled. He sat down next to Kendall. "Hey, it's time to get up. Time for breakfast."

Kendall groaned. "Not hungry."

"Too bad. I made you a smoothie. Now come on," James said, pulling the blanket off.

Kendall pulled the pillow over his head.

"Remember what happened the other day? I have no problem carrying you downstairs," James threatened.

"Go away," Kendall mumbled under the pillow.

"Last warning," James told him. Not getting a response, he put his arms under his friend and threw him over his shoulder.

"James, stop it!" Kendall squeaked.

James headed out the door with Kendall hitting him with the pillow. Carlos and Logan looked at each other and grinned, following their two friends downstairs. James delivered Kendall to the kitchen table and sat him on a chair. Kendall hit him with the pillow and he grabbed it.

"Breakfast?" Antonio smiled, setting the glass in front of Kendall.

Kendall blew his bangs out of his eyes and glared up at James.

"Hey, I warned you." He smiled, sitting down next to him.

Carlos and Logan sat down and the boys poured themselves some cereal and ate their breakfast.

James leaned over and whispered in Kendall's ear. "You don't have to eat, but at least drink that, okay? It's just fruit and milk, that way you can take your antibiotic."

Kendall looked at him and rolled his eyes, but drank a little of the smoothie.

"Are you feeling a little better today?" Antonio asked Kendall.

Kendall nodded.

"Good. Carlos, can you go knock on Jen's door so Katie can get ready for school?" Antonio asked.

"Sure thing," Carlos said and jumped up.

Kendall took another sip of his smoothie and then got up.

James grabbed his hand. "You need to finish this."

Kendall took a large sip and then pulled away.

James went to follow him, but Antonio put a hand on his arm. "It's okay, take the rest up to him in a minute."

"But..."

"James, it's okay."

James sat back down and nodded. He hated feeling so helpless, and he especially hated the feeling that Kendall was growing more distant with each passing day.

∞

Kendall went upstairs and closed the bathroom door. He sat on the floor, leaning against it, grateful that no one had followed him. He loved them all so much, but he didn't deserve everything they were trying to do for him. He was so tired, but no amount of sleep seemed to help.

He knew Deesie was dead, but he constantly felt his presence. He could hear his voice, the words, and the humming. He could feel his touch and it made him feel dirty and disgusting, and the memories made him want to vomit. Now he had hurt his sister and he was terrified he would hurt someone else. He was supposed to take care of them, protect them, and not hurt them. He felt completely useless. He sat there on the floor, just wanting it to all go away.

A few minutes later, James knocked on the bathroom door. "Kendall, are you okay?"

Not getting an answer, he knocked again. "Kendall... please let me in."

He tried the door and it was locked. Now he was worried. "Kendall! Open the door!" James pounded on the door. "Kendall!"

The handle turned and he pushed it open. Kendall was sitting on the floor. James knelt down next to him. "Are you okay?"

Kendall nodded. "Sorry, I just came in here because I didn't feel very well and I must have fallen asleep."

James grabbed him and hugged him tightly. "You scared me to death, don't ever do that again!"

Kendall hugged him back. "I'm sorry, James. Please don't cry."

"What? Who, me cry? Pshhhhhh," he said, still holding onto his friend. He rubbed his eyes on his arm. "I'm serious, don't EVER do that again. Are you feeling better now?"

Kendall nodded.

"Let's get you off the floor then," James said, pulling the smaller boy up with him.

"I need to shower," Kendall told him.

"Fine, but don't lock the door."

Kendall nodded and went to grab some clothes.

James took a deep breath and saw Antonio standing near the stairs. "Everything okay?" James nodded.

Antonio gave him a small smile and went back downstairs.

Chapter 64~ Enough Evidence at Last

Antonio walked back into the kitchen to find Jen and Katie sitting with Logan and Carlos.

"Good morning," he said, smiling as he kissed Katie on top of the head.

"Morning Papa G," Katie said.

"Good morning, Antonio. I thought I heard Kendall earlier. Did he eat?" Jen asked.

"No, but James fixed him a fruit smoothie and he drank a bit of that. James took the rest up to him. I think he's showering now."

"Hopefully Dr. Sharpe will have some ideas." Jen sighed.

"Jen, about the appointment... it might be a good idea if I go with you. If Kendall has a panic attack, you won't be able to hold him."

Jen smiled sadly and nodded. "I was going to ask you. I'm not even sure I should go."

"Yes, you should. Just be aware he might have some trouble going in and he may not want you in the room."

Jen nodded.

"Don't worry. He's known Anna Sharpe since he was four. It should be fine." Antonio said reassuringly.

"I hope so," Jen said.

∞

Upstairs, Kendall had finished showering and opened the door to find James waiting. "Thought you might need help with your shirt."

Kendall nodded. "Thanks."

James helped him pull the t-shirt over his head and went for his comb. Kendall put his hand up protectively on his head. "I can do it."

James smiled and nodded, but the minute Kendall removed his hand, James started combing out the blond locks.

Kendall sighed. "Owww."

"Conditioner," James said.

Kendall rolled his eyes and then smirked.

James noticed the look. "Don't even think about it," he said, pulling on a tangle.

"Ow!"

"You need a trim. If you want, I can do it tonight," James told him.

Kendall wasn't all that sure he wanted James whacking at his hair, but it was better than going in somewhere and having someone he didn't know touching him. "Maybe."

"There, all done. We need to get to school, but I'll see you this afternoon."

"Okay," Kendall said, going into the bedroom. Kendall pulled out his backpack with his schoolwork assignments and started on the next subject.

He was halfway through his social studies when Jen popped her head in. "Honey, we need to get ready to go. You have an appointment at ten with Dr. Sharpe."

Kendall shook his head.

"I know you don't want to go, but we need to get you checked out. We need to see if the pneumonia is clearing up and have her check your shoulder. Antonio is going to go with us, and

then I thought we could stop and get a burger and shake at the steak house. I need to check in, and we can sit in the banquet section."

Kendall sighed and then nodded.

Jen went to kiss his cheek but hesitated when he pulled back slightly. She smiled and kissed him on top of the head. "I love you, baby." She hurried downstairs before she started to cry.

Jen walked into the kitchen and Sylvia noticed the look on her face. "Are you okay?"

Jen nodded. "Just trying to remember that I need to go slowly."

"You're doing fine," Sylvia said.

"I hope so," Jen said.

∞

Kendall came downstairs. "You ready to get going?" Antonio asked.

Kendall nodded and pulled on his boots. Antonio helped him with his jacket and then put on his own. He grabbed Jen's coat and held it for her and the three of them left.

They arrived at Dr. Sharpe's office fifteen minutes later and walked into the building. Jen had already made sure the Appleton hospital had sent copies of Kendall's records to Dr. Sharpe, so she would be aware of what had happened, as well as letting her know about the incident with Dr. Graham.

Once they were in the office, Kendall took a seat furthest from the desk. He had his dark blue beanie pulled down as far as it would go without impeding his vision.

Antonio sat next to him as Jen signed him in.

She went and sat next to Antonio. "It should be just a few minutes."

Kendall's hands started clenching and unclenching, so Antonio took the hand closest to him and held it. A couple of minutes later, the nurse called Kendall's name and he just sat there.

"Come on, I'll go with you," Antonio said, pulling Kendall up. He wrapped his arm around the boy's shoulders and guided him through the doors. "It's okay. You've been coming here for years. Dr. Sharpe isn't going to hurt you," Antonio whispered.

The nurse smiled. "Okay, let's get your coat and boots off so we can get a weight."

Kendall looked at Antonio, who nodded. He helped the boy off with his jacket and Kendall pulled off his boots.

He stepped onto the scale and the nurse checked the balances and made a note. "Okay, let's get you into a room."

Kendall grabbed his boots and they followed her into an exam room.

"Have a seat," she said, patting the exam table.

Antonio helped him up on it and sat next to him. The nurse went to say something, but Antonio gave her a warning look.

She smiled and nodded. "Let's get your blood pressure and temperature."

Kendall shook a little, but Antonio stayed with him. The nurse smiled when she finished. "Dr. Sharpe will be right in."

"Thank you." Antonio smiled. "You doing okay?" he asked Kendall.

Kendall nodded.

Dr. Anna Sharpe came in a couple of minutes later. She was a tall woman in her late fifties, with shoulder length blonde hair streaked with grey. She had blue eyes that sparkled when she laughed. She was well loved by all her patients and had known the Knight's for almost ten years. Sylvia had recommended her to Jen and Will when their pediatrician had retired.

She smiled at Kendall. "I see we just need to give you a quick once over today. Make sure your lungs are clearing and check out an injured shoulder?"

Kendall nodded.

She looked at Antonio. "How's that boy of yours Antonio?"

"Carlos is fine, Anna. Thanks for asking."

She looked at Kendall. "Is it okay if I listen to your lungs?"

He nodded and she placed the stethoscope on his chest and then his back. "Well, you still have some congestion in there, so I think we'll be continuing with the antibiotics for a while. Now, can I check out your shoulder?"

Kendall looked at Antonio, who nodded and helped him pull up his shirt.

Dr. Sharpe was shocked to see all the bruises. Even though they were fading, they were still prominent on his pale skin. "So the left shoulder?"

Antonio nodded and she gently touched it.

Kendall pulled away. "Did that hurt?" she asked.

He shook his head.

"Okay, I should have warned you." She smiled. "Is it okay if I check it out now?"

Kendall took a deep breath and nodded. She gently palpated the area and could tell when she hit a tender spot.

"How far can you lift your arm?"

Kendall lifted it as high as he could before it started hurting.

"I see they sent home a shoulder stabilizer. Do you wear it?"

When he didn't answer, Antonio told her. "When he's up and around, he wears it. He hasn't been doing a whole lot the past couple of days."

"I want you to wear it for the next week, including at night. I know it's uncomfortable, but we need the muscles to start healing, which means you need to keep it still for now. We also need to get you in for some physical therapy. I'll give your mom the name of the therapist we use and she can call and make an appointment for next week."

Kendall nodded.

"You've also lost quite a bit of weight. You have lost nearly fifteen pounds, which is a lot for someone your age and build. Are you eating regularly?"

Kendall shook his head no.

"Do you get sick, or just no appetite?"

He shrugged, still not meeting her eyes.

"Okay, can you wait in here while I go write out your prescription and have a word with your mom?"

He nodded.

"Antonio..." she gestured for him to follow.

She asked the nurse to call Jen back.

"How long ago did he stop speaking?"

"Two days ago, after the incident with Graham," Antonio said.

"Is he speaking to anyone?"

"He talks to the boys, and he answers me when I ask him a question. Other than that, no. Last night was the first time I heard him speak a full sentence, and then nothing today."

Jen came in. "Hi Anna, how is he?"

"Hi Jen. First, I am very worried about the weight loss. If he doesn't start eating and gaining some weight, he is going to end up in the hospital. I am also concerned about the selective mutism he seems to be experiencing. You said you made an appointment with Dr. Jenkins for next week?"

Jen nodded, "It was the soonest she had available."

"Alright, see if the boys can keep him talking. Sometimes with selective mutism, the person will speak to certain people and no one else. For now, that's okay as long as he's talking to someone, and I would advise against pressuring him to speak. Dr. Jenkins should be able to help him with the rest. It's going to take time, but he's a strong boy." Dr. Sharpe smiled.

"What do I do about him not wanting to eat?" Jen asked.

"Let me talk to him. I think if we let him know where he'll end up, he might make more of an effort. I know he probably doesn't have an appetite, so try to get as many calories into him as possible. Maybe feed him several small meals throughout the day, instead of trying to get him to eat the traditional three meals."

"James made him a smoothie this morning and he drank most of that," Antonio said.

"That's perfect. Maybe add in a weight gain supplement, the kind they use for athletes who need to put on weight," Dr. Sharpe recommended.

"Good idea. I'll pick some up later today," Antonio told Jen.

"Okay, let me go chat with Kendall for a minute and I'll get the prescription written up for him," Anna said.

Kendall came out a couple of moments later and Antonio helped him on with his jacket.

"Let's go get some lunch." He smiled, putting his arm around the teen.

∞

Sally had tracked down the name of Dr. Graham's assistant, and Sheela Moore was now sitting at the station, waiting to be asked a few questions.

Sally smiled as she went into the interrogation room. She offered her hand. "Hello, my name is Officer O'Hara."

Sheela Moore shook her hand nervously. "What's this all about?"

"We need to ask you a few questions regarding Richard Graham."

"What about him?"

Sally went through the file she had brought in with her. "I understand you've been working with Dr. Graham for the last couple of years?"

Sheela nodded.

"You're a licensed nurse?"

Sheela nodded again.

"Are you aware of the laws regarding psychologists prescribing medications?"

The woman sighed. "Yes."

"So you know that Richard Graham has been prescribing these medications illegally?"

"Dr. Davis said we were to follow Dr. Graham's orders regarding prescriptions, and that he would take responsibility for it."

"Would you be surprised to find he's not taking responsibility?" Sally asked, looking at her.

When she didn't respond, Sally leaned forward. "Sheela, I believe you were just following orders, because you believed Dr. Davis and Graham were good people who would back up what they told you. The fact is, they aren't good people and they will throw you to the wolves to save their own skin."

"What am I supposed to do?" Sheela asked, tears in her eyes.

"Answer some questions truthfully and I'll speak to the DA about immunity."

Sheela took a deep breath. "What do you want to know?"

"Tell me about what he did to Kendall Knight on Tuesday."

Sheela looked like she might throw up. She had known what Dr. Graham was doing was wrong, but she needed her job. If word got out she had turned on a doctor, she would never work as a nurse again.

Sally watched the woman intently and knew she was struggling with doing the right thing and trying to salvage her career.

"If it helps, we already have a drug screen showing that Kendall was given a large dose of Lorazepam. That injection caused him to be rushed to the emergency room, where they had to place him on oxygen and give him something to counter the effects of the drug. I also have photos of the injection site where there is a large bruise. There were also bruises on his arm right above the elbow, clearly showing where fingers had held him tightly."

Sheela's face lost all colour and she started crying.

"So, I'm going to ask you one more time, what did Graham do to Kendall?"

Sheela took a deep breath. "He was speaking to Mrs. Knight in room three. He came out and told me to get Kendall and to tell him that his mother needed him and to bring him into room one. I went out into the waiting room and told him what Dr. Graham had said. He asked if

everything was alright and I told him that I thought so, but that it sounded urgent. He followed me back and we went into the room, and Dr. Graham handed me the syringe. He told me to be ready as Mrs. Knight had told him Kendall was becoming very unstable."

"Did you know what was in the syringe?"

Sheela nodded. "I watched him get the bottle from the cabinet."

"Are you aware Lorazepam injections are not intended for children under the age of eighteen, unless they're having a seizure?"

"No, I know it's used to stabilize someone suffering from an anxiety attack and as a pre-surgery sedative."

Sally nodded and made a notation. "What happened next?"

"Dr. Graham locked the door and Kendall asked him why. He told him because he didn't want him running away, because he wanted to talk to him. I could see Kendall was getting upset, the locked door seemed to set him off and he asked Dr. Graham to unlock it. When he refused, Kendall tried to get out the door, but Dr. Graham grabbed him and told him he needed to take his medicine like his mom wanted. He held his arm, and I gave him the injection. A couple of minutes later, Kendall collapsed and Dr. Graham went to get his mother." Sheela said, still crying.

"Okay."

"I thought he had Mrs. Knight's permission, but when she came into the room, she acted like she didn't know what was going on. Dr. Graham sent me out of the room then."

"Is that everything?" Sally asked.

"Yes, I think so."

"Let me speak to the DA and I'll be back in a few moments, alright?"

Sheela nodded.

Sally left the room and put in a call to DA Ryan. She waited a few minutes before going back in.

"Okay, DA Ryan has said to offer you a deal, it's a one-time offer and there are three conditions. First, you sign a statement with a transcription of what you just told me. Second, your license will be suspended for one year, at which time you will be allowed to take a reinstatement test before you're allowed to practice as an LPN again. Third, you're not to have any contact with Dr. Graham or anyone from the office regarding this case."

Sheela nodded. "I agree."

"I'll have them bring in the statement, and as soon as you sign it, you're free to go. I know this was hard for you, but I'm glad you chose to do the right thing," Sally said as she left.

∞

Sally got on the phone and called Antonio.

"Hey Sally, what's going on?"

"I just spoke with Graham's nurse."

"And?" Antonio asked, getting up and walking away from the table where Jen, Kendall, and he were having lunch.

"Based on her testimony, Ryan has given us the green light," Sally told him.

"Call Bennet and pick up Graham. I want him charged with everything," Antonio said.

"Will do." Sally smiled and hung up.

She dialed John's number. "I'm still on vacation until Monday," he whined.

"Do you REALLY want to miss this?" she asked.

"Graham?"

"Mhm."

"I'll be there to pick you up in ten," John said, going to the closet to get his uniform.

∞

Antonio dialed Brooke's cell. "Brooke Diamond."

"Hey honey, you asked for a call when we were getting ready to bring in Graham?"

Brooke smiled. "Thank you, dear." She hung up and grabbed her coat and purse.

Chapter 65~ Arrested

Richard Graham was not having a good day. First thing this morning he had been pulled over and given a citation for non-functioning taillights. The officer seemed especially cheerful giving him the ticket, even had the nerve to wish him a pleasant day.

On the way into the parking garage, he had hit a pothole and splashed mud onto the windshield, and when he turned on the wipers, red liquid came shooting out. The attendant had freaked out thinking it was blood. He called his mechanic and couldn't get his precious Mercedes in for a week to have it checked out. He had to either to leave it here or have it towed and stored at the garage.

The rest of the morning consisted of two appointment no-shows and now Nurse Moore had called in sick after lunch. At the moment, he was just going over the file of his next appointment, waiting for them to show.

∞

Brooke quickly placed calls to Sylvia and Joanna, and they agreed to meet in half an hour. Brooke would pick up the boys and run a quick errand, and Sylvia would pick up Katie.

Brooke stopped at the middle school. "Hello Tara, I need to run an errand with the boys, it shouldn't take too long."

Tara looked at Brooke. "Anything I should let Principal Lane know about?"

Brooke smiled broadly. "I don't think so, just helping the boys with a little closure. I'll have them back soon!"

Tara looked at her curiously but paged the boys to the office.

"How's Kendall doing? We really miss him," she asked while they waited for the boys.

"A couple of setbacks. Jen and the kids are staying with the Garcia's for the weekend. He has an appointment with his doctor today and a GOOD psychologist next week," Brooke said.

"I heard about what happened on Tuesday. Unbelievable. I really don't understand what is wrong with some people," Tara said sadly.

Brooke smiled and patted her arm. "Don't worry, dear, at least someone will be paying for his misdeeds."

Before Tara could ask her what she meant, the boys came into the office. "There are my boys! We have an errand to run, and then I'll bring you back to school."

"What's going on?" James asked.

"Justice, my love."

∞

A few minutes later, Brooke stopped at the same florist shop they had visited on Tuesday and she came out with another thirty brightly coloured balloons.

"Mom, what are we doing?" James asked as they squeezed the balloons into the back of her car.

"Celebrating, dear."

"What are we celebrating?" Logan asked.

"You'll see." She smiled as they drove off.

A couple of minutes later, Brooke had parked. "Follow me boys, grab the balloons."

They followed her around the block. "Hey, there's my mom!" Carlos yelled.

"Mine too... and Katie," Logan said.

Brooke crossed the street with the boys close behind.

"Mami!" Carlos said, hugging his mom. "What are we doing here?"

"Isn't this the building that we visited the other day?" James whispered to his mom.

She smiled. "Yes, darling."

A couple of minutes later, a patrol car pulled up and Bennet and Sally got out and went into the building.

"Are they..." Logan asked.

Brooke smiled. "Yes, they are."

∞

John picked up Sally at the courthouse, where she was waiting with the arrest warrant for Richard Graham. She also had a subpoena for Kendall and Jennifer Knight's records and the controlled substance log. They arrived at the St. Joseph Doctor's Building a few minutes later. John parked directly in front of the building and they went inside.

They got into the elevator and Sally pushed the button to the eighth floor. They didn't say anything on the ride up. The doors opened and they walked past the waiting patients to the desk.

"Dr. Graham, please, as well as these documents," Sally said to the receptionist, showing the woman the court documents.

"Uhhh..." the receptionist started.

"Where is he?" Bennet asked.

She pointed to the doorway. "Last door on the left."

Bennet started through the doors while Sally tapped the subpoena. "I want these waiting when we get back up here." She followed John down the hallway.

Bennet opened the door with Graham's name on it. "Richard Graham?"

"Yes, what is the meaning of this?" Graham demanded as he stood up.

Sally came in and showed him the warrant. "You are under arrest for illegal dispensation of prescription medications, medical fraud, prescription fraud, illegal shipping of controlled substances across state lines, illegal dispensation of controlled substances including injectable, falsifying controlled substance drug logs, assault and battery of Kendall Knight, including the injection of an illegally obtained controlled substance." Sally didn't even look at the paper as she listed the charges.

Graham was sputtering and yelling. "This is ABSURD, these charges are totally unfounded!"

"Yeah, we get that a lot," John said as he patted Graham down to check for weapons.

"Sally, would you like to do the honours?" Bennet asked, handing her his handcuffs.

"Certainly." She smiled and snapped the cold steel around Graham's wrists.

She pulled out a laminated card. "After all, we want to make sure this is done right," she said, smiling at Bennet.

She read Graham his rights.

"You have the right to remain silent.

Anything you say or do can and will be held against you in a court of law.

You have the right to an attorney.

If you cannot afford an attorney, one will be provided for you.

Do you understand these rights I have just read to you?"

When Graham didn't respond, John pulled him close. "She asked you if you UNDERSTAND these rights, so answer the question."

Graham nodded. "Yes, I understand my rights and I want my attorney."

"After you've been booked and processed, you'll be allowed to call your attorney. Now come on," John said, pulling Graham through the door.

Sally walked ahead of them, and when she got to the desk, looked at the receptionist. "Documents NOW." The receptionist handed her two folders and a large book marked, drug log.

"Thank you. I suggest you call and cancel any appointments Mr. Graham might have coming up. He's going to be detained for a little while," Sally told her.

The receptionist nodded and Sally took the paperwork and followed John and Graham to the elevator.

Graham continued complaining all the way down. "Whine, whine, whine," John said.

"Have you ever noticed the more educated people THINK they are, the more they whine about being held accountable for their actions?" Bennet asked Sally.

Sally smiled and nodded.

"I mean, if they were really so smart, they wouldn't be doing stupid things to begin with. Or at least be smart enough not to get caught."

Graham was now threatening them. "I will be SUING you and the police department for every cent you have. False arrest, false imprisonment, defamation of character!" he shrieked.

Sally and Bennet looked at each other and smiled.

"Just to be clear... the arrest is on a legitimate warrant, you're not actually in prison YET. In order to prove defamation of character, you actually have to show that you are NOT guilty of the aforementioned charges... so good luck with that," Sally told him.

"Don't you actually have to have character to be defamed?" John asked her.

"Good point," Sally smirked.

They arrived on the first floor and escorted Graham through the lobby and out the front door. The mothers, boys, and Katie were standing across the street, directly across from the patrol car.

Katie saw them come out and ran. "Katie!" Sylvia yelled, as she watched the little girl dash across the street. Luckily, traffic was light and no cars had been coming.

"I'll get her," Logan said, running after her.

Katie got across the street and ran up to Sally. "Is that him?"

"Katie, what are you doing here?"

"Is that him?" Katie asked again.

"This is Richard Graham," Sally told her.

"Who is she and what does she want?" Graham demanded.

Katie stomped up to him and crossed her arms. She looked him right in the eye. "SHE is Katie Knight. Kendall is my brother and you hurt him!"

"Prove it," Graham said smugly.

Katie glared up at him, and then slammed the heel of her foot into his kneecap. His leg snapped back and Graham yelled, almost falling, but Bennet kept him upright.

"NOBODY hurts my brother!"

Logan got to Katie just as she kicked Graham, and pulled her back. "Katie, don't EVER do that again! Running into the street like that, you could have been hit by a car."

Graham was having a difficult time keeping weight on his leg. "She broke my leg!"

"Really?" Bennet said and released his hold, but Graham remained upright.

"Nope, not broken," he said in a disappointed tone.

"Aren't you going to DO anything about this?" Graham yelled.

"Oh... sure," Sally said and looked at Katie. She held her hand up. "High five!" Katie slapped Sally's upraised hand, smirking.

"This weather, so many people tripping. You're lucky you didn't break your neck," John told Graham.

Graham glared at them as Sally opened the back door so they could put him in the back.

Graham looked across the street when something bright caught his eye.

He saw three women and two teenage boys standing there. The tall woman with short hair was holding a bunch of brightly coloured balloons that looked familiar. He realized where he had seen them before and glared across at them. He started yelling, "You won't get away with this! I will see to that!"

All five of them just smiled and waved.

"Just so you know... that's Kendall Knight's family. You know, the ones you said aren't REALLY his family," Sally hissed into Graham's ear as they put him in the car.

She waved over to the group, turned to Katie, and hugged her. "Be careful crossing the street next time."

"I will."

"Logan, tell Brooke and the others... good job." Sally smiled as she got into the car.

Logan nodded and smiled as the patrol car pulled away.

Chapter 66~ Being Processed

Antonio went back to the table and sat down.

"Is everything alright?" Jen asked.

"Everything is fine, Jen."

He looked over at Kendall, who was just picking at his food. "Come on, buddy. You heard Dr. Sharpe, you need to eat."

Kendall sighed and took a bite of his burger.

"I'm going to run back and talk to my manager for a minute," Jen said, getting up.

"At least drink your shake, honey. Denise made it extra thick, just the way you like it." She reached down, kissed Kendall on top of the head, and smiled when he didn't pull away.

"Getting tired?" Antonio asked him, to which Kendall nodded.

"I'm not sure Sally is going to be able to make it today, she had to help John with something. So maybe you and your mom can watch a movie and get some rest."

Kendall nodded again.

Antonio scooted closer to the boy. "Kendall, look at me."

Kendall looked up at him.

Antonio smiled. "You did good today, son. You made it through your doctor's appointment and you came out to lunch. I know it was hard, but you did it. I'm so proud of you."

Kendall smiled a little and looked back down.

Antonio put his arm around the teen's shoulders. "It's going to get easier, I promise."

Kendall lay his head on Antonio's shoulder and hoped he was right.

∞

Jen came out and felt a flash of sadness at seeing Kendall sitting there with Antonio. She shook it off and smiled. "Well, I'm going to have to start back to work next week. One of the girls is scheduled for vacation, and it wouldn't be fair to ask her to give it up."

"The kids can stay with us while you work," Antonio said.

"Is that alright with you, Kendall?" Jen asked.

He gave her a small smile and nodded.

∞

Brooke dropped the boys off at school in time for lunch.

They went to the cafeteria and sat down to eat, when Traci Nichols came over. "Hey Carlos, a guy asked me to give this to you," she said, handing him an envelope.

"What guy?" James asked.

"I don't know, I think he's a high schooler. He asked if I knew you guys, and I said yes, so he asked me to give this to Carlos," she said as she went to join her friends.

The boys looked at one another. "Carlos, let me open it," James said, holding out his hand.

"It's okay, I can do it," Carlos said. He tore open the top of the envelope and cautiously looked inside. He pulled out a folded piece of paper.

"Carlos..." James said, holding his hand out again.

Carlos' hands were shaking as he handed the paper to James.

James unfolded it and his face flushed as he read what was on the paper. "Come on," he said, grabbing his backpack and the envelope the paper had come in. He led the way to the office and told Tara that they needed to see Principal Lane immediately.

"I'm sorry, boys, she had a lunch meeting. What's going on?" Tara asked.

James handed her the paper and she took it and read it.

"Who gave this to you?" she asked.

"Traci Nichols. She said a high schooler asked her to give it to me," Carlos told her.

"She didn't know who it was?"

Carlos shook his head.

"Okay, Principal Lane will be back later, but I'm going to call your dad," Tara said, picking up the phone.

Antonio, Jen and Kendall had just gotten back to the Garcia home when his cell phone rang. "Garcia."

"Hi Antonio, it's Tara Shipley. I'm calling because the boys received another note today. Traci Nichols delivered it to Carlos in the lunchroom. She told them a high schooler asked her to give it to him."

Antonio walked into his study. "Are the boys alright?"

"They're a little shaken."

"Is the note anything like the other one?"

"It's pretty bad," she told him.

"I'm on my way. I'll want to speak with Traci."

"That shouldn't be a problem. Janice is at a meeting, but she should be back soon," Tara told him.

"Okay, I'll see you in a few minutes," he said, hanging up.

He came out of the study and Sylvia noticed the look on his face. "What's wrong?"

"The boys got another note at school. I'm going down to go check it out."

"Who the hell is doing this?" she asked.

"One of the other students said a high schooler asked her to give it to Carlos. I'm going to talk to her and see if I can track this guy down," he said, kissing her goodbye.

"Okay, let me know what happens," she said as he walked out into the living room.

"Is everything alright?" Jen asked as Antonio grabbed his jacket.

"Yeah, I just need to do a couple of things. You guys relax, watch a movie, and I'll be back in a little while."

"Okay." She smiled as he went out the door.

Sylvia and Jen exchanged looks. "How about I make some popcorn and hot chocolate?" Sylvia asked.

"Sounds great," Jen said. "Did you want to pick a movie, honey?" she asked Kendall.

He shook his head no.

"Okay," she winked at Sylvia. "Let's see... Ooh, how about An Affair to Remember?"

"That's a wonderful choice! I love a good romantic tragedy and I just adore Cary Grant," Sylvia said.

Kendall got a pained look on his face and rolled his eyes. He went over to the cabinet and pulled out the movie RV.

"That wasn't so hard, was it?" Jen smiled.

Kendall shook his head and rolled his eyes again. A few minutes later, Sylvia was sitting in Antonio's recliner, while Jen and Kendall sat on the couch. Half an hour later, he had fallen asleep, his head on the arm of the couch.

Sylvia got up and handed Jen a pillow. Jen laid it on her lap and gently pulled Kendall over until his head was resting on the pillow. Sylvia lifted his legs up onto the couch and covered him with a blanket and then went back to the recliner.

A few minutes later, Kendall had curled up and Jen had her arm around him. She was running her fingers through his hair with her other hand.

∞

Antonio got to the school and went to the office. He was beyond angry.

He walked in and saw the boys sitting there quietly, lost in their own thoughts. "Boys are you okay?"

They all nodded, but he noticed James' flushed cheeks, Logan's pale face, and Carlos' teary eyes.

Tara handed him the paper and paged Traci Nichols to the office. Antonio read the paper. It was just as bad as the first one Logan had found in his locker.

"Here's the envelope," James said, handing it to him.

Antonio took it. It was a plain white envelope with "Carlos Garcia" scribbled across it.

Antonio smiled. "Well, we have something to match handwriting against."

"That's good, right?" Logan asked.

"Yes it is. Did you all read this?"

"No, just James," Carlos said.

"Are you okay?" he asked the teen. James nodded. "Do you boys want to go home, or do you think you can make it through the day?" Antonio asked.

"I'm staying," James stated.

"Me too," Logan said.

"Same here." Carlos nodded.

Antonio smiled. "Okay, but I'll be here to pick you up after school."

"We have hockey practice," Logan told him.

"Alright, you boys go to practice and I'll pick you up at the rink," Antonio told them.

Traci Nichols came in. "Hi Tara, you called me?"

"Hi Traci, Officer Garcia needed to ask you a couple of questions."

"Did I do something wrong?" she asked.

"No, I just need to know who gave you this note for Carlos."

"Like I told the guys, I think it was a high schooler. I don't know his name, but I've seen him around before. What was in the note?" she asked.

"Just some inappropriate things," Antonio told her. "Would you know this guy if you saw him again?"

"I think so," Traci said.

"Tara, is there a way to get a copy of the high school year book so Traci can go through it?" Antonio asked.

"I think so. I'll call and see if they can send one over."

"Thank you. Traci, I want you to go through the book, and if you see the boy who gave you the note, tell Tara and she'll call me."

Traci nodded. "I'm sorry. If I'd known it was something bad, I wouldn't have taken it."

"You didn't do anything wrong. In fact, if you can identify that high schooler, it'll be a big help." Antonio smiled.

"I'll do my best," Traci said.

"I know you will," Antonio said. "I'm going to run to the station and drop this off and check on our newest addition," Antonio told the boys.

All three boys smiled at that.

He looked at them. "Do I want to know? Never mind, tell me tonight." He was pretty sure it had something to do with Brooke.

The boys nodded. "We better get to class," Logan said, hearing the bell ring.

"WAIT for me inside at the ice rink tonight," Antonio reminded them.

"Will do," Carlos said, hugging his dad.

The boys left for their classes.

"Tara, could you please let Janice know what happened and that I'll call her later?" Antonio asked.

"Of course. The high school is sending over a year book, so maybe we'll have a name by the time you call."

"Great! Thanks Tara, thank you Traci," Antonio said. He left and headed for the station.

∞

Richard Graham's day was not getting any better. He was sitting handcuffed to a table in an interrogation room, waiting to be processed. The police were taking their time doing it and he was getting angry.

"I want my attorney!"

"After processing," Bennet said.

"Then process me," Graham demanded.

"We're just making sure we have everything in order. Wouldn't want to have disrupted your day for nothing, now would we?" John smiled.

"You are delaying this on purpose!" Graham said.

"Now, WHY would we do that? You think I LIKE listening to you shriek like a banshee?" Bennet asked.

"Good word usage." Sally smiled.

"I thought so." John smirked.

"You two are going to be in SO much trouble when I get out of here. I will see to it that you PAY for this, one way or another!" Graham threatened.

Sally sat down across from him and stared, one eyebrow arched.

"NOW you did it," Bennet told him.

Graham looked at him and then at Sally. She put a finger to her lips, indicating he should be quiet.

"The longer you scream and carry on, the longer you will sit there. By LAW, we have seventy-two hours to book and process you, and I will see to it that you SIT there for seventy-one of those hours if you do not stop carrying on like a petulant child. You will be allowed your phone call after you have been processed, and the faster you SHUT THE HELL UP, the faster that will happen. By the way, you just added threatening an officer of the law to your list of charges," Sally said, her voice low.

John stood behind her, smirking at Graham. "Told you so."

Sally and John left Graham sitting in the interrogation room and went out into the main office. Antonio came in a couple of minutes later.

"How did things go?"

"He's not a happy camper." John smiled, putting his hand to his ear.

"Is that him?" Antonio asked.

"Yes, apparently he thinks if he yells loud enough, it'll move things along faster," Sally told him.

"Where are we at with it?"

"Still waiting to process." Sally smirked.

"Sounds like it's going to be a long night for him," Antonio commented. He handed Sally the note. "This was sent to Carlos at school. Someone asked one of his classmates to give it to him. I spoke with her and she thinks it was a high schooler, so she's going to go through the high school year book and see if she can pick him out."

Sally read it. "Oh my God, what the hell is wrong with people? Do you think this is a serious threat?"

"We're going to treat it as such. I told the boys to stay together and someone will pick them up from school or practice until we find who sent this. We also have this." Antonio handed her the envelope.

"Good, we can match the handwriting," she said, putting it in a plastic bag.

John read the note. "Did the boys read this?"

"James did, they all read the first one."

"I'll talk to them about it tomorrow. I'm meeting with them at your house after school," Sally told Antonio.

"Good. Thanks Sally."

"Does Kendall know about these notes?" she asked.

"No, and I want to keep it that way," Antonio said.

"Good, I really don't think he could handle it."

"Do you think he's EVER going to shut up?" John asked, still listening to Graham.

Sally looked at her watch. "I guess we can start processing him now. By the time we're done, the courthouse will be closed."

"Aw, he's going to have to spend the night." John pouted.

"Well, I seriously doubt the judge will come back down for a bail hearing tonight." She smiled.

"You know... let me make a quick call. Mike Duncan owes me a favour," Antonio said as he went into his office.

Sally and Bennet looked at one another. "What do you think he's up to?" John asked.

"Is that something you REALLY want to know?" Sally asked.

"Probably not... at least until later."

"I think that can be arranged." She smiled.

∞

Antonio got Mike Duncan on the phone. "Hey buddy, would you be willing to do a favour for me?"

"Anything. What do you need?" Duncan asked.

Antonio told him about Graham and what he had done to Kendall.

"What do you need me to do?" Duncan asked.

"How would you like to spend the night in a nice cozy cell? I'll throw in a steak dinner from the steakhouse tonight and every Friday for a month," Antonio said.

"Medium rare, two baked potatoes...I'm on my way," Duncan said.

∞

Antonio had met Mike Duncan ten years earlier when he arrested him. He wasn't a criminal per sey, he'd just needed money to help out his family, and working in a chop shop was the fastest way he found to get it. He used his time in prison to get his high school diploma and work towards his mechanic's certification. When he got out of prison, Antonio helped him get a job at Reger's Auto Repair Shop. Mike purchased the shop when Mr. Reger retired two years earlier. Antonio made sure that Mike got the contract to service the police vehicles and he was very grateful, not only for the work, but for their friendship as well.

∞

Antonio called Sally in and told her what he wanted done. She looked at him and smiled. "Can do, Boss."

"Thanks Sally. I'm going to run home and check on things there and then pick up the boys from practice. Call me if you have any trouble," Antonio said, pulling on his jacket.

"Oh, he won't give me any trouble," she said, smiling.

"You scare the hell out of me sometimes."

She arched an eyebrow. "Good." She smirked, walking back to the interrogation room.

∞

Two hours later, Graham had been processed, given his phone call, and taken to a cell. He was more than a little shocked to find he had a cellmate. Especially finding that cellmate was a 6' 7", 280-pound African American man, who was nothing but muscle. "Hey roomie, let me lay down some rules..." Mike Duncan growled as he stood over Graham.

Chapter 67 ~ Bullies

The boys met after last class and started walking the two blocks to the ice rink. They quickly caught up with the rest of their teammates, but Carlos noticed a group of four older boys lingering about half a block behind.

"Guys, I think we're being followed," he whispered.

James casually looked back and saw them. "I think they're high schoolers, the one in the red jacket looks familiar. Let's just stay with the rest of the team."

"I'll call Papi when we get inside," Carlos said.

The boys got inside the building and went to change in the locker rooms. Carlos called Antonio. "Papi, we're at the ice rink and I think there are four guys following us. James thinks he recognizes one of them."

"STAY inside and let Coach Banner know. I'll be there soon," Antonio instructed.

"Okay, we will," Carlos promised. He told the guys what Antonio had said and then went to find the coach

Antonio circled the block a few times, and not seeing anyone like Carlos had described, parked in front of the ice rink and went inside. He sat down and watched the team practice, cheering his boys on whenever they made a goal. An hour later, practice was over and the boys had showered and headed out for the car.

Antonio stopped to chat with Coach Banner for a moment, but kept his eyes on the boys as they walked out the glass doors.

The group of high schoolers were back, hanging out in front of the building and had started towards the boys. Antonio saw them and headed out the doors, Coach Banner right behind him. They stepped up behind the group as the one in the red jacket had started to say something.

Antonio cleared his throat. "Something you boys need?"

The four boys turned around. "Uh...no, just asking how practice was going," the one in red stammered.

"Do they know you?" Antonio asked.

"They know my brother," the teen replied, walking off.

"That's Brian Rickard. I think the rest of the boys are on the high school football team," Coach Banner said.

"Brian... is that Todd's brother?" Antonio asked.

"Yes it is."

Antonio nodded as he watched the group retreat.

Antonio opened the car doors and they all got in. "Coach Banner said the boy in red is Todd Rickard's brother. I want you boys to steer clear of them. Make sure you all stay together, better yet with a group. Someone will drop you off and pick you up from school until I have a little chat with their parents," Antonio said.

"Do you think he's the one that sent the note to Carlos?" Logan asked.

"I wouldn't doubt it," Antonio said.

After the movie, Jen had woken Kendall and he headed upstairs try and finish some homework. He managed to finish his social studies and had pulled out his chemistry homework.

Jen went up a little while later with a smoothie for him. "Here honey, try drinking this. I'm going to go pick up Katie. The boys are at hockey practice, so they'll be home later."

He nodded.

"Sylvia is downstairs if you need anything. Is there anything special you'd like for dinner?"

He shook his head.

"Please drink this for me?" she asked, pointing at the smoothie.

He sighed and nodded.

"Thank you. I'll be back in a little while." She smiled and kissed the top of his head.

∞

Kendall continued working on his homework and heard his mom and Katie get back about half an hour later. He heard a small knock at the door. "Kendall, can I come in?" Katie asked quietly.

"Yeah," he said, looking over at her.

She went in and stood next to his chair. "Are you feeling better today?"

He nodded. "How's your nose?" he asked quietly.

"It doesn't even hurt, really."

"Katie, I..."

"It was an accident. I shouldn't have jumped on you when you were sleeping."

"That's no excuse for me hurting you," he said, looking down.

"Do you remember last year when I was goofing around, jumping on the bed. I jumped too far and you caught me, but my foot pushed your finger back and broke it? You said THAT was an accident. Even though I was jumping on the bed when I wasn't supposed to."

"Katie, that's different."

"How?"

"I don't know it just is!" he said, getting frustrated.

"No, it's not. You forgave me because you knew I didn't mean to do it. Well, you didn't mean to hit me in the nose either. So if I forgive you, you have to stop blaming yourself," she declared.

He sat there for a moment. "I'm supposed to take care of you, that's what makes it different."

"You do take care of me. You're the best big brother ever."

"No Katie, I'm really not. I'm not the best anything," he said, turning back to his books.

Katie's eyes filled with tears and she walked out into the hall. She turned around and ran back to her brother, throwing her arms around him. "I love you."

"Katie..."

"I'm not letting go until you stop being mad at yourself."

"Katie, please!"

"NO!" she said, holding on tighter.

"You are such a pain in the butt," he said as he pulled her up onto his lap.

They sat there quietly for a few minutes. "I love you, Katie," he said as he hugged her, his chin on her head.

She smiled. "Are you going to stop feeling bad?"

"I'll try, okay?"

"Promise?"

"I promise. Now I need to get my homework done. I still have a lot to do."

"Okay, I have some to do, too," she said, hopping off his lap.

Kendall started back on his homework, but he couldn't concentrate, and after an hour, he gave up. He was going to have to wait for Logan. He realized the smoothie had melted, so he

drank a little, poured the rest down the toilet, and flushed. He decided to check the team's game times, so he turned on his laptop and pulled up the schedule.

Saturday at 10 am this week, next Saturday at 9 am. *Maybe I'll go next weekend, most of the bruises should be gone by then,* he thought.

He decided to lie down for a little while, but a couple of minutes later, he heard a ding, indicating he had a new email. He got up and checked it. He didn't recognize the sender and hesitated for a moment before opening it. He sat there in shock, looking at a picture of Deesie staring back at him.

The message read:

"Hey slut. Tell me, how did it feel having him touch you? You can deny it all you want, but I know you loved it. His hands, his mouth, all over you. Do you miss having him there, how his touch made you feel? All he did was love you and they blew his head off because of you. How many MORE people are going to get hurt because of you? It's not like anyone could love you now, you're damaged goods, just a worthless piece of garbage. You should do everyone a favour and join poor Mr. Deesie."

Kendall started shaking uncontrollably and backed away from the computer. He couldn't breathe and he was trying to fight the panic he felt building in his chest. He went into the bathroom and locked the door. He felt cold, so he turned on the shower, and when the water was warm, climbed in and sat in the tub, fully clothed. The warm water rained down on him, but he didn't feel any warmer. He sat there, rocking back and forth, wishing he had just died in the woods.

∞

Antonio and the boys got home a little while later. Sylvia kissed Antonio. "Dinner in ten minutes," she said. The boys nodded and ran upstairs.

"I need to call John and see if he wants to pay a little call to another student. I also want someone to drive the boys to and from school, same with Katie," he said as he went into his study.

Sylvia followed him. "Are you going to tell me what this is about?"

He nodded and picked up the phone and then he heard Carlos scream. "Papi!"

He ran upstairs and found James pounding on the bathroom door, yelling for Kendall to open it.

"What's going on?"

Logan grabbed Kendall's laptop and showed Antonio the message. He could hear the shower running and tried the door. "KENDALL, open the door!"

Not getting an answer, he listened for a moment. "Get back!" he told the boys and he kicked the door in.

"Stay here!" he ordered as he went to the shower and pulled back the shower curtain. He turned off the water, which was now ice cold, and pulled Kendall out. "James, hand me the towels."

James grabbed the towels from the rack and handed them to Antonio.

"I don't see any wounds," Antonio said, checking Kendall's wrists and arms. "Mijo, talk to me," Antonio said as he dried the boy's face with a towel.

When he got no response, he picked him up and carried him into the bedroom.

"Grab some dry clothes," he told Carlos as he started pulling off Kendall's wet ones.

Carlos handed him some sweats and Logan grabbed some blankets from the closet. Antonio got Kendall changed into the dry clothing and covered him with the blankets.

Sylvia, Jen, and Katie stood in the doorway. "Sylvia, please call John and tell him to get over here as soon as he can."

Sylvia nodded and went into their bedroom and called John. "He's on his way," she said.

Antonio nodded. "Logan, can you grab the thermometer and take his temperature? Carlos, take Katie downstairs, please."

Both boys hurried to do as they were asked. "James, sit there," Antonio said, pointing to the other side of the bed.

"Jen, sit here and talk to him. See if you can get him to respond. James, if he has a panic attack, hold him tight," Antonio instructed.

James nodded.

Antonio went in to change into his uniform. This was going to end tonight.

Logan came in, placed the thermometer under Kendall's tongue, and held it there until it beeped.

"What is it?" Jen asked.

"96.2... not too bad," Logan said.

She nodded and tucked the blankets in around him tighter. "Kendall, please wake up." Jen sat there stroking his hair and speaking to him softly.

"Logan, can you bring me the laptop please?" Antonio asked.

Logan grabbed it from the desk and took it to Antonio. "Do you recognize this email address?"

Logan shook his head. "No, but that picture is from the faculty photos they took for the yearbook."

"Okay, can you keep an eye on his temperature? If it starts dropping we'll need to take him in."

"I will," Logan said. He went and sat next to James.

Antonio went downstairs and put on his jacket. Carlos was sitting in his recliner with Katie on his lap, her head on his shoulder.

Antonio sat on the table in front of them. "It's going to be alright, I'm going to find out who's doing this and stop them."

"Are you going to arrest them?" Katie asked. She had stopped crying and looked at him with sad eyes.

"I am."

There was a knock on the door. Antonio grabbed Kendall's laptop and went to open the door.

Sylvia came out of the kitchen, having turned off the oven.

"I'm not sure how long we'll be. I probably won't be home until late," Antonio said, kissing her goodbye.

She nodded. "Get them."

"We will," Antonio promised.

∞

Logan took Kendall's temperature again. "97.6... almost normal."

Jen smiled at him. "Thanks honey. Why don't you grab something to eat, and then you boys can switch places."

"Good idea," James agreed.

"Okay, I'll be back in a few minutes," Logan said and went downstairs.

Kendall stirred a little. "Baby, please wake up," Jen said softly.

"Hmmm," he murmured.

"Kendall, can you wake up?" Kendall's eyes fluttered open for a minute and then closed. "Honey, please..."

"Mama?"

"Yes baby, it's Mama," Jen said softly.

"I'm tired."

"I know, but I need you to wake up for a little while."

"Don't wanna."

"Just for a little while."

"Hey buddy, you wouldn't believe what happened at practice today," James said.

Jen smiled and nodded at him.

"What?"

"Travis Miller tripped over his own feet and ended up with his head stuck in the netting. I swear he must be related to Jenny Tinkler."

Kendall smiled a little and then closed his eyes again.

"I think it's okay. He's a lot warmer than he was," Jen said.

James nodded.

Logan came in a couple of minutes later and traded places with James. He took Kendall's temperature again and smiled when it beeped. "98.4... normal."

"Are Katie and Carlos alright?" Jen asked him.

"I think so. They were working on homework when I went down. Maybe you should grab something to eat?" he suggested.

"I'll wait for James to come back up. Logan, what was on his laptop?"

"I really think Papi should tell you," Logan said.

"Okay," she sighed.

∞

James came up a little while later and Jen went down. Kendall was sleeping soundly and his breathing seemed normal.

"You think Papi will find who did this?" Logan asked.

James nodded. "Yeah, he'll find them."

"How is he?" Carlos asked as he came in and sat next to James.

"Doing a lot better, his temperature is normal," Logan told him. "Do you think it was those guys at the ice rink?"

"I don't know, maybe," James said.

"Papi will find them, whoever they are," Carlos said.

∞

A couple of hours later, the boys decided to turn in. The note, the guys at the ice rink, and now the message on Kendall's laptop, had them all worn out. They spaced themselves around the bed as they had done the night before and were soon asleep.

Carlos woke up around midnight and saw that Kendall was gone from the bed. He looked around and found that the bedroom door was open. He jumped up and checked the bathroom, but no one was there. He checked the guest room, but no one was there either, so he went downstairs, where he found the front door wide open.

"Oh no, he's sleepwalking!" He slipped on his boots and grabbed his coat. "James, Logan!" he yelled as he ran out the door, not waiting for them.

He followed the footprints in the fresh snow down the walk and across the street. They led to the park, and he looked around and sighed in relief when he saw Kendall sitting under the oak tree.

"Kendall, what are you doing out here? It's freezing!"

He ran up the small hill, slipping a couple of times and got to his friend. "Kendall..."

When he didn't respond, Carlos reached out and touched his shoulder. "Kendall, we need to get home. It's too cold for you to be out here."

He inhaled sharply when saw Kendall's sleeve pushed up and the knife lying next to him. Then he noticed the blood that stained the snow.

"Kendall!" he cried and grabbed his friend, trying to wake him. He held his hand over the deep cuts and screamed

Chapter 68~ Family of Bullies

Antonio decided to stop at the station first in hopes that Sally could track down who had sent the email. He had a pretty good idea of who it was, but he needed proof.

He and John walked in. "Sally, I need you to find out who sent this NOW, please."

Sally took the laptop, pulled up the message, and then sent it to her computer. "Damn!" she cursed when she saw the name R. Deesie come up when she tracked the name.

"What?" Antonio asked.

"It's a generic email created today. Let me see if I can track the IP."

"It's quieted down a bit in here," John commented.

"I don't think Mr. Graham is enjoying his cellmate's company." Sally smiled as she continued to work on the computer.

"Well, that's a crying shame." John smirked.

"Isn't it though?"

"Anything?" Antonio asked impatiently.

"It'll take a few minutes, but I should have it soon. Why don't you call home and see how they're doing while I finish this?"

He smiled. "Are you trying to get me out of your hair?"

"I love you, but yes. Now go call and let me know how they're doing. I can go over and help out tonight if they need me."

"Alright, alright. Have I told you today how fantastic I think you are?"

"No, but I know you do." She smirked.

∞

Antonio went into his office and called home. "Hello?" Sylvia answered.

"How's everyone doing?"

"Okay so far. The kids and Jen have all eaten and Kendall's temperature is normal and he's sleeping now. Have you found out anything yet?"

"Sally's working on tracking the IP right now. As soon as we have it, we'll be paying a visit to whoever sent it. She said if you need any help to let her know."

"I think we're okay for now. I'll give her a call later with an update."

"If anyone does need her, just call her cell," Antonio told her.

"We will. Tell her thank you. Let me know what happens, okay?"

"Will do," he said and hung up. He went back out into the main office and sat down next to wait.

"Got it! The IP belongs to... Paul Rickard," Sally told them.

"There's a surprise. Are you ready?" Bennet asked Antonio.

Antonio nodded. "Let's find out which of his sons, if not both, will be paying us a visit."

Sally got on the phone to Judge Warner and requested a search warrant to the Rickard home, which included all electronic devices on the property. "Judge Warner will fax a copy of the signed warrant in just a few minutes."

Antonio nodded, and as soon as the warrant came across, they headed out.

They arrived at the Rickard home a few minutes later. Bennet knocked on the door, and when there was no answer, he knocked again, louder.

Todd Rickard answered the door. "Are your parents here?" Bennet asked.

"Dad, cops are here!"

"What the hell for?" Paul Rickard demanded.

"How would I know? They asked for you!" Todd yelled. He turned and left as his dad came to the door.

"What?"

"We want to ask your sons a few questions regarding some notes and an email that was sent to a schoolmate," Antonio said.

"Come back tomorrow," Rickard said as he went to shut the door.

Antonio blocked it and handed him the copy of the search warrant. "I also need access to all your computers, cell phones, tablets, whatever else may have been used to send an email."

"What is this about?" Rickard asked.

"Your sons are being investigated for bullying and sending threatening messages to other students," Antonio said as he pushed past him. "Now, I suggest you call your sons down so we can discuss this."

"Todd, Brian... get your butts down here!" their dad called.

Both boys came down, glaring at the two officers.

"Have a seat boys. We need to have a little talk," Antonio said, pointing at the couch.

"Now, we can do this the easy way, where you answer our questions here, or we can do it the hard way, where you answer our questions at the station. At which point we confiscate EVERY piece of electronic equipment in your house, which means it'll take probably a month to get it back to you. It's entirely up to you," Bennet said.

The boys looked at each other. "What questions?" Brian asked.

"Which one of you sent the note to Carlos Garcia?"

"What note?"

"I should probably let you know the student that was asked to give him the note has already gone through the high school year book and guess who she identified?" Bennet asked, looking directly at Brian.

"You were also following Carlos and his two friends to the ice rink," Antonio said.

"That's where I've seen you before," Brian said.

"Oh, he's an observant one, isn't he? Considering that was what, only a few hours ago?" Bennet said sarcastically to Antonio.

"Very observant," Antonio said, staring the teen down.

"Who sent the email to Kendall Knight?" John asked.

"What email?" Todd smirked.

"Where's your computer?" Antonio asked Paul.

"Why?"

"Do we really need to go over this again?" Antonio asked.

Rickard rolled his eyes and pointed to a desk in the next room.

Antonio turned it on and pulled up the history. He found an email website and typed in R Deesie. "What's the password for this email?"

"Don't know what you're talking about," Brian said.

Antonio pulled out his cell and called the station. "Sally, I have the computer, but not the password."

"Give me a minute," she said. "Okay, I have it. These guys are so original. It's Deesie, all small letters."

Antonio typed it in and pulled up the account. "Who created this email address?"

"Anyone can make an email address and send an email from anywhere," Todd said smugly.

"True, but this one came from your DAD'S IP address. Know what that means, genius? Either one of you sent it, or he did," Bennet said.

"So what if one of them did send an email, who the hell cares?" Rickard asked.

"Have you ever heard of cyber bullying? Todd has. He took an immunity that was offered after the first email he sent to Kendall Knight," Bennet told him.

"So?" Rickard asked.

"So, that immunity has just been revoked and he's about to be charged. Same with Brian," Bennet said.

"Charged with what?" Rickard asked.

"Really? Okay, let's go over this again. They're being charged with three counts of harassment, two counts of bullying, and two counts of cyber bullying," Bennet said.

Antonio walked over. "Stand up," he said to Todd as he pulled his cuffs off his belt.

"Same with you, sunshine," John told Brian.

The teens were handcuffed and Mirandized. "You can meet them down at the station," Antonio told Rickard. He and Bennet escorted the two out to the police car and put them in the back.

"They're minors, you can't arrest them!" Rickard yelled, following them outside.

"Actually, they're over sixteen, so we can charge them as adults, which we are," Antonio told him as he got into the car.

"So they sent an email to the little fag. He probably had it coming anyway!" Rickard screamed, hitting the top of the car.

Antonio got out of the car and grabbed the man, pushing him up against the cruiser.

"Antonio..." John warned.

"You should be VERY careful about what you say," he growled, his eyes flashing. "Now I should arrest you right now for assault, but I'm going to give you ONE chance to shut up and get back into your house before I change my mind."

He released his hold on Rickard, who decided he should take advantage of the offer. Antonio watched him until he was inside and closed the door. He took a deep breath and got back into the car.

John looked at him with an eyebrow raised.

"What?" Antonio asked him.

"Not a thing, I was kinda hoping you'd arrest him. We could have had family night down at the jailhouse," John said as he pulled the car out onto the street.

Antonio smiled and shook his head.

∞

Two hours later, both Rickard boys were booked, processed, and waiting in a cell until morning when the courts opened. Their dad hadn't even bothered coming down.

"I'm going to check on our other prisoner, just to make sure he's settled in for the night," John said and turned on the video feed to the cell. "Aw, looks like it's going to be a long night for someone," he said, pointing at the screen.

Antonio walked over, looked at the screen, and had to laugh.

Mike Duncan had pulled both mattresses off the bunks and was stretched out across both of them. Richard Graham was perched precariously on the metal springs in a corner on the bottom bunk.

"Sally, can we take a picture of that and send it to my email?" Antonio asked.

"Sure thing, Boss."

"Well, I think we should both head home. Not too bad for a day's work. One crooked psychologist and two bullies locked away." John smiled.

"Especially considering you're both still on leave," Sally pointed out.

"Well, we can't let you have all the fun. Can you make sure Mike gets a really good breakfast in the morning?" Antonio asked.

"Will do. I'll stop and pick up something myself." Sally smiled.

"Thanks Sally. See you tomorrow, right?"

"Yup, session with the boys and Sylvia invited me to dinner."

"Good. I'll see you then."

"Night Boss, night John."

"Night Sally," Bennet said. "Hey, did you tell Sylvia who Samson is yet?" he asked Antonio.

Antonio just smirked.

"You suck." John sighed.

∞

John dropped Antonio off. The house was already dark and quiet. He looked at his watch to find that it was just after eleven. He took off his jacket and boots and walked upstairs. He checked in on the boys and found them all sleeping soundly. He smiled and closed the door.

∞

Two hours later, Carlos started talking in his sleep and then started thrashing around. Suddenly he let a out a blood curdling scream that woke the house. James jumped up and flipped on the light as Carlos shot up out of his blankets.

"Carlos!" James said as he tried to get a hold of his struggling friend.

Logan crawled over to Kendall, who had flung himself off the bed at the sound of the scream. He grabbed him, pulled him over, and held onto him. "It's okay, Carlos is having a nightmare," he whispered, trying to calm his trembling friend.

"NO! Kendall, why?! No, no, no!" Carlos screamed.

Antonio and Sylvia came running in. "What's going on?" Antonio asked.

"He woke up screaming," James said, wrapping himself around Carlos.

Sylvia went over to him and took his face in her hands. "Mijo, wake up. It's just a bad dream, baby. Please."

Carlos calmed at the sound of his mother's voice. "Honey, it's alright. It's just a bad dream."

Carlos was shaking. "No, no, he's dead! There's so much blood."

"Carlos, who's dead?"

"Kendall, he's dead. His arm's all cut up."

Sylvia looked at Antonio, who picked up his son and sat on the bed with him, rocking him back and forth. "Mijo, Kendall is right here, he's safe. You're all safe."

Antonio looked over at Kendall and motioned for Sylvia to check on him. She went over and sat next to them. "Kendall, it's okay, Mijo. Carlos is waking up, you're all safe."

Carlos had stopped crying. "Papi?"

"Yes, it's Papi. You had a bad dream, Mijo," he said, hugging his son.

"It was so real, I was so scared."

"I know, but you're all here and you're all safe," Antonio said.

Carlos looked around and saw Kendall curled up in Logan's arms. "I scared him," Carlos whispered.

"It's okay, he was just startled. He'll be okay as soon as he wakes up all the way," Antonio reassured him.

Carlos got up, went over to Kendall, and put his arms around him and Logan. "I'm sorry. I didn't mean to scare you."

James was sitting on the floor where Carlos had originally been, with his head in his hands.

Antonio went and knelt next to him, putting an arm around his shoulders. "Good job," he whispered, kissing James on the head.

"Why don't we all try and get back to sleep?" Sylvia said.

"Can you sleep?" Antonio asked James.

James nodded. "I think so."

Antonio went over and helped Kendall back into bed. His eyes were open, but he didn't say anything.

"Carlos, why don't you sleep up here with Kendall?" Antonio suggested.

Carlos nodded and climbed in next to his friend.

James and Logan rearranged the blankets, so one of them was by the door, the other by the closet. When Antonio checked on them half an hour later, Logan and James were sleeping head to head, and Carlos had his arms wrapped tightly around Kendall.

Chapter 69~ Snapped

Antonio crawled into bed, exhausted. "How are the boys?" Sylvia asked.

"Sleeping for now. I don't know how much more of this they can handle."

"What do you mean?"

"James is exhausted and looks like he's ready to drop. He's trying to take care of everyone else and ignoring his own needs. Logan can't concentrate and was having trouble at practice. He's taking his English lessons in the library now, because going into the classroom is too hard for him. Carlos... I just don't know. Maybe the boys should go home for a couple of days and get some real rest, some semblance of normalcy."

"You know perfectly well that none of them will be willing to do that. If you send them home, they'll just sit there worrying about everyone here," Sylvia told him.

"I know," he said, rubbing the bridge of his nose.

"Look, you got the bullies, so things should be easier at school. Tomorrow is Friday, so we have a nice dinner, watch a few movies, and just have a family night. Jo and Brooke are over, and I invited Sally to stay for dinner after she meets with the boys. Saturday, I think you should take the boys and Katie out for a while after the game—go to a movie, the mall, whatever. But ALL of you need to get out of this house and have a little fun," Sylvia said.

Antonio smiled. "You're right."

"Of course I am," she said, snuggling up to him.

Antonio sighed.

"What is it, honey?"

"I'm just worried. Kendall was doing pretty well today. He got through his doctor's appointment, went out to lunch and actually ate some of it, was working on his homework, now this. I'm not ashamed to say I was scared when I heard that shower running and we got no response."

"I know, but you got the bad guys and he's safe."

"For now."

"I didn't get much of a chance to talk to Jen. What did Anna say?" she asked.

"Anna said that if he doesn't start eating, he's going to end up back in the hospital. She's hoping Dr. Jenkins will help with the fact he's stopped talking. She called it selective mutism."

"What is that?" Sylvia asked him.

"I researched it a little. Apparently, it usually happens in younger children, but it's also a symptom of PTSD and can occur in older kids and adults. Basically, it's a self-defense mechanism. He's choosing to only speak to certain people he feels safe with. It's not something they actually diagnose until it's been going on for a month or longer," Antonio explained.

"So you and the boys are really the only ones he speaks to. He didn't say anything to me or Jen today."

"I know. It says that as long as he's communicating in some way, not to push it. After tonight, I don't know where that leaves us," Antonio said sadly.

"One day at a time, honey," she said.

He smiled and kissed her head. "One day at a time."

∞

Kendall heard Antonio open the door to check on them. Carlos still had his arms wrapped around him, and he felt safe, yet vulnerable. Carlos was having nightmares because of him. He could tell how tired James was, and Logan was jittery. He knew none of them was

getting enough rest, spending all their time either worrying about or taking care of him. He had heard Antonio talking about the bullies that were following and threatening his friends. He had put them in danger. Whoever had sent the email was right—the people he loved were getting hurt because of him.

I should have just stayed at the cabin with Deesie. If I hadn't run away, none of this would be happening now, he thought.

Carlos rolled over onto his back and relaxed his hold, so Kendall pushed his arm over and eased himself off the bed. He stepped over Logan and opened the bedroom door. Across the hallway, he saw the bathroom door frame splintered and cracked. He tried to remember what had happened there, but it was all fuzzy. He remembered being cold and hiding, and then nothing. He vaguely remembered someone yelling, and then his mom waking him up when all he wanted was to sleep. He went into the guest room and closed the door. He crawled onto the bed and curled up, trying to sleep.

A little while later he heard the bedroom door open and close, and suddenly someone was on top of him. He felt hands on him and warm breath on his neck. "I told you what would happen if you ran away." Suddenly, he was lying on his back on the ground in the woods, and he could her Antonio yelling for him.

"Not again," he pleaded, covering his ears. "No more, no more, no more," he chanted.

Logan heard something and looked around. The bedroom door was open and he looked and saw Kendall missing from the bed.

"Oh no... James, wake up," he said, shaking his friend.

"What?" James asked.

Logan pointed at the bed. "The door's open," he told James as he went out into the hall.

James followed him and Logan stopped. "Do you hear that?"

James nodded and opened the guest room door.

They could clearly hear Kendall whispering, "No more." James pointed to the bed and they both got down and looked underneath. Kendall was curled up in a ball, his hands covering his ears. James reached for him, but Logan stopped him.

"Don't grab him, let's move the bed." They got up and managed to push the bed over until they could see Kendall.

Logan gently touched his arm. "Kendall, you need to wake up now. You're having a bad dream."

James crawled to the other side of his friend in case he went into a panic attack.

"Come on, buddy, you need to wake up now," Logan whispered. He gently took one of Kendall's hands and pulled it away from his ear. Kendall inhaled sharply at the touch, but he realized it was Logan's voice. He opened his eyes and saw Logan sitting next to him, holding his hand.

Logan smiled. "It's okay. You were just having a bad dream. We need to get you back to bed."

"Come on, let's get you off the floor," James said, helping Kendall up.

"I'll stay in here with him," Logan told James.

"Okay. I don't want Carlos to wake up alone," James said as he went back to the other bedroom.

"You doing okay?" Logan asked as he sat down next to Kendall.

Kendall nodded and closed his eyes.

A little while later, Logan had fallen asleep and Kendall had curled up next to him.

∞

Antonio woke up at about 6 am and got up. He left Sylvia sleeping and went to check on the boys. He looked in Carlos' room and saw Carlos and James curled up together on the bed. He opened the guest room door and saw Logan and Kendall sleeping on that bed, which had been moved.

Kendall must have been sleepwalking. He sighed.

He closed the door and went downstairs to put on a pot of coffee. He found Jen already up and coffee ready.

"Good morning," she said.

"Good morning. How did you and Katie sleep?"

"Alright, I suppose. Antonio, what was on the laptop?"

"Are you sure you want to know?"

"No, but I need to know."

Antonio told her about the picture and what the message had said. She sat down and tried not to cry. "Why would anyone do that?"

"They won't be doing it again. We tracked them down and they're sitting in a cell as we speak."

"Good. Are they the ones who put the note in Logan's locker?" she asked.

"Yeah, they also sent one to Carlos yesterday. Luckily a classmate identified the boy who sent it, so we have a pretty good case against them," he told her.

"Good. So the boys should be okay?"

He nodded. "I still want someone to drop them off and pick them up until I'm sure. Same with Katie."

"I can drop them off this morning. I need to run home and pick up a few things anyway," she said.

"You might want to grab Kendall's nebulizer, just in case. Especially since we don't know how long he was in the cold water last night," he suggested.

"Good idea. Now, how about I make a nice breakfast for everyone? We'll let Sylvia sleep in and you can go read the paper."

He smiled broadly. "I think I'll take you up on that. I'll go wake the boys."

Antonio went back upstairs and first woke Carlos and James, and then went in and woke Logan. He gently shook Logan's shoulder. "Time to get up."

Logan yawned and nodded. "What about Kendall?"

"Let him sleep for now. I take it he was sleepwalking?"

Logan nodded. "He was under the bed. He just kept saying, 'no more.'"

"That's what I was afraid of. You boys are doing a great job." Antonio smiled.

"Thanks Papi." Logan smiled back.

The boys showered, dressed, and headed downstairs to find a big breakfast of blueberry pancakes, bacon, and scrambled eggs waiting for them. Katie and Antonio were already seated at the table eating.

"Yummy, pancakes!" Carlos squealed.

Jen smiled. "I thought I'd fix you boys a nice breakfast."

"Thanks Mama K," Logan said.

"No problem swe... honey." She smiled.

"Yeah, thanks Mama K," James said, kissing her cheek.

"You boys eat up. I'm going to make a smoothie for Kendall," she said.

"Jen, I picked up some of the weight supplement that Anna was recommending. It's supposed to be flavorless, so we can mix it in with almost anything," Antonio told her as he pulled the can from the cupboard.

"Thank you. I hope this helps," she said.

She read the label. "Wow, 255 calorie per scoop and two scoops per glass. If we can get him to drink at least three smoothies or shakes a day, that should help. It's supposed to chill, so I'll mix this up now and take it up later."

The boys finished eating and went to grab their backpacks for school. James checked on Kendall, who was still sleeping. He sat next to him for a moment then covered him with another blanket and followed the others downstairs.

∞

Sylvia woke up and went downstairs after Jen took the kids to school.

"What's this? You let me sleep in and breakfast is waiting?" she asked, kissing Antonio good morning.

"Well, I can take credit for letting you sleep, but Jen made breakfast," he said, handing her a plate.

"I'm going to wake Kendall and see if I can get him to drink this," Antonio said, pulling the smoothie from the fridge.

"How were the boys this morning?" she asked.

"I think they were a little tired, but they ate well. Kendall was sleepwalking and Logan found him in the guest room."

"Poor baby," she sighed.

"I think if we can get him to eat, he'd feel better and not be so tired. Then maybe he'd actually sleep peacefully," Antonio said.

"Well, I'm making pot roast for dinner and that's one of his favourites, so maybe he'll eat actual food tonight," Sylvia told him.

"I hope so," Antonio said as he went upstairs.

He started to the guest room when he noticed Kendall sitting on the chair in Carlos' room, staring out the window. "Hey buddy, I brought you a smoothie," Antonio said, sitting next to the teen.

Kendall just continued staring at the snow and Antonio put his hand on his shoulder.

Kendall looked up at him. "Try drinking this, okay?"

Kendall took the glass and went back to staring outside.

"We got the boys who sent the email, they won't be causing trouble anymore," Antonio told him, trying to get the boy to respond. "Kendall, look at me, please," Antonio said.

Kendall looked at him, his face expressionless. Antonio's heart dropped. "Just try drinking this, okay? Please… for me?"

Kendall took a sip and looked back out the window.

"Okay, I'll be back up in a little while. Maybe we can watch a movie later."

Antonio went downstairs and went into his study. He pulled out the file on Deesie's victims and looked at the pictures of the 12-year-old boy that Deesie had taken. The ones of him happy with his family and then the last ones.

Then he looked at the photos of the boys that he had sitting on his desk. All of them were smiling and happy. He tried hard not to cry as he realized that Kendall now looked like the little boy in the file. The light was gone from his eyes.

He called Sally. "Hey Boss, what's going on?"

"Do we have a time for arraignment on anyone there?"

"Not yet, waiting for a public defender for the Rickard boys, and Graham is still waiting for his attorney to call back," she told him.

"Call me as soon as you have a time."

"Will do. Everything alright?"

"No, it's really not. Were you going to meet with Kendall today?" Antonio asked.

"Yeah, early this afternoon. Did you want me to come earlier?"

"Can you?"

"Absolutely. Let me get everything finished here that I need to do, and then I'll be over."

"Thanks Sally."

"Not a problem," she said, hanging up.

∞

Sally took the breakfast she had picked up for Mike Duncan and put it in the interrogation room. She walked through lock-up to get to him. She shook her head and smiled as she looked in the cell. Mike was still stretched across both mattresses, singing an old Gospel tune.

Graham was sitting unhappily on the edge of the bottom bunk. "It's about time!" he shrieked.

"Problem?" She smirked.

"DO you NOT see this?" he yelled, indicating the very large man who was occupying most of the cell.

"Did you ask him to move?" she asked.

"Are you insane?"

"Well, did he force you to do anything?"

"Well, no! But do I look comfortable to you?"

"I can honestly say that your comfort is the very LAST thing on my mind," she said, opening the cell. "Duncan, you're free to go," she said and Mike jumped up.

He went over to Graham. "You look like you need a hug," he said, enveloping the much smaller man in his arms. Mike squeezed and rocked him back and forth for a minute before releasing Graham.

"Aw, that was sweet," Sally said.

Graham sat down quickly in shock. Sally closed and locked the cell behind Duncan. "You look like you should take a nap or something," she said to Graham and led Mike from the lock-up area.

She led him to the interrogation room, where a large breakfast of biscuits with sausage and gravy, half a dozen scrambled eggs, and a glass of freshly squeezed orange juice awaited him. "For you, sir." She smiled.

He took a seat and started eating the meal.

"You know, if you're not busy after breakfast, I know a couple of boys who could use a lesson in what it's like to be the victim of a bully," she said.

"I got nothing going on today," he said with a smile.

She smiled back and instructed Johnson to take Duncan back to "bunk" with the Rickard boys for a while.

∞

Sally headed over to the Garcia home. Antonio had not sounded good at all. She arrived and knocked on the door and Antonio opened it. She took a good look at him—he was pale and had dark circles under his eyes. He looked almost frantic.

"What's going on?" she asked.

He filled her in on the rest of what had occurred the night before and Kendall's behaviour this morning.

"He's slipping away and I don't know how to bring him back," Antonio said in a shaky voice.

"Where is he?"

"Carlos' room," Antonio said.

She nodded and headed upstairs. She knocked at the door. "Hey kiddo," she said, walking in.

Kendall didn't look at her, just continued staring outside.

She sat down and watched him for a minute. "What's so interesting out there?"

He shrugged.

"I could actually sit and watch it snow for hours, drinking tea, snuggled under a soft blanket."

She went over and sat next to him. "You all had a rough night, I hear. First the email, Carlos had a nightmare, and then you sleepwalking."

He looked down slightly when she mentioned sleepwalking.

"You weren't sleepwalking, were you? Maybe you just needed time alone and then had a bad dream after?"

Kendall looked back down.

"You know, it's okay to want time alone, right? I mean, you've pretty much been with someone for the last two weeks. Sometimes you just need time to yourself. You shouldn't feel guilty about that, or about the fact that everyone wants to be with you and make sure you're

okay. You're not a burden to them, you're someone they love and they know you'd be there for them."

Kendall just continued looking out the window.

"It's true that it's hard on everyone, but not because of you. It's because of Deesie, Graham, the bullies who have been harassing you all. NONE of that is your fault, and if you start believing it is, then they win. I know you and know that you're not a quitter. You're tired and you're hurt, but you're still a fighter. If you're too tired to fight for yourself, then you need to fight for Katie, your mom, the guys, Antonio, everyone who loves you. I know you can do that, because you always put them first."

Sally moved closer and picked up the glass. "You have to start by trying to take care of yourself, which means eating."

She handed him the glass. "Drink."

He sighed and took the glass. She sat there next to him, watching it snow. An hour later, he had finished the smoothie and was sleeping with his head on her shoulder.

∞

Antonio went up to check on them and smiled when he saw them sitting there. She looked over, smiled at him, and handed him the empty glass. He set it on the desk and then went over and picked Kendall up and laid him on the bed. Antonio sat next to him, brushing his bangs out of his eyes.

Sally stood next to him and put her hand on his shoulder. "It's going be okay, he's just tired and spending too much time with his own thoughts. We need to start getting his life back into a regular routine, so that he feels normal again."

Antonio nodded. "Tell me what we need to do."

"Let's go downstairs," she said.

∞

Antonio and Sally went into the kitchen, where Sylvia poured them some coffee. "Basically, he needs to feel normal again, and that means getting him back into some kind of routine. Make him take meals with the family, even if it means waking him up. Even if he doesn't eat very much, he needs to feel like he's part of the family unit. Have him watch TV with the other kids, if he falls asleep, leave him there. Let him wake up in a normal atmosphere, surrounded by the people who love him. Have him do homework with the other boys, etc. He needs to NOT be left alone to overthink everything, because when that happens, it starts to overwhelm him," she explained.

"Okay, so treat him like a kid," Antonio said.

"Exactly and when he doesn't want to eat, do what you and James did before. Sit there and bug him until he does. It annoys him, but the banter is good for him."

Antonio smiled. "That's true enough."

Sally's cell rang. "It's the station," she said, looking at the caller ID. "O'Hara." She listened for a moment and smiled. "Oh, that's a real shame. Guess they will have to wait until Monday. Thanks Johnson."

"What's up?" Antonio asked.

"Judge Warner is out with the flu and Judge Brown is stuck in Chicago due to weather. Looks like our little prisoners will be spending the weekend."

Antonio laughed. "How was Mike this morning?"

"Well rested, I think. He was eating breakfast when I left. I asked him for a favour and he said he would love to spend some time with a couple of bullies today. Which reminds me, I need to order him a good lunch." Sally smirked.

"I'm impressed," Antonio said.

"I learned from the master."

"Well, since there's not much going on at the station, why don't you take the rest of the day off?" Antonio suggested.

"Hmmm, there's a novel idea. I have a few things I could get done and then meet the boys back here," Sally said.

"Perfect. Bring your appetite," Sylvia said.

"No problem there. How about I stop and pick up dessert?"

"That would be great," Sylvia said.

"Okay then. I'll see you in a few hours," Sally said, heading for the door.

Antonio held her coat for her. "Thank you. Antonio, stay strong, we're not going to lose him."

"Thanks Sally."

"I would also recommend you take a nap, you look like crap."

"Thanks a lot."

"I calls 'em likes I sees 'em," she said.

∞

A few minutes later, Jen got back and she and Sylvia started getting things together for dinner.

He decided that Sally had a really good idea and went up to take a nap. He checked on Kendall and found him still sleeping. He went to his room and left the door open, just in case. He laid down and was soon asleep.

∞

About a half an hour later, Jen went up to check on Kendall. He wasn't in Carlos' room or the guest room. She pulled back the shower curtain in the bathroom, and when she didn't find him there, went to wake Antonio. She stopped at the door and smiled. There was Kendall curled up next to Antonio. She grabbed a blanket off of Carlos' bed and went in and quietly covered Kendall with it. She kissed him on the forehead and went back downstairs.

∞

A couple of hours later, Antonio woke up and found a small body next to him. He smiled and pulled Kendall closer. "Mijo, I need to get up. Why don't you jump in the shower and get dressed? Sally will be here soon to meet with the boys, and then we're having a family night."

Kendall stretched out and then curled back up against Antonio.

"Come on, time to get up," he said, gently shaking the boy.

"Uh uh," Kendall murmured.

"Shower, dress, now," Antonio said, pulling the blanket off. Kendall grabbed a pillow and pulled it over his head.

"Don't make me toss you in the shower with my pillow," Antonio said, pulling it away.

Kendall groaned and sat up.

"Come on," Antonio said, standing up and putting his hand out. Kendall hesitated a moment and then took it. He went into the other bedroom, grabbed some clean clothes, and went into the bathroom.

∞

Jen went and picked up the kids from school and dropped Logan and Katie off. James had to go in for a quick recheck with the dentist and Carlos had offered to go along to keep him company.

"Darn it, I forgot my book," Logan said.

"What book?" Katie asked.

"Les Miserables. I'm doing a report on it for extra credit."

"You volunteered to do EXTRA homework? Are you nuts?" Katie snorted.

"I like learning! I'm going to run home and grab it," Logan told her.

"Maybe you should wait for James and Carlos. Didn't Papa G say NOT to go anywhere alone?"

"Katie, I live like a block and a half away and the bullies are in jail. I'll be back in five minutes," he said, running out the door.

∞

Kendall was up in Carlos' room. He had showered, dressed, and put on the shoulder stabilizer. He was sitting at the window again, this time taking pictures as he had promised Sally he would. He took pictures of his mom driving up and Logan and Katie getting out and coming in. Then he saw Logan running down the walk and across the street.

∞

Logan ran across the street and cut through the neighbour's yard. He was halfway through the alley, when he heard Dylan Mason say, "Well, look what we have here. Little fag's friend decided to go out walking by himself. I thought you were the smart one."

Logan looked around and saw two other boys that he didn't know standing there with Dylan. "Look Dylan, I don't want any trouble," Logan said as he backed up.

"Should have thought about that BEFORE your little fag friend had my buddy arrested," Dylan said, pushing Logan up against a fence.

Logan was scared, but Dylan calling Kendall names was making him angry. "Kendall is NOT a fag. He was a victim of a freak. The fact that you're defending that pervert shows the level of your true mentality!" Logan yelled. "Your friend got himself arrested by sending that sick email to Kendall and being stupid enough to send it from home!"

"Oh yeah?" Dylan said as he shoved Logan again. The other two boys laughed and surrounded the younger boy.

∞

Carlos' room had a full view of the neighborhood, including the alleyway where Logan was now being threatened. Kendall had been taking another photo when he saw the three boys come out of nowhere. He saw them surround Logan and something inside him snapped.

He grabbed Carlos' hockey stick and ran down the stairs at breakneck speed, pulling off the shoulder brace as he ran. He ran out the front door and across the street, slipping once, but getting up and running again.

Katie had stood there in shock before she screamed. "PAPI!"

Antonio came running into the living room and Katie pointed out the door. He saw Kendall running through the neighbour's yard. "What the hell?" he said, as he took off after the boy.

Sally had just pulled onto the Garcia's street when she saw Kendall go tearing across the street as if he were being chased by the devil himself. He was barefoot and not wearing a jacket.

A moment later, Antonio came running out into the street after him. She pulled over, got out, and followed.

∞

Kendall got to the alley as Dylan hit Logan in the face. Kendall screamed and body slammed the other boy so hard that he fell. Kendall pushed Logan back and started swinging the hockey stick, catching one of the older boys in the knees. The boy cried out and fell and the other boy grabbed Kendall and pushed him into the fence. Kendall got back up and swung the stick catching one of the boys in the shoulder.

Dylan grabbed Kendall by the arm and threw him against the other boy who grabbed on. Kendall dropped suddenly to the ground and the boy lost his hold on him. Kendall kicked out catching the boy in the knee. He got up and Dylan backhanded him, and Kendall hit the ground, losing his grip on the hockey stick. Dylan turned back to Logan with a raised fist, but Kendall was back up and on him before he could throw the punch.

Suddenly, Antonio was there and pulled Kendall off the larger boy. He was trying to pull the younger boys to safety when Kendall pulled away and jumped on Dylan again. He was trying to pull the larger boy as far away from Logan as possible. He didn't even seem to realize Antonio was there.

Sally got there and pulled Logan over, away from the fence, and watched as Kendall finally got Dylan Mason on the ground. He screamed at the older boy and punched him in the face.

"YOU DON'T HURT MY BROTHERS!"

Antonio tried to get ahold of Kendall, but he was having difficulty maneuvering around them in the narrow alleyway.

"I HATE YOU!" Kendall screamed as he punched Dylan again.

Antonio finally just reached out, grabbed Kendall's arm, and pulled him back. "Kendall, stop! Stop it's okay now!"

Dylan had pushed himself up against the fence in shock. The other two boys had taken off running down the alley, and he got up to follow.

Sally pointed a finger at him. "STAY there. I know who you are, and if you make me chase you, I'll be pissed," she growled. He sat back down and stayed where he was.

Antonio had his arms wrapped around Kendall, who was still fighting him. "Shhhh, it's alright," he said, trying to calm the boy. He pulled him up off the ground and sat there for a minute. Kendall finally quieted and Logan rushed over and knelt next to them.

Logan's nose was bleeding and he had a bruise on his cheek. Logan pulled off his jacket and covered Kendall with it. "This is my fault. I shouldn't have gone after my book."

"It's not your fault, Logan, it's his," Antonio told him, looking over at Dylan. "You should be able to walk around your own neighbourhood in safety."

Kendall started shivering and Antonio picked him up. "Let's go home."

Sally had already called the station and a cruiser pulled up the street. "Back here! Arrest his sorry ass and find out who his two friends are," Sally ordered, pointing at Dylan. She put her arm around Logan, who grabbed Carlos' hockey stick, and they followed Antonio across the street.

Sylvia and Katie were standing on the porch and went back in when they saw Antonio carrying Kendall over. Sylvia grabbed a blanket and covered him with it as soon as they got in the door.

Antonio carried Kendall up to the guest room and sat on the bed with him. "Mijo, look at me."

Kendall finally looked up and suddenly everything that he had been holding in for the last two weeks surfaced. Tears started flowing from his eyes as a wave of sorrow came over him. He wrapped his arms around Antonio's waist and he started sobbing. Antonio held him tightly and let him cry.

Chapter 70~ Breakdown

Katie went to follow Antonio, but Sylvia took her arm. "Help me take care of Logan."

Katie nodded and Sylvia led Logan into the downstairs bathroom to clean up his face. "Oh Mijo." Sylvia winced as she washed the blood from Logan's face. The bridge of his nose was swelling and extended up to under his left eye. It was already bruising.

"Tell me what happened," she said as she rinsed the cloth and continued cleaning his face.

"I ran home to grab my book, and I guess Dylan and some other kids were hanging around. They saw me and started pushing me around. Dylan punched me, and the next thing I know, Kendall was there and..." Logan started crying. "It's all my fault. I should have waited. I thought it'd be okay since my house is close by."

Sylvia hugged him. "You listen to me. This is NOT your fault. The only ones to blame are those boys who beat you up. How did Kendall end up there?"

"I don't know. He just appeared out of nowhere."

"He came running downstairs a few minutes after you left. He had a hockey stick and pulled off his shoulder thing and ran out the door," Katie told them.

"He must have been looking out Carlos' window. You can see your house from there," she told Logan.

She pulled a bottle of Tylenol from the cabinet and handed two to Logan with a glass of water. "Take these. I'm going to get you an ice pack for your nose." She went to the freezer, pulled out a bag of peas, and wrapped it in another washcloth. "Come sit in the living room and keep this on your nose for twenty minutes. I'm going to go check on Kendall."

"I want to come," Katie said.

"You stay here and take care of Logan," Sylvia said firmly. She didn't know what condition Kendall was in and didn't want Katie there until she was sure he was okay. "Your job is to make sure Logan stays awake in case he has a concussion."

When Logan went to say something, she quickly shook her head and he understood she was just trying to preoccupy Katie for the moment.

"Okay," Katie said. She went and sat next to Logan and held his hand.

∞

Sylvia went upstairs and saw Sally standing in the hallway. She could hear Kendall sobbing in the guest room.

"Is he alright? Did he get hurt?"

Sally nodded. "He got hit a couple of times, but I think that's a secondary issue right now. From what I understand, this is the first time he's cried since this whole ordeal began. This could actually be a very good thing."

"'Do you know who did this?"

"They already picked up Dylan Mason, and with any luck, we'll be arresting the two boys who were with him soon. I need to call the station in a little while to see how things are going."

"Logan said Dylan hit him and Kendall just appeared out of nowhere," Sylvia said.

"I saw him run across the street and behind the house. Then Antonio came out, so I stopped and followed them. I have to tell you that for someone who has been so ill, he kicked

butt. He had Dylan pinned and was really letting him have it. It's amazing that this morning he was basically locked inside his own mind, barely communicating with anyone," Sally told her.

"He must have seen them through the window and his protective side took over," Sylvia said.

Sally nodded. "How's Logan?"

"He is going to have quite a bruise and his nose is swollen a little. Mostly, he's feeling guilty that he ran home to get his book."

Sally sighed. "As soon as James and Carlos get home, I'll have a chat with all of them. They need to stop blaming themselves for every little thing that happens."

"Thanks Sally. Do you think we should postpone family night?"

Sally shook her head. "No, I think you all need it. If Kendall's too worn out after this, then he should at least sleep well."

"Okay, then I should go check on dinner. Jen and the boys should be back soon, Brooke and Joanna will be here later."

"That reminds me, I have a lovely chocolate cake in my car, so I'll run out and grab that and then give the station a call," Sally said, walking down with Sylvia.

∞

Antonio just sat there, holding his godson as he cried.

Kendall had seen red when Dylan Mason hit Logan and found himself filled with rage. He had never been so angry. He couldn't see or hear anything but Dylan, and he knew he had to get him away from Logan. Finally, someone had pulled him away from the larger boy and was holding onto him. He fought them, trying to get away, and finally heard Antonio's voice, telling him it was okay. He realized it was Antonio holding him, and suddenly he was very cold. He heard Logan's voice and then saw his bleeding face, his eyes were full of fear and he was crying. He wanted to tell Logan it was alright, that he wouldn't let Dylan hurt him again, but it was all he could do to breathe.

He knew that Antonio was carrying him, and a moment later, he felt blankets around him and Antonio was telling him it was going to be alright.

Thousands of memories flooded his mind. Everything Deesie had done to him, the beatings, the touching, the kisses, the daily threats of more to come, all bombarded him. Graham, locking the door and holding him, while his nurse forced the needle into his arm. The notes, the looks, the whispers at school, his friends thinking he had betrayed them. His mother being angry and disappointed in him. Everything down to him hurting Katie.

Everything he had been holding in, all of the pain, fear, anger, and sorrow finally overwhelmed him and he could no longer hold back the tears. He cried for over half an hour and finally fell asleep in Antonio's arms, completely exhausted. Antonio stayed with him until he was sure he was sound asleep and then went into the bathroom and grabbed the first aid kit. Dylan had split Kendall's lip when he hit him, and Antonio gently cleaned the blood away.

"Is he okay?" Logan asked quietly from the doorway.

Antonio smiled and gestured for Logan to come in. "He's sleeping now. How are you doing?"

Logan sat next to him. "Okay, I guess."

"Logan, this wasn't your fault, and to be honest, this may have been a blessing in disguise."

"How so?"

"He's finally letting it all out. I think when he wakes up he'll be feeling a little better emotionally. Physically, I think he's going to be in a bit of pain. When he wakes up, we'll need to ice his shoulder down and get him to take something for the pain. Do you want to stay up here with him for a while? I need to go make a couple of phone calls and don't want to leave him alone."

"Of course," Logan said.

Antonio smiled. "Why don't you lie down for a while too? You look like you've been through the ringer. I'll wake you when dinner's ready."

"That actually sounds really good right now."

Antonio stood up and patted the bed. "Lie down then."

Logan did as Antonio told him and Antonio pulled off his boots and covered him with the blanket. He sat down next to Logan. "I'm going to say this once more, this was NOT your fault and I'm so proud of you." Antonio made sure the blankets were tucked around them. "Get some rest," he said as he closed the door behind him.

Logan's eyes teared up again and he rolled onto his side. He wrapped his arms around Kendall and pulled him close. Ten minutes later, both boys were sleeping peacefully.

Chapter 71~ Scared Straight

Antonio closed the door and went downstairs.

Katie went running up to him. "How is he? I want to see him."

He picked her up and hugged her. "He's sleeping right now, but I think he's going to be feeling better in the next couple of days. You can see him in a little while, after he's had a chance to rest. Logan is taking a nap with him."

Katie giggled. "A nap! I haven't taken a nap since I was four."

Antonio saw Jen's car pull up. "That's because girls grow up faster than boys. Now, can you do something for me?" he asked and kissed her on the nose.

Katie nodded.

"Let me tell your mom what happened so she doesn't get too scared."

"Okay," Katie agreed.

Jen and the boys came in. "Hey, I need to talk to you all for a minute," Antonio told them.

"What is it? Is everything alright?" Jen asked, concerned by Antonio's tone.

"Everything's fine, come and sit down. Boys, you too. We need to talk about something that happened a little while ago."

Sally came in and sat next to the boys.

"What is it, Papi?" Carlos asked.

"Well, Logan ran home to grab a book he needed and Dylan Mason and a couple of his friends cornered him in the alley," Antonio started.

"WHY did he go home alone? He knows he's not supposed to go out alone!" James yelled.

"James, calm down. He's alright and he should be able to go home and back safely. Getting angry isn't going to help the situation. He thought he would be safe and he SHOULD have been. We've already arrested Dylan and his friends," Sally told him.

"It was stupid! He should have waited for one of us." James was near tears.

"Honey, listen to me. He's okay and you need to stop being angry with him. He already feels guilty about it and he doesn't need anyone else coming down on him. I know you're trying to look out for him, but right now, he just needs you to be his friend, not his protector. He already has one..." Sally said, looking back at Antonio.

Jen and the boys looked at Antonio confused.

"Well, apparently Kendall must have seen them attack Logan from Carlos' window. He took off out of here like a bat out of hell with Carlos' hockey stick in hand. He got Dylan off of Logan and he..." Antonio said.

"HE WHAT?!" Jen yelled.

"Proceeded to beat the crap out of Dylan, as well as chase off the other two boys," Antonio finished.

Jen and the two boys looked at Antonio in shock. "What did you say he did?" Jen asked.

Antonio smiled at the expressions on their faces. "You heard me. He beat the crap out of him."

"Dylan is over six inches taller and eighty pounds heavier than Kendall," James said in disbelief.

"Yeah... that didn't really seem to work in Dylan's favour today. If anything, it made him a bigger target," Antonio told him.

"Is Kendall alright?" Jen asked.

"We got the boys home. I took him upstairs and he cried for quite a while. He's sleeping now and Logan is with him," Antonio told her.

"Jen, this really may have been the best thing that could have happened," Sally said.

"Really, how so?" Jen snapped.

"Honey, have you noticed he's shown very little emotion since he got home? He's been keeping everything locked up so tight inside himself that it was getting harder and harder to reach him," Antonio said gently.

Jen sighed and nodded.

"Now that he's been able to release some of these emotions, he should be able to move forward with his recovery," Sally told her.

"Did he or Logan get hurt?" Jen asked.

"They both have a couple of bruises, and Kendall got a small cut in his lip, nothing they haven't gotten at hockey practice," Antonio told her.

She took a deep breath. "Okay, so this might be a positive thing. And what if it's not?"

"Then we deal with it, but I really think this breakdown could be the best thing to have happened," Sally said.

"When will we know?" James asked.

"I don't know, maybe in a few days, maybe as soon as he wakes up later. However, how WE deal with it is just as important as how he does. Everyone has got to start treating him normally, help him feel like his life is getting back on track. He needs routine, consistency, and to know that he's safe, but NOT being put up on a shelf because everyone is so afraid he'll shatter. James, you and Antonio are the best at getting him to eat, so do what you did before—plop him in a chair and make him sit there until he eats something. Carlos, you're the best at cheering people up, you know how to make him smile... so do it," Sally said.

"What about me?" Katie asked.

"You are the best at getting him to do everything else. Make him play video games, read to you, whatever else he use to do, make him BE your big brother again."

The boys and Katie looked at each other. "I think we can do that," Carlos smiled, putting his hand out. James and Katie both nodded and put their hands on top of his.

"Alright, I'm going to go call the station and see how our new little residents are doing. Then, as soon as Brooke and Joanna get here, we're going to have a wonderful home cooked meal and watch movies and do whatever else you little monsters want to do," Antonio said.

∞

Mike Duncan was currently sharing a cell with Todd and Brian Rickard. He had stretched out on the bottom bunk and the boys were sitting together on the top bunk.

"So, why are you boys in here?" Mike asked in his deep voice.

When they didn't answer, he kicked the bottom of the top bunk, lifting the mattress several inches into the air. "I asked you a question. The polite thing is to answer."

"Bullying and harassment," Brian spat.

"Yeah, who were you bullying?"

"Some little freak at school, who totally deserves it."

"Why does he deserve it?" Mike asked, staring at the bottom of the top bunk intently.

"I told you, he's a little freak. Some teacher went all perv on him and took him for a while. Everyone says he's a victim, but I say he liked it. Even if he wasn't a freak BEFORE, he is now that he's damaged goods."

"Uh huh," Mike growled as he kicked up, and the mattress, with both boys on it, went flying off the bunk.

Mike stood up, took each boy by the throat, and held them against the wall. His fingers reached completely around each neck and he just stood there, not squeezing, but not allowing them to move. He got very close, so that his head was between the two of them.

"Let me tell you a story about two little boys who were BAD and ended up in jail. Do you boys know what HAPPENS to bad little boys in jail?" he asked quietly.

Both boys attempted to shake their heads.

"Bad MEN teach them a lesson," he growled. "Now does that sound like something you want to happen? Because if you want to find out what 'damaged goods' really means... I can show you."

Both boys whimpered and Brian's face turned red as the front of his jeans became wet.

"Little boy... did you just wet yourself?" Mike asked, looking down. "Do you need a diaper, little boy?" Brian just closed his eyes, trying not to cry.

Mike looked at Todd. "How about you, little boy, do you need a diaper too?"

Todd shook his head.

"The lesson today, boys, is to treat people like you want to be treated. Maybe your mommy and daddy never told you that, but you had DAMN well better listen to me. If I find out you have bullied ANYONE ever again, we WILL be spending more time together. If not me, then one of my friends. Do you understand what I'm saying?"

Both boys nodded.

Mike let go of them and they both crumpled to the floor and backed up against the wall. Mike looked at them and lay back down on the bunk. "Problem with today's kids is they don't go to church and they don't get enough whuppings."

He started singing an old Gospel song that his mother use to sing to him.

Chapter 72~ Family Night

Jo and Brooke arrived a few minutes later and Antonio filled them in on what had happened. Half an hour later, Sylvia and Jen finished preparing dinner and Antonio went up to wake the boys.

He gently shook Logan's shoulder. "Logan, wake up, Mijo, it's time for dinner."

Logan yawned and stretched. "Ow," he said, holding his nose.

"We'll get some more ice on that. Your mom's here and I already warned her about your nose," Antonio told him.

"Should we wake up Kendall?"

"I will. Why don't you go on down, say 'hi' to your mom, and grab an ice pack for your face?"

"Okay," Logan said, getting up and heading downstairs.

Antonio sat down. "Kendall, it's time to wake up, dinner's ready."

Kendall's eyes fluttered open and he curled up, groaning in pain.

"What hurts, Mijo?"

"Everything." Kendall's voice was raspy and hoarse.

"Your shoulder?"

Kendall nodded, his eyes squeezed tightly closed.

"Let me take a look," Antonio said and pulled up the boy's shirt. Kendall whimpered when Antonio touched it. Kendall's shoulder blade was swollen and hot to the touch. Antonio winced at the sight of the new bruises.

"Okay, I'm going to run down and get something to ice your shoulder and one of your pain pills."

Kendall nodded.

Antonio went downstairs and grabbed a bag of peas from the freezer. "Jen, do you have Kendall's pain pills?"

"Yes, they're in my bag," she said, going to get her purse. "Is he alright?" she asked, handing Antonio the bottle.

"His shoulder's acting up after using it, so we need to ice it and give him something for the pain," Antonio told her.

He went back up, sat next to Kendall, and handed him the pain pill and a glass of water. "Take this," Antonio said.

Kendall swallowed the pill.

"This is going to hurt at first," Antonio told him and then gently held the bag of peas to Kendall's shoulder.

Kendall jumped and squeezed his eyes shut again.

"I'm sorry. You'll feel better in a few minutes. What else hurts?"

Kendall opened his eyes. "My head and my hands."

Antonio took one of his hands and saw the bruised and scraped knuckles. "Okay, we'll take care of these next."

"What happened?" Kendall asked, looking at his hands in confusion.

"You don't remember?"

Kendall thought for a minute. "I don't know, I was dreaming someone was hurting Logan and... Oh God, it wasn't me, was it?"

"No Mijo, it was Dylan Mason. You saw him and a couple of his friends going after Logan in the alley and you went running out and took care of them."

"Huh?"

"What do you remember?" Antonio asked.

"I-I don't know. I remember this morning and Sally talking to me. Then I was dreaming about something bad and it went away. Then you were there and woke me up and told me to take a shower."

"And then?"

He shook his head, trying to clear it. He was confused, his thoughts were all jumbled. "Then... all I remember is being mad and hitting someone, and then it was cold. I saw Logan and his face was all bloody."

Kendall's eyes filled with tears. "Are you sure I didn't hurt Logan, because he was all bloody and crying?"

"Why do you think you hurt him?"

"I hurt Katie and didn't know it."

"Mijo that was an accident and you saved Logan. Dylan and his friends were pushing him around and Dylan had started hitting him when you showed up and pulled Dylan off of him."

"Are you sure?"

"I SAW it happen. You even had Dylan pinned and I had to pull you off of him."

Kendall visibly relaxed. "Okay, so I didn't do anything bad to Logan..." he said as he closed his eyes.

∞

A few minutes later, Jen went up to let Antonio know dinner was ready. He was still holding the cold bag to Kendall's shoulder. "You go eat, I'll do that," she said.

"Sounds good, probably needs another ten minutes. Let me take care of his hands first," he said, grabbing the first aid kit from the night table. He took some antiseptic and cleaned Kendall's hands with it. The teen whimpered when he cleaned the scrapes but slept on.

Jen sighed. "Is it wrong that I'm glad he hit that boy? I have always tried to teach the kids that fighting is not the way to solve problems. But this..."

"No, it's not wrong. You also taught them to defend themselves and each other. That's what he was doing."

"It just worries me. It's one thing after another and the kids are all getting so worn out."

"That's why we're having a family night tonight, and I'm going to take the boys and Katie out for a while tomorrow," Antonio told her.

"They'll like that. Now go eat before it gets cold." She smiled.

"You don't have to tell me twice. He took a pain pill, so he'll probably sleep for a while." Jen nodded as she stroked Kendall's hair.

∞

Antonio went downstairs. "Smells good!" He smiled, walking into the dining room.

"How's Kendall doing?" Sally asked.

"He's sleeping again. I gave him a pain pill, so he'll probably sleep for a few hours. His shoulder is pretty bruised again," he said. "So, what do you kids want to do tomorrow?"

"What do you mean?" Carlos asked.

"I thought after the game we could go do something fun. A movie, the mall, whatever you want."

"The new James Bond movie is playing at the mall," James said.

"Yeah! A spy movie!" Carlos said excitedly.

"Yeah, the mall!" Katie said.

"What about you, Logan?' Antonio asked.

"The movie sounds fine, and I can run to the bookstore too."

"The mall it is." Antonio smiled.

Jen came down a few minutes later and put the bag of peas back in the freezer. She sat down to eat with the others.

"Guess what, mom? Papa G is taking us to the mall and a movie tomorrow!" Katie said.

"He is? Wow, that's pretty ambitious!" She smiled.

They all sat around the table, enjoying their meal. After dinner, the moms cleared the table while the kids went into the living room and put in a movie.

∞

Kendall woke up a couple of hours later and went downstairs and into the kitchen unnoticed. The kids were on their second movie and Sylvia and Jo were in the kitchen getting ready to serve the cake Sally had brought. Kendall walked into the kitchen and stood there for a moment, trying to remember why he'd come downstairs.

"Come on, honey, sit down. I'll get you something to eat," Joanna said, leading Kendall to a chair.

She dished up a small plate of pot roast and vegetables and sat it in front of him. "Do you need something to drink?"

He nodded. "Please." His throat was scratchy and his voice was hoarse.

Sylvia poured him a glass of juice and put the teakettle on. "Here, drink this now. I'll make you some tea for your throat."

"Thank you," he said, taking the glass and drinking some of it.

Sylvia and Jo finished dishing up the cake and Sylvia put the plates on a tray and took it out to the living room.

Jo stayed in the kitchen with Kendall and smiled when he took a bite of his dinner. "Taste okay?"

"It's good," he said quietly.

Sylvia handed out the cake. "Kendall's in the kitchen, he actually spoke to us!" she said softly.

"When did he come downstairs?" James asked.

"A couple of minutes ago."

Jen went to get up and Sally stopped her. "We don't want to push him, so let him come in here if he wants to. If not, wait until it's time to clear the plates and then go in to see him."

Jen nodded and sat back down.

Joanna made Kendall a cup of tea and put some honey in it for him. He sipped at his tea for a few minutes, letting the warm liquid ease the pain in his throat. He soon found himself getting sleepy again.

"Why don't you go in and watch the movie with the other kids while I clean up?" Joanna smiled.

He looked at her and nodded.

Kendall walked quietly into the living room and James scooted over and patted the seat next to him. Kendall sat down next to his friend and started watching the movie.

"Did you want some cake, honey?" Jen asked.

"No thanks, mom."

Jen and Brooke got up and started clearing the plates. They took them into the kitchen, where Joanna pointed to the plate with the half-eaten food. "He ate on his own!"

"He's also talking a little." Jen smiled.

"Baby steps," Brooke said, hugging her friend.

Half an hour later, Kendall had fallen asleep and James pulled him over, so that his head was resting on his shoulder.

"Should we take him up to bed?" Logan asked.

Sally smiled and shook her head. "No, he needs this. Wake him when you're all ready to go up."

Logan nodded and they watched the rest of the movie.

Once the movie was over, James gently shook Kendall. "Hey buddy, it's time for bed."

"Hmm?"

"Let's get you upstairs," James said, pulling Kendall up. He wrapped his arm around his friend and helped him up the stairs, the other boys following. James helped him get into his pajamas and then grabbed the shoulder stabilizer.

"I hate that thing," Kendall said.

"I know, but you need to wear it, or your shoulder is never going to heal," James told him.

"Especially if you keep taking on bullies twice your size," Logan said.

"How's your face?" Kendall asked.

"Sore, but I'll live, thanks to you," Logan told him.

Kendall smiled and laid down. He was asleep in minutes.

Carlos smiled. "Tonight was a good night!"

"Yes it was," Logan said and James nodded in agreement.

The boys spaced themselves out like before and soon were all sound asleep.

Chapter 73~ A Good Night's Sleep

Brooke and Joanna got ready to go. "We'll see you at the game tomorrow," Brooke said, giving Sylvia a hug.

"Are you sure you want to take all four kids to the mall?" Joanna asked Antonio.

"Honey, I deal with hardened criminals for a living. I think I can handle four kids at the mall." He smiled, kissing her on the cheek.

All four mothers looked at one another and smiled.

"I'll have my phone on in case you need back up, Boss." Sally smirked, as she put on her coat.

"I am NOT incompetent, it's just a movie and a couple of stores," Antonio insisted.

"Of course it is, darling," Brooke said, patting him on the cheek.

"You're all SO funny tonight, aren't you?"

They all smiled and kissed his cheek as they left.

"Funny, funny ladies," he said as he went around, turning off the lights.

"What's that, dear?" Sylvia asked.

"Nothing... not a thing," he mumbled as he followed her upstairs.

Antonio checked on the boys before he went to bed to make sure they were all sleeping soundly. He went through the room and checked each boy to make sure they were covered and had enough blankets.

"Everyone alright?" Sylvia asked as he crawled into bed.

"So far."

"It was a good night, honey," she said, kissing his cheek.

"Yeah, it really was, considering the way the day started."

"I know, but things seem to be getting back on track. I was so happy I almost cried when I saw him standing there in the doorway, and then he spoke. I just hope they all sleep through the night and get some rest," she said, turning off the light.

"Me too. I can't believe it's only been two weeks. It feels like a lifetime," Antonio said, wrapping his arms around her.

∞

Kendall woke up around 1 am and looked around. He got out of bed and got onto the floor and crawled in between James and Logan and fell back to sleep.

∞

Sylvia got up around 2 am and went to check on the boys. She had a moment of panic when she didn't see Kendall in the bed. "Oh no!" Then she saw him lying next to the other boys and smiled. She grabbed the blanket from the bed and covered him up. She bent down and kissed each of them on the head and went back to bed

∞

The next morning, James woke up first and was surprised to find Kendall curled up next to him. "Hey, are you okay?"

"Hmmm?"

"Are you okay? Were you having a bad dream?" James asked.

"No, didn't like being up there alone," Kendall said, snuggling back under the blankets.

James smiled. "We have a game though, so why don't you get back in the bed. It's going to get cold down here on the floor. Unless you want to come to the game?"

Kendall shook his head.

"Okay, back in bed then," James said firmly.

Kendall buried his head in the blanket. "I'm comfortable."

James sighed. "Okay, I'm going to run and take a shower and then wake up Logan and Carlos. THEN you go back in the bed."

"Mmhmm," Kendall mumbled.

James smiled and shook his head as he got up. Twenty minutes later, he went back into the bedroom and found Kendall curled up next to Logan, completely covered by the blankets.

James went over to Carlos. "Carlos, time to get up," he said, shaking his friend's shoulder.

Next, he woke Logan.

"Why is Kendall down here?" Logan asked, looking at the lump next to him.

"He said he didn't like being alone," James told him.

Logan smiled. "Well he shouldn't stay down here."

"I know. I was just about to wake him up and make him move," James said.

"Okay, I'm going to jump in the shower," Logan said.

"No, me first!" Carlos yelled, jumping over his friends and running for the bathroom.

"Carlos, be careful!" Logan hissed.

"Sorry." Carlos grinned as he ran into the bathroom.

James shook his head. "Kendall, come on, back into bed."

The only response he got was Kendall pulling the blankets tighter.

"You know that's not going to stop me, right?" When he still didn't get an answer, he put his arms under his friend and lifted him up off the floor.

"James..." Kendall's voice was hoarse.

"Hey, are you feeling alright?" Logan asked.

"Meh troat 'urts."

"I'm going to grab the thermometer," Logan said and knocked on the bathroom door before entering. He grabbed the thermometer and took it back to the bedroom. "Put this under your tongue."

Kendall shook his head. "Kendall, I'm serious. We need to make sure you don't have a fever, especially since you ran out in the snow barefooted and with wet hair to SAVE ME. Do you want me to feel guilty and worry all day?"

Kendall glared at him but opened his mouth.

"Thank you." Logan smirked.

A minute later, it beeped and Logan took it out. "99.9...not too bad, but I'm going to get you some Tylenol."

Logan went back into the bathroom and grabbed the Tylenol and a glass of water. "Here, take these. I'm going to make you some tea with honey for your throat."

Kendall looked at the pills for a moment, shivered, and then looked up at Logan. He took the pills and swallowed them. "Thank you."

"No problem. Do you want me to stay home with you?" Logan asked.

Kendall shook his head. "I'll be 'kay."

"I'm going to go make you that tea now," Logan said and headed downstairs.

Logan went into the kitchen to find Jen and Sylvia making breakfast. "Morning Logan," Sylvia said.

"Good morning. Kendall has a sore throat, so I gave him some Tylenol and I'm going make him some tea," Logan told them, turning on the kettle.

"I'll go take his temperature," Jen said.

"I already did. It's 99.9, but considering he was outside yesterday with no shoes and wet hair, I thought it'd be a good idea to try and catch it before it turns into something serious."

Jen hugged him. "Thank you, honey. You are going to make a wonderful doctor."

Logan blushed. "Thanks, Mama K."

"I'm going to mix him up a smoothie for his breakfast. It should feel good on his throat too," Jen said, grabbing the ingredients.

Logan took the tea upstairs, while Jen mixed the smoothie. James and Carlos went downstairs after Logan went back up. Kendall was already sleeping again, so Logan left the tea on the night table and went to take his shower. He checked on Kendall again after he dressed, and his friend was still sound asleep, so he left the tea on the table with a glass of water. He went downstairs to join everyone for breakfast.

∞

After breakfast, the boys got their gear ready.

"Did you boys pack a change of clothing for after the game?" Antonio asked.

"Not yet," Carlos said, running upstairs, James and Logan behind him.

"Carlos, shhhh. Don't wake up Kendall," Logan said, grabbing his enthusiastic friend before he reached the bedroom.

"Sorry," Carlos whispered.

They quickly grabbed a change of clothing and Logan checked on his sleeping friend. He felt his forehead. "Not too warm."

They went downstairs and got ready to go.

"You know, maybe I should come home after the game. I hate to leave Kendall when he's sick," Logan fretted.

"No, you're going out and having fun today. You all need to get out for a while," Jen said.

"I know, but still..."

"Are you saying I can't take care of him?" Jen asked.

Logan looked horrified. "NO! I would never think that, honestly."

"I know that, I'm just giving you a hard time. He'll be fine for a few hours, and you will ALL do much better with some time away from the house," Jen told him.

Logan looked guilty.

"Honey, I know you just want to take care of him, but you need to take care of yourself too. I have your cell number if I need you, and if his temperature goes up, I promise I'll call you," Jen said, hugging him.

He smiled at her. "Okay. I know you're right. I just..."

"I know, honey, really, I do. Now you boys go win that game."

They all nodded and smiled.

"We'll see you all LATER this afternoon," Jen said.

"Yes you will." Antonio smiled as he ushered the kids out the door.

Chapter 74~ The Mall

Jen cleaned the morning dishes. She had insisted that Sylvia go and watch the game since it was only for a couple of hours.

When she was finished, she pulled the smoothie out of the refrigerator and took it upstairs. She decided to take Kendall's temperature again, so she grabbed the thermometer from the bathroom.

She knocked on the bedroom door. "Kendall, I need to take your temperature and I brought you some breakfast."

He was still sleeping, so she went in and sat next to him and brushed the hair out of his eyes. He yawned and started to stretch, but he quickly curled up realizing his mistake when the pain in his shoulder hit. "Ow," he whimpered into the pillow.

She rubbed his back until the pain passed. "Honey, let me take your temperature and then I'm going to get you a pain pill."

He let her put the thermometer in his mouth and it beeped a minute later. "Still 99.9. It's not going up though, so that's good," she said, kissing his forehead. "I'm going to run down and grab one of your pain pills. Do you want anything else?"

He shook his head.

She ran downstairs and came up a moment later. "Here baby," she said, handing him the pill and glass of water from the night table.

He stared at the pill a few seconds before swallowing it. "Thank you."

"I made you a smoothie. I thought it might feel good on your throat. I even put a bendy straw in it," she said, helping him sit up a little and handing him the glass.

"Thanks mom."

She smiled. "You're welcome. Do you want some company? I thought we could watch a movie or something."

"Sure," he said, giving her a small smile.

"What do you want to see?" she asked, going over to the TV.

"Whatever you want."

She smiled and chose Muppet Treasure Island and pulled a chair over next to the bed.

"You can sit here if you want," he said, scooting over. She smiled and sat down next to him.

He drank about half of his smoothie before the pain pill kicked in and he found it hard to keep his eyes open. Jen put her arm around him, and in a few minutes, he had curled up next to her, his head in her lap. She watched the rest of the movie, holding her son for the first time in far too long.

∞

The game didn't even last two hours. First, Carlos and then Logan spent a great deal of time in the penalty box, before all hell broke loose. One of the kids on the opposing team made a remark about Kendall under his breath and Carlos rushed to him, slamming the other boy into the boards. A little while later, the same boy repeated the remark to Logan, who let out an angry yell and threw himself at the boy's legs, causing him to fall backwards and over Logan.

Coach Banner was angry as he hauled Logan off the ice. "What is going on? Are you trying to lose this game on purpose?"

Logan told him what the other boy had said and he went over to speak with the other team's coach. Then he went and spoke with the referee. He came back a minute later.

"When your penalty period is over, feel free to continue with what you were doing," he said with his jaw clenched.

Half an hour later, both teams were in a full-blown fight and six players on each team were ejected from the game, resulting in a game misconduct call with neither side winning.

Antonio was waiting in the locker room with his arms crossed and his eyebrow raised as the boys went in to shower. "You want to tell me what that was all about?"

Logan spoke first. "They were calling Kendall names and it made me mad. Coach Banner went and spoke to their coach, but he LAUGHED at him and said that if we can't take a little name calling, we should take up ice skating."

"What did the referee say?"

"He said he didn't hear it, so he couldn't do anything about it. So when they started in again..." Carlos said.

Antonio sighed. "Alright, go get showered and changed and we'll get out of here."

"We're sorry, Papi," Carlos said.

"No you're not, and I don't blame you. Now go get changed."

The boys nodded and went to shower while Antonio went and explained what happened to their mothers. Twenty minutes later, the boys met Antonio and Katie outside.

He smiled at them. "Okay, let's get going, the movie starts at two, so I thought we'd grab something to eat and then hit the book store."

The boys smiled and got in the car, but they remained quiet.

"Boys, I know this is hard and it's really not fair, but try to not let it get to you too much. People say things because they know it'll hurt you and they try to use that to their advantage. Coach Banner said he told you guys to go ahead and do what you needed to do, so hopefully it's out of your system now."

The boys nodded.

"Now, the rest of the day is for fun. No more sad or angry faces."

Katie was smirking in the front seat.

"What's so funny?" Antonio asked her.

"ALL of my big brothers kicking butt in two days' time," she said.

He looked away, trying not to laugh, but in the rear view mirror saw all three boys break into wide grins.

∞

Sylvia got home and found the house quiet. She checked the downstairs guest room, but Jen wasn't there. She looked in Carlos' room and found Jen sitting up on the bed, her arms around Kendall as he slept.

She smiled and went in. "Hey, how's he doing?"

Jen just smiled back. "He asked me to sit next to him and then fell asleep."

Sylvia smiled. "See? Everything is going to be fine. I'm going to make us some lunch and I'll bring it up."

"You don't have to do that, I can help."

"You stay right there and don't move. I mean it," Sylvia said firmly.

"Thank you... for everything," Jen said.

"Honey, you don't have to thank me. We're family. Being there for each other is what we do," Sylvia told her.

Jen smiled and nodded. "Why are you back so early? Did the boys win?"

"Yeah... about that. I'll tell you later," Sylvia said.

"Why, what happened?"

"You know those boys of ours..." Sylvia said as she hurried out and headed downstairs.

Oh no, what did they do now? Jen thought to herself.

∞

Antonio and the kids got to the mall. "Okay where to first?"

"Food!" Carlos said.

"Alright, let's eat first, and then the bookstore for Logan?"

"The arcade!" Katie said.

"Well, I need to pick up some conditioner, I'm almost out," James said.

"One thing at a time, we have all day," Antonio told them.

They went to the food court, everyone headed to their favourite food counter, and they met at a table in the middle. Carlos had eaten his four corndogs before anyone else was finished and went back for seconds.

"Where does he put it all?" James asked.

"I have no idea. One day he managed to eat eight corndogs and then a large order of chili fries," Antonio said.

"With all the energy he expends, he needs it," Logan said.

"That's true," James agreed.

Carlos came back and everyone managed to finish their meal by the time he finished again.

"Alright, we still have an hour until the movie, so do you boys want to go and get your shopping done first and meet in front of the theatres?" Antonio suggested.

"That sounds good," Logan said.

"I want to go to the arcade!" Katie said.

"Me too!" Carlos said excitedly.

"Okay, I'll take you two to the arcade while James and Logan do their thing." Antonio smiled.

Katie and Carlos shrieked in delight and started for the escalators.

"Dad, I'm fourteen. I think I can handle going to the arcade on my own," Carlos called over his shoulder.

James and Logan both looked at Antonio and quickly shook their heads.

Antonio groaned. "Wait for me," Antonio yelled, running after the two. He finally caught up and couldn't believe how many kids frequented the arcade on the weekend. James joined them about fifteen minutes later, carrying two large bags.

"I thought you just needed conditioner?" Antonio asked.

"They were having a sale," James said as he went to join his friends.

Antonio sat on a bench with James' bags and soon found he was developing a pounding headache from all the noise. It's a wonder any of the kids today can even hear.

"Hey, why don't we go look around for a while?" he suggested.

"The pet store?" Carlos suggested.

"Sounds nice and quiet," Antonio said.

They went to the second floor and found the pet store. Carlos ran to look at the puppies while Katie visited the rabbit pen. "Don't you want to see the animals?" Antonio asked James.

"I'm not going in there with those two," James said.

"Why not?" Antonio asked, suddenly worried.

James smiled and pointed. Antonio looked over and saw Carlos had crawled into one of the kennels and the puppies were crawling all over him and he was giggling. He picked up the pups one at a time, kissing each one.

"Carlos, get out of there!" Antonio ordered.

"But Papi... they're so sweet!"

"You aren't supposed to get in with them. Read the signs, son."

"Just ONE more minute, PLEASE!" Carlos pleaded.

"No, get out now!" Antonio told him, as an employee walked up and informed Antonio that children were NOT allowed in with the animals.

"I know, I'm getting him," he told her.

"Is that one yours too?" she asked as she pointed across the room. Katie had opened the door to the rabbit pen and was currently trying to wrangle the three that had gone hopping out before she could stop them.

"Oh no," he groaned. "Carlos, OUT NOW! Go stand with James," he ordered as he ran to try to help catch the bunnies.

A few minutes and several apologies later, the bunnies were back in their pen. Antonio kept a firm grip on Carlos and Katie until they were well away from the pet store. He pulled out his cell and called Logan to let him know they would be at the theatre in ten minutes.

He looked at James. "Anyplace else we should avoid?"

"Yeah... there," James pointed across the mall to the candy store, where Carlos was already standing.

"Oh no," Antonio groaned again. He made his way over to the candy store when Carlos came running out.

"Papi, look what I found!" he said, running to his dad to show him what he'd found.

"HEY! YOU DIDN'T PAY FOR THAT!" an employee from the candy store yelled, following Carlos out.

"Carlos, you can't leave a store without paying!" Antonio told him as he pulled him back to the candy store.

"But Papi, I found Sour Belts. They're Kendall's favourite. Can I get them for him?"

"I'm so sorry. I'll pay for it, he was just excited," Antonio told the clerk.

The clerk mumbled something under his breath as he rang up the sale. Antonio paid him and pulled Carlos out of the store. "Carlos, you can't just leave a store without paying, it's stealing," Antonio told him.

"I'm sorry, I didn't mean to," Carlos said sadly.

"I know you didn't. Let's get to the movie before it starts."

Carlos smiled. "You're not mad at me?"

"No, you didn't mean to do it, just DON'T do it again." Antonio smiled.

"I won't," Carlos promised, hugging his dad.

Logan was standing in front of the movie theatre waiting for them.

Antonio bought the tickets and then handed Logan some money. "Katie and I will find seats. You boys get popcorn and something to drink."

"Okay, Papa G." Logan smiled.

Antonio and Katie found seats, and a few minutes later, the boys found them. The movie started and Antonio enjoyed the quiet as the kids became engrossed in the escapades of James Bond. After the movie, they went to the car with Carlos and James acting out some of the scenes.

"I want to be a secret agent," Carlos declared.

"How do you plan on doing that? You can't keep ANYTHING a secret," Logan pointed out.

"Can too!"

"Cannot!"

"Can too!"

"Boys! Please, be quiet while I'm driving," Antonio said.

The boys lowered their voices but kept up the argument. Antonio pulled up to his house and got out. They all went inside, Carlos running to give the candy to Kendall.

"So... how was the mall?" Sylvia smirked, taking note of her husband's tired and frustrated expression.

"Pshhh, piece of cake," he said as he went upstairs. "Honey, where's the ibuprofen?" he called down a minute later.

Chapter 75~ Denial of Guilt

Richard Graham was furious that he had to spend the weekend in a common jailhouse. His attorney had finally received his message and was on his way in for a conference with him.

First, he had the huge man for a cellmate, who took both mattresses and then had the nerve to hug him when he left. Then, when the officer had come to get him so he could meet with his attorney, his trousers had caught on the metal springs of the bunk and tore almost all the way down the leg. He was now wearing common jailhouse pants, which clashed horribly with his $2,000 suit jacket and silk shirt.

∞

Jonathan Reed was a 38-year-old trial attorney, who had been recommended to Graham by Dr. Davis. He specialized in malpractice lawsuits, and it sounded like Graham had a doozy. He was already annoyed with Graham because when he returned his message, Graham had thrown what amounted to a temper tantrum because he had been out of town.

He smiled and stood up when Graham was brought into the room. The officer attached the cuffs to the table and then left the room.

"Dr. Graham, it's..."

"IT'S ABOUT TIME!" Graham shouted. "I have been waiting for over twenty-four hours for you. Now they tell me there isn't a judge available until Monday, which means I have to stay here all weekend!"

"As I explained on the phone, Dr. Graham, I was out of town and the weather had the airports shut down in Madison. I'm here now, so why don't we discuss your case?"

"There is no case, the charges are fraudulent," Graham stated,

"Well, it says here that the charges are actually quite serious, including what could be interpreted as prescription drug trafficking. Did you have controlled substances illegally transported across state lines?"

"Don't be ridiculous. I purchased those drugs legally and simply had them shipped from my other office," Graham said.

"Your office in Louisiana?"

"Yes."

"You do realize that you're not licensed to prescribe drugs in Minnesota? That to have drugs shipped here, especially controlled substances, is in fact, illegal," Reed told him.

"Dr. Davis will back me up," Graham said.

"It's not really a matter of Dr. Davis backing you up—the law is the law. You've broken several drug enforcement laws and there's a good chance the DEA will get involved in this," Reed warned.

"Well, that's why I hired you, to FIX this."

Reed sighed. "Alright, tell me about these other charges. Assault and battery of a 14-year-old boy."

"Lies. I was trying to help the boy and he had a panic attack in my office, so the nurse gave him an injection of the drug, which had already been prescribed to help him with anxiety."

"The nurse gave him the injection?"

"Yes," Graham said.

"Under your direction?"

"Meaning?"

"Did you TELL the nurse to give him the injection?" Reed asked once more.

"Of course I did, he was having an anxiety attack."

"According to a witness, you locked the boy in a room, and when he tried to get out, you restrained him while the nurse gave him the injection of Lorazepam... which is a controlled substance. The witness claims the boy was not having an anxiety attack until you locked him in and then grabbed him."

"It's that damn nurse, isn't it? Trying to save her own skin!"

"Also, you did this WITHOUT a parent's permission or presence. Do you understand exactly how much trouble you're in?" Reed asked.

"The boy is a spoiled brat who defies authority. His mother cannot control him and asked me to intervene on her behalf," Graham stated.

Reed sighed. "You do know we have attorney/client confidentiality? You can tell me the truth and I can't tell anyone."

"Are you saying I'm lying?"

Reed just looked at him.

"Well?" Graham asked.

"Let's try it this way... you are guilty. You know you're guilty, I know you're guilty, the police and DA know you're guilty. The question is... what are we going to do to prevent you from spending a good portion of the rest of your life behind bars?"

"How dare you!"

"Dr. Graham, the DA has witnesses. They have subpoenaed all of your drug purchase records in Louisiana, as well as the records from the courier service that you use. They also have previous clients who have provided records and are willing to testify against you, including a family whose son committed suicide. The police also have photos of bruises on the boy that you forcibly gave the injection to."

"Those families signed release forms when we settled out of court!" Graham yelled.

"True, but those release forms were only good in the case of a civil suit. This is a criminal case, and the judge is allowing their testimony. So I strongly recommend that you agree to a plea bargain, if the DA is willing to offer you one."

"This is ridiculous," Graham sputtered.

"It is what it is, Dr. Graham. Or in this case, it is what YOU made it."

∞

Carlos ran upstairs, excited to show Kendall his gift. He went into his bedroom and found Jen and Kendall curled up on his bed. "Hi Mama K," Carlos whispered.

"Hi honey. How was your day at the mall?"

"It was good, the movie was awesome. Look what I found for Kendall!"

"What is it?"

"The candy store had Sour Belts in all kinds of flavours, so I got him one of each," Carlos said, showing her the bag.

"Carlos, those are his favourite. That was so nice!'

"How's he feeling?"

"I think he's feeling better. He took a pain pill and has been sleeping for a few hours now."

Carlos sat next to her. "Are you feeling okay?"

Jen smiled. "I'm feeling much better, today was a good day here too. Now, what happened at the game this morning?"

"Ummm... I think I hear my mom calling, I better go see what she needs!" he said, jumping up and running out the door.

"Carlos, no running on the stairs," Antonio said as his son flew past him.

"Sorry Papi," Carlos said as he slowed his pace.

Antonio shook his head and went to check on Kendall. "How are things going in here?"

"Good," Jen said, smiling. "How was the mall?"

Antonio shook his head. "Never again without back-up."

"We tried warning you."

"Yes you did," he admitted.

"So are you saying that a handful of teenagers are more difficult to handle than a hardened criminal?"

"I admit defeat only because I was at a disadvantage."

"Which was?"

"I was severely outnumbered."

"There were only three teenage boys and one little girl."

"True, but that little girl equals five teenagers and Carlos..."

Jen nodded. "I'd give you that, except each of us moms has managed all FOUR teenage boys and Katie with no problem."

"Ah, but you're forgetting the MOST important detail," he countered.

"Which is?"

"I am a man. I am not equipped mentally or physically to keep up with THAT many children. Especially in their own habitat."

"Meaning the mall?"

He nodded. "Whoever came up with the idea of malls was either a genius or completely insane. I'm inclined to think the latter."

Jen laughed at him. "I have to admit there are times I would agree with you. So, Carlos wouldn't tell me...What happened at the game today?"

Antonio sighed. "Just some unsportsmanlike conduct from the other team."

"How so?"

"I'll tell you later," he said, looking at Kendall.

Jen tightened her hold on her son. "Is this ever going to end?"

Antonio smiled. "Yes, it will. Especially when word gets out that Kendall single handedly beat the crap out of one of the toughest football players in school."

"It shouldn't be this way," Jen said sadly.

"No, it shouldn't. Unfortunately, it all too often is," Antonio told her.

∞

Graham was fuming. His fool of an attorney wanted him to plead out.

Ridiculous. Just because a few people disagreed with my treatment plans regarding a few stubborn, spoiled, rude little brats. They should be grateful that I even took the time to speak to them. If people knew the truth about how I have actually HELPED these people, he thought.

He smiled as an idea came to mind.

Chapter 76~The Haircut

Jonathan Reed shook his head as he walked into his office.

"Rough meeting?" his secretary, Tanya Sanders, asked.

"Richard Graham has to be THE most narcissistic person I've ever met. The man is completely oblivious to the trouble he's in, and he's in a LOT of trouble. Instead of agreeing to let me plead his case down, which could save him years in prison, he's trying to come up with a scheme to get himself off the hook. He doesn't seem to understand there's a good chance the DEA is going to become involved in this if he doesn't allow me to do my job."

"Bet you wish the airports had stayed closed," Tanya said.

"Yes I do. By the way, thanks for coming in on a Saturday."

"Not a problem, it's not like there was a lot to do here the two days you were gone." She smiled.

"Why don't you go ahead and take off? I need to research a couple of things and then I'll be going home, too."

"Okay, see you on Monday," Tanya said as she put on her coat.

"See you Monday," he said as he went and sat down at his desk, wondering what he was going to do about his troublesome client.

∞

Kendall stirred a little, so Jen decided to wake him up. "Kendall, it's time to get up. Everyone's home now and dinner will be in a little while."

He opened his eyes and groaned.

"Does it still hurt?" she asked, rubbing his back.

He nodded.

"Let me get you another pain pill."

He shook his head. "They make me feel funny."

"I know, but the doctor said you need to take them if you're hurting."

"Can I just have ibuprofen until bedtime?"

Jen nodded. "Alright, but if it gets to be too much, you'll need to take one. We also need to put some ice on your shoulder."

Kendall nodded.

"Okay, you wait here and I'll run and get the frozen peas and ibuprofen," she said..

"Can I take a shower first?"

She smiled. "Sure. I'll be back up in about twenty minutes."

He nodded and sat up, finding he was a little dizzy. He took a deep breath, stood up, and grabbed some clean clothes. He went into the bathroom and started the shower, and once the water was warm, got in. He almost screamed when it hit his shoulder and he felt slightly nauseated. He took few deep breaths and the warm, steamy air seemed to help.

He finished and got out and dried off. He sat down and pulled on his boxers and sweats, and then realized he still needed help with his shirt. He wrapped the towel around his shoulders and peaked out to see if anyone was upstairs. *Great,* he thought, not seeing anyone.

He walked over to the top of the stairs. "James, are you there?"

"Are you alright, honey?" Jen asked, starting up the stairs.

"I'm fine, I just need James," he said, backing towards the bathroom.

"I can help you."

"Mom, no!" he said as he closed the bathroom door.

Jen looked crestfallen as she went into the kitchen. "James, Kendall is calling for you. I think he needs help dressing."

James jumped up. "I have something for him anyway."

"What's the matter Jen?" Sylvia asked.

"He didn't want my help."

"Honey, he's fourteen. I can guarantee he didn't want you to help him get dressed BEFORE this happened," Antonio said.

She smiled sadly. "You're right. I'm reading too much into it. I'm not going to allow my fears to ruin the wonderful day I spent with him."

"Good girl," Antonio said. "Now, I'm going to go into public again with the other little monsters and get pizza for dinner."

Jen laughed at him. "Good luck!"

"I'll come with you, honey. Just in case you need back-up." Sylvia smirked.

"Funny ladies," Antonio said, shaking his head again.

∞

James knocked on the bathroom door. "Hey, it's me."

"Is my mom out there?"

"No, it's just me."

Kendall slowly opened the door and let James in. "I can't get my shirt on." Kendall sighed.

"I know, it's okay," James told him as he eased the long sleeved t-shirt over his friend's head.

Kendall flinched as he put his arm in the sleeve.

"Where's your stabilizer?" James asked.

"On the bed."

James grabbed it and helped Kendall put it on. He also brought out a small spray bottle. "I got this for you, it's spray-on conditioner. It helps do away with tangles and makes your hair soft as silk," he said as he sprayed Kendall's damp locks.

James grabbed his comb and ran it through his friend's hair. "See, what did I tell you? No pulling or pain." He smirked.

Kendall rolled his eyes.

"Admit it, I'm right," James said.

Kendall just looked at him.

"You're not going to say it, are you?"

Kendall shook his head and smirked back at him.

"You're so annoying sometimes. Did you want me to trim up these bangs a little? You're looking a little shaggy," James asked as he combed Kendall's bangs down to his nose.

"Sure, why not."

James looked in the drawers and found a small pair of scissors. "These should work for just a trim. Sit and stay still," James instructed as he combed Kendall's bangs forward.

Kendall closed his eyes as James started cutting. A few minutes later, James combed Kendall's hair up and then to the sides.

"What are you doing?" Kendall asked, opening one eye and trying to look up.

"Shhh, don't worry. Just let me work my magic," James said.

"What magic? You've never cut hair before," Kendall pointed out.

"That's why you should probably SIT still."

"WHAT did you do?" Kendall asked, suddenly very worried.

James smiled. "Gotcha... Next time you should ADMIT when I'm right."

Kendall glared up at him. "I'd rather my hair was cut wrong than admit you were right."

"I can arrange that, you know," James threatened.

"Do you really want to chance that?" Kendall asked, raising an eyebrow for emphasis.

James stared at him. "Touché. It would seem we are at an impasse for the moment."

"Yes it would." Kendall smirked, getting up. A wave of dizziness washed over him and he grabbed the counter for support.

"Are you okay?" James asked, putting an arm around Kendall's waist to steady him.

"I'm okay, just stood up too fast I guess."

"Did you eat today?"

"I had a smoothie."

"That's not enough!" James said.

"I know, but I took a pain pill and slept until just a little while ago," Kendall told him.

"Well you're going to eat something now," James said, still holding onto his friend.

He helped Kendall downstairs and led him into the kitchen. "He needs to eat," James said as he pulled out a chair for Kendall to sit on.

Jen grabbed some juice from the refrigerator and poured a glass. "Drink this and I'll make you something."

Kendall's hands were shaking as he tried to take a sip and James steadied it for him.

Jen quickly made him a sandwich. "Try eating this, baby, you're really pale."

He took a bite and swallowed. For a moment, he thought he was going to throw it back up, but it stayed down.

"Take another sip," James said, holding the juice glass for him.

Kendall did as James said and found he was feeling a little better. He took another bite, and soon the nausea passed.

"I should have made you wake up for lunch," Jen said. "Did you cut your hair?"

Kendall smiled. "James did."

"It looks great!"

James smirked. "Why thank you. At least SOMEONE appreciates my talent."

Kendall rolled his eyes again. He finished his juice and sandwich.

"Feel better?" Jen asked.

Kendall nodded.

Jen handed him two ibuprofen. "Here you go, honey. Why don't we ice your shoulder in the living room? The couch is more comfortable than the kitchen chairs."

He stared at the pills before taking them from her. "Thank you."

Kendall got up and James stood next to him, making sure he didn't lose his balance. Jen smiled at James and handed him the bag of frozen peas. "Thanks James."

James smiled back and nodded as he helped Kendall into the living room. They sat on the couch and James turned on the TV and handed Kendall the remote as he held the bag to his friend's shoulder. They sat there and watched a game until everyone got home, and then joined them all at the dinner table. Kendall wasn't hungry because he had just eaten, but James and Antonio got him to eat one slice of pizza.

After dinner, they went back into the living room, where they watched a movie. A little while later, Jen got Kendall a pain pill. He pouted but took it. About an hour later, he fell asleep and James grabbed a pillow and pulled him over so his head was in his lap. Logan pulled his feet up onto his lap and Carlos sat right below him on the floor, Katie leaning against him. They stayed that way for the rest of the evening.

When it was time for bed, Antonio carried Kendall upstairs, the others close behind.

Chapter 77 ~ Hide and Seek

The first thing he noticed was that he was freezing. He pulled the blankets over his head and tried finding warmth under the covers, to no avail. Finally, he gave up trying to sleep and got up to find a sweatshirt. He noticed he was alone in the room.

"Everyone must be up already." The bedroom door was open, so he went downstairs and realized that the reason it was so cold was the front door was wide open. There was no one in the living room, but he heard a sound in the kitchen and went to check it out. No one was there.

He heard whispering and went back into the living room. Still no one was there. Then he heard a scream coming from outside and ran for the door. He stepped out onto the front porch and listened. He heard the scream again coming from across the street and followed the sound. He kept running towards the screams, but it seemed the faster he ran, the further away they got.

Suddenly, he was standing in the middle of a grove of trees and the screams were close. Then he realized who was screaming and ran through the trees, desperate to reach him.

Something hit him and he landed on his stomach. He rolled over and tried to get up, but someone held him down.

"I finally figured out the BEST way to punish you," Deesie hissed into his ear.

Kendall looked in the direction of the screams and saw that Carlos was tied with a thick yellow rope, his arms above his head. The rope was thrown over a large tree limb and Deesie kept pulling the rope, yanking his friend off the ground, and then releasing it so Carlos fell to the ground.

Deesie tied the rope securely around the tree trunk, went over, and started hitting Carlos. Kendall screamed at him to stop, but the man just smiled his twisted smile and punched Carlos in the face. His friend's head snapped back and he stopped moving.

Suddenly Deesie was on top of him again. "How many times did I warn you, sweetheart? How many times did I tell you that you would be punished?" he asked, running his tongue along the boy's jaw line.

Kendall closed his eyes, and when he opened them, Deesie was gone and Kendall was back in bed. He tried to slow his breathing and sat up. He realized he was in the second motel room. He jumped up and ran to the door, frantically trying to open it.

"Where do you think you're going?" Deesie asked as he wrapped his arms around the teen, running his hands up and down his chest.

"Leave me alone!" Kendall screamed.

Deesie kissed his neck and pushed him into the bathroom. "Look what you did, sweetheart," he said, pointing to the bathtub.

Katie was lying in the bathtub under the water, her brown eyes open and staring up into nothing.

"NO!" Kendall screamed, trying to get to her.

"I don't think so," Deesie whispered as he pushed Kendall into the wall and put handcuffs on his wrists. Then he pulled his arm back and hit him hard.

Kendall fell to the floor and Deesie smiled. "Now, it's time for me to take a few pictures," he said as he turned out the light and closed the door.

Kendall got up and tried to open the door. He heard the clicking sound of a camera and then sobbing. "Please leave me alone."

"JAMES!" Kendall screamed and tried to break through the door. "Leave him alone!" Kendall screamed as he threw himself into the door once more.

The door broke and he fell through it to the other side. "You will ALWAYS be mine, sweetheart," Deesie whispered into his ear.

Kendall's eyes snapped open. His head was pounding and his heart felt like it was going to explode out of his chest. He got up, went into the bathroom, and closed the door. He got a drink of water and a wave of nausea hit him. He quickly knelt in front of the toilet and vomited. He flushed and sat there on the floor for a few minutes, shaking. Once he had calmed down enough, he got up and opened the door.

"Come out, come out wherever you are," he heard Deesie calling in singsong.

Kendall ran.

∞

James woke up slowly, thinking he had heard something.

He yawned and looked around. The hallway light was shining in his eyes. "Darn light," he mumbled as he got up and closed the door. Then he saw the empty bed and realized the bedroom door had been closed when they went to sleep.

He flipped on the light, looked under the bed, and then ran to the closet, tripping over Logan.

"Ow! Hey, what's going on?" Logan groaned.

"Kendall's gone! Get up and help me find him," James said.

"What do you mean he's gone?" Logan said, jumping up.

"He's not here either..." James said, closing the closet door.

"The bedroom door was open. I'm going to check the other rooms!" he said as he headed out the door.

"Carlos, get up!" Logan said, shaking him.

"I wanna sleep longer, Mami," Carlos said, pulling the blanket over his head.

Logan smacked his head. "I'm not Mami. Kendall is missing, get up!"

"What?" Carlos asked, bolting upright.

James came running back in. "He's not in the bathroom or guest room. We need to check downstairs!" he said, running for the staircase.

Logan and Carlos were right behind him. They turned on the downstairs lights and began searching downstairs room by room.

∞

Antonio heard something and went downstairs to find the three boys apparently looking for something. "What's going on?"

"Kendall's missing," James said as he checked the front coat closet for the second time.

"Were the front and back doors closed and locked?" Antonio asked.

"The front door was. I didn't check the back yet!" James said, running for the kitchen. "It's locked," he called out from the kitchen.

Antonio knocked on Jen's bedroom door. "Jen, is Kendall in there with you?"

He heard someone get up and Jen opened the door. "No, why?"

"The boys woke up and he wasn't in the bedroom with them."

"Oh my God!" she said.

"He has to be in the house, the doors were all locked," Antonio said calmly. "We just need to stay calm and not panic. Now, is there a chance he went into your room while you were sleeping?"

"I don't know, maybe," Jen said and went back into the bedroom. She quietly looked under the bed and in the closet, trying not to wake Katie. She came out and closed the door, shaking her head. "He's not in there."

Antonio went into his study and searched it while the boys rechecked the closets and cupboards.

"He's not anywhere," Carlos said, his voice rising in panic.

"Did you boys check behind all the furniture and the drapes?" Antonio asked.

They all nodded.

"Everyone take a deep breath. Did anyone check the basement?"

"I didn't," Logan said.

"Me either," James said and Carlos shook his head.

Antonio went and opened the basement door and flipped on the light switch. "Carlos, grab the flashlight in case we need it."

Carlos nodded and got the flashlight from the drawer. Antonio went down the stairs and looked around the nearly bare room. The boys use to play down there when they were younger and Antonio had planned to turn it into an actual recreation room in the next year.

"Okay, everyone go slowly and check everywhere," he said.

They all nodded, and once they had searched the main room, they checked the small laundry room and then the room the Garcia's used for storage.

Kendall was nowhere to be found.

Chapter 78~ Closed in Spaces

Dylan Mason was lying in a cell, fuming. His friends had been released into their parents' custody just a few hours after they had been picked up. Mostly due to the fact, they hadn't actually been seen assaulting anyone. They had been all too happy to point the finger at Dylan and claim neither of them had actually hit anyone. They would have to appear in court, but they hadn't formally been charged.

He had to wait until Monday, until the court opened, before he could get bail. That is, if his good-for-nothing parents even decided to pay the bail.

He had seen Todd and Brian as the officer had led him back to a cell. He didn't know what happened with them, but they avoided eye contact with him. He tried talking to them, but no one had answered.

There was an older guy in the cell next to his and all the guy did was whine and complain. He kept demanding to see his attorney, demanding to be released, demanding this and that.

Finally, Dylan had had enough. "Will you shut the hell up?"

"How dare you speak to me in such a manner! I don't know who you think you are, but I have had it with spoiled, ungrateful children!" Graham yelled.

"It's three in the morning and I am trying to SLEEP, you stupid prick!" Dylan yelled.

"So go to sleep then, you little imbecile. Who's stopping you?"

"You and your big mouth are!"

"So mind your own business, you impertinent little brat!"

One of the officers came back. "BOTH of you shut up or else!"

"Just you wait! When I get out of here, I am SUING this department, this city, the officers that allowed that Knight brat to kick me, as well as the wretched Knight family!" Graham screeched at the top of his lungs.

"What's that about the Knights?" Dylan asked, suddenly interested.

"That is none of your business," Graham said.

"Really? Because Kendall Knight is the reason I'm in here right now. The little freak can't handle a little teasing, and then when I'm talking to his little wimp of a friend, he comes out of nowhere and attacks me with a hockey stick. So they arrest ME all because his friend's dad is the chief of police," Dylan told him.

"Really? Well then, I think we might be able to come up with a mutually beneficial arrangement regarding our little problem child," Graham said, smiling.

∞

"Carlos go wake your Mami and search our bedroom. We need to search the house again. He has to be here somewhere. The doors and windows are all locked, he couldn't have gotten outside," Antonio said.

Carlos nodded and ran upstairs. "Mami wake up! We can't find Kendall and Papi says to search your room."

"Carlos... what?" Sylvia said, covering her eyes to shield them against the bright overhead light Carlos had switched on.

"Kendall's missing, we can't find him," Carlos told her.

"Okay Mijo," she said as she jumped up and they began searching the bedroom. Not finding him, they moved to the other bedrooms and searched them again.

"Where is he?" Carlos said as he checked the bathroom for the third time.

"We'll find him, Mijo," Sylvia said, hugging her son.

Carlos was trying not to cry, but he was scared. He knew the doors were locked, but what if Kendall managed to get outside anyway. He tried to block all the images from his dreams that flooded his mind as he raced down the stairs again.

"He's not upstairs, we searched everywhere!" Carlos said as a few tears spilled out of his eyes.

"Alright, everyone stop for a minute and think. When he was little, where would he go when he got scared?" Antonio asked.

"Kendall doesn't get scared," Carlos said, choking back a sob.

James went over and hugged his friend. "It'll be okay, Carlos. We'll find him. Remember, he always won at hide and seek."

Carlos buried his head in James' shoulder and started crying.

"Carlos is right, Kendall never acted scared when he was little," Jen said, her voice shaky.

Sylvia went to her friend and hugged her.

Suddenly Carlos pulled away from James. "Hide and seek!"

"What?" James asked.

"Remember when we were ten and played hide and seek and we NEVER found Kendall and he wouldn't tell us where he was?"

"Yeah," Logan and James said at the same time.

"Well, a few days later I asked him again... I know where he is!" Carlos yelled, racing to the basement door. He grabbed the flashlight and ran down the stairs, the others right behind him.

Carlos went into the room they used for storage, found the door to the little crawlspace under the stairwell, and opened it. He shined the flashlight, but he still couldn't see anything. He wiggled in a little and then backed out. "He's in there! I see his foot!"

"We need to be careful and not wake him too suddenly," Logan said.

Antonio and James pushed the boxes that were close to the door away and Antonio tried to look inside. "Damn it, I'm too big," he said. He looked at Logan. "You're the smallest and you were able to wake him carefully before. Do you think you can do it?"

Logan nodded and Carlos handed him the flashlight. Logan crawled through the small opening, which opened into a larger area, and saw Kendall curled up against the far wall.

He quietly moved over to where his friend was. "Kendall," he said softly. When he didn't respond, Logan moved a little closer. "Kendall, you need to wake up now," Logan said, gently touching his shoulder.

Logan noticed the stabilizer straps were loose, probably coming undone when Kendall had crawled in there. Logan sighed sadly. "You're going to be in so much pain later... Kendall, please wake up! We need to get out of here," Logan said again.

The walls were closing in a bit and he was a little freaked out by the thought of spiders and other creepy crawlies jumping on him. "Kendall... please wake up. We need to get out of here," Logan said, shaking him again.

Kendall opened his eyes. All he saw was a faint light surrounded by shadows. With the memory of the dreams still vivid in his mind, reality was blurred and he pushed away from whoever was touching him and screamed.

Logan backed away, trying to give his friend some space. "Kendall, it's me, Logan. It's alright, you're safe."

Kendall was shaking and started rocking back and forth, his eyes squeezed shut. "No more, no more, no more."

Logan risked moving closer and was soon sitting next to Kendall. He sat there quietly for a few moments, ignoring the fact that the room seemed like it was getting smaller. He put his hand on Kendall's shoulder, and when he didn't pull away, wrapped an arm around him.

The others were anxiously waiting in the storage room and jumped when they heard Kendall scream. James went to try to crawl in, but Antonio pulled him back. "You won't fit, Mijo. Let Logan handle this. If he needs help, we can break through the wall," Antonio said.

James nodded but sat at the entrance listening.

Kendall finally calmed down a little and sat next to Logan with his head on his shoulder. Logan noticed that Kendall was still shivering and that he felt very warm to the touch.

"Hey buddy, I think your fever's getting worse. We need to get you out of here," he whispered to Kendall.

Kendall shook his head. "He's here."

"Who's here?"

"He is."

"Kendall, nobody's here but me and people who love you. I promise, no one is going to hurt you," Logan said, his eyes tearing up at the fear in his friend's voice.

"He said he'd hurt them."

"Hurt who?"

"All of you."

"No one's going to hurt us, Deesie is dead. If he wasn't, Papi would protect us," Logan said, hugging Kendall.

"He killed Papi."

Logan's mind raced, trying to think of a way to convince his friend that everyone was alright. "If I show you Papi is alright, will you come out?"

Kendall thought for a moment and then nodded.

"Okay, I'm going to call out for him. He can't fit in here all the way, but he can talk to you."

Kendall nodded.

"Papi! Can you talk to Kendall and tell him that everyone is okay?" Logan yelled.

Antonio got on the floor and looked in the small door. "Logan, shine the light down here."

Logan did as he was told and he could see Antonio looking at them. "See, there's Papi," Logan said, pointing.

Kendall looked over and Antonio smiled at him. "Mijo, we've been looking for you everywhere. You need to come out so we can all get back to bed."

Kendall looked at Logan. "It was a dream?" he asked confused.

Logan nodded. "I think your fever might have caused it, you're really warm," he said, putting his hand on Kendall's forehead. "We'll get you some Tylenol and you'll feel better in no time."

Kendall nodded.

"You go first, so I can help you if you need it," Logan told him.

Kendall nodded again.

"Papi, we're going to come out now," Logan called out.

"Okay." He smiled and backed out of the doorway.

Antonio looked at the others. "They're coming out now. Why don't you all head upstairs so he isn't overwhelmed when he comes out?"

Jen and Sylvia nodded. Sylvia put an arm around Carlos. "Let's go upstairs and wait."

Jen took James' hand. "Come on, honey."

James looked at Antonio, who nodded at him. "We'll be up in a minute."

Logan shined the light ahead of them so they could see where they were going. Kendall was having difficulty crawling out with only one good arm, so Logan crawled next to him, his arm around his waist until the space narrowed.

Kendall stopped short of the door. "What's the matter?" Logan asked.

Kendall didn't say anything, but he didn't move either. He felt dizzy and tried to block the panic rising in his chest. He swore he could hear Deesie, even though he knew he was dead. He shook his head and backed up a little.

"Kendall, come on, we're almost there," Logan said, urging his friend forward. Logan had always hated small spaces, and he was afraid he was going to freak out if he didn't get out soon.

After a couple of minutes, Kendall took a deep breath and started moving again. He got to the doorway and Antonio offered him his hand and helped him out.

Logan rushed out right behind him, shuddering. "Are you okay?" Antonio asked him.

Logan nodded. "Just a little close in there."

"Good job," Antonio said, patting Logan's shoulder.

"Thanks Papi." Logan smiled.

"Let's get you two upstairs and everyone back to bed," Antonio said, wrapping an arm around Kendall's waist and helping him upstairs.

Chapter 79~ Self Doubt

Once they got back to the main floor, Antonio and Jen took Kendall back upstairs to bed.

Logan was still shuddering at being in such a small dark space. "You okay, buddy?" James asked him.

Logan nodded. "Remind me that I HATE hide and seek if we ever decide it might be a fun game to play if we're bored."

James' eyes widened as he saw a large spider crawl up Logan's arm. He smiled at Logan and quickly brushed the spider off as he put his hand on Logan's shoulder. "You did a great job though," he said as he pushed Logan towards the living room, stepping on the spider before following him.

They rushed upstairs after Kendall and the others.

Antonio and Jen got Kendall back into bed and Jen sat next to him. Logan grabbed the thermometer from the bathroom and Kendall allowed him to take his temperature. When it beeped, Logan took it out and read it. "102.7."

"I'll get some Tylenol," Sylvia said.

Jen nodded. "Thank you."

Kendall shivered and tried to pull the blankets around himself. "C-Can I have my sweatshirt?" he asked. The room was spinning and he felt so cold.

"No baby, we need to get your fever down," Jen told him.

"I'm cold," he whispered.

"I know, but if we bundle you up, your fever will get worse."

Sylvia came in with the Tylenol and a glass of water. "Here Mijo, take these. They'll make you feel better."

She held the glass for Kendall as he swallowed the pills.

"Thank you," Kendall said as he closed his eyes.

Carlos was sitting quietly at the foot of the bed, feeling completely useless. He got up, went downstairs, and sat in his dad's chair. James noticed the look on Carlos' face and followed him downstairs. He sat down next to him and put an arm around his shoulders. "Are you okay?"

Carlos nodded. "I was just... I just wish there was something I could do to help."

"What do you mean?" James asked softly.

"Logan was able to get Kendall out and can help him when he's sick. You take care of him when he has a panic attack and you can get him to eat. He doesn't need me..." Carlos said sadly.

James was shocked. He had no idea that Carlos felt this way. "Of course he needs you, we all do! Carlos, if it weren't for you, we wouldn't have even found him. No one knew about that crawlspace! He only told you about it and you remembered after all this time! Who knows what would have happened to him if he'd woken up in there all alone."

"I guess."

"Carlos, look at me."

Carlos looked over at James. "When this whole thing started who stood by him the whole time? YOU did. Logan and I... we let him down in the worst possible way. YOU never

doubted him. YOU never gave up on him, we did. You are the BEST friend any of us could ask for. The best big brother ever, and don't you EVER forget that."

"But..." Carlos started.

James' hazel eyes filled with tears. "I know it's been hard, but you always think of everyone else. Even down to remembering Kendall's favourite candy. The fact that you were so happy about it made everyone feel better. Sally's right, you can make anyone smile and feel better. I just wish I could do that for you right now," he said, hugging Carlos to him.

Sylvia had followed the boys, stood in the middle of the stairs, and listened. She thought her heart would break hearing the conversation between the two boys. They had all been through so much, and there was still such a long road ahead of them.

Deesie got off too easily, she thought for the thousandth time. She smiled when she saw James hug Carlos, turned, and went quietly back up the stairs.

∞

Jen took Kendall's temperature again. "102.2, it's coming down," she said, running her fingers through his hair. He was still shivering and had started coughing.

Antonio brought in his nebulizer and Jen hooked it up. "Honey, I need to put the mask on your face."

Kendall shook his head and pulled away.

"Kendall, please. You need the medicine, it'll help you breathe," she said, trying to put it on him again.

Kendall started to panic and moved further away from her.

"Let me try," Antonio said.

"Come on, Mijo, it's time for your treatment," Antonio said, sitting on the other side of the boy. Kendall looked at him and finally nodded. Antonio put the mask on him and turned on the nebulizer.

Jen sighed and Antonio looked at her. "Honey, don't. He's not feeling well and is confused because of the fever—we've already seen that. I sat with him at the hospital whenever they gave him a treatment, that's all this is."

She smiled sadly. "I know, I guess I'm just tired."

"Then go to bed. I can finish this, and Katie might get scared if she wakes up alone."

"Are you sure?" Jen asked.

"Of course I am, now go. By morning he'll be feeling better, you'll see," Antonio said reassuringly.

Jen smiled and kissed Kendall on the head. "Thank you, Antonio."

"No thanks necessary. Now get some sleep."

Logan had been sitting in the chair by the window and Antonio looked at him. "Logan, what did Kendall say down there?"

Logan went and sat next to Antonio. "Just that Deesie was here and he was going to hurt us all. He thought you were dead, that's why I wanted you to talk to him. He was really confused and afraid. I think the fever was making him dream again."

Antonio nodded. "You did really well tonight, Logan. I know you don't like small spaces, but you kept your cool and got him out. You boys have all done such a good job of being there for him and each other. I know it hasn't been easy for any of you."

Logan smiled. "It's what we do for family, right?"

Antonio ruffled his hair. "Yes it is. Why don't you go get your brothers, so you can all get back to sleep?"

"Okay," he said and went down to find James and Carlos.

∞

Sylvia came in and quickly told Antonio about the conversation between Carlos and James. "I think James got through to him."

Antonio nodded. "Alright, I think we'll put Carlos on 'night duty' tonight."

"Meaning?"

"Kendall needs someone with him at all times, and Carlos needs to be needed... Problem solved."

Sylvia smiled. "You really think it'll be that easy?"

"Of course it will be. You know your son, he lives in the moment and he lives for his friends."

"True," she agreed as the boys came up.

"Logan, can you take his temperature again?" Antonio asked as he removed the nebulizer mask.

Logan nodded and sat next to Kendall and held the thermometer in his friend's mouth. A minute later, it beeped. "101.9."

"Good, his fever's still coming down. Carlos, I need you to do something for me," Antonio said.

"What Papi?"

Sylvia pulled James aside and whispered in his ear. James nodded in agreement.

"I want you to sleep up here with Kendall, so he knows that he's safe. If he starts having a nightmare, wake up James and Logan, alright?"

"He might feel safer with James," Carlos said.

"Who did he call when he ran away from Graham?"

"Me."

"Who stayed with him in the hospital?" Antonio asked.

"Well, I did, but..."

"And who kept him calm that night, especially after we found him on the bathroom floor?"

"Me, but..."

"No buts, I need you to do this. Are you up for the job?"

Carlos nodded.

"That's my boy," Antonio said. "Now everyone to bed and try and get some sleep. Tomorrow we're going to try to take it easy. I'll be back in a couple of hours to take his temperature again."

"Okay, night Papi, Mami," Carlos said, kissing his parents goodnight.

"Night boys." Antonio smiled, closing the door behind him.

Logan and James decided to lie head to head across the floor in front of the door, and Carlos climbed into the bed next to Kendall. A few minutes later, they were all sleeping, and Carlos had curled up next to Kendall and had his arm curled around Kendall's head, his hand resting on his forehead.

Chapter 80~ Plots

Jen went downstairs and climbed back into bed next to Katie. "Mom, what's going on?" Katie yawned.

"Nothing honey, your brother has a fever and isn't feeling very well. We gave him some Tylenol and a breathing treatment. He's sleeping now."

"I thought I heard the guys down here."

"They were for a little while. I'll tell you all about it in the morning," Jen said as she hugged her daughter.

"Kendall's okay though, right?"

"He's going to be just fine, baby," Jen told her, praying it was true.

"What's going to happen when you have to go back to work?" Katie asked.

"Honey, can we talk about this in the morning? Mama's tired right now."

"Okay. Are we going to stay here or go home?"

"Katie..."

"What about Thanksgiving?"

"Katie, please!"

"Sorry mom."

"It's alright, goodnight Katie."

"Night mama."

"Are the boys going to stay with us?"

"Katie, seriously, go to sleep!"

It was quiet for a few minutes.

"Mom?" Katie whispered.

Jen sighed. "Yes Katie?"

"Can I sleep upstairs?"

"Why?"

"Just because."

"Katie, the boys are sleeping too," Jen told her.

"I know. I just want..."

"To be near your brothers?"

"Yes."

Jen smiled. "Alright, but be quiet and don't wake anyone up."

"I won't, thanks mom," Katie said as she jumped out of bed. Katie walked quietly upstairs and opened Carlos' bedroom door. She carefully stepped over James and Logan and climbed up on the bed next to Kendall.

∞

An hour later, when Antonio went in to take Kendall's temperature, he found Katie hugging Kendall around the waist and Carlos with his arm still encircling Kendall's head.

He moved Carlos' hand slightly and felt Kendall's forehead. He frowned when he found the boy was still too warm and gently placed the thermometer in Kendall's mouth. It beeped and he read it. *101.4, at least it's still coming down,* he thought.

He covered Katie with a blanket and quietly left the room, closing the door firmly behind him.

∞

A couple of hours later, Carlos woke up. Kendall coulsn't get comfortable and was whimpering in his sleep. "Kendall, are you okay?" Carlos whispered.

Kendall shook his head.

"What's wrong?"

Kendall's voice was weak and raspy. "Hurts."

"What hurts?"

"Everything."

"I'm going to get Papi so he can give you something for the pain, okay?"

Kendall nodded and realized someone was holding onto him on the other side. He looked down. "When did Katie come in?"

Carlos looked over. "I don't know. She wasn't here when I fell asleep."

Carlos got up and stepped over Logan and went to his parents' room, Antonio and Sylvia were sound asleep. "Papi," Carlos whispered. Not getting a response, he spoke a little louder. "Papi."

Sylvia woke up and looked at him. "Mijo, what's wrong?"

"Kendall says he hurts a lot, and I think he needs something for the pain."

"Okay, let Papi sleep. I'll get the thermometer and take his temperature. Then we'll get him a pain pill." She got up and Carlos went back into his bedroom.

He sat next to Kendall. "Mami's coming. She's going to help you."

Kendall nodded. "I'm sorry."

"For what?"

Sylvia came in, made her way around the bed, and sat next to Carlos. She felt Kendall's forehead. "Mijo, you're still so warm, put this under your tongue," she said, putting the thermometer in his mouth.

It beeped a minute later. "101.8, I think it's going up again. I'm going to get you some more Tylenol and one of your pain pills."

She came back a moment later with the pills and a glass of water. "Here Mijo, take these."

Kendall took the pills while Sylvia held the glass for him.

"Okay?"

He nodded, still shivering a little.

"Do you need anything else?"

He shook his head.

"Okay, well you boys try and get some more sleep. If you need anything, Carlos will come and get me," she said, kissing Kendall's forehead and then Carlos' cheek.

"Night Mami," Carlos said.

"Goodnight Mijo." She smiled and went back to her own bed.

Carlos lay down next to Kendall and rolled over on his side to look at his friend. "Kendall?"

"Hmmm."

"Why did you say you were sorry?"

"So much trouble," he said, his voice breaking.

Carlos hugged him and put his chin on Kendall's head. "You're NOT too much trouble. Don't ever say that again, I mean it. We all love you and you would do the same for any of us. Pretty soon you'll be feeling better and things will be like they should be."

"Sometimes I don't think that's ever going to happen, Carlos," Kendall whispered.

"It will, I promise," Carlos said, hugging his friend tighter.

Carlos tried to think of something to distract his friend. "Did I tell you about the puppies?"

"What puppies?"

Carlos went on to tell Kendall about the pet store and the movie. "Did you see? I found Sour Belts at the candy store and got you some. They had twelve different flavors, so I got you some of each. They're on the night table."

Kendall smiled. "No, I didn't. Thank you. Carlos, you're the best, I haven't had those in a long time."

"Anything for you, little brother." Carlos yawned.

A little while later, both boys had fallen asleep.

James had listened to most of their conversation and smiled. *At least Carlos is feeling a little better,* he thought.

∞

Back at the police station, Richard Graham and Dylan Mason had exchanged stories regarding Kendall, and both had ideas regarding their situations.

"The important thing is to discredit anything that can be used against us," Graham said.

"How do we do that?" Dylan asked.

"Your case shouldn't be that difficult. After all, HE attacked you with something that can be deemed a weapon. You simply get your friends to back up your story, then it will be your word against his."

"But Logan will back up Kendall," Dylan pointed out.

"Perhaps, but you weren't the one who was armed, and you can always claim that Logan misunderstood your intentions."

"Yeah, except I hit him."

"He provoked you."

"How?"

"Silly boy, make something up and have your friends back up what you say. Then NONE of you will be in trouble."

"Except my so-called-friends already turned on me," Dylan said bitterly.

"Well, perhaps a little monetary donation will make them change their minds. They can claim they were afraid of getting into trouble, especially since the father of one of Kendall's friends is the chief of police."

"Yeah, paying them off might work, except I don't have any money."

"No, but I do."

"Why would you pay them off?"

"It's quite simple, actually. I help you, and then you help me when the time comes."

"How?" Dylan asked.

Graham smiled. "I have a few ideas."

∞

Todd and Brian Rickard listened with interest to the conversation between Graham and Dylan. They looked at one another and smiled. "We could use this to our advantage," Todd whispered. His older brother nodded in agreement

Chapter 81 ∼ The Favour

Logan was the first to wake up the next morning, and he got up to check on Kendall. He saw Kendall lying on his right side with Katie cuddled up in front of him, her arms wrapped around his waist. Carlos was on the other side of Kendall, curled up in a ball. His hand was lying on the top of Kendall's head. Logan smiled and shook his head at the sight, wishing he could take a photo of the three. He thought for a moment and quickly grabbed the camera Sally had given him, took a quick picture and tucked the camera back into his backpack.

"You know you're not supposed to do that, right?" James whispered.

Logan jumped and suppressed a frightened squeal. "Don't DO that!" he hissed.

James just looked at him with one eyebrow raised.

"Don't tell, they just look so content right now and we ARE supposed to take pictures of our favourite things," Logan said.

James shook his head. "I'm pretty sure Sally told us NO photos of Kendall."

"I know, but LOOK at them," Logan said, pointing to their friends. "I won't show him, so please don't tell."

"I won't tell, but you're making pancakes for breakfast."

"Seriously, you're blackmailing me?"

"Chocolate chip pancakes, to be exact." James smirked.

"Fine, but you're helping," Logan told him.

James smiled up at him. "I don't think so."

Logan smiled back. "Fine. In fact, just to show you what a good sport I am, I'm going to make you a special pancake."

Logan headed downstairs still smiling.

James lay there smirking and then thought for a moment and jumped up, following Logan. "Wait, exactly what did you mean by 'special' pancake?"

Downstairs Logan started mixing up pancake batter, James watching his every move.

∞

Kendall felt arms holding him tightly and awoke with a start. His head was thick and he felt so cold. He opened his eyes and saw it was Katie holding onto him. He hugged her and then gently wiggled out of her grasp. He got up, went into the guest room, and climbed into bed there, pulling the blankets tightly around him.

A few minutes later, Carlos woke up, realized Kendall was no longer there, and jumped up in a panic. He shook Katie. "Do you know where Kendall is?"

She woke up. "What?"

"Do you know where Kendall is?" Carlos asked again.

She shook her head and looked around. "James and Logan are gone too. Maybe they're all downstairs together."

"Maybe. You check downstairs and I'll look around up here," Carlos said as he checked under the bed.

Katie nodded and went downstairs, where she found Logan making breakfast with James warily watching him.

"Is Kendall down here?" Katie asked.

"What? No, why?" James asked, getting up.

"Carlos woke up and he was gone. We saw you guys were up and thought maybe he was down here with you," she told him.

"Did you check the other rooms upstairs?" Logan asked.

"Carlos is looking now," Katie said.

"Okay, I'll go help Carlos check upstairs. I didn't hear anyone except you come down. Katie, you stay down here with Logan," James said, heading for the stairs.

"Why?"

"Make sure he doesn't put anything weird in my pancakes, okay?" James leaned down and whispered.

"Why would he do that?"

"Let's just say he kinda threatened to."

"What's in it for me?"

"What do you want?" he asked her suspiciously.

"Let's just say you owe me one."

"Fine, but my breakfast better be okay," James said as he went upstairs.

Katie shook her head. "Boys are so weird," she said to herself and went back into the kitchen.

∞

James went upstairs and checked Carlos' room. Not finding anyone, he opened the guest room door and found Carlos sitting next to Kendall on the bed. "Is everything okay?" James asked.

"I think so, but he still feels pretty warm."

James went into the bathroom and grabbed the thermometer. He tried to put it into Kendall's mouth, but the other boy groaned and turned his head. "Go 'way," he said.

"We need to take you temperature, buddy."

Kendall shook his head. "Leave me 'lone," he said, pulling the covers over his head.

"Kendall, I'm serious. It'll only take a minute," James said, trying to pull the blankets down a bit.

"I think he's feeling better," Carlos said.

"How can you tell? He won't let us take his temperature," James said in a frustrated tone.

'He didn't fight anybody about it last night," Carlos told him.

"Good point, but we still need to know what it is. Kendall, last chance to do this the easy way." Kendall didn't respond, so James grabbed the blankets and yanked them down.

"Why can't you just leave me 'lone? I wanna sleep," Kendall whimpered.

"Because," James said, putting the thermometer into his friend's mouth and not letting go.

"Because why?" Kendall asked. His voice muffled as James held his jaw firmly closed.

"Because there's no way you'd leave any of us alone if we were sick and being stubborn," James said, smiling. Kendall glared at him but stopped trying to open his mouth.

The thermometer beeped. "100.9. It's still there, but it's coming down," James said.

"Now can I sleep?"

"Yeah, go back to sleep. I'm going to make you a smoothie and bring it up later. Do you need anything now?"

Kendall shook his head and burrowed back under the covers.

"Come on, Carlos, Logan is making chocolate chip pancakes," James said.

"Yummy, chocolate chip pancakes!" Carlos squealed and ran out the door.

James shook his head and looked back at Kendall. "Hey, if you need anything, just call down, okay?"

"Okay, thanks James."

"No problem." James smiled and closed the door.

A little while later, Antonio woke up. He could hear the boys and Katie downstairs but doubted Kendall was with them. He went to Carlos' room, and not finding anyone there, checked the other bedroom.

Kendall was curled up under the blankets and Antonio pulled them down a bit to check on him. "Mijo, how are you feeling this morning?"

"Hmmm?"

"How are you feeling?" Antonio repeated, feeling the teen's forehead. "We need to take your temperature. You're still a little warm."

"James did."

"Do you know what it was?"

Kendall shook his head and pulled the blankets tighter.

"Okay, I'll go ask him and bring you some juice. We need to keep you hydrated. I'll be back in a few minutes. Do you want anything else?"

Kendall shook his head.

Antonio went downstairs to find everyone else sitting around the kitchen eating breakfast.

"Good morning!" he said, kissing Sylvia's cheek. "Smells good. What's for breakfast?"

"Logan made pancakes," Jen said.

"That was nice! Especially after last night," Antonio said.

Logan smiled and handed Antonio a plate.

"James, Kendall said you took his temperature, but he couldn't remember what it was," Antonio said.

James got up, went to the refrigerator, and pulled out a glass. "100.9. I mixed up a smoothie for him, since he probably doesn't feel like eating."

"You're probably right. I'll take it up in a minute," Antonio said.

"I can do it, you eat breakfast," James said.

Antonio smiled. "Thanks. Could you get him a couple of Tylenol too?"

James nodded and headed upstairs. He knocked on the door and went in. He sat next to Kendall and gently shook him. "Hey, I brought you a smoothie and some Tylenol. I thought if you're feeling a little better, you could come down and watch the hockey game with us. The Wilds are playing the Sabres."

Kendall stirred and tried to stretch out. "Ow," he groaned, curling back up.

"Your shoulder?"

Kendall nodded.

"Take the Tylenol, that'll help. Do you want a pain pill?"

Kendall shook his head no.

"Well, maybe a warm shower would help," James suggested.

"Maybe," Kendall said, trying to sit up.

James put an arm behind him and helped him. "Drink and take these," he said, handing Kendall the smoothie and Tylenol.

"Thanks," Kendall said, taking the glass. He swallowed the pills and looked at James. "What happened last night?"

"You don't remember?"

"Not very much. I had a bad dream and woke up, and I think I got sick. I must have still been dreaming though because I heard him calling."

"Who?"

"Deesie," Kendall whispered.

James put his arm around Kendall's shoulders. "I'm sorry, buddy. I wish there was something I could do. It's just not fair."

The boys sat there quietly for a few minutes, lost in their own thoughts. Kendall was trying to block the images from his dreams, and James was trying to fight down the urge to punch out a wall.

"Okay, finish your smoothie and then take a shower. You're coming down to watch the game," James said firmly.

Kendall smiled and nodded.

A few minutes later, Kendall had showered and James helped him with his shirt and stabilizer. He managed to avoid the comb by slipping past James as he reached for the conditioner bottle.

∞

The boys all settled on the couch and turned on the game. Joanna showed up during the second period and Logan jumped up to hug her.

"What are you boys up to?" she asked.

"Wilds against Sabres," Carlos said.

"Who's winning?"

"The Wilds, of course," Carlos replied excitedly.

Jo smiled and went into the kitchen, where Jen and Sylvia were sitting and discussing the upcoming week.

"Hi Jo, how are you doing today?" Sylvia asked.

"I'm doing well, just trying to get everything in order for Thanksgiving."

"Tea?" Jen asked, handing her a cup.

"Thanks Jen."

"Why don't you and Logan just come to my house? Sylvia and I already spoke to Brooke, and we can just have dinner there," Jen said.

"Logan is supposed to go to his dad's. I'm not sure he's going to want to go, though. I need to talk to him about it. He doesn't get to visit Alex that often," Joanna said.

"He should go," Jen said.

"I know. I also know that Alex would understand, and Logan could always visit for a few days during Christmas break. I also know Logan will feel guilty, whichever he chooses, because he'll feel like he's letting someone down," Joanna told her.

Logan came in a moment later, carrying a tray of empty mugs.

"Logan, we need to talk for a minute," Joanna said.

"Sure mom. What's up?"

"Honey, do you remember that you're supposed to go to your dad's on Wednesday?"

"Oh my gosh, Thanksgiving is this week? Mom, I can't just leave."

"Logan everything will be alright here," Jen told him reassuringly.

Joanna smiled. "It's up to you though, honey. You can always visit your dad next month for a few days, but if you're not going, we really need to let him know."

∞

Alexander Mitchell and Joanna Murphy met while attending the Minnesota State University in Mankato. Alex Mitchell was from a small town outside of Austin, Texas. His family had owned a ranch there for three generations and were not happy when their second eldest son decided to move away and study teaching. They were even unhappier when Alex and Jo married and decided to make their home in Minnesota.

He taught math at the local community college and she started her own real estate business. When Alex's dad had a stroke, they decided to move to Texas to help. A couple of years later, they had Logan and were thrilled with their little family.

Six years later, Alex's dad was doing better and his sister's husband was helping out, so the Mitchells moved back to Minnesota. Two years after that, they found themselves arguing more, mostly because Alex's parents were getting too old to run the ranch and they were constantly begging him to move his family back. Jo didn't want to leave her home or her business, which had become quite successful. She told Alex that while she loved her boy from Texas, she couldn't stand the thought of living there. It was too hot and his mother didn't like her. They parted amicably and remained good friends.

∞

Logan looked torn. "When do I need to decide?"

"Probably by tonight, honey. I know it's hard, but either choice you make will be fine," Jo said, hugging him.

Logan returned to the living room and sat down next to Kendall, who had nodded off and had his head on Carlos' shoulder. Logan sighed softly, trying to figure out what he should do. He really wanted to see his dad, but he really didn't want to leave his friends right now.

"What's the matter, buddy?" James asked, noticing Logan staring at the coffee table.

Logan smiled. "Nothing."

James raised an eyebrow. "Logan..."

"I forgot I'm supposed to visit my dad for Thanksgiving," he whispered, trying not to wake Kendall.

"So?" James said.

"I'm not sure I want to leave right now," Logan said, pointing to Kendall.

James smiled. "Logan, you don't get to see your dad that much. Kendall will be fine. We'll miss you, but it's only for a couple of days."

"I know. It's just... I know he'll understand, and I can always visit for a few days next month when Kendall's feeling better."

"It's up to you, but I'm sure everyone will understand, whatever you chose," James said.

"What does your heart tell you to do?" Carlos asked.

Logan thought about it for a moment. "I'm going to call my dad and ask if I can visit next month."

"Are you sure?" James asked.

Logan smiled and nodded. They went back to watching the game, and when it was over, decided to head to the pond to check if it was frozen enough to skate on. They put a blanket over Kendall and headed out.

Once they were gone, Kendall got up and headed upstairs. He found his cell phone and looked up a number.

"H-Hi, it's Kendall. I need to ask you a favour."

Chapter 82~ Snowball Fight

Carlos, James, and Logan walked to the park, glad to be out in the fresh air. It was cold and it looked like it would snow any minute. They got to the pond and Carlos ran to check the marker. "Almost five inches, it should be ready any day now!"

"Cool, maybe we can go skating on Thanksgiving," Logan said.

James looked at him. "Are you SURE you don't want to go visit your dad? You know everyone would totally understand."

Logan sighed. "Look, I really miss my dad and I know it's been months since I've seen him, but this is where I need to be right now. He'll understand and I'll call him on Thanksgiving too, then everyone can say 'hi' to him."

James smiled. "I know he'll understand. Papa M is pretty cool. It's too bad he's so far away. I haven't seen him for over a year."

"He said he was planning on visiting in January sometime. He wants to go skiing and thought we could all go up to the ski resort for a weekend," Logan told him.

"That would be awesome!" Carlos said.

James went and sat under the oak tree, Logan and Carlos following.

"What's the matter, James?" Carlos asked.

He shook his head. "I just think it's sad that a cool dad like Papa M lives so far away and then there's mine, who lives here, can't be bothered to even stop by half the time when he's supposed to."

Logan and Carlos put their arms around his shoulders. "Your dad's not a bad guy, he's just not as mature as he should be," Logan said.

James sighed. "Thanks Logan, but the fact is he's just selfish."

"That's why my Papi is your Papi too. He's Kendall's Papi because Papi K died, and he's Logan's Papi when Papi M isn't here," Carlos told him.

James smiled at Carlos. "Carlos, your Papi is the best, and I'm really glad you share him."

"Mami always says there's more than enough of Papi and me to go around. I'm not quite sure what she means by that though."

"It means you both have huge hearts and have enough love for everyone," Logan said tactfully.

"Or it means that you can both be an incredible pain in the butt. Especially when you have the 'who can smash the down door in helmets first' contests," James said.

"Mean!" Logan said, smacking James on the back of the head.

"Hey, I'm not the one who said that. I'm quoting Mama G."

Carlos just looked at him with smirk.

"What?" James asked as Carlos hit him in the face with a snowball. "Hey, not cool!" James said, scrambling to get up.

Carlos sprinted across the park and James followed, trying to hit his fleeing friend with snowballs that he made as he ran.

"I need new friends," Logan said, shaking his head as he followed the other two. He lost sight of them and rushed to find them. The next thing he knew, he was being pummeled from both sides, Carlos and James laughing hysterically.

"Oh, real funny!" Logan yelled.

The other two boys laughed as they continued launching snowballs at their friend.

"Time out!" Logan yelled after he had been hit about ten times. He caught Carlos' eye, jerked his head towards James, and made a little flying motion with his hands.

Carlos smiled and nodded.

Suddenly Logan jumped James, and a second later, Carlos landed on him as well. "REVERSE SNOW ANGEL!"

"NO!" James shrieked as he was pushed face-first into the snow. He had a friend on each side of him, forcing the rest of his body into the snow and then moving his arms up and down. Logan and Carlos took off running and made for the Garcia house before James could get up.

"You two are SO going to get it!" James yelled behind them, still spitting snow.

Carlos and Logan got to the house seconds before James and rushed inside.

"Boys, shake the snow off outside," Sylvia said.

They both shook their heads frantically. "James is going to kill us!" Carlos said.

"What did you two do?" Antonio asked as James came running in the front door.

"You two, outside now, so we can finish this!" James ordered.

Both boys hid behind Mama G.

"Boys?" Antonio asked.

"Well... we kinda helped him make a reverse snow angel," Logan said.

"Exactly what is that?" Sylvia asked, trying to get the two snow-covered boys away from her.

"That is where they push ME face first into the snow and sit on me, moving my arms to make angel wings," James said, making a grab for Carlos.

"Boys, that's enough," Antonio said, trying to hold back a laugh.

The front of James was covered in snow, which was quickly thawing and dripping onto the floor. "Outside, and take off your things," he said.

"And no more fighting!" Sylvia said, emphasizing her point by pushing Logan and Carlos towards the door.

James held the door open and smiled as Logan and Carlos carefully walked by him. He followed them out and closed the door behind him. A moment later, they heard shrieking from the other two boys, and Sylvia shook her head as she locked the front door.

∞

Kendall was upstairs in Carlos' room, sitting at the window. He felt awful that Logan was giving up time with his dad because of him. He saw Logan and Carlos come running up the walk and almost had a panic attack, until he saw James coming up behind them, covered in snow. He smiled, realizing they had probably been having a snowball fight, and took out the camera Sally had given him and snapped some photos of them.

He could hear them downstairs, and then suddenly, he saw them outside again, Logan and Carlos trying to outrun James. He watched James catch first Logan and then Carlos, and push them face first into the snow. He put the camera on video and recorded the whole thing.

∞

A little while later, the boys had finally come to a truce and shook off all the snow, before trying to go back inside. The door was locked, so they knocked, and when Mama G answered it with her arms crossed, they gave her their very best 'we love you' look.

She arched an eyebrow and inspected them before allowing them back into the house. They could hear Antonio laughing at them from inside the house, looked at one another, and nodded.Each had a small handful of snow tucked into their pockets, and after Sylvia allowed them inside, they went and stood next to Antonio, who was sitting in his chair, and put the snow down the front of his shirt.

He gasped in shock and looked at the boys, who all stood there smirking. "Oh, it's on!" he yelled, getting up and chasing them back outside.

Chapter 83 ~Logan's Dad

Jen and Sylvia were discussing how to manage the upcoming week. Jen and Antonio both had to return to work on Monday. Kendall couldn't be alone, and Jen had to work the morning shift on Monday and Tuesday. Wednesday wouldn't be so bad, as she worked the afternoon shift.

"I think you should just let them stay here. It doesn't make much sense to get them up at 5 am and drop them off here when they could just stay the night," Sylvia reasoned.

"I know, but I feel like I'm taking advantage of you. We were only home for a couple of days before we came back here after the thing with Graham," Jen said.

"Jen, Carlos stayed with you for over a month when my Papi died. Did YOU think I was taking advantage you?"

"Of course not!"

"Well then?"

Jen smiled. "I have to admit I feel much safer here than at home. I mean, I miss being in my own house, but..."

"You know you can stay as long as you want to. After Kendall's feeling better and is going back to school, things will go back to normal," Sylvia told her.

"Sometimes I wonder if that will ever happen." Jen sighed.

"Jen..."

"Not Kendall getting better, but the other kids at school. We've already seen the way some of them behave. I don't think I could take it if something happened because some bully went after him."

'That's a valid concern, but the other boys will be there, and the only kids who don't like Kendall are the bullies, and most of them have already been taken care of."

"Very true," Jen agreed.

"The other option is if you really want to go home, Carlos and I can come over by 5:30."

"No, there's no way I would ask that of you," Jen said.

"Thank goodness, I really hate getting up early!" Sylvia smiled.

"Alright, we'll stay until Tuesday when I get off work. The boys said they would work out which one of them will be staying with us, so I'll just leave that up to them. Thursday we'll have dinner at my house," Jen said.

"It's a plan then." Sylvia smiled.

"Oh no. I completely forgot about Kendall's appointment with Dr. Jenkins on Tuesday," Jen said.

"What time is it?"

"Ten, I don't get off until two."

"Don't worry, I can take him. Jo will be here tomorrow and Brooke will be here on Tuesday," Sylvia said.

"Alright, I'm not sure it would be a good idea for me to take him anyway," Jen sighed.

"Honey, will you please stop worrying and being so hard on yourself?" Sylvia said.

Jen smiled. "I'm just being realistic. I don't want him having a panic attack because I'm taking him to some stranger. It took Antonio to get him in to see Anna, and he's known her for nearly ten years."

"I understand. We'll work it all out, so don't worry, okay?"

"I'll try," Jen promised.

∞

After the boys had settled down and dried off, Logan went and called his dad.

"Hello," a gentle voice with a soft drawl answered.

"Hi dad. How are you?"

"Hey, how are you doing, Partner?"

"I'm doing okay."

"How's Kendall doing? Your mom has been keeping me updated, and I want you to know how proud I am of all of you. Kendall for being strong and surviving, and you and the other boys for sticking by him through all of this," Alex said.

"That's kinda why I called dad. I really miss you, and..."

"Logan, before you say anything, hear me out. I think you should stay there for Thanksgiving and come down here during your Christmas break for a few days. You can visit your cousins then, too. Emily and Jack will be coming down from Amarillo and we can have a small reunion of sorts."

Logan breathed a sigh of relief. "Really, you'd be okay with that?"

Alex chuckled. "Of course I would. I think you need to be there with your brothers right now. This way you can stay an extra couple of days, and then I'll come up and visit in January. What do you think?"

"I think you're the most amazing dad on the planet." Logan smiled.

After he got off the phone with his dad, Logan went up to check on Kendall and found him trying to get his chemistry homework finished.

"How's it going?" Logan asked, sitting next to him.

"I hate chemistry," Kendall said, erasing what he had just written.

Logan smiled. "Come on, I'll help you."

"Thanks Loges."

"No problem," Logan said and pulled up closer to the desk.

Kendall looked sideways at Logan. "So when do you leave for your dad's?"

"Ummm... I'm not going," Logan said. "Okay, a polymer is a chemical compound or a mixture of compounds created through the process of polymerization," Logan explained, trying to divert Kendall back to his homework.

"Why?"

Damn, Logan thought. "We decided next month would be better."

"Why?"

"Because they're having a small family reunion then and I can see my cousins that I haven't seen in three years," Logan said, not looking at him.

"Is that the real reason?"

Logan looked at him. "It's a big part of the reason. That and I don't want to leave right now, so this all works out perfectly."

"I'm tired. I'm going to take a break." Kendall sighed. He got up, went over, and sat on the bed.

"Kendall..."

"I'm sorry, Loges, I really am."

"Will you stop? You have nothing to be sorry for, and I would like to point out that you wouldn't leave either."

"You were looking forward to going, Logan, so don't try and tell me that you weren't."

Logan went and sat next to him. "Of course I was... I still am. The fact is, this is where I WANT to be right now, okay?"

Kendall looked at him and nodded. "I'm gonna take a nap," he said, lying down.

"Okay, we'll finish your homework later. I'm going take your temperature first, though," Logan said as he went to grab the thermometer.

"Open," Logan said and Kendall let him put the thermometer in his mouth. It beeped a minute layer. "99.4. It's still coming down, at least," he said and went and grabbed Kendall a couple of Tylenol.

"Here, take these, and hopefully your fever will be gone by tonight."

Kendall took the pills and swallowed them. "Thanks Loges... for everything."

Logan smiled. "Get some sleep."

"I will." Kendall yawned, closing his eyes.

∞

A couple of hours later, Jen went up to check on Kendall and to let him know dinner was ready. "Honey, it's time to wake up and come downstairs for dinner."

"I'm not hungry," he said, rolling over.

"Honey, have you been crying?" she asked, noticing his eyes were red and puffy.

She went to touch his cheek. "No!" he said, pulling back.

She smiled sadly. "You need to come down, even if you're not hungry."

"Why?"

"Because I'm your mother and I said so," she said, kissing him on the head.

"If you're not downstairs in five minutes, I'll send James up," she said as she went out the door.

Kendall sighed and got up. He went into the bathroom and rinsed his face with cold water. He looked in the mirror. The bruises were finally fading and the cuts had healed well. His eyes were red and puffy and had dark circles under them. He could still see Deesie's marks on his neck, and shivered.

"You're mine..."

"Just leave me alone!" Kendall hissed, his eyes tearing up again. He sat on the floor, pulled his knees up to his chest, and covered his ears. "You're dead, so leave me alone."

"Uh uh uh... What did I tell you?"

Kendall sat on the floor, rocking back and forth. "No more, no more..."

He didn't hear James knock on the door. "Kendall, are you okay in there?"

Not getting a response, he tried the door and was relieved when it opened. "Kendall?" He looked inside and saw Kendall sitting on the floor. James went in and closed the door behind him. He sat down next to Kendall and put his arm around his shoulders.

"What happened?" James asked softly.

"It's never going to stop, he's never going to leave me alone," Kendall whispered.

They sat there like that for a few minutes and Kendall leaned into James, who tightened his grip on him. "I don't know what to say. I don't know how to make this better. I can only tell you that he's dead and can't hurt you anymore, but I know you know that. I can't make the dreams go away and I would give anything if I could," James whispered.

"I know. I hate being like this."

"Like how?"

"Weak, scared all the time, not being normal."

"You're NOT weak, you're one of the strongest people I know. As for being scared, who wouldn't be? I'm scared, and I wasn't even there. As for not being normal... It's the situation that's not normal, not you. You didn't ask for any of this, none of us did. So we stick together and remember what's really important, US, and everything will be okay," James said.

"Promise?" Kendall said, choking back a sob.

"I promise little brother," James told him, fighting back tears of his own.

Chapter 84~ Injustice

About fifteen minutes later, Antonio knocked on the bathroom door and James opened it. "Everything alright?" Antonio asked.

James nodded. "I think so."

"Why don't I bring you boys a tray?"

James looked over at Kendall. "I think we can come down, right Kendall?" Kendall nodded and James helped him up. They went downstairs and James steered Kendall to a chair between him and Antonio. Logan and Carlos looked at James questioningly and he gave a slight shake of his head.

Antonio set a bowl of stew in front of Kendall and smiled. "Here you go."

James pushed a small plate with a biscuit on it next to the bowl of stew and smiled. "Eat."

Kendall rolled his eyes and picked at the bread for a while. Antonio picked up Kendall's spoon and handed it to him while telling Sylvia and Jen how he had managed to face plant Carlos into a snow bank down the block.

Logan and James started laughing at the expression on Carlos' face. "My OWN Papi tried to bury me alive." Carlos pouted.

Kendall took the spoon and took a bite.

"That's because you were the slowest," Logan pointed out to Carlos.

"Maybe, but it was YOUR idea to put snow down his shirt!" Carlos retorted.

Logan just smirked at him.

"Oh really?" Antonio said, looking at Logan.

"W-What... pshhhh, NO!" Logan stammered. "Why don't I clear the dishes?" he asked, grabbing empty bowls and heading to the kitchen.

Carlos smirked as Logan walked by him.

"Look, a volunteer to wash dishes," Sylvia said, smiling at her son.

Carlos groaned and got up and followed Logan into the kitchen. Kendall had set his spoon down, but Antonio picked it up and put it back in his hand, still talking to Jen and Sylvia.

Kendall took a couple of bites and tried to scoot his chair back, but he found James' arm around the back of his chair.

James looked over at him. "Going somewhere?" he asked with a smile.

Kendall rolled his eyes at him. A moment later, a thought came to him, but before he could move, James leaned over. "If you try going UNDER the table, I'll follow and spoon feed you."

Kendall gave an exasperated sigh and glared at his friend, but James just smiled back at him. "Eat at least half for me, okay?"

Kendall took another bite, and after a few minutes, managed to get most of it down. After dinner, everyone settled into the living room and watched a little television. James went upstairs, grabbed a pain pill for Kendall, and took it to him with a glass of juice. Kendall swallowed the pill and settled on the couch between James and Katie.

Katie wrapped her arms around Kendall and lay her head on his chest. He smiled and wrapped his arm around her and leaned against James.

An hour later, the siblings were asleep and Jen gently woke Katie. "Come on, honey, time for bed. You have school tomorrow." Katie opened her eyes and yawned, Jen took her hand and they went off to bed.

"We should all get to bed too, you boys have school and I go back to work tomorrow," Antonio said.

The boys nodded and Antonio went to help with Kendall.

"I've got him," James said as he put his arms under his friend and lifted him off the couch.

The boys went up and got Kendall tucked in for the night. They spread out on the floor around the bed. James and Logan lying head to head again, and Carlos lying right next to the bed, on the other side of Logan. Soon they were all sound asleep.

∞

The next morning, James woke up first and sighed in relief when he saw Kendall still sleeping soundly. He got up and went to take a shower, waking the other two boys before he left the room. They got ready for school and headed downstairs for breakfast.

Joanna had just arrived to spend the day with Sylvia and Kendall. "Hi mom!" Logan said, hugging his mom.

"Good morning, boys. How's everyone doing today?"

"Good, everyone slept through the night," James said, smiling.

"I'm so glad! Now go eat and I'll drop you all off at school," Jo said. The boys nodded and headed for the kitchen.

"Logan, did you call your dad yet?" Jo asked.

Logan nodded. "Yeah, I called him last night. He actually suggested that I stay here for Thanksgiving and go down next month, because Jack and Emily are visiting then, too. He also said he'll be visiting in January and we can all go skiing together."

"Good," Jo said.

"I know, isn't it great?" Logan smiled.

"Your dad's a pretty good guy," Jo told him. Logan grinned and nodded in agreement.

After breakfast, the boys grabbed their backpacks and gear.

"Mom, we have practice tonight and tomorrow because of the holiday, so we won't be home until later," Carlos said.

"Someone will pick you up, so stay inside until one of us gets there," Sylvia said.

The boys nodded and Joanna ushered the boys and Katie out the door.

∞

Sally was getting ready to transport Graham to the courthouse for his arraignment, hearing when Antonio came in.

"I thought you were taking this week off?" he asked her.

"I am, starting Wednesday. I want to make sure everything here goes smoothly today," she told him.

"What... you don't think I can handle it?" Antonio joked.

"You know as well as I do, the further you stay from the defendants, the better. Besides, we have two out with the flu, so I have Weaver pulling transport duty."

"Great," Antonio said.

David Weaver wasn't a bad person. He just wasn't the sharpest tool in the shed and had a tendency to get on Sally's nerves. The more experienced officers often referred to him as 'Barney Fife'. He was a little too eager about some things and much too ignorant about others, and already had two infractions on his record.

"Yeah, hopefully he doesn't screw it up. He has three runs to and from court, and he's already backed the SUV into a pole," Sally mumbled. She did not tolerate fools lightly, and Weaver just didn't seem to get it at all. She was close to losing her patience with him completely.

"Don't worry, it'll be fine," Antonio told her.

She looked at him with an arched eyebrow. "Sure it will. I can be optimistic, right?"

He laughed at her expression and then covered it with a quick cough. "Of course you can be," he said, hurrying into his office.

Bennet showed up a couple of minutes later. "Hey Sally... what's that look for?" he asked, noticing the expression on her face.

"Nothing, just me being optimistic."

"Well, that can't be good," he said as he headed for Antonio's office.

Sally followed him in. "Don't forget you two have a court date in Bloomington for the Barns' trial at ten," Sally told them.

Bennet groaned. "I hate testifying at domestic disputes."

"Same here, but what can you do?" Antonio said.

"They almost always end up dropping the charges or someone violates a restraining order, and we get called back for additional testimony, even if we weren't there," Bennet complained.

"If you quit whining about it, I'll buy you a lollipop," Sally said as she went to double-check on the arraignment times for Graham, Mason, and the Rickards.

"Someone's in a mood," Bennet said.

"Weaver," Antonio said.

"Oh... eww," Bennet said. He had even less patience than Sally when it came to the younger officer. "Guess I don't mind going to Bloomington after all."

Antonio shook his head. "Me either."

Antonio and Bennet headed out for Bloomington a few minutes later.

∞

Sally got Graham ready for transport and Weaver drove him to the courthouse. Once inside, Graham met with Jonathan Reed in one of the consult rooms. Try as he might, Reed could not convince Graham to try and plead down. When it was time for his arraignment, they took their places in the courtroom.

DA Ryan was there to handle the hearing personally.

Judge Warner was presiding, and the court was called to order.

"Charges," Warner asked.

Ryan read off the charges. "Illegal dispensation of prescription medications, medical fraud, prescription fraud, illegal shipping of controlled substances across state lines, illegal dispensation of controlled substances including injectable, falsifying controlled substance logs, assault and battery of a minor child, injecting minor child with an illegally obtained controlled substance, threatening two officers of the law."

"How does the defendant plead?"

"Not guilty," Graham declared arrogantly.

Reed sighed.

"Your Honour, we're requesting that bail be denied due to flight risk. Dr. Graham has a residence in Louisiana, he's also being investigated by the DEA for illegal prescription drug trafficking," Ryan said.

"Your Honour, we request bail be set and the defendant is willing to wear a tracking monitor until his trial," Reed countered.

Judge Warner looked over the paperwork in front of him. "Bail will be set at two hundred thousand and a monitoring device will be attached with random spot checks. You are to have no contact with the minor child or his parents, and you will maintain professional discretion. You are also not allowed to return to practice until such a time as you are found innocent of all charges," Warner ordered.

"Two hundred thousand... Is he insane? I'll have to put my house up as collateral," Graham complained.

"Well, you could always stay in jail until your court date," Reed said.

"Just arrange to have it paid," Graham hissed.

An hour later, Graham was fitted with the monitoring device and Reed drove him home.

∞

Weaver picked up Dylan Mason next and he met with the attorney his parents had called. They went into the courtroom and Judge Warner asked for charges.

"Assault and battery," Ryan said.

"How do you plead?" Judge Warner asked.

"Guilty with extenuating circumstances," Dylan's attorney said.

"We request bail be set at two thousand," Ryan said.

Judge Warner looked at the paperwork.

"Granted. Bail is to be set at two thousand, and the defendant is to be released into his parents' custody. Young man, you are allowed only to go to school and home. If you vary from these mandates, you will be fitted with a monitoring device. Is that understood?"

"Yes, Your Honour. Thank you," Dylan replied.

∞

Back at the station, Sally went to make sure the Rickard boys were ready to go.

"So... if we know something that could actually help Kendall, can we make a deal?" Todd asked.

Sally looked at him. "Such as?"

The brothers looked at one another. "We overheard that old guy and Dylan talking the other night, and they're planning on helping each other out," Brian said.

Sally crossed her arms. "How?"

"Can we make a deal?" Todd asked again.

"IF, what you tell me is true and IF it actually helps Kendall, then I'll speak to the DA about your case," Sally told them. "Now, what did you hear?"

∞

After Dylan was released, he went and spoke to his attorney again. His attorney did not look pleased as he went before Judge Warner.

"Yes?" Warner asked.

"Your Honour, my client is asking to have charges brought against Kendall Knight for assault and battery."

"What?" Ryan asked.

"Your Honour, he attacked my client with a hockey stick with no provocation."

"Your Honour, Kendall Knight was defending his friend, who had been surrounded and attacked by Dylan Mason, Brad Pruitt, and Adam Randall," Ryan stated.

"Your Honour, this is my client's word against that of Kendall Knight. He has every right to file charges."

Judge Warner sighed. "Mr. Ryan, please swear out a warrant and have the boy picked up for questioning."

He pointed his finger at Dylan. "However, if I find that you have perjured yourself and filed false charges, your bail will be revoked and I will see you prosecuted to the fullest extent of the law. Is that understood?"

"Yes, Your Honour," Dylan said politely.

"Your Honour, again I must protest..." Ryan said.

"Just have him brought in for questioning and we'll get to the bottom of this, I promise you that. I don't like this any better than you do, but the law is the law."

"Yes, Your Honour," Ryan said.

Ryan went and spoke with Weaver, who waited while the warrant was issued. Ryan knew Kendall was staying with the Garcia's. He also knew that Antonio was not going to be happy.

∞

Weaver called the station and asked for Sally. Johnson told him that she had been called to the scene of an accident but should be back soon.

"I've been ordered by the judge to pick up someone on a warrant he just issued, but should be back before the Rickards are due in court at two," Weaver told him.

"Alright, let me know if you run late," Johnson said.

"I will," Weaver said, hanging up.

∞

Kendall awoke at about 9 am and showered. He realized that only Sylvia and Joanna were there and was wondering what to do, when someone knocked on the door.

"You need any help honey?" Jo asked.

"Kind of," he said, opening the door. "I can't get my shirt on," he said shyly.

Joanna smiled and took the shirt. He got his bad arm into it first and she helped ease it over his head.

"Thank you."

"Come on, we have breakfast waiting," Jo said, taking his arm. Kendall went downstairs with her and they went into the kitchen.

"Scrambled eggs and bacon," Sylvia said, putting the plate in front of him.

He smiled. "Thank you."

"Is there anything you'd like to do today?" Joanna asked him.

He shook his head. "I still have a lot of homework to do," he said quietly.

"What kind of homework? Maybe we can help," Sylvia said.

"Chemistry."

Joanna and Sylvia looked at one another. "I think you're going to have to wait for Logan. If it were English or History, I could have helped," Jo told him.

"Same here," Sylvia said.

"It's not a problem, thanks though."

"How about a board game later?" Sylvia asked.

"Sure." Kendall nodded.

He was just picking at his food, so Sylvia did what Antonio and James had done and handed Kendall his fork. "Eat."

He rolled his eyes but took a bite.

"I'll tell you what. You don't have to eat all of it, IF you promise to drink a whole shake for lunch. You still need to eat a little though, okay?" Sylvia said.

Kendall nodded and took another bite. He managed to eat half of it, when he started to feel a little nauseated, so he stopped. "I'm sorry, I can't eat any more."

"Okay Mijo, why don't we watch a movie or something?" Sylvia smiled.

He nodded and they went into the living room.

"Anything in particular you want to see?" Joanna asked, looking through the video cabinet.

"Not really."

"How about this?" she asked, holding up Finding Nemo.

He smiled and nodded.

"Good, I love this movie," she said, putting it in the player. She sat next to him, and a few minutes later, Sylvia joined them. Jo put her arm around Kendall, and soon, his head was lying on her shoulder as they watched the movie.

Someone knocked at the door and Sylvia got up to answer it, only to find David Weaver standing there. "Good morning, Mrs. Garcia."

"Good morning, David. Why so formal?"

"I'm afraid I'm here on official business."

"Official business? What kind of official business?"

"Is Kendall Knight here?"

"Yes, WHY?" she said, crossing her arms and blocking the doorway. Something was wrong and she was not letting him into her house until she knew what was going on.

"I have a warrant for his arrest," Weaver said in a stern tone.

Sylvia arched her eyebrow at him. "For what?" she demanded.

"Assault and battery, please stand aside," he said, handing her the warrant.

"What's going on?" Jo asked, going to the door.

"He has an arrest warrant for Kendall," Sylvia told her.

"Don't be ridiculous, he's only fourteen. Why would you have an arrest warrant?" Joanna asked Weaver.

"For the assault and battery of Dylan Mason."

"Oh HELL NO! The boy who attacked MY son?"

Weaver was getting very nervous with both women staring him down, and forgot whom it was he was speaking to. "Ma'am, I'm going to ask you one more time to step aside."

"Or what?" Sylvia demanded.

"O-Or I will arrest you for obstruction of justice," he stammered.

Sylvia stared at him in shock.

"LEAVE them alone!" a voice came from behind them.

Kendall had already slipped on his boots and grabbed his jacket.

"Oh no! You are not going with him!" Jo said.

He pushed past her. "You leave them alone," he told Weaver.

Weaver took a hold of his arm and read him his rights, he took out his cuffs, but noticed Kendall only had one free arm.

"I guess we can forego the cuffs," he said. He took Kendall to the SUV and put him in the back.

Sylvia and Jo already had their coats on and were rushing for Jo's car. Sylvia was on the phone calling Antonio, but it went straight to voicemail. She left a message and tried calling Sally, but hers went to voicemail too.

"Damn it, where is everyone?"

"Calm down, we'll get this straightened out," Joanna said.

∞

Johnson was more than a little surprised to see Weaver walk in with Kendall. "What is going on?"

Weaver handed him the arrest warrant and led Kendall back to the cells, a firm grip on his arm.

"I can walk by myself, please stop touching me," Kendall said.

Weaver ignored the request and opened one of the cells. "Inside."

Kendall started to feel panic build in his chest as Weaver closed and locked the cell. "Please, couldn't I just wait in one of the interrogation rooms?"

"There's no one here to interrogate you yet, so... no," Weaver said, starting to walk away.

"Please don't leave me in here alone," Kendall said. Not receiving an answer, he sat down and pulled his legs up to his chest.

A few minutes later, the whispering returned.

Chapter 85~ Sally's Wrath

Sally finished taking statements at the scene of the accident and got back into her car. She called into the station to let Johnson know she was on her way back in.

"Sally, you better get back here quick. Weaver brought Kendall in on an arrest warrant," Johnson told her.

"HE WHAT?"

"Apparently that Mason kid is charging Kendall with assault and battery."

"Where's Kendall now?"

"I haven't been able to get to the back, but I'm assuming the small interrogation room."

"Is anyone there for him yet?"

"No, not yet."

"Alright, I'll be there in less than five."

Sally got off the radio and punched Ryan's number in on her cell phone.

"Somehow I knew you'd be calling," Ryan answered.

"What the hell is going on?"

Ryan told her about Dylan Mason pleading guilty with extenuating circumstances and then filing charges against Kendall.

"That is ridiculous and you know it!"

"I know that, but he's claiming that Kendall attacked him with a weapon, without provocation. Judge Warner issued the warrant and said to get Kendall's side of the story. It's the law, Sally. Dylan has a right to press charges. As soon as we show the charges are false, I will personally haul his butt back in and make sure his bail is revoked."

"On that note, the Rickard boys told me about an interesting conversation they overheard between Graham and Dylan the other night. I told them if it ends up helping Kendall and keeping Graham off the streets, you might be willing to cut them a deal," Sally told him.

"What did they hear?"

Sally relayed the conversation she had had with the Rickard boys to Ryan.

"If that's true and they're willing to testify to that in court, I'd be willing to offer probation with community service. They would be required to wear a monitoring device for a while, but after their community services hours are fulfilled, it would be removed," Ryan said.

"I think they'll go for that. I just got to the station, I'll call you later," Sally said, hanging up. She grabbed her phone and noticed she had three missed calls, all from Sylvia. "Damn!" she said. She went inside and found Sylvia and Jo both there arguing with Johnson.

"Sally!" Sylvia said.

"I know, I just heard. Go wait in Antonio's office and I'll bring Kendall up," Sally told her.

"Alright, thank you," Sylvia said.

"Johnson, get Antonio on the line, find out when they'll be back," she said as she headed to the smaller interrogation room. She opened the door and no one was there, so she checked the main interrogation room.

"Johnson, where did Weaver put Kendall?"

"I thought the small room."

"He's not there. He's not in the main room either."

"Maybe he put him in the women's ward?" Johnson said.

"Where's Weaver now?" Sally asked, heading for the prisoner cells.

"Patrolling."

"Call him and tell him to get his ass back here NOW!"

She went into the women's ward and Kendall wasn't there. "So help me God if he put him in the main cell ward, I will KILL him," Sally mumbled, hurrying to the other side of the building.

∞

Kendall sat there, huddled on the bottom bunk, trying to block out Dessie's voice.

He had tried calling the officer back a few times, but received no answer and was now close to a full-blown panic attack. He concentrated on controlling his breathing, but it felt like his heart was going to burst out of his chest.

"Hey kid, what are you in for? You're pretty cute. Wanna share a cell?" Someone laughed, clanging on their cell door.

"Tell them you're mine."

"Leave me ALONE!" Kendall screamed, covering his ears.

"That's not the way this works, sweetheart." Kendall could feel hot breath on his neck and then felt hands on him.

"Leave me alone!" he screamed again and crawled under the bunk bed, pushing himself until he was against the wall. He covered his head with his arm, trying to breathe, and then everything went black.

∞

Sally rushed to the main cell area and started down the row, checking each cell that had not been occupied that morning. She found one that was locked and didn't see anyone in it, but did see a jacket that she recognized lying on the bed.

Sally opened the door. "Kendall?" She looked under the bed and saw him curled up against the wall. "Kendall, it's alright."

Not getting a response, she crawled under, about halfway, and gently touched his arm. When he still didn't respond, she patted his arm. "Kendall, please come out."

"NO! Don't touch me!" He screamed. His hand lashed out, hitting her in the eye.

She quickly rolled out from under the bed so he didn't hurt himself. She grabbed her hand radio. "Johnson, when is Antonio due in?"

"He just pulled up."

"Send him back to the main cell ward as soon as he gets in the door. Did you get ahold of Weaver yet?"

"Yep, he should be here any minute."

"Good," she said through clenched teeth.

∞

Antonio and John walked into the station. "Boss, Sally needs you in the main cell ward now. She's looking for Kendall."

The two men looked at one another.

"Even Weaver wouldn't be stupid enough to put him in with the main population," Bennet said as they hurried to the back.

Sally stood at the cell door, waiting for Antonio, and a few seconds later, he and Bennet came running back. "He's under the bunk. I can't get him to come out."

Antonio lay down on the floor. "Mijo, it's alright. You need to come out now."

When Kendall didn't respond, he reached out and touched his arm, but the boy shrank back further.

After a few minutes of unsuccessfully trying to coax him out, Antonio stood up and tried pushing on the bunk bed.

"Antonio, it's bolted to the floor and the wall, there's no way to move it," John said.

"I'm afraid he's right, Boss. I think you're just going to have to pull him out from under the bed and we'll deal with the consequences once he's out," Sally told him.

Antonio nodded and got back down on the floor, reaching out for Kendall, but he couldn't get a grip on him. "Damn it, I can't really get ahold on him."

Sally thought for a minute. "John, give me your coat."

"Why?" he asked, taking it off.

Sally slipped it on and zipped it. "Okay, I'm going to crawl under and wrap myself around him. You two are going to grab the coat and pull us out when I say so, okay?"

The two men nodded.

Sally crawled under the bunk, careful not to touch Kendall until she was ready. She took a deep breath and wrapped her arms and legs around him. "NOW!" she yelled, holding the boy close.

Kendall screamed, fighting her. Antonio and John had pulled them out as soon as Sally had called out.

Antonio grabbed Kendall as John pulled Sally back away from the boy's flailing legs. Antonio wrapped his arms around the struggling teen and tried to calm him down.

"Kendall, it's alright, you're safe. No one here's going to hurt you," he said softly.

Once Kendall stopped struggling, he picked him up and sat with him on the bunk.

"We should get him out of here, maybe your office? Sylvia and Joanna are waiting there for you," Sally told him.

Antonio nodded and picked Kendall up and Sally covered him with his jacket.

"Sally, Weaver is here," Johnson radioed back.

"Good. John, I need you with me, please."

He nodded and they went up to the front, Antonio taking Kendall to his office, and John following Sally, wondering what she was going to do to Weaver.

∞

Antonio took Kendall to his office and lay him down on the small couch.

"Oh my God, is he alright?" Sylvia asked, sitting down next to him.

"He had a panic attack. It took a while to get him out from under the bunk. Damn fool Weaver, put him in the main cell ward," Antonio told her.

After a couple of moments, Antonio looked at the two women, who were obviously still shaken. "Can you tell me what happened?"" he asked Sylvia.

Sylvia took a deep breath and told him about Weaver and the warrant.

∞

"Where is Weaver?" Sally asked Johnson.

He pointed to the break room and she headed in, Bennet right behind her.

"You... come with me, NOW," she ordered, pointing at Weaver.

He just looked at her, deciding that he was in the right, and didn't move. She went over, grabbed him by the ear, and just started walking. Weaver yelped and had no choice but to follow his ear.

The other two officers in the room watched, knowing the younger officer must have done something bad to piss Sally off that much and they had no intention of getting in her way.

Sally went into the small interrogation room. "You sit there," she told Weaver, pointing to a chair.

"What's this about?" he demanded.

"John, remind me again WHO is the supervising officer here?"

"Why, I think that's you." He smiled.

Sally sat down and John stood behind her. "We need to go over a few things."

"Look, if this is about the Knight kid, I had to bring him in," Weaver said defensively.

She just looked at him.

"I had a warrant, the judge said to bring him in for questioning." When she just sat there, staring at him, he went on. "I had no choice!"

"What are the procedures when dealing with minors?" she asked quietly.

"What do you mean?" he asked nervously.

"John?" she said.

"Yes?"

"You want to help me out with some roleplaying?"

"In what way?" he asked.

"You pretend you're Weaver and actually ANSWER the questions I ask. Preferably with the correct answers."

"Sure." He smiled.

"Since we are a small town and do NOT have a juvenile facility, what is the proper procedure when dealing with minors under the age of eighteen but OVER the age of sixteen?"

"After they're processed, they can be held in a cell in the main ward, preferably away from adult prisoners."

Sally nodded.

"What is the proper procedure when dealing with minors UNDER the age of sixteen?"

"They are either kept in an interrogation room under supervision until a parent or guardian is present. If we're short-handed, they can be left, but the door must be locked."

"Very good. Do we ever put a minor UNDER the age of sixteen in the main cell area with the general male population?"

"NO... NEVER."

"What happens if we do that?"

"Very. Bad. Things," John said, looking pointedly at Weaver.

"Such as?" Sally asked.

"Well, first, it's against state and federal laws to place a minor child in with general male population. If they need to be placed in a cell, it's in the women's cell ward."

"Why is that?"

"For the safety of the child."

"What is the proper procedure when dealing with a child who is currently suffering from emotional, physical, or psychological trauma?"

"You make sure that you NEVER leave them alone."

"Why is that?"

"Because there's a possibility they can do harm to themselves or to others."

"How old is Kendall?"

"I think he had a birthday about three weeks ago, so fourteen."

"Where did we find him about twenty minutes ago?"

"In the MALE cell ward."

"And where was he?"

"Under the bunks after having suffered an emotional and/or psychological breakdown," John said angrily.

"Where is he now?"

"In the CHIEF'S office, where he and his wife are trying to bring him around."

Sally folded her hands. She had never stopped staring at Weaver. "What happens if his mother chooses to file charges against the police department?"

"Again, bad things. State investigations, possible disciplinary actions, including filing charges against the parties involved."

"Who would the involved parties be?"

"Why, I do believe that would be Weaver here."

"Weaver, how many infractions do you have on your record?" Sally asked.

"Two... WHY?"

"John, what do three infractions mean?"

"Three infractions earns you a week's suspension with pay."

Sally held out her hand. "Badge and gun please."

"Are you kidding? I was following the judge's orders!" Weaver yelled.

"Are you saying that Judge Warner TOLD you to put Kendall in the main cell ward and to leave him there alone?" Sally asked.

"Well... no," he said.

"Then why did you?" she asked quietly.

"I guess I wasn't thinking," Weaver admitted.

"Badge and gun, one week's suspension, and pray that's all," Sally said firmly.

Weaver took off his badge and his holster and handed them to her.

"Do NOT leave town until you hear from someone," Sally instructed.

"Yes ma'am," he said as he walked out of the room.

Sally sighed. "That idiot may have undone whatever progress Kendall's made since the LAST idiot."

John sat down next to her. "I know, but he's a strong kid. Maybe he'll be fine when he comes around."

"I hope so," Sally said, getting up.

"Whoa, what happened to your eye?" John asked, noticing a dark bruise forming around her left eye.

"What?"

"You've got quite a shiner there," he said, looking at her face.

"Oh, I freaked Kendall out when I first found him. We do NOT tell him. I'll put some makeup over it."

"Well, first we better get some ice on it. I'll go get you an ice pack," he told her and headed to the break room. A moment later, he brought her the ice pack and placed it over her eye.

"Thanks."

"No problem." He smirked.

"What?" she asked, noting the expression on his face.

"Not a thing."

She arched an eyebrow at him. "What?" she repeated.

"Just that you take on criminals and some cops twice your size and don't get a scratch. A fourteen year old kid gives you a shiner." He chuckled.

"Want one to match it?"

Chapter 86~ Lies and Lullabies

Antonio sat next to Kendall while Sylvia explained what had happened with Weaver. "He threatened to arrest you for obstruction of justice?" Antonio said quietly, his jaw clenched.

Sylvia nodded. "Then Kendall told him to leave us alone and went with him."

"Alright, I think Sally's talking to Weaver now. She'll get to the bottom of this."

There was a small knock on the door and Sally looked in. "How is he?"

Antonio shook his head. "Still out."

"Can I see you for a minute?" she asked quietly.

Antonio nodded and got up, and Sylvia took his place next to Kendall.

"First, I already spoke with Ryan. He said Dylan filed charges at the courthouse after his hearing, stating that Kendall attacked him with a weapon with no provocation. Second, the Rickard boys had already come to me asking for a plea bargain, because they had some information regarding a conversation they had overheard between Dylan and Graham the other night."

"What did they hear?" Antonio asked.

Sally told him about the conversation she had had with the two boys, as well as what Ryan had said.

Antonio nodded. "Weaver?"

"Third infraction, so I put him on a week's suspension at the moment. I told him to stay in town until he hears from someone."

"Thanks Sally," Antonio said. "Honey, what happened to your eye?"

"Nothing important."

In the office, Kendall whimpered and kicked out his feet, trying to turn over. His breathing picked up and he started shaking. "No more..." he cried and then tried to push off the couch.

"Antonio!" Sylvia yelled as she and Jo tried to hold onto the boy.

"Mijo, it's alright," Sylvia said, trying to comfort her godson.

Antonio and Sally rushed back into the room and he grabbed Kendall and pulled him up into his arms so he could hold him still. "Shhh, it's alright, Mijo, you're safe. You need to wake up now," Antonio said softly as he rocked the boy back and forth.

After few minutes, Kendall's breathing had regulated and he lay with his head against Antonio's chest. He finally opened his eyes and blinked, trying to focus his vision.

"Papi?"

"That's me." Antonio smiled.

Kendall curled up into Antonio's arms. "Make it stop, make him go away," he sobbed.

Sylvia and Joanna looked at one another, tears filling their eyes.

Antonio sat back and pulled Kendall as close as he could, his chin resting on the top of Kendall's head.

Sally was still standing in the doorway and was glad Weaver had already left, as she had an overwhelming urge to hurt him at the moment.

Officer Dane came walking in with Brad Pruitt and Adam Randall.

Now that's timing, Sally thought.

"Main interrogation room, please," she said.

Dane nodded and pushed the two boys ahead of him to the room. Sally quietly closed Antonio's office door and grabbed Bennet's arm, pulling him along with her to the interrogation room. "What, again?" he asked.

"Just come on... this'll be fun, I promise."

"Oh, well as long as you PROMISE," he said, following her.

"Don't make me hurt you," she retorted.

∞

Antonio sat there, holding Kendall for another ten minutes before the boy started to wake again. He shivered a little and hugged Antonio.

"Hey, how are you feeling?" Antonio asked him.

"My head hurts."

"I don't doubt that. Do you remember what happened?'

Kendall thought back. "Mama G and Mama M were watching a movie with me when someone came to the door. He said he was going to arrest Mama G if I didn't go with him. We got here, he made me go in a cell, and he locked the door. I asked him not to leave me alone, but he wouldn't come back. Then I heard other voices saying... stuff. Then I heard him whispering again. He won't go away."

Antonio hugged Kendall to him. "I know it seems that way now, Mijo. I don't know how to make it stop, or I would. I think it's just going to take time."

"I know," Kendall said. "Papi, am I in trouble?"

"No, you're not in trouble. Just people playing games again, but we're going to put a stop to it, I promise."

"Okay."

"I need to talk to Mami G for a few minutes, but Mami M is here. Will you be okay for a few minutes?"

Kendall nodded and Antonio smiled and helped Kendall lie back on the couch. Jo went and sat next to Kendall and held his hand.

Antonio and Sylvia went into the other room. She stood there, eyebrow arched and with her hands on her hips. "You don't have to keep him here do you? Because if you think I'll allow that..."

Antonio put his hands up. "No, he's NOT staying here, but I think we need to get an official statement about what happened that day. I'll have Sally or John do it as soon as they're free, and then you can take him home."

Sylvia visibly relaxed. "I'm sorry, honey, it's just..."

"Believe me, I know, but we're going to put an end to this soon," he said, hugging her.

∞

Sally and John let Brad Pruitt and Adam Randall wait alone in the interrogation room for a few minutes before going in.

Sally sat across from the boys and Bennet sat at the end of the table.

"WHY are we here?" Brad demanded.

"Don't you know?" Sally asked quietly.

"NO, the cop who brought us in didn't say anything."

"We just have a few questions we need to ask you," Bennet told them.

"About what?" Adam asked.

"Tell us about the arrangement you made with Richard Graham regarding Dylan Mason's case," Sally said.

Their eyes went wide. "We don't know what you're talking about," Adam squeaked.

Sally and John just stared at him for a minute.

"Really? Because your body language tells me differently," John said.

"Oh yeah, HOW?" Brad snapped.

"Your rapid breathing, profuse sweating, the fact that your voice goes almost an octave when you answer," Bennet told him.

"Whatever, I'm outta here," Brad said, standing up.

Sally looked at him. "Sit your ass back down before I lock you in a cell instead of giving you a chance to come clean."

He looked at her smugly, but after a moment, sat back down.

"Not as dumb as he looks," John remarked.

"Don't be too sure," Sally said.

She leaned forward, staring at both boys. "We KNOW you took money in exchange for changing your testimony, regarding what happened when you and Dylan attacked Logan Mitchell. We KNOW that Richard Graham is the one who paid you to change your testimony."

"I want my phone call," Brad demanded.

Bennet shook his head.

"I get a phone call!" he yelled.

Sally smiled. "Only if you've been CHARGED with something. You haven't been charged with anything, YET. You are here to answer questions, and I would strongly advise you to do so. You weren't charged in the assault on Logan, because he told us you never actually struck him. Now I hear you're saying that Logan taunted Dylan by calling him names and that Dylan lost his temper."

"Yeah, so?" Brad said.

"Also, that Kendall Knight came out of nowhere and attacked you all for no apparent reason?"

"Yeah," Brad said again.

Sally looked at them. "Do you know what perjury is?"

The boys looked at one another.

"That's where you lie in court," Adam said.

Sally nodded. "Not just in court, however. It's also when you lie while giving a sworn statement."

Sally pulled papers from a file. "Now, I have here your sworn statements regarding the case against Dylan Mason regarding his assault on Logan Mitchell. You read these and then you signed them. That means they are SWORN testimony, and if you knowingly lied while giving testimony, that means you perjured yourself. Do you know what the penalty for perjury is?"

The boys shook their heads.

"Up to five years in prison, and as you are both seventeen, you will be tried as adults. Therefore, I'm going to give you one more chance to come clean about this whole matter. Think about it, is it really worth up to five years of your life for a thousand dollars?"

Both boys looked shocked by the fact she knew how much they had been paid.

"What do you want to know?" Brad asked.

John smiled warmly. "Just the truth boys, that's all we want."

∞

Five minutes later, Sally and Bennet came out of the interrogation room and found Antonio waiting.

"Well?" he asked.

They both smiled. "Dane will be picking up Dylan Mason after dropping Brad and Adam off back at school. Ryan is revoking his bail," Sally told him.

"Good, one down-one to go," Antonio said.

Sally smiled. "There's no way Graham will beat the charges against him. Ryan tells me the DEA will also be filing charges as soon as we're finished with him."

Antonio nodded. "Good, I'm going to send Kendall home then, but I want you to get his statement about what happened that day so there are no more questions."

Sally nodded and headed for Antonio's office. She knocked before she opened the door and saw Sylvia sitting at Antonio's desk, while Jo sat with Kendall. "Hey kiddo, you up for answering a few questions for me?"

"About what?"

She went and sat on the other side of him. "About the day Dylan attacked Logan."

"I guess."

"Good. Can you tell me how you knew what was going on?"

Kendall thought back. "It was after you left, I think. Papi woke me up and I took a shower and then decided to try and take some pictures like I promised you."

Sally nodded.

"I was sitting in Carlos' chair at the window and saw my mom drop Logan and Katie off and then drive away. A few minutes later, I saw Logan cross the street and cut through the neighbour's yard into the alley. Then I saw Dylan, Adam, and... I can't remember the other kid's name, circle around Logan. I knew what they were going to do and I remember getting really mad, and then trying to keep Dylan away from Logan."

Joanna hugged Kendall a little tighter.

"Then I don't remember anything until I woke up and Papi was holding onto me."

"Very good, Kendall." Sally smiled, squeezing his hand. Then a thought occurred to her. "You said you were taking pictures? Do you know if you got any pictures of Dylan going after Logan?"

"I don't know, maybe. They'd still be on the camera."

"I'm going to stop by and pick up the memory card later, okay?"

Kendall nodded. "Can I go home now? I'm really tired."

"You bet you can. Kendall, I'm so sorry about what happened this morning. It never should have happened."

"Wasn't your fault," he said.

She smiled at him. "Why don't you go home and get some rest? I'll stop by later to pick up the memory card and say hi."

He smiled and nodded.

Sylvia and Joanna grabbed their coats, and Sally helped Kendall up and walked them to the door.

"Well?" Antonio asked after they had left.

"He remembered a good portion of it, and if we're lucky, actually got a photo or two of Dylan going after Logan. I told him I'd stop by later to get the memory card."

Antonio nodded. "Are you alright?" he asked, looking at her.

She nodded. "He's such a good kid. I'm just ready for all this idiocy to end, so your lives can go back to normal."

"Agreed, and your life too." He smiled.

She smirked at him. "You know I live for all this crap."

"Yeah, I know. That's what scares me." He smirked back.

∞

After they got back to the Garcia home, Sylvia and Joanna went to make some lunch, while Kendall laid down on the couch.

They came out a few minutes later and sat, watching the rest of Finding Nemo, and eating their lunch.

Kendall ate almost half a sandwich and drank most of his shake before he started feeling nauseated. He lay down and curled up, watching the movie.

Joanna moved over and pulled his head onto her lap, stroking his hair. She started singing her favourite lullaby to him... "Go to Sleep, My Little Teddy Bear."

Kendall's eyes closed as he listened to her sing. "I remember the first time you sang that to me."

"So do I. It was the first time you spent the night at our house. You were seven and Logan was so excited to have a friend over. You boys played and watched movies, and then Logan fell asleep, but you couldn't. I asked if you wanted me to read you a story, and you said no. Then I asked if you wanted me to sing you a song, and you said yes."

Kendall nodded.

"Soon, you were fast asleep, and the next morning, you were both re-energized beyond belief." She laughed.

Kendall sighed and snuggled in closer as she pulled a blanket over him.

Sylvia was watching and smiled at the two. She was relieved that Kendall had eaten and seemed to be doing better after the morning's ordeal. She was concerned about how Jen was going to take this, and wondered how they were going to tell her.

Chapter 87 ~ One Down

Kendall was still sleeping an hour later when Jen got back from work. She smiled at the sight of her son lying cuddled up with Joanna on the couch.

"Hey, how was your first day back?" Sylvia asked.

"Good. It was nice to be doing something other than sitting around and worrying," Jen said as she bent down and kissed Kendall on the cheek. "How did things go here?" she asked, sitting down.

Joanna and Sylvia looked at each other.

"What?" she asked suddenly concerned.

"He ate some breakfast and most of his lunch," Jo said.

"Good. What else happened?"

Sylvia sighed. "Come into the kitchen and we'll have some tea and talk."

Jen hesitated for a moment and then nodded and followed Sylvia into the kitchen.

Jo stayed with Kendall, hoping that Jen didn't break down completely.

Sylvia put the kettle on while Jen got the mugs down from the cupboard. She waited patiently until Sylvia was ready to tell her about the events of the morning. She took comfort in that Kendall was sleeping safe and sound in the living room, that he had eaten, and that he was allowing people close to him.

Sylvia handed her a cup of tea and sat down next to her. She took a deep breath and then told Jen what had happened that morning.

∞

Kendall woke up a few minutes later.

"Hey sleepyhead," Joanna said.

He smiled a little. "Did I hear my mom?"

Joanna nodded. "She got back from work a few minutes ago and is relaxing with some tea in the kitchen."

He stretched his legs out and yawned.

"Honey, can I ask you something? You don't have to answer me if you don't want to," Jo said, stroking his hair.

He nodded and curled back up.

"When you said he keeps whispering to you, what does he say?"

"Bad things." He sighed, closing his eyes.

"Are they things that he said to you when you were with him?"

Kendall nodded. "It's like that movie."

"Which movie?"

"The one where the scary guy dies, but he keeps coming back through dreams and hurting people."

"I hate those kind of movies," Jo said, wrapping her arm around him.

"Me too."

∞

Jen and Sylvia sat quietly in the kitchen, while Jen tried to absorb what Sylvia had told her.

She took a deep breath. "So, Dylan will be off the streets and unable to hurt the boys anymore?"

Sylvia nodded.

"What about Graham?"

"Sally said the DEA is investigating him too. He made bail, but he has to wear a monitoring device, and he is not allowed to contact you or Kendall. He's also not allowed to practice, and Sally said there is no way he will get off. The DA is unwilling to make any kind of deal with him."

"Well, maybe some good will come of this whole thing, because he won't be allowed to hurt anyone else."

Sylvia smiled. "That's the spirit! Kendall's doing fine right now, so let's just try and stay positive about things."

Jen smiled. "I'm trying."

"I know you are. Now, why don't we make a snack and see if we can get him to eat a little more?" Sylvia suggested.

Jen nodded and they made a plate of cheese and crackers and took it out for them all to share.

∞

Officer Dane came in with a handcuffed Dylan Mason, who was yelling at the top of his lungs.

"I'M GOING TO SUE ALL OF YOU!"

"Settle down, sunshine. You're giving me a headache," John said, smirking.

"I don't know kinda sounds like music to my ears. Definitely out of tune, but still music," Sally said, staring the teen down.

Dylan kicked out at Officer Dane and Bennet grabbed him by the front of his jacket and slammed him up against the wall. "You just added assaulting a police officer to the list of charges."

"Whatever!"

"You read him his rights?" Bennet asked Dane.

"Yes sir."

"Good, get him processed, give him his phone call, and put him in a cell."

Dane smiled. "Will do."

∞

After a while, things quieted down at the station, so Sally decided to run to the Garcia's and pick up the memory card and check on Kendall.

Sylvia answered the door. "Hi Sally. How are things going?"

"Very well. Dylan Mason was brought in and will be a guest in lock up until his trial."

"Good," Sylvia said.

"Hey kiddo, how are you feeling?" Sally asked Kendall, who was sitting between Joanna and his mom.

"Okay," he said.

"Good. I needed to pick up that memory card."

"It's upstairs."

She offered her hand and he took it and she helped him up. They went upstairs and he got the camera for her. She popped out the memory card. "I brought you a replacement," she said, putting the new one in.

"Thanks Sally. Oh, there's a video on there too. The guys were having a snowball fight the other day."

She smiled at him. "I'll get it onto a disc for you, okay?"

"Thanks," he said, looking a little closer at her. "What happened to your eye?"

Sally mentally cursed herself. She had forgotten to cover the black eye with makeup.

Kendall had a flashback to that morning. "I did that, didn't I?"

She sighed. "I promised you I'd never lie to you. When you were hiding under the bunk, I startled you. I shouldn't have touched you, but I did. You didn't know what you were doing. You didn't know who I was. You were just trying to get away."

He looked down and away from her. "I'm sorry," he whispered.

"Oh honey, please don't! There is nothing to be sorry for. It was my fault, and believe me, I've had worse."

When he didn't respond, she took his face in her hands. "Look at me. It was NOT your fault."

"So when does me hurting people become my fault again? First Katie, now you. That's not even counting how many times I've hurt the guys' feelings or ruined their plans."

"Okay, sit," she instructed, pointing to the chair.

He did as she said and she knelt in front of him. "Now you listen to me, this month has been one royally screwed up time. You are NOT responsible for Deesie, Graham, bullies, being sick, nightmares, or being afraid. Your FAMILY does not blame you for anything. The only one placing any blame on you is you, and that's because of who you are and who you have always been. You're a protector, and right now, you feel like you're letting everyone down because you need to be protected. That's a normal reaction, but you also have to understand that as much as you need to take care of them, they need to take care of you. You need to let them, because right now, you are vulnerable. I know that's a terrifying realization, but it's one everyone has at one point or another in their lives."

Kendall's eyes were tearing up and she reached up and brushed his bangs back a little.

"Honey, being scared doesn't make you weak and neither does crying. Things WILL get better, and while I know it feels like it's been an eternity since this whole thing started, it's only been two weeks. I've known adults, who went through a hell of a lot less than you have, that have taken months to recover. You have to give yourself some time and some credit, because you're an amazing kid who has an amazing life ahead of him." She smiled.

"How do you know that?"

"Oh, didn't I tell you? I know everything. Just ask Antonio or John," she said with a smirk.

He smiled a little.

"That's what I like to see," she said, squeezing his hand. "I know you have an appointment with Claudia Jenkins tomorrow. Would you like me to come with you?"

He nodded.

"Okay, I'll find out what time and meet you there."

"Thanks Sally."

"You're welcome. You call me if you need anything. I mean it, alright?"

He nodded.

"Okay, I need to get going now. I'll see you tomorrow though," she said, standing up.

They walked downstairs together.

"Jen, what time is Kendall's appointment tomorrow?" Sally asked.

"At ten. Why?"

"Since I know Claudia, Kendall would like me to meet him there."

Jen smiled. "That's so nice, thank you."

"Happy to do it. I need to get back to the station, so I'll see you all later."

"Sally, what are you doing for Thanksgiving?" Jen asked.

"Probably sitting at home in my fuzzy pajamas, watching sappy old movies. Why?"

"We're having dinner at my house and would love it if you joined us."

Kendall nodded. "Please come."

"I'd love to. Thank you," she said, giving Kendall a quick hug and then she left for the station.

∞

School was uneventful for the boys. After school, they walked to hockey practice with the rest of the team. Once they got there, they got into their gear and out onto the ice.

After warm-ups and about an hour of breakout and passing drills, the coach had them do some positional play drills. Carlos and James were playing on the defensive and Logan was playing perimeter offense.

After about ten minutes, Logan was attempting a breakout pass, when he collided with another player. They both slammed into the boards. Logan got up and felt something give in his ankle, and then the pain hit. He cried out as he went down to his knees and James got to him first.

"What's hurt?"

"I think it's my ankle," Logan hissed through the pain.

Carlos and the coach got there next and helped Logan back to the locker room. They got his skates off and saw that his right ankle had already swollen to twice its size.

"Wow, it's huge!" Carlos said, poking it with his finger.

"CARLOS! Don't touch!" Logan yelled, slapping his friend's hand away.

Coach Banner sighed. "Let's get you to the emergency room."

He and James helped Logan up and out to the car.

"James, finish running the practice drills. It shouldn't take us too long to get in to see a doctor."

James nodded. "See you soon, buddy."

Logan nodded, looking completely miserable.

After being x-rayed and having his ankle wrapped, Logan hobbled out on crutches to where Coach Banner was waiting. He handed him the paperwork the doctor had filled out.

"I have to stay off of my foot for at least a week, sorry Coach," he said, looking down.

"These things happen, son. Don't worry about it," Coach told him.

"I know, but we're already down a man with Kendall out for the season."

"It'll be fine. A week isn't that long, especially with the holiday weekend coming up. You and that logistical mind of yours can help out with the play strategies."

"Thanks Coach." Logan smiled.

"Alright, let's get back before your parents come to pick you up."

They got back to the rink just as Sylvia arrived to pick up the boys. She saw Logan walk up on crutches. "What happened? Did someone come after you?" she asked.

"No, Mama G. It was just an accident during practice. I sprained my ankle. I have to stay off of it for at least a week, and I'm supposed to get this prescription filled," he said, handing her the paper.

She released the breath she been holding. "Oh, thank God. I mean, I'm sorry about your ankle, Mijo, but I'm glad that's all it was."

He smiled at her. "Could be I'm my own worst enemy."

She smiled back at him. "Okay, let's get this filled and then get you home."

The other two boys came out, bringing Logan's gear with them. Sylvia stopped by the pharmacy to pick up the painkillers the doctor had prescribed and then took them home. Carlos helped Logan up to the house while James carried their gear. They got inside and Logan had to explain things all over again.

James and Carlos took their gear upstairs, and Logan looked at the staircase as if it were Mt. Kilimanjaro.

Kendall took his arm. "You go up first and I'll walk behind you."

Logan nodded and started slowly up the stairs, with Kendall one-step below, his hands held up, and supporting Logan's back.

Jen, Sylvia, and Joanna watched until they disappeared upstairs.

Chapter 88~ The Patient

Logan changed out of his hockey gear and into some pajamas. Kendall helped him get settled onto Carlos' bed and put a pillow under his leg to elevate it. "I'll get you an icepack. Do you need anything else?"

"Maybe my backpack? I still have homework."

"Okay, I'll bring it up with the ice," Kendall said.

"Thanks Kendall."

"No problem." Kendall smiled as he headed downstairs. He returned a few minutes later with a bag of peas and the backpack. He set up Logan's laptop on a tray and handed it to him. "This'll probably hurt," he said as he gently lay the bag of peas across Logan's ankle.

Logan grimaced in pain.

"Sorry," Kendall said. "Your mom is making you a tray for dinner."

Logan sighed.

"What?"

"Stupid accident," Logan said.

"At least it's not broken, and if you stay OFF of it, it should heal quickly," Kendall said.

"Still..."

"It'll be okay. You'll be up and around in no time," Kendall reassured him. "You want me to eat dinner up here with you?"

Logan looked at him. "Would you?"

"Sure, let me tell my mom," Kendall said and headed downstairs.

Logan stared after his friend and then smiled.

Kendall went into the kitchen. "Logan wants me to eat dinner with him, so can we make two plates to take up?"

"Uh... s-sure! Of course, we'll bring it up in a minute," Jen said.

"What's wrong?" he asked, looking at her expression.

"Nothing honey, I'm just glad you're taking such good care of Logan." She grinned.

"Okay..." he said and headed back upstairs.

James, Carlos, and Katie were all sitting around the kitchen table, their mouths open.

"He ASKED for dinner," Carlos said excitedly. James and Katie nodded and smiled at him.

"Maybe Logan spraining his ankle is a blessing in disguise," Jo said.

Antonio got home a few minutes later. He was still angry over what had happened that morning and was worried about what he was going to find when he got home. Sylvia had planned to tell Jen, and he was very worried about how she had taken it. Not to mention how the kids were going to react.

He sighed as he opened the door and was surprised to find that everyone seemed to be in good spirits. "So, what's going on?"

"Logan sprained his ankle," Sylvia said, hugging him.

"And we're happy about this, why?"

"Kendall asked if he could eat dinner with Logan upstairs," Jen said, smiling.

Antonio looked at them in confusion. "And?"

"Honey, Kendall ASKED for dinner so he could EAT with Logan," Sylvia said slowly.

"Wait, you mean he asked for actual food?"

"Well, I'm assuming that's what he meant when he asked if I could make up two plates." Jen smiled.

"So, he's doing alright even after this morning?" Antonio asked a bit shocked. He had fully expected to get home and find Kendall curled up in bed, hiding away from everyone.

The moms all smiled and nodded.

Antonio grinned. "Well, I'll be."

"Wait, what about this morning?" James asked.

"We haven't told them yet," Sylvia whispered to him.

"It's not important right now, I'll tell you later," Antonio promised.

James looked at him suspiciously but nodded.

A few minutes later, Antonio took the tray up for the boys. Kendall and Logan were sitting next to each other on Carlos' bed, and Logan was helping Kendall finish his chemistry homework. "Dinner anyone?" Antonio asked.

"Yes please, I'm starving," Logan said.

Kendall got up and awkwardly removed the tray that held Logan's laptop and Antonio replaced it with the dinner tray.

"How's your ankle doing?"

"It doesn't hurt as much right now." Logan told him.

"Good." Antonio smiled.

"How are you doing?" he asked Kendall.

"Okay."

"Good. Well, I'll leave you boys to your dinner and I'm going down to eat mine. Call if you need anything, okay?"

The boys nodded. "Thanks Papi," Kendall said.

Antonio smiled and went back downstairs. He sat down at the table with the others. "So, how was everyone's day today?"

"I sold over 45 tickets to the school play," Katie told him.

"Good job, Mija." He smiled.

"Papa G?" James asked.

"Yes James?"

"What happened this morning?"

Antonio sighed. He had a feeling he wasn't going to get out of this. "I'll tell you after dinner, okay?"

"Promise?"

"I promise."

After they had all finished eating and the table had been cleared, Antonio told them what had happened that morning.

James was beyond angry. "How could something like that happen? How could they let Dylan get away with something like that?"

"James, he didn't get away with it. He's back in jail until his court date, and that's where he'll stay."

"This is totally not fair," Carlos said.

"I know it isn't, but it's all settled now."

"Well, what about that cop? Is he in trouble?" James asked.

"Sally took care of Officer Weaver."

"He should get fired!" Carlos stated.

"Boys, I'm not any happier about what happened than you are, but things are under control now," Antonio said.

Kendall came in carrying the tray balanced against one hip. He looked at everyone sitting there. "What's going on?"

"Let me get that, honey," Jo said, taking the tray from him. She smiled when she saw one empty plate and one nearly empty plate. "Was dinner good?"

He nodded, still looking at the others. Antonio gestured for him to come over. Kendall went and stood next to him and Antonio put an arm around his waist. "We were just discussing what happened this morning."

"Oh," Kendall said, looking down.

"The point is that everyone is doing alright now," Antonio continued. "Right?" he asked Kendall.

Kendall nodded. "I told Logan I'd bring him some juice," he said and went into the kitchen.

"Is everyone okay?" Kendall quietly asked Joanna as he grabbed a bottle of juice from the fridge.

"Yes, they were just worried about you when they heard what happened," she said, taking the bottle and pouring a glass of juice for him.

Kendall sighed as he took the glass. "Thank you."

"You're welcome. Will you tell Logan that I'll be up in a few minutes to say goodnight?"

Kendall nodded and went back upstairs. "Here you go, buddy," Kendall said, handing Logan the glass.

"Thanks. God, I hate being so helpless," Logan complained and then looked at Kendall. "I didn't mean... Kendall, I just meant..."

"Will you relax? I know what you meant and I know how you feel." He smiled.

"Yeah, I guess you do."

"Your mom said she'd be up in a few minutes to say goodnight," Kendall told him.

"I guess I'll be going home tomorrow night. James said he wants to stay with you for a couple of days, and now I'm kinda out of commission."

"Only for a few days, and you can still stay over. Someone has to help me with all that homework." Kendall smiled.

"True, you'd be lost without me," Logan joked.

"You have no idea," Kendall said, thinking about how lost he would be without all of them.

Joanna knocked on the door. "Hey, I'm going to take off now. If your ankle is bothering you too much in the morning, stay home from school, alright?"

"Mom, it's just a sprained ankle. I think I can manage going to school."

"Leave it to you to throw away a perfectly good excuse to get out of going to school." Kendall smirked.

Joanna smiled at them. "I mean it, Logan. If it's hurting too much, stay home." She gave her son a hug and kissed him on the cheek.

"I'll see you later too," she said, kissing Kendall on the cheek.

"Okay, goodnight."

The other boys came up a little while later and got ready for bed. Logan went to get out of the bed, but Kendall pushed him back down. "Where do you think you're going?"

"To bed," he said, pointing to his place on the floor.

"I don't think so. You're staying there," Kendall ordered.

"You shouldn't sleep on the floor," Logan argued.

"Why not?"

"First, your shoulder. Second, your pneumonia."

Kendall just looked at him with a raised eyebrow. "I can use an extra blanket, and one night is not going to hurt me," Kendall told him, laying the blanket out on the floor.

James and Carlos were watching the interaction in amusement.

"I bet Logan wins, he's in doctor mode," Carlos whispered to James.

James shook his head. "No way, Kendall is in protective mode."

"Kendall, I mean it!" Logan said firmly, grabbing for his crutches.

Kendall snatched them away and leaned them against the wall on the other side of the room.

"You're staying in bed with your foot elevated, so deal with it," Kendall said, lying down on the floor.

"James..." Logan said, gesturing towards Kendall.

"No way dude, he's right. One night isn't going to hurt him, and you need to keep your foot up so that it heals."

"Carlos..." Logan begged.

Carlos looked at Kendall and then back at Logan. He shook his head. "James is right," he said, lying down on the other side of Kendall.

Kendall smirked up at Logan. "Goodnight Loges."

"I need new friends."

James smiled at him and then turned out the light. He double-checked to make sure the door was closed tight and then laid down in front of it.

∞

Richard Graham was furious that he was being treated like a common criminal. He sat in his home office and subconsciously scratched at the ankle bracelet. "Just another indignity I have to bear for trying to help that spoiled little brat," he fumed as he kicked back another shot of scotch.

He smiled when he thought of Dylan filing charges against Kendall Knight. Dylan's friends had been fairly easy to buy off, and with any luck, being arrested would send his former patient on a downward spiral. An inspired plan really, fueled on by his being forced to stay all weekend in a common jailhouse. Then again, if that stupid judge had not been sick, he wouldn't have met Dylan.

Tomorrow he would be implementing his plan to exonerate himself by winning popular favour. He had already made a few phone calls until he found someone willing to help him. He was sure his fool of an attorney would disapprove, but then again, he had wanted him to plead down.

"Yes, tomorrow will be a good day," he said with a chuckle.

Chapter 89 ~ Claudia Jenkins

Antonio went in to check on the boys at about two, almost tripping over James in the process.

James woke up. "What's wrong?"

"Shhh, it's just me. Sorry, I didn't know you were so close to the door," Antonio whispered.

"Okay," James said in relief.

"How's everything in here?"

"So far, so good." James yawned.

"Good." Antonio smiled. He went over and rearranged the pillow under Logan's leg, and then pulled another blanket from the closet and covered Kendall with it.

"Papi?" James whispered.

"Yes?"

"They can't hurt Kendall anymore, right?"

Antonio went and sat down next to James. "Who, Mijo?"

"Dylan, the Rickards, Graham..."

Antonio put his arm around him. "No, I don't think so. I think the Rickards have learned their lesson. Plus, if they act up, their probation will be revoked. As for Dylan and Graham, they will both stand trial. Dylan will probably be sent to the juvenile facility in Minneapolis, and Graham will most likely be sent to a Federal prison because of the drug violations."

"Good. I still don't think it's fair that Graham got bail though."

"I don't either, but everyone has rights. He's wearing a monitoring bracelet and isn't allowed to leave home without permission."

"I guess that's okay then." James yawned.

"Alright, back to sleep, you have school tomorrow," Antonio said, giving him a quick hug.

"Night Papi."

"Goodnight Mijo," Antonio said, closing the door behind him.

∞

The next morning, Logan woke up desperately needing to use the bathroom. He knew he couldn't reach his crutches and didn't want to wake up Kendall by calling out, so he threw his pillow at Carlos.

"Carlos," he whispered.

Carlos just rolled over and hugged the pillow to him.

"Unbelievable," Logan said to himself.

He swung his legs over the side of the bed and hopped over to where his crutches were. He finally made it, but then had to figure out how to maneuver around his sleeping friends. Finally, he just leaned against the wall and started poking Carlos with one of the crutches. Carlos kept trying to swat away whatever was poking him and finally just reached out and grabbed it.

"WHOA!" Logan yelled as Carlos pulled him over on top of him.

He landed on Carlos, who let out a grunt as Logan knocked the air from his lungs.

Kendall's eyes snapped open and he pushed himself away from the two and landed on James. James woke up and grabbed Kendall so he didn't hit the door. "It's okay, it's just me," James said.

Kendall tried to focus his eyes and saw Logan sprawled out on top of Carlos. "What are you two doing?"

Logan pushed himself up. "I have to use the bathroom and SOMEONE put my crutches clear across the room, so I had to hop over to them. Then I couldn't figure out how to walk around everyone, so I tried to wake up Carlos and he pulled me over."

"Did you hurt your ankle?" Kendall asked.

"No, I landed on my stomach."

"You mean you landed on MY stomach," Carlos said, pushing Logan the rest of the way off him.

"Because you pulled me over, genius," Logan retorted, smacking Carlos on the back of the head.

Kendall and James watched the two and started laughing.

"WHAT?" they both yelled.

"You should see yourselves," James said.

Logan's dark hair was sticking straight up on the back of his head from sleeping on his back all night, giving his head an odd square shape. Carlos looked like he had stuck his finger in a light socket with his hair standing up straight all over his head.

"Very funny," Logan said. "Now help me up, I have to pee!"

Carlos got up, put his hands under Logan's arms, and hauled him up. Kendall handed him his crutches, and James held the door open for him.

"I seriously need new friends," he muttered as he hobbled into the bathroom.

∞

After they got ready for school, the boys went downstairs for breakfast.

"Logan, are you sure you're up for a day at school?" Antonio asked.

"I'm fine. I took some ibuprofen and can get an icepack from the nurse."

"Alright. If your ankle starts bothering you too much, call and we'll pick you up."

Logan nodded.

"Kendall, your mom called. We need to stop by Dr. Sharpe's office to get you weighed," Sylvia said.

"Why?"

"Just to make sure you haven't lost any more weight. It's just a quick stop, not an appointment. We can go there first, before Dr. Jenkin's."

Kendall sighed miserably. He was already dreading going to see Dr. Jenkins, and now this.

"It'll be alright, Mijo," Antonio said, kissing him on top of the head.

"Come on kids, we're going to be late."

The boys and Katie gathered their things, and Sylvia walked them to the door.

"If you need me, call," Antonio told her. He was worried about how Kendall was going to react to the new psychologist, but Sally had told him she was going with them, so that helped to relieve some of the concern.

"I'm sure we'll be fine," Sylvia said, kissing him goodbye.

She went back into the kitchen, where Kendall was still picking at his breakfast. She handed him his fork. "Eat."

He took a few bites, but he was getting nervous about the appointment.

"It's going to be fine, Mijo. Remember, Sally is going to meet us there, and she's known Claudia Jenkins for years. She says she's very nice."

Kendall just nodded.

There was a knock at the door. "Besides, Brooke is coming with us, and you know she won't put up with any funny business."

Kendall smiled at that as Sylvia went to answer the door.

"How's our boy today?" Brooke asked, coming in and giving Kendall a kiss on the cheek.

"Okay."

"How about some coffee?" Sylvia asked her.

"That would be lovely." Brooke smiled.

"I should try and get some more of my homework done," Kendall said, getting up.

"Honey, you didn't eat very much," Sylvia said.

"I know. I'm just kinda nervous."

"Okay, but I want you to drink a shake for lunch."

He nodded and went upstairs.

∞

A couple of hours later, Sylvia went up to let Kendall know it was time to leave. Before she knocked on the door, she saw him sitting in the chair, looking out the window. He looked so alone and she felt herself tearing up.

She shook it off and knocked. "Hey, it's time to go."

He looked over and nodded. They went downstairs, he put on his jacket, and they headed out. They arrived at Dr. Sharpe's office and went in. Kendall sat down while Sylvia let the nurse know they were there. She sat down on one side of him and Brooke on the other.

A couple of minutes later, the nurse called and Sylvia stood up and held her hand out to Kendall.

He looked at it for a moment and then took it, getting up. He took a deep breath and followed the nurse.

"Hi Kendall, could you take off your coat and boots, please?"

Kendall slowly did as the nurse asked and then stood on the scale.

The nurse checked the balances and smiled. "Okay, if you could just wait here for a minute please."

"Is everything alright?" Sylvia asked.

"Dr. Sharpe just wanted me to let her know what Kendall's weight is before you leave, so that she can make any changes to his diet if need be," the nurse said with a smile.

Kendall looked at Sylvia and shook his head. He was terrified that Dr. Sharpe was going to try to put him in the hospital. He was so tired of all of this.

"It's fine, Mijo," Sylvia said as she helped him pull his jacket back on.

Anna Sharpe came out a couple of minutes later. "Hi Kendall. How are you feeling?"

He just looked at her and nodded.

"You're feeling okay?"

He nodded again.

"Are you eating enough?"

He nodded.

Anna looked at Sylvia.

"Honey, why don't you go sit with Brooke for a moment. I'll be right out," Sylvia said.

Kendall looked at her and shook his head.

"Mijo it's alright, I promise. Now go sit with Mama D and I'll be right out."

Kendall sighed, but he did as she asked.

"Is everything alright, darling?" Brooke asked as he sat down.

He nodded and looked down at his feet.

∞

"He's lost another pound and a half. How much IS he eating?" Anna asked Sylvia.

"There were a couple of rough patches. We had some other issues come up, but he's been eating pretty well the last couple of days."

"Sylvia, if he continues to lose weight, I'm going to have to insist we admit him to the hospital. His system cannot tolerate the continual weight loss."

"I understand. He actually did eat quite a bit yesterday. Last night he even asked for dinner, so if we could just give it a couple of more days?" Sylvia asked.

Anna nodded. "I want to weigh him again on Friday and I want to see that he's gained a little. If not..."

"Okay, we'll definitely be working on this," Sylvia told her.

"I don't want to have to put him in the hospital any more than you or Jen. However, if he loses any more weight, his body is going to start shutting down. He's too young and too slight of frame for him to lose any more."

Sylvia nodded. "I know, thank you, Anna."

"Is he still not speaking?"

"He's speaking to us at home, but I haven't been out with him until today. We're actually on our way to meet with Dr. Jenkins in a few minutes, so hopefully she can help him."

"I've heard good things about her," Anna said.

"That's a relief. Sally O'Hara from the station recommended her. She's going to meet us there because Kendall's nervous."

"I can't say I blame him there," Anna said.

"Thanks for everything, Anna. You have a nice Thanksgiving."

"You too. Tell Jen to call if she has any questions."

Sylvia nodded. "I will."

Sylvia took a deep breath and went into the waiting room. She smiled at Kendall. "She just wanted to tell me that you need to start gaining some weight. She wants to weigh you again on Friday, just to make sure it's going alright. Now I understand why you weren't hungry this morning, but this afternoon I need you to eat lunch, okay? This is really important, Kendall."

He looked at her and nodded.

"It's nearly time for your appointment with Dr. Jenkins," she said, holding her hand out for him.

He sighed and took it.

Brooke got up and wrapped her arm around his shoulders. "Don't you worry, darling. Everything will be alright, and we will be right there with you."

∞

A little while later, they pulled up in front of an older Victorian style house. There was wrap around porch with a porch swing near the side door and a rocking chair near the front door.

Sylvia smiled. "This is nice. I love it when they renovate these older homes."

She got out and opened the back door. "Come on, honey, it'll be alright," she said, holding her hand out to him.

He looked at her hand and shook his head.

She knelt down next to him. "Mijo, it's going to be okay, I promise. Please try."

He looked at her and she saw the fear in his eyes. "We'll just go in and meet her. If you don't like it here, we'll leave."

He bit his lower lip but finally took her hand. He got out and Sylvia put her arm around him. Brooke walked on his other side, holding onto his good arm. They slowly went up the walk and were almost to the front porch, when Kendall stopped.

"What is it, honey?" Sylvia asked.

He shook his head and started backing up. His breathing was becoming erratic and she could see the panic in his eyes.

"Kendall, it's alright. No one's going to hurt you," Brooke promised.

He shook his head again.

Sally pulled up just as Kendall pulled away from Sylvia and Brooke. She jumped out and ran up behind them.

"Hey kiddo, are you okay?" she asked, putting her arms around him.

"No, no, no," he said.

"Kendall, look at me," she said, taking his face in her hands.

After a moment, he made eye contact with her. "We're going to go back to the car, and while you wait there, I'm going to go talk to Claudia," she told him, walking him back to the car.

Sylvia and Brooke followed them and Sylvia opened the doors. Kendall nearly jumped into the back seat and scooted away from the door. He pulled his legs up and rested his chin on his knees.

Sally smiled at him as she closed the door.

"What are we going to do?" Sylvia asked her.

"I'm going to go talk to Claudia. She'll probably come out here to meet him, maybe talk to him if he's responsive."

Sylvia nodded and she and Brooke got into the front seat. "It's alright, Mijo," Sylvia said again.

A few moments later, Sally came out with a beautiful African American woman. She was tall, in her late thirties or early forties, with shoulder length hair cut into a sleek bob. They walked up to the car and Sylvia got out to greet them.

"Claudia Jenkins, I'd like you to meet Sylvia Garcia, Kendall's godmother," Sally said.

Claudia smiled as she and Sylvia shook hands. "It's nice to meet you, Mrs. Garcia."

"Please, call me Sylvia. I'm not sure what to do. He's terrified and won't come up to the house."

"Don't worry about it, a lot of children have problems being out of their comfort zone after a trauma. After reading Kendall's file, I can certainly understand why he doesn't feel safe in an unfamiliar place," Claudia said.

"Okay." Sylvia nodded, giving her a small smile.

"Is it alright if I sit up in the front seat for a few minutes? I'll introduce myself and see if he'll respond to me."

"Of course," Sylvia said, gesturing for Brooke to come out.

"Sally, why don't you sit in the back with him for a few minutes and get him use to the idea?" Claudia said.

Sally nodded and got into the backseat with Kendall.

Brooke came around and held out her hand. "Brooke Diamond. You must be Dr. Jenkins."

Claudia took Brooke's hand and smiled. "Please, call me Claudia. Why don't you and Sylvia go on inside for a few minutes. It's a little cold to be standing out here. There's tea and coffee inside, just to the right of the front door."

"That sounds nice, thank you," Brooke said. Then she took a step closer. "I don't want to be rude or anything, but the last so-called psychologist that hurt him, is now in jail."

"Brooke!" Sylvia said in shock. "I'm so sorry, Claudia."

"Don't be, I'm glad Kendall has people who will fight for him. You would be surprised how many children don't. It's frightening, really. I also respect a woman who's not afraid to speak her mind, so many stay silent."

"Brooke does NOT have that problem," Sylvia said as she took Brooke's arm and started up the walk.

Kendall watched as Sylvia and Brooke walked up to the house and got inside.

Sally was sitting next to him. "It's okay, honey. You don't have to go inside, but is it alright if Claudia says hello?"

When she didn't get a response, she scooted a little closer to him. He didn't move away, so she put her arm around his shoulders. "You don't have to speak to her, but it is cold outside, so can she sit in the front seat?"

He didn't look up but gave a slight nod.

Sally looked out and motioned for Claudia to get into the front seat. Claudia opened the door and quietly got in.

"Kendall, this is my friend Claudia." Sally smiled.

"It's nice to meet you, Kendall," Claudia said warmly.

Kendall didn't say anything, but he looked up quickly before looking back down.

"I understand you're not too sure about me, and that's okay. Trust is something that has to be earned and I hope you will give me that chance. Your godmother is very sweet and Mrs. Diamond... she's got your back if I do anything wrong," Claudia told him.

"Brooke is VERY special that way." Sally laughed.

"Yes, I heard SOMEONE gave Richard Graham a shock. God knows it was about time someone put that man in his place," Claudia said.

Kendall looked sideways at Sally. "Oh, you probably don't know about that, I'll have to tell you later. Your Mama D and brothers gave Graham quite a surprise."

"What did they do?" he whispered to her.

Claudia nodded to her so Sally told him about the pranks that Brooke and the boys had played on Graham. Kendall had slowly put his legs down and was sitting close to Sally as she finished.

"Well, I better get back inside. It was very nice to meet you. I'm hoping you might come back. Maybe next time you can come inside for a few minutes, no pressure though. If you would rather, we can sit on the porch or in the car again. You can bring whoever you want with you, if that makes you feel safer." Claudia smiled.

Kendall bit his lower lip, and looking up for a second, gave her a slight nod and a small smile.

Claudia got out. "I'll send the ladies back out and I'll see you later, Sally!"

"Bye Claudia thanks!"

Claudia smiled and waved goodbye to her as she went back to the house.

"Are you doing okay?" Sally asked him.

He nodded. "Sorry," he whispered.

"Nothing to be sorry for, you did great. Claudia is a wonderful person. I have known her for years and she's helped a lot of kids. I wouldn't have recommended her if she weren't the very best."

"I know. It's just hard..."

"I know it is, baby, you don't have to explain."

"I'm just tired," he said.

"I know you are. What do you say we try this again next week?"

Kendall thought about it and nodded. "Okay."

Chapter 90~ Stalker

Sylvia and Brooke were sitting in the waiting room when Claudia came in. "Wow, it is COLD out there!" she said, taking off her coat.

Brooke and Sylvia got up. "No, please sit for a minute." Claudia smiled.

"Is he alright?" Sylvia asked.

"He's doing just fine. He's sitting in the car with Sally. She was telling him about a surprise someone sent to Richard Graham," she said, sitting down.

"What kind of surprise?" Sylvia asked.

Claudia smiled, looking at Brooke.

"One that he had coming, I'm sure," Brooke said.

"You are one inspiring lady." Claudia laughed.

"I guess we should get going and maybe Brooke can let me in on this little surprise?" Sylvia said.

"Why don't you give Kendall and Sally a few minutes and we can have a little chat while you wait," Claudia suggested.

"Alright." Sylvia smiled.

"Now, I read the file and Sally filled me in on a lot of what's happened, but I'd like to hear from someone who's actually been there since this started."

"What do you want to know?" Sylvia asked.

"Well, Sally says that he doesn't eat much, doesn't talk to anyone outside his family unit, and has been having some pretty bad nightmares, which include sleepwalking?"

Sylvia and Brooke both nodded.

"Where's his mama today?"

"She had to go back to work this week, so the kids are staying with us while she's there," Sylvia told her.

"How's she doing?"

Sylvia and Brooke looked at each other. "It's a little hard to tell. She has a habit of keeping things locked up, but she's broken down a few times," Brooke said.

Claudia nodded. "Is she seeing someone to help her with this?"

"Not since Graham," Sylvia said.

"I'm going to give you the names of a couple of therapists who specialize in helping families deal with trauma. I would recommend she see one as soon as possible. They're usually pretty busy this time of year, but I can make a call and get her in sooner than later."

"That would be great," Sylvia said.

"Couldn't she just come and see you?" Brooke asked.

Claudia shook her head. "When it comes to cases like this, I prefer not to treat the child and the parent, unless it's for a family session."

"Why not?" Sylvia asked.

"Well, it tends to make the child less trusting, thinking maybe the therapist has discussed what happened during one of the sessions with the parent. Now, while I would never violate a patient's trust, it doesn't stop suspicions from coming up. I have also had the parent come in for a session and try to find out what was said during their child's appointment. It just

makes more sense to me to make sure the child feels completely at ease, and that's one of the things that helps."

"I understand," Sylvia said.

"I would like to meet with her though and talk a little about what's been happening. That way I have the parent's perspective on this."

"We'll have her give you a call," Brooke said.

"Can I ask... did he speak to you at all?" Sylvia asked.

Claudia smiled. "No, he didn't speak to me, but he did look at me a couple of times and even smiled a little. While I know that may not seem like much, it really is. By the time I was getting ready to leave, he had relaxed enough that he had stopped curling up trying to hide. He also spoke to Sally once while I was there."

"So, is there anything we should be doing?" Brooke asked.

"Just be there and let him know he's safe and loved. This is going take some time for him, for all of you, to get through. Just be patient with him and each other."

"What about going back to school?" Sylvia asked.

"Well, it doesn't look like he's physically ready to go back yet, and until he starts speaking to other people, it doesn't make much sense to send him."

"No, and Dr. Sharpe said that if he doesn't start eating more and put on some weight, she's going to want him admitted into the hospital. We have to take him back on Friday for another weigh-in," Sylvia said.

"I would definitely work on that first then. I don't think he'll emotionally handle another hospital stay very well at all. Is he eating anything?"

Sylvia nodded. "More so in the last couple of days. We were all thrilled when he came down last night and asked if he could have dinner with Logan. Logan sprained his ankle at hockey practice yesterday and was on bed rest. He does try when we ask him, but it seems like if he eats a lot he feels sick to his stomach."

"Probably from not eating for so long. Hmmm... See if you can find some real peppermint or ginger candies, both are good for nausea. He can just eat them throughout the day, but especially before a meal. When I was little, my granny would boil peppermint candy when we were sick, and we would drink the water. I know it sounds disgusting, but it really works. It also makes one less medication you have to throw at someone who is already suspicious of doctors. There's a little mom and pop store on Edgewood that carries them," Claudia told her.

Sylvia nodded. "Okay, we'll try that. I can't tell you how glad I am that we found you," she said while standing up.

Claudia smiled. "So am I and I look forward to meeting all of you at one point or another."

Brooke offered her hand and smiled. "I'm glad we found you, too."

Claudia took her hand and laughed. "I can't tell you how relieved I am to hear that."

Claudia walked the two women to the door. "Remember to have his mom call me. I can chat with her on the phone or anywhere she would like to meet."

"We will," Sylvia said as they left.

∞

Sally was still sitting with Kendall when she saw Sylvia and Brooke come out. He hadn't said too much more since Claudia had left and seemed like he was getting tired.

"Hey, I think you guys are getting ready to go," she said, pointing out the window. "Is it okay if I come and see you tomorrow? This time I'll bring my laptop so I can show you my photos."

Kendall nodded. "Okay. I think we'll be at my house though."

"Are you worried about being away from Antonio?"

Kendall shrugged, but she saw his eyes tear up a little. "Not just him," he said quietly.

"I know you feel safe at the Garcia's and having everyone around. They're still there for you though."

"I know."

Sally hugged him. "Too many changes in too short a time?"

He nodded.

"I know the feeling, honey, but I promise things will settle down."

He sighed. "When?"

"I wish I had a date that I could tell you, but all I can say is it WILL happen."

Sylvia and Brooke got to the car, so Sally hugged Kendall again. "I'll see you later, okay kiddo?"

He gave her a small smile. "Okay."

She got out. "Bye honey," she said as she closed the door.

"Things okay?" Sylvia asked.

Sally nodded. "I'll probably see you tomorrow. I'm going to come by to check on him."

"Okay, thanks for everything, Sally," Sylvia said, hugging her.

"No thanks necessary. I'll see you later. Goodbye Brooke," Sally said as she headed for her car.

"Goodbye Sally," Brooke said as she got into the car.

"We need to stop at the store so I can pick something up, and then we'll get some lunch," Sylvia told Kendall.

He nodded and leaned his head against the window. He saw Claudia Jenkins in the window and she waved goodbye, so he gave her a small wave as they pulled away. Claudia smiled to herself when she saw Kendall wave back at her.

∞

Sylvia found the little store that Claudia had told them about and ran inside. She found the little candies Claudia had recommended and bought all they had.

She got back to the car. "What do you stay we stop someplace for lunch?" she asked Kendall.

"I really don't want to go in anywhere."

"Drive-thru?"

"Sure," he said.

She found a nice little burger place she knew the boys liked and ordered lunch. By the time they got home, Kendall was asleep, his head still leaning against the window.

Brooke reached back and gently shook his leg. "Kendall, we're home." When he didn't wake up, she shook him a little harder. "Honey, it's time to wake up."

Kendall woke with a start and pulled away. After a moment, he realized where he was and relaxed.

"Are you alright? I didn't mean to scare you," Brooke said.

He nodded and sat up. "Sorry."

"Let's get inside and eat before it gets cold." Sylvia smiled.

Kendall nodded and got out.

Once inside, they sat down in the kitchen for lunch. Kendall ate most of his burger but left the fries. Sylvia had taken his shake and added some of the weight supplement to it. She pulled out the bag with the peppermints and ginger candy.

"Honey, are you still feeling a little sick when you eat?"

He nodded. "Usually."

"Claudia recommended these. She said they should help with any nausea. She said to just eat them during the day and make sure you have one before a meal."

"Candy?" he asked, looking in the bag.

Sylvia nodded. "They're made from real peppermint and real ginger. The lady at the store said they might be a little strong, but they actually taste good once you're use to them."

He looked at her dubiously. Usually when people say, "It's good once you get used to it," it means that it tastes awful.

He raised an eyebrow. "You first."

"It's just candy. You like candy canes, so you should like the peppermint ones. You like Chinese food so the ginger ones should be... okay," Sylvia said.

He looked at her and handed her the bag. "You first," he said again.

"Fine." She smiled and grabbed one of the hard candies from the bag and popped it in her mouth. "See, it's not that bad." She smiled.

He watched as her eyes started watering. "Oh my God!" she said and grabbed a glass of water. "Okay, maybe not the ginger ones, but the peppermint should be fine," she said, taking another sip of water.

He shook his head. "I don't think so."

Brooke reached into the bag and took a peppermint one.

Kendall and Sylvia watched her. "They aren't too bad, kind of like a stronger version of an Altoid."

Kendall looked in the bag and found a peppermint one. He sighed and tentatively put it in his mouth. It was strong but not unbearable. It sent a shiver down his spine though.

After a moment, he found the taste wasn't as bad. "These are okay after a minute."

"Okay, at least the peppermint will work," Sylvia said, getting another glass of water.

Kendall laughed a little at her expression.

"Oh, I'm glad you think it's funny!"

"Want a peppermint?" he asked.

"NO! Thank you," she said, holding up her hand.

"Why don't you take the rest of your shake and go put in a movie?" Sylvia suggested.

He smiled at her, grabbed his glass, and headed into the living room.

Brooke was smirking at Sylvia.

"What?" she asked.

"You really should have seen the expression on your face."

'Why don't you try one of the ginger ones?" Sylvia asked sweetly.

"I think I'll pass." Brooke laughed.

"I thought as much."

∞

Richard Graham was waiting for his guests to arrive and noticed someone sitting on a bench in the park across the street from his house. He looked a little closer and inhaled sharply when he realized who it was.

He got on the phone to the police department. "This is Dr. Richard Graham, I have a stalker! I want him arrested immediately!"

"Can you please hold, sir?" Johnson asked and hit the hold button.

"WHAT?" Graham screamed at no one.

"Sally..." Johnson smiled.

"Yeah?"

"Graham is on the phone, something about a stalker?"

"Aww, poor guy." She smirked as she picked up the phone. "Officer O'Hara."

"There is a man sitting on the bench across the street watching my house!" Graham screamed.

"Isn't your house across the street from the park?"

"Yes, so?"

"You do realize that people sit on park benches ALL the time?"

"It is that very large man that was in my cell," Graham hissed.

"Do you mean Mr. Duncan?"

"HOW would I know what his name is?"

"Mr. Duncan lives near the park and is perfectly within his rights to sit anywhere in a public park that he chooses. Sitting on a park bench is NOT illegal."

"He is STARING at my house!"

"That also is not illegal. Did you tell him where you live?"

"WHY WOULD I DO THAT?"

"Are you listed in the local directory?"

"NO!"

"Then I would suggest to you that he is just sitting in the park near his home, enjoying this beautiful day," Sally said.

"What beautiful day? It's overcast with snow expected and it's only twenty degrees outside!" Graham shrieked.

"But Mr. Graham, some people like winter," Sally said innocently.

"That's DOCTOR! Are you going to do something about this or not?" he yelled.

"I'd have to say no. We just don't have the manpower to send out a patrol because someone is sitting in the park. Tell you what though, if you get really nervous, just walk outside and go beyond your monitor's perimeter... and we'll come running."

She pulled the phone away from her ear as Graham screamed a string of expletives into the phone.

She hung up the phone. "That man simply has NO phone manners."

Chapter 91 ~ Graham's Lies

Jen got back from work at about 2:30, carrying food boxes from the steakhouse.

"What is this?" Sylvia asked.

"I thought I would provide dinner tonight." Jen smiled.

"You didn't have to do that." Sylvia smiled, helping her carry the boxes to the kitchen.

"Please, it's the least I could do. This way everyone can have a nice relaxing evening before we head home."

"Are you sure you don't want to stay longer?"

"I actually would, but we need to get home and try to get things back to near as normal as we can," Jen said. "Is Kendall upstairs?"

Sylvia nodded. "Brooke is helping him finish up some homework."

"How were his appointments?"

Sylvia sighed. "Anna said he's lost over a pound since last time and wants to weigh him again on Friday. If he isn't putting on weight, she said she'll want to admit him into the hospital."

"Damn it."

"He ate really well yesterday and he ate a good lunch today with a shake. I added some of the weight supplement to it and he drank it all. Claudia thinks part of the problem might be because he feels nauseated whenever he eats, so she recommended these," Sylvia said, and she handed her the bag.

"Candy? She recommended candy?" Jen said, shaking her head skeptically.

Sylvia nodded. "They're made from real peppermint and ginger and are supposed to help with nausea. She said just to have him eat them throughout the day, especially near mealtime. Hopefully we can avoid adding another medication."

"Did he try them?"

"We all did. The peppermint seems to be the most tolerable."

"How was he with Dr. Jenkins?"

"We got there and were walking up to the house when he panicked. Sally got there just in time and took him back to the car, and then she went in to speak with Claudia. They came out and sat in the car with him for a little while. She said it was a good first visit," Sylvia told her.

"How can it be a good visit if he wouldn't even go inside?" Jen asked frustration in her tone.

"She said it's normal for someone who's been through a trauma to panic once they're outside their comfort zone. She said that by the end of the visit, he was relaxing and even smiled at her. She wants to speak with you to get your perspective on what's been happening. She also gave me the names of a couple of therapists for you. She said they might be booked, but she can make a call and possibly get you in sooner."

Jen nodded and took the slip of paper. "I'll call them in a little while."

"It's going to be okay, honey. He did really well today."

"I'm going to go up and see him," Jen said, heading upstairs.

She saw Kendall and Brooke sitting at the desk. "Hey there, how's it going?" she asked, going in and kissing him on the head.

"Okay, almost done with the rest of my literature homework."

"Good job! Hey, I had the chef make roast chicken for dinner tonight. How does that sound?"

"Good."

"I'm going to make you a smoothie, okay?"

"I'm really not hungry, I ate lunch."

"I know you did, honey, but you need more calories."

"Mom..."

"Kendall, please don't be difficult again. We have to get some weight back on you by Friday. You can just sip it while you do your homework, alright?"

Kendall sighed. "Okay."

"Thank you," she said, kissing him again. She headed downstairs to mix it up.

"She's right, you know. We need to get some weight on you. I know you don't want to end up in the hospital with a feeding tube," Brooke said.

"No, it's just hard to eat when I'm not hungry though."

"I know it is, but just eat as much as you can. Hopefully the peppermint will help settle your stomach enough that you can eat a whole meal."

"Maybe. I guess I should try it."

"Yes, you should. Why don't I go grab them for you? At the very least it's an extra ten calories here and there." She smiled.

"Okay."

∞

Brooke went downstairs and got the bag. "He is trying, you know," she told Jen. She was a little irritated with the way Jen had spoken to Kendall and was worried she was starting to panic again.

"I know. I just don't want to see him back in the hospital." Jen sighed.

"I know you don't, none of us want that. I'm going to take these upstairs and we're going to see if it helps with his stomach."

Jen smiled. "Thanks Brooke."

"You know I'd do anything for you." She smiled.

"And then some." Sylvia smirked.

"What does that mean?" Jen asked curiously.

"I'll tell you later," Sylvia said.

Brooke just smiled and went back upstairs.

A few minutes later, Jen took the smoothie upstairs. "Here you go, honey. I'm going to go pick up Katie from school. Do you need anything while I'm out?"

"No, I don't think so. Thanks."

"Drink this, okay?" she said, handing him the glass.

He nodded and set it on the desk.

"Kendall..."

"I'll drink it in a few minutes."

Jen put her hands on her hips and raised an eyebrow. "Kendall, I'm serious!"

"Mom, I'm eating a peppermint right now," he said, sticking his tongue out to show her the white candy. "It's really strong and I don't think it will mix very well with berry and banana."

She laughed at his expression. He was speaking with a very pronounced lisp because his tongue was out, and then he crossed his eyes at her.

"Okay, I'll see you in a few minutes then." She kissed him on the cheek and left to get Katie, still laughing as she walked downstairs.

∞

Mike Duncan was sitting in the park across from Graham's house. He knew Antonio was worried about the man trying something once he was out on bail. Since they were down a few officers from the flu, and with the extra patrols that were always scheduled for this time of

year, he told his friend he didn't mind just keeping an eye out for any funny business. He lived just on the other side of the park, so it wasn't hard for him to take a few daily walks and check things out.

He'd helped the police out a few times before, keeping an eye on someone who was suspected of auto parts theft, walking a perimeter around the schools when a strange adult had been reported watching the schoolyard.

Sally had dubbed him their "mobile neighbourhood watch" and he liked knowing he could make a difference. He might not be able to arrest anyone, but he could report back and had even testified in court a couple of times with good results. Sally told him he should try for a private investigator's license. He had thought about it, but he liked working with cars too much to give it up.

He had seen the blinds move and figured Graham knew he was there, which was fine. He wasn't doing anything illegal.

After about half an hour, he decided to head home. It was starting to get windy out and the temperature was dropping. He would take another walk in a few hours and then again around eleven or so.

He was just getting up when he saw a van pull up in front of Graham's house and two people, a man and a woman, got out and walked up to the door.

He walked a little closer and read the words on the van.

He pulled out his cell phone and punched in a number. "Sally, two people from Minneapolis News just went into Graham's house."

∞

Katie and Jen got home a little while later and Katie ran up to see her brother.

"Hey Big Brother, what are you working on?"

"Just finishing up this part of my homework," he said with a yawn.

"Good, you can watch cartoons with me then!"

"Katie, I'm kinda tired."

"Please? You never do anything with me anymore," she said, pushing out her bottom lip.

He sighed. "Fine, but I get to pick the show. I am NOT watching the Power Puff Girls."

"HEY! Blossom is cool!" Katie told him.

"They're creepy! They have weird shaped heads with huge eyes, no noses, and stubby little arms," he said, getting up.

"Right and talking turtles who live in a SEWER aren't creepy at all," she retorted.

"First of all, they live in a STORM sewer, not a sewer sewer. Second, turtles are cool."

The argument continued as they walked downstairs together, Brooke shaking her head at them the whole way. Katie and Kendall settled in on the couch, and after having come to a compromise, turned on the Looney Tunes.

Brooke went into the kitchen and sat down with Sylvia and Jen.

"What's so funny?" Sylvia asked.

"Those two, arguing about cartoons." She smiled.

Jen sighed contentedly. "A nice, normal argument."

"It is nice," Sylvia agreed.

"So, the boys decided that James will stay with you through Thanksgiving, and then Carlos will take over through the weekend," Brooke told Jen.

"Poor Logan feels like he's letting everyone down," Sylvia said.

"Aw, he's such a swe... good boy, they all are. Maybe he can stay over on the weekend. Kendall will be getting next week's lessons and still needs help," Jen said.

"That might make him feel better." Sylvia sighed.

"What's wrong?" Brooke asked.

"It's silly."

"I doubt that," Jen told her.

"You know, when I was growing up we had a house full of family. Siblings, grandparents, cousins, you name it, and it's been nice having a lot of family around again. I know the circumstances are horrible and things have been completely chaotic, but I'm going to miss having everyone here. I don't know, I guess I just feel like if everyone is HERE, I know they're safe. God, that sounds selfish."

"No it doesn't," Jen said, hugging her. "The truth is I wish we could stay because I do feel safe here, and I know the kids do too. We're going to miss it, and it's going to be hard getting use to our own home again, but it's something we have to do. I do take comfort in knowing you're only a phone call away."

Brooke sniffled.

"What's wrong, honey?" Sylvia asked.

"No one is hugging me," she said, putting out her lower lip.

Sylvia and Jen laughed and pulled her into a big bear hug.

∞

Richard Graham was dressed very nicely in a dark blue, three-piece suit. He was wearing his black framed glasses and his hair was neatly combed, a far cry from his appearance yesterday. He listened carefully as Chelsea Waters explained how an interview is conducted. He smiled sweetly at her and nodded.

∞

Sally got off the phone with Mike Duncan and called Ryan. "There's a news crew at Graham's house right now."

"The man cannot be that stupid," Ryan said.

"He may not be that stupid, but he is that arrogant," Sally told him.

"Well, there's nothing we can do unless he discloses information about the case. Which news station?"

"KMAN."

"Alright, I'll be sure to watch the news tonight and tomorrow. If he mentions Kendall, or the case, he'll be in contempt of court and we'll bring him in. We can't do anything until then."

"I know, I just have a bad feeling about this," Sally told him.

∞

The boys walked to practice, and Logan was rethinking his decision to go. While the rink wasn't far from the school, it was difficult walking on crutches in the snow. Carlos and James walked on either side of him to make sure he didn't fall.

"Maybe this wasn't such a good idea."

"It'll be fine," James said.

"We're falling behind everyone and you're going to be late. I can call my mom and have her pick me up here," Logan suggested.

"No way are we leaving you alone out here," Carlos said.

"Carlos, take my gear," James said, handing him his bag.

"What are you doing?" Logan asked.

"Just give Carlos your crutches, you can ride piggyback," James said, taking the crutches from Logan.

"Are you crazy? What if you fall?" Logan protested.

"I'm not going to fall. We're almost there, and we need to catch up with the others. Now up," he said, patting his back.

James squatted down a little and Logan pulled himself up onto his back. They actually made good time, although Logan felt like a 4-year-old.

They got to the rink, and once inside, Carlos handed Logan his crutches. Logan went to find the coach while Carlos and James got their gear on for practice. Logan helped the coach with the strategy board while the team ran drills.

∞

Kendall fell asleep after watching cartoons with Katie for nearly two hours. Katie pulled the blanket down and covered him and channel surfed for a few minutes. Not finding anything good on, she went to her room to play her video game.

The moms started setting the table for dinner, when Jen heard a voice she knew on the television.

She walked into the living room, and there on the screen, was the smiling face of Richard Graham. "What the hell?"

"What's the matter, Jen?" Sylvia asked as she and Brooke rushed into the room.

Jen pointed at the television. Sylvia grabbed the remote, hit record, and then went to get the phone.

∞

"So Dr. Graham, in your twenty-six years of practice, have you ever had an issue like the one you are dealing with now?" Chelsea Waters asked.

"Well, you have to understand that in my line of work, you are always putting yourself on the line. As a practicing psychologist, I always run the risk that someone won't be happy with the results. What people fail to understand is that psychology is an inexact science, and you simply cannot cure everyone, at least not quickly. It can take months, even years to get any measurable results. Even then, some people will require continuing therapy, medication, and sometimes a stay in a facility with a more intense treatment plan."

"So you've had cases where people were unhappy because results were not instantaneous?"

"A few—usually parents of troubled teens that they simply cannot manage. As children get older, they tend to push boundaries more and more. If the parent does not establish early on exactly WHO is in charge, then problems arise."

"Have you had the problem of a parent caving to the demands of the child and destroying any progress they may have made?"

"Sadly, yes. I actually lost a young man when his parents failed to make certain that he was receiving his medication properly."

"How sensitive are the medications used in treating illnesses such as depression, anxiety, and other psychosis?"

"Very. Most take weeks to take effect and we usually start with a higher or, loading dose, and then cut back the dosage. They should never be stopped cold turkey."

"What happens if they do stop suddenly?"

"Depending on the medication, it can cause worsening depression, nausea, anorexia, heart arrhythmia, and can increase suicidal tendencies."

"You've been accused of medicating a child against his will and actually charged with assault and battery against this child. What can you tell me about that?"

"Well, a boy was brought in by his mother after he suffered a traumatic event. He was suffering from nightmares, delusions, and anxiety attacks. He was a danger to himself and to others, and his mother simply could not handle him. Before the event, he had a history of being willful, and he resents authority figures. I had seen him and prescribed an anti-anxiety medication for him, hoping it would help with some of his symptoms. At our first meeting, he was rude, disrespectful, and actually walked out of our appointment. His mother came to me the next day not knowing what to do. I told her I would speak to him about at least taking the medication until she could find a psychologist that he liked. I did as she asked and he had a panic attack in the office. He was having difficulty breathing, was non-responsive, so I had to make a snap decision, opted to put myself on the line, and ordered an injection of the same anti-anxiety medication that I had prescribed. It worked, and a few moments later, calmed down considerably and was breathing regularly."

"Did you believe that his life was at risk?"

"Not being able to breathe seems to be fairly life threatening to me."

"So, you basically saved this child's life and are now being charged for doing so. If you had to do it all over again, would you?"

"Absolutely. One child's life is far more precious than my career."

"And your freedom."

"Yes."

"This traumatic event included the child being taken by an accused pedophile after asking for assistance from this person. Is that correct?"

"Yes, although we never got into the actual treatment for this. I had thoroughly read the file and hoped I could help this young man."

"Do you think you could have helped him?"

"I certainly would have tried my best. Again, you have to understand that while I never actually had the opportunity to treat him, I had a few ideas which could have helped."

"Such as?"

"Well, there are several reasons as to why this man may have chosen this boy. Unfortunately, since he was killed, we have no way of really knowing. There was no indication that this man who took him was even interested in him until he asked for assistance."

"So you think this man saw it as a favour, so to speak, and thought he could call in that favour?"

"Possibly, or it could be that this was going on a little longer than originally thought and things just got out of hand."

"Meaning?"

Graham smiled sadly. "There is always the possibility that the boy knew what was going on from the start and was trying to use it to his advantage and things got out of hand. Boys without fathers have a tendency to act out more without the proper guidance."

"So you think he might have been using this man's predilection for children for his own personal gain?"

"There was the rumour that he was trying to acquire a better grade for himself and a friend. While I certainly hope that wasn't the case..."

∞

Brooke turned off the television and looked at Jen. Jen had sat down on the recliner and appeared to be in shock.

"Honey, it's okay. That son of a bitch just made a very big mistake," Brooke said, sitting down next to her and wrapping her arms around her.

She could hear Sylvia in the kitchen and knew she was speaking to Antonio.

Sylvia came running out of the kitchen. "Antonio's on his way to pick up the boys from practice and will be home in about twenty minutes. DA Ryan is trying to get ahold of Judge Warner to revoke Graham's bail, and as soon as he does, Sally and John will arrest Graham. It's going to be alright, Jen. He's not going to get away with this. Antonio said it's a clear violation of his bail."

All of the colour had drained from Jen's face, and she had tears streaming down her cheeks. Brooke pulled her closer and Jen wept into her shoulder.

Sylvia was rubbing Jen's back when she looked up. She inhaled sharply as she realized that Kendall was sitting on the couch, staring at them.

Chapter 92~ Two Down

Antonio was at the station just getting ready to head out for the ice rink, when Sylvia called.

"Honey, calm down... He WHAT?" he said, turning on the television in his office. A moment later, he found the television station. "Okay, I've got it on now... SALLY!"

Sally and Bennet came running in. "What's wrong?" she asked.

Antonio pointed at the television. "Honey, I'm going to pick up the boys and we'll be home soon."

Sally and John looked at the screen. "Son of a bitch. How the hell did they get this on the air that fast?" John asked.

"It's running live," Sally said as she got on the phone to Ryan.

A moment later, she hung up. "Boss, Ryan is going to find Judge Warner and have a warrant issued for contempt of court. As soon as we have it, John and I will go pick up Graham. Until then, I suggest we go and do a spot check on his monitoring device."

Bennet nodded. "Good plan."

"Make sure EVERYTHING is by the book. I don't want him getting off on a technicality," Antonio said, watching as Graham accused Kendall of asking for everything that had happened to him. "I need to pick up my boys and get home. Call me the minute you know anything."

"Will do," Sally said.

Sally and Bennet headed for Graham's house. "What is wrong with this guy? Does he think just because he didn't use Kendall's name that he'd get away with it?" John asked.

"I don't know, maybe. Or maybe he was trying to appear to be the persecuted hero," Sally said.

"How so?"

"Well, think about it. His story is he was trying to help a single mom, who couldn't control her teenager, who has had issues with authority. He asks the mom if he can speak to the kid about taking medication he says will help. When the kid conveniently has a panic attack, puts himself on the line and gives him an injection he knows can get him into trouble. Then he says that one child's life is worth more than his career or freedom. He's trying to win favour with the public."

"How is that going to help him?"

"Well, either it works and people on the jury take pity on him because of his so-called sacrifice, or he's trying to get a change of venue, claiming he wouldn't be able to get a fair trial because of the media exposure."

"How would changing venue help him? He still broke the law and Feds want him when we're through with him," Bennet said.

"I really don't know what he's thinking. Could be as simple as he knows he's going down, so he wants to take someone down with him."

Sally's phone rang. "O'Hara."

"Hey Sally, it's Claudia. I just saw Graham on the news and was wondering if you know how Kendall and his family are doing?"

"Hi Claudia. Sylvia called Antonio at the station and he's on his way home. Jen was near hysterics and I didn't hear anything about Kendall. With any luck, he was upstairs and didn't

see it. We're on our way to Graham's right now, just awaiting the judge's order to arrest him. I can give you a call once I know more."

"If it wouldn't be too much trouble, I just want to make sure Kendall's doing alright. I can clear up some time tomorrow if you think he needs help."

"I'll give you a call and let Antonio know when I speak to him. Thanks Claudia."

"No problem, sweetie. Let me know if they need anything. If Jen needs to get in someplace tomorrow, I'll call in a few favours and get her in too."

"I'll definitely let them know that. In fact, it might not be a bad idea to go ahead and arrange that. I know she was thinking about getting in to see someone, this way she doesn't have to wait."

"I'll make a couple of calls and let you know when and where once you get back to me."

"Thanks so much, Claudia, I can't tell you how much I appreciate this."

"You're welcome. I'll talk to you later."

"Bye Claudia."

"Bye Sally."

"Was that Claudia Jenkins?" Bennet asked.

"Yeah, she saw the news and wanted to see how Kendall and the family is doing. She's also going to call in a favour and get Jen in to see someone as soon as possible."

"She is one sweet lady," John said.

"Yes she is."

∞

Antonio drove to the ice rink with only one thing on his mind—get his boys and get home to make sure everyone was alright. Sally and John would handle Graham, so he was just going to concentrate on his family. He pulled up in front of the rink a few minutes later and took a deep breath before going inside.

The boys were just finishing up, and he found Logan sitting in the stands, checking notes on a clipboard.

"Hey Logan. How's your ankle doing?" he asked, taking a seat next to the teen.

"Hi Papa G. A little sore, but I can take some more ibuprofen once I get home. Is everything alright?" he asked, noticing that Antonio seemed a little off.

"Everything's going to be fine. I need to talk to you boys about something before we go home, though."

Logan felt panic rise in his chest. "Is Kendall okay? Did something happen with the new psychologist?"

"No, from what Sally told me, he did really well with her. It's about something else."

"Okay..."

"It's alright, Mijo, really," Antonio said, patting him on the back.

Logan nodded, trying to smile.

∞

John and Sally pulled up in front of Graham's house just as the news team was getting into the van. They got out and walked up to the door, and a smirking Graham opened the door.

His attitude swiftly changed when he saw the two officers standing there. "What?" he demanded.

"We're here to do a random spot check on your monitoring device," Bennet said, pushing his way inside.

"It's only been a day!" Graham yelled.

"And?" Sally asked.

"Lift your pant leg, please," Bennet said.

Graham lifted his right pant leg and Bennet checked to make sure it was secure.

Sally pulled out her phone and called the receiver line and the little red light blinked twice.

"Looks like it's working," Bennet said to her.

"Looks like."

Her phone rang. "O'Hara."

She looked at John and smiled. "Thanks Ryan, we'll bring him in now."

Bennet nodded and pulled out his cuffs. "Dr. Richard Graham, you're under arrest for contempt of court and violating the mandates of your bail."

"WHAT?"

Bennet turned him around, frisked him, and then snapped on the cuffs. He turned Graham around to face him.

"Sally..."

Sally stepped up next to him.

"You have the right to remain silent.

Anything you say or do can and will be held against you in a court of law.

You have the right to an attorney.

If you cannot afford an attorney, one will be provided for you.

Do you understand these rights I have just read to you?"

"This is outrageous!" Graham sputtered.

"Answer. The. Question," Bennet told him.

"Yes, I understand my rights!"

"Good, now let's go find you a nice cozy cell," Sally said. They walked out the door and escorted Graham to the patrol car.

The reporter jumped out of the van. "Why are you arresting Dr. Graham?" she asked, gesturing for her cameraman to follow her.

They ignored her and put Graham in the back and got in themselves. They pulled out and headed back to the station.

∞

Sylvia squeezed Brooke's arm and she looked up. Kendall was watching his mom and he got up and slowly walked into the kitchen. Sylvia and Brooke looked at each other, not sure what to do. Brooke stayed with Jen while Sylvia went after Kendall.

She found him pulling three mugs from the cupboard and saw he had already put the kettle on. "Kendall?"

He opened the drawer, pulled out three spoons, and set them on the counter near the mugs.

"Honey, what are you doing?"

"Making tea," he said quietly.

"Let me help you."

"I've got it, thanks."

"Let me get a tray then."

He nodded and she pulled a tray from the lower cupboard and set it on the counter. He took the mugs and set them on it. Sylvia handed him the box of assorted teas and he pulled out three bags and put them in the mugs. The kettle started whistling, so he turned off the burner and poured the water into the mugs.

Sylvia was very concerned by Kendall's demeanor. "Mijo, are you alright?"

He nodded.

"I spoke with Papi, and they're revoking Graham's bail and arresting him tonight."

"Okay."

"Kendall, look at me."

Kendall glanced up at her.

She put her hands on his shoulders. "Honey, I wish..." her eyes glistened with tears.

"Please don't cry. He doesn't matter."

"What?"

"He's just a bully. I knew that after I talked to him the first time. What bullies say doesn't matter, that's what Papi always says."

Sylvia looked into his eyes. "So, you're really alright?"

Kendall nodded.

"Oh, I was so scared!" she said, hugging him tightly.

"Mami... can't breathe."

"Sorry," she said, releasing him a little.

"We need to take care of my mom."

She smiled and kissed his cheek. "Okay baby, let's go take care of your mom."

Sylvia carried the tray out to the living room and Kendall grabbed the box of tissues from the counter.

∞

Sally called Antonio and let him know they had Graham in custody and were heading back to the station.

"Good job," he told her.

"Claudia Jenkins called me because she saw the interview and wanted to make sure everyone is alright. She's going to make a couple of calls so Jen can get in to see someone immediately, and she's clearing some time for Kendall tomorrow. Do you know how he is?"

"No, I need to call home before I talk to the boys."

"Okay, let me know if you need any help tonight. I can talk to the boys or take them out somewhere if they need to get out of the house for a while."

"I will, thanks Sally."

"Anytime."

Antonio hung up and called home. "Hi honey" Sylvia answered.

"Hey. How is everyone?"

"Jen's finally calmed down. She stopped crying a few minutes ago. Did they get Graham?"

"Yes, they picked him up a little while ago. How is Kendall? Does he know about the interview?"

"Yes, he was lying on the couch when it came on. He's doing surprisingly well, although he scared me for a minute."

"How so?"

"He didn't say anything and then went into the kitchen and started making tea. He told me that what Graham says doesn't matter because he's a bully... And that Papi always says that what bullies say doesn't matter."

Antonio smiled and sighed in relief. "I'm going to let the boys know what happened before I bring them home so they're prepared."

"Okay honey, we'll see you soon then."

∞

The boys were all quiet as Antonio told them about Graham's television interview.

"I know this is hard, but the positive side is that Graham will be locked up until his trial and we won't have to worry about him anymore," Antonio told them.

"How's Kendall?" James asked quietly.

"He's alright. He said it doesn't matter what Graham says."

"Really?" Logan asked.

"Really. Now, Mama K is another matter. She's having a really hard time with this, but Kendall's new therapist is going to get her in to see someone soon."

"Good," Logan said.

"Sally said that if you boys need to talk or just to get out for a while to give her a call."

"I think we're okay, right guys?" Carlos asked.

Logan and James nodded.

"Okay, then let's get home," Antonio said, helping Logan up.

∞

Sylvia went to warm up the dinner that Jen had brought home while Brooke finished setting the table.

Kendall sat with his mom in the living room. She had her head on his shoulder. She had stopped crying and was feeling better knowing that he was alright. Katie had come out of her room and Sylvia took her aside and told her what happened. She had cried a little and then gone in and hugged her mom and brother. Then she went to help Brooke and Sylvia.

Jen took a deep breath. "I'm going to go help with dinner," she said, kissing Kendall on the cheek and then hugging him tightly.

"It'll be okay, mom."

She smiled and just looked at him for a minute. "I love you so much."

"Mom..."

"What, I can't tell my son I love him?"

He rolled his eyes. "Yes."

"Good," she said as she went into the kitchen to help with dinner.

Kendall sat back and closed his eyes.

∞

Antonio and the boys got home a few minutes later. "Something smells yummy!" Carlos said.

"Shhh," James said, pointing at Kendall.

"I'm not asleep," he said, opening his eyes.

Carlos helped Logan off with his boots and then Logan hobbled over to the couch and sat next to Kendall.

"You doing okay?" Logan asked.

Kendall nodded as he pulled Logan's foot up onto the couch and placed a pillow under it. Logan winced. "I'll go get the ice," Kendall told him.

"You stay there, I'll get it and the ibuprofen," James said.

Kendall nodded and sat back down next to Logan. James came in a moment later with a bag of peas, the bottle of ibuprofen, and two glasses of water. He handed the peas to Kendall, who carefully wrapped it around the top of Logan's ankle. James poured out four ibuprofen and handed two to Logan and two to Kendall.

"Don't tell me you don't need it," he warned Kendall.

Kendall took the offered pills and water and swallowed them. "Thanks James."

James sat down and put his arm around him. "Are you really doing okay?"

Kendall nodded.

"Are you sure?"

"Yeah."

"At least he's locked up and can't hurt anyone now."

"I know." Kendall sighed.

"Dinner," Brooke said.

Kendall sighed again.

"You're eating, so deal with it." Logan smirked.

Kendall raised an eyebrow and then ran his finger down the center of Logan's foot.

"Don't do that! You know I have ticklish feet!" Logan shuddered. Kendall smirked and did it again. "Kendall!" Logan squealed.

"Come on, you two," James said, handing Logan his crutches.

"Thank you," Logan said, getting up.

"You WILL remember to wash your hands, right?" James asked Kendall.

"Hey!" Logan said.

"What? He touched your foot."

"You don't have to make it sound like I have the plague."

"The plague, really?"

"Alright you guys, go wash up for dinner." Antonio laughed.

After they had cleaned up for dinner, James steered Kendall to the seat between him and Antonio.

"I can sit on my own, you know," Kendall said.

"And?"

Kendall rolled his eyes at him.

"Here you go, honey," Jen said, putting a plate in front of him.

"Thanks mom."

After a couple of minutes, Kendall wasn't feeling too well. He looked at the plate and the smell seemed overpowering, so he pushed it away.

"No, you need to eat," James said, pushing it back.

Kendall shook his head. "I'll eat something else. I really don't want that."

"Honey you need to eat, it's one of your favourites," Jen said.

Kendall shook his head and tried to back up.

Antonio looked over and saw Kendall was pale and his breathing was becoming increasingly erratic. "Kendall, what's wrong?"

Kendall was shaking and desperately trying to back up when Antonio realized they had discovered another trigger. He quickly pushed the plate away from Kendall and pulled the chair back from the table. He pulled Kendall up from the chair and half carried him into the living room and sat with him on the couch. "It's alright, Kendall. Try and slow down your breathing."

James followed them. "What is it?" he asked, sitting on the other side of Kendall.

"Another trigger. Sit here with him."

Jen had come out behind James. "What happened?"

He put her arm around her and guided her back to the dining room. "I think it's another trigger. In Jaimeson, there's a diner that serves a chicken dinner much like this one. That's where they ate before Deesie took Kendall to the cabin."

Jen sat down. "This is never going to end."

"Jen..."

"NO! This is just going to keep going on and on!"

"Honey, calm down," Antonio said.

Jen was near hysterics, her fears, her guilt, her anger all rose to the surface, overwhelming her. "No, I'm not going to calm down! He won't eat and is going to end up in the hospital! He won't talk to most people! He can't sleep half the time without having a nightmare, and now he hides from us! He beat up a boy and doesn't remember half of what happened! I can't call my own son sweetheart or feed him what use to be one of his favourite dinners! Some freak goes on television and tells everyone that my son asked for what he got... after some other freak did God knows what to him, which he won't talk about either!"

Jen was crying and Antonio grabbed her by the shoulders. "JEN, STOP NOW!" he yelled, pulling her close. "You have to stop!"

"Mom! Shut up!" Katie screamed at her, covering her ears.

Carlos grabbed Katie and picked her up. He took her into the bedroom, Logan hobbling behind them.

Sylvia got up and went over to Antonio and Jen.

"Brooke, go get your car," Antonio said.

Brooke nodded and ran for her purse and coat.

"Mom," James said as she ran by.

"It's going be okay, James," she said.

"Jen, you need to calm down," Antonio said again.

Kendall had been breathing alright, so James had gotten up in case Antonio needed help.

"Why couldn't..." Jen sobbed.

"Why couldn't what, honey?" Antonio said softly.

"Why couldn't he have just finished the damn assignment? Then Deesie wouldn't have taken him, none of this would have happened, and everything would be alright!"

"Jen!" Antonio looked at her in complete shock.

She realized what she had said and covered her mouth with both hands, shaking her head. "No, no I didn't mean that! I didn't mean that!"

Antonio pulled her close. "We need to get you to the hospital, you need some help. James, can you grab her coat?"

James nodded and turned to go get her coat and stopped.

Kendall was standing behind him, watching his mom. His eyes were wide and filled with sorrow. He had heard the whole thing. "I'm sorry," he whispered and ran upstairs.

"Kendall... James go to him!" Antonio yelled.

James nodded and followed Kendall upstairs.

"What did I do?" Jen whispered.

"Honey, come on," Sylvia said, putting her coat around her shoulders.

Jen felt the world tilt and then go black.

Antonio caught her. "Stay here, make sure Kendall's alright," he told Sylvia.

∞

Kendall had gone into the guest room and locked the door. His mother's words resonated in his ears. She blamed him.

"This is all my fault."

"KENDALL!" James was pounding on the door. "Kendall, please open the door!" James said, nearing panic.

Sylvia came running up. "James?"

"He's locked himself inside. WHY did she say that?"

"Honey, she didn't know what she was saying."

"Kendall! Please..." James said, choking back a sob.

"Can you break it in?" Sylvia asked.

"I can try," James said as he started slamming into the door with his shoulder. After a few tries, the door gave and they went inside.

"No!" James yelled.

The window was open and Kendall was gone.

Chapter 93~ Missing

Antonio carried Jen to the car and got into the backseat with her.

"Is she alright?" Brooke asked.

"She fainted... We need to get her some help. She can't deal with this anymore."

Brooke nodded and pulled out and headed for the hospital.

He pulled out his cell and called home. It rang six times and then the machine picked up. "Sylvia, are you there?"

"Papi?" Carlos answered.

"Mijo, where's your mom?"

"Upstairs, she and James are trying to get into the bedroom."

"Why? Carlos, take the phone to Mami."

"Okay. Papi, is Mama K alright?"

"I don't know, Mijo. We should be at the hospital soon. She might be staying there for a few days."

"Like when Papa K died?"

"Yes Mijo, I'm afraid so."

"James, where are you going?" Carlos asked his friend as he ran past him on the stairs.

"What's going on, Carlos?"

"I don't know, here's Mami," Carlos said, handing the phone to Sylvia.

"Antonio, Kendall's gone!"

"What do you mean he's gone?"

"He locked himself in the guest room and James had to break down the door. When we got inside, we found the window open and his shoulder brace was on the bed. I think he climbed down the tree. James is trying to see if he can follow his footprints."

"Call the station and get Sally and John out looking for him. Ask the boys and Katie where he might go. Does he have a new key to his house yet?"

"I don't know. Antonio, we have to find him. He doesn't have his jacket or boots, only a hoodie with sneakers," Sylvia told him.

"Damn it! Alright, call Jo and see if she can stay with Katie and Logan, and then go check his house. He can't have gone too far yet."

"Okay. How's Jen?"

"Still out, we're almost to the hospital now. Make sure you have your cell so we can keep in touch. As soon as we get her admitted, I'll be there."

"Okay... Wait, James is coming back."

James came running up the stairs. "They've plowed the streets and I couldn't follow his footprints anymore. The sidewalks have all been shoveled. What are we going to do?"

Antonio could hear the panic in James' voice. "Tell him to take a deep breath, think about where Kendall might go, and then call Sally. Honey I have to go, we just got to the hospital."

"Okay, I'll call Sally now. Antonio, please hurry."

"I will. I'll see if Brooke can stay with Jen."

Brooke pulled up to the emergency doors and ran inside. She returned a moment later with nurses and a gurney. Antonio got out and lay Jen on it and the nurses took her inside.

"Brooke, can you handle this? Kendall ran away and we've got to find him."

"Of course. Call me when you hear anything, and I'll call you as soon as the doctor has checked her out," she said, handing him her car keys.

Antonio nodded. "Thanks honey," he said as he got into the driver's seat.

∞

Sylvia hung up. "James, do you have any idea where he might go?"

"Home, maybe. I'd say to one of our houses, but we're all here."

"Mami, what happened?" Carlos asked.

"We all need to talk," Sylvia said as she put an arm around each boy and ushered them downstairs. Logan and Katie were sitting on the couch. Katie had been crying and Logan was holding her.

"Okay, how much did everyone hear?" Sylvia asked.

"Everything," James said quietly. He knew it wasn't Jen's fault, but he was furious about what she had said and terrified that they wouldn't find Kendall.

The other three nodded. "We could hear her even though the door was closed," Logan said.

"Where's Kendall?" Katie asked.

James sat next to Logan and took Katie from him. "He got scared and climbed out the window. So we need to think about where he might go."

Katie's eyes filled with tears again. "Maybe he went home."

"We're going to check there first, Mija. Anyplace else?" Sylvia asked as she called Jo.

"Hello," Joanna answered.

"We need you here," Sylvia said.

"What happened?"

"I'll tell you when you get here. I need to call Sally."

"I'm on my way." Jo said as she ran out the door.

Carlos had a horrifying flashback to his nightmares. He jumped up, grabbed his jacket, and ran out the door.

"CARLOS! Where are you going?" Sylvia yelled.

James ran out the door after him. "I'll get him!"

Carlos ran as fast as he could to the park. Tears were burning his eyes and it was hard to take a breath. "Please, please don't let him be there," he chanted over and over.

"CARLOS!" James was yelling behind him. Even with his long legs, he couldn't catch up to his friend. He realized where Carlos was going and hoped Kendall was there, sitting under the oak tree. Then they would get him home, get him warm, and make him realize nothing that happened was his fault. Mama K didn't know what she was saying.

He got to the tree and found Carlos kneeling in the snow, crying.

"Carlos?" James said, softly kneeling next to him. "Everything's going to be okay, we're going to find him and bring him home."

Carlos grabbed onto James, sobbing. He was pointing to under the tree. James was confused. "Carlos, he's not here."

"H-He was," he said, pointing again.

James looked and could see sneaker prints going up to the tree. He looked closer, and right under the tree were dark spots in the snow. He grabbed his cell phone and opened it, the light from the screen illuminating the snow. His heart dropped as he realized the spots were red and appeared to be blood.

∞

"Sally, call on line two," Johnson said.

"Officer O'Hara."

"Sally, it's Sylvia."

Sally knew from Sylvia's voice that something was wrong. "What happened?"

"Jen had a breakdown and Antonio had to take her to the hospital. Before she fainted she said some things she shouldn't have, a-and Kendall's gone. He ran away and Antonio said to have you and John start looking for him."

"Oh God! What was he wearing?" Sally asked, jotting down some notes.

"Blue jeans, a long sleeved gray striped t-shirt, black sneakers, and a green hoodie. He doesn't have a jacket or boots."

"Any idea where he may have gone?" Sally asked.

"I'm going to head over to his house. Antonio's going to meet us after Jen is admitted."

The front door opened and Carlos and James came in. Carlos was still crying and James was pale and supporting Carlos.

"What happened?" Sylvia asked, looking at the two stricken boys. Carlos ran to her and she held him as he sobbed.

"Sylvia, what's going on?" Sally asked.

"Mijos?"

"The park, t-there's b-blood under the tree."

"Is Kendall there?" Sylvia asked.

He shook his head. "His footprints go up to the tree and away. T-There's blood under the tree."

"Sally..." Sylvia started.

"I heard. John and I are heading there now. Call me if you think of anyplace he might go or someone he might call."

"I will," Sylvia said, hanging up.

∞

Jo pulled up and ran into the house. "What happened?" Sylvia quickly told her what had happened as she put on her coat.

"I want to go," Katie said.

"I need you to stay here with Logan," Sylvia said gently.

"NO! I want to find my brother!" Katie yelled.

"Katie, please stay with me. I can't go either, but we can try and figure out where he might go and call Papi," Logan said. His brown eyes were full of tears.

She looked at him.

"Please... I don't want to be alone."

She nodded and sat back down with him, hugging him tightly around the waist.

Sylvia looked at Joanna and nodded. "Come on boys. Let's go find your brother."

∞

Sally and John got to the park. "Do you know what tree?" John asked.

"The big oak that overlooks the pond," she said, pointing to it.

They headed to the tree, carefully watching the snow for footprints. They got there and could see where the sneaker prints came up from the direction of the Garcia's house. "James said there's blood under the tree," Sally said, shining her flashlight on the ground.

"There," John said, pointing.

"It's not much. Maybe a nosebleed?" Sally said.

"Maybe. Which way is Kendall's house?" John asked.

"West of the park, so that way," Sally said, pointing.

"Footprints go that way," John said, pointing south. They followed them until they reached the shoveled sidewalk and they disappeared. "Fine time for park maintenance to start doing their job," John grumbled.

"You keep going this way, I'll cross the street," Sally said. He nodded and they slowly walked up the block looking for any sign of the missing boy.

Sally's phone rang. "Hey Boss. John and I are checking the streets around the park. It looks like he was at the oak tree and then headed south."

"Okay. If he's going south, he probably didn't go home. I'll have Sylvia and the boys look around just in case he doubled back. I'll meet up with you and John in about ten minutes."

"Okay, we'll see you soon. How's Jen?"

"I'm still waiting to hear from Brooke. She stayed at the hospital with her."

"Once things have calmed down a little, I'm going to call Claudia and see if she can get someone in to see Jen tomorrow."

"That's a good idea. She can't take much more. Graham and his damned interview pushed her over the edge."

"I know, but he can't hurt them anymore," Sally said.

"Sally, over here!" John called.

"Hold on, Boss, John found something."

She crossed the street. "What did you find?"

He pointed at two footprints that crossed a street median that hadn't been shoveled.

"Where is he going?" Sally asked. "Antonio, his footprints are going southeast now. Do you know anyplace he might go in that direction?"

"No, but maybe the boys do."

"I'll give Sylvia a call. I'll let her know you're on your way here too," she said.

"Okay, I should be at the park in a few minutes. I'll meet up with you then."

"Will do, Boss."

She hung up and called Sylvia. "Hello?"

"Sylvia, do you or the boys know where Kendall might go to the southeast side of the park?" Sally asked.

"I don't... Boys, does Kendall know anyone on the other side of the park?"

Both boys shook their heads.

"No, they don't. Is he heading to the downtown area?"

"Could be. He's heading away from the school and ice rink, so we can probably rule those two places out. I just got off the phone with Antonio. He said that since it doesn't look like Kendall went home, just to have you check it out, and he's going to head here," Sally said.

"Okay, we'll do that then. Sally, what about the blood?" Sylvia asked quietly.

"There was just a little, so it could have been from a nosebleed. There's no sign of blood as he was walking, so it is probably isn't very bad," Sally said reassuringly.

Sylvia sighed in relief. "Okay, I'll let the boys know. Thanks Sally."

"Tell the boys we'll find him."

"I will," Sylvia said.

∞

He couldn't escape his mother's words.. "Why couldn't he have just finished the damn assignment? Then Deesie wouldn't have taken him and everything would be alright!"

He choked back another sob. He pulled his hands up into his sleeves. He was so cold.

"What's the matter, afraid they'll all see the truth? That you ENJOYED your time with me? Just wait until I get my hands on you, sweetheart..."

He covered his ears and screamed, "Leave me alone!"

"Never, you are mine!"

Kendall turned and ran down the dark alley.

"You are going to be very sorry when I find you, you little shit!"

Chapter 94~ Can You Help Me?

Jen could hear voices around her and opened her eyes. She looked around and saw Brooke speaking to someone in a white coat. "What's going on? Where am I?"

"Jen, thank God. How are you feeling?" Brooke asked, taking Jen's hand.

"What happened?"

"You don't remember?"

Jen tried to think back and shook her head. "Everything is fuzzy."

"Mrs. Knight, you had a panic attack and fainted. I've run some bloodwork and you're suffering from dehydration and borderline exhaustion. Have you been sleeping well?" Dr. Davidson asked.

She looked at him. "I know you."

He smiled. "Yes, I was the one attending your son last week."

"My son." Her eyes filled with tears. "My son, my son...what did I do?" she sobbed. The monitors stared beeping as her blood pressure and heart rate increased.

Dr. Davidson looked at the nurse. "Valium please."

The nurse brought the bottle and Dr. Davidson pulled up 1cc of the drug and injected it into the IV port. A moment later, the monitors quieted as Jen's body relaxed.

"Oh God, Brooke, what did I do?" she asked, as she closed her eyes.

"It's going to be alright, honey," Brooke said, holding onto Jen's hand.

"We're going to need to keep her tonight, and I would recommend getting her in to see someone to help her deal with everything that's been going on," Davidson told Brooke.

She nodded. "I know she called a Dr. Thorne today. I'll find out when she's supposed to meet with him."

"Alright, we'll be taking her up to a room in a few minutes. We'll recheck her blood values again in the morning, but I'd recommend she stay at least through tomorrow. She needs fluids and rest right now, and she's going to need to watch herself so she doesn't end up back in here for a more serious condition."

Brooke nodded. "Thank you, doctor. I'll make sure that she takes it easy and has everything she needs once she goes home."

∞

Brooke called Antonio. "Garcia."

"It's Brooke. They're going to keep Jen tonight and recommend that she stay tomorrow. She's dehydrated and suffering from exhaustion. They had to sedate her when she woke up a few minutes ago."

"Damn it," Antonio said.

"What's going on with Kendall?" Brooke asked.

"He's run away and we're looking for him now," Antonio said.

"Any idea where he went?"

"Carlos and James found his footprints at the park, Sally and John are searching that area now. I'm on my way to meet up with them, while Sylvia and the boys check his house, although I don't think he went there."

"Why not?"

"John found a couple of footprints on the southeast side of the park, going away from home."

"How does he know they're Kendall's?"

"He's only wearing his sneakers and they match the ones at the tree."

"Why would he be going that way?" Brooke mused. "Wait... Antonio, isn't the cemetery on that side of town?"

"Yes... God I hope he isn't trying to walk that far in this weather!"

"Do you want me to help you search?" Brooke asked.

"Not right now, I think someone needs to be there for Jen. If she wakes up, don't tell her about Kendall running away. Hopefully we'll have him home soon."

"Alright, keep me updated and I'll do the same," Brooke said.

"I will, thanks Brooke."

Antonio saw Sally and John walking and pulled over.

"We haven't found anything else," John told him.

"Alright, keep looking here until you're sure there are no more signs. I'm going to head to the cemetery."

"Why would he go to the cemetery?" Sally asked.

"When he was ten, he was really missing his dad and walked all the way to the cemetery. I found him there, curled up on Will's grave."

"That's five miles outside of town," John said.

"I know, and it's getting colder," Antonio said as he walked back to his car.

Antonio called Sylvia. "Honey, anything there?"

"No, we checked all around the house and all through the inside. He hasn't been here. Antonio what are we going to do?" She was near tears.

"We'll find him. I'm going to check the road to the cemetery now. Sally and John are still searching around the park. Why don't you head over there and give them a hand?"

"Okay. Honey, why the cemetery?"

"Remember when he was little and went missing?"

"Antonio, that's a LONG way to walk with no jacket."

"I know. I'm heading that way now. Brooke called. The doctor said that Jen's suffering from dehydration and exhaustion. They're keeping her tonight and possibly tomorrow."

"Not again." Sylvia sighed.

"She'll be alright, Brooke's staying with her. How are the boys doing?"

"Not well... finding blood under the tree really scared them."

"Sally said it was just a little, though, so I don't think anything serious happened."

"I hope not. Maybe Jen's right, this is never going to end," Sylvia said, choking back a sob.

"Now don't YOU start with that! I'm serious, honey, I know we're all scared and tired, but we can't give up hope. The kids need us to be strong, and if we start thinking that way, then everyone will give up. Once we're all together and safe, then we can fall apart a little. Until then, we need to stay strong."

Sylvia took a deep breath and nodded. "You're right. We're going to head over to the park then. We'll see you soon."

"Alright love," Antonio said.

∞

Sally and John were still checking the sidewalks and street for any more footprints.

"John," Sally called. She pointed to half a footprint that led into an alley. They walked slowly into the entrance, John with his flashlight pointing down the alley, and Sally's on the ground.

"There!" she said, pointing at the footprints that went deeper into the alley. They followed them through to the other side, which opened onto another plowed street.

"Damn it," John cursed. "Exactly when did city maintenance start doing their jobs so efficiently?"

"I don't know. Okay, we have a fourteen-year-old with no jacket, no boots, suffering from pneumonia, and yet another emotional trauma. How far could he physically go?" Sally asked.

"I don't know. If it were anyone else I'd say not far, but Kendall..." John said, shaking his head.

∞

Antonio drove around the streets that led out of town towards the cemetery. Not seeing any sign of Kendall, he started down the rural road that led to the cemetery. It had been plowed recently, so he didn't bother looking for footprints. He just drove slowly, checking the road and keeping an eye on the fields. He got there and the gates were locked up tight, and there were no footprints in the snow around it. He walked the length of the fence, checking the perimeter just in case, and found nothing. He still wanted to have the grave checked, knowing if his godson were determined, he would find a way in.

He called the station and Officer Johnson answered. "Johnson, I need you to call the custodian at the Parkwood Memorial Cemetery and have him go check William Knight's grave for any sign of Kendall. I don't think he's in there, but I want to make sure."

"Will do, Boss. I'll call you back as soon as I hear."

"Thanks Johnson," Antonio said, hanging up. "Kendall, where are you?" he asked as he walked back to his car.

∞

He ran into the alley, having to stop and catch his breath halfway through. He coughed into his sleeve and the coppery taste of blood filled his mouth. His sneakers had very little traction and he had slipped as he had gotten to the tree in the park and reopened the wound on his lower lip. He wiped his mouth with his sleeve and continued walking.

He made his way out of the alley and tried to decide which way to turn. He finally got his bearings and started walking again. His mother's words haunted him, and he couldn't fight the overwhelming sense of hopelessness washing over him. He tucked his hands up under his armpits and tried to warm them—he could barely feel his fingers. It was getting colder and looked like snow.

He shivered and tried to fight the urge to curl up somewhere. To go to sleep and not have to worry about anything ever again. It would be so easy. No more fear, no more pain, no more hearing the disappointment in his mom's voice. No more hearing Deesie's voice or feeling him there when he wasn't. He felt a sob trying to escape his throat and choked it back.

He walked, lost in his own thoughts. "She's right. If I had just sucked it up and stayed up that night, I could have finished the assignment and never would have had to ask Deesie for more time. Mr. Crowley would be alive. John and the ranger wouldn't have been hurt. Everyone's lives would be normal, if I hadn't been so lazy. It's all my fault," he said.

After a while, it started snowing and he looked up. He realized where he was and stared at the house, wondering how he had ended up there. The lights were on and it looked so warm and inviting. After a few moments, he took a deep breath and crossed the street. He walked up the steps and stood at the door, trying to work up the courage to ring the bell. He finally pushed the doorbell and could hear it ring inside. After a moment, he heard footsteps coming to the door and then it opened.

"Baby, what are you doing out there in this weather?" Claudia Jenkins asked.

He looked at her and the tears began to fall. "C-Can you r-really h-help me?"

Chapter 95~ Breakthrough

Claudia had just finished up with her last appointment for the day and was getting ready to lock-up and start dinner, when the bell rang.

"Now who is that?" she asked herself and went to the door.

She was more than a little shocked to see Kendall standing there. He was shivering, and when he looked up at her, she could see the blood on his face. He wasn't wearing a jacket and looked to be frozen through.

"Baby, what are you doing out there in this weather?"

He looked at her and the tears began to fall. "C-Can you r-really h-help me?"

"You come inside right now," she said softly and took his hand. "Baby, you are so cold. How long have you been outside and where's your jacket?"

"I-I- d-don't k-know."

The shivering had turned into violent tremors and she risked putting her arm around him and escorted him into the living room where a large fire was roaring in the fireplace. "You sit here," she said, grabbing a blanket from the back of the couch and wrapping it around him.

She pulled off his wet sneakers and socks and set them next to the fireplace. She ran to the hall closet and grabbed a sweatshirt her brother had forgotten when he had visited the month before.

"Let's get that damp hoodie off of you, this is much warmer," she said as she unzipped the lightweight shirt and pulled it off him. She helped him get his arm into the oversized sweatshirt and then pulled the blanket back around him.

She went into the room across the hallway and turned the light back on. She grabbed a cup and poured some hot water from the water cooler into it. She put in a tea bag and went back into the living room.

"Hold this," she said, holding his frozen hands around the warm cup. She held his hands for a moment, trying to warm them. "What happened to your face, baby?"

"I-I f-fell."

"Okay, I'm going to get the first aid kit, you stay here."

He nodded and she went into the bathroom and grabbed the blue and white box. She sat next to him and cleaned the blood off his face. "Did you walk all the way here like this?"

He nodded.

"Are you feeling any warmer?"

He shook his head.

"Drink some of your tea, that'll help. I'll be right back."

He took a sip of the tea and she ran upstairs. She looked in her dresser drawer until she found some thick white sports socks.

She went back downstairs. "These should help," she said as she put the socks onto his feet. "Can you tell me what happened?"

His eyes teared up again. "M-my m-m-mom."

"What about your mama?"

"S-she... s-she..."

"Okay baby, let's just wait a few minutes until you've had a chance to warm up a little more. I take it your family doesn't know where you are?"

He shook his head and chocked back another sob.

"You know we need to call them, right? We don't want them going out of their minds with worry."

He nodded. "I-I j-just d-don't wanna go back r-right now."

"Why?" she asked softly.

"B-Because s-she was right, it is m-my fault."

"Who's right?"

"My m-mom."

"She told you that it was your fault?"

"S-She said s-she wished I h-had finished the d-damn assignment, because then D-Deesie wouldn't have taken me."

Claudia wrapped an arm around his shoulders and pulled him close. "Is that why you ran away?"

He nodded. "It's all m-my f-fault."

"Exactly what do you think is your fault?"

"I-If I'd finished the assignment on time, I wouldn't have had to ask for more time, and he w-would have left me alone. B-Because of me, everyone's lives are a-all m-messed up. Mr. Crowley is d-dead, John and Ranger T-Thompson got hurt, L-Logan got beat up, I h-hurt my sister and Sally. I let everyone down. I just w-wish..."

"What do you wish?"

"I j-just wish I h-had d-died there."

"What do you think that would have changed?"

"I c-couldn't hurt t-them anymore."

"You think your dying wouldn't hurt them?"

Kendall was quiet and stared into the fire. His expression had changed from sorrowful to introspective. "Only for a l-little while."

"I think you're underestimating how much you really mean to people. Do you think after having worked so hard to get you back and to keep you safe that ANY of them would be okay with you dying? Baby, they LOVE you and would do anything for you."

"They shouldn't," he said quietly.

"And why not?"

"Because I am damaged g-goods, nothing's right anymore."

"No... baby, no. Look, you might be hurt, tired, scared, and confused, but you are not damaged goods. Damaged goods are... a bag of chips that were crushed because the bagboy dropped a can of tomatoes on it. You're not bag of chips. You're just a kid who was in the wrong place at the wrong time."

Kendall shook his head. "No one would b-be hurt if I'd j-just stayed up and finished the assignment."

"Okay, let's say that you got that assignment done, turned it in, and Deesie breaks in and takes you. Whose fault is it then?"

"Why w-would he have done that?"

"Let's say because you have blond hair."

"Lots of p-people have b-blond hair."

"Alright, then because you have green eyes."

"That doesn't m-make sense," he told her, confused by the line of reasoning.

"Baby, that's just it. Deesie was psychotic and no one knows why he did what he did. From the first person he hurt, down to you, none of it had any rhyme or reason. He was an opportunistic abuser, and I have a feeling that even if you had turned in that assignment when it was due, he still would have obsessed about you."

"Why?" Kendall asked his voice breaking.

"I wish I could tell you, but with him dying, there's just no way to know for sure. Maybe you reminded him of someone he use to know. Maybe your voice, your smile. You DO smile, right?"

As hard as he tried not to, Kendall couldn't help but smile a little at the sudden question.

"I thought so. You should do that more often, it brings out your dimples more." She smiled.

He blushed a little and rolled his eyes.

"Baby the fact is, Deesie was probably a sociopath, and that means he didn't care who he hurt or why. It was all about him. They think he even killed his own brother, and people say he loved him."

Kendall remembered a conversation with Deesie. "He d-did kill his brother, he told me so. He said he loved him more than anyone, but n-needed his identity, so he killed him."

Claudia had a sudden realization. "His brother was older than he was, right?"

Kendall nodded.

"You're older than your sister?"

Kendall nodded again.

"You didn't get your assignment done because you stayed up taking care of her because she was sick?"

"Y-Yeah."

"Did you tell him that?"

Kendall nodded.

Claudia smiled. "Baby, I think I might know why he chose you."

"W-Why?"

"Well, from everything people said about the REAL Robert Deesie, he was a wonderful person. Stephen killed him and maybe he really did love him. Maybe he actually felt guilty for doing it. Robert was a great big brother and so are you, and not just to your sister. You and your friends look after the other kids in school and protect them from bullies. I think when you told him why your assignment would be late may have been what they call the 'stresser' and he started thinking about Robert. Then, when you got angry when he threatened Logan's grade, it kind of confirmed it for him."

"Confirmed what?"

Claudia looked at him. "Baby, when he looked at you, he was remembering his brother. As his mind deteriorated, he became more and more delusional. He realized what he'd done and then became increasingly violent and unstable, especially towards you."

"So it is because I asked for more t-time?"

Claudia shook her head. "No baby, I'm willing to bet he already knew all about you, and you asking for more time just gave him the opportunity he needed to try and make it happen. He probably would have tried something anyway. He was just waiting for the right moment."

"Are you s-sure?"

She hugged him. "I'm willing to bet my life on it. Now, I want you to lie down and try to get a little rest. I'm going to call Sally and let her know you're safe."

He nodded and curled up on the couch.

"Do you think you're ready to go home?"

He nodded again and then closed his eyes.

∞

Claudia dialed Sally's cell. "O'Hara."

"Sally, it's Claudia. Are you people missing someone?"

Sally stopped dead in her tracks. "Is Kendall there?"

"Sure is, he showed up about half an hour ago. He said he ran away because of something his mama said?"

"Yeah, Jen had a complete breakdown and Antonio had to take her to the hospital. She said some things she definitely shouldn't have, at least not in front of him. Is he alright?"

"He's doing much better. We talked for a while and he's resting now. Poor child was frozen clear through. He's lying on the couch next to the fire right now. He didn't want to go home at first, but I think we had a small breakthrough. I don't want anyone being mad at him for this, that's the last thing he needs."

"No one's mad, just terrified, and they're going to be so relieved to get him home. I'll call Antonio and have him pick him up."

"Okay, we'll be waiting," Claudia said. She went back into the living room and sat next to Kendall.

∞

Sally dialed Antonio's number and didn't wait for him to say anything. "Boss, Claudia Jenkins just called, Kendall's at her place," Sally said and gave him the address.

"Is he alright?"

"She said he's doing fine. They're waiting for you."

Antonio breathed a sigh of relief. "Alright, I'm on my way there."

He got to Claudia's house about ten minutes later and ran up the walk. He knocked on the door and she answered, smiling. "You must be Antonio, come on in."

He nodded and went inside.

"Is he alright?"

"I think he's going to be fine. I understand his mama said some things she didn't mean for him to hear, but I think we sorted through some of it."

"His mom's in the hospital right now, dehydration and exhaustion. It happened about a month after Kendall's dad died. If we're not careful, Kendall's going to end up there too," Antonio said.

"I think things are going to turn around a bit. Now, I don't want anyone coming down on him for this. He's extremely fragile right now, and I'd like to see him either tomorrow or Friday, if that's possible."

Antonio smiled. "Thank you so much for everything. He'll be here." Antonio went into the living room and sat next to Kendall. "Mijo, it's time to go home."

Kendall stirred a little and then opened his eyes.

Antonio looked at him and smiled, but there were tears in his eyes. "Mijo, I'm so sorry..."

Kendall looked at him and hugged him tightly around the waist. "P-Papi."

Antonio held him close. "Let's go home, Mijo."

Chapter 96~ Letting it Out

Antonio helped Kendall with his sneakers and was helping him off with the sweatshirt, when Claudia stopped him. "He's still cold and it's freezing out. Just bring it back next time."

"Thank you," Kendall said.

"It's just a sweatshirt, baby." She smiled.

"Not just for that."

"I know. You're welcome. Now I want a promise from you. If you ever feel like you need to get away from anything again, CALL me. I will come and pick you up wherever you are. I don't want you out walking like this again, understand?"

He nodded.

"Words, I'm not giving you any loopholes."

"I promise."

Antonio smiled at the two. "I need to call Mami and let her know you're alright and that we'll be home soon."

Kendall nodded and Antonio stepped into the hallway. Sylvia answered. "Do you have him? Is he alright?"

"Yes, we're just getting ready to leave now. How are the kids doing?"

"Much better now that they know he's safe. I made them some hot chocolate and they're warming up."

"Are they angry?"

"I don't think so. Why?"

"Claudia doesn't want anyone coming down on him for this. He wouldn't be able to handle it."

"I'll talk to them, but I think they're just scared. If they're angry at anyone, I think it's Jen."

Antonio sighed. "This isn't her fault either, but I know they're going to have a hard time processing this. Just tell them not to say anything about it unless Kendall brings it up. I'm not sure how long Jen is going to be in the hospital, but I AM sure he'll blame himself for this too. Maybe I'll tell him before we come home, that way Claudia's here if we need her."

"That's a good idea, and I'll talk to the kids," Sylvia told him.

"I don't suppose anyone's had a chance to eat?"

"No, not yet. I threw the chicken away since we left it out when everything happened. I'll find something."

"Why don't you call in an order to the steakhouse and we'll stop and pick it up on the way home?"

"That sounds good. I think we'll go with burgers though," she said.

"Good idea, maybe some soup for Kendall. He's still pretty cold and I think he'll be able to get that down."

"Okay honey, I'll call in an order now and we'll see you soon."

Antonio hung up and went back into the living room.

"Is everyone okay?" Kendall asked quietly.

He smiled and sat down. "Everyone's fine but hungry. So Mami's calling in an order and we're going to pick dinner up on the way home."

"I'm sorry."

"For what?"

"I ruined dinner."

"Child, you are bound and determined to blame yourself for something, aren't you?" Claudia asked, sitting on the other side of him.

"But, that was my fault. I freaked out and nobody got to eat."

"Alright, I'll give you that one, but that's the only one," Claudia told him.

"Which is not a problem, because everyone will eat as soon as we get home. There is something I do need to tell you before we get home though," Antonio said.

"What?"

Antonio took a deep breath. "We had to take your mom to the hospital, but she's doing fine now. Do you remember when she got sick after your dad died?"

Kendall nodded.

"It's pretty much the same thing. She's dehydrated and hasn't been getting enough rest, so she might have to stay a few days."

Kendall looked down and tried not to cry.

"Baby that might just be the best place for her right now. She'll be able to get all the rest she needs and they can keep an eye on her to make sure she does what she needs to do so she gets well," Claudia said.

"I know, that's not it," he said quietly.

"Then what it is?" Antonio asked.

"I-I'm..."

"Mijo, what is it?"

"I feel bad b-because..." Kendall stammered.

"Because why?"

"B-Because I'm glad she's not going to be there," he said, trying to choke down a sob.

He couldn't hold it in any longer and Kendall hid his face in his hands and cried. He couldn't believe he felt that way about his own mother, but he just couldn't take the sadness on her face or the disappointment in her voice anymore.

Antonio and Claudia looked at each other. "What do I do?" Antonio softly asked her.

Claudia smiled sadly at him and started rubbing Kendall's back. "Just let it all out, baby."

After a few minutes, he had calmed down. "Let me ask you something, when you were taking care of your sister that night, where was your mama?"

"W-What?"

"Where was your mama?"

"She had to w-work. Why?"

"Baby, don't you think it's possible she's blaming herself for this? I bet she's thinking that if she hadn't been at work then, you would have gotten your homework done, and you would have handed your assignment in on time. Where was she when Deesie broke into your house?"

"Work, but that's not her fault. She HAS to work."

"I know, but I know a lot of mamas, including mine, who have to work, and do you know what they say they hate the most about it?"

"No."

She took his face in her hands. "It's having to leave their babies. They want to be home with them more than anything, but sometimes there's just no choice. Baby, I bet your mama is really blaming herself for this whole thing, and maybe she just hasn't said anything. Or, maybe she hasn't even realized it yet, but it's starting to make its way to the surface."

"It's not her fault," he insisted.

"Of course not. It's not yours either, but you keep blaming yourself. The way I see it is the two of you are like peas in a pod. You both try to take care of everyone else and when

something goes wrong, you blame yourselves. What you both need to understand is there are just some things that you can't control, and not being able to control a situation doesn't mean that you're to blame for it."

"She's right, Mijo," Antonio said.

"Now, I know she said some things that hurt you, but I'm willing to bet that that wasn't the WAY she meant to say it. Sometimes when we're hurting and afraid, things just come out wrong."

"Maybe."

"Kendall, you know your mom would never hurt you on purpose. She was hysterical and afraid, she didn't know what she was saying. Claudia's right, your mom probably is blaming herself for this and she's been holding it all inside. It's what happened when your dad died and it's happening now," Antonio told him.

"Maybe the two of you do need a couple of days apart so she has a chance to come to terms with how she feels and to get some rest. You need rest too, and I want to see you eating. Unless you want to end up in the hospital with a feeding tube?" Claudia asked.

Kendall shook his head.

"I didn't think so. Tomorrow I want you to stay in bed and rest. I also want you to eat at least two full meals, or four small ones, if your stomach can't handle a lot of food at once. I also want you to let your family take care of you with NO complaints, understand?"

Kendall nodded.

"Okay baby, you two better get home and feed that family of yours. I have some free time tomorrow. Is it alright if I stop by just to say hello?"

Kendall nodded. "Yeah."

"I'd like to see you here on Friday, say 11 am?" Claudia said, looking at Antonio.

"We'll be here," Antonio told her.

"You'll come?" Kendall asked him.

"Of course I will." Antonio smiled.

∞

Sylvia went into the living room and sat down on the couch between Carlos and James. Logan was in the recliner with the footrest up and a pillow elevating his leg. Joanna was sitting at the other end of the couch holding Katie.

"That was Papi. He and Kendall will be home soon. They're going to stop and pick up dinner."

"How is he?" Jo asked.

"Antonio said he's doing much better. Claudia got him to talk after she got him warmed up."

"I can't believe he walked that far in this weather," Jo said.

"How far is it?" Katie asked.

"About three miles," Jo told her.

"That's not that far," Katie said.

"It is when you aren't dressed appropriately in this weather," Logan told her.

"At least he's safe and will be home soon. Antonio said that we shouldn't talk about what happened tonight until Kendall is ready. He's telling him about Mama K having to stay in the hospital before they come home, and we're not sure how he's going to take it."

"He should be glad. She won't be here to say mean things," Carlos said.

"Carlitos!" Sylvia said.

'It's TRUE! She said really BAD things, and he could have died climbing out the window and running away like that!" Carlos said angrily.

"Carlos, she's sick," James said quietly.

"But you heard her!" Carlos insisted.

"I also SAW her. She didn't know what she was saying, Carlos. I was really mad at first too, especially when I saw the window open, but that wasn't Mama K talking. She was like... a scared little girl," James told him.

"She was still being mean," Carlos said stubbornly.

Sylvia put an arm around each boy. "Yes she was, but she didn't mean to be. James is right. She's sick and needs our love and understanding, now more than ever. I understand you're upset, but I do not want you talking like this around Kendall. So go ahead and say whatever you need to now. No one is going to be angry with you. You're all allowed to feel how you feel."

"Logan, what about you? Do you need to get anything out?" Jo asked.

He shook his head. "I understand that she's not okay right now. I just want everyone well. Kendall running away, it just reminded me of when I hurt him and he ran away from me."

"From US. You weren't the only one accusing him that day," James reminded him.

"Us," Logan said.

"James?" Sylvia asked.

"Like I said, I was just scared when I saw the window open. It just seems like the harder we try to protect him, the worse things seem to get. I-I just didn't think we needed to protect him from one of us, much less his own mom. I wasn't ready for that."

"Carlos, anything else?"

He thought for a minute and sighed. "No, I just don't want any more bad dreams to come true."

"What dreams?" Logan asked.

"Before Kendall was taken, I dreamed we were trying to get away from somebody bad. A door closed between us and I couldn't get to him. Then I dreamed about the blood in the park. It's too scary to think about," he said.

"I remember the dream about the park, you saw blood on the ice," James said.

Carlos nodded.

"Katie, what about you, honey?" Jo asked.

Katie shrugged.

"Katie?" Joanna asked again.

"What do you want me to say? That I love my mom, but right now, I hate her? That she's hurt my brother twice now and BOTH times, he could have died? I mean, if I can figure out that it hasn't really been that long since he came home and he still doesn't feel well, why can't she? He's been trying really hard the last couple of days to eat and tries to do everything she asks, and it's still not enough! It's not his fault he has bad dreams or that he sleepwalks. It's not FAIR and I'm tired of it!" Katie yelled, angry tears filling her brown eyes.

James put his arm around her. "Maybe you should talk to Sally. She's really nice and is helping us deal with a lot of this."

"He's right, Katie. The next time Sally comes over you should tell her how you're feeling, it might help. I think we all forget you're only seven, because you're always so grown up about everything," Logan told her.

Katie hugged James. "Almost eight."

Logan smiled. "Almost eight."

Everyone was quiet for a few minutes, lost in their own thoughts.

"Does anyone need to say anything else?" Sylvia asked.

The kids looked at each other and shook their heads.

"I think I'm going to go call my mom and see how they're doing," James said, getting up.

∞

James went upstairs and dialed his mom's cell. "Brooke Diamond."

"Hi mom."

"Hello darling. How are you doing?"

He sighed. "Okay, I guess. Kendall and Papi are on their way home. How's Mama K?"

"She's doing better, the fluids have helped. The sedative they gave her is wearing off, so they're going to give her something so she can sleep through the night. I'll be over after that, since they won't let me stay because she's an adult."

"Okay, I'll see you then."

"James, tell me what's wrong, baby."

"Why do you think there's something wrong?"

Brooke stayed silent, and he could picture the look she was giving him in his head.

"I was just... worried."

"About what?" she asked softly.

"Everything... Everyone was so mad at Mama K, and then scared when we couldn't find Kendall. Sometimes it's just... hard, and I miss you."

"Do you want to come home tonight?"

"No, it's not that. I want to be here for Kendall, Katie, and the guys. I think it's just I miss getting to see you every day. I wanted you to know that, and that I love you," he said quietly.

Brooke smiled and felt tears stinging her eyes. "I love you too, darling, and I miss seeing you every day as well. Tell you what, I'm going to make it a point to come and see you every day that you're not home."

"It's okay. I know you're busy with the company this time of year."

"Now you listen to me, NOTHING is more important than my boy. I will be there to see you every day, no matter where you are."

James smiled. "Okay."

"James, I also want to say how very proud I am of you. All of you amaze me."

"Thanks mom that means a lot."

"Alright, I'll see you soon."

"Okay. I love you."

"I love you too. Goodbye darling," Brooke said.

∞

Antonio stopped by the steakhouse and quickly ran in and picked up their dinner. Kendall waited in the car. He was already tired and wanted nothing more than to sleep. He was worried about how everyone would react when he got home. He knew he had frightened them.

Antonio came back out and they drove home. They got to the house and Antonio carried the bags in one hand, while putting his other arm around Kendall. "It's alright, you know."

"I know." Kendall sighed.

They went up the steps and Carlos opened the door. "Hey," Kendall said quietly.

Carlos threw his arms around him. "I'm so glad you're home."

Kendall just hugged him back, trying not to cry again. "I'm sorry."

"You don't have to be," Carlos said as they walked in.

Antonio carried the bags out to the kitchen. "Alright, come and get it."

"Food!" Carlos smiled.

Kendall smiled back at him. "I'm glad some things never change."

Sylvia set out some paper plates and started handing burgers and fries around. She got a bowl for Kendall's soup and he sat down between James and Antonio. Everyone was quiet as they ate. "So, what happened at practice today? I didn't get there in time to see much," Antonio asked.

Carlos told him about some of the drills they had run and Logan jumped in with the new strategies he had had come up with. After a few minutes, everyone had relaxed and were enjoying their meal. Kendall was still working on his soup by the time everyone else had finished, so James stayed with him while the others went to finish homework and get ready for bed.

He put his arm around his friend and lay his head on his shoulder. "Don't ever scare me like that again," he whispered.

Kendall tilted his head, so that it was resting on top of James'. "I'm sorry."

"Don't apologize, just promise me."

"I promise," he said.

Chapter 97 ~Taking Over

Jen woke up and saw Brooke sitting next to her. "Where am I?"

Brooke sat on the bed next to her. "You're in the hospital. You fainted and Antonio and I brought you here. The doctor says you are suffering from exhaustion and that you are dehydrated. Jen, you promised us you would take care of yourself after the last time."

"That's ridiculous, I'm fine."

"Really? Then why are you here?"

"Because you all overreacted and I'm going home!" she said, trying to get up.

"Jennifer Rose Knight, you lie back down and stop acting like a child this instant!" Brooke demanded, pushing her back down on the bed.

"I TOLD you I'm fine!" Jen said, trying to get up again and failing.

"Really? Then why can I hold you down with one hand?"

"Because they drugged me," she said.

"That's right, they sedated you because you were getting hysterical again and your blood pressure was going through the roof. You are staying here until you're well, which means tonight and probably tomorrow, so stop being stubborn. It's not going to get you anywhere," Brooke said.

"I need to get home to my children!"

Brooke looked at her. "Your children need you well, not dropping from a sudden heart attack because you've let your health go. You need help, Jen, and you're not going home until you get it."

"That's not up to you, and I don't need any help. I am GOING home, so call the damn nurse!" Jen yelled.

Brooke watched the monitors and seeing that they remained stable, took a deep breath and counted to ten. She decided Jen needed to hear the truth. "Really, you don't need any help? Where is your son right now?"

"What?"

"I'll tell you where he is. He is FINALLY back home after climbing out a second story window and running away after what you said tonight. I know you didn't say what you said TO him, but he heard you essentially blame him for this whole thing. He was missing for over two hours, out in this weather, with no jacket, no boots, everyone desperately trying to find him. Now, I know that's not how you meant it, so does everyone else, but HE didn't."

Jen turned pale and lay back down. "Oh my God!" she said, covering her face with her hands. "It wasn't a dream?"

Brooke sighed. "No, it wasn't a dream. Now, I'm sorry I told you like this, but you needed to hear the truth. Kendall is back home and he's fine. I'll be going there after they kick me out of here. Jen, you really hurt him, and you need help dealing with this whole situation before you drive a permanent wedge between the two of you."

"I didn't mean it!" Jen sobbed.

"I know you didn't, honey, it all just came out wrong. But he didn't know that, and the fact that you're hiding these feelings means that you're not handling this well at all," Brooke said gently.

"Where did they find him? Did he go home?"

"No, somehow he ended up at Claudia Jenkins' place. She got him warmed up and helped him understand a few things, which is what you need," Brooke told her.

"He actually spoke to her?"

"Yes, apparently for nearly an hour. Then Antonio picked him up and took him home. Now, I know you said you called Dr. Thorne today. When did he say he could get you in?"

"Friday."

"We are going to make sure you keep that appointment. You need someone to help you with this as much as Kendall does, if not more. He at least confides in the boys and Antonio about some things. You haven't said a word to Sylvia, Jo, or I about how you're doing, no matter how often we ask. Did we not let you know that we're here for you?"

"Of course you did, I just..."

"Thought you could handle it on your own?"

Jen nodded.

"Because that worked out SO well when Will died. You gave us your word then, and from this moment on, you WILL be keeping your word. Understand?"

Jen nodded.

"Good." Brooke smiled as she pushed the call button. "The doctor ordered something to help you sleep through the night. After you're sleeping, I'm going to go and check on the children, and one of us will be back here in the morning."

Jen nodded. "Brooke, t-tell Kendall I'm sorry. Please?"

"Of course I will," Brooke promised as the nurse came in.

∞

Antonio found James and Kendall asleep at the table, Kendall's head still resting on top of James'. He smiled at the two. "Boys, you need to wake up."

James opened his eyes first and yawned. Kendall stirred a little when James moved.

"Come on boys, time for bed," Antonio said.

"Hmmm?" Kendall said.

"Time to get ready for bed."

Kendall sat up and groaned.

"It's your shoulder, isn't it?" James asked.

Kendall nodded.

"Come on," he said, helping Kendall up.

"Ow," Kendall said as he tried to straighten up.

"What is it?" Antonio asked.

"Everything hurts."

"Let's get you into a warm bath, and then you're taking a pain pill," Antonio said. He and James helped Kendall upstairs and Antonio ran warm water in the tub. Antonio helped Kendall off with his shirt. "If you need any help, just yell. I'll be next door, and the boys are across the hall."

Kendall nodded.

"I'm leaving the door unlocked, just in case you fall asleep. We're going to do a nebulizer treatment too, just as a preemptive measure."

"Okay," Kendall said.

Kendall finished undressing and climbed into the tub, submerging his cold and aching body into the warm water. He had been soaking for about fifteen minutes when someone knocked on the door. "Yeah?"

"Just checking. You doing alright?" Antonio asked.

"I'm okay, just getting tired."

"Why don't you get out and we can get you to bed?" Antonio said.

"Just a couple more minutes?"

"Alright, I'll give you five, but the water will be getting too cold if you're in there any longer."

"Okay."

Five minutes later Antonio knocked on the door again. "Time to get out."

"Okay," Kendall said, pulling himself out of the tub. He dried off and pulled on his boxers and pajamas bottoms. "Papi?"

"Do you need help?"

Kendall sighed. "Yes please."

Antonio went in and helped Kendall with his shirt. "Did that help?"

Kendall nodded. "Yeah, a little, I'm just really tired."

"I know, let's get you into bed."

Kendall went into Carlos' bedroom to find Logan already lying on the floor with his leg propped up under a pillow. He smirked at Kendall. "YOU are sleeping in the bed tonight."

Kendall rolled his eyes. "How are you going to get up on your own if you have to use the bathroom?"

"Simple," he said, pulling back the blanket to reveal his crutches lying next to him.

"Mmhm, let's see you get up with them," Kendall said.

"Not a problem," Logan said as he pulled up the crutches and tried to stand up... unsuccessfully.

"Carlos?" Kendall said.

"Yup," he said, jumping up and hauling Logan to his feet.

"You are NOT sleeping on the floor," Logan said.

"No, we'll sleep in the guest room tonight since it's got a double bed." Kendall yawned.

"Oh, good idea." Logan smiled.

Carlos grabbed the blankets and they all moved next door.

"Wait, what about Katie?" Kendall asked.

"My mom's staying over, so she's going to stay with her," Logan said.

"Okay, thanks."

James came in carrying Kendall's nebulizer. "Papi said you need a treatment before bed, and you need to put on your stabilizer."

"Okay," Kendall said as James helped him get the brace back on.

"It's never going to heal if you keep taking it off," James told him.

"I know."

A few moments later, Kendall was lying down with the nebulizer running and Logan with his leg elevated.

∞

There was a knock at the front door and Sylvia answered. "Brooke, how's Jen?"

"She's sleeping. I told her one of us will be there tomorrow. She's not happy about this, and I'm afraid I lost my temper with her a bit."

"Brooke, what did you do?"

"I told her the truth, something she NEEDED to hear, and then I made her promise that she will keep her previous promise to us."

"Did you tell her about Kendall?"

"Yes I did. She was throwing a fit, insisting that she was fine and was going to leave. Her heart rate and blood pressure were normal, so I told her exactly what happened and why."

"Brooke..."

"She won't listen to us when we try and be tactful with her, but she damn well listened when I told her what her lack of self-care caused tonight."

"Brooke!"

"Don't 'Brooke' me. She needed to hear it, and now she has and can move on. She cried, but it was better that she realized what had happened when one of us was there, as opposed to her remembering while she was there alone."

"She was really doing better?" Sylvia asked.

"Yes, and she has an appointment with Dr. Thorne on Friday, but I'm going to call Claudia and see if she can get him in to see her tomorrow sometime," Brooke said.

"Alright. How are we going to work this? Two of us need to be here with Kendall, and someone needs to be there with Jen," Sylvia asked.

"I'll go and stay with her in the morning, and we can work out the rest of the day. If she's doing better, they might release her."

"Okay and I guess we'll move Thanksgiving dinner here?"

"Sounds good. You know, we DO have a lot to be thankful for this year." Brooke smiled.

"I guess we do, sometimes it's just a little hard to see it."

"Yes it is," Brooke said, hugging her. "Is James upstairs?"

Sylvia nodded. "The boys are getting ready for bed. I think they moved into the guest room though."

Brooke went upstairs and knocked on the bedroom door before opening it. "Hello darlings, is everyone getting settled in for the night?"

"Hi mom!" James said, jumping up to hug her.

"Hi Mama D!" Carlos squealed as he hugged her tightly.

"Carlos, I need to breathe."

"Sorry." He smiled.

"How are my two invalids tonight?"

"I'm fine," Logan said.

"The swelling going down any?"

Logan nodded.

"Good. How about you, honey?" she asked Kendall.

"Mmm 'kay," he said, his voice muffled by the mask.

She sat down next to him and brushed back his bangs. "I just left the hospital, and your mom is doing better. She wanted me to tell you how very sorry she is and how much she loves you."

The boys were all quiet, not sure of how Kendall was going to react.

"'kay," he said, turning over and closing his eyes.

She reached over and kissed him on the forehead. "Goodnight darling."

She kissed each of the other boys and gave James a big hug. "I'll see you tomorrow, darling."

"Okay, thanks mom."

"I love you." She smiled.

"Love you too," he said, blushing.

She closed the door and went back downstairs.

∞

Antonio, Sylvia, and Joanna were in the kitchen discussing plans for the next couple of days.

"So, how did things go here?" Brooke asked.

"The kids are pretty upset with Jen, although after they talked, I think they were feeling a little better about everything," Sylvia told her.

"And Kendall?"

"That's what we were discussing. Claudia thinks they might do better with a couple of days apart. He broke down a little at her place. He was feeling guilty because he was relieved that she wasn't going to be here tonight," Antonio told her.

"I can't say I really blame him," Sylvia said.

"She can stay with either Brooke or I until things are a little less strained," Jo suggested.

"It's an option. I don't know how she'll take it though, she was already missing them tonight," Brooke said.

"I know, but we have to do what's best for everyone, and if Kendall can't handle being around her..." Antonio said.

"This is NOT going to be easy," Sylvia said.

"No. I love Jen like a sister, but Kendall has to come first right now. He has fought too hard, and I am not willing to let him lose any more ground. We'll make sure Jen gets all the help she needs, we'll be there for her night and day, but he has to come first. I know she would agree even though she's not thinking clearly right now," Antonio told them.

"It's what we promised each other," Sylvia said.

∞

Upstairs, Logan took the mask off Kendall and handed it to James. Kendall had fallen asleep, so they tried not to wake him.

"What do you think he's going to do if she comes home tomorrow?" Carlos asked.

"I don't know. I don't think he's really ready to face her," Logan told him.

"Let's try and get some sleep. We can deal with it tomorrow," James said.

They both nodded, and James turned out the light and settled onto the floor next to Kendall's side of the bed, Carlos lying on the other side of him.

"James?" Carlos whispered.

"Yeah?"

"Are we all going to be okay?"

"Sure we are. As long as we're here for each other, we'll be fine."

"Okay." Carlos smiled as he snuggled against James' side.

James smiled and put his arm around him, hoping he was right.

SARA ALLEN STEWART ∞ THOSE YOU TRUST ∞ PAGE 454

Chapter 98~ Restraint

Something woke Logan up, and he glanced at the clock on the night table to find that it was 4 am. He yawned and realized what had awakened him—Kendall was shivering. Logan pulled the blankets up over them further. "Are you okay?"

Kendall nodded, tucking his head under the covers.

"Are you sure?"

Kendall nodded again. "Just cold."

Logan had a feeling something still wasn't right and pulled the covers down from Kendall's head. "Kendall, what's really wrong?"

"I told you, I'm cold."

"Did you have another nightmare?"

When Kendall didn't answer, Logan put his arm around him. "I'm sorry, buddy. Can you tell me what it was about?"

Kendall shook his head.

"Kendall, you know you can talk to me, right?" Logan persisted when he got no response.

"I know."

"Was it about Deesie?"

"No."

"Graham?"

"No."

"Your mom?"

"I don't wanna talk about it right now."

"Okay, just as long as you know I'm here if you need someone to talk to."

"I know. I just don't want to talk right now."

"Okay. Do you need anything?"

Kendall shook his head.

"Hey, do you realize you woke up from a nightmare and didn't sleepwalk?" Kendall nodded and curled up more. Logan pulled his friend closer to him. "Try and get some more sleep."

"Okay."

"Night buddy," Logan whispered. He rested his chin on top of Kendall's head.

"Night Loges."

A few minutes later, both boys had fallen back to sleep.

∞

Antonio got up at about 6 am, showered, and got ready for work. He checked on the boys and was glad to see they were all sleeping peacefully. He went downstairs and started a pot of coffee, went out, and grabbed the newspaper, then went upstairs to wake the boys for school.

Sylvia heard him and got up. "Good morning, honey."

"Good morning." Antonio smiled, kissing her.

"Ewww. Mami, Papi!" Carlos complained as he headed into the bathroom.

"Ewww," Sylvia mimicked as she kissed Antonio again.

"Mami, stop! It's too early to see that!"

Sylvia smirked at her son and kissed Antonio again.

"Hey, I kinda like this game. Carlos, complain a little more." Antonio grinned.

Carlos groaned and Sylvia gave him a huge kiss on the cheek.

"Get ready for school while I make breakfast."

Twenty minutes later, the boys were all dressed and sitting at the kitchen table eating breakfast. Jo came out a few minutes later. "I think Katie needs a day at home. She didn't sleep very well and is still pretty upset with Jen," Joanna said.

"Probably a good idea—she can spend some time with Kendall. Sally's coming over later, so maybe they can talk," Sylvia said.

Antonio was finishing his breakfast and reading the paper when he suddenly folded it back up. "I need to get to the station. Can one of you take the boys to school?"

"Sure honey. What's wrong?" Sylvia asked.

"I'll call you later," he said, kissing her goodbye.

Sylvia and Joanna looked at one another, suddenly worried.

∞

Jonathan Reed was not happy. He had received a message from Richard Graham last night, saying that the police were harassing him and had arrested him again, on no grounds, of course. Reed had heard about the news interview and watched it online. Now he was heading to the police station to meet with his client and to let him know that he was considering requesting a termination of representation from the judge.

He pulled into the station parking lot and went inside. Officer Dane took him to the large interrogation room and went to get Graham. Reed sat there patiently waiting, and a few minutes later, heard Graham yelling at the officer and sighed. Officer Dane brought Graham in, attached the cuffs to the table attachment, and gave Reed a sympathetic smile.

"WHY didn't you call me back last night?"

Reed just looked at him. "Do you have any idea what you've done?"

"Yes, I gave MY side of the story."

"You've broken the bail terms that Judge Warner set down, as well as adding a few more charges to your already substantial list. Which means you WILL be spending the time before your trial in jail."

"Nonsense. I did nothing wrong, so get me out of here immediately!" Graham insisted.

"You contacted a news station from Minneapolis and gave an interview regarding the case, which means you failed to maintain professional discretion. You're also being charged with two counts of contributing to the delinquency of a minor and subornation of perjury, because you PAID two teenagers to lie about what happened in Dylan Mason's case."

"They can't prove anything," Graham said smugly.

"Do you know how far your voice carries? There were two witnesses who are willing to testify that they heard you and Dylan Mason come up with this hair-brained scheme."

"Do you really think they would take the word of two troublemaking teenagers over mine?" Graham asked.

"In a heartbeat."

∞

Sally was on her way to the station, hoping to get there before Antonio. She had called John, and he was already there waiting. He told her that Graham's attorney was there, and they were in a consultation in the main interrogation room. She pulled up and parked, grateful not to see Antonio's car yet.

She went inside and Johnson greeted her. "Didn't your vacation start today?"

She smiled. "Probably a little later."

She got on the phone to Ryan, and he started speaking the moment he picked up. "I already saw it and spoke to the editor—they know they're in trouble. I also contacted KMAN and let them know that we are filing an injunction. I also let them know we're looking into filing

charges against Chelsea Waters and the station for airing an interview regarding a case, which is still under investigation," Ryan told her.

"Good, but that doesn't undo what's been done."

"No it doesn't, but at the moment, it's all we can do," Ryan said.

She saw Antonio pull up. "Gotta go, keep me updated," she said, hanging up.

Antonio walked in. "Where is he?"

Sally stood in front of him. "Boss, I already spoke with Ryan and he's taking care of this."

"Where IS he?"

"He's meeting with his attorney. I'm not going to let you do anything you'll regret," she said, standing her ground.

John came running out. "She's right, Antonio, you need to take a deep breath and calm down."

Antonio inhaled deeply. "See, I'm calm, I'm very calm. Now, WHERE IS HE?"

"Antonio, you do NOT want to do anything that's going to jeopardize this case," Sally said, still standing in front of him.

"He is NOT going to get away with this!"

"Of course he's not. Neither is KMAN or the newspaper, but if you go in there and do anything to him, then HE wins," John told him.

Antonio took another deep breath. "His attorney is with him?"

"Yes," Sally said.

"Good," Antonio said. He took her by the shoulders, moved her to the side, and pushed past John. He opened the door to the interrogation room and went inside.∞

"Stay here in case I need backup," John told Sally as he followed Antonio.

∞

Reed looked at Antonio as he entered the room. "Yes?"

"Are you his attorney?"

"Yes, why?"

Antonio threw the newspaper on the table. "Are you aware of what your client's done now? Page three."

Reed picked up the paper and opened it to the page.

John had come in behind Antonio and removed Graham's cuffs from the table. He was attempting to get him out the door, when Graham started yelling at him. "How dare you interrupt a meeting between me and my attorney!"

"You just never know when to shut up, do you?" John hissed.

Reed stood up and walked over to Graham. "Is this your doing?"

Graham quieted down and looked at the paper. On it was his photo with the title, "Dr. Richard Graham: The Misunderstood Hero," and the article went on to say what he had said during the television interview. Only this time, it gave Kendall's name along with his school photo.

"IS. THIS. YOUR. DOING?" Reed asked again.

Graham stayed silent but smirked at him.

"Dr. Graham, I came here hoping to talk some sense into you, but I can see it will be a complete waste of time. After everything else, you have NOW disclosed the name of a minor child, who was the victim of a predator. I am hereby informing you that I am requesting a withdrawal of representation from the courts."

"What does that mean?" Graham asked.

"It means he's firing your ass," John explained.

"YOU..." Antonio said, grabbing Graham by the collar and pushing him up against the wall, "...are going to be VERY sorry for what you have done."

"Antonio..." John warned.

Graham looked at Antonio and went pale. "Antonio? Exactly WHO are you?"

Antonio smiled. "I guess we haven't been formally introduced yet. My name is Antonio Garcia, the Chief of Police."

"Y-You're..."

Antonio smiled again and nodded. "Kendall's godfather."

"I suggest you let me go immediately or I will sue," Graham blustered.

"You never learn," John said, shaking his head.

Antonio got very close to Graham. "Do you KNOW what you've done? How many people you've hurt or destroyed? Jennifer Knight is in the hospital because she collapsed after seeing your interview. Whether you admit it or not, you are already responsible for one child's death, and I will be DAMNED if we lose our boy because of you. You had better pray that you are convicted and sent away for a very long time, because if you're not, I am willing to go to prison for the rest of MY life to see to it that you never hurt another family. Do I make myself perfectly clear?" Antonio growled.

"You can't threaten me, I have witnesses!" Graham shrieked, looking at Reed.

Antonio stood back, smiled, and then put his fist through the wall next to Graham's head. "Do I make myself clear?" he asked again quietly.

"Did you see what he did?" Graham yelled at Reed.

Reed nodded and patted Antonio on the back. "That was a pretty big spider you killed there, Chief," he said as he walked out the door.

"John?" Antonio said.

"Yes, Chief?"

"Take this piece of... back to his cell."

"Will do," John said, pulling Graham out the door.

Antonio took a deep breath and pulled his hand out of the plaster.

Sally came walking in with an icepack. "Here," she said, wrapping it around his hand.

"How did you know I needed this?"

"You hit the wall so hard the room placard came flying off the other side of the wall. Are you alright?" she asked.

He nodded. "I'll fix that later," he said, looking at the wall.

Sally smiled. "Maybe we should leave it there as a warning to other ne'er-do-wells. We could put a frame around it."

"Sally, I'm sorry for losing it."

"Why? You're entitled. You've been through more hell than anyone else here."

"Still."

"Look, you didn't actually hurt him or break any laws, which surprises me. If it were me, I would probably be sitting in a cell right now. Why don't you go home and make sure everything is alright there? Get some rest, and if you need anything, call me. I'm coming over later to see Kendall and the boys anyway," she told him.

"That reminds me, Sylvia and Joanna think Katie might need someone to talk to about this. She's furious with Jen right now."

"Not a problem. Maybe I'll take her out for some girl time."

"I think she'd like that."

John came in. "That is the QUIETEST that man has ever been. How's your hand? Anything broken?"

"I don't think so," Antonio said, flexing his fingers.

"Good," John said as he inspected the hole. "Wow, another inch to the right and you would have hit the stud."

"Sally thinks we should frame it."

"That's an idea." John smiled.

"I'm going home," Antonio said, suddenly very tired.

"Can you drive alright?" John asked.

Antonio nodded. "It's not that bad."

"I'll see you later, Boss," Sally said.

"Thanks you two, for everything," he said as he left.

John sighed in relief. "I thought he was really going to hurt that idiot."

"He had me worried too. Come on, I'll buy you a cup of coffee," she said, smacking him in the arm.

"Ow," he whined.

"Oh, you big baby... at least it won't need stitches." She laughed.

"That is NOT funny!"

∞

Antonio got home and went inside. Sylvia, Jo, and Katie looked at him in surprise.

"Honey, what are you doing home? Is everything alright?" Sylvia asked.

He hugged her. "Everything's alright now. Katie, can you go watch television in my study for a few minutes?"

"Okay, but will you tell me later?" She was getting tired of people thinking they needed to protect her from everything.

"Yes Mija, when the boys get home. Now go, just for a few minutes."

She nodded and left the room.

Antonio sat down and told Sylvia and Joanna what had happened.

"You know, I think I'm just going to go pick the boys up now. Someone at school is bound to tell them about the article, and I don't want them hearing about it that way," Jo said, grabbing her coat.

"Good idea," Sylvia said.

Sylvia looked at Antonio's hand. "You punched a wall?"

"It was either that or his smug, self-righteous face," Antonio told her.

"I'm glad you chose the wall... kind of," she said, kissing him on the cheek.

"I'm tired. I think I'm going to go lie down for a while. Honey, can you explain this to the boys?"

"Of course I can. Get some rest, love."

He smiled and went upstairs. He changed out of his uniform and went to check on Kendall. He sat down next to him, and Kendall opened his eyes. "Papi, are you okay?"

"I'm fine, Mijo, just a little tired. How are you feeling?"

"I'm still a little cold and tired."

"I bet you are. Do you need anything?"

Kendall shook his head. "Mama G brought up some breakfast a little while ago."

"Did you eat?"

Kendall nodded.

"Good. I'm going to go rest for a while. Then we are going to have a good lunch."

"Are you sure you're okay?" Kendall asked, yawning.

"I'm fine, Mijo."

Antonio sat there for a couple of minutes, and then pulled another blanket out of the closet and covered Kendall.

A few minutes later, Sylvia went upstairs to check on them and found Antonio sound asleep next to Kendall. She smiled and grabbed another blanket and kissed Antonio's cheek as she covered him. She closed the door and went back downstairs.

Chapter 99~Trying to Cope

Jo drove to the middle school and went into the office. "Hi Tara, I need to pick up the boys."

"Is everything alright?" Tara asked.

Joanna smiled. "Yes, I don't know if you've seen the newspaper yet, but there's an article in it that we think is best that the boys hear about from us."

"No, I haven't read it yet. Is it bad?"

"It's not good, and the boys have been through enough without them finding out about it from someone here. We thought we'd get them home and get an early start to the holiday."

"I'll page them for you," Tara said, picking up the phone.

"No wait, a page might scare them and will definitely get people talking. Can you just tell me what classrooms they're in and I'll go and pick them up in person?"

"Sure," Tara said, pulling up the schedules on the computer.

"James and Carlos are in room 121, and Logan is in 202."

"Thanks Tara. Have a wonderful Thanksgiving."

"You too. Tell Kendall I said, hi."

"I will, thanks," Jo said, heading off to find the boys. She went to Logan's class first and knocked on the door. Ms. Benchley, the advanced algebra teacher, answered.

"Mrs. Mitchell, is everything alright?"

Joanna smiled. "Yes, I just need to pick up Logan a little early today."

"Logan," Ms. Benchley called.

Logan shoved his into his backpack and got to the door as quickly as he could. He had heard Jo's voice and found himself on the verge of a panic attack. "Mom, what's wrong?"

"Nothing honey, we need to get James and Carlos though."

"Something HAS to be wrong if you're pulling us out of school early," Logan insisted.

"Alright, the newspaper printed an article of Graham's interview, and Sylvia and I decided that we wanted you all home so we could tell you."

"Does Kendall know?"

"Not yet, he was still sleeping when I left."

They got to the chemistry room and Joanna asked for James and Carlos. They came out and she explained why she was there before they could panic. They got to the Garcia house and went inside. Sylvia and Katie were on the couch. Katie was trying to explain how to play Test Drive Unlimited to Sylvia, who kept crashing into walls, buildings, and other cars.

"Mama G, you're overcompensating at the turns."

Sylvia screamed as she crashed into yet another building.

"You're supposed to turn at, not drive THROUGH, the building." Katie laughed.

"Thank goodness, one of you can take over!" Sylvia said, dropping the controller.

"I will!" Carlos said, sitting next to Katie.

"Honey, can you pause the game just for a minute?" Joanna asked.

"Sure," Carlos said, hitting the pause button.

"Boys, sit down," Sylvia said as she sat next to Carlos.

Jo sat next to Katie and put her arm around her. "Katie, I explained a little about what happened this morning to the boys when I picked them up. In this morning's newspaper was Graham's television interview from last night."

"So? More people watch TV than read the newspaper. Why is it different?"

"Well Mija, they also printed a picture of Kendall and used his name, which isn't allowed. That's why Papi left so quickly this morning. He had a little... chat with Graham and his attorney," Sylvia explained.

"What kind of chat?" Carlos asked.

Sylvia and Joanna looked at each other. "Well, it's a little difficult to explain," Sylvia said.

"Why?" James asked. The boys were all very curious at this point.

"Well, Papi lost his temper, just a little mind you and..."

"And?" Logan asked.

"He punched out the wall next to Graham's head," Sylvia told them.

The boys all looked at each other in surprise.

"He punched a wall?" Carlos asked.

Sylvia nodded. "Put his fist right through it."

"Way to go Papi!" Katie smiled.

"Katie, Papi is NOT advocating violence. He's just been through a lot and seeing Kendall's picture in the paper this morning just..."

"Made him snap?" Katie asked.

Sylvia smiled. "Yes, just for a minute."

"Graham's just lucky he hit the wall instead of him," James said.

"We got the distinct impression Graham realized that as well," Jo said.

"Wasn't his attorney there though? Are they going to file charges?" Logan asked.

"Yes, his attorney was there, but after he read the article, he told Graham that he's requesting a withdrawal of representation from the court," Sylvia told him.

"What's that?" James asked.

"It means he's asking the court's permission to fire Graham as a client," Sylvia said.

"Why does he have to ask permission?" Katie asked.

"Because representation had already begun. They have already been to court once, and in some cases, it could hurt the defendant's case. So the judge has to decide if it's fair or not," Sylvia told her.

"Like he deserves any consideration," James said angrily.

"No he doesn't. Not from us, anyway," Joanna said.

"Kendall doesn't know about this yet, we're going to let Papi tell him. Hopefully he takes it as well as he did with the television interview and we can just get past this quickly," Sylvia said.

"Does Mama K know?" Logan asked.

"No, and I do need to call Brooke and let her know though," Sylvia said, getting up.

∞

Sylvia went to the kitchen and dialed Brooke's cell. "Brooke Diamond."

"Hi Brooke. How's Jen doing this morning?"

"She's still sleeping. Claudia got ahold of Dr. Thorne for me, and he'll be coming here to see her at about one today. How's everyone there?"

Sylvia quickly told her about the morning's events.

"I'll let Dr. Thorne know before he speaks with her. He can decide how to tell her since I'm assuming he will. It's not like we can keep something like this a secret forever, not in this town," Brooke said.

"Unfortunately not," Sylvia said.

"So the boys are home now?"

"Yes, we didn't want someone at school telling them about it," Sylvia explained.

"Maybe they should get out and do something fun today," Brooke suggested.

"I was thinking that too. Sally's coming over to meet with them in a little while, so maybe after that."

"How's Antonio doing?"

"He's tired. He got home and went to check on Kendall, and I found him sound asleep next to him a little while later."

"He's been through a lot too. We all rely on him so much."

"He loves you all though and wouldn't have it any differently."

"I know, and I hope that you know we all feel the same way about the two of you," Brooke said.

"We do." Sylvia smiled. "Has the doctor been in to see Jen yet?"

"Not yet, I'm expecting him soon though. Has Kendall said anything more about what happened?"

"No, I'm not sure how we're going to handle this. Hopefully Dr. Thorne has some ideas, and Antonio said Claudia is going to stop by to check on Kendall today, so I'll ask her as well," Sylvia said.

"Sounds good. Can you give James a hug for me and tell him I'll see him later?"

"Of course I will. Let Jen know we're thinking of her and will be by to see her later."

"I will," Brooke said.

"Bye Brooke." Sylvia hung up and went back into the living room.

Carlos and Katie had restarted the game, and James was sitting next to Carlos and watching. Logan was sitting next to the window, reading, and Jo was looking at her appointment schedule on her tablet.

Sylvia went over and sat down next to James. "Your mom said she'll see you later but wanted me to give you a hug," she said, wrapping her arms around him and squeezing him tight.

James smiled and hugged her back. "Thanks Mama G."

She kissed him on the cheek. "You're welcome, Mijo. So what do we want to do today?"

"What do you mean?" James asked.

"Well, you all have an extra day off, so you should do something fun. Sally will be over in a little while, so maybe after that we could go to a movie, or the mall, whatever you want to do."

"I can't really do a whole lot," Logan said.

"Maybe a movie then?" Joanna suggested.

"Sounds good," James said.

"I still need to pick up some things from the market for dinner tomorrow. Antonio and Kendall are asleep, so I think I'll make a quick run now and maybe stop by and see Jen for a few minutes," Sylvia said, getting her coat.

"I'll go with you," James said, grabbing his jacket.

"Anyone else?" she asked, looking at Katie.

Katie just continued playing her game, not answering.

"Carlos?"

"No thanks, mom. Tell her I said, hi, though."

"I'll go," Logan said, getting up. Sylvia smiled and James helped steady him as he put on his jacket.

"We'll be back in about an hour," Sylvia told Joanna.

She nodded. "Give Jen my love."

"I will," Sylvia said as they left.

"Katie, are you doing alright?" Jo asked.

"Yeah, I'm fine," she answered, still concentrating on her game.

"Honey, you know this isn't really your mom's fault, right?"

"Sure."

Joanna went and sat next to her and pushed the pause button on the remote. "Katie, Carlos, I know what's happened is hard to understand, but Jen loves all of you, and she needs us to be there for her."

"She doesn't listen," Katie said as she hit the play button.

Joanna hit the pause button again. "Honey, she has no idea how to deal with any of this, and she's getting help. You were just a baby when your dad died, but I remember it quite well. She has a habit of trying to take care of everyone else and hiding her feelings. She thinks it makes her look weak if people know she needs help. She tried to be supermom, and she failed this time. Honey, she's really sick and needs you."

Katie sighed. "I'm just really mad at her right now."

"I know you are. I think we all are to some degree or another. She's stubborn and was trying to be strong for you and Kendall. I know she ended up hurting him, but that's not what she meant to do. Think about it, if Antonio, who has had years of training to deal with situations like these, loses his temper and nearly punches out Graham, how is someone like your mom supposed to handle it?"

"You know, that does makes sense Katie," Carlos said.

"I guess. I just really don't want to see her right now, and I DON'T want her to hurt Kendall anymore."

"I understand, and we're going to try our hardest to make sure that no one gets hurt anymore," Jo said, hugging her.

"Okay," Katie said.

"So, maybe you'll call her tonight?" Joanna asked hopefully.

Katie thought for a moment and nodded.

"That's my girl," Joanna said, hugging her again.

∞

Sylvia and the boys finished up at the market and headed to the hospital. They found Jen's room and saw Brooke sitting next to the bed, talking to her.

"Hey. How are you feeling?" Sylvia asked, hugging Jen.

"Better."

"Hi Mama K," Logan said, using the railing to hold himself up so he could hug her.

James hugged her next and set a bouquet of autumn coloured flowers on the table next to her bed. She smiled. "Those are beautiful. Thank you."

"We hoped you'd like them," James said, standing next to his mom.

"So, has the doctor been in yet?" Sylvia asked.

Jen nodded. "He thinks I should stay here at least another night."

"Are you okay with that?"

She nodded and then her eyes teared up. "I miss my babies though."

"Honey, they miss you too. Kendall was sleeping when we left or I'm sure he would have sent you a message. I'll see if he's up to calling later, and Carlos said to tell you, hi," Sylvia told her.

"Katie must be pretty mad," Jen said, looking down at her hands.

"I think she's just confused by everything. She is only seven."

"I know. I just... screwed up so badly this time."

"If by screwing up, you mean you didn't take care of yourself, then yes, you screwed up. If you mean that you screwed up because you had a breakdown because of everything that's happened, then no," Brooke said firmly.

"Is Kendall really alright?" Jen asked.

"He's doing fine. He even ate all of his breakfast this morning. He's just really tired and he got pretty chilled last night, so Claudia told him to stay in bed today and rest," Sylvia said.

Jen nodded. "Will you tell him...?"

"Of course I will," Sylvia said, hugging her again.

"What are you boys doing out of school?" Jen asked.

"Umm... we were just tired after last night, and since there's not a lot going on because of the holiday, our moms decided we should stay home and maybe do something fun later," Logan quickly answered.

"That's nice. Will you make sure Katie gets out for a while?"

"Sure thing." James smiled.

"Thanks honey." Jen smiled back.

"Well, we better get back. Hopefully you'll be home for dinner tomorrow night. I'm making your favourite pie, and knowing our boys, there won't be any left," Sylvia said.

"Browned butter pecan?" Jen asked.

"Mmhm." Sylvia nodded.

"Well, that's definitely worth following the doctor's orders for." Jen smiled.

"Good. I'll call you later, okay?"

Jen nodded. "Thank you for everything."

"No thanks necessary, just feel better."

"I'm trying."

"I know you are. Now get some rest, and hopefully we'll see you home tomorrow."

Jen nodded.

Sylvia and the boys left.

"Katie and Carlos must both be upset with me," Jen said to Brooke.

"Don't start that again. Yes, Katie's upset, and Carlos probably just stayed home to keep her company."

"Probably," Jen said sadly.

"Get some more rest. I am going to run down and get some coffee. Do you want anything?"

"No thanks," Jen said as she closed her eyes.

∞

Antonio woke up surprised to find he was in the guest room. He noticed he was covered with a blanket and figured Sylvia must have come in to check on Kendall. His hand was throbbing, and he saw that it was now very bruised and swollen. He smiled when he saw Kendall still sleeping peacefully and slowly got up so as not to disturb him.

He headed downstairs to get some ice, and was surprised to see Carlos home, and then remembered that Jo had pulled them out of school early.

"Papi!" Carlos yelled as he hugged his dad.

"Carlitos!" he yelled back, hugging his son tightly.

"Mami said you punched a wall?"

"Not my brightest move," he said, showing Carlos his hand.

"I'll get the peas," Carlos said, running into the kitchen.

Antonio sat down in his recliner, and Katie went over and climbed on his lap. "How are you, Mija?"

She hugged him tightly and started crying.

"Honey, what's wrong?" he asked, looking at Jo.

"You hurt your hand, Kendall's sick, and I d-don't want to hate my mom," she cried.

"Mija, my hand is fine. I've hurt it much worse doing less important things than scaring some idiot who deserved it. Kendall is not any sicker than he was yesterday, he's just really tired, and Claudia told him to stay in bed today. She's coming over later and you'll meet her then. I think you're really going to like her. As for you hating your mom, you don't. You're just really upset right now, and no one blames you for that."

"But I-I don't even want to see her," Katie sniffled.

"Neither does Kendall, and that's normal. You'll both feel better about it soon, I promise."

"Really?"

Antonio nodded. "It's just a little too fresh in your mind right now. She scared you, and it's going to take a little time to get over that, but you will."

Carlos came back in with the bag of peas and sat it across his dad's hand. "Thanks Carlos." Antonio smiled.

"Is Katie okay?" he asked.

"I don't know. Are you feeling any better, Katie?"

She nodded.

"Good. You know Sally's coming over and thought maybe the two of you could go do something together. What do you think?" he asked Katie.

"Like what?"

"I don't know, she said you could have some 'girl time' together."

"That might be fun," Katie said.

"Sure it will. Sally is awesome! Ask her about the fish and onion," Carlos said.

"Why?" Katie asked.

"It's great!" He laughed.

Antonio arched an eyebrow at him. "Do I want to know about this?"

"Probably not," Carlos said.

∞

"Mr. Knight, have you finished your assignment yet?" Deesie asked, looking over his shoulder. "What did I tell you about assignment deadlines?" he whispered in the boy's ear.

Kendall found himself staring down at a notebook with a blank page. He tried to stand, only to find his hands cuffed to the desk. "No, no, no," he said to himself, trying to wake up.

"Now, I offered you a VERY fair trade for an extension, and I expect you to be grateful," Deesie said as his hands moved down to Kendall's shoulders. The boy tried to pull away, so Deesie tightened his hold. Deesie's mouth moved along Kendall's neck and his hands moved down Kendall's sides.

"Wake up, wake up, wake up," Kendall chanted.

"Did you want me to wait for your mother?" Deesie asked as he bit down on the teen's neck.

"Leave me alone!"

"Not going to happen. I told you that you're mine, and we haven't 'consummated' our little friendship yet," Deesie said, his hands moving to Kendall's belt buckle.

"NO!" Kendall yelled and slammed his head backwards into Deesie's face.

"You are pissing me off!" Deesie yelled, his face a bloody mess.

"Kendall, look at me! Don't think about it," Antonio begged. Kendall looked over and saw Antonio sitting there, his hands cuffed.

"We'll take care of HIS problems now!" Deesie said as he pointed a gun at Antonio and pulled the trigger.

"PAPI!" Kendall screamed.

Chapter 100 ~ Flashbacks

Dr. Eli Thorne was a nice looking man in his late forties. His dark hair was cut very short. He had chosen to start wearing it that way when his hair had started thinning ten years earlier. He had to shake his head whenever he saw men with the "comb-over" look. He believed in working with what you have and making the best of it.

He had been a psychiatrist for twenty-one years, and most of his patients adored him. He was soft-spoken and well mannered, but he had no problem telling you what he thought.

He got to the hospital a couple of hours early, because the patient that had been scheduled had cancelled because she had the flu. This was always a busy time of year for him, so many people got depressed during the holidays.

When Jennifer Knight had called him yesterday, he had cleared time for her on Friday because Claudia had already let him know about the situation. He had been surprised to hear from Claudia again, letting him know that Jennifer had been admitted to the hospital after suffering an emotional breakdown, and had asked if he could find time to see her today.

Then this morning, a friend of the family had called to let him know about the newspaper story regarding the Knight family.

He found her room and knocked on the door.

"Come in," a woman's voice said. He went inside and saw a petite woman with auburn hair lying in the hospital bed. Another woman with short brunette hair was sitting on a chair next to her. She stood up and walked over to him—her stride was strong and self-assured. She offered him her hand.

He shook it. "You must be Brooke Diamond?"

"I am, and you must be Dr. Thorne."

He smiled and nodded.

"Jennifer?" he asked, walking over to the bed.

"Hello, Dr. Thorne. It was so nice of you to come here, especially on such short notice," she said quietly.

He sat down in a chair next to the bed. "How are you feeling today?"

"A little better."

"Good. Perhaps Mrs. Diamond would excuse us for a while?" he asked, looking at Brooke.

"I don't think so. We've had issues with other 'professionals' lately, and I have no intention of leaving anyone until I'm certain that those who claim they're professional, are professional," she stated.

"Brooke..." Jen said.

"I'm staying, and don't think you can try using that bit about 'privacy laws' on me. Jen will tell me everything anyway, so you'll just have to deal with the fact that I'm here for the moment," Brooke warned him, sitting down.

"Well, if it's alright with Jennifer, I have no objections. Provided you promise to refrain from making any comments."

"Of course. Provided YOU don't cross any lines," she said sweetly.

"Brooke!" Jen said a little louder than she intended.

Brooke just sat back, arching an eyebrow at her.

"I'm so sorry, Dr. Thorne," Jen said.

"Don't be, Claudia told me about Mrs. Diamond. Your reputation precedes you," he said, smiling at Brooke.

"Just making sure that we're all on the same page," she said, smiling back.

"Understood."

"Brooke, please," Jen said again.

"It's alright, Jennifer, I'm glad you have someone strong by your side."

"Don't forget stubborn, opinionated, and has a tendency to speak before she thinks," Jen said.

Brooke smiled. "Don't be silly, darling, I ALWAYS think before I speak. It's simply that I believe in saying what I think, instead of beating around the bush. The fact that other people don't often care for what I have to say, is entirely besides the point."

Dr. Thorne smiled and turned his attention back to Jen. "What can you tell me about what happened yesterday?"

"Well, it was my second day back to work since everything started, and it went well. We're staying with our friends, the Garcias, because Kendall can't be left alone. I had the early shift, and we decided it would be easier to stay an extra couple of days, than to get the kids up so early and drop them off."

"How long have you been staying there?"

"Katie and I began staying there the night Kendall was t-taken. We were going to go home the day after we got him back, but..." Jen said as her eyes filled with tears.

"Take your time," Dr. Thorne said softly.

"It was time for bed and he'd fallen asleep on the couch, and w-when I went to wake him up, I called him 'sweetheart' by mistake and he woke up s-screaming. Antonio tried to wake him, but he started having trouble b-breathing, so he took him to the hospital and they kept him for the night. It was all my fault. I called him sweetheart out of habit, and Antonio told us t-that..."

"It's a word trigger?" Thorne asked.

She nodded.

"You blamed yourself because he ended up in the hospital that night?"

"It was my fault. I forgot and I scared him."

"You made a mistake by using a word that's common in your vocabulary. It is a term of endearment that you have always used when addressing your children. It wouldn't be easy just to stop using it. The good news is triggers aren't necessarily permanent, and Claudia is going to work with him on overcoming it."

"Okay," Jen said.

"Have you stayed at home at all since Kendall's been home?"

Jen nodded. "We stayed the rest of the weekend with Antonio and Sylvia, and went home Sunday evening. All the boys stayed over, and they were going to take turns staying with us. Kendall's pretty strong, and we were worried about what would happen if he had a panic attack or nightmare—I wouldn't be able to hold him on my own. It was around two or three in the morning when Carlos came and woke me. Kendall was having a nightmare and couldn't breathe. James and Logan were holding him, and after a while, he calmed down and fell back to sleep. I knew we couldn't go on like that, so first thing in the morning, I started calling around, trying to get him in somewhere." Jen stopped as the memories of that day came flooding back.

"That's when the two of you went to see Graham?" Thorne asked.

She nodded.

"Let's move on to something else. Why don't you finish telling me about last night?"

Jen nodded and took a couple of deep breaths.

"Take your time and just tell me what you can." He smiled.

"I got home from work at around 2:30, and Kendall was upstairs with Brooke doing some schoolwork. I asked Sylvia what Dr. Sharpe had said about Kendall's weight, and she said

he has lost over another pound, and that if he doesn't put on weight by Friday, he'll have to go into the hospital. Then she told me about his appointment with Claudia, how he panicked on the way to the door and had to go back to the car."

"Claudia told me. She also told me that she went out and sat with him in the car. She said he didn't speak directly to her, but responded when she spoke to him, and had relaxed by the time they were finished. It's quite normal for children who have been victimized to be suspicious of anyone new. Many don't respond for weeks, sometimes months. She said he even waved back to her when they drove off, and that's a very good sign," Thorne told her.

"Really?" Jen asked, hopeful.

"Really." He smiled. "Now, why don't you tell me about the rest of the day?"

"Well, after I spoke to Sylvia, I went up to check on him. I told him I was going to bring him up a smoothie before I left to pick his sister up from school, because he needs the calories. He said he wasn't hungry, but I insisted. I took it up a little while later and started to get upset when he just set it down."

She smiled a little.

"What happened then?"

"He said he'd drink it later, and when I started in on him again, he stuck out his tongue. There was a white candy on it and he started talking in a funny voice. He was eating a peppermint... Dr. Jenkins recommended them for nausea, and he didn't think the smoothie would taste very good with it. Then he crossed his eyes at me and made a goofy face... just like he used to."

"That was a good moment."

She nodded.

"There haven't been too many lately, have there?"

She sighed and shook her head.

"I can see you're getting tired, so why don't we skip forward to last night?"

"We were getting things ready for dinner and the television was on. I heard Graham's voice and went in to see what was going on. He was on the news, saying all of these horrible things about my son. I remember feeling so... violated, and thinking that this is never going to end. I can't believe I trusted him and that I forced my son to see him."

"And then?"

She took another deep breath. "I'd brought home a chicken dinner from the restaurant where I work. I thought not having to cook would be a nice surprise and we could just relax before we went home. We all sat down to eat. Kendall was sitting between James and Antonio. James is Brooke's son and always seems to be able to get Kendall to do things he doesn't want to. I think it's a family trait."

Brooke smiled over at her.

"We served dinner, and after a few minutes, Kendall pushed his plate away without having taken a bite. James pushed it back and told him he needed to eat, but Kendall said he didn't want it. Then he started shaking and trying to get up. Antonio asked him what was wrong, and then grabbed him and took him into the living room. James followed and stayed with Kendall, and Antonio said he thought the dinner was another trigger, and then I guess I lost it."

"How so?"

"I remember screaming about his weight and how he won't talk and can't sleep. I remember Katie screaming and hearing Antonio telling me that I need to calm down and t-then..." Jen said as the tears started down her cheeks.

"And then?" Thorne asked gently.

"I-I said I wished he'd just finished the damn assignment, so Deesie wouldn't have taken him. K-Kendall was there and he heard me. Then I don't remember anything."

Jen was sobbing into her hands now. Brooke got up, went, and sat next to Jen on the bed, holding her. "That wasn't w-what I meant t-though."

"What did you mean?" Thorne asked.

"If I h-had been home, D-Deesie couldn't have taken him."

"How do you know that?"

"He w-wouldn't have."

"How do you think you could have stopped him?"

"He wouldn't have tried it if he knew someone was home."

"Jennifer, why do you think that? From what I understand, Stephen Deesie had no problem killing people who were in his way. You would have been in his way, and I don't think he would have hesitated to use you to get to Kendall and then dispose of you."

"Are you saying I couldn't have protected my son from him?"

"I'm saying that he was a very dangerous man who gunned down a park ranger, strangled a man to death, as well as murdering his own brother. From what I understand, he even had control over Antonio at one point, handcuffing him while threatening Kendall, and HE is a trained police officer. So no, I don't think you could have protected your son from him. I think if you and your daughter had been home that night, you would both be dead by now. He fixated on Kendall for some reason, and no one was going to stand in his way."

"But..."

"He was a delusional psychopath, and I can promise you there was no way you could have stopped him that night. Now, I want you to do something for me."

"What?"

"Every time you start feeling that things are hopeless or there's another setback, and there probably will be setbacks, remember the moment with Kendall that made you smile. Hold on to it, and remember that things will get better, but it's going to take some time. Blaming yourself for not being able to protect him is not going to get us anywhere, just as Kendall blaming himself for drawing Deesie's attention isn't going to help him. You are a strong person, and you have a wonderful extended family, so use that and know you can and WILL get through this."

She nodded and gave him a small smile. "I'll try."

"Good. I already spoke with Claudia, and she told me what happened with Kendall last night. While it may not have been the ideal situation, he opened up to her, and that is a huge step forward for him."

"I hope so," Jen said quietly.

"It is," Brooke said.

"There's something else we need to discuss about Graham," Thorne said.

"What?"

He and Brooke looked at each other. "Mrs. Diamond called me to let me know about an article that was in this morning's newspaper."

"What article?"

"The local paper published Graham's interview with a very misleading title. They also published Kendall's name and photo."

"WHAT? How can they do that? Isn't that illegal? Did he see it?" Jen asked, nearing panic.

"Yes, it is illegal, and according to what Mrs. Diamond tells me, they've already been dealt with."

"Kendall doesn't know yet, Antonio's going to tell him a little later. Maybe while Claudia or Sally is visiting today. Kendall knows Graham is a bully, and that's why he didn't get upset about the television interview, so hopefully things will be alright. I have to say, I am very proud of Antonio though," Brooke said.

"Why?" Jen asked.

"He went down to the station and put the fear of God into Graham without breaking any laws. He almost broke his hand, but no laws," Brooke told her.

"How did he almost break his hand?"

"Apparently he punched the wall next to Graham and scared the hell out of him. Graham's own attorney is firing him after the stunts he has pulled. He won't be hurting any more families," Brooke stated.

"He punched the wall?"

"Apparently Sally wants to put a frame around it." Brooke smirked.

Jen put her face in here hands, and for a minute, Dr. Thorne and Brooke thought she was crying.

She looked up a moment later. "I wish I could have seen the look on that man's face!" She laughed.

∞

Sylvia and the boys got back to the house and unloaded the car. Sylvia went in to start lunch, while James and Carlos finished bringing in the grocery bags. Antonio and Jo followed Sylvia into the kitchen.

"So, how's Jen doing this morning?" Antonio asked.

"Better, but the doctor wants to keep her another night. She might be able to come home for Thanksgiving. Dr. Thorne is going to visit her today, so hopefully he will be able to help her deal with all of this. How's Katie doing now?"

"Well, I had a little talk with her, and then she cried on her Papi's shoulder," Jo said, patting Antonio on the back.

"She cried?"

Antonio nodded. "She was worried about my hand, Kendall being sick, and the fact she's mad at her mom. I think she got most of it out, and she's looking forward to going out with Sally for a little while."

"Good. Jen's worried that the kids won't forgive her. I'm glad James and Logan went to see her. They even picked out some flowers to take her," Sylvia said.

"I think they'll be okay. Kendall might still be uncomfortable around her, so we'll have to talk to him about it later," Antonio said.

"I think I'll make him some soup and a half sandwich for lunch. He did really well with the cornmeal porridge this morning. I was so happy when he ate all of it." Sylvia smiled.

∞

They were discussing plans for dinner the next day, when they heard a bloodcurdling scream, followed by a loud thump.

"Kendall..." Antonio said, running towards the stairs.

James and Carlos had been bringing in the last of the bags when they heard their friend scream. They both dropped the bags they had been carrying and ran up the stairs with Antonio right behind them.

James got to the door first and opened it, to find Kendall backed into the corner near the window.

"Kendall, it's okay, buddy," James said softly as he moved slowly towards his friend. Kendall was rocking back and forth, staring at something only he could see.

James reached out and touched Kendall gently on the shoulder. He screamed and lashed out with his hand, barely missing James' face.

"James, get back," Antonio instructed.

James did as he was told, and Antonio knelt down near Kendall. "Mijo, it's alright, you're safe here."

Kendall didn't respond, just kept staring at whatever it was that his mind was showing him. Antonio tried moving a little closer, and Kendall pushed himself back further against the wall.

"It's okay, we can sit here for a while," Antonio said softly.

Kendall started shivering and his breathing picked up. He would open and close his eyes, as if he were trying to clear his vision.

"Kendall..." Antonio said.

"No, no, no," Kendall whispered.

"It's alright, Mijo. Please wake up."

Suddenly, Kendall pushed himself up the wall and backed towards the window.

"Kendall, NO!" Antonio shouted as he grabbed his godson.

"DON'T TOUCH ME!"

Antonio pulled him away from the window, but Kendall swung his free arm out, trying to get away, and his hand went through the windowpane. Antonio pulled him back towards the middle of the room, and Kendall was fighting him the whole way. He managed to slip from Antonio's grasp for a second, but James grabbed ahold of him, wrapping his arms around him.

"NO!" Kendall screamed. "DON'T TOUCH ME! IT HURTS!"

He was still fighting and started kicking out, so Antonio grabbed his legs, trying to pin him down. Kendall continued trying to pull away, screaming at them to let him go.

James was now on the floor and pulled Kendall tightly up against him, and then wrapped his legs around the other boy, holding him firmly in place.

Carlos had run into the bathroom and grabbed some towels, and as soon as he could get ahold of him, grabbed Kendall's hand and applied pressure to the deep gash that ran from under his pinky finger and down to his wrist. Kendall screamed again and tried pulling away, but Carlos held his hand tightly.

∞

Claudia pulled up to the Garcia house and knocked on the door. She could hear something going on inside and the door flew open.

"Claudia... Kendall, second door on the right!" Sylvia said, pointing up the stairs.

Claudia could now hear Kendall screaming at someone to let go of him, and she raced up the stairs. She found the room and quickly took in what she saw.

One boy was holding Kendall tightly against his chest, and Antonio was practically lying across his legs. Another boy was holding Kendall's free arm and pressing towels against his hand. There was blood everywhere, and she could see the shattered window from the door. Kendall was still fighting them, seemingly frantic in his attempts to escape.

She walked over and knelt down next to them. She took Kendall's face in her hands. "Baby, look at me. Everything's gonna be alright, you just need to wake up."

"No, no it hurts," he sobbed, squeezing his eyes shut, trying to make the visions go away.

"Baby, we're gonna make the pain go away, but you need to wake up first. Focus on my voice. Everything's gonna be alright. Just follow my voice and you'll find me."

After a moment, Kendall opened his eyes and tried to focus on Claudia's face.

"There you are." She smiled.

Kendall collapsed against James, his chest heaving from the exertions.

"Okay, everyone's gonna relax their hold, except you, baby," she told Carlos. "You keep that towel pressed tight."

Carlos nodded.

Antonio relaxed his hold on Kendall's legs, and when he stayed still, got up and sat next to him.

"You too, baby," Claudia said to James.

James shook his head. "I'm not letting him go."

"I don't want you to let him go, just ease up a bit."

James relaxed a little and pulled Kendall up a little more, so his head was resting on his shoulder.

"Carlos, let me see how bad it is," Antonio said, taking Kendall's hand. "He's going to need stitches. Carlos, go have Mami get the car."

"I can drive you, my car is in your driveway," Claudia said.

Antonio nodded and went to pick up Kendall.

"I've got him," James told him.

"James..."

"Your hand is hurt, and he's not going anywhere without me," James said, pulling Kendall up further so he could stand.

"Alright," Antonio said and helped steady Kendall until James was standing. They went downstairs and Antonio grabbed the boys' jackets, and they headed out the door.

Sylvia followed them. "What happened?"

"His hand went through the window, and he might need stitches. I'll tell you everything when we get back. Make sure the kids are alright," Antonio said, helping James into Claudia's car.

Sylvia nodded and put her arm around Carlos, who had followed her outside. Carlos hugged her around the waist and watched as the car drove away. Sylvia and Carlos went back inside. Logan was sitting next to Katie with his arm around her. Joanna was standing behind them. Sylvia looked at them all and made a decision.

"Alright, boots and coats everyone."

"Why?" Carlos asked.

"We're going out for lunch, and then to do something fun. Whether it's a movie, the mall, whatever, we need to get out."

"But Kendall..." Katie said.

"Is going to be at the emergency room for a while getting stitches. I'll call Papi and tell him to call my cell."

"Sally?" Logan said.

"I'll call Sally and have her meet us."

"Mami, the window..."

"Close the bedroom door tightly. We'll worry about it later," she said, kissing his cheek.

"I can't get around too quickly," Logan said.

"Then we'll walk slowly or rent you a scooter. Now, no more arguments. Get ready to go."

They all did as Sylvia told them, and a few minutes later, were heading to the mall.

"A scooter would be fun," Carlos told Logan as they drove to the mall.

"If you're forty," Logan snorted.

His mom looked back at him. "Forty?"

"Uh, ummm fifty?"

"We could just lock him in the trunk," Jo told Sylvia.

"True." She smiled.

"Hey!" Logan said.

"Could we still rent a scooter?" Carlos asked.

∞

Claudia pulled into the emergency room parking lot, and she and Antonio got out. Antonio opened James' door. "Let me take him now."

James nodded and let Antonio take Kendall from him. They went inside and were led into a small room to wait. Claudia went out to make sure they pulled Kendall's previous file so the doctor was aware of his condition.

A few minutes later, a nurse came in to clean and evaluate the wound. "Looks like we're definitely going to need stitches. The doctor will be here in just a few minutes," she told them.

"Thank you," Antonio said.

"What happened?" Claudia asked once the nurse left.

"I'm not sure. He was sleeping soundly when I checked on him earlier. A little while later, we heard a scream, and it sounded like he hit the floor. When we got there, he was crouched in the corner as if he was trying to hide, and wouldn't respond to any of us. If we went near him, he would panic and scream. At one point, he stood up and was pushing himself against the window. I was afraid he was going to go right through it, so I grabbed him, and his hand went through the glass," Antonio told her.

"Who's hurting him?" James asked quietly.

"What's that?" Claudia asked.

"He kept saying it hurts. Is it Deesie?"

"I don't know, baby. Hopefully he can tell us when he's feeling a little better," Claudia said.

"He kept looking through us, like he was watching something else," James said.

"It could have been a flashback," Claudia said.

"Meaning he's remembering something that really happened?" James asked.

"It might be."

"So not fair," James said.

"No it's not, but he's lucky, because he has all of you here for him. That's more than a lot of people have," Claudia said, taking his hand.

The doctor came in and looked at Kendall's hand. He injected some lidocaine to numb the area, and Kendall started pulling away and began to hyperventilate.

"You're probably going to have to give him a mild sedative," Claudia told him.

"I was hoping we could get by without having to do that, but..." he said and called for the nurse. He ordered a half dose of Torbugesic. After he gave Kendall the injection, he said he would return in a few minutes.

A couple of minutes later, Kendall relaxed and closed his eyes.

"Come on, let's get you cleaned up a little and I'll buy you a soda," Claudia said to James, pulling him towards the door.

"I'm staying."

"Just for a few minutes. You don't want him waking up and seeing blood all over your face, do you?"

"I have blood on my face?"

She nodded, "And in your hair."

"Okay, blood is NOT a good look on me," he said.

"Oh, I don't know, kinda brings out the amber highlights in your eyes," Claudia teased as they went out the door.

Antonio's phone vibrated and he looked at it. "Hi honey."

"I just wanted to let you know that we decided to get the kids out of the house for a while. We're on our way to the mall, Sally's going to meet us there," Sylvia told him.

"Good idea. I'll fix the window after we get back."

"How are the boys?" she asked.

The doctor came back in and Antonio nodded at him. "The doctor's here to stitch up Kendall's hand now and Claudia's distracting James for a few minutes."

"Okay, let me know when you're home. We might see a movie if the kids want, so we won't be back until later."

"Take your time, honey. Tell the kids that Kendall is doing alright. Claudia thinks he was having a flashback and that's why he wasn't responding this time."

"Is that worse than a nightmare?" she asked.

"I'm not sure if it's worse, but it means he was seeing something that actually happened, and he was scared."

"I'm so glad Claudia showed up when she did," Sylvia said.

"So am I. I don't know how long it would have taken for him to come around otherwise. Honey, you all try to have a good time. Tell the kids we'll see them when you get home."

"Will do."

Claudia and James returned about twenty minutes later. James had cleaned the blood from his face and hair and as much as he could from his shirt.

Claudia was carrying two cups and handed one to Antonio. "Coffee, black."

"Thank you." He smiled.

"How many stitches?" James asked.

"Twelve. The cut was deeper on his wrist, so most of them are there. The doctor said it's okay to stay here until he wakes up."

"Are you going to tell Mama K?" James asked.

"Yeah, we need to. The question is, when?" Antonio said.

"No sense in putting it off. Isn't she here?" Claudia asked.

"Yeah, she is. I'm worried she'll want to come down and see him, and I really don't think he's ready for that."

"Then tell her that. You and James go on up, and I'll sit here with Kendall."

Antonio nodded. "Let's go see Jen."

"Okay, but you might want to stop and clean up a little first," James said, pointing to his hands and face.

"Good idea," Antonio said.

They left and Claudia sat in the chair next to Kendall. She got up a few minutes later, took a couple of paper towels from the dispenser, and soaked them in warm water. She gently cleaned the blood from Kendall's face and other hand.

He stirred a little, so she sat back down next to him. She stroked his hair and he slowly opened his eyes.

"Hi baby." She smiled.

"Hmm?"

"Don't move around too much right now. We had to bring you to the emergency room, because you cut your hand and the doctor had to give you a little something for it."

"Okay," Kendall mumbled. He shivered and curled up, so she pulled a blanket up over him.

"Do you remember what happened?"

Kendall didn't say anything, and then gave her a small nod.

"You know it's not your fault?"

He shrugged.

"Can you tell me what you were remembering?"

He stayed still, trying to remember, and then started shaking.

"What is it, baby?"

"We w-were in the t-tent."

"We? You mean you and Deesie?"

He nodded.

"Okay."

"He w-wouldn't s-stop."

"Stop what?"

"Touching m-me."

Claudia went over his file in her mind and recalled the statement sheet.

"Is that when he...?"

Kendall nodded.

"He wouldn't s-stop, and t-then he hurt m-me."

"You mean when he tied you to the tree?"

Kendall curled up tighter and shook his head.

"Baby, tell me what happened."

"He was m-mad because I h-hit him. He s-said I was p-pissing him off and t-there were things h-he could d-do to me that I wouldn't e-enjoy. Then he s-started... he w-wouldn't g-get off, and I couldn't b-breathe."

"Okay baby, just take a deep breath."

Kendall closed his eyes and tried to calm himself.

"Can you tell me what else happened?" Claudia asked softly.

"W-When he was... d-doing that, h-he p-put..." Kendall stammered.

Claudia's heart sank. "Baby, look at me. The doctor said that there were no signs of Deesie... going all the way. Is that true?"

Kendall nodded.

"Did he use something else?"

Kendall nodded again.

Claudia took a deep breath. "Okay baby, what did he use?"

"His f-fingers. It hurt so m-much, he w-wouldn't s-stop. I f-felt so d-dirty, I j-just wanted h-him to leave m-me alone!" Kendall sobbed.

"Oh baby, I'm so sorry," Claudia said, sitting next to him and pulling his head onto her lap. "You know we need to tell Antonio, right?"

He nodded.

"It's going to be alright," she said as she sat there holding him.

∞

Antonio and James returned about a half an hour later. Jen had been surprised to see them and taken the news about the stitches fairly well. She had asked Antonio to let Kendall know that she loved him and understood if he wasn't ready to see her yet.

"What happened?" Antonio asked, noticing the tear stains on Claudia's face.

She put her finger to her lips and carefully got up, so as not to disturb Kendall. "James, go sit with him."

"Okay," he said, giving Antonio a concerned look.

Claudia pulled Antonio out into the hallway and explained to him what Kendall had told her. He nodded and then sat down quickly. Claudia sat next to him and rubbed his back. "It's good he told us, because now we know what it is he's been repressing, and now he can start to heal."

Antonio nodded. "That son of a bitch. If he wasn't already dead, I would castrate him."

"I know, but remember, this wasn't easy for Kendall, and he's going to need you now more than ever. I told him that I needed to tell you and he agreed, but I don't think telling the other children is a good idea."

Antonio nodded. "We should get him home now."

She smiled. "He's pretty tired, but don't let him shut anyone out. I think someone should probably be with him at all times for now."

"That won't be a problem."

"I know it won't."

Antonio took a deep breath and stood up. "Okay, now we know what we're dealing with, and now we have you."

"That's a fact." She smiled.

They went back into the room and found James sitting on the bed next to Kendall. "Is everything alright?" James asked.

"Everything's fine, I just had a moment," Claudia told him.

"Okay," James said dubiously.

Antonio went over and carefully touched Kendall's shoulder. "Mijo, are you ready to go home?"

"Hmm?"

"Do you want to go home?"

Kendall nodded. James grabbed his jacket and helped him get it on.

"We forgot shoes, so..." Antonio said, picking Kendall up.

They got out to the car and Kendall sat in the back with James. He was starting to fall asleep again, as they reached the house, so once inside he went and laid on the couch. James went in and sat next to him watching TV, while Antonio and Claudia talked in the kitchen.

"So what do we do?" he asked.

"Just treat him normally. If he wants to talk, he will, but don't be surprised if he doesn't. He knows you know, and that might be enough for him right now. He knows you understand

these things and he trusts you. He knows if he needs you, you'll be there and won't judge him, and that is huge for him."

"Okay," Antonio said.

"I'll continue trying to draw him out more, but I think he's going to be alright. Think about how far he's come in just the last two days. It's not the most conventional way to do things, but it's worked for him. There's still a long way to go, but he took some pretty big steps forward."

"Yeah, he really did," Antonio agreed. "Would you like to stay for lunch? Nothing fancy, but I make a good sandwich."

"I love a good sandwich." She smiled.

A few minutes later, Antonio took a tray with soup and sandwiches into the living room. James woke Kendall and helped him sit up. "Here," James said, holding a glass of milk for him.

"Thanks," Kendall said, taking it with shaky hands. James steadied the glass while Kendall drank, and then set it back down on the tray. The soup was still hot, so James handed Kendall half a sandwich. There was a hockey game on, so they all watched while they ate.

Once they had finished, Antonio took the tray back into the kitchen. He came back out. "I'm going to go and replace the window pane."

"You want me to stay while you get glass?" Claudia asked.

"I already have a good supply in the basement. We learned when Carlos was younger, to stock up on things like window panes, door fixtures, railings, and band aids," he said, laughing.

"Do you need help?" James asked.

"No, it'll only take a few minutes, but thanks. Just relax and finish watching the game."

"Okay." James smiled.

Antonio went up and had the window repaired in less than twenty minutes. He grabbed the basket with cleaners, scrubbed the blood from the wall and floor, and pulled off the bedding.

Forty-five minutes later, the room looked as good as new, and he went back downstairs. He was surprised to see Kendall was still awake, although he was leaning against James. He saw Claudia watching them, smiling.

She followed him out into the kitchen still smiling.

"What?" he asked her.

"Sally's told me quite a bit about the kids and your families. Are they all still like that?"

"Pretty much." He nodded.

"That is a refreshing sight in this day and age. Too many kids grow up too fast and lose the opportunity just to be close to someone. Too many stigmas in society these days, discouraging such things."

Antonio nodded. "We want our kids to enjoy their childhoods and not be afraid to show affection to the people they love."

"Well, you've all done a fantastic job of that."

"Thanks," he said, a flash of sadness crossing his face.

"What?" she asked.

"Hmm?"

"That sad little look you just had," she said.

He sighed. "I'm just worried that their childhoods may have been cut short by all of this."

"I wouldn't worry too much about that."

"Why not?"

"Just look at them. Has anything changed in the way they act towards each other?"

"No."

"No, in fact, it may have made their bonds even stronger. They may have grown up a little, but they're still the same kids they were a month ago."

"I hope so."

She looked at him. "Was Kendall the most responsible one a month ago?"

"Yes."

"Was James the most protective one?"

"Yes."

"Logan the smartest? Carlos the sweetest? Katie a business mastermind?"

"Yes, but..."

"No buts. They may have had to face some grownup issues, but they are still the same wonderful kids they were before. They haven't lost themselves or each other, and that's what's important."

He smiled. "You're right."

"Of course I am. Do you know how much time would be saved if people just realized that from the beginning?"

He laughed and held up his hands. "Alright, I'm completely convinced."

"Well good, then we won't need to have this talk again." She smirked.

"No ma'am, we won't," he promised.

∞

The others got home at about five. Claudia had left around four, and Antonio and the boys were watching another game. Antonio heard the car pull up and opened the door for them.

"Papi!" Carlos said, throwing himself at his father.

"How's my boy? Did you have fun?"

Carlos nodded. "We played at the arcade, and Katie and Sally went shopping for girly things. Then we went and saw the James Bond movie."

"Again?" he asked.

"Papi, it's James Bond," Carlos stated, as if it were the most obvious thing in the world.

"Besides, Mami hadn't seen it yet," Sylvia said, kissing him as she walked in carrying pizza boxes.

Logan sat down next to Kendall. "How's your hand?"

"It's okay, just a couple of stitches."

Katie jumped on James' lap and hugged him and then Kendall. "Katie, next time WARN someone before you do that," James said in a pained voice.

"Sorry."

Antonio followed Sylvia into the dining room. "Too tired to cook?"

She just smiled and set the boxes on the table. "How's he doing?" she asked quietly.

"Much better. I'll tell you everything later," he said, getting some plates.

She nodded. "Alright, I worked hard making this wonderful dinner, so come and get it!"

They all went and sat down, Kendall sitting between James and Antonio again. Carlos and Logan were arguing about Carlos' decision to become a super spy, and Antonio was happy to see Kendall smiling at them.

Kendall managed to eat a slice of pizza and some of the salad, so James let him up.

The boys and Katie went back into the living room and found the Charlie Brown Thanksgiving special on. About halfway through it, there was a knock at the door.

Carlos started to jump up to get it, but Kendall stopped him.

"Logan, can you get the door?"

"Me? Why me?"

"Because I need you to get the door," Kendall said.

"You do realize that I'm the ONLY one here who has to use crutches, right?"

"Logan, just answer the door."

There was another knock, and Antonio came out to answer it.

"NO! Logan needs to answer it," Kendall insisted.

Antonio looked at him questioningly. Kendall just shook his head at him.

"FINE! Logan is answering the door," Logan grumbled. He hobbled over to the door and there was another knock. "I'm coming!" he yelled.

"I need new friends," he muttered under his breath.

"What have you done?" James whispered.

Kendall just shook his head, biting his lower lip.

Logan balanced on one foot as he unlocked the door. "Are you happy?" he asked as he opened it.

"I know I am," someone said in a soft southern drawl.

"D-Dad?" Logan stammered.

Chapter 101~ Alexander Mitchell

Logan stood there for a minute. "W-What are you doing here?" he asked in shock.

"Right now, freezing. So how about letting me in? It's a little colder here than it is in Austin," Alex said, grinning.

Logan stood there for a second and then stepped back so his dad could come in. "Don't I get a hug?" Alex asked, holding his arms open wide.

Logan stood there quietly for a moment and then launched himself into his father's arms. "Dad! How... When did you decide to come up? I missed you so much!"

Alex smiled, his brown eyes sparkling as he hugged Logan tightly. "I missed you too. So what's up with the crutches, Hopalong?"

"I sprained my ankle in hockey practice."

"Hello Alex, this is a lovely surprise," Jo said, kissing his cheek.

"Well, it is Thanksgiving and I figured since what I'm most thankful for is here, this is where I should be."

"How long are you staying, and when did you grow a beard and mustache?" Logan asked.

"I have a flight out on Sunday, and about four months ago. Got a little lazy around branding time."

"Papa M!" Carlos said, hugging him and Logan at the same time.

"Carlos, how's my favourite superhero?"

"Good!"

"Alex, it's been a while," Antonio said, shaking his friend's hand.

"Too long," Sylvia said, kissing his cheek.

"Yes it has," Alex said, kissing Sylvia back.

James got up and went over. "James! Looking as good as ever. You must have grown a good four inches since last year."

"Five and a half. We're so glad you're here," he said, hugging Alex.

Katie ran up and hugged him next. Alex picked her up. "Little Darlin', you're getting so big! Still taking care of business?"

"Of course!"

Antonio looked over and saw Kendall sitting there watching and went over to him. "Are you going to say, hi?"

He nodded and got up. Feeling a bit self-conscious, he stayed close to Antonio.

Alex smiled at him. "How's my favourite future center for the Wild's?"

"Good." Kendall smiled.

Alex walked over, his arm supporting Logan's weight, and pulled Kendall into a hug. "You doing okay?"

Kendall nodded and hugged him back.

"Have you eaten?" Sylvia asked.

"Just airline food, so no," Alex said.

"How about some pizza?"

"Sounds great!" he said, following her and Jo out into the kitchen. Logan followed them, grinning from ear to ear. Everyone else turned and looked at Kendall.

"What?"

"How did you know it was Alex at the door?" Antonio asked.

"I saw him through the window," Kendall told him, pointing to the big bay window with the sheer drapes.

Antonio walked over to the couch and looked out the window. "I suppose that's a possibility, but I have a feeling that's not the whole story," he whispered to Kendall as he walked past him and out into the kitchen.

Logan sat next to his dad as he ate. "So you get to stay until Sunday?"

"Yup, flight leaves at four in the afternoon, so we'll have the morning."

"Where are you staying?" Antonio asked.

"I made reservations at the River Inn."

"Nonsense, you can stay at the house," Joanna said.

Alex smiled at her. "Thanks Jo."

Logan's face fell a little.

"Or, you could stay here and spend some time with the boys," Antonio suggested, noticing the sad look on Logan's face.

Logan smiled and nodded.

"Yes, the boys can stay in the upstairs guest room, Katie can have Carlos' room, and you can have the guest room down here," Sylvia said.

"You sure about that?"

"Absolutely. Jen is going to stay with Brooke for a couple of days after she gets out of the hospital," Sylvia told him.

"How's Jen doing?"

"Better today. I spoke with Brooke earlier, and she thinks the doctor will release her tomorrow," Jo said.

"Which reminds me, we need to talk to Kendall about this," Antonio said, getting up.

"About what?" Alex asked.

"You want to fill him in while I talk to Kendall?" Antonio asked Sylvia.

She nodded. "Well, it's been a long week..." she started.

∞

Antonio went into the living room and sat on the table in front of the couch. "Kendall, I need to talk to you about your mom."

Kendall looked down. "What about her?"

James tapped Carlos on the shoulder. "Let's go see Papa M."

Carlos nodded and followed James into the kitchen.

"Well, they're probably going to release her from the hospital tomorrow and she's planning on staying with Mama D for a couple of days. But tomorrow is Thanksgiving, and I wanted to ask if you felt comfortable having her here for dinner. If not, it's perfectly alright, because Mama D has already made reservations downtown."

"But that means James wouldn't get to see his mom."

"No it doesn't. She plans on stopping by either way."

"I miss my mom, but I don't know how I feel about anything right now," Kendall said.

Antonio sat down and put his arm around him. "There is NO pressure either way. Your mom wants you to feel safe. She's the one who suggested that she should stay away for a few days to give you some time. I don't want you to feel guilty either way."

"I guess it's not like we'll be alone together, everyone will be here, and she hasn't seen Papa M in a long time either."

"True."

Kendall looked at his sister. "Katie, what do you think?"

Katie sat next to him and hugged him. "I was really mad at her, but Sally said mom was just confused and didn't know what she was saying, and it is Thanksgiving."

Kendall smiled. "Okay, I think we can handle it."

"Are you sure?" Antonio asked.

Kendall nodded.

"Okay, we'll let Brooke know when she stops by tonight."

Antonio went back into the kitchen. "Okay, two more for dinner!" He smiled.

"Really?" Sylvia asked.

Antonio nodded. "I think it'll be alright. He's nervous, but there will be enough going on to keep him distracted. We'll just make sure to keep a close eye on him for any signs of a panic attack."

"Has he had many of those?" Alex asked.

Antonio nodded. "Quite a few, plus a few nightmares, and today a flashback."

"I'm going to go watch TV with Kendall," Carlos said, getting up. James nodded and followed him.

"Why don't you go with the other boys? I want to talk to your mom and Mama and Papa G for a few minutes," Alex said, hugging Logan.

"Okay," Logan said, getting up. Alex smiled as he watched his son leave the room.

"So, why did you decide to fly up here?" Jo asked.

"I told you why." Alex smiled.

"Yes, now how about telling us the rest of the story."

"What makes you think there's more?"

She just looked at him. "Really?"

"I could never hide anything from you." Alex laughed.

"And things haven't changed." She smiled.

"Let's just say I got a call from a little bird Sunday afternoon," he said.

"Does that little bird's name start with a K?" Antonio asked.

"A solemn vow prevents me from saying little bird's true name," Alex said, nodding.

"Well, it was a wonderful surprise," Jo said, squeezing his hand.

∞

Carlos put in a movie and the kids were all sitting around watching it.

Kendall started feeling chilled. "I think I'm going to go take a shower," he said, getting up.

"You need something on your hand. You can't get the stitches wet. I have some non-latex disposable gloves in my bag," Logan said.

"Dude, why do you have disposable gloves packed in your bag?" James asked.

"Because you never know when you might need them, especially around the three of you," Logan said defensively.

Kendall smiled and shook his head. "Where are they?"

"I'll get them," Logan said, starting to get up.

"Just tell me where they are, I can get them."

"I don't mind, and this way I can rewrap your hand if needed," Logan told him.

"Okay, come along... Hopalong." Kendall smirked.

"Hey, don't call me that!"

"Why? It's cute!" Carlos said.

"It is not cute!" Logan told him.

"Sure it is. Maybe not as cute as Logie-Bear, but it's still cute," James said.

Logan hobbled over to the stairs. "I need NEW friends!"

"But Hopalong... WE love you," Kendall said, walking behind his friend.

"I should just fall on you," Logan mumbled as he went slowly up the stairs.

Logan found a glove for Kendall and helped him put it on. "There, that should keep it dry." Logan smiled.

"Thanks Loges," Kendall said as he took off the stabilizer.

Logan just looked at him.

"What?" Kendall asked, suddenly worried.

Logan threw his arms around Kendall, careful not squeeze too tightly. "I know you had something to do with my dad coming for Thanksgiving. Thank you so much," he said, his voice muffled by Kendall's shirt.

Kendall hugged him back. "You shouldn't have to choose."

Logan pulled away a little. "I WANTED to stay."

"I know, but you miss your dad and you don't get to see him very much."

Logan smiled. "Well, he's here now, and I get to spend Thanksgiving with my dad and my best friends."

"Yes you do." Kendall smiled. "I'm going to jump in the shower. I'm kinda cold and tired."

"Are you feeling okay? Be honest."

"Just kinda achy, and I have a little headache, that's all."

Logan put his hand on Kendall's forehead. "You're not warm, so that's good. I'll get something from Papi for your head."

"Thanks Loges," Kendall said as he went into the bathroom.

Kendall turned on the water and let it warm up. He undressed and stepped in and let the warm water flow over his tired and aching body. After a few moments, he lathered up his hair and realized how much his hand was throbbing. "Great... no working hands."

He stood under the water with his eyes closed and let it rinse the shampoo from his hair.

"Are you done in there, or do you need help drying off?"

Kendall's eyes snapped open. "What?"

"I asked if you're alright," Antonio said from the hallway.

"Yeah, s-sorry. I'll be out in a minute." Kendall got out and dried off. He pulled on his boxers and flannel pajama bottoms and then pulled on the button down top, but he had difficulty fastening all of them. He sighed wearily and opened the door.

"Are you okay? Logan said you have a headache."

"Just a little one," Kendall said.

"Take this then," Antonio said, handing him one of his pain pills.

"Thanks," Kendall said as he swallowed it.

"You look tired, Mijo," Antonio said as finished buttoning the top.

"I am."

"Let's get you into bed then," Antonio said.

Kendall nodded and went into the guest room.

"Where's your stabilizer?"

"Um, Carlos' bed." Kendall yawned.

Antonio went into the other room and grabbed it from the bed. He helped Kendall put it on and then tucked the blankets in around him. He sat next to him on the bed. "The other boys will be up soon, but I'm going to stay here with you for a while."

"Okay," Kendall said as he closed his eyes.

Antonio sat back against the headboard and smiled when Kendall rolled over and hugged him. He wrapped his arms around him and sat there with him until the other boys came up for the night.

"Is he okay?" James asked.

"He's fine, just worn out. He was supposed to stay in bed today, but that didn't happen. So tomorrow, I want him taking it easy. I'd like for one of us to be with him at all times," Antonio said.

"Not a problem!" Carlos said, hugging his dad.

"Because of Mama K?" Logan asked.

"Just... because," Antonio said.

They all nodded.

"Okay, who's sleeping up here?" Antonio asked, getting up.

"Logan," James and Carlos both said.

"I can sleep on the floor, my ankle is better," Logan told them.

James pointed at the bed. "Go."

"Fine," Logan said, making his way to the bed.

Antonio took his crutches and leaned them on the wall next to the bed within easy reach. He put a pillow under Logan's leg and then tucked him in.

"Thanks Papa G."

"You're welcome, Logan. You boys get some sleep. Tomorrow's going to be a busy day."

"Night Papi," Carlos said.

"Goodnight Carlitos, goodnight James."

"Night Papi." James smiled as he laid down next to the bed on Kendall's side.

Antonio turned out the light and closed the door.

∞

Downstairs, Sylvia had started making pies for dinner the next day while they all caught up.

There was a knock on the door and Antonio answered. "Hey Brooke, is everything alright?"

"Yes, I just wanted to stop by to kiss James goodnight after I got Jen settled in."

"The boys just turned in for the night. How's Jen doing?"

"Much better. I'm so glad Kendall wants her here for Thanksgiving."

"We need to take it slowly though," Antonio cautioned.

"I know, and I already told her that if he starts feeling uncomfortable, we're leaving."

"I think he'll be okay," Antonio said.

"Good," Brooke said as she went upstairs.

∞

Brooke knocked on the bedroom door. "Come in," James said.

She opened the door. "Mom, what are you doing here?" James asked, getting up.

"I promised you that I was going to see you every day, and I'm running a little late because they released Jen this evening. How are you, darling?" She smiled.

James hugged her. "Fine, but I saw you at the hospital, so I didn't think you'd come tonight."

"That didn't count," she said, kissing his cheek.

"How are the rest of my boys doing?" she asked as she bent down and kissed Carlos on the forehead.

"Good! Did you know Papa M is here?"

"Alex is here?"

Logan nodded as Brooke bent down and kissed him. "He decided to spend Thanksgiving here since I wasn't going down there."

"What a wonderful surprise!"

"It really is," Logan smiled.

"How's Kendall doing tonight?" she asked as she kissed the sleeping boy on the cheek.

"He's tired and had a headache, so Papa G gave him a pain pill," James told her.

"Poor baby. Well, you all get some sleep, and I'll see you tomorrow."

"Okay." James smiled as he walked her to the door.

"Mom?"

"Yes dear?" Brooke said, turning to look back.

"Goodnight and thanks for coming, it was a great surprise." James smiled.

"Goodnight darling." She smiled softly.

She went downstairs and went into the kitchen. "Alex! The boys told me you were here," Brooke said, hugging him.

"Hello Brooke. How are you? You're looking as amazing as always."

"Why thank you. I'm doing well. I need to get back to Jen, but wanted to say hello. I guess we'll see you tomorrow."

"Alright, you give Jen a hug for me," Alex said, giving her a kiss on the cheek.

"I will. We will see you all tomorrow. Antonio, give me a call if anything changes. I'm not going to cancel our reservations until I'm sure everything is a go."

"I will, honey," he said, walking her to the door.

Alex yawned. "Well, I think I'm going to go check on the boys and turn in," he said, getting up.

Joanna kissed him on the cheek. "I suppose I should head out myself. I'm glad you're here. It means a lot to Logan."

He smiled. "I can't think of anyplace I'd rather be."

He walked her to her car and then went upstairs. He looked in Carlos' room and saw Katie playing her handheld video game. "Hey there, little Darlin', shouldn't you be putting away your game and getting some sleep? Busy day tomorrow."

"Okay Papa M." She smiled and turned it off and set it on the night table.

He sat next to her as she snuggled in. "You doing okay?"

She nodded. "It's hard sometimes, but I think it's getting better."

"It's going to keep getting better."

"How do you know?"

"Because I know you're all strong, and together you can do anything."

"You're pretty smart for a grown-up." She smirked.

"Why thank you. I consider that a high compliment coming from you," he said, kissing her on the forehead. "Now go to sleep."

"Goodnight Papa M."

"Goodnight Darlin'. Door open or closed?" he asked as he went out into the hall.

"Open, in case Kendall needs something."

"Open it is." He smiled.

Alex knocked on the other door. "Come in," James said.

"I just wanted to say goodnight."

"Night dad!" Logan said.

Alex went over and sat next to Logan. "Goodnight son."

"I'm so glad you're here," Logan said, hugging his dad.

"So am I," Alex said, holding Logan tightly. "What do you say we do something while I'm here? Just you and me, doesn't have to be anything big."

"Really?" Logan smiled.

"Really."

"I'd love that."

"So would I. Now, I've been up since four this morning, so I'm going to hit the hay."

"Okay, night dad," Logan said, grinning.

"I love you, Logan," Alex said softly, hugging his son once more.

"I love you too."

Alex reached over and brushed the hair away from Kendall's eyes. "Alright, get some sleep now," he said, standing up.

He reached down and ruffled Carlos' hair. "Night, Trouble."

Carlos giggled. "Night Papa M."

"Night James," Alex said, patting him on the shoulder.

"Goodnight Papa M."

"I am so proud of all you boys," he said as he closed the door.

Logan smiled and looked over at his sleeping friend. He pulled Kendall over so that his head was resting on his chest. "Thank you," he whispered.

Chapter 102~ Thanksgiving

Kendall woke up at about one, feeling thirsty. He wiggled free from Logan and carefully stepped over James.

"Kendall, where are you going?" James asked.

"Sorry, I didn't mean to wake you. I was just going to get something to drink."

"You go back to bed and I'll get you some water," James said.

"I was going to get a glass of milk, and I can do that on my own," Kendall told him.

James sighed. "Fine, but if you're not back in ten minutes, I'm coming down."

Kendall rolled his eyes. "Okay, ten minutes."

He went down into the kitchen and pulled a glass from the cupboard. He got the milk from the refrigerator and went to pour it into the glass, but his hand wasn't steady enough and he ended up spilling most of it onto the counter.

"Great, I can't even get a glass of milk by myself," he muttered. He grabbed a sponge to sop up the mess, when the kitchen light came on and Kendall jumped.

"It's just me. Everything okay in here?" Alex asked.

"Sorry, I didn't mean to wake you up. I just wanted some milk, but apparently I can't even do that on my own," Kendall said as he finished cleaning up the milk.

Alex smiled and grabbed another glass from the cupboard, and then took the container, pouring a glass for Kendall and himself. He set the glasses on the table, pulled out a chair, and sat in another.

"Here you go."

"Thank you," Kendall said, sitting down.

"Hmmm," Alex said looking around.

"What?"

"Seems kinda silly to waste a perfectly good excuse to have cookies. I mean, why else have milk?" Alex said, getting up and grabbing the cookie jar from the counter. He set it on the table, took off the lid, and looked inside. "Chocolate chip!" He smiled, pulling out two and handing one to Kendall.

Kendall shook his head. "I'm not really hungry, thanks."

"The whole point of eating cookies isn't to eat them because you're hungry. You eat them because they're good and they're there. These are homemade, so even better," he said, still holding the cookie out towards him.

Kendall smiled and took the cookie, nibbling on it a little.

"You're gonna have to do better than that or I'll have the entire jar empty before you finish that one," Alex said as he took a second cookie.

Kendall dunked the cookie in his milk and took a bite.

"I want to thank you for calling and letting me know what was going on. I think Logan was pretty surprised," Alex said.

"He was so happy when he saw you." Kendall smiled.

"And so FRUSTRATED." Alex chuckled.

"He really was... 'Fine! Logan is answering the door!'... and grouching under his breath the whole way," Kendall said, shaking his head as he imitated Logan.

Alex laughed at him.

"He really misses you."

"I really miss him, too. I miss everyone," Alex said, smiling sadly.

"I wish you could move back."

"So do I, but unless one of my brothers or sisters takes over, I'm afraid I'll be living in Texas for a while. My parents just can't do it on their own anymore."

"Families are hard sometimes," Kendall said quietly as he picked at his cookie.

Alex watched him for a moment. "Yes they are. I'll tell you a secret though, but you have to promise not to say anything to anyone."

Kendall looked at him curiously. "I promise."

"My older brother, Sam, is thinking of retiring early and maybe moving back home in year or two. If he does, it means I can take some time away from the ranch and spend more time up here. Don't tell Logan though, I don't want to get his hopes up in case it doesn't happen."

"Really? That would be amazing!" Kendall smiled.

Alex smiled back at him. "Yes it would."

∞

James woke with a start and looked around. Kendall was not back in bed. He went down half an hour ago, James thought as he jumped up. He checked the bathroom and peeked into Carlos' room, and not seeing his friend, went downstairs. The kitchen light was on and he heard voices. He went in and found Kendall and Alex sitting at the table.

Alex looked over. "James, milk and cookies?"

James sighed in relief. "Do you KNOW what time it is? You were only going to be gone a few minutes," James said to Kendall.

"Sorry, I spilled the milk and woke up Papa M."

"James, calm down and have a cookie." Alex smiled.

"No thanks, I don't want a cookie. Kendall, you... Is that chocolate chip?" James asked, eyeing the cookie that Alex held out.

"Homemade."

James took the cookie and sat down. "You're still in trouble," he said to Kendall as he took a bite.

"James, I'm really sorry. We just started talking and I forgot about the time."

James looked at him. "It's okay, I'm just glad you're alright. Guess I kind of panicked."

Kendall smiled sadly. "Sorry."

Alex watched the two of them. "Alright, we have an important decision to make."

"What?" James asked.

"Should we finish off these wonderful cookies, which I haven't had in a really long time, or leave a few for everyone else?"

"I guess we should leave a few," Kendall said.

"Did I mention I haven't had these in a really, REALLY long time?"

James and Kendall smiled at him and each took another cookie. Fifteen minutes later, the cookie jar was empty and James put the dishes into the dishwasher as Alex wiped the table off.

"Alright you two, back to bed. I'll see you in the morning," Alex said, giving them each a hug.

The boys nodded and headed back upstairs. They got back to the bedroom and found Logan stretched out across the bed. "How does such a little guy take up so much room?" James asked.

Kendall just shook his head, and instead of waking Logan, curled up on the floor between James and Carlos. James pulled an extra blanket out and covered Kendall, who was already falling asleep.

∞

Carlos was the first of the boys to wake up, and was surprised to see Kendall curled up next to him. He got up carefully and headed downstairs. He found his parents, along with Jo and Alex, already in the kitchen.

"Happy Thanksgiving!" he said cheerfully.

"You're up early," Antonio said as Carlos hugged him.

"What's for breakfast?"

"Cornmeal porridge and toast," Sylvia said, kissing him on the cheek.

"Aww, but pancakes would taste SO much better," Carlos said sweetly.

"Well, I could make you pancakes instead of your favourite pies, homemade rolls, stuffing..." Sylvia said.

"Porridge sounds good," Carlos said quickly.

"That's what I thought," she said as she handed him a bowl of the hot cereal.

Katie wandered down a little while later and sat next to Carlos.

"Did you sleep well, Mija?" Antonio asked.

She nodded.

"What's the matter, honey?" Joanna asked.

"Nothing," she said.

"Katie..." Antonio said.

"I'm just hoping everything goes okay today," she said quietly.

"I don't want you worrying about that. Today's going to be a wonderful day with lots of good food and everyone we love here," Antonio told her.

"I just don't want..."

Antonio picked her up and sat her on his lap. "Nothing's going to happen. We are going to keep a close eye on everything. Your mom is feeling better. They even released her early. Kendall is going to be fine because one of us is going to be with him all the time to make sure of it. Okay?"

Katie nodded and smiled. "Okay."

"That's my girl. Now eat your breakfast while I go wake up your brothers."

She nodded and sat back down next to Carlos, who put his arm around her.

∞

Logan woke up and realized he was alone in the bed. He looked around and saw Kendall sleeping on the floor, curled up next to James. He crawled off the bed and shook James. "Hey, what's Kendall doing down here?"

James yawned. "He got up to get something to drink, and when we got back, you were stretched out and looked comfortable, and he didn't want to wake you up."

"We should get him back up on the bed. The floor isn't a good place for him."

James nodded. "Kendall, wake up."

"Hmmm?"

"You need to get back into bed," James told him.

Kendall opened his eyes and yawned. "What?"

"Back on the bed," Logan told him.

Kendall nodded and groaned when he tried to get up.

"You should have woken me," Logan said.

"I'm fine," Kendall told him as James helped him up.

Logan just looked at him.

"What?" Kendall asked.

Antonio came in. "I was just going to wake you boys. Breakfast is ready."

James handed Logan his crutches. "Come along, Hopalong!"

"Don't call me that!" Logan said as he took them from James. James just smirked at him as he walked out.

Kendall crawled back into the bed and pulled the covers up. Antonio sat next to him. "How are you feeling this morning?"

"Tired," Kendall said, closing his eyes.

"Logan, you go on down and eat. Your dad's up and your mom is already here. Can you ask Sylvia to send up a tray for Kendall a little later?"

Logan nodded and smiled. "Sure thing."

About twenty minutes later, Carlos came up carrying a tray with porridge and juice for Kendall. "Here's his breakfast." Carlos smiled.

"Thanks Mijo."

"Kendall, wake up, it's time for breakfast."

"Not hungry," he said from under the covers.

"Too bad, you need to eat," Antonio said, pulling the covers down a little.

Kendall groaned as Antonio helped him sit up. Carlos smiled and sat the tray on Kendall's lap. "Mami wants to know if you'd like some tea."

Kendall smiled a little. "That sounds good, thanks Carlos."

Carlos ran down to tell his mom and waited for the tea.

"Are you feeling alright? You still look really tired."

"I feel okay, just can't seem to wake up all the way," Kendall said.

"I think the last few days are catching up with you. When you're done eating, we can get you settled in on the couch. Katie has the parade on."

Kendall smiled and nodded.

Carlos came up a couple of minutes later with the tea. "Here you go! Lemon tea and Mami put honey in it just in case your throat is bothering you."

"Thanks Carlos," Kendall said, taking the mug. He almost dropped it, so Carlos kept his hand on it until it was safely on the tray.

"Is your hand bothering you?" Antonio asked.

"It's just a little hard to hold anything very well."

"I have an idea!" Carlos smiled and grabbed the mug. He headed back downstairs.

Kendall looked at Antonio. "What do you think he's doing?"

"I don't know, but I'm sure we'll find out." He laughed.

"That's what I'm afraid of."

Carlos came up a couple of minutes later holding a small cup with a lid and spout. "Here you go. Nothing will spill if you drop it now!" Carlos said proudly.

Kendall looked in shock at the bright red sippy cup that Carlos set on the tray. Antonio started laughing at the expression on Kendall's face.

"What? I thought it was a good idea," Carlos said, his face falling.

"It's a great idea, Carlitos. I was just surprised that you still have one is all."

Carlos grinned. "I hid them. This one even has a handle," he pointed out.

Antonio smiled. "Carlos, can you to stay up here while I go see if Mami needs any help?"

"Sure!" Carlos smiled, sitting next to Kendall.

A little while later, Kendall had managed to eat a little more than half of his breakfast before he started feeling nauseated. Carlos took the tray and the boys went downstairs. Kendall went and curled up next to Katie on the couch.

A few minutes later, he was sleeping with his head in her lap.

∞

At about eleven, James answered the door and Brooke and Jen came in carrying a couple of casserole dishes and a container filled with cookies. He took their coats and they carried the dishes into the kitchen.

"Jen," Alex smiled, going over and kissing her cheek.

"Alex, it's so good to see you!"

"You too, honey. How are you feeling?"

"Better now." She smiled. "How's Kendall doing? I saw him sleeping on the couch, but I didn't want to wake him."

"He's alright, just really tired."

"Are you sure he's okay with me being here?"

"Honey, relax, he's fine. He said he misses you, he's just really confused by everything right now."

She nodded. "I made the kids some gingerbread cookies."

Sylvia smiled. "That's great! Somehow over two dozen chocolate chip cookies disappeared overnight," she said, looking pointedly at Alex.

"Hey, you have FOUR boys in this house at the moment. Why point the finger at me?"

"Oh, I don't know. Maybe because I put them in the jar before turning in for the night, and then found the jar empty this morning and your room is down here."

"Could have been anyone," he said, opening the container of cookies and grabbing one.

"Mmmhmm."

"Would it make a difference to say Kendall had come down for a glass of milk and I convinced him that cookies were in order?"

"That depends," Sylvia said.

"On what?"

"Did he actually eat any of them?"

He nodded and held up three fingers.

"He ate three cookies in the middle of the night?" Jen asked.

Alex smiled and nodded. "Ask James. He came down because Kendall wasn't in bed." James nodded.

"By the way, James helped me to deplete the cookie population."

James looked at him in shock. "Tattletale!" he said and went out into the living room.

"Hmm, maybe I wasn't supposed to tell you that part." Alex laughed.

∞

Kendall woke up a little while later and stretched out, groaning.

"Here, let me help you," James said, putting an arm around Kendall's waist and pulling him upright.

"Thanks."

After the parade, Carlos put in Planes, Trains, and Automobiles, and they all settled in to watch it. Carlos was sitting on the other side of Katie, Kendall in between Katie and James, and Logan in Antonio's recliner with his foot elevated.

There was a knock at the door and James got up to answer it.

He opened the door and his jaw dropped. "Dad, what are you doing here?"

"Hello James. Can't a dad stop by and wish his son a happy Thanksgiving?" Michael Diamond asked, smiling.

"Yeah, you never have before."

"Well, it's about time then, don't you think?"

James nodded and stepped back to let his dad in. "Why don't we go into the dining room?" James said, walking into the other room.

Michael nodded and followed him.

"So what's really going on?" James asked his dad.

"What do you mean?"

James just looked at him. "Don't you usually go to Aspen with your new family for the holidays?"

Michael looked down. "I guess I deserve that... No, I know I deserve that. I haven't been a very good dad to you, and I'm sorry about that."

James listened quietly.

"The truth is I am a shallow, self-absorbed person. I will never be father of the year. I am glad you have someone like Antonio to show you what a REAL father is supposed to be like. I guess with everything that's happened with Kendall, it just got me thinking that it could have been you," Michael said, looking at James.

James looked into Michael's hazel eyes, and what he saw gave him hope that there might actually be a chance for a relationship with his dad.

"So, I have tickets to a game between the Vikings and the Bears on Sunday. Box seats at the Metrodome, I wanted to ask if you would like to go with me."

"You want me to go with you?" James asked, not quite believing his ears.

"I'll pick you up at eight. We'll drive there, have lunch at the game, and then stop for dinner on our way home. What do you say?"

"You're serious. You're not going change your mind?" James asked.

Then Michael Diamond did something he had not done in years. He wrapped his arms around his son and hugged him. "I swear I won't change my mind. I'm going to try to be a better dad to you, son, I promise."

James hugged him back, trying not to cry.

"Okay, Sunday morning. I had better say hi to your mom and everyone, and then I need to get home. Tiffany is having a few friends over for dinner."

"Okay," James said, smiling.

"I love you, son," Michael said.

"I love you too, dad."

James went into the living room to find everyone watching him.

"What happened?" Carlos asked.

James broke into the biggest smile. "My dad wants to take me to a football game Sunday!"

"Really? That's great!" Logan said.

"I know what you're thinking, I was too. In fact, I still won't believe it until we're actually on our way. But he promised!" James told them.

"That's great, James." Kendall smiled.

"I know! He said he's sorry he's been such a bad dad and that he's going to try and do better!"

∞

In the kitchen, things were a little more strained.

Brooke had seen him come in and immediately went for the throat. "What do you think you're doing here? Trying to ruin yet another holiday?" she hissed so the children didn't hear.

"No, I just came to wish James, and everyone, a happy Thanksgiving, and then go."

"That's all?" she asked, remembering all the other times he'd shown up and ruined her son's holidays, school recitals, and hockey games by being distant and dismissive, if he bothered to show up at all.

He nodded. "I also wanted to apologize to him for never being the kind of dad he deserves, and to try and salvage part of our relationship."

"How?" she demanded.

"I'm taking him to a game in Minneapolis on Sunday to start. After that, I am hoping he'll want to do more with me, and we'll go from there," he told her quietly.

There was an awkward silence in the room for a moment.

"Well, I think that's wonderful!" Sylvia said, hugging him. "Happy Thanksgiving, Michael. I'm glad you came by. Do you have plans for dinner?"

He nodded. "Tiffany made plans with some friends, so I need to get going, but thank you."

"Anytime."

"I'll walk you to the door." Brooke smiled, taking his arm.

They went out into the living room. "I need to get going, but it was nice seeing you kids again. James, I will see you Sunday," Michael said as Brooke opened the door for him.

"See you then, dad!" James grinned.

"I'm sure I don't need to tell you that if you disappoint him, I will hunt you down and gut you like a fish," Brooke said under her breath while smiling broadly.

He laughed and kissed her cheek. "No, you don't. Someone else has already made it quite clear that letting James down again, would be a very bad idea. Quite frankly, he worries me far more than you do at the moment," Michael said, being equally quiet.

She looked at him curiously. "Who?"

"Let's just say someone who had several very good points to make when he called me the other day," he said, his eyes looking over in James' general direction.

Brooke followed his line of sight and smiled. "Well, you have a lovely Thanksgiving. So glad you stopped by," she said, kissing his cheek.

After Michael left, James jumped up and hugged her. "He invited me to the game on Sunday!"

"I know, darling, I heard. I'm sure you will have a lot of fun. We brought some goodies. Can you go get them and bring them out for everyone?"

"Sure," James said, going into the kitchen.

She went over and sat next to Kendall. "How are you feeling this morning, darling?"

"I'm feeling okay." He smiled.

"Good," she said, hugging him. "I don't know how you did it and am trying to decide if I should be seriously impressed or envious... but, bravo," she whispered quietly, kissing his cheek.

"I don't know what you're talking about," he said, giving her a small smile.

"I'm sure you don't," she said, kissing his cheek again.

James came out carrying a tray with cheese, crackers, cookies, and a big pot of hot chocolate. Holiday tradition was that they snacked instead of eating lunch and had an early dinner.

He set the tray on the table and poured the hot chocolate. He handed a cup to Logan so he didn't have to get up. Carlos got up, ran into the kitchen, and returned a minute later with the sippy cup.

"Here, put some in here for Kendall," he told James.

James, Logan, and Katie looked at him and started laughing.

"What?" Carlos asked.

"A sippy cup... You still have a sippy cup?" Katie asked, giggling.

James was laughing so hard he was holding his sides.

"Kendall has a hard time holding a cup because of his hand," Carlos explained quietly.

"Dude, you're fourteen. Shouldn't you have gotten rid of those like ten years ago?" Logan asked, still laughing.

"Do you still have the stay-put munchkin bowls?" Katie asked.

"DON'T LAUGH AT HIM!" Kendall yelled, suddenly angry. "It was a GOOD idea because I spill everything I try and hold."

They stopped laughing and looked at Kendall.

"It's okay, they're just teasing. Maybe one of Mami's travel cups will work," Carlos said, trying to smile.

Kendall stood up. "NO, IT'S NOT OKAY! You at least figured out a way so I can do something on my own, without having to ask for help with yet ANOTHER thing I can't do! Do you know how hard it is to have to ask someone for help just so I can get my damn shirt on? Now I can't hold onto anything, Carlos figures out a way to help me out, and all you can do is LAUGH at him! So what if he still has a sippy cup? I don't see Logan getting rid of the little stuffed horse his dad gave him when he was two, or James getting rid of the fancy little mirror his mom got him! In case you forgot, his grandpa was really sick the last time he visited and couldn't hold a cup very well. Carlos gave him those sippy cups so they could sit and drink hot chocolate together without having to worry about him spilling and burning himself!"

The parents heard the commotion and went out into the living room. "What is going on out here?" Antonio asked.

Kendall looked furious. His face was flushed and his breathing had picked up. Katie, James, and Logan were all looking down, ashamed for teasing Carlos. Carlos looked like he was near tears.

"Nothing, I'm tired," Kendall said, his voice breaking. He ran up the stairs. Antonio followed him upstairs and the other parents looked at their children.

"Boys?" Alex asked, folding his arms across his chest.

"Katie?" Jen asked, arching an eyebrow at her youngest.

"We were teasing Carlos about the sippy cup and didn't know when to stop. Carlos, I'm sorry. I know you've been trying to think of ways to help him, and the sippy cup was a really good idea," James said.

"We're really sorry, Carlos, we were just goofing," Katie said, hugging him.

"I know, it's okay," Carlos said quietly as he hugged her back.

"It was pretty smart to think of a sippy cup. I mean the travel mugs are pretty heavy too, and with both his hands not working very well, it makes it easier for him." Logan smiled at him.

"Forgive us?" James asked.

Carlos smiled. "Of course I forgive you. I know you were just teasing. It's just... I thought I found a way to help him."

"You did. We were being stupid," Logan said.

"Well said," Alex told him.

"I didn't mind you teasing me so much. I just didn't want Kendall to feel bad because he was using one. He can't help it if his hand is hurting," Carlos told them.

Logan looked at him in shock. "Oh God, by teasing you for having one, we were actually teasing him for using one."

"Ding, ding, ding... we have a winner!" Jo said, standing in front of her son with her hands on her hips.

"I feel awful," James said, sitting down.

"You should. Today is supposed to be about being thankful for what we have and WHO we have in our lives. Instead, all three of you ended up hurting your two brothers," Alex said.

"We should go apologize to Kendall," Logan said to James and Katie. They both nodded. Katie looked like she might cry.

"I'd wait. I don't think he's feeling too well right now," Alex told him.

"I have an idea," Jen said.

"What?" James asked, hopeful.

"Why don't you make it up to Carlos and let Antonio take care of Kendall for now?"

"It's okay, they don't have to," Carlos said.

"Of course they do, right Katie?" Jen asked.

Katie nodded and smiled. "What do you want to do? We could play a video game, make a snowman, or have a snowball fight..."

Carlos smiled. "A snowball fight sounds like fun, but Logan can't with his ankle."

"Then he can referee," Jo said.

"Then the sides won't be even," Carlos pointed out.

"Well, since I'm not much help in the kitchen, I can help even out the teams. What do you say, Carlos, you and me against James and Katie?" Alex winked.

"Hey, not fair!" Katie said.

"Katherine Elizabeth Knight! Do you really want to go into what's fair right now?" Jen asked her.

"No mom, James is a great teammate," Katie said quickly as she put on her coat and boots and went outside.

The others followed her out.

∞

Kendall went into the bedroom and closed the door. He crawled into bed and pulled the covers over his head. He tried to calm down. He was near tears for yelling at everyone.

A moment later, he heard the door open. "Kendall?" Antonio said.

Not getting an answer, Antonio closed the door, went in, and sat next to the teen. "Kendall," he said again, pulling the covers down from around his head.

"I'm sorry," Kendall whispered.

"For what?"

"Getting mad and ruining everything."

"You didn't ruin anything, and you have every right to be mad. I heard most of what you said, and it seems like they were the ones being insensitive."

"They hurt Carlos' feelings and he was just trying to help me."

"I know, but I think they were just joking around. I don't think they meant for it to sound so mean. I was surprised you remembered about his grandfather and the hot chocolate. That was over six years ago."

"It was important. It was the last time Carlos got to see him," Kendall said in a quiet voice.

"Yes it was."

They sat there in silence for a few moments. "Tell me something?" Antonio asked.

"What?"

"How in the world did you get Michael Diamond, not only to show up, but promise to take James to the game on Sunday?"

"What makes you think it was me?"

Antonio looked at him. "I'm a cop. It's my job to know things."

"You have to promise not to get mad and not to tell."

"I promise."

"I told him that James is a great kid and he's missing out on all of it. Then I told him I didn't think it was fair that I got to spend more time with my dad in the short time I had him, then James has got to spend with him, and he's alive. I told him he was being selfish and should decide if he really wants to be a dad. If not, then to be honest with James so he doesn't keep hurting him all the time."

Antonio looked at Kendall, amazed by the teen's maturity. "I'm really surprised he listened."

"Well, that may not have been everything," Kendall admitted.

"What else did you tell him?" Antonio asked.

"Well... I might have also told him I met an FBI agent who likes to check out businesses, and if he decides he wants to be a dad and hurts James again, I'd call him," Kendall said, looking at Antonio sideways.

Antonio looked at Kendall, not sure he had heard him right. "You told him what?"

"I told him if he hurts James again, I'd call Agent Bower."

Antonio opened his mouth as if to speak and then closed it again. "I GAVE him a choice," Kendall pointed out.

"Well, I guess he should be careful then," Antonio finally said.

Antonio heard squealing and laughter coming from outside and went to the window. He smiled broadly. "Come here," he told Kendall.

Kendall went over to him, looked out, and saw James and Katie scrambling for cover as Carlos and Alex advanced across the yard. They stood there and watched for a minute. "Doesn't look like anything's ruined to me."

Kendall went to his backpack and pulled out the little camera and started taking pictures, and then put it on video, recording his friends as they pummeled one another with snow.

∞

Outside, the two teams had chosen their cover and started making their ammunition. Soon, snowballs were flying and Logan was keeping watch from the porch, making sure everyone was playing fair.

After about twenty minutes, Carlos and Alex conquered the other team's base and were declared the winners.

Alex was laughing. "What's the matter? Minnesota natives can't beat a Texas boy?"

James caught Carlos' eye and made little flying motions with his hands. Carlos nodded and looked at Logan, who smiled. Suddenly, Alex found himself lying face first in the snow, four kids on his back screaming, "REVERSE SNOW ANGEL!"

After practically burying Alex in the snow, James and Carlos each put an arm around Logan's waist and hauled him to the door as fast as they could. Katie opened the door and they rushed in, locking it behind them. They stood inside, giggling while they removed their jackets and boots.

Sylvia came out and looked at them suspiciously. "What did you do?"

"Nothing!" they declared simultaneously.

There was a knock at the door and they all jumped.

Sylvia walked over and the kids all moved to stand behind her. She opened the door and there stood Alex, snow covering the front of him. The snow clung to his beard, and he shook his head to remove as much as he could before stepping inside. Sylvia stepped back, trying to stifle a laugh. "W-What happened to you?"

The other moms had come out and started laughing.

"Oh, VERY funny. Exactly WHAT is a reverse snow angel?"

"It's where you push someone into the snow and move their arms and legs. It's a snow angel, just upside down," Katie explained.

"And whose wonderful creation was that?"

"Umm, actually Kendall came up with it about five years ago," James said, now hiding behind his mom.

"I see. Remind me to thank him later," Alex said quietly.

"Sure thing, dad!" Logan laughed, standing on one foot behind Joanna.

"Never mind, I think I'm going to go thank him now." Alex smiled as he headed upstairs.

"Alex, what are you going to do?" Joanna asked, still laughing.

He just smiled at her.

∞

Kendall and Antonio had watched the others face-plant Alex in the snow, and then watched as they ran for the door.

A few minutes later, Alex walked into the bedroom, still covered in snow. "So, I hear I have you to thank for this whole 'reverse snow angel' thing," he said as he walked towards Kendall with open arms. "Give me a hug," Alex said, grinning.

"No, I'm good," Kendall said, shaking his head and trying to hide behind Antonio.

"Don't drag me into this!" Antonio said as he tried to move away from Kendall.

Alex was still grinning. "Just ONE little hug!"

"No, I don't think so," Kendall said as he tried to stay behind Antonio.

"He just wants a hug," Antonio said as he quickly moved and pushed Kendall towards Alex.

"NO!" Kendall squealed as Alex pulled him into a big bear hug. Then Alex planted a large snowy kiss on Kendall's forehead and rubbed his beard on top of his head.

"Stop, you're all snowy!" Kendall said, trying to pull away.

"That's kinda the point, Champ!" Alex said, hugging him again.

Antonio was doubled over—he was laughing so hard. Kendall looked up at Alex and then looked over at Antonio. Alex nodded and they both grabbed Antonio and hugged him.

"HEY! What did I do?" Antonio asked, trying to push them away.

Sylvia had grabbed some towels and gone up after Alex. She stood in the doorway, laughing at the sight.

They looked at her and Alex smiled. "Oh Sylvia..."

She stopped laughing and looked at him sternly. "One more step and you can eat at Denny's."

He stopped.

"That goes for ALL of you," she said, holding out the towels. Alex took the towels and handed one to Kendall and one to Antonio. He kept two and started drying the snow from his clothes.

"That's better." She smirked.

"I'm going to go take off these wet things," Alex said, walking by her. He turned around, quickly hugged her and kissed her cheek, and then he ran down the stairs.

"Alexander Mitchell!" Sylvia shrieked as snow dripped down her cheek.

Alex went downstairs, laughing.

∞

There was a knock at the door and Carlos answered. "Sally!" he yelled, hugging her.

"Hey Carlos. Happy Thanksgiving!" She smiled, hugging him back

"Wow! You look really pretty today!" Carlos said, as he took her coat.

"Why thank you." She smiled. Her red hair, which was usually woven into a braid, was loose and fell below her shoulders in gentle waves. She was wearing an azure blue dress that matched her eyes.

"Sally, I'm so glad you could come," Sylvia said as she came downstairs.

"Thanks. I know you probably have a ton of food, but I made sweet potato pie. I also brought the fixings for some good old-fashioned Irish coffee, including a bottle of Greenore."

"My favourite." Sylvia smiled as she led the way back to the kitchen.

∞

Antonio and Kendall had dried off and then wiped up the floor. "You feel like going downstairs?" Antonio asked.

Kendall sighed. "I think I'll shower and change first."

"Okay. I'll be right next door."

"Thanks," Kendall said as he grabbed some clothes and headed into the bathroom. He managed to get the glove over his hand and quickly showered. He was almost finished dressing, when he heard a voice.

"Are you almost finished in there, sweetheart?"

Kendall closed his eyes. "Go away, you're not real."

"Keep telling yourself that, sweetheart."

Kendall took a deep breath and opened his eyes. He pulled off the glove and opened the door. "Papi?"

"Right here," Antonio said, coming out of his room.

He helped Kendall on with his t-shirt and then buttoned his flannel shirt for him. "You ready?"

Kendall nodded and they headed downstairs. The boys were sitting in the living room, watching a football game, and Katie was playing her handheld video game.

Carlos jumped up and hugged Antonio. "Papi, we made a reverse snow angel with Papa M!"

"I know... he shared."

"Come watch the game," Carlos said to Kendall as he pulled him to the couch.

"Hey," James said as Kendall sat next to him.

"Hey."

James put an arm around Kendall's shoulders. "We're really sorry."

"I know, it's okay."

"Dinner will be ready in a couple of minutes, so go wash up," Jen told the kids.

Everyone but Kendall jumped up and raced to the bathroom. Kendall took a deep breath, stood up, and walked over to his mom. "Happy Thanksgiving."

"Oh Kendall... Happy Thanksgiving, honey," Jen said as her eyes teared up. "Can I give you a hug?"

He nodded and she put her arms around him.

Antonio and Sally watched from the doorway. "Looks like it really is a good Thanksgiving," Antonio said.

"Looks like." Sally smiled.

"Dinner!" Sylvia called, walking past them into the dining room.

Everyone found a seat, Kendall in his usual spot between Antonio and James.

"Alex, would you give the Thanksgiving blessing?" Antonio asked.

Alex nodded and took Logan and Joanna's hands. They in turn took the hand of the person on the other side of them, until a circle was formed around the table.

"I think this simple quote by Ralph Waldo Emerson says it best. We are most thankful... for each new morning with its light, for rest and shelter of the night, for health and food, for love and friends, for everything thy goodness sends."

They started passing around dishes, Antonio and James making sure Kendall took a little of everything.

After about an hour, everyone was full, and the boys started clearing the table.

∞

After the table was cleared, the moms put away the leftovers while everyone else headed into the living room.

After a few minutes, Kendall looked around, realized Carlos wasn't there, and went to look for him. He hadn't seen him go upstairs, so he checked Antonio's study. Carlos was sitting on the small couch, watching TV.

"What are you doing?"

Carlos looked at him and smiled. "When I was looking for the other movie this morning, I found this DVD of Thanksgiving when we were seven."

Kendall sat next to him and started to watch. The first part was of the moms as they prepared dinner, Katie in her portable swing, people as they arrived.

Then images of the boys playing football in the snow. They were laughing and tackling each other, Logan running and screaming as James tried to tackle him when he didn't even have the ball. It was Logan's first Thanksgiving with them and he had never played football before, much less in the snow.

Then they heard a familiar laugh, one they hadn't heard in so long. Will Knight came onto the screen as he grabbed Logan and held him up out of James' reach.

"No fair!" James yelled, jumping and trying to grab ahold of the smaller boy. Logan was holding onto Will for dear life as the other boys started circling them.

Carlos and Kendall had each grabbed a hold of one of Will's legs, trying to pull him down. James grabbed ahold, and they managed to topple Will over into the snow as he held on tightly to Logan. Logan shrieked and ran the other way as the other three boys jumped on Will.

Antonio and Alex came onto the screen, laughing at their friend's predicament. "What's the matter Will? Three seven year olds too much for you?" Antonio laughed.

Will arched an eyebrow at the boys. They nodded and leapt up, chasing Antonio down and face planting him in the snow. Then they took off after Alex, who was running for dear life in the general direction of Sylvia, who was recording.

"You look like him. You even laugh like him," Carlos said.

Kendall just sat there quietly next to his friend and nodded.

Antonio noticed that the two boys were missing and went to look for them. He checked the kitchen and then heard sound of children laughing coming from his study. He opened the door slightly and saw the two boys curled up on the couch, watching the home video.

Kendall was lying with his head in Carlos' lap and Carlos had his arm wrapped around him. They were both crying quietly. He watched them for a moment and quietly backed out and closed the door.

Chapter 103~ Antonio's Fears

In the living room, the other kids were trying to decide on a game to play.

"Scrabble," Logan said.

"Too much like schoolwork," James said, shaking his head.

"Monopoly," Katie said with a smile.

"NO!" they both said.

"Why not?" she asked, crossing her arms and putting her lower lip out.

"We want to play something that we ALL have a chance of winning," Logan told her.

"That's why you chose Scrabble?" she asked.

"Where are Carlos and Kendall?" James asked, looking around.

"Kendall was a little tired, so he and Carlos went to watch TV in my study. I'll go get them," Antonio said, getting up. Antonio took a deep breath and knocked on the study door. "Hey, you two in here?"

"Hey Papi," Carlos said, quickly turning off the TV and wiping his eyes.

"The others are trying to decide on a game. Why don't you come join us?" Antonio smiled.

"Okay," Carlos said.

Kendall sat up. "I'm too tired."

"You can sit with me and watch then," Antonio said, offering his hands to the boys. They each took one and Antonio pulled them up.

"I need some water," Kendall said as they walked out.

"Okay, meet us out there," Antonio said, walking to the living room, his arm around Carlos.

Kendall went into the kitchen, grabbed a small cup from the cupboard, and filled it halfway with water. He drank it, took a deep breath, and went into the living room, where the others were still arguing over which game to play.

"Twister!" Carlos said.

"Logan can't play with his ankle," James pointed out.

"I'll call out the positions," Logan said.

"Twister it is." James smiled.

Kendall went over and sat with Antonio in his recliner, and they watched Carlos, James, and Katie contort into challenging positions, trying to keep from falling over. Logan called out right foot blue and James went down, taking Carlos with him.

"LOSERS!" Katie shouted triumphantly.

"You cheated!" James said accusingly.

"How can I possibly cheat at Twister, genius? Logan calls the same colour and move for everyone." She smirked.

"Because you're shorter than James, and when Logan called out left hand red, you picked up your hand and put it back down on the same red dot instead of moving to a new one, like you're supposed to," Kendall said.

"Trade secrets!" Katie said.

"I knew it!" James stated.

"Alright, how about dessert?" Sylvia said, laughing.

"Pie!" Carlos grinned happily.

They moved into the kitchen, and Sylvia and Jen pulled out dessert plates. "Okay, we have pumpkin, apple, brown butter pecan, and um... potato," Sylvia said, carefully trying to avoid the word sweet.

"Potato pie, what kind of pie is made from vegetables?" Carlos asked as he took a plate with a piece of pumpkin pie from his mom.

"Pumpkin," Sally told him.

"No way," Carlos said.

"Yes way, pumpkin is a squash," Logan told him.

"Ewww, I've been eating squash pie?"

"Well it sounds bad when you say it like that," Logan said.

"Sounds like a sneaky way to get someone to eat vegetables if you ask me."

"So, no pie?" Sylvia asked, taking the plate from her son.

"I never said I didn't like vegetables," Carlos said, grabbing the plate back.

"Well, I LOVE um... potato pie. My grandmother use to make it," Alex said, taking a slice.

"Kendall, I have green apple pie with cheddar cheese just for you." Sylvia smiled.

"I'm still full, but thanks," Kendall said.

"He'll take a small slice, and a small slice of the um... potato," Antonio said, smiling.

Kendall rolled his eyes and took the plate from Sylvia. "Thank you."

The kids took their dessert into the living room and the parents sat in the kitchen, and Sylvia made Irish coffee for them.

"So, how long are you here for?" Jen asked Alex.

"Until Sunday. How are you doing, honey?"

"Good," Jen said.

"Okay... Now, how are you really?" Alex asked again.

She sighed. "I'm doing better. I just wish I were handling this better."

"Jen, you're doing as well as can be expected, given the circumstances," Antonio told her.

"I made my son run away from me TWICE, so don't tell me I'm handling this well."

"He didn't say you were handling it well. He said you're doing as well as can be expected, and he's right. You just started therapy with a GOOD psychiatrist, and it's going to take some time. You and everyone have been through hell the last three weeks, but it's getting better. I know it seems like for every step forward, you take two steps back, but some of those steps forward have been huge. Kendall's gaining ground every day. He's eating, he's talking more, and he went to Claudia for help on his own," Sally told her.

"I know, but I'd give anything if I could change all of this," Jen said.

"Bargaining," Sally said.

"What?" Jen asked.

"Bargaining. One of the five stages of grief. While I don't necessarily believe the standard set down by the Kubler-Ross grief cycle, I do believe, depending on the circumstances, that we experience many of the stages described," Sally said.

"Isn't that for when someone dies? Kendall isn't dead," Jen said.

"Death isn't the only reason we grieve. You can grieve for any loss, any trauma, and any sudden loss of security that arises in your life. There are no rules and no deadlines. You can grieve for moments or for years. You can experience one stage or all of them. Everyone is different and every traumatic experience is different. You are experiencing this differently than Kendall. He most likely won't go through the denial stage, and he probably didn't go through the bargaining stage, he knew it wouldn't have done any good. He is going through the depression and anger stages, and they could last a long time for him," Sally explained.

"So how do I help him?" Jen asked.

"By helping yourself first. You know what happened when your husband died. You didn't take care of yourself and you ended up in the hospital, now it's happened again. Maybe

the reasons were a little different and you weren't in there as long this time, but you still wound up in there because you didn't take care of yourself like you should," Sally pointed out.

"She's right, you know," Sylvia said.

"You have an amazing family unit here, and you need to allow them to help you, as well as your children."

"Here's to the modern family." Brooke smiled as she held up her glass in a toast.

"Actually, more like the ancient families," Sally said.

"How so?" Brooke asked.

"You've heard the old proverb, 'It takes a village to raise a child'? Well, in most ancient cultures, this was true. Native American, African, Asian, and many European cultures believed that the tribe, clan, or in today's society, the family unit, were all responsible for one another. They helped feed one another, cared for each other when someone was ill, protected each other from outsiders. They all grieved when there was a loss among them. Only in the egotistical mindset of today do people believe they can do it on their own," Sally said.

"Tell me again WHY you're a cop?" Alex said.

"Because I get to wear a shiny badge and drive REALLY fast sometimes." She smirked.

Antonio laughed. "It's true, she likes to drive fast."

Jen smiled. "We should probably get going. I have an appointment with Dr. Thorne at nine tomorrow, and then I work the evening shift."

"Kendall has an appointment with Claudia at eleven and Anna wants to weigh him tomorrow," Sylvia said.

"God, I hope he's gained a little weight. I don't want him to end up back in the hospital. I don't think he can handle it," Jen said.

"He's been eating really well the last couple of days. There's no way he's lost any more," Sylvia reassured her.

"Maybe he'd want to have lunch with me tomorrow? My shift starts at two, so maybe we can meet before that. We can sit in the banquet room like we did before?"

"Well, why don't you go ask him?" Brooke said, pushing her towards the doorway.

"Antonio, maybe you could ask him?" Jen said nervously.

"Honey, this is something you need to do. It'll be alright."

Jen started towards the living room and then stopped. "Maybe next time."

Sally got up and took her by the arm. "GO," she ordered, giving Jen a little push.

Jen looked back at her. "NOW!" Sally said, pointing to the living room. Jen nodded and continued into the living room.

"Now, I get it. You like being a cop so you can boss people around," Alex said.

"Yeah, like being a cop is the ONLY reason she bosses people around," Antonio snorted.

Sally crossed her arms and raised an eyebrow. "Oh, really?"

"Uh, I mean..." Antonio stammered.

He reached over and punched Alex in the arm. "Ow, what was that for?"

"You always get me into trouble," Antonio said.

"How do you figure that?" Alex asked, rubbing his arm.

"Remember the time at the peewee hockey game when YOU threw the box of popcorn at the referee and then dove under the bleachers? Or the time at the Christmas recital when the boys were nine and you laughed at the soloist because his voice cracked in the middle of O' Holy Night, and you pointed at me when the teacher looked over?"

"Oh yeah! Good times." Alex laughed, ducking when Antonio went to smack him again.

"Children, don't make me separate you," Joanna said.

"I think that's enough Irish coffee," Sylvia said, taking their cups away.

"Hey!" Alex said, pouting.

"Not going to work," Sylvia said.

Jen slowly walked into the living room where the kids were watching The Polar Express on television. "So...Brooke and I are going to take off in a few minutes."

Katie jumped up and hugged her. "Happy Thanksgiving, mom. I'm glad you're feeling better."

"Thank you, honey." Jen smiled as she hugged her daughter back.

Kendall stood up and walked over to her. "Bye mom."

She smiled. "Goodnight honey. I wanted to ask if you would like to meet at the steakhouse and have lunch after your appointment tomorrow. I see Dr. Thorne at nine and my shift starts at two. We can sit in the back again, and I'll have the cook make your favourite burger."

"Okay," he said quietly.

"Really?"

He nodded.

"Okay. Well, I'll see you around one then." Jen smiled and held her arms open.

He nodded and hugged her.

"I love you, baby."

"I love you too."

The others came out from the kitchen. Brooke, Jo, and Sally all got their coats and said their goodbyes.

"It was a wonderful dinner! Thank you so much for having me," Sally told Sylvia and Antonio.

"Anytime Sally," Sylvia said.

"I'll stop by and see the boys tomorrow. Maybe see if Katie needs to get out again," Sally told them.

"Okay, thanks honey," Antonio said, kissing her cheek.

"Not a problem," Sally said.

"Kendall said he'd have lunch with me tomorrow around one," Jen said as she hugged Antonio and Sylvia.

"One it is, then." Antonio smiled.

Brooke hugged James. "I'll see you tomorrow, darling. I love you."

"Okay mom, see you tomorrow. I love you too," James said hugging her back.

Joanna hugged Logan and the other kids, and Alex walked the women out.

"I think I'm going to go up, I'm tired," Kendall said.

"Okay Mijo, get some sleep. Remember you have an appointment with Claudia in the morning and we have to stop by Dr. Sharpe's to weigh you," Sylvia reminded him.

Kendall groaned. "Do we have to?"

"Yes, we do," Antonio said.

"It'll be okay, you've been eating really well," Sylvia said.

"You'll eat a good breakfast before you go, that'll help," Antonio said, walking upstairs with him.

∞

Kendall got ready for bed and climbed under the covers, exhausted. He was asleep by the time the other boys came up a few minutes later.

The boys got ready for bed, and Logan found a place on the floor before Carlos and James were finished.

"What do you think you're doing?" James asked.

"I can get up and down just fine now, so one of you can sleep in the bed for a change."

"Prove it," James said.

Logan got up with relative ease. "See?"

"Okay, fine. But if you need help, wake one of us," James told him.

"I will," Logan promised.

Carlos settled in next to Logan. "We can take turns, so I'll sleep down here tonight."

"You sure?" James asked.

Carlos nodded. "Besides, this way if I want pie, I won't wake Kendall up."

"You and your stomach," Logan said.

"I'm a growing boy," Carlos said.

"You eat enough for three growing boys," Logan said.

"You say that like it's a bad thing."

Logan rolled his eyes and shook his head. "You're impossible."

Carlos just smiled at him.

James shook his head at the two and carefully climbed into the bed. Kendall stirred a little.

"It's okay, it's just me," James told him.

"Okay," Kendall said, not opening his eyes.

∞

Antonio checked on them about an hour later as he headed to bed. "Well, the boys are all sleeping soundly."

"Good, hopefully they'll sleep in a little," she said, kissing him goodnight.

"Hopefully."

"Honey, what are we going to do if Kendall hasn't gained any weight?" Sylvia asked a few minutes later.

"I'm sure he has, he ate quite a bit today and yesterday."

"But what if he hasn't?"

"Then we'll do what we need to do."

"What if Anna wants him in the hospital?"

"Honey, it's going to be fine. He has had to put on a little weight. If not, he can't possibly have lost any more."

"I guess. I am glad he wants to have lunch with Jen," she said.

"It's a step forward," he said, yawning. "Now go to sleep."

"Yes dear."

∞

It was a snowy day in mid-January when the call came over the radio. "Two car accident on Briarcliffe Drive, probable injuries. Emergency vehicles are on the way."

"Copy that," Antonio said.

His partner, Bill Blake, turned on the lights and siren and they headed to the scene of the accident. They arrived about five minutes later and found another patrol car there, already checking out the driver of the first car.

"How is he?" Antonio asked.

"Drunk," Jackson said.

"Where's the other car?"

"Over the embankment. Emergency units should be here any minute."

Antonio nodded.

"Garcia! Get over here!" Blake yelled.

"What is it?"

Blake pointed down the embankment at the SUV, which was leaning against a tree on the passenger side.

Antonio's heart dropped. "NO!" he yelled and started down the hillside.

"Antonio, stop! Wait for the fire units!" Blake yelled after him.

Antonio ignored him and continued down the hill, sliding most of the way.

"WILL!" he yelled, as he got to the car. He got to the driver's side and saw his friend of over thirty years unconscious. His head slumped to the side.

"Will, please be alright," Antonio said as he yanked on the door. When it didn't budge, he reached into his pocket for his keys and found Will's spare. He unlocked the door and pulled it open. "Will, please..." Antonio said, trying to waken his friend.

Will Knight had blood running down his face from a head wound and his breathing was laboured.

"Will, come on, buddy, wake up," Antonio begged.

Will turned his head slightly. "Tonio...what happened?"

"Drunk driver ran you off the road. Don't move, help is on the way. You're going to be okay."

"Tonio, g-get..." Will was having a hard time breathing and could barely speak.

"Shh, we're going to get you out. Just stay still and hold on, okay bro?"

Will shook his head. "Get K-Kendall out. Please, g-get my boy."

Antonio's heart nearly stopped as he jumped out and opened the back door. Kendall's car seat was strapped on the passenger side and he looked like he was sleeping. Antonio quickly climbed in and made his way over the broken glass to his godson. He felt for a pulse and found it was strong. He could hear the emergency vehicles as they arrived and knew they were heading down to the car.

"Kendall, can you hear me?" Antonio asked.

Kendall opened his eyes. "Papi? Daddy said to close my eyes. What happened?"

"It's going to be okay. Does anything hurt?" Antonio asked.

"My arm hurts... Where's my Daddy?" Kendall said, his green eyes filling with tears.

"He's right up front. It's going to be okay, Mijo. Which arm?"

"This one," he said, holding up his right arm.

Antonio saw blood flowing down his fingertips and reached over and found a large gash on the boy's arm, close to the elbow. He quickly applied pressure and smiled reassuringly at the frightened boy.

"It's going to be alright, Mijo, I promise. We're going to get you out of here and you'll be alright."

"O-Okay," Kendall said, trying to pull closer to Antonio.

Suddenly, Antonio was sitting in the woods, his hands cuffed, looking at Deesie as he pushed Kendall onto the ground. "What are you doing?!" he screamed at the man.

"We're going to give you a little show," Deesie said with a twisted smile.

Kendall screamed as Deesie started ripping open his shirt.

"Kendall, look at me. Please Mijo, just look at me," Antonio begged.

Kendall turned his head to look at him. "PAPI! Please!"

Deesie leaned down and said something to the boy. Suddenly, the look of terror was replaced by a quiet fury and Kendall looked up at the man.

"ANTONIO! Please save my boy!" Will screamed.

Antonio woke up with start—his heart felt like it was going to burst out of his chest. He got up, ran to the guest room, and quietly opened the door. He took a deep breath when he saw all of the boys sleeping peacefully.

He went back to bed and Sylvia woke up. "Is everything alright?"

He nodded. "Everything's fine, honey, just checking on the boys. I didn't mean to wake you."

"Okay, get some sleep," she said, kissing his cheek.

He nodded and lay down next to her, but sleep didn't come for hours.

∞

Antonio woke early, went down, and made a large pot of coffee. He was still shaken from the dream. He had never really had a nightmare before.

"God, if this is what it's like, no wonder Kendall's having trouble getting any real rest."

Alex came out a few minutes later. "Do I smell coffee?" He grinned.

Antonio nodded and handed him a cup.

"What's wrong?" Alex asked.

"Nothing, I just had a bad dream. It was a little disturbing."

"Wanna talk about it?"

"Not really, I'd rather just forget it."

"Let me know how that works for you," Alex said pointedly.

"You're such a smart ass, you know that?"

Alex just grinned.

"It started out with the accident that killed Will, and him telling me to get Kendall out of the car. Everything that happened almost word for word. It ended with Kendall, Deesie, and me in the woods."

"Was any of that part real?"

Antonio nodded. "Most of it."

"So what happened that day?"

Antonio took a deep breath. "After Deesie shot John, I was tracking them. I went into a wooded area and saw Kendall's backpack on the ground. Next thing I know, Deesie is standing there with John's revolver pointed at Kendall's head. I tried talking to him, but he was beyond reason. He told me to put my cuffs on and drop my radio, so I did. He told me to sit under one of the trees, and I thought he was just going to take off with Kendall, but that wasn't what he had planned."

Alex patted Antonio on the back. "I can't even begin to imagine what it was like. Kendall's lucky you were there."

Antonio shook his head as the memories flooded back. He hadn't really spoken to anyone about that day.

"He pinned Kendall down and started... I have never felt so helpless in my life. Kendall was begging me to help, and I couldn't do anything or Deesie would have shot him. I told him just to look at me, hoping he would be able to block out some of what was going to happen. He was looking at me and then Deesie said something to him, and he look in his eyes completely changed."

"How so?"

"At first he was scared, and then he seemed angry. He somehow maneuvered Deesie so his legs were free and he wrapped them around the bastard and pulled him down. He head bashed him, and when Deesie came back up, kicked him under the jaw. He must have flown off him by five feet. Kendall got up, grabbed a stick, and hit Deesie, but he grabbed ahold of the stick and threw Kendall into a tree. By that time, I was up and got to Deesie before he could reach Kendall again. We fought for a few minutes, and he managed to get the upper hand. He was just about to plant a hunting knife in me when Kendall came out of nowhere and landed on top of me. He still had the stick and held it up to keep Deesie back. It didn't stop the freak though. He came down on the damn thing and impaled himself."

"Damn, it's no wonder the two of you are having nightmares," Alex said.

Antonio nodded. "I just want... I just want him to be well. I promised Will I'd take care of him, and I nearly lost him."

"Tonio, you didn't almost lose him, you saved him. No one could have done a better job," Alex said, trying to comfort his friend.

"I don't know, sometimes it just feels like..."

"That things are beyond your control? I've got news for you, buddy—sometimes they are. You can only do what you can do and have to trust things will work out. You can't take away his bad dreams or his fears. You can only be there when he needs someone to reassure him that things WILL be better one day. That, my friend, you have done, and not just for him, but for everyone."

"Sometimes I wonder," Antonio said quietly.

"You wonder what?"

"What things would be like if Will were still alive?"

"They'd be different, but that doesn't mean this wouldn't have happened. I know you miss him. I didn't know him as long as you did, and I still miss him. He was a good man and didn't deserve to die like he did, but good men die every day. It's up to the good men who are left behind, like you, to hold things together and help their loved ones go on."

"When did you get so smart?"

"I was born smart. I just hide it very well beneath my fun-loving, hardened cowboy exterior." Alex smiled proudly.

"You hide it VERY well." Antonio smirked.

"I need to stop giving you ammunition."

"Do you really think it would make that much of a difference?"

∞

A few minutes later, Kendall wandered in, still half asleep. "What are you doing up so early?" Antonio asked.

"I don't know."

"Did you have a bad dream?"

Kendall nodded a little.

"You want go sit and watch TV for a while?"

Kendall nodded again. "Come on, Papa M, let's go watch some cartoons." Antonio smiled.

"Sounds good to me," Alex said.

∞

An hour later, Sylvia came down and found Alex snoring on the couch and Kendall curled up next to Antonio in his recliner.

"What's going on here?" she asked, kissing Antonio on the forehead.

"Bad dreams," he whispered.

Chapter 104~ Reprieve

James woke up and realized Kendall was gone. *Oh no, not again!* He thought. He checked the bathroom and Carlos' room and then headed downstairs. He breathed a sigh of relief when he saw Antonio and Kendall in the recliner.

"Hey James, what are you doing up so early?" Antonio asked quietly.

James yawned and pointed at Kendall. "He was gone."

"He came down a while ago because he had a bad dream. Why don't you go on back to bed?"

"It's okay, I'm up now. Maybe I'll jump in the shower before everybody gets up," he said, heading back up the stairs.

Half an hour later, James was showered and dressed, so he went back downstairs. "Is it okay if I go with you and Kendall today?"

"If you want to. Isn't there something else you'd rather do?"

"Not really, I'd rather just hang out with you guys today. Do you think we could stop by my house first, though? I need to grab something. It'll only take a minute."

"Of course we can." Antonio smiled.

Sylvia came out. "Breakfast for those of you conscious enough to eat," she said, standing directly over Alex.

He yawned. "Did I hear the word, breakfast?"

"Yes, we have waffles and fruit. If you want eggs, I can scramble a couple."

"Waffles sound good to me." James smiled.

"Me too, I'm not picky. I can eat pretty much anything," Alex said with a smug look.

"What is THAT supposed to mean?"

"Not a thing, Darlin'." He smirked.

Sylvia hit him with a throw pillow.

"What was that for?"

"Yesterday, for the snowy kiss and... you snore," she stated and went back to the kitchen.

"You better be careful. It sounded like you challenged her to me, and my wife does not back down from a challenge." Antonio laughed.

"Meaning?" Alex asked.

"You just MIGHT end up eating pretty much anything."

"Hmmm... Oh Sylvia, you know I love you, right?" Alex said, jumping up. Antonio and James laughed as Alex followed Sylvia into the kitchen.

"Mijo, time to wake up," Antonio said, gently shaking Kendall.

Kendall groaned. "I don't want to get up."

"I've got news for you—you got up almost two hours ago. Now it's time for breakfast. Mami made waffles."

Kendall groaned again.

"You need to eat, so come on," James ordered.

"No, go 'way."

"Come on, you need to eat before your appointment today," Antonio said.

"Don't want to go, tell her I'm sick."

James laughed. "You DO know she's a doctor, right?"

"Tell her I'm contagious and will contaminate everyone," Kendall said, curling up more.

"Then she'll just put you in the small exam room until she's ready to see you," James told him.

Kendall just curled up tighter with a stubborn look on his face.

"Come on," James said, taking Kendall's arm.

Kendall just pushed himself even tighter between the chair and Antonio.

"Kendall..." James said, warning him. Antonio stood up and got out of the way. James immediately reached down and pulled Kendall up and over his shoulder.

"James, put me down!"

"I gave you a chance, now it's time to eat."

Antonio followed them into the kitchen, where James deposited Kendall on a chair and stood behind him until Antonio sat down. James took the seat next to him and smiled.

"Well, there's something you don't see every day," Alex said, chuckling. Kendall glared at him.

"Stick around for a few days, I'm sure you'll see it again," Antonio said.

Kendall's eyebrow shot up as he looked over at Antonio.

"What?" Antonio laughed, holding up his hands.

"Here you go, honey," Sylvia said, putting a plate in front of Kendall and kissing the top of his head.

"Thank you."

"Syrup?" Alex asked, pushing the bottle towards Kendall.

He shook his head.

"Thanks!" James said as he opened the bottle and poured some syrup on Kendall's waffle and then his own.

"What are your plans for the day, Alex?" Antonio asked as he handed Kendall a fork.

"Not sure. Thought I'd see what Logan wants to do and go from there."

Kendall took a bite and put the fork down.

"His ankle's doing better, so he should be able to get around a little more," James said, handing the fork back to Kendall.

Alex watched the interaction between the three. "You guys are making me dizzy. What's the matter, Champ? Not hungry this morning?"

"No."

"Well, you need to eat before seeing Dr. Sharpe," James said.

Kendall sighed.

"Would you rather have a smoothie?" Sylvia asked him.

"No, it's okay, but thanks."

Antonio put an arm around him. "I know you're nervous, but it's going to be alright."

"Just eat a little more, okay?" James asked.

Kendall took a few more bites. "I can't eat anymore."

"Okay, why don't you go get ready?" Antonio asked.

Kendall nodded and got up.

"I'll be up in a few to help you," James told him.

"Thanks," Kendall said as he headed upstairs.

"He seems down today," Alex observed.

"He's afraid Anna's going to put him in the hospital," Antonio said.

"That, and he doesn't like going out in public," James pointed out.

"At all?" Alex asked.

"Not really. At first he said it was because of all the bruises, but they're pretty much fading," James told him.

"Maybe they haven't faded to him," Alex said.

"What do you mean?" James asked.

"Maybe he still sees them."

"I hadn't considered that. I think I'll give Claudia a call and talk to her about it," Antonio said, getting up.

∞

Kendall went into the bedroom and grabbed some clean clothes and the glove, trying not to wake Logan and Carlos. He went into the bathroom, closed the door, and turned on the shower. When the water was warm enough, he got in, closed his eyes, and let the water flow over his head. He was tired and sore and wanted nothing more than to climb back into bed and pull the covers over his head and sleep.

He washed and rinsed his hair and then just let the water beat down on his back.

"Squeaky clean yet, sweetheart?"

Kendall's eyes snapped open and he took a deep breath. He got out, dried off and pulled on his boxers and jeans.

"Hey, you doing okay in there?" James asked.

"Yeah," Kendall said as he opened the door.

James went in and helped Kendall on with his shirt.

"You look tired," James said as he grabbed the bottle of conditioner and sprayed Kendall's hair.

"A little," Kendall said as James combed out his hair.

"There you go." James smiled.

"Thanks James."

"I'm going to go with you today, okay?"

"You don't have to."

"I know I don't have to, but I want to."

"Okay, thanks." Kendall smiled.

"No problem, little brother."

∞

Half an hour later, the other boys and Katie wandered downstairs.

"Good morning, sleepyheads." Alex smiled.

"Morning, dad! Where is everyone?" Logan asked.

"Kendall's appointments. Mama G made waffles and they're in the kitchen waiting for you." Alex smiled as he ruffled Logan's hair.

"Waffles!" Carlos squealed and ran for the kitchen.

"That boy has a bottomless pit for a stomach." Alex laughed.

"Tell me about it," Logan said.

"The others will be back around two, so what do you want to do today?"

"I don't know whatever you want to do." Logan smiled.

"You're a BIG help."

"Decisiveness is NOT one of his talents." Katie smirked.

"Mean!" Logan said.

"Then CHOOSE something," Katie challenged.

"Fine, I will!"

"When?" Katie asked.

"After breakfast. I can't think on an empty stomach," Logan told her as he headed into the kitchen.

"You're just stalling," she called after him.

Alex shook his head and sat down in Antonio's recliner. "It's gonna be a long day."

∞

Antonio pulled up in front of the Diamond house and James ran inside. He returned a couple of minutes later with a black jacket. "Here, I know you don't want to go shopping, and your jacket's too small and it's not warm enough," he said, handing it to Kendall.

"James, that's your good ski jacket," Kendall said, shaking his head.

"It doesn't fit me anymore. It's a waste for it to just hang in my closet when you need a warm jacket," James told him.

Kendall smiled gratefully and took the jacket from him. "Thanks."

"You're welcome," James said, putting his arm around him.

"We have such good boys," Sylvia whispered.

"Yes we do." Antonio smiled.

They arrived at Anna Sharpe's office a few minutes later and went inside. Antonio walked on one side of Kendall with James on the other. Sylvia checked Kendall in while the others took a seat in the waiting room. The nurse called Kendall's name and Antonio stood up, pulling Kendall with him. He put his arm around him and walked with him into the back.

"Hi Kendall. Could you take off your coat and boots, please?"

Antonio smiled. "It's okay."

Kendall slipped off his boots and then took off his jacket. He got on the scales and the nurse checked the balances and smiled.

"Okay, let me tell Dr. Sharpe you're here."

They sat down to wait. Kendall was shaking a little.

The nurse came back. "Dr. Sharpe said to show you to a room so she can check out your shoulder."

Kendall looked at Antonio and shook his head.

"It's okay. She just needs to make sure it's healing alright. We should probably have her check your hand as well," Antonio said.

Antonio and Kendall followed the nurse into an exam room. "Dr. Sharpe will be right in," she told them and closed the door behind her.

"I'm just supposed to get weighed," Kendall said, trying not to panic.

"Mijo, calm down. It is time to recheck your shoulder, especially since we haven't been able to get you in for any physical therapy," Antonio said.

Anna opened the door. "Hello Kendall, Antonio. How was your Thanksgiving?"

"It was nice Anna. And yours?" Antonio smiled.

"Chaotic, but what can you do?" She laughed. "So, how are you feeling, Kendall?"

He moved closer to Antonio.

"Are you feeling any better?"

He nodded.

"Good. I wanted to check out your shoulder. Is it still painful?"

He nodded.

"Are you wearing the brace like you're supposed to?"

Kendall nodded again.

"Okay. Why don't you take it off so I can take a quick peek?"

He looked at Antonio, who nodded and helped him remove the stabilizer.

Anna smiled. "Is it alright if I touch your shoulder?"

He nodded.

She palpated it and stopped when she felt him tense up. "Okay honey, can I take a look at it?"

"It's okay," Antonio said as he helped Kendall pull up his shirt.

"It's still pretty bruised. I think it's definitely time to get you in for some physical therapy," she said, examining the area.

"Now, what's this about your hand?" she asked as she pulled down his shirt.

"He cut it the other day and had to have some stitches," Antonio explained.

"Okay, let's take a look." Kendall held out his hand and she took off the bandage. "Can you move all your fingers?"

He nodded.

"Can you wiggle them for me?"

Kendall did as she asked.

She smiled. "Good, it's healing well. Just keep it dry and we should be able to remove the stitches in about ten days."

He nodded.

She put another bandage on his hand. "Now, how's your appetite been?"

∞

In the waiting room, Sylvia kept checking her watch. "What is taking so long?" she asked nervously.

"It hasn't been that long," James told her.

"It's been over ten minutes. He was just supposed to be weighed. I'm going to make sure everything's alright," she said, getting up.

She asked the receptionist, who led her back to the exam room. She opened the door slowly. "Hi, just making sure everything is okay."

"Sylvia, come in. I was just asking Kendall about his appetite." Anna smiled.

"He's been doing so much better. He ate TWO pieces of pie last night," Sylvia said, sitting next to Kendall and putting her arm protectively around him.

"Honey..." Antonio said, shaking his head.

"Too much?"

"Just a little." He smiled.

Anna smiled. "Kendall, why don't you wait here while I speak to Antonio and Sylvia?"

Kendall looked at Antonio and shook his head.

"It's alright, we'll be right outside the door," Antonio said reassuringly.

Anna opened the door and they stepped into the hallway.

"Well?" Sylvia asked.

"He hasn't gained an ounce. He's exactly the same weight as he was on Tuesday. I'm afraid I'm going to have to recommend admitting him into the hospital, at least through the weekend."

"But he's been doing so well. He's eating so much more than he was!" Sylvia said.

"I understand that he's eating more, but it obviously isn't enough. When I examined his shoulder, I could see every one of his ribs. He's too thin."

"Damn it," Antonio cursed.

"I'm sorry, but I have to do what's best for him. I think a weekend on fluids and a high caloric diet through an NG tube is what he needs."

Antonio sighed. "I know you do. I just don't think he's going to handle this very well. Let me go talk to him."

Antonio went back into the exam room. Kendall looked up when Antonio entered the room and immediately knew what was going on.

"No, I don't want to!" he said, shaking his head frantically.

"Mijo, I know you don't, but Anna thinks you should go in just for a couple of days."

Kendall shook his head and felt the panic building. "NO! I won't go! Papi, please don't make me go!"

"Kendall, it's going to be alright."

"NO! I did what she asked. I've been trying so hard! Please don't make me go!" he said, choking back a sob.

Antonio tried to get closer, but Kendall backed away, shaking his head. "No, no, no!"

Antonio saw the fear in those green eyes and stopped moving towards him.

Out in the hallway, Sylvia and Anna could hear Kendall begging Antonio not to make him go. "Anna, please, just a couple of more days," Sylvia pleaded.

"Sylvia..."

"Look, you said he hasn't LOST any weight. Isn't that progress? It's only been a couple of days. I promise, by Monday he'll have gained some weight," Sylvia vowed.

Anna was listening to Antonio trying to calm Kendall down. She could hear the terror in the teen's voice and it broke her heart. "Alright. I have to speak to Jen about this first, but I

am willing to give him until Monday. I want at least half a pound on him by then, and I want him to start taking a good multivitamin. I want to start that off with an injection of B12 today, and I want to pull some blood on Monday as well."

"Thank you. I promise he'll have gained by then."

∞

As Antonio watched his godson back away from him in fear, he came to a decision. "I'm not doing this to you. I am NOT going to force you to do this after everything you have already been through. We will figure this out, I promise, Kendall. Please Mijo..." Antonio said, holding out his hand.

Kendall watched him for a moment and then took his hand. Antonio wrapped his arms around him and Kendall held onto him tightly.

∞

James got nervous when Sylvia didn't come back, so he got up and asked the receptionist where they were. She told him which room, so he went into the exam room area and saw Sylvia having a discussion with Dr. Sharpe.

"Mama G?"

"James." She smiled.

"Is everything alright?"

"Dr. Anna and I were just talking about Kendall. She's giving us until Monday to get half a pound on him."

"How are you, James?" Anna asked.

"Good. Where's Kendall?"

"He and Papi are talking. He got a little upset when he found out Anna wanted him to go into the hospital for the weekend."

"What? Why? He's been really good about eating, except this morning, but that's because he was scared about coming here. If you put him in the hospital, he'll really freak out! How is that good for him?"

"Mijo, she's giving us until MONDAY, so it's okay," Sylvia repeated.

"James, I'm not trying to be mean. I know he doesn't want to go. I know he's afraid, but if he doesn't start putting on weight, there's a good chance he's going to become very ill," Anna explained.

"Like how?" James asked.

"The added strain on his immune system means he's going to have a hard time recovering from the pneumonia. He can develop a heart arrhythmia and kidney problems. He's also still growing, so this could have severe repercussions on his joint and bone development."

"But he IS eating now, so if he starts putting on weight, he should be okay, right?" James asked.

"IF he continues eating and gets back to a normal weight, yes, he should be just fine," Anna said.

"Half a pound by Monday?"

Anna nodded.

"We can do that," James said.

Antonio opened the door to the exam room. "Anna, I need to talk to you, please."

She smiled. "I'll be right in. Sylvia, why don't you tell him what we discussed while I call Jen and get the B12."

Sylvia nodded and went to go into the room, but Antonio stepped out. "James, please go stay with Kendall." James nodded and went into the exam room and Antonio closed the door behind him.

"He's not going. I am NOT doing that to him," Antonio stated.

"Honey, we have until Monday. She wants him to put on half a pound and I know we can do this. Anna is calling Jen to talk to her. She wants to give him a vitamin shot, and then we can take him home."

Antonio took a deep breath and slowly exhaled.

"Honey, what happened?" Sylvia asked, noting her husband's red eyes and strained expression.

"He was afraid of me. He thought I was going to let them hurt him. That is NOT going to happen again. We will take care of him. He is not going into the hospital where they would have to put him in restraints to keep him there. I am not letting that happen, period."

"Okay, WE are not going to let that happen," Sylvia said, hugging him.

Anna came back with a small vial and a syringe. "Is everything alright here?"

"Yes, I think we're all just a little tired," Sylvia said, holding Antonio's arm.

"What is that?" he asked.

"Vitamin B12, he needs a boost and this should help."

He shook his head. "He's not going to let you do that."

"We need to try," she said.

Antonio nodded. "Let me talk to him first. Maybe if I'm holding him, it'll be alright."

"Okay." Anna smiled.

Antonio and Sylvia went into the exam room and found Kendall curled up, holding onto James. Antonio sat next to Kendall. "Mijo, we're going to go home, but Anna wants to give you a vitamin shot first. She said it'll help you feel better."

Kendall shook his head and clung more tightly to James.

"Mijo, you can look at the vial and watch her draw it up. It's just a little shot and then we're leaving, I promise."

Anna knocked on the door and Sylvia opened it.

"Anna, can I show Kendall the vial?" Antonio asked.

"Of course," she said, handing it to him.

"Kendall, see it's just a vitamin shot," he said as he held it out for the boy to see.

Kendall looked at the vial and shook his head.

"Kendall, the B12 will help you feel better. Then you can go," Anna said softly.

Kendall didn't respond.

"What if she gives me a shot first and then you? What do you say?" James asked, rolling up his sleeve so Anna could give him a shot.

"Are you sure?" Anna asked.

"I'm sure, it'll be fine." James smiled.

Anna drew up the B12 and swabbed James' arm. "See Kendall, nothing to it," he said as Anna gave him the shot.

Kendall looked at him and then at Antonio, who nodded. He sighed and sat up a little. James rolled up Kendall's sleeve for him and Anna and swabbed his arm and quickly gave him the shot.

"See, what did I tell you?" James smiled.

Antonio smiled. "Good job. Now why don't we get going? It's time to go see Claudia."

James nodded and stood up, pulling Kendall with him. He helped Kendall get his jacket on and they walked out of the room.

"Thanks Anna, really," Antonio said.

"You're welcome, but I do need to see him on Monday."

Antonio nodded and he and Sylvia followed the boys out.

Chapter 105~ Bruises

Once they got to the car, Antonio took a deep breath and then smiled. "Honey, why don't you drive? You can drop us off at Claudia's and then run home and pick up Carlos and Katie. We can go out for lunch and give Alex and Logan some time together."

"That's a great idea," she said and got into the driver's seat.

They got to Claudia's a few minutes later and Antonio, Kendall, and James went up to the house and knocked. "How are my favourite guys?" Claudia asked, answering the door with a smile.

Antonio shook his head a little, as they went inside.

"Babies, why don't you go and sit by the fire while Antonio and I get us something warm to drink?" Claudia said.

James smiled and helped Kendall off with his jacket and led him into the living room. Claudia walked back to the kitchen and Antonio followed.

"What's with all the sad faces today?" she asked, as she pulled out a box of tea and a tin of hot chocolate.

"We just left Dr. Sharpe's. She wanted to put Kendall into the hospital today."

"I take it that didn't go over very well?"

Antonio shook his head. "I went in and tried to break it to him gently, and he started panicking. He was afraid of me."

"I'm sure it wasn't you, just the situation."

"He was begging me not to make him go, and then he tried to get away from me. He hasn't said a word since we left," Antonio said.

"How did you convince her to keep him out?"

"Sylvia pointed out that he hasn't lost any weight and promised we'd get a half a pound on him by Monday. It wouldn't have mattered at that point anyway," he said.

"What do you mean?"

"I'm not doing that to him. I am not going to put him into a situation where he will have another attack. There is no way he would cooperate with them and he would end up in restraints, I'm not going to let that happen. He's been through enough and honestly, I NEVER want him to look at me in fear again."

"Well, I guess we better make sure he keeps eating then," Claudia said, pulling out a box of cookies and putting them on a plate.

"He's been eating, but his weight is the same as it was on Tuesday."

"Tuesday, isn't that the night he came visiting?" Claudia asked.

Antonio nodded.

"Well no wonder. He probably used up all the reserves he had been building, walking all this way in the cold. If it hadn't been for that, he probably would have shown a small gain in weight."

"I didn't think about that," Antonio admitted.

"With no jacket in this cold, he burned twice the calories he would have otherwise. So you see, things aren't as bad as all that." Claudia smiled.

"Are you sure?"

"Of course I am. What with the trauma of what happened with his mama that night, and then the flashbacks the next day, it's no wonder he's lost what he gained," she said reassuringly.

Antonio took a deep breath and smiled. "That makes sense."

"Good, now we're going to try this peppermint tea and see if it helps his stomach," she said, picking up the tray.

They went into the living room and Claudia set the tray on the table. She handed Kendall a cup. "Here baby, try this tea, it'll help soothe your stomach."

Kendall took the cup awkwardly. "Thank you."

"Hmm, hold on a minute," Claudia said and went back into the kitchen. She returned a moment later and poured his tea into an Eco cup with a screw-on lid and straw.

"Try this, baby. It should be easier to hold."

"Thank you."

"So, did you all have a good Thanksgiving?"

James smiled. "It was great! Logan's dad came up and my dad stopped by. We had a snowball fight, turned Papa M into a reverse snow angel, and had WAY too much food."

"What is a reverse snow angel?"

"Well, it's kind of like a regular snow angel, only you push someone into the snow face-first and move their arms and legs for them... and then you RUN," James explained.

Claudia laughed. "I'm definitely going to have to try that on someone."

She looked at Kendall. "How about you, baby, did you have a good day?"

Kendall smiled a little and nodded.

"Did your mama have dinner with you?"

Kendall nodded.

"We're actually going to go have lunch with her when we're finished here," Antonio said.

"Good," she said, smiling at Kendall. "Now, how about you and I go into the office while Antonio and James wait in here?"

Kendall nodded and followed her into the other room. She closed the door and sat down in one of the wingback chairs. Kendall sat down in the chair next to her and looked at his hands.

"I understand you had a hard morning, but it's gonna be okay. Antonio and I talked and figured out why you haven't gained anything, even though you've been trying so hard."

"Why?"

"You remember that little walk you took the other night? The one in below freezing weather and without a jacket?"

Kendall nodded.

"How many calories do you think your little bitty frame burned through that night?"

"Little bitty?"

"Baby, if a big northern wind blew through here, you'd become airborne at this point."

He rolled his eyes and smiled.

"Now that's what I've been waiting for."

"What?"

"For those dimples make an appearance."

Kendall blushed.

"Now, did the candy help your stomach at all?"

He nodded. "The peppermint. I never tried the ginger after Mama G almost died eating one."

"I guess I should've warned her they're a little hard on the taste buds."

"She figured it out pretty fast. You should have seen her face."

Claudia smiled. "So, there are a couple of things I want us to work on."

"What?"

"Well, we need to work on you being comfortable with going out in public again, and I think we should try and get you over the issue with your trigger word. How's that sound?"

"How do we do that?"

"Let's start with why you don't want to go out. Besides not wanting to be surrounded by too many people, which is normal. Is it because you think people are going to stare at you because of your bruises?"

Kendall nodded.

"Come with me," she said, standing up and holding out her hand.

He stood up and took her hand. She walked him over to the mirror and stood behind him with her hands on his shoulders. "Show me the bruises."

"What?"

"Point to the bruises people will notice."

He sighed and started pointing to his reflection in several places. "You see bruises in all those places?" she asked.

He nodded.

"Okay, now I'm going to show you where I see them." She pushed up his bangs a little to reveal the one he got from Deesie's face. "Right here is the only obvious bruise." She ran her finger down from his left eye to his cheek. "A faint one here. Also here, but those are the only ones," she said, pointing to the area where his lip had been split by Dylan.

He shook his head.

She looked at him and nodded. "Close your eyes, baby."

"Why?"

"Just do it."

He sighed but did as she asked.

"Now, I know you haven't known me very long, but I figure you must trust me a little to walk all the way in this weather just to talk to me, right?"

He nodded.

"Okay, I want you to think about how long it's been since you got those bruises. Don't you think they would've faded quite a bit by now?"

"I don't know."

"You've been playing hockey for most of your life and you don't know how long you stay bruised?"

"A couple of weeks."

"So it's been what, between two and three weeks now? Baby, they're almost gone. Now I want you to think about it and then slowly open your eyes."

Kendall took a deep breath and opened his eyes.

Claudia was smiling at him. "Well?"

He looked at his own reflection again. "I-I don't understand. Why?"

"A defense mechanism. It gives you a reason to stay away from people. Now, when you get home, I want you to ask someone there to point out the bruises they see."

"Why?"

"Because I want you to hear it from someone else you trust to reassure you that what I'm saying is true."

He pulled down his collar a little. "But these are still there."

She looked at the skin below his ear and saw several discoloured areas along his neck and shoulder.

"When did he give you these bruises?"

"They're not bruises," he told her, looking away.

"Oh... Well, sometimes those kinds of marks last a little longer than your typical bruising. But baby, no one can see those because of your shirt."

"But they're there."

"I know, and they make you feel... less than clean?"

He nodded.

She wrapped her arms around him, still smiling at him in the mirror. "Baby, the only one judging you, is you. You did nothing wrong, you did nothing to deserve this. That so called 'man' was a freak of nature and is lucky he got off so easily by dying, because he deserved so much worse. Now, I think we have done enough for today. I can tell you're tired and I want you to go have lunch with your mama and then go home and get some rest. Can you come back on Monday?"

"If they don't lock me in the hospital."

"I can tell you for a fact that's not going to happen."

"How do you know? Dr. Sharpe said..."

"Just between you and me, Antonio told me there's no way he's letting them put you in the hospital. As your psychologist, I agree it would do more harm than good and I'll tell them that."

"Really?" Kendall asked.

"Absolutely. But, you do need to keep eating and I would say a lot of bed rest through the weekend, okay?" She smiled.

He smiled at her and nodded.

"That's what I like to see," she said, still hugging him. "Next time we're going to work on getting you out in public a little, and we're going to try and give your mama back that word she misses so much."

Kendall nodded.

"Why don't we go finish our tea with Antonio and James while we wait for Sylvia?" she said, opening the door.

"Okay," Kendall said, following her back into the living room.

∞

Sylvia got home and found Carlos still in his pajamas. "Mijo, go get dressed, we're going to go have lunch with Mama K."

"Okay!" Carlos said, dashing upstairs.

"We thought we'd give you and Logan some time together," she told Alex.

Alex smiled. "That is if a certain someone can come up with anything to do."

"I'm thinking," Logan said.

"You've BEEN thinking for almost two hours." Katie smirked.

"Fine, how about lunch and then we can go to Edie's Ice Cream Shoppe?" Logan asked.

"Sounds good to me," Alex said.

"TWO hours and that's all you could come up with?" Katie asked.

"I LIKE ice cream," Logan told her.

"Alright you two don't make me plant you in a snow bank somewhere," Alex threatened.

Sylvia shook her head, laughing, and went into the kitchen.

Alex followed her. "So, you look a little frazzled. What happened?"

"Anna wants to put Kendall in the hospital. He started to panic when Antonio told him and wouldn't go near him. It really shook Antonio up and he's put his foot down. He said there's no way he's going to allow them to do that to Kendall. The problem is if Kendall doesn't start putting on weight, we're risking his health. I don't know what to do. Antonio was VERY adamant about keeping Kendall out of the hospital."

"She wants him in the hospital so they can put in a feeding tube?"

Sylvia nodded. "Alex, I'm getting really worried about how Antonio is going to handle any more of this."

"Let me check on something," Alex said, going into the study. He came out a few minutes later, smiling.

"What?" Sylvia asked.

"I'm gonna stay for at least another week to help out. I just spoke to my brother, Sam. He has a lot of vacation time coming, so he's gonna go down and take care of things at home."

"Alex, are you sure?"

He smiled. "A couple of years after my dad had his stroke, he got aspiration pneumonia because he was having problems swallowing properly. He wasn't allowed to eat anything for a couple of weeks, so the doctor showed me how to put in a nasogastric tube. We've had to do it a few times since then. It's not hard and there's no reason for Kendall to be in the hospital if he needs one. Anna might want to watch me do it the first time, but we can do this here."

"Are you serious? We can really do this at home?"

He nodded. "So, one problem solved."

Sylvia hugged him. "Thank you SO much."

"Does this mean you're going to forgive and forget my little comment this morning?" he asked.

"What comment?"

Carlos came running in. "All ready, Mami!"

"You and Katie go get in the car, I'll be right out."

He nodded. "Come on, Katie, we're leaving!"

"Thank you again, this is going to mean so much to Antonio and Kendall."

"Well, I can't let my best friend down now, can I?"

"I'm going to make you whatever you want for dinner tomorrow night," Sylvia said as she headed out to her car.

Logan came downstairs. "What was that all about?"

Alex smiled. "What do you think about me hanging around for another week or so? Antonio needs some back up, so I called your Uncle Sam and he's gonna take care of your grandparents until things have settled down a bit."

"Really? Dad that would be amazing!" Logan said, hugging him.

"Now, why don't we go get something to eat and maybe get in a little Christmas shopping?" Alex suggested, hugging him back.

∞

After hitting a few shops at the mall, Alex and Logan decided to eat at the food court. "So, how are you handling everything?" Alex asked his son.

"Okay. Some days are harder than others."

"Tell me," Alex said.

"Where do you want me to start?"

"How about the beginning?"

Logan looked down and sighed. "When this whole thing started, I didn't believe Kendall, and then when Deesie took him, I just wanted to die. I have never felt so badly about anything in my life. I didn't believe my best friend. Mama G had us listen to the recording Kendall made when he tricked Deesie into telling him what he wanted from him. Kendall did it all for us, because our friendship was that important to him."

"You do know he doesn't blame you for that, right?"

"I know. He made that clear on the recording. He only blamed Deesie and himself."

"He forgave you?"

Logan nodded.

"Then don't you think the fair thing is to forgive yourself?"

"He's still having so many problems though and maybe if we'd listened instead of judging him..."

"Things might have turned out differently?"

Logan nodded.

Alex shook his head. "No son, they wouldn't have. Deesie still would have taken him, he'd still be having problems, and you'd still find something to blame yourself for."

"How do you know that?"

"Because you boys are all so close, that when something happens to one of you, it affects ALL of you. Maybe in different ways and to different degrees, but you all come together with specific roles. That's the way you are."

"How so?"

"Well, James and Kendall become extra vigilant to the point of being over-protective. You become very nurturing, worrying about every little detail that comes along. Carlos tries to make sure everyone is happy by distracting them with jokes, games, or just being himself. Depending on who the one in trouble is, your roles shift a little."

"What do you mean?"

"Your mom told me that Carlos attacked a boy that helped Deesie, which isn't something he would normally do."

Logan nodded. "He really went after Jason. James and I had to get in-between them."

"When you hurt your ankle Kendall took care of you. He made sure you stayed off your foot, that you iced it, and had what you needed. He took over the nurturing role. Do you see where I'm going with this?"

Logan smiled and nodded. "I think so."

"Do you remember when Papa K died?"

Logan nodded.

"You boys were so young, but even then you did the same thing. You ALL threw a fit when they told you boys you couldn't stay in the hospital with Kendall. You ended up spending the night at Carlos'. The minute Kendall was home, you took turns staying with him. When Carlos' grandpa died and he was staying at the Knights', you and James were there every day. When Brooke and Michael broke up, you all stayed with James. The same when your mom and I broke up and I went back to Texas. You may not be blood, but you are all closer than most brothers I know, including your uncles and me. I was closer to Antonio and Will than any of my siblings, except maybe your Uncle Sam."

"Doesn't that make you sad though?" Logan asked.

"Sometimes, but I honestly wouldn't change a thing. You boys are lucky, don't you ever forget that. A lot of people can go their whole lives without finding one friend they can rely on completely. You each have three. Four if you count Katie."

Logan smiled. "I guess we can count Katie. Although she is bossy, scary, and really mean sometimes."

"Yes she is." Alex chuckled. "So stay on her good side. She's probably going to end up running the country one day."

"That's a fact."

"Why don't we head over to Edie's? I haven't had homemade ice cream in a long time," Alex said.

"Sounds good." Logan smiled.

∞

Edie's Ice Cream Shoppe was a little mom and pop place that had been there since the 1960's. It's décor reflected the old style ice cream shops from the 1950's, complete with a full-length counter with round barstools, large booths, and a vintage jukebox. They began making their own ice cream in the early 1980's and was a popular hangout for people of all ages.

∞

Alex and Logan went into Edie's and sat at a booth. Marcy Tinkler came up to take their order. Marcy was Jenny's older sister, and while they resembled each other physically, that was where the similarities ended. Marcy had spent years earning accolades in ballet and gymnastics, while Jenny could trip over the pattern on the floor. Where Jenny brought home straight A's, Marcy struggled to keep up her C average.

"Hey Logan, how's everything going?"

"Going okay, thanks. Did you all have a nice Thanksgiving?"

"Yeah, although Jenny almost put out her eye when she pulled on the wishbone with our cousin."

"Ouch," Logan said, wincing at the visual.

"What can I get for you two?"

"I think I'll have the raspberry cheesecake swirl," Logan said.

"I can't decide, so surprise me," Alex said.

"Mr. Mitchell?" Marcy asked.

"Yes."

"I didn't recognize you with the beard and mustache. Very distinguished." She smiled. "Any allergies?"

"Not a one."

"I'll have your ice cream right out," she said as she went to place their order.

Logan rolled his eyes.

"What?" Alex asked.

"Distinguished," Logan snorted.

"Watch it, junior, you could end up walking home," Alex warned.

Marcy came back with their ice cream a few minutes later.

"So, what flavour is this?" Alex asked.

"We call it the Happy, Happy, Joy, Joy. I don't name them...I just serve them. It's coconut ice cream with roasted almonds and chocolate chips," she said, smiling again.

"Sounds good, thank you."

"Is there anything else I can get for you?" she asked.

"Dad, could we order some chocolate chip cookie dough to take home?" Logan asked.

"Marcy, could we get two quarts of that to go?"

"Sure thing. I'll have it waiting for you at the counter when you're ready." She smiled, placing their ticket on the table.

"Thank you," he said.

Alex and Logan ate their ice cream and then decided to head home. They went up to pick up their order and pay the bill.

"That'll be $13.79," Marcy said, smiling.

"I think there was a mistake, you only charged me for one of the dishes," Alex pointed out.

"No mistake, yours was on the house."

"Why is that?" Alex asked.

"For trying our new flavour and for being the most distinguished looking gentleman here today!"

"Oh brother!" Logan muttered under his breath.

"Well, thank you!" Alex said as he took the bag with the ice cream.

"You're welcome! Please visit again," Marcy said as they left.

Alex smirked. "Distinguished."

"Barf!" Logan said, rolling his eyes.

Chapter 106~ Making Amends

Jen went to her appointment with Dr. Thorne feeling a bit more optimistic about things. Eli noticed the change in attitude and smiled. "So, how was your Thanksgiving?"

"It was nice. I've been staying with Brooke, but we went over to the Garcia's and had dinner there. Logan's dad, a friend we haven't seen in over a year, flew up for the holiday."

"How did you and Kendall do?"

"We did okay. He came up to me when I got there and let me hug him. Then when I was leaving, I asked if we could have lunch today and he said yes."

"Will it be just the two of you?"

"No, I think Antonio and Sylvia will be there since they're taking him to his appointments."

"How do you feel about that?" he asked.

"To be honest, a little relieved. I don't think that we're ready for any one-on-one time yet." She sighed.

"That's alright. You'll both probably feel a little more secure knowing that someone who loves you both will be there for you."

Jen nodded.

"How are you sleeping? Any bad dreams?"

"A couple, but not as bad as they were before. Instead of dreaming about Deesie hurting the kids, I dream about what's been happening with Kendall."

"Like what?"

"He runs away and I can't find him, or when he was in the hospital after he ran away from me the first time. When he woke up and saw me, he was so afraid I was taking him back to Graham, that he pushed me away. If Antonio hadn't been there, we both would have hit the floor."

"So you're basically reliving events that have happened?"

She nodded.

"Any variation on what occurred?"

"No."

"If you could go back, what would you do differently that day?"

"Everything," she said softly.

"You went back to see Graham because you thought he was trying to help you?"

"Yes."

"From what I've heard about Graham, he's very charismatic when he chooses to be. He has convinced many parents that he cares and has only their best interests at heart. From what I understand, there are several families who are going to be represented at Graham's trial, including one whose son died?"

Jen nodded.

"I know it's difficult, but I want you to forgive yourself for what happened."

"How?"

"By blaming the person responsible for this, Graham. He is as much a predator as Deesie was. He used your love and concern for your child to manipulate you."

"How can I forgive myself if my son can't forgive me?" she asked quietly.

"Did Kendall say he doesn't forgive you?"

"Well no, but how can he?"

"Have you asked him?"

"No."

"Why not?"

"I guess I'm afraid of what his answer will be."

"So, you are living with the assumption that your son hates you for this, causing you to emotionally and now physically distance yourself from him. Do you think that's fair to him or you?" Eli asked.

"I guess I never thought about that. After the incident in the hospital, my friend, Joanna, told me I was purposely distracting myself so I didn't have to deal with what had happened and to avoid getting close to Kendall."

"Do you think that's true?"

"Yes."

"So what are you going to do?"

Jen took a deep breath. "I'm going to start taking care of myself so I can take care of my children."

"And...?"

"I'm going to ask Kendall to forgive me."

"And if he doesn't?"

Tears filled her eyes. "I don't know."

He smiled and took her hand. "You're going to ask him again. I want you to try to put yourself in his shoes. If he came to you and asked for forgiveness, would you give it?"

"Of course, but he has nothing to be sorry for."

"Do you think he believes that, or does he believe that everyone's lives are in chaos because of him?"

"He's blaming himself," she said quietly.

"So, I want you to think about what we need to do to help him with that. Understand this is not going to be an easy or quick fix. It's going to take time for all of you to heal, and there will be times when it seems like things are moving backwards, and that's okay. Life doesn't always work the way we want it to, and that's why we need to deal with things as they come up. Not let them build up inside until we break, which is what you did."

"I know," she said, looking down.

"Jennifer, I'm not criticizing, I'm just stating the facts. You have an amazing support system. USE it. Do not feel ashamed or weak that you need help—everyone does at some point in their lives. Let your friends help take care of you like they're taking care of Kendall."

"I'm trying."

"I know you are. I also know it's not easy, and that's why I'm here. Things are probably going to get worse before they get better. Kendall is most likely going to continue having panic attacks and nightmares. He is going to relive some of the worst moments of his life, and he has no idea how to deal with them. Claudia was a step he chose to take, and hopefully he'll continue to let her in."

"I hope he does. Everyone really seems to like her. She even got Brooke's seal of approval."

Eli smiled. "How did I do in Mrs. Diamond's estimation?"

"I'm here without her, aren't I?"

"Yes you are." He laughed.

∞

Sylvia got to Claudia's house and they went up to the door and knocked.

Claudia answered. "Come on in, everyone's in the living room having tea and cookies."

"Cookies?" Carlos asked.

"Yes baby, go help yourself." She laughed, pointing to the room.

Claudia looked down at Katie and held out her hand. "I don't think we've officially met. I'm Claudia."

"I'm Katie and I'm glad my brother likes you, but if you do ANYTHING to hurt him, you'll have to deal with me," she stated, shaking Claudia's hand and then crossing her arms over her chest.

"Katie!" Sylvia said in shock.

Claudia raised her eyebrow and smiled. "Understood."

Katie followed Carlos into the living room.

"I am so sorry, Claudia," Sylvia said.

"Don't be... Are you sure she's not Brooke's daughter though?" Claudia laughed as she closed the door.

"Sometimes I wonder." Sylvia smiled.

Sylvia and Claudia went into the living room. "Hey, you guys ready to get going?" Sylvia asked.

"I think so," Antonio said.

James nodded and jumped up to grab their jackets.

"Let me help you clear up first," Sylvia said.

"No need for that," Claudia told her.

"Of course there is. Honey, can you get the tray?" Sylvia asked as she handed it to Antonio.

"Sure," he said, looking at her questioningly.

She took Claudia's arm and the three walked into the kitchen.

"What do you think they want to talk about?" Carlos asked.

"I don't know, but it's funny they think we can't figure that they want to talk without us hearing them," Katie said.

∞

"Okay, so what's going on?" Antonio asked his wife.

"Some good news." She smiled, looking at him.

"Well?" he asked.

"Alex is going to stay for another week to help out."

"He doesn't have to do that," Antonio said.

"YES, he does."

"Why?" Claudia asked.

"The reason he needs to stay is because he knows how to work a feeding tube."

"So?" Antonio said.

"So... that means if Kendall needs one, he doesn't have to stay in the hospital. Alex knows how to put them in. That means we can continue to take care of Kendall at home."

"Are you serious?" Antonio asked, not quite believing his ears.

"His dad has needed one a few times, and the doctor showed Alex how to do it. He said Anna might want to watch him do it the first time, but after that, everything should be fine. He can even show us how to do it," she told them.

"That IS good news!" Claudia smiled.

"Thank God." Antonio smiled in relief.

"See, everything is going to be alright. Now you better get going or Jen is going to think you stood her up," Claudia said, pointing to her watch.

Sylvia nodded. "Her shift starts at two. I hope her appointment with Dr. Thorne went well."

"He's a good man, I'm sure it went just fine," Claudia told her, walking them back to the living room.

"Come on, kids, we need to get going, Jen's waiting for us," Antonio said.

"Thanks for the cookies!" Carlos said, hugging her.

"Anytime, baby!" She smiled, hugging him back.

She looked at Kendall. "I'll see you on Monday, same time. Okay?"

Kendall looked at Sylvia, who nodded.

"Thanks Claudia," Kendall said quietly.

She hugged him. "Don't thank me, baby. You're the one doing all the work. Now remember, I want you to rest this weekend."

"He will," Antonio said, putting an arm around him.

Kendall smiled and leaned against Antonio as they walked out.

∞

They arrived at the steakhouse a few minutes later and went inside. Jen was waiting out front and smiled when she saw them all come in.

"I hope you don't mind, but Alex and Logan needed some time together, so we thought we'd all join you," Sylvia said, hugging Jen.

"No, I'm happy to see you all." Jen smiled.

She led the way to the back and they all sat around a table there. Kendall sat between Antonio and James, and Jen sat across from him. The waitress came in and took their orders and Jen asked her to put a rush on it.

"So, how did your appointment with Dr. Thorne go?" Sylvia asked.

"I think it went pretty well. I see him again Tuesday afternoon."

"Do you like him?" Antonio asked.

"I do, he's very nice. He listens instead of lecturing or pointing fingers. He was also quick to say exactly how important a good support system is. He believes in extended families and made me realize just how much I need you all. I'm so glad I have you," Jen said, tearing up.

Sylvia reached over and hugged her. "We're not going anywhere."

"No we're not." Antonio smiled.

"How was your appointment with Claudia?" Jen asked Kendall.

"Okay," he said quietly.

"Do you like her?"

He nodded.

"I'm glad, honey. I'd like to meet her, she sounds amazing."

"She is, you'll really like her," James said.

The waitress brought out their lunches and they started eating. Kendall took a few bites of his burger and found himself getting sleepy.

Antonio put an arm around him. "Hey, you need to eat a little more."

"I'm tired."

"I know, we'll get you home and into bed after lunch. Take a few more bites though, okay?"

Kendall nodded and took another bite.

Sylvia leaned over and whispered to Antonio, who nodded.

"So, would you like to hear some good news?" Sylvia asked Kendall and Jen.

"What good news?" Jen asked.

"Well, Papa M is going to stay another week," Antonio said.

"Logan will be happy." Kendall smiled.

"Yes, but that's not the only reason he's staying," Antonio told him.

"Why then?" Kendall asked.

"Do you remember why he moved back to Texas?"

"His dad got sick?"

Antonio nodded. "Well, it turns out that because of the stroke, sometimes his dad has problems with swallowing. Alex had to learn to feed him using a feeding tube. The doctor there showed him how to place and use them, so if you need one, he can do it."

"Wait, so Kendall WON'T have to go into the hospital?" James asked.

"I really don't think so. IF she wants Kendall to have a feeding tube, she might want to watch Alex put it in the first time, just to be sure he knows what he's doing, but then we would go home," Sylvia said.

"How do you put it in?" Carlos asked.

"Alex said it goes through the nose and down to the stomach. You mix up the formula, pour it into a special bag, and hang it. It just goes into the stomach through the tube," Sylvia explained.

"Formula? Like BABY formula?" Katie snorted.

Kendall glared at her.

"Katie, shhh," Carlos whispered.

"Katherine Elizabeth Knight! Do NOT say another word," Jen warned.

"Sorry Kendall," she said.

"So... it's a special mixture of nutrients and proteins based on the individual's needs," Sylvia continued.

"So I don't have to go to the hospital?" Kendall asked quietly.

"No, you don't have to go to the hospital. Let's try and make sure you don't need the feeding tube either," Antonio said.

Kendall nodded.

Jen smiled. "That's incredible. I'll give Alex a call later to thank him."

"Well, we better let you get to work," Sylvia said.

Jen looked at her watch. "Oh, yeah I better get ready. Thanks for bringing the kids," she said, hugging Sylvia.

"You're welcome. Why don't you come over for dinner tomorrow night? I told Alex I'd fix him whatever he wants."

Jen looked over at Kendall. "Is that alright with you?"

Kendall smiled a little and nodded.

"Okay then, I'll see you tomorrow," Jen said.

"Bye mom, see you later!" Katie said, hugging her.

"Okay, and I better not hear that you're teasing your brother, understand?" Jen asked her quietly.

"Yes mom, I'm sorry."

"Alright, I love you. I'll see you soon."

James and Carlos both hugged her and headed up front with Katie and Sylvia.

"Is it okay if I talk to you for a second, honey?" she asked Kendall.

He looked at Antonio, who nodded. "I'll meet you out front," he said and left the two alone.

"I wanted to tell you that I'm sorry about the whole nightmare with Graham. I should have listened to you, but I guess I wasn't thinking very clearly. I also want to apologize for what happened Tuesday night. What I said wasn't what I was trying to say."

"It's not your fault," Kendall said quietly.

"Yes it is. I wasn't doing my job, which is to take care of myself so I can take care of you. I promise I'm going to try my hardest to make sure it doesn't happen again. I also promise to listen to you when you're trying to tell me something. I know I'll make more mistakes, but I'm trying, baby, I really am."

"I know," he said.

"Kendall, I love you and Katie more than anything in the world, and I just want you to know that."

"I know you do, I just don't know..."

"Don't know what?"

"How to fix this."

"That's not your job. Your job is to feel better so you can start being a kid again," she told him.

"I don't know how to do that either."

She took a deep breath. "You start by forgiving yourself and realizing nothing was your fault."

Kendall looked down.

"Kendall, it's not your fault that I freaked out. It's not your fault Deesie chose you for some reason and did all the things he did. It's also not your fault Graham pulled what he did. Antonio said he has destroyed other families. I don't want our family to be one of them. I am completely out of my element in this, and I refused to listen to the people who love us most, but I am listening now. I'm praying it's not too late."

Kendall stood there quietly for a moment. "It's not. I never blamed you, but if you need me to, I forgive you."

Jen smiled and hugged him. "Thank you Kendall. I really needed to hear that."

He hugged her back. "I love you, mom. I'm just scared because I don't know what's going to happen next."

"I know, honey. So am I."

Chapter 107 ~ False Accusations

Jen walked Kendall up to the front of the restaurant, her arm around him. "Well, I better get to work, and you need to get some rest."

Sylvia had already taken the other kids to the car and Antonio was waiting for them. "Everything alright?"

Jen nodded. "Everything will be soon."

Antonio smiled. "We'll talk to you later and see you tomorrow."

Jen nodded. "Thank you, Antonio."

He kissed her on the cheek. "No thanks necessary."

"Bye mom," Kendall said.

"Goodbye honey, I'll see you tomorrow," Jen said, kissing him on the cheek.

Antonio and Kendall started walking out when Denise came running up to Antonio. "Hi Officer Garcia, I completely forgot to have you sign the credit slip for Mike Duncan's meals. Do you have time?"

"Not a problem. Thanks for taking care of that for me." He looked at Kendall. "You want to come back in or wait here?"

"I'll just wait here," Kendall said, sitting on one of the benches near the door.

"Okay, I'll be right over there. It'll only take a minute." Kendall nodded and tried to stifle a yawn. "Then we're going to get you home for a nap." Antonio smiled.

Antonio followed Denise back up to the counter and Kendall closed his eyes for a minute. He heard the door open, so he scooted further back on the bench. A moment later, he heard someone speaking. "I know you. You are that boy from the newspaper. You should be ashamed of yourself."

Kendall opened his eyes to find a very irate woman and someone, who was probably her husband, standing there staring down at him. He looked at her, confusion obvious on his face.

"First luring that misguided teacher into trying to acquire better grades, and now filing charges against a doctor who was only trying to help you."

Kendall shook his head and got up to go inside.

She moved and blocked his way in. "Oh no, you don't! I am so sick of smart-mouthed kids making trouble and thinking they shouldn't be held accountable for their actions. Well, I am going to give you a piece of my mind, whether you want to hear it or not. Maybe your parents don't care how you behave, but there are a lot of good, law abiding citizens who are tired of the trouble your kind causes."

"Sharon, that's enough," her husband said.

"It most certainly is not! You read what that article said, and now they have that poor doctor locked up because of him."

Kendall felt the panic rising in his chest as she closed the distance between them and he backed up as far as he could.

"What's the matter, don't like having people tell you what they think?"

Kendall started backing up towards the door, nearing a full-blown panic attack.

"It's YOUR kind that should be locked up, not decent men like Dr. Graham!" she said, her voice rising in volume.

Amanda, one of the other waitresses, came up. "Is there a problem?"

"There certainly is if you allow people like this to eat here!"

"I'm sorry, what?" she asked, looking at the woman in confusion.

She pointed at Kendall as she started advancing towards him again. "This... delinquent."

"JEN!" Amanda called out as Kendall continued backing towards the door.

"Sweetheart, that's enough," the man said.

Kendall started shaking uncontrollably and pushed himself back through the doors.

The woman continued after him. "They need to lock you up and teach you a lesson or two. You're a disgrace to this town!"

∞

The others were waiting in the car and Carlos looked over and saw Kendall come out, and then saw a mean looking woman who was shaking her finger at him. "KENDALL!" Carlos yelled and jumped out of the car.

"What the...?" James said and quickly followed Carlos. Katie jumped out to go after them, but Sylvia got out and grabbed her.

Kendall was still backing away from the woman and stumbled over the concrete bumper block. Carlos launched himself at his friend and managed to catch ahold of him before he hit the ground. Carlos pulled him close. "Stay away from him! What do you think you're doing?" he yelled at the woman.

"Giving that little brat a piece of my mind!"

James had been right behind Carlos and immediately got between her and his friends. "Back off!" he warned, holding his hand up.

Jen and Antonio came running out. "What the hell is going on here?" Antonio demanded.

Jen went over to Kendall. "Baby, are you alright?"

Kendall was shaking and he wouldn't look at her. Carlos pulled him tighter to him and glared at the screaming woman.

"HE'S YOURS?" she shrieked.

Jen turned and looked at the woman. "What did you say to him?"

"Just the truth! If you don't want to hear it, then maybe you should keep him locked away where he can't cause any more trouble."

Jen advanced on the woman, her fists clenched. "HOW. DARE. YOU!"

"Kick her butt, mom!" Katie yelled as Sylvia held the little girl back.

"How dare I!" the woman yelled. "I didn't give birth to a manipulative little monster who RUINED a man's life!"

Antonio got in-between the two of them and showed his badge to the woman. "I'm going to ask you one more time, what is going on?"

"What's going on is that good people are locked up and people like HIM are running around free."

Antonio took a deep breath. "Exactly what are you talking about?"

"I would think as a policeman that you would READ the newspaper."

"Are you talking about the article that was printed regarding the television interview Graham gave?"

"Yes."

"I see, and did you happen to read the RETRACTION the paper printed the next day? A retraction explaining how Graham was charged with contempt of court for discussing an ongoing investigation. Or their APOLOGY for printing Kendall's name and photo, which is AGAINST the law? Or perhaps the part where Graham is being charged with FOUR other counts of malpractice?" Antonio's tone was no longer neutral and his eyes flashed in anger.

"Well no, I didn't see that. It doesn't really change what he did, though now, does it?" she asked, pointing at Kendall.

Antonio looked over at the boys. "Take Kendall to the car and get him warm."

"He's with you?" she asked.

Carlos and James each put an arm around their friend and started back to the car. Carlos turned around and stuck his tongue out at the woman who was watching them leave.

"I suggest you make sure of all your facts before verbally assaulting someone again. The fact is you have no idea what you are talking about. That child has had to endure being forcibly taken from his family, beatings, threats of assault, and when he finally gets back home, exploited by a so-called psychologist. He's been bullied by schoolmates, and I will be damned if I'll tolerate him being bullied by another adult who should know better," Antonio said in a low voice.

"Now just a minute..."

"STOP talking before you get yourself into real trouble," Antonio advised.

"Sharon, I'd listen to the officer if I were you," her husband said.

"You never back me up!" she complained to him.

The manager, Gary, came out to see what was going on. "Jen, what's the problem?"

"This customer attacked my son! Called him names and sent him into another panic attack," Jen said, glaring at the woman.

"We've been loyal customers here for over ten years. We have recommended this restaurant to all of our friends and bring you a lot of business. Your waitress is rude and unprofessional, and I want her FIRED!"

Gary sighed and shook his head. "I see. Well, I would like to say this is a hard decision, times being what they are, but you have actually made it quite easy. Jen, I think you have customers waiting, unless you need the day off to be with your son."

"No, he's in good hands. Thanks though, Gary, I really appreciate it. Antonio, could you tell Kendall that I'll be over to see him after work, please?"

"Sure thing, honey."

Jen threw an icy glare at the woman and walked back inside with Gary.

Antonio stood there, staring at the woman. "Anything else you'd care to say?"

"NO, she's finished and I apologize for her behaviour," her husband said, pulling her away. The woman started yelling at her husband as he dragged her to their car and pushed her into the passenger side. "Just STOP talking before you get yourself arrested!" he yelled.

∞

Antonio shook his head and took a deep breath as he headed to his car. He got into the passenger side and looked into the backseat. Kendall was sitting between Carlos and James. His eyes were closed and his head was resting on Carlos' shoulder.

"Let's go home and get him to bed," Antonio said.

"What was that all about?" James asked.

Antonio looked back at him. "We'll talk about it later, okay?"

James nodded.

They got to the house a few minutes later.

"Kendall, we're home," Carlos said.

Kendall opened his eyes and James helped him sit up straight.

"You doing okay?" James asked.

Kendall nodded and sat there for a minute.

"Come on, boys, let's get inside," Antonio said, opening the car door.

Carlos climbed out and Antonio helped Kendall. He put an arm around the boy and they walked into the house.

"Let's get you to bed," Antonio said as he helped Kendall off with his jacket and boots.

Kendall nodded and headed upstairs. James and Carlos went to follow him, but Antonio stopped them.

"I need to talk to him, so give us a few minutes. I'll be back down once he's asleep and we'll talk about what happened."

They nodded and went into the living room.

Kendall went into the guest room and crawled into the bed, pulling the covers up. Antonio sat down next to him. "Can you tell me how that started?"

"I don't know. I was just sitting there. What newspaper article was she talking about?"

Antonio sighed. "You remember the television interview that Graham gave?"

"Yes."

"The next day, the newspaper printed a transcription of the interview, along with your name and school photo. Sally took care of it and they printed a full retraction the next day, stating they didn't have all the facts before running the story. They're also in trouble for disclosing your name and picture."

"So, everyone in town knows now? Why didn't anyone tell me?"

"I was going to tell you after it happened, but you had the flashback and hurt your hand. Then Alex showed up, and I guess I just let myself get distracted. The next day, they printed the retraction, but you were doing so much better by then, and I just wanted you to have a good day. I'm sorry, Mijo, I should have told you."

"It's okay. We did have a nice day."

"Yes we did." Antonio smiled.

"Is that why your hand is all bruised?"

"Yeah, I went down to the station and kinda let Graham know he wasn't going to get away with it."

"You didn't hit him, did you?"

"No, I hit the wall next to his head. Made quite an impressive hole, if I do say so myself."

"You punched the wall?"

Antonio nodded. "Knocked the placard on the other side clear across the room."

"That would have been something to see." Kendall smiled.

"It was. Sally wants to frame it."

"That would be cool."

"Speaking of, I thought your mom was going to punch out that woman today."

"I know. She didn't get into trouble, did she?"

"No, Gary came out, and when that woman gave him an ultimatum, he chose your mom without a second thought."

Kendall sighed in relief.

"Now you need to get some rest. I have to go to work in a couple of hours and try to get caught up on some things, but Papa M will be here."

"Okay. Papi, will you stay here for a little while?"

Antonio smiled. "Of course I will."

Kendal closed his eyes and Antonio sat back on the bed next to him. About half an hour later, Kendall whimpered in his sleep and then opened his eyes. "P-Papi?"

"I'm here. Are you alright?"

Kendall moved closer to him and Antonio wrapped his arm around him. "What's the matter, Mijo?"

Kendall took a ragged breath. "The other day d-did Claudia tell you about...?"

"Did she tell me what?"

Kendall tucked his head down, hugging Antonio tighter.

"About what happened in the tent that night?"

Kendall nodded.

"Yes, she told me. Were you having a bad dream about it?" he asked softly.

Kendall nodded. "W-Why did he do that?"

"I don't know, Mijo. You said he was going to show you how he liked it, so maybe that was something he liked," Antonio said. This was not an easy conversation, and Antonio was at a

loss as to how to explain it to the boy. He could only hope that Kendall was going to handle it alright.

Kendall was quiet for a couple of minutes. "It really hurts though, how can someone like it?"

"I'm not sure. Maybe after time people get used to it. Maybe you have to be older so things aren't as... sensitive. I wish I had an actual answer for you, but I honestly don't know. If you want, we can ask Anna about it, or find a doctor who specializes in that part of the anatomy."

Kendall shook his head. "I don't want anybody else to know."

Antonio sighed. "You know we should tell your mom."

Kendall shook his head again. "NO!"

"I'm not saying now, but eventually. I am hoping you can talk to Claudia more about what happened. I know it's not easy, I'm having a hard time with it, and I can't begin to imagine how difficult it is for you."

Kendall didn't respond.

"Mijo, was that the only time he did that?"

"I think so," Kendall whispered.

"Okay. Why don't you try and get some more sleep?"

"Papi?"

"Yes?"

"What if I keep remembering things that I forgot?"

"Well, if you remember something else, we'll deal with it then. There's no sense in worrying about something that may not even be an issue."

"I don't want to remember anymore," Kendall said.

"I know you don't. Hopefully there isn't anything else to remember," Antonio said, holding Kendall tighter.

"Papi?"

"Yes?"

"When you look at me, do you see bruises? Claudia said to ask someone else I trust."

"Well, I see the one here," he replied, touching Kendall's forehead. "Then a small one here by your lip, but most of them are almost gone."

"Okay," Kendall said, closing his eyes.

"Kendall, can I ask you something?"

"Mmhmm." Kendall yawned.

"Can you tell me what Deesie said to you, that day in the woods?"

"When?"

"When he had you pinned to the ground, right before you hit him. The look on your face completely changed when he said something to you. You were too far away for me to hear."

"Mm, he said when he was finished, he was going to kill you. It made me mad, so then I knew what to do."

"Okay, go back to sleep, Mijo. No bad dreams this time," Antonio told him.

∞

Alex and Logan got to the Garcia's a little while after the others got home.

James and Carlos were still sitting quietly in the living room. Sylvia had taken Katie into the kitchen and was trying to distract her by baking fresh cookies for Kendall and the boys.

"What's with the long faces?" Alex asked.

"Some crazy woman went after Kendall at the steakhouse," James said.

"What?" Alex and Logan asked at the same time.

James told him what they knew.

"Where's Kendall now?" Logan asked.

"He and Papi are upstairs. Papi said he'll tell us what he knows when Kendall's asleep," Carlos told him.

"Well, I better get this ice cream into the freezer," Alex said.

"Ice cream!" Carlos said.

"Yes, we got some of Kendall's favourite, but there's enough for everyone." Alex smiled.

"Provided Carlos doesn't get to it first." Logan smirked.

"I would only eat YOUR share," Carlos said, sticking out his tongue. Alex laughed and shook his head at the two.

He went into the kitchen. "How are things in here?" he asked as he put the bag into the freezer.

"We're making cookies," Katie said unenthusiastically.

"Don't sound so happy about it."

"We're just making them to keep me distracted, and so I won't ask too many questions," Katie told him.

"Ah, is it working?"

"Not really."

"Why do you need distracting?"

"Because of what happened at mom's work today."

"I see. You don't think it's because your wonderful Papa M loves fresh homemade cookies?"

Katie just looked at him.

"Okay, maybe not. You can be a very intimidating little girl," he told her.

She smiled broadly at that.

"That's it, Darlin', always be proud of your greatest strengths." Alex smiled back.

"She does NOT need encouragement in that area," Sylvia said.

Alex winked at Katie and tried to take a cookie from the tray. Sylvia slapped his hand away. "You've had enough cookies for a while."

"See Katie, Mama G's greatest strength is her mothering ability and her sense of responsibility to everyone's well-being."

"Not going to work." Sylvia smirked.

Alex stuck out his lower lip. "But I never get homemade cookies anymore."

"You ate two dozen the other night!"

"I didn't eat ALL of them, the boys helped."

"And almost a dozen gingerbread cookies yesterday," Sylvia pointed out.

"That doesn't count, it was Thanksgiving!"

"Go," Sylvia said, pointing to the doorway.

"But Sylvia!" he whined.

She shook her head. "Out!"

Alex left the kitchen still pouting.

The boys were laughing at him, having heard most of the conversation.

"So much for being 'distinguished,' right dad?" Logan smirked.

Katie followed Alex out and handed him one of the cookies she had managed to palm. "You were saying?"

"Unbelievable," Logan said.

Chapter 108~ The Gift

Antonio sat with Kendall until he was sure he was sound asleep. He carefully got up and went halfway down the stairs. "Carlos?"

"Yes Papi?" Carlos answered, jumping up.

"Can you go get your Mami for me?"

"Sure Papi!" Carlos said, going out to the kitchen.

"Everything okay?" Alex asked, getting up.

"Yes, I just don't want to leave Kendall alone."

Sylvia came in. "Is everything alright?"

"Yes honey. Could you sit with Kendall while I explain what happened today to the kids? I don't want him left alone. I can fill you in on everything when I'm done."

"Of course," she said, going upstairs.

"Thanks honey." He smiled and kissed her as she reached him on the stairs.

"Papi! Ewww," Carlos said.

"Oh look, he wants to play the game again," Sylvia said, kissing Antonio again.

"Mami, please! The guys can see you!"

Sylvia smirked, kissed Antonio again, and then went upstairs.

Carlos sat on the couch with his head in his hands. "You guys are SO embarrassing!"

"Hang in there, Carlos, someday you'll understand," Alex laughed, patting the boy on the back.

"Really? So you don't get embarrassed when your parents kiss?"

"Well, they don't really kiss anymore," Alex said and then shuddered at the images that suddenly popped into his head.

"Why not?" Carlos asked curiously.

"Yeah Papa M, why not?" Antonio asked, smirking.

"YOU stay out of this, or would you like to share the visual I just got thinking about MY parents?"

Antonio smiled and then shuddered. "Okay, new topic please."

Alex smirked at him. "You just had a picture of your parents making out in your mind, didn't you?"

"Shut up," Antonio told him.

"What's the matter, Papa G? Getting queasy at the thought of your parents locking lips?" Alex teased.

"DAD!" Logan said, smacking him on the arm.

"What?" Alex asked innocently.

"Gross!" Logan said.

"Okay, can we PLEASE not talk about any of our parents OR grandparents locking lips?" James asked.

"Agreed," Antonio and Alex said in unison.

"So what happened today?" Alex asked.

Antonio sighed. "Well, I guess we should start with Kendall's appointment with Anna. He hasn't gained any weight. He hasn't lost any more either though, but Anna wanted to put

him in the hospital. He had a panic attack in the exam room when I told him and wouldn't come near me. I just can't, I WON'T do that to him."

"Kendall will not do well if they put him in the hospital," Logan said.

"Well, luckily we don't have to worry about that because your dad knows how to use a feeding tube," Antonio told him.

"Wait, what?" Logan asked.

"Yup, when your grandpa has problems eating, we put one in and take care of things at home," Alex said.

Logan smiled. "So that's why you're staying?"

"ONE of the reasons," Alex said, putting his arm around his shoulder. "I miss you, I miss everyone, and since Sam can cover things at the ranch, I might as well take advantage of it."

"We still need to try and get some weight on him, though. Anna wants to see him gain half a pound by Monday. She's going to pull some blood then as well. Claudia pointed out that he probably burned through a lot of calories Tuesday night when he walked to her place," Antonio said.

"That's true, and those panic attacks take a lot out of him," Logan said.

"So, the plan is he rests and eats all weekend. I want someone with him at all times. If he has another violent flashback, we just hold on tight and try to get him to come around like Claudia did. I want to avoid having to go back to the hospital if at all possible."

They all nodded in agreement.

"So what happened at the steakhouse?" Alex asked.

"We were getting ready to leave and I went back in to sign my slip. Kendall said he wanted to sit on one of the benches at the door and wait for me. I should NEVER have left him alone," he said, shaking his head.

"Antonio, you didn't leave him alone. You were only a few feet away," Alex said.

"Still."

"You're starting to sound like Jen—blaming yourself for someone else's actions. That's not going to help anyone," Alex pointed out.

Antonio looked at him and started to say something but stopped. "You're right."

"Of course I am. Now what else happened?"

"Some foolish woman read the newspaper article and recognized Kendall from his photo. She laid into him about it. Apparently she believes everything she reads and only reads about half of what's out there. I heard one of the waitresses call for Jen and I saw her go running out, so I followed. By the time I got outside, Carlos and James were already there. Jen was asking the woman what she had done and the woman tore into her. Jen started giving it right back."

"I thought Mama K was going to hit her," Carlos said.

Antonio smiled. "So did I. I flashed my badge and sent the boys back to the car. She started on a tangent about how people like Kendall are the ones who need to be locked up, not decent people like Graham. I asked her if she had read the retraction the newspaper had printed the next day, and she said no. Amazingly, she took everything to heart that she read on page three the first day, and managed to completely skip the retraction about the story printed on page two the next day."

"The guy with her sure didn't look happy," James said.

"No, he didn't. Then Gary came out and asked what was going on, and the woman said she wanted Jen fired or the restaurant would no longer have their business. Gary told the woman he was sorry to see them go, and he and Jen went back inside."

"Thank God for that anyway," Alex said.

"Yeah, Gary's a good man."

"Well, we know what we need to do, and I think we can handle it," Alex said, looking at the boys.

They all nodded.

"I know we can." Antonio smiled.

"You're being awfully quiet, little Darlin'. What's on your mind?" Alex asked Katie.

She shrugged.

"Katie?" Antonio asked.

She sighed. "I was really happy to see my mom go after that mean woman, but it's scary seeing Kendall scared."

"You're not use to that, are you?" Alex asked, picking her up.

She shook her head. "I know he has bad dreams and they scare him, but he's not really awake when that happens. I've never seen him scared of anyone before."

"I don't think it's that he was scared of her. I think he was just freaked out by the situation. He was half-asleep when she started in on him about something he didn't know anything about, and that was my fault. With everything that's been going on, I never got around to telling him about the newspaper article, so he was a bit confused by the whole thing. We also know he's nervous about being out in public and he doesn't like it when someone he doesn't know invades his personal space," Antonio told her.

"I guess," she said sadly.

"Katie, he really only feels comfortable with us. He still won't talk to Dr. Anna, and he's known her forever," James said.

"He talks to Claudia and he just met her," she pointed out.

"That's a little different. Claudia hasn't tried to put him in the hospital or to medicate him with anything. While that might be the right thing to do medically, it doesn't mean it's the right thing to do for him emotionally," Logan told her.

"Plus, Claudia is one of those people that's just really easy to talk to, like Sally," James said.

Katie sighed. "Maybe, but what if he never gets better?"

"He will. It's just going to take time, and we have to be patient. You know, Sally's coming over today, and I think maybe you should talk to her about this," Antonio said.

"Okay, I guess I can do that."

"That's our girl!" Alex said, hugging her.

"Okay, I need to get to the station, so if you boys could arrange that one of you is with Kendall until he wakes up?" Antonio asked.

"I'll go first, I need to finish my book and get started on my paper," Logan said.

"Dude, it's Thanksgiving break. Why are you doing homework?" Carlos asked.

"Because my grade fell a little bit in English, so I'm doing work for extra credit," Logan said.

"What's the matter, your A+ fell to just an A?" James teased.

"Yes."

"It's not like they give you an A++ for giving up your break," James told him.

"Not the point," Logan retorted.

"You're such a nerd sometimes." Carlos laughed.

"Mean! I am at least making an attempt to remain on track. Did you happen to mention to YOUR parents what grade you got on your last paper?"

"What's this?" Antonio asked, looking at Carlos.

"Nothing Papi, really." Carlos smiled.

"Carlos, what did you get?"

"D."

"Carlos..."

"I'm sorry, Papi, it's just really hard to concentrate," he said, looking down.

"I understand that, Mijo, but I think you might want to consider doing a little extra credit too," Antonio told him.

"Yes sir," he said, still not meeting Antonio's eyes.

"How are your grades?" Antonio asked James.

"About the same." James smiled.

"Meaning?"

"C's."

"I know it's hard, but you BOTH need to start concentrating more on your schoolwork. Monday I expect to see all of you applying yourselves a little more," Antonio told them.

"Yes sir," they said.

Logan smirked at his friends.

"Well, since Logan is so concerned with your recent grades, I'm sure he'll LOVE to help you both with your studies," Alex said, patting his son on the shoulder.

"Dad..." Logan whined.

"Yes?" Alex asked pointedly.

"Nothing, I'd LOVE to help them with their studies."

"That's my boy." Alex smiled.

"Good. Now that we have that settled, could you go up and send your Mami down? I need to let her know what happened before I go," Antonio asked Carlos.

"Yes Papi," Carlos said and the boys headed upstairs.

∞

There was a knock at the door and Antonio answered, "Hey Boss! How goes it?" Sally asked.

"Just in time." He smiled.

"For what?"

"I was just going to fill Sylvia and Alex in on a few things. I think little Miss Katie needs to get out for a while."

"Is that so?" she asked Katie.

"Maybe a little," Katie admitted.

"What do you say to a little Christmas shopping? Then we can stop by the station and you can sell some of those Christmas program tickets that you need to unload."

"Perfect!" Katie grinned.

Sylvia came down. "Well, the boys certainly didn't look too happy."

"Yeah, we had to have a little talk about how their grades have slipped and how they need to start getting them up," Antonio said.

"Then why did Logan look so unhappy?"

"Because he 'volunteered' to help Carlos and James," Alex told her.

"Ah, that would explain the head smacking and comments about snitching and nerdiness." Sylvia laughed.

"Well, at least some things haven't changed," Alex said.

Antonio looked at Katie. "I know, I know! Can I please go watch TV in the study or upstairs so the grown-ups can have some tall talk," she said, walking upstairs.

"Tall talk?" Alex asked.

Sally laughed. "Yes, she's decided that since you all treat her like a child when she is obviously far more mature than the average 7-year-old, that she will refer to any mature discussions she's excluded from as 'tall talk' in protest."

"Interesting choice of words," Alex commented.

"Why is that?"

"What happens if one of the adults is really short?"

Sally just looked at him.

"What? It's a legitimate question."

"I think you've been thrown from one too many horses," she said, shaking her head.

Antonio laughed at the expression on Alex's face. "Don't even try to one up her, you will NEVER win, just ask John."

Sally smirked at him.

"Why don't we go into the kitchen? There are some things I need to let you know," Antonio said.

They followed him out and he sat at the table so he could see if anyone came downstairs. Antonio filled Sylvia and Sally in on what had happened at the steakhouse and then took a deep breath.

"There's something else I need to tell you. It's about the flashback Kendall had the other day. When we were at the hospital, he told Claudia what he had remembered. I don't want this to go any further than this room. He told Claudia in confidence and said it was okay if she told me. But I think it's important that we all understand what we're dealing with, so this is absolutely confidential," he told them, looking around.

They all nodded.

Antonio took another deep breath. Damn this is hard, he thought. "Do you remember what happened the night Deesie and Kendall camped out, the night before Ranger Thompson was shot?"

Sylvia and Sally nodded.

"I don't think I'm quite up to speed on everything," Alex said.

"That's right, you weren't here yet. Well, when Deesie started all of this, he told Kendall he was going to teach him his 'abc's' and made a sexual reference for them," Antonio said.

"Okay, do I want to know what they were?"

"Probably not. I know I didn't. Anyway, that night, he uh, he..." Antonio faltered.

"Boss, you want me to explain?" Sally asked.

He nodded gratefully.

"He performed oral sex on Kendall because he wanted him to learn how to do it the way he liked it. He got angry when Kendall told him that he wasn't paying attention. Then he punished him for it."

"He did w-what?" Alex sputtered.

"That's not all he did," Antonio said quietly.

Sylvia took his hand. "What do you mean that's not all?"

"Apparently, Deesie... violated him while he was doing that."

"Boss, Kendall said Deesie never... The doctor's report said there was no sign of trauma."

"He didn't use... He used... he used his fingers to..." Antonio faltered.

"Got it," Sally said quickly.

"Are you saying that that freak of nature got off on fingering a kid?" Alex yelled. His face had gone red and the veins on his neck were standing out.

"Come with me," Sally said, grabbing his arm and leading him out the back door. "Sit here and take a deep breath," Sally told him, pushing him down on the stoop.

Alex sat there and put his head between his knees, afraid he was going to vomit.

Sally sat next to him and rubbed his back. "It's okay. I know that was a shock, but we don't want the kids to know."

Alex took a few deep breaths of the cold winter air, trying to contain his anger.

Antonio came out and put Alex's jacket over his shoulders. He sat on the other side of him. "You okay, buddy?"

"No, and now I know why you're not okay. How can anyone do something like that to a kid?!"

"I honestly don't know," Antonio said.

Alex took another deep breath. "Okay, what else don't I know? If I'm going to help, I need to know everything."

Sally and Antonio looked at each other.

"Boss, why don't you get going, and Alex and I'll take a walk," Sally said.

"You sure?"

"Sure, if he's really up for it?" she asked, looking at Alex.

He nodded and stood up. "Okay, tell me."

They walked through the back gate and Sally filled him in on everything that had happened. They got back to the house about twenty minutes later and Alex felt like he needed a shower and a nap.

∞

Sally and Katie headed out, so Alex went upstairs to check on the boys. Carlos and James were in Carlos' room playing a video game.

"You boys doing okay?"

They both nodded. "Wanna play?" Carlos asked.

"Not right now, maybe later." He smiled.

He went to the guestroom and saw Logan sitting on the bed next to Kendall. "You still mad at your old man?"

Logan looked up from his book and smiled. "I'm not mad, they really do need help."

"Has he woken up at all?"

Logan shook his head. "He's really worn out."

"I don't doubt that. Why don't you and the other boys get out of here for a while, go to the park or something."

"It's a little hard on crutches," Logan pointed out.

"Then walk slowly. You boys need some fresh air."

"Are you okay?" Logan asked, noticing the tired expression on his father's face.

"I'm fine. Papa G and Sally just filled me in on some of what's been going on so I can be of more use around here."

Logan looked at him sadly. "It's not easy, is it?"

Alex sighed. "No it's not, but it's worth it. Now, you boys get out for a while and make sure you take your phones in case you need anything."

"But someone needs to stay here."

"Last time I checked, I'm someone. Now quit stalling and get some fresh air before it gets dark out."

Logan smiled. "Okay, I guess I could run home and get some clean clothes, maybe grab a couple of movies."

"There ya go." Alex smiled.

Logan got up and went into Carlos' room. A couple of minutes later, the boys headed downstairs and out the door.

Alex sat down next to Kendall, still trying to come to terms with what he had been told. He was still furious at what had happened, but he also felt guilty. He couldn't believe how relieved he felt that it wasn't Logan who had been taken. Sally told him it was normal to feel like this, but it didn't feel right to him. It felt like he was betraying Kendall. He loved all the boys, considered them all to be his sons. This was all so frustrating. "God, no wonder Antonio put his hand through a wall."

Kendall stirred next to him, whispering something in his sleep. His breathing picked up and he started to kick at his blankets.

"Kendall, wake up, son. You're safe at home," Alex said softly.

"Hmmm?" Kendall murmured.

"Hey, wake up, sleepyhead," Alex said, gently touching the boy's shoulder.

Kendall took a deep breath and opened his eyes. "Hi Papa M. Where's Papi?"

"He had to go to work, remember?"

Kendall nodded and closed his eyes. A couple of minutes later, he opened his eyes again. "Is it true you're staying longer?"

"Sure am." Alex smiled.

"Because of me?"

"FOR you, for everyone. Antonio needs to get back to work, and I miss being here."

"You can really use a feeding tube?"

"Yup."

"What's it like?"

"Well, it's not very comfortable until you get used to it."

"Does it hurt much?"

"No, it doesn't hurt. Just feels strange is all."

"Okay."

"Are you alright with this?"

Kendall nodded. "I trust you, not them."

"Well, with any luck you won't need it."

"My luck hasn't been the greatest though."

"Well, then it's time for a change, don't you think?"

"Maybe." Kendall smiled as he tried to sit up.

Alex put an arm around him and helped him up. "Maybe you should get some more sleep?"

"I'm tired of sleeping, plus I need to ask you another favour."

"Sure thing, what do you need?"

"Just a minute, I'll show you," Kendall said as he got up and went into Carlos' room. He returned a moment later with Carlos' laptop. He turned it on and pulled up a website for the restaurant, Casa D'Gabriel, in Bloomington.

"I wanted to do something for Papi and Mama G, and this is their favourite restaurant."

"Okay."

"I want to get them a gift certificate so they can go out for dinner, maybe tomorrow night?"

"That's a great idea! So what's the favour?" Alex asked.

Kendall pulled out his wallet. "I have eighty dollars saved. That should be enough for a good dinner, right?"

"That should about cover it."

"If I just give them the money, they won't take it. If I give them an actual gift certificate..."

"Then it's a gift and they can't say no," Alex finished.

Kendall nodded. "But, I don't have a credit card to buy one. So I was wondering if I give you the money, could you buy it online for me? Then I can print it up and put it in a card for them."

"I can do you one better. There is a beautiful hotel there. What if we got them a night's stay there as well?"

"I can't afford that."

"No, but I can." Alex smiled.

"I didn't mean for you to have to buy anything," Kendall said.

"I know you didn't, but I think it might be good for them to get away for a night, don't you?"

Kendall nodded.

"We can make it an early Christmas gift."

Kendall smiled. "It would be nice."

"It's settled then. You go ahead and make the reservations at the restaurant and I'll go grab my wallet," Alex said, getting up.

"Okay, thanks Papa M." Kendall smiled.

"Anytime Champ," Alex said as he headed downstairs. He returned, and a few minutes later, Kendall was printing up the gift certificates, restaurant reservation, and room confirmation sheets.

"I don't have a card," Kendall realized.

"Find a simple one online and print it up. I'll go get an envelope," Alex said.

Kendall nodded and Alex went back downstairs.

"Is everything alright?" Sylvia asked.

Alex smiled. "Everything's fine, I'm just looking for an envelope."

"There are some on the bookcase in the study. What are you up to?"

"Who me? What makes you ask that?" He smiled as he went into the study. He found an envelope and went back upstairs.

Kendall signed the card, folded up the gift certificates, and handed the card to Alex.

"What?" he asked.

"Don't you want to sign it?"

Alex shook his head. "This is from you."

"Uh, no," Kendall said.

"Yes, you can pay me back later," Alex said.

"How? It took me weeks to earn that much."

"We'll worry about the details later," Alex told him.

Kendall shook his head.

Alex sat next to him. "Let me do this, alright? When you're feeling better, you can work it off by helping Mama M around the yard this summer. I know she'd love to have a bigger garden, but she doesn't have the time."

Kendall looked at him. "Are you sure?"

"Absolutely, and tomorrow night we'll do something here with the other boys."

"Okay, thank you," Kendall said quietly.

Alex put an arm around him. "You want to go give it to Mama G?"

Kendall nodded. "Okay."

They went downstairs and into the kitchen.

"Kendall, how are you feeling, Mijo? Did you get enough rest?" Sylvia asked.

He nodded and set the envelope on the counter. "This is for you," he said shyly.

"What's this?" She smiled.

"Well, you'll probably find out if you open it," Alex teased.

"Keep it up and there will be NO more cookies for you at all," she retorted.

"I surrender," he said, holding his hands up.

Sylvia opened the envelope and read the card. She pulled out the reservations and looked at Kendall. "What did you do?"

"It's for tomorrow. You and Papi can go to dinner and have a nice evening. Papa M will be here, so you don't have to worry about anything."

"Honey, these are hotel reservations," she said, reading the second paper. "How did you do this?"

"Papa M helped me."

"Tomorrow you and Antonio will leave here about four, so you make it in plenty of time to check into the hotel. The dinner reservations are for seven," Alex said.

"I don't know what to say, this is too much. We can't accept this," Sylvia told him.

Kendall's face fell and he looked at Alex.

"Yes, you can. It's an early Christmas gift from your godson, so the both of you are going to get away for one night, period," Alex told her.

Sylvia hugged Kendall. "Thank you, honey, really."

He smiled and hugged her back. "You deserve it."

She looked at him. "Papi is going to be so surprised."

He smiled at her. "I'm going to go lie down on the couch for a while."

She nodded. "I'll bring you a smoothie in a minute."

"Okay, thanks." He yawned as he headed into the other room.

"As for you," she said to Alex.

"What did I do?"

"Thank you," she said, kissing his cheek.

"It was all his idea. He just needed a little help with it."

"Did you read the card?"

Alex shook his head.

Sylvia handed it to him.

Dear Mami and Papi,

This is to say thank you for everything you have done for my mom, Katie, and me. I don't really know what else to say except thank you for still loving me in spite of everything that's happened. Thanks for making me feel safe and treating me like I'm still normal, even if I don't always feel like I am.

Love, Kendall

Chapter 109~ Eavesdropping

Sally and Katie decided to head downtown and window shop there. There were several locally owned small businesses that Sally wanted to check out, and she much preferred shopping there than at the mall.

"So, what's going on with you today?" Sally asked.

"Papa G told you what happened at the restaurant?" Katie asked.

"Yes, I understand it kind of freaked you out."

"A little," Katie admitted.

"Do you want to talk about it?"

"I just don't get why people have to be so mean, especially since that stupid woman didn't know what she was talking about."

"Unfortunately ignorance runs rampant in much of the human population."

"I guess," Katie fumed.

"So, what made you angrier? The stupid woman or the fact Kendall seemed to be afraid?"

"I never said I was mad at Kendall."

"I didn't say you were mad at Kendall, I said angry at the fact he seemed to be afraid."

"Oh... I was mad at her for being mean to him."

"And?"

Katie sighed. "I was freaked out because it seemed like he was scared."

"Antonio explained that to you, right?"

"Yes, it just made me feel..."

"Sad, scared?" Sally finished.

Katie nodded.

"I hear your mom nearly went all ninja on her," Sally said.

"Yeah, it was great! She got right up in her face, and then Papa G came out and got in-between them." Katie smiled.

"You're pretty proud of your mom right now, aren't you?"

"Yeah, I really am. It's like my real mom came back, if that makes sense."

"It makes perfect sense. Your mom has been trying to keep her emotions under wraps, distancing herself, and today reacted like she used to."

"I just don't understand why she acted the way she did before," Katie said.

"Well, sometimes when people are scared and don't know HOW to deal with something, they hide from it. While they may not be able to actually run away from their problems physically, they can hide emotionally. That's what your mom was doing. She didn't know how to handle what was going on, so she hid from her problems."

"How?" Katie asked.

"Well, she kept herself busy doing things so she had something else to think about."

"Like cleaning and making cookies all the time?"

"Yeah, things that made her feel like everything was normal. Things that she could control."

"Maybe..." Katie said, her brow furrowed as she contemplated things.

"What are you thinking about?"

"Sometimes I feel bad because I wish..."

"You wish what?"

"Sometimes I wish Deesie didn't die."

"Why is that?"

"Then everyone would know WHO they're supposed to be mad at and stop blaming themselves and each other."

"Sometimes I think you're right."

"Really?"

Sally nodded. "But then we'd have to deal with a trial, testimony, and other things that might have actually made things worse. It's going to be hard enough with Graham's trial."

"I guess you're right, I never thought about that. Can I ask you something?"

"You can ask me anything."

"How come Kendall can talk to Claudia but not Dr. Anna? He's known her a lot longer than Claudia."

"Well, it could be because Dr. Anna's a medical doctor. I don't really know her, but from what I've heard, she's a very nice lady who cares a lot about her patients. It might be because she thinks it would be best for him to be in the hospital, and that's not something he's willing to do. He just doesn't feel safe away from home, which is perfectly understandable."

"But Dr. Anna would never do anything to hurt him."

"No, but right now he has some pretty big trust issues. Being in a place where strange people will be coming and going, different people touching and talking to him, is just a little too much for him to be able to handle right now," Sally explained.

"I guess that makes sense. She does seem nice, and she did get him to stop having the panic attack the other day. I guess if he's decided to trust her, she must have done something right."

"She's very good at what she does. I wouldn't have recommended her otherwise." Sally smiled.

Katie nodded. "I know. I just don't want anyone else to hurt my brother."

"I know you don't, and we're going to do everything we can to protect him."

"Just like he would do for me?"

"Just like that, honey." Sally smiled.

They walked for a few more minutes before they came to a little coffee shop. "How about some hot chocolate?" Sally asked.

"Sounds good," Katie agreed.

They sat down and ordered. After the waitress brought their drinks, Katie sat there, chewing at her lower lip. "Okay what's up, munchkin?" Sally asked.

"I was just wondering..."

"Wondering what?"

"What does fingering mean?"

Sally nearly choked on her cocoa. "Where did you hear that?"

"I was kind of sitting at the top of the stairs when I heard Papa M yell it."

"So you were eavesdropping?"

"Not really. I mean I couldn't actually HEAR anything unless someone talked loud, and he did."

"Katherine Knight, I am VERY disappointed in your behaviour."

"I'm sorry, but no one tells me anything and I want to be able to help my brother too!" Katie said stubbornly.

"I know you want to help him, but eavesdropping is wrong, and you know that."

"Yes ma'am," Katie said, looking down.

Sally looked at her for a moment. "Alright, do you promise NOT to eavesdrop anymore, or do I tell your mom and Papa G?"

"I promise... Will you tell me what it means though?"

Sally thought quickly. "Well, it's an old cop term that means picking out or choosing. A long time ago, they use to say 'the witness fingered the bad guy,' meaning he picked him out of a line-up."

"So it means Deesie picked Kendall out of all the kids?"

"Yes," Sally said.

"Okay, I guess that makes sense," Katie said.

"NO more eavesdropping, right?"

"Right."

"Good girl," Sally said.

They finished their cocoa and headed to the station so Katie could sell her tickets. Once they got there, Sally sent Katie to the break room to sell some of her tickets to a couple of officers who were taking a break.

She popped her head into Antonio's office. "Hey Boss, just checking in."

He smiled. "Have I ever mentioned I hate paperwork?"

"Only about a million times."

"How's Katie doing?"

"Better, but you should know your house has a little mouse who's listening to everything."

Antonio sighed. "What did this little mouse hear?"

Sally closed the door. "She overheard Alex yell when he found out what Deesie had done to Kendall. She asked me what 'fingering' means."

"What did you tell her?"

"The truth. That it's an old cop term meaning to pick out or choose."

"That was quick thinking."

"She really took me by surprise, though. I told her if she eavesdrops again, she'll be in big trouble."

"Okay, thanks Sally."

"No problem. I better go check on the little rugrat before Johnson and Shale end up signing their paychecks over to her."

"See you later." Antonio laughed.

∞

Sally collected Katie before she could do too much damage and they went back to the Garcia home. Kendall was curled up on the couch, half-asleep. "Hey kiddo, how are you feeling?" Sally asked.

"Okay, just tired."

"Look what I got for mom!" Katie said, sitting next to him. She handed him the vintage copy of Wuthering Heights.

He sat up. "Where did you find this?"

"The old bookstore downtown. Sally and I were looking around and I remembered mom loves this movie."

"That's great, Katie, she'll love it. You might want to put it away, though. Mom said she was coming by tonight."

Katie nodded. "Where's Logan? I want to show him."

"Papa M wanted the guys to get some fresh air, so they ran over to Logan's house so he could get some things. They might have gone to the park too, but they should be back any minute."

"Okay, I'm going to go put this upstairs so mom doesn't see it. You want to watch a movie with me when I come back down?" Katie asked, jumping up.

"Sure thing, Katie-Bug." Kendall smiled.

Katie stopped and looked at him. "What?" he asked.

She threw her arms around him. "You haven't called me that in a long time."

He hugged her back. "Maybe that's because you haven't been bugging me as much." He smirked.

"Whatever. I guess I'll have to work harder on that," she said as she went upstairs.

Sally smiled at the two. "Where's Sylvia?"

"She and Papa M are in the kitchen." He yawned.

"Do you need anything since I'm heading that way?"

"No thanks. Mama G already made me a smoothie."

"Did you drink it?"

He held up the nearly empty glass.

"Good job," she said as she headed into the kitchen.

"Hey, I brought the little munchkin back," Sally said.

"Did she have fun?" Sylvia asked.

"I think so. She found a couple of things for Christmas, and we stopped at the station so she could sell some tickets."

"Would you like to stay for dinner? We're just having left-overs," Sylvia said.

"Sounds great, thanks!" Sally smiled. Sally watched the doorway for a moment. "I need to let you two know something." She explained to them about her conversation with Katie.

"Do you think she bought it?" Alex asked.

"I think so, although with her it's hard to tell. I did warn her that if she does it again she'll be in big trouble."

"Well, we'll just have to be extra careful when discussing things from now on," Sylvia said.

"Yeah, like checking the stairwell, closets, cupboards..." Alex pointed out.

"All of those places, she's too smart for her own good," Sally said.

∞

A couple of minutes later, Katie joined Kendall on the couch after putting in a DVD of assorted cartoons. He was half lying on his right side, so he scooted up against the back of the couch so she could curl up in front of him. She curled up into the crook of his arm and pulled his right arm around her, hugging it tightly. A few minutes later, both were sleeping peacefully.

∞

The boys finally got back and James shushed them when he saw the siblings sleeping on the couch. They quietly removed their jackets and boots, and Carlos went over and covered the two with the blanket from the back of the couch.

Alex heard the boys come in and went to check on them.

"Did you get what you need?" he asked Logan.

"Yeah, first we went to check the ice level at the park, and it's ready for skating." Logan smiled.

"That'll be a neat trick on those," Alex said, pointing at the crutches.

"I shouldn't have to use them too much longer." Logan smiled.

"Aww, can we still call you Hopalong though?" Carlos asked sweetly.

Logan glared at him. "DON'T call me that!"

"Carlos, it's almost Christmas, don't call him Hopalong," James said.

"Thanks James." Logan smiled.

"We'll just call him Tiny Tim." James smirked.

Alex laughed. "Good one, James!"

Logan glared at him.

"What? It was funny!" Alex said.

"If the three of you are through tormenting poor Logan, it's time for dinner, so go get cleaned up," Sylvia said, shaking her head at them.

"Thanks, Mama G," Logan said.

"Anytime, honey," she said, patting his shoulder.

The boys went to wash up and Sylvia went to wake Katie and Kendall. She smiled down at her godchildren who were sleeping so contentedly, and decided not to wake them yet. She went back into the kitchen, and a minute later, the others joined her at the table.

"What about Kendall and Katie?" Carlos asked.

"Let them sleep a little longer. It's just leftovers, they can eat anytime," Sylvia told him.

Carlos nodded and they all sat around, enjoying their evening meal.

A little while later, Katie woke up hearing voices. She got up carefully, so as not to wake her brother, and followed the voices into the kitchen.

"Hey, are you hungry?" Sylvia asked.

"Starving." Katie smiled.

Sylvia handed her a plate. "I guess we should wake your brother so he can eat too."

"I'll get him." James smiled.

"This should be interesting," Alex commented.

James went out into the living room and sat next to his friend. "Kendall, it's time to wake up. Dinner's ready."

"Hmm?"

"Time to eat."

"Okay," Kendall said, not moving.

"Come on," James said, pulling the blanket off.

Kendall groaned. "James, quit!"

"Did you want a lift into the kitchen?" James asked.

Kendall opened his eyes and glared at him.

James just smiled.

"You're such a pain in the butt," Kendall said, trying to sit up.

"Yes, but I'm the best looking pain in the butt you know." He grinned, helping Kendall up.

"For now."

"What's that supposed to mean?"

"Not a thing." Kendall smirked.

"Kendall?"

"Yes?"

"What did you mean by that?"

"James, don't be blue."

"Why would I be blue?" James asked, confused. Then his eyes widened, "Did you do something to my shampoo?"

"Who, me?" Kendall said innocently as he went out to the kitchen.

"Kendall, I'm serious. What did you do?" James asked, following him.

"I don't know what you're talking about."

"Aw, I was looking forward to dinner and a show." Alex pouted.

Kendall looked at him, raising an eyebrow.

"What?" Alex asked. Kendall just shook his head.

"Alright you three, behave." Sylvia laughed.

She sat a plate in front of Kendall, who looked at it and sighed.

"Just try," she said, kissing the top of his head.

He nodded and took a few bites.

Katie quickly finished. "Logan, I want to show you what I got my mom for Christmas!"

"Why not us?" Carlos asked.

"It's a book," Katie told him.

"Ewww, what kind of present is a book?" Carlos asked.

"Some people LIKE to read," Logan said, smacking him on the back of the head.

"Boys..." Sylvia warned.

"Sorry," they both said.

"Anyway, it's in my bag. I didn't want my mom to see it when she stops by," Katie said.

"Okay, let's go take a look." Logan smiled, getting up.

"Nerd," Carlos whispered.

"D minus," Logan retorted.

"I thought you said you got a D," Sylvia told Carlos.

"Hey mom, I'll start the dishes for you." He smiled, jumping up.

"Aw, thank you, Mijo. Starting Monday, TWO hours of homework before anything else, and then you finish up the rest after dinner," Sylvia told him.

"But mom..." he whined.

"Yes?" she asked, her tone leaving no room for discussion.

"Nothing." He smiled.

James laughed at his friend's expression.

"Same for you," Sylvia said.

"Ah man," James whined.

"How are your studies coming?" Alex asked Kendall.

"I finished most of last week's assignments, but haven't turned them in yet."

"We'll take them in and pick up next week's for you on Monday," James told him.

"Thanks." Kendall smiled.

"You're welcome, buddy," James said.

"Well, since Logan is going to have his hands full with these two, I can give you a hand with your homework." Alex smiled.

"Okay, thanks Papa M," Kendall said gratefully.

∞

Upstairs, Katie and Logan were in Carlos' room and Katie pulled out the book for Logan to see. "Wow Katie, this is beautiful. Where did you find it?"

"At the old bookstore downtown."

"Harbisher's?"

"I think that's the name."

'Mama K is going to love it," he told her.

"You really think so?"

"Definitely, it's in beautiful condition," he said, running his fingers over the cover.

Katie smiled and then bit her lower lip. "Logan, can I ask you something?"

"Sure, what's on your mind?"

"Well, you know a lot about words and things, and I wanted to ask you what the word 'fingering' means?"

"I'm not sure. Where did you hear it?"

"Well, when I was waiting for Sally, I heard your dad use it. I asked Sally what it meant. She said it's an old cop word that means to pick out or choose."

"Hmm, I've heard that used in old movies when they said they fingered the suspect."

"Okay, I was just wondering because I think they were talking about Kendall. Sally said it meant Deesie chose Kendall."

"I guess that makes sense. Sally would know," Logan told her.

Katie smiled. "Good, because they like to keep things from me, and I just wanted to make sure."

"Were you listening when you weren't supposed to be?"

"Maybe..."

"Katie, you know you shouldn't do things like that."

"I know, I know. Sally already told me if I do it again, I'm in trouble."

"You know they don't keep things from us just because they can. If they don't tell us something, it's probably for a good reason. Because we probably couldn't handle it, and they don't want it getting around," Logan told her.

"Okay, I won't do it anymore," she promised.

"Good. Now, why don't you go see if Kendall's finished eating and we can watch one of the movies I brought over?"

"Okay." She smiled and headed downstairs.

Logan grabbed his laptop and typed in the word 'fingering.' He had heard that term used in old police movies, but he wondered why his dad had used the word.

The definition came up on the screen and he smiled. "Thank goodness," he said as he read the first definition. His good feeling faded though as he read the following definitions and his heart sank. "Oh my God."

Katie came running back up. "He's almost done. What movies did you bring?"

"Um, I thought we could watch The Nightmare Before Christmas tonight," he said as he quickly closed his laptop.

"I love that movie!" She smiled.

"Me too," he said as he got up. They went back downstairs together and Logan handed her the movie. "I'll go make popcorn."

"Okay!" She smiled and went to set up the movie.

Logan went into the kitchen. "Hey, Katie is setting up the movie."

"What are we watching?" Alex asked.

"The Nightmare Before Christmas," Logan told him as he put a bag of popcorn in the microwave and grabbed some bowls.

"How 'bout you, Champ, you ready to settle in for a movie?" Alex asked Kendall.

Kendall nodded.

"Good job with dinner, honey." Sylvia smiled.

"Thanks Mami," he said, getting up. He had managed to eat most of his dinner, but his stomach felt queasy and he wanted nothing more than to lie down again.

The other boys and Alex headed into the living room while Logan waited for the popcorn.

"Honey, I can do that," Sylvia told him.

"It's okay, I've got this. Why don't you go put your feet up and relax, I'll bring it out in a minute," Logan said.

"How can I say no to an offer like that?" She smiled, kissing his cheek.

"Sally, can I talk to you for a minute?" Logan asked before she left the room.

"Sure thing, kiddo, what's on your mind?"

Logan checked to make sure no one was within earshot. "Katie asked me what 'fingering' means."

"She asked you what?"

Logan looked at her. "It didn't mean what you told her, did it?"

"Logan..."

"I looked it up, and while your definition is the first, it isn't the only one," Logan said near tears.

"Damn it," she cursed.

"Sally... He did that to him, didn't he?"

She sighed. "Yes, that's what the flashback was about. I don't want you saying anything to anyone though, alright. If you need to talk about it, come to your dad or me. We don't want the other kids to know. You weren't supposed to know. "

Logan nodded and watched the bag of popcorn grow. He was trying hard not to cry.

Sally put her arms around him and rested her chin on his shoulder. "It's going to be okay, honey, I promise. I know it's a shock, but at least he's not repressing everything anymore. This means that he's actually starting to recover, and that's a good thing."

"Does Mama K know?"

"No, Kendall told Claudia in confidence while he was at the hospital getting stitches. He told her that she could tell Antonio, but he thought it was important we know so we can help

Kendall deal with it. Also, to understand there could be more flashbacks and how to handle them. Kendall doesn't know that we know, and we need to keep it that way for now."

Logan nodded, "I won't say anything, but it's going to be hard not to think about it."

"I know it will be. Try thinking of it as learning how to deal with doctor/patient confidentiality. After all, you are going to be a doctor someday." She smiled.

He smiled back. "I can do that."

"Logan, I'm serious about you calling if you need to talk, alright? You can call me at any time for any reason."

"Thanks Sally, I might have to take you up on that."

"I'll let Antonio and your dad know that you figured it out. In fact, although this is hard for you, it might work in our favour."

"How?"

"Well, you boys are with Kendall a lot of the time. If he has another flashback, we can go over methods on how to help pull him out of it."

"Like Claudia did?"

"Exactly. There are also a couple of other things that could help. Helping him control his breathing, reassuring him with key phrases that get through to him."

"Like what?"

"Well, we'll have to ask Claudia what she thinks will work best. Antonio said she got through to him right away when she came in. Maybe we can set it up where you can go see her and work with her on a few things."

"That's a good idea," Logan said as he pulled the popcorn out.

"Okay, I'll call her tomorrow and we'll set something up. Are you going to be okay?"

He nodded. "I can do this."

"I know you can." She smiled.

"Logan, you want to hurry up already?" Katie yelled from the living room.

"You can also keep an eye on the munchkin for me and make sure she keeps her little nose out of things," Sally told him.

"I can try, but she's awfully sneaky."

"I know, but I think together we might be able to keep one step ahead of her," Sally said.

"Maybe," Logan said doubtfully.

Sally took the popcorn and they headed into the living room.

"Took you long enough," Katie said.

"It's not like I can make the microwave pop the popcorn any faster than it does," he pointed out.

"It stopped popping a few minutes ago," she pointed out.

"I was waiting for it to cool down a little. I don't like steam burns."

She rolled her eyes at him.

"Katie, just start the movie," Kendall told her.

"Fine," she said and hit play.

Logan sat the popcorn on the table and sat down next to Kendall. "Are you still tired?" he asked quietly.

Kendall nodded.

"Here," Logan said and put a pillow on his lap.

Kendall smiled. "Thanks Loges," he said and curled up with his friend.

"Anything for you," Logan said softly as he draped his arm over Kendall.

Chapter 110~ Family Moments

Sally stayed and watched the first movie with them. She wanted to make sure Logan was handling everything alright, and couldn't help but smile at the way he had his arm wrapped protectively around Kendall. She glanced at Katie, who smiled over at her and then came over to sit next to her. Sally put her arm around the little girl as she snuggled in and saw Kendall smile at her. She winked at him and he smiled again. James and Carlos were sitting on the couch, Carlos next to Kendall with Kendall's legs resting across him, and James on the end. She smiled to herself and felt honoured that they had accepted her into their little family unit, especially since her family was less than loving. She had long since cut any ties with them, and in all honesty, she didn't really miss them.

She broke out of her introspection as Carlos squealed. "I want a dog like Zero!"

"Zero is a ghost," Logan told him.

"But he's really cool and he has a nose like Rudolph's," Carlos pointed out.

"That doesn't make him any less of a ghost," Logan said.

"There are advantages to having a ghost dog," Carlos told him.

"Like what?"

"You don't have to worry about feeding or cleaning up after him, and he could help me when I become a super spy," Carlos said.

"Don't you think the glowing red nose might give him away?" James asked curiously.

"I'm sure it turns off when he disappears," Carlos said.

"Probably." James nodded.

Logan shook his head. "There are NO such things as ghosts."

"Have you ever seen one?" Carlos asked.

"No."

"Then how do you know they DON'T exist?"

Logan opened his mouth and closed it again.

"You've gotta admit he's got you there." Alex smiled.

Logan rolled his eyes and sighed. "I need new friends."

"Aw Loges, where would you ever find anyone that challenges you the way we do?" Kendall asked, looking up at him.

Logan smiled at him. "Nowhere," he said as he reached over and smacked Carlos on the back of the head.

"Hey!" Carlos said, smacking Logan back.

"Boys! Don't make me come over there," Sylvia warned.

"Sorry," they said in unison.

After the movie, Sally got up. "Well, I should get going. I have a few things I need to get done. Thank you so much for another wonderful evening."

"Anytime Sally," Sylvia said, hugging her goodbye.

"Let me walk you out," Alex said, grabbing his jacket.

She smiled. "Well, thank you. Bye guys, Katie, I'll see you soon."

"Bye Sally," they said as she and Alex walked out.

"So, what's going on with Logan?" Alex asked.

"Katie went to him and asked him about the word and he looked it up and found the other definitions. He was pretty upset, but I told him how important it is for Kendall not to find out he knows. He and I are going to talk to Claudia about how to help Kendall if he has any more flashbacks."

Alex sighed. "Maybe I should see about staying here a little longer."

"Can you do that?"

"I'll give Sam a call later. I don't really want to leave knowing all of this is going on. Antonio's getting worn out, and it's only a matter of time before he snaps. Graham might not be so lucky if he pisses him off again."

"I know. I'm worried about him too. He's usually able to keep his temper under wraps, but with everything that's happened, his nerves are frayed."

Alex nodded. "I wanted to ask if you can make sure he's off by 3:30 or 4:00 tomorrow. Kendall wanted to do something special for him and Sylvia and got them reservations at their favourite restaurant in Bloomington. We also got them an overnight stay at the Inn there."

Sally smiled. "That's a wonderful idea! I'll go in and make sure he's out by three, just in case it snows again."

"Thanks, I appreciate it. Maybe a night away will help."

"You do know he'll be calling every couple of hours, right?"

Alex smiled. "Yup, but since there won't be anything bad to report, it'll be okay."

"Very optimistic."

"I try, although I did want to see about trying out a feeding tube on Kendall before his appointment on Monday. After they told me that my dad had to have one, I had them try it out on me, so I would know what to expect. It's not very comfortable and it's a pretty strange sensation to have something hanging down your throat. If he does have to have one and we show Anna that I know how to do it and he freaks out..."

"That's a good point, it might be better to get him use to it ahead of time," Sally told him.

Alex nodded. "I'll need Antonio or James to hold him just in case."

"Let me know if you need any help."

"I will. Thanks for everything, Sally."

"Not a problem. I told Logan I was going to let you know that he knows, in case he needs to talk about it."

"Okay. We'll get through this, right?" Alex asked hopefully.

"Of course we will." She smiled and handed him her card. "Call me if you need anything either way."

He nodded and closed her car door for her.

∞

Jen finished her shift and got ready to leave. She was still angry at what had happened and concerned about the repercussions. She knocked on Gary's door. "Hey, I wanted to thank you again for this afternoon."

Gary looked up from the supply reports that he was working on and smiled. "Not a problem, Jen. That woman was completely out of line."

"I just hope we don't lose a lot of business because of this whole thing. Maybe I should stop working here for a while."

Gary looked at her. "Jen, I want you to stop thinking like that right now. If people are going to act like that and judge a child for what an adult did to him, then I don't want their business. You've always been a dedicated and loyal employee, and I'd rather lose a hundred customers like that woman, than lose you."

Jen smiled gratefully. "You don't know what that means to me, Gary. Thank you."

He smiled back. "Shouldn't you get home to that son of yours and make sure he's doing alright?"

She nodded. "I called a couple of hours ago, and he and Katie were watching a movie together."

"Go home, I'll see you tomorrow."

"Goodnight," Jen said and headed out to her car.

She went to Brooke's first and changed out of her uniform. She was going to meet Brooke, and they would go over to the Garcia's together, so Brooke could see James. Brooke came home a few minutes later and Jen filled her in on what had happened that day. The look on Brooke's face made it clear that the woman should be grateful that Brooke was not in the vicinity when she went after Kendall. Jen had to make her promise not to hunt the woman down, and as soon as Brooke calmed down, they headed over to the Garcia's. They arrived a few minutes later and found everyone settled in watching a Christmas movie.

"Mom!" Katie said, jumping up and running to Jen.

Jen hugged her. "Hi baby. Are you having a good night?"

"Yeah. How was the rest of your day?"

"It was fine. What did you do this afternoon?" Jen asked.

"Sally and I went shopping downtown, and then we had hot chocolate, and then we went to the station and I sold twelve tickets to the Christmas program!" Katie said in one long breath.

"That was quite a day! Did you thank Sally?"

Katie nodded.

James got up and went over to hug Brooke. "How was your day today?" she asked her son.

"It was okay."

"Just okay?"

"I'll tell you later," he whispered as he hugged her again.

She nodded and then smiled broadly. "How are our other boys tonight?"

"Good! Even if Logan doesn't believe in ghost dogs," Carlos said as he hugged her.

"Carlos, there are no such things as ghost dogs," Logan said, exasperated.

"You only say that because you haven't seen one," Carlos retorted.

"No one has seen one because they DON'T exist!"

"You're fighting a losing battle," Kendall told him.

"I will PROVE they don't exist," Logan stated.

"How?" Carlos asked.

"I don't know, but I'll find a way," Logan said stubbornly.

Carlos just smiled at him.

"Oh, you're impossible!" Logan declared.

"Well on that note, how about dessert?" Alex asked.

"Sounds good!" Carlos grinned.

"I thought it might." Alex laughed, putting an arm around Carlos' shoulders and heading for the kitchen.

"How ARE you going to prove it?" Kendall asked Logan.

"I don't know, but I'll find a way."

"Good luck with that. He still believes in Santa Claus." Sylvia smiled.

Logan sighed.

"Come on, let's go get dessert." James laughed, holding his hands out to his friends.

Kendall sat up and shook his head. "I'm still full."

"It's your favourite ice cream, though we can make you a shake," Logan said as James pulled him up.

Kendall shook his head again.

"Okay." James smirked as he reached down and pulled Kendall up and over his shoulder.

"JAMES! Stop doing that! Put me down NOW!" Kendall yelled as James walked smiling into the kitchen. He deposited Kendall in a chair and stood behind him.

"Oh, it was an AFTER dinner show," Alex chuckled.

Kendall glared at him and tried to stand up, but James sat next to him and held the chair in place with his arm.

"He'll have a shake." James smirked.

Jen and Brooke followed them in and Jen sat on the other side of Kendall. "How are you doing?" she asked.

"Okay, if people would QUIT picking me up and carrying me around like a sack of flour."

"Make me," James told him.

"I will get even, you know." Kendall smiled.

"How?" James asked.

"You'll see." Kendall smirked.

James watched him for a minute, suddenly nervous.

Jen smiled at the two, shaking her head.

"Boys..." Sylvia said.

Kendall just smirked and James continued to watch him, wondering what his friend was planning. He was going to have to check his shampoo and conditioner bottles before using them again.

Sylvia handed out dishes of ice cream as Logan mixed a shake for Kendall with some of the weight supplement powder.

"So, did you manage to get any rest this afternoon?" Jen asked Kendall.

"Yeah, I fell asleep for a while. You're not in trouble at work, are you?"

"No, Gary wasn't happy with that woman. When I offered to stop working, he said he would rather lose a hundred customers like her, than lose me. So please don't worry about it."

He nodded.

"Honey, I'm serious. Everything is fine. You can call and talk to Gary if you don't believe me," she said, putting her arm around him.

He smiled a little. "I believe you. It just shouldn't be like this."

She looked over at Sylvia and Alex, not knowing what to say next.

"I hate to tell you this, Champ, but there are stupid people everywhere just looking for an excuse to get all self-righteous for whatever the story of the moment is. Good news is good people don't really pay attention to idiots like that," Alex told him.

Kendall looked at him. "Sure they don't."

"Meaning?" Alex asked.

"Nothing."

"Kendall..."

"I don't want to talk about it anymore."

Jen kissed him on the cheek. "Maybe you can talk about it with Claudia."

"Or maybe I can just NOT talk about things I don't want to talk about!" Kendall snapped.

"Fair enough," Alex said, giving Jen a small shake of his head.

Kendall sighed. "I'm sorry. I'm tired, please let me up."

James moved his arm and Kendall got up and went upstairs.

"He's a little tightly wound this evening," Brooke commented.

"Can't say I really blame him," Alex said.

Jen stood up and got the shake from Logan. "I'm going to take this up to him and say goodnight."

Sylvia smiled. "Good idea."

∞

Jen went upstairs and found Kendall sitting in the dark and looking out the window. "Hey, I brought this up since it was already made. I know you're probably full—Sylvia said you ate a good dinner and had a whole smoothie," she said, setting it down next to him.

"Thanks," he said quietly.

"I thought I'd say goodnight and see if maybe you want to have lunch again on Monday?"

"Like that worked SO well today."

"Well, I get off early on Monday, and we can go to a drive-thru, maybe sit in the car at the park?"

"Maybe."

"Honey..."

"I'm sorry mom, really."

"You don't have anything to be sorry about. I wish I could make you see that."

"Then why do I always feel like I do?"

"Because you're a good kid with a conscience. You always try and take care of everyone, and when you can't, you feel like you've let them down," she told him.

He sighed and continued looking out the window.

"Honey, can you tell me what you meant downstairs?"

"When?"

"Before you got upset and came up here. You don't have to, but if you need to let it out, I'm trying to be a good listener."

"I know you are."

They sat there quietly for a moment. "Good people do listen to things that aren't true. They do believe lies," he whispered.

"You're talking about Logan and James, aren't you?" she asked softly.

He nodded. "I'm not mad at them and I never blamed them, but good people do believe lies."

"But not for long," she said.

"Because they're my best friends and know me and what happened. Other people don't."

"That's true, but those are the people who'll forget it as soon as the next story comes along. Alex is right about that," she told him.

"Maybe."

"Honey, I wish I could make it all go away, but I can't. All I can do is tell you I love you and that it will get better. I know you hear that every day, but it's true. So many people love you, and you need to try and focus on them, not the fools like that woman today," Jen said as she wrapped her arms around him.

He leaned into her and they sat watching it snow.

∞

A few minutes later, Brooke came up. "Is everything alright?"

Jen smiled and nodded.

"Katie wanted to show you something before we leave," Brooke told her.

"Okay, I'll talk to you later," she said, kissing Kendall on the cheek.

"Night mom."

Jen smiled and headed down to see her daughter.

Brooke went over and sat next to him. "So, my darling, tell me about this woman who made such a nuisance of herself."

He looked at her. "Why?"

"Because Mama D needs to know just in case she tries getting your mom into any more trouble."

He arched an eyebrow at her. "You think she'd do that?"

"I believe in ALWAYS being prepared." Brooke smiled.

Kendall felt a chill go down his spine.

A few minutes later, Carlos came up. "Mama K said she's ready to go whenever you are," he told Brooke.

"Alright, I'll see you tomorrow," she said, hugging him.

"Night Mama D," Kendall said.

"Goodnight darling, I'll see you tomorrow too," she said, kissing him on top of the head.

After Brooke left, Carlos sat next to Kendall. "You okay?"

He smiled. "Yeah, I'm okay. Just..."

"Frustrated?" Carlos said.

Kendall nodded.

Carlos smiled. "You did eat really well today and drank some of your shake."

Kendall nodded. "You can have the rest. I'm too full, and it'd be sad for it to go to waste."

"Are you sure?"

Kendall smiled and nodded, and handed Carlos the half-empty glass.

"Thanks!" Carlos smiled.

"No problem."

"You want to put in a movie up here?" Carlos asked.

"Sure, that sounds good."

"Why don't you go get ready for bed and I'll set it up," Carlos suggested.

Kendall nodded and found some pajamas. He went into the bathroom, changed, and then brushed his teeth.

"I'm coming for you, sweetheart."

"No you're not, you're dead, so go away," Kendall said. He looked in the mirror at his face. The bruises were still faded, and he breathed a sigh of relief.

He opened the door slightly. "Carlos?"

"Yeah buddy?"

"Can you help me with this?"

"Sure," Carlos said and helped Kendall on with his shirt.

"Thanks."

"Anytime," Carlos said, looking at Kendall.

"What?"

"I'm just so happy you're home," Carlos said, hugging him.

Kendall hugged him back. "I've been back for a while now."

"I know, but I just want to make sure you know," Carlos told him.

"I do," Kendall said, hugging him tighter.

"The movie's ready. Let me get changed real fast."

"Okay," Kendall said, heading back to the bedroom. A few minutes later, he and Carlos were sitting on the bed, watching The Grinch.

James and Logan came up about half an hour later and found Kendall sleeping, curled up next to Carlos as he watched the movie.

"How is he?" James asked.

"Good, just tired." Carlos smiled.

"I told my mom what happened, and she's going to make sure that woman doesn't come near either Kendall or Mama K again," James told him.

"Good," Carlos said.

"Agreed," Logan added.

James and Logan got ready for bed and settled on the foot of the bed to finish watching the movie.

∞

Alex came up a little while later to check on them. "What are you watching?" he asked, sitting in the chair next to the bed.

"The Grinch." Carlos yawned.

"Sounds like you need to hit the hay." Alex smiled.

"Probably." Carlos yawned again.

"Alright you guys, lights out as soon as the movie's over," Alex said, getting up.

"Night dad," Logan said, hugging him.

"Night Papa M," James and Carlos said.

"Night boys," he said and closed the door behind him. He went back downstairs. "Well, they're almost out for the night," he told Sylvia.

"Good, hopefully they'll all sleep well."

The front door opened and Antonio came in.

"Hi honey, how was work?" Sylvia asked, kissing him.

"Very paper-oriented today." He yawned.

"Are you caught up?" she asked.

"Almost. Another couple of hours should do it."

"Good, because we're going out tomorrow night." She smiled.

"We are?"

She handed him the envelope. "What's this?"

"Just read it. Do you want something to eat?"

"No thanks, I grabbed something at work," he said, sitting down. He opened the envelope and pulled out the card with the gift certificate and confirmations. "What's this about?"

"Our godson gave us an early Christmas gift," Sylvia said, sitting next to him.

"How did he do this?"

"With a little help from an older friend," Sylvia said, looking at Alex.

"Hey, like I said, it was his idea and he paid for it. He just needed a little help ordering it." Alex smiled.

"We can't take this," Antonio said.

"Yes you can, unless you want to break his heart. He was so proud of finding something that he knew you'd enjoy," Alex said firmly.

"We can't just LEAVE for the night," Antonio said.

"Yes you can. I'm here, and if there are any problems, James is here as back up. You're going, so stop arguing," Alex ordered.

Antonio shook his head in disbelief. "Everything that's going on, even what happened today, and he's thinking of ways to give back."

"What do you expect? He's just like his dad," Alex said softly.

"Yes he is." Antonio smiled.

"Well, I don't know about you two, but I'm tired," Sylvia said, kissing Antonio.

"Me too." He yawned.

"You two go on up, I'll make sure everything is secure down here," Alex said.

"Thanks buddy." Antonio smiled.

"Oh, before I forget, I'm going to pick up an NG tube tomorrow. I think it might be a good idea to practice inserting it, so Kendall doesn't freak out in Anna's office if we do have to put one in," Alex told them.

"That's probably a good idea. If he fights it too much, she'll want him in the hospital for sure," Antonio said.

"We'll just make sure that doesn't happen then." Alex smiled.

Antonio nodded. "Goodnight Alex."

"Night you two," he said as he went to check the doors.

∞

A couple of hours later, Kendall woke up and eased himself off the bed. He went downstairs and found the little packet he was looking for. He smiled to himself as he took a coffee filter and doubled it, pouring some of the packet in between the layers. He doubled it

again and carefully put it in his pocket. He repeated the procedure and had just thrown the packet away when the light came on.

"Honey, are you okay? Do you need something?" Sylvia asked.

"Uh... no," he said.

"What are you up to?" she asked.

"Nothing," he smiled.

She crossed her arms. "Really?"

He smiled again, went over, and whispered in her ear.

She inhaled sharply and then smiled. "You wouldn't."

"Wanna help?" He smirked.

She thought for a moment and then nodded.

∞

The next morning, James got up first and went to shower. He double checked his shampoo and conditioner bottles and found them untampered with. He turned on the shower, let it warm up, and stepped inside. He lathered up and rinsed, taking extra care to get all the shampoo from his hair. He opened his eyes to pour conditioner in his hand and shrieked at the top of his lungs. His hands and body were a shade of bluish-purple. He looked in the mirror, found his face and hair the same colour, and shrieked again.

"KENDALL!"

Kendall had heard him get up and quickly got up and locked the bedroom door behind him.

Antonio heard the scream and jumped up. "James, what's wrong?"

James opened the bathroom door with a towel wrapped around his waist.

Antonio stared at him in shock. "W-Why are you blue?" he stammered before he burst into laughter.

"Ha-ha, REAL funny!" James said, stomping off to the bedroom. He found it locked and started knocking loudly. "Kendall, I know you're awake! Open the door!"

He heard laughter from inside. "I don't think so!"

"I will break this door down!" James yelled.

"No, you won't," Antonio said, grabbing his arm. He was still trying to contain his laughter but found it difficult looking at the blue boy.

"Look at what he did to me!" James shrieked.

"I know. I think we should probably figure out how to get you back to a normal colour, don't you?" Antonio chuckled.

"How?" James demanded.

Sylvia came out and looked at him. "Wow, you're really blue. I know something that will take it off. Go back into the bathroom and I'll bring it to you."

Sylvia went down to the kitchen and quickly mixed up a large batch of baking soda and water. She stirred in until it was the consistency of toothpaste.

"What's going on?" Alex asked, yawning.

"I believe Kool-Aid in the shower head." Sylvia laughed.

"Who?"

"James is a little blue right now." She laughed.

Alex started laughing. "Kendall did tell him not to be blue last night. Now I guess we know what he meant."

Sylvia went upstairs. "Here, scrub with this," she told James, handing him the bowl.

"What is this?"

"Baking soda and water. It's the only non-astringent that takes it off."

"Thank you," he huffed, shutting the bathroom door.

She knocked on the door.

"What?" he said, opening it.

"You might want to check the shower head BEFORE you get back into the shower," she recommended.

His eyes widened. "I knew that."

He closed the door and they heard him unscrew the showerhead. "You are in SO much trouble, Kendall!"

Kendall peeked out of the bedroom and then went into the hallway. "I TOLD you I'd get even. I even gave you a clue!"

"You better hope this works at getting this stuff off, or I'm going to throw you into a bathtub full of orange!" James yelled, scrubbing his skin.

Carlos and Logan were laughing hysterically in the bedroom. Antonio looked at Kendall, his arms crossed over his chest.

"What?" Kendall smiled sweetly.

"Which one of them helped you?"

"What do you mean?"

"There's NO way you could have gotten that shower head off alone. I know for a fact it takes two hands to get it off."

"I swear neither Carlos nor Logan helped me," Kendall said with his hand over his heart.

Antonio's eyes narrowed. "Katie's too short, so that leaves..."

They heard Alex yelling from the bathroom downstairs. Antonio looked at Kendall, who shook his head, and a moment later, Alex came stomping up the stairs. He was blue from head to toe.

"Alright, which one of you little monkeys did it?"

"Okay... so Alex didn't help you," Antonio said.

Logan and Carlos came out and nearly fell on the floor because they were laughing so hard at the sight of Alex standing there, looking very much like a fuzzy blueberry.

"Laugh it up. Once I get this stuff off of me, you're ALL in for it!" Alex said.

Antonio couldn't hold it in any longer and he started laughing as hard as the boys were.

"Come on, I'll go mix you up a batch of baking soda paste," Sylvia told him, pointing down the stairs.

"It better work," he fumed.

"It will." She laughed. She walked by Kendall and fist bumped him.

He smiled as she walked downstairs.

"Ahem," Antonio said.

Kendall smiled and quickly followed Sylvia downstairs.

Chapter 111 ~ Practice

Sylvia went down to the kitchen, Kendall on her heels. She smiled and kissed him on the cheek. "That was fun!" She pulled out the pancake mix and started preparing breakfast, whistling.

He looked at her curiously. "So, why did you want to prank Papa M? You know he thinks it was me, right?"

"Do you remember about six years ago when I cut my hair short?"

He thought back, remembering how she'd come to hockey practice with her hair cut much like Brooke's. While Brooke's style was ideal for her, it didn't really suit Sylvia.

He nodded. "I like your hair long."

"So do I. Anyway, Alex thought it would be funny to prank Papi, so he put caulking on the inside lining of a ski cap, thinking it was Papa G's. When I came back in from shoveling the walk, I found I couldn't get my hat off."

"Oh no!"

"Oh yes. I had to call Brooke so she could get me in with her stylist on such short notice. By the time he was able to even everything out, I had lost over eight inches of hair. I told Alex I'd get even some day and he just laughed at me." She smirked.

"But he thinks I did it," Kendall pointed out.

She smiled. "I know, honey, that's just a bonus."

"Wait, what? Why?" he asked, realizing he had been set up.

"Because you're young and he'll want revenge," she said, kissing his cheek.

"That is SO not fair!"

"I know, baby, but that's life." She smirked.

"Set up by my own godmother. I did not see that coming."

Sylvia smiled.

Antonio came in a moment later.

"Morning Papi." Kendall smiled.

Antonio arched an eyebrow. "Good morning. Is there a reason we have two blue people in the house?"

"Probably..."

"The reason would be?"

"I warned James, A LOT, and he didn't listen."

"Okay, fair enough... And Alex?"

Kendall looked over at Sylvia. "Collateral damage?"

"If he had been an unintentional target, collateral damage would have occurred if Alex had taken a shower BEFORE James in the same shower, not at the same time in a different bathroom," Antonio pointed out.

"Hmm, I should work on my vocabulary a little." Kendall smiled.

"I know you had help, and I'm pretty sure I know WHO your accomplice was," Antonio said, looking at his wife.

"Are you trying to suggest something?" she asked.

"No dear, not at all. You always bump fists with Kendall for NO reason." He smiled.

"Just supporting my godson in his endeavors."

Logan and Carlos came in. "That was GREAT!" Carlos said.

"You do know James is going to turn you orange if that stuff doesn't come off, right?" Logan asked.

"It'll come off," Sylvia told them.

"Too bad. I was kind of looking forward to seeing Kendall as an Oompa Loompa," Alex said, coming into the kitchen, towel drying his hair.

"Morning Papa M." Kendall smiled, standing behind Antonio.

"Don't hide behind me, go hide behind your ally," Antonio told him, pushing him towards Sylvia.

"I don't know what you're talking about," Sylvia said, pushing Kendall back toward Antonio.

"Hey!" Kendall said, quickly moving over to stand by Logan and Carlos.

"It's alright, I kinda figured it out." Alex smiled, looking at Sylvia. "I just never believed you'd find a way to get even."

"What's that supposed to mean?" she asked indignantly.

"It's okay. It's not your fault. It's just that girls aren't really cut out for pranks," Alex said.

"Oh really? Well it seems this girl did pretty well."

Antonio shook his head as Alex smirked. "So, you admit you did it?"

"Darn it," she said under her breath.

Kendall laughed and Sylvia looked over at him. He stood behind Carlos and Logan. "Hey, you tried to frame me for it!"

"Well let's not forget WHY I felt the need to stoop to the male level and get even in the first place. After all, you were able to wash my prank out in ten minutes. It took almost a year for my hair to grow back," she told Alex.

"True, true. I bow to the humanity and superiority of your prank," he said, making a low bow.

"Where is he?" James said, stomping into the kitchen.

"Now James, calm down," Antonio said, putting his hand up.

"Calm down? CALM DOWN! He turned me blue!"

"Yes, but now you're your usual beautiful self again, so how about some breakfast?" Sylvia said, pulling out a chair for him.

"Fine." James pouted as he sat down.

"Boys, sit down." Antonio laughed.

Logan, Carlos, and Kendall all took chairs on the opposite side of the table.

"This is SO not over," James told Kendall.

"I DID warn you," Kendall said.

"And?" James asked.

"Several times, in fact," he pointed out.

"So you turn me blue?"

"It washed out," Kendall told him.

James glared at him. "As soon as you're well, I am BURYING you in a snow bank somewhere."

"Here honey," Sylvia said, setting a plate of chocolate chip pancakes in front of him.

"Thanks Mama G."

"You're welcome," she said, kissing the top of his head. "Hmm, you smell like raspberry."

He sighed. "A very DEEP snow bank."

∞

Derek Manning was an attorney from Minneapolis that Richard Graham hired at an exorbitant rate. He had a high success rate of acquittals and wasn't above playing dirty to win. He was now waiting patiently at the police station for the officer to bring Graham up for their

first meeting. He smiled as he looked at his watch. At three hundred and hour plus travel time, he could afford to be patient.

Officer Dane brought Graham in, attached his cuffs to the table, and left the room.

"So good to meet you," Manning said warmly.

"Nice to meet you too, IF you can get me out of this situation," Graham muttered.

Manning smiled. "I petitioned the court, but they're adamant about keeping you in here until your trial. I am insisting on a timely trial, so you shouldn't be in here too much longer," he said confidently.

"So you really think you can get me out of this mess?" Graham asked hopeful.

"I don't see why not. I think our biggest problem will be with the DEA. I have a few contacts, and we can probably work out a deal on that end."

"Good. The last idiot I hired told me to plead my case down for less time," Graham said bitterly.

"Pleading down is admitting guilt, and we don't want to do that. What we DO want to do is plead guilty with extenuating circumstances, such as your need to assist the child who was having a panic attack. You KNEW you shouldn't have administer the drug, but did it for the greater good." Manning smiled.

Graham smiled back. "Exactly."

"Now, I have investigators looking into the families involved and have every confidence they'll turn up something useful, they always do. You'll just plead ignorance of the law regarding your interview, claiming your previous attorney didn't make it clear to you that you weren't supposed to discuss the case."

"That sounds good," Graham agreed.

"I have a few other ideas, so I don't want you to worry too much about any of this. That's why you hired me," Manning said, smiling broadly.

Graham smiled back, feeling confident for the first time in weeks.

∞

After breakfast, Antonio headed to the station to finish his paperwork while Alex ran to the pharmacy to pick up a nasogastric tube kit. They were going to practice inserting the tube once Antonio got back from the station. Kendall was nervous, but he agreed it would be better to get used to it at home, rather than chance having a panic attack in Dr. Sharpe's office.

Antonio got to the station just as Manning left.

"Who was that?" he asked Shale.

"Graham's new attorney," she said.

"He's not from here," Antonio said, watching the man drive away.

"A big law firm in Minneapolis," Shale told him.

"Did you catch his name?" Antonio asked.

"Derek Manning."

Antonio nodded as he went into his office. *I'll have Sally check up on this Manning,* he thought.

∞

Alex got back to the house and found the boys watching a game between the Penguins and the Sabres. "Who's winning?"

"No one yet," Logan said.

"No one's scored?"

"No, but there've been four penalties so far," James told him.

"They're how far into the game?"

"About half an hour," Logan said.

Alex smiled and shook his head, looking at the boys. Carlos was watching the game upside down, his legs hanging over the back of the couch, his head on the seat cushion. Logan was sitting on the floor next to him and tossing in popcorn whenever Carlos opened his mouth.

James and Kendall were sitting next to each other, James' arm around his friend, all apparently forgiven.

"Let me know if anything good happens." He laughed, heading into the kitchen.

"What's so funny?" Sylvia asked.

"Our boys."

"Enough said." She smiled.

Alex laid the kit out on the table and double-checked to make sure everything was there.

"Are you really going to be able to do this?" Sylvia asked.

He nodded. "It's not that hard, we just need to get him use to it."

"Okay, Antonio should be home by noon," she told him.

"Good, then we can try this and you two will still have plenty of time to get to Bloomington before dark."

She kissed his cheek. "Thank you again for helping Kendall with it. It was a lovely surprise."

"You two deserve it, although you do owe me a dinner now." Alex smiled.

"Whatever you want tomorrow night then," Sylvia told him.

"I'll have to give this some thought."

Katie came in and sat at the table. "What's that?" she asked, pointing to the tubing.

"It's a feeding tube," Alex told her.

"Why?" she asked suspiciously.

"We're going to practice, just in case."

"So we can do it at home?"

"Yes, so we can do this at home," he confirmed.

"Okay. It's not going to hurt him though, right?"

"No, Darlin', it doesn't hurt." He smiled.

She smiled back. "Good. Mama G, can I spend the night at Molly's?"

"I don't know. Is it okay with Judy?" Sylvia asked.

Katie nodded. "Molly asked me."

"Well, go call your mom, and if it's okay with her, then I'll take you over later."

"Okay!" Katie said, going into the study to call. She came out a couple of minutes later. "Mom said it's okay with her!"

"Alright, I'll call Judy in a little while to get details," Sylvia told her.

"Thanks Mama G! I'm going to go pack my backpack," she said, heading upstairs.

Alex heard the boys yelling in the living room. "Sounds like they're finally scoring," he said. He went in and sat down to finish watching the game with the boys.

∞

Antonio finished his paperwork and gave Sally a quick call.

"Hey Boss, what's up?"

"Graham's new lawyer was here today and I'd like you to do a background check on Monday."

"Sure thing. What's the name?"

"Derek Manning. Shale said he's from Minneapolis."

Sally wrote down the info. "Got it, I'll find out everything I can. Are you going to get out of there anytime soon? I promised Alex I'd make sure you were done by three."

"I'm actually finishing up now." He smiled.

"Good, drive safely and have a wonderful night. Tell Alex to call if he needs backup."

"Will do, Sally. Thanks for everything."

"You're welcome. I might stop by and check on the boys later. Did Alex tell you that Logan found out about what happened to Kendall?"

"No, I knew about Katie asking. How did he find out?" Antonio asked.

"Katie asked him about the word, and after he talked to her, he looked up the different definitions. He's not going to say anything to anyone else, but he was pretty shaken up. Alex knows that he knows, and I told Logan to call me if he needs to talk. I'm going to take him to see Claudia, since he knows he might be able to help if Kendall does have another flashback."

"Damn it, I was hoping we could keep this from all of them. They're too young to have to worry about this kind of thing."

"I know, but we need to face the fact that there's a chance they're all going to find out and decide how to deal with it. From what you said, James is already questioning why Kendall keeps saying it hurts when he has a panic attack," Sally told him.

"I know. I just HATE this."

"I know you do, and that's why it's important for you to get away for a while. Take advantage of the fact that Alex's here and can help. I have John on call as well."

"You think of everything."

"I know. that's why I get paid the big bucks."

"What big bucks?" He snorted.

"I've been meaning to talk to you about that." She laughed.

"Oops, look at the time, gotta go. Talk to you later!" He said, laughing.

"Mmhmm, that's what I thought. I'll talk to you later, Boss."

Antonio hung up and grabbed his jacket. "I'm going to be out of town tonight, so call Sally or Bennet if there's a problem. You can call my cell if there's a crisis," he told Shale.

"Will do. Have a great weekend, Chief." Shale smiled.

"You too," he said as he left.

∞

Antonio got home about fifteen minutes later and went upstairs to change. He was a little nervous about the feeding tube, but he knew Alex was right about trying to get Kendall use to it now. He went back downstairs and waited for the hockey game to end.

About half an hour later, it was over. "That was a disappointing game," Logan said.

"I don't know. It was kind of interesting upside down." Carlos smiled.

"You're so weird," Logan said, shaking his head.

Carlos put his finger in his mouth and then in Logan's ear. "Wet Willy!"

"Carlos, gross!" Logan shrieked, moving away from the other boy.

"Aw, what's the matter Logie-Bear, Carlos picking on you?" James smirked.

"Don't call me that," Logan said.

"Sorry, Tiny Tim." James smiled.

"Don't call me THAT either!"

"Hopalong?" Carlos said helpfully.

"Use my REAL name!" Logan insisted.

"Okay Hortense." Alex smiled.

Logan looked at him in shock. "You said you'd NEVER call me that again!"

"Oops, my bad," Alex said.

"They say 'my bad' in Texas?" James asked.

"It's not a third world country, ya know. Why we got us cable, internet, and all them new-fangled things down there. Might take us a while to figger 'em out, but that's why we send the young 'uns to them thar big city universities," Alex said in a pronounced southern drawl.

The boys laughed at him.

"Alright Champ, are you ready to give this feeding tube a try?" he asked Kendall.

"I guess." Kendall sighed.

"It'll be okay, it should only take a few minutes. I'll go get what we need. Why don't we do this upstairs?"

Kendall nodded.

Alex got up and went to grab the things from the kitchen.

Kendall got up and Antonio put his arm around him. "It's okay, Mijo." He smiled. The boy looked at him dubiously and they went upstairs.

Alex came out with the kit, stethoscope, and a glass of water with a straw. "James, why don't you come in case we need you?"

"Are you sure?" James asked.

Alex smiled. "It can be a little stressful."

James nodded and went upstairs with Alex. They went into the guest room, where Antonio and Kendall were waiting.

"Okay, so this is what we do," Alex said, taking out the long tube. "I'm going to measure this from your nose, around your ear, and down to just past your sternum."

Kendall nodded and Alex took the tube, measured it, and then marked the length with a sharpie.

"What now?" Kendall asked.

"What we do is we insert this through your nose and feed it down to your stomach. Once we get to your throat, I want you to start drinking the water."

"Why?"

"To help move the tube past your gag reflex since it feels really strange. Have you ever had a piece of spaghetti stuck in your throat?" Alex asked.

"I don't like that feeling, it makes me want to throw up," Kendall told him.

"I know. That's why you drink the water. Once it's in your stomach, it doesn't feel as weird. Once it's in, I take the stethoscope and listen while I use the syringe to push in a little air to make sure the tube is actually in your stomach."

"Then what?" Kendall asked nervously.

"Well, I think we should leave it in for a few minutes so you know how it's going to feel, so I'll tape it to your cheek. Then I'm going to flush the line with water, and after a few minutes, we'll pull it out and that's it." Alex smiled.

Kendall looked at Antonio, who smiled reassuringly.

"Okay, let's get this over with," Kendall said.

Alex nodded. "Let's sit on the floor, that way Antonio can hold you."

Antonio sat on the floor and Kendall sat in front of him. Alex looked at Antonio. "Just hold him."

He looked at James. "I want you to hold the glass of water for him, okay?" James nodded and sat next to Antonio, holding the glass.

"Are you ready?"

"No, but go ahead," Kendall said.

Alex nodded to Antonio, who wrapped his arms around Kendall. "Tip your head back just a little," Alex told Kendall.

Kendall did as Alex said. Alex opened the little packet of lube and dipped the tube in it. Then he put his left hand on the right side of Kendall's head to hold him steady, and with his right hand, slowly began inserting the tube into Kendall's right nostril. Kendall gasped at the intrusion and instinctively pulled back.

"Just hold still," Alex said softly.

Kendall was leaning back onto Antonio's chest, trying to hold still, but it felt really strange.

"Just close your eyes, Mijo," Antonio said soothingly.

The tube reached his throat and he started to panic.

"James, water," Alex said.

James put the straw up to Kendall's lips. "Here, just drink, buddy."

Kendall took a sip and felt the tube move a little further down and he gagged.

"Keep drinking," Alex instructed.

Kendall's breathing picked up and he tried to move his head.

"We're almost there," Alex said.

"I can't," Kendall said, panicking.

"Shhh," Antonio said, holding him firmly.

"Antonio, some help," Alex said, pulling his hand up to Kendall's head. Antonio held Kendall with one arm wrapped around his chest and the other firmly holding the left side of his head.

"No, no, no," Kendall said, trying to pull away.

"Keep sipping," Alex said.

Kendall tried, but it felt strange to have the water move the tube and he gagged again.

"Take another sip and we'll be there," Alex said.

Kendall took another sip, but he felt close to tears.

"There we go!" Alex said and quickly taped the tube to Kendall's cheek.

"I want it out," Kendall whimpered.

"I know, but we need to do this. That was the worst part, I promise," Alex said.

"It's okay," Antonio said, hugging him.

"Now I'm going to push some air into the line to make sure it's in the right place. You shouldn't feel anything with that," Alex told him. He pulled a few cc's of air into the syringe and then put the stethoscope in his ears. He uncapped the tube, attached the syringe, and put the stethoscope just under Kendall's sternum. He pushed the plunger and smiled. "It's in."

Kendall was trembling and pale. "It's okay, Champ, you did great!" Alex said.

"Here, drink a little more," James said. Kendall took another sip and tried to relax.

"Doing better?" Alex asked.

Kendall nodded.

"Okay, now I'm going to flush the line. You shouldn't feel anything except maybe a change in temperature, since the water is room temperature."

Kendall looked at him and nodded.

Alex pulled up a few cc's of water and attached it to the line. He slowly depressed the plunger and the water flowed through the line. Kendall shivered a moment later. "You okay?" Alex asked.

"Cold," Kendall said.

"That's normal," Alex said as he finished pushing the water in. He capped off the tube when he was finished. They sat there for a couple of minutes and Kendall's breathing slowed back down. His eyes started to droop and he was still shivering.

"James, can you hand me a blanket?" Antonio asked.

James nodded and grabbed a blanket from the bed and covered Kendall. A few minutes later, Kendall was sleeping in Antonio's arms. Antonio pulled him up and went to stand. "Here, let me get him," Alex said.

Alex took the sleeping teen from Antonio and laid him on the bed.

"What about the tube?" Antonio asked.

"I don't want to remove it while he's sleeping, so we either wake him now or let him sleep with it in for a little while."

"What do you think?" Antonio asked.

"Well, we want him to get used to it, so I say leave it in until he wakes up."

Antonio nodded.

"I'll stay with him," James said.

"You sure?" Alex asked.

"Of course." James nodded.

"Okay, let me secure the tube," Alex said, getting a piece of tape. He took the tube and taped it to Kendall's chest. "Don't let him pull on that, even in his sleep, and make sure the end cap stays closed," Alex told James.

"Okay."

"Call if you need anything," Antonio said.

James nodded and sat next to Kendall. He turned the TV on low and found another game to watch.

Antonio and Alex went back downstairs.

"Is he okay?" Carlos asked.

"Yes Mijo, he's just taking a nap now." Antonio smiled.

"How did it go?" Logan asked.

"It went alright. He panicked a little, but he got past it," Alex told him.

"That's good," Logan said.

"I need coffee," Alex said, heading for the kitchen.

Antonio smiled. "Me too."

Alex poured coffee into two mugs and handed one to Antonio. "So, how did he really do?" Antonio asked.

"Well, it's not a pleasant feeling, and given what he's been through already, I think he tolerated it well," Alex said.

"Good." Antonio sighed.

"What?"

Antonio shook his head. "He still gets so tired with the least amount of exertion."

"I think we're going to have to face the fact that, even if he puts on the weight, he's going to need the feeding tube," Alex told him.

"Why is that?"

"I think there's a good chance he's anemic. He's pretty pale, and that with the fatigue, nausea, and the headaches he's been getting, Anna may want him tube fed regardless."

"That won't go over very well, especially if he's put on the weight."

"I know, but the fact that he was malnourished before, coupled with the pneumonia, it's just taken a huge toll on his system. The good news is we can do this here."

Antonio nodded. "Thanks to you."

"You know I'd do anything for our boys or Katie." Alex smiled.

"I know you would."

"Shouldn't you be packing?" Alex asked.

"Probably." Antonio smiled.

"Well then?"

"I'm not sure I want to leave," Antonio said quietly.

"Antonio, you and Sylvia need this. It's only one night, and I'll be here. Sally and Claudia are a phone call away, and did I mention you need this?"

"I seem to recall you saying something along those lines," Antonio said.

"So go pack. Then we'll make lunch, wake Kendall, pull the tube, and you'll see everything's alright."

"You're right," Antonio said, getting up.

"I know I am." Alex smirked.

Antonio shook his head as he went upstairs. He looked in on the boys. "Everything alright in here?"

"Everything's good," James smiled.

"Okay, I'm going to go pack a bag, and then we'll wake him up for lunch."

James nodded.

Antonio went to his bedroom to find Sylvia had already packed most of what he needed. He put in a couple of more things and went back downstairs. Sylvia was already making lunch. "Thanks for packing my things, honey."

"You're welcome. I figured if I didn't, we wouldn't get out of here until tomorrow."

"You're a funny lady, you know that?" he said, kissing her.

"Well, you married the whole package you know. Beauty, intelligence, humour..."

"That I did. Little did I know what I was getting myself into."

"You..." she said, throwing a piece of cheese at him.

He caught it and smiled, taking a bite. "Of course, you didn't know what you were getting into either."

"That's true," she said.

"If you two lovebirds are done, maybe we should go pull that tube now," Alex said.

Antonio smirked at his friend. "What's the matter Alex, more visions of your parents locking lips?"

"What do you two talk about when I'm not around? On second thought, don't tell me, I don't want to know," Sylvia said.

Alex grinned at her. "Are you sure?"

"Yes."

"Because I'll be happy to tell you." He smiled.

"If you do, the next time it'll be actual dye that you'll have to try and wash off," she threatened.

"Hmm, might be worth it. I'll have to think about it a little longer."

"You do that and remember I have five very resourceful pranksters at my disposal," she reminded him.

"Maybe it's NOT worth the risk," he said reconsidering.

"Wise choice."

"Let's go wake up Kendall and pull that tube." Antonio laughed.

Alex followed him upstairs.

James looked up when they came in. "Is it time?"

Alex nodded.

"Kendall, time to get up," James said, gently shaking his shoulder.

"Hmm?"

"Time to get up," James repeated.

Kendall swallowed hard and then kicked out. His breathing picked up and James grabbed ahold of him.

"Kendall, wake up, it's okay."

Kendall managed to pull away and Antonio rushed to the other side of the bed and caught him before he hit the floor. "Kendall, wake up!" Antonio said, holding onto him.

Kendall was pawing at his face and coughing, trying to dislodge whatever was in his throat. Antonio held onto him as Alex came around and pulled the tube loose from Kendall's chest. Kendall was close to hyperventilating. He took the boy's face in his hands. "Kendall, I need you to focus and try to breathe," Alex said firmly. "KENDALL! Wake up," Alex said loudly.

Kendall's eyes opened and he tried to focus.

"Breathe," Alex said, still holding onto him.

Kendall took a shaky breath and coughed again.

"Can you hear me?" Alex asked him.

Kendall nodded.

"Good, now I'm going to pull out the tube. It's going to feel weird, so just hold on," Alex told him. Kendall nodded and Alex removed the tape from his cheek.

"Do you have him?" he asked Antonio.

Antonio nodded and Alex quickly pulled the tube out with one fluid motion.

Kendall gagged and started coughing again.

"It's alright," Antonio said, rubbing his back.

James came around with the glass of water. "Here, take a sip."

Kendall took a sip, and a couple of minutes later, had calmed down. He leaned into Antonio and closed his eyes.

"Are you doing better?" Antonio asked.

Kendall nodded.

"Okay, well I guess letting you sleep with the tube in is not an option," Alex said.

"You think?" James asked.

"Why don't you two go on down and eat. We'll be down in a few minutes," Antonio said.

"Are you sure?" Alex asked.

Antonio nodded.

Alex stood up. "Come on, James, let's go get some lunch," he said, taking him by the arm.

"Is he okay?"

"He's fine, they'll be right down."

"Okay," James said, unconvinced.

Antonio sat there with Kendall, waiting for his breathing to regulate. He put his chin on the boy's head and sighed. A few minutes later, Kendall put his arm around Antonio's waist.

"Are you alright, Mijo?" he asked quietly.

Kendall nodded. "Sorry, I started to wake up and something felt weird."

"I know. You did just fine though."

"I don't like it, Papi," Kendall said softly.

"I know. We'll get through this though."

"How?"

"Together."

Chapter 112~ The Date

Alex and James went downstairs and joined the others for lunch.

"Is everything alright?" Sylvia asked, noting their expressions.

Alex smiled. "Yeah, Kendall had a small panic attack when he woke up and felt the tube in his throat. He came around pretty fast though."

"Maybe we shouldn't go," she said worriedly.

"I already had this discussion with Antonio. You're GOING, period. You both need a night away, and we'll be fine," Alex told her firmly.

"But..."

"No 'buts,' you're going," he said, leaving no room for discussion.

"Alright, but you'll call if anyone needs anything?" Sylvia asked.

"No, because no one's going to need anything. Everyone will be just fine, so stop worrying."

"We can always call my mom or Mama D," Logan told her.

"That's right, and Sally, or Claudia," Alex added.

"Alright, alright," she said, putting her hands up in defeat. "What are you guys going to do for dinner tonight? I can make something for you to reheat, or there are leftovers."

"You'll do nothing of the sort. I was thinking take-out, maybe Chinese?" Alex asked the boys.

"Sounds great!" Carlos said.

Logan and James nodded in agreement.

Sylvia smiled. "Alright, I can take a hint."

"That was a hint? I thought it was more like a direct order." Alex smirked.

She arched her eyebrow at him.

"Katie, I'll take you to Molly's once you've finished with lunch," Sylvia told her.

"Okay, I'm almost done," she said. Katie quickly finished her sandwich and ran up to grab her backpack. She looked in the guestroom and saw Antonio and Kendall still sitting on the floor. "Is everything okay?"

Antonio smiled. "Yeah, we're just getting ready to go get some lunch."

Katie sat next to them. "I'm going to Molly's for the night, unless you want me to stay?"

Kendall smiled. "No, you go have fun. I'm fine."

"You don't look fine," she told him.

"I'm just tired."

"You're always tired."

"Katie, he still has pneumonia and tires easily," Antonio told her.

She hugged Kendall around the waist. "I know. I just want you to feel better."

"I will," he said, hugging her back.

"Okay, let's go grab some lunch. Do you have everything you need, Mija?" Antonio asked as he got up.

She nodded, still hugging Kendall as he tried to stand. Antonio smiled and pulled the both of them up. Katie grabbed her backpack and they went downstairs. Kendall held Katie's coat for her. "Thanks, Big Brother."

"You have fun tonight, okay?"

"I will. I'll call you before bedtime to say goodnight."

"Okay." He smiled.

"Katie, are you ready to go?" Sylvia called from the kitchen.

"All ready!"

Sylvia came out and Kendall held her coat out for her. "Thank you, honey. I'll be back in a few minutes. Is there anything you need while I'm out?"

"No thanks, I'm good." He smiled.

"Okay," she said, kissing his cheek.

"Bye Katie." He waved.

"Bye Kendall, I'll talk to you later!" she called out as she and Sylvia went out the door.

"Come on, let's go eat," Antonio said, steering Kendall towards the kitchen.

"I'm not really hungry."

"I know, but you need to try. Did the tube bother your throat?" Antonio asked.

"A little."

"I'll heat some soup up for you then. Do you think you can manage that?"

Kendall smiled and nodded. They went into the kitchen and James moved over and pulled out a chair. "Thanks James," Kendall said.

"No problem, little brother." James smiled as he put his arm around the chair.

Antonio warmed up some chicken noodle soup and set the bowl in front of Kendall. "Thanks Papi."

"You're welcome." He smiled as he sat down next to him and started eating his sandwich.

Kendall took a few bites and got a funny look on his face. He gagged a little and pushed the bowl away.

"What's the matter?" James asked.

"The noodles feel funny."

"Try chewing them," Logan suggested.

"Who chews soup?" Carlos asked.

"Not the broth, just the noodles," Logan said.

"No thanks," Kendall said.

Alex got up and took the bowl. He drained the broth into a mug and handed it back to Kendall. "Here, try this."

Kendall smiled. "Thank you."

"I'll make you a smoothie," James said, getting up and grabbing the items he needed.

Antonio finished eating and ran upstairs to grab the bags. He brought them down and set them near the door. He went back into the kitchen and sat down to wait for Sylvia. "So, what do you boys have planned for tonight?"

"Well, I thought we'd get take-out, maybe rent a couple of movies, and just hang around and relax," Alex said.

"Sounds good." Antonio smiled.

"Well, I want to finish my book," Logan said, getting up.

"Why don't you just watch the movie?" Carlos asked.

"Because the movie is NOTHING like the book," Logan told him.

"Is that a bad thing?"

Logan just rolled his eyes.

"Carlos, maybe you should read the book, watch the movie, and write a report on the differences between the two," Antonio suggested, trying to nip another argument in the bud.

"No, that's okay! I'll go grab your book for you, buddy," Carlos said, jumping up.

"Thanks, Papa G!" Logan smiled.

"Anytime Mijo." He laughed.

Sylvia got home from dropping Katie off. "You ready to go?" she asked Antonio.

He nodded.

"Jen's going to pick Katie up from Molly's tomorrow afternoon and do a little Christmas shopping. Then they'll come by here for dinner, which by the way, you still need to let me know what you want," she told Alex.

"Actually, I really miss your tamales."

"Do you mind turkey?"

"Sounds perfect to me."

"Tamales it is then!" She smiled.

"Okay, you two better hit the road," Alex said.

Antonio and Sylvia looked at each other and nodded. They all headed into the living room. "Okay, if you need anything at all, just call," Sylvia said as she put on her coat.

"We'll be fine, just go," Alex said.

"Thank you," she said, kissing his cheek.

"Bye Mami," Carlos said, hugging her tightly.

"Goodbye Mijo, you behave."

"I will," he promised as she kissed him goodbye.

Logan hugged her next. "Bye Mama G, have a great evening."

"We will. Thank you, honey. You boys have fun too."

James hugged her next. "Honey, don't forget your dad is coming to pick you up around eight in the morning."

"I won't, I just hope he doesn't forget," James said, kissing her on the cheek.

"He won't, Mijo," she said reassuringly.

He smiled.

She hugged Kendall and kissed his cheek. "You take it easy, get some rest, and make sure you eat. Call us if you need anything, okay?"

"I will, and we'll be fine."

"Thank you again, Mijo."

"You're welcome." He smiled.

"Alright, we better get going," Antonio told her.

She nodded.

"Bye Papi," Carlos said, hugging his dad again.

"Goodbye Mijo. Why don't you help me with the bags?"

"Okay!" he said and grabbed his jacket. He grabbed Sylvia's bag and followed his parents outside. Antonio opened the back door and they put the bags in.

"Carlos, I need you to do me a favour," Antonio told him.

"Sure, what do you need?"

"I want you to make sure that Kendall's never alone and that he eats, okay?"

"But James is better at that."

"James won't be here tomorrow and Logan is still on crutches," Antonio reminded him.

"Oh yeah. Don't worry, Papi, I'll take care of him," Carlos promised.

"That's my boy! Call if you need anything, and we'll call later to say goodnight," Antonio said, hugging his son again.

"Okay, bye Papi, bye Mami!"

"Goodbye Mijo," Sylvia said as she got in the car.

Carlos went back inside.

"Giving him something to do so he doesn't feel sad?" Sylvia asked as they drove away.

Antonio nodded. "He hates it when we're both gone, and having him look after Kendall lets him know he's needed."

She smiled. "Good idea. Are you ready to be away for a whole night?"

"Yes and no. I know we need some time, but that doesn't stop me from worrying." He sighed.

"I know. Me too, but Alex is perfectly capable of handling things, right?"

Antonio laughed. "Yes he is. I'm so glad he came home for a while."

"Me too. I wish he could move back," Sylvia said.

"I know. I really miss having him around."

"I know you do, honey. It's hard when your playmates move away." She smirked.

"Funny lady." He laughed, shaking his head.

∞

Carlos went back inside. "Are you okay?" Kendall asked.

He nodded, went over, and sat next to his friend. "I just miss them when they're gone."

Kendall patted Carlos' shoulder. "I know, but they need a break and we'll have fun."

"I know we will. Maybe we can rent James Bond movies and have a marathon." Carlos smiled.

"I'm up for that," Kendall said.

"Sounds good to me." James smiled.

"A James Bondathon it is then," Alex said. "Should we order dinner now, go pick up some movies, and then reheat dinner later?"

"That's a good idea," Carlos said.

"Okay, let's get jackets and boots on then," Alex said, standing up.

The boys got ready while Alex called in an order to the restaurant. They stopped at the video store first. Kendall didn't want to go in, so Logan stayed with him. The others returned about fifteen minutes later with a bag full of assorted movies.

"We got five Bond movies," Carlos told them excitedly.

Logan and Kendall smiled at him.

"We also got Zombie Plague and a cowboy movie with some old dude," James said.

"Hey! 'The Duke' is not just some old dude. He was one of THE best western actors that ever lived," Alex told him.

Logan rolled his eyes. "DON'T get him started. Just smile and nod."

The boys all smiled at Alex when he looked back. "I should let you know I have excellent hearing."

"Sorry dad." Logan smirked.

"Mmmhmm," he said as they pulled out and headed to the restaurant. He parked in front of the restaurant and ran in. He returned a few minutes later with four large bags of food.

"I hope you boys are hungry."

"Always!" Carlos told him.

"That's the truth," Logan said. Carlos stuck his tongue out at him. "What? It's true."

They got back to the Garcia house a few minutes later. James and Carlos helped Alex carry the bags in while Kendall walked closely to Logan. They went inside and Alex put the food in the refrigerator while Kendall followed him into the kitchen.

"I'm going to make popcorn. Does anyone want hot chocolate or tea?" Alex called out.

"Could I have tea please?" Kendall asked.

"Sure thing. Anyone else?"

"Hot chocolate," the other three boys called from the living room.

"Can I ask you something?" Kendall asked.

"Sure, what do you need?"

"Can we try the tube thing again?"

Alex looked at him. "Why? You did just fine."

"No, I didn't. I want to make sure we can do it with no problems so Dr. Anna won't..."

"Try and put you in the hospital?"

Kendall nodded.

"Kendall, honestly, you did fine. You did better than I did."

"You did?"

Alex nodded. "When I found out my dad had to have one, I had the doctor put one in so I'd understand what would happen. Let me tell you, I have a really strong gag reflex."

"So?"

"I threw up," Alex told him.

"You didn't say that might happen."

"Why put the thought in your head?"

Kendall thought about it a moment. "I still want to try again, if that's okay."

"Antonio's not here to hold you," Alex pointed out.

"James can do it."

Alex looked at him. "You really want to do this?"

"Please, I don't want to take the chance, and I just want..." Kendall faltered.

Alex looked at him. "You want what?" he asked softly.

"I j-just want to make things easier so Papi doesn't worry so much. I w-want to make him proud," Kendall whispered.

Alex put his hands on the boy's shoulders. "Look at me."

Kendall looked up and then back down. He was fighting to hold back tears again. He HATED not being able to control his emotions, and his hand went to wipe his eyes, but Alex's was there first. He pulled the boy into a hug and rested his chin on top of his head. "Antonio IS proud of you, we all are. We're proud of ALL of you, don't ever forget that."

"Sometimes it's just hard."

"I know it is, Champ. Let me go get what I need. We can do it down here, if that's okay," he said, turning off the stove.

"Thank you," Kendall said quietly.

Alex went into the bathroom and got the kit that he had already cleaned and prepped. He went out into the living room. "Hey guys, Kendall wants me to try the feeding tube again, so we're going to need a little help."

"Why does he want to do it again?" James asked.

"He wants to make sure he doesn't panic if Anna wants to see it done."

"Okay, what do we do?" Logan asked.

"Well, I'm going to need James to hold him, with you and Carlos as back-up. Carlos can hold the water for him, Logan you hand me what I need when I ask for it."

The boys nodded.

Kendall came in carrying a cup of water.

"Are you ready?" Alex asked.

Kendall nodded.

James moved the coffee table and sat on the floor in front of the couch. Kendall set the water on the table and then sat in front of him.

Alex sat everything on the table. "Okay, we're just going to put it in and then pull it out a minute later. Then we're going to watch movies, eat junk food, and then have dinner."

"What junk food?" Carlos asked as he picked up the cup of water and sat next to Kendall.

"I found out where your mom hides the cookies and assorted goodies." Alex grinned.

"Where?"

"Yeah, I don't think I should tell you that."

"But Papa M, I've been looking for that hiding place forever." Carlos whined.

"Really Carlos, FOREVER?" Logan asked.

"It FEELS like forever."

"Are you ready?" Alex asked Kendall.

Kendall took a deep breath and nodded.

"You don't have to do this if you don't want to," James said as he pulled him closer.

"Yes I do."

"Carlos, have the water ready and hold it up for him when I tell you," Alex instructed.

Carlos nodded and moved a little closer.

"James, do you remember how Antonio held him this morning?"

James nodded and wrapped his arms around Kendall, making sure he could move one hand if needed.

"I'm going to put it in your left nostril this time. Are you sure you're ready?"

Kendall nodded again and Alex took the tube. "Logan, can you open the lube packet please?"

Logan tore the little packet and held it up for his dad. Alex dipped the tube in the packet and put his right hand on the left side of Kendall's head. "Tip your head up a little."

Kendall did as Alex said, and Alex slowly started inserting the tube into Kendall's nostril. Kendall pulled back a little but forced himself to stop.

"You okay?" Alex asked.

"Yeah."

Alex continued feeding the tube in, until Kendall gagged. "Carlos, water please," Alex said.

Carlos put the straw up to Kendall's lips and he started sipping. Kendall felt the panic start to rise in his chest as the tube moved down his throat, but he forced himself to stay still and continued to sip at the water. James felt him tense up and tightened his hold a little. He rested his head on Kendall's right shoulder so he couldn't move his head too much.

"Almost there," Alex said.

Kendall closed his eyes, fought against the panic, and then heard Alex say, "We're there!"

Kendall opened his eyes. "Really?"

Alex smiled and nodded. "You did great! Logan, can you hand me the stethoscope and syringe?"

Logan handed him the items and Alex pulled up some air and placed the stethoscope just below Kendall's sternum. He pinched off the tube while he attached the syringe, then released it and depressed the plunger. "Perfect. Now I'm going to flush it, and then we'll pull it. We're going to do it the right way, not just yank it out this time." He smiled.

Kendall nodded again and took another sip of water, fighting off the overwhelming need to cough the tube out.

Alex pulled up the water and then reattached the syringe to the tube and flushed the line. Kendall shivered and James held him a little tighter.

"Okay, now I'm going to pull it," Alex told him.

Kendall nodded and Alex slowly inched the tube out. Kendall found the sensation worse than when it went in and his breathing picked up.

"Almost there, just drink," Alex said.

Kendall started sipping the water again, and a moment later, the tube was out. He started coughing and James rubbed his back until Kendall was able to stop.

"Well, I'd say that was a complete success," Alex said.

"I still don't like it," Kendall said, coughing.

"I know, but you DID it without panicking. I don't think there'll be a problem on Monday." Alex smiled.

"I hope not."

"Hey, you did WAY better than I did," Alex told him.

"Thanks Papa M," Kendall said, coughing again.

"Carlos, do you know if there's any cough syrup in the house?" Alex asked.

"I'll go check," Carlos said, jumping up.

"How about I go make that tea and hot chocolate?" Alex asked.

"That sounds good." Kendall smiled.

Alex got up, gathered the NG kit, and went back into the kitchen.

"That was awesome!" Logan said. Kendall and James just looked at him.

"What? I mean from a purely medical standpoint," Logan said.

Kendall rolled his eyes. "It doesn't feel awesome."

"I know, but it's still amazing the things that medical science has come up with! I mean, who thought up a feeding tube through the nose?"

"I don't know, but I'm sure you'll find out and bore us with the details later," James said, getting up.

He put his hands down to his two friends and pulled them up.

"How can you NOT be curious about things?" Logan asked.

"Oh, I am. Just not boring, annoying, scientific things like... who discovered boiling water."

"Well, if someone hadn't discovered HOW to boil water, you couldn't have hot chocolate," Logan pointed out.

"BORING. I only care about the fact that I can MAKE hot chocolate," James told him.

"Like YOU can boil water," Logan said, walking towards the kitchen.

"Hey, I can boil water. Just because I forgot about the kettle once, doesn't mean I can't boil water!" James said, following him.

Kendall shook his head at the two and sat down.

Carlos came running back down with a small bottle. "Cough syrup!"

"Thanks Carlos."

A few minutes later, James carried in a tray with hot chocolate, tea, and cookies for all of them.

"What do you want to watch first?" Carlos asked Kendall.

"You choose." Kendall smiled.

Carlos put in Goldeneye, and then sat back down next to Kendall. He handed his friend the cup of tea, holding his hand up in case he needed help. Kendall smiled at his friend's diligence. "Carlos, do you still have your sippy cup?"

"Are you sure?"

"Yeah, it's kinda silly for two of us to try and hold one cup."

Carlos smiled and took the cup, returning a moment later with a green sippy cup. "How many of these do you have hidden?"

"Enough." Carlos grinned.

Kendall smiled at his friend.

∞

Antonio and Sylvia arrived in Bloomington at about four. It had started snowing shortly after they left home, so they drove slowly. They checked into the hotel and went up to their room.

"This is so nice," Sylvia commented, looking around.

"It really is," Antonio agreed.

Sylvia went into the bathroom and came back out a moment later. "A jetted tub. There is a JETTED tub!"

"Well, why don't you take advantage of it? Dinner isn't until seven," Antonio told her.

She kissed him. "Can you believe this?"

"Not really." He smiled.

"Do you think we should call and check on the kids?"

"No, I think we can wait a couple of hours." He laughed.

"Well, I'm going to go fill that tub and soak for an hour. Feel free to join me..." Sylvia said, walking into the bathroom.

"An hour?" Antonio asked and then realized he had nearly missed the last part of her sentence. He smiled and followed her in.

∞

They arrived at Casa D'Gabriel at 6:45. The snow had made for several cancellations, so they were shown right to their table.

The headwaiter greeted them. "Because we haven't had the pleasure of your company in such a long time, a bottle of Zenato Amarone della Valpolicella, with my compliments," he said, showing them a bottle of wine.

"How sweet! Thank you so much, Affonso, it's been too long," Sylvia told him.

"Well, I expect business and that growing boy of yours keeps you very busy." He smiled.

"That's an understatement." Antonio laughed.

"I will bring you your menus in a moment," Affonso said as he opened the bottle of wine and poured it for them.

"Thank you," Antonio said.

Sylvia took a sip of her wine. "This is wonderful."

Antonio smiled. "You look beautiful tonight."

"Why thank you, so do you," Sylvia said.

She was wearing a red sleeveless evening dress with a matching short jacket. She had her hair down but combed back over one ear, and she was wearing the pearls he had given her for their tenth wedding anniversary.

He was wearing his black suit with a red tie that matched the colour of her dress.

Affonso returned with their menus and a basket of freshly made bread.

"I already know what I want," Sylvia said, setting the menu down.

"Well, I guess we're ready to order then," Antonio told Affonso.

"I would like the browned butter Mizithra with penne pasta," Sylvia said.

"I'll have the chicken piccata," Antonio said, handing the menus back to Affonso.

"Very good." Affonso smiled and went to place the orders.

The musicians started playing. "May I have this dance?" Antonio asked, getting up and holding out his hand.

Sylvia smiled and took his hand. They went on the dance floor, where two older couples were already dancing. Antonio took Sylvia in his arms and they began to slow dance. "We haven't done this in so long." She smiled.

"I know, we really need to start making more time for each other," he said, holding her close.

"We do. It's not easy with your schedule, hockey, school, and Carlos."

"No, but now that Carlos is older, we should start having a date night at least every couple of months," he told her.

"I agree." She smiled as she snuggled in closer to him. The song ended and they went back to their table, and their dinner came a few moments later. They ate their meal and enjoyed the music, dancing again once they were finished eating.

After the fourth dance, they sat back down. "We really should call the kids," Sylvia said, looking at her watch.

Antonio nodded, "I have an idea." He called Affonso to the table and handed him his phone. "Would you mind taking our picture so we can send it home?"

"Delighted." He smiled.

Antonio moved closer to Sylvia and put his arms around her. She leaned towards him and they both smiled. Affonso snapped the picture and handed the phone back to Antonio.

"Perfect, thank you, my friend," Antonio said.

"My pleasure."

Antonio sent a text along with the photo to Carlos' cell. "There, we can call them once we get back to the hotel," Antonio said.

"This was so nice."

"Are you ready to go?" He smiled.

She nodded and Antonio had Affonso bring their bill. They drove to the hotel and went back to their room.

Sylvia called home. "Hello," Alex answered.

"Hi Alex, we're just calling to check in and say goodnight. Did Carlos get our text?"

"He sure did, you both looked great tonight. I'll put Trouble on for you," he said as he handed the phone to Carlos.

"Hi Mami, you looked magical tonight!"

"Magical... I like that!" She smiled. "What are my boys doing?"

"We just finished dinner. Papa M got us Chinese, but Kendall wouldn't eat the noodles, so he had the rice. We're watching Die Another Day, because we're having a James Bondathon. We already watched Goldeneye, but I think we should watch the zombie movie next."

"That sounds like fun. Is everyone else doing alright?" She laughed.

"I think so. Do you want to talk to them?"

"Sure Mijo. Why don't you just put the phone on speaker?"

"Okay." Carlos set the phone down and pushed the speaker button.

"Hello boys, are you all having a good night?"

"Hi Mama G, we are," Logan said.

"Good. James, don't stay up too late. You need to be ready to go early."

"I won't," James said quietly.

"James?" she asked.

"Nothing, he just hasn't called yet, so I'm not sure we're still going."

"Oh Mijo, I'm sure you are. He promised, and I bet he just hasn't had time to call yet."

"Sure."

Kendall put his arm around James' shoulder. "She's right. He probably just had some things to finish up."

"Right," James said as he went back to sit down.

Kendall watched his friend and hoped his dad didn't let him down again.

"Kendall, how are you feeling?" Sylvia asked.

"I feel okay."

"You ate?"

"Yes, I ate."

"Good. Why don't you boys go back to your movie and put Papa M back on?"

"Okay, you have a nice night," Kendall said.

"Thanks to you we've had a wonderful night. Thank you again, honey."

"You're welcome, here's Papa M," Kendall said, handing the phone to Alex. He went over and sat next to James, leaning in towards him. James smiled and put his arm around his friend.

"He's not going to let you down," Kendall said quietly.

"Let's just drop it, it's easier that way," James said.

"James..."

"Look, it's just better if I don't expect anything from him. That way..."

"It doesn't hurt as much?" Kendall finished.

James nodded.

"You know we'll always be there, right?"

James smiled. "I know little brother. That's how I've made it this far."

"Look, if he doesn't show up for some reason, we can go do something," Kendall told him.

"Like what?"

"We could go skating since the pond is ready."

"You'd go skating? Out in public?"

Kendall rolled his eyes. "Yes, out in public. As long as you guys are there, it'll be okay."

"You can't go out with your pneumonia. You're supposed to stay quiet this weekend," James reminded him.

"We can go for a little while. I'll just bundle up really well."

"NO, you won't. But it makes me feel better knowing that you would." James smiled.

"You know I would," Kendall said.

"I know." James smiled again, lying his head on Kendall's shoulder.

"So gorgeous, you and the hubby having a good night?" Alex asked as he walked into the kitchen.

"We're having a lovely evening, thanks to the two of you. I'm worried about James if Mike doesn't show up. He seemed so sincere on Thanksgiving. I can't believe he'd do this to him."

"I hope he doesn't let him down too. I'll keep a close eye on James, and if Mike doesn't show up, I'll figure out something to do with him," Alex promised.

"We should be back late morning, early afternoon. Let us know what happens though, okay?"

"You know I will, but you two take your time and enjoy yourselves," Alex said.

"Okay, thanks Alex. We'll see you tomorrow."

"Goodnight honey. You two get some rest... or not." He smirked.

"Really? You do know you're impossible, right?" she said.

"I know. What can I say?"

"Goodnight." She laughed and hung up.

Alex went back into the living room and sat down to finish the movie. He glanced over at James and found himself wanting to throttle Michael Diamond. *James is such a good kid, he deserves a father that appreciates him,* Alex thought.

About half an hour later, he looked back over and saw that Kendall had fallen asleep and his head was lying on top of James'. James was still awake and watching the movie, Logan sitting on the other side of James, leaning against him. Carlos had pulled the blanket down earlier and covered all of them. He was sitting on the other side of Kendall, his legs curled up under the blanket. Alex smiled at the sight.

The phone rang at about ten and Alex got up to answer it. "Hello, yeah, just a minute. James... phone," he said, holding the phone out to the teen.

James looked at him. "Who is it?"

"It's your mom."

James sighed, carefully pushing Kendall towards Carlos and got up. He took the phone from Alex. "Hi mom. No, it's okay. It's been snowing all night, you stay home and I'll see you tomorrow. No, he hasn't called yet. I know, I'll see you tomorrow, okay? I love you too, goodnight."

James hung up and was going back to sit down with his friends when the phone rang again. James went back to answer it. "Hello... Hey dad. No, it's okay, I understand."

The others were listening and Alex's heart dropped when James told Mike it was okay. "Damn it," he cursed under his breath.

"No, I understand the meeting was running long." Suddenly James broke into a big smile. "Between eight and eight-thirty? Sure, I'll be ready. Okay, see you then!" James hung up.

"Well?" Alex asked.

"His meeting ran late tonight, so he couldn't call until now. He'll be here to pick me up in the morning."

"That's great, James! See, Mama G was right," Alex said.

James nodded. He hadn't felt this happy in quite a while and it showed in his eyes. He sat back down next to Kendall and finished watching the movie with his friends.

After the movie, they all headed up to bed. James carried Kendall, who was still sleeping soundly. Alex was going to sleep in Carlos' room in case he was needed during the night, so he went around and checked the doors and windows, and then headed upstairs.

Somehow, the boys managed to get Kendall into his pajamas, and a short while later, he and Carlos were sleeping in the bed, Logan and James next to it.

James was still smiling and Logan couldn't help but be happy for him. Michael Diamond had hurt James a lot over the years, but it seemed like he was finally making an effort

to spend time with his son. He snuggled into the blankets next to his friend and Logan was soon fast asleep, James soon to follow.

∞

James woke up early and jumped in the shower, checking the showerhead first. He showered, dressed, and headed down for a quick breakfast.

Alex heard him get up and followed him down. "You're up early, Sport." Alex smiled.

"Just want to be sure I'm ready to go."

"You're going to have a great day." Alex smiled.

"I hope so," James said.

"Why only hope?"

"I guess I'm just nervous. My dad and I haven't exactly spent a lot of time together. What will we talk about? It's a long drive to Minneapolis."

"The drive isn't that long, and I'm sure the two of you will think of something to talk about."

James nodded. "What are you guys going to do today?"

"I don't know. Antonio and Sylvia won't be back until later, so maybe we should try and replace some of those cookies we ate."

"You're going to bake?"

"Don't look so surprised. I'm sure we can figure out a simple cookie recipe," Alex told him.

"Good luck with that." James smirked.

"Smart aleck."

"I'm going to go shovel the walk while I wait." James laughed as he headed outside.

Twenty minutes later, he had finished and Mike Diamond pulled up. "Dad, you're early," James said.

"I want to take it slow today. It snowed quite a bit overnight and the weather report says more is expected. Are you ready to go?"

"Yeah, just let me tell Papa M," James said, going back inside.

Alex had seen Mike pull up and smiled at the grin on James' face when he came in to say goodbye. "You guys have fun, and don't worry. It's going to be fine."

James nodded. "I'll see you later! Tell the guys I'll see them after the game."

"I will, now go have fun."

James nodded and hugged Alex goodbye.

Alex watched them drive away and hoped things went well for the two.

∞

James and Mike got to Minneapolis about two hours later. Mike had decided to take it very slow and was relieved when they got there.

He loved his son, but he was never sure what to talk about, so they had discussed what was going on with Kendall and the rest of the boys. Mike had to admit he was impressed with his son and the other boys, coming together and standing together through it all. He knew he had basically thrown away his friendships with the other three families, and that they were not happy with his treatment of James. Kendall had made that VERY clear when he had called, and Mike had done a lot of thinking since that talk.

He smiled, remembering Kendall telling him what an idiot he was to throw away a great son like James. That James deserved better than he had gotten from him. What could he say? Kendall was right, James was a great kid and he DID deserve better. Mike just hoped he could salvage part of their relationship. He had never been close with his own dad, but he remembered WANTING that closeness.

God, I have turned into my father, he thought. He parked in the reserved parking lot at the Metrodome and he and James walked inside. They walked around for a while before heading up to the boxed seats that his company owned.

James looked at him smiling. "This is awesome! I've never been up here before. You can see the whole field!"

"Yes you can," Mike said, smiling back.

James pulled out his phone and snapped some pictures.

"Hey, how about a picture of the two of us?" Mike asked. James smiled and put his arm around Mike's shoulders. He smiled and snapped the picture and then looked at it. It was a great photo of the two, both smiling with the field in the background. The game started soon after and they sat down to watch.

Later, Mike called down and ordered hotdogs, sodas, and a pennant for James.

Mike kept watching his son, who was seemingly mesmerized by the game. He realized he had never actually taken his son to a game before and promised himself that would change.

Halftime came and James called the Garcia's home phone.

Kendall checked the caller ID and answered. "Hey James, how's it going?"

"We're having the BEST time! I took some pictures. This box seat is amazing, you can see everything!" James told him.

Kendall smiled. "That's great! I'm glad you're having fun. Is your dad doing okay?"

"Yeah, he's doing fine. It was hard trying to talk all the way here, but we managed."

"Good, I'm really happy for you. You guys have fun and we'll see you later today. I want to see the pictures then."

"Okay, I'll see you guys later!" James smiled and hung up.

The second half finished about two hours later, the Bears winning by six points. The two waited until most of the crowd had dissipated and then headed to the car.

∞

Sylvia and Antonio had a restful night and woke up late. They called home, found James had already left, and Alex and the other boys were planning on hanging around the house for the day.

"I think we're going to try and get some Christmas shopping in, if that's okay?" Sylvia asked Alex.

"Of course it's okay, take as long as you want."

"Thanks, we should be home around three or four then."

"Alright, we'll see you then," Alex said.

Sylvia and Antonio went to a few small shops around town and then stopped for lunch. Antonio looked at his watch and saw it was close to two. "We better get going after lunch."

"Alright with me, I'm ready to be home again."

"What, one night away and you're already tired of me?" Antonio teased.

"Yes, that's it," she said, rolling her eyes.

"I knew it. The honeymoon is over."

"What honeymoon? In case you've forgotten, our honeymoon was a weekend in Minneapolis because SOMEONE had to be back for a trial."

"Ouch... Sure, bring THAT up." He smiled.

"I just mean, how can the honeymoon possibly be OVER if we haven't even had one yet?" she said, kissing him.

"Oh, that's what you meant. I guess I can live with that."

She rolled her eyes at him again. "We should probably get home before the kids do something to Alex."

"True, but do we really WANT to save him?"

"Good point."

They were on the road a little while later. It had started snowing again and traffic was slow. They had been driving for about half an hour when it came to a standstill. After waiting twenty minutes, Antonio got on the radio to the station. "Hey chief, what do you need?" Shale asked.

"Can you give me the traffic report on I-494 about fifteen miles outside of Bloomington?

"Sure thing, let me pull it up," she said, typing the request into the computer. "Looks like a twelve car pile-up, truck jack-knifed. Rescue vehicles should be there in about ten minutes."

"Thanks Shale," Antonio said. He reached into a bag in the back, pulled out the magnetized portable patrol car lights, and put them on top of his car. He pulled in-between the lanes and drove up as far as he could, to see if he could help.

"What a mess," he said, looking at cars that had slid off the road into each other.

"Oh God, I hope no one is badly hurt," Sylvia said, seeing the large semi that had folded in on itself.

Suddenly, Antonio slammed on the brakes and their car slid to a stop.

"What?" she said.

Antonio jumped out of the car and raced to the side of the road. She watched him go over the slight embankment towards a gold SUV.

"No!" she choked out as she jumped out and followed him.

She ran over to where Antonio was trying to get the passenger door open.

"Stay there!" he ordered as he moved to the rear passenger window and started hitting it with a large rock. The window finally cracked and then shattered. He reached in and unlocked it. He got out after unlocking the front door and pulled it open.

He looked at the driver, who was groaning and trying to free himself from his seatbelt. "Mike, don't move around. Stay still, help is on the way," Antonio said firmly.

He looked down at the unconscious teen in the passenger seat. "James, Mijo, please wake up."

Chapter 113~ The Accident

Alex looked around the kitchen and took in the scene. Every bowl was dirty and nearly every inch of the counters and floor were covered in flour and various other ingredients. Carlos was popping any stray chocolate chips into his mouth.

Logan was reading Sylvia's cookbook. "Dad, I don't think we're doing it right."

"How can making chocolate chip cookies cause such a mess?" Alex asked.

"These aren't too bad." Carlos smiled, eating one from the first batch. They were completely flat because they had forgotten to add the baking soda. The next batch had all of the ingredients, but they had forgotten to turn on the oven timer. They had baked for forty minutes and were as hard as hockey pucks. The third batch had just turned out wrong somehow.

"You're the smart one. Why can't we make a simple batch of cookies?" Carlos asked Logan.

Logan looked at him, biting back a retort. Then he closed the cookbook. "Too many cooks in the kitchen, so I'm going to go finish reading my book."

"Oh, no you don't! No one is leaving this sinking ship," Alex told him.

"We could always do what my mom does," Kendall offered.

"What's that?" Alex asked.

Kendall opened the freezer and dug through to the back. He pulled out a tub of pre-made cookie dough and smiled.

"You couldn't tell us this TWO hours ago?" Alex asked.

"I was sleeping when you started."

"You've been awake for nearly an hour," Alex pointed out.

"Nobody asked." Kendall shrugged.

"Nobody asked..." Alex muttered, shaking his head as he took the tub from him.

"Well, no one did!" Kendall smirked.

An hour later, the kitchen was nearly clean and the dishes washed. The fourth batch of cookies were nearly through baking when the phone rang. Kendall looked at the caller ID and answered. "Hello."

"Kendall, can you put Papa M on?" Sylvia asked.

"Sure, is everything alright?" Kendall asked, worried by the strained tone in her voice.

"Yes Mijo, please get Alex."

Kendall took the phone out into the kitchen. "It's Mama G. She needs to talk to you."

"Hey gorgeous, you two going to be home soon? Okay, yeah sure. Not a problem." He smiled as he walked into the study and closed the door.

"What's going on?" Carlos asked.

"Something's wrong," Kendall said under his breath.

"He's smiling, everything's okay," Logan said, although he could tell from his dad's initial expression that it wasn't.

Kendall shook his head. "Something's wrong," he repeated.

∞

Mike and James had been six cars back and one lane over when the semi hit a patch of ice and started to slide. The cars directly behind the truck swerved to avoid hitting it and ended up off the road with the cars behind them swerving and slamming into them. Mike had seen the

truck start to turn and started pumping his brakes. He had nearly come to a stop when a car in the other lane slammed into the rear door on the passenger's side, forcing them into oncoming traffic. He threw his arm up across James' chest as he hit the gas to avoid the cars coming at them, and then threw the car into reverse to avoid a pick-up that was sliding out of control towards the front end of his SUV.

"DAD!" James screamed.

"Close your eyes, Jamie!" Mike yelled as he slammed the car back into first and headed for the embankment, away from traffic.

They went over the slight incline and Mike slammed on the brakes, turning the wheel right, hoping it would be the driver's side that hit the trees. The SUV spun around twice and then came to a stop on the two tires on the driver's side, just short of the towering pines.

After staying suspended in air for a few seconds, the SUV came back down on all four tires. Mike and James were whipped back and forth inside the car and Mike hit his head on the driver's window when the SUV first went up, and again when it came back down. He put his arm out, still trying to secure his son in his seat and then lost consciousness.

James was thrown first towards his father and then towards the dashboard, his seatbelt preventing him from going through the glass. He had put his hands up against the dashboard to stop himself from going forward and felt a terrible pain in his side as the seatbelt pulled him back.

"Dad..." he whimpered, looking over at Mike. He reached over to shake his dad, but the pain in his side made it hard to breathe. A moment later, he closed his eyes and the darkness claimed him. He was still holding onto Mike's arm.

∞

Mike heard a cracking noise and tried to open his eyes. There was a terrible, blinding pain when he moved his head, but he forced himself away from the window.

"J-Jamie?"

"Mike, don't move. You're going to be alright," a voice said.

"Antonio? Where's my son? Please save my son," Mike said, his eyes tearing up.

"He's fine. We're going to get you both out of here, but you need to stay still. You hit your head pretty hard and probably have a concussion," Antonio told him.

"James..."

"I'm okay, dad. Please stop moving," a soft voice said.

"I thought I lost you," Mike said as he closed his eyes.

Sylvia was sitting next to James, holding his hand and softly stroking his hair. She had grabbed the emergency blankets from their car and covered him with one. Antonio had gotten the driver's door open and covered Mike with another. They waited for the medics to get to them.

"Is h-he o-okay?" James asked, shivering.

"I think he's going to be fine. Where are you hurt?" Antonio asked.

"My s-side hurts, I think something's wrong with my r-ribs," James told him.

"Honey, did you hit your head?" Sylvia asked.

"No, I d-don't t-think so."

"Your dad did a pretty good job of avoiding the other cars." Antonio smiled.

"I-I didn't see what happened. He t-told me to c-close my eyes."

They heard the sirens getting closer, so Antonio ran back up to the road to let them know they had a man with a head injury off road. A few minutes later, the medics had a neck collar on James and put him on a backboard. They carried him up the incline and got him into an ambulance. "I'm NOT leaving without my dad!" he screamed.

"Mijo they're getting him, just hold on," Sylvia said.

A moment later, Mike was placed in the ambulance next to James. "He's right here next to you," the medic told James.

"Is he okay?" the teen asked, tears now flowing freely from his eyes.

"He's unconscious but stable, all of his vitals are normal. We're going to get you both to the hospital so the doctors can take care of you."

"It's going to be okay, James," Antonio said.

"Papi, please don't leave me!" James cried.

Antonio showed the medic his badge and got in. He sat next to James. "It's alright, Mijo, I'm going to ride in with you. Mami is going to follow us after she calls Papa M. We're going to have him pick up your mom and meet us at the hospital."

James put his hand out and Antonio took it. "Please d-don't let her b-blame my dad. It w-wasn't his fault and we h-had the best day."

"She won't. Now tell me about the game," Antonio said as the ambulance pulled away.

∞

Alex came out of the study and turned off the oven. He pulled the cookie sheet out and set it on the counter. He looked over and saw three pairs of eyes watching his every move.

"What's wrong?" Kendall asked.

"Are Mami and Papi okay?" Carlos asked, holding onto Kendall's arm.

"They're fine. There was an accident on the interstate between here and Bloomington. They stopped to make sure everything was alright."

"But?" Kendall said.

Alex took a deep breath. "They saw Mike's SUV off to the side of the road. They got out to check on them. Mike hit his head pretty hard and James might have some cracked ribs. They're on the way to the hospital now, so we're going to go and pick up Mama D and take her there."

Kendall went into the living room and started getting his boots and jacket on.

The others followed.

"Does she know?" Logan asked.

"Not yet. I called Jen and she said Brooke got home just as she was leaving to pick up Katie. They're going to meet us at the hospital."

"She's going to blame Mr. Diamond," Logan said.

"No she won't. It was a twelve car pile-up due to a jack knifing semi," Alex told him.

"That won't matter," Logan said.

"Let's just worry about it when we get there," Alex suggested as they headed out the door.

They arrived at Brooke's house five minutes later. "Stay here, we'll be right out," Alex told the boys.

Carlos was still holding onto Kendall's arm and watched his friend as he stared out the window. "Papa M said they're okay," Carlos said quietly.

Kendall didn't respond, lost in his own thoughts. Carlos looked at Logan, concern evident in his warm brown eyes.

"You doing okay, buddy?" Logan asked.

Kendall nodded, continuing to look out the window.

A moment later, Brooke came running out, Alex trying to keep up with her. She got into the passenger side. "Please hurry!" she called out to Alex.

Alex got into the driver's side and looked at her. "Put on your seatbelt, honey."

"Oh, that's right," Brooke said and tried to pull it around. When it kept catching, she gave an exasperated sigh. "Can we please just GO?"

Carlos quickly undid his seatbelt and popped up between the two front seats. He gently pulled the belt and latched it. He sat back and put his own back on.

"Thank you, darling."

"You're welcome." He smiled.

Alex winked at Carlos and backed the car out of the driveway.

They arrived at the hospital about twenty minutes later, and Brooke jumped out and rushed in. Alex opened the back door to help Logan out. "You better catch up with her, I'll help Logan," Carlos told him.

Alex nodded. "See you boys inside."

Logan got out, leaning on the door, and Carlos handed him his crutches. He looked over at Kendall, who was still sitting there. He undid Kendall's seatbelt. "Come on, buddy," Carlos said, pulling his friend out the door.

Carlos walked in between the other two boys as they made their way inside. Once inside, they looked around for someone they knew.

"Mijos!" they heard Sylvia say.

"Mami!" Carlos said as he threw his arms around her. "Are they okay?"

She nodded. "Come sit down," she said, putting an arm around Carlos and the other around Logan, trying to lend him some support against the slippery floors. Kendall walked behind them. They went into a small waiting area that was designated for families and sat down.

"James is alright. He just has some bruised ribs and possibly a case of whiplash. They're going to keep him overnight for observation, but he'll be able to go home tomorrow."

"What about Mr. Diamond?" Logan asked.

"They're doing an MRI. He hit his head pretty hard on the driver's door window."

They looked up as Antonio and Alex came in.

"Where's Brooke?" Sylvia asked.

"They took her to see James. I'm going to go pick up Tiffany, she doesn't know yet," Antonio told her.

"Oh my God, I forgot all about her," Sylvia said.

"Let me do it, you stay here," Alex said.

"Are you sure?"

"Yeah, I'll be back soon," Alex said as he left.

A few minutes later, Jen and Katie arrived. "How are they?" Jen asked.

"James is fine. Mike has a concussion, they're doing an MRI to see how bad it is," Antonio said.

"I was listening to the radio and they said there was one fatality and seven injuries that required transport to the hospital," Jen said.

Antonio nodded. "A car in the second lane went under the semi as it turned. The driver died instantly."

"Maybe we shouldn't talk about this now," Sylvia said quietly as she glanced at the children.

Katie sat down next to Kendall and wrapped her arms around his waist. He had his arm around her, not really looking at anything in particular. Logan sat to Kendall's left and Carlos was sitting next to Katie.

"When can we see James?" Carlos asked.

"I'm not sure, honey. Let's wait until Brooke comes out," Sylvia said.

A few minutes later, they heard shrieking and sobbing as Alex led Tiffany up to the nurse's desk. He left her there, went in, and sat down next to Logan. He shook his head. "She has quite a set of lungs on her, my ears are still ringing."

"Is she alright?" Jen asked.

"Damned if I know. She has been like that since I told her what happened. Not a coherent sentence out of her. Of course, that could be due to the champagne she was guzzling," Alex told her.

"I'll go stay with her," Jen said, getting up.

"Are you sure?" Sylvia asked.

"Someone should, and we should probably keep her and Brooke apart, so I'll take her to the waiting area on Mike's floor."

"Okay, call if you need us," Sylvia said.

"I will," she said as she headed in the direction of the hysterical woman. Jen shook her head at the sight of the tall blonde woman who was now shrieking insults at the nurse.

"Come on, I'll help you find Mike's room and we'll wait there," she said as she took Tiffany firmly by the arm.

"But, but, but," Tiffany hiccupped as Jen led her away.

"I know, it'll be alright, you'll see," Jen said in a soothing tone. The nurse threw Jen a grateful wave as they walked to the elevators.

Brooke came in about half an hour later. Her mascara was smudged from crying, but she was smiling now that she had seen her boy.

"How is he?" Sylvia asked.

Brooke sat down next to her. "He's going to be just fine. Bruised ribs and a little sore from the accident, but he's fine. He's just really worried about his dad right now. Has anyone heard anything yet?"

"Not yet, honey. It'll probably take a couple of hours after they run the MRI," Antonio said.

"Can we see James?" Carlos asked.

"The doctor said two at a time, so why don't you decide who goes when?" Brooke smiled.

"I think one grown up with one kid is the best plan," Antonio told them.

"Go ahead, Carlos," Logan told his less-than-patient friend.

"Are you sure?" Carlos asked.

Logan and Kendall nodded.

"Come on, honey," Sylvia smiled, holding out her hand. Carlos jumped up and took his mother's hand and they walked to James' room together.

"How are you holding up?" Alex asked Brooke.

"Much better now that I know he's alright. He'll be much better once he knows his dad is alright," she said.

"He was stable at the scene and on the ride in. I think he'll be fine," Antonio told her.

"I hope so," Brooke said.

"Just so you know... Tiffany is here. Jen took her up to wait in Mike's room," Alex said.

"As long as she stays away from my boy, everything will be fine," Brooke told them.

Sylvia and Carlos returned fifteen minutes later.

"Go ahead," Kendall said quietly to Logan.

"Maybe you should go next," Logan said, concerned by his friend's demeanor.

Kendall shook his head.

"Okay," Logan said, getting up.

Alex and Logan headed for James' room and Carlos took Katie down to find a snack machine. The adults were talking, but Antonio kept glancing over at Kendall. He started to get up to go speak with him, but Brooke stopped him. "Let me."

Brooke went over and sat next to Kendall. "So, you're pretty quiet and I think I know why."

Kendall looked up at her and then away.

"Come with me," she said, taking his arm and pulling him out of the waiting area.

Antonio watched them, concern in his eyes.

Brooke led him down the corridor until she came to a door marked chapel. She opened the door and pulled him inside. They sat on one of the benches. "It's quiet in here and people will leave us alone."

His heart clenched knowing what she was going to say. It was his fault Mike had taken James to the game, and if he had just stayed out of it, neither of them would be hurt right now. James would blame him too once he found out, and their friendship would be over. Especially if Mike didn't recover.

He sat there looking at his hands, trying to hold back the tears.

He felt an arm go around him and pull him close. "I don't blame you for anything. You did a wonderful thing by calling Mike. You should have seen James' face when he talked about the day they had together. I haven't seen his eyes light up like that in so long."

"B-But," Kendall started, confused.

"No, we're NOT going to play the blame game here. It was a car accident caused by bad weather and bad luck. It could just as easily have been Antonio and Sylvia in an accident. They were right there and you did give them a night away. They wouldn't have been on the road if not for that, which means Antonio wouldn't have seen Mike's car and got to them before something worse happened. He made sure the medics knew Mike had a head injury. Without that, he could very well have died."

"But if they hadn't gone to the game, then..."

"Then James wouldn't have had the best day he's EVER had with his dad. He wouldn't know exactly how much Mike does love him, and maybe Mike wouldn't know it either. Antonio said when Mike came around he had only one fear, that he had lost James. I think finally realizing how much his son does mean to him was worth a bump on the head to Mike."

"So J-James isn't mad at me? You d-don't hate me?" Kendall asked, choking back a sob.

She pulled him close. "Honey, James loves you so much. You're his little brother and nothing is ever going to change that. You boys might argue and do some pretty stupid things sometimes, but you're also always there for each other. As for me, I admit I was a little upset when Mike first told James that he wanted to try to be a better dad, but that has nothing to do with you. Mike and I don't have the best relationship, and I guess I was a little worried if James started doing things with his dad, he wouldn't need me as much. Today I realized just how selfish that is. There are times I would like to run Mike over with his little blonde bimbette's Mercedes, but there was a time when we DID love each other. I try and remember that when I look at James, because he's the one good thing we did together that's lasted."

"What if Mr. Diamond doesn't get better?" Kendall asked quietly.

"Oh please, that man has one of the hardest heads around. He'll be just fine." She smiled. "Now, I need to ask you a favour."

"What?"

"I have a very important meeting with some out-of-town investors tomorrow and the other boys go back to school. I need you to keep an eye on James after he gets out of here."

"He can still stay with us?"

"Of course, where else would he go? Now, can you make sure he stays quiet and does what the doctor says?"

Kendall nodded.

"Good. I know you have an appointment with Claudia tomorrow, and he really likes her, so maybe he can go with you?"

"That sounds good," he said.

"Alright then. Now that we have all of this settled, why don't I take you to see him?"

"Okay. Are you staying the night here?" Kendall asked.

"I am. Do you want to stay?"

"Will they let me?"

"Oh darling, that won't be a problem at all."

∞

Brooke and Kendall waited for Logan and Alex to finish with their visit and then went in to see James. James was lying there quietly and smiled when he saw them. Logan had mentioned Kendall seemed like he might be in shock, so James was ready.

"Hey, little brother. How are you feeling?"

"I'm not the one who was just in the middle of the worst accident of the season," Kendall said.

James smiled. "You also didn't get to see one of the BEST games of the season."

"Are you okay?"

"Just a little sore. Nothing worse than after getting dog piled in a game. I'll just be glad when they finish my dad's tests."

"He'll be fine, darling." Brooke smiled.

"I hope so," James said.

There was a knock on the door and Antonio walked in. "Hey, I'm going to grab dinner for everyone, that's not hospital food. The nurse said you can have whatever you want, so what would you like?" he asked James.

"Whatever you guys decide." James smiled.

Antonio looked at Brooke and made a motion towards Kendall. She smiled and gave him a little nod.

He smiled. "How about you, Kendall?"

"It doesn't really matter to me."

"Katie was asking for pizza. How does that sound?"

"Sounds good," James said.

"Okay, I'll be back in a little while," Antonio said.

"Thanks Papi." James smiled.

"Why don't you come with me? You can eat with James when we get back," Antonio said, putting an arm around Kendall's shoulders.

"Okay."

The two walked out together, Antonio holding onto the teen. "How are you doing, Mijo?"

"I'm fine."

"Are you sure?"

Kendall nodded. "Mama D said I can stay with James tonight, if that's okay."

"Of course it is. Do you think you'll be okay here, though? This isn't one of your favourite places."

"I'm not the one who has to be here this time."

"Very true," Antonio said.

They went to a nearby pizza place and Antonio ran in to pick up their order. They went back to the hospital and Antonio carried a plate for James back to his room. Brooke went back to the waiting area so that Antonio and Kendall could spend a little more time with James.

The nurse came in to check on James and gave him his pain meds. He started to nod off a short time later, and Kendall pulled his tray away from the bed. He pulled the blankets up further, and James was sound asleep within minutes.

"Your mom and I are going to stay in the family waiting area tonight, so if you need anything, just tell the nurse and she'll come and get us," Antonio told Kendall.

"Okay, thanks Papi."

Antonio hugged him. "Tomorrow we'll go home and get everyone settled back in. James can show you his pictures and tell you all about the game."

"I have my appointment with Claudia tomorrow."

"I know. I'm taking tomorrow off, so I'll go with you."

"We have to see Dr. Anna too."

"It'll be okay. Don't forget she wants to take some blood too, but try not to worry about it too much."

"Sure."

Antonio smiled again. "Alex is prepared to show her that we can do this at home if need be."

"I know, I just..." Kendall sighed.

"I know. It's getting pretty old, isn't it?"

Kendall nodded.

"Well, why don't you try and get some sleep?" Antonio recommended, pointing to the other bed. Kendall nodded and pulled off his boots. Antonio helped him up into the taller bed. "Hold on," he said as he pushed the bed over next to James'. "How's that?"

"Perfect, thanks Papi." Kendall yawned.

"You're welcome, Mijo. Get some sleep," Antonio said, pulling the blanket up over the boy. Kendall nodded and rolled over on his right side, so he was facing James.

Antonio waited with the boys until Brooke returned, and then went back to the waiting room. He went back to check on them a couple of hours later, and found Brooke sleeping on a cot the nurse had brought in for her. Kendall had crawled out of his bed and curled up next to James, careful to avoid touching his friend's ribs, and both boys were sound asleep. Antonio smiled and grabbed the blanket from Kendall's bed and covered him with it. He made his way back to Brooke, pulled her shoes off, and covered her. Then he carefully removed her tablet from her hands and put it in her bag.

He looked at the boys, smiled again, and then headed back to the waiting room to try to catch a couple of hours of sleep.

Chapter 114~ The Diamonds

The nurse went in to check on James during her two o'clock rounds and was surprised to find Kendall curled up next to him. She reached over to wake him, and James took ahold of her hand. "Don't touch him."

"I'm sorry, but he can't stay there with you. He needs to go back into his own bed."

"If you wake him up like that he'll freak out. I NEED him here, he's fine," James told her.

"If he moves wrong he'll injure your ribs, so he needs to move back to his own bed," she insisted.

"He doesn't move around, he's always quiet."

"Be that as it may, he needs to go back to his own bed," the nurse said, reaching for Kendall's arm again.

"My brother STAYS here or we both leave," James said firmly as he put his arm around Kendall.

"This is against hospital policy, he really shouldn't even be here," she told him.

"Fine," James said as he started to pull at his IV line.

"Don't do that," the nurse ordered, holding her hand over the line.

"Then leave us alone. He's not hurting me, and I want him with me. So either he stays where he is, or we both leave," James stated.

The nurse gave him an exasperated sigh. "I'm going to have to wake your mother if you don't start cooperating."

"His mother IS awake and I suggest you leave my boys where they are and move on to your next patient," Brooke said.

"Mrs. Diamond..." the nurse started.

Brooke stood up. "Yes?"

The nurse took a step back. "This is against hospital policy, and I'm simply looking out for my patient's well-being."

"YOUR patient is my son, and he told you that he needs his brother with him, and that is where he will stay."

"I have to follow hospital policy, and he needs to move back to his own bed or leave," the nurse said, standing her ground.

Brooke looked at her, arched an eyebrow, and smiled. "Let's discuss this in the hallway so my boys can get the sleep they need," Brooke said, opening the door.

The nurse walked out and Brooke followed her. "I understand you're just trying to do your job and that you're probably very good at what you do. However, my boys have been through hell this last month and separating them is NOT an option. James told you Kendall isn't causing him any pain, and you need to listen. Just because it's policy doesn't mean it's right for every situation. Kendall suffered a severe trauma earlier this month and needs to be with his brother."

"I read all about his 'trauma,' and I cannot allow him to stay unless he goes back to his own bed," the nurse said stubbornly.

Brooke's eyebrow went higher and she smiled at her. "Well, I say he stays where he is. If you still have a problem with that after what I just told you, then I'll speak to your supervisor," Brooke said, her tone growing colder by the second.

"Rules are rules."

"Oh really?" Brooke asked, her eyes narrowing. "We'll see about that," she said as she headed for the head nurse's station.

The nurse followed right behind her.

"Excuse me, who is in charge here?" Brook demanded.

An older nurse looked up and smiled. "I'm Nurse Feltman. What can I do for you?"

Brooke pointed at the other nurse. "This 'nurse' is trying to eject one of my boys from the room, and DON'T think I missed the tone you took when you said that you'd read about Kendall's trauma," Brooke growled at the first nurse.

"Perhaps you could explain in a little more detail?" Nurse Feltman asked.

Brooke took a deep breath. "This nurse came in to check on my son, who's here for observation after a car accident. His brother and I are staying with him, and Kendall crawled into bed with James. He's not even touching him and this... person, is insisting he leave. James explained that he wants him there, and I've tried explaining that the boys shouldn't be separated because of a trauma that Kendall's been through recently, and she's STILL insisting he cannot stay."

Antonio heard the commotion and came out when he heard Brooke's voice. "Brooke, what's going on, honey?"

Before Brooke could answer, the other nurse commented.

"What you haven't mentioned is that they're NOT really related and he shouldn't have been allowed to stay in the first place," the other nurse snapped.

Brooke turned on the nurse. "I have just about had it with you. I don't know who you think you are, but you don't even know these boys. They are closer than most blood relations I know, and have been to hell and back together."

"Alright, please. Nurse Reiner, continue with your rounds and I'll assist Mrs. Diamond," Nurse Feltman told the younger nurse.

Nurse Reiner gave Brooke a derisive little snort and a smug look as she turned and went to check on her next patient.

"Why, you little..." Brooke growled, heading after her, fists clenched.

"No!" Antonio said, grabbing ahold of her arm and pulling her back.

"Did you see what she did?" Brooke asked him.

He nodded. "I know, honey, but you can't hit her."

"Why not? I have an excellent attorney and can afford the fines," Brooke said.

Before he could respond, Nurse Feltman walked over and patted Brooke comfortingly on the shoulder. "I do apologize for any misunderstandings. Nurse Reiner is new and apparently having trouble with her bedside manners. I will be having a discussion with her later."

Brooke looked at her. "I will be having a discussion with Edward Brice tomorrow. Perhaps you've heard of him? He's the hospital administrator here, as well as a good friend of the family."

"Brooke, please, this isn't helping anything," Antonio said.

"I understand you're upset, and with good reason. No one is going to make anyone leave. Maybe you should try to get some more sleep. Now, is your son alright, does he need anything?" Nurse Feltman asked in a soothing tone.

"No, he has everything he needs," Brooke said, folding her arms across her chest.

"Good." The older woman smiled. "You must be exhausted after the day you've had, and should try and get some rest."

"Alright, but I don't want that so-called nurse near my boys again," Brooke told her.

"I'll take care of your son myself," the older woman said as she put an arm around Brooke's waist and led her back to James' room.

Antonio followed and made sure that everyone was alright before going back to the waiting area.

"What happened?" Jen asked.

"Nothing. Brooke was just going to kill a nurse."

"Oh." Jen smiled as she closed her eyes again.

∞

The rest of the night was uneventful and Nurse Feltman kept her word and checked on James at 5 am and again at 7 am. James woke up when she was checking his IV line. "How are you feeling, dear?" she asked.

"Okay. Has anyone heard anything about my dad?"

"I think he's on a different floor. What's his first name? I'll call and find out."

"His name is Michael Diamond," James said, wincing as he sat up.

"Are you in a lot of pain?"

"No, just stiff and sore. I've felt worse after a game." He smiled.

"Game?"

"We play hockey," James told her.

She smiled again. "I use to play girl's hockey in my younger days."

"Really?"

She nodded. "Left wing, we went to the nationals in '77."

"Wow, that's amazing. How did your team do?"

"We came in fourth. Now, what would you boys like for breakfast?"

"When can I go home?" James asked.

"As soon as the doctor comes in and checks you out. Probably between eight and nine."

James groaned and Kendall woke up. "Are you okay?"

"Yeah, I'm fine. I just want to go home." James smiled.

Kendall smiled and tried to straighten out.

Nurse Feltman went around and pulled the other bed away from James', and then went to help Kendall sit up. Kendall pulled back from her. "It's okay, honey, just giving you a hand." She smiled.

"It's okay," James whispered. Kendall looked at her and nodded. She put her arm around his waist and helped him sit up.

"How about some hot cereal and toast for the both of you?" she asked.

"That sounds good." James smiled.

"Alright, I'll put the order in and give a call to find out how your dad's doing." She smiled.

"Thanks a lot."

"You're welcome. I'll have them send some coffee up for your mom too."

"That's a good idea," James agreed, looking over at his sleeping mother.

Nurse Feltman smiled and went back to the nurse's station to make the calls.

Brooke turned over, giving a loud snore.

James eyes widened and Kendall smothered a laugh.

"Shhh, do NOT tell her she snores," James told his friend.

"Would she believe me if I did?"

"You have to swear NEVER to mention this to anyone."

Kendall looked at him and raised an eyebrow. "Really?"

"Really."

"I solemnly swear I will never mention that Mama D sounds like my granddad when he use to fall asleep in his chair."

"She doesn't sound that bad," James insisted.

Kendall just looked at him.

"Okay, she does sound that bad. But you can't say anything or she'll try and find some surgeon to fix it."

"I promise I won't say anything. I wouldn't do that to her," Kendall told him.

"Thanks." James sighed in relief. Brooke snored again and the boys looked at her.

"That doesn't mean the entire hospital won't hear her though," Kendall pointed out.

"Mom, are you awake?" James asked loudly.

"What? Honey, what do you need?" she asked, sitting up.

"Nothing, just saying good morning." He smiled.

"Good morning, darlings. Did you both sleep well?"

The boys nodded.

"Good." She yawned.

"The nurse is going to have them send up some coffee when they bring breakfast," James said.

"WHICH nurse?" she asked, instantly awake.

"Uh, the nurse that came in this morning," James told her.

Brooke got up and slipped on her shoes. "Was she younger or older?"

"Older... Why?"

She smiled. "Nothing, darling."

Nurse Feltman came in a few moments later. "I spoke to the nurse on your dad's floor, and he's doing just fine. He's allowed visitors, so I'll bring you a wheelchair after your breakfast."

"Wheelchair," James groaned.

"Hospital rules." She smiled.

Antonio and Jen came in a few minutes later. "How are you feeling this morning?" he asked James.

"Just a little sore."

"Did you sleep alright?" Jen asked.

He nodded. "Yeah, whatever they gave me helped."

"How about you, honey?" she asked Kendall, giving him a hug.

"I slept okay."

The nurse's aide came in with breakfast trays for the boys. Kendall pulled James' table tray over for him and went to sit on the other bed. Jen set the other tray next to Kendall on the bed, and he just looked at it.

"I don't think so," he said, looking at the bowl of lumpy, gray oatmeal.

"Honey, you need to eat. You have your appointment with Anna this morning," Jen told him.

He pushed it away. "I can't eat that."

"It's not really that bad," James told him as he took a bite.

Kendall shook his head again.

"Try eating the toast," Antonio said. Kendall picked up a piece of the toast and nibbled on it. "You're going to have to do better than that, Mijo," Antonio said.

Kendall sighed, took a bite, and forced it down. Jen handed him a carton of milk and he drank it.

James ate quickly so he could go see his dad. As soon as he finished, James pushed the tray away. "I'm finished. Can I go see my dad?"

"I'll go get the wheelchair," Brooke said and went down to the nurse's station. She came back with a nurse, and James got up carefully. With Antonio's help, he was soon sitting in the chair. The nurse attached his IV bag to the pole behind the chair.

"I'll take him," Kendall said, jumping up.

"We'll take him, AFTER you finish that toast," Antonio told him.

"Hurry up," James said.

Kendall rolled his eyes but managed to choke down the last of his toast. He pulled his boots on, and a moment later, the three of them headed for the elevator.

∞

They took the elevator up to the fourth floor and quickly found Mike's room. Antonio knocked first before pushing James through the door. Mike was lying in the darkened room, a bandage on the side of his head.

"Hey dad," James said quietly.

"James, how are you feeling? Are you doing alright?" Mike asked, smiling.

"I'm fine. I get to go home today. What did the doctor say?"

"I have a moderate concussion, so I'll be staying here for a couple of days."

"You're okay otherwise?" James asked.

"Yes, no broken bones, just a little cut on my head."

"Good," James said, relieved.

"Thanks for all your help, Antonio," Mike said.

"No thanks necessary. I'm just glad you both are going to be alright." Antonio smiled.

"How are you doing, Kendall?" Mike asked.

"Okay," he said, staying close to Antonio.

Tiffany came in after having gone to the cafeteria. "They have absolutely NOTHING worth eating down there," she complained.

"Please, not so loud," Mike said.

"Sorry baby, I keep forgetting." She smiled.

"It's okay, just a little quieter," he told her.

She smiled again. "Hi James. How are you feeling?"

"I'm fine, going home soon."

"Good... What are you doing here?" she asked, looking at Kendall.

Kendall moved closer to Antonio.

"Tiffany," Mike said in a warning tone.

"It's his fault you're here! If he'd kept his nose out of things, you wouldn't have gone to Minneapolis!"

Antonio wrapped his arm around Kendall and pulled him close, and James started to stand up. Antonio put a hand on his shoulder and shook his head.

"That is ENOUGH! We have already talked about this. I think you should go home now," Mike said firmly.

"But..."

"NOW!" he yelled and then put his hands up to his head.

She stuck her bottom lip out. "But baby," she cooed.

"I am not joking. Go home and get some sleep," he ordered.

The nurse came in and Mike pointed at his wife. "Please send her home." The nurse nodded and escorted a protesting Tiffany out the door.

Kendall tried to pull away, but Antonio held him tightly. "It's alright. Don't pay any attention to what she said."

"James, please come over here and bring Kendall with you," Mike said.

Antonio pushed James next to the bed and stood next to the wheelchair, still holding onto Kendall.

"Kendall, come over here, please," Mike said.

Kendall looked at Antonio and shook his head. He looked like he was going to have a panic attack. James reached over, took Kendall's arm, and pulled him over to him.

"What did she mean?" James asked.

Kendall's eyes filled with tears. "I-I'm sorry. I j-just wanted you to be happy."

Mike held out his hand. "Come here."

Kendall looked down and Antonio gave him a little push towards the bed.

Mike pulled Kendall over into a hug. "The accident was NOT your fault, and I can't thank you enough for the phone call." He held onto Kendall with one arm and put his other hand out to James, who took it.

Mike looked over at James. "Kendall called me a few days before Thanksgiving and gave me what for. He told me exactly what I was missing by not including you in my life, and he was right. When I think about what happened and what could have happened, it makes me sick. I took a long, hard look at myself and the way I have been living my life and I... I'm not very proud of myself. James yesterday was the BEST day I've had in a long time, even if it didn't end the way I planned."

"Me too." James smiled, squeezing his dad's hand.

"We have you to thank for that," he said, looking at Kendall.

Kendall looked at him and over at James, who smiled and nodded.

"So, as soon as I'm doing better and the doctor gives his okay, we're ALL going to do something together," Mike said.

"That would be great, dad," James said.

"What do you think, does that sound okay to you?" he asked Kendall.

Kendall nodded and Mike smiled at him. "It's a plan then. You boys think of what you'd like to do, and as soon as I'm able, we'll do it."

Antonio smiled at him. "We'd better let you get some rest. I'll bring all the boys by later to visit."

"That sounds great. Thanks Antonio, for everything."

"That's what friends are for." Antonio smiled.

Mike smiled and nodded. "Okay, I'll see you boys later then."

"Bye dad," James said, reaching over and hugging him.

"Bye," Kendall said quietly and went back to Antonio.

Antonio backed the wheelchair out of the room and they headed back to the elevator. Kendall was clinging to him, so he pulled him in front of him so he could hold onto the wheelchair.

"Are you okay?" Antonio whispered.

Kendall nodded but didn't say anything.

They got back to James' room and Antonio helped James back into bed.

"How's your dad?" Brooke asked.

"He has a concussion, so he has to stay for a couple of days, but he's okay," James said quietly, watching Kendall.

"Is everything alright?" Jen asked, noticing that Kendall was still staying close to Antonio.

"Everything's fine, just too many people around," Antonio told her.

The morning resident came in. "Rumour is you want to get out of here." She smiled, looking at James.

"Please."

"We'll wait outside," Antonio told him.

"Okay, thanks Papi."

Antonio, Kendall, and Jen went into the hallway. A few minutes later, the doctor came out. "He's good to go." She smiled.

"Thank you, doctor," Antonio said.

They went back in and James was already dressed and trying to pull on his boots. Antonio went over. "Sit," he said as he reached down and pulled the boots onto the teen's feet.

He quickly tied them and helped James stand. "Thanks Papi, it's not easy to do that without bending over."

"I know. I've been there." He laughed.

Kendall pushed the wheelchair over and James sat down in it. Antonio pushed him, and they all went out together. Brooke bent down and kissed James on the cheek. "I'll be by after my meeting, make sure you get some rest."

"I will, mom," James said.

Antonio helped James up into the SUV and Jen ran the wheelchair back in.

Kendall climbed in next to James. "So, are we on for lunch?" Jen asked.

"Sure," Kendall said quietly.

"Okay honey, we'll work out the details later. I traded shifts with Elaine so I could have this morning off. I don't have to be to work until three."

"Okay," Kendall said.

She closed the door. "Is everything alright?" she quietly asked Antonio.

"Everything will be fine. I'll tell you about it later."

"Alright, call me after he sees Anna?"

"I will. Just to confirm, you DON'T think he'll do well in the hospital?"

She shook her head. "Not at all."

"Okay honey, I'll call as soon as we're through. Are you sure you don't want to go?"

"No, I think it's better if I wait."

He nodded. "Okay, we'll talk later then."

She smiled and nodded to the boys as they drove away. They got to the Garcia's and Antonio helped James out and up to the house. Kendall followed them up the walk. Sylvia opened the door and smiled. "How are you feeling, honey?" she asked, helping James off with his jacket.

"I'm fine, really."

"Mike's doing fine too," Antonio said as he kissed her good morning.

"Thank God."

"Why don't you boys sit down and relax for a while. We don't have to be at Dr. Anna's until ten," Sylvia said.

"Sounds good to me," James said, heading for the couch. Kendall followed and handed him the television remote.

"You didn't eat enough, so I'm making you a smoothie," Antonio told Kendall.

Kendall nodded and sat in the recliner.

"What's going on?" Sylvia asked quietly, pointing to the two boys.

"Kitchen," he said, walking into the other room.

He gathered the ingredients for a smoothie. "Where's Alex?"

"He drove the kids to school and went to the market to get the rest of what I need for his tamales tonight," Sylvia said.

Antonio put the ingredients into the blender and told her about what had happened at the hospital with Tiffany.

"That little bleached blonde twit," Sylvia hissed.

"It's alright, Mike made her leave. I think James was surprised to find out Kendall had called Mike, but I think it was a good surprise. Kendall was a little shaken up and hasn't snapped out of it yet. I think the accident and Tiffany's big mouth have him a little unnerved."

"Worrying about his appointment with Anna probably isn't helping either."

"No, but he'll be fine. I made sure Jen agrees that going into the hospital is not in Kendall's best interests."

"Good," Sylvia said, handing him a glass. Antonio poured the smoothie into it and Sylvia put a straw in it.

Antonio took it out to Kendall. "I'm going to jump in the shower, and then you can shower and change."

"Okay, thanks Papi."

Antonio went upstairs and James looked over at his friend.

"Kendall?"

Kendall looked over and James patted the seat next to him. Kendall picked up his smoothie and went to sit next to his friend.

"I can't believe you called my dad, especially since you don't like talking to anyone but us."

"I didn't mean to."

"To what, give my dad a reality check? Yesterday was the BEST day I've ever spent with him, and it's because you cared enough to tell him off."

"But, he's in the hospital and you..."

"Just shut up and let me say thank you, okay? Like my dad said, the day may not have ended the way we wanted, but it was worth it," James said as he put his arm around his friend's shoulders.

"You gave me back my dad. I don't know how long it's going to last, hopefully forever. Even if it doesn't, I had ONE great day with him, and that's more than I ever had before. I just wish I could do the same for you."

Kendall lay his head on James' shoulder. "Me too."

Chapter 115~ Second Reprieve

Antonio showered and dressed. He was going over every possible scenario, trying to mentally prepare himself, for what could happen at Anna's office this morning. "Please just let him be alright and let us keep moving forward," he prayed.

He went downstairs and smiled to see the two boys curled up together on the couch. They had both fallen back to sleep and Sylvia was covering them with a blanket.

"They're so tired," she whispered as she kissed his cheek.

"I know. I wish they could both sleep longer, but we need to get Kendall up so he can get ready to go."

"James can stay home with me," Sylvia said.

He nodded and knelt down next to Kendall. "Mijo, time to get up."

Kendall opened his eyes and groaned.

"I know you're tired, but you need to get ready. You can take a nice long nap when we get home."

Kendall sighed and got up.

"I'll be up in a few minutes to help you," Antonio said as he steered the boy towards the staircase.

"Okay," Kendall said quietly.

Kendall went up and grabbed some clean clothes from his bag. He went into the bathroom and started running the water. He undressed and got in, letting the warm water run over him. He finished showering and had just started dressing when he heard a voice.

"You need to learn your lessons, sweetheart. What did I say would happen if you ran away from me?"

"You're dead, leave me alone," Kendall said.

"I don't think so."

"Leave me alone!" Kendall yelled again.

Antonio was in his room waiting for Kendall when he heard him call out. He knocked on the bathroom door. "Kendall, are you alright?"

Not getting an answer, he turned the doorknob and slowly pushed the door open. "Kendall?"

Kendall was half-dressed, sitting on the floor rocking back and forth, hugging his knees up to his chest.

"Kendall, what happened?" He knelt down next to the shaking teen. "Mijo, what is it?" he asked gently.

Kendall was looking at something in front of him, not responding to Antonio. Antonio took a deep breath, reached over, and took the boy's face in his hands. "Kendall, look at me," he said firmly.

A moment later, Kendall looked up and finally focused on Antonio. "What is it, Mijo?"

"H-He won't go a-away," he stammered.

Antonio sat next to him and pulled him close. "Yes he will. It's going to take some time, but he will. Until then, just remember he can't hurt you anymore and we're all here for you."

Kendall leaned against Antonio and they sat quietly for a few minutes. "Okay, let's finish getting you ready," Antonio said, standing up and holding his hand out. Kendall took his hand and Antonio pulled him up.

He helped him on with his shirt and the stabilizer. "You doing alright?"

Kendall nodded and they headed back downstairs.

∞

James was still sleeping soundly on the couch, so Antonio grabbed Kendall's glass and they went into the kitchen. Alex had gotten back and was sitting at the table, talking to Sylvia.

"Hey, I hear Mike's going to be alright in spite of his shrilly voiced wife."

"He's doing much better. I told him I'd bring the boys around for a visit later." Antonio smiled.

"How are you doing, Champ?" Alex asked Kendall.

"Okay," he said quietly as he sat down next to Antonio.

Alex looked at Antonio, who gave a slight shake of his head and mouthed, "Later."

Alex nodded.

Sylvia was looking in the refrigerator. "What happened to all the eggs?"

"I don't know, maybe you used them all?" Alex suggested, looking at Kendall, who raised an eyebrow at him.

"I'm sure I had two dozen eggs in here before we left," Sylvia said, digging to the back.

"Well, we should probably get going. We can stop at the market and pick some up for you," Alex said, getting up and going to living room.

"James wanted to go," Kendall said.

"Okay, let me wake him up and see how he's feeling." Antonio smiled.

Kendall nodded and followed Antonio into the living room.

"Where's all the flour?" Sylvia asked, looking in the container.

"I'll just go warm up the car," Alex said, grabbing his jacket and heading out the door.

Kendall shook his head at him.

Antonio looked at him. "I take it Papa M had something to do with the disappearances in Mami's kitchen?"

Kendall looked at him and smiled.

"I see," Antonio said.

James was still sleeping soundly. "It's okay, just let him sleep," Kendall said.

"Are you sure?"

Kendall nodded.

"I'll give Mama G a call when we're finished at Dr. Anna's and see if he's awake. If he is and feels up to going to Claudia's, we'll swing by and pick him up."

"Okay."

"Are you ready to go?" Antonio asked.

"No."

"It'll be okay. Alex has the NG kit if we need it, and I already talked to your mom. She doesn't want you in the hospital for this either."

"Okay," Kendall said as he pulled on his boots. Antonio held his jacket for him and they headed out to the car.

They arrived at Dr. Sharpe's office a little over fifteen minutes later. Kendall sat in the back, staring at the back of the front seat, so Antonio opened the door and held out his hand. "It's going to be alright, Mijo."

Kendall nodded and took Antonio's hand. Antonio put his arm around him and they walked into the building.

Kendall sat in the chair closest to the door while Antonio signed him in. Alex sat next to him. "It's okay, Champ. We'll be outta here before you know it."

Antonio sat next to Alex, and a few minutes later, the nurse called Kendall's name. He sat there, staring at his hands, and Antonio went over and pulled him up by the arm. "Come on." He smiled.

Alex followed them back.

"Hi Kendall. Are you feeling alright today?" the nurse asked.

He nodded.

"Can you take off your jacket and boots and step on the scale, please?"

Kendall sighed and Antonio helped him take off his jacket. Kendall reached down, undid his boots, and then stepped on the scale.

The nurse moved the balances and made a note on his chart. "Now I'll take you back to an exam room and we'll get your temperature and blood pressure."

"Thank you," Antonio said.

They followed her into an exam room and Kendall sat on the table, Antonio next to him. The nurse took his temperature and then went to put the blood pressure cuff on his arm.

Kendall pulled back from her. "It's alright," Antonio said.

Kendall let her get the reading and then scooted closer to Antonio.

"Dr. Sharpe will be in soon," the nurse said as she left room.

Kendall leaned against Antonio and closed his eyes. He was trying to fight down the panic he could already feel growing.

Anna came in a few moments later. "Good morning! How's everyone doing today?"

Kendall opened his eyes and tried to get closer to Antonio. "Hey, you're going to knock me off the table." He laughed.

"Alex, it's been a long time," Anna said.

"Too long. How have you been?" He smiled.

"Busy, especially this time of year. How's Logan's ankle doing?"

"Much better, he'll be in later this week to have it checked out. He hates those crutches."

"I bet. I had a report come in that James was in an accident?"

Antonio nodded. "He and his dad were in that pile-up on I-494 yesterday. He has some bruised ribs, but seems to be doing alright. His dad will be in the hospital for a couple of days with a concussion."

"It never rains, but it pours." Anna smiled.

"That it does," Antonio said.

"How are you feeling, any better?" Anna asked Kendall.

He nodded.

"Good. Well you managed to put on almost nine ounces," Anna said.

Kendall looked at Antonio, who smiled. "See, I knew you could do it!"

"I still want to run some blood work, starting with a CBC and PCV, which I can run in-house. I'll put a rush on the other tests, and we should have the results by tonight, tomorrow at the latest," she told them.

A nurse came in holding a tray with various tubes. Kendall saw the syringes and backed up a little more. Antonio put an arm around him. "It's alright."

Anna smiled. "Why don't we use your left arm since you're not using it much anyway?"

Kendall just looked at her, not moving.

"It's alright. It'll just take a minute." Anna smiled reassuringly.

Kendall shook his head and pulled his legs up.

"Give us a minute?" Antonio asked.

Anna nodded and she and the nurse left the room.

"Kendall, it's okay, Anna isn't trying to hurt you. You've had blood drawn before, so I know you can do this. Just take a deep breath, and it'll be over with before you know it, and then we can get out of here."

Kendall looked at him and nodded.

"Are you ready?"

Kendall nodded again.

"I'll get her," Alex said and went out to find Anna.

They came back a minute later. "Are you doing okay?" Anna asked.

Kendall looked at Antonio and then nodded.

"Okay." She smiled.

She undid the Velcro that held his forearm in place and tied a tourniquet around it. Kendall held onto Antonio with his other arm and buried his face in his shirt. Antonio held him as Anna placed the needle and drew the blood. She filled four 10cc red top tubes and two purple tops, and then taped a piece of gauze of the puncture site. She released the tourniquet and pushed Kendall's arm up a little so the blood would clot.

"You did great, honey." She smiled.

Kendall didn't look at her but started to feel dizzy. His breathing picked up a little and he started shaking.

"Kendall, let me see your face," Anna said and turned his head so she could see him. He had turned very pale, so she grabbed the bottle of juice she had brought and opened it. "Drink," she said, holding it up to his mouth.

Kendall took a drink and squeezed his eyes shut.

"Drink again," she said, holding it back up.

He took another sip.

"Okay, lie down for a few minutes."

Antonio stood up, helped him lie back, and sat down next to him. After a few minutes, the colour had returned to his face.

"Are you feeling better?" Anna asked.

He nodded.

She handed the juice to Antonio. "Make sure he drinks all of this. I'm going to see how close we are to having results."

Antonio nodded and took the bottle. A few minutes later, Anna opened the door and gestured for Antonio to follow her. Kendall was still resting, so Alex took Antonio's place next to him.

"I have the initial results of his CBC. I sent the rest to the lab for a more concise reading. His hematocrit is about 34 percent, when it should be closer to 42 percent."

"Meaning?" Antonio asked.

"Meaning his white blood cell count is too high and his red blood cell count is too low, even for an active infection such as pneumonia."

"What do we need to do?" Antonio sighed.

Anna looked at him. "I think the best thing we can do is hospitalize him. That way he can be on fluids with necessary electrolytes, a feeding tube, and 24 hour monitoring."

Antonio shook his head. "I know that's the best solution, but it's also the worst. Yes, he'll be on fluids and a feeding tube, but he'll also be in restraints and most likely sedated."

"Antonio..." she started.

"Please, hear me out. We can do the feeding tube at home. Alex has had to administer tube feedings to his dad for years now. He knows how to put them in, how to do the actual feedings, how to care for the equipment, and most importantly, Kendall trusts him. Jen and his psychologist both agree that he won't handle being hospitalized well at all."

Anna sighed. "Alex really knows how to do this?"

Antonio nodded.

"Alright, let me call Jen. If she agrees, then I need to watch him place a tube, and then I want to take an x-ray to make sure it's placed properly. If all goes well, I'll prescribe a high protein formula with an iron supplement, as well as vitamins C and B12."

"Thank you, Anna." Antonio smiled.

"Don't thank me until I'm convinced this will work. There's a big difference between placing a tube in an elderly man, who's had a stroke, and a teenage boy who can fight back."

Antonio nodded. "I'll go wait with Kendall while you call his mom."

Anna smiled and nodded as she dialed Jen's cell number.

Antonio went into the exam room. "Well?" Alex asked.

"She wants him in the hospital, so I told her you can do the tube feedings. She wants you to show her and then take an x-ray."

Alex nodded.

Antonio sat next to Kendall. "Mijo, wake up. Dr. Anna wants Alex to show her that he can place the feeding tube. Are you ready for this?"

Kendall groaned.

"I know, but if we don't do this, she's going to put you in the hospital. I'm just glad we practiced this ahead of time," Antonio said.

Kendall nodded and Antonio helped him sit up.

Anna came in a couple of minutes later. "Alright, I have Jen's okay with this. So, show me what you can do," she said to Alex.

He nodded and pulled out the NG kit.

"You came prepared." She smiled.

"I picked one up the other day and we already measured it out. I'll need a glass of water with a straw," Alex said.

Anna nodded and went to the cupboard. She filled a paper cup and put a straw in it for him.

"Thank you. Do you think you could hold it for him?" Alex smiled.

"Of course," she said, standing to the side.

"You ready for this, Champ?"

Kendall took a deep breath and nodded.

Antonio sat down and Kendall sat in front of him. He wrapped his arms around the teen as Alex prepped the tube. He set everything he needed on the tray and pulled it over.

"Okay?" He smiled.

Kendall nodded and tilted his head back a little.

"We're going to use your right nostril," Alex said as he put his left hand on the right side of Kendall's head. He inserted the tube and Kendall closed his eyes as Alex continued to push the tube in.

Kendall started gagging. "Water please, Anna."

Anna put the straw up to the boy's lips and he took a sip.

"Keep drinking, we're almost there."

Kendall squeezed his eyes shut and tried to focus on just swallowing.

Antonio held him close. "You're doing great!" he whispered.

"Okay, we're there!" Alex said as he taped the tube to Kendall's cheek. He grabbed the syringe and stethoscope and pinched off the tube. He attached the syringe and pushed the plunger. "Sounds like it's in to me." He smiled, handing the stethoscope to Anna.

She put it in her ears and he pushed a little more air in. She nodded. "I still want an x-ray to confirm."

Alex nodded and taped the tube to the top of Kendall's shoulder for added security.

She went out to have the technician set it up.

"Why do we need an x-ray?" Kendall asked quietly.

"She just wants to make sure the tube is where it's supposed to be," Alex told him.

"She can't tell?"

"She's just making sure that we're doing everything right," Antonio said.

She came in a moment later and handed Antonio a gown. "Okay, they're ready for you, but we need you in this, though you can keep your jeans on." She smiled.

Kendall looked at Antonio and shook his head.

"I'll wait outside so you can change," Anna said, going out into the hallway.

"It's alright, we just need to switch your shirt for this," Antonio said as he helped Kendall off with his shirt. He held the gown up and Kendall slipped his arms in. Alex was quiet —he hadn't seen Kendall without his shirt and was a little shocked to see there were still quite a few marks on him.

"Are you ready?" Antonio asked.

"No," Kendall said.

"It'll only take a couple of minutes," he said as he opened the door.

They followed Anna down the hallway to the other end of the building. They went into the x-ray room and the technician smiled. "Hi, so I hear we need a couple of pictures to check a tube placement?"

"That's right," Anna said.

The technician smiled and gestured for Kendall to follow her.

Kendall grabbed a hold of Antonio's arm and shook his head. "It's alright, you've had plenty of x-rays," he said, walking the boy over to the table.

"If you could sit here for a moment while I take a couple of measurements?" the technician asked.

Antonio helped Kendall up onto the table.

"Go slowly," Anna instructed the technician, who smiled and nodded.

"I'm just going to place this ruler on your side so I can measure for the machine settings."

Antonio held his hand while she took the measurements.

"Just one more," she said as she moved it up a little. "Okay, all done with that. Now if you could lie down for me?"

Kendall looked at Antonio and sighed. He laid down and the technician covered him from the waist down with a leaded half apron. "I need you to step out, this'll only take a moment," she told Antonio.

He nodded. "I'll be right outside, Mijo." He and Anna went to stand in the hallway and the technician adjusted the angle of the x-ray machine and then went to stand in her booth.

"Okay, can you take a breath and hold it for me?"

Kendall did as she asked and the machine dinged.

"Once more please."

He took another breath, trying not to cough as the tube tickled the back of his throat.

The machine dinged again. "Good job!" she said, coming out of the booth. She lifted the apron and he sat up while she went to let Antonio and Anna know they were finished.

"I should have these in about five minutes," she told Anna.

"Thank you." Anna smiled.

"Is it alright if we go back to the room?" Antonio asked.

Anna nodded. "I'll be right there."

Antonio and Kendall walked back to the exam room, where Antonio helped Kendall put his shirt back on.

"How did it go?" Alex asked.

"Alright," Antonio said.

Kendall was swallowing a lot. "This feels funny."

"I know, Champ, you'll get used to it." Alex smiled.

Kendall looked at him as he swallowed again. "I don't think so."

There was a knock on the door and Anna came in holding the x-rays. She put one up on the x-ray viewing box and switched on the light. "I have to say, I'm impressed. The tube is perfectly placed," she said, pointing to a white line that ran from the esophagus down to the stomach.

"So... we're good to go?" Alex asked.

"One week, and then we need to run another blood panel. If his numbers are better and he continues to gain weight, then you can continue doing this at home. If they haven't improved or have gotten worse, then it's the hospital, period."

"Thanks Anna." Antonio smiled.

"I'm also concerned by this," she said, pointing to the lung area. "There's still have quite a bit of congestion in his lungs, so I'm adding an antibiotic in addition to the amoxicillin. I also want him drinking lots of fluids, preferably orange or grapefruit juice. The vitamin C will help with the anemia. Stay away from tea right now, the tannin in it can block iron absorption."

Kendall nodded and looked over at Alex. He pointed to the tube and made a pulling motion. "Is it alright if we take the tube out now?" Alex asked.

"Yes, although it might be easier to leave it in. I want you tube fed twice a day for now, on top of whatever you can eat on your own. I'll go get your prescriptions written up and meet you out front." Anna smiled.

"Thanks again, Anna," Antonio said.

"You're welcome."

Alex removed the tape from the tube and handed Antonio the glass of water. He flushed the tube and then started to slowly pull it out. Kendall started coughing and Antonio held the water up for him, rubbing his back until he stopped.

"Okay, let's get out of here," Antonio said as he helped Kendall on with his coat.

They went out front and Anna met them with the prescriptions. "Azithromycin, one once daily. I called this and the formula prescription in to the pharmacy downstairs, so they can add the iron and vitamins. It should be ready in about an hour."

Antonio nodded. "We'll stop back by and pick it up after your appointment with Claudia."

Kendall nodded.

"I'll see you in a week." Anna smiled.

Kendall nodded and gave her a small smile.

The three of them headed for the car and Antonio called home.

"Hi honey, how did it go?" Sylvia asked.

"We can do the feedings at home, but Anna wants him back in a week for more blood work. He's anemic, and she added another antibiotic because his lungs are still pretty congested. Is James awake? Did he want to go with us to Claudia's?"

"Yes, he's already showered and changed," Sylvia said.

"Okay, we'll be there in about fifteen or twenty minutes," Antonio told her.

"He'll be waiting."

Chapter 116~Therapy

"Did they say how his appointment went?" James asked after Sylvia hung up. He had woken up not long after the others had left. Sylvia had told him they would call before going to Claudia's, so he showered and changed so he was ready. He needed to ask if they could stop by his house on the way back, to pick up a new package of contacts. They had removed and thrown away the ones he had been wearing at the hospital, so he was wearing his black rimmed glasses. He didn't normally like going anywhere wearing them, but he didn't really have a choice at the moment.

"He's anemic, and Dr. Anna wants him tube fed, but she's letting us do it here. He's still pretty congested too, so she's adding another antibiotic."

"Like he hasn't been through enough," James sighed.

Sylvia sat down next to him. "I know, Mijo, but he is getting better. These are just little bumps in the road."

"Bumps or ditches?" James asked.

"It seems like that some days, doesn't it? You know, I'm pretty sure Claudia wouldn't mind if you wanted to go see her on your own."

"Maybe. I'll think about it."

"Just let me know, and I'll give her a call so we can set something up."

James nodded.

She sat down and finished writing up a grocery list. "Well, while you're all out, I need to run to the market and pick up some eggs and flour. I'd still like to know what happened to all of it, although I'm pretty sure Alex has something to do with it."

"Probably. I think he gets into as much trouble as we do." James laughed.

"Yes he does, sometimes more." She smiled.

"Do you think he'll ever move back?"

"I don't know. I know he wants to, so maybe someday."

"That would be cool, Logan would be so happy. Do you think he and Mama M would get back together?"

"I don't know. You're sure full of questions this morning."

He smiled. "I guess."

"Does this have anything to do with your dad?"

James shrugged. "I know he and my mom will never get back together, which is probably a good thing. But Mama and Papa M just seem like they go together."

"They do, don't they?" She smiled.

He nodded.

"Well, you never know, maybe someday they will," she said, patting his shoulder.

∞

Kendall had fallen asleep a few moments after they left Dr. Sharpe's office. Alex and Antonio were speaking quietly so as not to wake him.

"So what happened this morning?" Alex asked.

Antonio shook his head. "I'm not sure if he was having a panic attack or another flashback. I was waiting so I could help him finish dressing, and I heard him yell. I found him sitting on the bathroom floor, staring at nothing. He wouldn't answer, so I did what you and

Claudia did. I grabbed him and told him to look at me. After a minute, he came around. He said Deesie won't leave him alone."

"What does that mean?"

"Every now and then he hears Deesie saying things to him. Usually when he's tired or stressed out more than usual."

"Damn, how do we get him over that?"

"I'm not sure, but I'm hoping Claudia can help with it. It isn't happening as often as it did, unless he's just not saying anything, which is a possibility," Antonio said.

"He really doesn't talk to anyone else, does he?"

Antonio shook his head. "He also doesn't like anyone he doesn't know close to him and panics if they touch him unexpectedly."

Alex sighed. "I didn't realize he still had so many bruises. I guess the anemia isn't helping with that."

"Probably not. He's actually looking a lot better than he did when he first came home. He was nearly covered head to toe in bruises or marks of one kind or another."

"Son of a bitch," Alex muttered.

"My sentiments exactly."

Alex glanced back at the sleeping teen. "Well, the protein rich formula should help. He'll probably have a lot more energy, and if he's not so tired, maybe the bad dreams will stop."

"I hope so. I'm not sure how much actual rest he's getting. I know Anna would give him something, but there's no way he would take it. Not after what happened with Graham."

"Maybe Claudia can recommend something," Alex said.

"Possibly. He does seem to trust her, and she might be able to convince him to at least try something."

"It never hurts to ask," Alex said.

"True. I'll talk to her about it and see what she says," Antonio agreed.

∞

Antonio's cell rang. "Garcia."

"Hey Boss, is this a good time to let you know what I found out about Derek Manning?" Sally asked.

"Sure, go ahead."

"He graduated from the University of Michigan Law School in '85. Grades were unremarkable, but he maintained his grade point average of 3.1 and somehow managed to pass the bar on the first try. He started out working in real estate law, and then made the switch to criminal law about ten years later. He was given a position at Riker, Goode, and Metcalf in '96 and made partner five years ago."

"Anything we should worry about?" Antonio asked.

"Well, he has a high acquittal rate on cases that seemed open and closed. He has a history of digging into witness's pasts and using it to discredit testimony. The firm has a lot of investigators and other resources at their disposal, so yeah...I think we should be a little concerned."

Antonio sighed. "About?"

"I've spoken with the other families in this case, and most of them have had problems before and after their dealings with Graham. Things like divorce, bankruptcy, alcoholism... things that a lot of families deal with on a daily basis."

"But things that can be used against them in court to destroy their credibility," Antonio said.

"Exactly."

"Have you talked to Ryan about this?" Antonio asked.

"Not yet, I faxed what I have over to him, but he's in court right now. I left a message for him to give me a call when he has a chance."

"What about the feds, have you heard of any concerns with their case?"

"No, and there shouldn't be. They have all the drug purchase records from Louisiana, as well as the courier service records. What he did was clearly against federal drug laws, and the feds are pretty unbendable on cases like this. He'll be doing at least fifteen to twenty years on those charges alone," Sally told him.

"At least that's something."

"I'll let you know what I hear from Ryan. How are the boys today?"

"James is home from the hospital. He's a little banged up, but not too bad. We just finished up at Dr. Sharpe's and are heading to Kendall's appointment with Claudia next."

"Let me know if you need anything," Sally said.

"Will do, thanks Sally," Antonio said, hanging up.

"Trouble?" Alex asked as he pulled into the driveway.

"Not yet," Antonio said as he got out. A moment later, he returned to the car with James.

"Hey Sport, that's a new look," Alex said.

"Yeah, the hospital threw my contacts out and I was hoping we could stop by my house so I can pick up another pair?" James asked.

"Sure thing." Alex smiled.

∞

They arrived at Claudia's a little while later.

"Kendall, time to wake up," James said, gently shaking his friend.

Kendall opened his eyes. "James?"

"Yeah."

"Where did you come from?"

"Papa G stopped by to pick me up like ten minutes ago. You've been sleeping the whole time."

"Ow," Kendall said, sitting up straight.

"We need to call and get you in for some physical therapy too," Antonio said as he opened the back door.

Kendall and James got out and they all walked up to the house.

Claudia answered the door smiling. "How are my babies today?"

Kendall smiled. "Okay."

"Good," she said while holding the door open.

They went inside and Claudia led them into the living room.

"Claudia, this is my best friend, Alex Mitchell. He's Logan's dad and visiting for the holidays, among other things," Antonio said, introducing the pair.

"Well it is wonderful to make your acquaintance. I've heard a few things about you." She smiled, taking his hand.

"Should I be worried?"

"Not yet, but I'm sure the time will come."

"Probably!" He laughed.

She looked at James. "I like the new look. Shouldn't you be in school?"

James smiled. "Thanks, not today. My dad and I were in a car accident yesterday, and I didn't get out of the hospital until this morning."

"Are you doing alright?"

"Yeah, just some bruised ribs. My dad has a concussion, but he's going to be okay too."

"I'm glad to hear that, baby. Antonio, you want to help me bring in the kettle and some cups. Then you gentlemen can help yourselves to something warm to drink."

"Sure." He smiled, following her back to the kitchen.

"So how did things go this weekend?" she asked, turning on the stove.

"It was a good weekend, with the exception of the accident yesterday. We just got through with Kendall's appointment with Dr. Sharpe, and while he has put on the half a pound, he's anemic. She wants him on tube feedings but agreed to let Alex do them after she watched

him place one. She'll have the rest of the bloodwork back tonight, and she said we have a week for his numbers to improve, or she's going to insist on admitting him."

"How's he doing otherwise? Any more panic attacks or flashbacks?"

"Well, after we left here on Friday, we had lunch with Jen. It went well. He and Jen had a good moment. Then some stupid woman went after Kendall while he was waiting for me to pay my tab. She had read the article about Graham's television interview and went right for the throat. He was trying to get away from her and ended up outside. Luckily, the other boys saw him come out and got to him before something worse happened. I saw Jen go flying out the door, and by the time I got there, she was giving the woman what for, and I had to get in-between them. The boys took Kendall back to the car, but he wasn't responding to anyone at that point. We took him home and he slept for the better part of the afternoon."

She shook her head. "Stupid people are always the most self-righteous. Anything else?"

"It seemed like he was starting to have one this morning, but he came out of it quickly. He still hears Deesie's voice, and I'm worried he's not really getting enough rest. I'm sure Anna would give him something to help him sleep, but I doubt he'd take it."

"Probably not. There are a few things we can try though."

"Like what?"

"Well, I know he didn't care for the ginger candy, but ginger tea can help with insomnia. But if he's anemic, he can't have tea, can he?"

Antonio shook his head.

"Okay, try hot lemonade, unsweetened. Or even better, hot grapefruit juice. Have him sip on it an hour before bedtime. Also, a warm bath right before bed can help," she suggested.

"Okay, we'll try that." He smiled.

She poured the hot water into the teapot and put it on the tray along with some tea bags and hot chocolate tin. Antonio picked it up and carried it back into the living room.

"Are you ready to get started?" she asked Kendall.

He nodded and followed her into the room across the hallway.

"I hear you all had a good weekend, except for an incident on Friday and the accident yesterday?"

He nodded.

"Do you want to tell me about what happened on Friday?"

He shrugged. "Some woman was mad because of what she read in the paper and started yelling at me. I tried to get away, but she kept following me, and then her husband said something, but I don't remember what."

"You don't remember what he said?"

He shook his head.

"Was he yelling at you?"

Kendall thought back. "No, he was telling her to stop... and then it's gone."

"I hear that you and your mom are doing a little better?"

He nodded. "Lunch was nice, and she apologized for what she said again. Then she came by that night to see how I was doing and we talked a little more. I was worried she was going to lose her job, but she said Gary told her there's no way he'd fire her."

"Did that make you feel any better about the situation?"

"Yeah, it wouldn't have been fair if she lost her job because of that," he said, looking down.

"Antonio tells me that Dr. Sharpe agreed to let you do the tube feeding at home. Do you think you'll be able to handle it?"

"I think so. Papa M and I practiced a couple of times before today. It feels really weird, but I don't want to go to the hospital," he said.

"Good." She smiled. "You seem tired. Are you getting enough sleep?"

He sighed. "It seems like that's all I do, but it's like I can't stay awake half the time."

"Are you sleeping through the night, or are you still having bad dreams?"

"Sometimes I think I dream," he said, biting his lip.

"You think you dream?"

"Sometimes I can't tell if I'm awake or asleep. It's really creepy."

"Do you still hear Dessie's voice?"

"Sometimes," he said quietly.

"Every night or just sometimes?"

"I think every night. I can't always remember."

"Have you remembered anything else from the time you were with him?"

He shook his head.

"Are you sure?"

"Sometimes I think I remember things, but then they're gone. I don't know if I'm just dreaming or not."

"That's pretty frustrating, isn't it?"

He nodded.

"Have you lost your temper or gotten upset over something that you normally wouldn't have?"

"Why?"

"Well, sometimes when people have been through a traumatic experience, they find it difficult to control their emotions. Sometimes people cry at something they normally wouldn't, like a sad movie or a song they hear. Sometimes they get angry about something that wouldn't have really bothered them before," she explained.

"I got mad and yelled at Katie, Logan and James on Thanksgiving because they were teasing Carlos. Then I get mad because people keep telling me to 'talk' about things I don't want to talk about."

"I bet you feel pretty bad about it afterwards."

He nodded, looking down.

"Just so you know...it's perfectly normal for that to happen. All those bottled up feelings are going to make their way out somehow."

"Great."

"That's not a bad thing, but the more you talk about things, the less it will happen."

"Okay."

"Now, today I thought we could work on getting you use to that word. We'll just work on it for a few minutes because I know you're tired. Does that sound okay?"

He took a deep breath and nodded.

"I'm going to combine a couple of techniques. So, what I'd like to do is have one of the others come in and sit with you so you feel safe."

"Okay."

"Who would you like me to ask? It should probably be Antonio or Alex, since James is probably still pretty sore."

"Papi?"

"Okay, let me go get him." She smiled.

She went across the hallway and returned a moment later with Antonio and he took a seat next to Kendall.

"Okay, now what we're going to do is gradually introduce that word back into your vocabulary. The way we do this is I'm going to have you sit with Antonio so he can hold you if you get scared. Then I'm going to have you follow my finger as I move it and we're just going to talk. Every now and then, I'm going to say a version of the word, but I want you to just concentrate on following my finger. If you get too uncomfortable, we'll stop. Any questions?"

"How does that help?" Kendall asked.

"Well, having Antonio here will give you the security you need. You feel safe with him and know he won't let anyone hurt you. Just having a normal conversation and introducing the word slowly means you know it's coming, but that no one here is trying to use it to hurt or

scare you. Following my finger gives you a little diversion, so that you aren't completely focused on the conversation, and therefore, the word."

"Okay," Kendall said.

"Are you ready?"

Kendall nodded.

"Where do you want me?" Antonio asked.

"I think right next to him for now."

He nodded and put his arm around Kendall, who scooted closer.

Claudia pushed her chair so she was seated in front of them and smiled. She put her index finger of her right hand up. "Now follow my finger with just your eyes," she instructed as she moved her hand back and forth.

Kendall took a deep breath and did as she said.

"Now, what did you have for Thanksgiving dinner?"

"Uh, turkey, mashed potatoes, corn, rolls..."

"That sounds good, any sweet potatoes?"

Kendall shook a little. "Candied yams, but Sally brought a pie."

"Did you try any of it?"

"Yeah, that one and green apple."

"Was it sweet potato pie?"

"Y-Yes."

"I LOVE sweet potato pie. My granny makes the best, homemade crust and all. Not very many people make a crust from scratch anymore. Did you have anything else sweet, like cranberry sauce?"

"I d-didn't," Kendall said, scooting closer to Antonio.

"Were there marshmallows on the yams? I like them sometimes, but usually they're just too sweet for me. I prefer a little butter and a sprinkling of brown sugar."

"Um, yeah there were marshmallows. Carlos really likes them and sometimes we have marshmallow spitting contests."

"That sounds like fun. Who usually wins?"

"Katie, because she cheats."

"You're telling me that sweet little sister of your cheats?"

"All the time."

She laughed. "I guess I can see that. She can be VERY intense, can't she?"

"You have no idea."

"I bet there are times she's just a little rascal?"

"Definitely."

"Yeah, I have a sister like that. One minute a she's a little monster, the next she's a little sweetheart, you just never can tell. But I love her just the same."

Kendall tensed at the word sweetheart and Antonio tightened his hold.

"Y-Yeah, s-she can be a handful sometimes."

"I bet she can, I also bet you wouldn't trade her for anything in the world," Claudia said as she slowly stopped moving her hand.

"No, I really wouldn't."

"There. That wasn't so bad, was it?" She smiled.

"No, not too bad."

"You did great, and I think getting use to that word will be easier than you think."

"I hope so."

"It's when you're sleeping that you seem to have the worst reaction to it," Antonio said.

"I don't want to do this while I'm sleeping," Kendall said.

"We won't, baby. I think once it isn't bothering you while you're awake, it won't bother you when you're asleep," Claudia told him.

"I hope not."

She smiled again. "Well, I think that's enough for today. You should get home and get some rest."

"Good idea. How about I call your mom and just have her come to the house for lunch?" Antonio asked.

Kendall nodded. "That sounds good."

"How about you come back on Wednesday, same time?" Claudia asked.

"He'll be here," Antonio said as they stood up.

They walked back to the living room. James had just nodded off, so Alex reached over and tapped him on the shoulder.

"Hey Sport, time to go."

James yawned and stood up, wincing.

"I think after lunch you both need some sleep," Antonio said.

"Sounds good to me. It's hard to get enough beauty sleep in a hospital bed," James said.

Kendall rolled his eyes. "Beauty sleep?"

"Hey, this does not come without a strict routine," James said, pointing to his face.

"Don't feel green with envy because other people are sleeping better than you." Kendall smirked.

"Ha-ha... Wait, what? What are you up to now? Because so help me if I wake up another colour, I will shave your eyebrows," James threatened.

"Okay, nobody is dyeing anyone a different colour or shaving anything, understood?" Antonio said firmly.

"Yes sir," they both said.

"What goes on at your house?" Claudia asked.

"Do you really want to know?" Alex asked, shaking his head.

"No, probably not." She laughed.

They made their way out to the car. "I'll see you on Wednesday!" Claudia said.

Kendall smiled and waved at her.

They drove off, and a moment later, a common model, blue sedan pulled out and followed.

Chapter 117~ Watched

Alex ran into the pharmacy to pick up Kendall's prescriptions and a couple of extra feeding lines and bags. Both boys had fallen asleep, so Antonio woke James once they got to his house. Jen's car was still in the driveway, so Antonio went in to talk to her about Kendall's appointment.

"Did he do alright with Alex placing the tube?" Jen asked.

"He did great, and Anna was very impressed with Alex's abilities, so with any luck we'll keep him out of the hospital." Antonio smiled.

"She's going to call with the rest of his results. I'm just hoping there isn't anything else going on," Jen said.

"I'm sure he's fine, honey. I was thinking since he and James are both pretty tired, maybe we could just have lunch at my house today?"

"Perfect. I'll follow you over." She smiled.

"Are you doing alright?"

"I'm doing much better. Dr. Thorne is very nice, and he's helping me with some calming techniques. He thinks I should spend some more time with Kendall, but I'm still a little nervous. I just don't want to hurt him again."

"I'm sure he'll be fine. You have had some good visits since your breakdown, and you're taking care of yourself. The trick is to continue taking care of yourself after you're back home."

She nodded. "I know. I also know that Sylvia, Brooke, and Jo won't leave me alone until they're sure."

"No they won't. Does that bother you?"

"No, I know they're just looking out for me, like the boys look out for each other. I don't feel quite so alone then," she said with a sad smile.

He hugged her. "Honey, you're not alone. I know it's been hard since Will died, but we all love you and are here for you and the kids."

"I know and I am so grateful to all of you. It just always feels like I'm taking and never giving back."

"Friendship is give and take, but it's NOT about keeping score. We all know you're here if we need you, so you need to get those kinds of thoughts out of your head."

She smiled. "That's what Dr. Thorne said."

"Well, he sounds like a wise man, so LISTEN to him."

"I'm trying," she promised.

"Okay, we'll see you at home for lunch."

She nodded. "I'll get ready for work and be right over."

Antonio and James went back to the car and they headed home. A few minutes later, Jen left and headed for the Garcia's. A couple of minutes after she drove away, a blue sedan pulled out and followed her.

∞

Alex pulled into the Garcia driveway and James woke Kendall. They went inside and Antonio went into the kitchen to start lunch. He read the note Sylvia left and laughed.

Alex had followed Antonio, laid everything out on the table, and started to read the formula label. "What's so funny?"

"Sylvia went to the market and said to keep you out of the kitchen so she doesn't have to restock everything again. She also said she's onto you because there were more cookies in the bin when we got back then there were before we left. Exactly what does that mean?" Antonio asked his friend.

"I have no idea."

"I'm not sure I believe you," Antonio told him.

"Aren't MORE cookies better than LESS cookies?" Alex asked as he went back to reading the instructions on the label.

"I think it depends on who you ask.," Antonio laughed.

∞

Jen pulled up to the Garcia's and went up to the door. She knocked and Kendall looked through the peephole and then opened the door. "Hi mom." He smiled.

"Hi honey, how are you feeling?" she asked, going inside.

"Okay," he said as she hugged him.

"Really?"

He nodded. "I'm just a little tired right now."

"It was a long night."

"Yeah, it was. Papa G's in the kitchen," he told her.

"Shall we go help him make lunch?" she asked, putting her arm around his shoulder.

"Sure," he said and they walked in together.

"Hey Jen," Alex said, looking up.

"Hi Alex. How are you doing?"

"I'm doing fine, just going over the instructions here."

"Is this what you need for the feeding tube?" she asked, looking at the items on the table.

"Yeah, Anna had them make a few additions to the formula, so I want to make sure I reconstitute it right."

Kendall picked up one of the bags. "How does it work?"

"Well, I mix up the formula and pour it in through this top cap. This line will attach to the feeding tube, and we use the clamp here on the infusion tubing to control the flow. Up is open, down is closed. Then we hang it high up and let gravity do its job." He smiled.

"How long does it take?"

"It really depends on how fast a flow your stomach can handle. We'll probably start out slow for the first couple of times and then increase it a little. It should take between one and two hours. When my dad needs one he's actually on a pump that's programmed for feeding times, and we leave the feeding tube in for a couple of days at a time before switching sides," Alex explained.

"It doesn't sound too complicated," Jen said.

"It's not once you get used to it. The question is, when do we want to start this, now, or tonight?" he asked Kendall.

"Tonight?" He smiled.

Alex looked at him. "Tell you what. We'll start it tonight IF you eat a good lunch now."

"Define good."

"As in everything put on your plate, as well as smoothie later," Alex told him.

"Who's putting the food on the plate?"

"I am, smarty pants," Alex said.

"Fine." Kendall pouted.

"Don't look so happy." Jen smiled, kissing his cheek.

He rolled his eyes and went back out to sit with James.

Alex laughed, shaking his head. "Kids."

"Funny, Sylvia says the same thing about you," Antonio said.

"Hey now," Alex protested.

"Boys, be nice," Jen said.

∞

Sylvia pulled into the driveway and went to get the bags from the trunk. She looked down the street and glanced at the car she had passed just a moment ago. She grabbed two bags, carried them up to the door, and started to put her key in the door when it opened.

"Need some help?" James asked.

"Thank you, Mijo, but you're not carrying anything." She smiled, walking in.

"I'm sure I can manage a couple of grocery bags."

"No, and that's final. I want you to stay inside," she said, closing the door behind her.

She carried the bags out to the kitchen. "Kendall, can you go and make sure James does NOT go out and get the groceries?"

"Sure... ya know, if you want to have grown-up talk, all you have to do is say so." He smirked.

"Just go," she said, swatting at him as he passed.

She watched him for a moment to make certain he was out of earshot. "Antonio, I think someone's watching the houses on this block."

"Why, what happened?"

"There's a blue, four door Chevy Malibu parked down the street. It was there when I took the kids to school, but it was gone when I got back. There's a man in the driver's seat and he's just sitting there."

"Okay, stay here. Alex, you want to help me bring in the rest of the bags?" Antonio asked.

"Sure thing."

The two men headed for the door and Antonio locked the door before he closed it. Sylvia and Jen followed them into the living room, Sylvia carrying the phone in case she needed to call the station.

"What's going on?" James asked as Sylvia stood to the side of the bay window watching.

"We don't know yet, honey," Sylvia told him.

Jen sat down next to the boys and put an arm around each of them.

Antonio and Alex walked out to the car talking. Antonio glanced down the street and saw the car as he opened the trunk. Alex moved in front of him and Antonio bent down to take a bag and took a longer look at the car. With Alex standing in front of him, the driver couldn't see Antonio watching him.

"Well?" Alex asked.

"He's watching alright, but I can't make out the license plate," he said, grabbing a bag. Alex grabbed the other two and Antonio closed the trunk. They went back up to the house and Sylvia opened the door as Antonio started to turn the knob. The two men went inside and Sylvia closed it behind them.

They carried the bags into the kitchen. "Well?" Sylvia asked.

Antonio nodded as he put a call into the station. "Hey Boss, what's up?" Sally answered.

"I've got a late model, blue Chevy Malibu watching the houses on my street. Driver is male, Caucasian, mid to late thirties, brown hair, closely trimmed. He's wearing sunglasses and a dark coloured jacket."

"Do you want me to send a patrol car or drive by in a personal vehicle?"

"Can you drive by in your car and see if you can get a plate? He's almost a block down and I can't read it. Have a patrol car standing by a couple of blocks over though, just in case."

"Will do. I'll be by in ten," Sally said, hanging up.

"What is going on?" Sylvia asked.

"I'm not sure. Sally's going to drive by and get the plates so we can run them."

"What about the kids?"

"Call the schools and tell them to have the boys and Katie wait inside until one of us picks them up. Tell them not to let them outside, period. Tell them to also keep the Meyer and Picket kids in. I'll have the station get ahold of their parents and make sure someone picks them up as well," Antonio said, handing her back the phone. He headed out to the living room and grabbed his jacket.

"Where do you think you're going?" Alex asked.

"I'm going to go out back and see if there are any footprints around the back gate or in the alley."

"Not without me you're not," Alex said, grabbing his jacket.

"What's going on?" Kendall asked.

"I'm not sure yet. There might be someone casing the neighbourhood. Tis the season for home break-ins. A couple of neighbours have been away for the holiday, so I want to make sure their houses are secure," Antonio said reassuringly.

Antonio and Alex headed out the back door. The back yard was surrounded by a seven foot, solid board fence, so they couldn't be seen from the front. Antonio unlocked the back gate and carefully opened it. He looked around and saw boot prints go up and down the alley, but none at the gate. He and Alex walked slowly down the alley in the general direction of the sedan.

"The Meyers yard isn't fenced, so we might be able to get a better look at this guy," Antonio said. Alex nodded and followed behind him closely.

They walked four houses down and tried looking for the car, but it was parked towards the center of the house, so they couldn't see it.

"Damn it," Antonio cursed.

"Who do you think this guy is?"

"I don't know, but I intend to find out," Antonio told him.

Chapter 118~ Piñatas and Creepy Clowns

Sally quickly changed and started towards the Garcia home. Bennet had taken Shale, and they were going to wait two blocks over, just in case.

She went the long way around and then pulled onto the Garcia's street. She saw the Chevy parked a few houses down from Antonio's and called the station, where Johnson was ready to take down and run the plates.

She drove slowly and could clearly read the plates about three houses down. "Johnson, Minnesota plates... Howard, James, Charles, four, four, one."

"Got it," Johnson replied, typing the number into the state database.

She drove past and glanced at the driver, who was just sitting there looking up the street in the general direction of the Garcia's. She drove another block down and turned the corner. She parked on the next street over, waiting for Johnson.

"Okay, Sally, got it. It's licensed to a rental agency called Rent-A-Dent, in Minneapolis. I called, but they won't release the name of the customer who rented it without a warrant."

She sighed. "Thanks Johnson. I'll think of something."

She started the car and called Bennet. "John, the car's a rental. They won't give us a name, so I'm going to try something," she said, driving back around the block.

"What are you up to?" he asked.

"Just answer your phone when I call, just in case I need you."

"Will do."

Sally drove back up the street behind the car and pulled into the driveway of the house where he was parked. She called John. "Okay, I'm going to put my phone in my pocket, so hang tight." She got out and grabbed her purse, making as if to go to the door, and she looked over at the car. She smiled and walked over to the driver's side and gestured for him to roll the window down.

"Can I help you with something?" she asked, smiling.

"Uh, no. I just needed to let the engine cool off. It was starting to overheat, so I pulled off the main street."

"Do you need me to call someone for you?" she asked, pulling out her phone.

"No thanks, I'm good. It's been a few minutes, so I should be good to go soon," he said, smiling back.

"You're not going to get too far if your engine keeps overheating. My neighbour down the street is great with cars. Why don't I call him?"

"No really, I don't want to bother anyone. I'll find a mechanic and have it checked out."

She could tell he was starting to get a little nervous, so she pressed him a little more. "Are you sure? Because he's always happy to help, and I'm pretty sure he's home today."

He nodded and turned the key. "See, it's doing fine now. I'm sure I can make it someplace to have it checked out before it happens again."

"Okay, well Reger's is a great place. Mike, the owner, is a friend. Just tell him Sally sent you and he'll see to it you get what you need right away." She smiled again.

"Reger's... got it. Thanks a lot."

"Not a problem. If you just go down to Verling, that's the next main street, and take a right, you'll see his shop about three miles down."

"Thanks again."

"Good luck!" she said as she started walking back to the house.

He pulled away and started down the street, taking a right on the third block down.

Sally waited until he was out of sight and got back into her car. "He's heading south on Verling Avenue," she told John.

"Got it. You going back to the station?" John asked.

"After I talk to Antonio."

"Okay, we'll see you later then," John said.

"Can you let me know where he goes?"

"Sure thing," John told her.

Sally looked at her phone and clicked play on the video she had just taken. She smiled when she saw it had worked, and pulled out of the driveway. She parked where the Chevy had been, got out, and walked to the Garcia house. Sally knocked on the door and Antonio opened it and let her in. The boys, Sylvia, and Jen were sitting in the dining room eating lunch.

"Hi Sally. Would you like something to eat?" Sylvia asked.

"No thanks, I'm good." She smiled.

"Well?" Antonio asked.

"Johnson ran the plates, and the car's a rental from Minneapolis. They won't give us a name without a warrant."

"Great," Antonio muttered.

"John's tailing him, and I managed to get a short video," she said, pulling out her phone and handing it to him.

Antonio hit play and watched it. "I don't know him."

"I've never seen him before either, but I'll see if I can get a clear enough photo from here and send it through the DMV data base," she told him.

"Good job, Sally. Are you sure you don't want something to eat?" Antonio asked.

She shook her head. "I ate at the station, and I want to get this into the computer as soon as possible. I'll let you know if I find anything. I was planning on meeting with the boys later today, so hopefully I'll have something by then."

Antonio nodded. "When you get to the station, could you have Johnson call the elementary and middle schools and explain what's going on? Have them get a hold of Jeff Meyer and Dana Picket, and have them either pick their kids up from school, or call us and we'll pick them up with our kids."

"Sure thing, Boss. Good idea," Sally said as she opened the door.

"I'll talk to you later," he said, walking her out. "Where's your car?"

"I left it parked in front of your neighbour's house in case that guy came back."

"Good thinking."

"I do my best." She laughed.

∞

Antonio went back inside and he and Alex joined the others at the table

"So what's going on?" James asked again.

"I'm not sure yet. Sally said the guy told her he was having car trouble, so it could be as simple as that." He smiled.

"Then why are you having the neighbours pick up their kids?" Kendall asked.

"Just a precaution. I don't want to take any chances—it's a cop thing," Antonio said reassuringly.

Kendall raised his eyebrow but didn't say anything.

"Well, I should get to work. I'll give you a call after my shift ends," Jen said to Kendall.

"Okay." Kendall smiled.

She kissed him on top of the head. "You get some rest too," she told James, kissing his cheek.

"I will, thanks Mama K," James said.

"I'll walk you out," Alex said.

"Thanks!" She smiled.

They walked out together. "Look honey, if you need anything at all, just call me," Alex told her.

"You've already done so much. I cannot thank you enough for this. He would not do well if we had to put him in the hospital."

"I'm just glad it's something I can do. Plus, it gives me a chance to hang around a little longer." He smiled.

"Something we're all happy about."

"Yeah, remind Sylvia of that, will ya?" He smirked.

"There are some things you are on your own with." Jen laughed.

"Great," he said, pouting.

"You know... you should call Joanna. Maybe stop by the steakhouse for dinner one night," Jen suggested.

"What excuse would I give?"

"You're friends, who needs an excuse?"

"Very true."

"I'll see you later. Thanks again, Alex," Jen said, getting into her car.

"You're welcome." He smiled.

∞

Bennet got back to the station just a few minutes after Sally. "Well?" she asked.

"He went through a drive-thru coffee place and then headed out of town. Apparently, he's staying at the Best Western out by the airport, at least that's where he stopped. What did you find out?" he asked.

"Not a lot. I sent a photo I took to the DMV data base, but that's going to take a while."

"Great. Maybe we should put the schools on alert," he said.

"Not a bad idea, just in case," Sally said, picking up the phone. Ten minutes later, all of the schools and licensed daycares had been notified about a possible predator driving a blue Chevy Malibu.

∞

After lunch, Kendall and James both headed up to get some sleep. James was starting to feel the effects of being jostled around so violently, and was getting stiff and achy. Sylvia gave him some Tylenol because he didn't want to take a pain pill. He wanted to be able to visit with his dad again, and he was worried the pills would knock him out.

"You go ahead and sleep on the bed," Kendall said.

"There's enough room for both of us, just like we've been doing," James pointed out.

"Yeah, but you hurt when you move now," Kendall said.

"Look, you didn't bother me last night and you're not going to bother me now."

"Okay, but if I do, let me know."

"I will," James promised.

Ten minutes later, both boys were sound asleep, worn out by the events of the last two days.

∞

Downstairs, the adults were talking. Sally had called to give Antonio an update and let him know they had put the schools on alert.

"So, any idea what this guy is up to?" Alex asked Antonio.

"No, and all we can do is guess until we find out who he is," Antonio said.

"I can't believe the rental agency wouldn't give you a name," Sylvia said.

"All these new privacy laws make it hard for us to do our job sometimes. He wasn't breaking the law, so we can't get a warrant. All we can do is hope we get a hit from the DMV on the photo Sally took."

"Do you really think he was casing the neighbourhood for houses to break into?" Sylvia asked.

Antonio shook his head. "That just doesn't add up. Most thieves don't rent cars and then drive to another city. They either steal one, or use an old beater they can easily dispose of. They also don't usually rent motel rooms and stay around."

"Well, I guess there's nothing we can do about it right now. I'm going to go pick up the kids. I'm dropping Nattie Picket off at her mom's office, so I'll be a little longer than usual," Sylvia said.

"Okay honey," Antonio said, giving her a kiss.

"I'll go with you," Alex told her.

Antonio gave him a small nod.

Sylvia and Alex arrived at the middle school about ten minutes later. They found all of the teachers out, one stationed at each bus, and two at the student pick-up area. Janice Lane was standing just outside the front doors, keeping an eye on everything. The teachers were all holding small radios the school had invested in a few years earlier, so they were in constant contact with Principal Lane.

Janice smiled and waved when she saw Sylvia and Alex walk up.

"It's good to see you're well-prepared." Alex smiled.

"Hello Mr. Mitchell, Logan said you were visiting. Yes, the entire staff has had security training, and most just finished a refresher course after what happened last month."

"Well you're doing a great job." Sylvia smiled.

"I'm not about to let another student be victimized if I can prevent it."

"You know none of that was your fault. You did everything right, even went above and beyond what most people would have done," Sylvia told her.

"And yet it wasn't enough," Janice said sadly.

Sylvia patter her arm. "Sometimes it seems that way, but there are just some things beyond our control."

"She's right, you know. We can only do our best, and then you have to hope that the rest works out alright," Alex said.

Janice smiled and then noticed a student walking off on their own. "We have a wanderer by bus three," she said into the radio. Alex and Sylvia followed her gaze and the nearest teacher ran for the student and escorted him back to the bus area.

"It's alright, he didn't understand the buses are giving rides to all the students who normally walk home," the teacher radioed.

"Thanks Erika," Janice said. "The boys are waiting inside," she told Sylvia and Alex.

"I'll go get them," Alex said.

"Janice, call me if you need to talk," Sylvia said.

She nodded. "How's Kendall really doing?"

"He's getting better. Hopefully he'll be able to come back to school soon."

Janice smiled. "Good, because as much chaos as those boys cause, I adore them all."

"I know you do. I'll tell him you said, hi. Maybe you should stop by and see him. The boys are all staying with us for now. He may not say much, but we need to get him use to being around people again, and it might be easier with people he knows," Sylvia suggested.

Janice nodded. "Maybe... I just keep remembering the last time I spoke with him. I didn't believe him and he looked so... betrayed."

"He doesn't blame you for that. He doesn't blame anyone except Deesie. Don't let what Deesie did make you doubt yourself. You are a wonderful principal and an incredible person. All of the kids adore you."

"Well, thank you for that. Maybe you could ask him how he'd feel about a visit, that way he doesn't feel uncomfortable."

"I can do that." Sylvia smiled.

Alex and the boys came out a couple of minutes later. "Mami!" Carlos yelled, hugging her.

"Carlitos... What is that?" she asked, looking at a large round thing with a head and tail feathers.

"It's a turkey piñata! Jenny made it in art and her mom wouldn't let her bring it home, so she gave it to me. She even filled it with candy!"

"That was nice... but why?" she asked with a pained smile.

"No reason, except her mom didn't want Jenny trying to whack something hanging from the ceiling with a big stick while she was blindfolded," Logan told her.

"Ah." Sylvia nodded.

"So WE get to!" Carlos squealed.

"Remind me to call and THANK Mrs. Tinkler," Sylvia told Alex.

He laughed. "Sure thing, but look at that face. Doesn't he look happy?"

"Yes, he does. Sometimes he amazes me with how little it takes to make him happy."

"He's a good boy." Alex smiled.

"Well, we better go pick up Katie and Nattie," Sylvia said, looking at her watch. "I'll talk to you later," she told Janice.

"Have fun with your piñata." She laughed.

"I will!" Carlos smiled, waving goodbye.

They picked up the girls and dropped Nattie off. They got home about twenty minutes later and Carlos ran in to show his dad his piñata.

"So, why did they put the school on alert?" Logan asked as he slowly made his way up the walk.

"There was a strange car hanging around, so they did it as a precaution," Alex told him.

"That's all?"

"Right now, that's enough," Alex said, helping his son up the steps. "By the way, I made an appointment to get your ankle checked after school tomorrow."

"Good, hopefully I can get rid of these crutches." Logan smiled.

"Hopefully, Hopalong!" Alex said.

"Dad..." Logan whined as they went inside.

Carlos and Katie were in the kitchen getting a quick snack. "Can we hang up the piñata after dinner?" Carlos asked.

"I guess that depends on how quickly you get your homework done," Sylvia told him.

"But Mami..."

"D minus."

"Okay," he said, grabbing his backpack. He and Logan went up to his room to get started.

"I think I'll get the formula ready and we can do this as soon as Kendall wakes up." Alex said.

He measured out the powder and then added lukewarm water to the blender. He mixed it until it was completely blended, and then poured it into the bag. He screwed the cap on tight and then opened the clamp on the bag to make sure it was flowing properly. "Okay, this is ready to go."

"That looks gross," Katie said.

"I know, but don't say anything like that to your brother, alright?" Alex asked.

"Okay, but can I watch?"

He looked at her. "I'm going to say no for now."

"But why?"

"Two words... baby formula," Sylvia told her.

"Oh, I forgot about that. I'll be nice, really." She smiled sweetly.

"Yeah, I don't think so," Alex said.

"I'll only tease him a little, and only when he's better," she promised.

Sylvia put her hands on her hips. "Don't you have homework to do?"

"I never get to do anything fun," Katie said as she pulled out her homework.

∞

There was a knock at the door and Antonio answered it. "Hi Sally. Any news?"

"Well, the guy hasn't been issued a Minnesota driver's license, so I expanded the search to include North and South Dakota, Illinois, Wisconsin, and Iowa. It's going to take a while, but hopefully I'll have something tomorrow."

"Okay, not much we can do until then," Antonio said.

She shook her head. "Are the boys around?"

"Carlos and Logan are doing homework upstairs. Kendall and James were both sleeping last time I looked," Antonio told her.

"How are they doing?"

"James is pretty sore right now. I should actually wake them up, since he wants to go see his dad, and we need to get a feeding tube placed for Kendall," Antonio said, starting upstairs.

"Is he doing okay with that whole thing?" Sally asked, followiing him.

"He's not happy about it, but he also doesn't want to go into the hospital."

"I don't blame him," she said.

Sally knocked on Carlos' door as Antonio went to wake the other two boys.

"Sally!" Carlos said, jumping up and hugging her.

"Carlos, you are SO strong!"

He grinned proudly.

"What are you guys up to?"

"Homework," Logan said.

"TWO hours of homework, just to start," Carlos whined.

"It's your own fault for not letting me know you needed help studying," Logan told him.

Carlos rolled his eyes.

"Alright you two... since you're pretty busy, why don't I just pick up your memory cards? I'll put them on a disc and we can look at them next time."

"Okay," Carlos said, grabbing his camera. He pulled the card out and handed it to her.

"Thank you," she smiled, handing him a replacement. "What about yours?" she asked Logan.

"Umm, if I tell you something, will you promise to not get mad?"

"Of course."

"I kind of took a picture of CarlosKatieandKendall, after we found him hiding in the crawlspace."

"Come again?"

"They were so sweet, all curled up on the bed together, and I couldn't help it. He was asleep and doesn't know I took it," Logan said, looking down.

"Honey, we explained why we didn't want you doing that," Sally said softly.

"I know, I just..." Logan started.

"Okay, we'll just make sure he doesn't see it."

"Thanks Sally. I'm sorry."

"Don't be sorry, it's not something you should have to think about. Just don't do it again, alright?"

"I promise."

"Okay." She smiled.

"Umm, Sally," Carlos said.

"Not you too?"

He nodded. "He and Katie were sleeping on the couch Friday and they looked so happy."

Sally sighed. "Okay, same with you. No more photos of Kendall until he's ready."

They both nodded.

"Carlos, can you go and ask James where his memory card is?"

"Sure," he said, jumping up and going next door.

"Okay, I spoke with Claudia and she thinks it's a great idea for you to help out with this. Would you be able to meet with her tomorrow?" Sally asked Logan.

"I think so. I have an appointment to get my ankle checked after school, so maybe after that?"

"Give me a call and I'll meet you there." She smiled.

"Thank Sally."

Carlos came running back in with James' memory card. "Thank you. Can you give him this one?" she asked, handing him a replacement.

"Okay, thanks Sally," Carlos said, hugging her again.

She hugged him back, not letting go for a moment. "I LOVE your hugs."

"Thanks!" He grinned.

"No, thank you!" She smiled. "I'll see you two later."

"Bye Sally," they both said.

She went downstairs and went to the kitchen to say goodbye. "Hey, I'll see you all later."

"Thanks for everything, Sally," Sylvia said.

"Not a problem. I'll call and set something up with the boys for later in the week, after things have settled down a bit."

"Good plan." Sylvia smiled.

"I'll walk you out," Alex said.

"Why, thank you."

They walked out to her car. "So what's on your mind?" she asked.

"I'm getting a little worried about Antonio. The night away was great for them, but then there was the accident. Now there's this strange guy hanging around. It's like it never stops."

"I know. It's a lot to handle. That's why I'm glad you're here. He needs the back-up."

"I'm not sure it'll be enough," Alex said.

"Well, you handling the tube feedings is going to help. It makes him hand over a little bit of control to someone else, because he can't do it all."

"Yeah, but I've known him for a long time, and he gets obsessive about making sure that everyone is safe to the point of ignoring what they might actually need."

"You mean like flat out refusing to allow Dr. Sharpe to put Kendall in the hospital, not that I disagree. I don't think he'd handle it well, but I've heard that tone before," Sally told him.

"Yeah, like that."

"Well, right now I think he needs Kendall as much as Kendall needs him. Maybe it's because of his friendship with Kendall's dad, maybe he thinks he let him down when Kendall was taken. It could be he saw losing Kendall as losing Will all over again. Right now Kendall feels safest with Antonio, and if we can transition some of that over to you, it would help. In all honesty, it hasn't been that long and they both witnessed some horrific things together."

"True, and maybe if he actually gets back to work, things will calm down for him," Alex said.

"It'll also help if Kendall keeps opening up to Claudia. Get him over some of these panic triggers and get his life back on track. Speaking of Claudia, she thinks it's a good idea to meet with Logan, and since he's going to be out tomorrow afternoon anyway, maybe we can meet there after his doctor's appointment?"

Alex nodded. "Good plan. Maybe she can give me a few tips on how to help out around here a little more."

"Give me a call when you're done and I'll meet you there," Sally said, getting into her car.

"I will, thanks Sally."

"No problem. I'll see you tomorrow."

He waved goodbye and went back inside.

∞

James was already downstairs and helping Katie with her homework.

"Kendall still upstairs?" Alex asked.

"Yeah, I think they're waiting for you," James said.

Alex smiled and went to gather everything from the kitchen.

"Do you need help?" James asked as Alex headed upstairs.

"It's okay. I can have one of the other boys hold the water."

"I can do it!" Katie offered.

"No!" both Alex and James said.

"Fine," she huffed, crossing her arms. Alex shook his head, laughing at her expression. He went up and found Kendall and Antonio waiting in the guest room.

"You ready to do this?"

"If I say no, can we start tomorrow?" Kendall asked.

"Nice try," Alex said.

He went into the bathroom, got a glass of water, and asked Carlos to come hold the glass for them. He prepared the tube, and a couple of minutes later, had placed it successfully.

"We're getting faster at this." He smiled.

"Yay?" Kendall said.

"Okay, why don't you sit back and make yourself comfortable," Alex told him.

Kendall sat back against the headboard, trying to get comfortable. Alex hooked the formula bag on a hanger and then hung it on a temporary hook they had attached to the wall about two feet above the bed. Alex attached the infusion tube to the feeding tube and made sure the connection was tight.

He sat down next to Kendall. "Okay, this is going to feel a little strange at first. It's room temperature, so it's going to feel a little cold going in. I'm going to start it off slow and then increase the flow gradually."

Kendall nodded and Alex rolled the clamp until it was about a third of the way open. After a minute, Kendall shivered, so Antonio pulled the blanket up over him.

Ten minutes later, Alex opened the flow to halfway. "Let me know if that's too much for you."

"How will I know?"

"You'll know." Alex smiled.

A couple of minutes later, Kendall started swallowing a lot. "I'm going to throw up."

Alex immediately cut the flow back. "That's how we know. Take a couple of deep breaths."

Kendall did as Alex said and sat very still for a few minutes with his eyes squeezed shut, worried he was going to puke. After a few minutes, his stomach stopped doing flip-flops and he relaxed a little more.

"Better?" Alex asked.

Kendall nodded.

Sylvia came up. "Dinner is ready. Are you almost done?"

"Not for a while... you go eat," Alex told Antonio.

"Are you sure?"

"Yeah, I can eat when we're through here."

"Or, I can bring you up a plate," Sylvia said.

"That'll work too." He smiled.

"I don't have to eat, do I?" Kendall asked.

"No, you don't have to eat tonight," Alex told him.

"Good, because I will seriously puke," Kendall said, closing his eyes again.

"Hang in there, Champ, you're doing just fine," Alex said, patting his shoulder.

Sylvia made up a plate and took it up for Alex. "Here you go, call down if you need anything."

"I will, thanks." Alex smiled.

"Are you sure he doesn't need to eat tonight?"

"We'll see how he's feeling later," Alex told her.

Kendall shook his head. "I'm NOT hungry."

Alex handed Kendall the remote. "Find something to watch, it'll help distract you."

Kendall took the remote, flipped through channels, and finally stopped it on the cartoon channel. Alex ate his dinner, and then sat next to Kendall watching TV with him.

An hour later, the bag was nearly empty. "Do you want me to open it up all the way for the last few drops?"

"Sure." Kendall sighed.

Alex rolled the clamp, and a moment later, the bag was empty. Alex pinched off the tubing and disconnected the two lines.

"Okay, I'm going to flush the line and we'll take it out in about half an hour."

"Why that long?" Kendall asked.

"What do you think will happen if I pull the tube out and it tickles your throat right now?"

"Oh... yeah, I don't want that."

"I didn't think so." Alex smiled. "Good news is we can go downstairs if you want to."

Kendall shook his head. "Not with this in."

"Okay."

∞

Antonio had taken the other kids to see Mike while Alex and Kendall were busy with the feeding. They got back after a short visit. Mike had quite a headache and wasn't allowed visitors for more than a few minutes.

After finishing his homework, Carlos asked if they could hang the piñata. Antonio smiled. "In the basement, where there's nothing breakable."

Carlos grabbed the piñata, and a few minutes later, he and Antonio had it hanging from a hook in the ceiling. Antonio found an old hockey stick and padded it with a dishtowel, just in case.

"Are you ready?" he asked Carlos.

"We need Kendall," he said, running upstairs.

Alex had just finished pulling the tube and Kendall was having a coughing fit. Alex rubbed Kendall's back for a couple of minutes while Carlos held the glass of water for him.

"Guess what we get to do?" Carlos asked excitedly.

"What?" Kendall asked his grinning friend.

"Jenny gave me a piñata, and Papi hung it in the basement so we can hit it!"

"Why did Jenny give you a piñata?"

"She made it in art and her mom wouldn't let her take it home. She even filled it with candy for us!"

"That was really nice of her." Kendall smiled.

"I know! So come on!" Carlos said, pulling his friend along with him.

"Carlos, not so fast!"

"Sorry," Carlos said, slowing down.

The boys and Alex went down to the basement where the others were waiting. "About time," Katie said, hugging Kendall.

"Okay, who goes first?" Antonio asked, holding up a blindfold.

"Carlos," everyone said.

Antonio laughed as he tried to put the blindfold on the excited boy. "Okay now, not too wild," Antonio said, placing the stick in his son's hands.

"Okay Papi!" Carlos said as he started swinging at air.

Antonio quickly moved back as Carlos continued trying to find the piñata with the stick. He connected once and it swung up and hit the ceiling but didn't break. "Okay, someone else's turn," Antonio said after two minutes and grabbing ahold of Carlos.

"Aww," Carlos said.

"Who's next?" Antonio asked.

"Logan can go next," Katie said.

"How am I supposed to hit it on crutches?"

"I'll hold on to you," Alex said.

Antonio blindfolded Logan and Alex held Logan around the waist so he could hit at the hanging turkey. He connected twice and it cracked but didn't break.

"Next?" Antonio asked.

"Katie, you go. I don't think I can swing very well right now," James said.

"I didn't think about that... We should have waited," Carlos said.

"Don't worry about it, buddy. This way I get candy and don't actually have to work for it." James smirked.

Antonio blindfolded Katie and positioned her under the piñata. He stepped back. "Okay, go for it!"

She listened for a minute and then swung the stick up slowly. The stick gently connected with the piñata, and she grinned before taking a huge swing and connecting with it again. The piñata cracked and small colourfully wrapped candies came flying out.

Carlos and Katie both squealed, diving for the floor. James carefully bent down and picked up a few pieces, and Alex helped Logan sit on the floor so he could reach a few.

"Shouldn't you get in there?" Antonio asked Kendall.

"I really don't think bending down is a good idea right now."

Antonio smiled and grabbed a few pieces and handed them to Kendall. "Thanks Papi." Kendall smiled.

"Okay, make sure you get all of it. I don't need mice down here," Sylvia instructed as she headed up the stairs.

After a few minutes, Katie and Carlos had found every piece of candy, and they headed upstairs.

Sylvia had warmed up some unsweetened lemonade and handed Kendall the cup. "Claudia said to try this and see if it helps you sleep a little better."

He took a sip and shuddered. "What is this?"

"Hot lemonade."

"This is not good."

"I know. It's an acquired taste, but try it, okay?"

"Okay, I'll try."

"James, take this," Sylvia said, handing him one of his pain pills.

"It's going to be hard to wake up."

"I think another day off to rest will do you some good." She smiled and kissed his cheek.

"I'm not going to argue," he said, swallowing the pill.

"Somehow I didn't think you would," she said.

An hour later, James and Kendall were both sitting on the couch and nodding off.

"Alright, bedtime," Sylvia said.

The kids headed upstairs and got ready for bed. James and Kendall climbed into bed while Carlos and Logan took their places between the bed and door. Half an hour later, Sylvia checked on them and they were all sleeping soundly.

∞

At about midnight, James started to toss and turn in his sleep.

He was inside when he heard someone calling his name. James went out into the backyard and saw a piñata hanging from the tree.

"James, come and play with me," Carlos said.

"Sure thing, buddy." James smiled, heading over to his friend.

"It's your turn," Carlos told him, putting the blindfold over his eyes. James swung the stick and missed. "Go again!" Carlos yelled.

James swung again and connected. Suddenly, there was a maniacal laugh coming from beside him. He pulled off the blindfold and screamed. A very large clown was standing next to him. He was very tall, and his face was done in white paint with a gruesome red smile painted on.

"Go on, James, swing again!" The clown giggled, clapping his hands.

James backed away from the clown, swinging the stick at him to keep him back. "Stay away!" James warned.

"But Jamie, don't you want to play with me?" the clown asked, honking a little horn.

James looked at him and backed away.

"I want to play with you!" the clown giggled, opening his arms and walking towards the teen.

"NO! STAY BACK!" James screamed.

Kendall woke up to James murmuring in his sleep. "James, are you okay?"

James shot straight up screaming, and Kendall fell backwards off the bed.

The scream woke Logan and Carlos. Carlos jumped up, ran to the other side of the bed, and pulled Kendall away from the bed. Logan got up carefully and got to the bed a few seconds after Carlos.

"James, wake up!" Logan said.

James started swinging his arms and hit Logan in the eye. The boy landed on his rear, and Carlos tried to get ahold of James' flailing limbs.

"JAMES!" Carlos yelled.

James was still swinging and caught Carlos in the face. Antonio came running in and launched himself at James. He caught ahold of him and held him tightly. Alex was there a moment later and pulled Logan and Carlos away from the bed. "Where's Kendall?"

Carlos pointed to the other side of the room, Alex went over, and found Kendall curled up in a ball, covering his ears.

He picked him up. "Out in the hall," Alex told the boys.

Carlos grabbed Logan and helped him out into the hallway. Alex lay Kendall next to them and went back in to help Antonio.

Sylvia grabbed a washcloth and held it up to Carlos' split lip. Logan was covering his right eye with his hand.

"Let me see, honey," Sylvia said.

Logan took his hand away to reveal an already swollen eye. "Okay, we'll get you some ice."

Carlos was holding onto Kendall, who hadn't moved since Alex put him down.

"Is he alright?" Sylvia asked.

"I think he fell off the bed," Carlos said. His lip was already swollen to twice its normal size.

"Kendall, are you okay?" Sylvia asked, carefully touching his arm.

He pulled himself closer to Carlos and his friend put his arm over him. "It's okay, it's just a bad dream," Carlos told him.

∞

Antonio and Alex were trying to hold onto James so he didn't hurt himself.

"Mijo, wake up. It's alright, it's just a bad dream," Antonio said soothingly.

After a couple of minutes, James relaxed.

"James, wake up, Sport," Alex said, brushing the boy's hair back off his forehead.

James opened his eyes—they were glazed and unfocused.

"James, can you hear me?" Alex asked.

James was suddenly alert. "Where is he?"

"Where's who, Mijo?" Antonio asked.

"The clown."

"Clown?"

"He was right here!" James said, looking around.

"James, there's no clown, it was a nightmare," Alex told him.

"It was so real," James said, looking around in confusion.

"That's why they call them nightmares," Antonio said.

"Where is everybody?" James asked, noticing the other boys were not in the room.

"I sent them out into the hall," Alex said.

"Is everyone okay? I scared them all, didn't I?" James asked, starting to panic.

"Everyone is going to be just fine. I think we might want to cut back on your pain meds, though," Alex said, noticing the way James kept blinking his eyes.

"Yeah, I don't think I want them anymore," James agreed.

"I think maybe you should bunk with me tonight, in case you have another bad dream," Alex said.

"Okay."

"Can you walk?" Antonio asked as he relaxed his hold.

James nodded.

"Let's get you to bed," Alex said, taking the boy's arm. He helped James stand up and then put an arm around his waist. Antonio went to his other side, and together they got him downstairs. Alex tucked him into one side of the double bed.

"I'm going to go check on everyone. I'll be right back," Antonio said.

"Okay." James yawned.

∞

Upstairs, Logan and Carlos were each sitting with an icepack on their face. Katie had come out, and Kendall was still lying on the floor, but his head was now in her lap.

"How is everyone?" Antonio asked.

"One split lip, one black eye, one bruised hip," Sylvia said.

"Is James okay?" Logan asked.

"He's fine. He just had a bad dream about a clown."

"Clowns are creepy." Carlos shuddered.

"I know, but he should sleep alright now. Will you boys be able to get back to sleep?" Antonio asked.

Carlos and Logan nodded and Sylvia helped Logan up. Antonio went over to Kendall. "Are you alright?"

Kendall nodded and Antonio gave him a hand up. A few minutes later, all three boys were tucked in on the bed.

"Nobody's going to fall out of bed, are they?" Antonio asked.

"We'll be fine, thanks Papa G," Logan said. He was sleeping on the right side, Carlos on the left, with Kendall tucked in safely between them.

"Goodnight Mijos," Antonio said as he turned out the light.

Sylvia was in Carlos' room, sitting next to Katie. "Are you going to be alright?"

Katie sniffed and nodded. "Why can't I sleep with Kendall?"

"Mija, there's no more room on that bed." Sylvia smiled.

She looked at the 7-year-old as she clutched Carlos' fluffy puppy. "Would you like me to sleep with you for a while?"

Katie nodded.

Antonio smiled from the doorway. "Why don't you two take our bed and I'll sleep in here?"

"Are you sure?" Sylvia asked.

"Yes, now go."

Katie and Sylvia went across the hallway and Antonio climbed into Carlos' bed.

Soon the house was quiet and everyone was sleeping.

∞

Two houses down, in the back ally, the man in the Chevy sedan waited until the lights were out and finished making a few notes.

Ten minutes later, he drove away.

Chapter 119~ Hortense

Alex woke up around 5 am. He stretched out, trying to work a kink out of his neck from sleeping in the chair. He looked over and saw James was sleeping peacefully after having tossed and turned for a better portion of the night.

He got up and quietly went into the kitchen, leaving the door open in case James needed anything. He started a pot of coffee and sat down to call home.

"Hello," his mother answered.

"Hi mama, just calling to check in and see how things are going."

"Things are fine here. How about up there?"

"A few complications, but we're handling them alright," Alex said.

"How's that grandson of mine?"

"He's doing just fine and looking forward to seeing everyone soon. Is Sam around?"

"Let me call him."

Sam was twelve years older than Alex and the only sibling he actually felt close to. He, his wife Elena, and their son, Eric, had moved to California about fifteen years earlier. Sam was an architectural engineer and had started up a business in San Jose with a friend of his from college. It surprised everyone, because out of all the Mitchell offspring, Sam seemed the most likely to stay and work the ranch. He knew everything there was about running a successful cattle ranch. From the best feed for each breed of livestock, to what direction the stock market trends were heading. He had made several improvements and modernizations that had increased profits, thereby providing their parents with a strong safety net.

He heard her call his brother's name, and a moment later, Sam answered. "Hey there, baby brother. How are things going up there?"

Alex smiled. "Hey Sam, they're going slowly. That's what I was calling about, would it be possible for you to stay a little longer? With everything that's going on, I think Antonio's getting a little overwhelmed, and I hate to leave him like this."

"No problem, I can work from home for now, and I think being here will do Eric some good. He was getting a little too big for his britches in San Jose. A few chores and some time with his grandma should help set him straight."

"That just might do it," Alex agreed. He loved his mother, but she was a harsh taskmaster, and his 16-year-old nephew was no match for her.

"How are the boys?" Sam asked.

"Alright, given the circumstances. James and his dad were in a car accident on Sunday, but they're both doing fine now. It seems like one thing after another." Alex sighed.

"Unfortunately that's the way life seems to work," Sam said.

"True. At least we have Kendall at home, and we did the first feeding last night. He handled it alright, so hopefully things will be better by his next appointment."

"Good. How's that nephew of mine?"

"He's on crutches, at least through today. He got slammed at hockey practice last week and sprained his ankle pretty badly."

"He's pretty tough for a little guy." Sam laughed.

"That he is. Good thing with all that's happened."

"They're all strong boys, and they'll come through this just fine," Sam said reassuringly.

"I hope so. They try and hide it, but I can see this whole thing is taking its toll."

"It's bound to. I wish there was more I could do to help."

"You coming down and taking care of daddy is more than enough. I don't know what I would have done otherwise. You know how he feels about having strangers take care of him."

"That I do, and he's stubborn as a mule about it." Sam laughed.

"When do you need to be back?"

"You take as long as you need. I've only got a few things I need to finish before the end of the year, and I can do that from here."

"Thanks Sam, I can't tell you what this means to me."

"Don't worry about it, baby brother. You do what you need to and give that boy of yours a hug from his old Uncle Sam."

Alex laughed. "I'll do that, old man. Thanks again."

"You're welcome, baby brother."

Alex finished his call and jumped into the shower. After he dressed, he went out, grabbed the paper from the porch, and stood there, stretching out for a minute, taking a quick glance up and down the street. Not seeing anything out of the ordinary, he went back inside.

He went into the kitchen and started making breakfast.

∞

Antonio came down a few moments later, dressed for work.

"You're up early," Antonio said.

"Actually, back home this would be late," Alex pointed out.

"True. How did you sleep?"

"James was pretty restless for a couple of hours, but he finally settled down. Hopefully he'll sleep until later this morning."

Antonio nodded. "Poor kid, he's been terrified of clowns since we took the boys to the carnival when they were five."

"What happened?"

"Well, you know those funhouses that you walk through?"

Alex nodded.

"We had just gotten through the hall of mirrors when this clown comes out of nowhere. The boys all screamed and ran the wrong way, the clown right behind them. Once they hit the hall of mirrors, it looked like a hundred clowns were after them. James tripped, and the clown was just trying to help him up, but being five and seeing some huge guy wearing a painted face with a red nose and frizzy orange hair, pretty much sent him over the edge. Carlos and Kendall realized James wasn't with them and turned around and attacked the guy. Carlos grabbed him by the arm and was trying to drag him back, while Kendall kept hitting him with the glow stick he had won. We finally got them all calmed down and out of there. It took almost two hours for James to stop shaking. Turns out there weren't even supposed to be clowns in there. He was just taking his girlfriend through on his lunch break. When he realized he'd scared the boys, he tried to stop them from running and hurting themselves, not considering the fact he was still in costume."

"Well, I have to say I agree with James. Clowns are scary, and I don't get why people think they're fun," Alex said.

"Me either," Antonio agreed.

Alex handed Antonio a plate with some scrambled eggs and toast. "Breakfast?"

"Thanks buddy. Are you keeping a headcount on the eggs?"

"Ha-ha, VERY funny."

"Just so you know, Sylvia found another hiding spot for the treat bin," Antonio said.

"So I get to play detective too?"

"Not unless you want to be a different colour permanently," Sylvia said, walking in.

"Good morning, gorgeous." Alex smiled.

"Not going to work," she said as she kissed Antonio.

"Good morning, honey. How did you and Katie sleep?" Antonio asked.

"Alright, she fell asleep a few minutes after we went to bed. How was James?"

"He slept alright after a couple of hours... I really don't think those pain pills agree with him," Alex said.

"I'll give Anna a call and see what she recommends and make sure they put he has a bad reaction to the Codeine in his file." She sighed.

"That's a good idea," Antonio said as he got up.

"Are you going in early?" Sylvia asked.

Antonio nodded. "I want to see if anything's come through about that Chevy, and then make the rounds to the schools. Make sure the kids know to stay inside until one of us is there."

"I will," Sylvia said.

"I'll pick the kids up this afternoon and then run Logan to his appointment with Anna," Alex said.

"Thanks buddy. I'll talk to you later. Do you need me to stop by to help with the feeding tube?" Antonio asked.

Alex shook his head. "I think we'll be okay. He's not fighting it too much, and James is here if I need him."

"Okay, call if you need me, though."

"I will," Alex said.

Antonio headed out and Carlos, Logan, and Katie came wandering down a few minutes later. Alex cooked up some more eggs while Sylvia made toast.

"How's James?" Logan asked his dad.

"He's okay. I think you and Carlos got the worst of it," he said, looking at his son's black eye and Carlos' swollen lip.

"He's going to feel awful," Carlos said.

"It wasn't his fault the medication made him have a bad dream," Sylvia told him.

"I know, but he'll still feel bad," Carlos said.

"I know, Mijo," Sylvia said, kissing the top of his head.

"Is Kendall still sleeping?" Alex asked.

Logan nodded. "I was going to wake him up before we left, but he's still pretty tired."

"I'll go up. Should I take him some breakfast?" Sylvia asked Alex.

He nodded. "It'd be best if we can get him to eat on top of the tube feedings."

She nodded and took a small plate with scrambled eggs and toast up for him while Alex mixed up the formula. She looked in and smiled at the sleeping teen. She set the plate on the night table. "Kendall, it's time to wake up."

He pulled the blankets tighter.

"Kendall," she said, tapping his shoulder.

"Huh?"

"It's time to get up, Mijo."

"Okay," he said, not moving.

Sylvia took the blanket and pulled it down. "Breakfast!"

Kendall groaned.

"Come on, sit up."

He sighed and pushed himself up. "Ow."

"Is it your shoulder or your hip?"

"Both."

"I'm going to call and get you in with a physical therapist for your shoulder. Let me take a look at your hip," she said, tugging on the blanket.

"NO!" he squealed, pulling the blanket tightly around him.

"Oh, for goodness sake, it's just your hip. I use to change your diaper, you know."

"Mama G!" he said, pulling the blanket even tighter, his face flushed red.

She rolled her eyes. "Really?"

"It's fine!" he insisted.

She sighed in exasperation. "Fine, you eat while I go get a bag of peas so you can ice it."

"Deal," he said, eyeing her warily.

"The kid moons the entire opposing team in front of dozens of people and won't let me check his hip," she mumbled as she went back downstairs.

Kendall waited until she was out of sight before scooting closer to the night table.

Downstairs, Sylvia was still mumbling as she got the peas from the freezer.

"What's wrong?" Carlos asked.

"Kendall's hip is bothering him and he won't let me check it."

"You're actually surprised by that?" Alex chuckled.

"If he's hurt, it needs to be checked."

"I'll see if he'll let me take a look later," Alex told her.

"Alright," she said, heading back upstairs.

Carlos groaned and shook his head.

"What's the matter, Trouble?" Alex asked.

"Parents are SO embarrassing!"

"That we are." Alex laughed.

∞

Sylvia took the peas up and handed them to Kendall. "Do you need anything for pain?"

"I'm fine, thanks." He smiled. "How's James, is he okay?"

"He's still sleeping, but Papa M said he slept alright."

"Good."

"So, how are you going to do with a physical therapist?"

"I don't know. What do they do?"

"Well, when Papi had to go when he dislocated his shoulder, they used a therapeutic ultrasound, hot and cold treatments, and massage therapy. Then they gave him some exercises to do at home."

Kendall shook his head. "I don't want to go."

"I know it's a little intimidating, but we want your shoulder to heal. If we don't do something, the muscles will start to atrophy."

"Can't we just do the exercises at home?"

"I don't know, honey, we'll have to see what they recommend."

Kendall sighed, looking miserable.

"We'll figure it out." She smiled.

"Okay."

"I'm going to take everyone to school. Alex is downstairs if you need anything," she told him, kissing the top of his head.

He nodded.

"Finish eating for me?"

"Okay."

She went down, and a few minutes later, had the kids loaded into the car. They stopped and picked up Nattie Picket on the way.

∞

Kendall finished eating, grabbed some clean clothes, and jumped in the shower. He finished a few minutes later when a voice called out.

"Come out, come out, wherever you are."

Kendall closed his eyes and took a deep breath. He called downstairs. "Papa M?"

"Morning Champ. Whatcha need?"

"I can't get my t-shirt on."

Alex went up and helped Kendall get his shirt on. "Thanks," Kendall said.

"No problem. Are you coming down?" Alex asked, taking the small plate.

"Yeah, in a minute. I just want to grab my homework."

"Okay." Alex smiled and headed back down.

Kendall went back into the bedroom and threw his pajamas in the hamper. His cell phone rang and he picked it up. Weird, he thought, looking at the caller ID.

"Hello?" he asked quietly.

"You're mine, sweetheart."

Kendall looked at the phone in shock. "You're not real," he said, closing his eyes.

"Guess again." The voice laughed and the line went dead.

Kendall sat down quickly, trying to stop the panic from rising in his chest. He checked the phone, but the only number on it was his. He put it back on the table and tried to get his breathing under control, but he couldn't stop shaking.

"Kendall?" Alex asked.

The teen jumped. "W-What?"

"Are you alright? You look like you're going to be sick," Alex said, feeling his forehead.

"Yeah, sorry. I bent down and stood up too fast, I guess."

"Okay, well come on down. I have the formula mixed up, and we can put the tube in as soon as Mama G gets back."

"Huh?"

"Look at me," Alex said.

Kendall looked up, but he was still fighting down the panic.

"Are you sure you feel alright?"

Kendall nodded. "I think I'm just still tired."

Alex watched him for a moment. "I think we'll do the feeding downstairs, since everyone will be gone. That way I can keep an eye on you and James."

Kendall nodded and grabbed his backpack, following Alex downstairs.

∞

Sylvia returned home a few minutes later and found James eating breakfast and Alex helping Kendall with his homework. "How are you feeling?" she asked James.

"Okay, just tired. Are Carlos and Logan really okay? Papa M said they just have a couple of little bumps."

"They're fine, really. Don't worry about it. You boys have given each other worse rough housing."

"Okay," James said as he finished his breakfast.

"Are you still sore?" she asked.

"Just a little, no more than after a really long game."

"Alright, I think we'll just stick with ibuprofen or plain Tylenol for now. Unless you need something stronger?"

He shook his head. "I'm fine, really. Can we go see my dad today?"

"Of course we can."

"Why don't you help me with the feeding tube, and I'll stay here with Kendall while you two go visit Mike," Alex suggested, helping himself to a piece of fruit.

"I just ate breakfast," Kendall groaned.

"And now you're going to have some formula... yummy!" Alex said, tousling the blond's hair.

"Not fair," Kendall complained.

"Did I forget to mention that you have to do BOTH?" Alex smirked, taking a bite of his banana.

"Yes!"

"Ah, my bad." Alex smiled.

James laughed at the expression on his friend's face.

Kendall glared at him and then reached over and pushed Alex's hand, so the banana smashed into his face. Sylvia covered her mouth so she wouldn't laugh. James didn't bother. He just started laughing at the sight.

"You're a funny little guy, aren't ya?" Alex asked Kendall.

Kendall just sat there with one eyebrow raised past his bangs. "My bad." He smirked.

"Okay, I guess I had that coming," Alex said as he wiped the banana off with a napkin. "I'm gonna go wash this off and then we'll get started," he said, going into the bathroom.

"Kendall!" Sylvia chastised.

"What? He had it coming," Kendall said defensively.

"He really kind of did," James said.

"I know, but still." She laughed.

Alex came out a couple of minutes later, banana free. "Are you ready?"

Kendall sighed. "Can't we do it later?"

"We need to do two feedings a day for now, so we should space them. Unless you want to do one right after the other?"

Kendall shook his head.

"Do you want to do this in the living room, so you can just rest and watch some TV? We can finish your homework later," Alex said.

Kendall nodded and got up.

Alex grabbed everything they needed. "James, can you hold him and we can have Mama G hold the water?"

"Sure," James said, following him.

Alex went over, picked up the coat rack, and moved it behind the couch. They took their positions in front of the couch and Alex had the tube in place a couple of minutes later.

"See, we're getting better at this," Alex said.

Kendall rolled his eyes.

"Alright, why don't you sit on the couch and we'll hang this from the coat rack."

Kendall nodded and James helped him up. Alex attached the tubes and started the flow out at one third of the way open. "I think we'll leave it at that flow, you seem to be able to handle it best."

Kendall nodded and sat back.

James sat next to him and handed him the remote. "You'll be done before you know it."

Kendall smiled at him. "Tell your dad, hi."

"I will. Hopefully he'll get out soon. If not, maybe you can visit with me tomorrow?"

"Maybe."

"Are you ready to go?" Sylvia asked James.

He nodded and grabbed his jacket.

"We'll be back in a little while. Call if you need anything," Sylvia told them.

"We'll be fine," Alex said.

James and Sylvia left. Down the street, a man in a tan SUV jotted down a few notes and pulled out.

∞

Kendall tried finding a comfortable position on the couch, but between his left shoulder and his right hip, found it nearly impossible. He sighed in frustration.

"Can't get comfortable?" Alex asked.

"Not really."

"How bad is your hip?"

"Just bruised, but it's sore."

Alex took a couple of pillows and laid them at the end of the couch. "Okay, scoot down to the end while I move the coat rack."

Kendall did as Alex said, and a moment later, he was lying down at about a forty-degree angle.

"Better?"

Kendall nodded and smiled. "Thanks."

"You're welcome."

"Do you want to watch your movie?" Kendall asked.

"I don't want you falling asleep with the tube in." Alex smiled.

"What makes you think I'd fall asleep?"

"Just a hunch. What do you want to watch?"

"Anything's fine," Kendall said.

Alex went through the shelf. "How about this?" he asked, holding up Jurassic Park.

"Sure, I haven't seen that in a while."

"Hard to fall asleep with dinosaurs eating people and it's almost two hours long."

Kendall smiled. "Papa M, I was wondering something."

"What's that Champ?"

"Why did you and Mama M name Logan, Hortense?"

Alex smiled. "That's actually a bittersweet story."

"Well?"

"You really want to know?"

"I think we all do."

"It's simple, really. You see, Jo was pretty much raised by her grandparents. Her dad died when she was little. Her mom... well, her mom had other things on her mind besides raising a little girl. So, Mama M spent a lot of time with her grandparents, Logan and Teni."

"Teni?"

"It's a nickname for Hortense."

"You named him after his grandma?"

"Well, technically he was supposed to be a she. When we found out we were expecting, they did an ultrasound and told us the baby was a girl. About that time we found out Teni had terminal cancer, and Jo wanted to name the baby after her. I thought it was a great idea. I loved Teni and thought we could just call the baby by her nickname. Her grandparents were so happy because we wanted to use both of their names, hence Hortense Logan Mitchell. Time went by and Teni got weaker, and about the time they did the next ultrasound, she took a turn for the worse. That's when they told us the first ultrasound was wrong and that our baby girl was a baby boy. When we went to tell Teni... well, we just couldn't. She was so happy to have a new life given her name. She died two weeks after Logan was born. We never did tell her that he was a boy. We actually have a couple of really nice photos of her holding him."

Kendall was quiet for a moment. "Have you told Logan this story?"

"Yeah, when he was younger. He still hates the name though. I can't really blame him for that."

"I think it's a good name," Kendall said.

"So do I." Alex smiled.

Chapter 120~ No More

Antonio got to the station and found Sally and Bennet were already there. "Anything?" he asked.

"I had Dane staking out the motel for a few hours this morning, and whoever it is, left around 6:30 and headed out west on I-35," Bennet said. "The clerk couldn't give us a name, but he did confirm that he'd checked out. He said he'll be happy to give us a call if he checks back in."

"Okay, maybe it's all just a coincidence after all," Antonio said.

"Possibly. I'll rest easier once we get an ID confirmation from one of the DMV data bases though," Sally said.

"Let's keep the schools on alert in case we hear something then," Antonio said, going into his office.

"Will do, Boss," Sally said.

∞

James and Sylvia got to the hospital and went inside. They went to Mike's room and found him sleeping, so James quietly sat down in the chair next to him. "I'm going to call Papa G and see if they've found out anything yet," Sylvia whispered.

James nodded and Sylvia went out into the hallway. "Garcia," Antonio answered.

"Hi honey, I was calling to see if you've found out anything yet. I kept an eye out for the car, but didn't see it this morning."

"John had someone watching the motel, and the guy checked out and left town early this morning."

"Thank goodness."

'We're still waiting to see if we can get a name from the DMV. Once we find out who this guy is, I'll know if I should lift the school alerts."

"You think he might come back?"

"I don't know, honey, there's probably nothing to it, but I don't intend on taking any chances. Where are you now?"

"I brought James to visit Mike. Alex is home with Kendall doing a morning feeding," Sylvia told him.

"How's Mike doing?"

"He was sleeping when we got here. I'm not sure if James is going to wake him up or not."

"Well, tell him hi for me. I'll probably be home around five tonight. If anything comes up, I'll let you know."

"Okay, we'll see you then," Sylvia said.

She went back in and smiled at James. "Are you going to let him know you're here?"

"I'm not sure if I should wake him up or not," James whispered.

"Yes, you should," Mike said, opening his eyes.

"Sorry, I didn't want to bother you if you were tired." James smiled.

"You never bother me and, yes, I'm tired, but I can sleep later." Mike smiled.

"How are you feeling?" Sylvia asked.

"Better. The doctor says I can go home tonight or tomorrow depending on how bad my headache is."

"How is it?" James asked.

"Much better, especially since it's now quiet."

"Antonio said to tell you hi, and he hopes you're feeling better," Sylvia told him.

"Tell him thank you, I really appreciate it," Mike said.

"I will." She smiled.

"How are you doing today?" Mike asked James.

"I'm okay. I'm not nearly as stiff as I was yesterday. My ribs are still a little sore, but nothing worse than I've had before."

"Ah, to be as resilient as a kid again," Mike said.

"No kidding." Sylvia laughed. "So, how's Tiffany handling all of this?"

"Well, the doctor kicked her out because she can't maintain a low volume on her voice, which is why my headache is doing better," Mike told her.

"I'm sure she was terrified," Sylvia said.

"I know. She's never had to face the possibility of losing someone, other than leaving them, before."

"Luckily she doesn't have to worry about that anymore," James said.

"True." Mike smiled.

"How many times has she been married?" Sylvia asked curiously.

"Just once before," Mike said, sitting up.

"Do you need anything? I can run down to the cafeteria if you need real food," Sylvia offered.

"I would love a coffee, but I can't have any."

"What about decaf? I can ask the nurse for you."

"I think I'm okay for now, but thanks. I might take you up on that later though."

"Anytime."

"So, what about hockey? Are they going to let you play?" Mike asked James.

"I don't see why not. We have practice tomorrow, so I'll have to see what coach says."

"When's your next game?"

"Saturday, but I think it depends on if we have enough players. Kendall and Logan are both out, and we've had a couple of other guys out with the flu."

"How is Kendall doing?"

"He's doing better. He said to tell you, hi. Papa M is staying, so we can do tube feedings at home instead of him having to go to the hospital. If you're still here tomorrow, Kendall might come with me to visit."

"I'd like that," Mike said.

"Well, we should let you get some rest now. I meant when I said if you need anything to just call," Sylvia said.

"I know you do. I can't thank you enough for being here for James and me," Mike said quietly.

"That's what friends are for. Now you get some rest and we'll see you later," Sylvia said, kissing his cheek.

"I'll see you later." Mike smiled.

"Bye dad, I'll give you a call later," James said, carefully hugging him.

Mike hugged him tightly. "I love you, son."

"I love you too, dad," James said, smiling.

∞

At about nine, Richard Graham received a visitor from the law firm of Riker, Goode, Metcalf, and Manning.

Danielle Regent was a new graduate from the Loyolo University of Law in Chicago. She had interned with the law firm the previous two summers and been hired as an associate once

she had graduated. She was currently assigned to work with Derek Manning and would be assisting him with Graham's case. Sally took her to the small interrogation room while Johnson went to fetch Graham.

A few moments later, Johnson came in leading Graham and attached the cuffs to the table. "Is that really necessary?" she asked.

"Sorry, it's regulations ma'am," Johnson replied politely and left the room.

"Stupid yokels," Graham muttered.

"Dr. Graham, my name is Danielle Regent, and Mr. Manning sent me to check on you and see if there's anything you might need," she said, smiling.

"Well, it would be nice to get out of here," Graham said.

"I understand. I really wish there was something we could do about that, sir, but the judge refused. On a bright note, Mr. Manning is pushing for an early court date and is hoping your case will be on the docket within the next couple of weeks."

"WEEKS! Do you understand what hell it is in here? My practice will be non-existent by the time this is through!"

She moved to the chair next to him and lowered her voice. "I understand the frustration, truly I do. Unfortunately, Mr. Manning doesn't set the court dates, but he is calling in a couple of favours to get your trial date moved up. He also said to tell you he has many people working on this and that the DA's case won't be nearly as strong as they think it is. He IS working on this case from all angles," she said reassuringly.

Graham relaxed. "Well, at least he's doing something about this. My last attorney was an idiot. He actually accused me of being guilty, saying this entire thing was MY fault!"

She smiled and patted his hand. "Don't you worry about that at all, Mr. Manning has everything under control."

∞

Kendall and Alex were watching the end of the movie when Sylvia and James got back.

"How's your dad?" Kendall asked.

"He's doing a lot better. They might let him out tonight or tomorrow. He said to tell you, hi!" James said, sitting next to Kendall.

Kendall smiled and then yawned.

"Are you getting tired?" James asked.

"A little."

Alex checked the bag. "Almost there, and then you can take a nap."

"Okay." Kendall smiled.

There was a knock at the door and James went to answer it, but Alex stopped him. "I'll get it. Why don't you sit down and rest?"

"Okay," James said in confusion.

Alex looked through the peephole and opened the door. "Well, this is a nice surprise," he said, letting Joanna in.

"It's good to see you, too." She smiled and kissed his cheek. "I thought I'd bring lunch and give Sylvia a hand, since things have calmed down at the office."

Alex smiled and took the bags from her. "What's in here?"

"Sandwiches and other assorted goodies."

"Yum," he said, taking the bags out to the kitchen.

"Hi Mama M," James said, giving her a hug.

"How are you feeling, honey?"

"I'm okay."

"How's your dad?"

"He's doing a lot better." James smiled.

"Good and how are you?" she asked, walking over and kissing Kendall on the forehead.

"I'm doing okay."

"Really?"

He nodded.

"Good. I'm going to go and help get lunch ready," she said, heading out to the kitchen.

James sat next to Kendall. "I think they're still freaked out about that car."

"Probably," Kendall agreed.

∞

"How are you doing?" Joanna asked Sylvia.

"Antonio and I had an absolutely lovely evening Saturday, thanks to Kendall and someone else," she said, looking at Alex.

"I'll say it one more time, it was ALL Kendall."

"I know, but you helped him, and we really appreciate it," Sylvia said.

"I'm glad it all worked out and you both enjoyed it." Alex smiled.

"We did!"

"So, what have you been up to?" Alex asked Joanna.

"I spent most of the weekend helping set up Christmas trees and decorating houses for showings." Jo sighed.

"Seeing how a house looks during one of the happiest times of the year does help sell them," Alex said.

"I know, it just makes it so hard to want to decorate at home sometimes," she said.

"Well, I spoke to Sam this morning, and he can stay through the end of the year. So, if you and Logan want help decorating, I'll be happy to help."

"Are you serious? You can stay that long. What about your dad?"

"Sam's got it under control. He knows how important it is for me to be able to help out here right now. He also said Eric's been getting into some trouble at home, so he's under grandma's thumb right now."

"If that doesn't straighten him out, nothing will," Jo said.

"True enough," Alex agreed.

"Papa M, I think this thing is done," Kendall called.

"I'll be right there."

'How's he really doing with this whole thing?" Jo asked.

"He's actually handling it pretty well, as long as we keep him awake for it," Alex told her.

"That reminds me, I need to call and get him an appointment with the physical therapist this week," Sylvia said, looking for the numbers that Anna had sent with Jen.

"How do you think he's going to handle that?" Jo asked.

"Not well," Sylvia said as she picked up the phone.

Alex went in and checked the bag. "Yup, you're done."

He pinched off the NG tube as he removed the infusion line and then flushed it. Kendall yawned again. "Are you going to be able to hold out for another half an hour, or do you want to chance pulling it now?"

"I'll wait," Kendall said.

"Okay. Did you want a sandwich? Mama M brought all different kinds from the deli."

"No thanks, I'm not hungry."

"We'll save you one." Alex smiled.

Joanna set the sandwiches out on a platter while Sylvia grabbed the bowl of fruit. They set them on the dining room table. "Lunch is ready," Joanna said.

"Do you want me to eat in here with you?" James asked Kendall.

"If you want to."

James went in and made up a plate, taking an extra half sandwich in hopes he could get Kendall to eat. He went back in the living room and sat next to Kendall, who was flipping channels.

"Anything you want to watch?" Kendall asked.

"Not really," James said.

Kendall found a channel with some Spongebob reruns and left it there.

"Hey, I brought an extra half in case you get hungry. It's roast beef." James smiled.

Kendall smiled but shook his head. "I don't think I could eat with this thing in anyway."

"I guess that would feel pretty strange."

"You have no idea," Kendall said, shaking his head.

∞

Sylvia and Alex filled Jo in on what had happened the day before with the blue Chevy. "But he's left town?" Joanna asked.

"So far as we now. Antonio said they're still waiting for a name from the DMV," Sylvia said.

'Well, hopefully it was nothing." Joanna smiled.

"Hopefully," Sylvia said.

Kendall got up and went to find Alex. "Could we take this out now, please? I don't think I can stay awake much longer."

"Sure thing, Champ," Alex said, getting up.

A couple of minutes later, Alex had removed the tube and Kendall curled up on the couch. James finished eating and sat next to Kendall. "Hey, look!"

"What?" Kendall yawned.

"The Incredible Hulk from TV is going to be at the comic con in St. Paul next week."

"He's Carlos' favourite," Kendall said.

"I know. It would be so cool if he could meet him."

Kendall smiled. "Maybe he could."

"How?" James asked.

"Maybe an early Christmas present?"

James smiled. "It's a thought...the tickets are only $12 for juniors, $24 for adults."

"So if we got Carlos and Papi each a ticket, it would only be $36."

"Do you really think Papa G would want to go?"

"Sure he would! He always watches the reruns with Carlos, and it'll give them a chance to do something fun together," Kendall said.

"Good point," James agreed.

"Maybe I can talk Mama G into stopping by the ticket place tomorrow after my appointment with Claudia."

"I'm paying for half," James told him.

"Okay, I guess we should ask Logan if he wants to go in on it too."

"He probably will," James said.

"This'll be so cool." Kendall smiled.

"It will," James agreed.

The boys settled onto the couch and were still watching cartoons when Sylvia, Jo, and Alex joined them. "What are we watching?" Alex asked.

"Spongebob," James said.

"Interesting. What ever happened to the Jetsons or the Flintstones? Good cartoons from when we were kids."

Both boys looked at each other and then at him. "I think they're on the channel that shows old fashioned cartoons," James said.

"Old fashioned... What's that supposed to mean?" Sylvia asked.

"I think it means they're old." Kendall smirked.

Alex snickered and both women looked at him. "You're the one who brought them up," Jo pointed out.

"True, but you should have seen the look on your faces." Alex laughed.

"NO more cookies for you," Sylvia said.

"Not fair. THEY are the ones who called you old, not me," Alex whined.

"Did we call them old?" James asked Kendall.

"I think it was implied."

"But he DID bring it up," James pointed out.

"Adults... What can you do?" Kendall asked, shaking his head.

All three parents stood there and looked at them.

"What?" they both asked innocently.

"I have a feeling we lost in that conversation," Alex said.

"Do you think so?" Jo asked him sarcastically.

∞

Sally received a report from the Illinois DMV at about two. She ran the name through the system and it came up clean. She knocked on Antonio's door. "Hey Boss, we got an ID on that driver from yesterday."

"And?"

"One Chad Taylor, age thirty-eight. Driver's license was issued in Illinois. His residence is in Chicago. No trouble with the law, not even a parking ticket."

"What the hell was he doing here then?"

"I'll run a full background check and should know more by the end of the day."

"Thanks Sally. Let's leave the school alerts in effect until you find out more."

"Will do, Boss."

∞

At the Garcia's, both boys had fallen asleep watching TV. Sylvia had covered them with a blanket and the parents were all talking quietly, catching up on the events of the last few days.

Alex noticed the time and grabbed his jacket, getting ready to pick the kids up from school. "Do I need to pick up Nattie?"

"No, her mom's getting off early and will get her. Thanks though." Sylvia smiled.

"Okay, I'll drop Carlos and Katie off and then take Logan in to get his ankle rechecked."

"Why don't I come with you?" Jo said. Alex smiled and held her coat for her and they headed out. He got to the middle school and saw the teachers were still on alert. He parked and they walked in and found the boys waiting inside the doors.

"Hey guys, you ready to hit the road?"

"Hi dad. Hi mom, what are you doing here?" Logan asked, getting up.

"I'm free for the next couple of days, so I thought I'd hang around, if that's okay?"

"Mom, you know I'm happy to see you," Logan said.

"I know," she said, kissing his cheek.

"Hi Mama M," Carlos said, hugging her.

"Hello Carlitos. How are you today?"

"Good." He smiled.

Alex grabbed Logan's backpack and they headed out.

∞

A few minutes later, they had picked up Katie and dropped her and Carlos off. The check-up with Anna was quick. Logan's ankle was no longer swollen and it felt alright when he walked on it, so she told him to just wrap it and take it easy for a few days.

Alex called Sally while Logan was getting his boots on. "Hey, we're heading over to Claudia's in a few minutes."

"Okay, I'll meet you there," Sally said and hung up. "Johnson, I have to run out for a few minutes. Could you call me if anything comes through about Chad Taylor before I get back?"

"Sure thing." He smiled.

"Thanks," she said, grabbing her coat and heading out the door. Sally met up with the Mitchells and they went into Claudia's together.

Sally introduced Jo and Claudia to each other. "It's so nice to meet you. You were there the day we took Kendall to the emergency room?"

Joanna nodded. "I'm afraid we weren't formally introduced then."

"Well, it's nice to meet you officially." Claudia smiled.

"Same here," Jo said.

"So, I understand you found out something that you really didn't want to know," Claudia said to Logan.

He nodded.

"Am I missing something?" Joanna asked.

"Yeah, you are, honey," Alex said.

Sally looked at Alex. "Do you want me to tell her?"

"Please." He nodded.

"It seems that what Kendall had last week wasn't a panic attack but a flashback to his time with Deesie."

"Okay," Joanna said.

"Antonio told you about what happened in the tent one night?"

Joanna nodded and her heart clenched. "Why?"

Sally looked at Claudia, who took over. "Well, when we were waiting for Kendall to wake up after the doctor put stitches in his hand, James and Antonio went up to tell his mama what had happened. He woke up a bit and I asked him if he remembered anything. He didn't say much at first, just nodded, but after a couple of minutes told me what he had remembered. It seems that while Deesie was... doing what he was doing to him, he also used his fingers to..."

"Oh my God." Joanna paled and put her arm around Logan.

"Exactly my reaction," Alex said.

"Antonio thought it was important that we know, because chances are he's going to have more actual flashbacks. He told us in confidence, but apparently, Katie had been listening, and when she and I were out shopping that night, she asked me what it meant. I told her it was an old cop term meaning to pick out or choose. I thought that'd be the end of it, but apparently she wanted to confirm what I told her and asked Logan what it meant," Sally explained.

"Honey," Joanna said, looking at him.

"I looked it up on the internet because I didn't understand why dad would use that word. Then I found out it had more than one meaning. I didn't tell Katie, though," he said quietly.

"Oh honey, I'm so sorry," Jo said, her eyes tearing up.

"Sally thought I might be able to teach Logan how to help Kendall come out of a panic attack or flashback, and I think that's a good idea. Especially since the boys are all together so much," Claudia said.

Joanna nodded.

"So what do we do?" Logan asked.

"What we have to do is to get his attention away from whatever it is he's seeing. I did that by going up to him and taking his head in my hands and calling him softly. When he finally responded, I told him he needed to wake up and that everything would be fine. The trick is to be able to get his attention and hold onto it. So just speak to him and let him know he's safe. That seemed to work for him, and once he does respond, just hold on until he comes out of it all the way. Now, if he's having a panic attack, a good technique is to take ahold of his hand and put it on your chest. Then you take your other hand and put it on his, if you can. Then you speak calmly but firmly and tell him to breathe with you. You take steady, calm breaths, and after a few minutes, he should be able to do the same," Claudia told them.

"How do we know the difference?" Logan asked.

"It's not easy, and it really depends on the severity of the panic attack. Usually with a panic attack, they can still hear you and they can feel it building up inside them ahead of time. He and I will be working on that a little bit tomorrow. A flashback, on the other hand, is something he can't control. It's as if he's reliving whatever happened, and he can't see or hear you. It's harder to get through, and sometimes the only thing you can do is just hold on until it passes. After it's over, it's going to take a while for him to calm down, so we do whatever it takes to let him know he's safe."

Logan nodded. "I can do that."

"I know you can, baby." Claudia smiled.

"I'm getting a little worried about Antonio, too," Alex said.

"It does take a toll." Claudia sighed.

"How can I help him out so he's not the only one having to deal with all of this?" Alex asked.

"You're taking care of Kendall while Antonio's working, right?"

Alex nodded.

"And you're the one doing the tube feedings?"

Alex nodded again.

"I think those two things will be more help than you realize. If he knows you're there with Kendall, then he knows he's safe. Kendall feels safest with Antonio, but the fact that he's letting you do the feedings, means he's going to be transitioning some of those feelings of security over to you. Right now, the slower we can go, the better, and that means with both of them. It's going to take some time, but right now if Kendall needs Antonio, that's who he should be allowed to go to. I've seen too many kids being forced away from people they feel safest with because others thought it was time for them to move on before they were ready. Now, that doesn't mean that life shouldn't go on. Antonio and Sylvia going away for the night was a great idea. The fact it was Kendall's idea and that Antonio actually went, means they both know they can trust you and they both realize they do need to keep moving forward."

Alex nodded. "Okay then, just keep doing what we're doing."

"There's no quick fix, there's no easy way to do this. It is what it is, and unfortunately, it's not going to be something that gets better overnight. I still need to talk to Jen about some of this, but I know Eli has been meeting with her and they have made some progress. It's going to take some time for Kendall to trust her completely and for her to forgive herself. Hopefully they will be able to go home together soon and try to get their lives back to some semblance of normal. Until they're ready, meeting for meals, appointments, or just speaking to each other on the phone is going to help."

"Maybe we should suggest to Kendall that he call Jen every night to say goodnight," Jo said.

"That's a good idea, but don't force him if he doesn't want to." Claudia smiled.

"Well, what do you think Logan?" Alex asked.

Logan nodded. "I think it makes a lot of sense and that we can do this."

"I agree." Alex smiled.

"If you have any more questions, just give me a call," Claudia said as she walked them to the door.

"We will, thanks Claudia," Alex said.

"My pleasure." She smiled.

She looked at Logan. "Same goes for you, baby. You call me anytime if you're worried or have any questions, alright?"

"I will, thanks Claudia."

"You're welcome, baby."

∞

They got back to the Garcia's and found Carlos and Katie finishing their homework. Logan went in and sat with them at the table.

"Aww, does this mean we can't call you Hopalong anymore?" Carlos asked, noticing his friend walking without his crutches.

"YES!" Logan said firmly.

"It's okay Carlos. We can still call him Tiny Tim." Katie smirked.

"Mean, mean, mean," he grumbled.

"Hey, maybe we can go skating after dinner," Carlos said.

"I don't know, Logan just got rid of his crutches," Joanna said.

"I can keep it wrapped, and the skates actually give more support to my ankle than my shoes," Logan said.

"We'll see," she said.

Sylvia had started dinner and asked Carlos and Katie to set the table. They all moved their books into the living room and had it ready within minutes.

Antonio got home and Carlos ran and hugged him. "Papi!"

"How's my boy?" Antonio smiled.

"Good. Logan doesn't have to use crutches anymore, so can we go skating at the pond after dinner if Mama M says he can go?" Carlos asked.

"How's the homework coming?" Antonio asked.

"Good, I already have most of it done, and I'm working on some extra-credit math problems."

"Well, I think if Mama M says it's okay, then we can probably go skating," Antonio said, hugging him.

Sylvia went in and kissed Antonio. "How was work?"

"Uneventful, thank goodness. Sally got a name on the driver, but it looks like he has a clean record. She's running a thorough background check just to be sure."

"Thank God."

"I'm going to run up and change."

"Dinner's ready when you are." She smiled.

Alex went over and woke James and then Kendall. Kendall just pulled the blanket tighter. "Not hungry."

"You need to eat just a little. We'll do the other feeding before bedtime," Alex told him.

Kendall groaned.

"Want me to get him?" James smiled.

"You stay out of this," Kendall warned.

"I don't think you should be picking up someone who can bruise your ribs any more than they already are," Alex told James.

Kendall smirked.

"So..." Alex said as he bent down and picked Kendall up, throwing him over his shoulder.

"NOT FAIR!" Kendall shrieked.

James pulled out a chair and Alex sat Kendall on it. James quickly scooted over and put his arm around the chair, holding it in place. Antonio came in a moment later. "Dinner and a show?" he asked Alex as he sat on the other side of Kendall.

Alex smiled and nodded.

Kendall glared at them both.

Logan and Carlos were both laughing and Kendall looked at them. Katie was sitting in between them, raised both of her hands, and made a pinching, twisting motion. They both covered their ears and tried to stop laughing.

"Alright, let's be nice," Sylvia said.

They passed around the serving dishes and Antonio put a little of everything on Kendall's plate. "You don't have to eat it all, Mijo, but eat what you can."

Kendall sighed and nodded. Half an hour later, they had finished eating. Kendall had taken a couple of bites of everything but left the rest.

The boys cleared the table, were rinsing the dishes while Jo ran home and grabbed Logan's ice skates, and then stopped by James' house to get his.

Kendall went back in and sat on the couch while the others got ready to walk down to the park. Carlos went and sat next to him. "I wish you could go."

Kendall smiled. "Maybe next time. You guys have fun and keep an eye on Katie, okay?"

"We will," Carlos promised.

Antonio, Alex, and Jo were going to go and watch the kids skate. Sylvia wanted to stay with Kendall, so she insisted Joanna go, especially since she and Logan hadn't seen much of each other over the weekend.

"Alright, we'll be back in about an hour or so," Antonio told Kendall.

"Okay." Kendall smiled.

"Maybe next week you'll be well enough to go."

"Maybe."

"Have fun," Sylvia said as she walked them to the door. She made sure to lock it behind them. Sylvia went and sat next to Kendall. "Are you okay about not being able to go?"

He shrugged. "Not much I can do about it."

She hugged him. "You'll be out there on the ice in no time."

"I hope so. I think I'm going to go up and get ready for bed, since we have to do the tube thing when Papa M gets back."

"Okay. If you need help, just call me," she said with a smile.

∞

He smiled and headed upstairs. He turned on the bedroom light and grabbed a clean pair of flannel pajamas. He had just buttoned up the top as far as he could when he heard a sound. His phone was ringing. He picked it up and looked at the screen. It showed only his number.

"Hello," he said quietly.

No one answered.

"Hello?"

"I'm waiting for you, sweetheart. Did you miss me?"

"Leave me alone, you're dead!"

"Wrong again sweetheart! Did you actually see me die?"

Kendall started shaking and dropped the phone. He backed away from it until he hit the closet door. He quickly opened it and went inside. He pushed himself as far back as he could and curled up tightly on the floor chanting to himself, "No more, no more, no more."

Chapter 121 ~ Ice Skating and Snowballs

The group headed to the park. Logan was walking carefully so he didn't slip and re-injure his ankle, and James sticking close by just in case. Katie and Carlos were running ahead, throwing snowballs at one another.

Antonio, Joanna, and Alex were walking a little behind them, talking. "Hey you two wait for us," Antonio called out to Katie and Carlos.

The pair stopped and waited for the others to catch up. They got to the park a few minutes later and the boys and Katie put on their skates and went out on the ice.

"Go slowly at first," Alex said to Logan.

"I will." He smiled.

A few minutes later, they were skating around. Katie was doing some intricate twirls and spins while James held her hand.

"Look at those two!" Jo smiled.

"She's really good at those fancy moves," Alex said.

They nodded and watched as Katie tried to show Carlos how to spin. She held his hand and slowly showed him what to do.

"Then there's my boy." Antonio laughed as he watched Carlos spin and land in the snow bank.

Katie shook her head and left him there.

"Like father like son." Alex smirked.

Antonio looked at him.

"What?"

"Not a thing, old friend." Antonio smiled as he reached down and grabbed a handful of snow. He started patting it into a snowball, still smiling.

"Now Antonio, be nice," Alex said, backing up.

Antonio just continued smiling as he launched the snowball at his friend.

It hit him in the forehead and Alex just stood there for a minute. He brushed the snow out of his eyes and looked at Antonio and Jo, who were both laughing. "Thought that was funny, did ya?" he asked as he grabbed a handful of snow.

"Extremely!" Antonio said, backing away.

"Uh huh, and you, my Darlin'?" Alex said, looking at Jo.

"Now Alex, don't you dare!"

"Sounds like a challenge to me," Antonio pointed out.

Alex tossed the snowball back and forth in his hands, trying to decide who to throw it at. He had just decided when another snowball caught him in the side of the head. Carlos was laughing as he skated further out onto the ice.

"Hey!" Alex yelled.

Another snowball hit him in the shoulder and Antonio stood there smirking. "You were saying something about like father like son?"

"No fair ganging up!"

"Aww, what's the matter, cowboy? Can't handle a little snow?" Antonio asked.

Joanna laughed at the two, shaking her head.

"Oh, I can handle a little snow. The question is, can you?" Alex asked as he threw the snowball. It caught Joanna in the chest.

She gasped and looked at him in shock. "Alexander Jebediah Mitchell!" she shrieked.

"Jebediah?" Antonio asked.

"What?" Alex asked as he picked up another handful of snow.

"Jebediah?" Antonio repeated, as he grabbed another handful of snow and backed up.

"Yes, Jebediah! Why, what's your middle name?" Alex asked as he moved towards his friend.

"Eduardo."

"Pshhh."

"What?"

"Boring," Alex said as he hurled the snowball at Antonio.

Antonio dodged it and threw his, hitting Alex in the leg. "I admit it doesn't bring up visions of say, BANJOS playing, but at least it flows when you say it." Antonio smirked.

"Really? A 'Deliverance' comparison, that's the BEST you could do?"

"It works for me!" Jo said as she hit him in the back of the head with a large, loosely compacted snowball.

∞

Kendall hid in the closet, curled up tightly as he tried to block Deesie's voice.

"Where are you, you little shit? I'm going to make you pay when I find you!"

Images flooded his mind and he squeezed his eyes shut and tried to control his breathing. He had nearly calmed down when he felt someone pressing down on him and a voice whispered in his ear. *"Hello, sweetheart."*

"No, no, no," he whispered.

"I told you what would happen."

Kendall felt a hand closing around his throat as another moved down his side. He started to hyperventilate, and a few seconds later lost consciousness.

∞

Sylvia was in the kitchen finishing the dishes when the phone rang. "Hello?"

"Hi Sylvia, I was just calling to check on everyone and to let you know that the rest of Kendall's blood work was normal," Jen said.

"That's good news." Sylvia smiled.

"I know. I was so worried she might find something else wrong. How is he doing? Are the tube feedings going alright?"

"So far so good. They did one last night and another this morning. They're going to do another one tonight after they get back from the park. Antonio, Alex, and Jo took the other kids down to go skating. I think Kendall was feeling a little down about it."

"My poor baby. Hopefully he'll be doing well enough by next week and he can go then."

"Hopefully."

"Do you think he'd want to meet for lunch after his appointment tomorrow? I get off at two, so I thought we could meet then. Maybe just get something to go and sit in the car at the park."

"I'm sure he'd love to. He went upstairs to change, so hang on and I'll go get him."

"Okay, thanks."

Sylvia set the phone down and went upstairs. She knocked on the guest room door. "Kendall, your mom's on the phone."

She didn't get a response, so she knocked again. "Kendall?"

Still not getting a response, she opened the door. The light was on, but he was nowhere in sight. "Mijo, where are you?" she asked as she checked Carlos' room. Not finding him there, she checked the bathroom and then her room.

She went back into the guest room and looked around. She saw his shoulder stabilizer still on the bed and the clothes he had been wearing in the hamper. "Kendall?" she called softly as she checked under the bed. She saw his phone lying there, picked it up, and set it on the bed.

She went to the closet and opened the door. "Oh my God. Kendall!" She knelt next to him and carefully touched him arm. "Baby, wake up."

His hair was damp with sweat and his face was hot to the touch. She put her arms around him and managed to pull him out of the closet a little. "Mijo, please wake up."

When she couldn't get him to respond, she grabbed his cell and called Antonio.

∞

After Jo and the kids ganged up on Antonio and Alex, they came to a momentary truce and the kids went back out on the ice. Alex was shivering because Logan and Carlos managed to get two snowballs down his shirt.

He had gotten most of it out. "I WILL be getting even with you two little monkeys!"

They laughed and skated out of reach.

Jo wrapped her arms around him. "Poor baby. Did those mean little kids get you all snowy?"

He nodded with a sad pout on his face.

Antonio laughed at the expression on his friend's face and felt his phone vibrate in his pocket.

"Garcia." His smile quickly disappeared. "Honey, what? He's where, what happened?"

Jo and Alex listened as Antonio tried to find out what had happened.

"Is he breathing alright? Okay, I'm on my way, I'll be there in a couple of minutes," he said as he started running towards home.

"Antonio?" Alex yelled.

"Stay here with the kids and let them finish skating. I'll call you when I get home," he yelled back.

Antonio raced home and let himself in. He ran upstairs to the guest room and found Sylvia still trying to wake Kendall.

"What happened?" he asked, kneeling down next to them.

"I-I don't know. He came upstairs to change so he would be ready when Alex got back to do the feeding. I was finishing up in the kitchen when Jen called to let us know the blood results. Oh no! She's still waiting on the phone."

"Tell her he's had a panic attack and we'll call her as soon as he's awake."

Sylvia nodded and went into their bedroom and got on the extension.

"Kendall, wake up, Mijo," Antonio said, brushing his hair back off his forehead. He didn't get a response, so he picked him up and laid him on the bed. "Kendall, it's time to wake up," Antonio said a little louder.

Sylvia came back in. "She's on her way over."

Antonio nodded. "Honey, you didn't hear him scream or say anything?"

She shook her head. "No, not a sound. I came up to get him so he could talk to Jen and couldn't find him. I checked all the rooms before looking under the bed and in the closet."

"Did he respond at all?"

"No, he was curled up in the back of the closet and I pulled him out because he felt so hot."

Antonio felt Kendall's forehead. "He's not hot now, so it could be because he was closed up in there."

His cell rang and he looked at the screen and handed it to Sylvia. "Tell Alex what happened. I told them to stay at the park and let the kids skate."

She nodded and answered while Antonio continued trying to get Kendall to respond. "He said they'll be heading back in a few minutes."

Antonio nodded.

There was a knock at the front door. "That's probably Jen," Sylvia said, heading downstairs. She let Jen in and they headed upstairs.

Down the street, a tan SUV pulled out and drove away.

∞

Upstairs, Kendall started whimpering and pulled away when Antonio touched his cheek. "Kendall, it's Papi. You're safe, but you need to wake up now."

Kendall's eyes fluttered open and he started screaming and tried to pull away.

"Kendall, WAKE UP! You're safe with us," Antonio said, grabbing ahold of him. He held the boy tightly to him, trying to calm him.

Jen sat next to him. "Baby, it's alright. Please wake up."

"HE'S HERE! He's going to hurt you, you have to run!" he screamed.

"Kendall, there's no one here that's going to hurt us. You need to wake up!" Antonio said firmly.

"NO, you don't understand, he's in the house! You have to run!"

"Jen, take ahold of his head and make him look at you," Antonio instructed.

She nodded and put her hands on both sides of Kendall's head and forced him to look towards her. "Kendall, you're okay. You have to wake up!"

Kendall continued fighting them, trying to pull away.

"KENDALL! Wake up!" Jen said firmly.

After a moment, his struggles slowed and his eyes started to focus. "Mama?" he said weakly.

"Yes baby, it's mama." She smiled.

He closed his eyes and collapsed against Antonio. Antonio laid him back and checked his breathing.

Sylvia heard the door open downstairs. "The kids are back."

"Why don't you two go down and let them know everything's alright? I'll stay here in case he has another attack," Antonio said.

They nodded and Jen reached over and kissed Kendall on the forehead. "It's going to be okay, baby."

They went down and Antonio sat next to Kendall. "Mijo, can you wake up?" he asked softly. Kendall stirred a little. "Kendall, wake up."

Kendall opened his eyes and groaned.

"It's alright," Antonio said.

"Papi?"

"Yeah, it's me." Antonio smiled. "Can you tell me what happened?"

Kendall looked at him. "I don't know. I remember changing and then I-I heard his voice."

"It's alright, don't worry about it right now," Antonio said softly.

Kendall sat up and hugged Antonio tightly. "Papi, why won't he leave me alone?"

"I don't know, Mijo," he said, pulling the boy close.

"I can't do this anymore," Kendall sobbed.

"Yes you can."

Kendall shook his head.

"Mijo, you're not alone. I know you're tired and this is hard, but we're NOT giving up. Do you understand?"

Kendall nodded.

"Okay, look at me," Antonio said.

Kendall looked up.

"I don't know how to make this stop. All I can do is be here. That's all any of us can do right now, but this is where we want to be. So when you start feeling scared or overwhelmed, I want you to promise me you'll tell one of us."

Kendall nodded.

"Use your words, no loopholes." Antonio smiled as he quoted Claudia.

"I-I promise," Kendall said quietly.

Antonio looked up and saw Alex standing in the doorway.

"That's my boy. Now I want you to rest for a little while. You and Papa M still need to do another feeding."

"Okay," Kendall said, lying back down.

Alex walked in and sat down on the other side of Kendall. "Hey Champ."

"Hi Papa M," he said as he closed his eyes.

Alex patted Antonio on the back. "It's going to be okay, buddy."

"I hope so," he said quietly.

Chapter 122~ Making Sense of it All

After Kendall had calmed down a little more, Alex went downstairs and mixed up the formula.

Logan followed him into the kitchen. "Is he okay?"

"I think so. He's just really tired right now. We need to get this done so he can go to sleep for the night."

"What happened?"

"I'm not sure. Hopefully he'll be able to tell us a little more later on." He finished filling the bag. "Do you want to give me a hand?"

"Sure," Logan said, grabbing a glass of water. They went upstairs, where Antonio and Jen were sitting with Kendall.

"Hey Champ, you ready to do this?"

Kendall sighed and nodded.

Antonio helped him sit up and Jen got up. "I'm going to go down and check on your sister," she said, kissing his cheek.

"Okay," he said quietly.

Antonio moved and pulled Kendall in front of him and Alex inserted the NG tube. A few minutes later, the formula bag was hung and flowing, while Kendall was still resting in Antonio's arms.

After about half an hour, Kendall had relaxed more but was starting to get sleepy. Logan put in a movie to help distract him and sat next to him on the other side of the bed.

"I need to run downstairs for a few minutes, Mijo," Antonio said.

"Okay."

Antonio shifted so that Kendall could lie back against the headboard, and Alex went to sit next to him.

"I'll be right back," Antonio told him.

Kendall gave him a small smile and nodded.

Antonio went downstairs and started for his study. "How is he, Papi?" Carlos asked as he followed him.

"He's alright, Mijo, just tired. Are you okay?"

Carlos nodded. "Can I go up and see him?"

"Sure. I'll be back up in a few minutes. I want to give Claudia a call and talk to her about a few things."

"Okay," Carlos said.

"Did you have fun tonight, though?"

Carlos smiled. "Loads. Maybe by next week Kendall will feel better and we can all go."

"Maybe." Antonio smiled.

Carlos went upstairs while Antonio closed the door to his study and dialed Claudia's number.

"Hello."

"Hi Claudia, it's Antonio Garcia."

"Hey Antonio, what can I do for you?"

"Kendall had another panic attack tonight, and it took him awhile to come around. I'm getting really worried about his state of mind. He said Deesie won't leave him alone and that he can't do this anymore, and I'm not sure he can."

"Okay, why don't you tell me how it started," Claudia said.

"I really don't know. We had taken the other kids to the pond to go skating and he stayed here with Sylvia. She said after we left, he went up to change so he would be ready for Alex to do the feeding when we got home. Jen called to tell us about his blood results and to ask him about lunch tomorrow, so Sylvia went up to get him. She couldn't find him at first, and then she found him curled up in the back of the closet. He was completely non-responsive, so she called me. It took me a couple of minutes to get home and another few minutes for him to come around."

"Do you know what happened?" she asked.

"No, Sylvia said he never made a sound, but when he finally started to wake up, he was screaming that 'he was here and going to hurt us.' It took a few minutes to get him to wake up from that and to stop fighting us, and then he passed out."

"How is he now?"

"Better. Alex put the feeding tube in and we're about halfway done. He's exhausted, but we can't let him sleep with it in," Antonio told her.

"I heard that didn't go so well when he woke up with it in the first time you practiced it."

"No, he said it freaked him out when he woke up and felt something in his throat."

"I don't blame him there. Alright, I'm coming over and we'll get this figured out."

"You don't have to do that."

"I'll see you in about ten or fifteen minutes," she told him, hanging up.

Antonio smiled and hung up. He took a deep breath and went out into the living room. "I called Claudia and she's on her way over. She should be here in a few minutes."

"Do you want us to send her up or call you down?" Sylvia asked.

"Could you call me? I think we're going to try and figure out exactly what happened tonight, and she'll probably want to talk to us first."

Sylvia nodded.

∞

Antonio went back upstairs. "How are things going?"

"Everything is just fine." Alex smiled, getting up.

Antonio went over and took his place next to Kendall. "Are you feeling any better?"

"Just tired," he said, leaning against Antonio.

Antonio put his arm around him. "I know, this shouldn't take too much longer," he said, looking at the bag.

"Do you want me to try and open the flow a little more?" Alex asked.

Kendall shook his head. "I don't want to puke."

"Good choice." Alex smiled.

"What are we watching?" Antonio asked.

"Harry Potter and the Goblet of Fire," Logan told him.

"Is it good?" Antonio asked.

"I like the first one the best," Logan said.

"How many are there?" Alex asked.

"Four so far," Logan said.

"So far? How many are they going to make?"

"Well, there are seven books."

"They better hurry if they're going to turn them all into movies," Alex said.

"Why?"

"Those kids aren't going to get any younger."

Logan rolled his eyes.

"What?"

"The books follow Harry as he gets older and learns to control his powers while trying to stop the evil Lord Voldemort from conquering the world."

"Ah, good to know," Alex said, giving Antonio a confused look.

"Don't look at me, I just smile and nod when they try to explain it to me." Antonio laughed.

Logan rolled his eyes.

"Hey, that's what you said to do when Papa M starts talking about cowboy movies," Carlos told Logan.

Antonio laughed.

"Carlos!" Logan said.

"What? He heard you in the car," Carlos pointed out.

"He's right, you know," Alex said.

Logan crossed his arms and sat back against the headboard. "I'm not explaining anything to either one of you anymore."

"Promise?" Carlos asked with a smirk.

"Yes, and remember that when you need help with your homework, genius."

"Boys..." Alex chuckled.

∞

Claudia got to the Garcia's and knocked softly. Sylvia answered. "Claudia, thank you so much for coming."

"It's not a problem. How is everyone?"

"I think we're all fine. Antonio wanted me to get him when you got here," she said, heading upstairs.

Jen stood up and walked over. "Hi, I'm Jennifer, Kendall's mom."

Claudia smiled and took her hand. "How are you doing? The boys told me you're feeling better."

"I am thank you. I also want to thank you for getting me in to see Dr. Thorne so quickly. He's wonderful." She smiled.

"He's a very nice man and very good at what he does."

"He is, I'm so lucky to have someone like him to talk to," Jen said.

Antonio and Sylvia came down. "Hi Claudia, thanks for doing this."

"James, Katie, maybe you—" Antonio started.

Katie stood up and rolled her eyes. "I know, come on James. They're going to have tall talk," she said, making air quotes with her fingers.

"Tall talk?"

"Just come on," she said, pulling him by the arm.

Antonio smiled and shook his head.

"Are you sure she's ONLY seven?" Claudia asked.

"Seven going on forty-two," Jen said.

"I believe that." Claudia laughed.

A moment later, Alex came down. "We have about another twenty minutes before the bag is empty."

"Why don't we go into the kitchen and I'll make us some tea," Sylvia said.

Claudia nodded and they all went out and sat at the table. "So, what happened?" Claudia asked.

Antonio held his hand up and went back into the living room. He listened for a moment and then called up the stairs. "Katherine Knight, go watch TV with your brothers." He shook his head as he heard the sound of little footsteps moving quickly down the hall. "Carlos?"

"Yes Papi?"

"Please make sure Katie stays with all of you."

"Okay, Papi!"

Antonio went back into the kitchen.

Alex laughed. "Little imp."

"Yes she is." Jen sighed.

Sylvia poured hot water into the mugs and passed them around. She set the kettle on the trivet in the middle of the table and set the basket with assorted teas next to it. Once everyone had their chosen tea steeping, she sat down.

"Alright, so who wants to start?" Claudia asked.

"I guess I should, since I was the one here with him," Sylvia said.

'Why don't you start from when everyone else left?" Claudia suggested.

Sylvia nodded. "Well, he seemed a little down that he couldn't go skating, which I thought was a good sign, since he hasn't wanted to go anywhere."

"He loves skating?" Claudia asked.

"Skating and hockey are a huge part of his life. He's skated almost since he could walk," Jen said.

Claudia nodded.

"After a few minutes, he said he was going to go up and put on his pajamas, since Alex and he were going to do another feeding once they got home. I should have checked on him when he didn't come right back down."

"Honey," Antonio said, shaking his head.

"What? We agreed we wouldn't leave him alone. I should have told him to come right back down. Instead I lost track of time finishing up the dishes."

"Blaming yourself or anyone else isn't going to help. It's also not going to change the fact that he had a panic attack. What we can do is try to figure out what triggered it," Claudia told her.

Sylvia nodded.

"What happened next?" Claudia asked.

"Jen called to tell us about his blood results and to ask if he'd want to have lunch with her tomorrow. I went up to get him and couldn't find him at first. I checked all of the rooms and then went back into the guest room. I saw his shoulder brace was on the bed and his clothes were in the hamper. I looked under the bed and then checked the closet. He was curled up in the back and wouldn't wake up when I called him. I tried again, and when I touched his cheek, he was hot. He still wouldn't wake up, so I tried to pull him out of the closet and called Antonio."

Claudia looked at Antonio. "You said it took a few minutes to get him to come around and then he started screaming about Deesie being here. Did he say anything else?"

Antonio thought back. "He said that he was in the house and that we needed to run."

"That's odd. Has he ever said that before?"

"No, he's said that he's here before, but never that he's in the house."

"Why would he think that?" Claudia asked.

"Not a clue. He's had dreams where we were still in the woods, that's when he's told me I needed to run. Deesie had told him he was going to kill me when he was... finished with him," Antonio said.

"Maybe he was thinking back to when Deesie first took him from our house," Jen suggested.

"Possibly, but what would have caused that line of thinking?" Claudia asked, trying to come up with a common denominator.

"Dad?" Logan called.

"Yeah Partner, what do you need?"

"The bag is finished. What do you want me to do?"

"On my way! I'll be right back," Alex said, getting up. Alex went upstairs, disconnected the tubing, and flushed the line. "How are you doing, Champ?"

"Tired."

"Just a little while longer, okay?"

Kendall nodded. "Why is Claudia here?"

"Papa G called her to let her know what happened, and she wanted to stop by and make sure you were doing alright," Alex told him.

Kendall sighed.

"We'll pull the tube in half an hour, and then she'll come up and see you. Do you think you can stay awake that long?"

"I'll try."

"We're just in the kitchen having tea, so if you need anything, just holler."

Kendall nodded and laid his head on Logan's shoulder.

Alex winked at Logan and then headed back downstairs. Everything going okay?" Jen asked as he sat back down.

"Perfect, he's becoming a pro at this. I told him we'll pull the tube in half an hour and that Claudia would go up and say hi then."

Claudia smiled and nodded.

"So, have we figured anything out?" Alex asked.

Antonio shook his head.

"So what do the panic attacks have in common?" Claudia asked.

"His last panic attack was on Saturday when he woke up with the tube in. The time before that was Friday when that woman accosted him at the restaurant," Antonio said.

"So, what those attacks had in common was he was sleeping and was startled by something. First the woman screaming at him, and then the tube in his throat. He came out of those fairly quickly though, right?"

Antonio nodded.

"This time it took a while for you to get through to him, so maybe it wasn't a panic attack, maybe it was a flashback. Sylvia, you said he was hot to the touch when you first found him?"

Sylvia nodded.

"So it's possible he started hyperventilating and that could be why he passed out. The surplus of oxygen would cause him to overheat as well. When was the last time he hid while he was awake?"

"When he hid in the crawlspace, but he had a high fever then, too," Antonio told her.

"Maybe we're complicating this... maybe it's something simple," Jo said.

"Like what?" Jen asked.

"Well, for the last couple of days everyone's been worked up about this blue car hanging around the neighbourhood... worried enough by the thought that this guy is a predator, that all of the schools were put on alert. Maybe with everything that's gone on, it put him in mind of Deesie," Joanna said.

"What blue car?" Claudia asked.

"There was a Chevy Malibu that looked like it might be casing the neighbourhood the other day. Sylvia had seen him come and go, and when Alex and I went to check it out, he was just sitting in the car, watching the street," Antonio told her.

"Did you find out who he is?"

Antonio nodded. "Sally had pulled into the neighbour's driveway and pretended to live there. When she asked what he was doing there, he told her that his car had overheated, but it was suddenly running fine when she asked him about it. She got his photo with her phone and sent it to the databases. She finally got a hit and his record is clean, so she's running a background check on him, because some things just don't add up."

"The kids knew about this?"

He nodded. "We put the schools on alert because he was an unknown, and we weren't about to take any chances."

"That makes sense, and Joanna's right that might be what caused this. I'll think I'll wait until tomorrow to see if he remembers anything else. I don't want to stress him out anymore tonight, "Claudia said.

∞

Upstairs, Kendall kept nodding off, so James ran downstairs to get Alex. "Papa M?"

"Yeah Sport?"

"I don't think Kendall can stay awake much longer."

"Okay, I'll be right up."

James went back upstairs. "He's on his way."

"Thanks James," Kendall said quietly.

"Katie, why don't you go get ready for bed while Papa M pulls the tube?" James suggested.

"Okay," she said, going into the other bedroom.

"Are you doing okay?" James asked Kendall.

"Just tired and I have a headache."

Alex came in. "You ready?" he asked, sitting next to Kendall.

Kendall nodded and James sat down next to him. He pulled him over so he could hold him while Alex removed the tube. Logan held the water for Kendall, and a minute later, Alex had pulled the tube and waited for Kendall to stop coughing.

"You okay, Champ?"

Kendall nodded.

"He has a headache," James told him.

"Is it bad?" Alex asked.

Kendall nodded.

"Okay, let me double check with Antonio to see what you can have," Alex said, getting up.

"Thank you," Kendall said quietly.

Alex went downstairs and there was a knock at the front door. He looked through the peephole and opened the door. "Hi Brooke. James is upstairs," he told her, kissing her cheek.

"Thank you, darling. Is Kendall alright? I saw Jen and Claudia's cars out front."

"He had another panic attack and Claudia stopped by to check on him. We've been trying to brainstorm to see if we can find anything in common between the attacks."

"Did you figure anything out?"

"Well, there's a chance tonight it was a flashback instead of a panic attack. He's pretty wiped out right now, so she's going to wait until tomorrow to talk to him about it. I do need to find out what he can have for a headache, though," Alex told her, walking to the kitchen.

"Poor baby," Brooke said, following him.

"Brooke, how are you tonight?" Sylvia asked.

"Just fine. I hear things were not so good here?"

"Everyone's better now," Jen said.

"Good. Well, I'm going to go up and say goodnight to the kids."

"I'll walk up with you so I can say hi to Kendall," Claudia said, getting up. The two women walked up together and Brooke knocked on the guest room door.

"Mom!" James smiled.

"Hello, my boy," she said, hugging him. She went over and kissed Kendall on the forehead. "Hello darling. Alex said you have a headache?"

Kendall smiled a little and nodded.

"Antonio's getting something you can take for it."

"Okay."

Claudia walked in behind Brooke and Carlos jumped up and hugged her. "Hi Claudia!"

"Hello baby. Sally's right, you do give the best hugs."

"Thanks!" He grinned.

She sat next to Kendall. "How are you doing now, baby?"

"Better, but I'm tired."

"I know you are. I just wanted to pop in to see if you needed anything."

He shook his head. "I think I'm okay."

"Alright. If you need anything, you call me. It doesn't matter what time."

"I will." He smiled.

"No you won't, and that's why I'm putting the other boys in charge of that. If he needs anything, call me," she said, handing her card to Logan.

"We will," he promised.

"Alright, I'm going to let you all get to bed. I'll see you tomorrow," she said to Kendall.

He nodded.

"Alright babies, you all get some sleep," she said, standing up. "I'm going to say goodnight to that adorable little sister of yours."

"She's next door." Kendall smiled.

She nodded. "Goodnight."

"Night Claudia."

"Well, I'm going to get going too. I'll see all of you tomorrow night," Brooke said as she kissed them each goodbye. She went downstairs and into the kitchen. "I'm going to head home for the night. Call if anyone needs anything."

"I should get going too," Joanna said.

"I'll walk you two out," Alex said.

"I'm going to say goodnight to the kids," Jen said, getting up. She went up and found Katie already in bed. "Goodnight, honey," she said, kissing Katie goodnight.

"Night mom." Katie smiled, hugging her.

She smiled at her daughter and tucked her in. "Light on or off?"

"Off please, but can you leave the door open?"

"Of course," Jen said as she turned off the light. She went next door and sat next to Kendall. "Goodnight, honey. Please call me if you need anything. Did you want to meet for lunch tomorrow if you're feeling better?"

"Sure." He yawned.

"Okay, I get off at two, so we'll decide what to do then."

He nodded and she tucked the blankets around him. She kissed him on the forehead and then reached over and kissed Logan's cheek.

"Goodnight Logan."

"Goodnight Mama K."

She got up, kissed James and Carlos each goodnight, and went downstairs.

Claudia was saying goodnight to Sylvia and Antonio.

"It was so nice meet you, and thank you for everything you're doing for Kendall," Jen said.

"It was nice meeting you too, and I would love the opportunity to sit down and talk to you, when you have time." Claudia smiled.

Jen nodded. "I'll call and set something up."

"Good, I look forward to meeting with you soon, then."

Alex came back in. "Let me walk you two ladies out."

"Security duty tonight?" Jen asked.

"Why let Antonio have all the fun?" He smiled as he walked them out.

∞

Antonio went upstairs and grabbed the Tylenol from the bathroom cabinet. He took two and a glass of water in to Kendall. "Here you go." He smiled.

"Thank you," Kendall said as he took the pills. He was shaking a little, so Antonio held the glass for him.

He laid back and Antonio sat the glass on the night table. "You get some sleep now, Mijo."

"Okay." Kendall yawned.

"If you need anything, just yell," Antonio said.

"James, why don't you take the bed?" Logan asked as he got up.

"I'm fine down here," James said.

"You really shouldn't sleep on the floor with bruised ribs," Logan pointed out as he laid down next to Carlos on Kendall's side of the bed.

"Are you sure? What if I have another clown dream?"

"Have you taken any more of those painkillers?" Logan asked.

"No."

"Then go." Logan pointed.

James got up and climbed under the covers on the other side of the bed. Antonio smiled at them. "Goodnight Mijos."

"Night Papi!" Carlos said, jumping up and hugging him.

"Goodnight Carlitos," Antonio said, kissing the top of his head.

"Goodnight Papa G," Logan said.

"Night Logan."

"Night Papi." James yawned.

Antonio smiled and closed the door.

∞

Derek Manning's phone rang. "Hello."

"Hello Mr. Manning, it's Danielle. I just wanted to let you know that I met with Dr. Graham and reassured him about everything. I also heard from our man, and he said he's managed to find quite a bit of information on the Waters and the Pearsons, and he'll be sending that along tomorrow. He hasn't found much on the Raymonds or the Tanners, but he's still looking."

"Good. Tell him to keep digging until he finds something. The more dirty laundry we can air, the less likely the jury will be to take their testimony seriously. If they testify at all."

"Yes sir."

"He's still working on the other matter?"

"Yes, he said he's staying on top of it and that things seem to be progressing nicely."

"Good. I should hear about a court date sometime tomorrow, so he might have to step things up a bit."

"I'll let him know," she said with a smile.

Chapter 123~ First Generation Pranksters

Kendall woke with a start. He lay there quietly listening, his heart pounding. After a moment, he relaxed and closed his eyes and fell back into a fitful sleep.

"Remember, I want it all!"

Kendall woke again in a cold sweat, trying to control his breathing. He carefully got up so he didn't disturb James and stepped around Logan and Carlos. He opened the door, went into the bathroom, and got a glass of water.

He closed his eyes and took several deep breaths. He opened his eyes and jumped at his reflection in the mirror. "Stupid, stupid, stupid," he chastised himself.

He turned out the light, went to the bedroom, and looked in. James had stretched out and was sleeping soundly on the bed. He smiled a little and decided to go downstairs, quietly closing the door. He went down into the living room and opened the drapes a little so he could look outside. He curled up in Antonio's recliner, staring outside. It was snowing lightly and the streetlamp made the snow shimmer and sparkle as it fell to the ground.

∞

Carlos woke up at about three to use the bathroom. He went back into the bedroom and noticed James was alone on the bed. He looked around the room, went to the closet door, and opened it quietly. "Kendall, are you in there?"

Not finding him there, he quickly checked under the bed. He tried to wake James, but he just rolled over, still exhausted from the events of the last few days. He thought about waking Logan, but decided to check out the rest of the house first. He went into his room where Katie was sleeping and checked under the bed and in his closet.

He went back into the bathroom, checked the tub, and then headed downstairs. He noticed a faint light shining through the window and his dad's chair turned and facing it. "Kendall?" he said softly.

The chair moved slightly. "Hey Carlitos. What are you doing up?"

"Looking for you. Can't you sleep?"

"Not really," Kendall said, moving over so Carlos could sit next to him.

"You need to get some rest, though."

"I know. I just can't seem to stay asleep."

"Are you having bad dreams?"

"I don't know," Kendall said quietly.

Carlos put his arm around him. "We can just watch it snow."

Kendall smiled and Carlos pulled him a little closer. "If you get tired, just go to sleep. I won't let anyone hurt you," Carlos promised.

"I know," Kendall said, smiling at his friend.

The two sat there quietly for several minutes and Kendall's eyes started drooping. Carlos pulled him over so his head was resting on his shoulder and he quietly started to sing the lullaby that Antonio use to sing to him.

Buenas noches, mi niño, No llores tú hoy por mi, Sueña con los angelitos Pero no te alejes de mi, Cierra ya tú tus ojitos, Que te veré al amanecer, No te preocupes, Que yo estaré aquí, Por lo bueno y por lo malo, Jamás te dejare ir, Buenas noches, mi niño

∞

Antonio got up to check on the kids at about 3:30. He looked in on the boys and saw Carlos and Kendall were gone, so he went downstairs. He smiled when he heard his son singing softly and walked quietly over to his chair. Kendall was sleeping and Carlos was still singing, even though he was half-asleep.

Antonio grabbed the blanket from the back of the couch and gently covered the boys. Carlos opened his eyes and smiled. "Hi Papi," he yawned.

"Are you comfortable there?"

Carlos smiled and nodded.

"Here," Antonio said, pulling the lever so that the footrest came up.

He tucked the blanket in around the two boys. "You're sure you're okay there?"

Carlos nodded again. "We're fine."

"Alright Mijo, I'm going back to bed. If you need me, just call up the stairs."

Carlos nodded and Antonio kissed him on the head. He reached over, felt Kendall's forehead, and smiled when he found it was still cool to the touch.

"Is he sick again?" Carlos asked.

"I don't think so. I think he's just really tired."

Carlos nodded and yawned again.

"Get some sleep," Antonio said as he headed back upstairs.

"I will, Papi."

Antonio climbed back into bed. "Is everything alright?" Sylvia asked.

"Everything's fine. Carlos and Kendall are downstairs sleeping, though."

"Why, did Kendall have another nightmare?"

"I'm not sure, but they're fine now, so I left them there."

"Goodnight honey."

"Goodnight." He smiled as he wrapped his arms around her.

∞

James woke up about five and realized Kendall wasn't in the room. He jumped up and checked the closet, and was looking under the bed when he realized Carlos was also missing. He shook Logan. "Hey, do you know where Kendall and Carlos are?"

"Carlos, stop it!" Logan said, swatting James' hand and pulling the blanket tighter.

"I'm not Carlos! Do you know where they are?" James asked again.

"'Los, go 'way!" Logan mumbled.

James rolled his eyes. "Unbelievable."

He went to check the other rooms, and not finding them, went downstairs. He started for the kitchen when he saw something in his peripheral vision. He looked around and saw his two friends sleeping soundly in the recliner. Carlos had his arm wrapped around Kendall, who was sleeping with his head on Carlos' chest, Carlos' chin was resting on Kendall's head.

James sighed in relief.

He tapped Carlos on the shoulder. "Carlos, what are you guys doing down here?"

Carlos yawned, opened his eyes, and smiled. "Hi James."

"What are you doing down here?" James repeated.

"I woke up a while ago and Kendall was gone. I found him down here looking out the window," Carlos told him.

"Are you guys okay?"

Carlos nodded and closed his eyes again.

James shook his head and smiled. He pulled the blanket back up around his friends and went to lie down on the couch. He pulled the other blanket down and was soon fast asleep.

Logan woke up a few minutes later and realized he was alone in the room. "Guys?" he asked, looking around. He looked at the clock and saw it was just a little after five. He got up, and seeing the bathroom door was open, headed downstairs.

He saw James sleeping on the couch and his other two friends in the recliner. He went over to James and shook him. "James, what's going on?"

James opened his eyes. "NOW you're awake?"

"What?"

"Nothing. Kendall couldn't sleep and Carlos found him down here. I woke up and saw they were gone and TRIED to wake you up, but you called me 'Los and slapped me. I came down here and found them. Now I'm going back to sleep."

"I slapped you?"

James nodded and then closed his eyes, trying to go back to sleep.

Logan yawned and laid down on the other end of the couch, pulling the blanket towards him. James pulled it back and Logan yanked on it again. James gave it one last tug and the blanket was pulled out of Logan's reach.

"Really?"

He scooted down closer to James and pulled the blanket gently until it covered him half way. A few minutes later, he realized he was cold, so he scooted down more until the blanket covered his torso.

Soon all four boys were sleeping soundly.

∞

Alex got up around six, started a pot of coffee, and mixed up the formula for the morning feeding. Since Kendall had an appointment with Claudia, he wanted to try to get it done early. He jumped in the shower, dressed, and went in to start breakfast.

Antonio had awoken a few minutes after six, showered, and dressed for work. He could smell coffee and knew his friend was already up. He went downstairs and had to laugh. James was sound asleep, his arms wrapped around Logan's lower legs and he was using his feet as a pillow. The only parts of Logan he could see were his feet. A blanket covered the rest of him. He checked on Carlos and Kendall, who were still curled up together.

He heard Alex out in the kitchen and went to get him. "Hey, come look at this."

"What?"

"Just come on."

Alex followed Antonio out into the living room.

Antonio pointed at the couch and Alex stifled a laugh. Alex grabbed his cell and took a quick picture of the two. Antonio put his finger up to his lips and got a pen from the table. He walked behind the couch and over to where James' head was resting. He took the pen and gently touched the bottom of Logan's foot. Logan twitched in his sleep and James hugged his legs tighter.

"Do it again," Alex whispered, grinning.

Antonio nodded and lightly ran the pen along the bottom of Logan's foot. Logan mumbled something and his foot twitched again.

James yawned and snuggled his cheek against Logan's foot.

Antonio and Alex were both trying not to laugh.

Alex held up a finger. "Do it again," he mouthed.

"Wait," Antonio whispered, pointing at Carlos and Kendall. He went over and gently shook Kendall. "Mijo, time to wake up," he whispered.

"Hmm?" Kendall murmured, opening his eyes.

"Shhh," Antonio smiled and whispered into his ear.

Kendall smiled and Antonio woke Carlos. "Morning Papi."

"Shhh, watch," he whispered and went back over to the couch. Antonio lightly ran the pen along Logan's foot again and the sleeping teen mumbled something in his sleep.

"Again," Alex whispered.

Antonio nodded and clicked the pen open. He rolled the pen along the bottom of Logan's foot, hard enough to leave a mark.

Logan shrieked and tried to yank his feet away, but they were still being held firmly in James' grasp. James squealed when he felt something moving against his face and released Logan's legs, pushing him away. Logan fell off the couch, still wrapped up in the blanket.

Antonio, Alex, Carlos, and Kendall all broke into laughter as James nearly pushed himself over the back of the couch and Logan thrashed around in the blanket until he finally managed to free himself.

"What?" they both yelled.

"That was great!" Kendall smirked.

"What the heck are you doing?" Logan asked his dad.

"Who me? I didn't do a thing."

Logan looked over at Antonio. "Hey, he told me too!" Antonio said, pointing at Alex.

"Excuse me? The pen idea was ALL yours. I was in the kitchen innocently making breakfast when YOU called me in here."

"True, but you have to admit James hugging Logan's feet to his cheek was adorable," Antonio said.

"I was hugging his feet to my cheek?" James asked in horror.

"Like a soft and cuddly pillow," Alex told him.

"Oh my God," he shrieked, getting up.

"Where are you going?" Logan asked.

"To WASH my face, where do you think?" James said.

"Hey, YOU wouldn't give me any of the blanket!"

"So you sleep with your feet in my face?"

"They weren't in your face when I went to sleep. You must have pulled them up. After all, YOU were the one hugging them," Logan said defensively.

"Just gross, dude," James said, heading upstairs.

"Hey, I wash my feet, you know!"

"Not enough to touch my face!" James yelled down.

Alex was still laughing when he reached down and helped Logan up.

"Real funny, dad." Logan pouted.

"At least you're not blue," Alex pointed out. "Now, how about some breakfast?"

"What's for breakfast?" Carlos asked, getting up.

"Bacon, eggs and toast," Alex told him.

"Yay!" Carlos yelled, heading for the kitchen.

"We better hurry or there won't be anything left," Antonio said, holding his hand down to Kendall.

Kendall took it and Antonio pulled him up and they walked into the kitchen.

Sylvia came down a couple of moments later. "What is going on down here?"

"Kendall couldn't sleep, so he came downstairs and I woke up and found him in Papi's chair, so we sat there and watched it snow, and then we both fell asleep. Papi woke us up because he and Papa M were tickling Logan's feet with a pen, and Logan screamed and James pushed him because he was hugging Logan's feet, and then James screamed because Logan's feet were touching his cheek, so he ran upstairs to wash his face and Papa M made bacon and eggs!" Carlos rushed out in between mouthfuls of food.

"He must have amazing lung capacity," Alex said to Antonio.

"That's my boy." Antonio smiled.

She looked around at all of them and went to say something but stopped. "I'm going back to bed, wake me in an hour," she finally said and turned around and went back upstairs.

Chapter 124~ Voices

James scrubbed his face and then jumped in the shower. Twenty minutes later he was dressed, his hair dried and combed to perfection. He moisturized his face after the scrubbing he had given it and shuddered at the thought of snuggling with Logan's feet. He went into the bedroom to put away his things and noticed Kendall's cell on the dresser with the low battery light blinking. He checked Kendall's backpack and found the charger, plugged it in, and headed downstairs for breakfast.

"All squeaky clean?" Alex asked as James walked into the kitchen.

Kendall shivered and dropped his fork.

"Ha, ha," James replied sarcastically.

"Are you okay?" Antonio asked Kendall.

"Sorry, I guess my hand still isn't working very well."

Antonio looked at him. "Well, with any luck the stitches can come out on Monday."

Kendall nodded.

Logan got up. "I'm going to go jump in the shower and scrub my feet."

Alex and Antonio snickered as James asked, "What is THAT supposed to mean?"

"Not a thing." Logan smirked, going upstairs.

James raised an eyebrow and glared at Alex and Antonio.

"What?" Antonio asked innocently.

"Nothing at all," James said, giving them a sweet smile.

"Uh oh," Carlos said.

"Uh oh, what?" Alex asked.

James looked at Carlos and shook his head. "Nothing, I better go get ready for school," he said, getting up.

"Carlos?" Antonio asked with a worried look.

"Yes Papi?" Carlos smiled.

"What does 'uh oh' mean?"

"I'm not sure, I'll go ask Logan," he said, running for the stairs.

"On that note, I'm going to head to the station." Antonio smiled as he got up.

"Sure, leave me with the plotting little monsters," Alex said.

"Hey! I am NOT little," James said.

"Aw, poor Papa M," Antonio teased.

"It was YOUR idea and now you're jumping ship?"

"Absolutely!" Antonio grinned. "I'll meet you at Claudia's. Try and eat a little more for me," he said to Kendall.

"Okay." Kendall nodded.

"James, do you boys have hockey practice today?" Antonio asked.

James nodded.

"You take it easy and don't overdo it. I want you boys to wait for one of us to pick you up," Antonio told him.

"I will, thanks Papa G." James smiled.

"See you later, buddy," Alex said.

Antonio smiled and nodded. "Try and not get into too much trouble."

"I'll do my best, but you know me."

"That's what worries me." Antonio laughed.

∞

Katie came down a few minutes later. "Hey Big Brother," she said, hugging Kendall.

"Hey Katie. Did you sleep alright?"

She nodded.

"Breakfast?" Alex asked, sitting a plate in front of her.

"Thanks Papa M."

"You're welcome, Little Darlin'. Kendall, we need to get the tube in before the boys leave for school," Alex told him.

Kendall groaned.

"I know, but we need to get it done before your appointment today."

"Okay."

"You ate pretty well too," James said, pointing to Kendall's half-empty plate.

"I'm trying." Kendall smiled.

"I know you are. Pretty soon your appetite will be back to normal and you won't need the formula anymore," James said, getting up.

Kendall nodded.

Katie giggled.

"What?" Kendall asked.

"Sorry, it just sounds funny," she said, her cheeks turning red.

"Katie..." Alex warned.

"I said I was sorry," she said, looking down.

"It's okay, Katie, it does sound funny. I'm going to go get dressed," Kendall said.

"Do you want to do the tube upstairs or down here?" Alex asked.

"Down here's fine," he said, heading upstairs.

Logan and Carlos were both dressed and gathering their things. "Hey, I can help you with your homework tonight," Logan said as he and Carlos headed downstairs.

"Okay, thanks Loges," Kendall said, grabbing some clean clothes.

He went into the bathroom and closed the door. The water was still warm, so he quickly undressed and pulled on the glove. He got in and showered. He still had a bit of a headache and the warm water felt good. He turned off the water, got out, and dried off. He pulled on his boxers and black jeans and attempted to dry his hair with the one hand. He brushed his teeth and grabbed a comb for his hair. The mirror was all steamy, so he wiped it with his hand.

Kendall saw someone standing behind him.

"Miss me?"

He dropped the comb and squeezed his eyes shut and felt someone kiss his neck. "NO!" he yelled and dropped to the floor, holding his hands over his ears. "You're not real, you're not real!"

Sylvia had just finished dressing and was getting ready to head downstairs when she heard Kendall yell. She knocked on the bathroom door. "Kendall, are you alright?" She tried the handle and found the door locked. "Kendall?" she called, knocking louder.

A moment later, the door opened. "S-Sorry, I d-dropped the comb and slipped."

"Are you hurt?" she asked, looking him over.

"No, I'm fine," he said, pulling the towel tight around his shoulders.

"Are you sure, honey? You're shaking."

He nodded.

"Everything okay?" James asked. He had heard Sylvia calling Kendall and ran upstairs.

"Yeah, I just can't hold onto anything," Kendall said.

James looked at Sylvia, who was looking a little uncertain. "Let me help you with your shirt and get your hair combed out."

"Thanks James," Kendall said quietly.

"No problem." He smiled, going into the bathroom and grabbing Kendall's shirt. He helped him get it on and then found the comb. He sprayed Kendall's hair with the conditioner and then combed it out. "See, no pulling if you use conditioner."

Kendall rolled his eyes.

"Okay, we better go down so Papa M can put the tube in before I leave."

Kendall nodded and followed James downstairs.

Sylvia watched the boys, still wondering what had happened. She had noticed Kendall shaking and how pale his face was when he opened the door. She followed the boys downstairs, making a mental note to mention it to Claudia.

∞

Alex got the tube placed and Sylvia ran the kids to school. He hooked up the bag and he and Kendall settled down to watch a movie while the formula ran.

"How are you feeling this morning?" Alex asked.

"Okay, just a little tired."

"I can imagine."

"That was great, with James and Logan this morning." Kendall smiled.

"Yes it was. They can both really hit the high notes." Alex chuckled.

"That's for sure."

Alex looked sideways at Kendall. "So, Sylvia said you slipped in the bathroom. Did you hurt yourself?"

Kendall looked down. "No."

"You know what I love about all of you kids?" Alex asked.

"Our appreciation of the older generation?"

"Good one! No, your inability to lie very well."

"Oh," Kendall said, biting his lower lip.

"What happened?"

"I just scared myself by looking in the mirror too fast."

"And?" Alex asked, sitting next to him.

"I-I thought I saw somebody standing behind me."

Alex put his arm around Kendall's shoulders. "You know you can tell us these things, right? You NEED to tell us so we can help you. Keeping it bottled up, it isn't going to help."

"I know, I just..." Kendall said.

"Just what?"

"Sometimes I don't know what's real anymore," he whispered, his eyes tearing up.

Alex took his hand and squeezed it. "THIS is real. Being here with the people who love you is real. I'm not going tell you that I understand how you feel, because I don't. I can tell you I know what it's like to be scared and to feel alone, and to tell you it's okay to feel that way, as long as you know that you're NOT alone."

Kendall nodded and Alex pulled him over so his head was resting on his shoulder. "If you need to cry, scream, throw things, that's okay, too. Nobody in this family is going to judge you for anything, and you need to stop judging yourself, do you understand?"

Kendall nodded.

"Good. We all love you Champ. Just remember that and everything will be alright."

∞

Sylvia got home a few minutes later and found Kendall and Alex sitting together watching TV. "Everything okay?"

"Everything's fine," Alex told her.

"Does anyone need anything?"

Kendall shook his head.

"I think we're good. Why don't you sit down and watch... what is this again?" he asked Kendall.

"Rat Race."

"Watch Rat Race with us," Alex said.

"In a few minutes. I need to get some laundry started," she said, heading upstairs. Sylvia gathered the clothes from the hampers in the bedrooms and heard a phone ring. She saw Kendall's cell on the dresser, charging.

"Hello?" There was a click as the caller hung up. She shook her head and sat the phone back on the dresser. "Rude."

∞

Antonio got to the station. "Hey Boss," Sally said.

"Good morning. Have you had anything come through about this Chad Taylor yet?"

"Not yet, should be anytime now, though. How are things at home?"

"Kendall had a possible flashback last night, and Claudia came over to help us try and figure out what's triggering them."

"Is everyone alright?"

"Yeah, he was pretty tired after everything, but he was doing okay this morning."

"Did you guys come up with anything?"

"Jo brought up it could have been all the talk about this car and the schools being put on alert."

"That would make sense."

He nodded. "I'm going to leave a little early for lunch and meet them at Claudia's for his appointment."

"I'll make sure you get out of here on time," Sally told him.

"Thanks." He smiled, heading into his office.

A few minutes later, the phone rang and Johnson answered. He wrote a couple of things down and thanked the caller. "Sally, the clerk from the Best Western called to let you know that the guy with the blue Chevy checked back in last night."

"Really?"

Johnson nodded. "He checked the registry this morning and saw his name. He's driving a different car, though."

"Do we know what?"

"He saw him drive off in a tan SUV this morning."

"Okay, call the schools and let them know to be on the lookout for a tan SUV. Hopefully we'll know more soon," she said.

"Will do," he said, picking up the phone to notify the schools.

She knocked on Antonio's door. "Boss?"

"Yeah Sally?"

"Clerk from the Best Western called. Chad Taylor checked back in last night and is now driving a tan SUV. We're notifying the schools now."

"Okay, thanks Sally."

"I should have more on him before ten."

"Good. I'd like to know what this guy is up to," he said.

"We'll figure it out."

At about nine, Sally got an email regarding Chad Taylor. She scrolled through the information and found nothing terribly interesting. She printed everything out and put it in a file, still waiting to hear from her contact at the social security administration. She took what she had and knocked on Antonio's door.

"So, we got some info on Taylor. Fairly unremarkable. No arrests, not even juvie. Average grades in high school, which improved once he got to college. A graduate from Greenville College in Illinois. Photos ALL match, double checked that, just waiting on the info from social security to get an employment history."

"Then what the hell is he doing sniffing around our neighbourhoods?"

"No idea, but if we find him just sitting around again, I think we should do a Terry stop."

He nodded, "Let everyone know, but have them call in first."

"Will do, Boss."

∞

Sylvia started the laundry and went to watch the movie with Alex and Kendall. "So, I made an appointment for you with Joel Riggs tomorrow at one," she told Kendall.

"Who's that?"

"He's a physical therapist that Dr. Anna recommended."

"I don't want to go," Kendall groaned.

"I know, honey, but you're going to lose the use of your arm if we don't do something."

"She's right, it'll be okay," Alex said reassuringly.

"Tomorrow's just an evaluation. We'll talk to him about what we can do at home," she promised.

"Okay," Kendall said, unconvinced.

"Do you feel up to meeting your mom for lunch after her shift today?" Sylvia asked.

"I guess so. I think she said she gets off at two."

"I think so, but we'll call and double check." Sylvia smiled.

"Before we meet her, do you think we can stop by the arena?" Kendall asked.

"Sure. Why do you want to go to the arena?" she asked.

"James, Logan, and I want to get Carlos an early Christmas present, and that's where they sell the tickets."

"What are you getting him?" Sylvia asked.

"The Hulk is appearing at the Comic Con in St. Paul next weekend, and we wanted to get tickets for him and Papi."

"The Hulk?"

"He's a comic book hero."

She shook her head.

"There was a TV show about him a long time ago."

She looked at him.

"He's really big and muscly."

She looked at him, still confused.

"He's green."

"Oh, the GREEN one."

Kendall rolled his eyes.

"Carlos went as the Hulk three Halloweens ago," Kendall said.

"Is that when he went around posing and I had to stop him from smashing the pumpkins?"

"Yes."

"I thought it was a wrestler."

"No, he's one of the Avengers."

"Avengers?"

Kendall looked at Alex for help.

"Yes, we can stop at the arena." He laughed.

"Thank you," he said, relieved that someone understood what he was talking about.

"There's a condition though," Alex said.

"What?" Kendall asked suspiciously.

Alex looked at Sylvia, who nodded. "You have to go in with us to buy the tickets."

"What if I can't do it?"

"Honey, you handled the hospital just fine, and there were a lot more people there than there will be at the ticket office," Sylvia said.

"You can do this, Champ. If there are people there, we'll wait for it to clear out a bit," Alex told him.

'I don't have to go in alone, do I?"

"We'll be right by your side," Sylvia promised.

"Okay, I'll try."

"That's my boy." Sylvia smiled and kissed his cheek.

Alex checked the bag. "Time to flush the line and we'll pull the tube in a little while."

Kendall nodded and Alex pinched off the line and disconnected the tubes.

"I think what we'll do is have Sylvia pull the tube while I steady you," Alex said.

"Wait, you want ME to pull the tube?" Sylvia asked.

"Why not?"

"I've never done it before."

"So, I guess BOTH of you will be trying something new today." Alex smirked.

Kendall smiled at that.

"What if I hurt him?" she asked.

"You won't hurt him. You just pull it slow and steady. It's actually pretty easy."

"I guess it would have to be," she said, patting his cheek and heading to do another load of laundry.

He smiled and then realized what she had said. "Hey!"

Kendall laughed.

"Laugh it up, she's pulling the tube out of your nose, not mine," Alex pointed out.

∞

Half an hour later, Sylvia sat nervously in front of Kendall and Alex. "What do I do?"

"Pinch off the tube and then just ease it out slowly. Don't worry when he coughs, it's just because the tube is tickling the back of his throat, so it's normal."

She looked at Kendall and gave him a small smile. "Here we go," she said, pinching off the tube and began to slowly pull it. A minute later, the tube was out and Alex was rubbing Kendall's back to ease his coughing fit.

"Great job! We should work on teaching you on how to insert one," Alex told her.

"I don't think so."

"You'd make a great back-up," Alex said.

"No, and we need to get ready to go."

"You're no fun." He smirked.

"Can you NOT push it?" Kendall asked him.

"You're no fun either," Alex said.

"On second thought, I'll be happy to learn how to do it," Sylvia said.

"Really?"

"IF I can practice on you." She smiled.

"You know, I think we're good."

"I don't know. I kinda like her plan." Kendall smiled.

"You be quiet," Alex said.

Sylvia laughed at him.

"Honey, are you ready to go?" she asked Kendall.

"I need to grab my wallet," he said, going upstairs. He went into the bedroom, got his wallet from his backpack, and grabbed his phone from the dresser. He went back downstairs and the three of them left for Claudia's.

∞

"Hey Boss, time for you to get going," Sally told Antonio.

He looked up from his paperwork. "Thank God, I don't think I can take any more of this."

"Don't worry, you're almost caught up, and then you and John can hit the mean streets again."

Antonio laughed. "Mean streets? Have you been watching old movies again?"

"What can I say?"

"Alright, I'll see you in a couple of hours. Call me if you find out anything more on Chad Taylor," he said as he put on his jacket.

"Will do. I should be hearing something soon. They're a little slow because of the holiday last week, but I have everyone on alert for the SUV."

"Thanks Sally," he said, heading out the door.

∞

Antonio got to Claudia's first and went inside to wait. "So, how did the rest of last night go?" she asked.

"Alright, I guess. Kendall got up and went downstairs in the middle of the night because he couldn't sleep. Carlos found him after he woke up and realized he was gone. The two of them spent the night in my recliner."

"Did he say anything else?"

Antonio shook his head.

"How was he this morning?"

"In fairly good spirits. I woke him and Carlos up because Alex and I played a prank on the other two boys, and I didn't want him to wake up to someone screaming."

"What did you two do?"

Antonio told her about James and Logan sleeping on the couch and how he had woke them up.

"It is never dull at your house, is it?" She laughed.

"Rarely." He smiled.

"Everyone else is doing okay?"

He nodded, "I think so."

"Good. Jen is sweet and she seems like she's doing alright," Claudia said.

"She's doing much better, although she's still nervous about approaching Kendall about anything. I was glad she called to ask him about lunch, and when she showed up after Sylvia told her he was having a panic attack. I had her do what you did by taking his head and making him look at her, and he responded to her."

"That's a very good sign." Claudia smiled.

"I think so, too."

There was a knock at the door.. "I think the rest of the gang is here," Claudia said.

She opened the door. "Hello baby, how are you feeling this morning?"

"Okay." Kendall smiled.

"Good. Come on in out of the cold," she told them.

They went inside and a tan SUV drove past and turned the corner. He parked on the opposite side of the street so their cars were facing the opposite direction.

"How about Kendall and I get started and you all can sit in here next to the fire and have something warm to drink? How about you baby, do you want something to drink?" Claudia asked.

Kendall shook his head.

"Are you sure?"

He nodded. "My stomach's all sloshy."

"Sloshy?"

He nodded.

"We did the formula before coming here," Alex told her.

"Well, if you change your mind, just let me know." She smiled.

They went into the office and sat down. "So, are you really feeling better this morning?"

Kendall nodded.

"Can you tell me what happened?"

He sighed. "I don't know, I just remember hearing his voice and then it was like he was there. I tried to hide, but he found me, and then I couldn't breathe."

"Did you see him?"

"No."

"But you could hear him?"

"Yes."

"Could you feel him there?"

Kendall didn't say anything—he seemed lost in thought.

"Kendall?"

She snapped her fingers and he jumped. "Sorry baby, but you were kinda spacing out there for a minute."

"Sorry."

"Don't be sorry. Can you tell me what you were thinking about?"

"I don't know."

"Do you hear him every day?"

Kendall nodded.

"When?"

"Sometimes in the shower, sometimes at night. He was on the phone the other day."

"On the phone?"

Kendall nodded. "Sometimes I think I'm going crazy."

"Tell me about the phone."

"It rang and when I looked at it, it was just my number on it. Then he was talking to me and he laughed, and then the phone was dead."

"Do you have your phone with you?"

He nodded and pulled it out of his jacket.

She looked at the screen for received calls. "Is this your number?"

He looked at it and nodded.

"And it rings?"

"I think so."

"You think so?"

"Sometimes I don't know what's real and what I'm imagining," he sighed.

"Has anyone else heard the phone?"

"No."

"You never spoke to him on the phone, did you?"

Kendall shook his head.

"Have you told anyone else about this?"

He looked down and shook his head.

"Alright, anything else?"

"T-This morning after I showered I thought I saw him in the mirror behind me. Then it felt like he was touching me."

"Did he say anything?"

"He asked if I missed him."

"Did you tell anyone about this?"

"Papa M."

"Okay, that's good. I don't want you keeping all of this locked up inside."

"This way everyone knows I'm crazy," Kendall said.

"You're not crazy. I have a strong suspicion that you are suffering from PTSD, and that's why you hear him and have these flashbacks. It's also why you won't talk to anyone outside of your family or go out in public."

"I have to go out today."

"Why is that?"

"James, Logan and I want to get Carlos an early Christmas present. Mama G and Papa M said we could go get it, but I have to go in with them."

"Where are you going?"

"The arena. They sell the tickets there and we want to get Carlos and Papi tickets to Comic Con next weekend."

"Well, that shouldn't be too bad. It's not usually crowded there."

"I know," he sighed.

"You could always get him something else later on."

"He has to go! The Hulk is going to be there and he's Carlos' favourite," Kendall said.

"Well, then I guess you'll make that happen." She smiled.

Kendall nodded. "I'll try."

"I know you will, baby, and next week I think we're going to try going out someplace else."

"Where?"

"Someplace with not a lot of people, but enough to start getting you use to going out again. They're going to be baby steps, but we are going to take them."

He nodded and sighed.

"Relax, it's not like we're going to the mall or anything."

"Okay."

"Now, how about we work on that trigger word again?"

He nodded.

She got up and went across the hallway. "Antonio, do you want to help with the word exercise?"

He smiled and got up, following her into the office.

"Okay, same as last week," she said, pulling her chair so she was facing Kendall. "Are you ready?" she asked, holding up her finger.

He took a deep breath and nodded.

"Okay." She smiled and started moving her finger back and forth. "So I hear that James and his dad are both doing better?"

"Yes," Kendall said.

"Antonio told me that you actually asked to stay in the hospital with James?"

"Yes."

"That was a really sweet thing to do."

Kendall started shaking and Antonio pulled him close.

"My mama had to go into the hospital a couple of months ago for a heart evaluation. Her doctor was so sweet though. He made sure she had a private room."

Kendall squeezed his eyes shut. "No! I don't want to do this."

Antonio looked at Claudia as he pulled the teen closer. "Mijo, it's alright."

"No, no, no," he said, burying his face in Antonio's chest. He was close to hyperventilating.

"Baby, look at me," Claudia said.

Kendall didn't respond.

"Kendall, look at me," she said firmly. He opened his eyes and looked at her, but wouldn't let go of Antonio.

"What's wrong?"

"I don't know! I don't know! I don't know!"

"Alright, we're not going to do the exercise this time, but you need to tell me what's going on."

"I don't know. I just keep hearing him. He won't leave me alone, and I don't know how to make him go away."

"When you hear the word, what happens? Do you start seeing what happened then?"

Kendall was quiet for a moment. "No, it's more like everything here is the same but different."

"Different how?"

"It's l-like everything here is like you see it, but he's there in the corner or in the closet..."

"Or in the mirror?"

Kendall nodded.

"Mirror?" Antonio asked.

"I saw him standing behind me in the mirror this morning," Kendall said quietly.

"He's also been hearing him at night, in the shower, and on the phone," Claudia said.

"Mijo, why haven't you said anything?"

"I-I just..." Kendall said, not looking up.

"I know you don't want to hear this, baby, but I really think we need to get you on something very mild for your anxiety," Claudia said.

Kendall shook his head.

"Listen to me. I'm not talking about a medication like the one Graham prescribed. What I'm recommending is diphenhydramine. Do you know what that is?"

He shook his head.

"It's also called Benadryl and it's an antihistamine that's used mostly for allergies. Do you know anyone with allergies?" she asked.

He shook his head again.

"Well, they've also found it can help with anxiety in children. It's over the counter. You don't even need a prescription, just like with Tylenol or ibuprofen. However, we do want to check with your doctor to make sure you can take it and what the dosage would be. I actually take it when I go visit my cousin in Georgia because I'm allergic to the pollen down there."

"That might be a good idea. What do you think, Mijo?" Antonio asked.

Kendall shook his head again.

She took his hand. "Baby, I know you're scared of taking anything, but we need to do something. You can't keep going on like this. If it doesn't help or makes you feel strange, you just don't take it anymore. You need real rest and you need peace, and what we have tried so far hasn't helped. I think the only side effect is that you might get a little sleepy."

"We can try it a few times, and if you don't like it, we can stop, but I really think it's worth a try," Antonio told him.

"You know we only want what's best for you, don't you?" Claudia asked.

Kendall nodded.

"Then can we try this? Only for a week, and if it isn't helping, you don't have to take it anymore," she said.

Kendall looked at Antonio, who nodded.

"Okay," he said quietly.

"That's my baby. I'm going give Dr. Sharpe a call and see what she says, alright?"

He nodded.

Claudia got up and walked into the adjoining room. She returned a few minutes later. "Dr. Sharpe thinks it would be a good idea. She said to pick some up at the pharmacy and to start you out on 25mgs twice a day for now. We can bump it up or down a little if we need to."

"Thank you," Antonio said.

Claudia smiled. "We'll try the word exercise next time. Can you come on Friday?"

Kendall looked at Antonio, who nodded.

"Same time?" she asked.

"Okay," Kendall said.

"If you hear him, whether it's in the shower, when you're sleeping, whenever, I want you to tell someone, alright? In fact, I want you to write it down, the time, the place, what he

says, everything you can remember," she told him, getting up and going to her desk. She pulled out a small notebook and handed it to him.

"Can you do that for me?"

Kendall nodded as he took the notebook.

"It might do some good if you started keeping a journal as well."

"A journal?" he asked.

She nodded, "Just take a few minutes every day and write down what you're thinking or feeling, just for you. You can even type it up and just keep it on your computer."

"I don't have it."

"I'll get it back from Sally," Antonio told him.

"Okay."

"Are you doing a little better?" Claudia asked.

Kendall nodded.

"Are you going to meet your mama for lunch today?"

"I think so."

"Good, she's very nice. Eli says she's doing much better. Do you talk to her every day?"

"Not every day."

"What would you think about calling her every night just to say goodnight?"

"I can do that."

"Hopefully you'll both be feeling better soon and you can start spending more time together."

Kendall nodded.

"I think that's enough for today. You go run your errands and start the Benadryl today, alright?"

"Okay," he said.

"It's going to be alright. It's just going to take some time, and you have GOT to start communicating with us a little more."

"I know, I'll try," he said quietly.

"I have to say I am a little disappointed, though," she said.

"Why?"

"I haven't seen those dimples yet today."

He rolled his eyes and smiled.

"That's what I'm talking about," she said, kissing his cheek. "Now you go and have a good day."

"Okay."

"Come on." Antonio smiled, standing up. "Thank you, Claudia."

"I'll see you on Friday." She smiled, walking them out.

Sylvia and Alex saw them come out and stood up. "Everything alright?" Sylvia asked.

"Everything's going to be fine," Antonio said.

They walked out to the cars. "I have to get back to work, but I'll see you this evening," he told Kendall.

"Okay, bye Papi," he said, getting into Sylvia's car.

"Honey, we need to pick up some Benadryl for him. Claudia talked him into trying it. She called Anna and she said 25mgs twice a day to start," Antonio said.

"Benadryl? Isn't that an allergy medication?"

"Yes, but I guess they use it for anxiety in kids, and Anna said we can try it. He actually agreed to it."

"Okay, I'll stop and pick some up on the way home," she said, kissing him goodbye.

"Give him one when you get home. I'll tell you what happened, tonight."

She nodded. "We'll see you tonight, honey."

Antonio pulled out and headed back to the station while Sylvia, Alex, and Kendall headed for the arena.

They arrived about fifteen minutes later. "Okay, are you ready for this?" Sylvia asked, turning around to look at Kendall.

He looked out the window at the larger building and took a deep breath. "Yeah."

Sylvia and Alex got out and Sylvia opened Kendall's door and held her hand out for him.

He took it and got out.

Alex came around and they walked toward the building. They were almost to the door when Kendall stopped.

"Are you okay?" Alex asked.

Kendall took a deep breath and nodded. Sylvia put her arm around his shoulders and they got to the doors.

Alex opened them. "All clear." He smiled.

They walked in and the woman at the counter smiled. "Hi. How may I help you today?"

Alex smiled and took Kendall's arm. "Hello Tina, this young man need to purchase some tickets for a gift," Alex said, looking at her nametag.

"I can help you with that. What is it you were looking for?"

"It's okay, Champ, you can do this," Alex said quietly.

Kendall's heart was pounding in his chest and he closed his eyes for a few seconds and visualized Carlos getting to meet his favourite superhero. "I-I," he stammered.

"Maybe you could point to what you're looking for?" she asked softly.

He nodded and moved closer to the counter. She unfolded a flyer with a list of upcoming events and held it out to him. He smiled shyly and took it.

"It's alright, take your time, I'm in no hurry," she told him.

He nodded and read the flyer until he found the listing for Comic Con and went back up to the counter, pointing to the listing.

"Comic Con?" she asked.

He nodded.

"How many tickets would you like?"

He held up two fingers.

"Adult or juvenile?"

He looked at Alex. "What's the cut-off age for juvenile?" Alex asked.

"Sixteen."

Kendall held up one finger and then held it up again.

"One of each?" She smiled.

"P-Please," he said quietly.

She typed in the order and printed up the tickets. "That'll be forty dollars with tax and venue fees," she said.

Kendall got out his wallet and handed her two twenties.

"Perfect." She smiled.

She put the tickets into an envelope. "This is a gift?"

He nodded.

"For friends?"

He nodded again.

"Well, then I have something special you can give them," she said, opening a drawer. She pulled out two other tickets and showed them to him.

"They gave us ten of these to hand out. Most ticket sellers get twenty, but since we're so small, this is all they gave us."

He took them and read them. "What?"

"These are the equivalent of backstage passes. While everyone will get to see the Hulk, these will ensure that your friends get to meet him. They'll also get a t-shirt and an autographed photo," she told him.

"Really?"

"Really! I'm sure they will have blast. I went last year and got to meet the Invisible Girl/She's my favourite."

"Thank you." Kendall smiled and then looked down.

"You're welcome. You have a great day."

"Why don't you two go to the car? I want to ask about tickets to the Nutcracker," Sylvia said.

Alex shuddered.

"What? It's a wonderful story," Sylvia told him.

"Yeah, guys dancing around in tights is not my idea of fun."

"Just go," she said, handing him the car keys.

"Come on Champ, before she tries to talk us into going." Alex smirked, ushering the teen out the door.

Sylvia went up to the counter. "I don't know how you did that, but thank you."

"I'm sorry?" Tina asked.

"You got him to respond to you. Not very many people have been able to do that lately."

"I can imagine. I saw the interview on TV with that Graham guy and then read the article in the paper the next day. To answer your question, my 5-year-old is autistic, and when he's having a bad day, I have found by just taking it slow and letting him go at his own pace, he usually does alright in uncomfortable situations. We once spent half an hour in an aisle at the market because some rowdy kids scared him. When he finally calmed down and didn't feel threatened anymore, we finished our shopping."

Sylvia smiled. "I cannot thank you enough. He was so worried about coming here and you made it such a positive experience."

"My son and I have had the displeasure of meeting several so-called doctors, psychologists, psychiatrists, and teachers who were supposed to be there to help. I understand what you're going through, and I hope things get better."

"They already have. I just wish more people were as patient and understanding as you are," Sylvia said.

"People are afraid of what they don't understand and too impatient to learn. They also have a tendency to believe whatever they hear on television, instead of reasoning things out for themselves."

"Very true," Sylvia agreed.

"I hope his friends have fun. Especially since he braved coming down here to buy the tickets. I know this wasn't easy for him."

"No, it wasn't, but it was important to him. Thank you for the passes too, Carlos is going to be so happy to get to meet this Hulk person."

"Not a superhero fan?" Tina laughed.

"I really don't know very much about them. I guess I should try to learn a little more. I thought the Hulk was a wrestler," Sylvia admitted.

"It can get pretty confusing, but kids love them. My little one loves Wolverine from the X-Men," Tina told her.

Sylvia shook her head. "I guess I better start reading up on these things."

"There's actually a website that lists the top superheroes and it gives a brief synopsis on each one," Tina told her, writing down the name of the website.

Sylvia smiled and took the paper. "Thank you."

"Superheroes are important to kids. Sometimes by pretending to be them, they feel a little more empowered. I use to pretend to be the Invisible Girl because she could project a

SARA ALLEN STEWART ∞ THOSE YOU TRUST ∞ PAGE 674

force field to protect people. Whenever my friends or I were confronted my bullies, I imagined a force field and it gave me the courage to stand up to them."

"How did that work when they actually hit you, though?" Sylvia asked.

"Oddly enough, they never did. Maybe the confidence I felt shined through and they decided it wasn't worth it. Most bullies are cowards anyway and don't like it when someone stands up to them."

"Very true. Thank you again, and I hope your son continues doing well," Sylvia said, offering her hand.

Tina smiled back, taking Sylvia's hand. "Thank you, he's doing great. I hope your boy's recovery keeps moving forward. Let me know how they enjoyed the show."

"I will," Sylvia promised.

∞

Sally was going over the information she had received from the social security administration, and then tracked down his business license.

"Hey Boss, how was Kendall's appointment?" she asked without looking up.

"Difficult," he sighed.

"Why is that?"

"He's still having nightmares, and apparently he's been hearing Deesie a lot."

"He hasn't said anything?"

"He's told us a few times, but it's been happening every day now. He thought he saw him in the bathroom mirror this morning."

"Damn it."

"On the bright side, Claudia talked him into trying Benadryl to help with the anxiety. We're really hoping that helps."

"I'm surprised he agreed."

"He's exhausted and just wants it to stop. I think he trusts Claudia and that helps. We told him he can stop taking it if it isn't working or if it makes him feel strange."

"Good. I think I'll try and stop by and see him tomorrow," she said.

"I'm sure he'd like that." Antonio smiled. "What have you got there?"

"The info on Chad Taylor. He has a business license as an independent contractor, but it's confusing as to what it is he actually does."

"Why?"

"Most independent contractors state what their line of business is, but he doesn't. He has to be getting work solely by word of mouth."

"Now what?"

She started typing at her computer. "Now I call in a couple of favours."

"Do I want to know?"

"Probably not." She smiled.

"That's what I thought. Let me know what you find out."

"Will do, Boss."

About ten minutes later, Sally received a message from her contact at the FBI. She read through the material and then pulled up Taylor's collegiate file. "Son of a bitch," she cursed. She grabbed the paperwork and knocked on Antonio's door, opening it before he answered.

"Yes?"

"So, our little friend Taylor majored in audio/video technology at Greenville College."

"So?"

"Well, I decided to bypass the IRS, because it takes forever to get through all the red tape, and contacted my friend at the bureau. She ran a check for me, and guess what Taylor's independent contract specialty is?"

"What?"

"While none of the files come right and say so, I'm betting surveillance."

"Why do you think that?"

She handed the papers over to him. "While there are a few clients who hired him for weddings or special occasions, most of his clients are law firms from Illinois, Michigan, and Minnesota. Guess who's hired him three times in the last two years?"

"I don't need to guess," he said, standing up.

"Where are you going?" she asked, following him.

He didn't say anything but headed back to the main cell ward.

"Chief?" she asked, following him.

"What?"

"What are you doing?" she asked, picking up her pace so that she was in front of him. She turned to face him and then stopped.

"I'm going to have a little discussion with one of the prisoners," he said through gritted teeth.

"No you're not," she said, holding up a hand.

"Sally," he warned.

"Antonio, I'm serious. If you do anything, HE wins. Is that really what you want after everything that's happened? How do you think your family will deal with YOU being brought up on charges?"

"He..." Antonio growled.

"I know, but if you think about it, we could use this in our favour," she told him.

"How?"

"Taylor has taken great care in keeping his profession under wraps. The only reason WE know is because I have a friend who knows what's been going on and she has access to more information than we do."

"Go on," he said, folding his arms.

"He doesn't know that we know his identity, or that he's back in town, correct?"

"Yeah, so?"

"So, we know what he's driving and where he's staying, which means we can follow him. We know he's not a predator, so we pull the alerts from the schools. He's most likely trying to dig up something they can use in court, but there's nothing there. So we wait, we watch, and the minute he crosses the line, we haul his ass in for unlawful surveillance."

"Which won't do us any good if Graham's lawyer actually hired him."

"Wrong. While he might be licensed as a private contractor, he STILL needs an investigator's license to actually be able to gather evidence for them."

"Mike does that for us all the time," Antonio pointed out.

"Not exactly. He watches and reports if something illegal is happening and then testifies as a private citizen. If Taylor is actually following people and taking photos or recordings to be presented in court, that's illegal surveillance. Which makes everything he has inadmissible in court, and it means we can actually charge him if we catch him in the act. Which we will."

Antonio sighed. "Why do you have to make sense all the time? I just want to hit Graham ONCE!" He pouted.

"Aw, I'm sure you'll get your chance," she said, patting him on the back.

"Promise?" he said as they headed back to the office area.

"I promise. If anyone gets to hit him, it'll be you." She smiled.

Chapter 125~ A Day in the Park

Sally called the schools and daycares to let them know they were removing the predator alert. Then she got on the radio and let the patrols know that they were no longer to do a Terry stop, but to call in if they spotted the SUV and to give the location.

She decided to give Ryan a call and let him know what was going on. He was in court, so she left a message.

She knocked on Antonio's door. "I called off the alerts at the schools and let everyone know not to pull over the SUV, but to give us a location. I also left a message for Ryan to let him know what's going on and to see about getting a warrant for when we catch Taylor in the act."

"You seem pretty confident that we'll actually catch him."

She smiled. "We'll catch him, and when we do, whatever Manning has been planning as a defense will go straight down the toilet."

"Good, I'd like to see that," he said.

"I'll let you know when we find the SUV and what Ryan says," she said, turning to leave.

"Sally, about earlier..."

"Don't worry, you'll still be the one who gets to hit him," she promised.

"Thanks, but that's not what I meant." He laughed.

"I know what you meant."

"Thanks."

"You're welcome." She smiled as she closed the door.

∞

Sylvia stopped at the pharmacy and ran in to pick up some Benadryl.

Kendall was sitting in back, looking at the tickets and passes, smiling. "I can't believe they get to meet The Hulk."

"Pretty impressive," Alex said.

"I know. Carlos is going to be so surprised."

"Yes he is, but that's not what I'm talking about."

Kendall looked up. "What do you mean?"

"Do you even realize what you did? Not only did you go into a public place, but you also spoke to someone new. It was amazing!"

"I needed the tickets for Carlos."

Alex laughed. "I know, but you won't even talk to Dr. Anna. Who was the last stranger you actually spoke to?"

Kendall thought back. "Claudia."

"You did great today, Champ. I'm proud of you."

"Thanks, Papa M." Kendall smiled.

Sylvia got back to the car. "Okay, so you take one of these twice a day. We'll wait until we get home, because they might make you sleepy."

"Okay," Kendall sighed.

"It's okay, I have to take an antihistamine at the beginning of spring when I'm up here," Alex told him.

"I talked to your mom, and we're going to meet her at the park. I told her we'd stop at the deli and pick up some sandwiches. She's bringing some feed for the ducks. Does that sound good?" Sylvia asked.

"Sounds fine." Kendall smiled.

Sylvia pulled out and they drove to the little deli close to the park. She ran in and picked up the order she had called in earlier, and then they headed to the park.

They got to the parking area in the park and waited. Jen arrived a couple of minutes later and got into the backseat with Kendall.

"How are you feeling today, honey?" she asked, kissing his cheek.

"Okay." He smiled.

"Tell her what you did," Alex said.

"What did you do?"

"We bought Comic Con tickets for Carlos."

"Who bought them?" Alex asked.

"Logan, James and I." He smirked.

"Funny little guy," Alex said, shaking his head.

"Am I missing something?" Jen asked.

"Your son went up to the ticket counter and bought the tickets himself," Alex smiled.

"Honey, really?" she asked.

"Papa M was with me."

"Baby, I'm so proud of you!" she said, hugging him.

"Mom, all I did was hand her the money."

"That's not completely true. You spoke to her a couple of times," Alex pointed out.

"You spoke to her?" Jen said, kissing his cheek again.

"Mom, please!" Kendall said, turning red.

"Hey, did you know your ears get red first, and then it spreads to your cheeks?" Alex asked, grinning at Kendall.

"At least I'm not blue," Kendall retorted. "Or purple," he said under his breath.

"What was that?" Alex asked.

"Nothing." Kendall smiled.

"Why don't I believe you?" Alex asked.

"Not a clue," Kendall said.

"I'd be checking the shower heads from now on if I were you," Sylvia advised.

Alex looked back at Kendall. "You wouldn't do that to me, would you?"

"Who, me?" Kendall smiled innocently.

Alex raised his eyebrow. "Kendall, do you really want to be tossed in a tub of orange Kool-Aid? Because I'm pretty sure James will help me."

"I won't put purple Kool-Aid in the shower head," Kendall promised.

"Or any other colour," Alex insisted.

"Or any other colour of Kool-Aid," Kendall said.

"In the shower head," Alex continued.

"I solemnly swear I will not put any colour of Kool-Aid in the shower head. Happy?"

"Not really, but I'm satisfied for now," Alex said.

"Are you two finished?" Sylvia asked.

"He started it." Alex pouted.

"Did not!"

"Keep it up and you'll BOTH be getting a time out," Jen said.

"Yes ma'am," Alex said.

Kendall laughed at the look on his face.

"That goes for you, too," Jen said to him.

"Yes mom."

Alex looked back and smirked.

Jen arched her eyebrow. "Alexander Jebediah Mitchell, stop gloating."

"Jebediah?" Sylvia and Kendall both said.

Alex sighed as they both broke into laughter.

"Alright, shall we actually eat lunch?" Jen suggested.

"Good idea," Alex said, handing her a bag with two sandwiches.

Jen took one out and handed it to Kendall along with some napkins.

"We have ice tea, and I got an orange juice for you Kendall," Sylvia said, handing it back to him.

"Thank you," he said, taking the bottle.

"Let me open that for you, honey," Jen said, twisting the top of the bottle.

"Thanks mom." He smiled.

"How was your appointment today?"

"Okay," he said quietly.

"Claudia's very nice."

"She really is," Kendall said.

"Dr. Thorne, Eli, is very nice, too. I think you would like him."

"Good," he said with a smile.

They finished eating their lunch and Alex gathered the trash and ran it to the trash bin.

"I brought some duck feed in case we wanted to go feed the ducks," Jen said.

"Sure, we haven't done that in a while." Kendall smiled.

She handed him his gloves and zipped his coat the rest of the way up. "You really shouldn't be out in the cold, but a few minutes won't hurt as long as you're bundled up."

"Okay."

She pulled off her scarf and wrapped it around his neck.

"Mom," he complained.

"Yes?"

"Nothing," he said, rolling his eyes.

They got out and Jen got two small bags of feed from her trunk and handed one to Alex. They all walked the short distance to the small pond that was just east of the large pond used for ice-skating. The park employees kept the ice broken up so the ducks and other wildlife would have access to water at all times.

∞

Chad Taylor was parked half a block away, but with a clear view of the park. He was making notes in a small notebook. After the neighbour had confronted him in front of her house that day, he had returned the Chevy to Minneapolis and rented the SUV, complete with tinted side windows. As far as he could tell, no one had noticed him, and he meant to keep it that way. He took a few photos of the group, but nothing interesting was really happening.

"They don't let that kid out of their sight for very long. Good thing I like a challenge," he said to himself. His employer was very clear about what they needed, and so far, he had been unsuccessful at getting anything.

∞

Jen opened the bag of feed and Kendall scooped some out and sprinkled it around for the ducks who made a mad dash for the seed. They started flapping around and some got out of the water, risking getting close to the humans for the treats. Kendall put a small amount in his hand and squatted down. Two of the smaller ducks got close, and when the teen didn't move, started eating the seed out of his hand.

Jen held the bag down so that Kendall could get more of the seed. "So, I was thinking that maybe you, Katie and I could spend some time together this weekend. Just for a couple of hours?" Jen asked, biting her lower lip.

"Doing what?"

"I thought we could go home for a while. Maybe watch a movie or play a game?"

"That sounds good," Kendall said, smiling up at her.

"We can decide what we want to do later."

He nodded and watched as the ducks ate the last of the seed. He stood up and stretched, "It feels good being outside."

"I know you miss it. With any luck, your lungs will be clear soon and you can go out more often," Jen said, taking his arm. She rested her head on his shoulder and he smiled.

"Hopefully," he said.

The ducks were milling around their feet, squawking for more seed. Alex and Sylvia joined them and their bag of seed was soon empty as well.

"The poor little ones in the back didn't get any," Sylvia said, pointing at a group of younger ducks that had joined the others.

"We used up all of ours too," Kendall said.

"I have a couple of more bags in the car, but then we need to get you in out of the cold," Jen said as she turned to go to her car.

"I'll get them," Kendall offered.

"Are you sure?" she asked, handing him the keys.

"Yes, I think I can handle two little bags of duck feed."

Kendall walked back to the car and opened the trunk. His phone rang and he pulled it out of his pocket and looked at the caller ID. "Hey James. I got the tickets for Carlos, and you're not going to believe what the lady gave me for him!"

James didn't respond. "James, are you there?" Kendall looked at the screen and it showed they were still connected.

"James?"

"What were the rules again, sweetheart?"

"You're dead, you're not real."

"You're going to be very sorry when I find you!"

Kendall started shaking and dropped his phone.

Jen, Alex, and Sylvia were talking and trying to avoid angry nips from the more assertive ducks. "We're not going to need the seed at this rate," Alex said as two ducks started yanking on his bootlaces.

Jen looked back at her car and saw the trunk open. "He's getting it. Don't worry, we won't let the mean duckies eat you," she teased.

"Very funny, but they bite hard when they want something," Alex said.

Jen shook her head, still laughing at him. "Kendall, did you find it, honey?"

Alex yelped when one of the ducks grabbed ahold of his finger when he tried to brush it off his boot.

"They really like you," Sylvia told him.

"Ya think?"

Jen looked back at her car. "I better go help him," she said, heading back to her car. She reached the front of the car. "Kendall, did you find it?"

She walked around to the back and found him on the ground rocking, back and forth, his eyes squeezed shut. "Baby, what happened?" she asked softly.

"No more, no more," he whispered.

"Kendall?" she said, touching his shoulder.

"NO!" he screamed, pulling away.

Alex and Sylvia heard Kendall scream and ran for the car.

∞

Down the street, Chad Taylor was smiling as he snapped several photos of the scene.

Chapter 126~ Surveillance

James was on his way to final period when his phone vibrated. He looked at the caller ID. "Hey Kendall, what's up?"

There was no answer. "Hello? Hey buddy, are you there?"

The bell rang. "Stupid cell reception. Look, if you can hear me, I'm heading into class now. If you need me, call the office and have them page me. Otherwise I'll call you when I get out." James hung up and went into his class.

∞

Ryan got out of court at about two and called the station asking for Sally.

"Sally, DA Ryan is on line two for you," Johnson told her.

"Thanks." She smiled, picking up the phone.

"Hey Ryan, thanks for getting back to me so soon."

"Not a problem. What can I do for you?"

"We might be having an issue with Richard Graham's case, and I wanted to let you know that we're going to need a warrant for one Chad Taylor from Chicago."

"Alright, who is he and why do you need a warrant?"

"He's a private contractor who's been trying to keep his profession a secret. He graduated from Greenville College in Illinois about thirteen years ago, majoring in audio/video technology."

"And?"

"He's been hanging around our town, more specifically the Chief's neighbourhood for a couple of days. I went in civilian dress and asked him what he was doing, and he told me his car had overheated."

"Could that have been true?"

"Not likely. Sylvia Garcia had seen him around the neighbourhood at different times during the day. He was definitely watching their house. At first, we thought he might be casing the neighbourhood or be a possible predator—we even put all of the schools on alert. He's been staying out at the Best Western by the airport, and after I spoke with him, he traded his sedan in for an SUV of some kind. Since we didn't have enough for a warrant, I sent his photo through the DMV and got a hit on his name. I did some more checking and found that he has worked for quite a few law firms, including the one Graham just hired. Given his vocation, it's my belief he's here doing surveillance for Graham's attorney, who has the reputation of scaring off witnesses," she told him.

"Plays dirty, huh?"

"Absolutely."

"Is this Taylor licensed?"

"Only as a private contractor. There's no record of him having an investigator's license."

"Alright, let me know when you need the warrant and I'll get it pushed through."

"Thanks Ryan. What are the chances that anything he's gathered will be admissible?"

"If he's not a licensed investigator, none."

"Good. Thanks again, Ryan. I'll give you a call once we have something."

"Alright, I'll let my office know in case I'm out."

"Okay, talk to you later," Sally said, hanging up.

She got up and knocked on Antonio's door. "Hey Boss, everything's set up with Ryan. Once we catch Taylor doing something he shouldn't be doing, he'll push the warrant through."

"Good. Thanks Sally." Antonio smiled.

"Also, I double checked, and nothing Taylor has recorded or noted will be admissible in court."

"That's very good news. Now hopefully we can find him and catch him in the act."

"I don't think that's going to be a problem. If no one spots him in town today, then we'll start tailing him in the morning. I have patrols driving by the motel every hour or so, and once he's back, I'll put a permanent unmarked patrol unit on him," she said.

"Sounds good. Make sure someone lets me know when they find him," Antonio said.

"Will do, Boss."

∞

Jen knelt down by Kendall. "Honey, it's alright. Can you tell me what happened?"

He just continued rocking back and forth, his eyes closed tightly.

Sylvia and Alex came around the car. "What happened?" Alex asked.

"I don't know, he was like this when I got here. He screamed when I touched him, so I stopped," Jen said.

"Hey Champ. What's going on?" Alex asked quietly as he moved to the other side of the teen.

Kendall was shaking, and the minute Alex went to touch him, he screamed. His eyes flew open and he tried to move away. Alex grabbed him and wrapped his arms around him, holding on tight.

"Get the door, we've got to get him out of the cold," Alex said.

Jen nodded, unlocked the back door, and held it open.

Kendall was still fighting Alex, who nearly lost his hold, so he tightened his grasp. "Sylvia, call Claudia, tell her what's going on and that we're heading back to her place."

Sylvia nodded and pulled out her cell. She saw Kendall's glove and phone on the ground and picked them up as she dialed. "Claudia, it's Sylvia. Kendall is having a panic attack and we can't calm him down. We're at the park, so we're heading to your place now."

"I'll be waiting," Claudia told her.

"How can someone his size and who's been so sick, be so strong?" Alex said as he tried to pick up the struggling teen. He finally managed to get him into the backseat and Jen closed the door.

"Kendall, you're safe! You need to calm down," Alex said firmly.

"NO! Don't touch me, let me go!" the boy shrieked.

Jen got in the driver's seat.

"Go slow, I can't get a seatbelt on him," Alex told her as he wrapped his arms and legs around Kendall, securing his hold on him.

She nodded, took a deep breath, and pulled out.

Sylvia got into her car and followed.

By the time they reached Claudia's, Kendall had stopped struggling and was just lying in Alex's arms, unresponsive. Alex carried him up the walkway and Claudia opened the door and pointed to the couch by the fire. Alex carried Kendall in and laid him down on it.

"What happened?" Claudia asked as she started to pull off Kendall's boots.

"I don't know. We had lunch and then went to feed the ducks. We ran out of seed, so he went back to the car to get the other bags. I looked over and the trunk was open, but I thought he was just having trouble finding them. I went to help and found him on the ground. He was saying something like, 'no more,' and when I touched him, he screamed," Jen said.

"Did he say anything else?"

"Yeah, after I got ahold of him, he started screaming 'don't touch me, let me go.' He was fighting me almost the whole way here, and then he just stopped," Alex told her as he pulled off Kendall's jacket.

Claudia grabbed a blanket and covered Kendall as she sat next to him. "Can you dim the lights?" Claudia asked, pointing to the switch.

Sylvia nodded and turned the knob halfway. "I'm going to call Jo and have her pick Katie up after school."

"Thank you. What about the other boys?" Jen asked.

"They have practice today, so we don't need to worry about that until five," Sylvia told her.

Jen nodded.

Claudia was sitting, quietly watching Kendall. She brushed back his bangs. "What's going on with you, baby?" she asked quietly.

Sylvia went into the hallway and called Joanna.

"Hello."

"Jo, can you do me a favour and pick Katie up from school? She gets out in about fifteen minutes."

"Sure. What's going on?"

"Kendall had a panic attack while we were having lunch with Jen at the park. We brought him back to Claudia's, and we're waiting for him to come around."

"No problem, I can get the boys after practice too," Joanna told her as she grabbed her coat.

"That might help," Sylvia said.

"I'll just take Katie to run a few errands with me, and then I'll get the boys and take them to your house."

"Thanks Jo, we'll see you there."

Sylvia took a deep breath and dialed Antonio's cell.

"Hi honey, what's up?"

"We're back at Claudia's. Kendall had a panic attack at the park and hasn't come around yet."

"I'm on my way," he said, grabbing his jacket.

He headed towards the front door. "Sally, call me if you hear anything."

"Is everything alright?"

"I don't know yet. I'll call you later," he said as he left.

∞

Chad Taylor watched as the man fought to get the teen into the car, snapping a few photos of them. He watched as they finally got him into the back of the car and as they pulled out. He saw the other woman get into the second car and follow them. He waited a few minutes before pulling out and driving in the direction they had taken.

∞

Last bell rang and James dialed Kendall's cell as he walked to his locker. It rang six times and went to voicemail. "Hey buddy, just returning your call. Reception must have been bad earlier. Logan, Carlos and I are going to be heading to practice in a few minutes. If you call back and I don't answer, just leave a message and I'll call when we're done. If you need me before then, call the rink and have them come and get me. See you soon."

∞

Antonio got to Claudia's a few minutes after leaving the station. He ran up the walkway and knocked on the door and Sylvia answered.

"How is he?" he asked, kissing her cheek.

"Still out," she said as they walked into the living room.

"What happened?"

Sylvia and Alex caught him up on what had happened.

Claudia was still sitting next to Kendall, monitoring his breathing and every little sound or movement he made. "I think he's going to sleep for a while. Why don't I go make us

some tea? Jen, why don't come with me and we can have that chat now?" Claudia said, getting up.

Jen smiled and nodded.

Antonio went and sat next to Kendall. "I don't understand this. He should be getting better, not worse. These attacks have to have something in common. Maybe we need to sit down and write it all out, mark the similarities, and see if we can find the trigger," Antonio said.

Alex nodded. "That might help. They can't possibly be as random as they seem."

"I hope not," Antonio said quietly.

∞

Taylor had followed and parked down the street. He watched Alex carry Kendall inside, took a couple more photos, and then he pulled out and drove away.

Two blocks back, Bennet was sitting in his own car, watching the SUV. He had been on his way home when he saw the vehicle driving back towards downtown and followed it. It wasn't until the SUV parked that he realized they were a few blocks down from Claudia Jenkin's place.

He saw the SUV pull away after a few minutes and followed it. He got on the phone and dialed the station and Johnson answered. "Johnson I need to speak to Sally or the chief."

"Chief just ran out, but here's Sally."

"What's up, John?" Sally asked.

"That SUV we've been looking for just left Claudia Jenkin's place. It's an Escalade, Minnesota license 333, shark, hammer, cat. I'm still behind him, but I saw Sylvia and Jen's cars in front of Claudia's."

"That must be where he went," Sally said.

"Who?"

"Antonio got a call and took off. He said he'd call and let me know what happened later."

"Okay, well I'm going to go ahead and follow this guy until we can get a patrol on him."

"Which direction is he headed?"

"He's heading north on Spencer Street."

"Sounds like he might be heading back to the motel. I'll just send a unit there. If he turns off before then, let me know and I'll have someone intercept."

"Will do," Bennet said, hanging up.

Chapter 127~ Phone Calls

Kendall felt chilled to the bone as he tried to block Deesie's voice from his mind. He hugged his knees to his chest, trying to make himself smaller. He heard someone calling to him in a gentle voice, but Deesie's voice broke through, overwhelming his mind. Someone touched him and he heard himself scream. The gentle voice broke through for a split second, and then it was gone.

Another voice got through, calling to him. This one was strong and caring. He sensed movement and tried to back away in a panic. Suddenly, strong arms enveloped him and he heard himself scream again. He struggled against them and was almost free when they caught ahold of him, holding him tight. He felt himself being half pulled, half carried, and then he heard a door close and he realized they were moving. He continued to struggle and screamed again, begging them to let him go.

The second voice was telling him he was safe, but he could sense that was something wrong. He just wanted to hide, but they wouldn't let him go. His chest hurt and it was getting harder to breathe. He felt himself getting weaker and finally gave into the darkness.

∞

Claudia pulled out the tray and set some mugs on it. She squeezed Jen's hand. "How are you doing?"

"I don't know. We were having such a wonderful time and now this. My little boy is so scared, and I don't know how to help him."

"Fear is a hard thing to understand, even harder to overcome. All we can do is be there and let him know that he's safe and loved," Claudia told her.

"I know...I'm not used to seeing him afraid. He's never been one to hide under the covers because there were monsters under the bed or in the closet. Kendall has always the one who is there comforting Katie when she's afraid. He tells her stories or sings her silly little songs until she falls asleep. He even takes care of me when I have a bad day or if he senses I'm missing his dad. He makes me sit down to rest and brings me tea. He'll put in an old comedy and sit and watch it with me, even if he's seen it a hundred times," Jen said quietly.

"Unfortunately the real monsters are the ones who walk among us in the daylight, wearing false smiles, and saying all the right words. We never know they're there until it's too late," Claudia told her.

"It's not fair!" Jen said angrily, slamming her hand down on the counter.

Claudia watched her for a moment. "No it's not."

"I had just asked him about spending some time together this weekend. Eli recommended trying some one-on-one time with the kids. I thought we could go home for a couple of hours, watch a movie, or play a game. Just to try and get used to being with one another again as a family with no pressure."

"That's a great idea. What did he say?"

"He said it sounded good and he smiled at me. He let me hold his arm and we watched the ducks for a few minutes," she said, her voice breaking.

"Can you tell me exactly what happened leading up to the panic attack?" Claudia asked.

"We'd finished the bags of seed and he offered to go back to the car and get the others. Several ducks were attacking Alex, and we were so busy laughing at him, that I didn't realize he

hadn't come back right away. I looked over and the trunk was open, so I thought he was just having a hard time finding it, so I went to help."

"That's when you found him on the ground?"

Jen nodded.

"Was there anyone else around?"

"No, I don't think he would have volunteered to go back to the car if there had been."

"You didn't hear anything?"

"No."

Claudia put the kettle on the tray. "Alright, we're going to figure this out. Something is setting off triggers and we need to find out how and why."

Claudia took the tray into the living room and set it on the table. She looked over at Kendall. "Any sign he's waking up yet?"

Antonio shook his head. "Not yet. Why the hell does this keep happening?"

"Something's triggering them and we're going to figure out what," Claudia said. She went into her office and grabbed a notebook and pen. "Alright, let's track the last few attacks and see what we can come up with."

"Where do we start?" Jen asked.

"Let's start from today and move backward," Antonio suggested.

Claudia started making notes. "Okay, let's write down the events of the days that led up to the attacks. Today, he saw Deesie in the mirror and heard him. Then he started to panic when we worked on the word exercise. What happened after that?"

"We went the arena where he did remarkably well. He even spoke to the lady at the ticket counter," Sylvia said.

"He what?" Antonio asked.

"She was amazing with him! She let him go slowly and point at what he wanted. He said 'please' and thanked her when she found what he was looking for."

"Did he seem stressed by it?" Claudia asked.

"No, he was excited and it didn't even seem to register what he'd done," Alex told her.

Claudia nodded and wrote it down on the list. "What next?"

"We went to the pharmacy and then the deli. He stayed in the car with Alex," Sylvia said.

Claudia looked at Alex. "He was fine, seemed happy, and after I pointed out what he'd done at the arena, even a little proud of himself."

"Then we met Jen at the park and ate lunch in the car. He and Alex were even joking around. When we finished, we went to the small pond and fed the ducks," Sylvia said.

"Then you ran out of seed and that's when he went back to the car?" Claudia asked.

Jen nodded.

"Last night he had another one," Claudia said, writing down everything they had talked about the night before.

"Before that was Saturday, after he fell asleep with the feeding tube in," Alex said.

"What happened up until then? Do you think it was just the feeding tube?"

Antonio nodded. "He said he freaked out when he woke up and felt something in his throat."

"That's understandable. What happened before that?"

"Well, he wasn't very happy about it when we first put it in, but he calmed down after a few minutes," Alex told her.

"Before that?"

"The boys watched a hockey game, and earlier that morning is when some people were turned blue," Sylvia said.

"He instigated that prank, didn't he?" Claudia asked.

"Yes, and I kinda, sort of, maybe, helped him just a little." Sylvia smiled.

"That's something he would have done before?"

"Absolutely," Jen said.

"The one before that?" Claudia asked.

"The steakhouse on Friday when that stupid woman went after him," Antonio said.

"You said he was half asleep?"

Antonio nodded.

"He didn't have one on Thursday, but he lost his temper with the other kids?" Claudia asked.

Antonio nodded. "Not badly, but they kind of crossed the line and had it coming."

"But it was something he might have let slide before?"

"He probably would have handled it differently," Antonio said.

"The rest of the day went well?"

"I did find him and Carlos crying in the den after dinner," Antonio told her.

"Why were they crying?" Jen asked.

"They were watching the home movie of the last Thanksgiving we had with Will. They didn't know I saw them. I just closed the door and let them cry it out," Antonio said quietly.

"It was probably good for them," Claudia told him.

"Alright, so what do we have?" Antonio asked.

"I really don't know. It seems like something different triggers it every time," Claudia said, going over her notes.

"Or, we just don't know everything that happened. He was alone today, yesterday, and last Wednesday when he had the flashback," Antonio said.

"He was sleeping when he had the panic attacks on Friday and Saturday," Jen said.

"Okay, let's try this another way. Let's list all of the things we KNOW set it off," Claudia said.

"That word," Jen said.

Claudia smiled and wrote it down. "Someone touching him unexpectedly, waking him suddenly, strangers, public places, certain foods. Then there are the times he dreams about Deesie or what happened."

"The fact that he sees or hears him all the time now," Antonio said.

"When did that start?" Jen asked.

"I don't know. He said this morning it's like Deesie is always there. He hears him in the shower, when he's sleeping or trying to, on the phone. He said he saw him in the bathroom mirror this morning," Antonio told her.

Claudia nodded. "That's when he agreed to try the Benadryl to help with the anxiety."

"Wait, did you say he hears him on the phone?" Sylvia asked.

Antonio nodded. "Why?"

"At the park, I found his phone on the ground with one of his gloves."

"It might have fallen out of his pocket when I tried to get him into the car," Alex said.

Sylvia shook her head. "It was already lying there. This morning when I was getting the laundry from the bedrooms, his phone rang. I answered it and whoever it was didn't say anything, just hung up. Last night when I was looking for him, I found his phone under the bed, as if it had been dropped. I called Antonio with it when I couldn't get Kendall to wake up. Oh God, what if it's another bully doing this to him?"

"Where's his phone now?" Antonio asked.

"In my car," Sylvia said, getting up and heading for the door. She returned a couple of minutes later and handed the phone to Antonio.

Antonio looked at it and scrolled down. "He has a message from James at about 3:00, James called him 2:37, there are no other numbers."

"That doesn't make sense. Who called him this morning?" Sylvia asked.

"None of this makes sense," Antonio said, scrolling through incoming and outgoing calls.

"What time was the call this morning?" Antonio asked.

"Between 8:30 and 9:00."

He scrolled back through incoming calls and shook his head. "Nothing, it only shows his number."

"Try calling his number from his phone," Claudia suggested.

Antonio punched in Kendall's number. "It goes to voicemail options."

"What does the incoming number show?"

Antonio looked at the screen. "Nothing."

"Try hitting redial—does it show a number then?"

He hit redial. "It shows his number."

"You don't really think he's calling himself and hearing Deesie?" Jen asked.

"I'm just trying to eliminate possibilities," Claudia explained.

"That wouldn't make sense though, because he was downstairs with the feeding tube in when his phone rang this morning," Sylvia pointed out.

"You didn't hear his phone ring at the park?" Antonio asked.

"No, we couldn't have heard it over the ducks anyway," Jen told him.

Antonio pulled his own phone out and scrolled down. "It shows that I received a call from his phone last night, and that's the only outgoing call there is, except for Alex and Mike's numbers from over a week ago."

He dialed Kendall's number from his phone. Kendall's phone rang and he looked at the screen. "My number shows up on his, but that's the only one besides James' and then his own."

Antonio dialed another number on his cell. "Sally, I need you to track any and all numbers going to and from Kendall's cell."

"What's going on, Boss?"

"I don't know, but we need to find out as soon as possible. Are you going to need his phone there?"

"Not right away, I can just pull his call records. What are we looking for?"

Antonio explained about the discrepancies with the call logs.

"That doesn't make any sense."

"Any ideas?" he asked.

"Not a one, but I'll figure it out," she promised.

Chapter 128~ Handling It

Joanna and Katie had run a couple of errands, stopped for a snack, and arrived at the ice rink half an hour before practice ended. Katie had been upset when she'd first been told about Kendall, but calmed down once Jo reassured her that he was at Claudia's and would be fine. They sat up in the bleachers and watched the boys.

Carlos saw them and stopped in his tracks.

"Carlos, what are you doing?" James yelled as he narrowly missed hitting his friend.

"Something's wrong! Papi was going to pick us up," he said, pointing in Joanna's direction.

"Maybe she wants to see Logan again."

"Why is Katie here?" Carlos asked as he skated towards the bleachers.

Jo saw the boys heading in her direction and took a deep breath. "Stay here, honey," she told Katie.

"Hi Mama M. Is everything okay?" Carlos asked.

"Don't you guys still have practice time left?" She smiled.

"What happened?" James asked.

"What, I can't pick my boys up from practice every now and then?"

They both looked at her, and a moment later Logan joined them. "Hey mom, what's going on?"

"Why do you boys think there's anything going on?"

Logan looked at Carlos and James, and then back at his mother.

"Alright, Kendall had another panic attack at the park and they took him back to Claudia's to try and figure out what's going on."

"Is he okay?" James asked.

"Honey, he'll be fine, they might even be home before you're done here. Now go finish practice before the coach makes you do extra skating drills."

"You're sure everything is okay?" Logan asked.

She smiled and nodded. "Now go."

∞

Kendall could hear voices speaking in soft murmurs around him. They were muted, as if he was listening through water. He tried to focus on them, but it was so hard and his head hurt so badly. He was cold and everything ached. He tried to stretch out and felt someone next to him and pulled away, trying to curl up.

Antonio felt Kendall shift slightly. "Mijo, can you wake up?"

Kendall started shaking and tried to push himself closer into the back of the couch.

"Kendall, it's alright. We need you to wake up now," Antonio said, brushing back his bangs.

Kendall whimpered and his breathing became erratic.

"You keep forgetting rule number four!"

"NO! Leave me alone! Don't touch me, it hurts!" he screamed, trying to push Antonio away.

Antonio grabbed ahold of him before he pushed himself off the couch. He held him tightly to him. "It's alright, Mijo. It's Papi. I won't let him hurt you. You're safe here with us," Antonio whispered as he rocked the teen gently.

"No, no, no," the boy sobbed.

"Shhh," Antonio said soothingly.

Jen sat next to Sylvia, who put her arms around her—both had tears in their eyes.

Alex watched the two and started shaking with anger. His face was red and he seriously thought he might lose it.

Claudia noticed and took his arm. "Let's gets some air."

He let her led him outside. "Take some deep breaths," she instructed.

He did as she said and then sat down on the porch. "You haven't seen that before, have you?"

"Not like that, not that bad," he said in a shaky voice.

"It's not an easy thing."

"He's reliving what the son of a bitch did to him, isn't he?"

"I think so," she said quietly.

"How do they do it? How do they stay so calm? I just want to hit something!"

"From what I hear, Antonio did hit something. Sally said he put his hand through a wall at the station when Graham made the mistake of crossing him."

"That sounds like a good idea," Alex said, standing up. He walked over to the large willow tree in the front yard and punched it.

"Alex! You're going to hurt yourself!" Claudia said, grabbing his arm before he could hit it again. She took his hand and saw the knuckles were split and bleeding. She wrapped her scarf around his hand and led him back to the porch, sitting next to him.

He looked at her, his eyes filled with tears. "I've known that little boy for over half his life, and the first thing that comes into my head is it could have been MY son! How selfish is that? I love that kid like he's my own, but all I can think about... is what if it had been Logan? How am I supposed to help Kendall when I'm thinking like that?"

She hugged him. "Of course you're going to think of Logan, how could you not? It's what any and every good parent would do. Do you think Carlos and James' parents haven't thought the exact same thing? Everyone has had their moments of fear and regret, it's natural."

"Well it feels wrong!"

"Of course it does, because you're a good person, and the fact that you feel this way proves it. Antonio has had years of training and there are times he has difficulty handling this. He has had his moments of anger, fear, guilt, and just plain hatred for the people who have caused all of this trouble. Hell, when Kendall first told me what happened to him, I sat there and cried like a baby, and I've been doing this for nearly twenty years now."

"How do you do it?" he asked.

She sighed, "I think about the alternative. What if these amazing children had no one who cared? No one they could just talk to. When I was in college, the younger brother of a friend of mine was having some trouble. He was sixteen, no father and a mama who worked all the time. He made a lot of wrong choices. She tried to help him, but being over 500 miles away wasn't easy. They found a psychologist who said she could help him. She said all the right things at the initial consultation. She helped get him on anti-depressants, and for a while, he seemed like he was doing better. Turns out, she was a lot like Graham, like too many so-called psychologists out there. Just treated the symptoms, not the underlying problems."

Alex shook his head. "Poor kid, that had to have been hard."

"I went home with my friend over spring break and that child was so confused by everything. On one hand, they're giving him a mood-altering drug, but not actually looking for the reasons as to WHY he was feeling the way he did. He didn't understand why he would feel such deep sorrow or have moments of intense rage. The psychologist never once spoke to him about why he was having those feelings. He and I talked a lot that week, and I found out some

older kids had been bullying him. He was feeling guilty about his dad leaving, even though he was only two at the time. Then I discovered the biggest issue was that he was dyslexic. His classrooms had over thirty-five kids per class and not one teacher caught it in all that time."

"No wonder he was having problems. What happened to him?" Alex asked.

"I spoke with my friend and we found him someone to help him with his reading. We convinced his mama to start telling him about his dad, and called in a favour with a couple of REALLY big football players from the school to deal with the bullies. He's a teacher at an elementary school in Milwaukee, working with special needs children." She smiled.

"So he was your first case?"

"Unofficially, and it helped me to decide what direction I wanted to take in life."

"I'm glad you took that direction," he told her.

"So am I." She smiled. "Now, are you feeling any better?"

He nodded.

"Good, because I'd really hate it if you hurt my tree. I like that tree. I was thinking of hanging one of those old-fashioned plank swings from it this spring."

He shook his head and smiled. "I promise I won't hurt your tree again."

"Well, we should probably get your hand cleaned up. If you ask me, it looks like my tree won that round," she said, examining his hand.

"Probably. I just need another few minutes, though."

"Alright, I'm telling you now though, it's gonna sting when I clean it."

"You know, I think it feels just fine," he said, trying to flex his fingers.

"Mmhmm, we'll see about that."

∞

Antonio sat, holding Kendall tightly until he stopped struggling. He eased his hold on the boy and sat back, pulling him over so he was resting against him. He had his arm around his shoulders, and Kendall's head was resting on his chest. He was running his fingers through his hair and he could feel him relax as the boy listened to his heartbeat.

Kendall was still shivering, so Jen grabbed the blanket and gently laid it over him. "We should go check on Alex," Jen said quietly.

Antonio nodded, so Jen and Sylvia got their coats and went outside. They found Alex and Claudia sitting quietly on the steps. Jen sat next to Alex and put her arm around him. "How are you doing?"

He shook his head. "Wondering why it is you have to ask me that. I'm sorry. I was kinda losing it in there."

"You don't have to tell me. I was the one who ended up in the hospital, remember?"

"Yes, but he's your child. I should be..."

"Stronger, more stoic, better able to handle it because you're an adult? Been there, it didn't work for me either. The fact is this is just hard, some days impossibly so. We can go from having a nice day, to a complete breakdown in a matter of moments. I'm not just talking about Kendall breaking down either."

"She's right," Claudia said.

"So what do we do?" he asked.

"Right now, we let Antonio handle this. Kendall trusts him the most and Antonio knows what he went through. It bothered me at first, a lot, that I couldn't help him when he has these attacks, but Eli has helped me realize how selfish that is. Believe me, it is not easy giving up control to someone else. Not even to someone I love and trust, but it's what's best for my son right now. They went through something together that I can't even begin to understand, and I'm so grateful that Antonio was there, that he's here now. I'm grateful for ALL of you," Jen said, taking his arm.

She looked at the scarf wrapped around his hand. "What happened?"

"A tree jumped out and hit him." Claudia smiled.

∞

Antonio's cell vibrated and he shifted slightly to get it from his pocket. "Garcia."

Kendall stirred a little and then curled up closer to Antonio.

"Hey Boss, I'm going to need Kendall's phone. The call log is making absolutely no sense. I need the phone to try and figure out why it's doing what it's doing," Sally said.

"Okay, I'll get it to you as soon as I can."

"Are you still at Claudia's?"

"Yeah, Kendall's still out of it."

"Do you want me to swing by and pick it up? It might be faster that way."

"Why don't I have Sylvia drop it off? It'll be even faster that way."

"Okay, I'll be waiting. Also, Taylor is back at the motel. John saw him parked near Claudia's and followed him. I have an unmarked car watching the motel, and they'll follow Taylor wherever he goes."

"Why was he watching Claudia's?"

"I don't know, but John saw your cars there when he drove past."

"Son of a... Alright, keep me informed."

"Will do, Boss."

He hung up, looked down at Kendall, and sighed. "No, no Mijo," he said as he pulled the boy's hand away from his mouth. He looked at the tip of Kendall's thumb, which was bleeding from where he had been biting the nail.

He called Sylvia's cell. "Honey, Kendall's sleeping, so I didn't want to disturb him. I need you to run his phone down to the station. Sally's waiting."

"Okay, I'll be right in."

"We're going to find out what's going on," Antonio promised his sleeping godson.

Chapter 129~ Getting Close to an Answer

Sally was on her computer studying the call log for Kendall's cell. Several incoming calls from his own number and she couldn't figure out HOW. She had the same cell service and tried calling her own number from her cell, but it went straight to her mailbox. She checked the outgoing call list and his number wasn't on it, although it did show up on redial. She called the customer service number for her cell service and they told her there was no way to call your own cell and have it go through.

"Damn it, Taylor has to be behind this somehow," she mumbled.

Sylvia arrived a few minutes later with Kendall's phone. "Thanks Sylvia, I appreciate you getting it here so fast."

"Anything to help figure out what's going on. Any ideas?"

Sally shook her head. "Not really. I've tried a couple of things, but they didn't work."

She scrolled down Kendall's call lists and double-checked them against the call log on her computer. "Everything matches, this doesn't make any sense. Antonio said you answered Kendall's phone this morning and whoever it was hung up?"

"Yes," Sylvia said, sitting in the chair next to Sally.

"What time?"

"Sometime between 8:30 and 9:00."

Sally scrolled down the list and found the call. "8:51."

"That sounds right."

"They didn't say anything?"

"No, after a few seconds they hung up. I remember thinking how rude people can be."

"Next incoming call was from James at 2:37 and then another at 3:00 when he left a message," Sally said. She picked up Kendall's phone, hooked up a USB cord, and plugged it into her computer.

She downloaded the message and played it. "Hey buddy, just returning your call, reception must have been bad earlier. We're going to be heading to practice in a few minutes. If you call back and I don't answer, just leave a message and I'll call when we're done. If you need me before then, call the rink and have them come and get me. See you soon."

"Did he say he was returning Kendall's call?" Sally asked.

Sylvia nodded.

Sally pulled up the call log again and then checked Kendall's phone. "There's no record of him calling James. Where's James now?"

"The boys are at hockey practice."

"Do you think he'd allow me access to his phone?"

"Of course he would. Do you want me to run and get it?"

Sally shook her head. "I can access it from here, I just need permission."

"He'll give it to you."

"I want this to be completely legal before I do anything. I don't want them to be able to throw it out. Can you call Brooke or his dad and get permission?"

Sylvia nodded and dialed Brooke's number. "Brooke Diamond."

"Brooke, Sally needs your permission to access James' phone records."

"Why, what's going on?"

"Something's going on with the boys' phones. Kendall's been getting calls from his own number and we think someone is deliberately doing this."

"Of course, whatever you need," Brooke said.

Sylvia handed Sally her phone. "Hi Brooke, I just need confirmation that you're giving me permission to access James' phone and call logs."

"Absolutely. Is there anything I can do?"

"Not right now, but I'll let you know. Thanks Brooke."

She handed the phone back to Sylvia and typed in the request for James' call logs. As soon as they came up, she scrolled through them. "Call received from Kendall's number at 1:55, and it lasted for a little over thirty seconds. Where were you guys at that time?"

"We were in the car on our way to meet Jen."

"He didn't call anyone?"

"No."

Sally went over the boys' call logs again. "This shows that James only called Kendall once, at 3:00 when he left the message. Kendall's records show James called him at 2:37 and that call lasted for almost a minute. Where were you guys then?"

"In the park. We'd finished eating and were feeding the ducks."

"Could that have been when Kendall went back to the car?"

"It's very possible," Sylvia said.

Sally went through the call logs again. "There was a call last night at about 6:45 that lasted for almost a minute. What time did Kendall go upstairs to change?"

"Everyone left the house around 6:30, so probably around then. Do you think that's what happened last night?"

Sally nodded. "There's also one yesterday morning that lasted about thirty seconds."

"What time?" Sylvia asked.

"7:50."

"I was taking the kids to school at that time."

"Who was home with him?"

"Alex and James, but James was still sleeping."

"Okay, I might have an idea about what's going on, but it's going to take me a little while to figure it all out."

Sylvia nodded. "I'm going to head back to Claudia's. Hopefully Kendall's doing better and we can get him home."

"Thanks for all your help, Sylvia. Can you tell Antonio I'll be over as soon as I have this all worked out?"

"Sure. Thanks again, Sally. We'll see you later."

"Hopefully soon," she said as she continued going over the phone records.

Sylvia was on her way out the door when David Weaver came in after finishing his traffic patrol shift. She arched an eyebrow at him. "Officer Weaver," she said politely and started out the door.

"M-Mrs. Garcia?"

She sighed and turned around, not really in the mood for a confrontation with the young officer. "Yes?"

"Ma'am, I just wanted to apologize for my behaviour that day. It was unprofessional and rude. I'm afraid I let my nerves get the better of me and I'm sorry. Very sorry and it will NEVER happen again," he promised as he nervously twisted his hands.

Sylvia looked at the young man and could see he was being sincere. "I accept your apology, David. Thank you."

"Thank you, ma'am, I really appreciate it."

"You're welcome. Have a nice evening, David." She smiled.

"Thank you, ma'am," he said, smiling back. He held the door open for her and headed back for the lockers.

"Weaver?" Sally called.

"Yes sir? I-I mean ma'am," he stammered.

Sally continued working on the computer. "First, it's O'Hara or Sally, not ma'am and never sir."

"Yes ma'am, I mean Sally," he said, mentally cursing himself.

Sally continued. "Second, well done. It takes character to apologize, and I know that wasn't easy for you. I'm glad to see you took the initiative."

"Thank you, Sally." He smiled.

"I'll see you tomorrow, David."

He nodded and continued on to the locker room.

"I think you made his year," Johnson commented.

"He's been towing the line so far, and I think it's important to let him know when he's done something good. God knows he hears about it when he does something wrong."

"True enough. So how long is his probation?"

"Six months."

"Think he'll make it?"

"It's anyone's guess. If he continues like this, probably. He told me he was going to write her a note, and I have to admit I'm impressed he actually worked up the courage to speak to her in person."

"A sign he's maturing?" Johnson asked.

"Here's hoping." She smiled.

∞

Claudia, Alex, and Jen had gone back inside and Claudia was working on Alex's hand. "Ow," he complained as she cleaned his knuckles with a mild antibacterial soap.

"I told you it would sting." She smirked.

"You don't have to act like you're enjoying this."

"Hey, you're the one who hit my poor defenseless tree," she pointed out.

"Defenseless? My poor hand is mangled and that poor tree doesn't have a mark on it."

"That tree is one of God's beautiful creations and you hurt its feelings."

"Now I hurt its feelings? What do you want me to do, apologize and bring it chocolates?"

"Don't be silly, bringing a tree chocolates. Whoever heard of such a thing? No, I think she'd like some pretty little pansies."

"You want me to bring your tree flowers?" Alex asked in disbelief.

"Pansies," she repeated. "The pretty purple ones with the blue centers and the little yellow dots."

"I don't even know how to respond to that."

"Just say alright." She smiled. "There, all done. How does that feel?"

Alex looked at his cleaned and bandaged hand. "You're finished?"

"It's amazing what a little distraction can do."

"Oh, you're good," he told her.

"You don't have to tell me." She smiled. "Remember, purple pansies around the first of May."

"They'll be here." He laughed.

Antonio was still sitting with Kendall and Jen was sitting on the chair next to the couch. "Antonio, can I ask you something?"

"Sure, what's on your mind?"

"What's he talking about when he says it hurts? Is he remembering when Deesie was beating him?"

"Honey, I can't tell you right now," he said.

"How can I help him if I don't know what happened?"

He looked down at Kendall and then back at her. "We'll talk later."

She smiled sadly and nodded.

∞

Sylvia got back to Claudia's and softly knocked on the door. Claudia answered, "Everything go alright?"

Sylvia nodded. "Sally said she might have an idea about what's going on."

"Did she say what?" Antonio asked.

She shook her head. "She said she'll be over as soon as she knows more. Apparently it's happening to James' phone too."

"James'?" Antonio asked.

She nodded. "She's going through all the call logs now."

"Jo will be picking up the boys any time now," Antonio said.

"Maybe I should run home and meet them and get dinner started," Sylvia said.

"That's a good idea. Make sure they're doing okay. We'll be home as soon as Kendall's awake."

She nodded. "Alex, did you want to come with me or stay here?"

"I'll stay, if that's alright?"

"Of course it is." Claudia smiled.

"I'll come with you. I need to spend some time with Katie and make sure she's doing okay," Jen said, getting up. She bent down and kissed Kendall on the forehead. "I'll see you later, honey."

They left and Alex sat in the chair next to the couch. "How are you doing, buddy?" Antonio asked.

"Better. How about you?"

"I'll feel better once we figure out what the hell is going on."

"Knowing Sally, she'll have it all figured out soon," Claudia said.

Antonio nodded. "Jen was asking me why Kendall was saying it hurts. She should know, but I don't want to send her over the edge again. I also need to tell her about the photos, because I'm sure that issue will come up."

"Why don't I give Eli a call and ask him how he thinks she'll do?" Claudia asked.

"That might help. If he thinks she can handle it, I can tell her everything tonight," Antonio said.

Claudia nodded and went into her office to give Eli Thorne a call.

"What did he do to his hand?" Alex asked, looking at the Band-Aid on Kendall's right thumb.

"He was biting his nail in his sleep and tore it down too far."

"Didn't he do that after Will died?"

Antonio nodded. "It took almost a year for him to stop. Jen had to buy his pajama tops a size larger so she could tie the sleeves closed."

Claudia rejoined them. "Eli said he thinks she can handle it. Her imagination is probably coming up with things far worse than the truth. He said he'll keep his cell with him, and if you need him to call." She handed Alex a slip of paper with Eli's number on it.

"Thanks Claudia," Antonio said.

She smiled. "Should we try waking him up again?"

Antonio took a deep breath. "Kendall, it's time to wake up, Mijo." When he didn't respond, Antonio gently shook his shoulder. "Mijo, time to get up."

Kendall could hear someone calling to him and knew it was Antonio. He fought to follow his voice out of the darkness. Kendall took a deep breath and stirred. His eyes fluttered open and then closed again, but he tightened his hold on Antonio.

"Kendall, can you wake up?"

"Hmm?"

"You need to wake up now. I know it's hard, but you have to try," Antonio said softly.

"M'kay."

Antonio breathed a sigh of relief and smiled. "Come on, we need to get home soon."

Kendall took another deep breath, opened his eyes, and stretched his legs out. "Papi?"

"Yes?"

"Where are we?"

"We're at Claudia's."

"I thought we left?" he asked, confused.

"We did. Something frightened you and we had to bring you back. What's the last thing you remember?" Antonio asked, looking over at Claudia.

"I don't know, my head hurts," Kendall whimpered.

"How bad, baby?" Claudia asked.

"Bad," he said, closing his eyes against the light.

"I'll get you some ibuprofen," she said, heading to the bathroom.

Antonio pulled Kendall up a little so he was half sitting. "It'll be alright, Mijo."

Kendall rested his head on Antonio's shoulder, holding onto his arm tightly.

Claudia came back, sat next to Kendall, and put the pills in his hand. "Thank you," he said his voice shaky.

She held the glass of water for him and he managed to swallow the pills. "Can you tell us what the last thing you remember is?" she asked softly.

"We bought tickets and then had lunch. Is my mom okay?"

"She's fine, she went to see Katie. Why?" Claudia asked.

"She was here?"

"For a while, Mijo. She and Mami went home because the boys are going to be getting back from practice soon," Antonio said.

"Okay," Kendall said, still confused.

"Are you worried about your mom?" Claudia asked him.

"She was mad?"

Antonio looked at Claudia. "No Mijo, she's not mad. She's worried because you aren't feeling well, but that's all."

"That was before," Kendall said quietly to himself.

"What was, baby?" Claudia asked.

"She was mad before, I just got it all mixed up."

"Nobody's mad, baby, just worried. What else do you remember?"

He thought back. "We ate sandwiches and Papa M's middle name is Jebediah."

"That he remembers," Alex said.

"Anything else?" Claudia asked, laughing a little at Alex.

"There were ducks and my mom didn't want me to get cold."

"Kendall, this is really important... Do you remember getting a phone call?" Antonio asked.

"Phone call?"

"At the park, on your cell?"

"James called me. Only it wasn't James... it was him. He won't go away," Kendall sobbed, burying his face in Antonio's arm.

"Listen to me, it wasn't him. We think someone is calling and pretending to be him," Antonio said, trying to comfort the boy.

"Why?"

"I don't know, but Sally's working on it now. We're going to find whoever it is and they're going to be VERY sorry," Antonio promised.

Sylvia got home and Jen pulled in behind her. They went inside and Sylvia started making dinner. "How are you doing?" she asked Jen.

"I'm doing alright. I just want to know what's going on and who could do something like this."

"Sally will find out, and Antonio will make certain that they never hurt anyone ever again."

"I know. it just makes me so angry."

Sylvia smiled.

"Why are you smiling?" Jen asked.

"You sound like your old self."

Jen smiled back. "I feel like my old self, and whoever is doing this had better pray that Antonio gets to them before I do."

"Good girl!" Sylvia said, still smiling.

∞

Joanna and the kids pulled up to the Garcia house a few minutes later. "Looks like they're home." Jo smiled.

They got out of the car and went inside.

"Hi mom!" Katie said, running up and hugging Jen.

"Hi Katie, how was school?"

"Okay. Is Kendall upstairs?"

Jen looked at Sylvia. "No baby, he's still at Claudia's resting. He and Papi and Papa M should be home soon."

Katie's face fell.

Jen hugged her. "It's going to be alright."

"Do you know what he needed?" James asked.

"When honey?" Jen asked.

"When he called me. Reception was bad, and when I tried calling him back, it went to voicemail."

"Boys, sit down," Sylvia said.

James, Carlos, and Logan all took seats at the table. Jen and Joanna both sat down, Katie on Jen's lap. Sylvia took a deep breath. "Someone's been calling Kendall's cell for the last couple of days pretending to be Deesie."

"WHAT? Who would do that?" James asked.

"Did they get a number? Do they know who it is?" Logan asked.

"No, whoever is calling is somehow making it so that Kendall's number shows up as the incoming call," Sylvia told them.

"How is that even possible?" Logan asked.

"I don't know, but Sally's working on it, and she said she might know what's happening. She will be over as soon as she has it figured out. What I want to know is if any of you have had any strange calls, maybe claiming it's a wrong number or just someone just hanging up?" Sylvia asked.

They boys all shook their heads.

"From each other?"

"What do you mean, Mami?" Carlos asked.

"Kendall's phone shows that James called him twice today and that he never called James," Sylvia explained.

"He called me when I was on my way to last period, and I called him once, after last period," James said.

"We know. Did anyone say anything on the call you received from Kendall?" Jen asked.

James shook his head.

"Sally got permission from your mom and accessed your call records. There are quite a few strange things going on with it, but I bet Sally will have it figured out in no time."

"Is Kendall okay?" Carlos asked.

"He will be. He's just really tired after everything that's happened." Jen smiled.

∞

Kendall had calmed down and was sitting quietly with Antonio. The sharp pain in his head had dulled to a steady ache.

"Do you feel like going home yet?" Antonio asked.

"Yeah," Kendall said quietly.

Alex grabbed his boots and helped him on with them. Antonio helped him stand and get his jacket on.

"Baby, if you need me, just call. I mean it," Claudia said, hugging him.

"Thank you," Kendall said, hugging her back.

"I'm going to call you tomorrow just to see how you're doing, and I'll see you on Friday."

Kendall smiled. "Okay, thanks Claudia."

"You're welcome, baby. Now you go home and get some rest and let your family take care of you."

"I will," he promised.

"Thanks Claudia. I'll let you know what Sally finds out," Antonio told her.

"Good. Give him two Benadryl before bed tonight, and then go to one, twice a day tomorrow."

Antonio nodded.

"Good night," Alex said, kissing her cheek.

"You have a good night, too. Take care of that hand."

"I will." He laughed.

They went out to Antonio's car. "Can you drive?" he asked, handing Alex his keys.

"Sure thing," Alex said, opening the doors.

Antonio got into the back with Kendall and Alex drove them home. "Looks like Jen and Jo are still here," Alex said as he parked.

"Good. Hopefully they're staying for dinner," Antonio said.

Antonio opened the door and got out. He reached down and helped Kendall out. "We need to get you fed and to bed."

"I'm not hungry."

"I know. You don't have to eat, but we do need to do the formula tonight. We don't want to lose any ground we've gained."

Kendall sighed and nodded.

"We'll get it done as soon as we get in, so you can get to bed," Alex told him.

"Okay."

They walked up to the door and Carlos opened it before Antonio had his key in the door.

"Papi!" he said, hugging Antonio.

"Carlitos! How was school?"

"Okay. How are you feeling, Kendall?" he asked, putting his arm around his friend.

"I'm okay." He smiled, letting Carlos led him inside.

"Dinner's almost ready. Mami made sloppy joes!"

"I'm not hungry, Carlos."

"You need to eat or you'll get sick again," Carlos said in concern.

"Papa M is going to do the formula thing. Papi said it's enough for tonight," Kendall said reassuringly.

"Okay, but you need to eat breakfast in the morning."

"I will," Kendall promised.

Alex went and gathered what he needed for the feeding, while Kendall went to change into his pajamas. Antonio walked up with him. "I'll be changing in my room if you need anything."

Kendall nodded. "Thanks Papi."

Kendall went into the bedroom and closed the door. He changed into his flannel pajamas with the button-up top. He managed to get the lower buttons done up, but needed help with the upper ones. He sighed, opened the door, and jumped to find James standing there.

"Need help?"

"Please," Kendall said.

James smiled and finished buttoning up the shirt.

"Thanks James."

"Are you okay?" James asked.

Kendall nodded and went to leave the room, but James stood there, blocking the doorway.

"Are you okay?" James asked again.

"I'm fine," Kendall said, trying to smile.

"Don't make me ask you a third time," James said, arching his eyebrow.

"James, please..." Kendall said quietly.

"Are. You. Okay?"

Kendall's eyes filled with tears as he tried to push past James.

James pulled Kendall to him and hugged him tightly. Kendall tried to pull away, but after a moment, he let James hold him as he started to cry.

Antonio heard the boys and saw James led Kendall back into the bedroom and sit on the bed with him. James was holding him closely and Kendall was sobbing.

Antonio sighed in frustration and headed back downstairs. His cell rang. "Garcia."

"Look at your caller ID," Sally said.

"What?"

"Look at your caller ID," Sally repeated.

Antonio looked at his screen and saw that he was supposedly calling himself. "How?"

He had just reached the landing when there was a knock at the door.

"Open the door and I'll show you."

He opened the front door and Sally was there, smiling broadly, John standing next to her.

"Wait until you see what I can do."

Chapter 130~ Setting the Trap

James sat back against the headboard, holding Kendall close as he cried. "It's okay, Papi and Sally are going to figure this out, and until then, I'm not leaving your side."

"James, you can't..."

"I can't what? Do my schoolwork here with you? Skip hockey practice? Wrong, I can and I am so deal with it. Why didn't you say anything about getting phone calls?"

"I-I didn't know they were real. I thought it was like when I hear him at night or in the shower. I feel like I'm going crazy."

James sighed. "From now on, you tell me when you hear him. You're not going crazy, somebody is doing this, and Papi will stop them. Now promise me you'll tell me if you hear him again."

"I promise. Claudia wants me to write it down for her too," Kendall said.

"Good. Now Papa M is going to put in the feeding tube soon, and then you're going to get some sleep."

"Yes mom."

"Very funny," James said.

A few minutes later, Kendall started to nod off and woke with a start. "I need my wallet," Kendall said.

"Why?"

"We stopped at the arena and I got the tickets for Carlos today. You won't believe what the lady gave me for him."

"Is it in your jacket?"

Kendall nodded. "It's in the inside pocket."

"I'll go get it once Papa M comes up. What did she give you?"

"Two passes so they actually get to meet the Hulk. They get a t-shirt and an autographed photo, too."

"You're kidding, that's amazing! Carlos is going to love that!"

"I know. She was really nice. She said they gave her ten passes to hand out and gave me two when she found out they were a gift," Kendall told him.

"I'll find a card and we can give it to him later."

"Okay."

∞

"You figured it out?" Antonio asked.

Sally smiled. "That I did, and you're not going to believe how it's done."

"Sally!" Carlos squealed, hugging her.

"Carlos, how's the best hugger around?"

"Good. Did you really find the bad guy?"

"Not exactly."

"Meaning?" Antonio asked.

"Meaning I know HOW he did it, but proving he did it is another thing."

"But... we have a plan," John interjected.

"Oh boy," Antonio said.

"Let's just start with how he did it," Sally suggested.

"Good idea," Antonio said.

"First I tried hacking into the cell accounts. The problem with that is you're basically just accessing the account, which means you can't call the number FROM the number."

"Okay."

"So I did a little more research and it's frightening how simple it is. I really cannot believe it's even legal given all of the laws that can be broken using it. People who have restraining orders against them, stalkers, bullies can all bypass the legal system with this."

"Are you going to actually TELL me what it is?" Antonio asked.

She smiled and handed him a piece of paper.

"What's this?"

"This is my Spoof ID call account."

"Your what?"

She set her laptop on the table and opened it. She typed in a website and showed him. "It's called spoofing. Most people use it to make prank calls, but it can do so much more."

"How does it work?" Antonio asked.

"You either call that number or go online to the website. Then you put in the number you want to call and then the caller ID number that you want to show up," she explained as she punched in Antonio's cell number again. His phone rang and she pointed to his caller ID.

"It also works on landlines," she said as she punched in the Garcia's home number and Antonio's cell number. The phone rang and he checked it.

"Okay, so we've got him then," Antonio said.

"Not exactly."

"Why not?"

"Now I've already got a call into Ryan for a subpoena to get Taylor's credit card and cell records. The issue is, when I track the calls from the boys' phones, it goes to the automated call center for the spoof site."

"And?"

"And that's where it ends, because in order to make the spoofed call, you have to call that number and then the ACTUAL call out is routed through the call center. That, coupled with the fact he's probably making the calls from a disposable cell, makes it nearly impossible to trace."

"But if he charged it on his credit card?" Antonio asked.

"A couple of problems with that. One, we can't actually prove he used the spoof card unless he's calling the number from his own cell. If he's not, he can always claim that the spoof card was stolen."

"Damn it."

"Language," Sylvia said. "Sally, John are you two hungry?"

Sally shook her head.

"I am," John said.

"When are you not hungry?" Sally asked.

"He's like me." Carlos grinned.

"Yes he is, minus the adorable grin and high metabolic rate," Sally said.

"Hey!"

Sally continued, "You know how they say it's nearly impossible to go off the grid in today's society? They're wrong. Now, if I were the one doing this, what I would do is first buy a disposable cell, paying with cash. Then I would buy a disposable credit card, because they don't require any ID. All you need is the pin number they give you when you buy the card. You never have to give your name, address, anything. It's the same with some of the disposable cells. Then I would sign up online for a spoof account, because they don't require any verification of ID, you can put in any name."

"So what do we do?" Antonio asked.

"We're going to go with the assumption that he used ALL disposable methods available to him, and then we set a trap."

"How?"

Sally smiled. "Well, the only way to prove he's the one calling is to record his voice. So we set Kendall's phone up to be answered through the computer and record him."

"I'm sorry, but I won't allow Kendall to answer any more calls," Jen said firmly.

"He doesn't have to. I'll record him saying 'hello,' as well as his normal greetings for the boys. The chances are he'll try using Logan or Carlos' numbers next, since he's already used James'. When a call comes through with Kendall's number, we set that greeting up to answer. If he gets a call from James' number, then we use that greeting, and so on."

"Okay." Jen nodded.

"How does he know when to call and how did he get our numbers?" Logan asked.

"Well, I was concentrating more on the incoming and outgoing calls, but when I checked the missed calls, there were quite a few there as well. Mostly mornings about the time you guys are on your way to school, and mid-afternoon. If someone else answers, he just hangs up, like he did when Sylvia answered this morning. As for how he got your numbers, thirty dollars can buy access to any number of websites that specialize in collecting and selling that kind of information. Plus, Manning's law firm probably has a real investigator on retainer, and they just use Taylor because he specializes in the audio/video field."

"What about last night?" Alex asked.

"I think he was probably watching the house and saw most of you leave. Once he saw the light go on upstairs, he took a chance and called."

"And this afternoon?" Jen asked.

"I saw his car driving north about a mile from the park. He was probably watching, and as soon as Kendall went to the car, called him," John said.

"But how does he sound like Deesie? It's not like there's a recording of his voice around," Antonio said.

"I don't think he necessarily has to sound like Deesie. Remember what happens when Kendall hears a trigger word. Manning has access to all of Graham's files, as well as what Graham has told him. The hospital files from Appleton mentioned the trigger word as well as a few other things that Dr. Talbot discovered and recorded. That, with the information sheet that Jen filled out when they first went to Graham, was probably enough."

"So he just repeats some of the things that Deesie said?" Sylvia asked.

Sally nodded. "Probably speaking in a quiet, deliberate voice."

"So you get a recording of what he's saying, and then what?" Alex asked.

"Then we send it, as well as a second recording that we'll have Taylor make after we arrest him, to Minneapolis where they have an audio forensic lab."

"What if he refuses to make a recording?" Jen asked.

"Then we make sure he knows that it's in his very best interest to cooperate," Sally said in an icy tone.

"Wow, I think you're as scary as Brooke," Sylvia said.

"Why, thank you." Sally smiled.

"Alright, so what's the plan?" Antonio asked.

"The plan is business as usual with a few slight adjustments. I'm going to be here at about 5:30 in the morning. I'll come through the back gate. It'll still be dark, so make sure your security lights are off. I'll spend the day here with Kendall and make sure everything's alright on this end. Do you think any of your neighbours would allow an officer to watch the street from their house? Preferably one at both ends, that way if the SUV comes back, we can watch him without worrying he'll spot the tail?"

"The Pickets would, maybe the Henricksens. Let me give them a call and ask," Antonio said, going into his study. He returned a few minutes later. "They both said yes. I told them I'll call them with the details a little later."

"Good, that'll definitely help."

"Kendall has an appointment with the physical therapist tomorrow. What do we do about that?" Sylvia asked.

"Just go, business as usual. I'll stay here and monitor any calls. If he follows you, the unmarked patrol unit will follow him," Sally told her.

"Why are they doing this?" Jen asked.

"Could be for a couple of reasons. We won't know for sure until we find out exactly what Taylor's instructions are. Ryan did tell me that Manning's filing for an early court date because Graham's business is suffering."

"Isn't that just too damn bad," Alex mumbled.

"Unfortunately he does have the right to a speedy trial. The issue is there is no way Kendall is ready to testify, and he won't be for quite a while. Ryan isn't too keen about putting him on the witness stand anyway, but the defense could insist that he be questioned via video remote. As he still isn't really speaking to anyone outside his family, the defense could use that as an excuse to insist on an outside mental evaluation."

"A what?" Jen asked.

"They can request that the court allow their expert to examine Kendall. Most likely the court will refuse, but would use a court appointed expert instead," Sally told her.

"So they'll try and force a kid who's suffering from PTSD to talk to someone he doesn't know and possibly testify?" Alex asked angrily.

"There's always that possibility. I'm not saying it's going to happen that way, with any luck we arrest Taylor and convince him that he should turn evidence. If he does, and he's been doing what I think he's been doing, that should be enough to convince Manning to take the plea bargain Ryan will offer him."

"And if he doesn't?" Antonio asked.

"Then we stall," Sally said.

"How?"

"Let's just say that Ryan knows the law just as well as Manning, if not better. He has a few tricks up his sleeve, and if we need to use them, we will." Sally smiled.

Chapter 131~ Telling Jen

"Well we better get this feeding done so Kendall can get some sleep. I'll send James down so he can eat dinner," Alex said, getting up.

"Thanks Alex." Jen smiled.

"No problem. Carlos, do you want to hold the water for me?" he asked, grabbing the tube kit and bag of prepared formula.

"Sure," Carlos said, getting a glass and straw.

Alex went upstairs and found Kendall curled up asleep next to James. "Hey Sport, you want to help me with this?"

"Sure," James said. "Kendall, come on little brother, we need to put the tube in."

Kendall groaned. "Later."

"No, later is for sleeping. The sooner we get this done, the sooner you can go to sleep," James told him.

"Fine," Kendall said, trying to sit up. James helped him up and then pulled him over in front of him. A couple of minutes later, the tube was in place and Alex had the bag hung and flowing.

"Why don't you boys go eat dinner," Alex said.

"I'm good," James said.

"James, go eat," Kendall told him.

"I told you I'm staying with you," James said stubbornly.

"Carlos, why don't you get Logan and bring dinner up for all of you? That way you can eat together," Alex suggested.

Carlos nodded and headed downstairs.

"James, are you alright?" Alex asked.

"I'm fine. I'm just not leaving Kendall alone until they catch this guy."

"Okay, well Sally and John are downstairs now. They figured out how he's doing the thing with the phones and are setting something up to catch him as we speak," Alex told him.

"Good."

"James..." Alex started.

"Look, I don't care what anyone says, I'm staying with him. That means I'm not going to school or practice. I'll do my schoolwork here with Kendall and the team is just going to have to understand."

"That you're being stubborn?" Kendall asked.

"Yes," James said.

"Alright, we'll talk about this later. Let's just try and relax and have a quiet evening," Alex said.

Kendall looked at Alex sadly and sighed.

Alex winked at him. "Everything will be okay. I don't think it'll hurt for James to stay home for a couple of days. Besides, with any luck they'll arrest this guy soon."

Carlos went into the kitchen. "Logan, Papa M said we should have dinner upstairs with James and Kendall because James won't come downstairs."

"Okay. Why won't he come down?" Logan asked.

"He said he's not leaving Kendall alone."

Jen looked at Sylvia. "It'll be alright. After they catch this guy, things will settle down," Sylvia told her.

"I hope so. The kids shouldn't have to worry about these things," Jen said sadly.

"Let's just be glad that they care enough to worry," Jo said, patting her arm.

Sylvia smiled and made a tray for the boys to take upstairs.

"Can I eat upstairs with the guys?" Katie asked.

"I don't know... Can you NOT say anything about the formula?" Sylvia asked.

"Katie, have you been doing that again?" Jen asked sternly.

"Only once, and it was an accident. Please, I promise I won't say anything about the formula or the tube or anything," Katie pleaded.

Jen looked at her. "Pinky swear?"

"Pinky swear!" Katie said, grabbing her mom's little finger with her own.

"One word though, and you're grounded for a month, understand?" Jen asked.

"I understand." Katie smiled.

"Okay, behave!" Jen called after her as Katie ran up the stairs.

"What can you do? She loves her big brother," Joanna said with a smile.

"That she does." Jen smiled back.

∞

Antonio, Sally, and John were in his study finishing up the plans. He had arranged for two undercover officers to stay at his neighbour's houses during the day, so that both ends of the street were being watched. Sally was going to stay at the Garcia's during the day and monitor the phones. Sylvia would call John before they left to go anywhere, and he would make sure he got there before they did. Another unmarked patrol unit would be following Taylor at all times.

∞

Jen knocked on the study door. "Dinner's ready. The kids are eating upstairs tonight."

"Thanks Jen." Antonio smiled.

"Do you have it all worked out?"

"I think so." Sally smiled.

"Antonio, after dinner could you tell me what happened with Kendall?" Jen asked.

"Are you sure you want to know right now?"

"No, but I think I need to."

"Alright, after dinner."

"Thank you," she said going back to the kitchen.

"What does she want to know?" Sally asked quietly.

Antonio sighed. "Why Kendall says it hurts when he's having an attack."

"Oh."

"Yeah, I need to tell her about the photos as well."

"That's not going to be an easy conversation," Sally said.

"That's putting it mildly."

"Look, why don't I take her someplace and I can tell her?" Sally offered.

"I don't want you to have to do that."

"You had a hard time telling Alex. How do you plan on telling his mother?" Sally asked.

"She has a point," John said.

"Why don't we leave it up to Jen? She might not feel comfortable discussing this with you either," Sally said.

"Okay, let's do that," Antonio agreed.

They went out into the kitchen and sat down to eat. After dinner, Sally was helping to clear the table. "So Jen, Antonio said he needs to tell you about some things, and I was wondering if you think it might be easier if we talked about it instead."

"Is it that bad?"

"It's just that I've had more experience working with families in these kinds of cases, and sometimes it's easier speaking to a woman about things. Especially if you have questions, plus I've been working with Claudia and Kendall," Sally explained.

"Okay, that might be better."

"Do you want to take a walk, or maybe make an ice cream run?"

Jen smiled nervously. "Why don't we go pick up dessert for everyone?"

Jen and Sally went and grabbed their coats. "We'll be back in a little while," Sally said.

"If the kids ask, can you tell them we just ran to get ice cream?" Jen asked.

"Sure thing, honey," Antonio said, opening the door for them. "Thank you," he whispered to Sally.

She smiled and nodded and the two women left.

"What's going on?" Sylvia asked.

"Jen wants to know what happened to Kendall, and Dr. Thorne thinks she can handle it. Sally's going to tell her about the night in the tent and the photos Deesie took."

"Oh God, what if she breaks down again?" Sylvia asked.

"I don't think she will, but Claudia gave us Dr. Thorne's cell number just in case."

"She's seemed stronger the last few days," Sylvia said.

"She'll be fine. If she needs us, she knows we're here for her," Joanna told her.

∞

Sally drove because she was pretty sure after hearing what had happened, that Jen wouldn't be in any condition to drive. She drove until they reached Edie's Ice Cream Shoppe and she parked in the side parking lot. "Okay, Antonio said if you feel ready, to tell you the rest of what happened. Are you really ready, and what do you want to know first?"

Jen took a deep breath. "I think I'm ready. There were some things Antonio didn't tell me before because I asked him to stop. I guess what I need to know first is... Is Kendall remembering when Deesie was beating him when he says it hurts during his panic attacks?"

"Do you remember when you were in the hospital and he had the flashback?" Sally asked.

Jen nodded.

"When Antonio and James went up to tell you that Kendall was there getting stitches, he came around and told Claudia what he'd remembered. She asked him if she could tell Antonio, because she knew he would understand and needed to know in order to help him."

"Okay," Jen said, suddenly filled with dread.

"Do you remember what Antonio told you happened the night that Deesie and Kendall were camped out in the woods?"

Jen thought back, wondering if she wanted to hear any more. "Yes."

"Apparently that wasn't the only thing that happened. Do you know what the term 'fingering' means?"

Jen shook her head.

"It's a sexual term meaning that someone is using their fingers to..."

"Oh my God!" Jen said, paling. She put her head in her hands and took a few deep breaths.

Sally rubbed her back. "Just breathe. I know this is hard, if you need to stop, we will."

Jen sat there quietly for a few minutes and took another deep breath. "Okay, what else?"

Sally looked at her. "Are you sure, because we can do this later? You read some of this on the statement sheet, but not all of it. Some of it Kendall's told us, some of it Deesie communicated at the time."

"I'm okay. I need to know what happened so I can help my son."

Sally continued, "After that happened, Deesie got very angry with Kendall because he refused to cooperate. So he cuffed his hands and took him to a tree, where he had attached a climbing rope. He put the rope between Kendall's hands and threw the rope over a branch and

he would pull him up off the ground and then release the rope. The way the rope was set up, it pulled on the center of the cuffs and he would be hanging by them until Deesie released the rope. This was right after he used the needles on the muscles in his shoulder. After a while, Deesie went back into the tent, leaving Kendall standing there, still tied to the branch."

"Okay."

"At some point during the night, Deesie went out and hit him and Kendall was knocked out. That's how he got the black eye and the cut above it."

"Go on."

"The next morning, Deesie tied him up and ran some errands, leaving Kendall in the tent. This is when Ranger Thompson found him. After Deesie shot Thompson, he cleared camp and drove to a motel, where he made Kendall shower and change."

"Why?" Jen asked quietly.

"Deesie wanted to get even with Janice Lane for questioning him a-and he was trying to break Kendall." Sally turned to look at her again, remembering when she had first seen the photos.

"Sally?" Jen asked softly.

"Sorry, just having a moment," she said, her eyes tearing up.

Jen patted her shoulder. "Take your time."

Sally smiled. "I'm supposed to be comforting you, remember?"

"It can't be easy, doing what you do, seeing what you've seen. I know I could never do it, and I appreciate it more than I can say."

"Thank you," Sally said.

"Is this the last thing you need to tell me?"

"Yes, and for some reason it's the hardest. Maybe because I know why Deesie did it, and it infuriates me beyond belief."

"What did he do?"

Sally took a deep breath. "He made Kendall sit on the bed and then posed him for photos. He took twenty-two of them, each one worse than the last. He undressed him a little more for each photo until he was naked. Then he sent them as an attachment with a message to Janice. She opened it, saw the first photo, and got hysterical. Tara went in when she heard her scream and she called me. She was in hysterics by then, too."

"That's why you told the kids not to take any pictures of Kendall?"

Sally nodded. "I'm sorry, I wish we'd found them sooner. I wish we'd gotten Kendall from home before going after Deesie that night, but Dessie said that Kendall had until Monday to make a choice."

"Sally... you, Antonio, John, and everyone else did everything they could and brought him home. Things could have turned out so differently—I could have lost him forever. Things have been so hard, and I admit there were days I gave up, but I'm not giving up anymore. My son fought to get home, and I'm going to fight to get us back to normal. I know it's not going to be easy and that it's going to take a while, but I know we can do it. I just need to remember that disgusting monster is dead and concentrate on helping Kendall get over what he did to him. As for that other pathetic excuse for a human being, I can only hope they put him away for the rest of his life."

"We're going to do our best to see that happens," Sally said.

"I know you are." Jen smiled.

Sally took a deep breath. "Antonio thought it was important for the adults to know what happened, so that we're better prepared to help him when he has flashbacks. Kendall doesn't know that we know, and we need to keep it that way."

Jen nodded.

"Also, Katie was eavesdropping when Antonio told us and overheard Alex use the term 'fingering.' She asked me what it meant and I told her it's an old cop term. Apparently, she decided to get a second opinion and asked Logan what it meant. He told her he had heard the

phrase used in old detective movies and she was satisfied with that. However, he couldn't figure out why his dad would be using it and looked it up online. He found the other definitions and came to me, and I had to tell him the truth."

"Oh no, poor Logie," Jen said.

"I know, but he, Alex, and Joanna went to meet with Claudia and she explained how to help Kendall when he's having a flashback or a panic attack. Claudia thought it would be a good idea, since Kendall is usually with the other boys at night and on the weekends."

"That makes sense," Jen said.

"It might be a good idea for you to talk to Claudia or Dr. Thorne about some of the techniques they use. Claudia got through to him pretty quickly that day, and I think Antonio actually had you use one of them last night."

"When I took his head and made him look at me?"

Sally nodded.

"Okay, I'll do that. It did seem to help."

"Is there anything else you want to know?"

"Is that pretty much the worst of it?"

"Yeah." Sally nodded.

"Okay, then I'm going to speak to Eli about it at my appointment tomorrow and then I'll give Claudia a call."

"There's one other thing we need to do," Sally told her.

"What's that?"

"Get ice cream before the shop closes," she said, looking at her watch.

∞

Carlos and Logan took dinner up for everyone, Carlos put Star Wars in, and they all settled in. "I remember this movie coming out when I was about your age," Alex told the boys.

"Wow, I didn't know this movie was that old," Carlos commented.

"Hey now!"

"Good one," Logan said high-fiving Carlos.

"Keep it up, you two," Alex warned.

"Or what?" Carlos asked curiously.

"You'll find out." Alex smirked.

"Yeah, he's got nothing," Logan said.

"You'd be surprised at what I can come up with."

"Like what?" Carlos asked.

Logan got up and whispered into James' ear. James smiled and nodded. He whispered to Kendall, who smiled and shook his head. Logan whispered in Carlos' ear and he nodded enthusiastically.

"What are you monkeys up to?" Alex asked, watching the boys carefully.

"Papa M, have you ever been introduced to the tickle bug?" James asked, wiggling his fingers.

"I'm not ticklish," Alex said, as the three boys moved to surround him.

"Are you sure? Because I'm pretty sure mom said you are," Logan said.

"Now boys, be nice," Alex said, trying to back up towards the door.

Carlos got behind him and closed it.

"Now boys, I'm serious!"

All three boys advanced. Logan attacked first, poking Alex in the ribs while Carlos wrapped his arms around his legs.

"No, no, no!" Alex yelped as he went down in a heap. All three boys started tickling his ribs and then Logan yanked off one of his shoes.

"No, no, not the feet!" Alex screeched. He managed to push Carlos and James off and tried to crawl for the door, but they grabbed his legs and pulled him back.

Downstairs, Sylvia and Joanna heard a thump and Alex yelling at the boys. "What the heck?" Sylvia said as she ran up the stairs with Joanna right behind her.

They heard the boys giggling and Alex laughing hysterically.

Sylvia opened the door to find all three boys sitting on top of Alex. Logan was sitting on his legs and tickling his feet mercilessly.

"Help!" he yelled when he saw them standing there.

Sylvia and Joanna looked at each other and quietly closed the door.

Antonio and John went running up a moment later. "Is everything alright? I thought I heard someone yell," Antonio said.

"Everything's fine, the boys are just torturing Alex." Joanna laughed.

"Thank God. Should we help him?" Antonio asked as he heard his friend shrieking at the boys to stop.

"You can try if you want to, but I'm not going in there. The tickle bug is on the loose," Sylvia said, kissing his cheek.

She and Joanna went back downstairs.

Antonio looked at John, who shook his head, "I'm not going in there."

They listened for a few more seconds and then followed Sylvia and Joanna back downstairs.

Chapter 132~ Planning

Sally and Jen got back to the house a few minutes later carrying four quarts of different flavoured ice cream. They took the ice cream into the kitchen and Sylvia grabbed some bowls. "Are you okay, honey?"

Jen nodded, "I'll be fine."

Antonio came in. "We have everything set up. Someone will be watching Taylor at all times."

Jen went over and hugged him. "Thank you for everything."

He hugged her back. "It's going to be okay."

"'I know." She smiled, wiping her eyes.

"Are you alright?" he asked.

"No, but I will be. Now I'm going to take some ice cream up to my son and send the other kids down for their dessert."

"Tell them to hurry or there won't be any left," he said.

She laughed as she headed upstairs. She knocked on the door. "Hey, Sally and I went and got ice cream, so you better hurry before Papi eats it all."

"Ice cream!" Carlos squealed and jumped up.

"Hey! Wait for me!" Katie yelled, close on his heels.

"What happened to you?" she asked Alex, noting his disheveled appearance.

"Three evil little monsters who shall rue the day..." he threatened.

"Bye!" Logan said, following Carlos.

"You better run!" Alex laughed as he gathered the NG items together and followed his son.

"James, we got vanilla bean for you."

"Maybe later, thanks though."

"James, go get some ice cream," Kendall said.

"I told you..."

"I know what you told me, but you're still in the same place I am. Just... please go get some ice cream and grab my wallet, okay?"

"Are you okay, honey?" Jen asked James.

"I'm fine, I just..."

"He's not fine, he's freaking out and it's because of me." Kendall sighed in frustration.

"That's not true," James said.

"James, go down and get some dessert. I want to spend a little time with Kendall, and I promise I'll call down if we need you," Jen said.

James sighed. "Alright, but I'll be back up soon."

"Thank you, honey."

"I'll ask Mama G for a card, too," James told Kendall.

"Okay, thanks James." Kendall smiled.

"How are you feeling?" Jen asked, sitting the bowl of ice cream on the table.

"Okay, just worried about James."

"He'll be fine. He's just in big brother mode. I know it's driving you crazy, but let him take care of you."

"He said he's not going to school or practice."

"We'll worry about that later. I'm sure it'll be fine if he misses a couple of days of school."

"The team needs him though," Kendall said.

"We'll talk to him about that later. Now, eat your ice cream," she said, handing him the bowl.

"I'm not really hungry."

"I know, but try to eat some anyway." She smiled, sitting next to him. "Are we still on for this weekend?"

"Sure."

"Sylvia said you have an appointment with the physical therapist tomorrow. Are you nervous?"

He nodded.

"It'll be okay. Hopefully we can do most of it at home."

"I hope so," he said quietly.

"Try eating a little, it's your favourite."

Kendall took a bite. "Thanks mom."

"How's your headache?"

"A little better, I'm just really tired."

"What else?"

"What do you mean?"

"Are you just worried about James, or is there something else?"

"It's James, Papi, you, everyone. No one is living their life because of me. Everything is different and nothing is ever going to be normal again. I'm just tired of it all," he said quietly.

She reached over, brushed his bangs back, and sighed. "I know you are, but Papi, Sally, and John are going to catch this person and things will get better."

"No they won't."

"Why do you say that?"

"Because there's always going to be something else."

"It certainly seems that way, doesn't it?" she said sadly.

He nodded.

"We're going to get through this, and someday this will be a distant memory," she promised.

"I'm sorry, I can't eat anymore," he said, setting the bowl on the night table.

She sat closer and a moment later, put her arm around him.

"Can you stay with me for a while?" Kendall asked quietly.

"Of course I can," Jen replied, kissing his forehead. He laid his head on her shoulder and she smiled. "Try and sleep, baby."

Kendall closed his eyes and was soon asleep.

Jen sighed sadly, as she held him tightly. "Everything will be alright, I promise."

James came back up a few minutes later and handed her two pink pills. "Mama G asked me to bring these up for him."

"What are they?"

"Benadryl, Claudia said they might help with anxiety," he said as he went to the bathroom and got a cup of water.

"Hey honey, you need to wake up for a minute and take these."

"What?" Kendall murmured.

"You need to take these before you go to sleep," Jen said, showing him the pills.

He shook his head.

"You promised Claudia you'd try them, remember?" Jen asked.

He groaned and James helped him sit up. He took the pills and swallowed them. "Thanks James."

"No problem. I have your wallet, too."

"The tickets are on the inside," Kendall told him, closing his eyes again.

"Mama G gave me a card for him," James said.

"Can you sign it for me?"

"Sure."

James quickly signed Kendall's name and put the tickets and passes into the envelope. Kendall was already asleep by the time he finished. "Carlos is going to love this!" James grinned.

Jen smiled. "You boys are incredible, you know that?"

"Why?" James asked.

"You just are. You're always thinking of each other." She smiled.

"We couldn't let Carlos miss seeing the Hulk."

"No, you couldn't and that's what I mean. In spite of everything, you still try and make things good for one another."

"Thanks Mama K."

"I'm so proud of all of you, standing by Kendall through everything. I know it hasn't been easy, and I don't know what we would have done without all of you."

"Where else would we be?" James asked.

"Are you doing alright though?" Jen asked him.

"I'm fine."

"James, I know you're worried about leaving Kendall alone, but you still have other obligations," Jen whispered.

"I can do my schoolwork here with him."

"The team?"

"They'll just have to understand."

"How about we make a deal?"

"What kind of deal?" he asked suspiciously.

"You can stay home from school, but you go to practice and the games."

"But..."

"Honey, listen, Kendall already feels like he's interfering in your lives. He needs to know some things are still normal, and you continuing with hockey is important to him. He won't be here alone. Sally is even staying through the day until they catch this guy. You'll only be gone for a couple of hours, and you can call and check on him."

James sighed. "I don't want him to feel guilty."

"Good, then you'll go to practice and the games?"

James nodded.

"Thank you, James. It'll mean a lot to him."

"You're welcome. I still don't like leaving him alone, though."

"I know you don't, and I can't tell you how much that means to me," Jen told him.

"I just want to make sure he's safe," James said quietly.

Jen smiled. "Why don't you go give Carlos his gift?"

"Are you sure we shouldn't wait until Kendall's awake?"

"No, I think you should give it to him now. It might cheer you up a bit. Carlos' smile can make anyone happy."

"That's true." James smiled.

"You can tell Kendall all about it in the morning."

"Okay. I'll be back up in a few minutes."

Jen nodded and pulled the blanket up around Kendall.

∞

James went downstairs and whispered in Logan's ear. Logan smiled and nodded.

Carlos was sitting at the kitchen table finishing his homework, and they took a seat on either side of him. "Hey Carlos, are you almost finished?" James asked.

"I think so," Carlos sighed.

"Good. So we kind of have an early Christmas present for you," James said, handing him the Christmas card.

"What is it?" Carlos asked.

"Maybe you should try opening it and find out," Logan told him.

Carlos grinned and tore the envelope open. He opened the card and the tickets fell out. "No way," he said quietly as he read them.

"Yes way! It's next weekend in St. Paul AND the lady gave you two passes so you and Papi actually get to meet the Hulk," James said.

"NO WAY!" Carlos squealed. He jumped up and grabbed James, squeezing him tight.

"Carlos, ribs!" James gasped.

"Sorry," he said, hugging him again. He turned around and grabbed Logan. "Thank you!"

"You're welcome buddy, but I need air!" Logan said, trying to inhale.

"This is totally AMAZING! I can't believe we get to meet the Hulk!" Carlos was bouncing up and down from the excitement. "LOOK Papi! We get to meet THE HULK!"

"I see that! That's a pretty special gift, thank you boys." Antonio smiled, and then winced as Carlos bounced into the refrigerator.

"Oops! Sorry, guess I'm just a little excited," Carlos said, grinning.

"You think so?" Alex laughed.

"I need to go thank Kendall," Carlos said.

"He's asleep right now, buddy, you can thank him in the morning," James said.

"Speaking of, you have school tomorrow, so maybe you should head up for bed," Sylvia said.

"Okay, night Mami!" Carlos said, kissing her cheek.

"Goodnight Carlitos."

"Night Papi!" he said, hugging Antonio. "We get to meet the Hulk!"

"I know, but try and get some sleep." Antonio laughed, kissing Carlos on top of the head.

The boys started to head up when there was a knock on the door. Carlos went to answer it when Antonio stopped him. "I'll get it, Mijo."

"Okay," Carlos said, continuing up the stairs.

Antonio looked through the peephole and opened the door. "Hello Brooke. How are you tonight?"

"I'm doing fine. How is everyone here?" she asked, stepping inside.

"Better now. The boys just headed up to get ready for bed."

"So what did you find out about the phones? Sally called asking for permission to access James' phone records."

Sally's in the kitchen, why don't you let her explain?" Antonio said.

Brooke nodded and went into the kitchen. Sally told her what they'd found and what their plans were.

"Well, if you need any help, just let me know." Brooke smiled.

"I will definitely do that," Sally told her.

"Where's Jen?" Brooke asked.

"She's upstairs spending some time with Kendall," Sylvia told her.

"We told her the rest of what happened when he was with Deesie. She handled it alright, but could you keep an eye on her tonight?" Sally asked.

"Of course," Brooke said.

"Dr. Thorne said to call him if she needs him," Sylvia said, handing her a piece of paper with his number on it.

She nodded and took it. "Well, I think I'll go say goodnight to James and the other kids."

∞

The boys had taken turns changing in the bathroom while Jen stayed with Kendall.

Carlos showed her the tickets, still grinning from ear to ear. "Did they tell you what they got me and Papi for Christmas?"

Jen smiled. "Yes they did, honey. I'm so glad you like it."

"I LOVE it! We get to meet the Hulk in person!"

"Carlos, shhh," Logan said, quietly pointing to Kendall.

"Sorry." He smiled.

"It's okay, I think he's out for the night," Jen said with a smile.

"Is he doing better?" Carlos asked, sitting on the other side of Kendall.

"I think so. Hopefully he'll get a good night's sleep and feel better in the morning. I should go tuck Katie in and let you boys get some sleep," Jen said, carefully getting up.

"Night Mama K," Carlos said.

"Goodnight Carlos," she said, kissing him on the forehead. She kissed Logan and James goodnight and went to say goodnight to Katie.

Brooke got upstairs as Jen was going into Carlos' room. "Hi honey. How are you?"

"I'm doing okay, just saying goodnight to the kids." Jen smiled.

"Same here. Have you eaten yet?"

"Yes, I ate with the kids," Jen told her.

"Alright, when we get back to my house you're going straight to bed. You've had a long day and need your rest."

"Yes mom." Jen smirked.

"I'm going to ignore that as long as you promise to do what I say," Brooke said, crossing her arms.

"I promise I'll go straight to bed once we get to your house." Jen laughed, holding her hand over her heart.

"Good," Brooke said, turning to go into the guest room.

"You're welcome... mom."

"I heard that," Brooke said.

"Hi mom," James said, hugging Brooke.

"Hello my boy," she said, kissing his cheek.

"Hi Mama D," Carlos said, hugging her as well.

"Hello darling. How are you tonight?"

"Great! I get to meet the Hulk!"

"That's nice darling. Who's that?"

Logan grabbed Carlos and pulled him back. "We'll explain it later. Otherwise you'll be here all night."

"Alright, you can tell me later," Brooke said, winking at Carlos. He smiled and nodded.

She went over and kissed Kendall on the cheek. "Goodnight darling. Alright, you boys get some sleep and I'll see you tomorrow."

"Goodnight mom." James smiled, kissing her cheek.

"Goodnight honey," she said and headed downstairs.

James closed the door. "Carlos, why don't you sleep on the bed tonight?"

"Are you sure?"

James and Logan nodded, so Carlos got into bed next to Kendall. James moved his blanket and pillow so he was lying right in front of the door.

"Why are you doing that?" Logan asked.

"He's not getting by me again," James said as he pulled his blanket up.

"You do know you're going to get stepped on by whoever comes through the door?"

"And?" James asked.

"Just pointing out they might step on your head because you're so close to the door."

James thought about it for a moment and got up. He went to his backpack, pulled out a notebook, and wrote, "I'm sleeping just inside the door. DO NOT step on my face. - James. "He took it and taped it to the door and laid back down.

Carlos was still too excited to sleep. He kept going over in his mind what he would say when he met the Hulk. After about an hour, he finally started to nod off.

Kendall started whimpering a little later and Carlos pulled him close. "It's okay, buddy, it's just a bad dream." After a minute, Kendall settled back into a deep sleep and Carlos fell asleep, keeping a tight hold on him.

∞

Downstairs, the adults were still discussing the plans for the next few days. Once it had all been sorted out, Brooke and Jen headed out.

Sally and John got ready to leave next. "Here's a key to the back gate, just knock on the back door," Antonio said, handing it to Sally.

She nodded. "Okay, I'll be here at about 5:30."

"I'll have coffee waiting." Alex smiled.

"Good, because I'm not a morning person."

"You hardly sleep, how can you NOT be a morning person?" John asked.

"I'm a night owl, not an early riser."

"Common sense says if you go to bed earlier, you can get up earlier," he pointed out.

"Yeah, it doesn't work that way."

"So what you're saying is you don't have any common sense?" He smirked.

"Do you really want me to answer that?" she asked, arching an eyebrow at him.

He looked at her and took a step back. "No, not really."

"Wise man," Joanna said.

"If he were wise, he wouldn't keep getting himself into these situations." Sally smirked.

"That is very true." Antonio laughed.

"Well, we better get going. I'll see you in the morning," Sally said.

Antonio nodded. "Thanks Sally."

"Not a problem. I'm just glad we figured it out." She smiled.

"Me too," he said, walking them to the door.

A few moments later, Jo got up. "Well, I better get home too. I'll be here tomorrow to give you a hand," she told Sylvia.

"Thank you," Sylvia said, hugging her.

"I'll walk you out," Alex said, holding her coat for her.

"Why, thank you." She smiled.

He grabbed his jacket and walked Joanna to her car. "So, I was thinking maybe you and I could go have dinner while I'm in town. Maybe catch up a little?"

"Are you asking me out?"

"Well, technically we would be going out to dinner, so y-yes," he stammered.

"You're so cute when you get flustered."

"I am not flustered," he told her.

She just looked at him.

"Alright, maybe just a little, but can you blame me? It's not often I get to ask a pretty lady out to dinner."

"Alex, we were married and have a son, why are you nervous?"

"Because you haven't said yes?"

"Yes, I would love to have dinner with you," she said, kissing his cheek.

"Okay then." He smiled.

She looked at him. "Well?"

"Well what?"

"WHEN do you want to have dinner?" she asked, rolling her eyes.

"Oh, um, this weekend sometime?"

"Alright, we can discuss the details later." She laughed.

He opened her door and she got in. "I'll see you later."

"Okay." He grinned.

She shook her head as he closed the car door.

He waved as she pulled out.

∞

Chad Taylor sat in his motel room and took another swig of his beer before he called Derek Manning.

"Yes?" Manning answered.

Taylor rolled his eyes at the smug, superior tone Manning used. "The phone calls seem to be working quite well. I'll be sending you some photos I took in a few minutes."

"Good. I have a meeting with the judge tomorrow to request a court date in the next week or so. I want you to take it up a notch. I don't want anything that brat says to be taken seriously in court. It would be even better if he weren't able to testify at all."

"If today is any indication, he won't be," Taylor reassured him.

Chapter 133~ Motions and Denials

Antonio got up at about 2 am to check on the boys. He saw the note on the door, smiled, and shook his head. He carefully pushed the door open and found it would only open a few inches.

"James, why are you sleeping so close to the door?" Not receiving an answer, he reached through and tapped James on the forehead. "James, open the door."

James mumbled in his sleep, slapping at Antonio's hand.

"Mijo, I need to check on Kendall," Antonio said a little louder, as he pulled at the teen's ear.

"What the?" James yelped, sitting up.

"James, open the door," Antonio repeated.

"Oh, sorry Papa G," he said, moving back.

"What are you doing sleeping so close to the door?" Antonio asked.

"Just making sure Kendall doesn't go wandering off."

"Are you doing alright, Mijo?" Antonio asked, sitting next to James.

"I'm fine. Why?"

"You've had a hard week with you and your dad being in the accident, and now this thing with the phones. It can be overwhelming, and I want to know that you're doing alright."

"I'm fine, really. I just need to make sure that Kendall's okay, that's all," James said.

"I understand your concerns, but we're going to catch this guy. Until then, either Sally, John, or I will be here as well. I don't want you worrying so much about this—we can handle it."

"I know you can, but I'll take care of Kendall while you take care of the bad guys."

Antonio looked at him. "James, you getting worked up about this is just going to stress Kendall out even more. If you keep this up, you're going to end up making yourself sick and he'll blame himself for that, too."

"I'm not going to get sick, and I already promised Mama K that I'll keep going to hockey practice and the games. I just need to do this because I have to make sure he's safe. Does that make sense?"

Antonio smiled and put his arm around him. "It makes perfect sense. Just remember there's more to keeping him safe than making sure there are no bad guys around."

"What do you mean?"

"A part of being safe is feeling safe, and if you're in panic mode, then he will be too."

"Like when Mama K lost it?"

Antonio nodded. "I know it's hard, and since Sally is going to be here, I really think you should talk to her about this."

"Okay," James sighed.

"Now, let's move you away from the door. You don't want to be sleeping there if Carlos suddenly needs to get up and use the bathroom."

"I didn't think about that," James said, moving his blankets closer to the bed.

"Are you doing better now?" Antonio asked as he tucked the blankets around James.

"I think so." James yawned.

"Good, now get some sleep, Mijo."

"I will."

Antonio smiled when he saw Carlos with his arms wrapped protectively around Kendall. He pulled the blanket up over them and then checked on Logan.

"Goodnight James," he whispered as he made his way back to the door.

"Night Papi," James said softly.

Antonio went out and closed the door behind him. He went across the hall to his bedroom and climbed back into bed.

"Boys alright?" Sylvia asked.

"I think so. It's starting to wear on James, though. Maybe he should see Claudia too." Antonio sighed.

"That's probably a good idea."

"I'll talk to Sally about it in the morning. He promised he'd talk to her, so we'll see what she says."

"Okay darling, try and get some sleep," Sylvia said, kissing him goodnight.

"I'll try. Goodnight honey," he said, wrapping his arms around her. A few minutes later, he was asleep, snoring softly.

∞

At about 5:15 am, Sally packed up her laptop, one of the department laptops, three extra two-way radios, as well as a disposable cell she'd picked up for Kendall. She loaded up her car and headed over to the Garcia's. She radioed the unmarked patrol unit and they told her Taylor's SUV was still parked at the motel.

She parked two streets over, walked down the alley behind the Garcia's, and opened the back gate. She relocked it and knocked on the backdoor. Alex answered, smiling and holding a large mug of hot coffee.

"Bless you." She smiled.

"I thought you said you aren't a morning person? You look wide awake to me," he said, taking her backpack.

"That's because I didn't go to sleep. I do better that way for the first couple of days."

"There's no way I could do that," Alex said.

"That's because you HAVE to get up on the ranch by a certain time every day," she pointed out.

"True enough."

"How did everything go last night?" she asked.

"Alright, I think. No one came downstairs and no one had any nightmares."

"Good. These poor kids need a break," she said.

"Yes they do," he agreed.

"I'm going to set up the department laptop in Antonio's study," she said, going into the other room.

Alex followed. "So what's the plan?"

"Basically we wait for Taylor to call and get a recording of his voice. I need to get Kendall to record his greetings for me once he's awake. Then I sync his phone up with the computer, and when a call comes in, it will play the appropriate greeting. If it comes from Logan's number, then it'll say 'Hi Logan,' or however Kendall would answer. The computer will be recording the entire time."

"How do we prove it's Taylor?"

"I'll have a trace running on it, but it most likely won't give us anything. That's why we need to be watching Taylor. If we can SEE him call when a call comes through, then we can question him about it."

"And if we don't see him calling?"

"Ryan should have those warrants for us as soon as the courts open. Once as we have those, we check to see if he used his credit or debit card to purchase a spoof account and a disposable cell. If he did, we can pull him in right away."

"If he didn't?" Alex asked.

"Then we watch him while he watches the house, and if he follows Kendall to more than one stop, we arrest him for stalking and harassment. We don't want to do that until we have a recording of his voice, though."

"So he needs to make at least one call to Kendall before you can do anything?"

"Pretty much, unless he was stupid enough to purchase the spoof card and then call from his own cell."

"You don't think he's that stupid?"

"It would be nice, but no, I don't think he's that stupid."

"Too bad," Alex said.

"Yes it is."

∞

Antonio woke up a little after 5:30 and jumped in the shower. He quickly dressed and went downstairs, where he found Alex and Sally sitting in the kitchen and drinking coffee.

"Morning Boss." Sally smiled.

"Good morning Sally. How about some breakfast?" Antonio asked, opening the refrigerator.

"As long as it's not Cheerios," she said.

"What's wrong with Cheerios?" Alex asked.

"First, they taste like cardboard. Second, my aunt taught my cousin to aim by throwing Cheerios in the toilet and telling him to try and hit them."

"Eww," Alex said, making a face.

"Exactly."

"How about eggs and toast?" Antonio asked.

"That sounds good." Sally smiled.

"Sally, could you talk to James for me today?" Antonio asked.

"Sure. What's going on?"

"He's being overprotective, and says he won't leave Kendall's side. Jen talked him into going to hockey practice and the games, but he refuses to go to school. I think this is really starting to get to him."

Sally sighed. "Yeah, I'll talk to him. I know he and Logan are still feeling guilty about not believing Kendall when this whole thing started, and it's going to be hard for them to get over that. James sees himself as the protector of the group, and not being able to protect Kendall when yet another threat presents itself is liable to send him over the edge."

"They're too young to have to worry about this," Alex said.

"Yes they are, so the sooner we catch Taylor, the better. We need to try to keep this low key where the kids are concerned, which will not be easy. Also, Taylor needs to see that Kendall's alone so he calls," Sally told him.

"Which means Taylor needs to see all of the boys go to school, and James can't go with Kendall to his physical therapy appointment," Antonio said.

"Yeah, he's probably not going to take that well," Sally said.

"No, he's not," Antonio sighed.

∞

Kendall woke up and found Carlos holding onto him. His head felt thick and his mouth and eyes were dry, and he desperately needed a drink of water. He tried to wriggle free from Carlos' grasp and finally succeeded. Carlos grabbed his pillow and hugged it to himself. Kendall shook his head and smiled at his friend—he didn't know anyone else who grinned in his sleep like that.

He went to step over James when a hand grabbed his ankle. He yelped in surprise.

"Where are you going?" James asked.

"Don't do that!" Kendall hissed.

"Where are you going?" James asked again.

"To get a drink of water, now let go."

"Fine, but come right back."

"I'm awake now, I'm going downstairs," Kendall said, walking to the door.

James got up and went to follow him.

"James, go back to sleep. I'm sure Papa M is up by now."

"I'm awake too," James said.

Kendall rolled his eyes and opened the door. "Fine."

The boys went downstairs and wandered into the kitchen.

"You two are up early," Alex said.

"I fell asleep really early," Kendall yawned.

"Breakfast?" Antonio asked.

Kendall shook his head.

"Didn't you promise Carlos you'd eat a good breakfast?" Antonio asked.

Kendall sighed and went to get a glass of water. He finished it quickly and poured another glass.

"Thirsty?" Alex asked.

Kendall nodded. "I don't know why."

'Did you take the Benadryl last night?" Sally asked.

"I think so."

"He did, Mama G gave him two," James told her.

"That'll do it. Drink slowly though, or you'll get sick," she said.

Kendall nodded and set the glass in the sink.

"After breakfast we need to record you saying 'hello' so I can set the computer to answer your phone," Sally told Kendall.

"Okay," he sighed.

"I brought you a disposable cell until this is over, and we can get your number changed again."

"Thank you."

"Not a problem, kiddo."

"So James, there might be a problem with the schedule. If you stay home..." Antonio started.

"I'm NOT going to school and leaving Kendall alone," James insisted.

"Calm down, we just need to figure this out. The problem is Taylor needs to think Kendall's alone so he'll call. If he knows you're here, he might not call. So, if you stay home, you can't go to his physical therapy appointment," Antonio said.

"But..."

"James, the faster we catch Taylor, the faster this is over. You can stay here and help me with a few things," Sally said.

"Okay, but I don't like it."

"I know you don't, Mijo, but it's for the best," Antonio told him.

"I could not go," Kendall suggested.

"You're going," Alex and Antonio said at the same time.

Kendall sat back and pouted.

"Not going to work. You're going to lose the use of your arm if we don't do something," Antonio told him.

"I don't want some stranger touching me."

"I know, but one of us will be with you the whole time," Antonio promised.

"We'll do the feeding tube at about eight or nine, that way it's not too close to breakfast or lunch," Alex said.

"Yay," Kendall said, pouting again.

"Don't look so happy about everything," Alex said.

Kendall just looked at him.

"You know, you and your sister share some scary looks," Alex pointed out.

"That they do." Antonio laughed, setting a plate in front of Kendall. He handed another to Sally and then one to James. He sat down on the other side of Kendall and handed him a fork. "I'll meet you at the physical therapist's office and then head back to the station."

"Okay." Kendall sighed as he took a bite.

"So, I'll stay here until they get back?" James asked.

Antonio nodded. "Why don't you call and see how your dad is doing? We can take you to see him later."

"How are we going to do this? If Taylor is watching before the kids go to school, he'll know James isn't with them," Alex said.

"Good question," Antonio said.

"I can go with them and Mama G can let me out around the corner and I'll come through the back," James suggested.

"By yourself? I don't think so," Alex said.

"You can see all the way down the alley, so you can be out back waiting for me," James pointed out.

"That might work," Sally said.

"Here's a thought... Why don't you just go to school?" Kendall asked.

"I promise I'll go to hockey practice and the games, but I AM staying close to you until they catch this guy," James said.

Kendall sighed and put his fork down. "James..."

"It's alright, Mijo. James needs some time, and while we're at your appointment, he and Sally can talk," Antonio said.

"Please don't be mad. I need to do this," James said softly.

"I'm not mad."

"Good, then eat." James smirked, putting the fork back in his hand.

Carlos and Logan came wandering in a little while later.

"Morning Papi!" Carlos smiled.

"Good morning Carlitos. Are you hungry?"

"Do you really even need to ask that question?" Logan asked.

Antonio laughed. "No, it's just a habit."

Carlos stuck his tongue out at Logan and took Antonio's seat next to Kendall. He hugged his friend. "Thank you so much for the Christmas present!"

"You're welcome, Carlos. We knew you'd love it."

"I can't believe we get to meet the Hulk!" he said, bouncing up and down in his chair.

"Don't start dancing around and bumping into the appliances again." Alex laughed as he handed Carlos a plate.

"I won't." He grinned.

Kendall smiled at Carlos. "You're not excited, are you?"

"No, he's not excited at all," Antonio said.

"Papi, in NINE days we get to meet the Hulk!"

"My God, he's done the math!" Alex laughed.

Carlos grinned as he started to eat. He picked up Kendall's fork and handed it to him. "You promised."

Kendall rolled his eyes and smiled.

A few minutes later, Katie and Sylvia came down. Katie sat down while Sylvia poured herself a cup of coffee.

"Good morning, Little Darlin'. How are you today?" Alex asked Katie as he sat a plate in front of her.

"Okay."

"Did you sleep well?"

She nodded.

"Not a morning person either?" Sally asked.

"No," Katie said.

"Well, you're in good company." Alex smirked.

Katie and Sally both stared at him.

"I think the temperature just dropped twenty degrees," Alex said, stepping back.

"One day you'll learn," Sylvia said, patting his arm.

"No he won't." Logan laughed.

"YOU, I can handle," Alex said, pointing at him.

"What, who, me?" Logan stammered.

"Yes you, smart aleck."

"That's not what I saw last night," Sylvia said.

"Hey, there were THREE of the little monsters ganging up on me," Alex pointed out.

"Aw, poor Alex." Sylvia smirked.

"Don't think I'll forget about you and Jo just leaving me at their mercy either," Alex told her.

"Really, what do you plan to do about it?" she asked.

"You'll see."

Antonio started laughing at the two of them.

"Don't forget about your best friend, who heard you shrieking through the door and just left you," Sylvia told him.

Alex looked at Antonio.

"What, did you really think I was going to risk being attacked by the tickle bug, too?" Antonio asked.

"I need new friends," Alex muttered.

Sally's phone rang. "O'Hara. Okay, thanks, Shale. Just follow and let me know where he goes."

"Taylor?" Antonio asked.

Sally nodded. "He just left the motel. Dane and Peters should be at your neighbours' houses by now."

"Good," Antonio said.

"How about we get that recording done?" Sally asked Kendall. He nodded and followed her into the study. Ten minutes later, she had recorded him saying "hello" as well as his normal greetings to the other boys.

"How does that work?" he asked.

"Well, I have your phone line synced with the computer. When someone calls, it will answer according to caller ID. So if a call came from James' number, then the computer will answer with your greeting for James. If there's no caller ID or it's from your number, then it'll answer with just hello," she explained.

"Think it'll work?"

"Yes I do." She smiled.

"Good."

"Are you doing alright?"

"Yeah, I just want this to be over."

"I know you do, and with any luck Taylor will be in jail by the end of the day."

"Why would someone do something like this?"

"I don't know, honey. There are a lot of bad people in this world, and it seems that most of them are for hire."

"It's not fair," he said quietly.

"No, it really isn't," she said, putting her arm around his shoulders.

"I just want things to be normal again."

"They will be. I know you're tired of hearing this, but it's just going to take some time."

∞

Chad Taylor pulled up and parked two blocks down from the Garcia's. He had been very careful after the encounter with the neighbour and was confident that no one had spotted him yet. He sat there and waited for someone to take the kids to school, and then he would make his morning call.

Officer Laura Peters was watching him from the Henricksen living room. She got on the radio. "Sally, I've got the tan Escalade parked about two houses up from here."

"Can you see the driver?"

"Negative, side windows are tinted and there's a glare on the windshield."

"Okay, let me know if he moves."

"Copy that," Peters said.

Sally looked at Antonio. "We don't have a visual on the driver, so we're going to have to hope we get that warrant soon."

Antonio nodded. "Let's hope we can at least get his voice."

"We will," she said reassuringly.

"Well, I better get to the station," he said.

"Okay honey," Sylvia said, kissing him goodbye.

"I'll meet you at the therapist's office. Make sure you call John before you go anywhere."

"I will."

∞

Kendall headed upstairs to shower and dress, James followed him a moment later. Kendall grabbed some clean clothes and found James standing in the hallway.

"What are you doing?"

"Waiting for you," James said.

"I can shower by myself."

"I know. I'll just be here to help you with your shirt when you're done."

Kendall rolled his eyes. "Fine, but I can comb my own hair."

"No, you really can't."

Kendall rolled his eyes again and closed the bathroom door.

"Don't lock it," James called from the other side.

"Yes mom," Kendall retorted.

"I heard that!"

"You were supposed to," Kendall pointed out.

Kendall finished showering and was dressing when James called through the door. "Are you almost done?"

Kendall shook his head and smiled. He opened the door and handed James his t-shirt. James helped him pull it on. "Thank you."

"No problem. I better hurry so I can ride with Mama G," James said as he threw on some clothes.

"You're not going to shower or do your hair?" Kendall asked in shock.

"I will when I get back," he said, pulling a beanie onto his head. He ran downstairs and Kendall followed him.

"If you want this to look realistic, you're going to need this," he said, handing James his backpack.

"Oh yeah, thanks!" He smiled as he headed out the door.

Kendall shook his head as he locked the door.

Alex went out into the backyard and unlocked the gate to wait for James.

"You doing okay?" Sally asked him.

"He's going to drive us both crazy," Kendall said.

"Hopefully we get this guy today and he can stop worrying so much."

"I hope so," Kendall said quietly.

Alex and James came back in a couple of minutes later and James headed back upstairs to shower. Alex started mixing up the formula and Kendall groaned. "Sorry, Champ, but we gotta do it."

"I know," Kendall sighed.

Sally's cell rang. "O'Hara."

"Hey Sally, you've got the warrant for Taylor's cell and credit card records. I'm heading to court now. Manning has requested an Omnibus Hearing."

"How do you think that'll go?"

"Depends on what they're requesting. If it's a change of venue, I doubt they'll get it. If they're requesting a speedy court date, I don't know. Given Kendall's age, physical and emotional state, I doubt the judge will allow them to force that issue."

"I hope not—there's no way he's ready to testify. I'll go through Taylor's records in a few minutes and see what I find there. If we can tie him to Manning it may be a moot point."

"Okay, let me know what you find out," Ryan said.

"Will do. Thanks Ryan."

Alex and Kendall were looking at her.

"We got the warrant, so I'm going to go work on his records," Sally told them, going into the study.

"I'm going to have to testify?" Kendall asked, panic in his eyes.

"We're doing everything we can to avoid that, honey. If you do, it won't be for quite a while, I promise," Sally said.

"It'll be okay, Champ. What do you say we go and put the tube in, watch a movie, and relax?" Alex asked, putting his arm around him.

Kendall tried to calm his breathing and nodded.

"Everything will be alright, please don't worry about it now. If everything goes according to plan, Graham will plead guilty and there won't be a trial," Sally told him.

"Okay," he said quietly. He and Alex went into the living room, and as soon as James came down, put the feeding tube in and they all settled in to watch a movie.

James noticed something was a little off with his friend. "You okay?"

"Just more fun coming in the future," he said sarcastically.

James put his arm around Kendall's shoulders and looked at Alex. "It'll be okay," Alex said.

James tightened his hold on Kendall a little, who leaned against him. "I'll be here no matter what," James promised.

"I know." Kendall smiled.

∞

Down the street, Taylor watched Sylvia as she drove the kids to school. He waited ten minutes and punched in Kendall's number twice.

The phone rang twice, "Hello."

"Hello sweetheart. Miss me? You and I are going to have so much fun together," Taylor hissed into the phone.

At the Garcia's, Sally smiled as the computer recorded the conversation and then hit end call on Kendall's phone. "Got you, you son of a bitch."

She pulled up the link for Taylor's cell and found no calls to Kendall or James' phone. She pulled up his credit records next and found a charge for twenty-five dollars to the Radical Spoof site. She also found a charge to the Minneapolis Rent-a Dent, as well as one for Thrifty Car Rental Agency.

She called Antonio's cell. "Garcia."

"Hey Boss, he called and I got a short recording of his voice. We also have the warrants for Taylor's records, no cell activity to the boys' phones, but there's a charge to a spoofing site as well as to two different car rental agencies in Minneapolis. I'm going to check to see if he's

made any calls to Manning or his office next. I think it might be a good idea to try and get another recording that way the lab has more than enough to work with."

"Do what you think is best, and make sure to keep me informed. Thanks Sally."

"Will do, and you're welcome."

∞

Ryan took his place at the prosecution table in court. Derek Manning came in a few minutes later and smiled at him. "Good morning."

"Good morning, counselor," Ryan said, smiling back.

The guard brought Graham out dressed in the blue jumpsuit worn by inmates and escorted him to the defense table.

The bailiff ordered them to rise and they all stood as Judge Paige Brown entered. She took her seat and called the court to order. "Defense has called for an Omnibus hearing to examine findings and eligibility of evidence. Before we get to that, are there any pre-trial motions?"

"Yes, your Honour. Defense requests a change of venue, as we believe it will be difficult to find an impartial jury in this case," Manning said.

"Based on what?"

"Based on recent publicity regarding the case. We request that the trial be moved to the Minneapolis court."

Judge Brown looked over the files that had been provided. "Are you talking about the newspaper article and television interview regarding the case?"

"Yes, your Honour."

"Objection," Ryan said.

"State your objection, please."

"Chelsea Waters with KMAN news has confirmed that Mr. Graham contacted them about doing an interview, not the other way around."

"Your Honour, my client was not aware of the restrictions regarding the case when he agreed to speak to the news about it. His last attorney failed to make it clear that he was not allowed to talk about the case," Manning said.

"I see. Mr. Graham, you are an educated man?"

"Yes, your Honour."

"Do you understand what professional discretion means? I believe it's a common term in your chosen profession, is it not?" Judge Brown asked.

"Yes, your Honour, but it was my understanding that I could speak about the case as long as I didn't reveal names."

Judge Brown looked at him. "Motion denied."

"Your Honour, I must protest..." Manning began.

"Motion DENIED. It is my belief that your client was well aware of what would happen if he revealed details about this case. The fact that the victim's name and photo were in the newspaper the next day proves what his intentions were. Even if he did not provide them, he instigated the investigation by the newspaper. Any other motions?"

"My client requests a speedy court date, as his business and personal life are suffering from his absence," Manning said.

"Mr. Ryan, any objections to setting the court date within the next week?"

"Yes, your Honour. Kendall Knight is currently unable to testify due to physical and emotional issues brought around by first the kidnapping, and then the trauma suffered at Mr. Graham's hands."

"Objection. My client's guilt in this matter had not been proven."

"Your Honour, Mr. Graham has admitted to injecting Kendall with Lorazepam, a drug NOT indicated for someone his age and for the physical condition he was, at that time, suffering from. The hospital report will confirm that he was overdosed with the drug and suffered side effects for several days after."

Judge Brown went over the paperwork and found the hospital reports. "Is he still suffering from pneumonia?"

"Yes, your Honour, in both lungs, as well as anemia. He is currently on a tube-feeding regimen and is scheduled for another round of blood work next Monday. I have submitted the records from his psychologist. He's also suffering from post-traumatic stress disorder and selective mutism."

Judge Brown nodded and went through that file. "Any ideas as to when the child will be well enough to testify?"

"Not at this time, your Honour."

"Your Honour, I object. Prosecution could drag this on for months, at which time my client's business will be non-existent and his reputation damaged beyond repair. He has a right to a speedy trial," Manning said indignantly.

"I am well aware of the defendant's rights, Mr. Manning, and I'm sure that you are aware the prosecution has a right to expect all of their witnesses to be able to testify. According to the doctor's reports, as well as those from his psychologist, Kendall Knight is physically and emotionally unable to do so at this time."

"We request that he be made available for an interview with our psychiatric specialist," Manning said.

"Objection, relevance? Dr. Jenkins is a licensed child trauma psychologist, who has worked with the courts on several cases. She's also acted as Guardian ad Litem in over thirty cases, and her professionalism is beyond reproach," Ryan stated.

"Relevance would be that she WORKS for you," Manning snorted.

"Enough, motion denied. Dr. Jenkins has an excellent reputation with these courts, and while she may be currently counseling a witness for the prosecution, she puts the welfare of the child first," Judge Brown said.

"We have a right..." Manning started.

"Motion denied. I will not have either side badgering this child in any way. When he is declared well enough to testify, then we will reconsider your request. Any other motions?"

"We are still waiting for a decision on a speedy trial. We would be willing to acquiesce to a video testimony," Manning said.

Judge Brown sighed. "How would you propose to do that if the child is suffering from selective mutism?"

"As I understand it, selective mutism means that he speaks to certain people. The court could ask the questions through one of these people and he could answer via camera," Manning said.

"Mr. Ryan, any thoughts on this?" she asked.

"No, your Honour. I will allow the police, doctor, and psychologist reports speak for themselves regarding this matter. If you will note, one of the things the child was forced to endure during his time with Stephen Deesie was to be photographed in several degrading poses. Dr. Jenkins has instructed everyone he knows NOT to take his photo until they have worked through this. Recording him on video would most likely send him into a panic-ridden state."

Judge Brown nodded. "Motion denied."

"Your Honour, we would be willing to allow questions be submitted on a statement sheet that he can answer at home with an officer of the court present," Ryan said.

"That does not allow for cross examination," Manning countered.

"Well, it seems like you have a choice to make then, Mr. Manning. You can choose to have a speedy trial with the statement sheet, or you can wait until such a time, as Kendall Knight is able to testify in court or on video," Judge Brown said.

"May I have some time to consider this?" Manning asked.

"Take all the time you need, but you are the one requesting a speedy trial," she pointed out.

"Who would the court officer be, and why does the prosecution think he would do any better answering questions in this manner?" Manning asked.

"Because he doesn't have to speak in order to fill out the statement sheet. He just writes his answers down," Ryan told him.

"Would we be allowed to submit questions?"

"After I have gone over them, yes," Judge Brown said.

"And if we need to cross examine on some points?"

"Then I will consider a second statement sheet, depending on the questions," she told him.

"May I have a moment with my client?"

The judge nodded.

"This is ridiculous," Graham hissed.

"Actually, this might work in our favour. If he's not in court, he can't win a jury's sympathy. Besides, according to my sources, it's going to be quite a while before he'll be in any condition to testify." Manning smiled.

"Fine, do what you think will get me out of this the fastest," Graham said.

"Your Honour, we would be willing to submit questions for a statement sheet, provided that he not be coached on how to answer them."

"That is why there is a court officer present during the time the statement is taken," Ryan told him.

"Yes, but I understand that his godfather is the chief of police?"

"Chief Garcia will not be the court officer present," Ryan said.

"We request that the statement be taken at the police station with at least two court officers present," Manning said.

"Mr. Ryan, will there be a problem with that?"

"No, your Honour, not at all. In fact, we could do it in your chambers and you could be the presiding court officer." He smiled.

She smiled back. "Any objections to that, Mr. Manning?"

"No, your Honour," he replied with a pained smile.

Chapter 134~ Taking Control

After the hearing, Ryan called Sally. "How did it go?" she asked.

"Manning asked for a change of venue, but it was denied. Asked that their psychiatrist be allowed to examine Kendall, denied. Asked for testimony by video, denied. Asked for a speedy court date, granted if they're willing to accept Kendall's testimony from statement sheets. Otherwise they're going to have to wait until he gets an all clear from his pediatrician and Claudia."

"Excellent. I managed to get a short recording of Taylor's voice. We're going to try for a second, so that the lab has enough to work with."

"Get as much evidence as you can against him, and we can use that as leverage against Manning. With any luck, he'll convince Graham to settle and we won't have to put these families through any more hell."

"Doing what I can. It would be easier if Kendall could actually answer the phone and draw the conversation out a little longer, but there's no way," Sally said.

"What if someone else answered pretending to be Kendall?" Ryan suggested.

"I thought about one of the other boys, but I don't think it'd work. He knows Kendall's voice by now, and the only one who comes close to sounding like him is James, and he's heard his voice too."

"What if James spoke quietly and answered with just one or two words?"

"That might work, but I really don't want to expose him to this. He's already on edge, and if he lost his temper on the phone, we could blow our advantage," Sally said.

"Okay, let me know if you need anything else and I'll do what I can."

"Thanks Ryan, I really appreciate it."

∞

Sally went into the living room and sat next to Kendall. "So, some good news. The judge isn't going to make you testify. She told Ryan if the defense wants a trial now, we can use the statement sheets instead."

"If they don't want one now?" Sylvia asked.

"Then they have to wait until Kendall is physically and emotionally able to handle it, which he won't be for quite a while."

"When will we know what they decide?" Alex asked.

"Soon, although the faster we take Taylor down, the faster we can force their hand."

"What else do you need? You already got a recording of his voice, right?" James asked.

Sally nodded. "We're going to try and get another one just to make sure we have enough for the lab to work with. Unfortunately, he doesn't say much without someone answering him back. In fact, I have an idea on how to get him to call back this afternoon."

"What?" Kendall asked.

"If Alex stays here, then it would just be you and Sylvia going to your physical therapy appointment. Antonio will be meeting you there and then he'll go back to the station. If you stopped somewhere on the way home and Sylvia ran in without you, then Taylor would see you alone and probably call again."

"I would never leave him alone," Sylvia said.

"You and I know that, but Taylor doesn't. Let's say you stop at the pharmacy on your way home. He would think you're just picking up a prescription. You would only be in there for a couple of minutes, that's all it would take for him to call. John would be waiting there before you arrive and Shale would still be tailing him, so there'd be two police officers right there."

"But wouldn't he see that Kendall doesn't have his phone?" James asked.

"No, because he takes the one I got for him and I'll call him as soon as the call from Taylor comes through. Taylor sees him answering and hopefully says a lot more. Then John and Shale arrest him," Sally explained.

"What if he doesn't call or say anything else?" Kendall asked.

"Then we work with what we have," Sally told him.

"I could always just answer the phone for real. He said a lot more when I talked back to him," Kendall said.

Sally shook her head. "I'm not going to put you in that position. I don't want you having a panic attack because of this."

"I won't. I know I'm not just hearing things and that he's not Deesie," Kendall said.

"No way!" James shook his head.

"James, please. Kendall, he still uses the trigger word, and I really don't think it's a good idea," Sally told him.

"But I'm awake, so it won't bother me as much. Claudia and I've been working on it, and if we do this, it could be over with today," Kendall said.

Sally looked at Sylvia and Alex. "Well, thoughts?"

"I don't know. Mijo, do you really think you can handle it?" Sylvia asked Kendall.

He nodded.

"Alex?" Sally asked.

He sighed. "Kendall has a point, but I don't like that he'd be there alone."

"But I wouldn't be alone. John and the other officer would be right there," Kendall said.

"We could also have Antonio follow and he'd be there too," Sally mused.

"You're not seriously considering letting him do this?" James yelled.

"James..." Alex started.

"NO! No way, this is SO not alright!"

"Well it's NOT up to you!" Kendall snapped.

"Kendall, you are NOT doing this! It's too dangerous!" James told him, panic evident in his eyes.

"I want this over with and if this helps, then I want to do it," Kendall stated.

"Kendall..."

"NO, I am tired of it! I'm tired of ALL of it! I just want everything to be normal again, including YOU!" Kendall yelled, pushing past James and running upstairs.

James went to follow, but Alex grabbed his arm. "Sit, I'll go. I need to pull the tube anyway."

"But..." James stammered, tears in his eyes.

"I know, it's going to be alright," Alex said.

"Honey, he's not really mad at you. He's just frustrated and scared," Sally told him.

James sat next to her. "I didn't mean to upset him. I just..."

Sally put her arm around his shoulders. "I know that, and so does he. He's just worried about all of you right now and he's tired of having to deal with all of the idiots who keep pulling this crap. Imagine how you would feel if you lost control over almost every aspect of your life. Good and bad people making all the decisions about everything, not giving you a say in it. How would you feel?"

"I just want him to be safe," James said quietly.

"I know you do, and he wants the same thing for you. Right now he sees you giving up everything for him and he feels like he's failing you."

"That's crazy, how can he fail anybody?"

"I'm not saying he's failing anyone, I'm saying it's how he feels."

"But why? None of this is his fault."

"Because he keeps having panic attacks, because it's taking a while for him to heal physically, because everything he feels or thinks is compromised by his memories of Deesie. He's use to being strong, to taking care of his family, of you guys, and right now he can't. Whether it's his fault or not, he blames himself," Sally told him.

"So what do I do?" James asked, choking back a sob.

"Be there for him, but let him have his space when he needs it. Also, I think you should talk to Claudia. I really think she can help you deal with this a little better, and she can give you some tips on how to better help Kendall."

James nodded. "I'll try."

∞

Kendall ran upstairs and locked himself in the bathroom. He looked at himself in the mirror and wanted to scream. He was still pale, his eyes were red and watering, and that stupid tube was still attached. He peeled the tape from his cheek, yanked the tube out, and threw it into the sink. He sank to the floor and hugged his knees to his chest, coughing and crying.

"Kendall?" Alex called, softly knocking on the door.

"Go away!"

"Son, please let me in."

"No! Leave me alone," Kendall sobbed.

"I'm not going to do that, so open the door. We need to talk about this," Alex said.

"What's the point? Nobody cares what I think anyway."

"That's not true. James is just really freaked out right now and Sally is talking to him. Please Kendall, open the door."

Kendall reached up and unlocked the door.

Alex opened it and went inside, sitting next to Kendall on the floor. He saw the tube lying in the sink. "Well, I guess you took care of that. Let me see you."

Kendall looked up at him but wouldn't meet his eyes.

"Does it hurt?" Alex asked quietly.

"A little."

"I bet. You're supposed to take it out slowly and at a specific angle," Alex said, putting his arm around his shoulders.

"I'm sorry."

"Don't be sorry, I'm just glad you didn't hurt yourself. Now, we need to talk about what happened downstairs. You do know James wasn't trying to be mean or anything, right? He's just really scared right now."

"I know, but he shouldn't be scared or worried. He should be home with his mom, who shouldn't have to come over here every night just to see him. Logan should be home with his mom, his books, and science stuff. Carlos should be able to sleep in his own room and have his parents to himself. You shouldn't have had to come all the way up here just to put a tube in my nose every day. Papi should be able to go to work and stay there, he should be sleeping through the night. My mom shouldn't be afraid to be at home or around me. My sister should be at home with her own stuff and able to see her friends whenever she wants."

"Okay, so what you're saying is that you've ruined everyone's lives? That adds up to eleven people. That's quite an accomplishment for someone your age, don't you think?"

"It's not funny," Kendall said.

"I'm not laughing. I am, however, very worried because I know you believe what you just said."

"That's because it's true," Kendall said, hugging his knees tighter.

"Damn, those people have done quite a number on you, haven't they?" he whispered, pulling Kendall closer.

"I just want to make things right again," Kendall said quietly.

Alex sighed. "Do you really think you can handle another call from this guy?"

"I want to try."

"Fair enough, but what happens if you do have a panic attack? There won't be anyone in the car with you."

"I've been alone when I've had them before and Papi and John will be close by."

"Do you understand WHY James is against this?"

"Yes."

"Why?"

"Because he won't be there to protect me."

Alex nodded. "He almost lost you once, and he's terrified he could still lose you. He feels like he failed you because he didn't believe you at first and then it turned out that Deesie really was a monster. Logan feels the same way, although I guess he lost it before you got back home, so he's handling it a little better right now."

"I never blamed them for that," Kendall said, his eyes tearing up again.

"I know you didn't, but think about it. How would you feel if the roles were reversed? If it were one of the other boys that had been threatened and taken. How would you feel if you didn't believe them and couldn't protect them?"

"Bad," Kendall said, sniffling.

"You'd do anything you could to protect them, wouldn't you?"

Kendall nodded.

"What would it take to make you feel better?"

"Making sure they were okay."

"Now I want you to stop thinking that you've ruined anyone's lives, because it's not true. I admit, some things have been hard, but that is NOT your fault. Just think...if it weren't for you, I wouldn't have come up here, even if it does mean I get to put a tube in your nose. James and his dad wouldn't have spent a great day together, and are actually trying to mend their relationship. Brooke is concentrating on spending more time with James instead of concentrating on just business. Logan and I get to spend more time together than we have in years. Carlos, he's like Sylvia—happy to have a full house and getting to spend time with all of his brothers. Antonio may not be at work as often as he was, but he's doing what he promised your dad, his friend and brother, what he would do. What your dad promised Antonio HE would do if anything happened to him. He's taking care of his family, his children. Your mom, she needs to work through things in her own way, also not your fault or responsibility."

"I miss my dad," Kendall said quietly.

"I know you do so do I," Alex said, resting his chin on Kendall's head.

There was a soft knock at the door. "Kendall?" James said quietly.

Alex looked at Kendall, who nodded. He got up and opened the door. "Come on in."

James walked in and Alex went out, closing the door behind him.

"Hey," James said.

"Hey."

James sat down next to Kendall. "I-I'm sorry, I didn't mean to..."

"Don't, it's not your fault."

"I'm just worried that something might happen if you do this," James said.

"I know. I shouldn't have gotten mad at you. I'm just tired of feeling so useless all the time."

"You're not useless. I wish I could make you understand that."

"You try having everyone you know take care of everything when you're not use to it," Kendall told him.

"I guess it would get kind of old, but we just want to be there for you."

"I know, but I can do some things for myself. Even if I can't, I still need to try. Can you understand that?" Kendall asked.

"Yeah, I get it. Can you understand that I'm not going to stop trying to take care of you until you're better and this is over?"

"Yeah," Kendall said, smiling a little.

"So... Are we good?"

"Yeah, we're good," Kendall said.

∞

Alex went downstairs. Sylvia and Sally looked at him. "How are they?" Sylvia asked.

"They're talking now, but I really think we need to let him do this," Alex told them.

"We need his mom's permission first. I'm also going to call Claudia and see if we can get James in to see her today or tomorrow. I think I'll have a chat with Carlos and Logan too. It wouldn't hurt for them to go see her as well," Sally said.

"That's probably a good idea," Alex said.

Sally went into the study to call Jen and talk to her about Kendall and the phone calls. She came out a few minutes later. "She says it's fine if we set Taylor up to call by having Kendall alone in the car, but she doesn't want him answering the phone."

"Will just seeing Taylor call be enough?" Alex asked.

"I think so. It would definitely be better if we could get his voice on a longer recording, but we can work with two shorter ones."

"At least James will feel a little better about it," Sylvia said.

"Let me call Claudia and see when she can get them in," Sally said, dialing Claudia's number.

"Hello," Claudia's cheerful voice answered.

"Hey Claudia, I was wondering if you'd have time to see the other boys this week?"

"Of course! What's going on?" she asked.

"James is having a really hard time right now, and I think it might be good to set up a group session between the three of them."

"Aw, my poor babies! Can you bring them tomorrow after school?"

Sally looked at Sylvia. "How about tomorrow after school?"

"They have hockey practice until about five."

"Is after five okay? They have hockey practice tomorrow," Sally relayed to Claudia.

"That's just fine. Bring them on over when they're finished."

"Thanks Claudia. I'll give you a call later." Sally smiled. "She said to drop them off after practice tomorrow."

"Good. I think it'll help them deal with everything a little better," Alex said.

"How was Kendall doing?" Sally asked.

Alex sighed, "Feeling like he's interfering with everyone's lives, and tired of not having any control over his own life."

"Well, hopefully giving us a hand nailing Taylor will help with that."

"I hope so too, because he's really down about all of this," Alex said.

"I know. It'll get better once this whole thing with Graham is over, though. Until then, we just have to help him and the other kids through it as best we can," Sally told him.

"Well, I'm going to go make some lunch so he can eat before we go to his appointment," Sylvia said, getting up.

"I'll go tell Kendall what the plan is, and I finally have my photos to show him," Sally said, grabbing her laptop.

∞

Sally went upstairs and knocked at the guest room door. "Hey, you guys doing okay?"

"Yeah, we're good," James smiled.

"Good. Could you give Kendall and me few minutes? I wanted to go over his photos and talk to him a little about what the plan is today."

James looked at Kendall, who nodded. "Okay, I'll go help Mama G," James said.

"Thanks kiddo," Sally said.

"What about today?" Kendall asked.

"Well, your mom agreed to let you wait in the car alone, but she doesn't want you answering Taylor's call. So, we'll just go with the first plan and it'll work fine. John and Shale will see him make the call and we arrest him."

"But it would be better if we caught him saying more stuff," Kendall said.

"Honey, two short recordings should be more than enough for the lab to work with."

"But..."

"Your mom was very clear about this and I'm going to respect her wishes."

Kendall sighed in frustration.

"I know you wanted to do more, but this'll work just fine. It could be he'll talk longer just because he sees you. That's why I'm going to call you on the disposable cell as soon as he calls. Then I'll give you a few instructions, depending on what he says."

"Like what?"

"Things like, look around, or hunch down in the seat. Simple things that would be normal reactions if you were actually answering the call yourself."

"Okay."

She sat next to him and opened her laptop. "I have your photos on here and I made you a disc as well," she said, pulling out a disc case and handing it to him.

"Thanks."

She pulled up the file marked "Kendall" and opened it. "So, what can you tell me about your pictures?"

"I don't know. I was just taking pictures of the guys outside."

She clicked on a photo. "Well, let me tell you about these photos. You actually got three of Dylan and his buddies going after Logan. Ryan showed them to Dylan and told him if he pled guilty to the assault charges, he would drop the charges of perjury. He agreed and will be going to a facility in Minneapolis that specializes in troubled, violent minors for at least six months. He was also given five years' probation after he gets out. If he crosses the line, he goes to prison."

"I guess that's good," Kendall said.

"It is. The facility has a high success rate in helping kids like Dylan. Hopefully with the proper counseling, he'll come around."

"I hope so," Kendall said.

"You're a good kid, you know that?"

"Why?"

"You just are." She smiled.

After going through Kendall's photos and discussing them, She showed him how to try and interpret the mood of the photos.

Kendall started looking through Sally's. "You take a lot of nature pictures."

"That I do."

"Why?"

"I don't know, personal preference, I guess. Taking photos of nature helps me to remember there's beauty in this world, in spite of everything that goes on in it."

"That makes sense."

"Plus, I've tried taking photos of people, and they just never look right."

"Why?"

"I don't know. They just never seem right to me."

"Maybe because people stress you out and nature makes you happy?" Kendall suggested.

"That could very well be," she said with a smile.

∞

About half an hour later, Alex knocked at the door. "Hey, lunch is ready."

"I'm not hungry," Kendall said.

"Oh, so what you're saying is you want a lift downstairs?" Alex asked.

"We'll be down in a minute." Sally laughed.

"Okay." Alex smiled.

Kendall was still looking at the photos and looked sideways at Sally. "I thought you didn't like taking pictures of people?"

She looked at the screen. "Crap, I thought I pulled all of those. You're not allowed to tell anyone about that."

Kendall raised an eyebrow. "Why?"

"Because I said so," she said, closing the file.

"But you guys are so cute together." He smirked.

"Kendall..."

"But Sally, why not?" he teased.

"Because it would NOT be good. Do I have your word?" she asked in a serious tone.

"I won't say anything," he promised.

"Thank you. I trust you to keep your word."

"I swear, I won't say anything to anyone."

"Thank you," she said.

"So do you guys love each other?"

"Kendall..."

"What?"

She looked at him. "Yes, now can we please drop it? Let's go get some lunch."

Kendall smiled at her.

"What?" she asked.

"Nothing."

"I CAN trust you, right?"

"Yes, you can trust me," Kendall said, getting up.

"Alright, let's go eat. Your appointment is in a little over an hour."

"Yay," he said unenthusiastically.

"It'll be okay."

"Sally?"

"Yes?"

"The last picture was happy?"

She smiled. "Yes it was."

∞

They went downstairs and joined the others for lunch. Kendall picked at his food, nervous about the appointment.

"Try and eat a little more," James said.

"I'm not hungry and we did the formula just a little while ago."

"Just half of your sandwich, okay?"

"Okay," Kendall sighed, picking it up.

"So, Papa M and I are going to stay here with you?" James asked Sally.

She nodded. "Kendall and Sylvia will meet Antonio at the therapist's office, and then they'll stop at the pharmacy. John will be waiting there, and Antonio and Shale will be right behind them."

"What if Taylor doesn't follow us?" Kendall asked.

"I don't think that's going to be an issue."

"So then when Taylor calls Kendall's cell, the computer will pick up and you'll call Kendall?" James asked.

"That's the plan."

"If my mom had let me answer, how would it have worked with the phone being so far away from the computer?" Kendall asked.

"It's still synced to the computer and it'll stay that way until I disconnect them. Why?"

"I just didn't think about it until James said something. So the spoof site is someplace he calls into and then dials in the numbers that he wants?"

"Yeah, that's what makes it so hard to trace without his phone. Once we arrest him, the spoof number should be on the phone he's calling from, and then we can subpoena the call records from the company. That will give us a list of the numbers he has called."

"Well, we better get going," Sylvia said.

Kendall groaned. "I don't want to go."

"I know, Mijo, but it's just an evaluation today," Sylvia reminded him.

"It'll be over before you know it," Alex said, putting his arm around him.

"Right."

"James, why don't we go over your photos while we're waiting for them to get back?" Sally suggested, setting the laptop on the coffee table.

"Okay." James smiled and went to sit next to her.

Alex held Sylvia's coat for her and then zipped Kendall's jacket. "It's going to be okay, Champ."

"My throat's still dry, I'm going to grab some water," he said, heading for the kitchen. He returned a couple of minutes later with a bottle of water and he and Sylvia left.

Peters called Sally to let her know the SUV followed Sylvia a couple of minutes after they left.

∞

They arrived at the physical therapist's office about fifteen minutes later. John was already waiting in the dentist's parking lot across the street, with a clear view of the building.

Antonio arrived a couple of minutes later. "Hi honey," Sylvia said, getting out of the car.

He kissed her and then went around and opened Kendall's door. "Come on, Mijo," he said, holding his hand out. Kendall sighed and took it. They walked inside and took the elevator up to the third floor.

Shale radioed John. "Taylor is pulling up on the east side of the building."

John looked to his right. "I see him, just stay back and keep him in sight."

"Copy that."

∞

Sylvia, Antonio, and Kendall reached the therapist's office and Sylvia signed Kendall in. "You doing okay?" Antonio asked him.

"Yeah."

"We won't be here that long today, and after the stop at the pharmacy, I want you to go home and rest, okay?"

"Okay," Kendall said, laying his head on Antonio's shoulder.

A couple of minutes later, the assistant called Kendall's name. "Come on," Antonio said, standing up.

Kendall sighed and took Antonio's hand and they followed her through the doors to the back.

The assistant led them through an exercise area and to a small room. She handed Antonio a gown for Kendall and smiled. "Joel will be right in."

"Thank you," Antonio said.

"I'm not wearing that," Kendall said.

"He has to be able to look at your shoulder. You only need to take off your shirt."

"Papi..."

"Kendall, please. We need to get your shoulder checked out, and I'll be here the whole time."

Kendall sighed and started to take off the stabilizer. Antonio helped him with it and then helped pull his shirt over his head. Kendall slipped his arms into the gown and Antonio tied it. Antonio sat on the table next to Kendall, who was hugging his arms tightly to his chest.

"It's okay, Mijo," Antonio said softly.

There was a knock at the door and then it opened. A pleasant looking man of about forty came in carrying a file. "Hi, I'm Joel Riggs, and I understand we need to do an evaluation of a shoulder injury?"

Antonio nodded. "His left shoulder was injured almost a month ago. He's been ill, so we haven't been able to get in until now."

Joel smiled and nodded, reading the doctor's notes. "Okay Kendall, why don't we take a look?"

Kendall looked at Antonio and shook his head.

Joel smiled. "It's okay, we'll go slowly. So, you've been wearing the stabilizer for nearly three weeks now?"

"Yes," Antonio answered.

"Day and night?"

"Yes. He actually re-injured it about two and a half weeks ago. That's when Dr. Sharpe said to wear it at night too."

Joel nodded. "Okay, unfortunately I do need to see it," he told Kendall.

Kendall scooted a little closer to Antonio. "It's okay, Mijo."

"Tell you what, why don't I stand over here and you just turn, so I can see it for a minute? I won't come any closer until you're ready," Joel suggested.

"Come on," Antonio said, pulling Kendall around to face him a little more. He untied the gown and pushed it off his left shoulder.

"That's still pretty bruised. Can you use your arm at all?"

Kendall shook his head.

"Can you show me how high you can lift your arm?"

Antonio steadied him while Kendall lifted his arm to about six inches above his waist.

"Can you not raise it any higher, or is it just too painful?"

Kendall tried lifting it higher, but he couldn't do it.

"I don't think he can raise it any higher," Antonio said.

"Okay. I'm going to need to palpate it to see how tightly the muscles are locked up," Joel told him. Kendall shook his head and could feel the panic starting to build.

"Breathe, in and out," Antonio said, softly holding Kendall's right hand to his chest.

Kendall closed his eyes and did as Antonio said. "That's my boy. It's going to be okay. I'm right here," Antonio said, taking Kendall's other hand.

He nodded to Joel, who took a couple of steps closer. Joel saw Kendall tense up and stopped moving. "Okay, I'm going to try my best to stay at just under an arm's length away, but I do need to touch your shoulder," Joel said.

Kendall took a deep breath and Antonio nodded again.

Joel got a little closer. "I'm going to touch your arm now, so try and relax." He touched Kendall's arm and stayed still for a moment. "I'm going to touch the top of your shoulder and then your shoulder blade."

After a moment, he gently touched the bruised area and Kendall jumped. "Did that hurt?"

Kendall shook his head.

"Okay. Are my hands cold?"

Kendall nodded.

"Sorry about that." He smiled. "Okay, I'm going to apply a little pressure. Let me know when it starts hurting."

He gently pressed the area surrounding the scapula and then moved his fingers to the center. Kendall flinched and pulled away.

"Did that hurt?"

Kendall nodded.

"Okay, just a little more and then we're done." He palpated the area where Deesie had inserted the needles and Kendall whimpered and pulled away. "That's really sore, isn't it?"

Kendall nodded.

"I think that's enough for now. I'm going to research a couple of things. You can get dressed while I'm doing that. I don't want you wearing the stabilizer for now, unless you're going to be doing something strenuous," he said as he left the room.

"Are you okay?" Antonio asked.

Kendall nodded and Antonio helped him on with his shirt. "At least I don't have to wear that thing anymore."

"See, something positive already." Antonio smiled.

Kendall rolled his eyes.

Joel returned a few minutes later. "Well, the muscles are locked up about eighty percent. I don't think you've developed adhesive capsulitis yet, but you're getting close."

"Capsulitis?" Antonio asked.

"It's also known as frozen shoulder syndrome. It's more common in older people, but with a severe enough trauma, children have been known to develop it."

"What do we do?"

"Treatment consists of massage therapy, therapeutic ultrasound, stretching exercises, and then stamina building exercises. Possible steroidal treatment and trigger point dry needling therapy has been shown to be very helpful in these types of cases."

"What is that?" Antonio asked.

"An acupuncture needle is used to relieve the stress of the muscle or joint."

Kendall shook his head frantically.

"That is NOT an option in this case," Antonio told him.

"I understand, but we do need to come up with a treatment plan, and soon. I would recommend starting off with the ultrasonic and massage therapies. I can show you some stretching exercises and these can be done at home."

Kendall looked at Antonio and he pulled the teen close. "It'll be alright, we'll figure this out. Why don't you go sit with Mami? I'll be right out."

"It's to your left and through the double doors," Joel told Kendall.

Kendall nodded and went to find Sylvia.

"The thing is, he panics if anyone he doesn't know touches him," Antonio explained.

"I noticed that. The problem is that the type of therapy he needs involves a lot of touching. I'm not sure what to do about this, but you can definitely do the exercises at home. Maybe I can give you a quick lesson in massage therapy, but it won't be nearly as effective. Let me check into a couple of things and I'll give you a call later. For now, no brace and have him lift his arm as high as he can for about twenty repetitions twice a day. Also, if he'll allow someone to rub a pain relieving ointment onto the area, that would help. It would also get him use to someone touching him."

Antonio sighed. "Thank you. We'll start with that tonight and wait for your call."

"We'll figure something out." Joel smiled.

"I hope so," Antonio said, shaking Joel's hand.

∞

Antonio went out and sat with Sylvia and Kendall. "He's going to give us a call later after he looks into a few things."

"Okay. I already called John to let him know that we'll be leaving in a couple of minutes," Sylvia told him.

"Good. I'll follow about five minutes after you leave."

She nodded and stood up. "Okay, let's get this over with."

Kendall stood up and they went to the elevator. Antonio put his arm around Kendall's shoulders. "Sally will call you as soon as Taylor calls your phone. Just follow her instructions and everything will be alright."

Kendall nodded.

They walked out to the car together and Antonio kissed Sylvia goodbye. "I'll be right behind you."

She nodded and got into the car and pulled out of the parking lot. "Are you sure you're going to be okay doing this?" she asked Kendall.

"Yeah, I'll be okay."

"I'll be right inside the doors and Papi and John will be right there."

"I know, it'll be okay."

She pulled into the pharmacy parking lot and took a deep breath. "I am SO not comfortable with this."

"It's fine, really." Kendall smiled.

"How can you be so calm?"

"Because it's going to be over with soon."

She smiled. "Yes it is."

She kissed his cheek and took another deep breath before getting out of the car. She hit the lock button on her key lock and went inside.

John was parked four spaces down on the passenger side and had a clear view of Kendall. He had watched Taylor pull in on the other side of Sylvia's car about six spaces down. Shale was four spaces down from Taylor, parked on the other side of the building, facing Taylor's SUV.

John watched Antonio pull in on the far end of the parking lot and he radioed Sally.

"We're in place."

"Okay, now we wait," she said.

∞

Taylor watched Sylvia go inside and waited a couple of minutes before dialing the spoof call center. He punched in Kendall's number and then Logan's.

"He's calling," John said into the radio.

"Copy that," Sally said.

Taylor waited for the numbers to go through the call center and then it started ringing through.

Kendall answered the phone on the first ring. "Hey Loges. What are you up to?"

Chapter 135~ Taking Taylor Down

Manning was furious—the judge had denied EVERY motion he had put before her. Now he had to either agree to a written testimony or wait until the Knight kid was able to testify, which would probably take months.

While Manning didn't particularly care one way or the other, Graham wanted out, and it made the most sense to agree to the statement sheets. He was hoping he could appeal and argue that they should be thrown out because the court officers were prejudiced, and then that damn DA had to suggest the judge preside over it. Manning dialed Taylor's number.

"Yeah?"

"Step it up. I don't want that kid to be able to function," Manning ordered and then hung up.

Taylor shook his head. "There better be a healthy bonus in this."

∞

He had watched the Garcia woman take the kids to school and come back that morning, but nothing had happened since then.

So he waited patiently, listening to music on his MP3 player and surfing the internet on his phone while he waited. Finally, Mrs. Garcia and Kendall came out and got in the car. He watched them drive away and then slowly followed. He never noticed the silver Subaru parked two blocks back pull out and follow him again.

Taylor followed them to a medical building and watched as Officer Garcia met them and they all walked in together. He waited for nearly an hour before they came out and Garcia went back to his own car. Mrs. Garcia pulled out, drove off through the west end of the parking lot, and took a left. He waited a couple of minutes and followed them. He hadn't noticed John leave five minutes earlier, nor did he see the silver Subaru following him two blocks back.

Taylor continued following them and parked across the street when he saw them pull into the pharmacy parking lot. He saw Mrs. Garcia get out and go in alone, so he quickly pulled into the parking lot and parked a few cars down. He smiled when he saw Kendall sitting in the car alone, and after a minute, dialed the spoof call center and punched in Kendall's number. He chose to use Logan's number this time, because he was worried the kid wouldn't pick up if he saw James' number again.

After a minute, the phone rang through and he smiled when he heard Kendall answer.

∞

Sally went into Antonio's study once John radioed and waited by the laptop. She had put the disposable cell number into her phone on speed dial so she could get ahold of Kendall quickly. The computer showed Kendall's phone receiving a call from Logan and she hit the speed dial number. First, she heard the ringing come from the phone lying on the desk, and then she heard Kendall's voice as he answered his cell.

She grabbed the cell from the desk and realized what he had done. "Oh no!"

Kendall answered the phone on the first ring, because he knew Sally had the computer set up to answer on the second. He looked at the caller ID and took a deep breath. "Hey Loges. What are you up to?"

No one answered, so he looked at the screen. "Logan, are you there?"

"What's the matter, sweetheart, don't you want to talk to me?"

Kendall took a deep breath. "No, you're not real."

"Want to bet?"

"You're dead," Kendall said quietly, sinking a little lower in the seat.

"Then how do I know what you're wearing, sweetheart? That's a nice black ski jacket. I love the matching beanie."

"You're not real."

Sally listened as Kendall spoke to Taylor and quickly called John on his cell. She did not want Antonio hearing this. "John! Kendall has HIS cell. He's speaking to Taylor himself."

"He's what?" John asked, looking over at the car.

"He switched the phones. He's the one talking to Taylor."

"He seems to be doing alright so far. Let me know if the conversation takes a turn—I'm just a few cars away from him," John told her.

"Copy that."

James and Alex heard Sally yelling and went in to see what was wrong.

"What's going on?" James asked.

"Your little brother seems to have taken matters into his own hands," she said, listening to the conversation.

"What?" James said.

Then he heard Kendall's voice on the computer. "What did he do?"

"He switched the cell phones. Probably when he came back for the bottle of water."

"Calm down," Alex told James, steering him to the small couch.

"Calm down?" James yelled.

"Yes, as in stop yelling. There's nothing we can do about it now. This was the original plan, and remember he has three officers right there, including Antonio," Alex said calmly.

"Oh, he is SO going to get it!"

"James, he seems to be doing alright. And I get dibs on letting him have it if anything goes wrong," Sally told him.

She continued monitoring the computer and prayed that this didn't send Kendall into a total breakdown.

∞

"We're going to have so much fun together. I've missed you so much."

"You're dead, so leave me alone," Kendall said, trying to control the panic building in his chest.

"The things I'm going to do to you will make you scream..."

Kendall sat the phone on the seat, trying to control his breathing.

∞

Sally was still listening and shook her head in disbelief. "He got him to threaten him."

"That's a good thing?" James asked, shaking with anger at Taylor's words.

Sally smiled and nodded. "That's a very good thing."

Alex put his arm around James' shoulders. "It's okay, this is what they needed."

She put a call over the police radio channel. "We've got him! Arrest his sorry ass, and someone get to Kendall now."

"Copy that," John said, getting out of his car.

Shale got out and walked towards the pharmacy entrance. Taylor was too busy watching Kendall to pay any attention to her.

Antonio went towards Sylvia's car as Shale and Bennet started for Taylor's. Shale saw John come up behind the car and nodded to him. She unzipped her jacket so she would have easy access to her pistol and knocked on the side window.

Taylor looked over, annoyed. "What?" Shale smiled and made a rolling motion with her hand. "What?" Taylor repeated, rolling down his window.

"I think you've got a flat on your rear passenger tire," Shale said pleasantly.

"Are you kidding me?" Taylor asked, exasperated.

"It doesn't look completely flat, but you won't get too far on it."

Taylor shoved his cell into his pocket and got out.

∞

Kendall closed his eyes and tried to take a few deep breaths. He was shaking and desperately trying to keep himself from panicking.

He jumped when his door opened. "Are you alright?" Antonio asked.

Kendall nodded. "I'm sorry."

"For what? You did great!"

"I-I need to tell you something, Papi. Please don't be mad," Kendall begged. His eyes tearing up as the events of the morning began to overwhelm him.

"I won't be mad. What is it, Mijo?" Antonio asked, concerned with Kendall's state of mind.

"I-I s-switched the phones. I was the one talking to him," Kendall told him.

"You what? Why would you do that to yourself?"

"I j-just wanted it to be over and..."

Antonio looked up when he heard John and Shale yelling.

He pushed Kendall to the floor. "Stay there!" he said as he shut the door.

∞

Taylor had gotten out and walked to the back of the SUV, Shale behind him. Taylor turned the corner and saw John standing there. "Chad Taylor, you are under arrest. You are being charged with..."

Taylor flew at John, swinging. He hit him in the face, just under his left eye and he went down. Shale drew her firearm and yelled at Taylor to stop. Taylor ignored her and kept running. Shale looked at John, who waved her on and she took off after Taylor.

Antonio saw Taylor heading his way and ran for John's car. He got around to the far side and when Taylor got there, he used his forearm and hit Taylor in the throat. Taylor went down and rolled to the side. He tried to get up, but Antonio was there and had him by the shirt before he could run.

Antonio pulled Taylor around and slammed him against John's SUV. Taylor tried to punch Antonio, but he blocked it and slammed him against the SUV again.

"YOU LIKE TERRORIZING KIDS! YOU THINK IT'S FUNNY TO HEAR THEM BREAK DOWN, YOU SICK BASTARD!" Antonio yelled, punching Taylor in the face. Taylor kicked at him and Antonio hit him again, and this time Taylor went down. Antonio pulled back to hit him a third time, but someone grabbed his arm and pulled him back.

"Let go," he ordered.

"No, he's down. We need to do this right or it was all for nothing," John said, holding his partner back. Shale cuffed Taylor and pulled him up and away from Antonio.

"Mirandize him, get him to the station, and turn O'Hara loose on him," Antonio said.

"You got it, Chief," Shale said, pulling Taylor towards her unmarked patrol car.

Antonio looked at John. "Are you alright?"

John nodded. "Just caught me off guard. I didn't think he'd be one to hit and run."

"We better get some ice on that eye."

"It can wait until I get back to the station. You better get back to Kendall," John said, pointing to Sylvia's car.

Antonio nodded and ran back to the car. He looked inside and saw Kendall where he had told him to stay, so he opened the door. "It's alright, it's just me."

Kendall was curled up on the floor of the car, shaking.

"It's alright, Mijo, we got him," Antonio said softly as he put his hand down to help the boy up. Kendall took his hand and got out. Antonio wrapped his arms around him and hugged him tightly.

Sylvia came running out as soon as she saw Antonio get back to her car. She threw her arms around him and Kendall.

"It's alright, honey. We got him," Antonio said, kissing her cheek.

"Is John alright?" Sylvia asked. She had seen him get hit and then get back up.

"He's fine, just a black eye."

"Are you okay, Mijo?" she asked Kendall, who was hiding his face in Antonio's jacket. He nodded.

"Now what's this about the phones?" Antonio asked him.

"I switched them," Kendall said, his voice muffled by Antonio's jacket.

"Why did you do that?" he asked softly.

"Because I-I wanted it to be over with, and this way, Sally got a longer recording and we don't have to do this anymore."

"You know your mom was against that, right?"

Kendall nodded.

"She's probably not going to be very happy about this," Antonio told him.

"I know."

"Look at me," Antonio said.

Kendall shook his head.

"Kendall, look at me," Antonio repeated.

Kendall sighed and pulled away a little, looking up at Antonio.

"I may not be very happy with what you did, but I understand WHY you did it. I'm very proud of you."

"Why? You should be mad at me," Kendall said quietly.

"Because I know talking to him wasn't easy, but you did it, and because of that we have a good case against him," Antonio said, hugging him again.

"What exactly are we talking about?" Sylvia asked.

"Your godson switched the cell phones, and when Taylor called pretending to be Deesie, Kendall answered."

"You what? And why is he MY godson when he does something like this?"

Kendall shifted so Antonio was closer to her. "I took my phone and left the disposable one."

She looked at him. "Honey, why?"

"Because he had to," Antonio told her.

"Alright, but I'd probably avoid Sally and your mom for a while," she said, kissing Kendall's cheek.

"That's probably good advice." Antonio smiled.

"Let's get home, you need to get some rest," Sylvia told Kendall.

"Why don't I take him home while you pick the kids up from school?" Antonio suggested.

"I asked Jo to pick them up, since we didn't know how long his appointment would last. She's going to stay for dinner and spend some time with the kids," Sylvia told him.

"Okay, then why don't I stop and pick up dinner on the way home? That way everyone can relax tonight."

"That sounds perfect." She smiled.

"I'll be home early. You take a nap when you get home," he told Kendall.

"Okay."

"We'll see you soon," Sylvia said, kissing Antonio goodbye.

"A couple of hours at the most," he said.

Kendall got into the car. Antonio secured his seat belt and then reached over and took the cell phone. "We'll get this back to you later."

"I'm in no hurry," Kendall said.

Antonio kissed him on top of the head. "You did well today, but you're still going to have to face your mom."

"I know."

"I'll see you later."

"Bye Papi."

Antonio closed the door and waved as Sylvia pulled out.

∞

Sylvia and Kendall got to the Garcia's a few minutes later and walked up to the house.

Sally opened the door, crossed her arms over her chest, and arched an eyebrow at Kendall. "Well?"

Kendall moved behind Sylvia. "Hi?"

She just looked at him. "Come here."

He shook his head and stayed behind Sylvia. "I'm not going to save you," she said, pushing him in front of her.

"What were you thinking?" Sally asked quietly.

"That I could help more if I actually talked to him?"

"What part of 'we're going to respect your mother's wishes' did you NOT understand?"

"Actually, you said YOU were going to respect her wishes. I never promised her," Kendall pointed out.

"You KNEW she didn't want you speaking to him," Sally said firmly.

"Yes, I know it was what she wanted. It's always what she wants, or what somebody else wants. What about what I want?" Kendall said defensively.

Sally sighed. "Honey, everyone is..."

"Trying to look out for me, I KNOW. But when there's something I can do to actually help, nobody listens to me."

Sally took a deep breath. "You're right."

"What?" he asked in surprise.

"You're right, people don't always listen. What you need to remember is you're fourteen and that the adults here make decisions based on what they truly believe is best for you. Not because they're trying to be mean or don't think your feelings count. What the adults need to remember is that you're not a typical 14-year-old."

"So... Are you mad at me or not?" Kendall asked.

"Furious. How do you think it makes me look to be outsmarted by a kid?"

"We don't have to tell anyone else."

"Nice try, but that's not going to work. YOU get to explain to your mom what happened," Sally told him.

"Couldn't you just arrest me or something?" he groaned.

"Sorry, now I need to get to the station and have some fun with our new resident."

"Thanks Sally," Sylvia said.

"I'll see you later." Sally smiled as she headed out the door.

Kendall felt someone behind him and turned to find James staring at him.

"James..." Kendall started.

His friend grabbed him and pulled him close. "I'm really glad you're okay, but as soon as you're well I am going to find a VERY deep snow bank and plant you in it."

"Deal," Kendall said, hugging him back.

Chapter 136~ Cutting a Deal

Kendall went upstairs to lie down for a while. James grabbed his homework and followed him.

"The bad guy is in jail, you don't have to worry so much," Kendall told him.

"I'm not worried. You know Papi wants someone close by when you're sleeping," James told him as he put his books on the small desk.

Kendall smiled. "Thanks James."

"Are you really doing okay?" James asked.

"Yeah, I'm just tired. The stupid Benadryl makes me sleepy."

"What do you think your mom's going to say?"

Kendall sighed. "I don't know. She'll probably be mad for a while. I guess I should call her and get it over with."

"That might be a good idea, and then you can just get some sleep."

Kendall nodded and went to get the phone from Antonio and Sylvia's room. He called Jen's cell.

"Hello."

"Hey mom, it's just me."

"Hi honey, what's up?"

"Um, I don't know if Papi called you, but they caught the guy making the phone calls."

"Thank God! No, he hasn't called yet. He's probably really busy at the station. Are you okay? Did everything work out alright?"

"Yeah, I'm okay. I kinda need to tell you something, though. Remember how you promised you'd listen when I need to tell you something?"

"Okay, what is it?" Jen asked, her voice betraying her concern.

"Well, you know how you told Sally that I could sit in the car but not answer the phone?"

"Yes," she said, already worried about where this was going.

"I know you didn't want me to talk to him and I understand why, but I might have switched the phones and took the call."

"You might have what!" she yelled.

Kendall flinched at her tone. "Yes, and I'm really sorry I didn't do what you wanted, but I needed to get him to say more so that we didn't have to do this anymore. Nobody else knew I was doing it, and Papi and Sally already talked to me about it. I'm really sorry, please understand that I had to do it," Kendall begged her.

"Kendall William Knight, I was VERY clear about this and I am very angry right now!"

"Mom, I'm really sorry, but..."

Jen tried to take some calming breaths like Eli had showed her, but her fear and anger overrode the attempt. "Why should I listen to your excuses when you won't listen to my concerns?" She snapped angrily.

Kendall held the phone away from his ear—she was yelling so loudly.

"Mom, please!" Kendall said his voice breaking.

James could hear the tone in Jen's voice and ran downstairs to get Alex and Sylvia. "Kendall's trying to explain what happened to Mama K and she's freaking out on him!"

"Oh no," Sylvia said.

"This can't be good," Alex said, running for the stairs, James and Sylvia behind him.

Alex got to the guest room and Kendall was sitting on the floor, the phone in his lap. Alex could hear Jen still yelling and grabbed it. "Jen, calm down," Alex said in a quiet but firm voice.

"Alex, do you KNOW what happened?"

"Yes, we found out about it after the call had begun," he said, leaving the room.

"This is unbelievable! How was he able to switch the phones?"

"Jen, listen, the important thing is that he's alright. He wasn't in any danger and he didn't have a panic attack. I know you're not happy about this, we weren't either, but the fact is it's over and he's fine," Alex said, trying to reason with her.

"He's fine now, but who's to say he won't break down later?"

"Honey, he was actually doing really well until now," Alex told her.

"What's that supposed to mean?" Jen asked angrily.

"Listen to yourself, your tone of voice. You're panicking and it's spilling over and affecting your son. You need to try and calm done before you make yourself sick. I think you should call Dr. Thorne and tell him what's going on so he can help you deal with this," Alex said gently.

"He shouldn't have done this," Jen said, a sob escaping.

"He knows he shouldn't have done it, but it's something he felt he had to do. He's willing to accept the consequences of his actions, but screaming at him isn't going to help."

Jen took a deep breath. "Can you put him back on the phone, please?"

"Let me get back to him," Alex said, opening the door. Kendall was still sitting on the floor, Sylvia on one side of him, James on the other. He squatted down next to Kendall. "Hey Champ, your mom want to talk to you."

Kendall shook his head.

"Come on, it'll be okay," Alex said, holding the phone out.

Kendall shook his head again.

Alex sighed. "Okay."

"He doesn't want to talk to me, does he?" Jen asked quietly.

Alex got up and went back out. "He's already half asleep, honey. I'll have him call you later, or maybe you should come over after you've had a chance to rest and the two of you can talk. Please think about calling Dr. Thorne and see if he can help you with this. I know it scared you, and I don't blame you for being upset about it, but I'm really worried about you right now."

"I'll be okay. I think I will give Eli a call and I'll talk to you later," Jen said, hanging up.

Alex went back into the bedroom. "She's going to call Dr. Thorne. She knows she's not handling this well and feels really bad about how she reacted."

"Brooke had meetings today, so I think I'll head over and stay with her." Sylvia said.

"That might be a good idea," he agreed.

"Come on, Mijo, let's get you into bed. You need to get some rest," Sylvia told Kendall.

Kendall just sat there until James got up and pulled Kendall with him. "Get some sleep," he ordered, pushing his friend onto the bed. Kendall moved back and then curled up, closing his eyes.

"Can you stay here with him?" Alex asked James.

James nodded and sat down next to Kendall.

Alex and Sylvia went downstairs.

"She's not handling this well at all. I think she was on the verge of a panic attack herself," Alex told Sylvia as he helped her on with her coat.

Sylvia nodded. "I'll make sure she calls Dr. Thorne and let you know what's going on."

"Okay. I think I'll give Antonio a call and let him know too," Alex told her.

Sylvia nodded. "Jo should be home with the kids in a little while. Antonio's going to bring dinner home, so tell her not to worry about cooking."

"Will do." He smiled.

∞

Sally got to the station and checked in with Antonio. "Hey Boss, you holding up okay?"

"Much better now that we have that piece of garbage behind bars."

"I hear you had to hit him a few times."

"Only twice, then John made me stop." Antonio pouted.

"That's probably a good thing."

"Probably. I was wishing he had been a little slower getting to us. Then I remembered that Taylor gets to deal with you next and it made it all better." Antonio smiled.

"Well, I hope I don't let you down. I'll give Ryan a call and see how he wants to play this."

∞

Sally called Ryan. "Hi Sally. I hear you got him."

"Yep. Calling to see if you want in on the questioning."

"You bet I do. I'll be there in ten minutes."

Ryan arrived and they gathered in Antonio's office to discuss strategy. "Well, we can offer him immunity if he helps us bring down Manning," Ryan said.

"No way is he getting off scot-free. He needs to do time for what he did to Kendall, period," Sally said.

"Okay, so we offer him a reduced sentence based on what he has to offer us. He's looking at ten years for aggravated stalking and harassment with intent to do harm. Another two for each count of assault of a police officer, and two for resisting arrest. Can you work that?" Ryan asked, smiling.

"It's a start."

∞

Sylvia got to Brooke's house and knocked. Jen answered—her eyes were red from crying. She was on the phone talking to someone. "I know you're right, I'm just so upset with him right now. Alright, I'll try. Yes, I'll see you tomorrow morning. Thank you Eli." She hung up.

"Jen..." Sylvia started.

"Please don't. I know I shouldn't have yelled at him. I feel bad enough!"

"I was going to ask if you wanted me to make you a cup of tea." Sylvia smiled.

"That sounds nice," Jen said as they walked into the kitchen. Sylvia put the kettle on as Jen pulled two mugs down from the cupboard.

"How is he?" Jen asked quietly.

"Sleeping. He's taking the Benadryl like he promised and it makes him tired. He had his appointment with the physical therapist and he's going to call us later with some options."

Jen nodded.

"Antonio said they're going to have to figure something out, because the therapy he needs involves massage and ultrasonic, and since he can't stand to be touched, it's going to take some research."

"Is the therapist nice?" Jen asked.

"Yes. I wasn't in the room, but Antonio said he went slowly and let Kendall know before he was going to touch him."

"Good."

"Jen, maybe you should lie down and get some rest. Why don't you come and have dinner tonight?" Sylvia asked.

"I don't know. I'll have to think about it."

"Jen, isolating yourself isn't a solution here."

"What is the solution? Every time I turn around, I end up doing something wrong! Something that hurts my son."

"That's not true and you know it. What did Eli say?"

"He said to do my calming exercises, make sure I take my medication, and focus my energy on healing, not anger."

"Sounds like good advice."

"Easier said than done," Jen snapped.

"Come on, you're going to lie down and get some rest," Sylvia said, taking Jen's arm.

"I can't sleep. I have too much on my mind."

"Too bad, you're going to try," Sylvia ordered.

"Fine," Jen said.

Sylvia got Jen tucked in, grabbed a book, and sat in the easy chair in the guest room.

"I don't need a babysitter."

"Go to sleep," Sylvia instructed as she settled in.

A few moments later, Jen was sleeping, so Sylvia stepped out and called home.

Carlos answered. "Hi Mami! Is Mama K alright?"

"She's fine, Mijo. She's sleeping now, so I'm going to stay until she wakes up or Mama D gets home. How's Kendall doing?"

"He's upstairs sleeping. Logan is staying with him for now."

"Okay. Can you put Papa or Mama M on for me?"

"Sure, bye!"

"Bye baby."

"Hey, how's Jen doing?" Alex asked.

"I'm not sure. She was talking to Dr. Thorne when I got here, but she's having trouble dealing with everything right now. She has an appointment with him tomorrow morning, so hopefully he can help her. She feels awful about getting angry with Kendall, but I think she's having trouble controlling her emotions right now."

"I don't doubt that."

"She's sleeping now, so I'm going to stay with her until she wakes up or Brooke gets home. I asked her to come over for dinner, but she's not sure she wants to. Is Kendall doing any better?"

"He's sleeping now. I had to put him in one of my shirts and tie the sleeves closed. He was biting his thumb in his sleep and got it bleeding again."

Sylvia sighed. "He hasn't done that in so long, and it took forever to break him of it."

"I know. We'll get through this, though," Alex promised.

"I hope so. Some days I just want to cry, it's so frustrating. Please don't tell Antonio that."

"I won't, but I'm sure there are times he feels that way as well."

"I know, but at least he gets to punch the bad guys."

"Life just isn't fair sometimes," Alex said, smiling.

∞

Sally went into the large interrogation room carrying a folder and a small laptop. She nodded to Shale and took a seat opposite of Taylor. She didn't say a word as she was going over the papers. Taylor watched her and had a funny feeling he knew her from somewhere.

After a moment, she looked up and tsked at him. "Mr. Taylor, it seems you've gotten yourself into quite a bit of trouble. Aggravated stalking and harassment with the intent to do harm to a minor, cyber stalking, illegal surveillance, two counts of assaulting a police officer, one count attempted assault on a police officer, resisting arrest, the list goes on and on."

"I know you," he said, still looking at her.

"Do you now?"

"You're that neighbour."

Sally smiled. "What neighbour?"

"The one that asked if I needed any help."

"Well, we're a tight-knit little community here and usually offer help where we see it's needed."

"You're a cop?"

"You're observant. What was your first clue?"

"What's going on here?" he demanded.

"What's the matter, did you really think we didn't know what was going on?" she asked in a cool tone.

"I don't know what you're talking about."

"Really? Then let me enlighten you. You were hired by Derek Manning to follow and terrorize Kendall Knight. We have been watching you since you were first spotted driving a Chevy Malibu. You have been staying at the Best Western out by the airport, left for a day and came back driving the Escalade. Did you really think that a seasoned cop's family wouldn't notice anything out of the ordinary in their own neighbourhood?"

"You can't prove anything," Taylor said, shifting uncomfortably in his seat.

She sat back in the chair and gave him a small smile. "Are you absolutely certain about that? Because I have a file here that says I can, and before you use those four little words, 'I want my attorney,' the DA is willing to make you a deal. Me... I'm against it because we have enough to charge both you and Manning, putting you BOTH away for a long time. Ryan though, he thinks it would be nice to offer you the chance to redeem yourself, since you've never been in trouble with the law before. Just be aware that everything you say here will be on record."

There was a knock at the door and Ryan entered. "Sorry I'm late."

"Not a problem. Ryan, this is Chad Taylor. You know the charges."

Ryan nodded and took the seat next to Sally. "So where are we at?"

"Just getting to the fact that you're willing to cut him a deal," Sally told him.

Ryan nodded and went over his notes. "Mr. Taylor, are you aware of how much trouble you're in?"

Taylor looked at him. "I was just doing my job."

"Exactly what is your job?"

"Surveillance."

"I see, but do you have a private investigator's license which IS required in the state of Minnesota?" Ryan asked.

"I'm a private audio/visual technician."

"I'm afraid that's not enough. In the state of Minnesota, most states actually, you are required to have an investigator's license in order to record people and legally obtain admissible information about them. Otherwise, you're just a private citizen breaking the law."

"I work for an attorney."

"Yeah, that doesn't matter. In fact, if it were me and I realized that an attorney had hired me to break the law, I'd be worried he was setting me up to be the fall guy," Sally said.

Taylor was quiet.

"I'm willing to offer you a plea, if you're willing to testify against Derek Manning. This will include any and all conversations, recordings, and documentation you've had with him regarding his employment of you in regards to this case," Ryan said.

"If not, you will be charged on all counts. So you're looking at about twenty years, minimum, in a state prison," Sally told him.

"Twenty years?" Taylor yelled.

Ryan nodded. "Ten years minimum for aggravated stalking and harassment, five years for cyber bulling, two years for each count of assault on a police officer and another two for resisting arrest."

"That's not counting illegal surveillance, causing emotional anguish to a minor child, and whatever the judge would throw at you for causing a citywide predator alert." Sally smiled.

"You can't prove any of that."

Sally smiled again and plugged a flash drive into the laptop. She clicked on a file and Taylor's voice came on.

"Then how do I know what you're wearing, sweetheart? That's a nice black ski jacket. I love the matching beanie."

"Proof that you've been stalking Kendall Knight."

She clicked on fast forward. "The things I'm going to do to you will make you scream..."

"Proof that you threatened Kendall Knight, a fourteen-year-old child."

Taylor had gone pale and was starting to sweat.

"So tell me, Mr. Taylor, exactly HOW were you going to make him scream?" Sally hissed.

"Look, I was just going off of a list of things that Manning gave me to say. Apparently, he got a list from his client's records of things that this guy said to the kid. He told me to speak in a low voice and use the word 'sweetheart' first," Taylor said quietly.

"And you thought this was okay, why?" Sally asked.

"I told you I was just doing my job."

Sally shook her head. "That's not good enough, and I don't think we should offer you a deal at all. I think you should pay for what you've done, period."

"Sally, let's hear what he has to say. If he can help us with Manning, it might be worth it. This is the first time he's been in trouble with the law and you know Manning's done this before," Ryan said in a calming tone.

"Fine, but he better have more than 'he told me to' before you give him a deal," Sally said, crossing her arms.

"I can prove he told me to," Taylor said.

"How?" Ryan asked.

"I record all of my conversations with my clients, just in case."

"Recordings made without the other parties' knowledge are not admissible in court," Sally told him.

"That's why I put that, I reserve the right to record any and all conversations regarding the contracted job, in my contracts," Taylor said.

"Are you saying Manning signed such a contract?" Ryan asked.

"No, Mr. Riker did the first time I worked for the firm. My contract specifies that I can be hired to do jobs for anyone employed by the firm and the contract applies to everyone that hires me."

"Prove it," Sally said.

"I have the contract in an office safe back in Chicago, but I scan everything into my computer."

"Can you access it with your tablet?" Sally asked.

Taylor nodded.

Sally looked at Shale. "Could you please bring Mr. Taylor's electronic equipment in?"

Shale nodded and went to get it.

"So are you telling us that you have a recording of Manning telling you what to do to Kendall?" Ryan asked.

Taylor nodded. "I have all of them."

Shale returned and handed Sally the items. She pushed the tablet across the table. "Show us, and then I want your permission to retrieve the actual contract from your office."

He nodded and turned on the device. He typed in a few things and then pushed the tablet back to Sally. She read the scanned documents and then handed it to Ryan. Ryan smiled and handed it back to Taylor. "I think we can work with this. Can we hear the recordings?"

Taylor nodded and pulled up the files. "This is the one from this morning."

Manning's voice came on. "Step it up. I don't want that kid to be able to function."

Sally looked at Ryan and nodded.

"Okay, you plead guilty to the charges of aggravated stalking, cyber stalking, and illegal surveillance. We drop the charges of assaulting a police officer and resisting arrest, with the understanding that you can be charged with those crimes for the next five years," Ryan said.

"How much time would that be?"

"You're looking at about five years, but you can knock that down to four with about a year off for good behaviour."

Taylor shook his head. "I want a better deal."

"Such as?" Sally asked.

"No prison time and I give you everything I have, as well as testify."

Sally leaned forward. "You terrorized a fourteen year old kid because someone 'told you to.' I think five years is pretty good, considering it could be over twenty."

"Sally..." Ryan said, getting up and walking across the room. She followed and they spoke too low for Taylor to hear. She shook her head and started gesturing angrily. He looked over at Taylor and whispered something else to her. Finally, she nodded and they went and sat back down.

"Alright, this is the final offer and it's not up for negotiation," Ryan told him.

Taylor looked nervously from him to Sally, who was glaring at him. "What?"

"You do two years in a minimum security facility. With time off for good behaviour that would be about twenty months. Then ten years' probation, during which time if you're arrested for anything, probation will be revoked and the additional charges of assault and resisting arrest will be reinstated," Ryan told him.

"Also, your private contractor's license in the technical field will be revoked for a period of five years. If at any time you're found committing illegal surveillance again, you lose it permanently," Sally said.

"How am I supposed to make a living?"

"Go back to school or learn how to make license plates, your choice," Sally hissed.

"Can I think about it for a few minutes?"

"Absolutely, and I'd recommend finding an attorney to help you with this. If you need one, we can get a public defender in here for you," Ryan told him.

"Maybe he should just hire Manning," Sally said.

"I think I'd like a public defender," Taylor told them.

"I'll call and get someone down here for you," Ryan said.

"Thank you," Taylor said quietly.

Ryan and Sally left the room. "You're really good at playing bad cop," he told her.

"Who said I was playing?"

"Remind me to never piss you off," he said.

"I would think that was a given." She smirked, heading for Antonio's office. She knocked on the door.

"Come in."

"Hey Boss, we've got him. He has recordings, documentation, everything we need to take Manning down. Ryan's going to request another hearing to present the evidence and hopefully convince Graham that he should plead out."

"Great job! Tell Ryan thanks for me," he said, looking up.

"Will do. Shouldn't you be heading home about now?"

"Yeah, I promised I'd stop and pick up dinner. Alex called and Jen didn't handle the news about Kendall taking the phone call well at all. Sylvia's staying with her now," he said, getting up from his desk.

"I was afraid that might happen," she said.

"She's just scared. I'm sure once she realizes he's alright, she'll feel better. Sylvia said that Jen already set up an appointment with Dr. Thorne tomorrow morning."

"That's good. At least she realizes she needs help dealing with things now," Sally said.

"I hope so. Hopefully this news will help."

"We'll see you in the morning," Sally said.

"Have a good night, Sally," he said as he headed out.

∞

Logan was sitting next to Kendall as he read his book. He reached over and pulled Kendall's hand away from his mouth as he chewed at the fabric of Alex's shirt. A few minutes later, Kendall started murmuring in his sleep and tried to curl up more.

"Hey, are you okay?" Logan asked.

"Hurts, please stop," Kendall whimpered.

Logan's heart clenched at the words and he gently shook his friend's shoulder. "Kendall, wake up. You're having a bad dream."

"No, no," Kendall whispered and Logan saw tears begin to fall from Kendall's closed eyes.

"Kendall, wake up. You're safe here at home. Pease open your eyes," Logan pleaded.

When Kendall didn't respond, Logan was torn between running and getting his dad or just staying where he was in case Kendall woke in a panic. He opted to stay where he was and pulled Kendall over to him. He ran his fingers through his friend's hair, hoping to comfort him. "It's okay, nobody's going to hurt you, buddy. Please wake up."

After a moment, Kendall relaxed. "Hmm?"

"You were having a bad dream."

"Don't remember," Kendall murmured.

"It's okay. You know if you ever need to talk about anything, I'm here for you."

"I know, thanks Loges," Kendall said as he curled up closer to his friend.

∞

Antonio stopped at the Peking Palace to pick up dinner and then headed home. He arrived a few minutes later, right behind Sylvia.

"Hi honey," she said.

"Hey. How's Jen doing?"

"She was still sleeping when I left. Brooke got home and I told her what happened. She'll give us a call later."

He nodded. "Sally and Ryan got a confession from Taylor. He's going to testify against Manning and Ryan is hoping that'll convince Graham to take a plea."

"Thank God. I really don't think Jen can handle a trial," Sylvia told him as she took a couple of bags from him.

"I know, I think we're all ready for this to be over."

They walked up the walkway and Carlos answered the door. "Mami! Papi! FOOD!"

"Well, at least we got top billing." Antonio laughed.

"This time," Sylvia said.

They carried the bags into the kitchen where Sylvia and Jo started pulling out plates and silverware. Carlos and James helped to set the table and Antonio headed upstairs to change and get the other two boys.

He looked in the guest room. "Hey, dinner's ready."

Logan looked up. "Okay," he said quietly.

"Everything alright?"

Logan nodded. "He was just having a bad dream earlier."

"Are you okay?"

Logan nodded. "I just kinda wish I didn't know."

"Know what?" Kendall asked quietly.

Logan looked at Antonio, panic in his eyes.

Antonio went in and sat next to Kendall. "That you took such a big risk today. You know what a worrier Logan is."

"Everything's okay, though." Kendall yawned.

"Yes it is. Now come on, you two get ready for dinner. I'm going to go change," Antonio said as he stood up.

Kendall went to sit up. "What the?" he said, looking at his hands.

"Yeah, you were kind of biting your thumb, so my dad put his shirt on you and tied the sleeves closed," Logan explained as he undid the knots.

"I was?"

Logan pointed to his hand. "I think so."

"Great," Kendall said, looking at his bandaged thumb.

"Come on, let's go eat," Logan said, pulling him up.

"I'm not hungry."

"I don't care, you're eating anyway," Logan said, pulling Alex's shirt up and over Kendall's head.

"Fine." Kendall pouted.

"Hey, you took a big chance today, so we're allowed to be overprotective and baby you for at least a week."

"I don't think so," Kendall said.

"Well, we voted and it's three to one, so deal with it." Logan smirked.

"That's not fair!"

"We also agreed that we don't care if it's fair or not. You're just going to have to put up with it," Logan said as he pulled Kendall out the door.

They went downstairs and James guided Kendall to his chair and sat down next to him. A moment later, Antonio joined them. Sylvia started passing around containers of food and James would put some on his plate and then Kendall's.

"I can do that, you know," Kendall told him.

James just smiled.

Kendall rolled his eyes and sighed.

A few minutes later, everyone was talking and enjoying their meal. Kendall would take a bite and set his fork down, and a moment later Antonio or James would hand it back to him. He sighed and gave up and continued to eat.

∞

Manning tried calling Taylor for the third time since receiving a call from the bailiff, telling him that Ryan had requested another hearing for tomorrow. He hung up in frustration when the call went straight to voicemail.

He called Danielle. "Hello."

"Have you heard from Taylor today?"

"No sir, why?"

"Ryan's requested another hearing for tomorrow, and I want to know where we stand on the Knight kid's ability to testify."

"Is he not answering?"

"If he were answering, would I be asking you if you've heard from him?" he snapped.

"Well, I'm sure there's a reasonable explanation. Why don't I drive there and find out what's going on?" she asked.

"You do that and get back to me as soon as you find out," he growled.

"Yes, Mr. Manning. I'll call you as soon as I find him."

Chapter 137~ Feeling Bad

Jen opened the door to find Sylvia and Joanna standing there. "What's wrong?" she asked, noting the tears in their eyes.

"Honey, we need to get to the hospital. Antonio called and Will was in an accident," Sylvia said.

"What happened?" she asked as she grabbed Katie's coat. Joanna took it from her and quickly dressed the toddler.

"A drunk driver ran him off the road. They're on their way to the hospital now," Sylvia told her.

"What about Kendall?"

"Antonio said he has a cut on his arm. We need to go now, honey," Sylvia said, putting her arm around her and pulling her out the door.

The next thing she knew, she was standing in the hospital next to a bed, looking down at her husband. His eyes were closed and he wasn't moving—they had turned the monitors off.

"I'm so sorry, Mrs. Knight. The thoracic trauma was too severe," the doctor had told her before leaving the room.

"No, no," she sobbed as she brushed the blond hair back from his forehead.

"You can't die! We're supposed to raise our children and grow old together. You can't leave us, I need you! Please Will, open your eyes. I can't do this alone!" she begged as she sat down next to him. She sat there and cried into his shoulder until she felt strong arms pull her up and close.

"You're not alone, we'll get through this together," Antonio promised.

She sat next to her son's bed after he was out of surgery. A piece of metal had punctured his right arm and nicked the brachial artery. They had to go in to repair the damage. He had lost a lot of blood by the time Antonio got to him, but applying pressure until the medics got there had saved his life. He was so small and pale. His right arm had a thick bandage on it and he had small cuts on his face from flying glass. She looked around the room at the paintings of baby animals on the walls. The primary coloured borders, the brightly coloured fleece blankets that the hospital provided for children to cuddle up with. It was a cheerful room, but all she felt was sorrow and an overwhelming sense of despair.

Sylvia and Joanna were sitting on the other side of the room, Katie sleeping in Sylvia's lap, curled up in one of the blankets. She was aware of Brooke coming in and handing her a cup of something warm, but she set it down on the table next to the bed.

The nurse had come in and told them that only family could stay through the night, but the combined looks from all the mothers quickly caused her to change her mind. Alex had taken the boys to the Garcia home. They had all been crying because they wanted to stay with their friend. Antonio was in the hallway, finishing his reports so that the drunk driver could be processed as soon as the hospital released him.

Kendall stirred and Jen moved to sit next to him. "Baby, can you wake up?"

Kendall's eyes fluttered open and then closed again. After another moment, he opened his eyes. "Mama?"

"Yes baby."

"Where's my daddy? I want my daddy!"

She was standing in the cemetery. Her friends and family were surrounding her as the pastor read the 23rd Psalm. Alex was holding Katie, and Kendall was standing between her and Antonio, holding their hands.

Suddenly, she was alone and the winter wind was blowing, causing the snow to swirl around her. She heard Katie crying and tried to figure out which direction the cries were coming from.

"Katie, where are you!"

Then she heard Kendall. "Mama, I'm scared! Please come, we need you!"

"I can't find you! Where are you, baby?!" she screamed, running towards the sound of his voice.

The next thing she knew, she was in her kitchen. It was in shambles, dishes on the floor, the towel rack ripped from the wall, and blood all over the floor. "KENDALL!" she screamed, running out the back door. She heard a man's laughter and then her son scream.

"LEAVE HIM ALONE!"

"You can't save him, you never could. Why do you think he turns to outsiders? You're too weak, you failed to take control before you lost it all," the man's voice taunted.

Kendall screamed again. "PAPI!"

"No, not Papi. I can help you, please let me help you!" Jen sobbed, falling to her knees.

"Too late, looks like I broke him," another voice taunted. She saw Kendall lying on the ground, bruised and bloody.

"Looks like you failed again! You should have listened to me. I could have helped you take control, to protect your son. Instead you've lost everything to the people you thought you could trust," the first man's voice called out.

∞

Brooke nearly jumped out of her skin when she heard Jen scream. She ran into the bedroom and Jen was sitting up in the bed, clutching her chest.

"Jen, what is it?"

Jen looked at her before jumping out of bed and heading out the door. "I need to get my babies."

"Okay, Jen calm down. I'll drive you over there," Brooke said, following her.

Jen ignored her and grabbed her coat as she ran out the front door.

"Damn it," Brooke cursed as she got into her own car. She called the Garcia's home number and Sylvia answered. "Sylvia, Jen's on her way over and I'm not sure what's going on. She woke up screaming and saying that she had to get her babies and rushed out of here. I'm not even sure she's completely awake."

"She's driving?" Sylvia asked.

"Yes, I'm going to follow her now."

"Drive carefully," Sylvia said.

"What's wrong?" Joanna asked.

"That was Brooke. She said Jen's on her way over after she woke up screaming. She's not sure what happened."

"Maybe we should call Dr. Thorne after what happened this morning," Jo suggested.

Sylvia nodded and went to get the number from her purse.

The kids were watching a Christmas special on TV. "What's wrong, Mami?" Carlos asked.

"Nothing, Mijo. Have you all finished you homework?"

"Almost," Carlos told her.

"Why don't you finish watching the program upstairs and then do your homework?"

"Are you sure everything's alright?" Logan asked.

"Everything's fine, now go."

They all got up and headed up to Carlos' room.

"Okay, what's up?" Alex asked as soon as the kids were out of earshot.

"I'm not sure, but it sounds like Jen is having some kind of panic attack. She's driving over here. Brooke couldn't stop her, so she's following her over. I'm going to call Dr. Thorne to find out what we should do."

∞

Jen couldn't stop the feeling of desperation that was overwhelming her. Her heart was racing and she kept replaying the nightmare over and over in her head. She choked back a sob.

"Everything is so wrong. How did I ever let it get this bad?"

She pulled up in front of the Garcia's and got out. The lights were on and everything looked so cheery, so normal.

"Why are our lives so far from this? Why did you leave us, Will?" she sobbed out loud.

She walked up to the door and Antonio opened it. "Honey, what's going on? You shouldn't be out driving in this condition," he said, putting his arm around her.

"I-I need to see my children."

"Why don't you come and sit down first," Sylvia said gently.

"No, I want my children," Jen insisted.

There was another knock at the door and Antonio opened it and let Brooke in.

"Are you insane driving that fast in this weather?" Brooke yelled at Jen.

"The important thing is everyone made it here safe and sound," Antonio said, shooting her a warning look.

Brooke took a deep breath. "Yes, we did."

Logan came downstairs. "Dad, were you going to put the tube in soon? Kendall's supposed to take his Benadryl and it makes him sleepy."

"Yeah, I'll be up in a few minutes, Partner."

"Is everything okay?" he asked, looking at the adults in concern.

"Everything's fine, honey, now go back upstairs," Jo told him.

"Can you tell Kendall and Katie to come downstairs, please?" Jen asked him.

"Um, sure."

Antonio looked at him and shook his head. Logan nodded to him and went back upstairs.

"Jen, we need to talk," he said calmly.

"Why?"

"We're worried about you," Sylvia said.

"I'm fine. I just need to get my kids and we'll all be okay."

"Jen, look at me," Antonio said.

Jen looked at him. "What?"

"You need to talk to us. We can't help you if you don't let us know what's going on."

"There's nothing wrong," she insisted.

Brooke took her by the arm and started walking toward the kitchen. "Then WHY were you screaming in your sleep?"

"I just had a bad dream, now let me go."

"No, now sit down and talk to us," Brooke ordered, pushing Jen down onto a chair.

The others followed them. Sylvia sat on the other side of Jen and took her hand. "Jen, I know you're upset about what happened today, but everything's fine."

"It is NOT fine! Nothing is fine! Now I would like to get my children and go home," she said, standing up.

"Jen, Dr. Thorne thinks he might need to adjust your medication," Sylvia said gently.

"You CALLED my doctor?"

"Yes, because we're worried about you," Sylvia told her.

"Well, you can stop worrying. I'm perfectly capable of taking care of myself and my kids!"

∞

The kids heard the yelling and went down to see what was wrong. "Mom, what's going on?" Kendall asked.

"Kendall, you and Katie go get your things, we're going home," Jen ordered.

Antonio shook his head. "Kids, go back upstairs for a few minutes."

James put his arm around Kendall and they headed up the stairs.

"How dare you! I told them to get their things!"

"You need to calm down and think about this," Antonio told her.

"I don't have to think about anything! They are MY children, not yours. You don't have any right to keep them from me!"

"Honey, nobody is keeping them from you. You're not thinking rationally right now and you need to CALM down!" Antonio said.

"I'll get them myself," she said, pushing past him.

"Call Dr. Thorne," Antonio told Sylvia as he followed Jen. The others were right behind him.

"KENDALL, GET DOWN HERE RIGHT NOW! WE ARE LEAVING!" Jen screamed.

Antonio blocked the stairway. "Jen, you need help."

"I don't need anything from you! You're trying to steal my son!"

Antonio looked at her in shock. "Jen, that's not true."

Jo grabbed Jen and whirled her around so she was facing her. "You are going to STOP this nonsense right now! That is NOT true and you know it! You're completely out of control."

"Let go of me!" Jen yelled.

Sylvia came in. "Honey, Dr. Thorne thinks we should take you to the hospital."

"I am NOT going to the hospital! I want my children!"

∞

The kids were in the bedroom with the door closed, but they could hear almost everything. Kendall was holding Katie as she cried. Kendall looked around at his friends. James and Logan were sitting on the other side of the bed. Logan looked like he might cry, but James looked angry. Carlos was sitting next to Logan and he was crying. "Why does Mama K hate us?"

Logan put his arm around his friend. "She doesn't, buddy. She's just really sick right now."

"But she said Papi's trying to steal Kendall. Why would she say something so mean?"

"I don't know, but it'll be okay," Logan said, hugging Carlos.

That was enough for Kendall. He pushed Katie into James' arms and went out the door. He went downstairs and saw his mom screaming at her friends, who were still trying to calm her down.

"STOP FIGHTING!" he demanded, stomping his foot.

There was instant silence as the adults looked at him.

Kendall walked over to Jen. "Mom, you need to go to the hospital like the doctor said."

"We are going home."

Kendall shook his head. "You need help."

"What I NEED is for you to go get your things so we can go home!" Jen yelled.

"No, I'm not going with you. Do you even care that Katie and Carlos are upstairs crying right now? Do you care that all ANYONE here has done is tried to help us?"

"Damn it! I said to get your things!" she yelled again, grabbing him by the arm.

"No," he said quietly.

"Jen, let go of his arm," Antonio warned as he moved towards them.

"I will NOT let go! I will never let go. He's my son, not yours!" she sobbed as she suddenly pulled Kendall towards the door.

Kendall screamed in pain as she pulled his arm up further than it could go.

She released him when she realized what she had done. "Honey, I..."

"You want to know why I don't want to go with you? Because you're the ONLY one who makes me feel bad about myself! You're the only one who makes me feel like I DID do

something wrong! Today I did something you said you didn't want me to do, but at least I didn't LIE to you about it! You promised you would listen when I tried to tell you something, but you didn't. Now you're accusing everyone who loves us of trying to take us away from you. You're wrong. You're the one pushing us away!" Kendall yelled. He was clutching his arm and his face was flushed with pain.

Everyone was silent, not quite sure what to say or do at that moment.

"Honey, I'm sorry," Jen sobbed as she reached out for him.

He pulled away from her and ran upstairs. He went into the bathroom and slammed the door behind him.

Jen looked around at her friends. "I'm s-so sorry. I don't know what's wrong with me."

Alex put his arm around her. "It's alright, we're going to take you to the hospital now. Dr. Thorne thinks there might be something off with your medication dosage."

Jen nodded and Joanna put her arm around Jen's waist and they led her to the door. "Antonio..." Jen started.

"It's alright. I'm going to go check on Kendall," he said softly.

Jen nodded. "Thank you. Please tell him I never meant to hurt him. I-I never meant to hurt you either."

Antonio nodded as Alex and Joanna guided her out the door.

∞

Antonio turned and ran up the stairs. He tried the bathroom door, but it was locked. He could hear Kendall retching inside. "Kendall, please open the door when you can."

The bedroom door opened and Carlos looked out. "P-Papi?"

Antonio held his arms open and Carlos ran to him, hugging him tightly. "It's alright, Mijo. Mama K is going to the hospital now. They'll be able to help her there."

Kendall unlocked the bathroom door and Antonio opened it. Kendall was sitting on the floor, clutching his arm. Antonio didn't say anything, just sat down next to him and pulled him close. Kendall leaned into him and Carlos sat on the other side of Antonio, who put his other arm around him. They sat there in silence for a few minutes, and then Katie came in and wrapped her arms around Kendall's waist. After another minute, James and Logan followed her, Logan sitting on the other side of Katie and James by Carlos.

Sylvia found them like that a few minutes later. She sat down next to James and put her arm around him. "Your mom's downstairs," she said, kissing his cheek.

James sighed and nodded.

"Come on, let's all get off the floor and get ready for bed," she said, getting up and holding her hands out to James and Carlos.

They each took one and got up.

"Come here, Mija," she said, picking Katie up. Logan got up and followed them.

"We need to check out your shoulder," Antonio told Kendall. He put his arm around the teen and helped him up. Kendall quickly leaned against the counter. He was afraid he was going to throw up again. "Are you alright?"

Kendall took a couple of deep breaths and then nodded.

"Is it bad?" Antonio asked.

Kendall just nodded.

Antonio opened the medicine cabinet and pulled out the Tramadol, Benadryl, and a tube of Icy/Hot. He poured out one of each of the pills and got a glass of water. He handed the pills to Kendall.

"We still have to do the feeding tube, and they make me sleepy," Kendall said.

"I think we can skip a night."

Kendall nodded, took the pills, and swallowed them.

"Okay, let's get your pajamas on and then I'm going rub some of this ointment on your shoulder."

Kendall nodded again, went into the bedroom, and grabbed his pajamas. Antonio left the bathroom so he could have some privacy.

Kendall opened the door, clutching his shirt.

Antonio went in and squeezed some of the ointment onto his hand. "You've used this before. Let me know if I'm pressing too hard."

Kendall nodded and flinched as Antonio rubbed the ointment onto the top of his shoulder and then gently worked his way down to the bruised area. Kendall inhaled sharply at the sensation.

"Are you alright?"

He nodded. "Just really sore."

"Well this should help it feel better in a little while."

When he was finished, he helped Kendall pull his shirt on. "I'm sorry she said those things to you, Papi."

"It's not your fault, and I know she didn't really mean them. She's just confused right now. Dr. Thorne thinks there's something wrong with her medication dosage. She'll be doing better once they get it figured out."

"It still isn't right."

"I don't want you worrying about any of that. This is between your mom and me, and we'll work it out."

"But..." Kendall started.

"No buts, I'm serious about this. This is not your problem—you have enough of your own. Your mom and I will work this out. I want you to talk about all of this with Claudia tomorrow, though. Can you do that for me?"

Kendall nodded.

"That's my boy," Antonio said, hugging him.

Carlos came upstairs. "Mami's making hot chocolate!"

He took Kendall by his right arm and steered him towards the stairs. They went down and sat with the others on the couch. Katie got up, scooted in between Kendall and James, and wrapped her arms around her brother. "It's okay Katie-Bug," he said, kissing her head.

"No it's not."

"It will be," he sighed.

∞

Sylvia, Brooke, and Antonio sat in the kitchen discussing what had happened.

"What happened after I left?" Sylvia asked Brooke.

"She was still sleeping and then woke up screaming. She said she had to get to her babies and ran out the door. I don't know what she was dreaming about, but she scared me half to death when she screamed."

"I hope it's just the dosage being off. I don't think anyone can take much more," Sylvia said.

"We'll have to trust that Dr. Thorne can get through to her and it's just the medication needing adjusting," Antonio said.

"And if he can't and it's not?" Brooke asked.

"Then we do what's best for the kids. We'll file for temporary custody if we need to," he told them.

"God, I hope it doesn't go that far," Sylvia said.

"So do I, but she's in no condition to take care of Kendall and Katie right now. We all promised each other before we even had kids, the children ALWAYS come first."

"I know. It just seems so... wrong somehow."

"Yes it does, but I'd rather have her hate me for the rest of her life than risk their well-being." He sighed.

"He's right," Brooke said.

"I know. I just hate all of this!" Sylvia said, holding back a sob.

Antonio put his arm around her. "So do I, but we have to stay strong for the kids. They're all feeling this a lot more than we are right now and they have no idea how to handle it."

"I know. I'm sorry, I just..." she said, burying her face in his neck.

"Me too," he said, holding her tight.

∞

Alex drove to the hospital. Jen and Joanna were sitting in the backseat. Jen was crying into Jo's shoulder.

"It's going to be alright, Jen. Dr. Thorne is going to meet us there and they're going to figure out what's going on."

"I hurt him," Jen cried.

"Yes you did, but he'll be alright."

"The things I said to Antonio, I didn't mean them."

"He knows that, but you need help right now. We'll worry about all of that later."

Alex pulled up to the hospital and got out. He opened the door and helped Jen and Jo out. They stood on either side of Jen, supporting her as they walked inside. Alex checked her in and after a few minutes, her name was called. She grabbed Jo's hand. "Please come with me."

"Of course I will."

"I'll wait here," Alex told them.

"Thank you," Jen said.

"You're welcome, honey."

The nurse led them back to an exam room and took her temperature, heart rate and blood pressure. "The doctor will be here in just a few minutes."

"Thank you," Joanna said.

Dr. Lerner came in a few minutes later. "Can you tell me what happened tonight?"

Jen told her about the nightmare and waking up in a panic.

Dr. Lerner nodded. "You are currently taking Effexor for depression?"

Jen nodded.

"Okay, we need to pull some blood and check your levels. Your blood pressure is also a little high, so I think we're going to keep you overnight."

"Okay," Jen said.

"When did you take your last dose?"

Jen thought back. "I can't remember."

"That might be the problem. The nurse will be in to pull the blood and then we'll get you settled into a room for the night," Dr. Lerner said.

"Thank you," Jen said quietly.

Half an hour later, Jen was taken to a private room. Jo went and got Alex and they followed her up. A few minutes later, there was a knock on the door and Eli walked in.

"Hello Eli," Jen said quietly.

"I hear you had a pretty bad day," he said, walking over to her.

She nodded. "These are my friends, Joanna and Alex Mitchell."

"How do you do?" He smiled, shaking Alex's hand.

"We should probably go," Alex said, looking at Jo.

"No, please stay. It's alright, really," Jen said.

"Okay honey," Alex smiled. He and Jo sat in the chairs by the window while Eli sat in the one next to the bed.

"Can you tell me what happened?"

"After I spoke with you?"

He nodded.

"Sylvia came over and we talked for a few minutes, and then she made me lie down. I told her I wasn't tired, but I must have been, because I remember drifting off. Then I was dreaming, and I woke up feeling like there was something terribly wrong."

"Do you remember what the dream was about?"

Jen started trembling. "It w-was the night Will died, starting with Sylvia and Jo coming to tell me he'd been in an accident. They drove me to the hospital, but I was too late!" she sobbed.

"Too late for what?"

"He was already gone. I didn't get to say goodbye!"

"Oh Jen," Joanna said, moving to her friend's side. She held her while she cried. After a few moments, she calmed down.

"Was that all?" he asked gently.

She shook her head, "Then we were in Kendall's room, waiting for him to wake up from surgery."

"He was in the car?"

She nodded. "At first I told him he couldn't go because they wouldn't be back until well after his bedtime. He wanted to go with his daddy so badly and Will promised he would get Kendall up in the morning and deal with a grumpy little boy, so I said yes."

"Kendall and his dad were close?"

Jen nodded.

"Antonio saved him then, too," she realized.

"What's that?" Eli asked.

"Antonio. He was called to the scene, saw Will's car down the embankment, and went down before the emergency vehicles got there. If he hadn't done that, Kendall would have bled to death. Oh my God! I said the most terrible things to him."

"We'll worry about that later," Eli told her. "Was there anything else?"

"Then we w-were at the cemetery and the pastor was reading from the Bible. Then I was alone... everyone else was gone. I heard Katie crying and then Kendall was calling for me, but I couldn't find them. Then I was in my kitchen and everything was broken and t-there was blood everywhere. I ran out the back door and heard Kendall screaming. There were voices everywhere."

"Did you recognize the voices?" Eli asked.

"I heard Graham telling me that I failed again, that I should have listened to him. Then Kendall screamed and someone else said that he broke him. Kendall was lying there in the snow, not moving, and there was b-blood everywhere. Then Graham repeated what he said and I remember waking up and knowing that I had to find Kendall and Katie."

"Jennifer, have you been feeling dizzy, nauseated, or has your heart felt like it was racing?" Eli asked.

She thought about it and nodded. "A little."

"Have you been taking your medication on time?"

"I don't remember. I think I forgot this morning and maybe last night."

"We decided to go with a fast acting anti-depressant because you have so many things to deal with right now. This means the medication is stronger, and if you don't take it like you're supposed to, you're going to have even worse side effects and the beginning signs of withdrawal."

"I was running late and just forgot."

"I know it happens, but some of the side effects include paranoia, hostility, panic attacks, and suicidal tendencies. It is VERY important to take it when you are supposed to. Now I want you to pick up one of those little pill boxes, the ones that have the days of the week on them. Pre-fill it, that way you'll know if you've taken it or not."

"Okay."

"I think your blood chemistry is off because of the inconsistency with which you've been taking the medication. The blood work will tell us where we're at with it, and then you HAVE to start taking it properly, alright?"

"I will," she promised.

"I want you to get some rest now. The doctor is going to give you a little valium to help you sleep. I will be back in the morning to see you again. If you need anything before then, just call my cell number and I'll get back to you."

She nodded. "Thank you."

He stood up. "Alright, you get some rest now," he said, patting her hand.

"I will. Thank you Eli."

Alex stood up and walked out with him. "So, do you really think it's just because she isn't taking her medication like she's supposed to?"

He nodded. "Effexor is a very strong medication, and if she's just taking it on and off, it's going to have a negative effect on her blood chemistry. Sylvia told me a little of what was going on when she called me, and that is definitely what it sounds like has happened. How's her son dealing with this?"

"I'm not quite sure. He heard her yelling, came downstairs, and told everyone to stop fighting. He told her to go to the hospital like you wanted, and that he wasn't going home with her. At one point, she grabbed him and hurt his arm when she tried to drag him to the door. I'm sure she'll tell you the rest, but basically he told her that she's the one who's making him feel badly about himself."

"Do you think that's true?" Eli asked him.

Alex nodded. "I'm afraid I do."

∞

Alex and Joanna waited for Jen to fall asleep and then they left. Jo held onto Alex's arm as they walked to the car. "Have I told you how glad I am that you're here?"

He smiled. "Not in so many words, but I know you are."

"How did everything go so wrong?"

"Dr. Thorne's pretty sure it's the medication. If that's the case, she should be doing better in a few days."

"I hope so."

"So, about dinner this weekend. I'm picking you up Saturday night and we're going to go to that little Mexican place you like," he told her.

"Do you really think we should with everything that's going on?" she asked.

"We still have to eat and haven't had a chance to just sit down and talk since I've been home."

She smiled.

"What?"

"You said, since you've been home."

He sighed. "I may be living in Texas right now, but this is my home."

She hugged his arm tighter. "We miss you."

"I miss you too," he said, kissing her cheek.

∞

"We better get the kids to bed," Antonio said, getting up. Sylvia and Brooke followed him into the living room.

The kids were all sitting closely together on the couch. Katie was still holding onto Kendall tightly and James had one arm around them. His other arm was around Logan, who was sitting on the other side of him. Carlos was on the other side of Kendall, curled up as close as he could get to his friend. Kendall's head was resting on top of Carlos'.

Kendall was already sleeping, the medication having finally done its job.

"Hey guys, time for bed," Antonio said.

Carlos sat up carefully so he didn't jostle Kendall too much.

"James, can you get Katie?" Antonio asked.

"No, I want to stay with Kendall," she said.

"You can sleep with him tonight, but you have to let go so we can get him upstairs," James told her.

She nodded and released her hold on her brother. James picked her up and headed upstairs. Antonio picked Kendall up and followed James, the other two boys right behind them.

They got Kendall and Katie tucked into the bed, and the other three boys laid their blankets out next to one another on the floor. James lay in the middle, and the other two boys curled up next to him. Antonio tucked the blankets in around them.

"Papi?" Carlos asked.

"Yes?"

"Does Mama K hate us?"

"No Mijo, she's just very sick right now."

"Is she ever going to get better?"

"Yes, now go to sleep," Antonio said, kissing his son's forehead.

"Okay," he said, turning over and snuggling closer to James.

Antonio smiled. "Are you two doing okay?"

James nodded.

"I'm okay," Logan said.

"Good. I think it'll be okay if you want to stay home tomorrow."

"We have practice though," Logan said.

"You can go to practice in the afternoon. We'll see if Claudia can get you in before Kendall's appointment tomorrow."

"That sounds good," James said.

"Okay," Logan yawned.

"Get some sleep now."

"Goodnight Papi," they both said.

"Goodnight Mijos," Antonio said as he closed the door.

Chapter 138~ Another One Down

Antonio went downstairs and called Claudia. "Hello?"

"Hi Claudia, it's Antonio. Do you have a minute?"

"Of course I do. What's going on?"

"I just wanted to see if it would be possible to get the boys in earlier tomorrow. We had a difficult evening here and I told them they can skip school."

"Can you have them here by nine?"

"We'll be there. Thanks Claudia."

"Baby, you sound exhausted. Do you want to tell me what's happened?" she asked in a motherly tone.

"Do you know what happened with Kendall today?"

"Sally called and asked if I could see the other boys tomorrow, but she didn't give me any specifics. She just said that they're all starting to show signs of PTSD."

"Yeah, James has been super protective and he and Kendall got into a little bit this morning. I'll let Kendall tell you what he did today, but it's what happened with his mom tonight that has us all concerned."

"What's happening with Jen?"

"Apparently she hasn't been taking her medication like she's supposed to and basically had another meltdown. She came over here and was insisting that Kendall and Katie go home with her. She was screaming and wouldn't really talk to us. Sylvia called Dr. Thorne and he said we should take her to the hospital."

"Oh Lord," Claudia said.

"I told the kids to stay upstairs because she was saying some pretty hateful things, but I guess they could hear what was going on. At one point, Kendall came flying down the stairs and told her to do what the doctor said. He told her she was making Katie and Carlos cry. When she told him to get his things, he told her no. She grabbed his bad arm and tried to pull him out, but let go when she realized she had hurt him. Then he really let her have it," Antonio said sadly.

"Oh no, what happened?"

"He told her she's the only one who makes him feel badly about himself. She makes him feel like he did do something wrong. Then he pointed out that she promised she'd listen to him and that she wasn't."

"Where's Jen now?"

"Alex and Joanna took her to the hospital. Dr. Thorne is meeting her there."

"How are the kids doing?"

"They're finally sleeping. I gave Kendall a pain pill and his Benadryl and we skipped the feeding tonight. He got sick to his stomach after confronting her and he's in quite a bit of pain because of his shoulder."

"My poor babies. You bring them over and I'll clear the whole morning, just in case," she said.

"I really appreciate that."

"It's not a problem. Now what about you, how are you doing?"

"Just worried. I need to talk to Alex and Jo when they get back and get their thoughts on it. Sylvia, Brooke, and I discussed things, and if Jen continues spiraling out of control, we're going to file for temporary custody."

"That's pretty drastic," she said.

"I know, and it's definitely going to convince her that she was right about me."

"What do you mean?"

"She thinks I'm trying to steal Kendall from her. At least that's what she said."

"She must be having some real issues if she's thinking that kind of nonsense," Claudia told him.

"She is. We're all really worried about her state of mind right now."

"I know you are, but she needs to do the work to get better, just like Kendall is."

"Neither of them deserve this," Antonio said bitterly.

"No they don't, NONE of you do. Now why don't you try and get some rest and I'll see you in the morning," Claudia said.

"Will do. Thanks Claudia."

"Not a problem. Call me if you need to talk again."

"I will. Thanks for everything." Antonio smiled.

"Goodnight baby," Claudia said, hanging up.

He hung up and went back into the kitchen. "She can see them at nine tomorrow."

Sylvia nodded. "Good."

"Are you alright?"

"No," she sighed, laying her head on his shoulder.

"Me either," he said, kissing the top of her head.

∞

Alex and Joanna returned a few minutes later.

"How is she?" Brooke asked.

"She was doing better. The doctor gave her something to help her sleep," Joanna said.

"Any idea what this was all about?" Brooke asked.

"She hasn't been taking her anti-depressant like she's supposed to. She had a terrible nightmare that sent her into a panic attack, which was exacerbated because of it," Alex told her.

"Did she say what the nightmare was about?"

Joanna nodded. "It started with Will's death and ended with Kendall lying in the snow, covered in blood. She said she heard voices taunting her, one was Graham's and I assume the other was Deesie's, telling her that he broke Kendall. She said Graham told her she'd failed Kendall again."

"No wonder she was panicking," Sylvia said.

"Dr. Thorne told her that she needs to start taking her meds on time. He recommended getting one of those pill boxes that you can pre-fill," Alex said.

"That's probably a good idea," Sylvia said.

"I'll pick one up on the way home," Brooke told them.

"We were discussing what to do if Jen continues on like this," Antonio said.

"What did you come up with?" Alex asked.

"Filing for temporary custody. It may be the only way to keep Kendall and Katie safe," Antonio said.

"Are you sure you want to do that?" Joanna asked.

"No, but we may not have a choice. She could have been hurt or hurt someone else driving in the condition she was in, and then hurting Kendall like she did," Antonio told them.

"She didn't mean to hurt him," Joanna said.

"No, she didn't, but she couldn't control herself or what she was doing. Whether it's because of the medication or because she's having a panic attack, she's unable to take care of herself, and that means she can't possibly take care of them," Antonio said.

"He's right. Kendall still needs the tube feedings, his therapy sessions with Claudia, physical therapy, and doctor's appointments. What was she planning on doing about those?" Alex asked.

"But taking the kids away from her?" Jo asked quietly.

"No, not taking them away from her—taking care OF them. Being able to make the legal decisions to ensure their safety and well-being," Antonio said gently.

"I know you're right. It's just, I know how I'd feel if someone tried to take Logan away from me," Jo said, her eyes tearing up.

Alex put his arm around her. "Honey, Antonio's right. It's not taking the kids away from her. It's making sure her kids are safe and cared for. Everyone agreed a long time ago that the kids will ALWAYS come first, regardless. If it were me, I'd be grateful to know someone cared enough to put my son first, because that's the way it should be."

"Well, hopefully it won't come to that. Hopefully she'll start taking her medication the way she's supposed to, and with therapy she'll be feeling better soon," Sylvia said.

"She'll be taking her medication like she's supposed to. I'll see to that personally," Brooke promised.

"Well, that's one problem solved." Alex smiled.

"I called Claudia, and she said we can take the boys in at nine tomorrow," Antonio said.

"Kendall's appointment is at eleven?" Alex asked.

Antonio nodded.

"Why don't you want to drop the boys off on your way to the station while I stay here and do the tube feeding with Kendall? Then you can meet us there at eleven and I'll pick up the other boys and bring them home," Alex said.

"Sounds like a plan." Antonio smiled.

"I'll pick Jen up if they release her tomorrow. If not, I'll stay and visit for a while. I don't expect the kids are going to want to see her that soon?" Jo said.

"I doubt it," Sylvia said sadly.

"Dr. Thorne said he was going to stop in to see her in the morning and they should have her blood results by then," Joanna told them.

"She was doing so well before today. I just hope once she starts taking her meds properly that she recovers quickly," Antonio said.

"Antonio, she did want us to tell you how sorry she was for what she said. She really didn't mean it," Jo told him.

"I know she didn't. Unfortunately, if she doesn't get better, it's going to turn out to be true."

Brooke watched Antonio for a moment, noting the dark circles under his eyes and the extreme sadness she knew he was trying to hide, and made a decision. "Well, I should get going and make a few arrangements for Jen. If I need to, I'll hire a nurse to stay with her twenty-four hours a day," Brooke told them.

"Oh, she'll love that," Alex said.

"I'm really not in a mood to worry about what she will or won't like," Brooke said, standing up.

"Brooke, if you're mad at her, maybe she should stay with me," Joanna suggested.

"I am not angry with Jen. I am furious that she has allowed something like this to happen, but I blame Graham. I am just finished with this whole thing, and she WILL start doing what she's supposed to do, period. She will NOT be having another episode like she did tonight."

She took Antonio's arm. "Walk me out?"

"How can I refuse?" He smiled.

He held her coat for her and they walked to her car. "I want you to know I'm behind you one hundred percent, in whatever we need to do to keep everyone safe. Anything you or the kids need, just let me know," Brooke told him.

"Thanks honey, that really means a lot to me."

"We're all in this together and we will get through this. Now, you get some rest tonight," she said, kissing his cheek.

"Will do." He smiled as he closed her door.

∞

"I should probably get going too," Jo said a little while later.

"We'll see you tomorrow?" Sylvia asked.

Joanna nodded. "Call me if you need me before then."

"Thanks Jo," Antonio said.

"I'll walk you out." Alex smiled.

He helped her on with her coat and they went outside. "Don't forget, Saturday around seven?"

"How could I possibly forget?" she asked, smiling.

"Just making sure."

"You are so cute when you get nervous." She smirked.

"Cute? Who said I'm nervous?"

She just smiled at him.

"Keep it up and it'll be the dollar menu at McDonald's," he threatened.

"As long as it's with you, that'll be just fine with me." She smiled, getting into her car.

"Imagine how much money I could have saved on dates all those years ago if I'd known that back then."

"Who said it would have been alright back then?"

"I'll let you in on a little secret though... It was worth every penny." He smiled, closing her door.

She laughed and shook her head and he waved as she drove away. He went back inside, still smiling to himself.

"So, did you ask her out?" Sylvia asked.

"Why do you ask?"

"Because you look like a smitten teenage boy," Sylvia said.

"What? I don't know what you're talking about."

"You're grinning like an idiot." Antonio smirked.

"Am not!"

"Are too!" Antonio said.

"Am not!"

"I'm afraid you really are," Sylvia told him.

"You two are impossible," Alex said.

"So did you ask her out or not?" Sylvia asked.

"We are going to have dinner 'out' someplace, so technically we'll be going out."

"Alex has a date," Antonio teased.

"We're friends going out to talk about things," Alex told him.

Antonio just grinned at him.

"Oh shut up, I'm going to bed," he said, heading for his room.

"We really are terrible," Sylvia said to Antonio as they headed upstairs.

"Yes, but he makes it so easy." Antonio laughed.

"Very true," she said.

Sylvia checked on the kids, making sure that they were all tucked in safe and warm, and then headed to bed.

∞

A couple of hours later, Antonio got up to check on them again and found Kendall sleeping, blood all over his pillow from biting at his thumb. He mentally cursed himself. *Damn it, I forgot the other shirt.*

He went into the bathroom, grabbed a washcloth, and ran it under the warm water. He went back into the bedroom and gently pulled Kendall's hand away from his mouth and started wiping the blood from the boy's face.

"Kendall, wake up. We need to put the other shirt on you."

Kendall didn't respond, but Katie stirred.

"Papi, what's wrong?" Carlos asked, yawning.

"Kendall's chewing on his thumb and I need to get him cleaned up and the other shirt on him."

"I can help," Carlos whispered, getting up.

"Thanks Mijo." Antonio smiled.

"What do you need me to do?"

"Why don't you grab his pillow and the shirt and we'll take him into your room so we don't wake anyone else up," Antonio said, lifting Kendall up from the bed.

Carlos nodded, grabbed the pillow and shirt, and followed Antonio.

"Kendall, can you wake up?" Antonio asked again.

"Hmm?" Kendall murmured. His eyes fluttered open and then closed again.

"Why won't he wake up?" Carlos asked.

"It's just the medication. Let's get him cleaned up and make sure he can't get at his fingers anymore."

"Why does he do that?" Carlos asked looking at his friend's bleeding thumb.

"It's just a nervous habit. He did it after Papa K died too."

"I remember that."

Antonio finished cleaning up Kendall's face and hand. "Carlos, can you get the first aid kit, please?"

"Sure." Carlos went and grabbed it from the bathroom.

"Thanks." Antonio smiled when Carlos handed it to him.

"You're welcome."

Antonio bandaged Kendall's hand and then pulled off the pajama shirt. Carlos handed him Alex's shirt and Antonio got it onto Kendall and tied the sleeves closed. Then he threw the pillowcase into the hamper, went to the linen closet, and grabbed another.

"Now let's get the two of you back to bed," Antonio said.

Carlos nodded and grabbed Kendall's pillow while Antonio carried him back to the guest room. He lay him back on the bed, while Carlos put the pillow under his head.

Kendall stirred a little. "Hmm, Papi?"

"Yes, everything's alright. Go back to sleep," Antonio whispered.

"Okay," Kendall mumbled.

"What if he bites through the shirt?" Carlos asked.

"I don't think he will."

"What if he has to use the bathroom?"

"I don't think that's going to be a problem tonight."

"But what if..."

"Carlos, why don't you sleep on this side of him, that way if he needs help with anything, you'll be the first to know?" Antonio suggested.

Carlos smiled and grabbed his pillow from the floor. Antonio tucked him in. "Better now?"

Carlos smiled and nodded. "Night Papi."

"Goodnight Mijo. I love you."

"I love you too, Papi."

Antonio smiled as he closed the door.

"Is everything alright?" Sylvia asked as Antonio climbed back into bed.

"Yeah, I completely forgot to put the longer shirt on Kendall and he was chewing on his thumb. Carlos woke up and helped me bandage Kendall's hand and then get him into the shirt. He's sleeping next to him, just in case Kendall wakes up needing anything."

"Is he okay?"

"He will be." Antonio yawned.

"Get some sleep, honey," Sylvia said, kissing him.

"You too." He smiled as she snuggled up closer to him.

∞

Ryan woke early and arrived at his office by seven, and started going over the evidence that Sally had sent over the night before. The hearing was scheduled for eight and he wanted to have everything in order by then. Sally and John arrived about half an hour later. They were going to accompany him to court in case the judge had any questions regarding the evidence.

They walked to the courthouse and arrived ten minutes before eight, Sally and John sitting in the back. Manning arrived a couple of minutes later with a younger woman, who took a seat at the table next to him. A moment after that, a guard brought Graham out and seated him at the defense's table. The bailiff came out and ordered the court to rise promptly at eight.

Judge Brown entered the courtroom and called the court to order. "So prosecution has called for this Omnibus hearing regarding evidence gathered over the last couple of days?"

"Yes, your Honour." Ryan smiled. He handed the documents to the bailiff, who took them to Judge Brown. She put on her reading glasses and went through the files, at one point glancing up at Manning.

"Is there anything else?" she asked.

"Yes, your Honour, we have several recordings as well. I have them downloaded onto my laptop if you would like to hear them."

"I will. As to the rest of this, these are very serious charges. I trust your witness is reliable?"

"Yes, your Honour. He documented or recorded everything," Ryan said.

"Please hand these to Mr. Manning," Judge Brown said, handing the file to the bailiff.

The bailiff nodded and took them over to the defendant's table. Manning took the offered file and started reading through it. After the first page, his face got very red—by the third, he was pale.

"Your Honour, I have no idea how prosecution came by this, but these are all lies fabricated by Chad Taylor. He used to do some work for my firm, photos and such, and obviously became disgruntled after he was released from his contract," Manning sputtered.

"Exactly when was he released from his contract?"

"I'm not sure of the exact date. My colleague, Ms. Regent, will call the offices and have it sent right over," he said, nodding to Danielle, who moved to stand.

"Not necessary, your Honour. I have already taken the liberty of contacting Mr. Manning's office, and they confirm that Mr. Taylor was still employed with them yesterday afternoon. It's noted on the last page in the file," Ryan told her.

Judge Brown arched an eyebrow at Manning. "What do you have to say for yourself?"

"What the hell is going on?" Graham hissed.

"Shut up," Manning said under his breath.

"Your Honour, because Mr. Graham is entitled to fair representation, I notified the law offices of Riker, Goode, and Metcalf and Mr. Riker has graciously agreed to take over this case. He should be arriving shortly."

"Very good. Guard, please take Mr. Graham to one of the holding rooms until Mr. Riker arrives," Judge Brown ordered.

The guard nodded and pulled Graham up and away from the table. "What is going on?"

"I'm sure Mr. Riker will explain everything as soon as he arrives," Judge Brown told him.

"I would like to hear these recordings," she said as soon as Graham was out of the room.

"Your Honour, conversations recorded without BOTH parties knowledge and consent are not admissible," Manning said.

Ryan smiled. "I have a copy of the contract between Taylor and the law firm, and it clearly states that he reserves the right to record any and all conversations regarding ANY case that he's contracted for."

"I never signed any such contract," Manning said.

"No, Mr. Riker did when he originally hired Mr. Taylor. I'm surprised you haven't learned that you should read all contracts before hiring someone." Ryan smirked.

"Mr. Ryan, please," Judge Brown said, smiling a little. "Mr. Manning, do you have anything else you would like to say?" she asked.

"No, your Honour."

"Mr. Ryan, please play the recordings," she instructed.

Ryan nodded and clicked to open the first file, which had the first conversation between Taylor and Manning. He was instructing Taylor to find anything he could use against the families back in Louisiana and convince them that they shouldn't testify. They listened to a total of seventeen recordings, the last being Manning instructing Taylor to make sure that Kendall wasn't able to function.

Judge Brown folded her hands and stared at Manning. "Well?"

"I have nothing to say, your Honour."

"Your Honour, we also have recordings of the phone calls that Taylor made to Kendall Knight per Mr. Manning's instructions."

"Let's hear it."

He nodded and opened the file. They heard Kendall's voice as he answered. "Hey Loges. What are you up to?"

"What's the matter, sweetheart, don't you want to talk to me?"

"No, you're not real."

"Want to bet?"

"You're dead."

"Then how do I know what you're wearing, sweetheart? That's a nice black ski jacket. I love the matching beanie."

"You're not real," Kendall repeated.

"We're going to have so much fun together. I've missed you so much."

"You're dead, so leave me alone."

The adults could hear the strain in the boy's voice and could tell he was fighting back a major panic attack.

"The things I'm going to do to you will make you scream..."

There was silence in the courtroom as Judge Brown contemplated what she had just heard. "How many calls were made to the child?"

"There were several made, but Kendall only answered five times, two of which sent him into a panic attack," Ryan told her.

"What happened during those times?"

"The first time he was found hiding in a closet, unresponsive. It took over half an hour for him to come around. The second time he and his mother were at the park and they had to take him back to Dr. Jenkin's so she could help bring him around. That attack lasted nearly two hours."

"Mr. Taylor is willing to testify to all of this?"

"Yes, your Honour."

"Very well. Mr. Manning, to say what you have done is reprehensible would be a massive understatement. If I were a cursing woman, your ears would be burning right now. You

have managed to victimize a child and his family, who are already trying to recover, first from an attack by a predator, and then from an unscrupulous therapist."

"Your Honour..." Manning began.

"SILENCE!" she yelled, banging her gavel.

"It is my order that you be remanded into custody for charges to be filed by the DA's office in regards to this case."

"Your Honour, we've already filed charges against Mr. Manning and are prepared to take him into custody now," Ryan said, handing the warrant to the bailiff.

Judge Brown read the warrant and nodded. "I will also be filing a grievance with the State Bar Association and see that you are brought up on charges before them as well," she told Manning.

Ryan looked back and nodded at Sally and John, who both stood and walked over to Manning. John pulled him up and turned him around so that Sally could handcuff him.

"This is outrageous!" he yelled.

John just smiled and pulled out the laminated card and read it.

"You have the right to remain silent.

Anything you say or do can and will be held against you in a court of law.

You have the right to an attorney.

If you cannot afford an attorney, one will be provided for you.

Do you understand these rights I have just read to you?"

"I'm an attorney. Of course I know my rights!" Manning yelled.

"He knows his rights," John said to Sally.

"Good, then we won't have any misunderstandings." She smirked.

They pulled him towards the door.

"I'll be right behind you after I confer with the judge about the list of charges," Ryan told them.

Sally smiled and nodded. They went out the door and started walking.

"Where are we going?" Manning asked.

"To the police station," John said.

"We're walking?"

"Looks like." John smiled.

Danielle was following them but stopped suddenly and turned around, heading back to the courthouse. A car was parking in a spot reserved for court employees and attorneys, and a tall man with white hair got out. He gave a disapproving glare to Manning and shook his head.

"Owen, you have to get me out of this!" Manning shouted to Owen Riker.

Riker walked towards them.

"Uh oh, your boss looks pissed," John said, still smiling.

"In case you haven't figured it out, you're FIRED!" Riker hissed as he walked by.

"You can't fire me, I OWN one quarter of that practice!"

"Come on," John said, pulling Manning down the street.

"You are ALL going to regret this!"

"Here we go... bitch, bitch, bitch," John said, rolling his eyes.

"Maybe we should put him and Graham together. They might lose their voices trying to out-whine each other," Sally said.

"There's a thought." John smiled.

"I am going to have your entire department under investigation by the time this is over!" Manning threatened.

"Investigate away. Maybe you can discuss how with your little surveillance expert after we book you. After all, you're going to be neighbours for a while," Sally told him.

"Yeah, I'm sure he'll be thrilled to see you there." John laughed.

"I want a private cell!"

"Good luck with that," John said, laughing again.

Manning continued to complain on the short walk to the station.

"I'd shut up now if I were you," John said.

"Why is that, exactly?" Manning snapped.

"See, that very calm looking officer standing there at the door?"

Manning looked to where John was pointing and saw a dark haired police officer standing at the entrance to the station with his arms folded across his chest.

"That officer is Chief Antonio Garcia."

"So?"

"Kendall Knight is his godson."

"You really didn't listen to Graham or read the reports that Taylor provided you with, did you?" Sally asked.

"They say ignorance IS bliss," John said.

"True, but I think they also say ignorance of the law is no excuse," Sally pointed out.

"Good point," John said, pulling Manning to the station doors. He smiled and waved at Antonio.

Antonio looked at them, arching his eyebrow.

"Good morning, Boss!" Sally smiled.

"It is now," he said as he opened the door for them.

Chapter 139~ We're Getting There

Antonio woke up before Alex for once and he quickly showered and dressed. He checked on the kids, who were all still sleeping and smiled at Carlos holding onto Kendall's wrist so he couldn't bite on his fingers. Katie was sound asleep on the other side of Kendall, her arms wrapped around her brother's waist. James was sleeping on his back and Logan was curled up close to him, the only thing visible from under his blanket was a tuft of dark hair.

He quietly closed the door and then went downstairs and started a pot of coffee.

A few minutes later, Alex came out. "What are you doing up so early?"

"Too much on my mind, I couldn't sleep."

"Anything I can do?"

Antonio smiled. "You're doing it."

"Any more nightmares?"

Antonio shook his head. "Right now my bad dreams are all too real."

"You know I'm here if you need to talk, right?"

"I know, but you pretty much know everything so far."

"Somehow I doubt that," Alex said.

"What do you mean?"

"I think what Jen said really bothered you."

"A little," Antonio admitted.

"Because she hurt your feelings or because you're afraid it might be true?"

Antonio sighed. "I don't know, maybe a little of both. At first, I thought I was just trying to protect Kendall, to make sure everyone was alright. Now I just don't know. When Deesie first took him, all I could think of was getting to him before he killed him. Then as we got closer to finding them, it was praying that Deesie didn't do anything that would permanently damage him."

"When you found him?"

"It was getting him to safety and then medical attention, but even that was complicated. After we got to the hospital, there was this idiot of a doctor who started to cause more problems, until Doc took care of him."

"Doc? He's the vet you stayed with?"

Antonio nodded. "He's a great guy. He's the one who saved our lives that day. Deesie was coming at us after he impaled himself, and Doc shot him. He took care of Kendall at his clinic until he was stable enough to go to the hospital."

"I think I'd like to meet him." Alex smiled.

"Yes you would. In fact, he has invited us to his place this summer. The boys can go fishing, hiking, horseback riding. Remind me to show you the pictures of Kendall with the baby horse."

"You mean foal?" Alex laughed.

'Whatever," Antonio said, rolling his eyes.

"It sounds like fun." Alex smiled.

"I'm sure Doc wouldn't mind having one more."

"We'll see," Alex said with a smile.

Antonio sighed. "Maybe Jen's right. Maybe on some level I am trying to keep Kendall here. I do worry about what will happen once he goes home"

"That's normal. I think we're ALL worrying about that. You wanna know what I think?"

"Sure."

"I think you did your job. You found your godson and brought him home. I think there have been extenuating circumstances and that this has affected everyone far more than anyone realized. Graham, Manning, and Taylor have complicated everything even more, and it sent Jen over the edge. I think Kendall is getting better and he's doing his best to recover, even if he does have moments of regression. He handled yesterday amazingly, both the phone call and then the confrontation with Jen."

"He did, didn't he?"

"Tonio, don't start doubting yourself now. Kendall needs you. Whether she wants to admit it or not, Jen knows that, and she needs you too. She was doing really well before what happened yesterday, and I really think not taking her meds like she's supposed to is what caused this. Dr. Thorne said it's a strong drug, and had warned her that she needs to take it regularly or there would be side effects."

"Maybe."

"There's no maybe about it, and since Brooke is taking charge of it, I think we'll see that. You can bet Jen will be taking her meds on time and doing what she's supposed to be doing. I also think a big part of this is she's just plain scared. She doesn't know how to handle it, and she knows that Kendall needs the kind of help she can't provide."

"I hope so," Antonio said quietly.

"Would it surprise you to find out that Kendall is having the same concerns?"

"About what?"

"After he and James got into it yesterday, he told me it's not fair that the other boys are giving up so much for him. He mentioned that Carlos should be able to have his own room back and have his parents to himself. I think he's worried the other boys might start to resent the attention he's getting at some point. He thinks he's ruining everyone's lives. That's why he needed to help yesterday."

"They would never resent him for this." Antonio sighed.

"That's what I told him. I pointed out to him that it's because of his call that I'm here getting to spend time with everyone. Because of him, James and Mike spent a great day together, and with any luck, can build a good relationship. He said something about his mom being afraid of him and home, which I think is true. He's also worried about you and Carlos."

"It shouldn't be this way," Antonio said sadly.

"No, it shouldn't."

Antonio noticed the red light flashing on the phone and checked the messages. "Damn it, I missed the call from Joel Riggs last night."

"Who?"

"The physical therapist," Antonio told him as he listened to the message. Antonio sighed. "Great, there's really no substitution for the massage therapy that Kendall needs."

"How are we going to work that?"

"Joel says he can teach me a little, but he really needs a professional."

"Maybe if we learn a little and get him use to it, it'll help with transitioning him to someone else," Alex said.

"I hope so. I'll give Joel a call in a little while. I think his office opens at seven."

"We should be able to figure something out between the two of us," Alex said.

Antonio smiled wearily and nodded.

∞

Kendall woke to a sharp pain in his shoulder and a throbbing pain in his hand. His throat was dry and his eyes felt like they had sand in them. He gently wiggled free from Katie

and Carlos and stepped over Logan as he made his way to the door. He opened the door and went into the bathroom for a drink of water, but for some reason couldn't get his hands free.

He made his way downstairs and wandered into the kitchen, where Antonio and Alex were just finishing breakfast.

"Hey, look who's up," Alex said.

Kendall just stood there, rubbing his eyes.

"Or not," Alex said.

Antonio reached over and pulled Kendall towards him. "Hey, are you awake?"

"Hmm?" Kendall murmured.

"I think you need to go back to bed." Antonio smiled.

"Meh, throats dry."

"Benadryl," Alex said, getting up and getting Kendall some water. "Here ya go, Champ," Alex said. He went to hand the cup to Kendall and realized he couldn't take it because the sleeves were still tied closed.

"Meh, hands don't work," Kendall said, trying to figure out what was going on.

"Here." Antonio chuckled as he untied the sleeves.

"S'not funny."

"No it's not," Antonio said, wincing at the sight of the blood soaked bandage.

"I'll get the first aid kit," Alex said, heading for the bathroom.

"Come on, sit," Antonio told Kendall. He sat Kendall in the chair next to him and carefully unwrapped the boy's thumb.

"Ow, ow," Kendall whimpered.

"I'm sorry, Mijo. I know it hurts," Antonio said softly.

"What'd I do?"

"You were biting your nails in your sleep," Antonio told him.

Alex came back in, set the first aid kit on the table, and handed him a warm washcloth.

"Thanks buddy," Antonio said as he wrapped the cloth around Kendall's hand.

"Ow," Kendall cried, trying to pull his hand away.

"I know, Mijo. We have to get it cleaned up, though."

Over half of Kendall's thumbnail was gone and the cuticle was torn in three places. Alex sat on the other side of Kendall and put an arm around him to help hold his arm steady. Antonio started cleaning around the thumb and then gently dabbed the cloth onto the nail bed.

"No, no, Papi stop!"

"It's going to be okay," Alex said, holding tightly onto Kendall's wrist.

Antonio grabbed the antibiotic ointment and squeezed a fair amount onto the teen's thumb, and then gently rewrapped it.

∞

Carlos woke up thinking he heard Kendall cry out and realized his friend was no longer next to him. He jumped up and quickly checked the bathroom and then his bedroom, before running downstairs. He heard voices coming from the kitchen and went in. Antonio had just finished bandaging Kendall's hand.

"There we go, all done," Antonio said.

"Here, drink," Alex said, holding the cup of water for Kendall.

Kendall took a sip of water.

"Are you alright?" Antonio asked.

Kendall nodded.

"Morning Papi, Papa M," Carlos said.

"Carlitos, what are you doing up so early?" Antonio asked.

"I thought I heard Kendall crying and woke up. He was gone, so I came downstairs."

"He came down a little while ago. We had to change the bandage on his hand," Antonio told him.

"Are you okay?" Carlos asked his friend.

Kendall nodded.

"How did you get past all of us?" Carlos asked.

"I don't know," Kendall yawned.

"I think you need some more sleep," Antonio told him.

Kendall shook his head.

"Did you have a bad dream?"

"Don't remember," Kendall said his eyes half closed.

"Why don't we go in the living room and you can lie down on the couch?" Antonio asked.

"Okay."

Antonio put an arm around him and one around Carlos and they went into the living room. Antonio sat down, Kendall on one side, Carlos on the other. Carlos turned on the TV, found a channel with some cartoons, and settled in next to Antonio. Carlos lay his head on Antonio's shoulder, watching TV. Within minutes, Kendall was sleeping, his head lying against Antonio's chest.

Alex smiled and covered each boy with a blanket. "I'm going to go start breakfast for the kids and mix up the formula."

Antonio nodded. "Thanks buddy."

"No problem."

"What are we having for breakfast?" Carlos asked.

"Whatever you want." Alex smiled.

"Can we have chocolate chip pancakes?"

"Sure we can."

"What's this 'we'? Didn't you just eat breakfast?" Antonio asked.

"There's always room for chocolate chip pancakes," Alex told him.

"I'll help! I like to put in the chocolate chips!" Carlos said, jumping up.

"Do not use two bags this time, and make sure MOST of the chips get into the batter." Antonio laughed.

"But Papi more is better."

"Do you want to explain that to Mami?"

"One bag's fine." Carlos smiled.

"Come on, Trouble, let's get to work." Alex laughed.

He and Carlos went into the kitchen and Alex pulled out the box of pancake mix, while Carlos found the chocolate chips.

"Papa M, can I ask you something?"

"Of course you can. What's on your mind?" Alex asked as he mixed up the batter.

"I was wondering if Papi's okay." Carlos said as he poured the chocolate chips into the bowl.

"Why don't you ask him?"

"Because he'll tell me everything's fine and not to worry."

"I guess he would," Alex said.

"So, is he?"

"He's worried, but he's doing okay. I think he'll feel a lot better after they arrest Graham's crooked lawyer."

"Is he sad because of what Mama K said?"

"A little."

"I know you said it's because of her medication, but she doesn't really think that, does she?"

"I don't think so. I think she's just really scared and confused right now. Carlos, can I ask you something?"

"Sure."

"Do you ever feel like your Papi is spending too much time with Kendall?"

"What do you mean?"

"Do you feel like you're being left out or that he's ignoring you?"

"No. Why would I feel like that?"

"Can you keep a secret?"

Carlos nodded.

"I think Kendall's worried that you might think he's trying to take your dad away."

"Why would I think that?"

"Well, he's having a lot of problems right now, and Antonio is the one who's helping him deal with them. It doesn't really leave a lot of time for much else," Alex explained.

Carlos thought for a moment. "If it had been Papi who died and Papa K who lived and this happened to me, would Kendall feel that way?"

"That's an interesting way of looking at it. Do you think he would?"

"No, because he'd want to protect me and make everything better. Papa K was like my dad, just like you are. Papi is like a dad to Kendall, James, and Logan, and that's the way it's always been. I like having them here. I just wish it were for a happy reason. I just hate that everybody is so sad, and I want Kendall to get better. I miss him," Carlos told him.

"You see him every day."

"I know, but it's not the same. It's like part of him is gone, still hiding somewhere, and I can't find him. Does that make sense?"

"Yeah, it does," Alex said sadly.

"I just want everyone to be okay, and I feel better knowing we're all together," Carlos said.

"You're one amazing kid, you know that?" Alex said, pulling him into a hug.

"We all are." Carlos smiled, hugging him back.

"Yes you are." Alex smiled.

Alex and Carlos finished making the pancakes, and then Carlos ran upstairs to wake the others. "James, Logan, pancakes!" Carlos squealed as he pulled off their blankets.

"Carlos!" they both yelled.

"We made chocolate chip pancakes and Papa M will eat them all if you don't hurry," Carlos told them as he gently shook Katie's shoulder.

"What?" she asked in an irritated tone.

"Chocolate chip pancakes!"

She looked up at Carlos and put her arms up. He smiled, picked her up, jumped over the other two boys, and ran for the stairs.

"How much do you want to bet that he put most of the chocolate chips in the first few pancakes?" Logan asked James.

James looked at him, threw his blanket over Logan's head, and jumped up, following Carlos downstairs.

Logan untangled himself from the blanket. "James! Not nice!"

He got up and then smiled to himself. He grabbed his clothes, went into the bathroom, and proceeded to take a very long hot shower. Logan got downstairs just as the others were finishing their breakfast.

"Where were you, Partner?" Alex asked as he pulled a plate out of the oven for his son.

"I decided to get dressed first so there wouldn't be a long line after breakfast."

"Good thinking." Alex smiled as he set the plate in front of Logan.

"Thanks dad!" Logan grinned.

Carlos and James looked at each other. "Dibs on the shower!" they yelled at the same time.

"Me first!" Carlos said, getting up.

"No, me! It takes me longer to get ready," James told him.

"Which is why I should go first!" Carlos said, running for the stairs.

James raced after him. "NO running up the stairs!" Antonio called after them.

"Sorry Papi!" they both called down.

"Hmm?" Kendall murmured.

"Your brothers are racing up the stairs. Now, how about some breakfast?"

Kendall shook his head and pulled the blanket tighter.

"You know that's not going to work, right?"

"I'm still tired."

"I know, but we didn't do the formula last night and you didn't keep your dinner down. Papa M and Carlos made chocolate chip pancakes, and I'm willing to bet they hid a couple for you."

Kendall tried to sit up and groaned.

"Your shoulder?"

Kendall nodded.

"After you eat, I'll get you some ibuprofen. I don't want you taking it on an empty stomach."

"Okay."

Antonio helped him up and they went into the kitchen. "Look who's up." Alex smiled.

"Hey buddy, how are you feeling?" Logan asked.

"Tired."

Alex pulled another plate from the oven and set it in front of Kendall.

"Thank you."

"You're welcome." Alex smiled.

Kendall sat there for a minute, then picked up his fork, and awkwardly cut into his pancake. He took a bite and put the fork down. Logan reached over, cut up the rest of the pancake for his friend, and handed him his fork.

"Thanks Loges."

"No problem." Logan smiled.

"We'll put the feeding tube in before everyone leaves, so we can do the formula before your appointment with Claudia," Alex told Kendall.

"Okay."

James and Carlos came back down. "You used ALL the hot water!" James said accusingly to Logan.

"No I didn't."

"Yes you did," Carlos said, shivering.

"No, I didn't," Logan repeated.

"Boys..." Antonio said.

"I can prove I didn't use all the hot water," Logan told them.

"How?" James asked.

Logan smirked and got up. "I'll show you."

He headed upstairs and went into the bathroom, James and Carlos right behind him. He opened the cupboard under the sink and turned a valve. He stood up and turned on the faucet, and after a minute, warm water was running from the tap. "Next time, be nice." He smiled as he walked out the door.

"Boys, what are you doing?" Sylvia yawned.

"Saving hot water." Logan smiled as he went back downstairs.

"I say we plant him headfirst in a snowbank and sit on him," James said.

"I'm with you, buddy," Carlos said.

"I'm going to pretend I didn't hear that," Sylvia said as she walked into the bathroom and closed the door.

∞

The phone rang and Antonio answered it. "Hi Sally. How's it going?" He listened to what she was saying and smiled. "I'll meet you there."

"Well?" Alex asked.

"Ryan has a warrant for Manning and they'll be arresting him after they present the evidence at the hearing."

"Good. I take it you want to be there to greet him?"

Antonio nodded and smiled.

"Then will it be over?" Kendall asked.

"We're getting there, Mijo," Antonio said, sitting down next to him.

Logan came in and sat down next to Kendall, grinning.

"What did you do?" Alex asked.

"Just teaching rudimentary plumbing to James and Carlos." He smirked.

"That can't be good," Alex said, shaking his head.

"Everyone should know where the shut off valves are in case of emergency," Logan told him.

"You turned off the hot water, didn't you?" Kendall asked.

"I turned it back on." Logan smiled.

"Good thing, because Mama G hates cold showers." Antonio laughed.

"How do you boys think these things up?" Alex asked.

"This coming from someone who thought it'd be funny to wake James and me up by tickling my foot with a pen," Logan said.

"Oh, it was funny." Antonio laughed.

"Hilarious, but again, it was his idea," Alex said, pointing at Antonio.

"I can't eat anymore," Kendall said.

"You did pretty well, almost two whole pancakes," Logan told him.

Kendall smiled and pushed his plate over to Katie. "Thanks big brother."

"You're welcome."

"Why don't we put the tube in, since everyone needs to get going soon?" Alex asked.

"Okay, but can I have the ibuprofen first?" Kendall asked.

"Sure," Antonio said, getting up. He went into the bathroom and came back with the pills. "Here you go."

"Thanks Papi," Kendall said, taking them.

He tried to pick up the cup of water and Antonio steadied it for him. "Stupid hand."

"Doesn't make it easy, does it?" Antonio asked.

"No, my thumb hurts and the stitches itch."

"I know, I forgot about the longer shirt when you went to bed," Antonio said.

"It's not your fault I bit my nails," Kendall told him.

"At least you get your stitches out on Monday." Antonio smiled.

"Yeah, that's good," Kendall said.

Kendall and Antonio went into the living room and Logan followed with the water.

A few minutes later, Alex had the tube in place and Antonio and the boys headed for Claudia's. They got to her place and went up the walkway. She answered the door before they knocked. "Good morning. How are my babies this morning?"

"Claudia!" Carlos said, hugging her tight.

"You can brighten the darkest day. You know that, baby?" She smiled as she hugged him back.

He smiled up at her.

"How are you two?" she asked James and Logan as she put an arm around each of them.

"Okay," James said quietly.

"Same here," Logan agreed.

"Well, I think we have a few things to talk about, so why don't you go on in and make yourselves comfortable."

They nodded and followed Carlos into the living room.

"How are you this morning?" she asked Antonio.

"A little better." He smiled.

"Is that the truth?"

He nodded. "I'm actually heading down to the station, since Sally and John will be bringing Manning in soon."

"Good, one more sorry excuse of a human being off the street. Now don't you do anything that you'll regret."

He smiled. "I won't. Alex will be dropping Kendall off at eleven and picking up the other boys. I'll meet them here as soon as I'm finished at the station."

"We'll see you then."

He nodded as he went back to his car.

∞

Antonio arrived at the station a few minutes later and went inside. He finished some paperwork and Johnson knocked. "Sally and John are walking Manning over now."

"Thanks Johnson," Antonio said, getting up. He went to the doors and watched as Sally and John escorted Manning to the building, and went outside when they were about half a block away. He stood there patiently, his arms folded across his chest as he waited. He could tell Sally and John were talking and smiled to himself, knowing they were probably baiting Manning.

His eyes turned dark and his expression grew stern as they got closer, and he knew Manning could see him. He watched as John said something and then waved at him and he arched his eyebrow, wondering what his partner had told the man.

Manning wasn't speaking anymore, but Sally and John were still talking as they reached the building.

"Good morning, Boss!" Sally said in a cheerful tone.

Antonio opened the door for them. "It is now." He followed them inside. "Book him, process him, give him his phone call, and then throw his ass in a cell," Antonio ordered.

"Yes sir," Sally said, grinning.

"What are you all so happy about?" Manning snapped.

"Remind me to show you a piece of framed art we have in our main interrogation room. I think you'll find it very interesting," John told him as he pulled him along to the processing room.

Chapter 140 ~ How It Is

Owen Riker was furious. It was all he could do to not punch Manning in the face when he passed by him at the courthouse. Thirty-two years as an attorney, and now one of his associates does something so stupid that he is arrested. He never liked Derek Manning, had voted against giving him partnership, but Diana Goode and Harvey Metcalfe had outvoted him, and now they were in this up to their eyeballs. He had already put his foot down with his remaining partners and Manning was on his own in this. He had agreed to take over Graham's case and had already ordered the rest of Manning's cases divided amongst the other associates.

He followed the guard into the holding room, where Richard Graham was waiting for him. He had gone over Manning's notes and then the actual case files, and already knew how he was going to deal with this case. He entered the room and saw Graham sitting there, cuffed to the table and speaking with Danielle Regent. He looked at her. "Get out, and when you get back to the offices, be prepared to defend your behaviour in this case."

Her eyes grew wide. "M-Mr. Riker I can assure you..."

"Out and leave those papers," he said, pointing to a file she was holding.

She nodded and quickly exited the room.

"Mr. Graham, I'm Owen Riker. I'm taking over your case for Derek Manning."

"Good, then you can tell me what the HELL IS GOING ON!"

"You will watch your tone and your language, or you can find yourself another attorney. I think Manning was a fool to take this case, but as he's committed my firm to your defense, I will defend you to the best of my ability."

"What is going on?" Graham asked through clenched teeth.

"It would seem my former partner decided it would be alright to break the law in regards to this case. None of which is your concern, unless of course I find out that you knew about it?"

"I knew nothing about it," Graham sputtered.

"That had better be the truth," Riker said, staring at Graham.

"All he told me was that he was working on my case and I didn't have anything to worry about."

"Very well, but if I find out differently be forewarned, I will turn over any such evidence to the courts and you will be held fully accountable for it."

"It's true." Graham glared.

"Good. Now as for your case, we're going to accept the plea the DA has graciously offered," Riker told him.

"WHAT? Are you insane, do you know how long they'll send me to prison for?"

Riker just looked at him. "Far less time than you'll do if we go to trial. You ARE guilty of what you are accused, and the prosecution has more than enough evidence to send you to prison for well over twenty-five years. That is NOT including the fact that the DEA is planning to bring you up on charges as soon as they are finished with you here. However, if you cooperate, try, and at least appear remorseful, they may be willing to offer you a deal too. You WILL be going to prison, but at least there would be a chance that you'll be out before you're too old to enjoy the rest of your life," Riker told him.

"Manning told me that he could get me off," Graham fumed.

"Yes, well Manning is an idiot and the two of you could very well be spending some quality time together in prison," Riker snapped.

"That's not fair!"

"FAIR? Let's discuss how fair it was to further traumatize a child after he was kidnapped and brutalized by a psychopath. Let's discuss how fair it was to try to talk his mother into drugging him, without his consent or knowledge. Or how fair it was to forcibly inject this child with a drug that could very well have killed him! Not to mention the fact you spoke about this case on television and helped to reveal a minor's identity to the public. Or perhaps we should discuss how fair it was that his mother was taken to the hospital after collapsing because of what your antics have caused," Riker growled.

"Now just a minute!"

"This is also not including the four cases from Louisiana, which may also be included, ALL of which are admissible in this case. If you do not plead, you will be spending the rest of your life in prison, period. Of course, if you'd rather find another law firm to represent you, I am more than happy to pass this mess along to the next person," Riker told him.

Graham sat back and stared at Riker. "What are they offering?"

"You plead guilty to simple first degree assault and battery, illegally dispensing a controlled substance, and contempt of court. They drop the charges of first degree aggravated assault and battery and illegally administering a controlled substance to a minor."

"What difference would that make?" Graham asked.

"The difference between simple and aggravated assault and battery is about twenty years. It would be up to the judge to determine the exact length of time, but my recommendation is to request a sentencing hearing by jury," Riker said.

"Why?"

"You'd have a better chance of getting a shorter sentence, because you'd be allowed to have people speak on your behalf, asking for leniency. That is, if you actually know anyone reputable who would be willing to do that. Also, the odds are there might be at least one person out of twelve who feels some sort of empathy towards you, especially since I doubt that you've managed to impress the judge at all."

"Wouldn't that be the same thing as a trial?" Graham asked.

"No, you're admitting you're guilty of the charges but asking the court's leniency in sentencing in exchange for not forcing the victims to go through the emotional and physical turmoil of a trial. Just be aware that victims and their families are also allowed to speak and can sway the jury and you could end up doing the maximum time."

"Victims," Graham muttered.

"Yes, victims. That is what YOU made them, and I suggest you lose the 'holier than thou' attitude, it does not impress anyone," Riker said sternly.

"I thought you were supposed to be on my side?"

"I may be your attorney and honour bound to represent you, but I am not on your side. You've preyed upon families who came to you in a time of personal crisis for your help and made a fortune doing so."

"I most certainly have not!" Graham yelled.

"Don't bother denying it. Between what you charged the insurance companies and the prescription benefits, you more than reaped the rewards from their misfortune. Now, do I go to Ryan and try to come to some sort of agreement, or do you find different representation?"

Graham sat there quietly. "You really think the DEA would be willing to make a deal if I plead out here?"

"It depends on how you comport yourself at the hearing. I would also advise you to start behaving yourself while you are incarcerated in the local jail. Any negative reports will not reflect well upon you. I also recommend offering financial restitution to the families involved."

"You want me to pay them off again?"

"No, reimburse them for the hardships they've suffered as a result of your inept treatment. I would recommend setting up a college fund for each of the children involved. I'm not saying you need to pay for their entire education, but a small stipend might help to convince people that you're remorseful for what you've done," Riker told him.

"How much?"

"I would normally say to let your conscious guide you, but I'm afraid that would be a short journey. I would recommend ten thousand per child. It certainly won't break you, and it's enough to give each of them a good start. I would also recommend that you offer to cover the cost of Kendall Knight's therapy with his new psychologist. His mother is a single parent and has lost quite a bit of work because of all of this. They may not accept it, but it shows that you are willing to make amends. Now, do I go speak to Ryan about a plea bargain, or do I speak to him about finding you a public defender?"

"Make the deal," Graham said quietly.

Riker nodded and stood up. "You've made the right choice."

∞

Claudia joined the boys in the living room. "So, how are you all doing this morning?"

"I'm doing okay, but I'm worried about Papi," Carlos said.

"Why are you worried about your dad?"

"I think he's sad about Mama K. She wasn't very nice to him last night."

"That's an understatement," Logan said.

James nodded in agreement.

"Alright, what did you all hear?" Claudia asked them.

"Pretty much everything," Logan told her.

"Why don't you start from the beginning?"

"It started when Kendall called to tell her what he'd done and she started screaming at him," James said.

"What did Kendall do?"

"Do you know about the phone calls he was getting?" James asked.

She nodded. "Sally told me."

"Well, they were trying to set this guy up and decided the best way to do it would be to record him when he called Kendall again. Only no one wanted him answering the phone because of the panic attacks."

"Okay, that makes sense," she said.

"Well, Kendall thought it'd be better for him to answer the phone, so that this guy would actually talk more, and then they could arrest him and it'd all be over with."

She nodded. "That makes sense too."

"So he and I got into a fight because I didn't want him doing it, because it was dangerous. I was scared he would have a panic attack and he would be all alone there. He got mad at me, told me it wasn't up to me, and ran upstairs. Papa M went up and talked to him and Sally tried to explain things to me," James told her.

"What did she say?"

"That Kendall's frustrated and scared. That he's tired of everybody else making all the decisions about everything and not giving him a choice. She said he feels like he's failing everyone because of his panic attacks and because of Deesie," James said, his voice breaking.

"Do you think she's right about that?"

James nodded. "At first I thought that was just stupid, but when I think about everything that's happened, I don't know how he does it."

"Does what?"

"Faces everything that he's had to face. I couldn't do it," he said quietly.

"Baby, why you think that?"

"Because I couldn't."

"I think you're wrong. I think you are all strong. The fact is no one knows how much they can take until they're put to the test. Look at how strong you have all been since this whole thing started. You have stuck together and been there for each other every day. Do you really think Kendall could have done this alone?"

"But..." James started.

"No baby, he told me the only reason he's gotten through any of this is because of all of you. When he was with Deesie, all he thought about was getting home to you. You are his strength and inspiration. Now, what happened after you talked to Sally?"

"I went upstairs and talked to him. He told me he was tired of feeling useless all the time because everybody was trying to take care of him, and that's why he needed to help. I told him I would try to understand as long as he understands we're going to keep taking care of him until everything is better. We both agreed and he said we're okay."

"What happened after that?"

"Sally called Mama K to get her permission and she said he could be in the car, but that he couldn't answer the phone. I knew he was upset about it, but I didn't think about him switching the phones."

"What do you mean switching the phones?"

"They were getting ready to leave for his physical therapy appointment, when he said he needed to get some water. He went back into the kitchen to get a bottle of water. The study is right there, and he went in and switched the phone Sally brought him yesterday, for his."

"That little sneak." She smiled, shaking her head.

"So that's how he did it!" Carlos chuckled.

"What's so funny?" James asked.

"Nothing, I just don't know why people got so upset."

"Maybe because it was a risky and possibly dangerous thing to do," Logan said.

Carlos kept smiling.

"Why are you smiling like that?" James asked.

"Because."

"Because why?" Logan asked, exasperated.

"Don't you get it? That's the first normal thing Kendall's done in a long time."

James and Logan looked at him, and then at each other. "He's right." Logan laughed.

"I guess he is," James agreed.

"So what you're saying is, that switching the phones so he could do what he thought was right, is something he would have done before?" Claudia asked.

"Absolutely," Logan said.

"Yeah, it's too bad Mama K went off on him like that, though," James said quietly.

"What happened?"

"After they got home, Kendall called his mom to tell her what happened. It didn't go very well, she wouldn't listen to him, and then she started screaming at him. I ran down and got Papa M and Mama G, and when we got back upstairs, he was just sitting on the floor. You could hear her screaming from the hallway. Papa M took the phone and tried to calm her down. He brought the phone back in because she wanted to talk to Kendall, but he wouldn't take it. I don't know what she said to him, but he didn't say anything for a long time. He finally fell asleep and slept for a few hours after that," James told her.

"Yeah, my dad had to put one of his shirts on him so we could tie the sleeves closed. He's biting his fingers in his sleep and making them bleed. He did that before too," Logan said.

"When did he do that?"

"After Papa K died," Carlos said.

"He also had a bad dream. It took a few minutes for him to wake up," Logan said, looking at her.

"About Deesie?"

"I think so. He was crying in his sleep and said it hurt," Logan told her, hoping the other boys wouldn't ask any questions. Claudia saw the look in his eyes and knew what Kendall had been dreaming about.

"Maybe he was dreaming about when Deesie hurt his shoulder, since he went to the physical therapist?" Carlos asked.

"That may very well be," Claudia agreed.

Logan gave her a small, sad smile.

"Can you tell me what happened when Jen came over?" she asked.

"I think Mama D called first, because my mom said we should go upstairs and finish watching TV, and then do our homework," Carlos said.

"I went back down to ask my dad when we were going to put the feeding tube in, because the Benadryl makes Kendall sleepy and the feeding takes a while to do. Mama K told me to have Kendall and Katie come downstairs. Papi was standing behind her and shook his head, so I just went back upstairs," Logan said.

"What else did you hear?"

"I closed the door, but we heard pretty much everything," James said.

"She said Papi was trying to steal Kendall," Carlos said, his eyes tearing up.

"We know that's not true," Logan said, putting his arm around him.

"I know, but it made Papi sad, and he's already sad because of everything that's happened," Carlos told them.

"It's just because she forgot to take her medication. It's really strong, and if you don't take it right, there are side effects," Logan told him.

"It's always something, isn't it?" James asked quietly.

"What's that, baby?"

"I don't know. I've been defending her since the first time she accidentally woke him up by saying 'sweetheart.' Then again, after he ended up in the hospital because Graham gave him that shot. I even defended her when she lost it after Kendall had the panic attack at dinner and then ran away. There's ALWAYS an excuse! She knows what she's supposed to be doing and she's not doing it," James said bitterly.

"Why do you think that is?"

"I don't know, but I'm tired of her hurting Kendall and Katie," James said.

"What do the two of you think?" she asked Logan and Carlos.

"I think she's scared," Carlos said.

"Why do you think she's scared?"

"What happens if everybody does what they're supposed to, but things never get back to normal?" Carlos asked.

"That's a good question. So it might be possible that by creating these little situations, it delays her having to actually face it."

"But if that's true and she really doesn't want to go home, why would she blame Papi for trying to steal Kendall?" Logan asked.

"That way she doesn't have to blame herself for pushing him away, just like Kendall told her she was," James said.

"That actually makes a lot of sense," Logan agreed.

"So are you all angry at her?" Claudia asked.

Carlos nodded.

"Yes," James said.

"A little. I just wish there was something we could do to make it easier," Logan said.

"That's understandable, but I'm going to tell you what I told Antonio. Jen has to do the work to get better. As much as people want to help, they can't do it for her."

"I know," Logan said quietly.

"So, how about I go make us some hot chocolate?"

"I'll help!" Carlos offered.

Claudia smiled. "I would love that!"

They went into the kitchen and Claudia got some mugs and started the kettle.

"Can I ask you something?" Carlos asked quietly.

"Of course you can. What's on your mind?"

"Papa M told me something and I wanted to ask you about it, but he said it's a secret."

"Well, as your therapist, I can't tell anyone else. What's it about?"

"Kendall."

'What about him?"

"Papa M said Kendall's worried that I'll think he's trying to take Papi away because of all the things Papi's helping him with," Carlos told her.

"Do you?"

"No, but how do I let Kendall know that?"

"I'm not sure. Maybe you should just tell him."

"Then he'll know somebody talked to me about it."

"What if you talked to him about it and tell him you're worried about what he might be thinking because of what Jen said?" Claudia suggested.

"That's a good idea," Carlos said.

"I have my moments." She smiled.

They carried the tray into the living room and Carlos handed out the mugs. "So, anything else on your minds?" she asked.

"What happens if Mama K doesn't get better? What if she keeps doing things like this?" James asked.

Claudia sighed. "Can you ALL keep a secret?"

They looked at each other and then nodded.

"Antonio said if she keeps on this path that he and Sylvia will file for temporary custody. All of your parents have agreed to stand with them on this."

"That won't be an easy thing for them to do," Logan said sadly.

"No, but unfortunately sometimes the right thing isn't always the easiest. Kendall and Katie will need your support more than ever, and so will your parents," Claudia told them.

"They have it," James said.

"We stick together, no matter what," Carlos said.

"To the end," Logan agreed.

"Good, because if this does happen, it won't be easy for any of you," Claudia said.

"You'll be there though, right?" Carlos asked.

"To the end." She smiled.

∞

Antonio called Joel Riggs and set up an appointment for Kendall later that afternoon. Joel was going to show Antonio a little of the massage therapy and work with Kendall on a few exercises.

Sally knocked on his office door. "Hey Boss, Ryan just called with some good news. Manning's former partner got Graham to agree to take a plea. There won't be a trial, but he is requesting a sentencing hearing by jury."

Antonio smiled. "That is good news. I'll let everyone know when I meet them at Claudia's."

"Speaking of, aren't you suppose to meet them there at eleven?" she asked, pointing at her watch.

"Yeah, just finishing up," he said, getting up.

"Do you think Katie would want to get out later?"

"I think she'd love it," Antonio said.

"I'll be by later this afternoon then."

"Thanks Sally."

"No problem. I'll see you later."

"We'll see you then." He smiled as he headed out the door.

∞

Joanna arrived at the hospital and walked to Jen's room. She had stopped by Brooke's and picked up Jen's prescription for her. She and Brooke had discussed things, and if Jen didn't start doing exactly as she was supposed to, they would take action. Jo had decided she wasn't going to let Jen off so easily this time.

She knocked on the door and went in. "Good morning. How are you feeling today?" she asked as she sat in the chair next to Jen's bed.

"I feel like I'm hung over," Jen said.

"Probably the Valium."

"Probably."

"We need to talk."

"I know," Jen said quietly.

Joanna showed her the prescription bottle. "I brought your medication."

"Thank you."

"You have one month's supply?"

"Yes."

"You said you may have missed a couple of doses?"

Jen nodded.

"You've been taking it for two weeks now, so there should be thirty-two pills left?"

"Yes, why?"

"There are still forty pills in the bottle, which means you missed four days."

"That can't be right," Jen said.

Jo handed her the bottle. "Count them."

Jen looked down. "I believe you."

"Eli explained to you what happens if you don't take it correctly."

"Yes."

"So what happened?"

"I don't know, I just forgot," Jen said.

"Don't hand me that, you're not a forgetful person."

"I don't know why I forgot. With everything that's been going on..."

"STOP! You're not going to use that as an excuse anymore."

"But..."

"No. I'm sorry, Jen, but there is absolutely NO excuse for your behaviour. You know you need to take your meds. Eli told you before you started them what would happen if you didn't take them properly. Because you didn't do what you promised, you managed to hurt most of the people who love you. You physically injured your son and made him run away from you for the THIRD time."

"Oh my God is he alright?" she asked as she remembered his cries.

"Do you really care?"

"What's that supposed to mean?" Jen asked.

"It means... do you really care? Because your words and your behaviour last night told him, and everyone else, differently."

"He took a risk he wasn't supposed to, and I admit I lost it," Jen explained.

"That wasn't until yesterday, therefore not an excuse for missing four days of medication."

"I don't know," Jen said quietly.

"Jen, we've been friends for over twenty-five years and I love you like a sister. Which is why I feel I can tell you what I truly think and feel. I love your children as if they're my own, and what you did last night was inexcusable. You accused Antonio of trying to steal your son. You hurt him and Sylvia with your hateful words. The children, OUR children, were upstairs and could hear every word. They were crying and angry. Your son tried to reason with you and you

screamed at him for the second time that day, and then you injured his arm. Do you even remember what he told you?" Jo asked, tears pooling in her eyes.

"No."

"He told you that you're the one who makes him feel badly about himself. That you make him feel like he deserved what happened! Is that what you really think?"

"Of course not!" Jen sobbed.

"Then why do you continually keep him at arm's length? Yes, you have had a couple of good days together, but you still treat him as if he's a stranger. He's your child and everyone can see that you're afraid to be with him."

"It's not him, it's me! What happens if he has a flashback or a panic attack and I can't help him? What if I'm not strong enough to help him through this?"

"You haven't even given it a chance! It's as if you gave up on him before you even tried, and now you're accusing the people who ARE there for him of trying to take him away from you. He's not a possession, he's your child! Now grow up and start acting like his mother, because this isn't about you and what you can or cannot handle. You're a parent... you HAVE to handle it all. You also know that we're here for both of you, so instead of acting as if you're all alone in the world. Open your eyes and see the people who are here and love you! I know you miss Will, I know this is hard, but you are NOT alone, unless you continue pushing everyone away. Can you even see what progress he's made? He's working to get better and he's fighting back against the people who've hurt him. Unfortunately right now, that includes you."

Jen was sobbing into her hands and Joanna reached over and took her by the shoulders. "Look at me!"

Jen looked up into her friend's soft blue eyes.

"I love you, we all love you, but you need to get your act together and you need to do it now. If you don't, you will lose your children and it will be because of you, and no one else."

"Tell me what I need to do," Jen said quietly.

"First, you will take your medication like you're supposed to. Brooke is ready to hire a nurse if she needs to. If you think you can do without one, I'll make sure you take your morning dose, and Brooke will make sure you take your evening dose. I know you're going to your therapy sessions, and I really hope you're being honest with Eli, because if you're not, there's really no point in you going. We will be calling him with any issues that arise, and if that makes you angry, that's just too damn bad. You need to find a way to reach out to your children before it's too late, so I suggest you have a long talk with Eli about how to do that."

Jen nodded.

"I'm not trying to hurt you, but enough is enough. What happened last night will NOT happen again. Understood?"

"Yes," Jen whispered.

"You also need to make this right with Antonio. I've never seen him so hurt."

"I will."

"I hope so, because he really didn't deserve what you said to him," Joanna said firmly.

"I know. None of you did."

Jo handed her a tissue. "Let it all out, because afterward we have a lot of work to do. I'm going to stay with you today and we're going to figure out how to make things right again."

"Why do you put up with me?" Jen asked.

"Because you're like a sister to me, and like it or not, you're stuck with me."

"Like our kids?" Jen asked.

"Just like our kids." Joanna smiled.

Chapter 141 ~ Emotional Overload

Antonio got to Claudia's and knocked.

"Did everything go alright?" she asked as she let him in.

"Perfectly." He smiled.

They went into the living room and he sat down next to Carlos. "How are my boys doing?"

"Good," Carlos said in a subdued tone.

"It doesn't sound like it," Antonio said, putting his arm around his son.

"We were just talking about Mama K," Logan told him.

"She'll be alright. It's just going to take some time."

"She's not really the one we're worried about," James said.

Antonio looked at the boys and realized they were worried about him. "Hey, I promise I'm okay. In fact, I have some good news, which I'll tell you as soon as Kendall and Papa M get here."

"Is it about the lawyer?" Carlos asked.

"Yes, but there's more, so let's wait for Kendall and Papa M."

"How about some coffee?" Claudia asked.

"That'd be great. Let me help you," Antonio offered. She smiled and they walked back to the kitchen. "So, how are they really doing?" he asked.

"You know I can't give you specifics, but they're worried about you and angry at Jen," she told him.

"I was afraid of that."

"I can't really say I blame them. Jen seems to be subconsciously undermining any attempts to move forward in her recovery."

"I know. Brooke said that if Jen doesn't straighten up, she'll hire a nurse to follow her around and make sure that she does what she's supposed to," Antonio told her.

"She certainly won't like that."

"No, she won't. I just wish she would stop being so afraid and realize the damage she's causing before it's too late," Antonio said quietly.

"Tell me something, has she ever really been on her own before?"

Antonio thought back. "Not really. She went from living at home with her parents to sharing an apartment with Sylvia while we were all in college. We were all always together, even then. She and Will married after graduating and they were happy until he died."

"How were her parents? Does she have any brothers or sisters?"

"Her parents were very nice. Her dad died during her first year in college, and her mom died about four years ago. She was an only child and they were very protective, maybe too protective."

"So the first time she ever had to face anything on her own was when her husband died, but even then she's had all of you?" Claudia asked.

"I guess so."

"What about Will's family?"

"His mom died about ten years ago. His dad's still living but moved back to High River after Will died."

"Where's High River?"

"Alberta. Will's grandparents emigrated from there and settled here before they started their family."

"Why did he go back there with his grandchildren still here?"

"People thought it was because he couldn't handle losing Will—they were really close. I have a feeling it was more about Will's brother, Thomas, though."

"He had a brother?"

Antonio nodded. "He wasn't the nicest guy in the world. No one here has heard from him since right after Kendall was born."

"What was his problem?"

"No one really knows. Will's parents were always loving and supportive, but it didn't seem to really matter to Thomas. No matter what they did for him, it was never enough."

"That's sad. So do you think his dad went back to Alberta to find him or avoid him?"

"I really don't know, but let's just say that no one here misses Thomas," Antonio said.

"That bad?"

"I just don't understand how two brothers can be so different," Antonio told her.

"Unfortunately it seems to happen all too often."

"Very true," Antonio agreed.

There was a knock at the door. "Sounds like the other boys are here." Claudia said with a smile.

She answered and let Kendall and Alex in. "How are you doing, baby?" she asked Kendall.

"Okay, just tired."

"Are you taking the Benadryl?"

He nodded. "I think that's why I'm tired."

"It'll take a while for your system to adjust to it."

He nodded again.

"Well, I think Antonio has something to tell everyone, so why don't we go see what it is?" she said, putting her arm around him.

They joined the others in the living room and Kendall sat down next to James, and Alex sat beside Logan.

"Are you going to tell us now?" Carlos asked Antonio.

Antonio smiled and put his arm around Carlos. "Sally called and they arrested Manning. The DA and Judge Brown are going over the charges now. Also, they called in one of Manning's partners and he's convinced Graham to make a deal, so there won't be a trial."

"So this is all good news?" Logan grinned.

"Yes it is." Antonio smiled.

James noticed that Kendall wasn't saying anything and put his arm around him. "Are you okay?"

Kendall nodded.

James looked over at Claudia. He saw she was watching them and she gave him a small smile. "Why don't we get started?" she said and held her hand out to Kendall.

He took it and followed her into her office. "So, how are you doing today, really?"

Kendall shrugged.

"Antonio and the boys told me some of what happened yesterday. Can you fill me in on the rest?"

"Not really much to tell," he said quietly.

"Really? That's not what I heard. I heard that you decided to do what you thought needed to be done and handled it very well."

"I think it depends on who you talk to."

"Well, this is from Antonio, Sally, and the boys. Carlos was very impressed and proud of you. In fact, he pointed out that switching the phones was something you would have done before all of this happened."

"Maybe."

She went over and sat down next to him. "What's going on in that head of yours today?"

"I don't know. Not much, I guess."

"Can you tell me how you're feeling right now?"

"Tired."

"No baby, I mean emotionally."

"Tired," he repeated.

She looked at him and smiled softly. "I bet you are. What do you think about what's going on with your mom?"

"I think we hurt everyone who loves us, and I don't want to talk about it anymore," he said, not looking up.

Claudia looked at him. "Kendall, look at me."

He sighed and looked up.

"You cannot close yourself off again—you've made too much progress. I also noticed that you used the word 'we' when I asked about what your mom did. You are NOT responsible for your mother's actions, and I'm not going to let you take the blame for them."

"We're both to blame," he said quietly.

"You're a child, and you're not responsible for the fact that your mom is having a hard time dealing with this. It's her responsibility to do what the doctor says and she knows it. You are doing what you are supposed to be doing. You've worked very hard to get better, and I will NOT allow her to stop your progress."

"But..."

"No 'buts.' Baby, this is HER responsibility, not the other way around. She needs to step up to the plate and start doing her job, period."

Kendall sighed. "I don't know what to do anymore."

"You do what you have to so you keep recovering. If that means you can't be around your mom right now, that's okay. Believe it or not, it's alright to not want to be around people who make you feel badly about yourself, even if it's someone you love. Sometimes we just have to take a step back before we can move forward again. Your mom needs to realize what she's done and SHE needs to fix it, and it's up to her to figure out how to do that."

Kendall's eyes filled with tears as he looked back down. "You don't understand."

"Then tell me," Claudia said gently.

"She s-said Papi is trying to steal me."

"I know she did."

"She's wrong. It's more like...," he said, choking back a sob.

"Like what, baby?"

"Like I'm t-trying to t-take Papi away from Carlos," he said, covering his face.

Claudia put her arm around his shoulders. "Why do you think that?"

"Because I d-don't have a dad and I want mine back. I m-miss him so much," Kendall sobbed.

She pulled him close. "Of course you do, especially now. I can understand why you might be worried about this, but I can promise you that's not what Carlos thinks at all. He loves you and wants you close, so that he knows you're safe."

"I'm just so tired of everything," Kendall said.

"I know you are, baby, and having your mom take a step backwards isn't helping."

"I-I don't trust her anymore. I don't know if I even like her. What kind of person does that make me?"

"It makes you normal. You can dislike someone for the way they're behaving, while still loving them as a person. Believe me, when I was growing up, there were lots of times I didn't like my mama, even though I loved her more than life itself. It was the same with my brother and sisters. You can be angry at the person, but that doesn't mean you don't love them."

"I just want my dad," he sobbed.

"I know, baby. Let it all out," she said, rubbing his back comfortingly as he cried.

∞

"So is there going to be a trial for Manning?" Alex asked Antonio.

"Probably, but I don't think that's going to have anything to do with us. Taylor has turned over all of his records, and that should be enough to convict him. It's also enough that the courts will probably be reopening a few of Manning's cases that Taylor told Ryan about."

"Nothing like opening a can of worms," Alex said.

"True enough."

"But Graham pleading guilty means that Kendall and Mama K don't have to testify, right?" Logan asked.

"Right, but the defense is asking for a sentencing hearing by jury," Antonio told him.

"What does that mean?" James asked.

"It means that instead of the judge deciding how long Graham goes to prison for, a jury will."

"Is that good?" James asked.

"I don't think it's going to be a problem." Antonio smiled.

"Well, we should probably get going. You three should try and get your schoolwork done," Alex said to the boys.

"Aww. Shouldn't we celebrate instead?" Carlos asked hopefully.

"You can celebrate by keeping your grades up," Antonio teased.

"Papi..." Carlos pouted.

"Alright, why don't we all meet for lunch after we're done here? I think Claudia wanted to try to get Kendall out in public today, so maybe she will join us. Then he has another appointment with the physical therapist."

"Can I go?"

"How much homework do you have?" Antonio asked.

"Not that much." Carlos smiled.

Antonio looked at him and then at Logan. "How much?"

"Just a two-page math assignment and a short essay in English. I can help him finish it up this weekend." Logan smiled.

"Alright, bring your gear and I'll drop you off at hockey practice afterwards."

"Thank you, Papi!" Carlos said, hugging him.

"Give us a call when you know what you're doing and we'll meet you," Alex told Antonio as he handed the boys their jackets.

Antonio nodded. "Thanks buddy."

∞

Jen and Joanna sat and talked until Eli arrived.

"How are you doing today?" he asked.

"Better. I have some things I need to talk to you about," Jen said, looking down.

"I thought you might," he said gently.

"Well, I should let you two talk," Joanna said, getting up.

"No, please stay," Jen asked.

Joanna looked at Eli, who nodded, so she sat back down.

"I haven't taken my medication in four days. I really don't have an excuse."

"Alright, why did you stop?" Eli asked.

"I don't know. I was feeling so much better about things that I thought I didn't need it anymore. Then I started having bad dreams and feeling anxious again. I didn't want to start taking it again, because I thought as soon as it was out of my system, it would all stop."

"I understand you were feeling better, but you do understand it was because the medication was doing its job? You cannot just stop taking this type of medication cold turkey. You have to taper off of it slowly, or things like what happened yesterday, happen," Eli told her.

"I know. I wasn't thinking very clearly."

"And now?" he asked.

"I'll be taking it the way I'm supposed to," she said.

"Jennifer, if you don't want to be on medication, you don't have to be. However, we need to take you off it the right way. I don't want you thinking that I'm making you take it," Eli told her.

"I don't think that. I'm the one who asked for something to help me deal with all of this."

"Alright, how do we make sure that what happened yesterday won't happen again?" he asked.

"My friends will make sure that I take it properly," she said, smiling at Joanna.

"Yes we will," Jo replied.

"Alright." He smiled. "Have you spoken with Kendall since this happened?"

Jen shook her head.

"What about your daughter?"

"No," she said quietly.

"What would you say to them if they were here right now?"

"I don't know. I don't know how to talk to them anymore."

"Things were going well before the episode yesterday?"

"Yes, I think so. I don't know. I keep having these horrible thoughts and feelings. I can't get them out of my head, and I haven't told anyone about them, not even you," she said, looking out the window.

"What kind of thoughts?"

"I can't," she said, shaking her head.

"Jennifer, if you don't tell me, I can't help you," Eli said gently.

"I'm a terrible person, and I don't deserve to be a mother," she said quietly.

"Honey, you made a mistake. We'll get through this," Joanna said, looking at Eli.

Jen shook her head, still looking out the window. "I don't think so."

"Why not?" Eli asked.

"What kind of mother looks at her child and thinks...?" she said, tears now falling.

"Thinks what?" Eli asked.

"Thinks that it would have been easier if he'd never been born. Or t-that he wouldn't be in so much pain if... if he hadn't made it," Jen sobbed.

Jo looked at her in shock. She opened her mouth to speak, but Eli looked at her and shook his head. He reached over and took Jen's hand.

"Those are actually very common thoughts when a life-altering crisis like this occurs. We see our loved ones in pain and wish for an end to it. It's more common when dealing with a family member who is suffering from a debilitating illness, but it's also common in an intense emotional crisis."

"You're telling me it's NORMAL that I wish my son were dead?"

"No, I'm saying it's normal to wish for the pain to end. You don't really wish Kendall hadn't survived. You wish the pain and fear were no longer there for the both of you."

"I don't know," she said quietly.

"He's right," Joanna said sadly. "Remember when Teni was dying? At first I was hopeful that she'd beat it, but as she got weaker and weaker, I just prayed for it to end."

"Teni was dying from cancer and in pain from the treatments, not recovering from being kidnapped by a psychopath," Jen snapped.

"Kendall's in pain and he's trying to recover. The only difference is that he CAN recover and he's working hard towards that," Jo told her.

"You really think that you're wishing that your terminally ill grandmother's pain would end is no different than me wanting my injured child's to end?" Jen asked, her temper flaring.

"No, what I'm saying is that you want YOUR pain to end, just like I wanted mine to end. The only difference is that Teni died and is at peace, while your son is alive and still trying to deal with all of this. The only difference is you CAN'T give up because he needs you!" Jo told her, wiping angry tears from her eyes.

"What if I have given up though?" Jen asked.

Joanna stood up. "Then to hell with you!" Jo grabbed her coat and purse and ran from the room.

Eli pointed at Jen. "I will be right back. We are not finished discussing this." He then followed Joanna out. "Mrs. Mitchell, please stop!"

She stopped and he caught up with her. "Are you alright?"

"No, I'm not. How are we supposed to tell Kendall that his own mother has given up?"

"She hasn't really given up, it's just a combination of her fears and the withdrawal from the medication. Once she's back on track with it, she'll be doing much better," he said reassuringly.

"I'm not sure I can deal with her anymore," Joanna told him.

"Then by giving up, she wins."

"What?"

"Don't you see what she's doing? She is trying to push you all away, because she believes that her children would be safer with someone else."

"They ARE with someone else. They have been since day one!"

He nodded. "If they stay there, she doesn't have to face any of this anymore. She can close herself off from everyone and not have to deal with it. She doesn't understand how to do this, and instead of trying to figure it out, she's taking the easy path and hiding from it."

"Well, it's working! She has hurt almost everyone who loves her. How are we supposed to reach her if she keeps this up?"

"By NOT letting her get away with this. She has actually led a fairly sheltered life. Always having someone there to deal with problems as they arise. First her parents and then her husband. From what I understand, it took over a year for her to be able to fully function after he died."

"That sounds about right."

"She had all of you there to help her?"

Joanna nodded.

"This time what we need to do is make her take control of her own life."

"How do we do that?"

"First, we need to get her back on her medication, and that means someone needs to make sure she's taking it. After that, she needs to go home and start taking care of herself."

"Not with the children," Jo said firmly.

"No, not right now. She needs to learn how be on her own and how to take care of herself first. This includes her therapy sessions, and I am going to see about getting her into a support group. There are a couple of support groups for families of violent crime victims in Minneapolis. I think getting an outside perspective might help her realize that this, unfortunately, is not an isolated incident and there are a lot of people who understand what she's going through."

"Do you really think that'll help?"

"I do." He smiled. "How were the children doing this morning?"

"I haven't been there yet. Logan, James, and Carlos all have an appointment to see Claudia this morning. Kendall's appointment is after theirs."

"If anyone can help them through this, it's Claudia."

"I hope so—she's very sweet. All of the kids seem to like her, even Katie."

"She's a hard person not to like."

"What do we tell the kids about Jen?"

"Maybe a simplified version of the truth," he suggested.

"Such as?"

"Tell them we're getting her back on her meds and keeping a close eye on her until she's regulated. Then we'll be increasing her therapy sessions and including a support group."

Jo nodded.

"I know this isn't easy, but she really needs to learn to survive on her own. Until then, I would recommend making arrangements for Kendall and Katie to be away from her for a while."

"We were actually discussing that last night. Antonio and Sylvia are their godparents and would be their legal guardians if something happened to Jen, so they're prepared to file for temporary custody."

"That might be something to go ahead with."

"Antonio was worried it would confirm what she said to him last night—that he's trying to steal Kendall from her, but we all agreed the children come first."

"That's the way it should be. I will be working with her on all of that, so you do what you need to. Maybe you should go and spend some time with your family."

"I think I will. Thank you," Joanna said.

"You're welcome. Now I need to get back and have a little talk with Jennifer."

"Please tell her I'm sorry for what I said."

"Are you?"

"No, not really," she sighed.

"I'll tell her that you're alright and you'll talk to her later."

"That sounds good," she said with a smile.

"Try getting some rest too," he suggested.

"I will," she promised.

∞

Joanna got to her car and sat there for a minute before pulling out. She drove to the Garcia's, lost in thought, and pulled up into the driveway behind Alex's car. She went up to the door and knocked. Sylvia answered.

"You know you don't have to knock."

Joanna gave her a small smile and walked in. The boys were sitting at the dining room table working on their homework. "Hi mom!" Logan smiled.

"Hi honey. How was your visit with Claudia?"

"Good."

"Are you okay, Mama M?" James asked, noting her red eyes.

"I'm fine, honey," she said, kissing his cheek as she walked by him and into the kitchen.

The boys looked at each other and Logan went to get up, but Sylvia put her hand on his shoulder and shook her head. "Go get your dad."

Logan got up and ran to the guest room, where Alex was finishing a phone call with Sam. "Dad, I think mom needs you."

"What's going on?"

"I don't now, she looks funny. She's in the kitchen."

"Okay, you boys finish your homework upstairs."

"But..."

"Now," Alex said firmly.

Logan told James and Carlos that Alex wanted them upstairs. The boys gathered their things and started upstairs as Alex went into the kitchen.

"Hey, is everything alright?" Alex asked.

Sylvia looked up at him and shook her head. "I don't know what's wrong," she whispered.

"Jo?" he asked, sitting next to her. She looked over at him and then threw her arms around his neck, sobbing.

"Hey, honey, what's wrong?" he asked, holding her tightly to him.

"J-Jen, what she said, it's all wrong. How can you just want your child dead? Eli said she didn't mean it, but how can she say that?"

"What? Honey, I don't understand."

Sylvia grabbed a glass and poured some water for Jo, which she handed to Alex.

"Thanks Sylvia. Here, drink," he said, holding the glass up for Joanna.

Joanna took a sip and then a deep breath. "I'm sorry."

"Honey, don't be sorry. Just tell me what happened," Alex said.

Jo took another deep breath and then told them about the conversation between her, Jen and Eli. She had stopped crying by the time she was finished, and they all sat there quietly. She was sitting with her head on Alex's shoulder, and he kissed her forehead.

"Come on, you need to get some rest."

"But..."

"No buts, you're going to lie down for a while and then we'll get this all figured out," he told her, pulling her up. He walked her to the guest room and she laid down. He covered her with a blanket and sat down next to her. "Everything will be alright."

∞

Sylvia sat there for another minute before making a decision. She grabbed the phone and called their attorney's office.

"Hello, this is Sylvia Garcia. I need to speak with Mr. Christopher, please."

A moment later, a friendly voice came on the line. "Good morning, Sylvia. What can I do for you today?"

"Hi Mark. I need you to draw up some papers for us," she said, trying not to cry.

Chapter 142~ Good News and Bad News

Claudia held Kendall as he cried. After a few minutes, his sobs decreased and he took a few ragged breaths. "I-I'm so tired of being such a big baby all the time."

"There's nothing wrong with crying. When most people cry, it's usually for a good reason. It helps us move through the pain or sorrow, and Lord knows you have had your share of both. The bad thing is when you try to keep it all inside, because then it can turn to poison, "Claudia said gently.

"I know."

"Are you feeling any better?"

Kendall nodded.

"I think we'll skip working on the word exercise today, but we are going to go out somewhere."

"Where?"

"Well, I'm running low on a few things, so I thought maybe we'd go to that little market I sent Sylvia to," she told him.

"The one with the candy that nearly killed her?"

"Yes, that one." She smiled.

"What if there are a lot of people there?"

"It's not usually crowded, especially in the middle of the day. You don't have talk to anyone, and Antonio will be there, too."

He sighed. "Okay."

"You did great at the arena ticket counter the other day, so I know you'll do just fine."

"There was only one person there," he pointed out.

"Yes, and you SPOKE with her on your own. When you think about it, you've actually accomplished quite a bit this week."

"Yay, I spoke to a stranger," he said, rolling his eyes.

She took his chin in her hand and looked him in the eyes. "Do NOT downplay your progress. That was a huge step for you and you should be proud of it—I know everyone else is."

"I use to be able to talk to anybody."

"You will again, I promise. If you think about it, you actually spoke to two strangers, because you took the call from the man that was making those phone calls. Something you chose to do on your own, even though not everyone else agreed that you should."

"I guess."

"Thinking back on what you use to be able to do is good, but only if you use those memories as a goal. If you think back and start feeling badly because you're not to that point yet, it's just going to make it harder for you."

"Okay, that makes sense," he said, smiling a little.

"Are you ready to give this a try?"

He nodded and they went into the living room, where Antonio was waiting. "So, we're going to take a little field trip to the market today," Claudia told him.

"Sounds good. The boys wanted to meet us for lunch afterward, and we'd love to have you join us." Antonio smiled.

"Well, how can I turn down lunch with six of my very favourite guys?"

"Is my mom having lunch with us?" Kendall asked.

"No Mijo, she's still in the hospital," Antonio said, putting his arm around his shoulders.

Kendall nodded, feeling guilty at the small surge of relief he suddenly felt.

"Then we have another appointment with the physical therapist," Antonio told him.

Kendall groaned.

"He's just going to show me a little of the massage therapy so we can work on your shoulder at home. He's also going to work with you on a few exercises."

"Fine."

"It's just not your day, is it?" Claudia smiled.

"No," Kendall replied with a trace of a pout on his lips.

"It won't be that bad." Antonio said, chuckling.

Kendall raised an eyebrow and just looked at him.

"I get the distinct impression he doesn't believe you," Claudia said.

"I'm getting that feeling too." Antonio laughed as he handed Kendall his jacket.

Kendall rolled his eyes. "Grown-ups, thinking they're so funny all the time," he mumbled as he put his jacket on.

"What's that?" Claudia asked.

"Nothing," Kendall said with an innocent smile.

"Mmhmm, that's what I thought."

∞

The boys had gone upstairs and were waiting in the guest room. Katie had been in Carlos' room playing a video game and joined them when she saw them come upstairs.

"What do you think happened?" James asked.

"I don't know, but it must be bad if my mom was crying," Logan said, trying not to panic.

"Wasn't she visiting my mom?" Katie asked.

"I'm not sure. I know she was planning on seeing her sometime today," Logan told her.

"I'm sure everything's okay. Why don't we play Ice Castle Blaster?" he asked Katie as he grabbed his laptop.

"You're just trying to distract me, aren't you?"

"No, I'm trying to distract me," Carlos said as he logged into the game.

"Fine, but I don't want any complaining when I kick your butt," Katie told him.

"You wish," Carlos retorted.

"I know," Katie stated.

After a few minutes, Katie and Carlos were engrossed in the game.

"I'm going to go see if I can find out anything," Logan whispered to James.

James nodded.

Logan went downstairs and made his way to the kitchen. Alex and Sylvia were sitting at the kitchen table, talking quietly. "Dad, is everything alright? Where's mom? Is she okay?"

"Hey Partner. She's fine. She's just tired. We finally got her to rest for a while, so you guys try and keep it down, okay?"

"She went to see Mama K, didn't she?"

Alex patted the chair next to him and Logan sat down. "Jen's not doing very well right now. She's having a really hard time dealing with all of this, and it turns out she hasn't been taking her medication for a few days."

"So she's going through withdrawal?"

Alex nodded. "Her doctor said it's going to be a few days before she gets back on track."

"Is she going to be okay?"

"Sure she will. Once she's taking her meds like she's supposed to, Eli's going to find her a support group. He thinks it'll help her to realize that she's not the only parent going through something like this."

"What about Kendall and Katie?"

"They'll be staying here with us, just like they have been," Sylvia told him.

"Look Partner, after Sylvia and I talk to Antonio, we'll sit down and tell all of you everything we can. Right now, let's just try and keep this on the quiet side."

"What do I tell the others? They know I came down to find out what was wrong."

"Just tell them that your mom's exhausted and we'll all talk later, okay?"

"Okay."

"It's going to be alright. I don't want you worrying about this," Alex said.

"That's easier said than done," Logan said sadly.

"I know it is. But it's really important that we stay strong for each other, especially right now."

"We will," Logan promised.

"That's my boy," Alex said, hugging him.

"I'll go tell them what you told me," Logan said, getting up.

"Can you ask Katie if she wants to go have lunch with us?"

"Sure thing." Logan smiled as he headed back upstairs.

∞

Antonio and Kendall followed Claudia to the little market on Edgewood. They parked in the small parking lot and Antonio got out. Kendall counted seven cars besides Antonio and Claudia's and sat there trying to take deep, even breaths.

Antonio opened his door and held out his hand. "Come on, you can do this," he said with a smile. Kendall nodded and took Antonio's hand, and they met Claudia at the door.

"Are you ready?" She smiled.

"If I say 'no,' can we go home?"

"Nice try," she said, opening the door. Antonio chuckled and they walked inside.

Claudia pulled out a cart and started down an aisle, Kendall and Antonio beside her. "I do a lot of my shopping here. The owners are a lovely married couple who opened this place about forty years ago," Claudia told them.

"I've only been in here a couple of times before, but it's a nice little place." Antonio smiled.

They passed a woman who was pushing a cart loaded with groceries and had a toddler strapped into the seat of the cart. The little girl giggled, happily waving around a binky attached to her coat with a cord. The woman smiled and said 'hello' to the trio.

"Hello. How old is this precious little one?" Claudia asked the woman, smiling broadly.

"Almost eighteen months."

"Well, she's adorable," Claudia told her.

"Thank you. I try and remember that when she's up at two in the morning teething."

"It's always something at this age," Claudia said.

"Very true. I don't mind losing the sleep so much, but she's always so uncomfortable and the drooling is non-stop. The little toys you freeze for them to chew on just don't work."

"Well, I'll tell you something that my sister does. You get some of those frozen waffles and let her chew on those. They aren't as hard and won't hurt her gums, and as an added bonus, they absorb the drool," Claudia told her.

"Really? I'm definitely going to try that. Thank you," the woman said, smiling gratefully.

"You're welcome. I hope it works for her."

"So do I." The woman laughed as she continued down the aisle.

"See, nothing too scary here," Claudia said gently to Kendall.

He smiled at her but clung tightly to Antonio.

"Here, why don't you push the cart so you have something to lean on? Antonio and I will walk on either side of you," Claudia suggested.

Kendall nodded. He moved to take the cart and froze. *"You push so you have something to lean on."* Kendall felt the man's hand squeezing tightly on his shoulder as the man continually told him to, *"behave or else."*

Kendall was shaking and trying to get the images out of his head. He vaguely heard someone calling to him.

"Baby, what is it?" Claudia asked, trying to get the boy to respond.

Kendall closed his eyes and fought against the panic as the memories washed over him. He opened his eyes and found himself looking into Claudia's worried brown eyes. He realized Antonio had his arms around him and had pulled him away from the cart.

"Can you tell me what happened?" Claudia asked.

"We w-were at a store in that town and he t-told me to p-push the cart and behave or else."

"Deesie?" Claudia asked.

Kendall nodded.

"In Jamieson?" Antonio asked.

"I don't know. Is that where Doc lives?"

"Yeah, it is," Antonio told him.

"Is that all that happened?" Claudia asked.

"I think so."

"Okay, why don't we go? I can finish shopping later."

Kendall took a couple of deep breaths. "No, it's o-okay."

"Are you sure?"

He nodded.

"Alright, but let me know if you feel like you need to get out of here," she told him.

"I will."

Antonio put his arm around Kendall's shoulders and smiled at Claudia. "We should decide what we want for lunch, so I can call Alex. Knowing my boys, they're probably all starving to death by now."

"True enough. When we were growing up, I swear my brother could eat his weight in food every day." Claudia laughed.

"That's Carlos," Antonio said.

"What about you, baby, what are you hungry for?" Claudia asked.

"It doesn't really matter to me," Kendall said.

"You're a big help," Antonio said.

"Why don't you call home and see what the boys want?" Claudia laughed.

"Good idea, since I'm getting no help on this end."

Kendall rolled his eyes as Antonio pulled his cell from his pocket and called Alex's number. "Hey Alex, you want to ask the boys where they want to go for lunch?"

"Sure thing, hold on a minute," Alex said.

Claudia grabbed a couple of boxes of Oreos and tossed them in the cart. "Can't disappoint Carlos now, can we?"

Kendall smiled and shook his head.

Alex got back on. "The boys said pizza sounds great, but since Kendall won't want to go in anyplace, maybe we should just get one to go and eat at the park? He should be okay if he bundles up, and he really loved being outside the other day."

Antonio looked at Kendall. "Pizza in the park sound good?"

Kendall smiled and nodded.

"Why don't you call in the order and we'll stop and pick it up? We'll meet you there in about thirty minutes?"

"Sounds good. We need to talk about something too, so it's good Claudia will be there," Alex told him.

"Okay, we'll see you there. Can you remind Carlos to bring his gear?"

"Sure thing," Alex said.

"We'll stop and pick up lunch and meet everyone at the park," Antonio told Claudia and Kendall.

"I haven't been on a winter picnic in years!" Claudia smiled.

"We usually have one a couple of times a year," Antonio said.

"Well, I think I have everything I need, so we should probably get going," Claudia told them.

They headed up to the checkout, where there were a few people in line. Kendall clung tightly to Antonio and he moved the boy in front of him, so he was between him and Claudia.

Claudia greeted the checker as she placed her items up on the counter. "Hello Mrs. Hanssen. How are you today?"

"Hello Dr. Claudia! I can't complain. And yourself?" the elderly woman smiled.

"It's a beautiful day outside and I'm off to have lunch with six very special guys," Claudia told her.

"Are these two of them?" she asked, smiling at Antonio and Kendall.

"Yes they are. This is Antonio Garcia and this is Kendall," Claudia said, patting Kendall on the shoulder.

"It's nice to meet you." Antonio smiled.

"It's nice to meet you, too. How are you today, young man?" she asked Kendall.

Kendall pushed himself back until he was underneath Antonio's arm.

"Kendall's the one that I recommended your candies for," Claudia said.

"Oh good, did they help?"

Kendall looked at her and nodded a little.

"I'm glad. Nothing better than a nice piece of peppermint to soothe an aching stomach," she said, smiling gently.

Kendall smiled back a little.

She reached under the counter and winked at Claudia. "In fact, these just came in. All natural, just in time for Christmas," she said, holding a candy cane out to Kendall.

Kendall saw the people in the next lane over staring at them and shook his head as he tightened his grip on Antonio. "It's alright, Mijo. She's a friend of Claudia's."

Claudia noticed the woman staring at Kendall. "Is there something I can help you with?"

The woman snorted and shook her head.

"Like maybe a lesson in manners, or did you just major in being rude?" Claudia said loudly. The woman turned red and quickly paid for her purchases, then she ushered the children with her out the door. "Sorry about that," Claudia said.

"Mrs. Kline always has been a little uppity, as my mother would say," Mrs. Hanssen said, shaking her head sadly. "Here honey, it's alright. It's just an early Christmas gift," she said, holding the candy cane out again.

Kendall looked at Antonio, who smiled and nodded. Kendall reached out and took it. "Thank you," he whispered.

Claudia smiled at Antonio, who hugged Kendall. "That's my boy!"

Mrs. Hanssen smiled and continued to ring up Claudia's items.

"I'll see you again soon," Claudia said as she paid for her groceries.

"Looking forward to it, Dr. Claudia. Maybe we'll see you too?" she asked, smiling at Antonio and Kendall.

"I think there's a good chance of that," Antonio told her.

"Good. You have a nice lunch."

"We will." Antonio smiled.

She smiled at Kendall and waved.

He smiled back. "Bye," he whispered.

They went out to the cars and Antonio helped Claudia load her bags in the car. Kendall took a deep breath and grabbed the cart, pushing it back to the store entrance, and putting it with the other carts. He ran back to Antonio and grabbed onto his arm again.

Antonio put his arm around him and they walked back to his car. "I'm so proud of you!"

Kendall smiled as he got into the car.

∞

"Come on guys, we gotta get going," Alex called up the stairs.

"Coming, we're just getting our gear packed up for practice later," Logan yelled down.

"Are you sure you don't want to come?" Alex asked Sylvia.

"No, I'm going to run to Mark's office and pick up the papers."

"I think I'll go with you," Jo said. She had awoken half an hour earlier and was worried if she saw Kendall right now, she would burst into tears again.

"Okay honey," Alex said, kissing her cheek.

The kids came running downstairs. "Ready!" Carlos said.

"Here, take this extra scarf for Kendall. I want you to make sure he stays warm," Sylvia said, handing Carlos a blue scarf from the closet.

"I will, I promise." Carlos smiled, taking it from her.

"You guys have fun, and Carlos, you behave at the physical therapist's office. NO playing with the equipment," Sylvia told him.

"Mami, would I do that?" he asked innocently.

"Carlos..."

"I promise," Carlos said.

"Thank you, Mijo."

Katie smirked. "You do know he's going to get into trouble there?"

"Probably, but I got the promise out of him. The rest is up to Papi."

Katie nodded. "Smart."

Sylvia smiled at her. "I have my moments. You have fun, Mija."

"I will," Katie said, hugging her.

"Call if you need anything," Alex said as they headed out the door.

"We will," Joanna said.

Sylvia waited for Alex to pull away and then grabbed her coat. "Might as well get this over with. Brooke's going to come over after work so we can all discuss this."

"What did you tell her?" Jo asked as she put on her coat.

"Enough for now, but not everything."

"That's probably a good idea," Joanna said.

Sylvia nodded and they headed out to Mark Christopher's office.

∞

Alex and the kids were on their way to the park when James' cell rang. He looked at the caller ID and smiled. "Hi dad. How are you feeling?"

"I'm feeling a lot better. How about you?" Mike asked.

"Doing good, we're just heading to the park to have lunch and then hockey practice later."

"What time is your game tomorrow?"

"Nine, why?"

"I thought I might come and watch. If that's okay?"

"Really? I'd love that!" James said.

"Why aren't you in school today?"

James told him about what had happened the night before and about their appointment with Claudia that morning.

"Well, I was going to see if you boys wanted to come over after the game tomorrow. I thought we could do something here, since Kendall doesn't like going out."

"That would be great. We're meeting him and Papa G at the park, so I can ask him then. What about Tiffany, though? I don't want her saying anything bad to him," James told him.

"That's not a problem. James, let me get back to you. I have an idea, and if it's okay, I'll stop by later and tell you what it is."

"Sure. Practice will be over at about six, and we should be back to Papa G's a few minutes after that."

"Okay, I'll see you this evening then," Mike said, hanging up.

"Is your dad doing okay?" Logan asked.

"Yeah, he's coming to our game tomorrow, but he said he's going to stop by tonight."

"Why?" Carlos asked.

"He invited us over tomorrow, but said he has an idea and he'll stop by later and tell us about it."

"I wonder what it is," Logan said.

"I guess you'll find out tonight," Alex told them as he pulled into the parking lot next to Antonio's car. They got out and Carlos ran over to Antonio's car as Antonio got out.

"Papi!"

"Carlitos!" Antonio smiled, hugging Carlos tightly. "Are you ready for lunch? It's going to get cold soon."

"I think the question is when is Carlos NOT ready for lunch?" Logan smirked.

"At breakfast and dinner," Carlos retorted, sticking out his tongue.

"You keep that up and your tongue is liable to freeze like that," Claudia said.

Carlos quickly pulled his tongue back in. "Really?"

"You never know."

"NO! You're not going to see how long it takes for your tongue to freeze like that!" Logan ordered, noting the curious expression that suddenly appeared on Carlos' face.

"You're no fun." Carlos pouted.

"Fine, go ahead and try it. Just remember that if your tongue freezes, you won't be able to taste anything," Logan told him.

Carlos pondered it for a minute. "It might be worth it just to see how long it does take," he said, sticking his tongue back out.

"Did I mention that you wouldn't actually be able to EAT either?"

Carlos quickly pulled his tongue back in. "Okay, that wouldn't be worth it."

Claudia laughed at the two of them.

"What?" Carlos asked.

"The two of you are like twins."

"Maybe mirror twins," Logan said.

"What's a mirror twin?"

"Twins who are the complete opposite of each other," Logan told him.

"So I'd be good looking and you'd be ugly?" Carlos smirked.

"No, I'd be smart and you'd be stupid."

"That's not quite the way it works. It means that you would be identical, but one of you would be left-handed and the other right-handed. Your hair might part on the opposite side, or if you had a birthmark, it would be the same, but on the opposite side," Claudia told them.

"I still say I'd be the good looking one," Carlos said.

"And stupid, don't forget stupid," Logan told him.

"Boys are all stupid," Katie stated, shaking her head.

"Too bad one of you couldn't be the tall one," James piped in.

"Hey!" they both yelled.

"Boys..." Alex warned.

"Sorry," they all said.

"On that note, let's eat before lunch does get cold." Antonio laughed.

Antonio had taken the emergency blankets and laid them across the benches, so they would all stay dry. Carlos ran back to Alex's car, grabbed the extra scarf, and put it around Kendall's neck.

"Carlos, I'm already wearing a scarf."

"Mami said to make sure you wear it so you stay warm."

Kendall rolled his eyes. "I'm not cold."

"And now you won't be." Carlos smiled.

They all sat down and Alex handed out paper plates and napkins. James sat down next to Kendall and put a slice of pizza on his plate. "You need to eat."

Kendall rolled his eyes and picked at the food.

Antonio sat on the other side of him. "You better eat, or I'll let James feed you."

"I'm still full from this morning."

"That was hours ago," Antonio told him.

"We did the formula before we went to Claudia's," Kendall reminded him.

"Just one piece, please?" Antonio asked.

Kendall sighed, picked it up, and took a bite.

Claudia smiled as she watched the three of them.

They all finished their lunch and the boys cleaned up the table.

"Papi, can we go skate?" Carlos asked.

"Did you all bring your skates?"

"We packed up our gear just in case we were running late," Logan told him.

"Alright, but just for a few minutes. Kendall still has his physical therapy appointment."

"We didn't bring any skates for Kendall," Carlos realized.

"It's okay, I'm not supposed to skate anyway," Kendall said.

"Which is why I brought your camera. You can take some photos if you want to," Logan said, handing him the small camera.

"Thanks Loges."

"That's a good idea. Why don't you go take some pictures of the boys and Katie skating?" Alex suggested.

"Fine, but just so you know, we can tell when you guys are trying to get rid of us so you can talk," Kendall told him.

"Wise guy," Alex said.

Kendall smirked and followed the others to the pond.

"What happened?" Antonio asked quietly after the kids were out of earshot.

Alex relayed what had happened at the hospital with Jen. "Sylvia and Jo ran to your attorney's office to pick up the papers," Alex told him.

"She said that she wished he hadn't made it?" Antonio asked in disbelief.

Alex nodded. "Jo was so upset that she broke down once she got to the house."

"Damn it! I was really hoping we wouldn't have to do this," Antonio said miserably.

"I know, but if Eli is saying to go ahead with it, then we probably should," Alex told him.

"Alex is right. So far everything's been alright when it comes to Kendall and Katie having what they need, but if Eli is saying to file for temporary custody, then you need to," Claudia said sadly.

"I know," Antonio sighed.

"Look, maybe you should let Jo and I do it. That way we don't have to worry about her blaming you for anything," Alex suggested.

Antonio shook his head. "No, I made a promise to Will and Jen that we'd take care of the kids if need be. We already have the original papers that we had drawn up after the kids were born, stating we would become their legal guardians. We all signed them, so it shouldn't take much to get this pushed through."

"We're here for you," Alex told him.

"Thanks buddy, we're going to need you."

"If you need any help with a recommendation, I can give you one, too. As his psychologist, I would definitely recommend that Kendall stay with you for his own well-being, and that's without what happened last night and this morning," Claudia said.

"Thanks. We may need you to do that," Antonio said.

"I'll write it up and have it waiting for you, just in case."

"Thanks Claudia, I really appreciate it. What do we tell the kids?" Antonio asked.

"The truth. That Jen's sick and is going to be getting the treatment she needs," Claudia told him.

"Yeah," he said as he watched the kids. The boys and Katie were out on the ice and Kendall was standing there, watching and taking some pictures.

"Look on the bright side, he did really well today—they all did. If we focus on the good moments, then things won't seem so hopeless," Claudia pointed out.

"Yes they did, and you're right." Antonio smiled.

"You should probably have Eli right up a statement, saying that he recommends you go ahead with the request for custody," Claudia suggested.

Antonio nodded. "I'll call him when we get home."

"They look like they're enjoying themselves," Claudia said, watching the kids as they skated. Kendall was now sitting on a bench close to the pond and taking a video of Katie doing some spins.

Antonio nodded and looked at his watch. "Unfortunately we need to get going. Kendall, it's time to go, buddy!"

Kendall sighed when he heard Antonio call him. He didn't want to go to physical therapy. All he really wanted to do was stay and watch the boys and Katie skate. "Bye guys," he said as he headed over to the cars.

"Wait, I'm coming with you!" Carlos called after him. He got off the ice, quickly changed back into his boots, and took off after Kendall.

"Carlos, you don't have to come. Why don't you stay here and have fun?" Kendall asked as Carlos caught up with him.

"Being with you is fun," Carlos said, putting his arm around Kendall's shoulders.

"Not at physical therapy."

"But they have all kinds of cool equipment and stuff!"

Kendall smiled and shook his head. "You can make any place and anything sound fun."

Carlos grinned and ran up to Claudia and hugged her. "Bye Claudia!"

"Goodbye baby, I'll see you soon. There's a treat for you in the car," she whispered.

"For me?"

"Just for you, although you might want to share it with your dad and Kendall."

"I will!" he promised as he hopped in the back seat. "Oreos!" he squealed.

She laughed. "Well, at least I can make him smile. I'll see you soon. If you need anything, call me," she said to Kendall.

"I will. Thanks Claudia," he said, hugging her.

"You're welcome, baby. Same time Monday?" she asked, kissing his cheek. He nodded and got into the car next to Carlos, who was already munching on the Oreos.

"Same with you, if you need anything, call me," she said to Antonio.

"Will do, thanks for everything."

"Anytime. Let me know when you want the boys to come again."

"We'll give you a call tonight." He smiled as he got into the driver's seat.

She waved as they pulled away and looked at Alex. "How are you doing?"

"Better than he is."

"Antonio?"

Alex nodded.

"He's a strong man and he has all of you standing by him. He'll do what needs to be done and get through this alright."

"Yes he will," Alex said, smiling sadly.

∞

Antonio pulled up to the medical building and they got out and went inside. Kendall and Carlos took seats in the waiting room while Antonio signed Kendall in. About ten minutes later, they called Kendall's name and Antonio stood up, pulling Kendall with him.

"It won't be that bad."

"Yeah, it'll be fun!" Carlos smiled.

Kendall rolled his eyes and shook his head.

They followed the assistant back into the gym area and then into an exam room. "There's a gown on the table for you, if you could please put it on. Joel will be right in." She smiled as she closed the door behind her.

Kendall groaned.

"I'll help you," Carlos said, grabbing the gown.

Kendall tried to unbutton his shirt, but he was having trouble lifting his left arm, so Carlos helped him with the upper buttons. He slipped the shirt off, Carlos held the gown up for him, and he slipped it on. "Thanks Los."

"No problem." Carlos smiled as he went to tie the gown around Kendall's neck. He stopped and looked at Antonio and gestured for him to come over.

Antonio went over and Carlos pointed to Kendall's shoulder. It was badly bruised and swollen again, and there was now a small lump near the center of the bruise.

"What's wrong?" Kendall asked.

"Mijo, is your shoulder hurting like it did before?"

"I guess."

"Kendall, why didn't you say something?" Antonio asked.

"I just thought it was because my mom pulled on my arm. Why?"

There was a knock at the door. "Come in," Antonio said.

Joel went in and closed the door behind him. "How are we doing today?"

"I think we have a problem," Antonio told him.

"Why?"

Antonio went to pull the gown back, but Kendall pulled away. "Mijo, stop. He needs to take a look at it."

Kendall shook his head.

"Kendall, please, this is important. Now let Joel look at it," Antonio said firmly as he moved in front of the teen and pulled him into his arms. Kendall buried his face in Antonio's chest as Joel gently touched his shoulder. Kendall whimpered as a sharp pain went across his back and down his arm.

"What happened?" he asked.

"His mom pulled on his arm last night," Antonio said.

"Why would she do that?"

"She was upset and wasn't thinking. He wasn't wearing the brace, so I think she forgot that he's injured," Antonio told him.

"We need to get him upstairs for an ultrasound to see how bad it is. Let me go give the radiologist a call."

Kendall shook his head and clung tighter to Antonio. "It's alright, Mijo. Let me go talk to him and find out what he's thinking. Stay here with Carlos, I'll be right back," Antonio said as he steered Kendall to a chair.

"Carlos, take care of your brother."

"I will Papi," Carlos promised as he sat next to Kendall.

Antonio left the room and looked for Joel. He found him in an open office area, just getting off the phone. "They can take him right in, it's just two floors up."

"What do you think is wrong?" Antonio asked.

"I'm concerned he has a stage three tear now," Joel told him.

"What exactly does that mean?"

"It means that the muscle is now torn completely, and depending on the location and severity, Kendall may need surgery to repair it."

"Just because she pulled on his arm?" Antonio asked.

Joel nodded. "Considering that the muscle was already compromised, yes."

"Does it have to mean surgery?"

"Sometimes we can treat this type of injury medically, but you've already been doing that for a month and it didn't heal enough to withstand any additional trauma. The good news is they can debride any scar tissue when they repair the muscle. He will need to wear another type of immobilizer for a few weeks and then physical therapy. However, that means he'll recover a lot faster and that the muscles will be stronger than they would be otherwise."

"He is not going to do well in the hospital," Antonio said.

"It's very possible they can do an arthroscopy instead of an open incision surgery. He can probably go home the same day."

"How will they decide that?"

"The orthopedic surgeon will discuss that with you after he sees the results of the ultrasound. I know Kendall's scared, but if he needs surgery and doesn't have it, he could very well lose the use of that arm permanently," Joel told him.

Antonio nodded. "We'll do what we need to do."

Chapter 143~ Betrayals and Breakdowns

Eli walked back to Jen's room and found her still staring out the window. "Is she alright?" Jen asked quietly.

"She's going home to rest," Eli said, sitting down.

Jen nodded.

"Do you really think pushing everyone away is going to solve your problems?"

"I'm not trying to push everyone away."

"Lying to yourself is not going to help," he told her.

"I am not lying!"

"Then look at me and tell me that's not what you're doing."

Jen looked at him. "I'm not lying," she said, looking away.

He sighed. "Alright, let's try this a different way. Which is the truth... that you're grateful to Antonio for saving Kendall's life both times, or that he's trying to steal him from you?"

Jen just looked at her hands, not responding.

"Do you really wish Kendall had never been born or that he'd died on either of those occasions?"

"Of course I don't wish Kendall had died," Jen said quietly, still looking at her hands.

"So when you said that before, you were just trying to hurt Mrs. Mitchell?"

"Of course not!"

"Then why did you say it?"

"I don't know! I am so confused. I don't know how to do this!" Jen said, her eyes tearing up.

"So you think by pushing everyone away it will get easier?"

"Maybe."

"Why? So you don't have to deal with how everyone else feels. You are not the only one frightened and confused by this whole nightmare. Everyone who loves you and Kendall are trying to deal with this and have been doing their best to help you both. You being cruel to them is not fair to them or to you."

She hung her head. "I know."

"I understand you've never had to deal with something like this before—most people don't. That's why after you're feeling a little more stable, I want you to start attending a support group."

"What kind of support group?"

"One for families of victims of violent crime. You need to see that you are not alone. There are thousands of people out there trying to deal with exactly the same issues that you're trying to deal with."

"Really, thousands of people have had their child taken and abused by some freak and then had them come home just to have to deal with more freaks?" she asked bitterly.

"No, not the exact same situation. What I am telling you is there are people out there who understand what you're going through and how you're feeling. There are also people who have had their loved ones taken from them, and they either died or were never seen again. People whose loved ones were killed or brutalized in the most horrific ways imaginable. You

are not alone in this, and you have the opportunity that so many never did. You got your son back and he is actually making tremendous progress in his recovery. So instead of trying to hide from the world and crying that it isn't fair, think about what else could have happened to him and be grateful that it didn't," Eli said firmly.

"I don't know how."

"That's why I'm here, to help you figure this all out. I know your parents were older when they had you and that you were an only child. Did they have a tendency to be overprotective of you?"

"I guess so. Why?"

"Sometimes as parents, we try and protect our children from all the bad things in the world. Unfortunately, sometimes when we do this, we prevent them from learning how to take care of themselves. It's good to have someone there for us, but we all need to learn to pick ourselves up when we fall."

"Meaning?"

"Meaning you need to learn to take care of yourself, so you can take care of your children the right way. This includes learning how to deal with this situation and stop placing blame where it doesn't belong. Your children, your friends, and you deserve better."

"How do I stop feeling like this?"

"First, you start taking your medication properly. Second, you realize that the bad people are either dead or behind bars. They are not the people who love you and who have been there for you since day one. Third, you take responsibility for hurting your son and realize it's probably going to be awhile before he trusts you again."

"How do I fix this?" she asked, her eyes tearing up again.

"You have to do one of the hardest things there is to do. You have to grow up and take control of your own life."

∞

Carlos sat with his arm around Kendall as they waited for Antonio to return. "It'll be okay," Carlos said reassuringly.

"Sure it will."

"I'll stay with you the whole time," Carlos promised.

"What if they won't let you?"

"Let them try and stop me." Carlos smiled. Kendall shook his head and smiled a little.

"Isn't an ultrasound what they use to look at babies?" Carlos asked.

"Yeah, I think so," Kendall said, remembering the little video of Katie that his parents had brought home before she was born.

"You never know, it might be kind of cool," Carlos said.

"Somehow I doubt it."

Antonio went back into the exam room and sat down next to the boys. "We need to get an ultrasound of your shoulder. Joel thinks your muscle may have torn all the way through."

"What does that mean?" Kendall asked with a sinking feeling.

"It means we need to find out how bad it is, so they know how to treat it. They're going to do the ultrasound, and the orthopedist is going to take a look at the results and let us know what we need to do."

"I'm staying with him," Carlos stated.

"I'm sure that'll be okay. I'll explain that he needs you there." Antonio smiled.

There was a knock at the door. "Come in," Antonio said.

Joel handed Antonio a slip of paper from the clipboard he was carrying. "Okay, you're all set. They will do the ultrasound, and then Dr. Jackson will give you a call as soon as he has gone over the results. Before that though, I need to ask Kendall a few questions. You can just shake your head or nod, if that's easier for you," he said, sitting on a rolling stool by the counter.

Kendall looked at Antonio. "It's alright, Mijo."

"Did you hear a 'pop' when your arm was pulled?"

Kendall shook his head.

"Did you feel a burning sensation?"

Kendall nodded.

"Okay, good. Now can you tell me if it felt kind of like a rubber band being snapped? First tight and then loose?"

Kendall thought for a moment and then nodded.

Joel made a few notations on the paper. Then he rolled the stool over until he was in front of him. "I need you to try something for me. I want you to squeeze my hands as hard as you can, okay?" he asked, holding them out in front of him.

Kendall shook his head and pushed closer to Antonio.

"It's alright. I'm not going to hold onto you. I just need to see how strong your grip is," Joel said gently.

Kendall shook his head.

"Kendall, please?" Antonio asked.

Joel rolled the stool so that he was in front of Carlos. "How about you? Maybe you can show Kendall that it's okay?"

"Sure!" Carlos smiled and took his hands.

"Squeeze as hard as you can for five seconds."

"As hard as I can?"

Joel smiled and nodded.

Carlos squeezed on his hands and counted to five. "Wow, that's quite a grip you have." Joel laughed, shaking out his hands.

"Are you okay?" Carlos asked.

"I'm fine. Luckily, I get a lot of practice at this." He smiled. "Do you think you could give it a try now?" he asked Kendall.

Kendall sighed and nodded.

Joel smiled and rolled the stool so that he was in front of Kendall again and held out his hands.

He reached up with his right hand, but his left wouldn't go up and out far enough.

"Is that as far as you can lift your arm now?"

He nodded.

"I'm going to move just a little closer," he told him and rolled the stool a few inches forward. He held his hands out a little further until Kendall was able to take them.

"Squeeze for five seconds, just like Carlos did." He smiled.

Kendall looked at Carlos, who smiled and nodded. He squeezed down and immediately released his hands as a sharp pain shot across his back and down his arm.

"Are you alright?" Antonio asked.

Kendall's face was flushed with pain and he shook his head. He was taking deep breaths and desperately hoping he wouldn't throw up.

"Is it a burning pain that goes all the way down your arm?" Joel asked.

Kendall nodded.

"Can you show me how his arm was pulled?" Joel asked Antonio as he stood up.

"I think so," he said, standing up. He took a hold of Joel's arm, just below the elbow, with both of his hands, and pulled it up and forward.

"So almost straight out?" Joel asked.

Antonio nodded as he sat back down next to Kendall.

Joel made some more notations and then looked at Antonio. "Okay, if you can head up as soon as Kendall can move comfortably, they'll get you right in."

"Thanks Joel," Antonio said, shaking his hand.

"You're welcome."

Carlos grabbed Kendall's shirt. "I'll help you get dressed when you're ready."

"You might as well keep the gown on. They'll just have you put on another one anyway. They'll send it back down here when they're done," Joel told them.

After a few minutes, Kendall was able to sit up straight and he leaned against Antonio. "Are you ready to head up?" Antonio asked. Kendall sighed and nodded. Carlos grabbed Kendall's jacket and put it around his friend's shoulders.

"It's going to be alright," Antonio said as he put an arm around each boy.

∞

They headed for the elevator and took it to the third floor. Antonio went to check Kendall in at the desk.

"We're actually ready for him now," the receptionist said with a smile.

He looked at her and gestured slightly for her to come closer. "I don't know if Joel told you, but Kendall's recovering from severe emotional trauma and has a fear of being touched. So I'm not sure how this is going to work."

She nodded. "He did. They also sent his file up. He will be in with Rachel Macintosh— she is our main pediatric radiologist. She's very sweet and tries to work at a pace comfortable for the child."

"Would it be possible for his brother to stay with him? I think it would help Kendall stay calm," Antonio said.

"I don't think that will be a problem."

"Thank you." Antonio smiled.

Antonio walked back over to the boys. "They're ready for us now."

"Did you tell her that I have to stay with Kendall?" Carlos asked.

"Yes Mijo, she said that's fine."

"See, I told you everything would be alright." Carlos smiled as he pulled Kendall up.

Kendall raised his eyebrow and looked at him, unconvinced.

"Come on, it'll be fine," Antonio said, putting his arm around him.

They followed the assistant back to a large exam room that contained several different kinds of equipment. "Rachel will be right in."

"Thank you," Antonio said.

They sat down and Kendall started taking deep breaths, trying not to panic. "It's going to be okay," Antonio said.

"I don't want to do this," Kendall told him.

"I know, but we need to know what's going on. Your shoulder is really bruised and swollen right now, and we need to know how to take care of it."

"It'll be okay," Carlos said, scooting his chair closer to him.

The door opened and a blonde woman about thirty years old came in. "Hi, my name's Rachel and I'm the technician who'll be doing your ultrasound today."

"Hi Rachel!" Carlos smiled.

"Well hello and you are?"

"I'm Carlos, this is Kendall," Carlos told her, smiling at his friend.

"Hi Kendall." Rachel smiled.

Kendall pushed himself closer to Antonio.

"You must be Antonio," Rachel said, holding out her hand.

"Hi, yes I am." Antonio smiled, shaking her hand.

"I see that we need to do an ultrasound of your left shoulder?"

Kendall looked at her and started shaking.

"It's alright, we'll go as slowly as you need," she said reassuringly. "When did the original injury occur?" she asked Antonio.

"It happened close to a month ago."

She nodded and made a notation. "It was reinjured last night?"

"Yes," Antonio said.

"I bet you're pretty sore," she said to Kendall.

He gave her a slight nod and tightened his grip on Antonio's arm.

"Do you know how an ultrasound works?"

Kendall shook his head.

"First, I put some clear gel on the area, and then I use something called a transducer and move it over the area that I'm scanning. It bounces sound, or sonar waves, off of what I scan and sends the information to the computer. Then the images are displayed on a screen."

"Isn't sonar what bats use to fly?" Carlos asked.

She nodded. "It's also how dolphins and other toothed whales get around in the ocean."

"That sounds so cool!"

"It's very cool." She laughed.

"It's too bad Logan couldn't come, he'd love it here," Carlos said.

"Yes he would." Antonio smiled.

"Logan?" Rachel asked.

"He's our friend. He's going to be a doctor someday," Carlos told her.

"Really? Well, maybe someday he can come visit and I'll show him around."

"He'd love that!" Carlos told her.

"Well, you give me a call and I'll make it happen," she promised.

"Thanks!"

"You're welcome! Now, can I take a look at your shoulder?" she asked Kendall.

Kendall looked at Antonio. "It's alright, Mijo."

Kendall nodded and Antonio pushed the gown down off Kendall's shoulder. Rachel got a little closer and noticed Kendall tense up. "Could you turn towards Antonio just a little?"

Kendall did as she asked.

"I'm going to lightly touch your shoulder now," she said gently.

Kendall tightened his grip on Antonio. She reached over and barely brushed across his skin and he pulled away.

"Once more," she said, touching him with a little more pressure.

He inhaled sharply and tried to pull further away.

"Does it really hurt when someone touches you?"

He nodded.

"Okay, let's try something," she said as she went to one of the machines and picked up something about six inches long and two inches wide. "This is the transducer, and I want to press it against your hand so you can tell me if you'll be able to handle the pressure on your shoulder. Can you do that for me?"

Kendall extended his right hand and she placed her left hand under it and gently placed the transducer on his palm. "Now I'm going to start applying the same amount of pressure that I'll need to apply to your shoulder."

He nodded and she started moving the transducer back and forth across his palm, pressing down a little more with each movement. "This is about how hard I need to press down. Do you think it's going to be too much for you?"

Kendall nodded and pulled his hand away.

She looked at Antonio. "Why don't we go discuss our options?"

He nodded and went to stand up, but Kendall wouldn't release him. "It's going to be alright. We'll be right outside the door. You stay here with Carlos and I'll be right back."

"It's okay, I've got you, buddy," Carlos said, putting his arm around him. Antonio smiled as Carlos pulled Kendall over to him and followed Rachel out of the room.

"There's no way we can do this without some type of sedation. It's far too painful for him. The good news is we have a few options," Rachel said.

"What are they?"

"The ideal choice is to sedate him and do the ultrasound, but I don't think he'll go for that."

"No, he won't," Antonio sighed.

"I say we start with a topical anesthetic. The only problem I can see is it may not work if the pain is too deep seated."

"What if it doesn't work?"

"Then we can opt for either a conscious sedation with an oral sedative, or an IV sedation."

"Okay, let's start with the topical and pray it works," Antonio said.

"Is he taking anything at all for pain?"

Antonio nodded. "They gave him a prescription for Tramadol and I gave him one last night. Usually he just takes ibuprofen, because he doesn't like medication that makes him sleepy."

"If we just go with the topical, give him a Tramadol when you get home, because once it wears off, he's going to be in quite a bit of pain just from the ultrasound."

Antonio nodded.

"Let's go give this a try."

∞

"I want to go home," Kendall told Carlos.

"I know, but it shouldn't take too long. Do you think she'll really let Logan come visit and see all of this cool stuff?" Carlos asked, trying to distract his friend.

"I guess if she said so, she will."

"He would really love this!"

"Yeah, he would," Kendall said, smiling a little.

"Maybe before we leave, I can ask her when he can come and surprise him."

"That's a good idea."

Antonio held the door for Rachel and they went back into the room. He went back over to the boys and sat down next to Kendall. Rachel sat on a stool in front of them.

"Okay, so what we're going to do is try a topical anesthetic gel to numb your shoulder. If it's not enough though, we'll have to use a mild sedative, but we're going to hope this works."

Kendall looked at Antonio in abject misery.

"I'm sorry, but we have to do this, Mijo."

"Are you ready?" she asked.

Kendall leaned against Antonio, holding onto his arm. Antonio nodded to Rachel.

"We can actually do this while you're sitting up, which means you and Antonio can stay right there," she said, getting up and going over to one of the machines on the other side of the room. She rolled it over to them and then went to a cabinet, where she pulled out some surgical gloves and a small jar. She sat down on the stool again as she pulled on the gloves.

She opened the jar. "This is lidocaine. I'm going to gently rub it onto your shoulder. You might feel some tingling in a few minutes, and your shoulder should be fairly numb in between five to ten minutes."

Antonio pulled Kendall a little closer as she gently rubbed the gel onto his shoulder. Kendall took deep breaths. He was fighting down the panic he could feel building as Rachel applied the gel. He was shaking and Antonio held him tightly.

After a couple of minutes, he felt the tingling she had told him about and he tightened his hold on Antonio. "It's okay," Antonio said softly.

Rachel set up the machine while waiting for the gel to take effect. After about ten minutes, she sat down in front of Kendall again. "Is your shoulder feeling any differently?"

Kendall nodded.

"Okay, I'm going to touch it with my hand and you let me know if you can feel anything." She brushed her fingers across the bruised skin and Kendall didn't react. Next, she touched with her fingers, applying a little more pressure. "Can you feel that?"

He shook his head.

"I think we're good to go. I'm going to need you to sit up straight and I'll have Antonio hold your arm where I need it."

Antonio nodded as he helped Kendall sit up more.

"I'm going to clean the rest of the lidocaine off and apply a different gel, and then we'll get this done. Let me know if you start feeling any pain."

Kendall took a deep breath and nodded.

"I'm going to take your arm and show Antonio how I need it held, okay?"

Kendall nodded and she gently took his arm, had moved it down, and back a little. "If you could just place your hands where mine are and hold his arm steady for me?"

Antonio did as she asked and she picked up a baby wipe and cleaned off the lidocaine. Then she squeezed a fair amount of clear gel onto the area. She picked up the transducer and adjusted the settings. "Okay, here we go. Try and hold as still as possible," she instructed as she started moving the sensor along his shoulder.

Kendall closed his eyes and concentrated on his breathing. He could feel pressure but no pain, and the sensation was a little unnerving.

"Are you doing okay?" Antonio asked.

Kendall nodded slightly.

"You're doing great. A few more minutes and we'll be done," Rachel said.

Carlos was watching the screen. "What is all of that?"

"Those are the muscles, tendons, and blood vessels in Kendall's shoulder," she said, smiling.

"They look weird."

"They do a little."

"Is this how they see babies?"

"Yes it is."

"Do you think Logan could come and visit soon?"

"Sure. When we're finished here, I'll get my appointment book and we can set up a time."

"Thanks! He's gonna love this!" Carlos smiled.

"Kendall, could you take a deep breath and hold it for three seconds?" Rachel asked.

Kendall inhaled and counted to three. She clicked a button on the machine's control panel. "Perfect. Okay, we're done," Rachel told them. She wiped off Kendall's shoulder and pulled the gown back up for him.

"Do you think it came out alright?" Antonio asked.

She nodded. "I'm going to email this to Dr. Jackson right away, and he'll give you a call as soon as he looks at it."

"Okay, I'll make sure you have all my numbers before we go."

She handed him a clipboard and he wrote them down for her.

She looked at Kendall. "Is your shoulder still numb?"

Kendall nodded.

"The lidocaine can last anywhere from twenty minutes to about four hours, so don't worry if it's still numb later. I already told Antonio that you need to take something for pain when you get home, because you're going to be sore after this."

Kendall nodded again.

"You did a great job. I know it wasn't easy keeping still in that position." She smiled.

He gave her a small smile.

"Why don't you go ahead and dress and Antonio can come with me to arrange a time for your friend to visit?"

"I'll help you," Carlos told Kendall, grabbing his shirt.

Antonio followed Rachel out to the main desk.

"Dr. Jackson will probably call you within a couple of hours. I saw what appears to be a rather large tear running laterally along the subscapularis."

"Could you explain, so that I know what you're talking about?" Antonio smiled.

"Sorry, it means the tear isn't up and down, it's actually tearing lengthways, and there's a good chance it'll continue to tear unless we do something."

"Meaning surgery?" Antonio sighed.

"I'm not the doctor, but I'd say that's what he's going to recommend. The problem is that if we don't stop the tear, it's going to end up compromising the bicep tendon as well."

"Damn it," Antonio said quietly.

"The good news is that I'm pretty sure Kendall's a candidate for arthroscopy. Which means they can probably do the surgery on an outpatient basis and his recovery time will be considerably shorter."

Antonio nodded. "We'll do what we have to. Thanks for being so patient with him. He responded well to you."

"I love working with kids, and I know going to the doctor's and having tests done can be pretty scary. Which reminds me, we should make arrangements for their friend to visit," she said, grabbing an appointment book from the desk. She looked through it. "I actually have students from the community college coming for the day on the fourteenth. Do you think Logan would like to sit in on an actual training day?"

"I think he'd be blown away." Antonio smiled.

"Good. I'll write him in, and if you could tell him to be here at nine that morning, he can spend the day with me."

"Thank you, I'll make sure he's here."

"I'll see you then." She smiled.

Antonio nodded and headed back to the exam room. He stopped outside the door and called Sylvia's cell.

"Antonio?"

"Yeah honey, it's me. Alex said you were going to pick up the papers from Mark. Did you get them?"

"I have them here."

"We need to get them signed, and I need to get them into court today."

"What's going on?"

"Kendall probably needs surgery, and we need to be able to take care of him. Can you do me a favour? Call Eli, and have him fax a letter to the station saying that he recommended we file for custody because of Jen's mental state? We're probably going to need it."

"I'll call him as soon as we hang up. What did the doctor say?"

"I haven't spoken to the doctor yet, but the ultrasound technician told me it looks like Kendall has a pretty severe tear and that the doctor is probably going to recommend surgery. I just want to be prepared and make sure we can legally do this."

"Okay, I'll call Eli and Claudia. Are you coming home soon?"

"We'll be on our way in just a couple of minutes. I need to drop Carlos off at the rink first, and then I'll bring Kendall home."

"Alright, I'll see you soon."

"It's going to be alright," he told her.

"I hope so," she said sadly.

He found Carlos and Kendall waiting for him. "Can we go home now?" Kendall asked.

"Yes we can," he said, putting an arm around each boy. "Rachel said Logan can come on the fourteenth and spend the day, because she's actually teaching a class here that day."

"He's going to be so excited!" Carlos grinned.

"Yes he is," Antonio agreed.

"It was a great idea, Carlos," Kendall said.

"Thanks!" Carlos said, grinning.

They got to the car and the boys got in the back. They arrived at the skating rink a few minutes later. Carlos got out and grabbed his bag. "Bye Papi, bye Kendall!"

"Bye Mijo. Papa M will bring you home after practice."

"Okay!" he said, closing the door.

Antonio waited until Carlos was inside and then pulled away. "Well, we've had a busy day today."

"Yeah," Kendall said quietly.

"Are you tired?"

"A little."

"What are you thinking about?"

"I have to have surgery, don't I?"

"We haven't heard from the doctor yet, but if you do, I'll be right there," Antonio promised.

Kendall didn't say anything, just sat looking out the window.

"Are you alright?" Antonio asked.

"Yeah, just tired."

"When we get home you're going to take a pain pill and then lie down for a while. We'll worry about the rest once we hear from the doctor."

"Okay."

Antonio pulled into the driveway and got out. He opened Kendall's door and helped him out and they walked in together.

"I'm going to go grab you some juice. Why don't you head on up to bed?" Antonio told Kendall as he helped him off with his jacket.

Kendall nodded and headed upstairs.

Antonio went into the kitchen, where Sylvia and Joanna were talking. "Hi honey. Where's Kendall?" Sylvia asked, kissing Antonio.

"I sent him up to bed. He's exhausted and will probably be hurting more as soon as the topical wears off. I'm going to give him a Tramadol and hopefully he can get some rest."

"Why don't I take it up? I can sit with him until he falls asleep," Jo offered.

"Thanks honey, but I need to talk to him about us filing for custody. Could you stay with him after that, though?"

"Of course. What do you think he's going to say?" Joanna asked.

"I really don't know, but Claudia says he'll do better here right now, so he must have said something to her. I just don't want him blaming himself for this too."

"Claudia said to call her if we need her," Sylvia told him.

Antonio nodded. "We probably will. Is Katie with Sally?"

"Sally picked her up about half an hour ago," Sylvia told him.

"We'll need to let Sally know what's going on too," he said as he headed upstairs. He went into the bathroom, got a pain pill for Kendall, and then went to the guest room, but Kendall wasn't there.

"Kendall?"

"I'm in Carlos' room," Kendall answered in a quiet voice.

Antonio opened the door and found Kendall sitting at the window. "Did you want to stay in here?"

"I'm just looking out the window."

Antonio smiled and sat down next to him. "It is a nice view," he said, handing him the pill.

"Thank you."

"Is your shoulder still numb?"

"It's starting to wear off," Kendall told him as he took a sip of the juice.

"Let's get you into bed."

Kendall got up and climbed into bed. Antonio sat next to him. "You did so well today, Mijo. I'm so proud of you."

Kendall gave him a small smile. "Papi?"

"Yes?"

"If they have to do surgery, will it be because of what happened last night?"

"I don't know, but I'll find out more when I speak to the doctor, okay?"

"I just... If it is, can we not tell my mom that part?"

"Why not?"

"She's already sick because of all of this. I just don't want to make it worse."

"First of all, it's not you making it worse. But if you don't want to tell her, then we won't, unless it's necessary."

"Okay."

Antonio took a deep breath. "There's something else I need to talk to you about, buddy. When Mama M was visiting your mom this morning, she spoke to her doctor. He told her that your mom isn't stable enough to take care of you or Katie. So we need to make arrangements so that we can legally take care of you both."

"What does that mean?"

"It means Mami G and I need to file for temporary custody, just until Eli says that your mom's well enough to take care of you. Are you going to be okay with that?"

"I am, but she's going to blame you for this!" Kendall said.

"Maybe at first, but once she's feeling better she'll realize the truth."

"That's not fair! It's not your fault, it's mine," Kendall said in frustration.

"Now you listen to me, NONE of this is your fault and I want you to stop thinking like that. This isn't something that either of us could control. Your mom chose to stop taking her medication. It wasn't because she forgot. She hasn't been taking it for a few days because she was feeling better and thought she didn't need it anymore. She didn't realize the side effects would be so bad. She also hasn't been completely honest with Eli. I know it's hard, but she needs to start taking responsibility for her own recovery. Until then, there's nothing we can do to help her."

"I just don't want her to hate you," Kendall said, looking down.

"I'd rather do this and have her hate me, than to risk your or Katie's well-being. Besides, it's not just me. Papa and Mama M and Mama D all agree that this is the best course of action right now. This is between the adults, and I don't want ANY of you kids blaming yourselves."

"It's still not fair," Kendall said quietly.

Antonio hugged him. "Nothing about this last month has been fair, Mijo, but we'll all get through it. Now I need to run to the station for a bit, but Mami M is going to come up and sit with you for a while. I want you to get some sleep."

"I will," Kendall promised.

Antonio went downstairs.

"How did he handle it?" Sylvia asked.

"He's worried she's going to hate us. I told him what Eli said and that we're all in agreement on this."

"I'll go on up and sit with him," Joanna said.

"Thanks Jo, he's in Carlos' room."

She nodded and went upstairs. She knocked on the door and went in. She saw Kendall sitting in the chair by the window. "I thought you were lying down?"

"I was."

"How are you doing?" she asked, sitting down next to him.

He shrugged. "Okay, I guess."

"It's been a long day, huh?"

He nodded.

"Are you worried about what the doctor's going to say?"

"I don't want to have surgery."

"I know, honey. Maybe you won't have to."

"Yes I will."

"Well if you do, then I'll make sure you have all the ice cream you can eat," she promised.

"Isn't that for having your tonsils out?"

"I firmly believe that ALL surgeries mean you should get all the ice cream you can eat." She smiled.

"What if I'm not hungry?"

"That's the good thing about ice cream—you don't have to be hungry, it's just meant to be enjoyed. Plus it's easily turned into liquid form, so it doesn't really matter if you're hungry or not."

"Now you sound like Carlos and Papa M."

"Carlos is wise beyond his years and Papa M has years of experience." Jo smiled.

Kendall yawned and covered his mouth with his hand.

"Alright, back to bed with you," she said, taking his right arm.

Kendall got up and went back to bed. She tucked him in and sat down next to him. "I don't want you to worry about anything. Whatever you need, we'll be here."

"I know, I just..."

"Just what?"

"I just wish things would go back to normal."

"They will, honey. It's going to take some time, but they will."

"Can you do me a favour?"

"Of course, anything."

"Would you sing to me?" he asked quietly.

"I would love to sing to you." She smiled, brushing his bangs back. "Go to sleep, my little teddy bear...

∞

"Did you get a hold of Eli?" Antonio asked.

Sylvia nodded. "He already had something written up and said he'd fax it to the station. He said to let him know if we go through with this and he will go in and tell Jen. He recommended that she stay in the hospital at least through tomorrow so her medication has a chance to start working. Claudia is sending a statement too."

"Did you sign the papers yet?"

"I signed them at Mark's office so he could witness it. He already notified the court and will meet you there, so all you need to do is sign them and wait for the judge's ruling."

"Okay honey, thanks. I better get down there and get this over with," he said, picking up the file from the counter.

"I'll give Eli a call and let him know then. Do you think we're doing the right thing?"

"Yes, I do, especially if Eli told us to go ahead with this. We need to be able to take care of the kids, especially now with Kendall probably needing surgery."

"You're right. I just hate that's it's come to this."

"So do I," he said, kissing her cheek. "I'll be back soon. Let me know what Eli says."

"I will."

Sylvia took a deep breath and called Eli's number.

"Hello, this is Dr. Thorne."

"Hi Eli, it's Sylvia Garcia."

"Hello Sylvia. How's everything going there?"

"Not well. We're waiting to hear from the doctor, but Kendall most likely needs surgery. Antonio's on his way down to the courthouse to file for emergency custody."

"Alright, I'll head over to the hospital and let Jen know what's going on and why."

"Do you think she's going to be alright? Antonio and I both hate that it's come to this, but we don't know what else to do."

"I know this is hard, but you are doing the right thing. She's in no condition to care for her children and won't be for a while."

"She's going to hate us."

"She's going to be hurt and probably angry, but she's really left you no choice. She needs to learn to take care of herself before she can care for her children properly."

"So you really think we're doing the right thing?"

"Yes, I know you're doing the right thing," he said gently.

"Thank you for all your help. Could you let Jen know that we love her?"

"Of course I will. I'll call you later and let you know how she's doing."

"Thank you."

"You're welcome."

Sylvia hung up and went up to check on Kendall. She smiled as she heard Joanna singing. She looked in and saw that Kendall had fallen asleep. Jo was still singing quietly, running her fingers through his hair, tears falling down her cheeks.

Sylvia went in and put her hand on her friend's shoulder. Jo looked up and smiled. "He's so tired."

"I know he is," Sylvia said, putting her arms around her friend. "I spoke to Eli, and he said he's going to the hospital to tell Jen that we're filing for custody."

Joanna nodded.

There was a knock at the front door. "That's probably Brooke," Sylvia said. She went downstairs, looked through the peephole, and then opened the door. "Hi Brooke."

"I managed to finish up early today. Where are we with things?"

"We're still waiting to hear from the doctor, but Kendall probably needs surgery. Antonio's going to court to file for emergency custody and Eli is on his way over to tell Jen," Sylvia told her.

"Damn. Where's Kendall now?"

"He's upstairs sleeping. Jo's with him right now."

"I should go say hello to her," Brooke said.

Sylvia took her arm. "Give her a few minutes. Come on, I'll make some coffee and tell you everything that happened today."

∞

Eli arrived at the hospital and went up to Jen's room. He knocked at the door. "Come in," Jen said. "Eli, I wasn't expecting you back until tomorrow." Jen smiled.

"How are you feeling?"

"Still kind of off, I guess."

"It's going to take a few days for the medication to start working properly. That is why I think it's a good idea for you to stay here for a couple of days. I need to speak with you about something," he said, sitting down in the chair next to the bed.

"What is it?" she asked nervously.

"You know your friends love you and only want what's best for you and your children?"

"Yes, I know that. Why?"

"You understand that right now you aren't emotionally stable, especially while dealing with the side effects from the medication?"

"I know."

"Your son might require surgery to repair the damage to his shoulder, and because of your emotional state, by law, you can't sign off on any legal documents."

"What are you saying?" Jen asked.

"A surgical release form is a legal document, and I've recommended to the Garcia's that they file for emergency custody, so Kendall can get the medical care he needs."

"I see," she said, looking at her hands.

"This isn't because you're not a good mother—you are. You and Will chose the Garcias to take care of your children, should anything happen to you, because you trust them and you love each other like family. They chose you for the same reasons."

"I know."

"They're very concerned about your state of mind, and Sylvia is terrified you'll hate them for this. I want to make sure you understand that I am the one who recommended this. Someone has to be able to legally care for Kendall and Katie until you're well, and your families chose each other before your children were even born."

She nodded. "I know."

"I'm not convinced that you're alright with this."

"It's hard, but I'm trying," she told him.

He watched her for a couple of minutes. "So you're alright?"

She nodded. "Why?"

"I'm a little concerned by the fact that I just told you your son might need surgery, and you haven't asked about him once."

"That's because I know he's in good hands."

Eli looked at her unconvinced and stood up. "We'll discuss this again tomorrow, after you've had a chance to rest. You have my number if you need me. The nurse's station has it there as well."

"Thank you, Eli." Jen smiled.

"Get some sleep."

She closed her eyes and started to nod off, when she felt her heart start to race. Her mind replayed the conversation first with Jo and then with Eli. "I'm losing my babies," she sobbed.

She woke up in a complete panic, got out of bed, and quickly dressed. She found her cell and called for a cab to meet her outside the hospital. She opened the door and looked down the hallway. Not seeing anyone, she made her way to the elevators and took one down to the main floor. She went out front and the cab arrived a couple of minutes later. She gave them the Garcia's address.

"No one's taking my children away from me," she said to herself.

∞

They arrived at the Garcia's a few minutes later and Jen paid the driver. Her car was still parked out front and she checked her purse to make sure she had her keys. "I'll just get Kendall and Katie, and we'll go home, and everything will be alright."

She went up to the door and knocked.

Sylvia answered. "Jen, what are you doing here? Are you alright? How did you get here?"

"I'm fine, thank you. Well enough to take care of MY children," she said, pushing past Sylvia.

Sylvia closed the door and moved to stand in front of the stairway. "Did you speak to Eli?"

"Yes. He told me you think you need to file for custody, because I'm not well enough to take care of my own children."

Brooke came out of the kitchen. "You're supposed to be in the hospital until tomorrow, at the earliest."

"Well, I decided that I don't need to be in the hospital and I want my children."

"Not this again," Brooke said. "Jen, I'm taking you back to the hospital, and you're going to stay there until Eli releases you."

"Wrong. I am taking my children and we are going home. If Kendall needs medical care, I will see to it that he gets it. Now, where are they?"

"Katie is out and Kendall is sleeping. They're staying here," Sylvia said firmly.

"KENDALL! COME DOWNSTAIRS RIGHT NOW!" Jen yelled up.

Jo was still sitting next to Kendall when she heard Jen call for Kendall.

"What the hell?" She got up and went out into the hallway, where she could hear Sylvia and Jen arguing. She closed the bedroom door, went into the master bedroom, and grabbed the phone. She called Eli's cell.

"Dr. Thorne."

"Eli, this is Joanna Mitchell. Did you release Jen from the hospital?"

"No. In fact, I just left her there a little over half an hour ago. Why?"

"She's here at the Garcia's and screaming for Kendall again."

"Alright, give me the address and I'll be there shortly."

Joanna gave him the address and then headed downstairs. She stood next to Sylvia. "Jen, what are you doing? Kendall isn't feeling well and needs to sleep."

"He can sleep at home."

"Like it or not, THIS is his home until you're better," Brooke stated as she moved and stood on the other side of Sylvia.

"You're supposed to be my best friend and you're trying to steal my children!" Jen screamed at Sylvia.

"Jen, that's not true and you know it."

"You always wanted a big family, and because you can't have any more kids, you're trying to take mine!"

Sylvia looked at her in shock before pulling her hand back and slapping Jen across the face. Her brown eyes were filled with sorrow. "I may not be able to have any more children, but unlike you, I would have given anything for my little Analeigh to have lived. I NEVER once wished she hadn't been born just because it would have been easier on me, no matter how much it hurts. Can you say the same? What you said about Kendall this morning is unforgivable!"

"That wasn't what I meant! I never meant I wish he'd died!" Jen cried, holding her cheek.

Sylvia took a deep breath and pointed at the door. "Get out!"

"I am not leaving without my son."

"That's what you think!" Brooke growled. She grabbed Jen by the arm and pulled her to the door. "You're going back to the hospital until Eli releases you. You're not welcome here until you get your head out of your ass and stop being so cruel to the people who love you!" Brook opened the door and hauled Jen through it, slamming it behind her.

Jo followed them. "Brooke, Eli will be here any minute! He can take her back to the hospital."

"I'm not waiting. Tell him he can meet us there!" Brooke said as she shoved Jen into the passenger's side.

Joanna nodded and went back inside. Sylvia was holding onto the banister, shaking. "Sylvia?" she said softly.

Sylvia looked at her and dissolved into tears.

"Come on, honey, let's splash some cold water on your face and then we'll call Antonio," she said, putting her arms around Sylvia and leading her to the downstairs bathroom.

∞

Kendall awoke thinking he heard yelling. He listened for a moment and realized his mom was yelling and he could hear the other moms' voices as they tried to reason with her. He ignored the pain in his shoulder as he got up and opened the bedroom door.

He listened to Jen screaming at her friends, went into the master bedroom, and found the phone. He called Antonio's cell, but it went to voicemail.

"Papi, my mom is here and she's saying bad things again. Mami G needs you... she hurt her. I'm sorry this is all my fault," Kendall sobbed as he hung up.

He got up, went back into Carlos' room, and grabbed a tablet of paper. He scribbled a quick note and placed it on the pillow. He went into the bathroom and grabbed something from

the medicine cabinet. He quietly walked down the stairs and could hear Sylvia and Joanna in the downstairs bathroom. He quickly slipped on his boots and grabbed his jacket.

He could hear Sylvia sobbing in the other room. "I'm sorry," he whispered as he slipped out the front door.

Works Cited

Chapter 102~Thanksgiving

Emerson, Ralph Waldo. "Father, We Thank Thee". (1803-1882)

Chapter 123~First Generation Pranksters

Vela, Erika, and Gonzalez, Dani. "Goodnight-A Lullaby." (2015)

Coming soon:

Those You Trust: Learning to Trust Again

Surviving a predator was the first step in a long journey for Kendall and his family. They find that staying strong for each other gets more difficult with time. Will they all be there to the end?

Made in the USA
Middletown, DE
15 October 2015